Teaching
British Literature

Teaching
British Literature

A Companion to

The Longman Anthology
of British Literature

SECOND EDITION

David Damrosch
General Editor

Christopher Baswell
Anne Howland Schotter
Constance Jordan
Clare Carroll
Stuart Sherman *with* Cynthia Wall
Peter J. Manning
Susan J. Wolfson
Heather Henderson
William Chapman Sharpe
Jennifer Wicke
Kevin J. H. Dettmar

New York   San Francisco   Boston
London   Toronto   Sydney   Tokyo   Singapore   Madrid
Mexico City   Munich   Paris   Cape Town   Hong Kong   Montreal

NOTE REGARDING WEBSITES AND PASSWORDS:

If you need a password to access instructor supplements on a Longman
book-specific Website, use the following information:

Username: awlbook
Password: adopt

Vice President and Editor-in-Chief: Joseph Terry
Senior Supplements Editor: Donna Campion
Electronic Project Management and Page Makeup: Dianne Hall

Teaching British Literature: A Companion to The Longman Anthology of British Literature,
Second Edition, by David Damrosch et al.

ISBN: 0-321-11584-8

12345678910–MV–05040302

CONTENTS

The Middle Ages
Before the Norman Conquest

After the Norman Conquest

The Early Modern Period

The Restoration and the Eighteenth Century

The Romantics and Their Contemporaries

The Victorian Age

The Twentieth Century

General Editor's Preface

Extensively revised along with the new edition of *The Longman Anthology of British Literature*, this companion volume carries farther the ambitious aims we set for our first edition. First, it has been written directly by the editors responsible for each period. Second, it discusses every major author or combination of authors in the anthology, opening up possible lines of approach, indicating fruitful connections that could be made, and sketching important trends in scholarly debate. Our third goal has been to be suggestive rather than prescriptive, and we have hoped to inform people who are new to some of this material while also intriguing people interested in a fresh take on familiar works. Our whole effort in the body of the anthology has been to construct exciting and teachable conjunctions of classic and newly current works, and this volume gives us a chance to expand on the reasons behind our choices, and to indicate ways that we have found these materials to work best in class.

An Evolving Collaboration

In revising this teaching companion, we have taken advantage of responses and suggestions from many people who have been using the anthology in the classroom. Their advice and comments guided us in revising existing entries and in planning out our additions of new authors and clusters of works for this edition. This revised companion volume includes new entries for all our major additions, and we have also created a new opening section of sample syllabi. Several of these have come to us from people who responded to an invitation via our e-mail newsletter; others are syllabi developed by members of our editorial board as we've taught from the anthology ourselves. Naturally, these syllabi give only a sampling of some of the ways the anthology can be used, but it can be interesting to see how people at other institutions have approached teaching with the anthology. I would like to expand this section in future, and so I welcome syllabi from other users of the full anthology or its individual volumes. The present selection concentrates on giving an example each of several different kinds of course, but next time round it would be interesting to include creative alternatives for similar courses.

I also welcome suggestions for improvements to the anthology itself. Teaching texts normally go into new editions every few years, with the editors making a few cosmetic changes to justify the new edition. We view *The Longman Anthology* quite differently, much as we view the British literary canon otherwise than as a fixed series of timeless monuments. Our anthology is meant as a resource for teachers in an evolving and growing field, and our second edition gives new attention to a variety of authors and topics currently receiving substantial attention in literary studies: vernacular religion in the medieval period; "England in the New World" in early modern times, "Imagining Childhood" in the Victorian era, to name a few. Our new entries in this companion volume address these new features of the anthology, and revisions to existing entries suggest new ways to approach works already included in the first edition. Going forward, I would be delighted to hear what things you would most like to see added in the next edition, and to learn what existing combinations work best for you, what others might better be rethought. I can be reached by e-mail at dnd2@columbia.edu or by letter at the Department of English, 602 Philosophy Hall, Columbia University, New York NY 10027.

Typo Alert!

At a more local scale, I would be very grateful if you would let me know of any typos you find in the anthology (or indeed, in this manual). There is a great deal of new material in this edition, and we have made revisions to existing introductions and notes throughout, so typos are always a concern. Every page has been proofread both by the editors and by in-house proofreaders, and no errors have turned up to match the most memorable typos the first time round—a pair of quivering limbs turning into quivering lambs; Beckett's *Texts for Nothing* turning into some sort of travel promotion, *Texas for Nothing*; the Nietzschean transvaluation of Wordsworth's *Immortality Ode* into the *Immorality Ode*—but some typos are probably still hiding in the six thousand pages of the anthology. So please let me know of any lingering errors that you encounter, as well as sending in broader ideas and suggestions of all sorts.

Using the Anthology

A distinctive feature of our anthology is the grouping of works in Perspectives sections, in clusters illustrating a work "and Its Time," and as companion readings where there is a direct link between two texts. Together, these groupings are intended to set works in cultural context for students, and these groupings have a strategic pedagogical function as well. We had observed that in other anthologies, brief author listings rarely seemed to get taught. Added in with the laudable goal of increasing an anthology's range and inclusiveness, the new materials too often would get lost in the shuffle, hemmed in between the major author listings. Our groupings of works cluster shorter selections in ways that make them more likely to be taught, creating a critical mass of texts around a compelling literary or social issue.

At the same time, we expect that our various contextual groupings will be used variously by different people. As our sample syllabi show, a Perspectives section can be taught entire as a freestanding unit, or it can share a week with an important work or major author. Thus, the Early Modern section on "Government and Self-Government" can be taught directly along with More's *Utopia*, which it follows, or can be used as a general resource for explorations of political issues in such works as *The Faerie Queene*, *The Tempest*, and *Paradise Lost*. Alternatively, individual works within that Perspectives section can be paired with works elsewhere: for example, those selections that treat government within families, and specifically discuss relations between husbands and wives, can be used as context for discussions of the politics of gender in several of the period's writers. In the Twentieth Century, "Regendering Modernism" makes a highly teachable unit in itself, but stories within that Perspectives section can also readily be used in different conjunctions. Several stories could be brought together to make a cluster of short fiction, including stories by Joyce, Lawrence, and Wodehouse; or the stories by Sackville-West, Forster, and Mansfield with colonial settings could be taught together with *Heart of Darkness* and Graham Greene's *A Chance for Mr Lever*.

Particularly in the case of our fuller Perspectives sections, like the Romantic-era section on the abolition of slavery and the slave trade, it can be productive to assign different readings to different members of the class, with people working in teams to explore contrasting viewpoints; these can then be debated in class, or presented as written projects. Students interested in exploring Perspectives section issues in greater depth should be alerted to the extensive bibliographies at the end of each volume; Perspectives sections, as well as individual author listings, have bibliographies which can lead students farther into the primary sources.

Students will also find many current leads on our website, located at www.awlonline.com/damrosch, which has been greatly revised and augmented. A particularly useful new feature is an interactive time line, which gives information and directs students to web resources on a wide variety of authors, works, and issues.

Obviously, the several Perspectives sections and the clusters of texts on a work "and Its Time" are only a few of the many groupings that could be created. We wouldn't want any student to come away from the course with the misconception that these were the only issues that mattered in the period in question. Rather, these groupings should be seen as exemplary of the *sorts* of literary and cultural debate that were current in an era. Students can be encouraged—individually or in small groups—to research and develop their own perspectival clusters of materials, using as a point of departure some text or some issue that has particularly intrigued them. They could then present their own "Perspectives" section to the class as a whole, or write it up and analyze it as a term project.

Our broader groupings are similarly intended to be used in various ways. Thus, in the medieval period, we have included *Mankind* in our section on "Late Medieval Allegory," but it could also be taught directly together with the medieval cycle dramas earlier in the period. In our section on the Romantics and their contemporaries, the "Literary Ballads" can be taught as a unit, or Burns, for example, could be paired with a variety of other poets, from Blake to John Clare.

On a larger scale, we have followed custom in dividing the anthology according to the period divisions that have become ubiquitous in modern literary study, but there is no reason that a survey course should treat them as sacrosanct. Even within a generally chronological presentation, it can be interesting to have some cross-cutting sessions or weeks, such as an overview of the sonnet, or a section on travel writing, or one on the short story. Such groupings can bring together material from two, three, or even more sections of the anthology. One advantage of our six-volume format is that different combinations of volumes can also be used: Peter J. Manning, for instance, has been teaching a course in the long eighteenth century using a pairing of volumes 1C and 2A to explore the period from 1660 through 1832. Our greatest hope is that teachers and students alike will use our table of contents as a starting-point for ongoing explorations and reconfigurations of their own.

Reading the Illustrations

The hundred black-and-white illustrations in our first edition are now joined by the color images we've added for each period. These are very much conceived as part of the anthology's teachable material, and the extensive captions for the color images, and for many of the black-and-white ones, are intended to signal effective avenues of approach to them. Many of the images work directly with particular authors or works, but valuable points can be made with images of more general import. The cover illustrations for our two big volumes can serve as cases in point. The illustration for Volume 1, the frontispiece to John's Gospel in *The Book of Kells*, gives a haunting image from one of the masterpieces of medieval Irish art. This eighth-century manuscript testifies to richness of medieval Celtic culture and the vitality of early Irish Christianity, even as its intricate designs show the ongoing ebullience of pagan visual forms and motifs. The picture is also one of many medieval representations of books and writing. Poised to write the gospel his viewer is about to read, the Evangelist is framed within an intricate border that itself is the body of Christ—the Word of God with whom John's gospel begins. This Word-made-flesh has hands, feet, and head, yet as one modern commentator notes, he is "more suggested than described, the painter trying to convey by this device the unknowable character of God" (Françoise Henry, *The Book of Kells: Reproductions from the Manuscript in Trinity College Dublin* [Knopf, 1974], 194).

The cover to Volume 2 gives J. W. Waterhouse's painting *Destiny*. Painted in 1900, near the end of the Victorian era and at the beginning of the new century, *Destiny* shows the medieval heroine Isolde poised between her own past and future. About to sail from her native Ireland to marry King Mark of Cornwall, whom she has never met, she unwittingly drinks a love potion that will inaugurate her fatal love affair with her escort, Tristan. Waterhouse combines pre-Raphaelite medievalism with concerns that the modernists would soon make their own. Ambiguity and illusion predominate in the presentation: what at first seems to be a window is in fact a mirror, reflecting sailing ships that are behind the viewer rather than behind Isolde. Whose destiny is really being shown? In *Idylls of the King*, Tennyson had returned to Arthurian myth as a way to reflect, or refract, Victorian concerns with personal faith and faithlessness. Just one year before Waterhouse painted his picture, Conrad had evoked old ships in an imperial context in *Heart of Darkness*, having Marlow preface his tale by speaking of the Thames, "crowded with memories of men and ships it has borne. . . . from the *Golden Hind* returning with her round flanks full of treasure . . . to the *Erebus* and *Terror*, bound on other conquests." Emblematically, the book in front of Isolde turns into a globe in the mirror's reflection, as world and text intertwine.

Reading and Listening

A important addition to our anthology's resources is our new pair of audio CDs, which can show students how literature has played out in the larger aural culture of its times. Our CDs feature eloquent readings of poems and prose texts by such actors as Richard Burton and Clare Bloom, and we have commissioned recordings of several previously unrecorded works, particularly by recently rediscovered women. We also present a range of modern authors reading their own writing, from Tennyson and Yeats to Dylan Thomas, Ted Hughes, and Eavan Boland.

We also include a range of musical selections, both song settings of poems in the anthology (such as Robert Burns's beautiful A Red, Red Rose and his lusty, satiric The Fornicator) and other music that develops themes and issues in the anthology. So, for example, we include the famous Purcell setting of If Music Be the Food of Love, a poem that takes up Shakespeare's theme only to turn it on its head.

Like the anthology itself, the CDs regularly group works in teachable clusters: a speech by Queen Elizabeth on the sentencing of Mary, Queen of Scots is followed by a selection from Thomas Tallis's haunting Lamentations of Jeremiah, in which Tallis—both a loyal servant of Elizabeth and a devout Catholic—mourns Mary's fall through the figure of Jerusalem, "once a queen of provinces, now subject to others." On the second CD, stirring wartime speeches by Winston Churchill, recorded by the BBC as he delivered them, lead into selections of postwar poetry on themes of loss and endurance, including Sylvia Plath's "Lady Lazarus" with its startling use of Nazi imagery.

Individual tracks, and clusters of tracks, can be played in the classroom for a variety of purposes: to illustrate the sound of Anglo-Saxon, Middle English, and Middle Scots; to emphasize the intense drama of Shakespeare's sonnets and Robert Browning's dramatic monologues; to show directly the play of dialogue in Wilde and in Shaw; and to stimulate discussion of the ways performance entails interpretation. Students can also use the CDs as they study the works in the anthology. Most of the selections appear in the anthology itself; in some cases we have also taken the opportunity to extend the anthology's range by including a compelling recording of a work not contained in the anthology, and in these cases we include the text in the liner notes. So all these works can be studied as they are heard. Finally, the CDs are a pure pleasure simply to listen to—a salutary reminder of the degree to which literature is an art of the ear as much as it is a presence on a printed page.

In Closing, a Poem

For all the worldliness of literary study today, we never want to forget the beauty of literary language and the shaping force of literary form. One of the great pleasures of working on this anthology has been living so closely with so many beautiful works. All of the editors can testify to the ways in which our teaching, our reading, and our own writing have been invigorated by the process of work on our anthology, and nothing pleases us more than when we hear from the book's users

that teaching from it has been similarly stimulating as well. It seems fitting to close
with a poem that William Chapman Sharpe was moved to write in the course of
long summer weeks of work on his period introduction as we prepared the first
edition. I had assured my co-editors, with a mixture of naivety and guile whose proportions should perhaps be left unexplored, that this task would involve little
more than writing up an introductory lecture to a period survey course. It proved
to be much more, as you will find as you work with the period introductions and
the other editorial matter throughout the anthology. Bill's experience crystallized
in the form of this poem:

Introduction to the Victorian Period

> I bequeath days, weeks to it. The light
> stains the windows sun-green, rainy office
> gray. These are black-and-white people, written off
> as history, profiles smeared by time. Their legacy
> is inky mud, sepia and soot. Then one day, enterprise
> and moral crisis bring them round. They nudge me
> with their phobias and peccadilloes, afraid
> to eat sex, drink Darwin, not wear black.
> They beg me for some color, pale rose
> for cheekbones, a blaze of prim teeth pearly
> against tight lips–or maybe June dust gilded
> with pollen on their riding clothes, an ankle
> chafed red-raw by a stiff irreproachable boot.
> I bend in their service, try to tint the crease-lines
> of laughter, the unruly hair of ministers' wives. But
> they clamor for the whole box of crayons:
> one has a favorite crimson ribbon, another eyes
> bluer than death by cold, a third lost a child
> who brightened only when his rainbow prism
> danced faeries round the room. They importune
> now by the dozens, they get up petitions, charter
> trains, hire halls to fulminate in. Men break
> ground for brooding monuments, women chain themselves
> to the railings of my monochrome brain. What can
> I do but promise to colorize their lives if they will only
> stop their endless keening and make a poem
> Edenic as a Morris print? It's not enough. To ease
> their gloom, they make me swear
> to chromo mournful souls at Dover Beach,
> retouch the yellowed shade of Robert Browning.

This poem expresses the engrossing quality that this project has taken on for all of
us during the years we have worked together on its first and now its second edi-

tions. We expect that this new form of the anthology, revised in its selection of works and in its visual and aural accompaniments, will continue to engross its readers as well. It is certainly impossible to "cover" so much rich material in a single course, but it may be possible to *uncover* it with some real success. This companion volume can be a point of departure for the process of classroom exploration and discovery; my heartiest welcome to all who now join in teaching with the second edition of *The Longman Anthology of British Literature.*

—David Damrosch

Sample Syllabi

The purpose of this section is to offer some examples of effective approaches to different sorts of courses that can be taught with the anthology in its various versions. Given here are a two-semester survey sequence using all six period volumes (or the two big volumes); a one-semester survey using our Compact Edition; two cross-period courses that use materials from two of the period volumes together; and two focused treatments of particular themes or genres within a single period. Several of the following syllabi have been contributed by adopters of the book, whose contributions we gratefully acknowledge; others are syllabi developed by members of our editorial board as we've taught from the anthology. We have revised the sample syllabi where appropriate to take account of the new offerings in our second edition. Syllabi are presented here in summary form, for convenience, by week rather than by individual class session, and without full listings in all cases of individual works assigned from an author. Instructors also often assign the period introductions, and sometimes include individual author introductions on the syllabus as explicit assignments, though we don't show this on these summary syllabi. Each syllabus is accompanied by a version of its catalogue description or a commentary by the instructor. We plan on expanding this section of sample syllabi in the future, and would be very pleased to receive samples from anyone who would like to share their approach to teaching with the full anthology or any of its component parts. These should go to David Damrosch at the Department of English, 602 Philosophy Hall, Columbia University, New York, NY 10027, or can be sent electronically to dnd2@columbia.edu.

Page references in the following syllabi are to the starting page of a selection as it appears in the second edition of the anthology, either volumes 1A–C or 2A–C, as appropriate (or in the Compact Edition, in the case of the third sample syllabus). For the first two syllabi, items that can be heard on our audio CDs are labeled *CD.

1: A fall-semester survey of British literature, beginnings through the eighteenth century

Prof. Roxanne Kent-Drury, Northern Kentucky University.

Week 1: Introduction; Bede, 132; hyperlink to *Caedmon's Hymn*, audio version, with glosses. Wanderer, 150; Wife's Lament, 154
Week 2: *Beowulf*, 27 (*CD); hyperlink to kennings in *Beowulf*
Week 3: *Sir Gawain and the Green Knight*, 192

Week 4: *Canterbury Tales*: Prologue, 301 (*CD); Miller's Tale, 321
   hyperlink to modern translation of the selections
Week 5: "Vernacular Religion and Repression," 514; Margery Kempe, 529
Week 6: Intro to Renaissance period and to sonnet form. Wyatt (*CD) and
   Petrarch, 670; Sidney, 1043; Elizabeth I, 1078 (*CD)
Week 7: Shakespeare sonnets, 1225 (*CD)
Week 8: Lanyer, *Salve Deus Rex Judaeorum*, 1098; "Tracts on Women and
   Gender," 1496
Week 9: Metaphysical Poets: selections from Donne, 1647 (*CD), Herbert,
   1685, Phillips, 1738
Week 10: Pepys, 2086 (*CD); poetic conversations between Rochester, 2280,
   and Behn, 2130, and between Swift, 2370, and Montagu, 2568 (*CD)
Week 11: Behn, poems, 2213; Coterie Writing, 2224; Astell, *Reflections upon
   Marriage*, 2357
Week 12: Behn, *Oronooko*
Week 13: Pope, *Rape of the Lock*; *Essay on Criticism* selection (*CD)
Week 14: Gay, *The Beggar's Opera*, 2588 (*CD)
Week 15: Sheridan, *School for Scandal*, 2888

Professor Kent-Drury comments: The course is approximately half undergraduate
English majors and half students of other majors. In general, although I try to
expose students both to works and to forms they need as background to later
period courses, I avoid a monolithic "great books" approach and rely as well
upon providing "backgrounds" that highlight important cultural ideas. My
choices for the medieval period provide opportunities to analyze how
medieval ideas about religion, gender, heroism, etc. differ from those of the
present. Because of my classroom demographics, I elect not to teach a
Renaissance play; English majors will get a course in Shakespeare, whereas
teaching one Shakespeare play to non-majors is of doubtful value. Instead, I
teach the sonnet as reflective of a highly structured, hierarchical world view;
this also ensures students get some exposure to formal poetry. I am also interested in literature as a conversation and discuss literature by Behn, Finch,
Leapor, Rochester, Swift, Montagu, Pope, and Gay. My overall philosophy is
that I can't teach students everything about the periods of study, so I try to assign works that provide insight into how people perceived their worlds and
the function of literature as an imaginative space for exploring and resolving
conflict. My teaching is informed by Jean Joseph Goux's notion of "symbolic
economies"—that human institutions and relationships can be seen as negotiated through parallel systems of exchange, including the political, social, gendered, legal, religious, and monetary. Another concept I find important is
Raymond Williams' idea of the "residual" and "emergent" in culture; this idea
provides a way to approach the "strange" and the "familiar" that coexist in any
work of literature.

2: A spring-semester survey of British literature, nineteenth through twentieth centuries

Prof. Anne Fernald, Depauw University

[Course description]: 201 years in 41 days: this course needs to cover 4.8 years every time we meet. Faced with such a task, we have to consider what is truly important. This course focuses on a selection of the greatest, most exciting, and most influential writing to come out of Britain since the French Revolution. It will acquaint you with some of the major figures and works of Romantic, Victorian, modernist, postmodern, postcolonial, and contemporary literature in Britain, but it is more than just a road map or itinerary. Since we will focus on only a few representative writers each week, there will be plenty of opportunities for in-depth discussion. We will read plays, novels, short stories, nonfiction, selections from journals, some letters, and lots and lots of poetry. Through these many literary forms (and these many authors) we will develop a sense of the literature, culture, and history of Britain in the last two centuries. Themes and images—of nation and empire, of social class, of women's rights, of education, of capital, of the individual, of civic rights and duties, of war, of religion, and of beauty—will appear, disappear, and re-emerge transformed. Fifteen weeks from now, you will have a sense of both the breadth and depth of English literature in the 19th and 20th centuries.

Week 1: Selections from "Perspectives: The Rights of Man and the Revolution Controversy," 56 (Burke, Wollstonecraft, and Paine) and from "Perspectives: The Abolition of Slavery," 159 (Equiano, Prince); Barbauld, "Mouse's Petition" (*CD); Dorothy Wordsworth, *The Grasmere Journals*, 478; William Wordsworth, several Lyrical Ballads, 337 (*CD)

Week 2: Wordsworth, "Tintern Abbey," Immortality Ode, 454; Coleridge, poems, 520; "Perspectives: The Sublime, the Beautiful, and the Picturesque," 496

Week 3: Shelley, "Mont Blanc," 754, "Ode to the West Wind, " 771; Keats poems and letters, 877 (*CD)

Week 4: "Perspectives: The Industrial Landscape," 104; Dickens, *Hard Times* (new Longman Cultural Edition)

Week 5: E. B. Browning, Sonnets from the Portugese, 1108, Aurora Leigh, 1112 (*CD); Tennyson, poems, 1146 (*CD); Arnold, "Dover Beach," 1551

Week 6: Hopkins, several poems, 1679; Wilde, "Decay of Lying," preface to *Dorian Gray*, Aphorisms, *De Profundis*, 1864ff.; (*CD for Wilde and Gilbert and Sullivan)

Week 7: Secret lives: Kipling, "Without Benefit of Clergy," 1749; Stevenson, *The Strange Case of Dr Jekyll and Mr Hyde*, 1821

Week 8: Yeats, poems, 2246 (*CD); Joyce, "Araby" and "The Dead," 2274; *CD for Joyce reading "Anna Livia Plurabelle"

Week 9: "Vorticist Manifesto," 2169, Rebecca West, "Indissoluble
Matrimony," 2594, Wilfred Owen, poems, 2188, T. S. Eliot, "The Waste
Land," 2356 (*CD)
Week 10: Virginia Woolf, *Mrs Dalloway*, 2386 (*CD)
Week 11: "Perspectives: Regendering Modernism" (Forster, Rhys), 2582;
D. H. Lawrence, poems and "Odour of Chrysanthemums," 2640.
Week 12: Dylan Thomas, *Return Journey*, 2762; Beckett, *Krapp's Last Tape*, 2771
Week 13: Tsitsi Dangarembga, *Nervous Conditions* (separately ordered novel)
Week 14: Walcott, "The Fortunate Traveller," 2951; Caryl Churchill, *Cloud
Nine*, 2839

3: A one-semester survey, beginnings through the twentieth century, using the Compact Edition

Prof. Anne Schotter, Wagner College

[Course description]: What constitutes the canon of English literature, and
who decides? What were the literary consequences of Britain's complex colonial past, starting as a land invaded and conquered (by Germanic tribes, the
Vikings, and the Normans), growing to be a world empire that colonized
others, and recently, losing the empire but leaving the English language to its
former subjects? In this long history of military conflict, what role did women
play? The themes of love and war and love as war will help to focus these
questions as we survey over a thousand years of British literature, reading such
classics as *Beowulf*, *Paradise Lost*, and *Emma*, as well as postcolonial writers such as
Seamus Heaney and Derek Walcott.

Week 1: *Beowulf*, 27; *Judith*, 94; "The Wanderer," 104; "Wulf and Eadwacer,"
107; "The Wife's Lament," 108
Week 2: "Arthurian Myth and the History of Britain," 109; *Sir Gawain and
the Green Knight*, 143
Week 3: Chaucer, *Canterbury Tales*, General Prologue, 220, Wife of Bath's
Tale, 275
Week 4: Shakespeare, *King Lear* (Longman Cultural Edition)
Week 5: Donne, poems, 665 Lovelace, poems, 683; Marvell, "To His Coy
Mistress," 677, "Horatian Ode upon Cromwell's Return," 691; Horace,
three Odes (xeroxed)
Week 6: Milton, selections from *Paradise Lost*, 785
Week 7: Pope, "The Rape of the Lock," 1165; Swift, "A Modest Proposal,"
1138
Week 8: "Perspectives: The Rights of Man" and Wollstonecraft, selections
from the *Vindication of the Rights of Woman*, 1471
Week 9: Jane Austen, *Pride and Prejudice* (Longman Cultural Edition)
Week 10: Poems by Blake, 1389, Wordsworth, 1520, and Shelley, 1702
Week 11: Poems by Keats, 1749, Tennyson, 1922, Browning, 1957, and
Arnold, 2020

Week 12: Poems by Wilfred Owen, 2301; Horace Ode III.2 (xerox); Eliot, "The Waste Land," 2425

Week 13: Two stories by Virginia Woolf, plus selections from A Room of One's Own, 2445; Joyce, "The Dead," 2362

Week 14: Yeats, poems, 2327; "Perspectives: Whose Language?" selections from Heaney, Ní Dhomhnaill, and Walcott, 2575ff.

4: A one-semester survey of medieval and early modern literature, using vols. 1A and 1B

Prof. Linda Troost, Washington and Jefferson College

Week 1: Early Irish verse, 111; *Judith*, 120; *Dream of the Rood*, 125; *Beowulf*, 27

Week 2: *Gawain and the Green Knight*, 192; Marie de France: *Lanval*, 179

Week 3: Chaucer, *Canterbury Tales*: Prologue, 301; Wife of Bath, 337; Pardoner, 384

Week 4: *Second Play of the Shepherds*, 488, and *York Play of the Crucifixion*, 507

Week 5: Middle English Lyrics, 549; Dunbar, Lament for the Makars; 588; Malory, "The Day of Destiny," 269; Late Medieval Allegory, 597: John Lydgate and Christine de Pizan

Week 6: Sidney, *Astrophil and Stella*, 1043, Spenser, *Amoretti*, 954; *Faerie Queene* opening canto, 793

Week 7: *Faerie Queene*, continued

Week 8: Marlowe, *Faustus*, 1143; Shakespeare, sonnets, 1225;

Week 9: Shakespeare, *The Tempest*, 1292; "Perspectives: England in the New World," 1354

Week 10: Jonson, "To Penshurst," 1630; Lanyer, "Description of Cookham," 1093; Jonson, *The Alchemist*, 1530

Week 11: Mary Herbert, psalms, 1072; Donne, lyrics and Holy Sonnets, 1662; Herbert poems, 1686; Herrick, secular and religious poems, 1674, Marvell lyrics, 1726

Week 12: Lecture on the Civil Wars and the Interregnum. Katherine Phillips, "Upon the Double Murder of King Charles," 1741; Marvell, "Horatian Ode upon Cromwell's Return from Ireland," 1735; Milton, early poetry, 1812

Week 13: Milton, *Paradise Lost*, Books 1–2, 1836

Week 14: *Paradise Lost*, selections from Books 4, 9, and 12. "Perspectives: Spiritual Self-Reckonings," 2029

Professor Troost comments: This course emphasizes the importance of the intellectual climate of the past on a text. We try to read the works as someone from the time might have read them and focus on issues that were central at the time (as opposed to emphasizing issues that are central in our own time). Since Christianity pervades British culture and politics, I have included a fair bit of religious material so that the students get some grounding (I do not expect them to know too much about medieval Roman Catholic doctrine). I have placed Anglo-Saxon religious poetry like "Judith" and "The Dream of the Rood" before pagan heroic verse to drive home the point that the audience for *Beowulf* was Christian. The medieval plays, Book 1 of *The Faerie Queene*, and lyric poems lead us to the Everest of religious literature: *Paradise Lost*. I want students to understand that the writers work within traditions, not vacuums, so we consider European literary fashions and the English authors who write in them. We study the Arthurian romance of the Gawain poet, Marie de France, and Malory; the Petrarchan tradition developed in the love sonnets of Sidney and Spenser; the Ruins-of-Time (as well as the anti-Petrarchan) tradition developed in Shakespeare's sonnets; neoclassical "imitation" in Donne ("The Apparition") and Jonson ("To Penshurst"), and metaphysical poetry (Donne and Herbert). Finally, I wish to make clear to the students that literature adapts itself to a changing society. We see drama reshape itself to accommodate political and financial pressures, as well as respond to particular political events: the conquest of the Spanish Armada (*Doctor Faustus*), for example. We see various power bases depicted in poetry and drama: the landed ("To Penshurst," "To Cookham") and the mercantile (*The Canterbury Tales* and *The Alchemist*) showing us that the monarch's court does not have the lock on patronage. The final weeks of the course follow the contradictory impulses authors and audiences grappled with during the Civil Wars, the Commonwealth, and the Restoration. I finish with *Paradise Lost*, partly because of the wonderful momentum that teaching the work creates, but also because it pulls together the many threads woven into the course.

5: A 10-week survey of medieval and early modern literature, using vols. 1A and 1B

Prof. Renée Pigeon, California State University, Santa Barbara. First part of a three-quarter sequence.

[Course description]: This course is a general introduction to English literature from the early Middle Ages to 1640. Because it is a survey course encompassing several centuries of literature, it allows students to sample some of the great works of the Middle Ages and the Renaissance, and to develop a broad sense of the historical and intellectual context of the works read, providing the background necessary for more specialized study. The web page for this course is located at http://mail.csusb.edu/~rpigeon/230.html.

Week 1: "The Wanderer," 150; *Beowulf*, Introduction and lines 1–1883, pp. 27ff.
Week 2: Chaucer, *Canterbury Tales*: General Prologue, 301; Miller's Tale and Merchant's Tale (Coghill translation, Penguin discount)
Week 3: *Canterbury Tales*: Knight's Tale; *Sir Gawain and the Green Knight*, 192
Week 4: *Gawain* continued; Marie de France, *Lanval*, 179; Dafydd ap Gwilym, poems, 579
Week 5: Poems by Wyatt, 670, Raleigh, 1092, and Marlowe, 1124; Spenser, *Faerie Queene*, Book 1, Letter & Cantos 1–2 (790)

Week 6: *Faerie Queene*, continued
Week 7: Sidney, *Arcadia*, 1009; Shakespeare, Sonnets, 1225
Week 8: "Perspectives: Tracts on Women & Gender," 1496; Whitney, poems,
1051; Jonson, poems, 1628
Week 9: Poems by Donne, 1648, Wroth, 1669, Herrick, 1674, Marvell, 1726
Week 10: Browne, from *Religio Medici*, 1767; Burton, from *Anatomy of
Melancholy*, 1771; Milton, "L'Allegro," "Il Penseroso," sonnets, and selec-
tions from *Areopagitica* (1812-35)

6: A course focused on Victorian Poetry and Criticism, using Volume 2B

Prof. William Sharpe, Barnard College

[Course description]: This course is designed to explore the changing position
of poets and artists in modern society, and particularly their participation in
the construction of the elaborate gender roles and social codes we know today
as "Victorian." Special emphasis will be given to the interaction between the visual arts, literature, and their social context.

Week 1: Poems by Tennyson, 1139; paintings by Millais and Hunt; drawings
from the Moxon edition of Tennyson's poems
Week 2: Poems by Tennyson, including selections from *Idylls of the King*,
1196, and *In Memoriam*, 1165; photographs by Julia Margaret Cameron;
paintings by Morris, Burne-Jones, and others
Week 3: Robert Browning, poems, 1308
Week 4: Nightingale, "Cassandra," 1498; selections from "Perspectives:
Victorian Ladies and Gentlemen," 1515; Mill, from *The Subjection of
Women* and "Statement Repudiating the Rights of Husbands" (1095)
Week 5: E. B. Browning, *Aurora Leigh* (entire; Penguin discount)
Week 6: *Aurora Leigh*, continued, plus selected *Sonnets from the Portuguese*,
1108; Matthew Arnold, poems, 1550; selections from Clough in
"Perspectives: Religion and Science," 1283
Week 7: Arnold, poems, 1550; selections from "The Study of Poetry," 1593.
Slide lecture on pre-Raphaelitism and painting
Week 8: Dante G. Rossetti, poems, 1601. Pre-Raphaelitism and photography:
photographs by Julia Margaret Cameron, C. L. Dodgson, and others;
photos of Jane Morris posed by Rossetti
Week 9: Christina Rossetti, poems, 1612. Illustrations by Dante Gabriel
Rossetti. William Morris, poems, 1634, Guenevere (painting), wallpaper
and fabric patterns, stained glass, furniture, book design
Week 10: Swinburne, poems, 1652
Week 11: Hopkins, poems, 1679. Walter Pater, from *The Renaissance*, 1665.
Visual Arts: Neo-classicism to Art Nouveau
Week 12: Whistler, from "Mr. Whistler's 'Ten O' Clock' " in "Perspectives:
Aestheticism, Decadence, and the Fin de Siècle," 1945; paintings by
Whistler, including "Symphonies," "Arrangements," and "Nocturnes."

W. S. Gilbert, "If You're Anxious for to Shine in the High Aesthetic
Line" (1943, and on CD)

Week 13: Wilde, poems and selections from "The Decay of Lying" and from
"The Soul of Man Under Socialism"; Preface to *The Picture of Dorian
Gray*, Aphorisms, excerpts from the trials (1862ff). Selections from
"Perspectives: Aestheticism, Decadence, and the *Fin de Siècle*" (Alfred
Douglas, Arthur Symons, "Michael Field," etc)

Week 14: Bram Stoker, *Dracula* (separately ordered)

7: An upper-level course on "Modernism and Its Enemies," using Volume 2C:

Prof. David Damrosch, Columbia University

[Course description]: British modernism was less a movement than a series of
heated arguments. This course will explore the aesthetic and cultural stakes in
the radically varied constructions of modernity by such opposed figures as
Woolf versus Bennett, Barnes versus Woolf, Wilde versus Shaw, Kipling versus
Conrad, Conrad versus Wells, Eliot versus Hardy, *Blast* versus itself. Texts will
be *The Longman Anthology of British Literature*, volume 2C, plus three novels
(Wells, *Tono-Bungay*; Bennett, *Riceyman Steps*; Barnes, *Nightwood*). In addition, a
photocopied course pack will include essays, reviews, and letters by authors
commenting on one another.

1: Aestheticism, Decadence, and Realism
  Week 1: Poems by Wilde, Douglas, Yeats, and Field; Kipling, "Without
    Benefit of Clergy," Beerbohm, "Enoch Soames" (all xeroxed; or avail-
    able in vol 2B of the anthology)
  Week 2: Wilde, preface to *Dorian Gray*; "The Decay of Lying"; *Salomé*
    (coursepack)
  Week 3: Conrad, preface to *The Nigger of the 'Narcissus,'* 2018; *Heart of
    Darkness*, 2020; Henry Morton Stanley on the Congo, 2076, Woolf on
    Conrad (coursepack)

2: Conflicts: Class, Gender, and the Great War
  Week 4: H. G. Wells, *Tono-Bungay*; Wells on Conrad, James, and Bennett
    (coursepack)
  Week 5: Shaw, *Pygmalion*, 2085; P. G. Wodehouse, "Strychnine in the
    Soup," 2675
  Week 6: *Blast*: Vorticist Manifesto, 2169, Rebecca West, "Indissoluble
    Matrimony," 2594. War poems by Hardy (2161), Brooke, Sassoon,
    Rosenberg, and Owen (2183ff)

3: The Heights of Modernism
  Week 7: Yeats, poems, 224; Eliot, "The Waste Land," 2356; David Jones,
    from *In Parenthesis*, 2195; Auden, "In Memory of W. B. Yeats," 2790

Week 8: Joyce, *Dubliners* stories, 2274, and "Nausicaa," 2312. Forster, "The Life to Come," 2583; Rhys, "Mannequin," 2626

Week 9: Essays pro and con: Eliot, "Tradition and the Individual Talent," 2374; Arthur Waugh, "Cleverness and the New Poetry," 2350; Pound, "Drunken Helots and Mr Eliot," 2352; Lawrence, "Surgery for the Novel—or a Bomb," 2671; Woolf, "Mr Bennett and Mrs Brown" (coursepack); Bennett, reviews of the modern novel (coursepack)

Week 10: Woolf, *Mrs Dalloway*, 2386; excerpts from *Diaries*, 2535

Week 11: Arnold Bennett, *Riceyman Steps* (Penguin)

4: Afterechoes

Week 12: Djuna Barnes, *Nightwood* (Faber, with Eliot's preface)

Week 13: Joyce, selections from *Finnegans Wake*, 2338; Wyndham Lewis, from *Time and Western Man* (coursepack); Beckett, *Krapp's Last Tape*, 2771, and "Texts for Nothing," 2777

Week 14: Graham Greene, "A Chance for Mr Lever," 2688; Caryl Churchill, *Cloud Nine*, 2839

The Middle Ages

Before the Norman Conquest

Beowulf

Students are often intrigued to learn that the author of *The Hobbit* and *The Lord of the Rings*, J. R. R. Tolkien, was a medievalist who drew inspiration from *Beowulf* for his fictions. In fact, his classic article, "*Beowulf*: the Monsters and the Critics" (1936), which insists on the poem's aesthetic coherence, set the tone for criticism of the poem for almost fifty years. Such coherence is rather elusive to first-time readers, students and professors alike, and much ingenuity has gone into demonstrating it. Fred C. Robinson argues that despite its disconnected appearance, the poem implies meaning through its juxtaposition of its most minute parts: "the compounds, the grammatical appositions, the metrical line with its apposed hemistichs" (*Beowulf and the Appositive Style*, [1985], 24–25).

The view of *Beowulf* as a highly-wrought work of art would seem to presuppose a literate and self-conscious poet. The literacy of the *Beowulf*-poet, however, was challenged by the proponents of the "oral-formulaic" theory adapted from Homeric studies, which held that the poem was orally composed by an illiterate bard or "scop," who would have had neither the learning nor leisure to strive for literary effects. Although much controversy raged betwen proponents of these two views in the 1960s and '70s, it is now generally agreed to have been a false dichotomy: a poem can be formulaic without having been orally composed, and therefore can have been artistically shaped by a literate poet.

Nevertheless, an understanding of *Beowulf*'s oral background can help students to understand many of its most puzzling aspects. Its structural use of alliteration, which Tim Murphy's translation captures brilliantly, would have been a mnemonic aid to a poet who performed, if he did not compose, orally. Students should understand the poem as being orally performed, to an audience of aristocrats or clerics; they should experience it themselves, preferably in Old English; Tim Murphy reads the poem's concluding dirge, both in Anglo-Saxon and in his translation, on our audio CD. Finally, the poem's oral origins help to explain its digressive, non-linear style, the feature that students find most difficult.

Whatever the origins of *Beowulf*'s digressive style, there are a number of fruitful ways to analyze it. New Critics have shown the relevance of apparent digressions to the main thread of the narrative, by way of comparison and contrast or foreshadowing and echo. The visual art of the period also provides stylistic analogies. John Leyerle shows that the poem's interwoven strands of narrative can be understood as "the visual analogue of the interlace designs common in Anglo-Saxon art," particularly in manuscript illumination, metal work, and stone carving (rpt. in R. D. Fulk, ed., *Interpretations of Beowulf: A Critical Anthology*, [1991], 146). His illustrations include the gold belt buckle from the Sutton Hoo ship burial and the so-called carpet pages from the Lindisfarne Gospels. More recently, recognition of the mutual influence of Celtic and Anglo-Saxon art suggests that the patterns in the Ardagh chalice (color plate 3) and the Book of Kells are equally relevant examples of the "Insular" or "Hiberno-Saxon" interlace style (see p. 10).

Another aspect of *Beowulf* which causes confusion for students is its apparently conflicting references to Christianity and paganism. Scholarly discussion of this has ranged from the earlier contention that the Christian "coloring" contaminates the pagan Germanic purity of the epic to the argument that the poem is a full-fledged Christian allegory, with the hero either a figure of Christ or a deeply flawed materialist, unaware of the transience of earthly wealth and glory. At present, the poem is most often seen as thoroughly Christian, but literal rather than allegorical, with the poet looking back with regret at his pagan ancestors of centuries earlier, admiring their nobility while recognizing their ultimate damnation.

Although the New Critical tendency to resolve the contradictions in *Beowulf* is useful for teaching, it has been recently questioned by critics influenced by post-structuralism, who see it as imposing more coherence on the poem than is actually there. Rather than look for balance and closure in the poem, they stress its anomalies and discontinuities, as well as the social and historical context in which it was produced. Gillian Overing, in *Language, Sign, and Gender in Beowulf* (1990), links the poem's non-linear style to "the irresolution and dynamism of the deconstructionist free play of textual elements" and suggests teaching students to deconstruct the binary, hierarchical oppositions in the poem, such as Christian and pagan, good and bad, weak and strong. In the process of challenging formalist readings of the poem, some critics are returning to earlier approaches such as philology and literary history. Teachers may want to stress the poem's status as a product of a manuscript culture, starting with the miracle of its survival in The British Library manuscript Cotton Vitellius A. xv, and the difficulty of deciphering it through the burn marks. Its manuscript context points to an interest in tales of the exotic and the monstrous on the part of the compiler and his audience. Joseph Harris argues that *Beowulf* itself is an anthology of genres like the *Canterbury Tales*, reflecting the poet's reading of earlier literature. A recognition that the poem contains "genealogical verse, a creation hymn, elegies, a lament, a heroic lay, a praise poem, historical poems, a flyting, gnomic verse, a sermon, and perhaps less formal oral genres," then, should serve as an antidote to fixation on the poem's "unity" (in Fulk, 236).

A recent approach to *Beowulf* which takes social context into account is feminist criticism. Critics may disagree as to whether the women are presented as heroic or victimized, but they all agree that the role of women is important to the poem. Overing, among others, discusses their status as "peaceweavers," which she sees as mere objects of exchange: "the system of masculine alliance allows women to signify in a system of apparent exchange, but there is no place for them outside this chain of signification; they must be continually translated by and into the masculine economy" (p. xxiii). Both male and female students are often drawn to the feminist approach because it addresses the way female experience is slighted in this most masculine of epics.

Beowulf can be effectively taught with other works in a medieval literature course or a British literature survey. In the Old English period, it can be linked not only with such heroic Christian works as Judith and The Dream of the Rood, but also with The Wanderer, whose concentration on the dark side of heroic violence links it to Beowulf's elegiac passages, such as the elegy of the "last survivor." Wulf and Eadwacer and The Wife's Lament, elegies which focus specifically on the effect of such violence on women, can illuminate such doomed women as Wealhtheow and Freawaru, as well as the tragic Hildeburh.

In the Early Modern period, two major works which offer comparison with Beowulf are Hamlet and Paradise Lost, both of which criticize the heroic code. Hamlet, which derives in part from a Germanic heroic legend recorded in the twelfth-century Saxo Grammaticus' Historia Danica, can be read as the story of a Renaissance university student resisting an injunction to fulfill a pre-Christian code of blood vengeance. In Paradise Lost, the tension is between Renaissance Christian values and the ancient Greek heroic code, represented by Satan, who mouths the sentiments of Achilles. Although Beowulf also criticizes the code of vengeance, it does so with considerably more ambivalence.

While Beowulf is less likely to be taught with twentieth-century works than with medieval and Renaissance ones, familiarity with them can serve as a useful point of comparison for upper-level English majors. Experience with Woolf's or Joyce's "stream-of-consciousness" technique might incline students to patience with Beowulf's non-linear style. Students might also be interested to know that Joyce makes a connection between his narrative technique and Insular manuscript style when he writes of the Book of Kells, "some of the big initial letters which swing right across a page have the essential quality of a chapter of Ulysses. Indeed, you can compare much of my work to the intricate illuminations."

The Táin bó Cuailnge

For all the challenge of its antiquity and alien culture, The Táin speaks easily to modern readers in its evocation of epic battle, heroic achievement, struggle for social prestige, and tragically divided loyalties. Yet The Táin may be most useful in the classroom as a moment in which to reconsider our acquired expectations of "literature," and to explore the encounter of orality and literacy. And in its celebration of pagan society and its series of influential women, it offers a kind of epic strikingly different from the elegiac, largely male-dominated world of Beowulf.

Origins: Pagan Tale and Clerical Transmission The selections of The Táin in this anthology are translated from a version ("Recension II") first written down in the early twelfth century, in the "Book of Leinster." That manuscript contains a fascinating collection including ecclesiastical texts, as well as secular material such as the story discussed in the editorial headnote, and an Irish translation of a Trojan War narrative attributed to "Dares the Phrygian." It reflects the extent to which vernacular, secular culture in Ireland, whose stories often carried distant echoes of a pagan past, had achieved a rapprochement with Christian institutions and the technology of writing that they had promoted.

The rapprochement of pagan and Christian cultures developed across the centuries as the church encountered a long-established and socially prestigious class of native scholars, some of whom entered clerical orders; and it aided the survival of a large body of ancient traditional learning, mostly derived from oral sources, that embraces law, mythology, and epic such as *The Táin*. Ambivalence toward native Irish culture remained, though, nicely implied in this quote from the late eighth-century *Martyrology of Oengus*: "Paganism has been destroyed though it was splendid and far flung." Consider too the double closing to *The Táin*. Despite this final note, the tale itself is fully engaged in its pagan, secular world. This might be contrasted with the echoes of the Old Testament in *Beowulf*, and its persistently elegiac regret for a world long lost.

The Táin derives from stories of gods, heroic cattle raids, and symbolic beasts that stretch back perhaps as far as the early centuries A.D., orally transmitted by generations of the Irish learned class. Some scholars think that an early, now lost version of *The Táin* may have been copied even in the seventh century during a flurry of vernacular writing prompted by a period of plague and social upheaval. It has had a huge influence on later Irish literature, both topically and in exaggerations of the highly adjectival, somewhat florid style of "Recension II".

The Keeper of the Tales   The hero Fergus (discussed below) is at once a warrior and poet/prophet in *The Táin*, which only reflects how important was the class of men and women who preserved and transmitted the stories and social lore of medieval Ireland. Their place is made explicit in a passage from an eighth-century legal collection, the *Senchas Már* ("The Great Old Knowledge"):

> The *Senchas* of the men of Ireland, what has sustained it? The joint memory of the old men, transmission from one ear to another, the chanting of the *filid*, supplementation from the law of the letter, strengthening from the law of nature, for these are the three rocks on which are based the judgments of the world.

This provides a nice framework for discussion of the emerging position of writing in a still largely oral culture. It is difficult to re-imagine today a society in which the tale-teller had so eminent a place. In a society finely attuned to public pride and shame, the *fili*'s praise recorded and upheld a king's prestige, but equally, his satire and malediction had the power to undo it.

The *filid* are tale-tellers, keepers of cultural memory and hence social order; to call them poets inadequately conveys the range of their roles. Indeed, most medieval Irish tales that survive through writing are largely in prose, with poetry used at moments of great emotion, prophecy, or eulogy. At the same time, "Recension II" may be influenced by writing (and by the declining need for strict memorization) in its occasionally florid style, tending to pile up synonymous or almost synonymous nouns and adjectives. Nonetheless, *The Táin* retains many elements of its oral background: formulae, dialogues formalized through repetition and refrain, key phrases repeated verbatim (like the boasts of Ailill and Medb), structurally identical descriptions of warbands and their leaders.

Epic and Heroism   *The Táin* has epic force both in its evocation of military glory and in its historical reach and geographical breadth, covering much of the northern half of Ireland. The lists and apparent digressions that are equally part of its epic reach, though, can frustrate students. One might sketch out the epic genre first as a kind of oral encyclopedia, with catalogs of genealogy, geography, battle cohorts, etc. Narrative aside, what bodies of knowledge get raised as the story proceeds? Consider Medb's genealogy or her brief summary of her courtship, the review of a king's property, the catalogs of the Connacht and Ulster forces, or the verbal map of the march toward Ulster. These lists and apparent digressions can then be understood as part of the way *The Táin* draws together a system of values and knowledge for a whole society, a project even more ambitious than its narrative.

The narrative itself has epic dimension, as two great alliances slowly move toward a climactic battle. *The Táin*, however, is unlike many epics of race or empire that students may know (like the *Iliad* and *Aeneid*), in the ambitions that animate it. *The Táin* is an epic of raid, not of territorial expansionism or a whole people's might. Its tribal kings, whose highest claim is to dominate a province, gain their prestige by the control of movable wealth, especially cattle, and by triumphing in combats that are highly ritualized, though often mortal. Narrative discontinuities, like the shift from a competition between Ailill and Medb to their joint foray against Ulster, make richer (if not clearer) sense seen as an anatomy of the sources of power and glory in early Irish society.

The impulse to create a long, more or less continuous and self-contained narrative, though, may also reflect influences that arrived in Ireland through writing and the church. Before the Carolingian revival on the continent, Ireland was the center of clerical learning in northern Europe, including study of Latin secular literature. As noted above, the "Book of Leinster" contains a story of the Trojan War in Irish; and in the period that produced "Recension II" clerical scholars were also retelling Virgil's *Aeneid* and Statius's *Thebaid* in Irish. The latter, with its story of military alliances and strife between close relatives, could have been particularly resonant for an audience of *The Táin*.

Cú Chulainn   Individual heroic figures, though, both men and women, provide the crucial focus for *The Táin's* sense of glory, and for a poignancy that sometimes borders on the tragic. Chief among these is Cú Chulainn. Consider the complex and multiple sources of his power. It certainly includes magic in weapons like the *ga bulga*, and superhuman strength, but also (in episodes not included here) arcane knowledge of taboos and writing, and diplomatic skill in negotiating a series of single encounters. Cú Chulainn first enters with his description by the woman poet, Feidelm. Feidelm's poem emphasizes Cú Chulainn's youth and beauty, but also mentions the monstrous transformation that comes upon "the distorted one" in his battle rage.

Cú Chulainn compares interestingly to other large or heroic figures in epic. Like Beowulf he protects a weakened realm; but like Grendel too he is at moments monstrous, capable of uncontrolled violence. His powers in battle are often compared to those of Achilles. Like Hercules, he has qualities of the trickster (and, elsewhere, an enormous sexual appetite), yet lapses into excess and frenzy. His emphatic boyishness, and the Ulstermen's slow recovery from their torpor, may link him to a seasonal god of the returning year. Whatever remnants of pagan divinity may reside in his character, though, Cú Chulainn's appeal is thoroughly human. This may be clearest when he is badly wounded, physically restrained from battle, and calls upon his charioteer, who gives him news of the conflict in a series of dialogues that are at once highly formalized and very intimate ("friend Láeg," "little Cú"). Yet note how this same narrative strand ends when Cú Chulainn bursts his restraints with an explosive force that literally alters the landscape.

Cú Chulainn is a continuous presence in Irish legend and literature, increasingly a unifying national hero as Irish resistance to British colonialism grew. He appears in many retellings of ancient legend produced during the Irish Renaissance (by Lady Gregory and W. B. Yeats, for instance). This adoption of an Ulster hero by the entire Irish Republic is reflected in the statue of Cú Chulainn, commemorating the Easter Uprising of 1916, now in the General Post Office in Dublin. Frank McCourt treats Cú Chulainn worship more humorously in his recent memoire *Angela's Ashes*.

Medb Equally powerful is Medb, the queen of Connacht who sparks the entire conflict as she seeks to equal her husband's wealth by obtaining the Brown Bull of Cooley. She and other women such as Feidelm dominate many episodes in *The Táin*. Medb echoes an Irish goddess of sovereignty through whose power Ailill became king of Connacht. She is often seen purely as an amoral figure, a source of conflict both military and sexual, stemming from her semi-divine origin. What about her motivation, then, of achieving equal status with Ailill?

Medb's ambition, while extravagant, is coherent with the position of some women, especially heiresses, in the clan society of early medieval Ireland. While women had little status in the highly developed system of law, they did have inheritance rights within the clan, especially in the absence of a son (as in Medb's case). Further, social prestige and power within marriage were closely connected to wealth, primarily estimated in terms of cattle. So the somewhat comic "pillow talk" with which "Recension II" opens is also a scene of Medb laying serious claim to equal power in the marriage, which she is then unable to prove through equal possessions. Medb's sexual history has a considerable political logic as well. As the ex-wife of the Ulster king Conchobor, she may reflect the shift of dynastic power toward the kings of Connacht; her affair with the warrior poet Fergus is crucial to retaining his allegiance; and she offers her body (and other rewards) to the owner of the Brown Bull of Cooley before she resorts to armed force.

Fergus Perhaps the most complex heroic figure in *The Táin* is Fergus mac Róig. In some ways a secondary character, Fergus is at once a warrior and poet-prophet, and an exile with poignantly divided loyalties. Once king of Ulster, Fergus was deposed and then further betrayed by his clansman Conchobor. He fled to Connacht and entered the clientship and service of Ailill, whom he serves both as a fighter and an interpreter of mysteries. The events of the *Táin* are a slow crisis of loyalties for Fergus, torn between the bonds of clan and clientship. As was the case with Medb, this enacts, on a heroic scale, a real conflict inherent in the ordering of early medieval society in Ireland. Finally Fergus encounters his own foster-son, Cú Chulainn. That bond of family triumphs, Fergus turns from the battle, and Medb's allies from beyond Connacht go with him. To an extent, then, the epic turns on this moment of Fergus recalling the profound emotional links of fosterage, even within a clan whose leader has betrayed him.

Geography and Nature *The Táin* has a rich sense of geography, and of places becoming saturated with meaning from the events that occur upon them. In legend, Ireland was divided into five provinces ruled by high kings: Ulster in the northeast, and (counter-clockwise) Connacht, Munster in the south and Leinster in the southeast, with Meath—politically a somewhat vague area—toward the center. These provincial divisions correspond more to notions of cosmic order, and legends of prehistoric settlement, than to historical reality. Both centers and boundaries take on great symbolic importance. Cú Chulainn's heroism is established as he protects the borders of Ulster; and then the climactic battle of *The Táin* occurs toward the center of the island, in Meath between the rivers Shannon and Boyne. The human story subsides as Medb's forces retreat into Connacht, only to be followed by a sort of coda in which the two great bulls fight and the loser's body is deposited in pieces across Ireland. One episode after another results in the naming of a place, as if the story itself called the places into being.

Natural beings too are perceived, though unsentimentally, as agents of power and beauty, from the bulls (possibly an echo of bull-worship), to the natural forces by which the Ulster army is described, to the painstaking descriptions of Feidelm and Cú Chulainn. Totemic animals are present, too, as in the very name of Cú Chulainn, "the Hound of Culann," given him as a boy when he had miraculously killed the savage watchdog of Culann and then volunteered to guard Culann's property in its place.

Epic and Social Order We already noted that the epic enfolds certain norms of social order in early medieval Ireland (many of which survived into the era of "Recension II"), and thus validates them through heroic exemplars and antiquity: clientship, the links of wealth and rank, prestige gained through combat. It also explores tensions inherent within that social order, such as the conflict between clientship and clan loyalty. *The Táin* is dense with such occasions.

Early Irish social order was almost entirely rural, organized by kinship groups or chiefdoms, as many as 150 at the beginning of the Christian era, with no larger political structure except for a vague idea of high kings. Each such *túath* was headed by a petty king, chosen by election (aided by force) among any men related within four generations to an earlier king. The king gained followers, even from beyond his clan, by entering into client relationships, usually through the loan of cattle in exchange for services and the ultimate return of the loan. The power of the king hence resided in his cattle, and was increased either through clientship or cattle raiding. This system of wealth and military prestige is enacted in *The Táin*, especially in the crisis of rank in the comparison of Medb's and Ailill's cattle, and the extended raid that ensues.

This however is only the core of a range of ways that society is modelled within the epic. Others include fosterage, the bride-price, a marital system much broader and more flexible than that sponsored by the church, and the complex obligations of guest and host. If *The Táin* enfolds much of its pre-Christian mythic past, it also uses the glamor of heroism and legend to underwrite social power in its own era.

Early Irish Verse

For all their cultural distance, the early medieval Irish poems selected here speak to us in very direct ways in their wit, affection, and rueful longing for times and people lost. I have found, too, that their directness and relative brevity make a good change for students who have just weathered *Beowulf* or the *Táin*. Except for "The Old Woman of Beare," all are short enough to read in class. This is useful since, as I suggest below, each of these poems offers a rich context and comparison for texts from much different places and times in the Middle Ages.

While they are a wide-ranging group, several of these poems can be approached as versions of elegy, "Findabair Remembers Fróech" speaking for erotic loss (and the sheer beauty of Fróech), and "A Grave Marked with Ogam" coming from the tradition of heroic lament. Each offers a version of solitude, looking back at two kinds of joyous companionship. Combining all these themes, and much more, "The Old Woman of Beare" is one of the most powerful and unflinching evocations of old age and mortality in any language. The fearfulness of the survivor can be compared with that in the Old English "The Wanderer" (pp. 150-53) and Taliesin's "The War-Band's Return" (pp. 148-49).

By contrast, solitude can be a pleasure in other poems here that are linked by their fascination with the written word: its acquisition, the technology of its transmission, and the challenge of its interpretation. "To Crinog" has aspects of riddle. Crinog is at once the poet's former lover, a wise crone, and a chaste friend, but in all forms she is a teacher. Taken all together, her attributes suggest she is a book, perhaps a primer or prayer book, which were often the same thing. Yet even tough manuscript books can fall apart; both the poet and the book face their mortality at the poem's end. "A Grave Marked with Ogam" and "Writing in the Wood" feature two kinds of writing, in stone and on parchment. And "Pangur the Cat" plays on the delights of the difficult, the skill of unwrapping a textual problem, like the cat on its hunt. The pleasure these poems take in indirection and technical skill bears comparison with the Anglo-Latin and Anglo-Saxon riddles later in this volume.

The episodes from *The Voyage of Máel Dúin* (here in their slightly cryptic, evocative verse form) offer a Christianized version of a long tradition of secular narratives of miraculous voyages. The encounters with the uncanny compare effectively with those in Arthurian works in this anthology, especially Marie de France's *Lanval*, which Marie explicitly claims to have come from the Celtic world of the Breton *lai*. At the same time, Máel Dúin receives a kind of moral test and education in the course of his quest, comparable to that received by Gawain in *Sir Gawain and the Green Knight*.

The longest and richest of these early Irish poems is "The Old Woman of Beare." The challenge and beauty of the poem lies in the unresolved complexity of the speaker. She is one of a powerful group of female figures and voices in medieval Irish literature, among them the woman warrior Medb and the poet Feidelm in the *Táin*, or the elegiac Findabair and the multifaceted Crinog in this group. Not unlike Crinog, the Old Woman of Beare moves (in her memory at least) through youth and old age, secular sexuality and sacred prayer. She seems to have encountered generations of splendid and generous heroes; and indeed she derives in part from female sovereignty figures, whose sexual favors at once gave power to a new king and rejuvenated themselves. Yet she is insistently mortal and decrepit in this version, squarely facing a religious life she does not truly want and a Christian death that saves, yet comes too soon. Even in her decline, the Old Woman connects herself to a whole created world: seasons, tides, sap, the "stricken oak" (l. 100), arms, bones, skin, and hair. She is decrepit but insistently physical, bodied. Never married, and long abandoned by the men of her past, the Old Woman nonetheless praises them in comparison with the self-serving courtiers of the present. "The Old Woman of Beare" is a wonderful poem to read in combination with two other solitary female voices from very different cultural settings, the speaker of the Anglo-Saxon "The Wife's Lament" (pp. 153–55) and Chaucer's Wife of Bath (pp. 337–64). And she combines in one figure the wife and the crone whom Gawain encounters in *Sir Gawain and the Green Knight*.

Finally, note that "Pangur the Cat" is translated by the distinguished contemporary Irish poet Eavan Boland. It reads interestingly with Boland's own work. Her own title for the translation is "From the Irish of Pangur Ban," as if the original speaker were the cat ("Ban") itself. It is a playful version of the many serious ways in which Boland explores the voices of people and issues often left silent.

Judith

As the poem which immediately follows *Beowulf* in the unique manuscript, *Judith* has most often invited comparison with that poem, particularly by critics concerned to stress *Beowulf*'s Christian nature. As a heroic narrative with a warrior hero who triumphs over the enemies of God, Judith gives support to reading the pagan Beowulf in that way. Critical approaches to *Judith* itself have often gone beyond its literal celebration of Old Testament Hebrew heroism to a more allegorical interpretation. They have used its putative sources—the Book of Judith in the Vulgate Bible and Latin commentaries on it—to interpret the heroine's victory as that of the Church over the devil or of female chastity over lust.

Recently, however, many critics have tended to stress the poem's literal meaning rather than its timeless Christian significance, placing it in its historical context, whether political or feminist. According to these views, the poem reflects the resistance of the Christian Anglo-Saxons to the invading pagan Danes in the tenth century, and was perhaps even written to inspire rebellion against them (see Alexandra Hennesy Olsen, "Inversion and Political Purpose in the Old English *Judith*," *English Studies*, 63 [1982], 289-90). *Judith* is seen as a symbolic depiction of the contemporary ethnic and religious conflicts which are more literally expressed in the *Battle of Maldon*, the poetic account of the doomed struggle of a band of Anglo-Saxons against the Danes. The poem can thus remind students that in this early period Britain was colonized and invaded rather than colonizing; it can be instructively read, in volume I, with "Perspectives: Ethnic and Religious Encounters," which includes King Alfred, Ohthere, and Bede, and in volume II, with the postcolonial works of Conrad and Forster.

The feminist approach intersects with the political in focusing on Holofernes' attempt to use rape as a method of humiliating and intimidating the enemy. Karma Lochrie sees the poet's replacement of the Vulgate's reference to Holofernes' desire with the statement that he "meant to defile the noble lady with filth and with pollution" as the exposure of the patriarchal violence inherent in a warrior society: "Carnal desire proves to be a function not only of Holofernes' pride and drunkenness, but of a masculine warrior economy bound by a homosocial network and a code of violence that does not always succeed in masking the sexual aggression it sublimates" ("Gender, Sexual Violence, and the Politics of War in the Old English *Judith*," *Class and Gender in Early English Literature*, ed. Britton J. Harwood and Gillian Overing, [1994], 8). She argues that poet implicates the Anglo-Saxons themselves, and not just the Assyrians and the Danes, in this use of sexual violence as an instrument of war.

Students often find *Judith*, with its strong female hero, refreshing after *Beowulf*, with its focus on masculine heroic behavior. Those who come to the course with expectations formed by feminist theory or the works of nineteenth and twentieth-century women writers, however, often have difficulty in seeing that Judith is not acting on her own but is rather empowered by God's grace. It is useful to point out to them that while actual Anglo-Saxon women of the aristocracy wielded more power than most fictional depictions of them—such as Hrothgar's queen Wealhtheow and her daughter Freawaru in *Beowulf*, or the anonymous speakers of *Wulf and Eadwacer* and *The Wife's Lament*—they generally did so as religious leaders, such as abbess Hilda of Whitby, rather than as independent secular figures. (See Christine Fell, *Women in Anglo-Saxon England*, [1986]).

The Dream of the Rood

When taught following *Beowulf* and *Judith* in a two-semester survey course, *The Dream of the Rood* effectively rounds out a first view of Old English heroic poetry. It also leads naturally into a study of the three elegies included in the volume—*The Wanderer, Wulf and Eadwacer,* and *The Wife's Lament*—and suggests connections with the Anglo-Latin and Old English riddles.

The Dream of the Rood's affinities with heroic poetry are particularly striking. Students familiar with the depiction of the suffering Christ in the late Middle Ages will be surprised by the way in which the poet transforms Christ into a bold Germanic hero. It can be seen from *Judith* that Old English poets were drawn to the subject matter of the Old Testament, which is not surprising given its focus on the history of a tribal warrior people. The New Testament, however, has little to inspire heroic narrative, and *The Dream of the Rood* has been traced to no exact biblical source. Widely regarded as the finest poem on the Crucifixion in English, it may have been inspired by contemporary theological controversies over the humanity versus the divinity of Christ; it certainly achieves an almost perfect balance between these two aspects. In this it can be contrasted with a Middle English lyric on the Crucifixion included in this volume, *Jesus, My Sweet Lover*, which exemplifies the late medieval tendency to humanize—even sentimentalize—Christ's Passion (see J. A. Burrow, "An Approach to *The Dream of the Rood*," *Old English Literature: Twenty-Two Analytical Essays*, ed. Martin Stevens and Jerome Mandel, [1968], 254–56).

Although the heroic treatment of Christ in *The Dream of the Rood* reflects the early medieval view of Christ generally, the poet gives it a particularly Anglo-Saxon resonance by employing the specific language and conventions of Old English poetry. He describes Christ as a Germanic warrior girding himself for battle, like Beowulf. The Cross presents itself "as a loyal retainer in the epic mode, with the ironic reversal that it must acquiesce and even assist in its Lord's death, unable through its own command to aid or avenge him" (Stanley B. Greenfield and Daniel G. Calder, *A New Critical History of Old English Literature*, [1986], 196). Finally, the poet envisions heaven, in the manner of Old English poets, as a feast in a mead hall.

The Dream of the Rood has affinities not only with *Beowulf* and *Judith*, but also with the Old English elegies, to the extent that the dreamer presents himself as an exile longing to join his friends in the home of "the high Father." In addition, as an inanimate object granted speech, the Cross recalls the speaking objects in Old English and Anglo-Latin riddles, several of which also recount their origin as plants or trees. The poem can be contrasted with such Middle English treatments of the Passion as Julian of Norwich's mystical *Book of Showings* and the Crucifixion lyric mentioned above, which portray Christ in the suffering rather than the heroic vein. A dramatic exception, however, is *Piers Plowman* (B. *passus* 18), which presents Christ as a knight going to joust with the devil for the right to human souls. A poem of similar length that bears comparison is William Dunbar's late medieval Easter hymn *Done is a battel*.

Finally, the rich use of Christian paradox in *The Dream of the Rood* (e.g., "I saw the God of Hosts stretched on the rack") suggests comparisons with the Holy

Sonnets of John Donne, whose tension, irony, and paradox so fascinated the New Critics. His Sonnet 2 ("Oh my black soul! Now thou art summoned"), on the pilgrim-speaker's longing for release from wretchedness, and Sonnet 9 ("What if this present were the world's last night") on the Crucifixion, are particularly relevant.

PERSPECTIVES

Ethnic and Religious Encounters

All the texts included in this perspectives section concern the emergence of the idea of Englishness, an English people, and an English nation, with the rather varied implications of those phrases. In millennial America they are unlikely to be read as preliminary ventures toward Great Nationhood or a prehistory for empire, although the life of King Alfred and the works of Bede have both been exploited that way with varying degrees of subtlety. (*Rule Britannia*, almost an imperial hymn, was first performed in *Alfred: A Masque*, [1740].)

Still, it is good to emphasize how tentative are the notions laid out here; how differently they approach communal identity (through language, class, religion, as well as race); how their working categories often contradict one another; and how they construct identity by marking off "others" through distinctions that use ethnicity but do not end there. One might locate some moment in each entry along a gamut (admittedly fuzzy) of tribe, race, and nation. Even if discussion centers on this area, however, these passages are only pieces of bigger texts that often have rather different primary objectives, like Bede's slow and measured exploration of history within the scheme of salvation. They also bring students into contact with some key moments in earlier English history that continue to echo in the minds and texts of writers working when nationhood and empire were indeed powerful concepts.

The interactions, production, and power of language provide an independent issue, richly present in these excerpts but only sometimes germane to the construction of identity by ethnicity and religion. Literacy and illiteracy, the claims of Latin and vernacular, books as mere records or talismanic objects, and the magical force of words (in contexts both pagan and Christian), all have their moments here. Students might be asked to gather instances. Together, they can be connected to similar convergences of issues in *The Táin*, *The Dream of the Rood*, and later medieval literature.

Bede

Bede's gift for storytelling, his economy and pacing, are clear in these passages. He has a terrific sense of the image or scene that will pull in the reader: Edwin's counsellor and his poignant image of a sparrow flying through the mead hall, Imma's bonds repeatedly loosed, Caedmon's dream in the cow byre. The emotional pull (even sentimentality) of his stories, though, should not mask their considerable complexity.

In each of the three incidents here, Bede shows us a key moment in cultural transformation or encounter, not through didactic moralizing (a historiographical habit we do encounter in *The Anglo-Saxon Chronicle*) but through a series of implicit and explicit positions of speakers and audiences. Sometimes these are pretty straightforward, as when King Edwin hears from a warrior noble, a pagan priest, and a Christian missionary. The strategy is more complex when the positions are implicit in a range of audiences for any one event or linguistic moment. Coifi has an audience first of wavering king and nobles, then of common people (who think he's gone crazy), and always of Bede's Christian listeners. This compares to the implicit audiences of *Beowulf* (pagans within the tale, Christians now hearing it in England), or even the doubled responses to an Old Testament poem like *Judith* which has shifting implications seen from the old law or the new. Caedmon too shifts audiences within his story: first his angelic visitor, then his fellow lay brothers and the reeve, finally the abbess Hild herself and an audience of monks. And Imma's story of loosing from bonds is at the center of a tangle of verbal powers and audiences: a mass for a soul that gets literalized by loosing Imma's restraints, and is then confused (from a pagan perspective) as verbal magic.

For all the uncertainty about the relations between language and the new Christian faith, each story shows a stable sense of class hierarchy. In the story of Edwin's conversion, Bede puts one of his most moving similes into the mouth of a pagan nobleman; the argument for conversion of his priest Coifi is very different in tone and self-interest. The impression of Coifi's madness results from a breach of class behavior. Note too the wholesale conversion of Edwin's nobles, and the more limited change by his commoners; the unifying community of Christendom arrives here from the top down. The pagan *gesith* who holds Imma prisoner may wholly misunderstand the powers behind the loosing of the bonds, but noble identity seems to be transparent between religious faiths, and he sees right through Imma's effort to appear a peasant. (The *gesith* proves his own nobility, and respect for words, by honoring a promise not to injure Imma.) And in addition to his holiness, Caedmon shifts rank, from a laboring lay brother to a monk in holy orders.

Language and its modes of transmission add still another angle to these moments in the making of a Christian "English People." Edwin is converted not just by the fulfillment of a prophetic dream, but also by the eloquence of his counsellors and Paulinus. Caedmon moves into the "learned" monastic community, but does he ever become literate? How does he learn the biblical stories he retells so powerfully in Anglo-Saxon verse? What does this suggest about Latin and vernacular in religious life as Bede imagines Hild's monastery? What motivates Bede's apology for his Latin translation of Caedmon's poem? Caedmon's divine gift isn't literacy or Latin, but singing in the inherited vernacular in such a way as to make it sacred. Consider Caedmon's song of the origin of things in contrast to the song of the *scop* in *Beowulf* about the same subject. Caedmon's other subjects echo the creation of a corpus of Anglo-Saxon biblical poetry, such as *Judith* and *The Dream of the Rood*.

Imma's loosing from his chains prompts a suggestive sequence of reactions to language: a Christian readership is invited to see it as the impact of the new faith, and especially of the Latin mass; Imma's captor takes it to be the result of pagan "loosing spells." Is there a certain ironic humor in the scenes of misdirected masses, meant to free Imma's soul, but in fact undoing his literal bonds? Why the detail about the name of his brother the priest (Tunna) and *Tunnacæstir*? A Christian myth now stands behind a place-name, in ways comparable to the pagan myths of place in *The Táin*.

Bishop Asser

The very presence of the Welshman Asser at Alfred's court has a certain paradox. Alfred hoped to restore to the Anglo-Saxons the glory of a somewhat mythicized pre-Viking past, including its Latin learning. Because of the state of education south of the Humber, though, Alfred had to import teachers from Wales and from the continent. Further, however, Asser wrote his *Life of King Alfred* in part for a Welsh audience, which may suggest participation in a project of state-building based on geographical contiguity, not race or language. In fact by the time he wrote the *Life*, Welsh leaders had submitted to Alfred.

Asser was a serious biographer although his own Latin is awkward. He used written sources like *The Anglo-Saxon Chronicle* for Alfred's earlier years, and he knew continental models of laudatory biography like Einhard's *Life of Charlemagne*. (Alfred himself was connected to Carolingian kingdoms through his mother.) At moments, though, he is more a praise poet in the tradition of Taliesin, whose work was certainly circulating in Asser's native tongue. The intimate scenes of a dependent court around Alfred especially invite comparison to Taliesin's evocation of royal glory yoked to a powerful emotional bond.

Asser marks Alfred as a king by a series of more or less conventional attributes: his good looks and the universal affection he gained as a boy, his love of books and wish to overcome illiteracy (very like Einhard's Charlemagne), his hunting skills, patronage of craftsmen, and support of religion. Alfred establishes that kingship as a fighter, though, in a series of conflicts and final triumphs against the Viking invaders, which culminate in their conversion and expulsion into the Danelaw in the northeast.

Kingship and ethnicity thus might appear to converge nicely. Asser makes the situation more complex, however. For Asser, religious practice becomes the fundamental ethnic divide; his Alfred makes a nation against "assaults of the heathen." Compare this to Bede where complex religious differences seem not to have affected other kinds of ethnic coherence between Imma and his imprisoner. Further, Asser implies a royal court that embraces many races, even beyond those of the court scholars, and thus probably many languages. He sees Alfred's vernacular reading as specific to his Saxon race, but not as part of a boundary of participation in the state. Asser even aligns literacy and faith. It was the heathen invaders that prevented young Alfred from getting a better education, although Alfred's love of "Saxon poems" is a key sign of his youthful promise.

The story of Alfred memorizing poems in exchange for the promise of a book locates him in a crossing place of oral and written culture comparable to Caedmon and the mixed linguistic heritage of vernacular poetry and Latin literacy. (Indeed, from this perspective their real difference is one of class, not faith or talents.) Compare too the story of how the "whole *Táin*" was recovered (see the headnote), and how that elides books and oral transmission. Alfred desires the book as an icon, not for its words but the beauty of its decorated initial.

King Alfred
Preface to *Pastoral Care*

Asser's preoccupations, especially his elision of Christianity and ethnicity, contrast significantly with Alfred's own justification in translating *Pastoral Care*. Alfred constructs his alignment of ethnicity and kingdom from two perspectives, history and language. First, he invokes a nostalgic regard for the glories of an unspecified past he wants to emulate. Second, he wants to restore learning to a people among whom Latin has steeply declined, through the medium of Anglo-Saxon, "the language which we can all understand." Who make up that "all," at a court populated, Asser told us, by many nations? This evocation of a somewhat homogenized "Anglo-Saxon" people is echoed in charters of about the same time, in which Alfred is styled "king of the Anglo-Saxons."

At the same time, the idea of translation links Alfred's realm to other great nations of the past, moving in a roughly westward direction. This movement of learning and power (*translatio studii, translatio imperii*), with its implications of a chosen people and justification of empire, will be very important in the more secular history writing of Geoffrey of Monmouth, and throughout Arthurian tradition, especially *Sir Gawain and the Green Knight*. Ironically, it will be invoked by the spokesmen of the Anglo-Saxons' conquerors, the Normans.

Ohthere

The report of Ohthere's journeys records a rather different encounter, not only with the "exotic" peoples of northern Scandinavia, but also between Alfred's Anglo-Saxons and their own geographical past. Even while he was fighting Viking insurgents, Alfred also maintained trade ties with other Scandinavians, and brought some to his court. Ohthere is one of these, and his travels are introduced almost like a report on tribal groups of varying levels of primitiveness. There is little concern with religious practice here, but with the geography of far northern Scandinavia and with the region's languages, social habits, settlement patterns, and trade. Ohthere's own society is an object of curiosity, too, and his story includes details about farming and the measure of wealth in his own country. The emphasis on deer herds suggests the difficulty Ohthere had in explaining concepts of wealth based primarily on moveable possessions, not land. (This may be compared to wealth in *The Táin*.) Alfred also seems interested in aspects of his people's historical identity and their origins around the Baltic, accessible through the memory of a Norwegian trader—an interest consistent with the intense, even elegiac nostalgia of *Beowulf*.

The Anglo-Saxon Chronicle

If King Alfred promoted the idea of a language to link all Anglo-Saxons, the *Chronicle* helped that occur. Initially distributed to a number of monasteries (as were some of Alfred's translations), the *Chronicle* was extended at some of them, right up to the Norman Conquest in 1066, and in a few cases even beyond that date. This passage reflects an achieved sense of ethnic nationhood in its uncomplicated assumption of the "English people" who oppose Harold of Norway and William of Normandy. Nowhere is the tone of loss and lamentation at the fall of Anglo-Saxon kingship more acute than here. The *Chronicle* depicts Harold moving feverishly between an old enemy, the Norwegians (who had maintained close relations between their own country and the Danelaw), and the new invaders, the Normans. Yet the *Chronicle*, especially in these passages, also adopts a much wider perspective of divine disfavor, cosmic signs, and punishment for "the sins of the people." It sees the Normans as an alien invading force, but even more as God's punishment for Anglo-Saxon corruption. The latter notion echoes historiographical ideas developed out of biblical narrative, but used more recently by Welsh historians explaining the triumphant incursions of the Anglo-Saxons themselves. Both in biblical history and in notions of *translatio imperii*, a people could lose their favored status. This excerpt of the *Chronicle* ends with an appeal not to nationhood but to the will of God.

Taliesin

One job of poetry in the oral tradition is to preserve its culture's whole knowledge, especially the history and legends that generate social identity, in the absence of written texts. This can generate a sort of literary superabundance (from the perspective of an audience accustomed to books) involving catalogs and digressions whose presence has more an encyclopedic than an immediately narrative relevance. Aspects of this were noted in *Beowulf* and *The Táin*. On the other hand, such a cohesive culture creates an audience well informed about its great communal stories. This also allows the poet to work in forms of extreme economy, using only the most glancing references to the narrative setting of a poem. This resource of an orally derived poetry is found in Anglo-Saxon laments like *The Wanderer* and *The Wife's Lament*, but is even more extreme in the emotionally charged narrative allusiveness of Taliesin.

Militant heroes on the order of Beowulf, Cú Chulainn, Urien and Owain dominate this oral tradition, but poets themselves are charismatic figures, especially in Celtic culture where their talents are also linked to prophecy and even verbal magic. Feidelm in *The Táin* provides a good instance, as does the warrior poet Fergus mac Róig. So it is not surprising that Taliesin himself becomes the focus of tales of marvel in later Welsh culture, nor that a growing group of poems are attached to the prestige of his name.

Taliesin celebrates cattle raids that recall *The Táin* in *The War Band's Return*, but in the very next stanza he evokes the fragility of a realm so dependent on warrior kings, and imagines the disaster of his king's death. This fearful glance toward dispersal and isolation invites comparison with the Anglo-Saxon elegies as well as with a number of moments in *Beowulf* where celebration is interrupted by the poet's reminder that it is soon to be followed by disaster. The poem's final stanza at once insists on Urien's power and registers (in the repetition of "foes") how it is challenged on every side. Taliesin's sense of glory in the prospect of defeat is not purely conventional; the Welsh kingdoms of the northwest were in fact being slowly swallowed up by the Irish to the north and Angles to the east and south.

Taliesin uses powerful repetition (note "gaiety" and "riches" in the poem *Urien Yrechwydd*), but also meaningful omission, as when he describes only the results of warfare in the final stanza of *The Battle of Argoed Llwyfain*. The ravens here typify his power with very brief visual images. This same technique has its high point in *Lament for Owain Son of Urien*, when it switches from the "sleep" of easy triumph to that of death. This poem also displays Taliesin's quicksilver shifts of tone, possible only in poetry of such economy, in the unresolved moves from Christian consolation to heroic ferocity and back again.

The Wanderer

In the past there has been much controversy as to the relation between the pagan and Christian elements in *The Wanderer*: was it composed by a Christian poet, or by a pagan poet and later reworked by a Christian one? (It is unlikely that it was ever purely pagan, given that writing was not introduced to England until the Christian conversion.) Anne L. Klink gives a succinct summary of criticism on this subject, including the exegetical reading of D. W. Robertson, Jr. (*The Old English Elegies: A Critical Edition and Genre Study* [1992], 30–35). The debate offers an opportunity to talk about the tensions between exegetical and literal or historical interpretations which have later relevance to the work of Chaucer.

In fact, most contemporary students have difficulty appreciating poetry which recommends stoicism of any kind, whether pagan or Christian, and so teaching *The Wanderer* poses something of a challenge. This is perhaps best met by comparing the poem to other works, primarily from the Old English period, but also from Middle English and later. To this end seeing the poem's structure as divided into the three sections of exile, the ruin, and the *ubi sunt* motif can be helpful. In the opening section about exile, *The Wanderer* can be compared to the elegiac elements of *Beowulf*, a poem which, for all its celebration of heroic values, reminds us of the loss which follows from their violence (this is clearest in the endless tribal warfare presented through digressions in the second half of the poem). *The Wanderer* explicitly laments that loss, as the exiled speaker longs for his lord, his companions, and the mead hall. Lyric portions of *Beowulf* that can be compared with *The Wanderer* include Hrothgar's "sermon" warning Beowulf against pride in his youthful prowess, and the so-called "elegy of the last survivor," who buries useless treasure in the dragon's cave. In addition, the dreamer's presentation of himself as an exiled Germanic warrior in *The Dream of the Rood* bears comparison with the voice of the exile in *The Wanderer*.

The section of the poem where the speaker reflects on ruins,

old walls stand, tugged at by winds
and hung with hoar-frost, buildings in decay.
The wine-halls crumble, lords lie dead,

can be compared to other poems which meditate on ruined buildings and monuments as symbols of transience, whether in medieval Welsh (Dafydd ap Gwilym's
Ruin) or nineteenth-century English (Shelley's *Ozymandias*). And the related *ubi
sunt* passage that laments the fleeting joys of the Germanic warrior's life—"Where
has the horse gone? Where the man? Where the giver of gold?"—can be related to
two later medieval lyrics, the anonymous Middle English *Contempt of the World*,
which asks, "Where beth they biforen us weren?", and more generally, William
Dunbar's *Lament for the Makers*, which regrets Death's claiming not only poets, but
also strong warriors and beautiful ladies.

Wulf and Eadwacer *and* The Wife's Lament

Male-voiced elegies like *The Wanderer* are the norm of exile poetry, expressing the
dark side of heroic experience—the painful loss of the joys of the hall with the warrior band that is the predictable consequence of tribal warfare. Female-voiced elegies reflect a double exile, from the ties between men in the comitatus as well as
from lover or husband. These women are not agents but objects of exchange with
the role of "peace-weaver and mourner for the dead produced by feud," being "part
of the treasure dispensed by the victorious ruler" (Helen T. Bennet, "Exile and the
Semiosis of Gender in Old English Elegies," *Class and Gender in Early English
Literature*, ed. Britton J. Harwood and Gillian Overing, [1994], 45). In suffering the
pain of separation, the speakers of *Wulf and Eadwacer* and *The Wife's Lament* may
be compared to the doomed Freawaru, Hrothgar's daughter, and the tragic
Hildeburh in *Beowulf*.

The importance of the female voice in these elegies has long been recognized.
(Some earlier editors, however, tried to efface it by emending the feminine endings
on some of the adjectives, reading the poems as conventional elegies spoken by an
exiled warrior.) It should be stressed, however, that these poems were more likely
written by men constructing a female persona than by women. Marilyn Desmond
has suggested that they may nevertheless be added to the female canon, arguing
that in cases of anonymity, voice rather than authorship should be the determining factor ("The Voice of Exile: Feminist Literary History and the Anonymous
Anglo-Saxon Elegy," *Critical Inquiry*, 16 [1990], 572-90). Certainly *Wulf and
Eadwacer* and *The Wife's Lament* can be compared with the anonymous Middle
English laments on pregnancy and rejection (such as *The Wily Clerk* and *Joly Jankin*),
and later poems written by women themselves, such as Mary Wroth, Aphra Behn,
and Anne Finch.

The feminist approach to this material is rather new, for students of Old English
literature have been skeptical of literary theory of any kind until recently. (Roy
Liuzza characterizes the approach generally as asserting "I am Woman, let me read

The Wife's Lament".) But in fact, several theoretical approaches in recent years have challenged the earlier new critical, oral-formulaic, and exegetical concerns. (See the preface to Katherine O'Brien O'Keeffe, ed., *Old English Shorter Poems: Basic Readings*, [1994].) Like feminist criticism, many of the new approaches attempt to restore Old English poetry to its social context. One of these is the study of manuscript context, which seeks to gain insight into the work through the tastes of the compiler.

The female elegies are a particularly good place in which to practice such critical modes, as well as the more traditional ones of close reading and philology. Because of their short length, they enable a close attention to the text which is difficult with a longer narrative like *Beowulf*. Starting a British Literature survey course with these poems, together with *The Wanderer* and the riddles, lets the teacher raise these issues at the outset while at the same time allowing students to finish *Beowulf*.

One might expect students to be engaged by the feminist implications of *Wulf and Eadwacer* and *The Wife's Lament*. What is surprising, though, is that they are also drawn to the very ambiguity which so frustrates editors, translators, and critics. As with Emily Dickinson's poems, they seem to relish the liberty offered by so many gaps in the text. *Wulf and Eadwacer* is so cryptic that it was earlier thought to be one of the riddles, which it in fact precedes in the Exeter Book. While some things are clear from the translation in this anthology (by Kevin Crossley-Holland)—Wulf is the speaker's lover, by whom she has a child, Eadwacer is her husband, and she has lost her lover and may lose her child—much else remains murky. The ambiguities may be explored by giving students a photocopy of the original Old English (see Anne L. Klinck, *The Old English Elegies: A Critical Edition and Genre Study*, [1992], 92, also useful for its introductions and notes) and another translation (perhaps S. A. J. Bradley, *Anglo-Saxon Poetry*, [1982], useful because it follows the order of the manuscripts). One question of translation concerns the repeated phrase "on threat" (lines 2 and 7), which Crossley-Holland translates "with a troop":

> Wulf is on one island, I on another,
> a fastness that island, a fen-prison.
> Fierce men roam there, on that island;
> they'll tear him to pieces if he comes with a troop.

Bradley, however, translates "on threat" as "under subjugation":

> Wulf is on one Island; I am on another. That island
> is secure, surrounded by a fen. There are deadly cruel
> men on the island; they want to destroy him if he comes
> under subjugation.

Depending on which translation is chosen, the line "They will kill him if he comes *on threat*" means that Wulf will either threaten or be subject to violence. Either way, the exercise is a good way to illustrate Old English and problems of interpretation to students who don't know the language.

Even more than *Wulf and Eadwacer*, *The Wife's Lament* is a teachable text, per-haps as much because of its riddling qualities as its female voice. The speaker tells of her husband's departure, his kinsmen's fomenting enmity between them, and her husband's ordering her into a friendless exile. Again with photocopies of Klinck's text and Bradley's translation, students can be shown a difficult crux. At the end of the poem, Crossley-Holland translates a passage as follows:

> Young men must always be serious in mind
> and stout-hearted; they must hide
> their heartaches, that host of constant sorrows
> behind a smiling face. . . .

This appears to be a general statement with particular application to the speaker's husband, with whose sorrows she sympathizes. There is an alternative reading of the passage as a curse, however, aimed at a young man, not previously mentioned, who has implicitly caused the couple harm:

> For ever shall that youth remain melancholy of mind and
> painful the brooding of the heart. He shall sustain, as
> well as his benign demeanour, anxiety too in his breast
> and the welter of incessant griefs.
> (Bradley, 385)

If we translate the subjunctive *scyle* in "A scyle geong mon wesan geomormod" (line 42) as "*may* a particular young man know mental anguish," the speaker is cer-tainly wishing ill luck on someone. Thus, *The Wife's Lament*, which has been called "perhaps the 'hottest' text" among the lesser studied Old English poems, can be used to show students who will never study the language the value of old-fashioned philology.

Riddles

The riddles from the Anglo-Saxon period reflect many spheres of activity—agri-cultural, domestic, and sexual—which are generally ignored in the more canoni-cal genres of Old English poetry. Of those selected here, however, all but one deal with literary activity, playing on the power of writing or the miracle of books. They reflect the high level of Christian scholarship in England and Ireland before the Norman Conquest. (See also the image of St. John the Evangelist with the tools of a scribe, the pen and the book, from the *Book of Kells* on the cover of this volume.)

Students' love of deciphering should draw them to the intricacies of the Anglo-Latin riddles of Aldhelm. The "seventeen sisters" are the alphabet, while the "six bastard brothers" are the letters h, k, q, x, y, z, which are regarded as illegitimate because not native to the Latin alphabet. For more detailed correspondences, see the notes of the editor and translator, James Hall Pitman, *The Riddles of Aldhelm*, (1925). A recent study is by Nancy Porter Stork, *Through a Glass Darkly: Aldhelm's Riddles in the British Library ms. Royal 12.c.xxiii*, (1990).

The Old English Riddles from the Exeter Book are doubtless aimed at the same elite literate audience as the Latin ones, and reflect similar philosophical concerns. The answers to the speakers' implicit questions "what am I?" here include a Bible, a bookworm, and a reed pen. The sense of awe at the technology of writing in these riddles is remarkable. In the riddle whose answer is "A hand writing," the poet moves from four earthbound creatures to the image of the quill pen to evoke the freedom of a bird in flight:

> I watched four curious creatures
> travelling together; their tracks were swart,
> each imprint very black. The bird's support
> moved swiftly; it flew in the air,
> dived under the wave.

The marked respect for the process of writing in such riddles contrasts sharply with later medieval observations on the technologies of writing and printing. Students might compare Chaucer's despair, 400 some years later, at the incompetence of his copyist (in *To His Scribe Adam*), or, even more remarkably, William Caxton's relative indifference, in his Preface to Malory's *Morte Darthur*, to the print technology which less than fifty years later Rabelais was to recognize as revolutionary.

The last riddle to be discussed reveals one aspect of human activity notably repressed in Old English literature—sexuality. The Exeter Book is known for its "double-entendre" riddles which offer simultaneously a prim and a pornographic solution. (See Craig Williamson, trans., *A Feast of Creatures: Anglo-Saxon Riddle Songs*, [1982], 22.) The "onion/penis" riddle included here has a nearly perfect form, because almost every detail points to two possible solutions. Part of the riddle's charm comes from the fact that the onion-picker, "a good-looking girl, the doughty daughter of some churl" is presented as attractive, though of middling status.

Other double-entendre riddles are neither so consistent in their corresponding details, nor so positive about sexuality. Many treat it as characteristic of the lower classes and of ethnic outsiders, as described in John W. Tanke's "*Wonfeax wale*: Ideology and Figuration in the Sexual Riddles of the Exeter Book" (*Class and Gender in Early English Literature: Intersections*, ed. Britton J. Harwood and Gillian Overing, [1994], 31–32). Students interested in pursuing such riddles further may also consult Anne Harleman Stewart, "Double Entendre in the Old English Riddles," *Lore and Language* 3 (1983), 39–52.

After the Norman Conquest

The Arthurian Myth in History and Romance

Ask any classroom of undergraduates who Etiocles was, or even Hercules or Alexander the Great, and we are likely to get responses that are hesitant, fuzzy, and uncertain about the broader legendary context of each name. Ask about biblical characters, Old Testament or New, and there may be more answers, but usually from particular communities of believers, and their reactions are likely to be somewhat constricted by inherited religious interpretations. Ask that same class about Guinevere or Lancelot or Morgan, though: students speak right up, better informed, with some sense of how the names connect in narrative, and unhindered either by the inhibiting prestige of classical antiquity or the constraints of their varied orthodoxies.

Of all our great inherited story clusters in western culture, the Arthurian tradition remains the most vital, widespread in popular as well as "high" culture, and thus among the easiest legends through which to reach back to its very different manifestations in a distant past. Now as in the Middle Ages, the Arthurian myth has room for a free play of response among its audiences and its users. This puts right in the teacher's hands a wonderful energy and ease that can help carry students, at any level, to the challenges of medieval English literary culture.

The selections in the following two sections show the Arthurian legend emerging in a range of key genres—history and heroic narrative, letters, and several versions of romance—across three centuries. They also provide a setting in which to examine the tremendous flexibility of the tradition and its exploitation by a series of cultural and political agents who make efforts (never fully resolved) to define and underwrite their social and religious visions through an ancient national hero who is widely admired, but not universally nor absolutely so. Further versions and reactions to the Arthurian legend also appear in Chaucer's Wife of Bath's Tale and the series of ironic references in his Nun's Priest's Tale.

Before his story attains an elaborated narrative coherence in Geoffrey of Monmouth, Arthur does appear widely in Celtic sources such as the Welsh Mabinogion and in those Latin chronicles that concern themselves with the surviving British communities after the departure of the Romans. Students whose interest goes beyond the very brief sketch in the editorial headnote can be directed to the first three sections of The Romance of Arthur, (ed. James J. Wilhelm [1994]), which also provides further bibliography. For these and other topics, too, they should know about The New Arthurian Encyclopedia (ed. Norris J. Lacy, [1991]).

It's good to keep reminding students of the changing cultural and historical settings in which these texts operate, and the many roles that Arthur and characters around him play therein. The Arthur of the Welsh retains (as in the Mabinogion) strong elements of sacral, semi-divine kingship. He brings young warriors into his cohort through ritual actions, and battles totemic beasts that carry at least some echoes of pagan gods. In the early Latin chronicles, some of this remains in Arthur's high kingship, but he is increasingly a figure of political and military resistance to post-Roman incursions. Geoffrey of Monmouth uses both the uncanny and the stories of British resistance around Arthur, but draws him into international settings of world history, Roman and European empire, and the more local tensions between Celtic and Mediterranean cultures, and Welsh and Norman powers. English kings like Henry II, Edward I, and Edward III invoke Arthur (through history and imitation) to buttress their own royal claims and ambitions, yet a poet like Marie de France (probably connected to the court of Henry II) uses a minor Arthurian episode to evoke a very different reaction to royal power, and to make place for dominant women, eroticism and the uncanny. *Sir Gawain and the Green Knight*, whatever its extraordinary craft and its connections to surviving Celtic culture, also implies the ambitions and anxieties of a traditional chivalric class under great pressure in its own time, the fourteenth century. At about the same time (and using an analogous tale) Chaucer's Wife of Bath uses the Arthurian court to deliver a protest against the violence and bias supporting that same chivalric ideal. And Malory works under the pressures of extended civil war that darkly echoes the eruptions of strife in Arthur's Britain. New ethnic, cultural, and political settings make constantly new demands on these materials.

Despite the protean vitality of the Arthurian tradition, it is also a good idea to keep reminding students of two qualifications. First, there has been continuous doubt and debate about the very existence of a historical "Arthur" with anything like the attributes he quickly attracted in the tradition. Geoffrey of Monmouth's encyclopedic gathering of Celtic Arthurian material was met by dismissive skepticism (even outrage) in his own time. Does this limit, or enhance, Arthur's potential roles in cultural imagination? Second, in "literature" narrowly defined, the Arthurian legend bulks smaller in England than in France, with its enormous outpouring of verse narratives and prose cycles in the twelfth, thirteenth, and fourteenth centuries. By the later Middle Ages, the materials of secular story had been codified as the three "matters": the Matter of Troy (or Rome, and embracing a wide range of classical story), the Matter of France (Charlemagne and his twelve peers, including Roland), and the Matter of Britain (Arthur and his knights); the Arthurian legend was only one of these, and not always pre-eminent. Nonetheless, as a king on British soil with lingering echoes of the divine and uncanny, he invited a remarkable range of uses—to encode social order, faith, and private psychology—as no other legendary figure did.

PERSPECTIVES

Arthurian Myth in the History of Britain

This section provides several looks at the story of Arthur as used in fairly immediate contexts of supporting dynastic power. It also asks students to look at history, topography, and the formal letter as self-conscious literary genres. The section thus can also be used to challenge and broaden received notions of what makes up "literature" in cultural settings not immediately our own.

Geoffrey of Monmouth

In his *History*, Geoffrey links the Celtic myths of King Arthur and his followers to an equally ancient myth that England was founded by descendants of the survivors of Troy, and makes his combined, largely fictive but enormously appealing work available to an Anglo-Norman audience by writing it in Latin.

Feudal tenure, the centralization of power, and the establishment of bureaucracy were the worldly means by which the Norman and Angevin rulers established their power in the generations after 1066. They also, however, exploited a subtler mode of influence in the ideological underpinnings of history and literature produced under their patronage. The early Norman conquerors had promoted narratives of their ancestral founder Rollo, like the *Roman de Rou*. Geoffrey of Monmouth dedicated his *History of the Kings of England* to Robert Duke of Gloucester, uncle of the future Henry II. Soon after, Henry's Angevin court was supporting the "romances of antiquity," poems again in French that narrate the story of Troy (the *Roman de Troie*) and its aftermath (*Roman d'Eneas*), thus creating a secular typology for the Normans and their westward conquest of England.

Geoffrey of Monmouth himself led a mixed Celtic-English life. He is linked by name and geographical information to the area of Monmouth, though he may actually be Breton in family background. Geoffrey's name also appears, though, on legal documents around Oxford in the second quarter of the twelfth century. The title he uses in some of those charters, "Magister," suggests an elevated role in the intellectually active schools that were the forerunners of the university. Geoffrey was thus in an unusual but certainly not unique position to mediate between Celtic traditions and the Latin learning of the schools, and between the local culture of his upbringing and the international, Mediterranean-derived studies of classical and patristic literature. It may be this double affiliation that led Geoffrey to imagine a dialogue of Celtic and Norman perspectives in his *History*. If he makes the Anglo-Saxons God's instruments in punishing the sins of the Britons, he also makes them scapegoats, unwanted intruders; the focus of hostility on them creates a space in which to imagine ethnic conciliation with the Normans.

Language provides Geoffrey's most daring gesture in his construction of a British historiographical perspective. By basing his story on a "very ancient book written in the British language," he inverts the usual hierarchy of prestige among Latin and the vernaculars. Whether that book was real or fictive, the "British language" here is seen as an ancient tongue, an alternate focus of historical inquiry. He presses this point further, later on, when he explains that the language of Brutus and his followers was Trojan or "crooked Greek," and the origin of Welsh.

As noted above, references and episodes about King Arthur had been circulating in Welsh and Breton culture for generations before Geoffrey's day. An "ancient book" could well have come into his hands, but it probably would have offered disconnected pieces of Arthurian story in the form of quasi-mythic episodes, genealogies, and king-lists, the genres of Celtic narrative. It was almost certainly Geoffrey's own inspiration to combine these materials in a linear story, linked with the Trojan origins of Britain, and exploiting the style and themes of history writing which was among the most distinguished genres in twelfth-century England. Geoffrey wrote a broadly conceived history of ethnic glory; corruption (especially illicit erotic desire) and declining power; divine punishment through human agents, and the vague promise of redemption. He lends weight and coherence to the events of his story by aligning them with the chronology of ancient and biblical history. His repeated emphasis on the disaster of political infidelity and division must have struck deep chords in an England mired in civil strife in the 1130s.

Note the details of Brutus's voyage to Albion. Geography and other details recapitulate, invert, and undo the Greek triumph over Troy; they then widely overlap Aeneas's wanderings, echoing the glamor of Brutus's great-grandfather and the founder of the Roman empire. Consider also the original name of London, "New Troy." Geoffrey dramatically re-centers England in the context of ancient history. He makes it part of the Trojan diaspora and potentially an imperial counter-balance to Rome. He also provides it with a heroic, exiled founder like that of the Romans.

Centuries later, Arthur is born from a lineage that involves both British kings and a Roman imperial family, the Constantines. But Geoffrey's Arthur is more than a bearer of genealogy. He is a fully delineated epic and heroic figure, combining single combat and personal leadership of a national force. His later career also involves telling links to the Normans: Arthur seeks territorial expansion on the continent, and settles retainers in Anjou (Kay) and Normandy (Bedivere)—an inverse prehistory of the Norman conquest. This also helps produce, nonetheless, a legend in which the Norman conquest is a return to a place of genealogical origin, exactly the claim that Virgil makes for Aeneas's right to inhabit Latium.

Women and erotic desire play a key role in the *History*, but students will need to discard expectations of courtly love play. Arthur's life begins and ends with transgression of the marriage bed: Uther's adultery with Ygerna, and Mordred's with Guinevere. In this respect, Geoffrey still occupies the world of early Welsh stories, where women are taken, and (except maybe Guinevere) mortal women lack will. Uther's desire for Ygerna is specifically physical. His lovesickness can be cured not by her affection but by the possession of her body. Ygerna lives happily with Uther after he kills her husband, though he pays for his transgression with a lingering illness. Arthur chooses Guinevere because of her Roman lineage. Is there anything like romantic love or emotional eroticism in the *History*?

Another area in which Geoffrey's imagination inhabits Celtic traditions is his depiction of Merlin, the prophet and magician. Like priests and some poets (such as Taliesin) in Celtic myth, Merlin can shape-shift. And like the high poets of early Wales and Ireland, he can mock and criticize his king with impunity. But even his magic serves Geoffrey's broader themes. Stonehenge, which Merlin magically transports from Ireland, is assembled as a memorial to dead heroes in the British struggle against the Saxons. As in *The Táin*, myth lends significance to a place surviving in the writer's time. The episode is typical of Geoffrey's double reach, rewriting a very ancient site as a symbolic space of the Arthurian line, but also drawing the even more ancient and uncanny ambience of Celtic tradition into his story.

Gerald of Wales

Beginning even before Geoffrey of Monmouth, Arthurian legend has a common thread of the unknowable, undiscoverable body of Arthur, or sometimes of his tomb. It is easy to see how this theme was attracted into parallels with the life of Christ. Both stories derive from a myth of immortality, a never-quite-lost savior of an oppressed people, and the promise of his return. Whatever hope this gave the Welsh, it also made Arthur not a forerunner but a potential opponent for the Norman and Angevin kings. The episode of Henry II helping the monks of Glastonbury uncover the true tomb and authentic body of Arthur is a cunning moment in the political co-optation of a powerful legend. The tomb, which was a sign of marvel and uncertainty in Arthur's end, here provides ocular and textual proof of his death. Note how carefully Gerald sets up his story as opposed to "legends." Yet the uncovering of the "real" body retains its evocative mystery, only now under the patronage of Henry and (not coincidentally) to the considerable benefit of the abbey, which writes itself ever more firmly into Arthurian myth.

Edward I

Edward's silences in this letter are as interesting as his claims. He doesn't grapple with the absence of documents to back his story of ancient lordship, giving just a vague assertion of "other evidence." Edward uses Geoffrey of Monmouth's narrative of the Trojan origins of England. What details get left out? Why? Unnerving details about irregular marriage, patricide, and exile simply disappear. Edward's letter does tell the story of the division of the island among Brutus' three sons, but adds the crucial detail of Locrine retaining "royal dignity" as first born. He thus deploys the Trojan myth to underwrite primogeniture and an ancient claim to the overlordship of Scotland.

The Scots' reply, reported second-hand to Edward by his agents at the Papal court, is a dazzling piece of legal critique and counter-mythology. The Scots begin with the issue of the textual sources of power. What will dominate? Traditional tales, oral and written, or the non-narrative force of charter and bureaucratic record? Just in case their audience feels some attraction for foundation myth, the Scots offer their own. They answer a narrative of fathers, and English claims of primogeniture, with a story of female foundation and clan-like partition of land among several heirs. Scota comes to Scotland via Ireland—is hers also implicitly a more Celtic foundation than that of the Trojan Britons?

Marie de France
from Lais

Marie de France's *Lanval* marks a distinct shift in tone and theme from the "historical" Arthurian materials. Yet Marie's originality, and the complexity that lurks behind her restrained style, seem to emerge best by being taught in comparison with Geoffrey of Monmouth and Gerald of Wales.

Prologue

The Prologue to the *Lais* is intriguing quite on its own, as a statement by a poet in contact both with the Latin classical tradition and with tales emerging into French and English literary culture from the Celtic vernaculars. Why tell us about her abandoned translations of classical story? Is Marie leveling the respective importance of texts derived from the institutional learning of the church-sponsored schools and those from the more popular and oral performances she has heard? Compare this with the linguistic moves in Geoffrey of Monmouth's *Dedication*.

What kind of independence does Marie imply for the composer or translator? Note the way her attention shifts from a responsibility for spreading the word of God to just spreading words. Does the notion of textual obscurity give a certain power to the reader as well? Is Marie willing (or even eager) "to speak quite obscurely" herself?

Marie's prologue could be part of a more ambitious look at how medieval writers take positions in regard to older cultures, both Latin and Celtic and, in later medieval England, French. This might include King Alfred's Preface to *Pastoral Care*, Geoffrey of Monmouth's *Dedication*, the opening stanzas of Chaucer's *Parliament of Fowls*, Caxton's Prologue to Malory's *Morte Darthur*, and the copyist's comments in *The Tale of Taliesin*.

Lanval

Marie's innovativeness is clearest when she is compared to her rough contemporary Gerald and to her predecessor by about a generation, Geoffrey of Monmouth. All have links to the highest levels of the royal court, all tell Arthurian stories. Like Geoffrey of Monmouth, Marie de France draws explicitly from a Celtic-language tradition, although Marie's source is explicitly Breton and oral. One might compare the quite different audiences implicit in their emphasis on written vs. oral sources and their divergent target languages, Latin and French. Mostly men, or women? Mostly lay people, or clerics?

Discussion might begin by considering the space for alternate, even dissenting perspectives, that Marie creates by these choices. Oral attribution frees her from textual control and the kinds of critique Geoffrey had indeed met. The decision to tell only a brief incident separates her from the broader historical perspectives of Geoffrey's search for beginnings, or Gerald's search for endings (or even from the broad historical reach implied by the Trojan references that open and close *Sir Gawain and the Green Knight*). What else does Marie's narrower focus allow her to bring into her *lai*?

Social Setting The complex implications of Marie's laconic style and story of fairy marvel may be clearer if approached through the realistic social and political setting within which she situates these events. Marie's Angevin audience would recognize the setting of territorial battle, the poverty that could result from ambition at court and, later on, details of legal procedure. Unlike the Arthurian romances of Chrétien de Troyes, Marie does not begin with a court held in peaceful cele-bration and in conscious pursuit of some marvel. Instead her *lai* is set in a brief respite from war, when Arthur is battling an invasion of Scots and Picts. Even Lanval's plight is socially sited, almost banal. Lanval's initial social isolation does not result from any lack of noble birth or martial bravery; he just hasn't enough money. The episode of courtly eroticism and adulterous intrigue grows out of this setting, as does Lanval's contact with the Celtic otherworld. Both elements imply powerful counterforces to the imperial aims, economic hierarchy, and militant order of Arthur's world.

Paradoxically, the instant when the fairy world and the Arthurian realm briefly cross one another occurs in the context of a highly formalized legal procedure co-herent with practices in the reign of Henry II. Indeed, this period produced one of the first detailed texts on legal procedure, *The Treatise on the Laws and Customs of the Realm of England Commonly Called Glanvill* (ed. C. D. G. Hall, [1965]). There is a formal accusation; Arthur consults with a baronial court; Lanval is free pending trial in exchange for pledges; and witnesses are demanded in court. In particular, an Angevin audience would recognize, in the murmurs of Arthur's barons, a sense of how the strict rituals of legal procedure can serve to mask wrongdoing. Arthur is to some degree trapped within the very legal structures that underpin his power. The fairy mistress, when she does arrive, is at once an irrefutable witness and a sort of mounted champion in one alternative to court procedure, the trial by battle.

Fairy World   From his isolation within public society and from the city of Carlisle, Lanval retreats to the less stable and morally uncertain world of the field and the streamside. The sudden emergence of the fairy world, and the magical lady's reappearance at Arthur's court, produce the powerful attraction of the *lai*. Part of Marie's resonance, however, derives from her extreme economy in intro-ducing these elements, the deft but almost laconic flatness with which she sets out her narrative. Yet Marie's imagery is distinctly enriched and concrete at moments that open into the fairy world: Lanval's trembling horse, the ladies with their golden basins and towels, the luxurious tent of the fairy mistress, even the dark marble stone from which Lanval vaults behind her onto her horse.

The setting of the streamside boundary is reminiscent of moments in much earlier Celtic literature where women of uncanny beauty and power suddenly emerge as if from nowhere, for instance the appearance of Feidelm in *The Táin*. Other details echo the Celtic otherworld, such as the ritual washing after which Lanval can move into this new realm. Yet Marie also leaves open the possibility that the fairy world is an interior state. The ladies approach in what could be Lanval's dream. His lady promises to be with him "when you want," and appar-ently anywhere—perhaps in his imagination?

The world of Lanval's fairy mistress, though, is also an elaborate mirror world to that of Arthur's court. It is a world in which superabundant wealth is linked to eroticism, not militant conquest; and a world in which a woman's loyalty is en-dangered by a man's transgression of his oath, whereas Arthur's loyalty to the marriage bed is endangered by Guinevere's adulterous desire. The counter-world of Lanval's lady echoes but inverts regal symbols of the Arthurian frame: the eagle on her tent, her ermine and purple cloak, her lavish gifts which all reward obedience to love, not the feudal tie.

Knighthood, Women, and Sexuality   Historicizing versions of the Arthurian story tended to emphasize strong kingship, powerful knights, and Arthur's preoccupations with territorial battle and the maintenance of aristocratic order. In Geoffrey of Monmouth, women and romance play a very small role, and even marvels and prophecy tend to be linked with national destiny. By contrast, while strong men like Gawain and Yvain are not absent in Marie de France, neither are they central to her tale. Can we even speak of a "hero" in *Lanval*? Lanval himself is rather passive, compared to knights of either the histories or later romances. Unlike many heroes of Arthurian romance, he has no specific ambition or quest to fulfill. Instead, he and the focus of the *lai* move from a public setting and imperial ambition to private erotic fulfillment and a very different realm of being.

Compared to the relatively passive mortal women in Geoffrey of Monmouth, Marie de France's Guinevere stands out in bold relief. She is not an attractive character, but she has a powerful will of her own. Her desires imply a private erotic existence which she is willing to lead outside the marriage bed. Guinevere's power in *Lanval*, however, is not especially subversive of the broader social order. Unlike Geoffrey's Guinevere, whose affair with Mordred undoes Arthur's campaign of continental empire and finally his insular realm, Marie's Guinevere is relatively harmless, operating within the canons of social order, through a cunning manipulation of legal procedures.

The scene of courtly ritual play in which Guinevere approaches Lanval lies somewhere between the world of Arthurian militancy and the rural haven of the fairy mistress. Can it be seen as a context where Arthurian order and the erotic power of the fairy lady may dangerously mix? When rejected by Lanval, Guinevere accuses him of homosexuality. This makes sexuality a central issue, as it might interrupt the order of Arthur's public world. It is an accusation sufficiently threatening to knightly identity that it alone pushes Lanval to betray his promise of secrecy to his fairy mistress.

Lanval ends with the knight's return to the mysterious place that has been the space of magic and female power in prior tradition. Lanval abjures the Arthurian court, apparently forever. Are we asked to view this in a negative or positive light? And does Lanval's departure really transform the Arthurian realm? Or rather, has the fairy lady been accommodated simply as a witness leading to Lanval's exoneration within an unaltered legal structure?

Sir Gawain and the Green Knight

Romance and Chivalric Ideals   The outlines of the genre we loosely call romance emerged in Arthurian narratives and retellings of classical story, in French and Anglo-Norman verse of the middle and later decades of the twelfth century. Their name derives from their use of the romance vernacular, as opposed to Latin. What draws these highly varied works into a related group is their exploration of complex individual consciousness through narratorial comment, through interior monologue and dialogue, and through a kind of projection of the psyche upon the landscape. The romance hero, in quest or flight, often encounters a series of versions of the self–sometimes a "version" of his own reputation. (Consider Gawain's assertion "I am not he," line 1242 and Bercilak's "You are not Gawain the glorious," line 2270.) Equally he may meet up with some form of the other (especially in an erotic partner) who may either help achieve the quester's ambitions or subvert the quester's identity and social position.

Romance helped create, as much as it reflected, the cultural ideals of chivalry. Growing out of ancient social realities of the male battle cohort, chivalry celebrated the armed knight but also placed his militancy within more controlled structures such as the tournament. In the thirteenth century and after, these were increasingly theatricalized and ritualistic; in literature, arms and tournament often carried symbolic weight, as seen in Gawain's shield in *Sir Gawain and the Green Knight* (hereafter *SGGK*). The social ideals of chivalric loyalty had their private counterpart in the conventions of courtly love (again often highly ritualized and artificial), and spiritual counterpart in religious chivalry. This was expressed not just in the knight's individual faith but also in the ideals of crusade and the religious orders of knighthood like the Templars. If courtly love was often thought to elevate the knight, though, its adulterous implications clearly transgressed Christian faith; romances variously skirted or thematized this conflict. All these concepts had a highly variable and sometimes tangential relation to political reality, yet such was their power that they could be exploited for political ends. In the fourteenth century, for instance, kings across Europe sponsored chivalric orders in efforts to shift chivalric loyalty from local magnates to the crown. (The motto of Edward III's Order of the Garter is invoked at the end of *SGGK*.)

Romance is also typically concerned with the ways that the individual relates to social order, often moving from episodes of alienation or conflict to a restored harmony. Typically, too, it involves an adventure, especially a quest into the unknown or uncanny, that takes the hero away from an initial social setting, into a private confrontation or crisis (be it erotic, martial, or spiritual), and then returns him to that initial setting. Both hero and society are usually altered–improved or compromised–by these events.

Social Setting   It is exactly because of the double reach it shares with the most ambitious romances–toward the private crisis but also toward its societal implications–that *SGGK* is so powerful and challenging a text. Its poetic structure is so finished as to seem separate from mundane events, yet it was written (according to scholars' best guesses) during the later fourteenth century in the midst of royal and baronial crises in which the Trojan and Arthurian legends were again being exercised.

Troy and Arthur were inextricably mixed into political ambitions. Both Edward III and Richard II had interest in models of strong kingship and invoked their legendary Trojan and Arthurian genealogy. Edward III had refounded a Round Table in 1344 (but hadn't carried through). The French prose *Brut*, virtually a national chronicle that greatly expands on Geoffrey of Monmouth, was translated into English in the later fourteenth century and was enormously popular. The Mortimer family, who had royal ambitions, owned the "Wigmore Manuscript," which includes a Latin *Brut* and a genealogy linking Brutus, Arthur, and themselves. Middle English versions of the Troy story were written in alliterative verse, in the same general time and area that produced *SGGK*, and likely for the same provincial courts, which were rather conservative and loyal to the crown. And Geoffrey Chaucer wrote his *Troilus and Criseyde*, an episode of the Troy story, while working within the government of Richard II.

While *SGGK* is a celebration of Christian chivalry, its celebration is perhaps overdetermined because of the real stresses that the abstract notion of chivalry was facing in the later fourteenth century. By this time, some urban merchants had grown richer than knights, and mercantile families had risen into the aristocracy. The older model of aristocratic power based on provincial land tenure was shifting as nobles around the king became more like a paid bureaucracy. The military importance of the mounted knight was declining under new military technology that enhanced the effectiveness of archers on foot.

Regionalism and Alliterative Form   The alliterative meter which is *SGGK's* most distinguishing poetic feature is the great form of traditional heroic narratives in the second half of the fourteenth century. Like several other heroic tales in alliterative verse, it is associated with the northwest midlands—Cheshire and Lancashire, precisely the areas whose nobles came into the favor and patronage of Richard II during his repeated conflicts with the southern magnates after 1385. Cheshire nobles in his retinue moved back and forth to London (and the continent) as a result, which opened up lines of cultural mobility between the urban center and their provincial courts. And Richard and his retinue spent periods in the midlands. At the same time, English as a literary language was on the rise in Richard's reign. These elements, combined with Richard's own interest in history and imperial genealogy, provide a possible political setting for *SGGK's* yearning if fragile idealism and its exploration of courtly behavior. It has even been suggested that the poem's locales and themes involve some echo of Richard's famous Christmas Court at Lichfield in 1398–99.

Celtic Elements   This regional aspect involves another cluster of associations in *SGGK*. The territory between Chester, Wirral and North Wales was very well-known to the *Gawain* poet, as is clear in the geography of Gawain's wanderings (esp. lines 691 and after). The poem derives to some degree, then, from the culturally permeable border lands between the English and the Welsh. It was a multilingual area, including Welsh speakers who used English and *vice versa*, and (as everywhere in England) users of surviving specialized kinds of French, such as that of the law courts. *Gawain's* alliterative meter derives from English models, but it has other features of metrics and form, rhyme, assonance, and repetition of key words, which also have correspondences in Welsh poetry. These bear comparison with the Welsh-influenced "Harley lyrics" such as *Alisoun* included in this anthology. (For more details and bibliography, consult Jeffrey Hunstman, "The Celtic Heritage of *SGGK*," Miriam Y. Miller and Jane Chance, ed., *Approaches to Teaching SGGK*, [1986], 177–81; it contains several other fine essays.) Celtic influences are especially dense in the description of the Green Knight himself; "in fact, the *dyn glas* 'grey-green man' is a familiar figure of Welsh folklore, the pivotal winter figure who represents simultaneously the dying of the old year and . . . the birth of the new" (Hunstman, 180). And of course, "Morgan the Goddess" is a figure from pre-Christian Celtic myth.

Form, Balance, and Pedagogy   Exquisite as they are, the formal symmetries and highly accomplished craft of *SGGK* offer temptations to the critic that it may be well to resist, or leave behind at some point in classroom discussion. So elaborate are the poem's mirrorings, repetitions, and inversions—structural as well as thematic—that they may tempt the reader permanently into the New Critical stance of unresolvable ambiguity.

Discussion might start by laying out the poem's structural densities. Explore repetition at the level of key words: accord, contract, covenant, game; adorn, array; knot, lock, bind/bound; leap, hurtle; figure, sign, blazon. Unpack some of the numerical associations. Consider the brilliant balancing and pacing of Bercilak's three hunts and the Lady's three love dialogues with Gawain.

Approached these ways, the poem is indeed a monument to its own artifice, a celebration of its craft. In this respect it has been rightly compared to the metaphorical cut-paper castle in the description of Bercilak's own castle (lines 801–02). That metaphor is only one in a sequence of narrative celebrations of craft that are also worth pausing over: the decoration of the Green Knight's garb, even of his weapon, the arming of Gawain, the elaborate ritual of Bercilak's hunt, the almost equally formalized rules of love-play between Gawain and the Lady. Even highly emblematic description, though, is balanced by lively movement; Bercilak's gothic castle, metaphorized as cut paper, is followed by Bercilak himself, nervily leaping about to make Gawain at home and honor his presence.

Even these celebrations of the achievements of human craft and social ritual, though, have their inverses in the natural world within the poem. Death itself makes an early and frightening appearance in the agreement to exchange ax blows; and the lapse of time through the seasons, beautiful but transient, occupies one of the poem's most moving moments. The world of nature, beyond the reach of human artifice, becomes ever more frightening, raw, and abandoned as Gawain approaches his second meeting with the Green Knight.

These elements are certainly crucial to a poem that asserts its own craft (it is "fashioned featly," line 33); moreover, they provide pedagogically elegant ways to articulate the poem's complexities and formal dexterity. Yet it is also important to investigate *SGGK*'s narrative loose ends, unresolved themes, and anxious gaps and silences. So after considering the elements of "formal perfection," the brilliant pacing and the sheer narrative engagement of the tale, one might (as the editorial headnote hints) begin to read backward in a way more alert to other elements that the poem equally includes.

Felix Brutus, Bliss and Blunder   The pressure on an idealizing reading of the poem is probably greatest at the very points where its circularity is most emphatic, in the references to Troy and Brutus with which it begins and ends. That same circular echo also insists upon a kind of broad-scale history on the model of Geoffrey of Monmouth, in which British glory is repeatedly compromised by British sin and decadence, and in which Arthur's reign (for all its splendor) is only a brief British revival against encroaching invaders. Further, the poet seems to present Aeneas as a compromised dynastic founder, a betrayer of his own city. Hence any betrayal among Arthur and his knights has an implicit genealogical foundation, and an unnerving place in a bigger story of national rise and decline. The poem's internal narrative of a youthful and idealistic Arthurian court receives a dramatically broader, and darker, historical perspective at these moments.

Asymmetry, Loose Ends, Thematic Threads   Upon further examination, indeed, some of the poem's symmetries and mirrorings are more apparent than real; at key places, images and narrative remain significantly imbalanced or unresolved. There is, as suggested in the headnote, a female-centered narrative that emerges retrospectively after Gawain's second encounter with the Green Knight. This is important, but does not counterbalance the longer narrative of martial adventure and knightly quest. Bercilak's revelation of Morgan's identity and the prior cause of the story scarcely rewrites the impression and reflections of male Christian chivalry that a reader has gained up to this point. Similarly, the green girdle and the pentangle, neatly as they carry mirrored concepts, are not symmetrical signs. SGGK also presses at its limits by ironizing certain key, even formulaic terms at carefully chosen moments. What is the impact of "Gawain the good" when he is about to accept the green girdle?

Some of this asymmetry, and the thematic issues it raises, emerge in a comparison of the courts of Arthur and the lord later identified as Bercilak. Bercilak is explicitly more mature than Arthur, and his court appears more sophisticated and challenging, though it also proves to be more seductive and dangerous. This may be because Bercilak's court (which turns out to be really Morgan's) seems to be more in touch with aspects of mortality that Arthur's court, in this poem, leaves aside: women appear in extreme old age as well as youthful beauty, and the hunt is as violent as it is ritualized. Yet the forces of mortality and creaturely excess, while more apparent at Bercilak's court, are also controlled. Both the Green Knight and Bercilak, for all their size and power, are proportioned and orderly, bigger than life but never monstrous.

Other symmetries seem to raise questions by their very neatness. As they have agreed, Bercilak and Gawain exchange winnings after each of three hunts. Bercilak gives Gawain his day's quarry; Gawain responds with the kisses he has received from the Lady. The kiss, by itself, has no particular erotic valence, except for the covenant that they exchange *exactly* their winnings. Does Gawain transmit exactly the explicitly romantic kiss he had received (in a rather static and feminized posture) from the

Lady? Here the narrative is so attentive to its ritual that the reader is left to wonder at the apparently melting boundaries between chivalric male bonding and sexual exchange. Is Gawain's perfect knighthood the only quarry, or also his manhood?

Repeatedly, the poem's somewhat brittle formalism and depiction of social lightness give way to deeply engaging and disturbing themes. The courtly games of Arthur's New Year suddenly turn into the Green Knight's mortal "game" (line 273) of ax blows. This in turn takes up language of covenant, whose fulfillment offers a serious challenge to the self-image of the Arthurian court. And again, the game-covenant at Bercilak's court turns into the deepest challenge to Gawain's "truth." Gawain begins by playing out a courtly ritual, but finds himself painfully balancing obligations to his host and to the Lady. The elaborate love-play in which Gawain half-heartedly engages in turn produces the deepest temptation, and the one he does not resist: the temptation to be alive. (Bercilak's most appealing line may be "you loved your own life; the less, then, to blame," 2368.) When Gawain accepts the green girdle from the Lady, then holds it back in the third exchange with Bercilak, he enacts one of the poem's asymmetries, the unbound knot by which we grasp the poem's serious issues. Another emerges with the incompletely explained identity of "Morgan the Goddess" and her plot against Guenevere, discussed in the headnote. The rage Gawain feels when his failing is known, and his misogynist diatribe (lines 2413 ff.) carry these asymmetries further.

Does, finally, Arthur succeed in reintegrating the "loose end" opened by Gawain's adventure? If the girdle is, as the poet says, a "sign of excess" (line 2433), is it successfully restrained? Can the reader react to the laughter and game of the Arthurian court with the same delight as before? Can the reader choose between the poem's claims as a heroic romance and a moral fable?

Sir Thomas Malory
Le Morte Darthur

The plot and elegiac tone of the Arthurian legend in English literature, from the late Middle Ages until today, was largely created by Sir Thomas Malory. Prince Arthur's fleeting appearances in Edmund Spenser's *Faerie Queene* derive partly from Malory's episodes of Arthur's youth and initial military successes; Malorian names are used by John Milton when he mentions the legend. *Le Morte Darthur* (hereafter *MD*) became significantly influential again in the early nineteenth century, when it was reprinted in the wave of late romantic medievalism led by Sir Walter Scott and Robert Southey, and in the Victorian period when it was retold in numerous versions. The most prominent was Tennyson's *Idylls of the King* (1859–85) from which three episodes appear in the second volume of this anthology, as does William Morris's *The Defence of Guenevere* (1858). Malory and his Victorian followers were in turn mined (or parodied) in late nineteenth- and twentieth-century versions like Mark Twain's *A Connecticut Yankee in King Arthur's Court* (1889), T. H. White's *The Once and Future King* (1958), and their theatrical and cinematic progeny. Malory remains among the most widely read of medieval authors; continuing popular and scholarly interest is reflected in many critical studies, most recently the excellent collection, A *Companion to Malory* (ed. Elizabeth Archibald and A. S. G. Edwards, [1996]).

The persistently elegiac, even apocalyptic tone we encounter in Tennyson's *Idylls* was not a Victorian invention. Malory's version, as suggested by its very title, is colored throughout by an awareness of the inevitable fragility of Arthur's world, which sometimes seems engaged in a communal push toward death. Malory's vision of the Round Table features brief moments of exquisite unity and knightly harmony, but they are always hedged by potential strife and violence, and by an increasingly explicit sense of the moral compromises by which Arthur assembles and preserves his court.

Malory's Life   There is a near consensus among scholars that Sir Thomas Malory of Newbold Revell was the jailed knight who wrote *MD*. This Thomas Malory began his adult life as a solid citizen of the provincial gentry, married to the daughter of another landowning family; he was a member of Parliament by 1445. In the early 1450s, though, Malory crossed the somewhat hazy line between local influence and local brigandage, perhaps responding to hostilities among the great ducal families and enjoying the protection of the Duke of York. His life thereafter was caught up in the disorder and political divisions of the Wars of the Roses. He was repeatedly arrested, for theft and rape among other accusations, though his long imprisonment without trial after 1452 probably resulted from being on the wrong side of power shifts. He was freed when the Yorkists invaded in 1460, and spent some years at liberty. Soon, however, Malory transferred his loyalties to the Lancastrians and was jailed again by the later 1460s, when he most likely wrote the *MD*. He was freed in late 1470 when the Lancastrians returned to power, and died soon after.

It is a paradox worth considering that Malory seems to have led the life of narrow self-interest, occasional violence, and unstable loyalty that he eloquently laments in Arthur's court, especially among the minor knights whose social place had analogies to his own. In the later episodes of *MD*, the greater knights fall away—dead, exiled, disaffected, or in holy orders—and key events turn increasingly on secondary figures, like Sir Pinel and Patrise in "The Poisoned Apple," or Lucan and Bedivere in "The Day of Destiny."

The Political Context   It can be reductionist to pursue too neat an analogy between *MD* and affairs in later fifteenth-century England. Nonetheless, students should be alert to the great disorder and shifts of influence that came with the weak king Henry VI and the Wars of the Roses. Also, as Felicity Riddy has recently stressed ("Contextualizing *MD*: Empire and Civil War," A *Companion*, 55–73), these events closely followed the final loss of England's lucrative (and violently-held) colonial territories in France, which had been regained in the brief military glory of Henry V. The noble and administrative class not only lost income from these setbacks, but even in Henry V's earlier triumphs they witnessed their military obsolescence as the yeoman archers became more and more lethal in combat. If the increasingly apocalyptic tone of *MD* is specific to Malory's version of the Arthurian legend, the explosive pressure on a paradigm of noble existence had real echoes in his own world: civil strife, the hostilities of two great clans, weak kingship, and especially the diffusion of power downward upon ever lesser figures.

Style   MD is a long work by modern standards, but it is brief in comparison to the French prose romances that were Malory's major source. The energy and engagement of his work can be traced in good part to two elements. First, despite his frequent and respectful references to "the book," Malory was very free with his sources. Malory moves his narrative along at a faster pace than most of the French versions he used, especially trimming off much of their explanations of uncanny events and their moralizing sermons. This pacing sometimes creates an almost dizzying sequence of events, banal or uncanny, whose unnerving similarities are thereby laid bare even while their mystery remains intact.

Second, Malory used a simple but rhythmically powerful prose style that derives from early English prose but also uses effects from the alliterative poems he clearly knew. (For more discussion, see Jeremy Smith, "Language and Style in Malory," A *Companion*, 97–113.) Malory generally uses a "paratactic" sentence structure, its independent clauses linked by simple conjunctions, and without the implicit explanatory logic of subordinate clauses. Events and speeches are set out, but much is left for the reader to connect. Sentences achieve a density and rhythmic drive through Malory's persistent use of repetition and, especially at moments of high emotion, alliteration: "'What sawest thou there?' said the king. 'Sir,' he said, 'I saw nothing but waters wap and waves wan'" ("The Day of Destiny"). Thematically key words pile up with an insistence that can be almost independent of narrative; students can be urged to trace a few such lines of repetition.

Caxton's Prologue

In Caxton's Prologue to his first printing of MD, print rears its ugly head, and with it comes a new kind of textual commerce, and an interesting social strategy by the maker and purveyor of books. Caxton's Prologue is not unlike a jacket blurb today, using the words of persons of prestige (usually highly edited) to promote the appeal or social utility of the merchandise. Note Caxton's insistence on the "noble and dyuers gentylmen" who press him to publish a full Arthurian narrative. It is through this elite, in indirect discourse, that Caxton argues the historical reality of Arthur. In his own voice, further, Caxton makes an implicit nationalist argument for his book: the French in one direction and Welsh in another have all the stories of Arthur, but the English "nowher nye alle." Caxton will supply the lack, though he does even this under the favor and correction of both lords and gentlemen. This insistence on a double audience is telling in a period of hierarchical distinctions between nobles and gentry. Does the London bookseller, with his considerable mercantile clientele, echo some yearning to join that higher class?

The Miracle of Galahad

Galahad's vision of the grail in this episode is almost redundantly represented in terms of the Eucharist, the mass as a repetition of the Last Supper (note also the twelve knights at Corbenic), and the transubstantiation of the wafer into the body of Christ. Other transformations are also taking place, though. Secular objects and agents are insistently sacralized. A bloody spear, so often seen in earlier knightly combats, here becomes part of the grail symbolism. The unity of the Round Table is superseded by a different meal and unity on another plane. In a swift sequence of encounters, Galahad's touch cools fires and heat that elsewhere are Malory's images of chivalric rage and battle. Similarly, Galahad heals a series of wounds or illnesses, but thereby frees their sufferers to die and leave this world, rather than rejoin it. The symbolic structure of the tale makes these all holy deaths into movements toward eternal life, but the sobriety of Malory's description also gives the impression of a tale thick with death and the wish for death. Corpses and burials litter its narrative landscape. Galahad's transforming touch, presented with little of the Christian exegesis of the French sources, also seems to undo structures that elsewhere uphold the Arthurian world. The one link he holds to, and that he encounters in almost breathless repetition, is the relation of father and son. Galahad's last words recall his father Lancelot, and attempt to call him from his entanglement in the world, his passion for Guinevere. Finally, Bors returns to Camelot, and his story to the court enacts his frequent role as mediator among forces greater than he. The writing of his story in "great books" is another in a series of occasions in the later episodes when Malory's own project is mirrored poignantly within his text.

The Poisoned Apple

The religious grail quest has been a disaster for the secular Round Table, and Bors returns to a mere "remnant" of the prior company. The surviving characters seem stuck in this diminished world, though, playing out old passions and hostilities with a sense of exhausted inevitability, banal but tragic. Lancelot retains some impression of his brief vision of the grail and the warning of his son Galahad, yet he takes up with Guinevere nonetheless, resuming an affair that we now witness only in a spiteful, weary argument. Their love has exactly the heat Galahad elsewhere extinguished. They try to keep it "privy" (a significantly repeated term), but the disembodied voices and sacred writings of the grail quest are now replaced by mutterings, gossip, and an unconvincing effort to preserve outward appearances.

This episode explores once again, more sadly than ever, a paradox at the center of MD: that desire for Guinevere is what keeps Arthur's best knight at court, yet that desire undermines the codes and cohesion of the court. Public celebration of the Round Table is only possible in silence about the affair, but sacred and profane revelation (Grail and gossip) place that silence under impossible strain. Petty, secondary hostilities begin to drive the plot. Something like open talk occurs only in private, as in the scene of Arthur and Guinevere alone, where Arthur seems to connive to retain Lancelot's service. Even here, though, they use the coded dialogue of a long marital truce.

Lancelot's return and triumph in a trial by battle is arranged again by Bors. Lancelot tries to limit scandal by stipulating that no mention of Guinevere be made on the tomb of Sir Patrise. Yet a report of the false accusation appears there nonetheless, told in an indirect discourse that melts indistinguishably into Malory's own narrative voice. Voices are abroad that will bring down Arthur's realm.

The Day of Destiny

The episode in which the text of MD finally enacts its title is itself littered with texts of death: fake letters announcing Arthur's death, tombs, inscriptions, tales of death, and most poignantly Gawain's letter, his dying effort. Here death converges with the very making of a text, and that death letter repeats, almost verbatim, the immediately preceding narrative paragraph. Malory folds his own cultural work into the final unravelling of the aristocratic model.

"The Day of Destiny" also sees the final conflict between feudal loyalty to Arthur and loyalty to clan, as Gawain seeks vengeance for Lancelot's killing of his kinsmen. Arthur's absence while prosecuting that kinship vendetta provides Mordred with the chance to seek the tale's most impacted bond of kinship: to supplant his incestuous father on the throne and in the bed of his stepmother, and to kill off (first by the fake letters, then in fact) his father. To some degree, however, this replicates the royal usurpation of a marriage bed (and murder of its rightful occupant) by which Arthur was born.

Throughout this final episode, the abandonment of the secular world witnessed in the grail quest is repeated, as one public character after another abjures the world, to become a hermit, a nun, or a man suspended near death on an unknown island. These changes carry little of the grail quest's sense of unification with an invisible world, however. Rather, they seem to be the nadir of the slow dispersal of central power and the chivalric paradigm under the pressure of conflicting and unstable loyalty.

Other mundane worlds are glimpsed in this final episode, however, and deserve attention. Sir Lucan reports the pillaging of knightly bodies in the moonlight after the battle. It is a chilling scene, but also one of the very few appearances of commoners in MD. A never-acknowledged source of Arthurian wealth recovers it, however repulsively, at the very close of the tale. In another strangely anomalous detail, Guinevere escapes Mordred by going to London on a fictive errand to buy her wedding needs. The world of mercantile activity opens, in a phrase, onto the death-throes of chivalry.

These two elements have converged in the literary past, for instance, when the mercantile Wife of Bath told a tale of a common girl raped by an Arthurian knight. And this moment may be considered, in turn, along with the conflict of values between Gawain and his guide (the sole presence of a servant in Sir Gawain and the Green Knight), when the guide tries to convince Gawain to flee his second encounter with the Green Knight. Together, they imply another perspective and position in the totalizing, if moving, value systems of the Arthurian legend.

Geoffrey Chaucer

The Chaucer industry—editions, scholarship, criticism, pedagogy—stretches back in a continuous tradition of nearly six hundred years. It can be said to start within a decade or so of Chaucer's death, with the production of luxury copies like the famous Ellesmere manuscript. (See the portrait of Chaucer from this manuscript, p. 281.) This already began to institutionalize Chaucer as a "great writer" and, in such beautiful manuscripts, to reserve him for the consumption of an elite audience. Contemporary writers went about a related project by imitating aspects of Chaucer's style, notably John Lydgate in a series of historical and moral works written under the patronage of King Henry V. Few writers since Virgil and Dante (both of whom Chaucer emulated) have been so swiftly made the unimpeachable objects of reverential study and imitation.

Ever since then, a range of audiences has appropriated Chaucer's prestige as an element, sometimes even a voice, of their interests and preoccupations, always aided by the still astonishing variety of ideas and attitudes implicit in his works. Chaucer has thus been an icon for royalty, democracy, the protestant reformation, even (in his skeptical vein) the Enlightenment. One after another, social and intellectual communities have registered their arrival on the textual and especially the academic scene by a usually reverent laying of hands on the Chaucerian text.

Appropriations of this sort should not be seen as perversions or crude exploitation of the Chaucerian text. Rather, it is how a literary community makes obeisance to a particularly layered and resonant body of work, and it is among the best reasons to continue the undeniable efforts involved in laying our own hands on books as linguistically and culturally distant as Chaucer's. For all the difficulty of the work, happily, the very fact of our continual grappling with Chaucer across the centuries has helped construct the many continuities of human experience through which we can still find links with his world.

The last couple of decades of critical and scholarly work around Chaucer make this a particularly challenging moment, but equally a very rich moment, in which to be reading him. Most of the major critical theories of the past three decades have generated important new statements on Chaucer. Some have been particularly fruitful or resonant because, for all their newness, they have encountered materials in earlier criticism or in medieval culture itself already engaged with their preoccupations. This is perhaps truest of deconstructive readings, whose play with polysemy has important precedents in medieval theories of interpretation, both the prescriptive notion of four-fold Biblical exegesis, and the much looser explorations of twelfth-century commentators like William of Conches and Bernard Silvestris.

The great critical deposit of the decades after mid-century has a continuing and important role in readings of Chaucer that go on today. The New Critics brought a fine-grained detail to their reading of Chaucer's poetry which remains profitable, not only in the classroom, but equally in the focus it gives to current readings in very different modes. For all their emphasis on the poetic text as a self-contained unit, comprehensible (and best enjoyed) independent of its historical setting, the New Critics also pressed readings of Chaucer past a divide that had opened between philological and related research, and literary "appreciation." It is not surprising that E. Talbot Donaldson, the great exponent of New Critical readings of Chaucer, trained a leading New Historicist Chaucerian, Lee Patterson.

One danger of bringing only the critic's fine ear to the reading of an early text, is that the critic may find largely him- or herself therein. And the Chaucer who emerges from some New Critical readings—liberal-minded, genial, open to change—can sound today like an enlightened voice of the 1950s or '60s. That Chaucer is generous-minded toward women, but sometimes (like those same liberal circles) rather condescending too.

An alternative, and in some ways a corrective, to this approach grew up in the same years in the exegetical or "patristic" criticism of Chaucer most often associated with the work of D. W. Robertson. The patristic school wished to read Chaucer as his contemporaries might have done; the model of medieval reading they used toward that end was the allegorical approach to interpreting the Bible, begun by the Fathers of the Church and developed (with less system and more variety than Robertsonians usually registered) at various times in the Middle Ages. This opened up a very rich body of medieval thought for Chaucerians, but a narrow one nonetheless, a view of dogma and social order that was conservative even in the medieval period. In the hands of flexible and complex readers, such as Robert Kaske, the patristic approach produced rich interpretations, nicely embedded in at least one important arena of medieval culture. Used by lesser minds, the results can be mechanical and often seem to support a sentimental and highly conservative, hierarchical view of the medieval past.

Recent scholars have used analogous procedures with more varied results. A great deal of research has been done on habits of secular reading in the schools of the Middle Ages, such as Alastair Minnis's *Medieval Theory of Authorship* (1988). This and related work in turn has been applied to Chaucer as a writer well in touch with the universities, as in Ann W. Astell's recent *Chaucer and the Universe of Learning*. Another approach to how Chaucer's near-contemporaries might have read him, in a more immediate and concrete way, is through study of medieval manuscripts of his work, and how they compare to contemporary copies of other texts. (One resource of this "codicological" approach is suggested in the entry on the Wife of Bath's Tale.)

The better-known critical theories of the past decades—deconstructive, psychoanalytic, Marxist, feminist, New Historicist—are all currently in use by some of our most learned and brilliant Chaucerians. What generates much of the current richness of Chaucer studies is the extent to which these approaches speak to one another and borrow from one another. The tone of armed encampments that surrounded a great deal of literary criticism in, say, the 1970s, has largely dissipated in favor of an eclectic but theoretically self-aware posture among Chaucerians. Peter G. Beidler's recent collection of essays on the Wife of Bath (1996), with introductory essays by Ross Murfin, offers students and teachers an accessible first look at these theoretical approaches.

So for instance the work of H. Marshall Leicester (*The Disenchanted Self: Representing the Subject in the "Canterbury Tales,"* [1990]) draws both from deconstruction and from post-Lacanian psychology. The "New Historicism" practiced by Lee Patterson is also informed by deconstruction's challenge to the idea of a natural, self-contained subject (*Chaucer and the Subject of History*, [1991]). Marxists like David Aers include gender in their analyses of class and alienation, profiting from the perspectives of feminism (*Culture and History, 1350–1600: Essays on English Communities, Identities, and Writing*, [1992]). The influential feminist work of Carolyn Dinshaw equally draws on psychoanalytic and historicist perspectives (*Chaucer's Sexual Poetics*, [1989]).

If the challenge of critical theory is rewarded with a stimulating array of readings, merely reading the Chaucerian text is a great challenge for most college students. The decision to present Chaucer in Middle English in this anthology, in a text only modestly regularized, was taken after considerable thought. In fact, Chaucer's English is very much more like our own than is that of many of his contemporaries, because he wrote in the London dialect that was also used by the government bureaucracy, and soon in print. His English has become ours, and if it is taught by starting with those continuities, a well-glossed text like that given here can become readable without great difficulty. Middle English can be a nice equalizer in class, too. Students who have English as a second language often find themselves deciphering Chaucer's English better than their peers who are accustomed to read English more transparently. Reading out loud helps a lot; so does spending some time making sure that the class is clear about the plot, then (of course) working through the syntax and vocabulary of brief passages. The selections from the General Prologue to the *Canterbury Tales* on our audio CD provide a lively gurde to the sound of Chaucer's verse. Students should also be urged to consult a good new CD-ROM, *Chaucer: Life and Times* (Primary Sources Media, [1995]). It provides a full text (from the Riverside edition) with pull-down glosses and notes; more important, the entire text is also in audio form, pronounced with accurate Middle English and (in some tales) considerable drama. Students can thus read as they listen—a more medieval practice than silent reading anyway—and use the audio for cues on syntax.

The Parliament of Fowls

The opening line of Chaucer's *Parliament of Fowls* (hereafter PF) almost makes us expect a self-reflexive poem about poetry itself ("the craft"); the second line suggests the theme of state-"craft" ("the conqueringe"). Only line 4 reveals Chaucer's announced topic: "Al this mene I by Love . . ." Even then, the very nature of Love (craft or conquest? dreadful or joyous?) slides around fascinatingly for the rest of the poem. And the PF turns out in fact to be about all three topics: poetry, the polity, and the many forms of divine, romantic, and sexual love. The poem also proves to be densely self-reflexive after all: a new book written about a dream of (earthly) love that comes to the narrator after he reads about (cosmic) love in a visionary dream written in an ancient book.

For all the resonances created by this mirroring structure, though, it is important to help students respond as well to the very worldly, realistic touches that fill the PF and animate its rich but rather traditional themes. In the poem's speaker,

Chaucer continues to refine and elaborate the somewhat fuzzy-minded, owlish narrator he had already used in his earlier *Book of the Duchess*. This character again knows the world mostly through books, but even his indirect quest for knowledge suggests a somewhat random, passive reader, picking up volumes almost by habit ("Of usage") and without fixed intent ("what for lust and what for lore," line 15), a seeker of bookish wisdom who remains unsatisfied but uncertain of just what he's looking for. In the end, though, this very range of reading provides the background for the poem's daring—and playful—combination of cosmic speculation and rarefied courtly artifice, even if the narrator leaves the poem only dimly aware of what complexity he has just encountered.

Book, Dream, Experience   The poem achieves its density and its play through the interpenetration and mutual questioning of book, dream, and experience. One always qualifies or comments on the other. The narrator encounters Scipio's visionary dream of the cosmos and its analogies to the state in his book "write with lettres olde" (line 19). His own dream of Venus' temple contains conventional personifications from the bookish courtly love tradition. Nature's parliament, in the same dream, features "natural" birds whose talk sounds increasingly like a debate of social classes in contemporary London, though the narrator has compared the whole scene to a famous book, Alan of Lille's *Complaint of Nature* (line 316). Nature and the search for generative sexuality comment on the frustrated love in Venus's temple, yet the tercel eagles speak the language of courtly love.

Occasion   The PF has a place in literary history as among the first (and possibly the very first) in the tradition of Valentine's Day poems. It may well be an "occasional" poem in a more interesting and thematically relevant sense, though. The counsellors of young King Richard II were actively seeking a politically advantageous wife for him in the later 1370s. The search went slowly. In 1380 negotiations began for an alliance with Anne of Bohemia, daughter of Emperor Charles IV. There were other suitors, though, and before a deal was struck, the future King Charles VI also made a bid for her hand. Richard was finally betrothed to Anne on May 3, 1381, and they married the following January. It has often been proposed that the debate of the tercel eagles for the love of the formel plays on this diplomatic competition to marry Anne, even down to the claim of the third eagle (lines 470-76) that while he may not (like the dauphin Charles) have been the longest in her pursuit, he can still love her as well as any. The year's delay may reflect the period of diplomatic activity before the match was settled.

Common Profit   The PF as a whole could certainly speak to a young king like Richard, already engaged with the arts at a sophisticated level, just at the age of romantic yearning and enormous physical desire, yet still under instruction in the work of the prince and the state. The poem returns again and again to the theme of "commune profit" (lines 47, 75) and the good of the group—the idea, that is, of the polity. *The Dream of Scipio*, through which this topic enters the poem, is the closing section of Cicero's *De Re Publica*, and itself involves the running of the state. Such "commune profit," here and elsewhere in the poem, occurs within a hierarchy, authorized and naturalized by the vision of the cosmos. The poem and its voices (and possibly the social perspective of its royal or any other reader) is suddenly expanded in the debate of the birds, but the debate ends with them paired "By evene accord" (line 668) and the closing roundel recapitulates in form and sound the "musik and melodye" of the spheres (line 62).

Medieval Traditions and Literary Backgrounds Anthologies too often edit out that side of Chaucer's career that does not look toward later literature, especially the rise of the bourgeois narrative that has been loosely connected with certain speakers in the Canterbury Tales. The PF is included in this anthology for its inherent appeal, but equally because it carries a whole range of older forms and themes that Chaucer helped bring into later English literature. At the same time, it suggests Chaucer's extraordinary powers of synthesizing continental traditions, yet innovating with a genuinely new colloquial tone from his own vernacular. To that extent, and especially in the debate of the birds, it also looks forward to the multiple voices and social perspectives that lend such energy to the Canterbury Tales. And the PF has an important influence on a whole Early Modern tradition of allegorical and political poetry, especially Spenser's Faerie Queene.

Most prominently, the poem draws on traditions of dream vision stretching back to antiquity. Its main narrative draws heavily on thirteenth- and fourteenth-century French dream visions. From these poems comes the slightly feverish garden of desire, populated by an almost allegorical set of love's agents and postulants, and the often rather arcane demande d'amour, a question regarding priority or propriety within the ever more elaborate conventions of courtly love. The earlier Book of the Duchess was almost a pastiche of such poems. By the time of the PF, though, Chaucer's range of reading and his ambitions as a writer were drawing in two other important textual traditions. First, contemporary Italian literature has an impact here. Study of Boccaccio and his poems in ottava rima (a stanza of eight 10-syllable lines) probably helped Chaucer realize the narrative resources of the related rime royal stanza; further, the temple of Venus in PF lifts elements rather directly from Boccaccio's Teseida. And while the garden of PF echoes the French Romance of the Rose (which Chaucer had translated into Middle English), the fearful inscription on the gate seems to recall the gate of Dante's Inferno. Further implications of this double tradition are explored in fine essays by Piero Boitani and David Wallace in The Cambridge Chaucer Companion, ed. Boitani and Jill Mann (1986).

It is from Chaucer's reading in a still earlier tradition, though, that the PF gains much of its philosophical resonance, its musings on statecraft and occasional echoes of neoplatonic cosmology. Chaucer was deeply engaged by texts and intellectual preoccupations surviving from the twelfth century. Cicero's Dream of Scipio was a favorite text of that era, always accompanied by the fifth-century commentary of Macrobius, which included long discussions of dream theory, the order of the cosmos and its reflection in the symbolism of number. Further commentaries were added in the twelfth century (especially by the influential William of Conches); this in turn influenced philosophical poets like Bernard Silvestris and Alan of Lille; and all these texts continued to circulate in England into the fourteenth century. One useful area of discussion is which of these two dream traditions carries more weight in the PF.

Love and the State   The narrator's move from reading in classical cosmology to the dream garden continues to startle readers. There is no reason to think it was not meant to, but a connection starts to emerge if students are reminded of the medieval commonplace that the universe itself was created by an outpouring of divine love. Consider, too, that it is the Roman general Scipio who brings the hesitant dreamer to the gate of the poem's love-garden and then pushes him in. In this perspective—informed by Plato's *Timaeus*, Boethius's *Consolation of Philosophy*, and their medieval commentaries—love is the force that binds the individually warring elements of the universe, and generates from them the kind of harmony that Scipio hears during his cosmic journey. And that model becomes part of medieval notions both of human love and of the state. (For a fuller discussion, consult Paul Beekman Taylor's recent *Chaucer's Chain of Love*, [1996].) This helps account for the PF's move from a text on the state, through a vision of courtly love, and into a love debate among birds that seem increasingly like members of a fractious human society.

Within the garden, love is by turns delightful, animating all nature, and then threatening, sterile. This begins with the unnerving double inscription on the garden gate. It is a good image to keep in mind; students often divide Venus's temple and Nature's hill into neat units, but it is important that they are in the same dream and same garden. The temple of Venus and its allegory of courtly love is only paces from Nature's fecund hill and the mating birds. The garden seems initially an earthly paradise, emulating the harmony—the "ravisshing swetnesse" (line 198)—of the spheres. But this soon gives way to the unfulfilled arousal of Priapus, and the superheated and frustrated atmosphere of Venus's temple with its sighing lovers. The gorgeous artifice of the temple only mirrors sterility. Yet the tragic lovers depicted on its walls (lines 284 ff.) are key figures from ancient history, particularly the Trojan war and its aftermath, which gave rise in turn to the legendary origins of Britain. A more immediate kind of England enters later in the colloquial debate of the birds.

The dream can well be approached through its obvious divisions, but its richness emerges best when connections between those moments are explored. This becomes quite clear when key words and images are tracked across the entire poem: number; accord, harmony, and noise; birds and fish; noble, cherl; array. These and others carry issues from the love garden and temple to Nature's hill and the debate of the birds. Consider how quickly the placid description of "noble goddesse Nature" gives way to the noise of the birds. (Is the adjective moral, or political?) Chaucer plays nicely in here with details that pull the reader between literal birds and figures of social class. Even noble Nature has trouble with her polity; the order of love choices she initially envisions is soon undone by strife, interruptions, and dismissive interjections like the duck's wonderful "Ye, queke" (line 594). Is the hierarchy of birds only social, or does it also echo the cosmic hierarchy of Scipio's vision, and at the same time compromise it as an image of the state? Note too the snobbery and mutual hostility from one class of birds toward another, and the slightly snivelling tone of the respectful turtledove ("oon the unworthieste," line 512).

Chaucer's attention to the voices and perspectives of a range of social classes, though, can be given too prominent a place in our reading of the poem. For all the colloquial chatter of the birds, with their non-aristocratic voices and attitudes, the parliament ends with the birds drawing themselves back into a harmony that suggests the music of the spheres, using the traditional lyric form and explicitly French tune of a roundel. To the small extent that the *PF* is working as a mirror for princes (or for one particular prince), it investigates social variety and disruption only to pull those elements back into a celebratory harmony.

Female Voices: Turtledove, Goose, and Formel Eagle   Finally, and as a turn toward the *Canterbury Tales*, one might spend time discussing the gender of voices in the *PF*. Powerful women are frequent presences in dream vision poems, often controlling the *demande d'amour*. But their power is specific to the courtly love context of most such poems. Chaucer begins at that point in the *PF*, with conventional figures like Venus (who is silent anyway) and Nature. With the parliament of birds, though, several highly characterized and occasionally obstreperous female voices come into play, and bespeak a social posture that extends beyond the dream. It is interesting to consider the convergence of such voices (prominently the turtledove and goose) and the entry of Middle English colloquialism. At the same time, as Elaine Tuttle Hansen has pointed out in an intriguing reading of the poem, the formel's delay, her very refusal to speak and her choice not to choose a mate, focus power on her. (See "Female Indecision and Indifference in the PF," *Chaucer and the Fictions of Gender*, [1992], 108–40.) And her year's delay extends the liminal moment of female influence and choice, both within the conventions of courtly poetry (that usually seeks a solution) and the social negotiations of marriage. This aspect of the *PF* looks forward significantly to the convergences of gender, class, and vernacular voice in the *Canterbury Tales*.

The Canterbury Tales
The General Prologue

The clearly fragmentary nature of the *Canterbury Tales* poses problems of interpretation that have tempted many critics to construct unifying schemes. The most influential of these has been the exegetical approach, which sees the pilgrimage as directed to the New Jerusalem as much as to Canterbury. To support this Augustinian view, D. W. Robertson, Jr. leans heavily on the General Prologue, which establishes the pilgrimage frame, and on the prologue to the Parson's Tale, which promises to show the way to "thilke parfit glorious pilgrimage / That highte Jerusalem celestial" (A *Preface to Chaucer*, [1962], 373).

Readers of various theoretical persuasions, however, have found this view reductionist. New Critics such as E. Talbot Donaldson point out that such a moralistic reading misses Chaucer's irony and complexity. Glending Olson, in *Literature as Recreation in the Later Middle Ages* (1982) questions Robertson on historical grounds, reminding us that there was a medieval theory justifying the use of literature for pleasure, as well as for instruction. He argues that the serious purpose of the pilgrimage (the "outer frame" of the *Canterbury Tales*) is balanced by the playful purpose of the story telling contest (the "inner frame"), which has been generally overlooked (156). For Olson, too, the General Prologue looms large, for it is here that the Host, Harry Bailey, most clearly articulates his view of the importance of pleasure in literature. While later on he appears naive or philistine in his insistence that pilgrims tell tales of "mirth," here the Host expresses a more balanced Horatian ideal of pleasure *and* profit, as he stipulates that the winner of the prize supper will be the pilgrim who tells "tales of most sentence and best solas." While the Host's aesthetic ideals will prove to be at odds with the puritanical ones of the Parson which conclude the *Canterbury Tales*, the fact that they have a precedent in the medieval theories of literature as recreation gives them a measure of credibility (Olson 157).

Historically oriented critics who view the *Canterbury Tales* in its social context, such as Stephen Knight, David Aers, and Lee Patterson, have also taken issue with Robertson's view that the ideal of hierarchy was universally accepted in the Middle Ages. In a recent article David Wallace speaks for all of them when he writes of Chaucer's struggle "to assess the possibilities of a complex, urbanizing, aggressive, post-bastard feudal society" ("In Flaundres," *Studies in the Age of Chaucer*, 19 [1997], 84). The historical critic who has particularly focused on the General Prologue is Jill Mann, in *Chaucer and Medieval Estates Satire: The Literature of Social Class and the General Prologue of the Canterbury Tales* (1973). She shows how Chaucer draws on the criticism in Estates Satire of all three estates—the nobility, the clergy, and the commons—for failing to perform their proper function.

Such satire is particularly sharp in the case of the clergy. The Prologue reflects the increasing insistence of the laity on a role in religion, an insistence exemplified by John Wycliffe, who challenged the efficacy of the Eucharist and the necessity of the priesthood as an intermediary between God and human beings. While not a follower of Wycliffe, Chaucer shares his objection to the hypocrisy of many of the orders of the Church, particularly that of the friars. The fraternal orders, the first of which was founded in the twelfth century as part of a reformist movement, claimed that they begged because they had given up property in imitation of Christ's apostles, but by the end of the fourteenth century they had in fact amassed a great deal of wealth.

While Mann shows Chaucer's debts to Estates Satire, she also shows how he goes beyond the genre with the ironic technique of the naive narrator. By refusing to dwell on the harm that his immoral pilgrims do—as when the friar and the pardoner lead unsuspecting souls to damnation with their empty absolutions and fake relics—this narrator appears to accept all the pilgrims at their own flattering estimation, leaving the readers themselves to supply the judgment. This becomes especially clear at moments when the narrator transmits a pilgrim's views in indirect discourse, but then slides into near-quotation, is if his voice (and mind?) were being taken over by that pilgrim; the effect is particularly egregious in the portrait of the Monk, lines 177–88.

E. T. Donaldson's influential distinction between "Chaucer the pilgrim"–an ironic literary persona–and "Chaucer the poet" (*Speaking of Chaucer*, [1970], 1–12) has been questioned, but clearly the sophisticated author of the *Canterbury Tales* could hardly have been as naive as he appears. It should be pointed out that the self-deprecating narrator is in fact part of a well-worn medieval literary convention, used by Boethius, Dante, and Christine de Pizan, among others.

Questions about narrators pertain not only to Chaucer the pilgrim, but also to the pilgrim narrators of each of the tales, enough of which are included in this anthology to explore their relation to the portraits of the pilgrims in the General Prologue. The influential theory of a consistent dramatic appropriateness of tales to tellers formulated by George Lyman Kittredge (*Chaucer and his Poetry*, 1915 [rpt. 1970]), it should be pointed out, has been somewhat discredited. Nonetheless, students can appreciate such relationships when they do pertain. For instance, the General Prologue's portrait of the Miller as a teller of "harlotries" is confirmed by his tale, and its reference to the Wife of Bath's boldness and deafness is dramatized and explained by her own prologue. (Inconsistencies also reward discussion, however, such as the fact the Prologue's detail of the Wife's clothmaking–of interest to feminist critics as a source of financial independence for a middle-class woman–is omitted from her own prologue. There, she attributes her wealth instead to inheritances from her husbands.) The Pardoner's portrait as a scoundrel in the General Prologue is particularly well-suited both to his prologue, in which he boasts of his skill at cheating his audiences, and to his tale, a gripping account of the punishment of greed, which concludes with his offer to sell absolution to the pilgrims themselves. It is equally intriguing, though, to consider occasions when Chaucer did not suit the teller to the tale: the virtually faceless Nun's priest–mentioned in the General Prologue simply as one of "prestes three" accompanying the Prioress–tells one of the most brilliant tales of all.

The Miller's Tale

Nicholas has just grabbed Alison by the crotch and she, for the moment, is having none of it: "Do way youre handes, for your curteisye!" (line 179). This is not just a key turn in the fabliau structure of the Miller's Tale, but equally a comic high point in the tale's extended parody of the verbal conventions of courtly love. In turn, it is a particularly sly part of the Miller's broader attack on the values of the aristocratic class who were the cultural consumers of courtly love.

Although the tale contains no explicit reference to contemporary political conflict among the classes, scholars point out the considerable if still obscure place that millers had in the discourse of the Peasants' Revolt. (See the fine discussion in Lee W. Patterson, *Chaucer and the Subject of History*, [1991], 254–58.) The famous letters of John Ball, a leader of the revolt, refer to an allegorical miller (see "*Piers Plowman* in Its Time: the Rising of 1381"). And millers were important throughout late medieval rural society as the first agent in the transformation of crops into goods, a crucial link then between farm and town.

Certainly Chaucer's Miller is openly eager to challenge hierarchy and social order within the confines of the pilgrimage community. He usurps the order of speakers that the Host is trying to stage-manage, and thereby alters the social meaning of tale telling. In one shout he imports values of verbal skill (his are immense) and liveliness in several senses, and displaces the Host's emerging plan of tale telling linked to social eminence and the archaic model of the three estates. (This point can be supported by turning to the General Prologue portrait of the Miller; note the implicit class challenge of carrying a sword and buckler, line 560.)

If the Miller's interruption generates a slippage among narrative orders in the pilgrimage fiction (loud voice versus social rank) it also opens a gap in the conventions of transmission of the textual product, the tales themselves. Chaucer has opened the Tales as a mammoth exercise of memory, repeating the tales he heard, implicitly out loud before a (presumably courtly) audience: "What sholde I more sayn . . . ?" his narrator asks, line 59. But now, seemingly shocked at the prospect of a "cherles tale," he urges modest readers, "Turne over the leef, and chese another tale" (line 69) in what must suddenly be conceived as a book.

The story itself, further, is a perfect example of strains between a teller and tale: how could a man as drunk as the Miller claims to be still manage a story so layered yet economical? It is brilliantly paced, full of brief and telling characterization that occasionally slows into beautifully managed description, especially of the body and dress of Alison.

The Miller's tale is a *fabliau*, with its typical plot of sexual competition and cuckoldry (and what genteel critics used to call "the nether kiss"), and its punning on terms like "queinte," "hende," and "privee." He thus uses a genre "of" the bourgeois—but does that mean "about" or "controlled by"? If we see it as a genre consciously manipulated by an artisan like the Miller, it invites celebration of the brilliant response with which he "quits" the class and worldview of the knight. If however the genre is seen as an aristocratic property, the audience can react with condescension toward the churls therein depicted. The narrator's ambivalence about even repeating the tale reflects some of this potential instability of reception.

Along with its complex internal plot, the tale also manages to parody the plot of the Knight's Tale. There, in a similar love triangle, two captive knights compete (finally in a tournament) for the attention of a young noblewoman whom initially they have not even met, and wait years for her favor. The Knight's lady, Emelye, is almost entirely passive; her one expressed wish (spoken only in prayer) is to have neither man, and that wish is denied.

The Miller's squabbling suitors parallel this romantic competition nicely, yet they couldn't be more different from the Knight's lovers. Nicholas spouts a bit of courtly vocabulary ("For derne love of thee, lemman, I spille," line 170) then grabs what he wants. Absalon's aping of courtship is more elaborate, but deflated by his very narcissism and apparent effeminacy. The tale's most powerful answer to the Knight, though, is the character of Alison. Her description draws in vast areas of plant and animal life, both domesticated and wild, through metaphor and analogy, overwhelming the conventional lily-and-rose beauty of Emelye.

But, feminist critics have wondered, is there a person residing in so global a range of reference? Can Alison be claimed as an agent in the tale, or is she rather an icon first of old John's wealth (note her costly clothing and her purse), and then of the broader social competition among men? Note how thickly bound up she is in all that restrictive clothing. On the other hand, consider how effectively she handles Nicholas' sexual approach, and how she sets up the conditions of any future sexual gift.

The figure of Alison engages a web of biblical reference in the tale. The situation of a young wife married to an old carpenter echoes the Nativity story, and Nicholas dupes old John with a tale of Noah's flood repeating itself. But this is particularly a version of Christian story and action as practiced within urban culture: attendance at liturgical celebrations, and civic productions of biblical dramas such as Noah, the Nativity, or the play of Herod in which Absolon acts (line 276). There are also quieter but equally emphatic echoes of the Song of Songs and other Old Testament imagery. This network of reference has invited some reductionist allegorical readings of the tale, but also subtler comments on the exploration of human and Christian love that at some points seems continuous in the tale. With old John tucked up in the attic, awaiting a second flood, Nicholas and Alison make love

> Til that the belle of Laudes gan to ringe,
> And freres in the chauncel gonne singe. (lines 547–48)

The tale's close is Saturnalian: pitch darkness, the hot coulter, the explosion of boundaries between attic and bedroom, private house and communal gaze. Along with the laughter here, a strain of male sexual violence and injury also emerges: John's arm broken, Nicholas's ass burnt by the traditionally phallic coulter. On the one hand, Alison is the one uninjured character at the end of the tale; on the other she does seem to be dealt out of a scene of violent physical (and comic) exchange among men. Indeed, even Absolon's effeminate delicacy seems effaced by his rage and his odd negotiation with the blacksmith. For all the tale's aim of filling up the limited perspective and erotic desiccation of the Knight's Tale, and for all its laughter, the Miller's Tale also closes with the violent underpinnings of male competition laid, literally, bare.

The Wife of Bath's Prologue and Tale

Dame Alison of Bath is a central focus of recent Chaucer criticism, yet (for all her garrulous sociability) a solitary and somewhat isolated figure in the pilgrimage community. There are two other women travelling to Canterbury, the Prioress and "Another Nonne," but both are in holy orders. So the Wife of Bath alone speaks for women in the secular world, in marriage, and in the unstable, socially striving mercantile class. The General Prologue portrait is one of Chaucer's great character sketches, exploiting traditional associations with dress, physiognomy, and social conduct. Her comically fashionable hat (as big as a shield, the narrator says) and her sharp spurs challenge male chivalry; her repeated widowhood challenges some notions of marriage; and her red face and hose suggest a bold sexuality that threatens the model of male erotic aggression. (These same details of her dress also underwrite associations made by some patristic critics between the Wife and the biblical Whore of Babylon.) The Wife is an eager participant, even a competitor, in the rituals of public culture. She attends mass often, but wants to be first in line at the offering. And she is an inveterate traveller on pilgrimages, a habit she has in common with historical women interested in aspects of the religious life, like Margery Kempe.

The Prologue   The Wife of Bath's Prologue is long and dense, spanning many episodes of her past. It is useful first to set out its main moments and interlocutors: the lengthy debate with an unidentified clergyman about a sixth husband, and the further clerical issues that accompany the debate; the three old husbands lumped into a single story (why?); the brief mention of her fourth husband the reveller; and the closing tale of her battle and peace with Jankyn. This is autobiography presented as a series of arguments with men in different kinds of authority, and suggests the way that Alison has created herself in constant battle with various male discourses. The question this leaves is whether she triumphs in that combat and creates a self that is her own; or whether, rather, she is trapped inescapably among versions of womanhood already present in those discourses. Recent criticism from several theoretical perspectives is selected and lucidly introduced in *The Wife of Bath*, ed. Peter G. Beidler (1996); the collection includes a well-glossed text and the editor's discussion of "Biographical and Historical Contexts."

The Wife's Prologue and Tale have been the object of a great deal of very productive critical research and reflection, especially by feminist scholars, in recent decades. For two major statements, see Carolyn Dinshaw, *Chaucer's Sexual Politics*, (1989), chapter 4, and Elaine Tuttle Hansen, *Chaucer and the Fictions of Gender*, (1992), chapter 2. Assessments of the Wife vary widely, nonetheless. Is she to be approached as a positive model of economic independence and a degree of self-determination? Or is Alison a kind of unhappy warning of the unavoidable costs of self-creation? Responses are based partly on the critic's estimate of Chaucer himself, and the degree of independence from the more conservative values of the era that is attributed to him. These estimates have also been informed by deconstructionism, with its lively attention to the limits imposed on verbal self-creation (authorial or personal) by the ideologies always embedded within language.

Consider Barrie Ruth Strauss's telling comment on the Wife's Prologue: "Her insertion of addresses to women inside addresses to men exposes the major requirement of phallocentrism—that masculine discourse enclose feminine discourse" ("The Subversive Discourse of the Wife of Bath: Phallocentric Discourse and the Imprisonment of Criticism," *English Literary History* 55 [1988], 531). One might add the question, *what* women? The Prologue speaks to "wise wives," but there aren't any others in the pilgrimage; and the Wife recalls her old gossip Alisoun, but she's now dead ("God have hir soule!"). The Wife does seem haunted by her male opponents; she can't stop arguing with them. She finally burns her last husband's book of misogynist texts, but many readers would recognize scraps from those very texts in the Wife's own story, especially in her manipulation of her first three husbands.

Jankyn's "book of wicked wives" is almost a fetish object of male power over the Wife: literacy. The Wife's own talk is thick with textual references, but they are often partial or slightly wrong; and they are just the kind of material that could be held in memory from the public culture of liturgy, sermons, and biblical drama that the Wife enjoyed. By contrast, Jankyn has a stable book with which to torment her. Yet the Wife's body itself is repeatedly figured as a text, a document authenticated with "sainte Venus seel" on it (line 610), or a book that Jankyn can "glose" (line 515) both sexually and textually. This textual struggle over control of the book and the body provides the climax of the Wife's Prologue.

Another way of approaching these issues of pilgrim voices, gender, and textual power is to look at the manuscript setting of the Prologue. If facsimiles of the Ellesmere Manuscript (ed. Daniel Woodward and Martin Stevens, [1997]) or the Hengwrt Manuscript (ed. Paul Ruggiers et al, [1979]) are available, show students one of the heavily glossed pages of the Wife's Prologue. The glosses provide, to a medieval reader of these manuscripts, the sources of much of the Prologue in the very Latin misogynist texts listed in Jankyn's book. So while the Wife is (orally) asserting her independence and triumphs, the book is (textually) asserting the priority and continuity of a hostile tradition. This displacement of opposition onto the glossed page leads back to the double conventions of poetry in Chaucer's time—at once a performed medium and one available for private reading in a book.

Critical focus on the Wife as a woman and a merchant has obscured an equally important and poignant aspect of her situation: mortality. The Wife of Bath experiences age (and, well past forty, the prospect of old age) with a humorous resignation that is very appealing. See especially her very moving speech, "I have had my world as in my time," lines 475–85. At the same time, she seems utterly disconnected from any of the comforts of the church or its promise of a life beyond the body.

The Tale If the Wife's Prologue asserts her position against a series of clerics and husbands, her Tale is a brilliant counter-version of a great bearer of aristocratic male values, the Arthurian tradition. She reverses a pattern of conventions encountered in the texts in "Arthurian Romance." Instead of a Guinevere who manipulates law as an instrument of unjust vengeance (as in Marie de France's *Lanval*), the queen of the Wife's Tale only seeks to have punishment come from the injured gender. The Wife's Arthurian knight ("chivalrous" only in the technical sense of "mounted") is a common rapist. Not only do women control most of the plot, further, but the central women—the raped girl and the crone—are commoners. The tale also explores the further irony that the discourse of true "gentillesse" comes from the mouth of the low-class crone. The knight's submission to the crone, and her miraculous transformation into a young lady both beautiful and faithful, mark the Wife's entry into a fantasy as complete as any in earlier Arthurian romance. But at least it is a fantasy for the pleasure of a female teller.

Franklin's Tale

If they come to the Franklin's Tale immediately after an encounter with the Wife of Bath, students should be informed of the earlier view that the Wife's Prologue initiates a group of four tales debating the question of rulership in marriage: those of the Wife, the Clerk, and the Merchant, and the Franklin. The Franklin's Tale was once read as Chaucer's ultimate resolution of the issue, a call for the relinquishing of sovereignty on the part of both husband and wife. As R. E. Kaske pointed out thirty years ago, however, this interpretation was based on the Franklin's stated ideals about marriage (ll. 53–70), rather than on the events of the tale, which show Dorigen, faced with the obligation to honor her rash promise to commit adultery, behaving like a child in need of wise guidance from her husband Arveragus ("Chaucer's Marriage Group," in *Chaucer the Love Poet*, ed. Jerome Mitchell and William Provost [1973]). More recently, feminist critics have rejected the argument that the Franklin's Tale portrays an ideal of marriage based on equality even more forcefully. Elaine Tuttle Hansen in the final chapter of *Chaucer and the Fictions of Gender* (1992) sees Dorigen's being handed back and forth between men—the husband who insists that she keep her promise and the suitor who releases her from it—as an explicit affirmation of male homosocial bonds based on the exchange of women. Susan Crane, in *Gender and Romance in Chaucer's Canterbury Tales* (1994), points out that Dorigen is constrained by the tale's genre—romance—which in its focus on courtship serves to limit female choice.

In addition to marriage, the issue of *gentillesse*—nobility—has received much attention from critics of the tale, being the quality for which the three men in the tale compete. The Suitor Aurelius, explaining to the clerk he employed as a magician why he failed to enjoy Dorigen's love, he says that though her husband had insisted out of "gentilesse" (l. 887) that Dorigen keep her promise, he himself, out of pity, sent her back again. The fact that each men had behaved "gentilly" (l. 900) to the other inspires the magician's own act of generosity, that of releasing Aurelius from his debt, an act he explicitly attributes to class ambition:

Thou art a squire, and he is a knight.
But God forbede...
But if a clerk could do a gentil dede,
As well as any of you...(ll. 901–04).

The sentiment that nobility is based on deeds rather than birth was frequently expressed at the time, when the bourgeoisie was attempting to acquire a voice, and formulate an ideology. While much has been said of the appropriateness of the idea to the Franklin, as a wealthy landholder possibly insecure about his status, this view is marred by dependence on a "roadside drama" theory of the relation of tale to teller. Perhaps more convincing is the tale's appropriateness to Chaucer himself, as a member of the upper bourgeoisie who nevertheless had extensive dealings with the aristocracy, and even royalty. (For further discussion by an historian, see Nigel Saul, "Chaucer and Gentility" in *Chaucer's England*, ed. Barbara Hanawalt [1992]).

A useful work to teach with the Franklin's Tale is the other Chaucerian romance included in the anthology, the Wife of Bath's Tale. It too deals with issues of gender and class, but because it shows women, uncharacteristically, as holding all the power, its emphasis is different. The knight in the Wife's tale, like Dorigen, faces an unwanted sexual encounter because of a blind promise: he must marry the old crone to whom he is obligated for saving his life. Since his death sentence had been for rape, however, there is some appropriateness to his lighter punishment, in contrast to the undeserved nature of Dorigen's obligation.

The Wife of Bath's Tale also treats the theme of *gentillesse* in a way that illuminates the Franklin's Tale. The wedding night "pillow sermon" with which the old crone seeks to console the knight about her age, ugliness, and low class status makes explicit the concept of nobility that is only implicit in the Franklin's Tale. Scorning the *gentillesse* that is descended from old wealth, she says, in a pointed reference to the knight's crime, that one often sees "a lordes sone do shame and vilainye" (1157) and that "vilaines sinful deedes maken a churl" (l.1164). Ultimately, she argues, "gentilesse cometh fro God allone" (l.1167), as she cites Dante's statements on the subject in the *Convivio*.

Finally, students should be reminded that Chaucer treats the issues of gender and class with his characteristic humor in the Franklin's Tale. The account of the heroine's recitation of chaste suicides from antiquity (concluding with "thus plained Dorigen a daye or twaye,/ purposing evere that she wolde deye," 1.750) is amusing from the perspective of fourteenth-century England, where few women killed themselves to preserve their honor. And the anomaly of the magician negotiating the cost of his services to Aurelius with mercantile exactitude ("lasse than a thousand pound he wolde nat have," 1.516) reminds us that by Chaucer's time money, rather than magic (or gentility), made the world go 'round.

The Pardoner's Prologue and Tale

Chaucer's Pardoner has exercised a creepy fascination on his audiences from the moment of the Canterbury pilgrimage to the reader of the late twentieth century. In that fascination lies his power, both as an agent in the church of his day and in Chaucer's text. The Pardoner moves along a fine and wavering boundary between the great force of language and its rhetorical underpinnings; by delineating that boundary he threatens to undermine the efficacy of clerical language and of the tale-telling project. The Pardoner is the *Tales'* great (and perhaps tragic) de-mystifier.

Scholars have expended a great deal of learning and effort trying to establish the Pardoner's exact physical status and his sexual relation to the Summoner who bears his singing a "stif burdoun." (For a full discussion, see Monica McAlpine, "The Pardoner's Homosexuality and How It Matters," PMLA 95, [1980], 8–22.) Is he a man born without testicles, or a eunuch, or a hermaphrodite (like the hare and goat to which he is compared)? This discussion is important, but to a degree it misses the point. The fascination with the Pardoner, as with any figure of extreme physiological difference, is largely generated by what is unknown, unasked, unspeakable. "What is he?" is probably a question asked (silently) as eagerly by the pilgrims as it is (loquaciously) by modern critics.

Just as important, and connected to physiognomy in the General Prologue portrait, is the sheer amount of stuff with which he has laden himself: clothes, pilgrim badges, pardons, fake relics. This only adds to the spectacle of the Pardoner, further exaggerated by his high but piercing voice. If this is freakish, it also has a certain pathos, like his efforts at fashionable dress. There emerges a sense of a compulsive and internally divided wish to be part of a group from which he will always be divided by physiology, by sexual practice, and equally by the self-isolation of the con man from his victims. Yet the Pardoner also exploits the fascinated gaze of this and his other publics, connecting the fascination caused by physiognomy to his verbal skill in holding their attention. (Regarding the Pardoner's isolation, see the superb and deeply involved discussion by Donald Howard in *The Idea of the Canterbury Tales* [1976], esp. 342–45.)

The Pardoner raises the religious question of whether true faith and salvation can derive from a corrupt clergy. Equally, though, he lays bare the rhetorical schemes by which the institutional church raises the money on which it has (like the hospital for which he works) become dependent. The Pardoner's prologue, and the tale he attaches thereto, are presented as a sample of his professional skill in sermonizing. They correspond neatly to the structure of many medieval sermons, which are elaborated commentaries on biblical passages (such as *radix malorum est cupiditas*), usually following a loose rhetorical division: (1) theme, (2) protheme, a further introduction, (3) dilatation, the fuller exposition of the text, (4) exemplum, an illustrative anecdote, (5) peroration or "application" of the exemplum, and (6) a closing formula. Parts 1, 4, and 5 are clearly present in the Pardoner's discourse, and perhaps 6.

The Pardoner's cynical exposition of his technique here is further exaggerated by two parody masses. He turns the pilgrims' road-side stopping place into the church-like setting for his sermon, but first he announces

> at this ale-stake
> I wol bothe drinke and eten of a cake.

Later, the rioters celebrate their riches and the murder of their companion, by consuming the wine poisoned by their victim when he was sent to fetch "breed and win ful prively."

The Pardoner's rhetorical force is fully equal to the attention his looks draw to him. His eerie tale of the three rioters is full of powerful and creepy episodes, that hold our attention exactly because (like his own body) they are evocative yet resist full explanation: the passing corpse, the bizarre exegetical mistake through which the rioters set out to find the person "Death," the old man encountered at a stile, the crooked way and the gold. The tale moves seamlessly from its "realistic" opening into an almost allegorical story.

The final ploy of the Pardoner's sermon is so daring that it may almost be inviting exposure: he asks for contributions. Harry Bailey responds with a degree of rage whose own excess may stem less from the Pardoner's religious cynicism than from his disentanglement of Harry's earlier equations of verbal and virile prowess. The Host reacts by speaking out loud exactly the absence which has so fascinated and silenced the rest of the pilgrims: that the Pardoner's "coilons"—testicles—are as phony as his relics. By naming the lack that had given the Pardoner such eerie power, the Host also silences him.

The kiss (intended to be a sort of "kiss of peace") imposed by the Knight at the very close of the tale rewards careful discussion. It is at once layered with paradox and emptied of meaning. It is the invitation to kiss the Pardoner's relics that invites the Host's explosion; the Host suggests that would be more like kissing the Pardoner's ass; yet that in turn raises the homoerotic kissing and sexual practice implied by the General Prologue. On top of all this the Knight tries to impose a kiss of social concord. Is it possible? Is any symbolic practice possible after the multiple exposures of the Pardoner's Tale?

The Nun's Priest's Prologue and Tale

Prologue   Given the Knight's urgent will to repair rifts in the pilgrimage community at the end of the Pardoner's Tale, it is worth discussing his decision to interrupt the Monk's Tale. In a sense, the Monk has told a series of tales, lugubrious and very much alike, under the general rubric of tragedy. This he defines in the most reductionist sense of the fall of men in good places, for reasons the Monk scarcely pauses to distinguish, with no hope of restoring their fortunes. It is a notion of genre the Knight summarizes in three lines, urging instead stories of "joye and greet solas" (lines 5–8). Is his alternate formula any more complex, though?

The Host, always respectful of social hierarchy, is almost too eager to agree with the big man and share in his authority. The Host repeats the Knight's terms but shifts his complaint: the Monk is putting him to sleep. When the Monk refuses Harry's request of a hunting tale, the Host turns instead to the Nun's Priest. His social coding continues; to the Knight and even the Monk, he used the respectful "Ye" and "you," but for the Nun's Priest uses the familiar form "thou." (Note the form of the second person that Harry uses at the end of the tale. What has led to the change? How else does the Host register his new respect for the Nun's Priest?)

The Tale   No other story among the *Canterbury Tales* exploits the echoes and possibilities of the frame tale as densely and playfully as does this. It is framed not only by the pilgrimage contest, but also by the domestic world of the widow and her cottage that surrounds the farmyard; and that yard and its events in turn frame Chauntecleer's three *exempla* defending his theory of dreams. The first of these innermost tales is about pilgrims, and thus mirrors the outermost.

Animal fable provides the initial genre from which the Nun's Priest plays. This was a widespread and popular form in the high and later Middle Ages, especially in school texts. Part of its appeal lay in the idea of reading on two levels at once, animal and human, or literal and moral. Chaucer explores this delightfully, in the jarring but funny movement back and forth between worlds of animal and human reference. Consider the nice moment when Chauntecleer's hens are said to be his sisters (typical in a domestic flock) "and his paramours" (line 102).

Upon this easily recognizable generic ground, the Nun's Priest adds an extraordinary range of generic and topical reference, pushing the little story of a rooster into ever bolder (or wilfully preposterous) extremes. The Nun's Priest makes the story an occasion for reflection on serious issues of the day: dream theory of course, but also free will and predestination, pride and flattery, and Boethian issues of contentment versus worldly goods. As events heat up and the rhetoric builds, it begins to suggest epic in details like the prophetic dream, the armed pursuit, the epic apostrophe and epic simile, and the use of long catalogues. Explicit comparisons are made between Chauntecleer's fall and the fall of Troy and Carthage. The language of tragedy enters, too, clearly parodying the Monk's Tale. Romance is evoked in terms like Chauntecleer's "aventure" (line 420) as well as references to stories like the "Book of Launcelot de Lake" (line 446). The gap between literal topic and referential language gets greater and greater, funnier and funnier, until the seams threaten to split, the whole thing burst open—which is exactly what happens in the plot.

Such gaps, or course, are the stuff of animal fable, bringing dissimilar things together. The Nun's Priest offers a very gentle social critique through his restrained use of the language of noble food and architecture in the description of the widow's cottage and life, which is extended by the far more exaggerated entry of the language of courtly love with Chauntecleer and Pertelote. Such modest social parody shifts to a more gendered analysis in the differing dictions of rooster and hen: his polysyllables vs. her monosyllables, Romance vs. Germanic diction (e.g., lines 201-07). Consider too the different cultural deposits from which their speeches draw. Pertelote uses medical precept, wives' tales, and reference to the quite elementary "Cato." Chauntecleer draws in arcane dream lore, saints' lives, and other men "more of auctoritee" (line 209).

Chauntecleer uses the language of courtly love as a source of power over his spouse. His merely decorative use of French and Latinate terms, citation of "auctoritee," his frequent use of enjambed lines and elaborate syntax, all signal man at his most culturally pretentious. This is most marked in his false translation of Latin. His style, though, is not primarily an expression of pomposity (for he is a brave beast) but rather an enactment of his power and learning as a means of exercising control in a world which has just been threatened. Like storytelling generally, Chauntecleer's language is a means of reorganizing a world that resists our logic and desires. Such language as a means of access to bravery and control is doubled by Chauntecleer's sexual desire. He faces any terror to show his love and virility to Pertelote.

The garden setting also takes on ever richer resonance as the story proceeds. It is first a chicken yard, but in Pertelote's prescriptions it soon takes on aspects of the medicinal garden. And it becomes a medieval love garden, by implication, when Chauntecleer starts invoking the language of courtly love. This in turn inevitably includes echoes of the garden of Eden. That association is enhanced by the red-and-black enemy who penetrates the garden and destroys (if only temporarily) the happy world of the man and wife who live there, through his powers of verbal persuasion.

The fox's rhetoric, and Chauntecleer's rhetoric of condescension, are only the starting places for an ever more parodic and self-reflexive rhetoric as the rooster's temptation and fall occur. The Nun's Priest uses the figure of apostrophe to address "destinee" and Venus who aided Chauntecleer's fall, and apostrophizes the rhetorician Geoffrey of Vinsauf for his skill in lamenting the death of Richard the Lion-Hearted. This hyperbole sets the stage for an inverse move of language into inarticulate shouts and yells, when the widow and all the barnyard animals set out to rescue Chauntecleer.

It is in this passage (lines 628–30) that the Nun's Priest makes a brief but much-discussed reference to human shouts, and murder, in the Peasants' Revolt. Following the tale's reference to historical cataclysm in ancient Troy, Arthurian and then Plantagenet England, the extreme concision of the reference is all the more interesting. Is this to be taken as a kind of anxious evasion? Or does it suggest a mild courtly indifference (by Chaucer himself) or clerical indifference (by the Nun's Priest)? It is relevant here to distinguish the job of this priest, serving a community of nuns, from the local parish work of the Parson, described in the General Prologue.

The Nun's Priest describes Chauntecleer's salvation from the fox as a turn of Fortune. But does Fortune have anything to do with it? Or rather does Chauntecleer use his tongue to get himself out of the fix that his tongue got him into? He uses the fox's own trick, guiling the beguiler. He escapes the dangers and temptations of this world through his own wit and craftiness. The pursuit is gaudy but irrelevant.

The frequent moral interpretations attached to animal fables have invited explicit moral, even allegorical readings of the Nun's Priest's Tale, particularly by patristic critics. Chauntecleer has been interpreted as a priest figure tempted by the devil in the form of the fox. Certainly there are enough details (as in the visual description of the fox) to invite some symbolic reaction. Yet much of the referential reach of the poem goes unregarded in such a reading. Nonetheless, the Nun's Priest begins to close his tale with a traditional and often-cited formulation of moral and allegorical reading, "Taketh the moralitee . . ." (line 674). Is this to be taken as the Nun's Priest's instruction on reading? Is it the only instruction? How seriously we take it has something to do with how firmly we draw a line dividing the tale (with its constant ironizing even of the most serious references), from the Nun's Priest's comments on that tale. If that line is very clear, then this may solicit a highly moralized reading. If it is unstable, could the Nun's Priest be voicing these commonplaces with the same sort of raised eyebrow he used in regard to the commonplaces about rhetoric or about Troy and Arthur? The value of such irony is that the reader can explore uncertainty without being forced to repudiate the story or rhetorical posture under scrutiny, or even the "moralitee." As is clear throughout the tale, one can parody what one also enjoys, even loves.

The Parson's Tale

Introduction   The exegetical interpretation that the entire Canterbury pilgrimage is directed to the New Jerusalem leans heavily on the Parson's offer in his prologue to show the pilgrims the way to "thilke parfit glorious pilgrimage / That highte Jerusalem celestial" (D. W. Robertson, Jr., *A Preface to Chaucer*, [1962], 373). According to this view, the Parson, as the ideal pilgrim, has moral authority and speaks for Chaucer. Other critics, however, have dissented, regarding the Parson as a fictional character who is treated ironically. His long treatise on penance, by his own account devoid of any poetic ornament, violates the Host's injunction to the pilgrims not to bore the pilgrims by preaching. By disdaining to tell a "fable," the Parson not only refuses to play by the rules of the tale-telling contest, but shows that he "confuses fiction with falsehood" (Gabriel Josopivici, *The World and the Book*, [1971]).

From the Tale: Remedy for the Sin of Lechery   While elaborate attempts have been made to demonstrate parallels between The Parson's Tale and specific Canterbury tales, these are in reality the chance correspondences one might expect when an exhaustive manual of sin and an encyclopedic account of human behavior are linked. (See E. T. Donaldson, *Speaking of Chaucer*, [1970], 164–74.) Nevertheless, the portion excerpted here throws some light on the tales' treatment of the ideal relationship of men and women in marriage, a theme of many of the tales. The Parson suggests marriage as the primary remedy for the sin of lechery, although he gives the avoidance of sleeping late its due. Woman's status in marriage is explained by the history of her creation in a much more subtle way than the stereotype of "Adam's Rib" would suggest. God made her neither from Adam's head (lest she rule over him in "maistrye") nor from his foot (lest she "be holden too lowe, for she can nat paciently suffre") but from his rib, so that she should be "felawe unto man."

This apparent statement of equality between the sexes, with its echoes of the concerns with "maistrie" in marriage which the Wife of Bath introduces in her Prologue, should be read in the context of what follows, however. For the Parson goes on to say that the woman should be subject to her husband, and that while married she "hath noon auctoritee to swere ne to bere witnesse withoute leve of hir housbonde that is hir lord." In fact, both views were considered orthodox in Chaucer's time: that a husband should treat his wife kindly because she was his companion, and that she should be subject to his rule.

One can see connections with some of the other Canterbury tales in the Parson's distinctions among the various reasons for sex between married people, and the degrees of sinfulness they entail. The first and second reasons—the engendering children and the "yielding the debt" of their bodies—are laudable, but the third—to avoid lechery—is a venial sin, and the fourth—"for amorous love . . . to accomplice thilke brenning delit"—a deadly one. By that calculation, two of Chaucer's most engaging characters are damned: the Wife of Bath's claim that "God bad us for to wexe and multiplye" will not save her, for she admits to enjoying sex and makes no mention of having had children, and

Chauntecleer's making love to his hens "more for delit than world to multiplye" is a deadly sin.

After reading even a short passage from the Parson's Tale, students might notice that, for all his moral rectitude, the Parson's tale is rather boring. And if they compare him with that other preacher, the Pardoner, they will be faced with the ironic contrast between a good man who tells a bad tale and a bad man who tells a good one, reflecting the vexed question of the relation between morals and esthetics which hovers over the *Canterbury Tales* as a whole.

Chaucer's Retraction

Even those critics most skeptical of Robertson's judgment of the individual tales tend to agree that The Parson's Prologue and Chaucer's retraction, and even his tale, should be taken straight. According to Alfred David, the retraction "is a deeply moving statement of the limitations of art," and of the difficulty in justifying literature for its own sake in a chaotic and corrupt world (*The Strumpet Muse*, [1976], 238). He sees the tension as transcending Christianity, having been expressed by Plato, Virgil, and Kafka, among others. Many, if not most, critics agree with the view that Chaucer is serious about abandoning the world of experience for the spiritual world, but students have great difficulty in accepting this. They often insist that he was insincere, making a cynical deathbed repentance. Nor are they convinced by being told retractions were common in medieval poems with any erotic content, such as Andreas Capellanus's *De amore* or Chaucer's earlier *Troilus and Criseyde*, for they see these too as ironic. But irony, in the end, may be too easy an explanation of the contradictions of writers from the past who frustrate us.

To His Scribe Adam and Complaint to His Purse

In *To His Scribe Adam*, Chaucer ruefully wishes a skin disease on a copyist who has failed to reproduce his words as he intended them. Now he must correct the manuscript himself, in a laborious process of rubbing and scraping the old ink off the parchment, in preparation for rewriting. In their volume of the Chaucer Variorum, George Pace and Alfred David point out the "poetic justice of the threatened curse on Adam's head," in that "he will have to scratch his scalp just as Chaucer had to scratch out Adam's mistakes" (Geoffrey Chaucer, *The Minor Poems* [1982], 26). While the poem is decidedly playful, it also points to a serious concern that Chaucer had for the transmission of his works to posterity, a concern endemic to writers in a manuscript culture.

The critical history of this lyric can give students insight into the range of interpretive stances—from the literal to the exegetical to the feminist—from which Chaucer can be approached. For the echoes of the first Adam in the scribe's name have tempted several critics to move beyond the literal interpretation mentioned above to read the poem as a Christian allegory. R. E. Kaske, for instance, sees the scribe as an Adam whose fallen workmanship mars the creation of Chaucer, who stands in the relationship of God to his literary work.

While such exegetical criticism, which affirms traditional gender hierarchy and attributes the Fall to Eve, would seem to be antithetical to feminist criticism, Carolyn Dinshaw actually relies on it in her analysis of *To His Scribe Adam*, the epigraph to her book *Chaucer's Sexual Poetics* (1989). In her project of illuminating "the varied and nuanced uses of gendered models of literary activity in Chaucer's works" (9) she cites Kaske and engages in similar allegorizing activity as she describes *To His Scribe Adam* as illustrative of Chaucer's complex relation to patriarchal language. Ringing changes on the poem's final word, "rape," which she translates as the modern "rape" as well as the more commonly glossed meaning, "haste," she argues that Chaucer presents himself as simultaneously rapist, with respect to the parchment, and rape victim, with respect to Adam, who violates his own work with his fallen language (10). Following the medieval tradition of pen as phallus, she argues that this word "points out that literary activity has a gendered structure, a structure that associates acts of writing and related acts of signifying—allegorizing, interpreting, glossing, translating—with the masculine and that identifies surfaces on which these acts are performed, or from which these acts depart, or which these acts reveal—the page, the text, the literal sense, or even the hidden meaning—with the feminine" (9).

While students may find Dinshaw's own glossing overingenious, they should be reminded that she too starts with a recognition of the poem's literal meaning. It reminds us that "literary production in the late fourteenth century is a social enterprise" and that Chaucer "is unavoidably dependent on the copyist for the accurate transmission, and indeed, the very intelligibility of his works" (3). Students might want to compare *To His Scribe Adam*, which makes such self-conscious reference to the conditions of a manuscript culture, to the riddles on the technology of writing from the Anglo-Saxon period. Chaucer's poem can be seen to resemble them more in its awareness of the medium, than in the judgment of it, however. For while the Anglo-Saxon authors, clerics in a culture that has only recently embraced literacy, marvel at the power and novelty of writing, the secular Chaucer, writing at the end of the Middle Ages, laments the corruptibility of the medium and its practitioners' incompetence.

The second Chaucerian lyric, *Complaint to His Purse*, illustrates another constraint on authors in the Middle Ages—their dependence on patrons. (See Richard F. Green, *Poets and Princepleasers*, [1980]). Chaucer is thought to have written his first major poem, the *Book of the Duchess* (1369–72) at the request of John of Gaunt, Duke of Lancaster, in commemoration of the death of his wife Blanch, and to a lesser extent he wrote for patrons as his career progressed. *Complaint to His Purse*, however, reflects his dependence on patronage as a civil servant rather than a poet. In 1399, the last year of his life, Chaucer faced the accession of a new king—Henry IV—after many years of depending on his predecessor, Richard II, for a pension. There is no record of Chaucer having sent this poem or of Henry having responded to it, although Henry did augment the earlier pension within the year.

This poem combines two conventional genres, the French begging poem and the love complaint, in a particularly witty way. To explore Chaucer's technique of parody, students might enjoy comparing it to some of Chaucer's other humorous twists on the courtly love complaint. Examples might be the speeches of the aristocratic birds in the *Parliament of Fowls* and of Chauntecleer in the Nun's Priest's Tale, and of Absolon in the Miller's Tale.

Both *To His Scribe Adam* and *Complaint to His Purse*, finally, reveal Chaucer's sophisticated awareness of the constraints on authorship under which he worked, whether material or economic.

William Langland
Piers Plowman

Piers Plowman is an exceptionally open, polysemous text, in several senses. First, despite fierce editorial efforts in the past three decades, the text itself remains a debated issue. Langland's poem swiftly gained popularity with a range of audiences, and its many manuscript copies—over fifty survive—were not always produced with much discipline. Second, Langland himself was constantly altering his text, through at least four major revises. (The selections here are translated from the B-text, written in the years before the Rising of 1381.) These revisions went on while earlier versions were being copied, and many manuscripts of one text also have portions copied from another. Further, Langland's use of protean and overlapping symbolic and allegorical characters, as well as his mysterious prophecies, have invited various emphases and interpretations, and have been appropriated by highly interested textual communities: the leaders of the Rising of 1381 for instance, and later on agents of the Protestant reformation. Langland still invites eager but often conflicting interpretations.

The Identity of "Will" William Langland's "identity" (a problematic term here) has been constructed mostly from hints and word-plays within his poems, such as "I have lyved in londe . . . my name is Longe Wille" (*passus* 15, line 152). He refers to the Malvern Hills in the southwest, and various districts in and around London, especially Cornhill, a poor district. And he mentions more glancingly his marginal work as a comforter in the homes of various patrons (which perhaps involved his own poetry), as well as professional mourner, praying for the dead. He also says he begs. A picture emerges of a man in a liminal world between clergy and laity, poor but educated, finding unstable and ill-paid employment, and involved in a life-long exploration of how social order should operate and how a Christian should live within it.

Do these elements derive from a historical person, though, or do they rather produce a largely fictive narrative "I" who is a character in a visionary fiction? The name "Will" carries moral overtones, and is an aspect of the dominant Aristotelian psychology of the later Middle Ages. Chaucer, we have seen, creates a rather bumbling and bewildered narrator, clearly distinct from the courtier bureaucrat known in his extensive life records. One note in an early manuscript of *Piers Plowman*, however, does suggest parallels, at least, between the *persona* Langland and the poet:

It is known that Stacy de Rokayle the father of William
de Langlond was generous and lived in Shipton under
Wichwood, holding from the lord Le Spenser in the county
of Oxford. The aforesaid William made the book that is
called Piers Ploughman.
(Translated in *The World of Piers Plowman*, ed. Jeanne Krochalis and Edward
Peters, [1975], xi.)

A poet who has spent time in the west country around Malvern Hills might well
choose to use the alliterative meter that was popular there (and used, to the north,
by the *Gawain*-poet); yet an audience in London might explain why the poem avoids
the kind of regional dialect found in *Gawain* and other chivalric narratives in alliterative verse. Despite the allegorical mode that seems archaic to modern readers, the
poem's persona corresponds intriguingly to romantic and later notions of the poet as
an eccentric genius, speaking from the social margin, and living in poverty (even, as
the narrator acknowledges, wearing odd clothes).

One reason that Langland's dreamer so engages us is that he so often implicates
himself in the very failures and social practices he castigates. So his initial
panorama of society in the Prologue attacks the unstable and phony hermits who
go off on pilgrimage (line 53 ff.) But he has already portrayed himself "In the habit
of a hermit unholy of works" (line 3), travelling in quest of wonders. He depicts
Meed as a figure of sexual license and financial corruption, but also acknowledges
that he is "ravished" by her dress and adornments (2.17).

Langland and Chaucer   The careers of Chaucer and Langland thus seem to overlap both in time and place, though they lived in very different social worlds and
worked in largely different poetic traditions. Scholars still wonder if they knew
each other's work; certainly they compare interestingly at moments such as the social panoramas of the Prologues to *Piers Plowman* and the *Canterbury Tales*. The audiences of *Piers Plowman* and Chaucer may have overlapped at certain points, such
as educated readers of the upper merchant class and some religiously serious members of the lower reaches of the court. Otherwise their apparent audiences largely
diverged; Chaucer was taken up by aristocrats and their supporters, and Langland
seems to have appealed to clerical and modest mercantile readers. The figure of
Piers Plowman was invoked by key figures in the Rising of 1381 (see "John Ball's
Second Letter" in "*Piers Plowman* in Its Time"), and by the "Lollard" followers of
the religious reformer (later declared a heretic) John Wycliffe. Both appropriations
overlook the complexities and deep conservatism that is clear in the B-text; certainly Langland's revisions and expansions in the C-text (after 1381) suggest that
he wanted to distinguish his position clearly from the Lollards and the 1381 rebels.

Genres and Traditions   Both the great appeal and the great frustrations of *Piers
Plowman* derive from the variety of genres within which it operates, often moving
among several simultaneously. Langland seems always to have been more concerned to pursue his twin social and spiritual concerns than to stay within any one
generic framework. The outermost structure of the poem is a dream vision, though

that generic setting fades in and out of our attention. It can be very important when, as at the start of *passus* 18, the narrator consciously seeks sleep as an escape from the mundane world and an access to vision. (Langland's use of this highly traditional form invites comparison with *The Dream of the Rood*, Caedmon's dream in Bede, Chaucer's *Parliament of Fowls*, and Arthur's dream in Malory.)

At the same time, the dreamer's encounters with the workings (or failures) of secular society regularly partake of satire and social complaint, which in turn give rise sometimes to passages of apocalyptic prophecy. The social world within a private dream is only one example, among many, of how Langland's poem tries to yoke together questions about the workings of public order and about the role and fate of the individual soul. Toward the latter end, he also borrows from the genre of the penitential manual, and from pilgrimage narrative internalized as private journey. Even the romance motif of a quest to discover or achieve personal identity may inform the persistent wandering of the narrator and his first dream vision. As a poem of pilgrimage and wandering, *Piers Plowman* has links as well to travel narratives; indeed in five of its manuscripts the poem appears along with Mandeville's *Travels*.

Both in the dream quest, and in the social encounters that emerge within it, Langland repeatedly exploits the varied resources of allegory. Allegory in the poem, though, is a strategic and highly flexible tool. To seek a single, continuing allegorical story or theme, is to invite frustration in the reader. Instead, Langland uses allegory as a form so naturalized and continuous with more "realistic" modes, that he slips easily among allegorical kinds, often playing with several at once. So in *passus* 18, the "human" dreamer watches four allegorical women derived from a line in the Psalms; these reflect typological thinking, in which moments in the Old Testament are fulfilled in the New. They then converse with an abstract personification "Book," and finally all fall silent and watch (with the dreamer) Christ arrive as an allegorical knight and rescue historical characters from hell.

Piers Plowman is so peppered with Latin phrases, and sometimes brief passages, that at times it is almost a macaronic poem. (For an example of that form, see "The Course of Revolt" in "*Piers Plowman* in Its Time.") These phrases derive from Latin poetry and from the liturgy, but most often from the Bible. The many ways that the biblical passages relate to the surrounding vernacular poem suggest Langland's deep acquaintance with traditions of four-fold exegesis: literal, allegorical (dogma and belief in this world), moral (action in this world), and anagogical (eternity, life beyond this world). Biblical quotations are hubs around which episodes often develop. So are individual allegorical characters, who may seem initially to close off or resolve an issue, but whose presence often sparks a more troubled and complex reaction in the dreamer. For instance, Hunger enters in *passus* 6 to force "wasters" to work in Piers' half-acre; but his presence in turn leads Piers to think about how to deal with those who still will not, or who cannot, work. And this in turn opens the reality of want even among those who do work.

Langland in His Time Langland's double preoccupations, as well as his mixture of dream, spiritual quest, and social satire, have led to a persistent divide in critical attention. Is the poem best approached in terms of moral behavior within a social structure set in current history? Or is it more truly a private quest, informed by secular history only in so far as that history points toward an apocalyptic end in which all people come under divine judgment? Critics often acknowledge both questions, but tend to concentrate on one or the other, as may be inevitable in a poem of such size and range. The historical setting of the poem, and its dense references to local places and recent events, have made it an exciting arena for the work of historicist and Marxist critics in recent decades. Two recent collections offer fine examples of these approaches: Steven Justice and Kathryn Kerby-Fulton, eds. *Written Work: Langland, Labor, and Authorship*, ed. Steven Justice and Kathryn Kerby-Fulton, (1997), and *The Powers of the Holy: Religion, Politics, and Gender in Late Medieval English Culture*, ed. David Aers and Lynn Staley, (1996).

Even if they are to be approached carefully, within the literary context of complaint, satire, and moral polemic, current social problems do bulk large in *Piers Plowman*. Weak kings and weak knights, corrupt officials and lazy peasants, indulgent clerics and their opponents, all come into play. The plagues and the shrunken labor market that resulted get their mention, and the early sections of the poem are deeply concerned with the changing place of the peasantry, and official efforts to legislate social stability in the face of that change. Again and again, the dreamer invokes conservative social models like the theory of the three estates, only to find them abandoned or inadequate to the social interactions he witnesses. The poem's central focus on a plowman engages the very classes where social competition, social change, and resistance to both, were being played out most openly and angrily in Langland's time. How effectively he reflected the tenor of his era becomes clear in the adoption of his chief character in the discourse of the Rising of 1381; how that is not the end of his aims is equally clear in the laborious revisions that adoption seems to have sparked.

The Prologue   It works very well to teach this along with the General Prologue to the *Canterbury Tales*. Both offer a social panorama, though in contrasting settings of the visionary "field full of folk" and the "realistic" tavern in Southwark.

From what posture does the narrator begin his journey? Is this initially a serious quest? What sort of "wonders" is he after? Given the many disguisings and fakery later on, how should we react to a narrator taking on a costume and a somewhat false identity? Note the "romance" language of magic and marvel, and the site of the dream by a stream, a frequent boundary with the uncanny, as in Marie's *Lanval* or even the second encounter with the Green Knight in *Sir Gawain*. The initial geography of the dream—the secular world, but bracketed by heaven and hell—is almost an emblem for the dual preoccupations of the rest of the poem.

Explore the swift and effective (if sometimes confusing) shifts in tone, mode, and address. A literal and "realistic" figure (e.g. the Pardoner) will suddenly engage in allegorical action (lines 74–75). Or the dreamer will shift from general address suddenly to "you" (lines 76). Or attention will move from a complex personified figure like "Lewte" to a narrative allegory like the rats and mice. Consider how these shifts correspond to modern notions of the associational logic of dreams.

The opening and closing scenes of the classes and their work have an engaging energy. Despite their mutual echoes, they seem also to shift from the allegorical landscape of the beginning to a more specifically urban scene at the end. Along with the corrupt and false clerics (lines 40 ff.) who mirror one aspect of the narrator, note also the minstrels and "word jugglers" (line 35) who correspond to another of his roles. Compare the friars here (lines 58 ff.) with the depiction of the Friar in Chaucer's General Prologue, especially their self-serving biblical exegesis; also the Pardoner in both.

The arrival of the king brings another of the estates into play, but also introduces the theme of national governance. Here, as often when he considers upper levels of government, Langland becomes a little vague, relying on quite traditional tripartite formulas, especially the three estates, and notions like "common profit" (also encountered in Chaucer's *Parliament of Fowls*). The lunatic clerk opens up more complex debate on the king and his role. He is the kind of marginal figure Langland often invokes, whose perspective reveals the limits of a prior model.

The story of the rats and mice may reflect baronial resistance to royal authority, but belling the cat doesn't involve any overthrow; rather it is a strategy to avoid wrath. Note how the narrator pulls away from interpreting the passage: an allegory so transparent can involve danger.

Passus 2   This *passus* opens with the dreamer in dialogue with Lady Holy Church, seeking grace but also a knowledge of "the false." She turns his attention to Lady Meed, then fades from the scene. If Meed begins (from Holy Church's perspective) as a personification of "the false," her implications swiftly become more complex and morally uncertain. She figures the role of money in an economy where cash was replacing the older ties of feudal and communal obligation; she is a relative of the king. As the story of Meed's marriage emerges, she becomes less of a moral agent, more a source of power whose users need to be chosen well. Efforts to determine her proper spouse carry with them a whole frame of legal reference, including the corruptibility of the justice system. The scene again shifts (as in the Prologue) from the unspecified dream place to the seat of royal justice at Westminster in London, and the wonderful visual spectacle of justice officers figured as horses, with Meed, her suitor False, and others riding on them.

Meed is a yet more complex figure, though. She also refers to Alice Perrers, the avaricious mistress of the aging King Edward III. Her red clothing has been taken to signify the biblical Whore of Babylon. At the same time, as Clare Lees has recently pointed out (in *Class and Gender in Early English Literature*, ed. Britton J. Harwood and Gillian Overing, [1994]), Meed's gender requires close attention. She is desired by practically all men, including the dreamer, though she is described in terms of her costly array rather than her body. And for all the bad influences attributed to her, Meed has little agency in the *passus*; she is carried from one suitor or judge to another as others decide who should best control her.

Passus 5   In this *passus* the seven deadly sins (and related characters) display themselves in a tavern scene, and repent their wrongs in a confession of Repentaunce, a priest. The passage quoted here describes in colorful terms the confession of the particularly unsavory figure of "Glutton."

Passus 6 This *passus* introduces the figure of Piers the Plowman, who will take on more and more resonance in the rest of the poem, until Christ, as an allegorical knight, jousts with death in Piers's arms in *passus* 18. It opens with the repentant sinners crying for grace to seek Saint Truth. They do not know how to find the way, but a plowman suddenly says he knows Truth well and gives them instructions and serves as their guide. Rather than the class of knights ordering society, it is the plowman who sets various agents to work along traditional lines of the three estates, and expresses his class's willingness to support the knights and clergy.

The narrative of repentance and the quest for Saint Truth, though, quickly give way under social pressures recognizably specific to Langland's time. The deadly sins return to some of their practices such as sloth, informed now by references to the rising expectations of peasants in the shrunken labor market after the Black Death. Equally the *passus* registers the oppressive legislation by which landowners tried to limit wages ("the statute," line 320).

Piers tries to mediate between these social forces. Knighthood is of no help to him, being too involved in good manners to enforce its own laws. Piers calls instead on the figure of Hunger, who gets people to work but then embodies a complicating factor of real want even among those who work.

The prophetic passage with which the *passus* ends pulls the poem into its occasional apocalyptic mode. Its general tone of foreboding may be more important than any specific prediction.

Passus 18 After much wandering and a period of wakefulness, the narrator again seeks sleep—but as an access to vision, or as an escape from the world? There follows a dense interweaving of Will's dream and the Easter narrative and its liturgy. Christ appears under a series of allegorical guises: as the Samaritan, as a knight in the arms of Piers, as a trickster beguiling the great beguiler, Satan. Repeatedly, though, at high points of the Easter story (Longinus at the Crucifixion, the Harrowing of Hell), the allegorical structure fades away into simple narrative.

The entire *passus* also uses the public culture of drama. At one point the dreamer looks from a window with Faith, as urban magnates looked at dramatic stagings of the Passion. There he listens to Faith's anti-Semitic diatribe, similar to attitudes found in the mystery plays and in images like that of Christ's tormentors in Winchester Psalter, color plate 5. When the dreamer withdraws in fear from the Crucifixion, he comes to another implicit stage setting, "He descended into hell." Here he draws into the shadows and witnesses another dialogue, between four allegorical women drawn from the Psalms. (Note how these allegorical figures offer different vantages, narrow and broad perspectives: Faith's close view of the trial and crucifixion, the four "wenches" and whole picture of Christ's conception, life, and death.) They in turn become the audience for a dialogue in hell, Christ shattering hell's gates, and his extraordinary (and doctrinally daring) speech promising to bring "all men's souls" out of hell at the Last Judgment. The four women then carol until Easter dawn.

This visionary episode, with its layers of allegorical audiences and dramatic spectacle, does not lead the dreamer to some elevated state. Rather, it ends with him waking into a domestic setting, calling his family to the universally available medium of human contact with the divine: church liturgy and the participatory acts of the Easter Service.

Piers Plowman and Its Time: The Rising of 1381   Despite its only incremental long-term effects, the Rising of 1381 must have seemed almost apocalyptic to London merchants and magnates at the time. It is an event difficult to imagine in contemporary America on quite such a scale, but students might be invited to recall the riots that followed the Rodney King verdict in Los Angeles, with their public disorder, burnings, and initially disorganized official response. The rioters had a comparable sense of righteous wrath and justice gone wrong, and a similar uncertainty about just who needed chastisement; the 1381 rebels, however, seem to have had a more elaborate (if highly plastic) program for change.

Are the reactions printed below, for all their variety, "subjective" in the sense of individual? Or do they rather reflect the interests and preoccupations of a particular group or class?

As noted earlier, Langland seems to have revised *Piers Plowman* after 1381, to distinguish his social complaint from that of the rebels. But in the earlier B-text, he had identified many of the social and ecclesiastical failures which the rebels also attacked. Despite the more complex position Langland did take, and despite the conservatism of much of his reaction, it is a useful exercise to pursue a "rebel reading" of Langland. Indeed, even some conservative elements in Langland would themselves have struck responsive chords with the commoners in 1381, such as his idealistic faith in the king. Both Langland and the rebels made him a figure above nobles, divinely ordained and a true friend of commoners.

All these texts focus, positively or negatively, on the phenomenon of peasants using various forms of public and written expression. John Ball uses overt references to a widely known and learned poem, *Piers Plowman*, and *The Anonimalle Chronicle* minutely records Wat Tyler's articulate if disrespectful dialogue with King Richard. At the same time, the *Chronicle* laments the more general "hideous cries and horrible tumult" of the commoners beheading foreigners. The rebels are even less human when the aldermen surround them "like sheep." In "The Course of Revolt" the rebels are "laddes lowde" who merely "schowte" (lines 17, 29). And Gower allegorizes them wholesale as beasts, whose sole speaker is a jackdaw, a bird that only mimics language. This is the treatment of the rebels as subhuman that informs the reference to them killing Flemings in Chaucer's Nun's Priest's Tale.

These and a wide range of related texts are magisterially discussed by Stephen Justice, *Writing and Rebellion: England in 1381* (1994). For a broader perspective, consult also Jesse Gellrich, *Discourse and Dominion in the Fourteenth Century: Oral Contexts of Writing in Philosophy, Politics, and Society* (1995).

The Anonimalle Chronicle   This passage centers on the Tower, the seat of royal authority in London, and a series of public confrontations between King Richard and the rebels at the borders of the city. The almost apocalyptic mood is emphasized by two different scenes when the king watches great secular and ecclesiastical houses burning, and in the writer's prediction of divine vengeance on the rebels. (The rebels attack church property as much as that of aristocrats; compare Langland's complaints, persistently divided between clerical and lay power.)

It is significant, however, that the *Chronicle* does not look to the traditional sources of royal force, the armed aristocrats, for action in the revolt. Note how the king's noble counselors are repeatedly depicted as confused, ineffectual, even (after Smithfield) cowardly. This bears comparison with the knight's useless intervention against Waster's laziness in *Piers Plowman* (6.159-70). Consider too the role of the mayor and armed aldermen—citizens, not noblemen—in the critical meeting of Richard and the rebels. Where do the chronicler's sympathies lie? Is there another sort of anti-aristocratic perspective at work here? (In this regard, too, consider Richard's unrecorded but long interview with the anchorite. Why emphasize it?)

These episodes from the *Chronicle* are wonderfully depicted, with a great sense of detail and the setting of scenes, such as the detail of a "wicked woman" raising the alarm and preventing the Archbishop's escape from the Tower, or the herald having to read the king's bill to the commons from an old chair. There is also a poignant sense of invoking ancient rituals, especially ecclesiastical, to resist disorder. Note the public procession from Westminster Abbey to greet the king, or the performance of the liturgy from which the Archbishop of Canterbury is dragged to his beheading. (This detail may consciously echo the martyrdom of Sudbury's predecessor, Thomas Becket, during mass at Canterbury.)

These moving but ineffectual ceremonies contrast sharply with the disordered encounters of King Richard and Wat Tyler at Mile End and Smithfield. Tyler is depicted as willfully insulting in speech and gesture. (The commons as a group, though, all kneel to the king.) Tyler's demands keep increasing; the king accedes, and the chronicler gives no hint here of how swiftly Richard will disavow all his promises and turn on the rebels. Indeed, the violence at Smithfield is attributed to no group, noble or common, but to individuals at the edge of each: Tyler and the king's valet from Kent.

Here and elsewhere in reports of the Rising, language and the written record are the objects of great but ambivalent attention. The rebels want a charter of their freedoms, on the one hand, but they also reject the king's first bill, then seek out and kill anyone who could write the kind of official writs that had brought such burdens of taxation upon them. The rebels are in turn hostile then naive in their trust of documents. They demand the physical presence and voice of the king at Smithfield, but accept his use of the very language of charters ("confirm and grant"). The chronicler himself implies considerable cynicism in Richard's manipulation of documents; Richard's first "bill" rewrites the Rising as a "desire to see and maintain their king," and he has a whole series of charters copied in an effort to appease the rebels. (His authentication of the bill with his signet seal is another invocation of traditional, but here insincere, ritual.) This bears comparison with Langland's emphasis on charters in the Lady Meed episode, or the corruption of letters by Mordred in Malory's *Morte Darthur*. By contrast, writing is never thematized in *Sir Gawain and the Green Knight*. Can this be related to that poem's general cultural conservatism?

John Ball's First and Second Letter   Beyond the clear echoes of Langland here, the poems use the tone and diction of the kind of prophetic passages found in *Piers Plowman* elsewhere. The rebels' ambivalent preoccupation with written language is discussed above. These poems and letters may be more significant for their efforts to appropriate written documents to the aims of the rebels, than for their specific content. For recent discussion, see articles by Richard Firth Green and Susan Crane in *Chaucer's England: Literature in Historical Context*, ed. Barbara Hanawalt (1992), 176–221.

The Course of Revolt   As with *The Anonimalle Chronicle*, the social alignment of *The Course of Revolt* is not immediately clear. The poem acknowledges the grievances of the commons under the poll tax, and speaks with them as "vs alle," prophesying vengeance; yet it calls the murdered treasurer, Sir Robert Hales, "that dowghty knyght" (line 33). The mixed Latin and English lines imply a fairly educated audience, though the English lines have sense without the Latin. What about the "Kyng" (lines 3, 45)? Can a poet positioned in sympathy both to king and commons be compared to the attitudes of the chronicler? If the rebels are nonetheless "ffoles" (line 13), is there any positive agent in the poem? Compare this troubled but unstable perspective to Langland's shifting sympathies and complaints. Who is the final agent the poem calls upon?

John Gower, *The Voice of One Crying*   Gower's tone in *Vox Clamantis* is clearer and more persistently hostile to the rebels than the selections above. He simplifies the class affiliations of the rebels, making them all peasants, and grouping all freemen with the nobles. Gower's text does not register the rebels as human, allegorizing them first as domestic animals then as wild beasts. Wat Tyler is not just a jackdaw but explicitly an agent of Satan, leading a hellish cloud to London. Further, the false rhetoric of the daw has an audience incapable of anything but mass response.

Gower's attack on plowmen contrasts almost entirely with Langland's more nuanced and complex picture of laboring society and its ills. Just as Tyler was defined in the absolute moral terms of the devil, so the proper role of peasants is assumed to be ordained by God, and immutable. Like Tyler, the resistant peasant is attracted into the wild animal world by comparison with a fox. Yet Gower's wish for a restored past is not very different from the desire of the peasants for a restored strong kingship and equal justice. Both project the social order they desire on a nostalgic myth of a better past.

Mystical Writings

For all their specialized language and eager search for a more immediate experience of divinity, these texts also connect to dominant themes and motifs in vernacular literature, religious and secular, of the later Middle Ages. Indeed, the "Middle English Mystics" make a less coherent group than their traditional title among scholars would imply. Rolle combines his ecstatic style with strong pastoral aims; *The Cloud of Unknowing* comes from an ancient Neoplatonic tradition; while

Julian of Norwich uses her visions only as the basis for a quite complex speculative theology. They have parallels to other literatures in the widespread idea of quest, pilgrimage as a means thereto, and interior transformation through contact with mysterious agencies. This is found not just in specifically religious literature, but in the Arthurian Grail quest and other romances. Langland's elaborate, semi-dramatic narrative of the Passion is echoed by Dame Julian's vision of the Crucifixion. And the metaphorical aspects of Langland's Will, as a mental quality and quester, are present in *The Cloud's* discussion of the soul and its role in mystical attainment. Behind even Chaucer's humor and deft social critique, let us remember, is the deeply serious model of pilgrimage and the spiritual accomplishment—the quest for the heavenly Jerusalem—it symbolizes.

Wolfgang Riehle's *The Middle English Mystics* (1981) remains a key study of these texts. Important work appears in the series *The Medieval Mystical Tradition in England*, ed. Marion Glasscoe (1980–92). The broader cultural and liturgical context is explored by Sarah Backwith, *Christ's Body: Identity, Culture, and Society in Late Medieval Writings* (1993). A fine recent essay is worth seeking out: Nicholas Watson, "Visions of Inclusion: Universal Salvation and Vernacular Theology in Pre-Reformation England," *Journal of Medieval and Early Modern Studies* 27 (1997), 145–87. Watson also contributes the chapter "The Middle English Mystics" to the *Cambridge History of Medieval English Literature*, ed. David Wallace (1999).

Julian of Norwich

Dame Julian of Norwich is an important figure in Middle English theology and mysticism. Equally, though, she is a major player in a movement among women across Europe to experience a more immediate and responsive religious faith (often within an even broader urge toward "affective piety"), and to find a verbal medium by which to communicate those and other experiences. This created considerable anxiety among the traditional controllers of language and of social and religious dogma.

Dame Julian, Chaucer's Wife of Bath, and Margery Kempe work very well when taught as a group of female voices within these movements right around the turn of the fourteenth and fifteenth centuries. One might begin, though, with a detail in *The Anonimalle Chronicle*, where a "wicked woman" among the 1381 rebels raises an alarm and prevents the Archbishop of Canterbury's escape from the Tower. Though the Wife of Bath is Chaucer's fiction, and Dame Julian and Kempe historical people, all three (and the wicked woman) leave behind a textual record through some medium of male language, both by using amanuenses and by necessarily negotiating with a whole language whose underlying ideology is (at best) ambivalent toward women. (Such problematic mediation of "female" perspective is found again in "women's songs" among the Middle English lyrics.)

One might discuss their connections of religious quest within domestic settings or secular quest in the context of religious action; their different strategies of language; differences of mobility and stability; their dialogue or negotiation with male agents of clerical authority; their apparent birth into the mercantile or modest gentry class; the connections of all three to kinds of public culture (liturgy, sermons, drama); and the imagery of marriage and domestic experience in all three. (In most of these regards, the three resonate intriguingly with the writing of the religious enthusiast Rebecca Jackson, a free African-American in Philadelphia before the Civil War. She too was from a modest bourgeois family, struggled with illiteracy, and experienced visionary dreams dense with domestic imagery.)

Dame Julian created a place for her spiritual ambitions, and a degree of social power, by choosing the life of an anchorite, which avoided traditional critiques of women's mobility and love of public display. (See just such accusations in the Wife of Bath's Prologue.) For all their enclosure and modest life, though, anchorites gained a certain prestige thereby. Consider the report, in *The Anonimalle Chronicle*. that Richard II made confession and talked with an anchorite right in the crisis of the Rising of 1381.

Julian explicitly calls herself "unlettered" (chapter 2), although whatever that means it did not preclude access to a wide variety of texts. Within what we might call her empowering humility, Julian uses two very daring linguistic strategies. First, her meditations are not centrally on Bible texts; rather, she uses her own early visions as "texts" for exegesis that went on for decades (such as her meditation on the "little thing" in her hand, chapter 5). Second, she imports the specific setting of traditional female experience in her class—household, wifehood, motherhood—as the fundamental metaphors of her religious thinking. From these she produces what Nicholas Watson rightly calls a "vernacular theology" ("Visions of Inclusion," 146).

Dame Julian's wish for "bodily sight" of the Passion is coherent with later medieval affective piety, and with visual representations of Christ as the Man of Sorrows. Her desire to experience an illness close to death literalizes ideas of dying to this life, found in monastic vows and in mystical texts. Conversely, the three wounds she desires are metaphorized as contrition, compassion, and longing for God. Julian deflects possible critique of these ambitions by acknowledging their eccentricity, leaving her wishes in the will of God, and by repeatedly asserting her orthodoxy. This deflection by reference to a male agent is persistent in Julian's early visions, as when her curate's crucifix stimulates her bodily vision of the Passion (chapter 4). This is balanced by her vision of the Virgin Mary and her "created littleness," later seen "high and noble and glorious" (chapter 25). (A similarly double vision of Mary appears in Middle English lyrics devoted to her.)

The extreme physicality of some of Julian's visions can be startling. Along with her compassion for Christ's complete suffering, she also separates his body and wounds into discrete units, which become sites for theological meditation. This is elaborated in her sight of the wound in Christ's side (chapter 24) as a space for the salvation of all mankind. She also controls rhetoric nicely at key points, by the building up of repeated phrases, such as Christ's "I am he . . ." in chapter 26, or the famous lines, Christ's response to Julian's long meditation on sin and its origin in chapter 27, "but all will be well." It is typical of Julian to place this expansive rhetoric in the mouth of Christ, not her own.

From this bodily vision and the domestic imagery of her meditations, Dame Julian constructs a theology of widespread salvation, rather than a program for individual vision. She is emphatic that her visions do not privilege her, and that the fruit of her exegesis does not depart from the dogma any Christian learns in church. She is writing not just for contemplatives, but for all believers. Chapters 60 and 61 especially explore Christ and humanity, and God and humanity, through a detailed narrative of mother's love: gestation, birth, nourishment, protection and chastisement. Breast-feeding, for instance, becomes the image for Mother Jesus and the Eucharist. Following traditions of polysemy in Biblical exegesis, Julian will move a single image toward a number of ends. The breast itself thus suggests the Eucharist, but elsewhere Christ's spear wound, and Holy Church. Gender is fluid, however; Julian's maternal imagery leads her reader into an ever richer sense of the implications of Christ's statement, "I am he whom you love." From the specifically gendered and hierarchicalized love of man for woman (a trope from the Song of Songs, spiritualized by centuries of Christian commentary), Julian expands the belovedness of Christ to include varieties of love within a family, especially love for the mother. The convergent languages of love and faith are also seen in many Middle English religious lyrics.

Studies partly or entirely devoted to Dame Julian include Frances Beer, *Women and Mystical Experience in the Middle Ages* (1992), and Denise Baker, *Julian of Norwich's Showings: from Vision to Book* (1994). The context of Julian's theology is set out in Caroline Walker Bynum, *Jesus as Mother: Studies in the Spirituality of the High Middle Ages* (1982).

COMPANION READINGS

Richard Rolle

Richard Rolle was enormously popular in the fourteenth and fifteenth centuries, and his works survive in as many as five hundred manuscripts. Rolle explores the major themes that appear in mystical tradition, but uses characterisitic imagery of warmth, sweetness, and song. He also borrows freely and quite openly from the Song of Songs (especially in imagery of thirst and longing) and the Psalms (for ideas of praise and song).

Rolle did not work in the immediate milieu of his contemporary John Wycliffe (though both were Oxford-trained) and the school of Bible translators who worked under Wycliffe's inspiration. Nevertheless, Rolle's call for an eager exile from the goods of the world was enthusiastically taken up by Wycliffe and his "Lollard" followers after Rolle's death. In fact, he is hostile to the involved questions and logic of university theology. And he does not reach toward (and even seems to deny) the highest aspirations to spiritual union found in some continental models such as Bernard of Clairvaux.

Rolle is an approachable writer in his emphatically personalized voice and in his very inconsistencies. The images of heat and sweetness particularly reflect Rolle's shifts of attention, sometimes between metaphorical and (apparently) literal language, from "real warmth" to "as if a real fire." And the text itself enacts Rolle's warning about slipping back into the concerns of the world. Repeatedly, his own memory of past wrongs (by himself or others) generates an episode of divided, sometimes still angry response.

Like many clerics going back as early as St. Jerome, Rolle had a deeply ambivalent attitude toward women. On the one hand, many of his English works were composed for the direction of recluses and nuns, among whom may have been his own sister; on the other hand he invokes traditional misogynist associations of women with instability and excess. By contrast, Rolle tends to imagine mystical accomplishment in terms of male action. In the story of his own spiritual awakening and withdrawal from the world Rolle speaks of "doughty warriors."

Compare the bodily experience of the divine here with the more intellectual approach in The Cloud, its avoidance of imagery of bodily desire. Rolle's imagery of food and drink is distinct from that in Dame Julian, linked more to the Eucharist than to Julian's domestic experience. Rolle's memories are usually warnings, calls from a world he wants to (and cannot) leave behind. Julian by contrast uses the memory of her visions almost as a text for exegesis. Compare too Rolle's initial spiritual experience in a chapel, Julian's in her family home, and Margery Kempe's often in public spaces such as cathedrals or roads.

The Cloud of Unknowing

This text uses ideas and imagery of neoplatonic Christianity going back to the so-called pseudo-Dionysius and his translator and commentator John Scotus Eriugena. This tradition moved into the high and later Middle Ages through the Victorines in Paris, who in turn had daughter houses and texts distributed in England. Hugh of St. Victor was widely read in England and Andrew of St. Victor spent years there as an abbot.

From this long-established mystical tradition, The Cloud of Unknowing creates a voice of restraint, calling for submission to authority even in private spiritual growth. It echoes ecclesiastical anxiety about undirected mysticism, lay access to the mysteries of faith, and any religious experience registered at the level of bodily sensation. The author connects the "false ingenuity" of interior quest to dangers of devilish deception. The dominant figure of the cloud and waiting in darkness avoids pleasurable senses like heat and taste, for the more abstract notions of light and dark. The Cloud is far more troubled and explicit than Rolle or Dame Julian about the limits of worldly language in expressing spiritual experience.

Note the persistently hortatory tone, and dependence on imperative verbs. The author works through instruction and warning, and avoids private experience. His emphasis on the great difficulties of spiritual progress may specifically counter Rolle's assurances of the ease with which the yearning Christian may achieve some experience of spiritual warmth and sweetness. Indeed he emphasizes forgetting as a prerequisite to contact with the divine, quite differently from either Rolle or Julian of Norwich. And he links spiritual improvement explicitly to the work of the whole church, since it aids all souls, even those in purgatory.

The Cloud's negative account of a soul wavering between the divine and "memories of things done and undone," is comparable to the very experiences

Rolle reports. Given the accompanying imagery of fire, this could even be a direct critique of Rolle and admonition to his followers. It offers explicit warning, if not about Rolle himself, then about the sensory experience of spiritual elevation Rolle describes.

Medieval Cycle Drama

Forms of play and public culture (a better term than "popular culture" in this context) were influential shapers of medieval experience, both sacred and secular. At a number of such cultural sites, the line between enactment and awesome transformation becomes highly porous. Clearest at the altar where the priest's words summon the transubstantiation of bread into the body of Christ, this porosity is less mysterious but present in the public performance of a poem, with the inevitable ventriloquism of voices that entails. Medieval public culture involved many mobile rituals in which one group's space and identifying objects moved temporarily into another's: secular events like formalized jousts and tournaments; royal entries into cities, often accompanied with recitations, music, *tableaux vivants*; and religious processions out of the church and into the spaces of commerce and production.

The great Middle English biblical dramas enacting the story of creation, fall, and salvation, were developed in the thriving but contentious towns of the East Midlands and north, that had been greatly enriched in the fourteenth century by trade (particularly with the Netherlands and Flanders) and especially by the export of wool. The mercantile bourgeoisie formed much of its identity by participating in a network of guilds, both religious (for the establishment of chantries and prayers for members' souls after death) and secular (for members of various crafts and trades). These guilds were only one site of contact, and strife, between the lay bourgeois and the clergy; their encounters were also more ritually enacted in the many public religious processions that moved from the parish churches and cathedrals into the settings of urban trade and manufacture. Public sermons had a similar, and even more hierarchicalized, impact.

Ritual processions were especially elaborate at the Feast of Corpus Christi, sixty days after Easter and close to the summer solstice, and this early summer holiday became a frequent occasion for the production of "mystery plays," a title derived from the continent and the Latin *mysterium*, referring to the trades or crafts organized in guilds. In medieval England, they were often called Corpus Christi plays, for the church holiday with which many were associated. These productions were a dense site of communal identity and contest; the urban craft guilds (and probably rural religious guilds) financed production and often supplied staging and actors directly, while the texts show every sign of coming from clerical hands. A particularly intense notion of identity is implicit in the spectacle of craftsmen and other workers of medieval England watching their opposite numbers in biblical history, and sometimes seeing one of their own guildsmen playing such a theatrical role.

The Second Play of the Shepherds

Especially in the work of the "Wakefield Master" who wrote, or revised from an earlier form, *The Second Play of the Shepherds*, the professional pride and discontent of contemporary laborers fold into the drama of salvation. (The play has its name because it began as an alternate play to the one already available—*Alia eorundem* the manuscript says, "another of the same.") The Wakefield Master, almost certainly a cleric, was a brilliant and innovative dramatist. He depicts complex and changeable characters in vigorous, colloquial dialogue, rich in proverbial interjections, and more "naturalistic" (if also less awesome) than was attempted in earlier drama like the York Cycle, and he engages these characters in evolving relationships that imply a past and a world beyond the play. This accomplishment is the more impressive in that the Wakefield Master uses a challenging nine-line stanza. He is not only a good poet, though. The play is theatrically brilliant; its scenes flow nicely together (in settings that lie close together on the stage), at once structured and related by repeated motifs like song, sleep, challenges at doorways, disguise and recognition.

The famous grumbling of the shepherds as the play opens, and Mak's hunger later on, are intriguingly similar to some of the laborers' grievances in the Rebellion of 1381, and to social satire widespread throughout the later Middle Ages. In addition to the hostile forces of nature (in which the audience would recognize the inheritance of Adam and the fall), the shepherds lament the bondage of servile tenure, marriage, and serving men of their own class. They complain about taxes and oppression by "gentlery men." Yet Shepherds I and II, for all their complaining, are not outside the system of oppressive service, as they abuse their own servant Daw. Hunger is present throughout the play.

That the shepherds voice their "moan" need not mean, however, that the play supports any rebellion on their part. Their complaints and violence disappear in the face of the Nativity of Christ, and they are drawn into a socially and musically harmonious expression of praise; their economic and class hostility turns to charity. The subversive comedy of the magician and sheep-stealer Mak is similarly attracted into a parodic echo of the Nativity by the end of the play. In both ways, the play ultimately draws these potentially subversive expressions into normative actions of faith.

This effect is only one aspect of the play's complex and subtle use of figural and typological thinking. In its narrow meaning as applied to biblical commentary, typological interpretation approached Old Testament events as historically real, but also as precedents or prefigurations that would only be fulfilled by events in the New Testament, especially the Incarnation of Christ. As Adam of St. Victor commented on Hebrews 10:10: "The Old Law is a shadow of future things." This kind of typological thought is frequently reflected in Langland's *Piers Plowman* and in lyrics like *Adam Lay Ibounden*. It was so influential a way of looking at history, though, that typology sometimes shaped extra-biblical legend and even views of secular history. One might even consider a kind of reverse typology, in which a person (say a shepherd) takes on his fullest significance as he participates, or witnesses the enactment of a prototype in sacred history.

The implications of an extended typology are most elaborately developed in
The Second Play of the Shepherds in the scenes of Mak disguising his stolen ram as a
newborn, swaddled baby and its discovery by the three shepherds. This extraordinary scene uses slapstick comedy at once to figure and to parody the transcendent
events of the Nativity that, in the economy of the play, are occurring simultaneously. The scene at Mak's house of course neatly doubles the Nativity scene with
the Lamb of God: the beast swaddled between Mak and Gill is replaced by baby
Jesus swaddled between two beasts. But the binding of the ram further draws in
the iconology of the Passion, and Mak's wife swearing to eat the sheep/baby if
she's tricked the shepherds also parodically forecasts the Eucharist.

The Shepherds (with their symbolic link to the iconology of Christ as good
shepherd, e.g. the Book of Luke 15:3-7) are the mediators between the audience
(whose social stresses they reflect) and the transcendent history of the Nativity (in
which they participate). They move repeatedly from conflict to harmony, both social and musical, a kind of middle ground between the comic disputatious household (and bad singing) of Mak, and the Holy Family and singing of the angels.
Their decision to toss Mak in a blanket (game as punishment) rather than deliver
him to his death as a sheep-stealer is the act of charity that qualifies the shepherds
for the angelic message that follows. Indeed the stanzas in which they make their
modest gifts to the infant savior, with the refrain of "Hail!", provide the dramatic
gesture that makes the baby into a holy icon.

These stanzas are also a high point in the Wakefield Master's craft, with their
tense yoking together of highly referential and idiomatic language. The density of reference within humble and literal objects in the play is especially touching in this
scene, in the gifts of the shepherds: cherries, a bird, and a toy ball. These are modest, but cherries appear in a number of legends of the Annunciation, the bird implies
both the ascent of mankind with the Incarnation and the dove of the Holy Spirit,
and the tennis ball may suggest an orb, symbol of the kingdom of heaven. Together
the three gifts echo Christ's sacrificial humanity, spiritual primacy, and lordship.

Mak is certainly the most complex and resonant character in the drama. His
unruliness and preference for theft over work suggest the hostile portraits of some
peasants found in writers like Langland and certain chroniclers of the Rebellion
of 1381. Mak is more eloquent about his plight than the wordy shepherds, for instance when he identifies himself as "a man that walks on the moor, / And has
not all his will!" (lines 196-97). As both a role-player within the drama (pretending to be a yeoman of the king and feigning a southern accent) and a magician, he
links ritual magic and theatricality. Mak is more broadly a speaker for the non-
Christian uncanny in his efforts to explain the monstrous "child" evoking a range
of folk belief: the child is bewitched, or a changeling switched by elves. This is not
inconsistent with the redemptive structure of the play, in which Mak may be seen
as a comic anti-Christ (named "Sir Guile" by his wife and having a "horned lad"
as his child), replaced by the higher "magic" of the Incarnation.

The play's convergence of secular and sacred, and its exploitation of typology,
are further supported by its conscious juggling of time schemes. Time collapses in
the overt anachronisms of the shepherds' and Mak's speeches, calling on Mary and

the Passion, and swearing by martyred saints, before they even witness the Nativity (e.g. "By him that died for us all"). This can be compared to the penetrability, or near disappearance of time in the Eucharist, where the body of Christ is present among the faithful. The play invokes a related overlap of places, Bethlehem and Britain, in the first shepherd's dream—"I thought we had laid us full near England"—and elsewhere. In such a context, could local and contemporary figures like the shepherds seem almost to enact, not merely mimic, the revelation of their forebears a millenium and a half earlier?

The Second Play of the Shepherds has attracted a large body of scholarship and critical interpretation; the collections by Beadle and Emmerson listed in the Bibliography give a good first look at the range of approaches. Earlier writing focussed on the play's links to typological thinking and contemporary iconology. Research has also interested itself in the socioeconomic setting of the plays in the urban public culture of the later Middle Ages. The material thus uncovered (much of it collected and edited in the Records of Early English Drama series, 1981-ongoing), though little is of direct relevance to the Wakefield Cycle, has provided a springboard for New Historicist critics, interested in the place of the plays in the wider drama of urban public culture. Feminist readers have been exploring the analogies between the characters of Gill and the Virgin Mary, and their connections to female speakers in other vernacular works like those of Chaucer and Langland.

The York Play of the Crucifixion

Like the Wakefield Master who wrote in a similar milieu of prosperous northern English towns, the "York Realist" was an inspired dramatic artist. His Crucifixion, though from a different cycle, when read with the Second Play of the Shepherds can give students a sense of the span of Christian history covered by the Corpus Christi plays (See Clifford Davison, From Creation to Doom: The York Cycle of Mystery Plays [1984]). Both plays present fallen human beings—the shepherds and Christ's torturers, respectively—with whom the audience can initially identify, but whose errors in misunderstanding Christ's message are revealed at the end. Students may be intrigued by the use of the blasphemous in both plays, and disturbed by the grotesqueness of the torture in the Crucifixion. Teachers might point out that according to Lawrence Clopper, the clerical authors included the grotesque elements in the cycle plays not to be subversive, but to co-opt the festive celebrations of the populace for sacred purposes ("English Drama: From Ungodly Ludi to Sacred Play," Cambridge History of Medieval English Literature [1999], p. 748).

The brutality of the portrayal of the crucifixion has often been explained as a reflection of the late medieval focus on Christ's suffering humanity, as opposed to His divine power. A similar expression of affective piety can be seen in the mystical and meditative works in this anthology, such as the writings of Julian of Norwich (e.g., when she sees herself as being drawn through Christ's wound) and the Middle English lyrics on the crucifixion (e.g., "Jesus, my Sweet Lover"). Nevertheless, as Ruth Evans has pointed out, the York Crucifixion lacks the nur-

turing feminine characteristics often associated with the late medieval view of
Christ that Carolyn Bynum has identified in *Jesus as Mother* (1982). Evans argues
that the suffering of Christ in this play is in fact masculine and heroic, in the tradition of the Germanic warrior giving his life for his people, as in the Old English
Dream of the Rood. She views Christ's silence in response to the taunts of his torturers not as passive and feminine, but restrained and stoic, emanating from a
knowledge of power ("Body Politics: Engendering Medieval Cycle Drama," *Feminist
Readings in Middle English Literature*, ed. Ruth Evans and Lesley Johnson [1994]).

The heroic and dignified image of Christ is enhanced by the poem's highly al-
literative style, a feature the York Realist is known to have added in his revision.
For alliterative poetry from Old English times to the early sixteenth century was as-
sociated with epic subject matter, as in the fourteenth-century alliterative *Morte
Arthure*. The alliteration helps to focus on Christ's power rather than his suffering
in this play, much as it does in the more military passages recounting his
Harrowing of Hell, such as *Passus* 18 of *Piers Plowman* and William Dunbar's
"Done is a Battell" (in addition to the *Dream of the Rood*).

Many critics have commented on the balance between the depictions of the
suffering "Gothic" and the heroic "Romanesque" Christ in the York Crucifixion.
Clifford Davidson draws explicit art historical parallels to this dichotomy ("The
Realism of the York Realist and the York Passion," *Speculum*, 50 [1975], 270–83).
It might be helpful to show students visual depictions of the crucifixion, starting
in this anthology with the passion scenes from the Winchester Psalter (color plate
5), and the image taken from "On the Passion of our Lord" (p. 515). (The double
image of the Annunciation to the Shepherds and the Nativity from the *Holkham
Bible Picture Book* [color plate 7] can similarly serve to illustrate the *Second Play of
the Shepherds*).

Vernacular Religion and Repression

The challenge of teaching the materials gathered here is to press beyond their
usefulness as cultural and historical background, and show students their literary merit and their critical role in the complex rise of Middle English. These are
indeed important backgrounds: they contextualize the urban piety of the Corpus
Christi cycle plays, the social and religious paranoia that led to much of the ha-
rassment of Margery Kempe, the critique of morally lax clergy in Langland and
parts of the *Canterbury Tales*. They are equally important, though, as examples of
translation, sermons, argumentative prose, and (no doubt heavily mediated)
spoken word.

These texts also greatly complicate any simple account of "the rise of Middle
English" as a single, centralized, or unimpeded climb to preeminence. Certainly,
by the last quarter of the fourteenth century, we encounter a group of poets writing in English who enjoy the favor and patronage of the aristocratic magnates and
royal court: Chaucer, John Gower, John Lydgate, and others. There was much
else going on, though. Further away from London, the prose translator John

Trevisa worked for Thomas, Lord Berkeley in the southwest Midlands. Alliterative poetry was produced by writers from the west Midlands and north, including the very popular work of William Langland (who lived in London and whose readership stretched across England), and some of the cycle plays from mercantile northern cities like York and Wakefield. Alliterative poetry splits across classes as well, however; the poet of *Sir Gawain and the Green Knight* apparently wrote for an aristocratic (but also pious) household in the area around Chester. In an era of strong regional dialects, some of this writing sounded strange in the ears (or minds) of distant readers.

Further, when the expressivity and broadened readership of Middle English came to serve the aims of religious dissent (which was also perceived as social dissent), as in some of the texts here, it was the object of official anxiety then official condemnation, even judicial murder as many Lollard preachers learned. In this regard, it is worth pausing with students over the passage from Henry Knighton quoted on page 515, and noting how his anxious hostility spreads across classes, educational levels, and gender. (This passage again becomes relevant when students encounter the hostility toward the very orthodox Margery Kempe, partly because her "holy conversation" came close to preaching without license, but equally because she was a woman doing so.) On the other hand, those same authorities promoted certain kinds of (uncritical) devotional writing for laymen in Middle English, like that of Nicholas Love. The Lollards had stolen a march on the church, though, partly because they so often used the widely comprehensible "Central Midlands Standard" dialect. The popularity of their efforts, even in the face of ultimate official condemnation, is reflected in the 240 (or more) surviving manuscripts of the Wycliffite Bible. This compares with 82 or 83 surviving *Canterbury Tales* manuscripts, and about 56 of *Piers Plowman*.

Altogether, this work of translation, vernacular religious writing, and debate over its value helped push Middle English prose to higher levels of flexibility, syntactic and rhetorical resources, and intellectual and theological nuance. The fruits of this process are seen in the rich imagery, moving cadences, and theological reach of Middle English mystics such as Julian of Norwich. The practices of oral preaching and debate also lie behind the prompt and (when necessary) highly organized responses of Margery Kempe in her many and sometimes dangerous moments of public confrontation and clerical questioning.

The Wycliffite translation from the Book of John is austerely restrained and carefully non-Latinate in its vocabulary. This contributes to the measured repetition that is part of its aural impact. The imagery of the good shepherd echoes in many directions across Middle English literature, perhaps most famously in the description of the hard-working Parson in the General Prologue of the *Canterbury Tales* ("He was a shepherd and nought a mercenarye," l. 516). Some further (or perceived) connection to the religious language movements represented in this section may be seen in the Parson's offer to tell a "merye tale in prose." The Wycliffite sermon based on this passage in John is similarly restrained; it is traditional in form if not in content. It works by going carefully through the biblical text and using it to criticize clerical abuses in the established church. Its emotional heightening derives again from conscious repetition of phrases and from alliteration. Chaucer's Pardoner, as seen in the General Prologue and the tale, has comparable concerns for the salvation or perdition of laymen in the afterlife. By contrast, the sermon's attack on clerical wealth can be read against Chaucer's portraits of the Prioress and Monk.

John Mirk's sermon, on a passage in the Second Letter to the Corinthians, is very different in tone and method, but also represents a widespread form of sermon. Mirk is out to entertain as well as instruct his audience. He leaves the text of the Bible passage behind rather quickly, and makes his points by appeal to popular sayings and, especially, by telling a good secular story, an *exemplum*, to drive home his point. Mirk tells his story with great relish; indeed it threatens to swamp the putative purpose of the sermon. His tale especially pulls on his imagination as he casts the wealthy lady as the villain; the knight is no worse than handsome and ambitious. (Interestingly, it is only another tale-teller, a harper, who keeps the knight's castle safe on the long-delayed day of vengeance, and it is only the harper who survives its conflagration.) This may be the sort of thing Chaucer's Parson refers to when he reproaches those who "tellen fables," in his Prologue l. 35. And it just the kind of sermon that Chaucer's Pardoner tells, cynically aware of how very effective it can be. Langland does something not dissimilar, though, in Passus 18 of *Piers Plowman*, when he introduces Christ as a knight on a quest. Nicholas Love is similarly interested in using drama and concrete detail to draw the attention (and meditation) of his readers. *The Mirror of the Blessed Life of Jesus Christ* combines biblical narrative with a good deal of legendary material to create an emotive, even sentimental picture of scenes from the life of Christ. And the simple but eloquent morals he draws from these scenes urge his readers to fairly passive virtues that do not threaten the *status quo*: poverty, meekness, and bodily penance.

The Statute "On Burning the Heretic" reflects the real anxiety that the Wycliffites were causing in official circles. It elides religious dissent and political subversion. And the *Confession of Hawisia Moone of Loddon* gives a glimpse of what the religious and political powers feared. It is worth asking, though, whether this is a straightforward "true report," or a heavily prompted confession by a frightened woman willing to feed the authorities what they wanted. Much of the specificity does suggest, though, the extent to which serious religious dialogue was occurring at the level of rural villages, and how a network of preachers spread the Lollard word. Moone's somewhat reductive recital of Lollard tenets can be recalled when students read Margery Kempe. Kempe eagerly pursues a whole list of practices condemned by the Lollards. This makes even more interesting (and perhaps paranoid) the frequent accusation that Kempe herself is a Lollard, and it suggests how any religious deviance or outspokenness was subject to such attack.

It is just this atmosphere of nervous official condescension to lay piety, and fearful attacks on many acts of religious dialogue, that informs the two orthodox defenses of writing and reading religious works in the vernacular. Many writers of clear orthodoxy nonetheless continued to support the idea of biblical reading in

English and its interpretation by laymen, as we see in "Preaching and Teaching in the Vernacular" and *The Holy Prophet David Saith*. Yet the first writer expresses real anxiety about the dangers he faces for holding such opinions, and appeals to a lay patron, not a powerful cleric, for protection.

Margery Kempe

If one measure of literary achievement is the capacity of a text to arouse passionate response, positive or negative, then Margery Kempe produced a great book; and the public expressions of her religious attainments that preceded that book for decades, judged by the same measure, had a similar greatness. No other single medieval text has enjoyed a level of engaged appropriation and reaction in the second half of the twentieth century equal to *The Book of Margery Kempe*.

Both in fifteenth-century Lynn and in twentieth-century scholarship, Kempe generated strikingly similar and similarly polar reactions. Is she a genuine holy woman (however eccentric), or is she a megalomaniac, almost a self-deceiving fraud? Students of mysticism have tended—more in their tone than their explicit judgments—to favor the latter position; more recently, feminist scholars have tended at least to accept Kempe's claims of religious experience at face value, and celebrate her achievement of a female voice and position (however limited) within the highly patriarchal hierarchies of the late medieval clerisy. Either view has seemed to focus more on exegesis and judgment of Kempe's personality than of her book. But recent readers have tried to move past these dichotomies and the pattern of dismissal or celebration. Instead, they see her book as the complex and divided product of a setting in which competitive secular ambition and religious accomplishment, bodily experience and mystical knowing, disruptive expression and clerical approval, cannot be disembedded one from the other. Particularly intriguing instances of such an approach are found in Sarah Beckwith, *Christ's Body: Identity, Culture, and Society in Late Medieval Writings*, (1993), chapter 4, and in Nicholas Watson, "The Middle English Mystics," in *The Cambridge History of Medieval English Literature*, ed. David Wallace (1999).

Since the rediscovery of her book in 1934, Margery Kempe has usually been studied in the context of the Middle English mystics (a category that is itself rather recent). Kempe clearly sought the kinds of direct, affective contact with the love and sufferings of Christ seen in Richard Rolle and the initial visions of Julian of Norwich. The mode by which she pursued these ends, though, was markedly different from Rolle or Julian; far from the persistent inwardness of private prayer and meditation, Kempe exercised several kinds of mobility. She expended tremendous energy negotiating with her husband and with ecclesiastical authorities to achieve a mobility within the hierarchies of marriage and clerisy, seeking abstention from the conjugal debt of sex and from certain foods, and requesting to wear special clothes and receive weekly Eucharist. But she particularly enacted her religious quest through mobility of place. Kempe repeated her contacts with the

Passion by engaging in pilgrimage, visiting both the site of its original occurrence and sites of its imitation by vision and martyrdom.

The late medieval clergy was increasingly threatened by the extent of unsupervised religious quest, unregulated lay preaching, and unorthodox or heterodox speculation within its own ranks. It reacted in a range of manners, from open-spirited negotiation (which Kempe occasionally encounters) to repressive hostility (probably more widespread). One result of this was Archbishop Arundel's Constitutions of 1409, which made illegal any theological speculation in the vernacular.

What produced perhaps the most trouble for Kempe, though, was her need (and, it appears, choice) to express her links with the Passion in highly public fashion, through her tears and sobbing roars, long before that expression painstakingly took the form of her book. (Even that book can be viewed as a crucial site of negotiated mobility, from oral expression to written, through protracted dealings with two priest scribes.) Where the site of Julian's speculation was the internal memory of her early vision of Christ's body, the principal site of Kempe's religious contact was her own mobile and usually public body.

Kempe's intensely somatic religious experience was not unique in her time. Her theatricalizing extends but is not wholly different from the public ritual and dramas of late medieval civic culture, in which she lived: costume, role playing, emotive experience of the joys of the Virgin or sufferings of Christ. Public religious rituals especially developed around the feast of Corpus Christi, a holiday that commemorates the last supper and Eucharist with which Kempe's religious expression is so closely identified. She describes her weeping reaction to a Corpus Christi procession in a chapter not included here (chapter 45). Many such events of public religious ritual come into the book, such as the great scene of Margery and John at Bridlington as they return from Corpus Christi day at York, and thus probably having seen the mystery plays there. In such plays Kempe would witness a melding of secular class strife and divine visitation comparable to her own unresolved mixture of life in and beyond the mundane world. Such themes are found in *The Second Play of the Shepherds* in this anthology.

What was radical in Kempe's relation to these public, emotive, and somatic expressions of faith was her persistent denial of a line between herself as audience and as actor. Repeatedly, in local ecclesiastical events or on pilgrimage, Kempe's expressivity makes herself the object of the public gaze and (to a degree that never satisfies her hopes) of public veneration. This behavior also radically inverts the usual role of the traveller. Rather than seeking in the foreign place (or the local holy site) some experience of marvel or the uncanny, Margery Kempe repeatedly makes herself the object of that wondering (or repelled) gaze. If her body at times registers and replicates the sufferings of Christ, it also seems to absorb and perform the holy marvels of exotic place.

The theatricality and persistence of her religious expression enraged many in Margery Kempe's own time, and their reactions in turn are folded into elements of betrayal, mockery, and abandonment that underwrite her program of imitation of Christ. Kempe's mobility extends even to selfhood. (She is also dressed as a fool and mocked—a scene often enacted in passion plays; she rides into Jerusalem on a donkey; finally she stretches her arms wide and writhes on Calvary.) So intense is her identification with the life and sufferings of Christ, so easily is it triggered by place, memory, or analogy, that Kempe's very body moves past imitation and virtually becomes Christ's body. As the *Book* progresses, the line between representation and literal presence of Christ to her senses, or even between analogy and literal presence (as in the infants and young boys over whom she weeps in Rome) is ever more permeable.

Yet it is exactly the will to such expression that gave Kempe her disruptive power, clear in her own time and little diminished today. The actual content of her visions and meditations is orthodox and very much in the tradition of such predecessors as Richard Rolle, whose work Kempe names in the *Book*. If Julian's safety lay in her stable enclosure and rhetoric of humility, Kempe's lay in her doctrinal conservatism and the detail with which she could, when pressed, articulate it under clerical scrutiny. Notwithstanding the spectacle of her piety and her insistence that she communicated directly with Christ, Kempe eagerly sought approval and authority from persons within the ecclesiastical establishment: from bishops and archbishops, mystical friars, and Julian of Norwich herself. Nevertheless, that very approval was sought by repeatedly travelling beyond the traditional geography of clerical authority, the parish. And the acceptance she often gained thereby provided Kempe with an even greater tool of disruption (or, just as unnerving, a greater alternative) to priestly religion, the authority of her intimate, direct "dalliance" with the three persons of the Trinity, especially the Son.

Middle English Lyrics

The many languages spoken and written in the British Isles from the thirteenth century on introduced a wealth of poetic traditions, and inspired a linguistic self-consciousness and a taste for word play that greatly enriched the Middle English lyric. The intricate rhyme schemes, alliteration, consonance, and assonance of two of the Harley lyrics included here, *Spring* and *Alisoun*, are thought to have been influenced by the highly sophisticated technique of medieval Welsh poets, since the Harley manuscript was compiled in Hereford, near the Welsh border. (See G. L. Brook's introduction to *The Harley Lyrics*, [1956], 1–26). Students might want to compare the poems of Dafydd ap Gwilym, whose translator tries to convey these features in modern English.

Middle English itself is so rich in homonyms that it provides an opportunity for word play, whether sacred or profane. The famous lyric *I Sing of a Maiden* praises the Virgin Mary as being "makeles"—which can be translated as "spotless" (from the Latin *macula*), "matchless," or "without a mate" (both from the Old English *ge-maca*, "equal" or "mate"). Far from being seen as frivolous, in the Middle Ages such punning was thought to reveal profound spiritual correspondences between word and thing, as Walter Ong has shown. (See Stephen Manning, "On 'I sing of a maiden,'" in *Middle English Lyrics*, ed. Maxwell S. Luria and Richard L. Hoffman, [1974], 331).

Ambiguous language is also used for humorous purposes in several of the Middle English lyrics. Church Latin or Greek—priestly code languages which the laity could not understand—are often shown as being used to deceive women. In the satirical *Abuse of Women*, a series of stanzas in mock praise of women—ostensibly denying the negative stereotypes familiar from Chaucer's Wife of Bath's Prologue—are punctuated by a refrain whose Latin portion reveals the speaker's real assessment: "Of all creatures women be best: / Cuius contrarium verum est." Liturgical Greek is used for the purpose of seduction in a more dramatic situation in *Joly Jankin*, by a clerk whose refrain—*Kyrie Eleison*—the female speaker takes to refer to her own name, Alison. Only at the end of the lyric does she reveal her pregnancy, and with it a new understanding of the refrain—"Lord have mercy upon us." Such love of word play, whether spiritual or humorous, recalls Langland's play on the names "Piers" and "Will," as well as Chaucer's flattering interpretation of Eve's guilt—*mulier est hominis confusio*—in the Nun's Priest's Tale and his puns on "hende" and "privitee" in the Miller's Tale.

Secular Love Lyrics

Middle English lyrics play with generic as well as verbal ambiguity. The imagery shared between the secular and religious lyrics is so pervasive that the distinction between them is often considered arbitrary. Both genres, in fact, are highly conventional, and of interest for the way they manipulate traditional motifs. The love lyrics' application of language appropriate to the worship of the Virgin Mary to the earthly lady give them a generally idealistic rather than sensual tone. The love complaint *Alisoun*, for instance, is hardly a seduction poem in the manner being able to love his lady ("An hendy hap ich habbe ihent!"), asserts its divine origin ("Ichot from hevene it is me sent"), and only at the end makes a timid request for her to listen to his plea: ("Herkne to my roun!"). In *Spring*, the speaker is even less direct in his address to his lady, for the most part celebrating the burgeoning of nature—the flowering of the meadow and the mating of animals—and only at the end contrasting it with the disdainful behavior of women:

> Wormes woweth under cloude,
> Wimmen waxeth wounder proude.
>
> [Worms woo under the soil,
> Women grow wondrously proud.]

While it has been suggested that the reference to the worms' wooing is a subtle reminder to the lady of the inevitable decay of her own flesh (Manning, 271), it hardly has the coercive force of the graphic "worms shall try that long-preserved virginity" in Marvell's *To his Coy Mistress*, the most famous of the Renaissance and seventeenth-century poems to revive the "carpe diem" rhetoric of the Ovidian love tradition.

Women's Songs

Greater cynicism is to be found, surprisingly, in the Middle English "women's songs" that express a female perspective on courtship. Students may be disappointed to learn that such lyrics were most likely written by men, and project a male idea of a woman's feelings. They tend to be more narrative than male-voiced lyrics, perhaps because they describe not the anticipation of sex, but its frequent consequences for the woman—desertion and pregnancy. The response these lyrics invite is more often ironic than sympathetic, suggesting that the audience as well as the authors were male (See John F. Plummer, "Woman's Song in Middle English and its European Backgrounds," ed. John F. Plummer, *Vox Feminae: Studies in Medieval Woman's Song*, [1981], 135–54). This is particularly true of women's songs in which the seducers are clerics—a group well-known for their cleverness and immorality. The speaker who laments her pregnancy in *The Wily Clerk* is impressed by her seducer's "gramery," translated as "magic", but carrying echoes of *grammatica*, one of the arts of the trivium which lay people found arcane. In the lyric *Joly Jankin* discussed above, both the clerk's play on *Kyrie eleison* as the speaker's name and the witty tone of the poem in general tend to distance the emotion in her cry, "Christ fro schame me schilde, / . . . alas, I go with childe!" The entire narrative has a tone of the fabliau, and recalls Chaucer's Miller's Tale in particular: the stock country woman's name (Alison), the courtship in church (Absolon), the successful clerical seducer (Nicholas). Such overtones suggest that these laments are not to be taken seriously, but ironically, at the woman's expense.

Religious Lyrics

In Middle English, the religious lyric is closely connected to the secular lyric, and can hardly be understood apart from it. Most obviously, as we shall see, it employs the language and imagery of courtly love poetry. But beyond that, poems in praise of Mary can be seen as inversely related to antifeminist lyrics and, occasionally, parodic of women's songs. Mariolatry—the worship of Mary as the one virtuous woman—reflects implicitly on all other women. In *Adam lay ibounden*, the assertion that the fall was fortunate rests on the assumption that Eve's fault was repaired by Mary's excellence in bearing the son of God:

> Ne hadde the appil take ben,
> The appil taken ben,
> Ne hadde never our lady
> A ben hevene quen.

Like the writings of Richard Rolle, Julian of Norwich, and the author of *The Cloud of Unknowing*, Marian lyrics are indebted to the mysticism of Bernard of Clairvaux, who worshipped Mary with the allegorized language of the Song of Songs. *In praise of Mary* states that no other woman is "so fair, so shene, so rudy, so bright," and begs Mary, "swete Levedy, . . . have mercy of thine knight" in language that recalls courtly lovers appealing to their ladies' mercy for more physical favors. Arguably the best of the poems to Mary in Middle English, *I Sing of a Maiden* describes the Incarnation in terms of Christ's courtship of her:He is said to have approached her "bower," and she to have graciously "chosen" him as her son. This nativity poem then concludes with the classic paradox of Mary as "moder and maiden."

Yet another poem in praise of Mary almost crosses the line into blasphemy as it plays with the idea that Mary is just another pregnant girl, explaining her plight. The male speaker tells of overhearing a maiden confess, "I am with child this tide," leading us to expect a lament such as *The Wily Clerk*. But we soon learn that this is a different situation altogether: the child's father is "ghostly" and embraced her "without dispit or mock." The maiden is rejoicing in her condition, and the refrain, "Nowel! nowel! nowel!" tells us that this is a nativity poem. Its use of sacred parody might be compared to the similar treatment of the nativity in *The Second Play of the Shepherds*.

Poems in praise of Christ use the language of the secular love lyric as much as those to Mary. The fact that *Sweet Jesus, King of Bliss* is preserved in the Harley manuscript, in the company of the love songs *Spring* and *Alisoun*, underscores the fact that the same audience might enjoy both genres. The speaker confesses that he is happily in bondage ("How swete beth thy love-bonde") and begs Jesus to draw him with his "love-cordes." More poignantly, in the shorter love song, *Jesus, My Sweet Lover*, the speaker identifies with Christ in his suffering on the cross, and asks that His love be fixed as firmly in his heart "As was the sphere into thine herte, / Whon thou soffredest deth for me." The imagery is almost masochistic, suggesting comparison with Donne's Holy Sonnet 10, *Batter my Heart, three-personed God*. (Teaching the two together can show students that Donne's erotic imagery is not so unusual as might appear, but has roots in medieval mysticism).

One final religious lyric takes a different tack, turning from love of Mary or Christ to the repellent subject of death. *Contempt of the World* is an *ubi sunt* poem that shows only passing regret for the worldly pleasures which must be relinquished. The speaker gloats that those who enjoyed wealth and pleasure on earth, "the riche levedies in here bour, / that wereden gold in here tressour," will suffer eternal damnation:

> Here paradis hy nomen here,
> And now they lien in helle ifere;
> The fuir it brennes evere.

His grim moral to the reader is to suffer pain on earth so as to earn the rewards of heaven. Students are likely to resist this poem, because, in sermon fashion, it urges an ascetic rejection of worldly goods. (See Rosemary Woolf, *The English Religious Lyric in the Middle Ages*, [1968]). It poses problems similar to those of Chaucer's Parson's Prologue and Retraction to the *Canterbury Tales*, with their ascetic rejection of poetry.

Taught in survey courses covering the Middle Ages through the eighteenth century, Middle English lyrics can be used to illustrate major shifts in the attitudes of the English with regard to the status of women, love, and religion. One approach would be to trace male-voiced love poems from the anonymous Middle English lyrics through Dafydd, Shakespeare, Donne, and Marvell. A study of woman's songs comparing *Wulf and Eadwacer* and *The Wife's Lament* with poems in Middle English would demonstrate the uniqueness of the first two as Old English love poems in a woman's voice, and contrast their dignity with the banality of the Middle English pregnancy laments. Furthermore, the difference between such anonymous women's songs and poems actually written *by* women—Mary Wroth, Aphra Behn, and Anne Finch, for instance—would be promising to explore. In addition, one might read pairs of male and female-voiced lyrics in Middle English—such as *My lefe is faren in a londe* and *Alisoun* with *A Forsaken Maid's Lament* and *The Wily Clerk*—as backdrop to a famous matched pair, written by two men: Marlowe's *Passionate Shepherd to His Love* and Raleigh's *Nymph's Reply to the Shepherd*.

Insight into attitudes toward sex and word play in two different periods can be gained from comparing two double-entendre poems: the Old English "Onion/Penis" riddle, and the Middle English *I have a Noble Cock*.

Religious poetry has a much longer tradition in English than love poetry, and it too has seen historical change. Since the worship of Mary developed only in the twelfth century and waned after the Reformation, the Marian lyrics included in this volume are primarily from the Middle English period. Poems devoted to Christ, however, have a much longer tradition. The Crucifixion, in particular, is imagined splendidly in *The Dream of the Rood, Now Goeth Sun under Wood*, Dunbar's *Donne is a Battell*, and Donne's Holy Sonnet 9 (*What if this present were the world's last night?*), all in ways reflective of their time.

The Tale of Taliesin

The Tale of Taliesin is a passage from Elis Grufydd's world chronicle. Written in the mid-sixteenth century, the text translated here is from a seventeenth-century manuscript in the National Library of Wales, but it was still being copied in the eighteenth century. One part of the tale's fascination is the way it invites us to rethink divisions in the cultural history of the British Isles that have largely been constructed from a specifically English perspective. In the setting of King Maelgwn's court, in the concept of the poet, and a range of mythic references, the tale reaches back to Celtic traditions thriving before the arrival of the Angles and Saxons. The forms of the poems continue practices that are pre-Norman. And yet the story was being retold with obvious relish (if with some rationalist doubt) long into the Early Modern era. It enacts the extraordinary continuity of texts and traditions in Wales, which has telling parallels in Ireland. The tradition is not ossified or archaic, though. Grufydd brings his Taliesin very much into his own time, not least by repeated assertions of a written source—a gesture by which he creates a useful distance from any narrative elements that challenge his sense of reason or orthodoxy.

Celtic Myth and Tradition   The figure of Gwion Bach/Taliesin comes from very early Welsh tradition, and reflects Celtic notions of poets as inheritors of priestly functions and keepers both of ethnic history and arcane mysteries. This can be compared to the prophetic poets Fergus and Feidelm in *The Táin*. As Patrick Ford writes, "The practice of poetry among the Celts had explicitly magical overtones, and the poet was understood to have supernatural and divinatory powers." (Ford provides a fine survey of the background of Celtic belief and the role of priest-poets, in the introduction to his edition, *Ystoria Taliesin* [1992].) As holder of his culture's whole learning and prophet of its future, the poet transcends time and place, and is heir or reincarnation of other great prophet-poets such as Merlin. Taliesin thus knows simultaneous events in other places (like Elphin's imprisonment), and when he reveals himself to King Maelgwn, he claims to have been present from the Creation onward and links himself not just to poets but also to angels.

Taliesin's magical birth, from a womb-like leather basket carried by the sea, is similar to stories of Merlin. His reincarnation from Gwion Bach draws upon a series of images of magical knowledge in Celtic myth: the salmon of wisdom, the three drops of knowledge, the magical cauldron. Taliesin reincarnates other modes of being as well as other poets: he has been a seed, is reborn through a hen, and comes from the sea in place of salmon. This is a way of literalizing (even allegorizing) the poet's learning, but also relates to pre-Christian Celtic beliefs in the transmigration of souls. Other aspects of the poet-prophet that emerge in the tale derive from a belief in the magical power of words, which can be exercised but must also be protected by habits of riddling and obscurity. Taliesin's song looses Elphin's fetters—just the sort of loosing spell that the *gesith* wonders about in Bede's story of Imma. One might compare how Bede moves verbal magic into an explicitly Christian context.

The poet's power with words has specific social functions. Taliesin sings the origin of the human race, in a performance that invites comparison to the *scop's* song of origin in *Beowulf*, and Bede's story of Caedmon. His praises of the king are not mere reports; they actually help call royal glory into being. Yet panegyric has a flip side in satire. The poet's attack can undo the pride of a king or, in this tale, literally silence unworthy competing bards.

Synthesis with Other Myths and Cultures   As imagined in this tale, Taliesin's reach goes far past the echo of ancient Celtic tradition, and links the Welsh to an extraordinary range of other peoples and cultures. This reproduces within the narrative the synthetic processes by which Welsh culture in particular managed to remain vital across centuries, even under great economic and political pressures. Taliesin operates in an explicitly polylingual culture, calling on poets and heralds to work in Latin, French, Welsh, and English. He expands the learning he demands of the bard to encompass the traditions that have by now infiltrated Welsh culture. His claim to knowledge beyond the bounds of place and time carefully enfolds the Christian universe and its quasi-magical figures (John the Prophet, the Cherubim), and classical heroes like Alexander the Great. His song of human origins links the Welsh to the survivors of Troy, an idea that had spread widely through the influence of another Welshman, Geoffrey of Monmouth.

Current Issues of Court Life and Money   For all his enactment of magic and learning, Grufydd's Taliesin moves in a court full of piquantly realistic detail. Consider his first poem, *Elphin's Consolation*. Taliesin begins to unwrap his wondrous powers, but is careful too to promise Elphin "Riches better than three score." The frame of the whole tale is Elphin's impoverishment by court life and being cut off financially by his father, a provincial squire. The situation is like that in Marie de France's *Lanval*. (Other developments—the return to court favor through wealth, the dangerous boast, magical protection—can also be compared to *Lanval*.) The salmon weir later links to the magical salmon of Celtic myth, but enters here strictly as an issue of economics, supporting Elphin's aristocratic ambition at court. Does the praise of Maelgwn by his courtiers derive from the world of panegyric, or is it empty flattery? Elphin's certainty that the finger with his ring is not his wife's borrows from very old tales, but is also a careful articulation of class as reflected in even the smallest part of the body. Finally, Taliesin silences the king's bards at just the moment when they present themselves for largess, and thus takes away their financial reward too.

Dafydd ap Gwilym

Writing in Welsh from the Celtic Fringe of the British Isles, Dafydd ap Gwilym is fellow to William Dunbar and Robert Henryson, although they wrote in the Northern English dialect of Middle Scots. He also looks back to the tradition of the early Welsh poet Taliesin, represented in the fictional *Tale of Taliesin* from Elis Grufydd's world chronicle. In this, Dafydd is heir to an exalted, almost sacred concept of the role of the poet. (See Patrick Sims-Williams, "Dafydd ap Gwilym and Celtic Literature," *Medieval Literature: The European Inheritance*, ed. Boris Ford, [1983], 313.) Dafydd in fact domesticates this tradition, retaining its exacting standards of craftsmanship, but substituting an ironic poetic persona for the bardic voice. For while Taliesin was a figure from the oral past, Dafydd was formed by a highly literate European lyric tradition. (See Helen Fulton, *Dafydd ap Gwilym and the European Context*, [1989]). Strangely enough, the poet to whom Dafydd is most often compared, his near-contemporary Geoffrey Chaucer, is not an influence at all, nor is Middle English poetry in general. Resemblances are due primarily to shared European influences.

Lyric genres from the continental European tradition provided Dafydd with models to play with and to personalize through reference to his own life. For instance, in *Aubade*, he takes the traditional dawn song, in which the lovers lament parting, and invests humor into it with the man's indifference to getting caught. After spending the night with his lover Gwen, he observes that

> Something started going wrong.
> The edge of dawn's despotic veil
> Showed at the eastern window-pale
> And there it was, the morning light!

> Gwen was seized with a fearful fright,
> Became an apparition, cried
> "Get up, go now with God, go hide!

His contribution to the *aubade* is his use of elaborate poetic comparisons known in Welsh as *dyfalu*, such as "dawn's despotic veil." These resemble John Donne's poetic conceits, such as his figuring the sun as an old busybody in *The Sun Rising*, one of the finest *aubades* in English. For more on this form, see Jonathan Saville, *The Medieval Erotic Alba: Structure as Meaning*, (1972).

Dafydd rings changes on other lyric genres as well. In *Winter*, he inverts the *reverdie*, or spring poem, investing it with local significance:

> Across North Wales
> The snowflakes wander,
> A swarm of white bees.

And in *The Ruin*, he gives personal meaning to the *ubi sunt* poem with the memory of a tryst. Looking at an abandoned house, the speaker says,

> Nothing but a hovel now
> Between moorland and meadow,
> Once the owners saw in you
> A comely cottage, bright, new.

Even while making an elegiac observation about the transience of life, he stops to recall moments of love:

> Life is illusion and grief;
> A tile whirls off, as a leaf
> Or a lath goes sailing, high
> In the keening of kite-kill cry.
> Could it be, our couch once stood
> Sturdily under that wood?

The topos of the ruin has a long tradition in Celtic, as well as Old and Middle English poetry; students might want to contrast Dafydd's palpable love of this world with the asceticism in the Old English *The Wanderer*.

The Girls of Llanbadarn personalizes not so much a genre as a topos from Roman literature that persists in later Christian European poetry—the pursuit of young women in a public place. Ovid in his *Art of Love* suggests the Roman theater as a promising locale; for Dafydd it is his local church in Llanbadarn, a town outside Aberystwyth:

> Every single Sunday, I,
> Llanbadarn can testify,
> Go to church and take my stand

> With my plumed hat in my hand,
> Make my reverence to the altar,
> Find the right page in my psalter,
> Turn my back on holy God,
> Face the girls, and wink, and nod.

In contrast to some of his boasting poems, this one confesses that his only reward is to be laughed at. His lack of guilt about pursuing love in church is striking; on the whole, Dafydd is less moralistic than Dunbar and Henryson, and even than Chaucer.

Dafydd's personal touch is also seen in *One Saving Place*, which describes his search through Wales to find his beloved Morvith:

> There at last I made the bed
> For my Morvith, my moon-maid,
> Underneath the dark leaf-cloak
> Woven by saplings of an oak.

The Morvith (Morfudd) who is frequently named in his love poems was a real woman; her husband, "the little hunchback" mentioned in a document of the time, is the "Hateful Husband" in the poem of that name (Sims-Williams, 306). Though Dafydd excoriates him in terms he could have borrowed from Ovid, he places him in a contemporary Welsh setting. The husband is a spoil-sport, who fails to respond to love or to the pleasures of spring:

> I know he hates play:
> The greenwood in May,
> The birds' roundelay
> Are not for him.
> The cuckoo, I know,
> He'd never allow
> To sing on his bough,
> Light on his limb.

Dafydd alludes to the cuckoo, traditional harbinger of spring (see the Middle English *Cuckoo song, Sumer is icumen in*), to refer to his own adulterous situation.

Finally, in the *Tale of a Wayside Inn*, Dafydd experiments with a narrative genre, the fabliau. He departs from the usual format, however, in telling the story in the first person, and thus creating a comic persona for himself. He describes an ill-fated assignation in the inn, where instead of the young woman, he finds three Englishmen in the bedroom:

> For, by some outrageous miss,
> What I got was not a kiss,
> But a stubble-whiskered cheek
> And a triple whiskey-reek,

> Not one Englishman, but three,
> (What a Holy Trinity!)
> Diccon, 'Enry, Jerk-off Jack,
> Each one pillowed on his pack.

As he clumsily makes his retreat, he prays to Christ to save him from harm, showing little concern for the sinful intent of his enterprise:

> So I clasped my crucifix,
> *Jesu, Jesu, Jesu dear,*
> *Don't let people catch me here!*

Though he expresses regret that he had "only God's" love that night, the speaker humorously prays that He will help "mend my wicked ways."

Teaching Dafydd in English translation, while it entails a loss, has the advantage of allowing students to sample his oeuvre without linguistic hurdles. He can easily be presented in the contexts mentioned above, particularly those focusing on Celtic background and literary genre. Though he wrote in the fourteenth century, Dafydd has certain resemblances to Elizabethan and seventeenth-century English poets, who had a more developed sense of poetic identity than most Middle English ones. His literary self-consciousness may have been sharpened by the Welsh treatise on poetry of Father Einion, which in some ways resembles Renaissance English arts of poetry (Sims-Williams, 307). In a course with an emphasis on form, Dafydd's *dyfalu* can be compared with Donne's conceits and the metaphors in Shakespeare's sonnets.

William Dunbar

Like the Scottish Henryson and the Welsh Dafydd ap Gwilym, Dunbar worked in the so-called Celtic Fringe, the northern and western edges of the British Isles which were less Anglicized than other parts. Unlike Dafydd, however, both Dunbar and Henryson wrote in a language—Middle Scots—which was not Celtic, but a northern dialect of Middle English. (It has been suggested that Gaelic was an influence on Middle Scots, but this has not been proven, and the Scots poets of the time refer to their language as "Inglis" so as to distinguish it from Gaelic.) While students often find Dunbar's language difficult, his poetry is worth teaching in the original, for it allows them to experience his virtuoso style first-hand. On our audio CD, Patrick Deer gives a riotous rendition of *In Secreit Place This Hyndir Nycht.* Dunbar has a colloquial Middle Scots diction which he augments with ornamental alliteration, with a musical and often onomatopoetic effect. (For a helpful analysis of Dunbar's poetics, see Denton Fox, "The Scottish Chaucerians," *Chaucer and Chaucerians,* ed. D. S. Brewer, [1967], 179–87.)

In the *Lament for the Makers,* Dunbar takes the traditional genre of complaint on the transience of earthly things and infuses it with a new sense of self-con-

sciousness about poetic identity. After speaking about Death's implacability to people in general—he spares "no lord for his piscence, / na clerk for his intelligence"—
he moves on to his primary subject, poets:

> I se that makaris among the laif
> Playis heir ther pageant, syne gois to graif;
> Sparit is nocht ther faculte:
> *Timor mortis conturbat me.*

He balances the conventional warning against pride typical of the *ubi sunt* poem with
a sense of affection for the poets he admires, past and present. First on the list is "the
noble Chaucer of makaris flour," whom he and the other Scottish Chaucerians
revered for bringing continental rhetorical sophistication into English poetry.

In addition to three southern English poets (Lydgate and Gower as well as
Chaucer), Dunbar pays homage to his northern English and Middle Scots precursors, many of them unknown to us today. Some of these, like the *Clerk of Tranent*,
author of *the Anteris of Gawane*, may have written in the alliterative style which flourished in the north of England and in Scotland long after it had died out in the
south, and in which Dunbar proved himself a master, with his bawdy *tour de force*,
the *Tua Mariit Wemen and the Wedo.* (See Thorlac Turville-Petre, *The Alliterative
Revival*, [1977], 115–21.) Dunbar's inclusion of twenty northern and Scottish poets
suggests a self-conscious regional, and even national pride, especially in the case of
the two authors of epics recounting resistance against England, John Barbour (the
Bruce, ca. 1376) and Blind Harry (*Wallace*, ca. 1475).

If the Latin refrain of *Lament for the Makers*, (*Timor mortis conturbat me*), from
the Office of the Dead, underscores the somber message of the poem, that of
Done is a Batell, (*Surrexit dominus de sepulchro*), from the liturgy for Easter morning,
conveys a contrasting mood of joy. It draws from the account in the apocryphal
Gospel of Nicodemus of the harrowing of hell—Christ's freeing of the Old
Testament souls to go to heaven—in portraying a triumphant Christ as military
hero victorious over Satan. The ornamental alliteration recalls heroic poetry in the
alliterative tradition, from *The Dream of the Rood*, to the fourteenth-century
Alliterative Morte Arthure, to *Piers Plowman* B-text *passus* 18, with its account of
Christ as a knight jousting against Satan for human souls:

> Dungin is the deidly dragon Lucifer,
> The crewall serpent with the mortall stang,
> The auld kene tegir with his teith on char.

One strategy for teaching religious lyrics is to group them thematically and
chronologically, matching a series of *ubi sunt* poems like *The Wanderer, Contempt of
the World*, Dunbar's *The Lament for the Makers*, and Dafydd's *The Ruin*, with a series
on the Crucifixion and Resurrection, like *The Dream of the Rood, Done is a Battell*,
and metaphysical poems from the Renaissance (like Donne's Holy Sonnets 6 and
9 and Herbert's *Easter*).

Proving Dunbar's extraordinary range of genres and modes, *In Secreit Place this Hyndir Nycht* takes a 180-degree turn from the preceding two poems, being a bawdy satire in the manner of Chaucer's fabliaux. One suspects that he found Chaucer as much an influence in satire and parody as in the more respectable area of "rhetoric" that he explicitly acknowledges. In this poem Dunbar adapts to his own purposes continental lyric genres which Chaucer had already naturalized. He parodies the *chanson d'aventure*, in which the speaker overhears a lament or a conversation between two lovers, opening in courtly fashion with the man complaining about the woman's aloofness: "I can of you get confort nane / how lang will you with danger dell?" It soon becomes clear from the lover's ugly appearance, his explicit language (her lovely white neck makes his "quhillelillie" rise), and the woman's willingness, that they are not courtly at all. We are reminded of Nicholas and Alison in Chaucer's Miller's Tale, a more attractive, but equally speedy, couple. (Dunbar's woman's giggle– "Tehe"–suggests that there may have been actual influence from the tale.)

In addition to the *chanson d'aventure*, *In Secreit Place* parodies the genre of woman's song within the dialogue. In analyzing Dunbar's more extensive account of woman's voice in the *Tua Mariit Wemen and the Wedo*, Maureen Fries argues that Dunbar's treatment of sexually willing or voracious women was antifeminist, used for the purposes of satire ("The 'Other' Voice: Woman's Song, its Satire, and its Transcendence in Late Medieval British Literature," *Vox Feminae: Studies in Medieval Women's Song*, ed. John F. Plummer, [1981], 164).

Robert Henryson
Robene and Makyne

Henryson earns his reputation as a "Scottish Chaucerian" in *Robene and Makyne* by parodying courtly modes and genres. The discussion of courtly love sentiments by rustics resembles the use of courtly language by chickens in the Nun's Priest's Tale (a poem to which Henryson was indebted in his adaptation of the Aesopian Fable, *The Cock and the Fox*). When Makyne tries to teach Robene the "ABCs" of love, she echoes the conventional attributes of the courtly lover in Pertelote's instructions to her henpecked husband Chauntecleer as to what women want:

> Be heynd, courtas and fair of feir,
> Wyse, hardy and fre;
> So that no denger do the deir,
> Quhat dule in dern thow dre, . . .
> Be patient and previe.

This wording also recalls Chaucer's use of courtly language for parodic purposes in the Miller's Tale. The adjectives "heynd" (gentle) and "previe" (discreet) echo the epithets applied in that work to Nicholas as a courtly lover, which are made humorous by the speed of his courtship. And Makyne's claim that she will die if she doesn't gain Robene's love—"Dowtless but dreid I de"—echoes Nicholas's protestation to Alison.

In addition to courtly language generally, *Robene and Makyne* parodies a number of lyric genres. As in Dunbar's *In Secreit Place this Hyndir Nycht*, it follows the pattern of the *chanson d'aventure* in which the narrator recounts a conversation overheard between two lovers. More significantly, it recasts the genre of *pastourelle*, in which a man of higher status or education tries to seduce a shepherdess, with or without success. The effects are amusing here, first because the genders are reversed in the seduction, with Makyne pursuing the bashful and uncomprehending shepherd Robene, and second because the *pastourelle*, well represented in Goliardic and troubadour poetry, is given a contemporary and local twist through allusions to the British wool industry. When Makyne makes her suggestion, Robene is too worried that his sheep will wander off to respond: "Peraventure my scheip ma gang besyd / quhill we haif liggit full neir." In an update of Andreas Capellanus's twelfth-century observation that love is unsuited to peasants because they lack leisure, Henryson seems to be poking fun at the work ethic of his middle-class audience. Students might want to compare this treatment with the satirical reflection of the sheep-raising economy in *The Second Play of the Shepherds*, where the shepherds visiting the infant Christ are rendered in contemporary fifteenth-century English terms.

Finally, Makyne's strong voice in the dialogue suggests affinities with the genre of woman's song. But although students may be drawn to her portrayal as a strong woman who boldly offers her love and her virginity ("and thow sall haif my hairt all haill,/ eik and my madinheid"), they should consider that Henryson may actually be antifeminist, satirizing Makyne in the manner of poems like *The Abuse of Women* and Chaucer's Wife of Bath's Prologue. (See Maureen Fries in *Vox Feminae*, 164.)

In addition to the poems mentioned above, *Robene and Makyne* can be taught with a famous matched pair highly indebted to the *pastourelle* tradition, Marlowe's *Passionate Shepherd to his Love*, and Raleigh's *Nymph's Reply to the Shepherd*. Further, Henryson's depiction of a bashful male shrinking from a sexually forward woman can be contrasted with a woman poet's depiction of a similar topic, Aphra Behn's *The Disappointment*. This could be an occasion for discussing the issue of woman's voice in male and female-authored poetry.

Late Medieval Allegory

Despite its immense popularity in the Middle Ages, allegory was generally held in low regard from the Romantic period into the twentieth century. Its appeal has revived somewhat, however, under the influence of modernists like Joyce and Kafka, and more recently, of magic realists like Marquez, Morrison, and Rushdie, all of whose work at times calls for an allegorical interpretation. Those students coming to late medieval allegory after experience with such writers might be more receptive to the mode than their fellows in the past. Nonetheless, allegory can be hard to grasp, even the simplest kind, personification allegory. Usually defined as "extended metaphor," it can also be explained as a narrative whose meaning consistently operates on a level other than the literal.

The purpose of allegory in the later Middle Ages was generally to make abstract concepts concrete and therefore understandable to a wide audience. It employed a number of recurrent images to convey spiritual truths, among them the journey, the interior battle, and the building. These tropes have a long literary tradition: Prudentius' fourth-century *Psychomachia*, which conveyed the battle between personified vices and virtues in epic terms, Fulgentius' sixth-century commentary on the *Aeneid*, which allegorized the poem as a spiritual journey, and Bishop Grosseteste's thirteenth-century *Chasteau d'Amour*, which popularized the metaphor of the besieged castle as a figure for assailed virtue. Another prominent trope, the female guide who enlightens the narrator, goes back at least to Boethius' *Consolation of Philosophy* in the sixth-century.

The three works in this section make use of many of the tropes mentioned above—the journey, the spiritual struggle, the building, and the female guide. Lydgate's *Pilgrimage of the Life of Man* combines all four, as the pilgrim, journeying to the New Jerusalem, is assailed by the Seven Deadly Sins, and defended and instructed by the lady Grace Dieu. The overall effect is rather wooden, however, giving some indication of the features that have given allegory a bad name. The morality play *Mankind*, in contrast, adapts the spiritual struggle in a much more dynamic way, as the colorful vices Mischief, Nowadays, New Guise, and Nought contend with the Priest Mercy for the eponymous hero's soul. Finally, Christine de Pizan's *Book of the City of Ladies* uses three female guides—Reason, Rectitude, and Justice—to comfort the heroine in her despair over the negative way that women have been portrayed in classical and Christian traditions, and to urge her to construct an allegorical building—a walled city—in their honor.

A great deal of work has been published on medieval allegory, some of it extending to the Early Modern period. Rosamond Tuve's classic *Allegorical Imagery: Some Medieval Books and Their Posterity* (1966) is exhaustive. It is strong on the late antique and medieval French traditions, including such allegories as Guillaume Deguileville's *Pèlerinage de la vie humaine* (the source of Lydgate's *Pilgrimage*) and *Le Roman de la rose*, even though her purpose is to show the influence of such works on Spenser's *Faerie Queene*. Carolynn Van Dyke offers a clear overview of allegory, paying particular attention to the popular tradition, with chapters on the morality play (including *Mankind*) and Bunyan's *Pilgrim's Progress*; she too ends with the *Faerie Queene* (*The Fiction of Truth: Structures of Meaning in Narrative and Dramatic Allegory* [1985]). Finally, Maureen Quilligan, in *The Allegory of Female Authority: Christine de Pizan's Cité des Dames* (1991), while touching on the earlier tradition of medieval allegory, is far more theoretical than the other two, providing a nuanced feminist analysis of Christine's work.

The texts in this section, then, look both backward and forward, to the medieval and Early Modern periods, having affinities with both *Piers Plowman* and the *Faerie Queene*. They thus lend themselves to being taught in either a Middle English literature course or in the first half of a two-semester survey of British literature.

John Lydgate

from Pilgrimage of the Life of Man

By contrast with the troubled and fractious debates about vernacular religious texts and translations during his time, Lydgate's texts mostly present an unruffled, morally conservative surface. Lydgate calmly (if, one wonders sometimes, swiftly) translates the sturdy allegorical imagery of pilgrimage, mirror, heavenly city, and ship. A good bit of this will be invoked (in some ways more radically) by Christine de Pizan. The failures that threaten the ship of religion, in this selection, are conservative: failures to observe the old ways, especially the rituals of the church; young folk "Keep not the observances / That were made by folks old..." (p. 600, ll. 36–37).

At the same time, Lydgate's work is also a vital part of the complex growth of Middle English as a dominant force in the cultural life of England. His work is not as crucial, perhaps, as the Wycliffite translation of the Bible, but Lydgate nonetheless brought a tremendous amount of medieval Continental culture, both Latin and French, to English readership. He was very much on the side of the central authorities, but he played an important role in the making of English as both a cultural and political force. Lydgate sees himself as an heir, perhaps *the* heir, to Chaucer, but he tames Chaucer a good bit, and makes the Chaucerian legacy more palatable to his nervous Lancastrian patrons.

Mankind

Everyman, the twentieth century's favorite morality play, is in fact not the most typically medieval; it is too reserved, psychological, and focused on the individual hero. Much more typical is *Mankind*, a farcical comedy with allegorical figures contesting for the hero's soul. While its difficult language and scatological subject matter makes it a challenge to teach, the effort is worth it, especially in a course on medieval English literature in which students have already developed their Middle English skills by reading Chaucer. Its language is a mixture of pompous Latinate English (and Latin) and an irreverent colloquial English that undercuts and parodies it. The language, in fact, is essential to the play's meaning, serving to focus the conflict between the Christian truth expressed by the self-righteous priest Mercy and the human carnality expressed by vice figures: Mischief, the three characters representing the world (Nowadays, New-Guise, and Nought), and the devil Titivillus.

Because of its earthy humor and puncturing of authority, *Mankind* is likely to have a strong appeal to students. The play opens with Mercy's pedantic and abstract 44-line sermon, first surveying man's fall and Christ's redemption, and then urging the audience to mend their ways:

> O soverence, I biseche yow yowr condicions to rectifye,
> Ande with humilité and reverence to have a remocion
> To this blissyde prince that owr nature doth glorifye,
> That ye may be participable of His Retribucion. (11.13–16).

Mercy is eventually interrupted by Mischief, however, who scorns his "predica-cion," and is soon joined by New-Guise, Nowadays, and Nought, who begin to en-gage in slapstick comedy. When Mercy proudly announces "'Mercy' is my name by denominacion./ I conseive ye have but a lyttl favour in my communicacion," New-Guise replies, "yowr body is full of Englisch Laten!" (ll.122–24). To Nowadays' sud-den interruption, New-Guise snaps, "*Osculare fundamentum!*" [kiss my ass] (l.142), in a parody of Mercy's Latinate speech. The play is full of this sort of irreverent and scat-ological word play; it moves beyond the merely verbal, however, when a character ap-parently defecates on stage (ll.782–86). Most critics see the low comedy as challeng-ing Church authority ultimately to affirm it. Students could be reminded of the similar burlesque elements in Chaucer's Miller's Tale, and asked how they function in a Christian morality play as opposed to in a fabliau.

Mankind's use of offensive language and behavior to make a serious point is in-debted to medieval sermon technique, which used grotesque realism in a way that often seems indecorous to modern readers. Preachers used concrete examples, such as the disgusting "Glutton" confessing his sins in *Piers Plowman*, to illustrate abstract moral principles to an unlettered audience, and the seduction of Mankind by New-Guise, Nowadays, and Nought can be seen as illustrating Mercy's opening warning against "thingys transitorye" (l.30). (For the influence of sermon tech-nique in it, see Michael R. Kelley, *Flamboyant Drama: A Study of the* Castle of Perseverance, Mankind, *and* Wisdom [1979]).

Most critics agree that by the end of *Mankind* the hierarchy that has been in-verted is restored, and Mercy has the last word: "Your body is your enemy. Let him not have his will!" (l. 897; see, for instance, Carolynn Van Dyke, *The Fiction of Truth: Structures of Meaning in Narrative and Dramatic Allegory* [1985]). The audience, after having been seduced by the antics of the vice figures, is, predictably, made to realize their error. Some commentators, however, have paid special attention to the subversive message within the play's orthodox frame, looking at the social con-ditions referred to in the play. Victor I. Scherb has discussed Mankind's profession as a farmer as not only a timeless reminder of the laboring Adam, but a contem-porary social reference, reflecting labor unrest in East Anglia. While for some members of the audience he might have a positive spiritual meaning, recalling the peasant hero Piers Plowman, for others he might be an alarming specter of rebel-lion (*Staging Faith: East Anglian Drama in the Later Middle Ages* [2001]). While Scherb asserts that the author was fundamentally conservative, giving temporary rein to license while still enclosing it within Mercy's sermon, he suggests that the play might not be able to contain the subversive elements on any given perfor-mance. Even more skeptical of the play's ability to contain social disruption is John Watkins, who sees *Mankind's* association of the vices with novelty—a distinct de-parture from the typical morality play—as a reflection of anxiety about new oppor-tunities for social mobility ("The Allegorical Theatre: Moralities, Interludes, and Protestant Drama," in *The Cambridge History of Medieval English Literature* [1999]).

Although allegory as a mode, with its focus on abstract truths supporting the existing social order, tends to be conservative, the nature of *Mankind* is slippery enough to call such conservatism into question. Students might be asked to consider the normative or subversive message of the other allegorical readings included in the anthology. In the section devoted to Late Medieval Allegory, Lydgate's *Pilgrimage of the Life of Man* is extremely conservative, while Christine de Pizan's *Book of the City of Ladies* supports the feudal status quo at the same time that it criticizes patriarchy. The earlier section on "*Piers Plowman* in Its Time" shows that Langland's allegorical criticism of specific social abuses, though conservative, was misunderstood by many of his contemporary readers.

   Mankind offers important insights into the development of the Elizabethan theater. David M. Bevington argues that it was the first example of professional drama in England, as llustrated by the characters' taking up a collection from the audience (ll.457–59; *From Mankind to Marlowe* [1962]). Furthermore, it seems to have had a socially mixed audience similar to Shakespeare's over a century later, as reflected in Mercy's address to both "ye soverens that sitt and ye brothern that stonde right uppe" (l.29). The play's loose structure and scatological language also illustrate the pre-Shakespearean dramatic tradition that observed neither Aristotelian unities nor classical levels of style. It would be useful to teach *Mankind* with a number of Elizabethan plays, starting with Marlowe's *Dr. Faustus*, whose Mephistophilis is descended from Titivillus, and which became tragedy upon dropping the morality play's happy ending. Shakespeare's plays could be selected for a variety of purposes. The buffoonery of the clowns and fools in his tragedies can be traced to *Mankind*'s vice figures, as can the evil of Iago, while Richard III can be seen as the vice figure merged with its human protagonist. There are also significant parallels between the foregrounding of the theater in *Mankind* and Shakespeare's self-conscious depictions of it, whether in the performance of Bottom and his company in *Midsummer Night's Dream* or Hamlet's negotiation with the traveling players. Finally, a course that used *Mankind*, *Dr. Faustus*, and some Shakespeare plays to explore the development of Elizabethan drama might include Ben Jonson's *Alchemist* as an example of the contrasting classical tradition.

Christine de Pizan
from Book of the City of Ladies

First, the hard part: Brian Anslay's English is a challenge to the reader, just like the complex, Latin-influenced syntax of Christine de Pizan's French original. We have modernized spelling, added a good bit of punctuation, and glossed generously. Students seem to have an easier time if they read out loud; the syntax emerges more clearly. Most find it's worth the effort, because Christine provides such an intriguing (if finally ambivalent) critique of textual misogyny. We think it's also worth it because Brian Anslay provides a good example of Early Modern English prose, and because his translation represents the kind of bridges that link the medieval and Early Modern eras. (If you want to move more quickly, there is a readable modern English translation by Earl Jeffrey Richards.)

   Then the more fun part: Christine's narrative suggests the ways that the most traditional allegorical vision can be dramatic, effective, truly innovative in its argument. Christine does this by dramatizing the scene so well, with telling details of gesture like leaning on the arm of her chair, the movement of her head, and the initially fearful hesitancy of her speech, the laughter of the ladies in response. The allegorical lady as wise counselor goes back at least to Boethius' *Consolation of Philosophy* (as does the imagery of blindness and renewed sight), but Christine makes her ladies vivid in the clear-headed logic they practice on her. And the building of a symbolic city is equally traditional, but Christine's city—a defensive place for women of virtue, where they can respect themselves and create their own literary heritage—is very new.

At the heart of Christine's argument is a confrontation already dramatically introduced by Chaucer's Wife of Bath: experience *vs.* authority. The emotional crisis that sets up the entire vision is the clash between Christine's direct knowledge of the goodness of most women she knows, and the persistent misogyny she encounters in the books in her library. The deeply "bookish" three ladies who come to her aid suggest three main strategies: Christine should trust her own perceptions; remember that even textual authorities often disagree; and when necessary, ignore the author's hostile intent and interpret texts in ways favorable to women.

Despite these traditional allegorical structures, Christine makes the vision very personal. There is a sense of special election in the ladies' choice of *her* to carry out their work. At the same time, Christine finds herself repeatedly tugged into tropes and comparisons with male action. Sometimes this is glorious, as when her work as a mason is compared to God building paradise, the New Jerusalem. At other times, it is more troubling. In her initial self-loathing, Christine wishes she had been born a man. Even as builder of a city for ladies, she is compared to an armed chivalric champion and defender of maligned women.

This sense that heroic roles end up being male (or cross-gendered) is interesting to compare, again, to the Wife of Bath, who similarly finds herself borrowing male rhetorical gestures of boast and aggression. Like the Wife, Christine finds herself talking back to male authority, and reconfiguring it to new ends, more favorable to her gender. Both women willfully choose to read and interpret selectively—to "translate" male-dominated traditions to new ends. And though they occupy very different ends of a wide spectrum, Christine and the Alison of Bath are both parts of a new world of the urban, bourgeoise business woman who must make her own way in the world, especially when widowed.

Given all this innovation at the intellectual level, it is also important to emphasize that Christine's social positions seem distinctly conservative. Her city will be ruled by the Virgin Mary, a figure of grace and dignity, but also of meek obedience to male will. Christine ends her work by turning to wives, virgins, and widows. She tells wives to suffer their subjection to their husbands, since freedom can lead to sin. Virgins should protect their chastity, which seems very prone to masculine temptation. Widows should be meek. In that regard, Christine would surely get her own backtalk from the Wife of Bath.

The Early Modern Period

John Skelton
Various Lyrics

Students need to begin by identifying the voices in these lyrics. Which can be heard as Skelton's own (or at least one with which he can be identified) and which must be assigned to another? To this end it might be helpful to ask a couple of students to read a few of these poems to the class: "Manerly Margery" would be particularly suited to this exercise. The poems also ask for an interpretation as satire. Is "Lullay" a poem that makes fun of a cuckold and also sympathizes with his adulterous mate? So-called "blazon" poems, in which the virtues of a beloved lady are celebrated in a list of attributes, are a frequent feature of medieval verse and Skelton resorts to this form in "Knolege, Aquayntance." He ends, however, with a strikingly Petrarchan reflection: he discovers that the absent beloved is present in his heart (lines 36–49; cf. Petrarch #140, #164). This is a figure to which Sidney will return to at the end of his *Astrophil and Stella* and which acquires an even more important function in Shakespeare's sonnets. Skelton's eye for physical detail is acute as well as whimsical. Consider the brief lyrics in *A Garland of Laurel*; what can the reader discover there about the poet's feelings and inward thoughts? With what kinds of images does he convey tenderness, affection, joy?

Sir Thomas Wyatt

The power of Wyatt's verse is, in some degree, a borrowed and reflected one: there are very few of his poems that do not gain immediacy, verve, and a certain argumentative brilliance when compared with those of Francesco Petrarca, known to English readers simply as Petrarch. Equally true is that almost every line of Wyatt's poetry exhibits his unique gift of meter and imagery: they make a virtue of a certain roughness that when set beside the work of later poets, such as John Donne, would become the antithesis of a polished style. Yet Wyatt's sturdy lines: "But all is turned through my gentleness / Into a strange fashion of forsaking; / and I have leave to go of her goodness, / And she also to use new fangledness," stand up well beside Donne's elegant wit: "I can love both fair and brown, / Her whom abundance melts, and her whom want betrays. . . . / I can love her, and her, and you, and you, / I can love any, so she be not true." The difference between these poets should remind students that Wyatt, true to his career as courtier and diplomat, wrote occasional poetry, designed almost by necessity to serve the exigencies of the moment. As Stephen Greenblatt's study on the "self-fashioned" poet shows, Wyatt exemplified a common habit of mind in this respect. (*Renaissance Self-Fashioning: From More to Shakespeare* [1980]).

The samples of Petrarch's verse included here as companion pieces provide a way of assessing Wyatt's diction. Where Petrarch says he will "stay with his lord (i.e., love) until the last hour," Wyatt says he will go "into the field with him to live and die"—a locution that preserves the martial imagery of the poem's opening. Sometimes Wyatt's English text works punning wonders that cannot be achieved in Italian. Where Petrarch writes of a beloved "cerva" (deer), Wyatt describes his pursuit of a "deer" who is also, obviously, a dear. The pun, with its companion "heart/hart," becomes commonplace in later English lyric.

Robert Durling's edition of Petrarch's verse notes tough passages in the poems and briefly runs through questions of style: Petrarch transformed what was called its *dolce stil nuovo* or "sweet new style" by addressing his lady in terms that suggest her divine nature (which Dante had done before him) but also imply his idolatry. By contrast, both Wyatt and his lady are represented as typically human. Disgusted by her fickleness, Wyatt rejoices that she will "lie weathered and old," complaining to the only thing that will listen to her, the moon. This toughmindedness defies the conventions of Renaissance love poetry—it can be compared with Shakespeare's sonnets repudiating his so-called Dark Lady as well as his bittersweet lines to the beloved young man who betrayed him. Students need to notice in Wyatt's poems the popular and related themes often referred to in Latin: *tempus fugit* or "time flies," *carpe diem* or "seize the day." These themes were so endlessly reworked they frequently became the pretext for satire, as here in Wyatt.

But Wyatt's moral voice needs also to be recognized. In addition to the short lyric *Lucks, my fair falcon*, Wyatt's imposing verse letter to John Poins conveys the poet's capacity for a stoic resignation when faced with misfortune. Like so many other poets whose principal work was to serve at court, Wyatt—accepting his exile from the center of power—turns to the poetry praising the virtues of simple country life. Jonson's *To Penshurst*, and Marvell's *On Appleton House* make useful comparisons with Wyatt's *Mine Own John Poins*: all these poems echo sentiments in Horace's verses to his Sabine farm.

Henry Howard, Earl of Surrey

Surrey was a courtier-poet, like Wyatt before him and Sidney after him. Executed at twenty-eight, he had neither chance to mature, as did Wyatt; nor to recover royal favor, as did Sidney. His verse is brilliant nonetheless. Surrey's sonnets should be compared to Wyatt's for their form (octet / sestet as opposed to quatrains and couplet) and to those of later poets for which they establish the form. Why is Surrey's solution better for English poets?

Surrey found many of his subjects in history and politics: *Th' Assyrians' King*, describing the suicide of a weak and effeminate king, implicitly asks readers to imagine one who is just. Students can look ahead to Perspectives: Government and

Self-Government to see how the idea of a good governor took shape later in the century. Politics became personal for Surrey when he was imprisoned for rioting in London; his poem on the occasion becomes a lament for past happiness, lost youth, and the death of the king's son and his companion, Henry Fitzroy. Their friendship exemplifies what has been termed a homosocial bonding, illustrated earlier and conventionally by Chaucer's pairing of Palamon and Arcite in *The Knight's Tale,* and later with radical shifts of character and intention by Sidney's cousins Pyrocles and Musidorus in *The Arcadia.*

Surrey's elegy to Wyatt probably overstates his connection to the older poet; there is no indication that the two were very close. Its importance is rather in its celebration of Wyatt as the new British poet who can replace Chaucer. The poem emphasizes Surrey's skill as a satirist and thus as a social reformer. This was not an unusual stance for a poet of his time. Sidney's *Apology for Poetry* and other contemporary treatises on poetry can point up the importance of the poet as moralist. Surrey's own satire on London—*London Thou Hast Accused Me*—harshly condemns the city for its hypocrisy and vice. It can be compared with another critique of London, the gently witty *In the Manner of her Will* by Isabella Whitney. Students can reflect on the poet's status (Surrey a nobleman from a powerful family, Whitney probably of the "middling sort") as an index to his or her point of view; this can become an opportunity to discuss how the reader's status affects his or her interpretation of the text.

Sir Thomas More

Utopia

More's longest and best-known prose work needs to be understood as an example of a typically humanist style known as "serious play" or *serio ludere,* and of the literature of courtiership that became so popular in the early modern period. To know more about works in this style, students can go to Erasmus's *Praise of Folly;* in the *Praise,* as in *Utopia,* the author criticizes aspects of his society—the monarchy, the church, the professions—but in the persona, a fictive narrator, of one who is not entirely reliable. More's *Utopia* is in effect a dialogue between two speakers: More, who takes the part of a practical statesman, and Hythlodaeus, who is a philosopher. Neither can be identified as representing an entirely credible position, although both speak a good deal of sense from time to time. Their names suggest they are each a type of fool: Hythlodaeus means "learned in nonsense"; More, as Erasmus pointed out in *The Praise of Folly,* stands for folly, as folly is *moria* in Greek. Students will need to be ready when reading and discussing this text to decide whether either, neither or both of the speakers is being foolish or sensible and if so why.

A good way to begin analyzing *Utopia* is to distinguish the difference between Books I and II. Book II was actually written before Book I and represents the form of society that the speaker Hythlodaeus regards as ideal. In this respect, the state of Utopia resembles other ideal commonwealths, notably Plato's *Republic.* It is also just an ideal (its name means "nowhere") and therefore it needs to be examined for assumptions it does not justify. Students should ask what Hythlodaeus does not recognize about human beings when he describes an entirely rational state, inhabited by entirely rational people. Why does Hythlodaeus equate political rationality with an absence of private property? Why does he see a rational government as one that lacks any kind of inherited office (a monarchy or nobility, for example), and actually gives little importance to personal taste and even to family ties? Is this folly? If it is folly, is it to be credited, as it is a fool who speaks it? Students should confront the so-called "Cretan liar paradox"—"All Cretans lie, a Cretan speaks this"—as the conceptual basis for the language and description of government in Book II.

It is also important to try to search for what might be called the inferential content in Hythlodaeus's account. This search will require some discussion of the historical setting and context in which Sir Thomas More wrote Utopia. Students should know that Sir Thomas More (to Roman Catholics also St. Thomas More) eventually (much after writing Utopia) opposed his faith as a Christian to what he saw as the ungodly rule of his king, Henry VIII, who sought to separate the English church from the papacy. Alastair Fox's biography, Thomas More: History and Providence (1983) has disturbed More's pious image, but not without evidence. More's history is complicated by the fact that as Lord Chancellor he dealt cruelly with heretics, doubtless from the same principles that led him to defy his king.

Discussion on the government of Utopia can begin by testing the assumption that sustains Hythlodaeus's politics: the belief that mankind is or can become entirely reasonable, rational, and free from greed. To Christians, this position was nonsense. It was a primary tenet of their faith that mankind had lost much of its capacity for rational and disinterested behavior after the fall from Paradise; and therefore that no human society can or should be based on the assumption that its members will be reasonable. Hythlodaeus blames private property for social ills; Christians asserted that it is human nature to err. To appreciate this distinction students can consider the writer More's description of Utopian religion: why the Utopians do not speak of sin and atonement but rather of guidance and enlightenment is a question that addresses the most enigmatic aspects of this rational state. Advanced students can explore the various interpretations of Utopia during this century, especially those that are indebted to Marxist politics. A quick look at the various editions published from 1945 illustrates the range of opinion on the practicability of Hythlodaeus's model state: especially useful is George M. Logan and Robert M. Adams' introduction to Utopia (1989), published in the series Cambridge Texts in the History of Political Thought.

Why the writer More created such an unfamiliar and in many ways uncongenial body politic as Utopia is a question that can be approached by way of Hythlodaeus's statement that the Utopians, although versed in logic, do not know "second intentions." A second intention is a conception gained by generalizing upon a first conception, an idea or notion that derives its content from a reflection upon a prior idea or notion. In other words, the Utopians, insofar as they think at all, are unable to reflect upon what they are thinking. This may be because, as perfectly rational beings, they do not need to do more than apprehend and then act; or it may be because they are themselves second intentions, the product of the writer More's reflection on the conception he has of an ideal state. In either case, they are creatures of fiction, either purely rational or a reflection of what that rationality might be.

Book I provides the rhetorical frame in which to place Hythlodaeus's foolish idealism in Book II. Book I in effect recovers much of the standing the writer More gives Hythlodaeus in the whole *Utopia*; we say recovers but in fact we mean establishes. It is as if the writer More decided that in a certain perspective he had to credit Hythlodaeus with both dignity and worth. Students might be asked to characterize the serious side of Hythlodaeus as it emerges in Book I, taking special account of his critique of social ills that More's readers would have recognized as afflicting their contemporary England.

As Logan and Adams observe, "*Utopia* is a pretty melancholy book," and the ills it identifies in England were real enough. They fall roughly into two categories: those created by bad policy, such as enclosures; and those created by human weakness confronting great power, for example, flattery, hypocrisy and power mongering. The latter category can provoke a discussion on the question of power. How does the writer More account for social and political power?

It should be possible to distinguish More's position from Hythlodaeus's: More represents the case for practicality and realism, Hythlodaeus for principle and truth. Students can assess these positions in light of their own politics and also to appreciate how More's first readers might have reacted. The difference between readings brings up the question of personal autonomy and freedom. Were the subjects of Henry VIII free to do what they thought was right, to act on principle? If they were the king's *servants*, how truthful could they be, given his immense authority? Treatises on the conduct of rulers and subjects often assumed that a head of state would appreciate the advice of his servants; quite a few hinted that he would not. Some of the issues implicit in Book I are raised again by texts in Perspectives: Government and Self-Government.

Finally, *Utopia* presents the reader with a frame that is only partly fictional. The writer More did go to Antwerp with a diplomat and friend called Peter Giles. He was on the king's service, and both abroad and at home a man of much business. How and where does the writer More begin to represent himself as a fiction, More the speaker? Clues abound early in Book I: Utopia is literally "No Place," and its physical features are non-existent. The writer More's representation of a nowhere land implicated in its irony and extravagance the whole genre of travel literature that in the first quarter of the sixteenth century stirred the ambition of European readers. Piqued by stories of great wealth, armchair explorers imagined how they might improve themselves were they to travel to the New World. How some real adventurers saw the Americas is represented in extracts from their accounts following Sir Walter Raleigh's treatise on Guiana (see "*The Discovery* and Its Time"). But the fact that Utopia is pictured as vaguely similar to England in being an island with its principal city near a river warns readers against imagining that anything they could encounter in the New World would be really new to them.

Hythlodaeus's account of his discovery suggests that wherever explorers go, they see a reflection of the world they have left, at least to some degree.

Government and Self-Government

This section is intended to complement the study of government in *Utopia*, which, we hope, will seem less curious when compared to the variety of opinion on the subject by other writers of the century. For readers new to this area, a couple of excellent surveys may be useful: J.W. Allen, *A History of Political Thought in the Sixteenth Century* (1928) remains a classic; and Quentin Skinner, *The Foundations of Modern Political Thought* (1978) is an indispensable guide to the subject. A briefer but excellent account is to be found in Quentin Skinner, "Political Philosophy" in *The Cambridge History of Renaissance Philosophy*, ed. Schmitt (1988). Students of literary history usually like discussing the political implications of early modern texts and their doing so often gives them a stake in the outcome that brings the whole period to life.

A beginning can be quite simple. To assume that because England was ruled by a monarchy it had no appreciation for the welfare of subjects; or that because the Bible declared that a woman should be in subjection to her father or husband, she had no chance to express herself entirely misrepresents the situation. As the few examples in this section suggest, some opted for an absolute and authoritarian government but others did not. Students can identify and test the assumptions supporting various positions. **Tyndale** thought that absolute government was justified by God, who spoke of rule in scripture; **Elyot** saw that it corresponded to the order of nature, as illustrated by such social creatures as bees. Others feared that to depart from this rule and order invited chaos. By contrast, those who, like **Ponet**, saw merit only in a government that caused the governed to prosper, were fearful of too much power in the hands of one person. He stressed not the anarchy of no rule but the tyranny of a rule designed to profit only the ruler. Especially striking is Ponet's insistence on property rights; here his argument needs to be compared to the comprehensive view of the "rights of man" which emerged during the Romantic period. In every case, it should be understood that just as the literature of our own period makes sense in relation to ideas of how society should function—ideas that are so common as not to need stating—so also was the literature of earlier periods understood in light of assumptions and beliefs that remained implicit rather than expressed.

Because the order of the household was thought to be the basis for the order of the state, domestic government was studied almost as much as political government. As Robert Cleaver noted, the household is a "little commonwealth" in which the husband is "cheef" and his wife a "fellowhelper" (*A Godly Form of Household Government*, 1598). The last ten years of studies on early modern women have turned up a wealth of information and debate. Students interested in the representation of women in literature should go to Linda Woodbridge, *Women and the*

English Renaissance (1987); for an introduction to theoretical arguments about woman's nature see Constance Jordan, *Renaissance Feminism: Literary Texts and Political Models* (1990).

Class discussion can begin by considering the conventionally constituted doubleness of the female character who was both man's equal and inferior, his soulmate and his servant. And then there was Elizabeth: Elyot, paying attention to the possibility that England might be governed by a woman in his lifetime, claimed that history supplied many exceptional examples to the general rule of female subservience. But the reality would be more astonishing than he imagined. Students interested in the terms of Elyot's defense of women can skip ahead to the Wollstonecraft controversy to see how the conversation on the nature of womankind developed into a full-fledged defense of their rights.

Religion, because administered by the church, a social institution with much wealth and power, also elicited statements on the best kind of government. Here too writers tended to focus either on the right to dissent, sometimes with bloody consequences (as **Foxe** did); or on the duty to conform, not without justification in natural law, the law which binds all human beings together irrespective of kind (as **Hooker** did). In each case, the writer resorts to language that suits his vision: Foxe is dramatic, while Hooker tends to abstractions. Embedded in the passages from Hooker is the germ of what would become a theory of social contract: the origins of government are in the human need to congregate in communities under law. **Hobbes** would elaborate the point in *Leviathan*.

But finally almost all commentary on government returned to a consideration of education. The formidable scope of a teacher's duties has recently been assessed by Rebecca Bushnell, *A Culture of Teaching: Early Modern Humanism in Theory and Practice* (1996)—an excellent study of the topic. Why was a teacher supposed to be so important? Because it was only with a self-governed citizenry that a civil society could function and become prosperous. **Castiglione's** treatise is directed specifically to the situation of the courtier and addresses the need to avoid affectation, an unattractive excess of fashion and display of self-worth. The practical comments of **Ascham** and **Mulcaster** on corporal punishment, the "quick study," and close-mindedness or prejudice may strike today's students as especially relevant to their own experiences in the classroom. Discussion of what Mulcaster understood by prejudice can lead students to an appreciation of how suspect were some kinds of intellectual inquiry in this period; the point can be made again when reading Bacon and Sir Thomas Browne.

George Gascoigne

The poems of Gascoigne exemplify the precarious situation of the Tudor gentleman who sought preferment at court. Students should be aware that Gascoigne's rank mattered; he was not the privileged character that the noble Surrey was, nor even of the status of knight, as Wyatt was. The difference points to the emergence in this period of the professional writer, one who saw himself primarily as a man of words. The politics involved in the creation of this class of writer were complex but they are usefully presented in a recent study of the booktrade: Cyndia Susan Clegg, *Press Censorship in Elizabethan England* (1997). For whether or not a writer was good at his work, as Gascoigne certainly was, he had to find ways to ingratiate himself with a powerful and rich patron who would give him a stipend in return for various services and help him to protect his work from press pirates seeking to publish it without authorization. In *Sonnets to Neville* and *Woodmanship*, Gascoigne represents his public career as a stunning failure. (As Clegg shows, his publishing career was even more vexed.) But he does so in terms that allow his reader to understand why and how he made his mistakes.

Students can analyze Gascoigne's candid self-portrait for its way of both blaming his own ambition, and warning others of how easy it is to let dreams of plenty and power obscure the hard realities of getting ahead in the world, especially one that is notoriously given to corruption, as was the Tudor court. But for all their implicit moralizing, Gascoigne's poems are wonderfully light-hearted; they show the quality Castiglione termed *sprezzatura* in his *Book of the Courtier*: a disdain for deliberate effects that was supposed to characterize the truly accomplished man. In his *Sonnets* Gascoigne transforms one truism—"if it be done, let it be done quickly"—into another, "haste makes waste," cleverly linking the sequence by repeating the last line of one sonnet as the first line of the next: the effect is to make the poet's descent into poverty appear to be the result of his cumulative decisions. *Woodmanship* suggests that it is not so much the poet but rather his courtly society which is to blame.

But are we to interpret without irony the "amendment" Gascoigne is supposed to want and expects to achieve? Is he to be seen as rejecting or capitulating to the temptations of ambition? The class might discuss how a sincere moralist, More's Hythlodaeus for example, would deal with the poet's dilemma. In any case, Gascoigne presents his reader with some of the choices many young men of the period faced: should they spend the resources they have at home to seek their fortunes in the city? Should they compromise their values for the sake of promotion?

Edmund Spenser

Spenser fashioned his poetic career in direct imitation of the poet his age considered the greatest, Virgil, who began his work with pastoral, the *Eclogues*, and ended with epic, the *Aeneid*. The belief pervasive among early modern writers that history can repeat itself, at least as far as general patterns are concerned, is illustrated by Spenser's conscious sense that his mission is like that of Virgil—like his Roman predecessor, he is to celebrate a national identity. With important differences, this is Milton's sense of his mission as well. As a habit of thought, such desire for imitation contrasts with twentieth-century ideas of authorship, which gains power to the extent that it is highly individualistic and an index of the supreme value of originality. By contrast, early modern writers felt a kinship with the past, the burden of its traditional wisdom, a love for its subjects and forms of expression. What they could not do was leave it alone; they had to revive it albeit in their own way.

It may be true, as C. S. Lewis has said, that no one ever stopped liking *The Faerie Queene*, but it is probably just as well to admit that very few have liked it right off the bat. It is therefore worth spending time coming to grips with Spenser's difficult diction. In the *Calendar* it is deliberately archaic, as if Spenser were reaching to the past to find a means of making his verse memorable; in *The Faerie Queene*, it is densely allegorical, a way of allowing his verse to develop in a dynamic way the various meanings that collect around its powerful images. Both texts confront readers with major difficulties in their interpretation, *The Faerie Queene* perhaps supremely so, and students need to be encouraged to persevere in their efforts to understand them. Fortunately, there is excellent criticism available. For a comprehensive view of the poem, see James Nohrnberg, *The Analogy of the Faerie Queene* (1976); and since 1990 readers have consulted the massive *The Spenser Encyclopedia*, edited by A.C. Hamilton, which identifies all Spenser's characters, comments on features of style and idiom, and includes mini-essays on various generic questions. Enthusiasm for Spenser has flagged periodically, in part because the poems are so complex; but recently interest has focussed on the poet's politics, especially when the nationalistic aspects of his work are under review.

The Shepheardes Calendar

The "Tenth Aeglog" is about the value of poetry, what it can and should do to make its readers members of civil society. In this sense, it is a kind of metacriticism; it reflects on its own means of persuasion. It is also pervaded with irony and a disbelief in its own mission: it can teach readers what poetry is but it also tells them how hard it is to write and, indeed, how poorly their age encourages poets. The poem itself illustrates how dialogue creates perspective, with both shepherds expressing points of view. Cuddie claims his moral verse is misunderstood and his heroic verse lacks proper subjects; Piers suggests that Colin might be the one to succeed because he is in love and love causes the spirit to ascend to see things in an "immortal mirror." Students can compare this image with Sidney's "idea," the foreconceit of the work from which all its power derives (see *The Apology for Poetry*). Cuddie counters by saying that Colin's inspiration is in fact no more than wine, an accusation that hints at the narrow and earthbound limits of pastoral vision. The image suggests that although the shepherd can gesture toward an epic intention with all the high seriousness that this entails, he cannot imagine the way to achieve it. This eclogue resonates with Virgil's seventh eclogue, which also represents a competition between two shepherds. Virgil's work is perhaps more subtle; Spenser's more directly keyed to passionate convictions.

The Faerie Queene

The "Letter to Raleigh" states Spenser's intention in writing *The Faerie Queene*. Comparing the project described in the "Letter"—the composition of a poem consisting of twelve books—with the actual text of *The Faerie Queene*, students will notice how much the poet failed to accomplish. By not writing more than six books, plus two cantos of a seventh, Spenser has prompted readers to seek for signs of frustration and disappointment in the work as it stands. In a general way, they may be implicit in the very program of the poem, particularly in its first two books, entitled "The Legend of Holiness" and "The Legend of Temperance."

Spenser's Protestantism is obvious in his attack on such stock figures as the wily Abbess Corceca, and the duplicitous and lavishly dressed Duessa, a figure of the doubleness of the Roman Catholic Church. Because Spenser's hero, Redcrosse, defeats Duessa, readers may think that the poet's conscience is clear; he achieved what he intended. But at a more profound level Protestantism is also registered in the poet's doubts about the very stuff of poetry: its language, its imagery, its music, its engagement with the senses and with the pleasures of the imagination. Patricia Parker's interpretation of the figure of "dilation" (in *Inescapable Romance* [1979]), the continuous amplification of a subject in an attempt to represent its meaning— an attempt which is never wholly successful—has opened up the rhetorical complexity of Spenser's poem. To read it as a reflection upon poetic language is now an established mode of its criticism.

Students can be encouraged to discover the varied but powerful meanings associated with Spenser's most malevolent character, Archimago. Literally "the chief of all images," the magician signals the deceptive potential of all signs and therefore of all systems of signification. True, by foiling his intrigues Spenser's Redcrosse shows that it is possible to read signs correctly—if the reader has the right moral stance toward the text. But Redcrosse is also often deceived, visually as well as by words and the histories people tell. Late sixteenth-century English Protestants sought to discriminate between signs of truth and falsehood, the latter candidates for iconoclastic destruction, the former for reverent preservation. But the task was a rigorous one. Spenser shows how hard it is: he represents Una, the truth, as constantly veiled except when she is simply in nature. Language, as a veil, can obscure but it can also hide, distort, mask, and give false indications. How does Spenser tell us whether his characters are understanding their situations correctly? Or is part of his technique to defer such disclosures for later and more dramatic revelations?

Allegory is, of course, a rhetorical trope that exploits the nature of language precisely as Una's veiling signifies it; what allegory says stands for what it implies. Unlike much medieval allegory, in which the writer actually tells the reader what a particular image means—"the black crow was the devil," a poet might say— Spenser requires that the reader make up his mind as to the meaning of his figures. As Milton would later insist, in *Areopagitica*, the knowledge of truth is wrested from illusion, deception, falsehood; it does not come of its own. And the meaning of Spenser's allegory, its figures and images, changes too. Readers need to read *contextually*, by assessing the situation each character is in.

Contextual reading is at the center of Spenser's semiotic program and what makes it memorable. Book I—"The Legend of Holiness"—addresses the difficulty of finding spiritual truth in the phenomenal world of time and history; Book II— "The Legend of Temperance"—deals with the challenge to maintaining a moral discipline in the natural world replete with sensuous pleasure, especially the pleasure produced by art. Just as what seems is not always what is in Book I, so what at first pleases is not always lastingly pleasurable in Book II. Rosemond Tuve's work on allegory as a mode of representation (*Allegorical Imagery* [1966]) made readers see that Spenser's allegory, what he refers to as its "darke conceit," was essentially dynamic; like the meanings of history, it changes with time and place. Students may be helped by being asked to visualize the poem's narrative form. Its allegory is punctuated by iconic moments of a highly pictorial character; it is moved along by interlaced plot lines that entail explanatory accounts of action, character, and dramatic setting. These two modes exist in a constant and almost perfect balance; readers have to appreciate both in order to interpret Spenser's allegory.

Spenser's verse is also intensely musical and students should be prepared to read it aloud, both to themselves and in class. A useful exercise is to read a stanza without emphasizing its rhymes and rhythms, that is, as prose; and then a second time as poetry. An ideal reading should avoid a sing-song beat yet convey the aural dimension of the verse. Spenser's stanza form (known as "Spenserian") is built on eight pentameter or five beat lines, rhyming *ababcdcd*, and a final hexameter or six beat line (known as alexandrine), ending in another *c* rhyme. Its effect is elegant and dynamic; it is also unusual. Influenced by the principal stanza form of Italian epic, the *ottava rima* (*abababcc*), Spenser intended his poem to show the versatility of the English language; despite its very different sounds, it too could produce a comparably dense and harmonious verse. A brief consideration of the quality of the English language reveals that his task was incomparably more difficult than that confronting his Italian counterparts (Boiardo, Ariosto and Tasso, for example); English has far fewer possibilities for rhyme and many more words consisting of two long or heavy accents which tend to slow down a poetic line than does Italian.

It is useful to point out that what would become the standard form of English narrative and dramatic poetry, the unrhymed pentameter line known as blank verse, did not get much representation before Marlowe and was made popular only by Shakespeare. A quick comparison of Spenser's neo-Italianate prosody with the quintessentially English blank verse of Milton makes the point. Students interested in Spenser's prosody can be referred to the excellent article on the Spenserian stanza in *The Spenser Encyclopedia*.

The following comments on each canto, though in no way exhaustive, are designed to facilitate discussion on questions of theme, imagery, and historical setting.

Book I—"The Legend of Holiness" Canto 1   Students should notice how often Spenser uses the word "seems" when he could have used the word "is"; this alerts readers to the problem of illusionistic deception that Redcrosse constantly confronts. He quite easily overcomes Error, the dragon of the dark wood, when Una is beside him: "add faith to your force" she says, and with that he skewers the beast. Later, this victory can be compared with Redcrosse's conquest of Duessa's dragon in canto 11. What is the difference between the two conquests?

Canto 2   The plot thickens rapidly about figures of mistaken identity; suddenly nothing is what it seems. Archimago dresses as Redcrosse and fools Una: why can't Spenser's image of truth know the truth? The example of another person's trouble—Fradubio's imprisonment—doesn't seem to help Redcrosse understand his own plight. Here is an instance of Spenser's complex allegory; Redcrosse's failure to learn from Fradubio is motivated at two levels: first iconically, as Redcrosse in the company of Duessa can see only falsehood; second dramatically, as Redcrosse seeing only falsehood cannot know the truth of his condition or realize that Fradubio's history is like his own. Duessa's account of her parents as rulers of the "wide West" will reveal that she is an exponent of the *Roman* church, as opposed to Una whose parents, she will relate, were rulers of East and West and hence governed the Universal church, although they are now imprisoned by a dragon of hell (cantos 5 and 7).

Canto 3   Una unveils in nature; a creature in nature, the lion, understands who she is. Why does Spenser make the natural world so hospitable a place for the truth when the social world of human beings finds her so doubtful? Does this suggest that nature retains its original purity when there is no human being to experience it? Consider, for a comparison, Milton's description of paradise before Adam and Eve sinned.

Canto 4   The House of Pride is one of the great set pieces of the poem. Students can recognize why it is built on sand (it recalls the house of the foolish man in Scripture); why it is surmounted by a clock may be intended to illustrate the irrelevance of worldly accomplishment in achieving holiness. The old-fashioned and rather static allegory of Lucifera and her six counsellors, who together represent the seven deadly sins, serves to point up, by contrast, the drama of Redcrosse's encounter with Sansjoy.

Canto 5   Sansfoy has been killed, Sansloy is still abroad, and Sansjoy resides in the House of Pride: what aspects of human history do their situations reveal? It's appropriate to discuss passages in which meaning seems indeterminate in such a way as to open up rather than close off interpretation. Perhaps the aspects of human history Spenser symbolizes here are first, that the historical fact of Christianity dispelled the absolute possibility of existing without faith; second, that social order nevertheless remains threatened by lawlessness; and finally that pride will always condemn the sinner to a life without joy. Consensus in cases so suggestive is not an indication that the text has been understood; sometimes some uncertainty is justified. For instance, although the canto represents a stock feature of epic, a descent to the underworld, it does so in the guise of demonic parody. Students may want to compare Duessa's descent into the underworld with another descent Spenser knew well: Aeneas's descent to Hades in Book 6 of the *Aeneid*. Particularly interesting is Spenser's treatment of the doctor Aesclepius. Unlike Virgil's philosophy of *metempsychosis* or the transmigration of souls, Christian doctrine denies that human beings, united in soul and body, can return to earthly life after death. Sansjoy does not in fact reappear in Spenser's poem at any point (at least as the poem exists today); nevertheless, here in Book I Aesclepius begins his healing work and readers see that Sansjoy is not quite dead but rather in a cloudy daze. Where would Spenser have ended this story?

Canto 6   Redcrosse leaves the House of Pride regretting that he has lost Fidessa / Duessa, and blaming Una for deserting him. Spenser proceeds to illustrate how Redcrosse's correction of one mistake does not mean that he eliminates the possibility of making others. A comparison of Lucifera with Orgoglio, who is waiting to attack Redcrosse, indicates further depths to Redcrosse's sin. What are the elements of each kind of pride? Spenser's beasts are usually iconic. Here the Lion symbolizes the purity in nature before truth; yet the Salvage nation of fauns and satyrs have quite a different response to Una. Why? Finally, how does a hybrid of nature and culture, as incarnate in Satyrane, respond to truth?

Canto 7   Redcrosse's pride in courting and making love to Fidessa / Duessa becomes manifest as Orgoglio, whose description conveys the psychology of pride, logically linked to falsehood and together with falsehood constitutive of the dreadful prison into which Redcrosse is thrown. Redcrosse's rescuer, Prince Arthur, has been identified as the knight of magnificence in Spenser's "Letter to Raleigh": he is powerful through his deployment of light, virtually always a sign of knowledge or enlightenment. His power differs from and complements Una's sunny essence: she who incarnates the truth itself is incapable of acting against Archimago; he who directs truth against falsehood can defy the magician and his works. Prince Arthur projects Spenser's narrative into the world of Arthuriana, familiar to English readers chiefly through Malory's *Morte Darthur* and ideologically important to the Tudor monarchs because of its association with a *British* identity (associated with Wales, where the Tudors were supposed to have originated) rather than an Anglo-Saxon one. Prince Arthur is traveling to Cleopolis, Gloriana's city, i.e., Queen Elizabeth's London. Students can admire the deft way all this imagery unifies historically discrete elements of English cultural experience: Arthurian Britain, Tudor Wales, and Protestant London. Una states that her parents are prisoners of a dragon of hell; how are they distinguished from Duessa's parents, described in Canto 4? Spenser alludes to what he considers the captivity of the true church in the structures of papal Rome; by contrast, the false church is papal Rome and its history is merely specious.

Canto 8   Prince Arthur conquers pride, different elements of which are incarnate in Orgoglio who is also, nevertheless, paradoxically insubstantial. The power of Arthur's shield is decisive. Redcrosse is freed from Orgoglio's palace and reunited with Una. But Prince Arthur and Redcrosse let Duessa go free. Here is another instance in which students can recognize Spenser's Protestantism: he requires that good be secured in a battle with evil; Duessa is essential to the education of a Christian.

Canto 9   Prince Arthur's history motivates his presence in Faerieland: he seeks its queen, Gloriana, whom he has seen in what might be called a living dream. She is both a figment of his imagination *and* a corporeal being who leaves a mark on the grass where she slept. Here Spenser gestures toward the truth of premonition; he makes the reader see that our aspirations, in being experienced in time and history, can be realized there too. It is especially appropriate that Redcrosse now face the temptation of suicide. He is at the lowest point of his self-esteem. Because he has been freed from pride, however, the truth does not desert him as Una tells him of God's infinite mercy and grace.

Canto 10   Dame Caelia's house provides the religious, moral, and psychological haven that will allow for Redcrosse's rehabilitation. The poem's allegory becomes explicit; the iconic figures of the three theological virtues who live in this house speak for themselves. Only the hermit Contemplation, turning Redcrosse away from his eventual home in the New Jerusalem, interjects a dramatic element to the narrative by counseling Redcrosse to face the challenges of earthly life. Contemplation's rationale is inherently Augustinian: on earth, Christians must live in two cities simultaneously, the city of man (here Cleopolis, which reflects but is distinct from the heavenly city) and the city of God, which is mystically present in time but really experienced only in eternity. It is appropriate that at this point Spenser identifies what for him was the historicity of Redcrosse. Only apparently a faery, Redcrosse is actually St. George, the patron saint of England. His Saxon inheritance complements Prince Arthur's British provenance: Spenser makes complementary the two principal elements in English national history. Redcrosse is also understood to have been translated from the world of dream, a theoretical projection of the ideal, to the world of history, the record of an actual past. Inasmuch as "The Legend of Holiness" apologizes for the creation of a Protestant church, Spenser's historicization of Redcrosse makes the sixteenth-century reformation of the church in England an event that was actually present, in some sense, much earlier in its history. In effect, it takes the novelty out of Henry VIII's divorce from Rome (always rather shocking in its motivation) and makes that event part of a providential unfolding of events in salvation history.

Canto 11   The rescue of Una's parents follows the rehabilitation of Redcrosse. The sequence of conquests by which Spenser imagines Redcrosse's progress toward a perfect faith is entirely logical. If Prince Arthur conquers Redcrosse's pride, Redcrosse restores what Una's parents stand for—the apostolic church reconstructed in Protestant England. Students should notice the scriptural and liturgical symbolism of Redcrosse's fight with Duessa and her dragon, its three days of struggle and its two restorative agents: the water of life and the tree of life. These are intended to familiarize readers with the universal nature of Redcrosse's victory: both water and tree are constantly present in the life of the faithful Christian.

Canto 12   Redcrosse is now free to be betrothed to Una; now she can take off her veil. Yet he cannot marry her any more than he can move out of time and history to live in the New Jerusalem. A certain threat remains: it is comprised in the duo Duessa and Archimago and is consistent with the terms of earthly life. Their weapon and medium continue to be semiotic, the systems of communication by which human beings understand themselves and others. Here their perversion is instanced in Duessa's lying letter. This pseudo-pledge is obviously comparable to the books and papers that Error has vomited in Canto 1. What has "The Legend of Holiness" revealed about interpreting signs, language, story?

Book II—"The Legend of Temperance" Canto 12   The action of this canto is generally reflective of the *Odyssey*, Book 10; ambitious students can compare the two stories. Spenser's allegory is again explicit—at least until he puts Guyon on Acrasia's island. Its features have always challenged interpretation. On the one hand, Guyon is deliberately styled as an iconoclast: he destroys objects of great art. On the other hand, he frees Verdant from the constraints imposed upon him by this art. It cannot therefore be unequivocally great. What's wrong with it? What are the assumptions sustaining Spenser's aesthetics? His theory of art is not, in any case, to be divorced from moral considerations. As Sidney will state in his *Apology for Poetry*, art educates society in civil behavior. Guyon's virtue of temperance must protect him from the illusionistic pleasures of a merely sensuous art. His mission is, in a sense, that of a critic of art: he must identify works that paralyze the will, making it incapable of moral indignation, and render the viewer or reader unable to take a stand against evil.

   Spenser's moralism has generated commentary on all sides. A. Bartlett Giamatti's *The Earthly Paradise and Renaissance Epic* (1966) places Acrasia's bower in a long tradition of magical and very dangerous gardens. Stephen Greenblatt's association of this beauty with the objects of English imperialism, Ireland and the New World (see *Renaissance Self-Fashioning*), has produced other historicist readings. In any case, Spenser's aesthetics have been recognized as absolutist and invite comparison with ideas more sympathetic to the culturally relativistic understanding of art common in post-modern commentary. Apart from simply historicizing his views of art's value and purpose, are there other ways to make use of Guyon's story as a way to think about poetry and why it is important?

Amoretti *and* Epithalamion

Spenser's sonnet sequence is an intricate formal exercise in both the entertainment of and escape from Petrarchism; it is also a betrothal gift to his prospective wife, Elizabeth Boyle. Students should look for evidence in Spenser's imagery for this double perspective, at once conventional and personal. The key to understanding the sequence as two-fold in another and strictly formal sense was discovered by Alexander Dunlop in his essay "Calendar Symbolism in the 'Amoretti'" (*Notes and Queries*, 1969). As he saw, the sequence follows two calendars or time-frames: the Roman (or pagan) and the Christian. Thus it celebrates two New Years, on January 1 when the Roman god Janus faces two ways on the gate between the past year and the one to come (in Sonnet 4), and on the Feast of the Annunciation when the Virgin Mary hears she will bear Jesus Christ (in Sonnet 62).

   These two moments organize the two kinds of experience the poet as lover describes in the course of the sequence. He is first the tortured pursuer of a disdainful and proud beloved, complaining (like Petrarch) of frustration and grief (especially in Sonnet 13) and caught in the temporal cycle of natural time. He is second a grateful lover who speaks to his lady of their shared humility, having been instructed by the example of a holy love supremely exemplified in the sacrifice of the "Lord of lyfe" (Sonnet 68, which marks Easter Sunday). This second experience generates the lover's sense of sacred time. The eternity it envisages is given an earthly correlative in the fame the poet's verse will give his lady (Sonnet 75) at the very end of the sequence. The trope of fame has already been treated in parodic form by Wyatt, who sought revenge on his lady's disdain by defaming her; it will be transformed by Shakespeare, who will seek to "eternize" the young man he extols and loves.

Students might be asked specifically to distinguish the Petrarchan elements of the first three sonnets of the Amoretti; the shift to sentiments of penitence and humility beginning with the Lenten season (in Sonnet 22); and finally the anti-Petrarchism epitomized by the union of lovers (in Sonnets 65, 66, 68). These distinctions can then form the basis for an understanding of Spenser's idea of love, as it is gradually emptied of the frustrations created by a desire to pursue and possess, and filled with the confidence that comes from mutual trust.

The Amoretti are concluded by the ceremony to which they have pointed: marriage. Like the Amoretti, Spenser's Epithalamion is organized by a scheme of time: its stanzas correspond to hours of the wedding day, beginning at one in the morning and ending at midnight. The poem transforms the most classical figures of the genre, which in its typical Roman form celebrates marriage as the basis for the generation of children and the preservation of the family, yet also resisted by boys and girls (represented by separate choruses) who want to hang on to their youth and freedom. By contrast, Spenser's bride is inspired by the female deities of place, the nymphs of the countryside, and although modest is not reluctant. This change from a classical to a Spenserian mood is in keeping with the tone of the Amoretti in which, as the poet relates, he has finally won his lady. Students may want to comment on Spenser's treatment of physical intimacy: on the one hand, he seems to encourage a kind of voyeurism, as he records how the bride is "stared upon" (stanzas 9 and 13); on the other hand, he describes sexual intercourse in figures, as Venus's "sports" and "merry play" (stanza 20).

If the class has read The Faerie Queene, the question of Spenser's prosody can be revisited. The Amoretti follow what since Surrey was a standard English sonnet form: a fourteen-line stanza showing six different rhymes: ababcdcdefefgg. The Epithalamion has a very complex and demanding form: its nineteen-line stanza is pentameter with the exception of the sixth, eleventh, and seventeenth lines, which are trimeter or three beat; and the concluding nineteenth, which is an alexandrine. The rhyme scheme is comparably difficult: ababccdcdeefggfhhii, with the last line of each stanza ending in the words "eccho ring." The aural effect of the verse is exquisitely musical and quite deliberately antiphonal, with the emotions of one moment answered by the next. These are characteristics that emphasize at the level of prosody the momentous union of bride and groom that is the poet's theme. Spenser refers to his poem as a bridal gift "in lieu of many ornaments": unlike a gentleman of property (which he most certainly was not), he could not "dower" his wife with land, moveables, or jewels of importance. What he had to his name was his ability to write verse of lasting beauty.

Sir Philip Sidney
The Apology for Poetry

Although Sidney's treatise is called a "poetics" it is not about poetry per se but rather what today we call fiction, whether that be expressed as poetry, drama, or prose narrative (short story or novel). Students should consider whether what Sidney says about fiction works equally well for art forms he could not have known: movies and performance art. Some distinctions may help to clarify the situation.

For Sidney, there is fiction on the one hand, and history and philosophy on the other. The latter are tied in certain obvious ways to what Sidney understood as reality: history to the facts of the past, philosophy to the authority of moral discourse. History narrates what was, but it cannot say anything about good conduct (as its examples are so frequently of bad conduct); philosophy discloses what men and women should do and say but it lacks the rhetorical power necessary to make its audiences seek the good. Fiction compensates for both kinds of defect by constructing narratives that—while not historically true—nevertheless promote good conduct; by brilliant figures of thought, charming descriptions, and powerful images, it moves audiences to right action. Neither history nor philosophy venture into the world of the ideal or, as Sidney says, a "golden world," as does fiction. This world is in many respects recreated by poets who write of the romantic Imagination—a look ahead to Coleridge's *Biographia Literaria*, Shelley's *Defence of Poetry*, and Keat's letters "To Benjamin Bailey" and "To George and Thomas Keats" will provide useful points of comparison. Students will notice that Sidney's poetics remains resolutely focussed on fiction as a cultural force designed to promote a moral and civil virtue. Another point of comparison is with an aesthetics that is, in a sense, de-moralized; the class can note relevant differences in "Perspectives: Aestheticism, Decadence, and the *Fin de Siècle*."

The supreme merit of fiction over history and philosophy is the point Sidney wants to press above all others. His *Apology* takes the form of a classical oration, however, and as such makes a complex argument that embraces various issues. A look at its organization is helpful. *The Apology* begins with an "Induction" which instructs the reader or listener in the terms of the debate and establishes the author's good character. It then represents the authorities which have defended poetry: the mythical status of poets, King David who wrote the Psalms, the works of Solomon and the parables of Jesus. Next is Sidney's comparison of poetry with other disciplines, followed by a refutation of arguments against poetry. A conclusion criticizes particular practices by English poets. Such faults do not, however, mean that poetry in general is to be dismissed as an abuse of good sense.

The tradition in which Sidney is writing his poetics is a rich one. Students may want to consult two excellent articles: "Renaissance Poetics" in the *Princeton Encyclopedia of Poetry and Poetics* (1974); and "Rhetoric and Poetics" in *The Cambridge History of Renaissance Philosophy* (1990). They may also want to go back to classical arguments on the status of poetry, especially Plato's, in *The Republic*, Book 10; and Aristotle's in *Poetics*. In a nutshell: Plato insists that poets imitate the truth but at a remove so far from it as to make their imitation of doubtful value; they make a "copy" (or picture) of a "thing" which is in turn a copy, in this case of a pure "idea" (*The Republic* 2.597). And he argues further that the distorting and distracting effect of poetry is compounded by its appeal to the senses: "it waters and fosters these feelings when what we ought to do is to dry them up" (*The Republic* 7.606). By contrast, Aristotle understands the poet's imitation to mean not the representation of realities or ideals, but rather "characters, emotions, actions" (*Poetics* 1447a28)—in other words, poetry does not represent the sensible world but rather the world as colored by human feeling. And, Aristotle adds, "poetry is something more philosophic and of graver import than history, since its statements are of the nature rather of universals, whereas those of history are singulars" (*Poetics* 1451b5–7).

Sidney's *Apology* obviously builds on Aristotle's. Yet perhaps suspicious that Aristotle's "universals" might not be sufficiently infused with the power to prescribe the good, Sidney emphasizes that the subject of poetry (what the poet imitates) is a world surpassing any that human beings experience; it is rather wonderful and impressive in the excellence of its figures and forms:

> The poet doth grow in effect another nature in making things either better than nature bringeth forth, or quite anew, forms such as never were in nature . . . Nature never set forth the earth in so rich a tapestry as divers poets have done . . . Her world is brazen, the poets only deliver a golden.

This golden world is the one that justifies the poet's work by making it express an intensely desirable ideal.

The Arcadia

This prose narrative represents Sidney's attempt to venture into the world of romance. What we print here is the first of five books of a first version, which was circulated in manuscript to a coterie readership in 1581 and printed only in 1912. Sidney continued to work on his romance (cutting some portions and adding many more to the first three books) which remained unfinished at his death in 1586. This amplified version was printed under the supervision of Sidney's sister Mary Herbert, Countess of Pembroke, in 1590; and, with the addition of the fourth and fifth books of the first version, again in 1593. This version was further amplified by Sir William Alexander, who wrote episodes that bridged the gap between the text of the third book of the 1593 version and the fourth book of the 1581 version, to produce a final version, printed in 1621. This much-emended text was the only text of the romance that was known for three centuries.

Sidney's dedication to Mary Herbert states that he wrote his romance as a "trifle": "Your dear self can best witness the manner, being done in loose sheets of paper, most of it in your presence, the rest by sheets sent unto you as fast as they were done." Students can speculate on to what extent this self-representation illustrates the *sprezzatura* or artlessness so much recommended to the courtier by Castiglione (see Perspectives: Government and Self-Government); in Sidney's case, there may be little affectation in his claim.

The genre of romance had a complex history in early modern Europe; its various types or models are lucidly summarized in the entry on "romance" in *The Spenser Encyclopedia* (1990). Perhaps most familiar to Spenser's contemporaries was chivalric romance, exemplified in this anthology by *Sir Gawain and the Green Knight*. Typically, chivalric romance represents the conflicts a knight encounters as he ventures between the court and the surrounding wilderness, often populated by weird or unearthly creatures who challenge his character and very existence. How he responds and survives reflects on his chivalry and the culture of his court. Spenser's *Faerie Queene* conforms to this type while adding a dimension of epic in its celebration of the character and historical mission of a particular people. A second but chronologically prior model derives its essential features from Homer's *Odyssey* which narrates a mythos or history of return: Odysseus leaves Troy an epic hero, but must then face the challenge of going back home—to a world that is both like and very different from the one he left. Typically, Greek romance features sea voyages, children lost and found, family or dynastic ruptures and successions, identities disguised and revealed, and a persistent focus on the future, which is often shadowed in enigmatic prophecies which are realized but in unexpected ways. Sidney's *Arcadia*, locating its action by persons of royal birth in a pseudo-pastoral setting, conforms loosely to the norms of Greek romance.

Book I invites discussion on a number of issues that are central to the rest of the romance and to some degree unique to the *Arcadia*. It begins with a prophecy, apparently of doom, that propels a king, Basileus, to become a recluse in an effort to avoid a dire future. He passes his royal responsibilities onto his minister Philanax. To Sidney's contemporaries this abdication was tantamount to misrule; students can turn back to Perspectives: Government and Self-Goverment to assess what Basilius has become.

Pyrocles's falling in love with Philoclea elicits a conventional critique of passion from Musidorus. It is the more remarkable in that this love is prompted by no more than a picture. Students can debate whether this figure exemplifies the power of art, even verbal art, alluded to in *The Apology*. Pyrocles's disguise as an Amazon, named Cleophila, provokes a debate on the woman question: Musidorus speaks the misogynist part; Pyrocles a standard defense of woman. The image of the androgyne is implicit in Pyrocles's assertion that he can seem to be a woman and yet be a man; is there a theory of gender here? For an analysis of contemporary gender theory, see Thomas Laqueur, *Making Sex: Body and Gender from the Greeks to Freud* (1990), but discussions of the topic are many; for applications of gender theory especially to theater, see Stephen Orgel, *Impersonations: The Performance of Gender in Shakespeare's England* (1996). Cleophila's "performance" of womankind provokes love in Basilius, but is detected as no more than a performance by Basilius's queen Gynecia. To what are these different responses to be attributed? Sidney leaves the answer to his reader.

Finally Sidney's text also plays with notions of rank and class, each categories that his contemporaries supposed were attached to qualities carried "in the blood" or (as we would say) genetically, at least to some degree. The shepherd Dametas and his entire family are stock characters known conventionally as "clowns." Does the fact that Musidorus, a prince and heir apparent, disguises himself as a shepherd, named Dorus, imply a theory of class? And finally, does the fact that both Pyrocles and Musidorus assume identities that mirror those of the women they love imply a theory of love?

The actions and attitudes of Sidney's characters are nothing if not passionate, generally impulsive, and often willful. They are in every way performative; they make things happen that otherwise would not happen. Sidney's characters don't seem to be victims of fate. And yet the prophecy that Basilius has sought to avoid seems to be coming true. Is there a sense in which Sidney's romance is also about writing history? Like so much literature of the early modern period, Sidney's *Arcadia* is enigmatic; it poses more problems than it solves. Students do not need to be alarmed that they have not arrived at an unambiguous interpretation of this text; it was probably designed to be provocative not definitive.

Astrophil and Stella

As would Shakespeare and Spenser, Sidney writes his sonnet sequence as the record of a courtship. Unlike them, he fashions his principal speaker as a dramatic character, the young and somewhat pretentious young man Astrophil; and he gives him a vocal antagonist who speaks in her own right, the lady Stella. Students can detect the wit in Sidney's names: Astrophil is literally the lover of a star, in this case Stella. The wordplay gives the reader a clue to the larger rhetorical program of the sequence. It is in some sense about the frustrations of a courtship: many literary historians have thought that it mirrored Sidney's own disappointment at the marriage of a lady he was said to love, Penelope Devereaux who married Lord Rich, perhaps the "rich" who is mentioned in the sequence. But throughout the sequence Sidney is also playing on a figure of thought, irony, that not only calls into question the speaker's sincerity and maturity of character (how self-indulgent is he?) but also the referential status of language itself.

Sidney takes both kinds of irony from Petrarch, although he deploys it to illustrate more forcefully than the earlier poet the difficulties inherent in poetic "Invention" or the discovery and voicing of a subject. The first sonnet is illustrative but it also requires a context. The speaker pretends to be without a subject that is wholly original and to find his path blocked by other feet (or measures of poetry). The reference is to Petrarch, who has pretended that his verse "walks in untrodden ways." Sidney's speaker Astrophil is therefore in a double bind: in seeking to be original, he cannot be original because "being original" has already been preempted as a poetic stance. As an "Invention," the claim to originality is old hat; by being original or looking away from books to the "heart," the poet is being conventional.

Sidney resorts to paradox to structure his representation of courtship throughout the rest of the sequence. Finally, he can love Stella only if she denies him, or, as Astrophil says, she is an "absent presence" (see Sonnets 60, 106, 108). (Students interested in post-structuralist language theory may wish to see in Sidney's rejection of reference an example of that theory's explanatory value.) Yet in a way, even as he follows the Petrarchan model, Sidney achieves originality. While Petrarch's

Laura is never present to him except in some figured form, as a figment of the poet's imagination, Sidney's Stella is represented as a forceful dramatic presence; because she actually speaks a part, the poet's frustration in losing her has an obvious reference. As a lover, his physical being is invoked as a kind of intransigence that stands outside the rhetoric of the poem and remains unaffected by it: "Desire still cries, give me some food" (71; see also 45).

The best way to get across to a class the performative dimension of the sequence is to have students identify the voices in "The Fourth Song" and "The Eighth Song" and then read the poems as a mini-play. There are two parts to "The Fourth Song" (Astrophil's and Stella's) and there should be three parts to "The Eighth Song": Astrophil's, Stella's, and that of the narrator who fills in with a description of the action between speeches. Such a reading will bring the poetry to life in a way that no amount of analysis can do. It will have the added benefit of allowing the class to experience Sidney's lyric musicality.

"The Apology" and Its Time   The debate about the value of fiction and particularly poetry can be understood as part of a larger cultural movement that sought to justify an aesthetics of pleasure in a society still largely dominated by religion and its primary imperative, the salvation of the individual soul. Moralizing attacks on poetry found an authority in Plato, who rejected fiction because it stirred the passions. Before poetry could be recognized as a legitimate art with its own requirements for excellence in diction and style, it had to be defended from accusations that it was morally derelict. In his treatise *Of the Genealogy of the Pagan Gods*, Giovanni Boccaccio had opened the way to such a defense by maintaining that from its earliest inception as myth, fiction had been the cover for deeper meanings that addressed morals and the spiritual life. But his argument was by no means universally accepted. Stephen Gosson's *The School of Abuse* illustrates the counter-case.

Puttenham's *The Art of English Poesie* was perhaps the best-known of the sixteenth-century treatises on the subject, in part because it contains a comprehensive discussion of the figures of rhetoric and it could thus be used by writers wishing to learn how to produce "copy"—that is, arguments that are as fully developed or "amplified" as the subject requires. In the portion of his treatise printed here are ideas on how to justify poetry as a means to a civil society: many of these ideas are echoed by Sidney.

Gascoigne's *Certain Notes of Instruction* is an eminently practical work that focusses on diction—the actual language a poet should use. It illustrates the extent to which *English*, as opposed to Latin or the other vernaculars, was seen as having become a language fully capable of expressing all kinds of thought. It is perhaps the first instance of an overt nationalism with respect to language. Gascoigne urges writers to use words of a single syllable because "most ancient English words are of one syllable" and writers who use them will seem "the truer Englishman." But his major preoccupation is with the virtues of simplicity and clarity.

Like Puttenham and Gascoigne, Daniel's *A Defence of Rhyme* is concerned with the craft of the poet. His sense of a national identity as the product of particular uses of language includes a consideration of what might be called historical relativism. He rejects a blanket endorsement of "antiquity" as authoritative. Each age, he insists, evolves the authorities appropriate to its culture: "we [i.e., the English people] are not so placed out of the way of judgment but that the same sun of discretion shineth upon us" as upon the writers of the past. Students interested in today's debates on the values of what is sometimes termed "the canon" and of up-to-minute literature from writers whose works constitute a multicultural field can appreciate Daniel's approach to the problem of authority.

Isabella Whitney

Not until students encounter the work of Aphra Behn in the next century will they have a chance to assess writing that relies so completely on self-taught skills. Both Aemilia Lanyer and Mary Herbert, Countess of Pembroke, benefited from instruction in the most sophisticated modes of expression and conduct. Whitney probably had no more than a dame-school education. She would have been taught to read scripture, write an italic script (the more complicated secretary hand was reserved for men), and perhaps do simple arithmetic. She would not have been taught Latin, history, rhetoric, moral philosophy, theology. Her acquaintance with classical literature was therefore acquired on her own.

Whitney's poem to London is remarkable for its control of tone. She writes that she had a bad time in the city; she speaks of its "cruelness." Yet she is able to lighten her disappointment, grief, and even anger by recourse to irony. She conveys her experience of poverty, what she has lacked in London, by imagining it as a kind of wealth, *what she leaves in (and to) London*. There is further wit in the poem: it is her will in two senses of the word. First, it is a testament distributing her wealth (her non-existent property standing for her prudent wisdom) to her descendants, those other women who will venture to try their luck in the city; and second, it is a record of *her choice to leave a place that has not treated her well* (an indication of her moral fortitude). In other words, she wrestles from defeat a kind of victory.

Whitney's plight needs to be understood in both gendered and social terms. Her work provides readers with an excellent opportunity to assess the extent to which conditions of class and rank qualify strongly the determinant of sex. In many respects, Whitney is closer in spirit to men of the "middling sort" like Defoe than she is to aristocrats like Mary Herbert, Countess of Pembroke. Slight as it is, Whitney's work introduces to British literature an important figure—the woman on her own in the world—whose future incarnations appear in the work of Behn and (much later) Charlotte Brontë and George Eliot.

Mary Herbert, Countess of Pembroke

It is doubtful whether Mary Herbert, sister of Sir Philip Sidney, would have made a mark in British literature had it not been for her brother's early death. Her final arrangement of the material in *The Arcadia*, then known as *The Countess of Pembroke's Arcadia*, and her completion of the translation of the Psalms were as much a tribute to Sir Philip as her own literary project. In any case, she is often described as in his shadow, devoted to his work and memory. This picture may be overly conservative. The antiquarian John Aubrey in his collection of biographies, *Brief Lives* (first published in 1813, much bowdlerized), recalls that as a child she was "very salacious": "she had a Contrivance that in the Spring of the yeare, when the Stallions were to leape the Mares, they were to be brought before such a part of the house, where she had a *vidette* (a hole to peepe out at) to looke on them and please herselfe with their Sport." But nothing of Herbert's saucy spirit emerges in her dedicatory poem to Elizabeth I or her elegy to Sir Philip, both of which are models of a devoted propriety and a suitably gendered deference to authority and command.

Herbert's rhetoric is remarkably practiced and deserves attention. *Even now that care* tropes throughout its eleven stanzas on the image of Elizabeth's heavy responsibilities or "care," which is offset by what the poet herself "dares" by way of compliment to the queen. The notion of "daring" is further registered in Herbert's tribute to her brother's service to England, which is also attributed to the powerful "care" the queen has for her country, her "moving all, herself unmoved." Students should notice Herbert's recourse to figures from scripture, her attribution to Elizabeth of the life of King David; this compliments the queen while at the same time it avoids a reference to King David's role as founder of a "house" or dynasty—in short, to a role Elizabeth I was supposed but unlikely ever to play. Richard Helgerson and Claire McEachern have recently drawn attention to the emergence of a concept of nationhood during the last quarter of the sixteenth century (in *Forms of Nationhood: the Elizabethan Writing of England* [1995] and *Poetics of English Nationhood: 1590–1612* [1997] respectively). Students may want to comment on Herbert's references to England as a nation and a people in *Even now that care*—evincing a nationalism almost certainly created not by the queen but by the memory of her brother's life and death—by contrast to her invocation of a transcendent realm in her elegy.

Herbert's translations permit several kinds of comparison; first, with the prose translations of the same psalm by Miles Coverdale; second, with the very somber verse translations of Boethius' *Consolation* by Elizabeth I. Herbert's rhymes are always deft and sometimes ingenious, her meters occasionally irregular but not unmusical—it is therefore a good idea to have students read her poems aloud in order to appreciate their curiously effective use of the sounds and tones of the English language. A comparison with Whitney ought to be instructive but not invidious: while Whitney's verse is often sing-song, Herbert's rhythms are generally quite subtle.

Whether or not *The Doleful Lay of Clorinda* is Herbert's poem, it performed the cultural work required by the death of a national hero. The figuration of the dead poet as shepherd is conventional in pastoral elegy; it practically always allows the poet-speaker a chance to reflect on the terms in which the dead are given an afterlife in both poetry (as an example to the future) and in heaven (as a reward for their faith). Herbert's invocation of her brother as the "shepherds' hope" which "is not dead, nor can it die" recalls the very imposing terms in which Milton will later describe Edward King, in *Lycidas*.

Elizabeth I

The poems and speeches of Elizabeth I will allow students to assess the ways they go about interpreting literature. Most of what they read from periods other than the present they will understand by relying on criteria that are largely personal and ahistorical: whether a poem or a narrative fiction is interesting, moves or persuades them, or presents a social problem that seems like one they have known. What their interpretations often lack is a sense of literary context: the generic and stylistic factors shaping the literary work; and of historical setting— the social, economic, and political world for which the literary work was originally intended. Considering the works of Elizabeth I, students can be encouraged to realize how much a knowledge of context and setting influences their understanding. Elizabeth I's poems provide an especially good test case for what critics call "reader response"; their interpretation will almost certainly depend on information that predates the experience of reading them. What that information is, how it has been derived (movies, novels, plays, history books, pictures), is worth discussing. Students may want to reflect on the nature of history itself: is what we know of history always based on facts, or does it depend on what a particular society or age thinks it needs to know in order to establish its own cultural norms?

Poems

The *Woodstock* poems are intentionally enigmatic; they convey only as much of Elizabeth Tudor's anxiety as she thought safe to disclose to the world. The references to fortune as blameworthy and to God as the power who will vindicate and revenge her wrongs makes Elizabeth's situation as the prisoner of Mary I a matter of universal meaning and importance; by refusing to make accusations, it also protects the speaker.

The Doubt of Future Foes expresses a resolution absent from the *Woodstock* poems. It is overtly political; in a sense it is a poem about affairs of state. How does our knowing that it is written by a ruling monarch contribute to our understanding of the meaning of such terms as "exiles," "subjects," "seditious sects," "peace"? These words not only have referents in the general sense of the term, they also indicate features and elements of a particular historical moment. *On Monsieur's Departure* is a frankly occasional poem that conveys the distress associated with maintaining a public persona in a time of personal anguish. Whether or not Elizabeth I's infatuation with the Duke d'Alençon was sincere or a mere ploy to distract her courtiers from other important affairs matters less than that it prompted her to write on a problem in statecraft. Students can identify the poem's Petrarchan conceits ("I freeze, I burn," etc.), heretofore a resource for male poets, and consider whether there is anything here to identify the writer as a woman.

As a historical document, the poem raises the vexed question of Elizabeth's marriage, a topic she discusses in her speech to Parliament. Here an excursion into the literature of contemporary political thought may be profitable. The concept of the monarch's "body politic"—her person as at one with that of the state and all its powers and representatives—is central to the poem's meaning. This "body" was supremely authoritative. But what would happen to it if the monarch were female and married a husband whom custom and religious doctrine said she had to obey? Would the obedience required of her "body natural" not compromise the authority of her "body politic"? The conflict between reasons of state and the dictates of the heart is sometimes supposed to be the reason for Elizabeth's refusal to marry.

Elizabeth's translations from the Psalms and *The Consolation of Philosophy* certainly reveal her interest in language and literature, but they also suggest states of mind. Each addresses ways to deal with different kinds of challenge or misfortune; in this respect, we may think that they are especially suited to advise a head of state. Boethius, although a Christian, wrote very much as a philosopher. Discussion can focus on the most obvious concepts: a person's "earthly flaws" rob him (or her) of the joy of knowledge, the discovery of the "sundry causes of hidden nature"; the prudent course is to cultivate a steady and virtually passionless state—"Chase joys," etc.; and, knowing that nature is constantly changing, be prepared for "sliding" in one's own life. Does the knowledge that Elizabeth wrote these philosophical poems at the very end of her life contribute to the way we read them? Does the poet's tone of regret seem sharper because the terms of her life—essentially so critical—limited her time for peaceful recreation? Compare this tone with the strained but confident assertions of the *Woodstock* poems.

Speeches

On Marriage needs to be read in conjunction with *On the Departure of Monsieur*, although it was written at a much earlier time: both speech and poem defend the position of a virgin queen regnant. Elizabeth was obliged to resolve the minds of her subjects on two topics primarily: first, that her commitment was entirely to her people; and second, that the kingdom would not lack for an heir. Cleverly, she calls on God's help to fulfill the latter claim; this suggests that she herself is not in a position to make a decision on the matter, much as if she were speaking not about getting married (understood to be a personal decision), but whether or not she, having married, would bear a child (traditionally considered an act of providence). Elizabeth was adept at such rhetorical sleights of hand. They often featured a figure of thought called a "concession," a point raised in order that it be rejected. In this case, she intended that her subjects both consider her marriage but also understand that she had set it aside for good and appropriate reasons.

Students can appreciate Elizabeth's skill as a writer in her speeches dealing with the subject of Mary, Queen of Scots, which date from 1586. (An eloquent selection can be found on our audio CD.) In one after another turn of phrase—"were we but as two milk-maids, with pails upon our arms"; "I have had good experience and trial of this world"; "we Princes, I tell you, are set on stages, in the sight and view of all the world duly observed"; "accept my thankfulness, excuse my doubtfulness, and take in good part my answer-answerless"—she exhibits the technique of an experienced writer and a brilliant thinker. The matter at issue was, of course, a very grave one. A knowledge of history is key to understanding why Elizabeth had to be so subtle and circuitous in her argument. The questions she had to answer were two: whether Mary was guilty of treason; and, if guilty of treason, whether she should be executed. Mary, having been accused of the murder of her husband, Henry Stuart, Lord Darnley after abdicating in favor of her son, James VI of Scotland (and later to be James I of England), was defeated by her rebellious subjects in June of 1567. She fled to England in 1568 where Elizabeth persuaded her to present her case before an English tribunal. This judicial body did not find Mary guilty as accused; nevertheless, she remained Elizabeth's prisoner for sixteen years. Evidence suggests that during this time she plotted to be released or to escape. But one such conspiracy, led by Anthony Babington, seemed to implicate her conclusively. She was tried for treason and condemned. Faced with commanding the execution of a queen and her cousin, Elizabeth at first refused to sign the death warrant; at last, however, convinced by her counselors of Mary's guilt, she did what the law required. The two speeches reprinted here illustrate how subtly Elizabeth could make a point when the issue she confronted was ambiguous. Her contemporaries called this style of government "policy"—by which they meant a style suited to government according to the demands of circumstance and contingency rather than principle.

In times of crisis, Elizabeth could be forthright and open, as her speech at Tilbury or her *Golden Speech* indicates. A comparison between her very political speeches to her council on the subject of Mary and her essentially popular speeches to her subjects can be the basis for yet another consideration of "reader response." What are the different rhetorical strategies that each situation calls for?

Aemilia Lanyer

Poems

Lanyer may be considered among the first generation of English woman to have written from a point of view not only clearly dependent upon her experience as a woman but also frankly engaged in pro-woman argument. The genre has obvious antecedents in what was called "the woman question" (or in France the *querelle des femmes*) and had produced a very considerable body of literature in France and Italy, some of it by women. The most notable work was that of Christine de Pisan, whose important treatise *Le Livre de la Cité des Dames* (1405) was translated into English by Brian Ansley in 1521. The terms of the debate were derived in the first instance from scripture in which the nature of woman is described both as the same as and also inferior to that of man (following accounts in Genesis); much pro-woman argument therefore focuses, as does Lanyer's, on the figure of Eve. Lanyer's treatment of Eve, expressed by Pilate's wife in *Salve Deus Rex Judaeorum*, is remarkable for its insistence on Eve's rational powers and its claim that she accepted Satan's temptation because she did not and could not know what would result. In effect, this replaces the meaning of the Fall as an index of sin and disobedience with something less charged: Eve is an exponent of reason and as such she can be and was misled. This change has the effect of establishing Eve as at least equal to Adam intellectually if not his superior; in Lanyer's account, it is Adam who exhibits passion and unreason when he follows Eve's example even after he knows what will happen.

The obvious comparison to make here is with Milton's account of the same event (*Paradise Lost*, 9). Students will notice that like Lanyer, although to a different end, Milton gives Eve rational powers: she takes what the serpent offers because he tells her he has eaten and still lives. In other words, she reasons from example. This feature of Lanyer's pro-woman argument had not been made before by an English writer; her insistence on a reasonable womankind underscores the beginnings of a feminist consciousness during this period. Other features of Lanyer's defense of women follow established strategies: to the charge that women were inferior, writers often countered with examples of powerful, courageous and brilliant women as Lanyer does in her letter "To the Reader." Yet these examples are countered by others less commendable.

Lanyer is very tough on women who study to be beautiful, pointing out how often in history beauty has led to misery, disaster, and even death. Her position is more critical than that often taken against privileging beauty as transient, earthly, and a distraction from moral and spiritual life. At the same time, Lanyer extols the virtues in Clifford that are conventionally reserved for women who occupy an exclusively domestic role: piety, motherhood, generosity. To a degree, therefore, her pro-woman argument wavers between two approaches: one that reflects a traditional emphasis on the subordination of women, and the other that presents the case for a reformation of these attitudes. Students who are interested in an overview of literature in English on "the woman question" can move ahead to Perspectives: Tracts on Women and Gender.

Lanyer's most brilliant expression of a burgeoning feminist consciousness is, however, not polemical but deeply personal. In her poem *The Description of Cookham* she testifies to what might be called a feminine sensibility quite independent of masculine influence. She locates her experience of this in a past that allowed her contact with Margaret Clifford, Countess of Cumberland who is featured as both a genius loci, the spirit of a place, and as a spiritual mentor. In this way, Lanyer combines the trope of description, usually restricted to objects such as houses, gardens, or landscapes with the history of a conversion, her own awakening to the life of the soul. As it is virtually impossible that as Lanyer wrote *The Description* she did not have in mind *To Penshurst*, Jonson's poem on the estate of Sir Robert Sidney, a comparison of the two may prove especially revealing. Lanyer's eye is constantly informed by her sense of the *presence* of Clifford; Jonson's eye takes in a varied landscape and sees it in the conventional terms of pastoral and georgic poetry. A particularly acute difference of mood can be gauged by comparing how Lanyer and Jonson build meaning around the image of the oak. For Lanyer it is a testimony to friendship infused with a kind of sanctity; for Jonson it is a marker of dynastic power. Finally, although the two poets both celebrate the virtues and character of a country house, Lanyer writes an elegy, a poem of a better past that cannot return; by contrast, Jonson writes what is generically an epistle, a poem that tells a present readership of a better past that remains, wonderfully and remarkably, in a landscape of a modernity that lacks and desperately needs an old-fashioned virtue.

Sir Walter Raleigh
Poems

Raleigh's poems fall roughly into two categories: erotic and elegiac. As categories, they are not always distinct; love and the loss of love and even life are themes that the poet weaves together in much of his verse. Like the literary output of his contemporary, Elizabeth I, Raleigh's poems come to the twentieth-century reader embedded in associations; these will condition a reader's response to the work, the more so if that work is obviously occasional.

To get a sense of Raleigh's tone, his blend of romantic lyricism with an almost philosophical realism, the class can begin with his reply to Marlowe's pastoral *The Passionate Shepherd*, printed here in our selection of Marlowe's work. While Marlowe writes in a manner entirely typical of pastoral—the adventurous student can skip ahead and read other examples of the genre in Barnfield—Raleigh recontextualizes the tropes suggestive of a Maytime carelessness so that they gain an ironic meaning in light of the passage of seasonal time, as May becomes December. This retrospectively transforms Marlowe's celebration of youth so that it becomes the prelude to a meditation on age. Considered as a pair, these poems can offer students yet another opportunity to discover how generic conventions both determine content, as in Marlowe's poem, and also create a certain conceptual space in which such conventional content can be made ironic.

Ambivalence also shapes the content of *As You Came from the Holy Land*, and *Nature that Washed Her Hands in Milk*, though in these poems the edge given to realism is sharper and more personal. Students should notice how the first of these poems treats antiphonally the voices of the pilgrim and the lover; the lover's complaint and the pilgrim's consolation (such as it is) situate love in the landscape of time and presage for all lovers its inevitable loss. The second poem is similarly charged with pathos, this time deliberately generated by the poet's representation of cause and effect: in the third stanza the poet suggests that his love will die because of the hard heart of his lady (however much a fantasied lady she is); but in the succeeding stanzas the causal agent is not human but rather time itself. The reader is left to determine whether the lover's classic complaint

of the loss of love is not actually a pretext to celebrate life, even life that is
charged with disappointment. For Raleigh, the loss to be feared is the loss of life.
Students who want to assess the scope of pastoral now have a good chance to entertain a retrospective of the genre: what are the salient differences between the
pastoral of Spenser, of Marlowe, of Raleigh? How do these poems compare with
the pastoral as represented in Sidney's *Arcadia*? Interested students can be
encouraged to read Virgil's *Eclogues* for insight into the function of pastoral as
political commentary. A fine recent study of the genre is Paul Alpers, *What is
Pastoral?* (1996).

In this selection, the subject of death is represented by *On the Life of Man* and
the poet's own epitaph, but his general view of it is best summed up in his conclusion of his unfinished *History of the World* (1614), and written during his second
long imprisonment at the order of James I. The passage, often anthologized, is
worth quoting because it not only epitomizes Raleigh's own end with an almost
prophetic canniness but also the mood of an age that had grown tired of its ambitious optimism:

> O eloquent just and mightie Death! Whom none could advise, thou hast
> perswuaded; what none hath dared, thou has done; and whom all the
> world hath flattered, thou only hast cast out of the world and despised;
> thou hast drawne together all the farre stretched greatnesse, all the pride,
> crueltie, and ambition of man, and covered it over with these two narrow
> words, *hic iacet*.

Death for Raleigh was not, however, simply a matter of the body. It might be more
accurate to say that insofar as his life was the politics of court, death was his exile
from his sovereign's favor. Students can begin with the overtly flirtatious *To the
Queen*, remembering that Elizabeth had determined that the norms of courtiership should be those of courtship. What figures of thought reveal that this poem
is not, in fact, to a beloved lady but rather to a sovereign? Students may want to
ponder Raleigh's recourse to such terms as "a saint . . . As all desire but none deserve." By contrast, *To Cynthia* is a poem closely keyed to the terms of Raleigh's
own bitter experience. Although it reports his disappointment at Elizabeth's indifference to his accomplishments, it could as well be seen as a reflection of a sovereign's disdain for her subjects. A comparison of Raleigh's language of reproach
with Elizabeth's eloquent embrace of her subjects' desires in her *Golden Speech* will
suggest how very broadly the queen imposed her protean personality on the society and people she ruled.

The Discovery of Guiana

The discovery of the pioneering scholarship of historians investigating the
European explorations of the New World, increasingly known as "the history of
contact," has provided students of literature with a new perspective in which to
place and consider such writing as Raleigh's account of his encounter with the
land and peoples of the Americas. The work of Anthony Pagden, John Elliott, and

Tzevan Todorov indicates how profoundly different European explorers found all aspects of the New World—how different and yet also how quickly they sought to understand their experiences in the terms they were familiar with, that is, in European terms. The literature of "contact" should be read both for its registration of what many explorers saw as "wonders" and "marvels," but also for the ways in which it could represent novelty as familiar.

Raleigh's dedication to Sir Charles Howard and Sir Robert Cecil outlines the conditions of his voyage; remarkable is his need to defend himself from detractors who apparently had claimed that he had not in fact gone to Guiana, and that he had enriched himself at the expense of the state. The dedication illustrates how easy it was to concoct fictions upon the bare suggestion of a trip to such distant and mysterious places. And Raleigh's address "To the Reader" reminds us that the desire to know the New World was almost invariably coupled with the expectation of gaining wealth. The lure of gold, most vividly expressed in the concept of an actual city of El Dorado, drove Europeans to the limits of sanity. Some of the fervour with which they pursued their mad dreams of wealth in the New World is implied by Raleigh's precise account of discovering gold ore: *el madre del oro*. Not gold itself, but the vast and hopeful promise of it. There was, of course, the presumption that the possession of gold meant control of the known world. As Raleigh says of Philip II, king of Spain:

> It is his Indian gold that endangereth and disturbeth all the nations of Europe, it purchaseth intelligence, creepeth into councils, and setteth bound loyalty at liberty in the greatest monarchies of Europe.

Raleigh's fixation on the power of gold calls to mind More's illustration of the Utopian economy, in which only the smallest children find attractive this in itself quite useless metal. For further discussion of the ideology of conquest that motivated both colonial powers, students could be asked to read the brief but very pithy attack on Spanish rule in New Spain by Bartolomé de las Casas entitled (in English translation) *The Devastation of the Indies*, first published in 1552. Clearly, how conquest and its methods were regarded was not entirely a function of national feeling; there were practices that persons from all quarters could feel were reprehensible.

Much of Raleigh's text registers a triangulated contest for power: Spanish agents, who had been operating in the region for decades, Raleigh and his English cohorts, and finally the Indians who actually possessed and had dominion over the region. Raleigh denounces Spanish rule, arguing that the English can win the allegiance of the Indians by cooperative dealings; he also—inconsistently—claims that the English can overcome the poorly defended Indians and whatever Spanish resistance develops to become lords of the territory.

But Raleigh also takes an inconsistent view of the Indians. He sees them as aliens and allies, often mixing fact and fiction in a single narrative or description. In this way he illustrates the European tendency to see the strangeness of the New World as the basis for making associative connections. The account he gives of the life of the Amazons, the warrior women of classical mythology, is largely derived from accounts in the *Geographica* of the Greek historian Strabo (c. 63 B.C.–19 A.D.) and in the glossator Servius's commentary to *Aeneid* 11. His respectful description of the King of Aromai represents this tribal chief as a gifted elder statesman, the sort of character who could have wandered to Europe from Utopia or some other hypothetical realm. And he is clearly fascinated by customs he observes in his travels—they allow him to recognize the civility of peoples he would otherwise regard as entirely foreign.

Raleigh's conclusion, which so optimistically points to a conquest of Guiana, was designed to convince Elizabeth that he, Raleigh, deserved praise and reward. Students can be asked to reflect on other texts of the period in which ambition is so clearly represented and also thwarted. The trope of ambition checked finds its commonplace representation in the wheel of Fortune but it also lends itself to ironic, moralized, and even tragic treatment. Here useful comparisons can be made with Gascoigne's youthful wish to climb the social ladder and the destructive illusions of Marlowe's Dr. Faustus.

"The Discovery" and Its Time   Something of the shock Europeans received as they saw and landed in the New World is summed up by Bill M. Donovan in his introduction to Las Casas's history of Spanish conquest, *The Devastation of the Indies* (see Raleigh, "The Discovery of Guiana"). In many ways, it was the shock that comes to readers when they encounter their subject in the flesh:

> Sixteenth-century Europeans sailed out into the world armed with knowledge from the ancients, above all Aristotle; with a long tradition of exotic European travel literature filled with strange people, fantastic geography, and mythic creatures; and with the Bible. From these texts, Europeans had constructed a complete cosmology, one that explained how the world had begun, how it would end, the types of people—good and evil—who had once inhabited the world, and the types of people still in it. Nowhere in that system did space exist for the variety of life they encountered in the Americas.

Class discussion of the texts included here can focus on the play between knowledge and ignorance, fact and fiction, reality and illusion that structures many of their representations of the New World. It is important to stress that accounts of very early contact, such as Arthur Barlow's, show the natives of North America as friendly and essentially without guile. These characteristics almost certainly suggested to readers that trade with natives would result in huge profits: for trinkets they would receive goods of great value. Barlow was, in a sense, doing a sales pitch. He was also interested in descriptive detail, much as a real estate agent selling property in a newly developed neighborhood might be. His and later accounts take care to describe in detail the clothing, weapons, dwelling places, and manner of life of the Indians; students should notice how important were records of *fact*, often itemized as if in a cultural inventory. The class can consider the difference between what might be called "tales of voyagers" and "colonial reporting." The two genres coalesce in places, to be sure, but they are nevertheless conceptually different, the first designed to intrigue armchair readers and the second to stimulate adventuresome entrepreneurs. Beyond these designs, students should be encouraged to find expressions of a genuine though perhaps unsophisticated sense of ethnography.

Laudonnière wants to explain by what systems of belief the Indians lived and how they communicated with each other. Hariot's account is remarkable for its interest in technology; obviously, he is looking forward to the means by which the English will manage to control a people who remain defenseless before the guns and powder of the colonists. His comments on disease and the devastation it caused to native populations which had acquired no immunity to the microbes the English carried with them have been considered by Stephen Greenblatt in an essay entitled "Invisible Bullets" in *Shakespearean Negotiations: The Circulation of Social Energy in Renaissance England* (1988); the essay is particularly useful for its analysis of the cultural importance of such technological expertise. The most astute of observations is that of Michel de Montaigne, who never went to the New World. There is no doubt that he intended to challenge European presumptions of civility by comparing their social and political practices with those of Brazilian natives, whose habits he learns by hearsay. But students might also be asked whether Montaigne does not also imply a supra-cultural critique of all practices that ritualize cruelty, vengeance, and a bloodthirsty delight in pain. Taken together, these texts will provide Raleigh's account of Guiana with a context in the beginnings of comparative ethnography.

Richard Barnfield

Poems

Barnfield's poems exploit the figures of pastoral that were so often a resource for poets of erotic and especially homoerotic verse in the early modern period. The practice began with the Hellenistic poet Theocritus (third century B.C.) who wrote idyllic fictions of the life and loves of shepherds, occasionally punctuated with sexually explicit passages. His characters establish the type of "pastoral naif"—the young shepherd lover who courts his beloved with the humble gifts of the countryside and imagines settling down to modest rural contentment. The type is presented in order to be mocked—gently and with sympathy for its untroubled dreams of happiness. It persists in pastoral through the poetry of Marvell, whose *Mower* poems illustrate the satisfaction as well as the danger attendant on thinking that a life in nature is simple and uncomplicated. Marvell's vision of pastoral is of course made problematic by its association with another and essentially alien genre: georgic, a literature devoted to the illustration of country life as the scene of rural labor. Marvell's mowers, while they celebrate nature and its bounty as opposed to human art and its products, are nevertheless workers on the land. Some might argue that their experience of work should have taught them to know better than to trust to nature. By contrast, Barnfield's shepherds live without material care: their interests are dictated by a desire for pleasure and include not only sex but all the pleasures of the senses.

Discussion needs to identify the triangle of lovers in *The Complaint of Daphnis for Ganimede* and what the speaker is claiming: that love between men is superior to that of love between a man and a woman. When Daphnis, urging Ganimede to love him not Queen Guendolin, states for a fact that: "I love thee for thy qualities divine," he is invoking a model of human relations that derives its cultural authority from the literature of Hellenic Greece, especially in such texts as Plato's *Symposium*. Students who have worked through Marlowe's *Hero and Leander* and have some acquaintance with Shakespeare's sonnets will already have a sense of how to look at early modern expressions of homoerotic feeling and its cultural history. It is important that they keep in mind the considerable difference between early modern notions of sexuality and our own: the former do not engage questions of identity as much as morality. What is important to a person's sense of himself or herself is not sexual identity but rather the control of his or her passions by the operation of reason and the intervention of grace. Poems of the kind Barnfield writes have the effect of setting aside, for a moment, such questions as the prospect of salvation (or damnation) usually pose in deference to a need to play. But their implied reference is nonetheless to the possibility of enjoying a licit passion, however this can be realized.

The Second Day's Lamentation of the Affectionate Shepherd is a continuation of many of the themes voiced in *The Complaint of Daphnis*. Once again, the poet pictures his beloved in images common to love poetry of the period—less Petrarchan perhaps than evoking the medieval blazon of beauty. Again, the speaker tempts his beloved with gifts that are suited to such rural activities as fit a life of ease: piping, fishing, trapping. It is remarkable for its recourse to tropes common in the poetry of heterosexual love. The Affectionate Shepherd urges his beloved to "Remember age," to "trust not to beauty's wings," and to "Serve Jove (upon thy knees) both day and night"—these are moral directives that all lovers need to keep in mind. They indicate how easily and with what little apology Barnfield's homoerotic message finds its place in contemporary culture. The sonnets from *Cynthia* render in a more formal manner the sentiments Barnfield also expresses in pastoral. Like Shakespeare's sonnets, they profess eternal love; unlike Shakespeare's sonnets, they are predicated on the hope of fidelity not the experience of betrayal.

Christopher Marlowe
Hero and Leander

Marlowe's source is the Greek poet Musaeus Grammaticus, who wrote the story of Hero and Leander toward the end of the fifth century A.D. Marlowe's tale is unfinished; according to Musaeus, the story ends with Leander drowned in a storm while swimming the Hellespont and Hero a suicide, having jumped from her tower in Sestos. But the spirit of Marlowe's poem owes much to Ovid's *Metamorphoses*.

Fascinated by the idea of the transformation of material creation, Marlowe, like Ovid, creates images of life in which what is only seems to be, and what seems to be is essentially what is. Students should notice how the imagery of the poem exploits deliberately conflated categories of existence. Hero's costume is both a dress and a kind of living work of art: "sparrows . . . Of hollow pearl and gold" perch on her boots of coral, and "chirrup" as she walks. The effect of these images is to create a fictive world very similar to the one Guyon destroyed in Book 2 of *The Faerie Queene*. In each case, it is art that is called into question, art and the power of the artist to rival the creativity of God.

The obvious homoeroticism of the poem needs to be discussed in frank terms. Yes, Marlowe's pen, for all its disclaimers, is actually engaged in describing the "loves of men" for men as well as for women. Leander is simply a beautiful youth, and as such he will attract the attention of the sea-god Neptune who, in allusive figures, makes love to Leander as he swims to meet Hero. Students puzzled (or troubled) by these images and what they signify can be directed to a wealth of current scholarship on sexuality in this period: an excellent study is Bruce Smith, *Homosexual Desire in Shakespeare's England: A Cultural Poetics* (1991). How Smith defines the scope of his subject is especially useful, as it establishes how different was the understanding of sexuality in the early modern period:

> In the sixteenth and seventeenth centuries, sexuality was not, as it is for us, the starting place for anyone's self-definition. . . . The structures of knowledge that impinged on what we would now call "homosexuality" did not ask a man who had sexual relations with another man to think of himself as fundamentally different from his peers. Just the opposite was true. Prevailing ideas asked him to castigate himself for falling into the general depravity to which all mankind is subject.

In other words, Marlowe's representation of Neptune's encounter with Leander, which is so suggestive of their sexuality, was written for an audience for whom passion, lust, and desire for *any* creature was a sign of a fall into sin, a loss of rationality, and was understood to be offensive to God. Thus on the one hand, assuming Marlowe was going to finish his poem according to Musaeus's model, Leander's career constitutes a warning to those who tend to lose their self-control. On the other hand, of course, his career also exemplifies an education into sexuality.

For most of the poem, Leander is a sexual innocent, a "novice" in Marlowe's words, who after merely "dallying with Hero . . . Suspected / Some amorous rites or other were neglected." The experience that educates and matures him is figured in Neptune's watery embrace; the pattern of his education into sexuality is ancient and derived, as Marlowe almost certainly knew, from the literature on friendship between men in Greek antiquity. Then, men and boys were expected to share sex as part of friendship; upon maturity and reaching a marriageable age, men were enjoined to treat women as bearers of children and guarantors of family and dynasty. Typically, at least as recorded in literature, a boy's relations with women followed his experience with men.

But just how serious is Marlowe being in any of his representations of sexuality? Class discussion may be able to bring to light a certain farcical element in descriptions of foreplay, as when Hero, to avoid Leander, dives into her bedcovers:

> With both her hands she made the bed a tent,
> And in her own mind thought herself secure,
> O'ercast with dim and darksome coverture.

Her downward movement recalls Leander's own earlier descent into the sea in the toils of the sea-god Neptune and reminds readers that the sea is traditionally the place where the most profound transformations occur. Marlowe celebrates the initiation into sexuality as such a transformation even as he makes light of it. The more imposing phenomenology of the poem remains Ovidian: like the Roman poet, Marlowe illustrates human experience as comprising sequences of change, some foreseen and deliberate, others mysterious and unaccountable. Art and nature coalesce, then become distinct: human life is as "sliding" as Neptune's oceanic body.

Dr. Faustus

A play-text is not a play-in-performance and most students will recognize this without being told—instructors who exploit the talent of their student actors by asking them to read scenes aloud to the class, or better yet, actually use the classroom as an impromptu stage in order to present a scene or two will discover that the play-text they are teaching immediately comes to life. The play-text becomes a play, however amateurishly performed. And after a rehearsal or two (outside class), student readings usually improve a good deal.

It's as well to begin with a discussion of some background. In the case of Marlowe's *Dr. Faustus*, an account of the legendary scholar who had acquired an impressive erudition and yet sought a power that no education could provide will give students a chance to identify the principal themes of the play. An initial focus on what the early modern period thought were the proper limits of knowledge is a good way to introduce the choice that Faustus makes. Students should know that although some kinds of knowledge were forbidden, the beginnings of a post-Copernican science were even at this early date calling such strictures into question. Speculation can center specifically on the question of authority, whose it is, and at what price it is purchased. Is it the case that at some level Marlowe is representing in the career of Dr. Faustus one that he himself idealized yet at the same time could not but condemn? A very different set of considerations will emerge much later, as writers and thinkers of the Victorian age debate the relationship of science (or knowledge) and religious faith and morals. Interested students can jump ahead to The Debate on Science and Religion in the Victorian section of the anthology.

Students can prepare for in-class dramatic readings by reviewing the text in relation to the particular roles being played. Stanislowski's questions for actors provide an excellent way to open up a character's nature and development over the course of the play. Students can imagine themselves playing a particular role and ask of themselves "Who am I?" (that is, the "I" of the role), "What do I want?", "What's in my way?", "What am I willing to do to get it?", "What do I do if I do or do not get it?" These questions will not address the literary aspects of the play but they will transform its words into living speech, endow them with a personality and a motivation, and create for the class a stage "society," a representation of human beings in conflict. It's helpful if students refrain from intellectualizing a character's nature and development especially at first; the play will not come to life unless they can see for themselves why, at a human level, characters behave the way they do. Thereafter, the refinements of meaning that come from an investigation of images, themes, allusions, and word play will enrich but not obscure what is basic to theater: an encounter with a virtual reality that has the power to make itself more real than the reality our daily lives can offer.

A few points to focus on in each of the acts:

Act 1   The status of magic was vexed in Marlowe's day. Some thinkers believed that there was a difference between an allowable white magic, which simply sought by natural yet powerful means (precious stones and metals, charms and signs) to alter the elements of life so that they became useful to man, and a forbidden black magic, which sought by diabolical aid actually to create a second nature and therefore to rival God. Marlowe constructs his first scene so that these distinctions are clear. Faustus is in love with power; his evil angel states: "Be thou on earth as Jove is in the sky." But when Faustus seeks the assistance of Valdes and Cornelius, he masks this ambition and they understand that he will pursue a study that is recognized as licit. They mention books and authors who were well-known to students (though not necessarily practitioners) of white magic: Agrippa, Bacon, Albanus. From that point on, the action of the play is predictable: Faustus seeks a forbidden art, he buys it at the price of his immortal soul, and he cannot repent of this choice even on the brink of death.

Act 2   The character of Mephistophilis is central to understanding Faustus's temptation. On the one hand, he identifies where he is (or exists) as "hell, nor am I out of it" (1.3), a reflection that Milton's Satan will later echo. Hell is, in other words, not a place but a state of mind, one presumably so inflated with ambition, pride, and self-love that it denies all other creation. On the other hand, Mephistophilis is also a fount of knowledge. He knows the elements of creation, the structure of the world (2.1). He also knows how to create an illusion of life so powerful that it passes for life: in this respect, he and his pupil Faustus appear divine.

Act 3   Mephistophilis has the power to transform Faustus into a heavenly creature, one who flies about the earth in a magic chariot, a kind of parodic angel. The reference to "Saxon Bruno" and his defiance of the Pope in favor of the Apostle Peter signals Marlowe's depiction of Faustus as diabolically irreligious. Bruno not only defies the Pope and is therefore on the side of the Protestants; but he is also a Lollard and therefore to be considered a heretic even by Protestants. Faustus's part in supporting Bruno suggests a complete rejection of the authority of religion: Faustus is at once an ally of Bruno against the Pope, both heretical by English Protestant standards, and a damned necromancer who uses diabolical means to further his ends, whether Protestant or not. The act ends with a comic scene in which characters who would usually have been termed "clowns" encounter Mephistophilis. Students can consider how this scene effectively debases the tragedy of Faustus's life, which appears more and more to engage trivia as the action of the play progresses.

Act 4   Faustus loses status rapidly in the aftermath of his triumph over the Emperor. He sees his own end is near; his magic becomes cheap, like that of a common street magician. This deterioration mirrors his soul's growing degeneracy. In effect, Marlowe reveals that what sometimes passed for black magic was nothing more than a sleight of hand; its credit depended entirely on the extent to which it was believed. Studies of early modern magic are plentiful, and curious students will benefit from reading Wayne Schumaker's introduction to his edition of Renaissance treatises on magic: *Natural Magic and Modern Science: Four Treatises, 1590–1657* (1989).

Act 5   Faustus is damned but up to what point could he have repented and been saved? What element in tragedy is represented by the scholars' decision to give Faustus "due burial"? As one of the damned Faustus does not deserve such respect. But is Marlowe hinting that sheer intellectual power and love of learning, however much they are perverted, need to be noticed and admired? That they are nevertheless the only avenues to true greatness that human beings can aspire to? If so— and it is a big if—Marlowe's play denouncing intellectual ambition as a form of pride is also a play that celebrates this ambition as utterly and not despicably human. And because God created humanity, such ambition, even after the Fall, cannot go entirely despised and unrecorded.

There are two texts of this play, the A text, published in 1604, and the B text, published in 1616. The text used here is primarily the B text, with portions of the A text included.

William Shakespeare
The Sonnets

The language of Shakespeare's sonnets is prismatic; like a crystal that separates white light into a spectrum of colors from purple to red, it opens up to multiple meanings. Which ones a reader chooses to focus on depends, to a degree, on his or her interest and point of view. In that sense, the sonnets provide a kind of mirror of the self—not Shakespeare's self but that of the reader. It's important to allow students to experience the reflexive quality of these poems. Although students may not be satisfied that they have understood what Shakespeare meant in any conclusive way, they can be confident that second, third, and even fourth readings will continue to engage their interest and ingenuity. The class can discuss how and why poetic language avoids being denotative and instead gets its power from suggestion, allusion, association and—most important—from puns.

Shakespeare was a master-punster and nowhere more so than in the sonnets. Their most acute readings are registered in the definitive edition by Stephen Booth, *Shakespeare's Sonnets* (1977), which has the added advantage of providing a facsimile of the 1609 quarto on facing pages. (Students who go to this edition will be alerted to the difficulties of editing an early modern text: what appears in all modern editions, including this one, is a version of an original which may itself be partly the work of the printer or compositor who was responsible for setting type from a manuscript which may itself have been more or less readable.) Especially useful in its discovery of ambiguity, often generated by Shakespeare's recourse to puns, Booth's exhaustive and detailed commentary illustrates the dense complexity of Shakespeare's language. Looking at one or two sonnets in detail is a practical necessity.

Particularly rewarding is the magnificent pair (numbers 123 and 124 in the sequence), "No, Time, thou shalt not boast that I do change," and "If my dear love were but the child of state." Here Shakespeare juxtaposes themes and images of time with the ways human beings have devised to arrest its passage and destructive changes. The poems build their assertions of timelessness on the poet's reaction to the young man's betrayal of faith. They claim that the poet's love is eternal, that it will survive all material structures, all strategies (that is, "policy") that have been designed to cope with contingency. This is a treatment of the image of Time and temporality quite different from that seen earlier in Wyatt, Spenser, Marlowe and Raleigh. Some of this difference can be gauged by exploring questions of tone, especially irony.

The sonnets can also be read as a dramatic sequence, despite the fact that their order is probably not Shakespeare's. The poet's own voice, the characters he refers to, are clearly expressive of particular personalities: the young man, who causes the poet at first to feel intense affection and at last profound disappointment; the rival poet, who insinuates himself into the young man's affection; and the poet's lady friend, evidently a woman with whom he has easy and rather unsatisfactory sexual relations. It is difficult not to read the sonnets as a set of cues for what could be, in a larger and more capacious setting, a drama of romance, conflict, and even tragedy.

The class may need to be reminded of the work it did on *Hero and Leander*, for like that poem Shakespeare's sonnets express erotic love between men. Students, particularly women students, may be dismayed by the poet's disdain for his "dark lady." His vitriolic denunciations of her diseased condition (probably syphilis) are especially remarkable; they stand out by comparison with the gentle forbearance the poet expresses in the face of the young man's infidelity. Lifted out of their place in the sequence, the sonnets on the "dark lady" can be seen to exemplify a certain misogyny that was perhaps more a feature of early modern culture than it was specifically an attitude of the poet. Feminist scholarship has now documented the most important elements of early modern misogyny and its origins in classical philosophy and Christian theology. For a study of early modern literature on and about women, see Linda Woodbridge, *Women and the English Renaissance* (1984); for contemporary doctrine on the nature of woman, see Ian Maclean, *The*

Renaissance Notion of Woman (1980); and for analysis of the debate on the woman question, see Constance Jordan, *Renaissance Feminism: Literary Texts and Political Models* (1990) and Margaret R. Sommerville, *Sex and Subjection: Attitudes Towards Women in Early Modern Society* (1995).

Twelfth Night; or, *What You Will*
(Folio 1623)

The title connects this comedy with holiday festivities and specifically with the feast of the Epiphany, which occurs on January 6, the twelfth day of Christmas. The Epiphany commemorates the appearance of Christ to the Magi, or the three wise men. In the medieval tradition of these holiday festivities, a Feast of Fools was celebrated in which hierarchical authority was flouted and general feasting and merrymaking was licensed. The play expresses the world turned upside down spirit of the twelfth night celebration in Sir Toby's challenge to the sanctimonious steward Malvolio, "Dost thou think, because thou art virtuous, / there shall be no more cakes and ale?" (2.3.90). Even the puritanical Malvolio, who expects everyone to go to bed early and work as hard as he does, is not immune to the spirit of folly; a letter forged by Maria leads him to believe that his mistress Olivia is in love with him. For a thoroughgoing recreation of this literary medieval festival world, now challenged as cultural anthropological reality by social historians, see Mikhail Bakhtin's *Rabelais and His World.* Such elements in *Twelfth Night* as the role of the Fool and the wonderfully comic ambiguity of his language unite Shakespeare's play with the celebration of the body and desire that Bakhtin calls the carnivalesque. The playfulness of the language in *Twelfth Night* has a comic and erotic resonance. As Viola says at 3.1.10, "They that dally nicely with words may quickly make them wanton." Crucial to this carnivalesque spirit is this sense of parody, a comic send-up that at once celebrates and derides what it makes fun of. The foolishness of erotic desire is both celebrated and mocked in the stories of Orsino, who self-indulgently pines for Olivia from a distance while she rejects him, and of Olivia, who is instantly infatuated with a youth (actually Viola in disguise) who rebuffs her. The students can be asked to test the limits of this approach to the play as an expression of parody in so far as it does not fully account for the mockery of Malvolio, which is closer to satire. How is the audience's response to Malvolio's ridiculous self-portrayal as the yellow cross-gartered and grinning lover he believes Olivia want him to be different from their response to Toby's, Maria's, and even the Fool's manipulation of Malvolio as a madman penned up in a dark house? What is the difference between folly and this staged madness? And if the carnivalesque is a festival spirit that includes everyone, why then are Malvolio, Maria, Toby, Sir Andrew Aguecheek, and also Antonio left out of the celebration at the end of the play?

Part of the answer to this question lies in the genre of the play as a marriage comedy, with its conclusion in happily paired couples closing down other possibilities that it has set in motion. To understand the role of marriage and gender in the play it can be historicized in relation to the social context of sex and gender roles in early modern England and in relation to the portrayal of such roles in dramatic history. Much of the criticism on *Twelfth Night* has focused on the impact of the single sex model prevalent in the early modern period according to which women were simply thought of as inverted or defective males (for which, see Thomas Laqueur, *Making Sex* [1990]). The indeterminacy of sex and gender in the early modern period as evidenced in an account of hermaphroditism is the point of departure for Stephen Greenblatt's "Fiction and Friction in *Shakespearean Negotiations* (1988). Jonathan Crewe has characterized the desire that circulates in the scenes between Viola/Cesario and Orsino, and Viola/Cesario and Olivia as "no more definitively homosexual or heterosexual." ("In the Field of Dreams: Transvestism in *Twelfth Night* and the *Crying Game*," *Representations* [Spring 1995], 101–121). To enable students to imagine this free-floating desire, they need to be reminded of the anachronism of homosexuality as a concept and subculture in the early modern period (Alan Bray, *Homosexuality in Renaissance England* [1982]). Students could instead be encouraged to examine the very different social construction of sex in early modern gender roles as exhibited in such texts as *Hic Mulier; or the Man-Woman*, and *Haec-Vir; or the Womanish-Man*, excerpts from which are included in *Tracts on Women and Gender*. The transvestism that these texts describe is also an issue in the costuming of boy actors for female roles. The students need to be reminded that on Shakespeare's stage Viola/Cesario would have been played by a boy, playing a girl, playing a boy. At the same time, Viola's dressing as a boy gives her a kind of freedom in her exchanges with Orsino that make her more his equal and more his friend. All of this is in keeping with the emerging early modern ideal of companionate marriage, an eloquent defense of which may be read in Rachel Speght's *A Muzzle for Melastomus*, excerpts of which appear in "Tracts on Women and Gender." Viola's defense of women's love against Orsino's misogynist judgment of their passion and fidelity as inferior to men's (as in 2.4) needs to be contextualized in relation to the more equal moral status of women within the notion of friendship in marriage.

Another issue in the representation of sex and gender in *Twelfth Night* is the tradition of the eunuch. At the outset of the play Viola asks the Captain to present her to the Duke Orsino "as an eunuch to him" (1.2.56). Her role as castrato would explain her high pitched voice, which Orsino refers to admiringly as "thy small pipe . . . shrill and sound." These references to the eunuch connect the play to a whole tradition of comedies about sexual masquerade and the role of eunuchs. This tradition stretches back to ancient Rome in Terence's *Eunuchus* and forward to the Italian Renaissance in two different versions of *Gl'inganni* (1547; 1592), which at *Twelfth Night*'s first performance was recognized as similar in plot, and Bandello's novella, which was the basis of Barnabe Riche's romance "Of Apolonius and Silla" (1581), the narrative source of *Twelfth Night*. Keir Elam, the editor of the Arden edition of *Twelfth Night*, describes the much more graphic depiction of sex and the more explicit representation of upward social movement in these Italian sources to point out the more "civil" in the sense of polite and sexually restrained character of Shakespeare's text and the more conservative character of the social milieu of the English manor house in which it is set. (See Elam's "The Fertile Eunuch: *Twelfth*

Night, Early Modern Intercourse, and the Fruits of Castration" *Shakespeare Quarterly*, Vol. 47, Issue 1 [Spring 1996], 1-36.). Allowing the students to read or hear you recount even a simple summary of some of the Italian texts that form *Twelfth Night*'s dramatic genealogy that Elam describes would enable them to understand the cultural translation involved in adapting this material in an English context. Elam points out how Sir Andrew Aguecheek and Malvolio also represent types of the eunuch. Unlike Viola, who follows a downwardly mobile path in her disguise that lands her in a better position by the end of the play, their upward striving ends in frustration as do their failed comic courtship of Olivia.

In addition to playing off of Italian romance and dramatic ancestors, *Twelfth Night* also draws on lyric sources. Orsino's love lament which begins the play is replete with the Ovidian image of himself as the hunter Actaeon turned into a stag pursued by his own "desires, like fell and cruel hounds" (1.1.20-22). The students can be asked to make the connection between the hunt of love in this allusion to Ovid and in Wyatt's "Whoso List to Hunt," which is a translation of Petrarch. The Petrarchan love sonnet is also the model for Viola/Cesario's wooing of Olivia. The suffering of the lover, the beauty of the beloved, and the transporting quality of that beauty all come into play. Viola's assumption of the role of desiring subject can be compared to that of a woman writer in the Petrarchan tradition, Lady Mary Wroth. How, if at all, does the woman's assumption of the voice of the lover in *Twelfth Night* and in Wroth's lyrics change the character of this poetry? In relation to the Petrarchan tradition, students can also be asked to consider love lyrics by Sir Philip Sidney, Drayton and Campion. Particularly interesting is the comparison to Shakespeare's *Sonnets* with the gender ambiguity of the beloved. The young man who is the love object of the first part of Shakespeare's *Sonnets* is not unlike Viola/Cesario. Another consideration is the social and political deployment of Petrarchan conventions with the court as a form of elaborate compliment to Elizabeth, described both in Greenblatt's "To Fashion a Gentleman" in *Renaissance Self-Fashioning* and in Tennenhouse's *Power on Display* (1986).

The songs of Feste that run throughout the play deserve special attention for their lyric brilliance and musicality. Students should know that these songs were set to music and could even listen to CDs of such settings, or could watch scenes of the video in which Feste sings. Our audio CD pairs Orsino's melancholy opening speech with Purcell and Heveningham's far more celebratory song "If music be the food of love, play on," vividly illustrating the ways in which British musical tradition continued to play on, and even against, Shakespeare's poetry.

Provocative questions for discussion include: How does the language of the play (especially in 1.5 and 2.4) show that Viola's role as a feminine man make her appealing both to Olivia and to Orsino? To what extent are we disturbed that Sebastian is willing to marry a woman he hardly knows, and that Olivia is open to a continued relationship with him despite the fact she finds out that he is not Cesario? Or do we suspend disbelief and simply celebrate the hilarious fun of this? How does the second title for the play, the only one in the Shakespeare canon, "What You Will" relate to the play's action and characterization? Consider that "will" in early modern English meant decision, wish, and irrational desire. The name Malvolio contains the Latin roots *mal-*, ill or evil, and *volere*, to will or to desire, a root also present in anagrammatic form in Olivia's and Viola's names. How does the exclusion of Malvolio, Maria, Toby, Sir Andrew and Antonio from the comic ending influence the way we feel about the conclusion of the play?

The Tempest
(Folio, 1623)

To a large extent *The Tempest* is about power. The dramatic presentation of the terrifying power of the tempest at the start of the play followed by the revelation of Prospero's power to create and quell it sets in motion an exploration of how his power as magus is analogous to the power of theatre to alter our view of reality. Ask the students to observe the meta-theatrical aspects of the text—for example, the way Prospero functions as author and director, with the help of Ariel as stage manager. Draw their attention to the anti-masque (3.3) where, as Prospero says, his "enemies are all knit up / In their distractions" (3.3.89–90), and to the marriage masque, which Prospero famously refers to as "this insubstantial pageant faded" (4.1.155). Explain to the students how these scenes staged within the play disrupt the audience's involvement in the action to reflect on the artifice behind it. As an example of the form of the masque, the students can be asked to consider Ben Jonson's *Pleasure Reconciled to Virtue*. Jonson's masque and the marriage masque in *The Tempest* share such elements as the iconography of the pagan gods, didactic moral allegory in verse, and the theme of conflict resolved. An important article on this topic is David Bevington's "*The Tempest* and the Jacobean Court Masque," in David Bevington and Peter Holbrook (eds.), *The Politics of the Stuart Court Masque* (Cambridge: Cambridge UP, 1998). The self-referentiality of the play is also symbolized in Prospero's "art" or "magic." This metaphor of magic for the power of drama can be compared and contrasted with the metaphor of alchemy as the power to transform reality in Jonson's *Alchemist*.

The Tempest is not only about the power of art but also about the power of government and of knowledge. The twin plots of Prospero's punishment of his brother Antonio who usurped his power over the dukedom of Milan and the comical insurrection of Caliban, Stefano, and Trinculo are concerned with questions about authority, the right to rule, and the responsibilities of the ruler. Gonzalo's famous speech about how he would rule the perfect "commonwealth" according to the model of the Golden Age (2.1.142–47), where there would be no work, poverty or need for formal government, is an example of utopianism, closely based on John Florio's translation (1603) of Michel de Montaigne's "Of the Cannibals." Gonzalo's claim that there would be no need for "sovereignty" in his commonwealth is shown to be naïve and unreal in contrast to the struggles over sovereignty that dominate the play as a whole. There is first of all Prospero's struggle over the dukedom of Milan, which is successfully resolved by the marriage of Miranda and Ferdinand. Second, there are Caliban's protestations of his rightful claim to the island as a native inhabitant: "This island's mine by Sycorax my mother, / Which thou tak'st from me" (1.2.332). Postcolonial readings of the play have sympathetically read Caliban's voice as a defense of the rights of indigenous peoples and a critique of slavery. Since his name is an anagram of cannibal, it links his portrayal with early modern ethnographic stereotyping of the inhabitants of the Americas as bestial man-eaters, without civilization, used to rationalize their subjugation under European colonialism. That the portrayal of Caliban both evokes this demonization and its contestation makes the reader aware of how knowledge is constructed and used to control power over the world.

If Prospero's power stands for the power of the stage and of the state, it also stands for the power of the father within the family. In this context, Miranda as daughter has often been seen by critics as merely her father's pawn, conforming to the ideals of chastity, silence, and obedience, prescribed for women by the conduct books of the time. For this reason, many editors from Dryden in the eighteenth century to Kittredge in this century have assigned the "Abhorred slave" speech (I.2.352–363) to Prospero rather than to Miranda. Ask your students how the editorial decision to reassign this speech to Prospero rather than to Miranda, as it is printed in the Folio, changes the meaning of the play. You can also ask them to look for other passages in the play where Miranda displays an independent spirit, most notably at the end of Act 1, scene 1, where she speaks out on behalf of Ferdinand to protect him from her father's charges. With the exception of the mention of Caliban's mother Sycorax, who is portrayed as a witch, mature women and mothers are absent from this play.

The play was originally listed in the 1623 Folio as a comedy, but modern critics have invented the category of romance for *The Tempest*, *The Winter's Tale*, *Cymbeline*, and *Pericles*. Romance refers to a more symbolical and fantastical plot as well as one that moves from one world to another. Romance also tends towards a more self-referential presentation. While there is much self-conscious artfulness and fantasy in *The Tempest*, there are also references to the contemporary world, especially to exploration and colonization (for more about which, see the Companion Readings to *The Tempest*). It is particularly important to note, as the Oxford University Press editor Stephen Orgel (1987) does, that the very serious issues raised by *The Tempest*, such as the desire for revenge versus the possibility of reconciliation and forgiveness, justice and mercy, death and rebirth, and the relation between power and authority, ally this text with tragedy as well. For this reason, the play is sometimes referred to as a tragic-comedy. You can ask your students to explore the limits of the generic labels comedy, romance, and tragic-comedy to a reading of the play.

COMPANION READINGS

William Strachey

from *A True Repertory of the Wrack and the Redemption of Sir Thomas Gates, upon and from the Islands of Bermuda (1625)*

The first companion reading is selected because it is one of a number of documents that recounts the shipwreck of the *Sea Adventure* in 1609, which was the inspiration for *The Tempest*'s initial scenes of shipwreck and providential deliverance, the subplot of a conspiracy to rebel, as well as the title of the play. The language of *The Tempest* also echoes the connections between hard work, temperance, chastity, and fertility on the one hand and sloth, riot, and famine on the other that characterize the colonial ethos of William Strachey's *A True Repertory of the Wrack and the Redemption of Sir Thomas Gates, upon and from the Islands of Bermuda.* Although this text was not published until 1625, it circulated in manuscript as early as 1610. The text relates how a hurricane caused the shipwreck of a group of 400 English colonists, who had been sent across the Atlantic to Jamestown, Virginia. This venture was funded by the Virginia Company which was founded by a royal charter in 1606, and then became a joint stock company in 1609. Prominent members of this company, such as the Earl of Southampton were known to Shakespeare and could have shared the manuscript of Strachey's account with him.

Recommended reading on the relation between *The Tempest* and travel literature includes: Charles Frey's "*The Tempest* and the New World," *Shakespeare Quarterly* 30.1 (1979), 29–41, as well as Stephen Greenblatt's "Martial Law in the Land of Cockaigne," in R. S. White (ed.), *The Tempest* (New York: St. Martin's Press, 1999). An interesting article that links the allusions to Virginia with the elements of the masque in the play and its performance at court for the wedding of the princess Elizabeth to the Elector Palatine is John Gillies' "Shakespeare's Virginian Masque," in *ELH* 53, 4 (Winter, 1986), 673–707. Gillies finds that the connections between chastity, temperance, and landscape in *The Tempest* connect it with "the Ovidian construct of Virginia, the temperate and virginal land whose chastity is threatened by her own 'ruder natives.'" A stimulating article which challenges Shakespeare's dependence on Strachey's letter and suggests as a more likely intertext James Rosier's *A True Relation of the most prosperous voyage made this present yeere 1605, by Captain George Waymouth in the discovery of the land of Virginia* is Arthur Kinney's "Revisiting The Tempest" *Modern Philology* 95.2 (1995): 161–177, reprinted in a generally useful collection edited by Patrick M. Murphy, *The Tempest: Critical Essays* (New York and London: Routledge, 2001).

Michel de Montaigne
from "Of Cannibals" (1603)

The second companion reading shows Montaigne at his skeptical best questioning whether New World cannibalism was actually less barbarous than the European practice of "eating men alive." Montaigne's portrayal of the cannibals' revenge as a form of a heroic martial code is part of his larger strategy of likening the Amerindians to the heroes of ancient Greece and Rome. Shakespeare's Caliban is not granted such heroic nobility but he does by virtue of lyrical beauty of the lines of verse that he speaks manage to capture the imaginative vision of the place more than any other character. You could ask students to explain whether or not they think *The Tempest* participates in Montaigne's questioning of European conceptions of civility versus barbarism. How and to what extent does Shakespeare's text allow the reader to question Prospero's power and endorse Caliban's curses upon him? For a recent comparative analysis of Montaigne and Shakespeare, see Arthur Kirsch, "Virtue, Vice, and Compassion in Montaigne and The Tempest," *Studies in English Literature*, no. 2 (Spring 1997), 337–52.

England in the New World

The contributions to this Perspectives section convey some of the complicated and at times conflicted images and impressions coming to the English reading public from their outposts in America during the first years of the seventeenth century. Reports from "Virginia," the name given to the territory along the Atlantic coast from Cape Hatteras to what is now Nova Scotia, illustrate experiences that were interpreted by particular interests in often opposed ways. The second book of More's *Utopia* provides a useful blueprint by which to assess the earliest examples of this literature. While Hythlodaeus represented a wholly rational society in which all property was common, a kind of up-to-date and Europeanized new world, exponents of American colonization (like Drayton) spoke of a Golden Age, both figurative and real. There Nature was entirely generous and the precious metal lay everywhere, just under the surface of the soil, ready to make the diligent colonist rich beyond his wildest dreams. But the reports of the men, and eventually the women, who actually crossed the Atlantic to colonize its coastal regions also depicted lives of dire hardship, near escapes, and backbreaking labor. Such harrowing narratives invoked scriptural models of endeavor, in which ordinary privation pointed to providential outcomes in the long run. Common to all the texts in this section is their preoccupation with new societies; while alienated in mind and body from their English origins, they are nevertheless entirely dependent on English sources for their understanding of what is happening to them.

Students can be asked to imagine how those who stayed at home in England read this literature. Did it convey an invitation to enjoy an effortless life of plenty or did it issue a command to pursue a strenuous regime of self sacrifice? And what had changed in the English vision of the New World and colonial enterprise between the first decade of the 1500s, when More constructed his state of a rational "nowhere," and 1608, when John Smith chronicled his experience in Jamestown? Raleigh's account of Guiana can usefully introduce students to the strange mixture of fantasy (the account of the Amazons) and reality (the portrait of the King of Aromaia) that so often characterizes early colonial literature. Raleigh makes little effort to distinguish what we would term a "fact"—can we infer that for him an experience could seem too strange to categorize as real? Or was he rather wishing to impress his readers with the exotic nature of this new world?

Drayton's "Ode to Virginia" recalls the terms in which Arthur Barlow couched his idyllic account of Virginia; by contrast, Smith's unblinking assessment of Virginia's actual trials of body and spirit minimizes the riches colonists could expect to extract from "Virginia" and stresses rather the need for hard work and an orderly society, one committed to the preservation of liberty but not to the promotion of license. His love of detail leads him to perform astonishing acts of ventriloquism, as he tells his readers what Powhatan said to him about the English presence on his land and their mission there. How far, can we judge, is Smith constructing an image of the Powhatans; and would his apparent sympathy for the Indian be interpretable at home? Students who have read *The Tempest* can be asked to reflect on the sense of mission, catastrophe, and deliverance conveyed by Strachey in his account of the wreck off the Bermudas and its later and most lyrical counterpart in Marvell's poem of that name. In what sense is *The Tempest* also a play of deliverance? and from what? The figure of Caliban may have struck English audiences as an archetype of the New World native: how does Caliban convey his status as a man and how are we to understand Prospero's terming him a "slave"? Montaigne's essay "Of Cannibals" can provide a interesting perspective in which to answer these questions.

Donne's sermon to the Virginia Company reveals yet another aspect of early colonial literature. With the Indian massacre of in 1622 doubtless on his mind, Donne sees the colony's future very differently than did Drayton just a few years earlier. Students can discuss Donne's moralized account of what caused the massacre of the colonists in Jamestown in 1622 and how it reflects his understanding of the apostolic mission in Acts. How does his sermon give a new meaning to the idea of "wealth"? And how does his vision fit with the triumphalism implied in earlier commentaries, especially that of Hariot, who spoke of how advantageous it would be for the English to represent themselves to the Indians as gods?

Ffrethorne's letter from Jamestown, Bradford's *On the Plymouth Plantation*, and Rowlandson's narrative of her captivity by the Pequot tribes in Massachusetts, although separated by time and place, all depict lives in the New World as informed by events recorded in Scripture. The figure of analogy leads these writers to an understanding of what is happening to them. The Psalms were a textual means by which to bind the present with what was taken to be divine history. Do these texts as a whole show that the Bible was thought of as providing a key to the code in which the real events of the world were represented? Does this belief affect how these writers represent human action? Students can compare Bradford's attitude toward the Pequots with Smith's toward the Powhatans. How are they different? Rowlandson suggests that she and her Indian captors engaged in a two-way traffic of material things and ideas: does her narrative suggest a kind of negotiation between the parties?

By comparing the narratives of Ffrethorne and Revel, students can identify the difference between an autobiographical account of a period of time, and its reconstruction as an element in a moralized history. The writer's point of view is key; while Ffrethorne has to contend with representing present dangers, Revel can place each event in a historical perspective and give a meaning to the whole from a point of view transcending those of particular moments. The question of which narrative, Ffrethorne's or Revel's, is more faithful to reality can provoke reflections on the kinds of truth conveyed in literature—historical, psychological, moral, and religious—as well as the ways in which the writer discovers and values each alone or in some combination of them. A number of useful studies that focus on English appreciations of the new world are now available: *America in European Consciousness, 1493–1750*, edited by Karen Kupperman, 1995, collects a number of essays illustrating how the experience of exploration and colonization refashioned English sensibilities and aspirations.

Thomas Dekker and Thomas Middleton
The Roaring Girl, or Moll Cut-Purse (1611)

Since students sometimes find the double plot of Sebastian Wengrave's mock court-ing of Moll Cutpurse and the complicated intrigues between Mistresses Gallipot and Openwork and their seducers Laxton and Goshawk confusing, you need to take some time at the outset to explain not just what is going on in each plot but the relation between the two plots. A helpful article on this topic is Viviana Comensoli's "Play-Making, Domestic Conduct, and the Multiple Plot in *The Roaring Girl*," *Studies in English Literature* 27.2 (Spring 1987), 249–66. You can ex-plain that both plots are about marriage. While Sir Alexander Wengrave is at first primarily concerned that his son marry a young lady who will bring with her a large dowry, he ends up settling for a marriage prospect who at least has a sure fem-inine gender. His outrage over what he perceives as the monstrosity of Moll can be connected with the tradesmen's wives' fear that their chastity should be questioned by their husbands. In all these marriages, chastity and all the behavior that it re-quires is a value. Such comments as Laxton's "money is the aquafortis that eats into many a maidenhead" (2.2), as he is lusting after Moll, further adumbrate the no-tion of a woman's sexuality as something that can be bought and sold.

Moll's famous speech in which she rebukes Laxton with "thou'rt one of those / That thinks each woman thy fond flexible whore" contests this view as does her in-domitable independence throughout the comedy. Her comment in this same speech "Better had women fall into the hands / Of an act silent that a bragging nothing" reflects back upon the concern of the female characters in *The Roaring Girl* with their public reputations. A useful article to consult for the examination of Moll's role as iconoclastic social critic is Jane Baston's "Rehabilitating Moll's Subversion in *The Roaring Girl*," *Studies in English Literature* 37.2 (Spring 1997), 317–335. The articles on *The Roaring Girl* in Susan Zimmerman's *Erotic Politics: Desire on the Renaissance Stage* (1992) are also an excellent source to consult in order to open up *The Roaring Girl* for discussion in terms of the representation of gender and sexuality.

The fact that Moll can back up her challenge to Laxton ("I scorn to prostitute myself to a man, / I that can prostitute a man to me") with a show of arms unites her with the female warrior Britomart in Spenser's chivalric epic *The Faerie Queene*. An important difference, however, is that Moll moves not in the aristocratic and sylvan romance world of Spenser's knights but in the streets of London. Not only must she overpower her opponents but she must constantly outwit them. And it is this element of cunning improvisation that she shares in common with Mistress

Gallipot, who convinces her husband that Laxton is suing her for pre-contract, and Mistress Openwork, who persuades her husband to ambush Goshawk. All three female characters show their power to manipulate the plot. It could be argued that they manipulate the plot for conventional ends—the two tradesmen's wives for the continuation of their marriages, and Moll for the successful suit of Sebastian Wengrave for the hand of Mary Fitzallard. Students can be asked to question how subversive this comedy really is since it promotes marriage, chastity, and the importance of a woman's reputation while it pokes fun at all three. Moll's refusal of marriage at the end of the play makes possible the conventional ending of comedy—the happy marriage of the lovers and their reconciliation with the older generation. Nevertheless, much is said along the way, not only by Moll, but also by the citizens and their wives to question the sentimental ending. Perhaps this city cynicism is nowhere better expressed than in Openwork's "What's this whole world but a gilt rotten pill?" Underlying this world-weary wisdom is an optimism about the street smarts of citizens.

The Roaring Girl and Its Time: City Life   This section provides a context for the literature of the city by presenting some observations on overcrowding, street slang, crime, weaving, shopping, theatre going, and tobacco smoking. More than covering these social topics, the selections in this section also give the students an idea of popular writing, as opposed to aristocratic or scholarly humanistic writing. Crime could be the object of a humorous story, as in Greene's *A Notable Discovery of Cosenage* and Thomas Dekker's *Lantern and Candlelight*, or the object of censorious diatribe, as in Barnabe Riche's *My Lady's Looking-glass* (1616), or even mock-serious invective, as in Thomas Nashe's broadly satiric *Pierce Penniless* (1592).

All of these readings work well with the drama. An excellent source for both the city and the drama is David L. Smith, Richard Strier, and David Bevington's *The Theatrical City: Culture, Theatre, and Politics in London* (1995). *The Roaring Girl*, which is set in London, makes frequent references to London low-life and even uses the canting slang recorded in Dekker's *Lantern and Candlelight*—especially in Act 5. The outrageousness of Moll's smoking a pipe can best be explained to students with reference to King James I's *A Counterblast to Tobacco* (1616), in which students can read that tobacco was imported from the New World and commonly known as a cure for venereal disease. The Crown attempted to prohibit the lower classes from using it.

The Alchemist also works well with this section. The sense of city people living by their wits can be seen both in the rogue literature and the drama—for example, Moll in *The Roaring Girl*, and Face and Subtle in *The Alchemist*. An excellent introduction to early modern rogue literature is Arthur Kinney's *Rogues, Vagabonds, and Sturdy Beggars: A New Gallery of Tudor and Early Stuart Rogue Literature* (1990).

Another topic which comes up in both *The Roaring Girl* and *The Alchemist* is trade and the market economy. From the ever-present concern of the characters with money in *The Roaring Girl* to the get rich quick dreams of the characters in *The Alchemist*, the constant drive to increase one's capital appears frequently in this period. Even such works in the high style as Milton's epic *Paradise Lost* are full of the metaphors of exchange. If Jonson's *Alchemist* is as a criticism of greed, its portrayal of worldly goods is a far cry from the simple morality of Chaucer's *Pardoner's Tale* which bears the motto *pecunia radix malorum est*. In response to the emergence of capitalism, such authors as Jonson comment on not only the exploitation and deceit but also the sheer genius involved in making money out of money, a process which Jonson more than once likens to the trickery of the playwright in convincing his audience that what is fictional is real.

PERSPECTIVES

Tracts on Women and Gender

Desiderius Erasmus
In Laude and Praise of Matrimony (trans. Richard Tavernour, 1534)

Two sources for contextualizing Erasmus's text and the other texts in this section are Linda Woodbridge's *Women and the English Renaissance: Literature and the Nature of Womankind, 1540–1620* (1986) and Constance Jordan's *Renaissance Feminism: Literary Texts and Political Models* (1990). The question of whether or not discourse on the nature of women before Mary Wollstonecraft's *A Vindication of the Rights of Women* (see Volume 2: *The Romantics and Their Contemporaries*) is feminist is discussed by Denise Riley in "*Am I That Name?*" (a book which takes its title from Desdemona's line in *Othello*). It is important for students to understand that the whole notion of companionate marriage is a middle-class and an early modern innovation. While Lawrence Stone has stressed the greater value given to marriage in Protestant culture, early modern Catholic authors such as Erasmus were also concerned with marriage. You can ask your students how closely Erasmus's view toward marriage resembles that of the many texts from the early modern period which focus on marriage—including Spenser's *Epithalamion*, Milton's *Paradise Lost*, and Dekker's and Middleton's *The Roaring Girl*. A further topic for discussion would be to compare and contrast the point of view of Chaucer's Wife of Bath with Erasmus's view in this moral essay.

Barnabe Riche
My Lady's Looking-Glass (1616)

This book falls into the genre of conduct book, and so can be compared with Castiglione's *Book of the Courtier*. The title *Looking Glass* refers to the Mirror of Princes genre; most early modern conduct books presented their middle-class audiences with a model for behavior adapted from that of the aristocratic court. The requirement that the lady should stay at home rather than gad about town can be applied to a reading of the female characters in Dekker's and Middleton's *Roaring Girl*, where not only Moll Cutpurse but even the shopkeepers' wives do not conform to the strict code of the quiet, stay-at-home, hard-working housewife. The Protestant trope of the Catholic Church as the Whore of Babylon is an example of how religious identity was symbolically represented through gender difference. See Frances Dolan, *Whores of Babylon: Catholicism, gender difference, and seventeenth-century print culture* (1999).

Riche's complaint against idolatry needs to be explained in terms of Protestant destruction of images in churches. See Eamon Duffy's *The Stripping of the Altars* (1992).

Margaret Tyler
Preface to The First Part of the Mirror of Princely Deeds (1578)

This argument in favor of women's writing and education can be compared to
Juan Luis Vives's comments on women's education in *Instruction of a Christian
Woman*. For a Spanish woman's defense of female literacy, see Sor Juana Inez de
la Cruz's letter (translated by Alan Trueblood, University of Oklahoma Press). It
is interesting to note that both Tyler and Elizabeth Cary moved in Catholic circles. Translation was a common endeavor for educated early modern women—perhaps because it was less adventuresome than original work. At the same time,
translation allowed women to display not only their ability to write but also their
knowledge of languages. See Betty Travitsky's comments on Tyler in *The Paradise
of Women* (1981).

The next three texts need to be considered as a group: **Joseph Swetnam,** *The
Arraignment of Lewd, Idle, Froward, and Unconstant Women* (1615); **Rachel Speght,** *A
Muzzle for Melastomous* (1617); **Esther Sowernam,** *Ester Hath Hang'd Haman* (1617).
Swetnam's comic diatribe was interpreted as a serious slander against women by
both Rachel Speght and the pseudonymous Ester Sowernam. Barbara Lewalski's
chapter on Speght in *Writing Women in Jacobean England* (1993) and her edition of
A Muzzle in Polemics and Poems of Rachel Speght (1996) are the best sources for background on Speght. Ann Jones's "Counterattacks on 'the Bayter of Women': Three
Pamphleteers of the Early Seventeenth Century" (Hazelcornand Travitsky,, eds.
The Renaissance Englishwoman in Print [1990]) gives insight into the more secular
view of Esther Sowernam. The notion of marriage as an economic market as portrayed in *The Roaring Girl*—for example, Sir Alexander's demand that his son marry
a wealthy girl—can be connected with Sowernam (see Megan Matchinske's article
in *ELR* 1994). For Speght and Sowernam, also see the introductions to their texts
by Simon Shepherd (1985).

Hic Mulier *and* Haec-Vir (1620)

These two texts parodying the outspokenness of the masculine woman and the
foppishness of the feminine man might be taken by students as purely fantastical. In addition to the historical Mary Frith, upon whom the Moll Cutpurse of
The Roaring Girl was based, there were many other examples of female trans-
vestitism in early modern England, notably among such aristocrats, such as
James I's cousin Arabella Stuart. Also, the issue of dress suitable to one's gender
was a serious issue for Protestant authors such as John Calvin and Philip Stubbes
who wrote in *The Anatomie of Abuses* (1583): "What man soever weareth woman's
apparel is accursed, and what woman weareth man's apparel is accursed also." A
letter by John Chamberlain of 1620 recounts how the clergy of London "had express commandment from the King to will them to inveigh vehemently against
the insolency of our women, and their wearing of broad-brimmed hats, pointed
doublets, their hair cut short or shorn." (See Valerie Lucas, "Hic Mulier: The

Female Transvestite in Early Modern England," *Renaissance and Reformation*. 24.1, [1988], 65–84). Woman's dress was viewed in the early modern period as an expression of woman's subordinate status to man. Hic Mulier's argument in *Haec Vir* that customs of dress change from place to place is no less than an attack on the notion of gender difference as ordained by the law of natural reason. These representations of cross-dressing can be connected to Viola's disguise as Cesario in *Twelfth Night*. You can ask students to what extent Viola as Cesario transgresses the limits set for a woman's conduct in the early modern period. These texts can be used to get the students to focus on dress as a discourse not only of sexuality but also of class. See, for example, Malvolio's dressing as Olivia's lover as a transgression of his role as servant. Students need to be informed of the sumptuary laws that restricted the use of the most expensive fabrics to the nobility. Deloney's story of Simon the Weaver's wife from *Thomas of Reading* (see *The Roaring Girl and Its Time: City Life*) displays a middle-class preoccupation with acquiring costly apparel similar to the fascination with lavish dress in *Hic Mulier* and *Haec Vir*.

Thomas Campion

One of the chief things to stress in teaching Campion is that his lyrics were written to be sung. Perhaps more than any other lyric poet of his time, Campion was profoundly influenced by such musicians as John Dowland and Philip Rosseter. If it is at all possible, bring a tape or CD to class to introduce the students to the sound of these lyrics sung to the accompaniment of the lute. For a helpful article explicating the relation between Campion's verse and music, see Stephen Ratcliffe, "Words and Music: Campion and the Song Tradition," in Patrick Cheney and Anne Lake Prescott (eds.), *Approaches to Teaching Shorter Elizabethan Poetry* (New York: MLA, 2000). A useful article for comparing Campion to Spenser and discussing the meaning of flower imagery in Elizabethan lyric poetry is Julia Reinhard Lupton's "Sex and the Shorter Poem," also in Cheney and Prescott (eds.), *Approaches to Teaching Shorter Elizabethan Poetry* (2000). For Campion's metrics and a commentary on *Rose Cheeked Laura Come*, see Seth Weiner, "Spenser's Study of English Syllables and its Completion by Thomas Campion," *Spenser Studies* 3 (1982), 3–56. In Drayton's *Observations on the Art of English Poesie* (1602), *Rose Cheeked Laura Come* is given as an example of "The English *Sapphick*":

> Dimeter, whose first foote may be a *Sponde* or a *Trochy*. The two verses following are both of them *Trochaical*, and consist of foure feete, the first of either of them being a *Spondee* or *Trochy*, the other three only *Trochyes*. The fourth and last verse is made of two *Trochyes*. The number is voluble and fit to express any amorous conceit.

You need to point out that Campion's work is heavily indebted to Latin poetry. *My sweetest Lesbia, let us live and love* is based on Catullus V, "Vivamus, mea Lesbia, atque amemus." *When thou must home to shades of underground* is based on Propertius II.xxviii. 49–52.

Michael Drayton

Drayton's *To the Reader* can be compared with Jonson's comments on style in *Timber* in *Perspectives: Emblem, Style, Metaphor*. Students can also be asked to compare and contrast Drayton's sonnets with Shakespeare's and Sidney's, and read the work of all three poets in relation to the Petrarchan tradition. For an article that takes up the influence of Petrarch upon Drayton's sonnet sequence, see Ted Brown, " 'When First I Ended, Then I First Began': Petrarch's *Triumph* in Michael Drayton's *Idea*" in David C. Allen and Robert A. White (eds.), *Subjects on the World's Stage: Essays on British Literature of the Middle Ages and the Renaissance* (Newark: U of Delaware P, 1995). You could design a whole unit on the sonnet that would take the students from Wyatt through to Drayton, having the students observe the English adaptation of this Petrarchan form. Beginning with Wyatt's early translations of Petrarch, you could have students examine how the sonnet is changed, both in terms of the topics it treats and the form it takes in English verse. The concreteness of the event described in Drayton's poetry and the masculine persona are not unlike that of Wyatt's poetry. The witty eroticism of Drayton's *To His Coy Love, A Canzonet* can well be compared with the tone of Donne's early lyric love poetry.

Ben Jonson
The Alchemist
(Quarto 1612, Folio 1616)

The Alchemist, which roundly satirizes a wide array of early modern professions and schools of belief, can usefully be connected with other texts in this section in relation to the following topics: magic as a means of transforming the world; self-referential allusions to the theatre and to the machinery of drama; the setting of the city of London. *The Alchemist* works extremely well when taught alongside *Dr. Faustus* and *The Tempest*, since all three plays are concerned with magic and connect it with the drive to know, control and profit from the world. Magic as secret knowledge is imbued with the enslaving power of the demonic in *Dr. Faustus*, and with the creativity of the demiurge and the absolute control of the monarch in *The Tempest*. In *The Alchemist*, however, magic is thoroughly debunked as a fraud and a scam. As Surly puts it in Act 2.3.180–1: "Alchemy is a pretty kind of game, / Somewhat like tricks o' the cards, to cheat a man / With charming." And yet almost everyone in the world of the play wants to play the game, whether to improve their luck at gambling, to make a killing in business, to realize dreams to untold wealth or to become a London wit.

The fraudulent and ridiculous character of the search for the philosopher's stone to transform base metals into gold is also underscored throughout by the nonsensical character of alchemical jargon, which is mirrored in the discourse of Puritan biblical exegesis as parodied by Dol in her fits, and the discourse of courtly amorousness as counterfeited in Spanish by the waggish Surly who manages for a time to best the scoundrel alchemists at their own game. If alchemy is sent up as a fraud, it is not condemned here. No one suffers that seriously as a result of these pranks. And no one learns much of anything either. If Faustus suffers for his hubristic pact with the devil to gain knowledge, and if Prospero ultimately has to renounce his magic in order for resolution to be achieved, Face returns to his initial role as Jeremy the Butler, only having amused himself and the audience and made a small profit that he must cede to his master Lovewit.

Andrew Gurr has suggested that Lovewit as one who profits from the hoaxes of Face and Subtle is a figure for Shakespeare as a joint owner of the Blackfriars Theatre where the play was first performed. See Andrew Gurr, "Who is Lovewit? What is he?" in Richard Allen, Elizabeth Schafer, and Brian Wolland, (eds.), *Ben Jonson and Theatre: Performance, Practice, and Theory* (London and New York: Routledge, 1999). The play abounds in theatrical jokes including Face's description of the costume of the Don (actually Surly) as like "Hieronymo's old cloak," (4.7) i.e. the costume worn by this character in Kyd's *The Spanish Tragedy* (1587). (Hieronymo is a role said to have been once played by Jonson himself.) By allowing the audience to witness costume changes, changes of character, and multiple exits and entrances, the play lays bare how the theatre functions.

That the play takes place during the season of the plague, during which Lovewit is out of town, is another significant meta-theatrical reference, since the theatres were closed during times of plague. The play abounds in references to the London of its day and can be read in conjunction with *The Roaring Girl* as a depiction of city life. Both plays depict the lowlife world of confidence men and prostitutes. *The Alchemist* juxtaposes the specialized pretentious jargon of alchemy against the street smart slang of the London underworld.

Useful articles to consult in order to contextualize the play include: Richard A. Burt, "Licensed by Authority": Ben Jonson and the Politics of Early Stuart Theatre," *ELH*, 54.3 (Autumn 1987), 529-560; Susan Wells, "Jacobean City Comedy and the Ideology of the City" *ELH*, 48.1 (Spring 1981), 37-60.

Poems (Folio 1616; Folio 1640)

Two excellent studies of Jonson's poetry are Wesley Trimpi, *Ben Jonson's Poems: A Study of the Plain Style* (1962), and Richard S. Peterson, *Imitation and Praise in the Poems of Ben Jonson* (1981). The first five poems printed here were all published under the heading "Epigrams" in the 1616 Folio edition of Jonson's *Works*. In May 1612, the printer Joseph Stepneth entered "A Book Called Ben Jonson His Epigrams" in the Stationers' Register, but the book was never printed. Most of these epigrams would appear to have been written before 1612. The collection was dedicated to William, Earl of Pembroke, a literary patron and the nephew of Sir Philip Sidney.

Jonson's classical model is Martial, and his concern throughout is with the praise of virtue and the criticism of vice. He adopts the perspective of an unsentimental moral critic and a worldly-wise satirist. *On Something That Walks Somewhere* mocks the pretensions of the ambitious in terms that focus on dress ("in clothes brave / enough to be a courtier") which makes it possible to connect this poem with the early modern discourse on clothing in such works as *Hic Mulier/Haec Vir*. This economical poem in four couplets of iambic pentameter ends on a savagely funny note: "Good lord, walk dead still."

In contrast with Jonson's satirical vein are the two profoundly moving and personal poems on his children, On My First Daughter and On My First Son. David
Riggs (Ben Jonson, A Life [1989]) calls On My First Daughter "an exercise in
Mariolotry" and so dates it "after Jonson's conversion to Catholicism in October
1598" (86). The contrast between the two poems makes for an interesting discussion in terms of the attitude toward death, and the metrical form that conveys
these differing attitudes. The greater metrical complexity, the almost halting character of the poem read aloud, and the greater use of enjambment in the poem on
his son need to be pointed out to students. There is an emphasis on the "mother"
in the poem on his daughter and an emphasis on the "father" in the poem on his
son. The complex association between paternity and writing in the poem on his
son make for an interesting analysis of gender in Jonson's writing. You can connect
the representation of paternity here with that in the Cary-Morison Ode.

Joseph Lowenstein's Responsive Readings: Versions of Echo in Pastoral, Epic and the
Jonsonian Masque (1984) is a good place to turn for the explication of Inviting a
Friend to Supper and Queen and Huntress from Cynthia's Revels 5.6.1–18. Both can be
discussed in relation to the topic of patronage, and Jonson's social position. David
Riggs (1989) asks about Inviting a Friend to Supper: "Does Jonson describe a meal
that he intends to serve or one that he wishes he could afford to serve?" The line
"we will have no Pooly or Parrot by") suggest the threat of spies, since Robert Poley
and Henry Parrot were just that.

To Penshurst, first published in The Forest as part of the 1616 Works, is one of
Jonson's major poems and since it is in the genre of the country house poem, you
can compare it with Herrick's The Hock-Cart. As Raymond Williams writes in The
Country and the City (1973): "These are not, in any simple sense, pastoral, or neo-
pastoral, but they use a particular version of country life as a way of expressing, in
the form of a compliment to a house, or its owner, certain social and moral values" (27). Williams points out the "definition by negatives" in To Penshurst which
reveals that the "forces of pride, greed and calculation are evidently active among
landowners as well as among city merchants and courtiers" (28).

To the Memory of My Beloved, The Author, Mr. William Shakespeare was printed
with the 1623 Folio of Mr. William Shakespeare's Comedies, Histories, and Tragedies.
The publication of the plays was important for Jonson whose own 1616 Works signalled that plays were meant to be read and criticized as texts as well as enjoyed as
performances. A provocative way to begin the discussion of this poem is to cite
Dryden's comment that it was "an insolent, sparing and invidious panegyric." Is
the praise here so equivocal as not to be praise at all but a covert kind of criticism?
What is Jonson saying about literary criticism in this poem? Notice Jonson's comparison of Shakespeare to classical authors and compare this with the importance
he gives to classical models in his literary criticism. See the selection from Jonson's
Timber in Perspectives: Emblem, Metaphor, Style.

Another panegyric which is much more than a simple poem of praise is To the
Immortal Memory of and Friendship of that Noble Pair, Sir Lucius Cary and Sir H.
Morison (1640), first published in The Underwood. The poems in this collection were
gathered by Jonson in the 1630s but not published until after his death, in the sec-

ond Folio of 1640, overseen by Sir Kenelm Digby. Lucius Cary was the son of Elizabeth Cary, author of *The Tragedy of Mariam*, and he wrote an elegy for Jonson. Lucius Cary's friend Sir Henry Morison was the nephew of the travel writer Fynes Morison, and died of small pox at the age of twenty-one. Jonson weaves into this panegyric, the first imitation of the Pindaric Ode in English, a subtle reflection upon his own writing and on paternity, which may be compared with On My First Son. Jonson refers to Lucius Cary as his "son." As David Riggs (1989) points out, the "Ben" at the end of line 84 might suggest to the reader that "the poet was referring to his first son Ben." Riggs compares the chiasmus in these lines to that in On My First Son: "rest in soft peace, and ask'd, say here doth lie / Ben Jonson his best piece of poetrie" (315).

Pleasure Reconciled to Virtue (1618)

Performed on Twelfth Night, January 6, 1618, this Masque celebrated the investiture of James I's son Charles as the Prince of Wales. Apparently Charles was a very straight-laced young man, unlike his father, who was known for his love of sport, sexual dalliance, and a general good time. An account of this masque by the Venetian ambassador tells of how the King was disappointed that there was not more dancing and complained, "Why did they make me come here for?" Point out to your students that while twentieth-century critics deem this masque to be great poetry, the original court audience was less than thrilled with it. Perhaps they understood the masque as a criticism of their own extravagance. Jonson used this masque as an opportunity to teach the court a lesson about virtue and portrayed the god Hercules, a Renaissance symbol of the choice of virtue over pleasure, as triumphing over his own desires.

It is interesting to note that at the second performance of the masque, Welsh rustics were substituted for the pygmies, and it was retitled *For the Honor of Wales*. That Jonson equated the pygmies with the Welsh peasants suggests the similarity between the early modern view of cultural others outside and inside the British Isles. The exotic peoples of other continents were on some level thought of as analogous to such cultural others as the Irish, Scots, and Welsh within Britain.

John Donne

Two of the most useful works for teaching Donne are the collection of essays edited by John Roberts, *Essential Articles for the Study of John Donne's Poetry* (1975), and Arthur Marotti's *Critical Essays on John Donne* (1994). Of the monographs on Donne the most useful for explaining the context in which he wrote his love poetry, published with his collected verse in 1633, is Arthur Marotti's *John Donne, a Coterie Poet* (1986). Marotti points out that many of Donne's poems, like Sidney's, were "coterie works, intended for an audience of close friends, clients, and family members" (3). Noting that the "book was an alien environment" for most sixteenth-century poetry, Marotti brings forth such evidence to prove his point as "the absence of all of Donne's *Songs and Sonnets* save one . . . from the important Westmoreland manuscript" as evidence of "the private character of the lyrics" (16). See also Alan MacColl, "The Circulation of Donne's Poems in Manuscript (in *John Donne: Essays in Celebration*, ed. Smith, [1972]).

Most students are unfamiliar with Neo-Platonism, which was a considerable influence on Donne. You need to spend time explaining key Platonic concepts such as the perception of beauty in the beloved as a remembrance of perfect beauty in the eternal realm (see Plato's *Symposium*). An excellent introduction to Renaissance Neo-Platonism is in the introduction to Rinaldina Russell's and Bruce Merry's edition of Tullia d'Aragona's *Dialogue on the Infinity of Love* (1997). She surveys the *trattati d'amore*, or treatises on love, which discuss the relation between soul and body in the experience and perception of love. Even before these issues are explained, perhaps the best first introduction to Donne's poems is simply to *hear* them, as in Richard Burton's mesmerizing performance of two of his lyrics, included on our audio CD.

The Good Morrow, usually taken to be an early lyric from the period of Donne's courtship of his wife Ann, is perhaps Donne's greatest expression of love as a little world, or microcosm. As A.J. Smith has pointed out in "The Metaphysic of Love" (in *Discussions of John Donne*, ed. Frank Kermode, [1962]) the background of this and many of Donne's other love lyrics is the Italian Renaissance treatises of love. Part of his audience was most likely made up not only of Ann but also of his male friends who were familiar with the Neo-Platonic philosophy of these treatises, which Donne challenges when he writes: "Love's not so pure, and abstract, as they use / To say, which have no mistress, but their Muse."

The Good Morrow is in the tradition of the alba or aubade, a poem celebrating the rising of the sun as the lovers awake, as are *The Sun Rising* and *Break of Day*. This is a type of poem that Ovid wrote, as did the medieval Provençal poets. The muscular syntax of *Break of Day* and its strong lines made up of one-syllable words (for example: "Nor hours, days, months, which are the rags of time") makes it an exciting poem to read aloud. As in *The Good Morrow*, the lovers' world here is everything. But the greater world is present in the poem as a form of hyperbole: "She is all states, and all princes, I." The notion that the man is to the woman as the prince is to his state is a political adaptation of Aristotelian metaphysics in which the male principle is form and the female principle is matter. And yet the next line presents both lovers as Princes ("Princes do but play us") and argues towards a blurring of gender boundaries in love.

The persona of the *Song* "Go and catch a falling star" is a young man confronted with competition in the world of sex and career. Both the search for a woman and the search for professional preferment lead to a sense of disillusionment. The tone of the poem is ironic and world-weary, with more than a touch of the resentment of a young idealist: "And find / what winde / Serves to advance an honest mind." The line "Teach me to hear Mermaides singing" was lifted from this poem by T. S. Eliot for his *Love Song of J. Alfred Prufrock*.

Manuscripts of Donne's poetry can be divided into several groups; in the second group, *The Undertaking* is entitled *Platonique Love*. Marotti connects this title with similar titles in the poetry of Donne's friend Sir Edward Herbert and sees the poem in part as Donne's witty teasing of Herbert's Platonism. The poem parodies Neo-Platonic conventions through exaggeration, or hyperbole.

The Indifferent is a marvelously complex poem from Donne's Inns of Court period in which the speaker often takes the role of a worldly libertine. Ovid's *Amores* 2.4 is the source for the first stanza, in which the speaker portrays himself as a bragging Don Juan. The students need to be asked to observe the change of audience from stanza to stanza—from his male comrades in sexual sport, to a female audience that seems at first plural then singular, to the voice of Venus speaking to all three previous audiences in an ironic and self-reflexive commentary on the whole poem up to this point.

The creation of what Marotti calls "a lively author reader dialectic" in *The Canonization* connects it with both *The Extasy* and *The Undertaking*, poems in which Donne appeals to a third party to witness his love. Like *The Undertaking*, *The Canonization* employs witty hyperbole. Not only do *The Extasy* and *The Canonization* rely upon witty conceit, but both employ rational argument, as does *Elegy 19, To His Mistress Going to Bed*. The self-confident and aggressively seductive charm of this poem often makes it a favorite with students. Donne imitates Ovid's *Amores* 1.5 here, but makes some changes that are worth getting your students to consider the effects of. Donne uses the present tense; the lady, unlike the scantily clad Latin lady, is elaborately dressed. And Donne's speaker, unlike Ovid's, conceals his nudity until the very end of the poem. Ovid is fairly witty to begin with; Donne is even wittier. To do a master comic erotic poet one better is a mark of Donne's achievement. Marotti puts great stress on the social conditions in which such poems as this were written, emphasizing the complex sexual and power relationships between rich city women and struggling ambitious young law students.

The Flea and *The Apparition*, both seduction poems, enact the speaker's desire for social and economic as well as erotic success. The real pressure that Donne and his contemporaries at the Inns of Court felt with respect to their economic dependence on patronage and their social subservience to an aristocratic code of Petrarchan love surfaces in these two poems. In *The Flea* the reference to the lady's disapproving parents may allude to the economic requirements parents had for their children's marriages (see Sir Alexander's disapproval of his son Sebastian's fiancée in *The Roaring Girl*) as well as their disapproval of premarital sex. In *The Apparition*, the speaker begins by making the Petrarchan concept of the lady's power to wound the lover a literal death, and then moves on to subvert a whole set of Petrarchan conventions. The beloved is not the young *donna angelicata* of Petrarch lyric but an experienced woman who, the speaker predicts, will be unhappy with future lovers who will be put out by her excessive sexual demands. You need to contextualize this poem in terms of literary history as the complete reversal of the conventional Petrarchan and Neo-Platonic pose of male deference to the lady, and the idealization of her as a thing of transcendental beauty leading the lover to moral perfection. Another poem in the anti-Petrarchan mode is *Love's Alchemy*, which is even more overtly misogynist: "Hope not for mind in woman."

The Bait is a mock imitation or parody of Marlowe's *The Passionate Shepherd to His Love*. Here the object of Donne's witty send-up is the pastoral. Just as Donne

had made fun of and challenged Petrarchan conventions by making them physically real, so in *The Flea* the naturalistic representation of the country setting de-
flates the convention of the pastoral idyll.

Helen Gardner's "The Argument about *The Extasy*" (in Roberts [1975]) sets out
two conflicting interpretations of the poem and attempts to reconcile them. The
first view is that the poem expresses "Platonism believed" (as Pound wrote in the
ABC's of Reading) and the second is that the poem presents "the case of a couple
who have been playing at Platonic love . . . and imagines how they would pass from
it to carnal enjoyment" (as Pierre Legouis wrote in *Donne the Craftsman*). Gardner
makes the argument that Donne's poem is about the conception of love as mutual
union, a common theme in much of Donne's other love poems, here illuminated
by a reading of Leone Hebreo's Neo-Platonic *Dialoghi d'Amore* (*Dialogues of Love*):

> And this, by affection and love, has transformed me into you begetting in
> me a desire that you may be fused with me, in order that I, your lover, may
> form but a single person with you, my beloved, and equal love may make
> of our two souls one, which may likewise vivify and inform our two bodies.
> The sensual element in this desire excites a longing for physical union, that
> the union of bodies may correspond to the unity of spirits wholly com-
> penetrating each other.

Given the philosophical, social and emotional complexity of Donne's lyrics it
is easy to lose sight of his innovations in prosody. Donne's verse is characterized by
a kind of directness and muscular syntax that owes a great deal to the verse of dramatic dialogue; he was surely a play-goer. His intellectual imagery is leavened by a
witty Ovidian streak, which gives his poems a kind of urbane sophistication and
erotic knowingness. His verse may at times appear misogynist to students, and
sometimes it is. But it is also important to get students to see that there is a self-
consciousness in Donne's verse which entails self-criticism of the speaker as male
lover. And in his most mature lyrics, such as *The Valediction Forbidding Mourning*,
which turns on the paradox of union in separation, there is a mutuality in the expression of love which transcends the division of lover and beloved. Containing
the memorable emblem of the "stiff twin compasses," this poem can be explained
with reference to Perspectives: Emblem, Style, and Metaphor.

Holy Sonnets (1633)

This edition follows the sequencing established by Helen Gardner, according to
the earliest manuscripts and the 1633 edition. She argued that the first twelve
poems of the 1633 edition are ordered according to the steps of spiritual meditation as set forth in Saint Ignatius Loyola's *Spiritual Exercises*. While most critics accept her ordering as based on solid evidence, some disagree with her grouping of
the *Holy Sonnets* into thematic groups—the first group of six sonnets devoted to
death, and the second group devoted to love. Douglas Peterson has found evidence
in Donne's *Sermons* that explains his own attitude toward the relation between fear

and love as "essential preliminaries to repentance" (see "John Donne's *Holy Sonnets* and the Anglican Doctrine of Contrition" in Roberts [1975]). Peterson sees Donne's *Holy Sonnets* as informed by the Anglican doctrine of salvation that insists upon a love of God which motivates hatred of sin. The theology of Donne's *Holy Sonnets* enacts direct confession to God and a profound belief in the resurrection of the body.

In terms of the representation of gender and sexuality, Donne's earlier flouting of male authority figures disappears in the *Holy Sonnets*, in which the speaker no longer seeks power but submission to a power greater than himself. In a reading which contrasts with that of Peterson's emphasis on love, Arthur Marotti, citing John Carey's interpretation of the *Sermons*, puts forward the notion that Donne's God is above all a God of power and wrath. Marotti mentions "Batter my heart three-personed God" as evidence of the speaker's masochism. Marotti more acutely expressed the tension in these religious poems as "the conflict between assertion and submission" (255). The struggle of the speaker throughout these poems bears careful examination. Students could be asked to comment on the erotic and visceral language in which Donne expresses religious devotion.

Devotions Upon Emergent Occasions (1624)

As William Mueller observes: "in these moving and magnificent devotions he brings to the reader a step-by-step account of the progress and regress of his malady—from his first awareness of its approach, to the coming of the physician . . . to the period of crisis and sleeplessness, to the tolling of the bells announcing the deaths of others, to the successful purging of his poisoned body, to the final warning to fortify himself against a relapse" (*John Donne: Preacher*, [1962]). As a work of spiritual self-examination and as a comment on human mortality, Meditation 17 bears comparison with the selections in *Spiritual Self-Reckonings*.

Lady Mary Wroth
Pamphilia to Amphilanthus (1621)

This collection contains 103 of the over 200 poems extant by Lady Mary Wroth. The first critic of Lady Mary Wroth's work was Dudley, third Baron North, who wrote in the introduction to his first book of poems: "I wish your Ladyship's authority would so abate the price that our poorer abilities might hold trade without straining." His appeal to her authority here taken in conjunction with his argument in favor of the style of "good sense and matter elegantly delivered" as opposed to "fancy and extravagancy of conceit" shows that he approved entirely of her poetry. Mary Wroth's poetry in many ways hearkens back to her uncle Sir Philip Sidney's. She writes in the Petrarchan manner with all its well-known features of sonnet form, oxymoron, and the persona of the suffering lover. The intellectual conceits and extravagant wit of the metaphysical style that we associate with Donne are not part of her work. However, Mary Wroth's poetry does have some of the melancholy and the world-weariness of early seventeenth-century poetry, and so may be read as a link between the Elizabethan style and that of Jonson, who was a great admirer of her verse.

The Pamphilia of the title may refer to the Latin woman poet of the Roman Emperor Nero's reign; none of her poetry has survived. Amphilanthus means "the lover of two," and has usually been taken to refer to Mary Wroth's first cousin, William Herbert. In *Urania* Wroth identifies Amphilanthus as Pamphilia's first cousin and has Amphilanthus recite a poem elsewhere attributed to Herbert. In some sense the poems in this sequence are autobiographical and document "her own fidelity and his lack of commitment" (Gary Waller, *The Sidney Family Romance*, [1993], 199).

The sonnet sequence begins with "When night's black mantle could most darkness prove, / and sleep death's image did my senses hire." The speaker dreams a vision of Venus placing a "heart flaming" into her breast. The poem contains the image of "night's black mantle" and "darkness"—colors that recur throughout the sequence (for instance, in number 17) to create a mood of melancholy. The subtle and frequent enjambment, the unobtrusive inversions of syntax, and the symbolic climax of the poem occurring at the end of the second quatrain that is a rhymed couplet, all make this a gorgeous poem.

Wroth's use of the Petrarchan style places her in a complex subject position—since the speaker of the Petrarchan sonnet is masculine and in conflict over the unwillingness of the lady to return his love. Even acknowledging such desire through writing pits Wroth against her social role as a woman because of the requirement for women to be chaste and silent. (See Perspectives: The Tracts on Women and Gender.) Josephine Roberts in the introduction to her 1983 edition of *The Poems of Lady Mary Wroth* has described the position of the speaker of Mary Wroth's poems as "a struggle between passionate surrender and self-affirmation." For the female speaker of Wroth's poem self-affirmation sometimes means fleeing the subjection of love: "Must we be servile doing what he list?" (#16). Love is apostrophized in the masculine gender; the beloved is absent, unlike the ever-present visual image of the beautiful beloved in the Petrarchan tradition. She shuns the world to engage in a dialogue with herself: "I with my spirit talk, and cry" (#26). As Gary Waller has written, "The poems thus present a fascinating gendered variation on a common Petrarchan paradox: she is trapped yet free...Pamphilia's speaking, even to herself, is like Wroth's writing itself, an act of self-assertion...the more agency is affirmed, the more she finds that, because she is woman, she must struggle in what the poems repeatedly term 'a labyrinth'" (1993, 204). See #77, "In this strange labyrinth how shall I turn?"

An excellent poem to focus on in order to show how Mary Wroth appropriates the gaze of the speaker of the Petrarchan sonnet for her own purposes is #39, "Take heed mine eyes, how you your looks do cast." The plural "selves" in "be true unto your selves" may at once refer to her and her lover and to the multiple facets of her own subjectivity. She is not the object of the gaze here but the one delighting in the gaze: "mine eyes enjoy full sight of love."

These poems need to be read in conjunction with the excerpt from *Urania* in The Development of English Prose. The concerns of constructing female subjectivity as evidenced in Wroth's poems can also be compared to that in Elizabeth

Cary's *Tragedy of Mariam* and Katherine Philips's love poems. In terms of her complex relation to the Petrarchan tradition, Wroth's appropriation of Petrarchism can be compared and contrasted with Donne's antagonism to the Petrarchan role of subservience to the beloved.

Robert Herrick
Hesperides (1648)

This volume of poems was dedicated to Charles, Prince of Wales. The title refers to the garden of the Hesperides, guarded by the nymphs of the same name. Juno planted the golden apples, given her as a wedding present by the goddess Earth, in this garden. The conceit appears to be that this text is a garden of poetry, as the first couplet of *The Argument of His Book* proclaims: "I sing of brooks, of blossoms, birds, and bowers / of April, May, of June, and July flowers." The memorable phrase "times trans-shifting" suggests that Herrick's subject is a world in constant motion, in the state of growing and becoming. This sense of the beauty of things in motion is continued in *Delight in Disorder*, which concludes on a self-reflexive note in which everything "neglectful," "flow[ing] confusedly," and "tempestuous" in the woman's dress "more bewitch the speaker, than when art / Is too precise in every part." The Ovidian dictum *ars celare artem*, or the art is to conceal art, comes to mind here. Again in *Upon Julia's Clothes* there is a similar delight evident in such words as "liquefaction," "brave vibration," and "glittering."

The *Hock-Cart, or Harvest Home* is part of the pastoral tradition of poetry. Raymond Williams comments on how *The Hock-Cart* in its directness lays bare the social relations which Ben Jonson's *To Penshurst* more subtly mediates: "It [*The Hock-Cart*] is crude in feeling, this early and jollying kind of man-management, which uses metaphors of rain and spring to see even the drink as a way of getting more labour (and more pain)" (*The Country and the City*, [1973], 33). For a contrasting point of view on Jonson's *To Penshurst*, see the poet Thom Gunn's essay in *The Occasions of Poetry* (1982): "It is difficult to put oneself into a time when admiration for rank was not snobbery, but we have to make the attempt, and if we do so then we have a chance of understanding the ideas that Jonson is trying to embody in the poem" (109). For Gunn, these ideas include "the responsibilities of rank" and "the admiration of chastity," values which Gunn claims are "genuinely Jonson's." Are these ideas present in Herrick's *Hock-Cart*, or does this poem, and for that matter Jonson's *To Penshurst*, merely attempt to please the gentry?

Another poem of Herrick's set in a pastoral landscape is *To the Virgins, to Make Much of Time* on the theme of *tempus fugit*, or time flies. This poem can be compared to a much more complex treatment of the same theme by Marvell, *To His Coy Mistress*, and a much more urbane and humorously erotic treatment of the theme by Donne, *To His Mistress Going to Bed*. For all Herrick's Latinity and admiration of Ben Jonson, there is an element of English country folk culture in his verse, as in the very local reference to the "whitethorn neatly interwove" in *Corinna's Going A-Maying*.

George Herbert
The Temple (1633)

One of the best places to look for close readings of Herbert's poetry is Helen Vendler's *The Poetry of George Herbert* (1975). Her chapter "Emblems and Allegories" contains sensitive explications of how Herbert's metaphors work. For instance, on *The Altar*, Vendler writes: "The 'allegory' seems too simple at first glance, as Herbert takes pains to elucidate it: the altar is a heart, the cement is tears, God is the stonemason, the altar is a place for sacrifice. But as soon as we begin to examine the terms in their interrelations, mysteries arise. A hard heart is not likely to spend its time praising God; neither is a hard heart one normally associated with tears. We decide that perhaps the heart used to be hard: after all, it is now 'broken,' presumably by God's 'cutting,' and God has used the tools of suffering, provoking tears, to re-establish the heart, not in its natural heart-shape, but in the shape of an altar" (61-62). Vendler focuses throughout on the creation of complex alternatives of meaning in Herbert's deceptively simple creation of poetic parables.

A more historicized approach to the question of how the emblematic metaphor works in Herbert's poetry can be found in the very useful article by Martin Elsky, "George Herbert's Pattern Poems and the Materiality of Language: A New Approach to Renaissance Hieroglyphics," *ELH* 50.2 (1983). Michael Rothberg's "An Emblematic Ideology: Images and Additions in Two Editions of Henry Vaughan's *Silex Scintillans*," (*ELR*, 80-94) contains perceptive comments about the relation between Herbert's and Vaughan's deployment of the emblem and places the whole question of emblematic representation in terms of the ideological differences between the Anglican approach to images and Puritan iconoclasm. Quarles's concept of emblem as "silent parable" (*Emblemes*, 1643) helps to explain how the visual effects of Herbert's poems generate meaning. You will want to pay great attention to the visual effects of such poems as *The Altar*, *Easter Wings*, and *The Pulley*.

The continued interest of contemporary poets in Herbert's poetry can be illustrated by reference to Seamus Heaney's lecture on his assumption of the Chair of Poetry at Oxford, *The Redress of Poetry* (1989). There are perceptive insights into both *The Pulley* and *The Collar* here. Heaney writes of *The Collar*: "The dance of lexical possibilities in the title, the way which the poem changes partners with the meanings of 'collar,' both as an article of clerical clothing and a fit of anger, the reversal of emotional states from affront to assuagement, the technical relish of postponing stanzaic composure until the last lines—it is all, as Seferis says, 'strong enough,' and can be hung out on the imaginative arm of the balance to take the strain of our knowledge of things as they are" (16).

The final poem by Herbert in this anthology, *The Forerunners*, is perhaps one of his most difficult. The line "Farewell, sweet phrases, lovely metaphors" would appear to mark this poem as a kind of poetic retraction, a turning away from "Lovely enchanting language," just as Chaucer had turned away from secular storytelling at the end of the *Canterbury Tales*. Paradoxically, *The Forerunners* itself depends on such metaphors, with the "harbingers" of the first line suggesting both the king's servants, and by extension God's messengers coming to announce his arrival. The tension in the poem between "sparkling" and "dullness," "brothels" and "Church," "thence" and "thither," "flame" and "bleak paleness," "the door" and what is "within"—all create what Heaney finds to be the great achievement of Herbert's poetry: how it "contains within itself the co-ordinates and contradictions of experience" (1993, 16).

PERSPECTIVES

Emblem, Style, Metaphor

The texts in this section offer perspectives on representation through similitude—the complex system of resemblances that connected words with the world in the early modern period. **Geoffrey Whitney's** *The Phoenix*, taken from his *A Choice of Emblemes* (1586), can be used to show students the tri-partite picture, motto, and poem that comprised a typical entry in an early modern book of emblems. Students need to see that such emblems appear frequently in English early modern poetry. One assignment that helps students concretely grasp the concept of emblem and to see its relationship and difference from metaphor, which Emmanuele Tesauro defines as a kind of visual transference, and allegorical symbol, which is exemplified in **Giordano Bruno's** chapter on Venus in *On the Composition of Images, Signs and Ideas*, is to have them read a selection of poems from this section and identify how the emblems in these poems work. Excellent poems for examination of how the emblem generates meaning would include **Richard Crashaw's** *To the Noblest and Best of Ladies, the Countess of Denby*, John Donne's *A Valediction: Forbidding Mourning*, and Katherine Philips's *Friendship in Emblem, or the Seal*. Milton's *L'Allegro* and *Il Penseroso*, which contain emblem, metaphor, symbol, are also excellent places to turn to get students to engage in close reading of how these different types of resemblance contain compacted forms of meaning that could not otherwise be expressed. Indeed Milton's sensuous imagery in these two poems hearkens back to Shakespeare and looks forward to the Romantics. Perhaps the best introduction to the mysteries of early modern symbolism can be found in the work of Frances Yates—both *The Art of Memory* and *Giordano Bruno and the Hermetic Tradition*. Broadening the discussion to include the difference between medieval allegory and early modern emblem and metaphor, you can ask students to contemplate the difference between the biblically governed symbolism in *The Dream of the Rood* and Chaucer's Nun's Priest's Tale with the more esoteric symbolism of the emblem. Milton's eschewal of allegory but employment of complex metaphors and similes for his telling of the Genesis story in *Paradise Lost* would be another example for students to consider in order to understand the dramatic shift from the medieval to the early modern similitude.

Richard Lovelace
Lucasta (1649)

You can have your students read Lovelace's poetry in relation to the texts in Perspectives: The Civil War, since To Lucasta, Going to the Wars was occasioned by his setting off to fight for the royalist cause. The aesthetic of his poetry owes something to the genealogy of Castiglione's Courtier in England, as the cavalier can be seen as a seventeenth-century embodiment of this type. Sir Walter Raleigh's poetry would provide an earlier point of comparison. Patsy Griffin's The Modest Ambition of Andrew Marvell (1995) explores the importance of Lovelace to the life and work of Marvell. In order to contextualize To Althea, from Prison, see Raymond Anselment's "'Stone Walls' and 'Iron Bars': Richard Lovelace and the Conventions of Seventeenth-Century Prison Literature," Renaissance and Reformation, 17.1 (Winter 1993). 15-34.

Henry Vaughan
Silex Scintillans (1650, 1655)

All of Vaughan's poems published here are from Silex Scintillans, or Sacred Poems and Private Ejaculations. An excellent article explaining the difference between the two editions is Michael Rothberg's "An Emblematic Ideology: Images and Additions in Two Editions of Henry Vaughan's Silex Scintillans" (ELR), 80-94. Rothberg particularly focuses on "The Author's Emblem (of himself)," which was deleted from the 1655 edition. Rothberg sees Vaughan's deletion of the emblem as "an overtly political move which does not signify retreat, but instead a pragmatic intervention in the 'tumult' of the discursive battles of the 1650s" (87). These battles included the very popular Eikon Basilike, attributed to and written in defense of Charles I, and Milton's Eikonoklastes in which he argued against the idolatry of the King. For these texts, see Perspectives: The Civil War. The problem for Vaughan would appear to be "not merely the letter...as opposed to the spirit, but also with the iconic or figural as opposed to the literal." This discussion raises important questions about the ideological meaning of the interpretation not only of visual emblems but of metaphors as emblems. See Perspectives: Emblem, Metaphor, Style. Turning to the poems, one could ask the students to consider if such images as "the pair of scales" in Regeneration, the "solitary lamp" in Silence and Stealth of Days, and "the fearful miser," in The World function as emblems. If so, how? If not, why not? Vaughan's imagery would seem to participate in Francis Quarles's definition of emblem as "silent parable" (Emblemes, 1643). Indeed, much of Vaughan's imagery displays a strong allusiveness to the New Testament, as in the "dazzling darkness" of They Are All Gone into the World of Light which recalls and extends the Pauline "through a glass darkly."

Andrew Marvell
Miscellaneous Poems (1681)

One of the best introductions to Marvell is still T. S. Eliot's essay in Selected Essays (1932) reprinted in Marvell: The Critical Heritage, edited by Elizabeth Story Donno

(1978). Defining the "wit" of which Marvell's *Horatian Ode* is a great example, Eliot wrote: "It is more than a technical accomplishment, or the vocabulary and syntax of an epoch; it is what we have designated tentatively as wit, a tough reasonableness beneath the slight lyric grace" (363-64). Eliot goes on to explain that if we do not usually associate this wit with Puritan literature, perhaps it is because we misunderstand the varieties of Puritans: "Many of them were gentlemen of the time who merely believed, with considerable show of reason, that government by a Parliament of gentlemen was better than government by a Stuart" (364). The historicity of Eliot's analysis separates it from the New Critics, with whom he is so often erroneously lumped, and shows the poet-critic's awareness of the tension maintained in Marvell's work between a French and Latinate poetic wit and a Republican politics.

You need to get students to recognize both the Latin form of the *Horatian Ode*, and the Latinate register of its language. At the same time, you will want to historicize a reading of this poem in relation to Cromwell's own account of his conquest of Ireland in his *Letters*, and the effects of this conquest upon the Irish, as registered in the Irish popular song, *Seán O'Dhuibhir an Ghleanna* (*Sean O'Dwyer of the Glenn*). See Perspectives: The Civil War, or the War of Three Kingdoms. An excellent close reading of Marvell's *Horatian Ode* as "a form of political commentary" is in Annabel Patterson's *Marvel and the Civic Crown* (1978, 63-68). She concludes: "In taking a position somewhat between *Eikon Basilike* and *Eikonoklastes*, the *Horatian Ode* mediates not between two political camps but between two interdependent theories (which rhetoric has always recognized as pathos and ethos) of how language works upon the human mind" (68). For these two texts, see Perspectives: The Civil War. Some of Patterson's readings will provoke debate. To what extent does Marvell unironically "shift responsibility for evaluating the Irish campaign to the conquered Irish" (Patterson, 64)? The poem was suppressed after its first printing in the 1681 edition until 1776, which, according to David Norbrook, caused readers to overlook Marvell's republicanism. Norbrook argues that Marvell "stresses the ideological, republican elements of the campaign." Admitting the possibility of some irony in the presentation of the Irish, he maintains that there is "generic precedent" for the Irish praise of Cromwell in the conquered Hannibal's praise of the Romans in Horace *Odes* 4.4 (*Literature and the English Civil War*, ed. Thomas Healy and Jonathan Sawday, [1990], 160). Thus, Marvell uses the praise of the Roman empire as a model for his praise of the English republic. Is the sympathy which Marvell evokes for the King's death merely a digression in this poem, or does it qualify the praise of the revolution?

For *To His Coy Mistress*, again turn to Eliot who explained how the wit of this poem "is not only combined with, but fused into, the imagination...it is structural decoration of a serious idea" (Donno, [1978], 366). Eliot compares the four lines that begin "But at my back I always hear" to "But, soone as once set is our little light, / Then must we sleep an ever-enduring night" (Catullus 5.5-6). Likening the *carpe diem* theme to that in poems by Herrick, Donne, Propertius and Ovid, Eliot also cites Ben Jonson's version of this in *Volpone*: "Cannot we deceive the eyes / Of a few poor household spies?" (3.7.176-7). To further explain the seventeenth-century concept of wit, turn to Tesauro's deployment of *ingenium* (Latin), or *ingegnio* (Italian) in his *Cannochiale Aristotelico* (*Through the Lens of Aristotle*) in Perspectives: Emblem, Metaphor, Style.

Katherine Philips
Poems By the Incomparable, Mrs. K. P. (1664)

Katherine Philips's poetry was first published in an unauthorized edition in 1664, the year that she died, and then was re-edited and expanded into the 1667 edition overseen by her literary executor Sir Charles Cotterell. As Harriette Andreadis has written "The Sapphic-Platonics of Katherine Philips" *Signs* 15.1 (1989), 64-60. "Philips' contribution was to appropriate the cavalier conventions of platonic heterosexual love, with their originally platonic and male homoerotic feeling and to use those conventions and that discourse to describe her relations with women" (37). *To My Excellent Lucasia on Our Friendship* needs to be read in conjunction with Donne's *A Valediction: Forbidding Mourning*. Not only does Philips use Donne's conceit of the compass, as an emblem of constancy, but she plays on the Neo-Platonism and the eroticism of Donne's poem through this allusion. Two other poems to Lucasia, or Mrs. Anne Owen—*Friendship in Emblem or the Seal*, and *To the Truly Noble and Obliging Mrs. Anne Owen*—further adumbrate the poetic representation of this passionate friendship. In the military metaphors of *To the Truly Noble and Obliging Mrs. Anne Owen*, Philips appropriates the masculine language of love as a conquest. In "Excusing the Breach of Nature's Laws: The Discourse of Denial and Disguise in Katherine Philips' Friendship Poetry" (*Restoration Studies in English Literary Culture 1660-1700* [1990]), Celia Easton has analyzed the complex way in which the speaker of Philips's poems both protects her beloved friend from the world and acknowledges her love's existence in the very world it transcends. Easton sees two kinds of tension in Philips's verse—a tendency to repress the physical in favor of the Neo-Platonic and a tendency for their transcendent love to be dependent on the vehicle of Orinda's verse. "Friendship discovered in the ideal realm is maintained by its verbal celebration" (5).

Two poems on historical events display Philips's royalist sympathies: *Upon the Double Murder of King Charles* and *On the Third of September 1651*. Philips's sympathy with the Stuarts can be compared to that of such other women authors as Aphra Behn and Lady Margaret Cavendish. As a female poet she denies her concern with politics ("I think not on the state") and claims that such a concern is a transgression of her position as woman ("the breach of nature's laws"). Much of her poetry, however, is indeed concerned with history and the political world.

The World calls to mind Vaughan's poem by the same title. While Philips was well-versed in Neo-Platonic thought, her poem upon the world is much more directly moral and political and less visionary and metaphysical than Vaughan's. Her final celebration of the "uncaged soul" is preceded by a meditation upon the vicissitudes of fortune, the "treacherous world," and contains the evocative simile of how "we run from what we hate / like squibs on ropes." The poem's concern with the relation between "tyranny" and self-imposed "bondage" can be compared with the state of

Milton's devils in Hell. Since the popularity of Philips's poetry continued after her death, with such readers as Dryden, Philips's poetry works well as a transition between the Early Modern Period and the Restoration and Eighteenth Century.

The Development of English Prose

Francis Bacon
Essays (1597, 1625)

Reprinted in 1598, 1604, and 1606, the 1597 Essays were revised by Bacon in 1612 and 1625. Not only did he cover a greater variety of topics but he also significantly revised the style or the original essays. To illustrate how Bacon revised his writing towards greater clarity of thought and greater fluency, you can ask students to do a close reading of the 1597 and the 1625 versions of Of Studies. You can ask them to determine which version is closer to the terse Senecan style, and which makes greater use of Ciceronian parallelism and variety. In which version do the sentences flow more smoothly from one to the other? An excellent introduction to Bacon's rhetoric is Brian Vickers's Francis Bacon and Renaissance Prose (1968).

Morris Croll's essays (in "Attic" and Baroque Prose Style, the Anti-Ciceronian Movement, edited by J. Max Patrick and Robert O. Evans [1966]), provide a useful analysis of Bacon's "Attic" style as a reaction against the emphasis in sixteenth-century prose on "words and forms," in favor of "maximal expressivity" and "the process of thinking" (163). As John J. Miller observes in "Pruning by Study: Self-Cultivation in the Essays" (Papers on Language and Literature, 339-361): "Though Of Studies is the first essay in the 1597 group often, in subsequent editions it appeared towards the end of the Essays...Nevertheless, Of Studies still appears as a kind of preface to the rest of the Essays, offering instructions on how to read, warnings against the misuses of reading, and particular recommendations regarding the therapeutic values of reading for various readers" (349-350).

In the dedication to the 1625 edition of his Essays, Bacon commented: "Of all my other works, [they] have been most current; for that, as it seems, they come home to men's business and bosoms." As a genre the Essays were indeed meant to speak to people in their daily lives and to impress upon them practical wisdom in a memorable form. Towards this end Bacon employs a rhetoric designed to hit home his message. Such rhetorical aspects of Bacon's style as the aphorism, a pithy maxim or sententia, and the syntactical symmetry, or parallelism of his clauses were major innovations in prose style. Point out to students that Bacon adapted these stylistic features from imitation of such Latin writers as Seneca (for concision) and Cicero (for parallelism and pleonasm or elegant restatement). A good example of the sententia is in Of Truth, where the argument is summed up by the aphorism: "A mixture of a lie doth ever add pleasure." This aspect of the Senecan style can also be seen in early modern tragedy—particularly in Elizabeth Cary's Tragedy of Mariam (see for example the senteniae of the Chorus at the end of each act).

An excellent source for Bacon as an author of philosophical discourse is Lisa Jardine's "The method of Bacon's *Essays*" in her *Francis Bacon: Discovery and the Art of Discourse* (1974). The end of this chapter contains a reading of the essay *Of Truth*. In order to explain Bacon's condemnation of dishonesty here, which runs contrary to Bacon's advice to politicians to use dissimulation, Jardine comments on Bacon's distinction between moral and civil instruction: "Moral instruction on the duty of individuals in a community does not teach policy, but persuades individuals to behave so as to uphold the 'bonds of society'" (247). Of the method of the *Essays* as a whole, she observes: "The individual essays are built up out of devices which Bacon believed to make non-rational appeal, and to sway the reader's imagination into a 'method of discourse' which ensures a favourable reception for the knowledge which they communicate" (248).

The skeptical attitude towards religion in *Of Superstition* can be compared with Sir Thomas Browne's view in *Religio Medici*. Bacon contrasts atheism which "leaves a man to sense, to philosophy, to natural piety, to laws, to reputation, all which may be guides to outward moral virtue, though religion were not" with superstition "which dismounts all these." Bacon is interested in separating religion from popular belief ("the master of superstition is the people") and from tradition. In contrast with Bacon, Browne has a much more accepting view of custom as a necessary part of culture and of conflicting traditions. Bacon's concern with "the stratagems of prelates for their own ambition and lucre" looks forward to the Puritan protests in the English Civil War. See the selections from Milton's *Eikonoklastes* and *The Petition of Gentlewomen and Tradesmen's Wives* in Perspectives: The Civil War.

Of Plantations can be discussed in relation to other texts on colonization in the early modern period such as Donne's *Sermon Preached to the Honorable Company of the Virginia Plantation*. Bacon's focus is largely economic: how to fortify the colony with food and supplies, how to use the land, and what type of colonists should inhabit the plantation ("rather noblemen and gentlemen, than merchants"). It is interesting to note that the native inhabitants of the territory to be colonized are nowhere mentioned.

The King James Bible (1611)

You will want to point out to your students that the English Bible was the most popular text in the early modern period. The interpretation of these two chapters defines early modern theology, and the discourse on gender. See Joseph Swetnam and Rachel Speght in The Tracts on Women and Gender. The choice of Genesis, Chapters 1 and 2, is also dictated by their relevance to Milton's *Paradise Lost*. The language of the King James Bible echoes throughout Milton's text as the notes to this edition illustrate.

Lady Mary Wroth
The Countess of Montgomery's Urania (1621)

The best source for this text is the superb edition of Josephine Roberts (1995), which contains a comprehensive introduction to the text's circumstances of publication and the literary traditions that inform it. Since this text falls into the genre of romance, it can be compared with such works as *Sir Gawain* and Spenser's *Faerie Queene*. Since it is a prose romance, *Urania* is a useful narrative to look at in terms of the origins of the novel, both for the trope of the woman reader and for the representation of the protagonist's introspection. See Perspectives: Spiritual Self-Reckonings.

Thomas Hobbes
Leviathan (1651)

As Charles Cantalupo comments: "Hobbes' infamous 'state of nature,' in which a person's life is 'solitary, poor, nasty, brutish, and short,' is nothing if not a conceit and Hobbes's own rhetorical elaboration on a philosophical convention found in Thucydides, Lucretius, and Horace." His pessimism is rooted in his reading of classical history and moral philosophy. The selection from this text, "Chapter 13: Of the Social Condition of Mankind as Concerning Their Felicity, and Misery" can be compared to the texts in Perspectives: Government and Self Government. David Johnston in *The Rhetoric of "Leviathan"* (1986) stresses both the roots of Hobbes's political thought in Renaissance humanism and the historical dimension of Hobbes's theory of the commonwealth which was based on an evolutionary view of human nature: "The prospects of the commonwealth as he envisaged it were vitally dependent upon the outcome of the struggle between superstition and enlightenment" (129). See Bacon's essay *Of Superstition*.

Sir Thomas Browne
Religio Medici (1643)

First published in the unauthorized edition of 1642, this text was published in an authorized edition in 1643. While Stanley Fish once disparaged Brown for his religious "middle way," and the introduction to the *Norton Anthology of English Literature* found him wanting for not taking sides in the Civil War, a new generation of critics is finding a plasticity in his rhetoric and a charity in his theology that makes his writing worth reading. For bibliography, see Andrea Sununu, "Recent Studies in Sir Thomas Browne (1970-1986)," *ELR* (Winter 1990), 118-129.

You can begin by contrasting Browne's curt style with Burton's more meandering one. Maurice Croll uses a sentence from *Religio Medici* 1.6 as an example of the *période coupée* (the curt period), the characteristics of which are short members, a mode of progression, and deliberate asymmetry of the members of the period: "To see ourselves again, we need not look for Plato's year...there was none then, but there hath been some one since that parallels him, and is, as it were his revived self." This six-member period is described by Croll as follows: "a series of metaphors flash their lights; or a chain of 'points' and paradoxes reveals the energy of a single apprehension in the writer's mind" ("The Baroque Style in Prose," in

"*Attic*" *and Baroque Prose Style*, 218-19). Croll traces this style to the model of Seneca and distinguishes it from the parallelism of the Ciceronian style. Whether the apprehension is always single is open to debate, as Victoria Silver's analysis of Browne's rhetoric argues for the multiplicity of its perceptions, in which a skeptical perspective allows for contradictory views to be held in tandem. See Victoria Silver, "Liberal Theology and Sir Thomas Browne's 'Soft and Flexible' Discourse" (*ELR* [Winter 1990], 69-105). At times, Browne's sentence structures do display a sonorous parallelism which C. A. Patrides connects with the parallelism of the Bible (see the Introduction to his 1977 edition of Browne's *Major Works*).

As a kind of autobiography on the order of Montaigne's *Essais*, *Religio Medici* can be compared and contrasted with the texts in Spiritual Self-Reckonings. Browne is known for his tolerance and acceptance of the difference of customs in different cultures. The flexibility of his viewpoint is mirrored in the flexibility of his style. As Victoria Silver (1990) notes: "Verbal contrivance and excess do not necessarily indicate a disregard for a sense of the reader's improvement: it can express skepticism about received categories of value and how we determine and propagate them" (105).

Robert Burton
The Anatomy of Melancholy (1621)

Revised editions of this text were printed at Oxford in 1624 and 1628, and there were five other printings up to 1676. E. Patricia Vacari (*The View from Minerva's Tower*, 1989) notes that Burton uses "the old rhetoric of the spoken language rather than the new rhetoric for writing that had developed significantly only after the invention of printing" (125). The speaking voice of Democritus is the uniting principle in this confusing text which contains an encyclopedic range of knowledge and a style which is foreign to the modern reader in its long, meandering sentence structure and dizzying allusivity.

The "Utopia of Democritus," an excerpt from the lengthy introduction, can be compared with the texts in Perspectives: Government and Self-Government as well as with Thomas More's *Utopia*. Burton's comment on civility versus barbarism can be connected with the texts in The Discourse of Ethnography, as well as with the excerpt from Florio's translation of Montaigne's *Of Cannibals* in "The Discovery" and Its Time. Burton's mention of Sir John Davies's *The True Causes Why Ireland Was Never Entirely Subdued* draws attention to the early modern portrayal of the Irish as barbarous. Burton's notion that those in Europe were "once as uncivil as they in Virginia" is not unlike Spenser's contention in *A View of the Present State of Ireland* that the English were once as uncivil as the Irish. You can explain to your students that this comparison of the European and English past to the Irish and Amerindian present is an example of what the anthropologist Johanes Fabian calls "the denial of coevalness." See Walter Mignolo, *The Darker Side of the Renaissance* (1995).

The Division of the Body, Humours, Spirits will give the students a sense of what the body of the text is like. Burton attempts to control the multiplicity of the text by dividing it into Parts, Sections, Members, and Subsections, according to the principle of dialect in Ramist rhetoric to form a kind of tree of knowledge spreading out from larger branches into smaller shoots. This chapter introduces students to the humoral theory of the body, the influence of which can be felt in everything from medicine to poetry and drama to political theory and to the discourse on gender. The description of the "spirit," or "subtle vapor" can be useful in explaining Donne's use of "spirit" in such poems as *The Ecstasy*. The most comprehensive and suggestive study of humoral theory and its importance for drama in early modern England is Gail Kern Paster's *The Body Embarrassed: Drama and the Discipline of Shame in Early Modern England* (1991).

PERSPECTIVES

The Civil War, or the War of Three Kingdoms

This section is intended to give students a way to contextualize the literature of this period in relation to perhaps the most momentous event of the century: the wars that raged not only in England but also in Scotland and Ireland. For a solid historical account, see Martin Bennet's *The Civil Wars in Britain and Ireland 1638–1651* (1997). The first two texts need to be read in tandem, since **Milton's** *Eikonoklastes* (1649) was written as a response to the King's *Eikon Basilike* (1649), which was actually ghost-written by **John Gauden**. According to Ernest Gilman this text "sparked an explosion of pity for the martyred king" (*Iconoclasm and Poetry in the English Reformation* [1986]). See Richard Helgerson, "Milton Reads the King's Book: Print, Performance, and the Making of a Bourgeois Idol," *Criticism* 29.1 (1987), 1–25. *The Petition of Gentlewomen and Tradesmen's Wives* (1642) gives some sense of the unrest in London in the early 1640s—including the economic hardships of the people as well as the complaints against the Bishops. This text also documents the English outrage at the outbreak of rebellion in Ireland, and the reports of massacres of colonists there. Events in Ireland had a great impact on the pressure to get rid of the monarchy, since Charles was perceived as a crypto-Catholic, and a potential ally of papists in Ireland. That women banded together to produce a petition is a striking example of women's communal political activity in the early modern period. You can point out to your students that women in Scotland and Ireland were also involved in the conflict. For comments on this see Martyn Bennett (1997).

To give students a sense of the conflict in Ireland, have them read **Oliver Cromwell's** *Letter of Sept. 17, 1649*. This letter can be used to do a symptomatic reading of Marvell's *Horatian Ode*. Cromwell's letter can also be read in connection with Spenser's *A View*, which, like many other English tracts on Ireland, proposed the military conquest of Ireland that Cromwell carried out. At the time of the confiscations, Spenser's grandson received a letter from Cromwell granting him his land and mentioning that Cromwell had actually read his grandfather's writing on Ireland. An Irish account of the confiscations, *Seán Ó Duibhir an Ghleanna* (John

O'Dwyer of the Glenn) (c. 1651) circulated orally from the time of the Cromwell, although it was not published until the nineteenth century. To read other poems by the many poets who wrote in the Irish language during the early modern period, see the anthology edited by Thomas Kinsella, *An Duanaire, Poems of the Dispossessed*.

For a sense of the dissent that arose within the Republican movement over discontent with Cromwell's failure to live up to the ideals of the English revolution, see **John Lilburne**, *England's New Chains Discovered* (1648).

Turning to Scotland, where the initial religious-ideological conflict broke out over the imposition of the Book of Common Prayer, the conflicts within Presbyterian Scotland can be witnessed in *The Story of Alexander Agnew, or Jock of Broad Scotland* from the newspaper *Mercurius Politicus*. Agnew was the first Scot to be publicly tried for atheism. Finally, **Edward Hyde's**"The Death of Montrose" from *The True Historical Narrative of the Rebellion* (1702-1704) shows the participation of some Scots in the royalist cause, with Montrose figuring as the hero of the highland Scots' support of the Stuarts. As one of the great English prose stylists, Hyde, usually referred to by his title Clarendon, can be read in connection with the texts in The Development of English Prose.

John Milton
L'Allegro *and* Il Penseroso (1638)

Written in 1637, these poems were first published in 1638. As companion poems they intricately mirror one another in their prosody and in their complex interwoven allusions to one another both by echo and antithesis. Both are written in octosyllabic couplets. Both express a whole orientation to the world through the description of place. Both poems are highly allusive—particularly to Shakespeare. Both poems draw upon the conception of humoral psychology as discussed in Burton's *Anatomy of Melancholy*.

Milton's earliest sonnets were written in Italian, so it is not surprising that he follows the precedent set by Petrarch of dividing the sonnet into octave and sestet. The one exception here is *To the Lord General Cromwell*, which ends on a strong English couplet. While this sonnet was not published until 1694, the other sonnets here were published in 1673. *How Soon Hath Time* was first printed in 1645. Milton's sonnet in praise of Cromwell, written in 1652, can be compared with Marvell's *Horatian Ode*. It makes sense to have the students carefully read the introduction to Perspectives: The Civil War in order to understand the network of events surrounding *On the New Forcers of Conscience under the Long Parliament* (1673).

Lycidas

First published as the last poem in a collection of poems entitled *Justa Edouardo King naufrago* (1638), commemorating the drowning of Milton's Cambridge classmate Edward King, *Lycidas* is considered to be one of the great elegies in the English language. A useful introduction for students is J. Martin Evans's *"Lycidas"* in The

Cambridge Companion to Milton, edited by Dennis Danielson (1989). A controversial view of this poem is expressed by the eighteenth century critic Dr. Johnson who complained that Lycidas "is not to be considered the effusion of real passion." Evans argues against the two main responses to Johnson: that Milton was not really writing about Edward King at all and that real grief is inarticulate and any poetic expression of grief must be artificial. Evans points out that "the verse form itself holds the key." The first 185 lines were modelled on the Italian *canzone*, while the last eight lines are written in the *ottava rima* that are the verse form of romance-epic. Thus, they function as a kind of call to action. Evans argues that the voice of the speaker subtly shifts from Milton himself lamenting his dead friend at the outset to the voice of Phoebus at line 76. After St. Peter's speech, a chorus of mourners appears. Evans reads the final dramatic shift at line 186 in autobiographical terms, as marking Milton's own farewell to a life of "retirement, chastity, and poetry." In order for students to understand this complex poem, you will have to lead them through observing these shifts of voice and perspective.

Areopagitica (1644)

Milton was one of the greatest prose writers of his age, and *Areopagitica* shows his writing at its most exciting—both for the striking deployment of metaphor and the innovative diction. The whole issue of freedom of the press can be explicated in relation to the context of the Civil War. This text can also be read in relation to the whole issue of censorship—both self-censorship and state censorship—not only in the early modern period but even today. Francis Barker discusses the context of this work as the shift to modernity, in which "the private citizen is constituted in reason and judgement as a self-policing entity" ("In the wars of truth: true knowledge and power in Milton and Hobbes" in *Literature and the English Civil War*, ed. Thomas Healy and Jonathan Sawday, [1990], 100). For Barker it is the move from censorship prior to publication to censorship after publication through state intervention that is of greatest interest in *Areopagitica*. Against the notion of "depoliticized private utterance," Barker sees the image of Truth as a militant warrior, "a figuration of true discourse not yet willing to surrender itself to private obscurity" (101).

Paradise Lost (1674)

Prior to the composition of *Paradise Lost*, the epic poem, Milton planned to write a tragedy about the loss of Paradise; there are four drafts outlining this work in the Trinity College MS. Knowing that Milton originally intended *Paradise Lost* to be a tragedy helps emphasize the tragic element of the work and suggests that the poem should perhaps be considered a tragical epic rather than a pure epic. Although *Paradise Lost*, as epic, contains within it a variety of genres (e.g., tragedy, pastoral, lyric—for a full discussion of *Paradise Lost* and its literary forms see Lewalski), the tragic mode warrants special consideration since the loss of Paradise can be regarded as *the* tragedy underlying all other tragedies. When considering Milton's decision to change the form of *Paradise Lost* from tragedy to epic it is profitable to recall that while Aristotle exalted tragedy over epic, most Renaissance commentators privileged epic as the highest literary form because it includes all other genres; only the poet who excels in every other form can attempt to write epic.

Nothing is known about the order in which the various parts of *Paradise Lost* were written, however, we do know the various textual forms *Paradise Lost* took in print. The most significant textual alteration *Paradise Lost* underwent during its publication history was the shift from the first edition version in 1667 of *Paradise Lost. A poem in ten books* to the second edition version in 1674 of *Paradise Lost. A poem in twelve books*. The change from ten books to twelve books involved a redivision of the ten existing books into twelve books while adding only fifteen new lines. This structural change is particularly significant in relation to its parallel thematic shift; the shift from scriptural or prophetic history (based on the Bible's ten books narrating the word of God: the Pentateuch along with the four Gospels and Acts) to political history (based on Virgil's *Aeneid*). Other textual alterations include the addition of the following preliminary matter (first included in the fourth issue of the first edition onward): "The Printer to the Reader"; the "Argument" (a single composite argument for the entire poem); Milton's note on "The Verse"; and the "Errata." Also, in the second edition, along with the change from ten to twelve books, two poems were added to the prefatory matter—S[amuel] B[arrow]'s *In Paradisum Amissam summi poetae Johannis Miltoni* and A[ndrew] M[arvell]'s *On Paradise Lost*—and the Argument was distributed to the beginning of each book. The two added poems offer a specific view of *Paradise Lost* and its author—Barrow's poem considers *Paradise Lost* a poem of disclosure, declaring it an epic of the highest magnitude and its author a national hero; Marvell initially discounts the notion of *Paradise Lost* being prophecy, but after proclaiming the trustworthiness and piety of prophecy, Marvell re-establishes *Paradise Lost* as prophecy and distinguishes Milton as a true prophet (one who does not use contrivances such as rhyme). The addition of these poems in 1674 (three years after the publication of *Paradise Regained* and *Samson Agonistes* and a few months before Milton's death) raises questions about the poem/author's initial reception and why the printer, Samuel Simmons, or Milton himself would have wanted it modified; who stood to benefit from these "authoritative" descriptions of the poem and its author?

From the very beginning of *Paradise Lost*, Milton introduces his readers to the audacity of his enterprise, and of the poem itself. In Book 1, lines 12–16, Milton announces his transgressive claim "to soar / Above the Aonian mount" (where Homer and Virgil locate their Muses) in order to receive his inspiration; thus surpassing the epics of Homer and Virgil in the process. The next transgressive aspect of Book 1 is Milton's decision to grant Satan the first words spoken in the poem, and to render his defeat to God sympathetic. Satan's defeated state corresponds directly to Milton's own state of political defeat; Milton was struggling with the failure of the English Revolution and the return of monarchy. As John Carey points out, "Milton's effort to encapsulate evil in Satan was not successful" (*Milton*, 1969). Satan's "Farewell happy fields" speech (lines 249–55), for example, sympathetically reflects the human condition; it is among the most poignant cries of agony as well as resilience ever written and its emphasis on the power of the mind is both revolutionary and conciliatory. Thus, Satan forces the question—perennial in Milton criticism since Dryden—who is the hero of *Paradise Lost?* Milton's decision to represent Satan as a Promethean figure in Book 1 (lines 44–9) further supports Satan's heroic stature—particularly since Satan's ultimate transgression and suffering clearly outweigh the trials of Prometheus. In Book 2, Milton continues to advance the notion of Satan's superior struggle and heroism, in relation to classical figures, by contrasting Satan's perilous journey with Ulysses's journey, and claiming Satan's way to be "harder beset / And more endangered" (lines 1016–7).

In the 1960s Milton critics were preoccupied with the issue of how to account for Satan's appeal in *Paradise Lost*. In *Surprised by Sin*, Stanley Fish deploys reader-response theory to acknowledge and then defuse the problem of Satan's appeal to readers. Fish locates the poem's meaning not in the structure of the text, but in the structure of the reader's progress through the text; thus, Fish circumvents the hermeneutical problem of authorial intention by placing the responsibility for the text's meaning in the reader. The main drawback to Fish's reading is that it dismisses narrative context and generalizes over individual differences. (For a thorough examination and rejection of Fish's argument, see the introduction to John Rumrich's *Milton Unbound*).

Another controversial issue in Milton studies centers on the depiction of women. In Suzanne Woods's essay, "How Free are Milton's Women?" (in *Milton and the Idea of Woman*), Woods concludes that Milton's women are not as free as his men, but that they are responsible for their actions; while Milton's male supremacy may be that of his time, as an author he is in subtle and complex ways moving toward greater liberty for women. It cannot be denied that the depth of subjectivity Milton grants Eve in *Paradise Lost* is certainly progressive for its day (as well as for Milton). Among the most compelling aspects of Eve's portrayal is the attribution of language, thought and intellect to a female character. Eve has her own history and is allowed to express it in her own words and using her own hermeneutic capabilities. Joseph Wittreich astutely points out in his essay, "'Inspir'd with Contradiction,'"that Adam more often than any other speaker in the poem is "responsible for bleaching Eve's story"—Wittreich argues that Adam is responsible for imposing a Gen. 2 or masculinist viewpoint on his account of creation in 8.250ff which is a retelling of Raphael's Gen. 1 or feminist account of creation told to Adam in 7.519ff—and that these self-aggrandizing attempts on Adam's part are exposed as such by the poem, thus causing "Adam [to] lose stature, not Eve."

It is rather difficult, however, to sustain the view that Adam loses stature in *Paradise Lost* rather than Eve, particularly in light of Eve's controversial, and, according to some critics, tainting dream in Book 5. The meaning and consequence of Eve's dream is difficult to assess. While Adam tries to comfort Eve by explaining that "[e]vil into the mind of god or man / May come and go, so unapproved, and leave / No spot or blame behind" (5.117–9), this assurance proves to be somewhat inaccurate based on Adam's proffered reason for why Eve should not part from him in Book 9: "For he who tempts, though in vain, *at least* asperses / The tempted with dishonour foul" (lines. 296–7; emphasis added). With the new information divulged by Adam in Book 9, and remembering that prior to Eve having her dream, Satan was found "squat like a toad" at Eve's ear "[a]ssaying by his devilish art to reach / The organs of her fancy, and with them forge / Illusions as he list, phantasms and dreams" (4.800-3), it is possible that Eve has already been inflicted by some tincture of corruption. Further evidence of the induction of Satan's evil into Eve in Book 4 is the fact that the only other time tears are shed in heaven, besides when Eve sheds a solitary tear after her dream (5.130), is when both Adam and Eve cry about their fallen state (9.1121); evil seems to be the cause for tears in both instances. If Eve is in fact the victim of foul play in the poem (be it by God or Milton), readers of *Paradise Lost* would benefit by considering what this indicates about the inherent nature of man and woman according to Milton, and/or his social milieu.

Numerous Milton critics, particularly the so-called Milton apologists, have argued that feminist renderings of Milton's writing are a product of anachronistic misreadings of his "progressive" representation of women. While proposing that Milton's depiction of Eve be considered in relation not to modern conceptions of feminism and marriage, but rather to Lawrence Stone's notion of the "companionate marriage" and seventeenth-century Puritan marriage doctrine, the apologists—e.g., Barbara Lewalski, Joan Webber, and Diane McColley—tend to overlook the egalitarian portrayals of women's role in marriage in existence during the period and written by members of society outside the realm of dominant culture (see the works of Elizabeth Cary, Rachel Speght, Ester Sowernam, and Mary Wroth).

Contrasting Milton's view of mankind's creation in Book 4 of *Paradise Lost* with Speght's *A Muzzle for Melastomus* may help clarify why feminist critics such as Mary Nyquist and Christine Froula argue against a feminist sensibility in Milton's thinking and writing. Speght argues that woman was created (like man) to glorify God, her creator, directly, and not God in man because "in the Image of God were they both created." This "radical" notion of woman's equity in creation immediately calls to mind Milton's bruisingly misogynous, "Hee for God only, shee for God in him" (4.299). However, it would be misleading simply to contrast Speght's egalitarian view of creation with this single misogynous statement made by the narrator of *Paradise Lost*—particularly since just a few lines earlier this same narrator makes the following observation:

> Two of far nobler shape erect and tall,
> Godlike erect, with native Honour clad
> In naked Majestie seemd Lords of all,
> A worthie seem'd, for in thir looks Divine
> The image of thir glorious Maker shon.
> (4.288-92)

How can one contend with such imbrications of competing viewpoints? According to Joseph Wittreich, "[t]his poem maps patriarchal, misogynous, and feminist discourses within a cacophony of competing but not equally authoritative voices, each of which marks a different state—and stage—of consciousness" ("'Inspir'd with

Contradiction'" in *Literary Milton*, 157) Thus, maintaining a certain degree of healthy skepticism and open-mindedness when confronted with any reading of Milton's poem is always advisable. The Miltonic "truth" concealed within the multiple perspectives on creation and gender provided in *Paradise Lost* can potentially be reached only by allowing the "cacophony of competing voices" in the poem to exist in dialogue with other ideologically relevant, contemporary voices.

Samson Agonistes (1671)

The date of composition of *Samson Agonistes* is uncertain and still contested. John Carey, in the Longman edition of the poem, sides with William Riley Parker's surmise of 1647–53 as the probable date of composition (*Philological Quarterly*, 28, 1949, and *Notes and Queries* 5, 1958), as opposed to the traditional dating of 1666–70 proffered by David Masson. In addition to controversy over the actual date of composition, the poem's publication history has more recently become a source of critical attention. *Samson Agonistes* was originally published in 1671 along with *Paradise Regained*. The title page of the composite 1671 volume—*Paradise Regain'd A Poem. To which is added Samson Agonistes*—allows for an interesting discussion of why Milton would have selected to pair these two disparate works varying in genre (poem versus drama), biblical source text (New Testament versus Old Testament), resolution of characters' agon (passive versus active). Since neither poem was published separately until 1779, the question of why these works were paired together is relevant not only with regard to Milton's intention, but also in relation to the poems' reception for over a century.

The immediate source text of *Samson Agonistes* is Judges 13–16; however, Milton takes numerous liberties with his redaction. Among the most criticized interpolations to the Judges story (all of which can be found in *Interpreting Samson Agonistes*), are those regarding Milton's treatment of the female characters, thus raising the issue of Milton's misogyny—an identification fostered by William Empson's description of Dalila as "a deeply wronged wife" (*Milton's God*). Milton excises from Samson's nativity tale the active role of his mother, who in Judges is the parent graced twice by the presence of an angel and, thus, first informed of Samson's expectant divine birth (Judges 13); instead, Milton offers an expanded role of Samson's father, Manoa. Also, Milton chooses to represent Dalila as Samson's wife which is not the case in Judges. However, this seemingly ennobling act on Milton's part is further elaborated with a poignant rejection of Dalila by Samson when she comes to seek forgiveness for her betrayal. This rejection (a scene which does not take place at all in Judges) takes on the significance of divorce in *Samson Agonistes* since Milton has accorded to Dalila the rights of a wife. Thus the elevation of woman's position through marriage (which Lawrence Stone attributes to the rise of Protestantism) in *Samson Agonistes* needs to be considered in conjunction with woman's ultimate rejection.

Milton's portrayal of divorce in *Samson Agonistes* can profitably be compared with his defense of divorce—for men—in his divorce tracts. Considering that Milton allows Dalila to articulate her own defense for betraying her husband, how has Milton's view of women's marital role changed since the composition of the divorce tracts? It is also useful to contrast Milton's depiction of divorce with Elizabeth Cary's in her closet drama, *The Tragedy of Mariam* (1613). What are we to make of the fact that one of the earliest literary references to divorce in the period is found in the writing of a woman and advanced by a female (albeit villainous) character, i.e., Salome? Is there a gendered perception of divorce in the period? How does the overall portrayal of women (Mariam, Salome, Dalila) differ in these two plays?

According to Jim Swan ("Difference and Silence: John Milton and the Question of Gender" in *The (M)other Tongue*), the steady negation of women in *Samson Agonistes*, as well as in Andrew Marvell's *The Mower's Song*, can be read as an attempt to maintain a sense of solitude—which provides both Samson and the Mower with a sense of identity. For Samson and the Mower, solitude—and thus their identity—is threatened and ultimately violated by a woman. As a result of this violation, Samson is driven throughout the poem by a desire to destroy all that is contrary in order to reachieve the oneness that affirms identity (note the numerous instances of repetition in the poem: Samson's birth is foretold twice by the angel, Samson marries twice and betrays his silence twice, and finally it is "two massy pillars" that Samson must pull down to put an end to all that is contrary). However, since life without contrariety is impossible in the post-lapsarian world of discourse (Milton himself writes in *Areopagitica* that trial purifies us in our fallenness, "and trial is by what is contrary"), Samson can only ultimately achieve singularity in death; at which point he becomes like the phoenix, a genus of one. The image of Samson after his death as "a secular bird" is read by Jackie DiSalvo ("Intestine Thorn: Samson's Struggle with the Woman Within" in *Milton and the Idea of Woman*) as an androgynous image—uniting the masculine eagle with the feminine phoenix (*Samson Agonistes*, lines 1695-1705)—which exposes Milton's rebellion against the exactions and contraries of gender, the psychic costs of patriarchy. (See Geoffrey Whitney, *The Phoenix* in Perspectives: Emblem, Style Metaphor.)

Critical debate over *Samson Agonistes* has centered on the question of how to perceive Samson's final act—i.e., as an act of divine justice or as personal revenge. Antiregenerationist readings of *Samson Agonistes* (e.g., Irene Samuels's, Joseph Wittreich's) interpret Samson's behavior as vengeful and unregenerate. Samson's unregenerate act is understood by such readings as fulfilling the Aristotelian requirement of tragedy—"by raising pity, fear, or terror, to purge the mind of those and such like passions" without having to experience them first-hand. Antiregenerationists view *Samson Agonistes* as contrary to a model of imitation. Alternatively, regenerationist readings of *Samson Agonistes* find a redeeming quality to Samson's behavior based on the mimetic nature of Milton's relationship to Samson. According to Mary Ann Radzinowicz, *Samson Agonistes* "imitates and concludes Milton's own intellectual development; it demonstrates the necessity of mental labor for tempering of the mind and control of the passions" (*Toward Samson Agonistes*, 7).

Finally, critical studies of *Samson Agonistes*, along with Milton's other Restoration poems—*Paradise Lost* and *Paradise Regained*—have generally de-politicized these works. Milton's experience of defeat has been interpreted by

Christopher Hill as a retreat from radicalism. Hill views the Restoration poems as acknowledging defeat while offering a means of coping with it; thus, for Hill, *Samson Agonistes* symbolizes the need to prepare for a future call to action. However, Laura Lunger Knoppers's recent study of Milton's Restoration poetry entitled *Historicizing Milton*, proffers an alternative, politicized view of Milton's later works. She reads Milton's experience of defeat as the writing of poetry under the constraint of censorship, not as an abandoning of contemporary politics. Citing Foucault, Knoppers notes Milton's use of "oppositional discourse" (particularly in relation to forms of spectacle) as a "competing source of authority" capable of challenging the reality of political defeat—a possibility which is overlooked by Hill. According to Knoppers, Milton's "turn inward does not eschew politics but evinces a complex internalization of Puritan discipline [regarding issues of punishment, conquest, martyrdom, joy and prophecy] that can carry on the Good Old Cause in the very theater of the Stuart monarchy" (12).

PERSPECTIVES

Spiritual Self-Reckonings

In *Hydrotaphia*, Sir Thomas Browne wrote: "Our days become considerable like petty sums by minute accumulations; where numerous fractions make up but small round numbers; and our days span make not one little finger." This section allows students to see quantitative representation of the economic and spiritual side by side in late seventeenth-century writing. The rise of capitalism and of the market economy along with developments in applied science combine to produce this sense of measured "reckoning." Reckoning functions as a method of introspection, a way of, as we still say, "taking stock" of things. In some respects it is similar to our own post-modern penchant for lists. See for example the financial accounts of **Ralph Josselin**'s *Diary* and the soul-searching accounts of **Daniel Defoe**'s protagonist in *The Life and Surprizing Adventures of Robinson Crusoe, of York, Mariner* (1719). The best source to contextualize representation through "reckoning" is Stuart Sherman's *Telling Time: Clocks and Calendars, Secrecy and Self Recording in English Diurnal Form* (1997).

The texts of Lady Falkland's daughter, **Anna Trapnel**, and **John Bunyan** focus more on the spiritual and the sense of the person as a self. While the three genres of these works—biography, testimony, and spiritual allegory—are distinct, all three share in the representation of the individual person. You can contrast the sense of interiority and individuality here with that in a medieval spiritual autobiography *The Book of Margery Kempe*, and the intellectual autobiographies of Montaigne and Bacon's *Essays*. *The Lady Falkland: Her Life, by One of Her Daughters* (composed 1643–49) is a helpful companion reading to Cary's *Tragedy of Mariam*. **Alice Thornton**'s *Book of Remembrances* (1629–60) gives a realistic portrayal of the difficulties women encountered in childbearing and sickness in the early modern period. Her strong reliance on the Bible as a text through which to interpret her life and her strong belief in salvation link her narrative with **John Bunyan's** *Pilgrim's Progress* (1678). Thornton's, Trapnel's and Cary's texts can all help explain what was at stake in the controversies over the nature of woman in The Tracts on Women and Gender.

You need to explain Anna Trapnel's *Report and Plea* (1654) with reference to the early modern discourse on witchcraft. You can point out that Sir Thomas Browne actually judged a case of witchcraft. One early modern account of a case of witchcraft, in Edward Jordan's medical pamphlet *Discourse on the Suffocation of the Mother* (1605), shows there was at least some attempt to explain that mental disorder was due to physiological and psychological causes rather than to sin or demonic possession. (For discussions of Jordan's work see Coppelia Kahn in *Rewriting the Renaissance* and Stephen Greenblatt's *Shakespearian Negotiations*.) You can also point out that Othello is accused of witchcraft by Desdemona's father Brabantio in *Othello*. The charge of witchcraft could be a way of branding the cultural other—whether a Moor or a fifth monarchist woman seen as a threat to the social order.

The final selection in this section, John Bunyan, *The Pilgrim's Progress*, is an allegory and so invites comparison with earlier versions of allegory such as Chaucer's *The Nun's Priest's Tale*, and Spenser's *The Faerie Queene*. Bunyan's introductory verses are worth reading carefully as a discussion of exegesis and allegorical representation. They provide a useful way to reflect back on the entire section—from Milton's eschewal of allegory in his adaptation of Genesis in *Paradise Lost*, to Herbert's and Vaughan's deployment of emblems as "silent parable," and the disputes over the interpretation of scripture in the work of Joseph Swetnam and Rachel Speght. As the most popular text in England and in the American colonies for at least a century after it was written, Bunyan's *Pilgrim's Progress* looks forward to the development of the novel, providing a way, for example, of contextualizing Moll Flanders's confessional narrative in Defoe's novel. The allegory of *Pilgrim's Progress* is also a useful point of comparison for the allegorical element in Swift's *Gulliver's Travels* and Johnson's *Rasselas*.

The Restoration and the Eighteenth Century

Ways In

Students are apt to find the eighteenth century more alien than the periods on either side. Shakespeare they have heard in high school, and the nineteenth century's presence persists in many forms: in lingering Romantic conceptions of art and celebrity; in innumerable representations of the novels on film and video (where the eighteenth century has figured less often, and fared less well). Survey courses rarely afford a pause for breath, but this may be the place for one, to choose short texts and assign small tasks designed to offer students a way in to this strange, intriguing world.

Some of the biographical prose (Pepys's accounts of the coronation and of his marriage; Carleton's *Case*; Cavendish's *True Relation*; Boswell's *London Journal*; Thrale's *Family Book*) can give students a particularly quick sense of the material and emotional textures of lives lived. So can some of Swift's poems (the two "Descriptions," the "Dressing Room") with their dense catalogues of debris. Most immediate and copious of all, perhaps, are the pictures: Bowles's *Medley*, the frontispiece of the section (how does it differ from the earlier frontispieces? what does it show and suggest about the culture it depicts?); the century-spanning portraits of women that punctuate the general introduction (what changes do they trace?); and above all the *Rake's Progress*, which tracks one fool through eight sites crucial to the culture (home, salon, tavern, square, church, gambling den, Newgate, Bedlam), and unfolds the story of his ruin in the plethora of people, texts, garb, and artifacts that surround him.

Students will move more confidently and perceptively through the literature of the period if they learn to recognize (even reproduce) some of the recurrent shapes in which writers cast their language: the periodic sentence; the running style; the heroic couplet. The writer of a polished period, with its intricately balanced structure and delayed resolution, performs a pointed mastery over information, arrangement, even time itself. The structure implies a kind of foresight: "I know what comes next, though you, the reader, may not." Plainer styles—simpler clauses,

---

Cynthia Wall (University of Virginia) wrote the sections on Behn, Rochester, Astell, Defoe, Swift, Pope, Mary Wortley Montagu, and "Mind and God." Steven N. Zwicker (Washington University in St. Louis) co-wrote the section on Dryden.

either clipped or strung together in long run-ons—embody a different take on time: "The content of this clause has been established, but *anything* may happen next." The periodic sentence can readily impart that "extensive view" of the world (*Vanity of Human Wishes*, l. 1) which Dryden, Pope, and Johnson often aspired to. The running style often facilitates what Samuel Richardson called writing "to the moment," that prose practice which prompted so many of the period's literary innovations, in newspapers, diaries, letters, essays, travel narratives, and novels. Students can get at the pulse of both these modes by reading aloud some specific examples (ask them to "predict" the sentence's end before they get there, or to snap their fingers when they hear a clause complete itself) and by casting some new sentences into these same shapes: sentences they've made up and sentences they've "translated" from other sources—conversation, songs, etc. Some periodic/running pairs for practice: *Rambler* No. 60's global opening sentence (2738) and the particulars from Aubrey's life of Bacon (2138); the *Female Spectator's* first paragraph on Seomanthe (2433) and the first passages from Pepys's and/or H. F.'s accounts of the plague (2090, 2380). (A useful aid in teaching this topic is Richard Lanham's chapter on "The Periodic Style and the Running Style," in his *Analyzing Prose* [Scribner, 1983].)

Imitation and translation are also among the surest ways of initiating students into the structures, challenges, and pleasures of the heroic couplet; for specific suggestions, see the section on Alexander Pope, below. Since hearing poetry always enhances the reading of it, a particularly useful tool for teaching is the series of *Penguin English Verse* cassettes: volume 2 (The Seventeenth Century: Donne to Rochester, ISBN 0140861319) and volume 3 (The Eighteenth Century: Swift to Crabbe, ISBN 0140861327) offer good performances of many of the poems in the anthology. Christopher Fox's collection of essays by many hands, *Teaching Eighteenth-Century Poetry* (AMS Press, 1990), includes pieces on many of the major poems and poetic topics (satire, couplet, landscape). Margaret Anne Doody's *The Daring Muse: Augustan Poetry Reconsidered* (Cambridge UP, 1985) bursts with original, eminently teachable insights on many, many poems.

For teaching the prose of the period, the resources are more scattered; see the suggestions under individual authors, below. Jeremy Black's *Illustrated History of Eighteenth-Century Britain* (Manchester UP, 1996) provides helpful cultural backgrounds and a terrific array of pictures. James Sambrook's *The Eighteenth Century: The Intellectual and Cultural Context 1700–1789* (Longman, 1990) is perhaps the one most valuable book to keep at hand. With clarity and grace, Sambrook presents a wealth of detailed information—as well as a superb set of short biographies and bibliographies—useful for teaching nearly every text in this section of the anthology.

Samuel Pepys

Students find Pepys's predicaments intriguing, but at first they sometimes think his prose a little chilly; it takes a while for them to hear how his reportorial style (clipped and run-on at the same time) encodes emotion, anxiety, and (often) comedy. One shortcut to such understanding is provided by Kenneth Branagh's recorded reading (Highbridge Audio, ISBN 1565111346): the voice in the text comes through live and clear. What Branagh's recording does for sound, Robert Latham's *Illustrated Pepys* (Berkeley, 1978) does for sight, providing useful pictorial ways in to the diarist's world.

Our distance from this diary is also worth confronting head-on: What is Pepys doing in his diary? How do his ideas of what a diary is for differ from our own? One useful way of answering these questions is to read Pepys alongside the selections from James Boswell and Hester Piozzi later in the anthology. Their diaries, dealing in passions openly stated and energetically (even psychoanalytically) explored, are of a kind more familiar to present readers, and help to highlight both the different narrative game that Pepys is playing and the cultural changes of the intervening hundred years, where Locke's mapping of the associative mind, and Hume's doubts as to the fixity of identity, partly displaced the Puritan and fiscal models of self-tracking that Pepys (and Ralph Josselin and Robinson Crusoe) are working from. The opening entries of Pepys's, Crusoe's, Boswell's, and Piozzi's journals can make for a particularly fruitful grouping, a good class hour of comparisons.

Whether alone or in conjunction with the opening gambits of other diarists, Pepys's first entries are worth some discussion (for a close reading of these entries, see Stuart Sherman, *Telling Time* [U of Chicago P, 1996] 29–76). They provide a key to the whole, a chance to identify and explore concerns, motifs, and methods that drive the diary, cropping up in almost every entry thereafter. I'll highlight a few of these elements here, and then discuss most of the entries in chronological sequence.

Time and motion   Pepys is fascinated by beginnings and endings. He commences his diary at the start of a new week, month, year, and decade, and he frames most subsequent entries in a neat enclosure that begins with "up" and ends with "to bed." But he treats these termini as useful markers for tracking a life of constant motion, in which time is both fluid and full. The flux is conspicuous in the opening paragraphs, where verb tenses shift from present to past to neutral (as they will throughout the diary) and where temporal perspectives change swiftly too, reading sometimes like current reportage, sometimes like projected history ("the condition of the state was thus"). The biblical text that Pepys quotes on New Year's Day is rich in implications for his own new enterprise: his diary performs the "fullness of time" by reporting (as apparently no diarist before had done) each day's full sequence, from wake to sleep, in an unbroken series. Of course this "fullness" is a textually managed illusion: in fact Pepys selects a few incidents, moments, and thoughts from each day, but by his abundant recurrent connectives (nearly endless *thens*, *thences*, and—above all—*ands*) he fosters a deep sense of continuity, of flow. He treasures not only the immediacy of the passing present, but also its ignorance. Though he often revised his entries days or even months after their date, he rarely suffuses them with foreknowledge: he prefers to perform the day's uncertainties, even when he knows how they have since resolved themselves. (For the richest account of the diary's composition, see William Matthews, "The Diary as Literature," in the first volume of *The Diary of Samuel Pepys* [U of California P, 1970], xcvii–cxiii).

Death and posterity The diary's first sentence touches on death; so will its last. Pepys recalls the "old pain" of his bladder stones, which prompted him to risk his life in an operation that (with fifty-fifty odds) ended up healing rather than killing him. Loss hovers too over the second and third paragraphs, where hopes of progeny vanish for the moment (Elizabeth Pepys never bore children, possibly—as Pepys perhaps already suspects—because of sterility induced by his surgery). From its first lines, then, the diary presents itself as a (surrogate?) gesture towards posterity, an attempt at self-perpetuation along new textual lines. For all its fascination with endpoints, Pepys's diary is an essentially open-ended structure: the series of entries will continue indefinitely, and in one sense with no conclusion. The diarist will not be able to record the day of his death—and this fact makes the diary's actual conclusion, nine years later, all the more interesting and intricate.

The public, the private, and the secret In the opening entry, Pepys modulates in a moment from the condition of his wife to the condition of the state, and concludes with a wildly unstable reckoning of his public status ("esteemed rich") and private agitations ("indeed very poor"); the sentence affords a hilarious introduction to a recurrent Pepysian dialectic, which proposes opposite extremes and ends up somewhere in the middle. As Pepys progresses chronologically through the day, he moves constantly among the public, the private, and the secret; the entries on Charles's coronation (23–24 April 1661) offer a rich instance of this motion, with Pepys carefully tracking his private connections (wife, patron) and releases (pissing, vomiting) amid the public festivities. The pressures of containment and the pleasures of revelation drive the diary between them: it operates at highest energy when depicting those moments (the fire, the domestic crisis of Deb Willett) where objects, feelings, and secrets burst forth from their enclosures. (For a subtle assessment of Pepysian secrecy, sexuality, textuality, and power in the diary, see James Grantham Turner, "Pepys and the Private Parts of Monarchy," in *Culture and Society in the Stuart Restoration*, ed. Gerald MacLean [Cambridge UP, 1995]).

Pleasure The phrase "with great pleasure" recurs with great frequency throughout the diary; so does the exclamation "But Lord! to see . . . " (whatever there is to be seen and recorded). The diary presents itself as a running catalog of pleasures, and above all (despite Pepys's passion for music and for food) as a chronicle of pleasures of the eye. The language of pleasure, first glimpsed in Pepys's attention to such matters as the New Year's turkey, is at its richest in the selections on "Theater and Music" (the backstage tour, though, prompts a mixture of pleasure, fascination, and horror: the diarist, for once, has seen too much).

In the entries on the plague year, two of the diary's deepest concerns—with pleasure and with death—come into highly charged convergence. Pepys comes up with an astonishing array of tactics—in his life and in his prose—for simultaneously *registering* his fear of death, and for keeping death at bay. Among the most striking of these: his purchase of tobacco to allay his alarm at seeing the red crosses on the quarantine houses of infected families (7 June 1665); his account of the children's game of levitation and "resurrection," complete with transcription of the French incantation (7 July); the nearly hysterical laughing session (10 September) with John Evelyn, whose puns on the words *may* and *can* suggest darker plague-time resonances (who will be permitted to live? what can anyone do to forestall death?); Pepys's dream of "dalliance" with Lady Castlemaine (15 August), which prompts him to recast Hamlet's suicide soliloquy in a more hopeful mode: Hamlet fears "what dreams may come" during the sleep of death, but Pepys devises a counter-fantasy in which those dreams perpetually sustain (even enhance?) the pleasures of real life. (Pepys's maneuvers here are so intricate as to be worth a good discussion, possibly with the text of Hamlet's soliloquy at hand.) Pepys invokes pleasure as though it were an operative antidote to plague—not merely a mode of enjoying life, but a means of prolonging it.

Pepys's entries on the plague invite—almost demand—comparison with the selections from Defoe's fictional *Journal* of the same *Plague Year*, published 1722 (2090). For Defoe's narrator, H. F., the plague is an agent of alienation, sundering each London denizen from all others, who may carry the threat of infection. For Pepys, by contrast, social connection itself works as a kind of plague preventative, albeit a precarious one. It is in his links with others (with Evelyn, with Captain Cocke, and in dreams with Lady Castlemaine) that furnishes joy and distraction; the mix of social pleasure, pride, and agitation is perhaps most vivid in his account of the wedding (31 July) which he himself has deftly arranged, and which prompts in him an interesting oscillation between misgiving and self-satisfaction. At the same time, Pepys's position as writer is more dangerous than that of Defoe's narrator. H. F. too supposedly wrote journal entries in 1665, but now, decades later, he recasts them in a running narrative as both a history and a warning to later generations. He *rewrites* as someone who has survived the plague (and must now make some sense of his own survival); Pepys writes as someone who may not—and must make some sense, and pleasure, from his own predicament. Taken together, the two texts may also prompt thoughts about genre—about the differences between the kind of "run-on" memoir, free-associative in structure and free-moving in time, that deeply interested Defoe, and the date-compartmentalized format that Pepys devised for his diary.

Pepys's account of the Fire of London, the most famous passage in the diary, may benefit from comparison with John Evelyn's entries for the same dates (included here as a companion reading)—and with the *London Gazette*'s account (2096–2100). Like Defoe's H. F., Evelyn rewrites his earlier memoranda in frank retrospect: "This fatal night . . . began that deplorable fire," which (so the *that* declares) is at the present moment of writing (ca. 1680) a familiar historical datum. Evelyn makes sense of the fire by casting it within even larger arcs of time, as a "resemblance of Sodom, or the last day," and as an echo of falling Troy (2 September). These last lines of this entry offer a rich and compact instance of typological thinking: Evelyn's way of interpreting London's destruction is to set the city into a patterned history (Sodom past, Judgment future) composed by God and embellished by authors classical and scriptural.

Pepys records at greater length more local data. As he does throughout the diary, he confines himself almost exclusively to reporting what he experienced and knew on the date of the entry (though the catastrophe of the conflagration prompts him to half-break this rule: he admits early on that he was unprepared for "such fires as followed"). Like Evelyn, Pepys seeks out pattern amid the chaos, but he finds it (or creates it) from immediate observations: the pigeons, like the people, cling to their homes until "the very fire touched them." While typology sets its stamp on Evelyn's account, a kind of proto-sociology pervades Pepys's. He is fascinated by the data about people's lives that the fire suddenly makes available, noting, for example, that perhaps one householder in three (to judge by the cargo in the rescue boats) possesses a "pair of virginals" (2098). Perhaps every diarist, in writing down the world, ends up making the world resemble the written record. In Pepys's account of the fire, the fire "works" like the diary: it provides an occasion for the exposing of secrets, the disclosure of domestic privacies. The fire entries attain their greatness in part from this carefully wrought empathy between the diarist and the occasion he records.

Where Evelyn casts his account from the vantage of distance (temporal, typological), Pepys takes pains to write from the midst. He emphasizes his role as middle man between those working on the blaze and the king and duke who supervise the labor; he contrives to bring both his person and his text "as near the fire" as he can, in language seemingly devised (whether consciously or no) to bring an imagined reader with him: "and all over the Thames, with one's face in the wind, you were almost burned with the firedrops—this is very true" (2098). The immediacy of the fire entries, often praised, is the product of careful work. Pepys inscribed these entries into his journal book a full three months after the events they record, working from memoranda drawn up during the fire which the pressures of the disaster itself forestalled him from expanding to his satisfaction. Like Evelyn, then, Pepys is *rewriting* events from a certain remove, but with a different purpose: not so much to set the catastrophe into a firm and larger framework, as to recreate—by choice of incident, by arrangement of phrasing and cadence—the intensities and uncertainties of the lived experience. Where Evelyn seeks fixity, Pepys attempts to recapitulate motion, and the movement of his long first entry (2 September) is so crucial to its impact that any class on the topic would do well to begin with a reading aloud (or the listening to a tape) of the entry whole, as a first step in understanding and savoring its many parts.

Pepys's intrigue with Deborah Willett proves so intriguing to students that it practically teaches itself; in fact, though it comes at the conclusion of the diary, it offers an excellent starting point, an easy way in (students will often appreciate earlier entries more after reading these). These entries focus and dramatize questions of gender that run throughout the diary. As a result of the crisis, Elizabeth Pepys's personal history and inner life (and to a lesser extent Deborah Willett's) occupy the imagination of the diarist, and the pages of his diary, as never before. (For an imaginative reconstruction of Elizabeth's inner life, see Dale Spender's antic *Diary of Elizabeth Pepys* [Grafton/HarperCollins, 1989]). The struggle for control and for autonomy is played out in the text, in ways that shed light on both gender and class: the negotiations between wife and husband, the differences in status (economic, amatory, imaginative) between mistress and maidservant. This section also brings to an intricate culmination many of the diary's most abiding concerns: with secrecy (all those revelations and counter-revelations, all that diving into the further secrecy and revelation of the *lingua franca*); with time (the crisis precipitates a heightened, agitated fluidity in the prose, and even a confusion about dates); with writing as a vehicle of truth and manipulation (see the stratagems involved in Pepys's break-off letter to Deb), with ending and with loss: Pepys is eager and reluctant to end the liaison, and writes and acts accordingly. Note especially the resonant ambiguities of the diary's last entry (31 May 1669), in which he visits the "World's End"; in which, having resolved upon fidelity, he pursues the pleasures of an old infatuation; in which he makes explicit the link between his writing and his *amours*; in which he proposes to end the diary and not to end it; and in which he leaves unclear whether it is the prospect of blindness or of concluding his diary that seems to him as frightening "as to see myself go into my grave." Even in this final fantasy of death, there persists the diarist's devotion to self-observation as a means of self-perpetuation: he not only goes into his grave, he gets to *see* himself do so.

Mary Carleton

Carleton writes with scorn and verve about the ordeals she's endured, the trouble she's caused, the fools she's thwarted, and the triumph she's enjoyed; students may well find much to say about her sardonically subversive autobiography.

Among the excerpts printed here, perhaps the most important is the fascinatingly convoluted paragraph beginning "What harm have I done in pretending to great titles?" (2115). Here Carleton almost (but not quite) confesses to having made up the story of her aristocratic origins that she steadily sticks to throughout the rest of the pamphlet (though "pretending" *could* just mean "laying legitimate claim"). The passage suggests something about the taste of the reading public for narrative that was neither patent fact nor patent fiction but hovered tantalizingly between the two (sensational pamphleteers and artful novelists would skillfully exploit this predilection). But Carleton goes on to argue that pretense, feigning, and fictive emulation are the very currency of the culture, indeed the language in which it couches its morality: "the best things are to be imitated." If she has perpetrated a deception (a very lively *if*, as she presents it here), at least she has thought hard about what she's doing, and has managed the trick with admirable panache. In her often comic courtship narrative, she makes clear that her accusers, the Carletons, are more obtuse. In exaggerating their status to deceive her, they are also (she strongly suggests) deluding themselves as to their own importance and power—their power (among other things) to trick this solitary and gullible young woman. Theirs, Carleton suggests, is the way of the world; her way, of seeing through deceptions even while perhaps perpetrating a few of her own, amounts to innovation—a new way out.

The innovation had analogues. Carleton's "case" has often been compared with that of the actresses newly arrived in the Restoration theater who, having impersonated aristocrats onstage, often moved among them offstage as the mistresses and (more rarely) wives of men in power. Pepys's dismissal of Carleton's acting (quoted in the headnote) may smack of ironic condescension: in the temple of impersonation, the great impersonator doesn't perform well at all. But the irony readily reverses. The trick she could not bring off onstage she had already managed triumphantly in the larger, more volatile venue of real life. In her autobiography, Carleton commutes her "case" into a critique of marriage in general (see her address "To the Noble Ladies") and of England in particular (see the closing paragraphs). In her impersonations and in her rhetoric, she pursues an autonomy which, as she angrily points out, neither the institution nor the nation makes available to women.

Carleton's case teaches well in tandem with the selections from Margaret Cavendish (for explicit comparisons, see Janet Todd, *The Sign of Angellica* [Columbia UP, 1989]; and Mihoko Suzuki, "The Case of Madam Mary Carleton: Representing the Female Subject, 1663-1673," *Tulsa Studies in Women's Literature* 12:1 [1993]: 61-84); with Pepys, that "very rising man" for whom her tale seems so highly charged (perhaps because so parallel in some respects); with Rochester, Dorimant (*Man of Mode*), and Macheath (*Beggar's Opera*), in whose company she moves interestingly as female libertine, pursuing schemes and autonomies normally reserved to men; and with Defoe (*Moll Flanders* and *Roxana*, as well as the anthology selections), whose copious narrative circumstantialities may derive in part from her own prose.

PERSPECTIVES

The Royal Society and the New Science

For a single session on this material, a few overarching questions may prove useful. First, the experimental method accorded new centrality to the data supplied by the senses. The Fellows of the Society, Sprat observes at one point in his *History*, feel surest when inquiring into "things" that can "be brought within their *own touch and sight*" (italics his); they feel less secure about experiments in which they are "forced to trust *the reports of others*." Yet from a reader's point of view, *all* writing consists in "the reports of others"; apart from the reader's use of sight to discern the letters read, prose makes no direct appeal to the senses. Hence a crux and a question: how does each of the writers here attempt to bring the senses into play within his prose? The answer is perhaps most obvious in Hooke's *Micrographia*, where our eyes take in directly the drawn-up data—even as the data, obtained by means of microscope, alert us to the *inadequacy* of human vision heretofore. The answer is only slightly less elusive in Aubrey, whose biographies deal so abundantly in *things* touched, smelled, tasted, counted (it is worthwhile, perhaps, to compile a quick catalog in class: Bacon's aversion to neat's leather, his strong beer, his snow-stuffed goose . . .). The *Transactions* seeks to build a sturdy chain of sensory testimony (the fetus-stone of the monstrous calf has been carefully palpated and repalpated in Hampshire, and pieces of it are being sent to Robert Boyle); and Sprat himself returns repeatedly to the dream (savagely mocked by Swift) of a method in which words attain the "nakedness," specificity, and palpability of *things*. Of course all these writers are inescapably involved in acts of surrogacy; even with Hooke we are looking not through a microscope, but at his drawings. The question concerns what strategies the Fellows devise to compensate for the surrogacy, to close the gap between their report and the thing itself.

The second question concerns another challenge to writers, intrinsic to the Society's agenda. In phrases key to this Perspectives section, Sprat emphasizes the importance of *incompletion* in the Fellows' work: "their purpose was to heap up a mixed mass of experiments, without digesting them into any perfect model," and to present their reports "not as complete schemes of opinions, but as bare, unfinished histories" (2127). How does each of these writers attempt to convey the sense of a heap, a mixed mass, an unfinished history, in the structure of his writing? In what ways—and for what reasons—do they complicate this agenda by insinuating order, hypothesis, point, and rhetorical flourish in their prose?

Thomas Sprat

At crucial moments, Sprat's prose famously seems at odds with his program. He is at his most ornately rhetorical when denouncing ornate rhetoric. His scornful rejections of "this vicious abundance of phrase, this trick of metaphors, this volubility of tongue," and of "all the amplifications, digressions, and swellings of style," are both instances of the Ciceronian tricolon (or three-parter), that amplification and swelling of style that had long afforded writers and orators the kind of prefabricated grandeur that putatively prompts Sprat's rage (students may enjoy seeking out other instances of such ornament). Sprat was uncomfortably conscious of the inconsistency: "The style in which [this history] is written," he confessed in his preface, "is larger and more contentious than becomes that purity and shortness which are the chief beauties of historical writings," but for this fault he blames the Society's detractors. So severe are their attacks, Sprat argues, that he must deploy all the rhetorical resources available to him.

Philosophical Transactions

The question of rhetoric recurs: Oldenburg's ornate introduction (an attempt, perhaps, to produce new converts?) contrasts with the plainer style of his reports (preaching to the already converted?). It may be worthwhile to read an excerpt of each aloud.

The newly developing genre of the periodical provided a near-perfect implementation of the "mixed mass" and the "unfinished history." The table of contents for each number blazoned an ostentatious variety of topics. In the matter of "the monstrous calf," erroneous observations in the first number are comfortably corrected in the second. Boyle's conjectures about ambergris, though erroneous in themselves, fulfill flawlessly the Society's agenda for inquiry: its proud dependence on information gathered by merchants and "mechanicks" engaged with the real world; its use of a manuscript "journal" (another mode of periodical) in which the data are recorded fresh, at the time and place of their first gathering.

Robert Hooke

Rhetorically, Hooke sustains a continual traffic between small things and great: he presents (in the first dedication) a "small present" to a great king; apologizes (in the second) for his own "faults" before an "illustrious assembly"; yet he makes clear, throughout his text that the microscope's minutiae have much to teach us about Creation and about the "true philosophy" in which Hooke and his colleagues are engaged. Like other modesty *topoi*, Hooke's is rich in potential inversion. He insists repeatedly on his subordinate status (real enough at the Royal Society) while all the while establishing his value as a discoverer. In a book where small things are made great on every page, his claim gains pictorial potency.

Hooke's preface highlights the double status of the human senses in the Society's agenda: the senses are all-important, and they are woefully inadequate. New instruments must be used to extend their reach and refine their grasp. Hooke promptly remakes this point, with subtle visual force, by showing us a printed period (or full stop) many times magnified in the book's first illustrative plate. In the text that accompanies the picture (indeed in every text we read) we have beheld numberless periods of ordinary size. The plate inducts us deftly into the book's central revelation: that the things we have looked at all our days, we have not fully *seen*. We are alerted both to the insufficiency of our senses, and (as Hooke emphasizes) to the inferiority, the imperfection, of works of "art" (human artifice) in contrast with works of nature. Once having seen the magnified period in the plate, we cannot look at the periods on the page in quite the same way again, and so we advance a little way into that collaborative process of skeptical inquiry which the Society so prized. Hooke draws us thither again and again by inviting us to do our own "work" on the plates he presents, as at the end of the commentary on the flea.

Hooke's depiction of the flea seems to have produced the most shock and fascination of any of his plates, partly because of the implicit violence of the image (see the metaphors of armor and weaponry that Hooke deploys in his description) but partly too because the picture was a foldout, glued into the book but four times the size of the book's normal page. Having perhaps become accustomed to the magnifications on early pages, the reader was confronted, here at the very end of the book, with expansion expanded—and with the implication that *Micrographia* and its attendant inquiries would prove an unending program, of which this first installment was a bare, unfinished history.

Among those agitated by the depiction of the flea was Margaret Cavendish, whose *Observations upon Experimental Philosophy* is in large measure a retort to *Micrographia*. The two texts make a useful pairing; see the section on Cavendish below.

John Aubrey

Aubrey's *Lives* are unfinished history incarnate: even in this copious array of notes *towards* biography, he leaves blanks that he never got around to filling in. The real question is what makes them so pleasurable as prose and so persuasive, in their own way, as biography. It may be best to hear a few items read aloud, some short (Bacon's "hazel eye"; Harvey's "young wench") and some longer (Harvey's involvement at Edgehill, with its striking train of narrative thought), and to ask, one by one, what effects Aubrey achieves in these items and how he achieves them. One key may lie in Sprat's recurrent praise of "naked" language (and "bare" history). Aubrey's anecdotes *seem* unadorned, unmediated, as though rawly reported in accord with the Beat credo, "first thought, best thought." At the same time, Aubrey is conspicuously and pervasively present, as gatherer ("Mr. Hobbes told me. . .") and as shaper: it seems clear, for example, that Aubrey admires both these men tremendously, though he does not directly say so. How, then, can we tell?

The *Lives* teach very well in concert with the selections from Johnson's *Lives of the Poets* or (closer in time) from Edward Hyde's *True Historical Narrative of the Rebellion*. The difference between Aubrey's clipped, simple sentences (and sentence fragments) on the one hand, and Hyde's and Johnson's polished periods on the other, embodies two prose-patterns and world-views in flux and sometimes conflict throughout the Restoration and eighteenth century (for more on this distinction, see the introductory section on "Ways In," above). To state the contrast over-simply: the period figures, as syntax, those "perfect [i.e., polished, completed] models" of thought and report that Sprat rejected; the running style embodies the provisional model, the sense of history unfinished, which he celebrated. To teach students the differences in the two modes is to enable them to make sense of much eighteenth-century writing (Fielding's periodic sentences and narrative structures work alike; so do Defoe's running sentences and provisional, improvisatory narratives). Yet writers, particularly in the Restoration, availed themselves of both modes. Pepys wrote ornate Ciceronian "public prose" (letters, speeches), but chose a far plainer style for the data-gathering of his diary.

This section on the New Science will work well in combination not only (as suggested above) with Hyde, Cavendish, and Swift, but also with Pepys and Defoe, whose prose styles and narrative tactics have much in common with Sprat's advocacy and Aubrey's practice. Two points of contact: 1) The close affinity between the seventeenth-century definitions of *experiment* and *experience* (the two terms were sometimes used interchangeably). To what extent can Pepys's or Defoe's records of private *experience* be understood as the bare unfinished history of a mixed mass of self-centered *experiment*: the gathering of data in the unending attempt to document and understand a single mind, a lived life? 2) The odd applicability of the term *micrographia*: what new bearings do small things have upon great in this emergent culture of magnified examination, copious documentation?

Margaret Cavendish, Duchess of Newcastle

In virtually every one of her works, from the shortest poem to the longest treatise, Cavendish oscillates energetically between the poles of self-deprecation and self-assertion. This doubleness has been variously interpreted: as a protective strategy in which Cavendish's true, outspoken self dons shyness as a disguise in order to move acceptedly through a patriarchal culture; as the moodswings of a narcissist; or as an inconsistency which Cavendish deliberately refuses to resolve, the polarity itself—

the containing of multitudes—being an essential element of her cherished "singularity" (see Eve Keller, "Producing Petty Gods: Margaret Cavendish's Critique of Experimental Science," *ELH* 64:2 [1997]: 447–471). Because the doubleness is difficult to explain away, and because it takes so many different forms in the different texts, it makes a useful touchstone in class discussions of Cavendish's work.

Cavendish's short poems *about* her poetry oscillate rapidly, in both their "arguments" and their metaphors. In the first, Cavendish prevails over the arguments of Reason against publishing her book, then promptly suffers misgivings (interestingly enough, in the poem's first edition Reason was gendered female, a "she" rather than a "he"). The second poem reverses the process: it begins as funeral for the poems (and the fevered poet?), but ends in hoped-for resurrection. In the third poem, the verse that was a corpse becomes her child: to publish poetry, then, is simultaneously to risk the death attendant upon disgrace and to court a perpetuity of admiration, to build a "pyramid of fame."

Is "poor Wat," the victim-protagonist in "The Hunting of the Hare," a further figure for the poet and her poems? Some have thought so ("I am as fearful as a hare," Cavendish once remarked). The condemnation of the male hunters who invade the natural world, rather than paying it the sympathetic attention that Cavendish here models, will surface again in her critique of experimental science. Virginia Woolf wove this poem into her eulogy for the Duchess: ". . . few of her critics, after all, had the wit to trouble about the nature of the universe, or cared a straw for the sufferings of the hunted hare. . . . Now, at any rate, the laugh is not all on their side" ("The Duchess of Newcastle," in *The Common Reader*, ed. Andrew McNeillie [Harcourt, Brace, Jovanovich, 1984], 77).

A True Relation, like so much of Cavendish's work, professes itself to have been written out of a mix of strength and fear. "There is nothing I dread more than death," Cavendish wrote in her *Sociable Letters*. "I do not mean the strokes of death, nor the pains, but the oblivion in death." As Cavendish makes clear in the final sentence of the *Relation*, that dread has driven her to write her autobiography. Men frame the narrative—her father at the start, her husband at the end—but women prevail between, in Cavendish's admiring portrait of her mother, and in the sustained self-reckoning that she carries out in her conclusion. Here she lays out the contradictions of her character as points of fascination and (intermittently) of pride—as the sources of her singularity. Cavendish's counter-offensive against oblivion seems to consist in an attempt to make herself wholly seen, in the hope (often frustrated) that she will win thereby a wholehearted approval (such as she receives from her husband), and thence immortality. The reader, as witness and judge, becomes indispensable to her schemes of redress and resurrection, of presence and permanence. A striking instance: her attempt to describe her handwriting, so that we "see" the original messy manuscript that lies behind the delusive neatness of our printed book. Her careening syntax has some of the same self-insistent effect—an index, she implies, of her teeming, speeding fancy. As chronicler of the self, Cavendish bears comparison with Pepys (he is not half so introspective), with Carleton (who constructs herself along the opposite vector: overwhelming confidence in pursuit of feigned aristocracy), with Mary Wortley

Montagu (whose fascination with Turkish dress collates interestingly with the Duchess's fashion-consciousness), with Hester Thrale (who shares some of Cavendish's anxieties as a woman writer), and with Boswell who (unexpectedly perhaps) turns out in some ways to be her closest co-practitioner, at once proud and distressed at his own exhaustively catalogued contradictions.

Cavendish's doubleness finds its most intriguing literary manifestation in her *Observations* and *Blazing World*–two works of very different kinds, pointedly yoked together. The *Observations'* attack on *Micrographia* can serve as a salutary reminder to students of how little-established, how precarious in status, how open to objection, the experimental method was among many of Hooke's contemporaries. Cavendish's particular objections collate interestingly with some late-twentieth-century modes of thought about the history of science (see Keller). She argues that the microscope, far from presenting an "objective" image, produces its own distortions, and that the notion of an objectivity achievable by instruments and machines is itself an illusion, an "artifice," a construct–perhaps a peculiarly masculine construct, propagated by the men of the Royal Society, whom she here depicts as boys playing uselessly with bubbles (interestingly, Cavendish describes the microscope's distortions themselves as "hermaphroditic," neither male nor female: half artifice, half nature). A question that may prompt much talk: what is Cavendish rightly seeing about Hooke's methods and intentions here, and what is she missing?

The preface to *Blazing World* ("To the Reader") has occasioned much comment, and rightly so. Cavendish here makes some amazing literary and conceptual moves, especially in the passage where she declares herself "Margaret the First." Catherine Gallagher's article, "Embracing the Absolute: The Politics of the Female Subject in Seventeenth-Century England" (*Genders* 1 [1988]: 24–39) remains the best way in to what is now a thriving debate about the import of Cavendish's gesture here. To couch part of the debate as question: To what extent do Cavendish's grand gestures, here and in her epilogue, ally her with her readers (and particularly her women readers), and to what extent does she set herself apart? Are we all to enjoy the privileges of "creating worlds," of producing imperial fictions–or only some of us, or Cavendish more than anyone? As for the *Blazing World* itself, it has been explored as utopian fantasy, feminist tract, philosophical treatise, and science fiction. It is also (as the excerpts here may help suggest) one of the most extraordinary pieces of self-portraiture–of autobiography–ever penned, and bears interesting comparison with the author's *True Relation*, as well as with all the other self-writing of the period and beyond.

John Dryden
Absalom and Achitophel

Of all the great English poets, Dryden seems at once the most transparent and the most resistant to the immediate pleasures of reading and contemplation. Part of the problem is surely the intense topicality of his great poems, and no verse presents that topicality in a more demanding fashion than *Absalom and Achitophel*; this is topical verse veiled beneath scriptural reference. One good way to begin is with selections from the scriptural story that Dryden uses (2 Samuel, 14.21–19.8). These passages will at least make the narrative outlines of the poem come clear; yet of course, the drama of the poem has only begun to be unfolded by the Scripture. Next, it will be necessary both to identify the contemporary players veiled by scriptural identities and to suggest the very contemporary drama of the Exclusion Crisis which the scriptural episode is made to narrate. A brief summary of that crisis appears on p. 2159; for fuller, but still usefully concise accounts, see Ronald Hutton's biography *Charles II* (Clarendon Press, 1989) 358–66; or J. R. Jones, *Country and Court* (Harvard UP, 1978) 200–02.

The real problem, of course, is how to set the historical materials into play with both the preface and the poem itself. Here, it's worthwhile to spend time first reminding the students of the gravity of the Crisis and of the virulent partisanship that surrounded all of the events and personalities involved, and then taking note of Dryden's careful insistence in the preface on modesty, moderation, and diffidence. Why, we might wonder, should the introduction to a poem that is after all virulently partisan so strenuously affect moderation? The answer to that question is in fact the key to the poetics of this whole enterprise: the rhetoric of political modesty in the preface; the frame of scriptural narrative; the seeming balance with which Dryden calculates the virtues and defects of the wicked characters; the structural counterpoint between the Hydra-headed cohort of the king's enemies (ll. 541–681) and the "small but faithful band" of the king's supporters (ll. 810–916); and the crowning oration that Dryden ventriloquizes for the king, who after the strain of long forbearance calls for the sword of the law. And here it will be good to point out that the excisive conclusion of the poem is foretold in the images of amputation hidden in the Latin quotation at the close of the prose preface.

Other features to note in unfolding the drama of this verse are the brilliant ways in which Dryden achieves ambivalence in the opening portrait of Davidic patriarchy, the inclusion of substantial echoes from *Paradise Lost* in the drama of Absalom's political seduction, and the startling gallery of portraits in which Dryden memorializes a cast of political thugs and operatives (the depiction of Zimri, ll. 544–68, provides an excellent short sample for close reading). It will also be worth noting that Dryden balances these brilliant figures with cooler and more integrated portraits of those who stood with the king. One of the points to make about these portraits is that in fact they are hardly as memorable as Dryden's satiric verse on the political operatives—surely the aesthetics here constitute a political argument that a well-ordered and affective commonweal can run only when a vaunting individualism is subdued to the interests of the whole.

Dryden's most astute student was Alexander Pope, and the mock-epic of the *Dunciad* absorbs and extends the lessons both of heroic satire and of punishing diminution. But it's worth noting that we should not reduce *Absalom* to the genre of mock epic, for Dryden assiduously avoids generic identity for this verse, pointedly referring on the title page to *Absalom and Achitophel* as "A Poem." Not only elevation but also generic combination is at issue, for what Dryden sets in motion with this epithet is the brilliant mixture of kinds that the verse captures: surely satire, but also heroic poetry, poetry of praise, poetry of civic debate, and verse of political theory.

One of the great puzzles that has interested readers of this poem nearly from the moment of its publication is Dryden's political position. Dryden gives us many indications of real forbearance and political moderation; just as surely he handles the rhetoric of moderation with studied brilliance. The portraits of Charles II's Whig enemies are devastating, often libellous. There was nothing moderate about this portraiture, nor was the poet's suggestion of political excision the solution of a moderate in this crisis. True moderation had suggested tempering the threat of a Catholic succession with limitations on the crown (Lord Halifax was a good example of this position), and in teaching this poem we do well to point out that Dryden's immediate contemporaries found nothing moderate in this verse, and responded in kind with outraged satires.

But another address to the question of political values might be formulated out of the passage on government (ll. 753-810) in which Dryden seems to speak in his own voice, posing possible solutions to the present crisis and ways of theorizing the State. This passage might convincingly open the whole problem of satiric argument and political values. Can a poet who seems devoted to demolition and all the offices of slander really maintain a balanced and judicious mind in matters of state, particularly in a culture in which so much was dependent on the will of monarchy? At this point it might be well to turn to the language of the monarch himself in the companion reading, *His Majesty's Declaration*, and to compare the rhetoric and the values of political proclamation and political poem. Like Dryden's David, Charles strikes the pose of breaking out from long forbearance into new and firm resolve; like Dryden himself in the poem's preface, Charles propounds a surgical strategy (to purge from the polity "the restless malice of ill men," [2186]) in place of the more extreme measures that cost the biblical David the life of his beloved son. Note Dryden's careful statement in the preface: "The conclusion of the story I purposely forbore to prosecute" (2161).

Mac Flecknoe

It is difficult for students (indeed for all readers) now to become engaged by the kinds of literary rivalry that clearly drove this poem. Indeed it is hard to believe that characters like Thomas Shadwell, Richard Flecknoe, Thomas Heywood, and James Shirley could really have posed a threat to a poet of Dryden's brilliance. And perhaps it pays to remember that our sense of their various reputations was certainly not the contemporary sense. Indeed, Dryden had to fight for patronage with Shadwell, for the brilliant satirist the Earl of Rochester, among others, preferred Shadwell's drama to Dryden's.

But this kind of contextualizing only goes so far in getting to the heart of Dryden's accomplishments in the poem. What students may respond to most readily is Dryden's arsenal of insult. Let them count the ways and means by which Dryden manages to put Shadwell down: by grotesque inflation (see the opening lines, which grandly and casually yoke Flecknoe and Augustus); by lewd and excremental association (the suggestive abbreviation Sh—; locations like Pissing

Alley; and the conflation of text with toilet paper [l. 101]); and by weirdly inappropriate intertextuality. Throughout *Mac Flecknoe*, Dryden applies Virgilian echoes of imperial succession to a debased literary inheritance; the poem was written ca. 1678, and it is important to remember that like *Absalom and Achitophel* this is in some ways a poem on the crisis of succession. Part of Dryden's art consists in the ways he conflates parturition with defecation, and repeatedly literalizes the "downwardness" implicit in lineal "descent" (see especially the closing lines). Other pleasures that this poem affords to late-twentieth-century readers include the brilliantly individual lines that manage both compactness and convolution ("But Sh——never deviates into sense" [l. 20]); and as always with Dryden, the subtle management of ironies that allow the poet to ventriloquize stupidity, all the while leaving the puppet (Flecknoe) clueless, and winking the reader into complicity with the humiliation.

The art of this poem points both to the more serious forms of Virgilian intertextuality that Dryden uses in the poem to Oldham (where in fact he reworks some of the same materials into eulogy rather than derision) and again to Pope's *Dunciad*, where Pope achieves such a triumph of competition and humiliation, and where *Mac Flecknoe*'s comparatively local crisis of literary mediocrity expands into apocalypse.

To the Memory of Mr. Oldham

The handful of lines that Dryden wrote in memory of a minor satirist, John Oldham, have come down to us as some of Dryden's most admired poetry. In teaching this poem, quoting some translations of the materials that Dryden himself adapts and translates in this verse will suggest how intimate the poet is with the texture of so remote an age as Virgil's, how Dryden made utterly contemporary to the late seventeenth century—in fact, utterly his own—such a distant poet, which in turn can serve to remind us of how seriously seventeenth- and eighteenth-century writers and readers took their communion with Augustan Rome: its language, its cadences, its political personalities, its forms of governance.

Dryden writes not only with Virgil and Catullus over his shoulder, but with Oldham himself. The poem seems almost as much competition as commemoration (hence the relevance of Nisus and Euryalus, whose friendship in the *Aeneid* [5.286-361; 9.314-449] merits a retelling—perhaps a reading aloud—as one of the central resonances in Dryden's poem); the particular art of this verse is to be able to hold the competition at bay in the service of commemoration. A pointed contrast with this double move is provided by Jonson's commemorative verse on Shakespeare, and Marvell's commemorative verse for the second edition of *Paradise Lost*.

Ode to Anne Killigrew *and* Alexander's Feast

Students can readily see what makes a Pindaric ode Pindaric, and quickly hear it too. No verse paragraph resembles any other in visible layout or in rhyme scheme. The poet leads the reader on a sustained journey whose next turn (even *within* each paragraph) is always unpredictable. By its copiousness and variety, the Pindaric ode is meant to display concurrently two opposite qualities: a mastery of verse technique and a susceptibility to strong emotion, even to poetic "possession" by the poem's stirring subject. The "conduct" of an ode, wrote the poet Edward Young, "should be rapturous, somewhat abrupt, and immethodical to a vulgar eye" (quoted by Margaret Doody, at the outset of a very useful close reading of the Killigrew ode: *The Daring Muse* [Cambridge UP, 1985] 249–55). The abruptness, and the seeming absence of method, attest the rapture.

It falls to the reader to detect the method within the rapture. Part of what distinguishes the ode is the broad range of its concerns. In both of Dryden's odes here, that range becomes a central attribute of the personage being celebrated: Killigrew the multi-faceted artist, Timotheus the infinitely versatile musician. Both Killigrew and Timotheus are seen mediating and modulating among many modes and moods, and at the end of both poems the very processes of art make possible a larger modulation, from the realms of poetry, painting, and music, to that of the Christian cosmos. On Judgment Day, Killigrew, "a harbinger of heaven," will lead the way from earth below to realms above. At the end of *Alexander's Feast*, St. Cecilia reverses this vector (and trumps Timotheus too): by inventing the celestial-sounding organ, she "drew an angel down" to earth.

The ode to Killigrew will read well in conjunction with the poem to Oldham (how do the poems enact Dryden's different attitudes to the commemorated poets?), with Gray's *Elegy*, with Collins's ode on Thomson, and (oddly but interestingly) with Swift's *Verses* on his own death. In all elegies, it is valuable to ask about the *I*, the *you*, the *we*, and the *they*: how does the speaker position him- or herself in relation to the lamented dead and to the communities they have inhabited together? *Alexander's Feast* pairs interestingly with Pepys's rapturous entry on the *Virgin Martyr* (2107) and with Pope's remarkable evocations of the poem in the *Essay on Criticism* (ll. 374–83, 483–93).

Fables Ancient and Modern

Teaching Dryden's last work allows us to appreciate his art as both a translator and a prose writer. One of the most notable features of Dryden's prose is a conversational quality that, more than any of his verse, makes him seem our contemporary. (For a lively, teachable close reading of the preface's first paragraphs, see Richard Lanham, *Style: An Anti-Textbook* [Yale UP, 1974], 41–43.) In fact, in the preface to the *Fables*, there is nothing in syntax or diction or stance to distinguish this late- seventeenth-century writing from modern prose. But casualness in this prose is not simply a sloughing off of Dryden's own time. The digressive and even irregular pace of the prose allowed Dryden to move with utter freedom among personal concerns, artistic ambitions, theories of translation, and the contemporaneity he felt at the end of his life with the spirits of all poets—with Ovid and Boccaccio, Homer and Chaucer. This improvisatory quality of the preface opens it up to a volatility of self-presentation, of literary stance, and even of personal identity. The superb economy of Dryden's prose makes it as artful in its own way as all the studied and managed brilliance of the preface to *Absalom*, and even of that poem's opening lines.

One figure particularly useful for teaching the *Fables* is the idea of transmigration—the transport of souls across time. Notions of reincarnation suffuse the collection. Dryden begins with a poem to the Duchess of Ormond, whom he figures at different points as the "second coming" of Homer's Penelope, Virgil's Dido, and Chaucer's Emily (from The Knight's Tale); near the end of the *Fables*, he recasts into heroic couplets Ovid's presentation "of the Pythagorean philosophy" of reincarnation (*Metamorphoses*, Book 15). Within the preface proper, reincarnation becomes something of a running argument. Dryden has been "emboldened" to translate and embellish Chaucer because "I found I had a soul congenial to his" (2209); when reading the *Canterbury Tales* "we have our forefathers and great grand-dames all before us" (2207); "Spenser more than once insinuates that the soul of Chaucer was transfused into his body" (2203). By this logic, imitation and translation—the chief activities of the *Fables*—are poetic modes of reincarnation. Dryden's confidence in these processes contrasts instructively with Pope's pithy, pessimistic line in the *Essay on Criticism*, in which he argues that changes in the volatile English language will always render great poets obsolete: "And such as Chaucer is, shall Dryden be" (l. 483, 2472). Dryden's figures, of still-vital souls "transfused" into new vessels, comfortably accommodate changes of language and form. For Pope, by contrast, to lose original form is to lose everything; only apocalypse can follow (see the simile of "treach'rous colors" and fading "creation" with which Pope elaborates the line on Dryden and Chaucer).

The Secular Masque

For classroom study of Dryden, or indeed of the entire Restoration, there can be no more powerful coda than this compact, evocative valediction forbidding mourning. The quickest way to help students feel its impact is to reckon up the deities Dryden brings on, the sequence in which he introduces them, and the proportions in which he distributes their utterances.

Janus comes first, the calendrical god of meshed endings and beginnings, with one face looking back, the other forward. He summons Chronos, the older, grander deity who presides over time's essence rather than its measure, and whose entrance commences the comedy: weary of bearing the world, he cannot muster the haste Janus urges. He sets down the globe, and time stands still, while we consider what it has wrought in England over the century now ending. But neither Janus nor Chronos turns out to be the deity designated to preside over that meditation. They are promptly upstaged by Momus, god of satire (his name means "blame"), ridicule incarnate. His first utterance is longer and more lively than theirs. They assent by echo to his closing proposition ("'Tis better to laugh than to cry"), and promptly set about, like anxious stage managers, to mount a "show" for his entertainment and ours.

The show consists of three more deities, each figuring a successive phase of the seventeenth century. Diana, goddess of chastity and of the hunt, embodies both the Virgin Queen Elizabeth and the ardent venator James I. Mars summons memories of the Civil Wars, and Venus conjures the amorous court life of the Restoration. Each phase works changes in the one before (Mars stains with blood Diana's fields; Venus heals what Mars destroys). Dryden punctuates all three vignettes with commentary by the three gods who came in first. Chronos's nostalgic response to Venus may have possessed autobiographical resonance for the old and dying poet, but he arranges things so that at every turn, retrospective celebration gives way to Momus's more derisive reckoning. The merry old England that in Diana's account was free from certain faults, was also (as Momus reminds us) remarkably "unthinking"; Mars's wars were worse than any conceivable alternative. In Momus's last speech, Dryden works with devastating simplicity, summing up both the century and the masque in four perfectly proportioned lines. Janus and Chronos echo the mocker once more, assenting at the last to the dismissal he has implied throughout. In a piece designed for the cusp of centuries, the final lines are remarkably neutral, and free of hope for the future (students may wish to compare their own reasonably fresh memories of millennial rhetoric). The last words' latent pun ("anew") may promise a fresh start, but the syntax avows only that the next age will be "a new"—and not necessarily a different or a better—one. Dryden's tone is both hypnotic and elusive; students will differ as to the proportions of mocking, mourning, and letting go.

"The Secular Masque" is eloquent even in its choice of genre. The masque was by now an old-fashioned form, far more characteristic of the century's first decades than of its last. Dryden couches his summation of the century in a form that, in 1700, would have made the whole epoch seem longer ago than it actually was; it evanesces as we watch. Dryden's "Masque" teaches well with his *Alexander's Feast* (another study in successive moods and intermittent mockeries); with Jonson's *Pleasure Reconciled with Virtue*; with the scene (4.1) in Shakespeare's *Tempest* devoted to the marriage masque and Prospero's dismissive peroration ("Our revels now are ended . . ."); and with Hardy's "Darkling Thrush," another poem poised on the cusp of centuries.

Aphra Behn

Poems

Behn seizes and adapts a number of conventional poetic tropes and positions that pay off fruitfully in discussion. Teaching "The Disappointment" in tandem with Rochester's "The Imperfect Enjoyment" (2280-82) is the most obvious opening strategy. Behn takes a different narratorial point of view, a different poetic form, a different set of images, and a notably different ending, to produce a poetic experience that, as its very title suggests, registers much more empty than "half-full." The narrator, unlike the speaker in Rochester's poem, is not one of the characters, and so has a different sort of authority about what really happens. The tidy ten-line stanzas (nine lines of fairly consistent tetrameter, with a tenth of emphatic pentameter) contrast with the insistent heroic meter of "The Imperfect Enjoyment" that is, typographically speaking, almost engulfed by its own lambasting stanzas. Behn's poem, like Rochester's "The Disabled Debauchee" (2279-80), uses military imagery to set up tensions of sexual power, and, according to the war/sex conventions, gives all power to Lysander: Chloris can "defend herself no longer"; she "wants power"; she breathes faintly; she admits "the conquest of [her] heart"; he, on the other hand, is "unused to fear" as well as "capable of love," and looks on her nearly naked body as "The spoils and trophies of the enemy." The power is *heaped* on Lysander and makes the "disappointment" (his? or hers?) all the more embarrassing; not even his obvious masturbating can put things right (ll. 89–90). Meanwhile, when Chloris, dreamily waiting for something nice to happen, accidentally-on-purpose lays a hand on the snake beneath the leaves, she's granted two more complete stanzas of her own in which her shock, confusion, disdain, shame, and death of love get full exposure. In the last stanza the narrator chimes in to grant Chloris experiential authority, allowing us to listen to Lysander's blaming everything and everyone, most especially Chloris, for his failure; and this narrator, unlike many male narrators in the "disappointment" tradition, leaves him, at least textually, in "the hell of impotence."

In "To Lysander at the Music-Meeting" Behn makes use of the narratorial position to reverse the usual terms of the (male) gaze, visually and descriptively eroticizing the female and, like Harriet as the "mask" in Etherege's *The Man of Mode*, constructs a little power-play of her own, for the pleasure of her (female) readers: "I saw the softness that composed your face, . . . Your mouth all full of sweetness and content / . . . Your body easy and all tempting lay, / . . . A careless and a lovely negligence, / Did a new charm to every limb dispense" (ll. 15–25). Like any male narrator, this speaker is wounded, slain, undone, dissolved in desire by this sight; but here the beloved object is a sexy young man in a suggestive pose.

As the introduction to Behn's works in context mentions, shaping the poems as letters (to Lysander, to Mr. Creech, to the fair Clarinda) gives them an almost voyeuristic intimacy for the reader, who seems to be reading the private, fairly explicit love letters of a stranger. The speaker creates a small, warm, close world that deliberately excludes the public, or draws attention to its own privacy by alluding to the larger, colder world of rules and conventions: "For sure no crime with thee we can commit," says the poet to Clarinda, since both are women, "Or if we should—thy form excuses it" (ll. 14–15). And in the cumulative effect of her love poetry, Behn creates an almost androgynous world, a more idealistic flipside to that of Rochester's speakers, who generally see a common ground—or common orifice—in everyone, man and woman, aristocrat and page, whore and linkboy. Behn's speakers play with the imagery, appropriate the positions, and claim the rights of the traditionally masculine position ("Or give Amynta so much freedom back: / That she may rove as well as you" [2219]) in order to imaginatively join "soft Cloris with the dear Alexis" (2223)—to join the feminine with the masculine not only in heterosexual or homosexual love, but in individual *identities*.

Aphra Behn and Her Time: Coterie Writing   Seventeenth- and eighteenth-century writers—both men and women—were intrigued by the combinations of "masculine" and "feminine" traits that could be found or encouraged (or discouraged, of course) in cultures, in arts, in languages, and in individuals. The writers represented in this section all share, with Behn and Astell and Lady Mary Wortley Montagu, a greater or lesser commitment to the basic idea that women's intellectual and spiritual abilities, if not their historical accomplishments, were equal to men's and ought to be given equal encouragement, granted equal voice. Some students find it difficult to see literary works or ideological positions within historical context and often want more from these writers than their own place in sheer history would permit—students want to see themselves in the past, not inadequate aliens. Emphasizing the historical and political weight of the patriarchal assumptions (not to mention laws) that constricted these early writers should give more dour resonance to Lady Chudleigh's opening lines, "Wife and servant are the same, / But only differ in the name." In some sense what might now be hyperbole was then a nearly literal truth.

Mary, Lady Chudleigh   By 1701 Lady Chudleigh was a public figure, with male as well as female followers, and Dryden, among others, a critical benefactor. Her poems were known for their classical learning, their knowledge of philosophy, natural science, and history. "To the Ladies" was apparently very popular among her contemporaries, especially the ladies themselves: the poem was frequently transcribed into other texts, such as one Elizabeth Brockett's First Folio of Shakespeare (see Margaret Ezell's introduction to Poems and Prose of Mary, Lady Chudleigh [Oxford UP, 1993]). This poem is a tight little compression of Astell's argument in Some Reflections upon Marriage published three years earlier; students might analyze the advantages that go along with the choice of poetic form, such as the emphatically closed couplets, the connotations in the choice of paired rhymes (same/name, tied/divide, speak/break, despise/wise), the choice of tetrameter, the suggestive assonance of the first and last words of the poem (wife/wise).

In "To Almystrea," on the other hand, that not-so-artless tribute to Astell, Chudleigh uses other strategies. Like many of Behn's poems and prologues, and Finch's "The Introduction" (2226), "To Almystrea" acknowledges, by its very gesture of humble second-bestness, an already rich literary tradition of women's writings. The intrinsic merit of Astell's writings has already created a space for Chudleigh's own, even if Chudleigh's Muse is (as she modestly claims) more heavy-footed; still, Astell's "exalted height" paradoxically beckons into print Marissa's "failures" to prove her love, and Almystrea's beamy brightness attracts others to follow in "the lofty roads of fame."

Anne Finch, Countess of Winchilsea   How does the very first line of "The Introduction" work? "Did I my lines intend for public view—"; we know that, unlike many such protestations in and about poems and letters, Finch pretty much meant this one—this poem was not published until this century. What kinds of things does the speaker allow herself to say in the privacy of her own writing-closet? There's clearly a will to "come out," to say these things aloud. The poem creates its own sense of audience (and, as manuscript poems circulated among friends, that imagined audience would come alive) through pronouns, among other things: the "I" of the first line quickly becomes "us" and "we" facing a hostile or contemptuous "they" who tell us things (l. 13). Finch's speaker then goes on to re-construct history, one rather different from those in which "[men] recount each others' great exploits" (Astell 2364), one which instead more objectively recognizes that, as in biblical history, women "with alternate verse, complete the hymn divine" (l. 32).

How does the dialogue structure of "Friendship Between Ephelia and Ardelia" work, like the use of pronouns in "The Introduction," to construct a world of friendship in the act of defining it? In "A Ballad to Mrs. Catherine Fleming," how does the valorizing of rural solitude combine with the classic country-house poem tradition of a pastoral bounty that flings itself gratefully back into human hands, to create that world of sturdy friendship, literary straightforwardness, and the inhabiting of a literary tradition?

Mary Leapor   "The Headache" offers its own take on the literary history angle. Leapor's poem calls in all the troops: the Restoration cuckolds, the pastoral swains and shepherdesses, the tropes of gallantry and insult, are all employed to highlight the poet's wryly comic perception of herself poised between the literary and the all-too-human worlds. The gossip, it seems, has a kind of durability, if not immortality, beyond that of the poet; in a wry twist on the *carpe diem* tradition, this speaker seizes her day in tolerant tandem with the "oral" tradition: "I'll still write on, and you shall rail" (l. 53).

"Advice to Sophronia" and "An Essay on Woman" might be read against Pope's *The Rape of the Lock*, particularly Clarissa's unpopular but apparently common-sensical speech (2520–21); "The Epistle of Deborah Dough" invites questions about perspective, choice of narrator, play of dialect, the ironic construction of a self-image, the poet's ability to inhabit other identities, to speak other voices.

Oroonoko

Oroonoko has, among its many other excellent qualities, the ability to excite and engage almost any student not in principle committed to sleep. It appeals to all the standard requirements of *dulce*—it's got action, adventure, romance, beauty, horror, treachery, exoticism, and familiarity. It borrows comfortably from the romance tradition in its high heroism; as George Starr argues, it is also grounded in an early anti-Hobbesian form of sentimentalism that "examines what it means to be powerless in a society where, despite Christian pretenses and protestations, power is everything, and the Beatitudes are a prescription for endless torment" ("Aphra Behn and the Genealogy of the Man of Feeling," *Modern Philology*, 87:4 [1990]: 362). Many critics place this work among early modern novels in its "real life" context of "true histories," vividly rendered physical and psychological detail, and occasionally plausible dialogue. It of course fits beautifully into late-twentieth-century interests in gender, class, and race studies. As Catherine Gallagher comments: "Each century seems to have been able to reconcile this one story with its ideas of what a woman writer should accomplish" (*Nobody's Story: The Vanishing Acts of Women Writers in the Marketplace 1670–1820* [U of California P 1994] 54 n. 11).

The narrator of *Oroonoko*, like Defoe's narrators, takes great pains to establish the truth of her story. Pretty much appearing as herself (Behn really was, as later twentieth-century critics confirmed in the face of earlier suspicions, the daughter of the late-intended lieutenant-governor of Surinam and present at the historical version of these events), the narrator repeatedly assures the reader that she was an "eyewitness" to most of the story, and the rest she fills in "from the mouth of the chief actor," Oroonoko himself (2236). But as a character, the narrator invites all sorts of questions. Although she remains largely shadowy in her narration of Oroonoko's and Imoinda's story, in her actions both as character within and writer of the story, she sometimes directly influences—by omission—the events. Because Oroonoko was sold to her own overseer (2255), she was able to know him, to establish friendship and trust—and to become the "female pen to celebrate his fame" (2257). At two points her absence seems to entail Oroonoko's fall: when Oroonoko calls the slaves to a sense of injustice and an act of revolt, "all the females [flew] down the river," and Oroonoko's capture was marked with a vicious cruelty that the narrator supposes she would have had "authority and interest enough . . . to have prevented" (2292). Upon Oroonoko's recapture after the sacrifice of his wife and unborn child, when the narrator departs down the river, reassured by the promises of Trefry and the servants to guard his life, she notes: "I was no sooner gone, but the governor . . . forcibly took Caesar, and had him carried to the same post where he was whipped," dismembered, and executed (2276–77). On the levels of plot and politics, the narrator sees herself unwittingly complicit in the white men's crime; on a more allegorical level, as Gallagher argues, the narrator defines herself in some ways as Oroonoko: "Like him, she arrives a stranger in Surinam but is immediately recognized as superior to the local inhabitants; like him, she appears a shining marvel when she travels to the Indian village; and like his words, hers are always truthful. . . . [A]s the story moves forward, narrator and hero polish each other's fame" (*Nobody's Story*, 68). At the end of the story, the narrator, like many seventeenth- and eighteenth-century writers anxious to negotiate the whole English literary tradition (cf. the last lines of Pope's *The Rape of the Lock*), puts herself-as-writer in a position of final and immortalizing authority: "Yet, I hope, the reputation of my pen is considerable enough to make his glorious name to survive all ages, with that of the brave, the beautiful, and the constant Imoinda" (2193).

Behn's treatment of race is a hot topic among critics; most notice that the descriptions of Oroonoko and Imoinda are both poised against and defined within contemporary European prejudices about "savages." Their actions conform entirely to European traditions of chivalric romance; their features, apart from pigmentation, are European; yet their very blackness, as Gallagher points out, is pointedly laden with linguistically positive connotations: "brilliant," "polished," "beautiful." And for much of the story, racial characteristics entirely disappear: Oroonoko's conflict with his grandfather over Imoinda is simply a human story of love, lust, jealousy, and revenge, with its own tradition on the Restoration stage.

The characterization of Oroonoko is also part of the seventeenth- and eighteenth-century interest in the basic nature of human beings. Oroonoko and Imoinda, along with their vast European sophistication (Oroonoko is learned in many arts and sciences and speaks several languages), are also classic models of the "noble savage." This text could be linked profitably to other analyses and satires of the human condition as European "civilization" has corrupted it, versus "the first state of inno-cence, before man knew how to sin" (2238). The English governor, for example, might in his treachery be a model yahoo for Swift's later Houyhnhnms. The Indians, believing only death would keep a man from his word, mourned for the death of the governor who promised to come; when he finally showed up, not dead, they asked: "what name they had for a man who promised a thing he did not do? The governor told them, such a man was a liar, which was a word of infamy to a gentleman. Then one of them replied, 'Governor, you are a liar, and guilty of that infamy.' They have a native justice which knows no fraud, and they under-stand no vice, or cunning, but when they are taught by the white men" (2238).

Other fruitful points of discussion: why is Imoinda's face carved (or her head cut) from her body? Gallagher links this to masks. What do Oroonoko's various dis-memberments imply? What, along with his body, is allegorically chopped up and/or kept whole? Why is it necessary to kill Imoinda when she becomes pregnant? What does it suggest when her name is the last mentioned in the narrator's account?

John Wilmot, Second Earl of Rochester

The chronicler John Aubrey recorded a contemporary evaluation of Rochester as poet: "Mr. Andrew Marvell, who was a good judge of wit, was wont to say that he was the best English satirist and had the right vein" (*Brief Lives*, ed. Richard Barber [The Boydell Press, 1982], 326). David Vieth, the editor of the standard edition of Rochester's poems (*The Complete Poems of John Wilmot, Earl of Rochester* [Yale UP, 1968]), suggests that "Rochester's poems possess value in three directions which are difficult to separate in discussion: historically, as a crucial contribution to the shaping of the new literary idiom which was brought to perfection by Swift, Pope, and their contemporaries; biographically, as part of a life-story so compelling that it constantly threatens to overwhelm his poetry; and artistically, as unique formu-lations of universal human experiences" (xxxiii). Discussion of the poems can use-fully sort through all three. Historical issues can include the development of satire as an increasingly dominant cultural form; the deliberate devolution of traditional tropes; the contexts of sexual and political promiscuity; the frequent presence of, shall we say, bodily fluids and earthly filth in the "highest" of Augustan art (Dryden, Swift, Pope). Aesthetic issues can address the choice of heroic couplets for unheroic matter—the constraints imposed, expectations established, and ironies created by rhymed iambic pentameter; the creation of *immediacy* (sensual and psychological) through the ironic intersection of multiple planes of experi-ence, as Vieth puts it.

But often the most compelling direction for students lies in an intersection of the biographical and aesthetic: analyzing the voices—the masks—of the various speakers in Rochester's chameleon poems. Bishop Gilbert Burnet, Rochester's ad-visor and biographer, relates of the poet: "He took pleasure to disguise himself, as a porter, or as a beggar; sometimes to follow some mean amours, which, for the va-riety of them, he affected; at other times, meerly for diversion, he would go about in odd shapes, in which he acted his part so naturally, that even those who were in on the secret, and saw him in these shapes, could perceive nothing by which he might be discovered" (quoted in *Complete Poems*, xlii). Although the poems are largely autobiographical, Rochester loved to play both personally and aesthetically with multiple identities, and the insistent "I's" of his poems are rarely the same. How is the "disabled debauchee" presented? Rochester frequently compares sexual with military conquests (an old tradition, of course), but his comparisons often emphasize the ironic distance between the traditional figuring of the one ("some brave admiral . . . pressed with courage still" [l. 1]) and the immediate rendering of the other ("I'm by pox and wine's unlucky chance / . . . On the dull shore of lazy temperance" [ll. 14, 16]). Who is his audience? Lines 37-40 suggest a lover, Chloris, as the immediate audience ("Nor shall our love-fits, Chloris, be forgot"); but the speaker obviously imagines a wider, later audience of rapt, advice-hungry lads to whom "With tales like these [he] will such thoughts inspire / As to important mischief shall incline" (ll. 41-42). But brave old admirals have a hard enough time telling their tales; the entire construction of the rake's world presumes that the impotent old sot has no audience: as the speaker in "Against Constancy" points out, "old men and weak . . . can but spread their shame" (ll. 9, 11, p. 2278).

The speaker in "The Imperfect Enjoyment" is yet another voice. This poem really demands to be taught with Behn's "The Disappointment" (2215-18); Behn's poem was originally published with Rochester's in his *Poems on Several Occasions* (1680), and both come from a tradition of poems describing sexual disappointment beginning with Ovid. Note how Rochester's speaker loses all sorts of control. The most startling, for students, is the linguistic shock: from warm but conventional euphemisms ("charms," "fire," "melting," "flaming," "Love's lesser lightning," "all-dissolving thunderbolt") the lines are first interrupted by—then consumed with—crude, graphic, and finally obscene language ("her very look's a cunt"). The erotic tradition dissolves into the pornographic, except that the shift, deliberately shocking, becomes *comic*.

Rochester loves the silly side of sex, as another textual slippage illustrates. The poem begins most definitely with two people in bed ("Naked she lay, clasped in my longing arms"), and "she" remains physically and textually embraced throughout the first two stanzas—but then, as his attention, his shame, his anger, and his dialogue turn to his penis, Corinna pretty much disappears, lost among the thousand "oyster-cinder-beggar-common whore[s]" and "ten thousand maids" who participated in his success. And by the last stanza, the speaker himself has more or less disappeared into his own penis (as women are so frequently reduced to "cunts"), and that figure itself overwhelmed: "And may ten thousand abler pricks agree / To do the wronged Corinna right for thee" (ll. 71-72).

The speakers of "A Satyr Against Reason and Mankind" and "Upon Nothing" offer yet another set of voices, of cultural and aesthetic issues, that teach well with the Perspectives: Mind and God section; with Pope's *Epistle to Dr. Arbuthnot* and the selections from the *Essay on Man*; and with Swift's *Verses on the Death of Dr.*

Swift. Whatever their ideological polarities, these works tend to agree at least on the strangenesses of "those strange, prodigious creatures, man" ("A Satyr," l. 2).

William Wycherley

It's a strange play. Restoration comedy is like no other, and *The Country Wife* is (particularly in its ending) like no other Restoration comedy. The trick in teaching the play may be to bring the students deeply enough into it to recognize what is familiar, funny, and compelling, while keeping them distant enough to grapple with what's strange.

For these mixed purposes, there is perhaps no handier companion than the relevant chapter in Judith Milhous and Robert D. Hume's *Producible Interpretations* (Southern Illinois UP, 1985). The authors adroitly catalogue the cornucopia of critical interpretations prompted by this play they deem "the best known, the most admired, and the most hotly disputed comedy of the period" (73). They speculate persuasively as to which interpretations might have worked for the original audience, and which are most likely to succeed with a contemporary one (even the readings they reject can prove useful in class discussion). Students enjoy becoming such an audience themselves; the video of a very fine production by the Stratford Festival of Canada, commercially unavailable but still get-attable, is worth incorporating into the course.

The Restoration and its theater, new to most undergraduates, was newish also for Wycherley's first audiences. Pepys's entries on "Theater and Music," coupled with the section of the period introduction on "Money, Manners, and Theatrics" (2066–74) can help capture both the exhilaration of the novelty and the particulars (scenery, sumptuousness, *actresses*) that prompted it. Two new handbooks to the period's plays (Deborah Payne Fiske, ed., *The Cambridge Companion to English Restoration Theatre* [Cambridge UP, 2000]; Susan J. Owen, ed., *A Companion to Restoration Drama* [Blackwell, 2001]) offer superb essays on playhouses, players, politics, and performance, as well as (in Fiske's book) some fabulous illustrations, worth circulating.

But the play itself, its suddennesses and surprises, will ultimately offer students the richest way into these new worlds. The prologue repays close attention. It depicts the playwright as an incorrigible but fearful aggressor (at first a "trembling" bully, then an incompetent general) launching repeated attacks upon an audience equally hostile but in the end more effectual: they beat up the bully, they defeat the general. The speaker, meanwhile, describes himself and his fellow actors as soldiers caught in abject panic between the two, weary of the playwright's commands, seeking "quarter" from the audience's "saving hands" (their applause), and ultimately offering a surrender that is at once military and sexual. "With flying colors," like a conquering army entering a defeated town, the audience will be permitted to invade the players' dressing rooms, taking into their power the "poets" (due no doubt for yet another punitive drubbing), the "virgins" and "matrons" who as characters have peopled the play, and (in the prologue's final gambit) the actresses who now, for the first time in the history of the English theater, are play-ing these female roles, and who (so the speaker insinuates) may make themselves available to any male bold enough to make his way backstage. (A brief detour to Samuel Pepys's diary entry of 5 October 1667 [2106-7] will supply some sense of what such backstage visits actually meant to the male gazer and theater addict; he sees the king's mistress "all unready," and rehearses cues with Elizabeth Knepp, who first played the role of Lady Fidget in the *Country Wife*.) The passage compactly conjures up an audience long engrossed in actual wars—the civil wars of the 1640s, the Dutch wars of the 1650s, 60s, and 70s—and deeply disposed to construe sex-ual encounters as the spoils of combat too. The prologue posits a relationship be-tween stage and spectator in which the pleasures of intimacy are barely distin-guishable from the perils of aggression.

That dynamic governs the play as well. At the play's first performances, the actor who spoke the prologue promptly reappeared as Harry Horner, and Horner's scheme partakes of the prologue's pugnacity. As he describes and then quickly demonstrates his "new unpracticed trick" for conquering new women by passing himself off as a eunuch ("a man unfit for women"), it becomes clear that sexual grat-ification is only part of the pleasure he is promising himself. He will also enjoy dup-ing and defeating the husbands who deliver their wives and relations into his hands under the misimpression that he is now a safe companion. He savors the game then as a means of establishing his superiority over other men; at the end of his first di-alogue with the doctor, he first voices a comparison that will saturate the play, be-tween himself and a "cunning gamester," between sex and gambling as enterprises where cheating can limit risk, but relentlessly requires the devising of fresh tactics (of "new unpracticed tricks"). Horner's very name expresses his intent, even his des-tiny: he is out to put the horns of cuckoldry on the heads of as many men as pos-sible (this seemingly ancient emblem of disgrace comes much closer to home if you remind students about the grade school tradition of holding two fingers above the head of a playmate for purposes of mockery at recess or in posed photographs; those imaged "horns" are the cultural residue of the old insult). Horner's name proves expressive in another way as well: it construes his enterprise as the competi-tive action of one male upon another, of cuckolder upon cuckold; the competition presumes the involvement of a woman, but leaves her notably invisible.

Wycherley devotes much of the first act to delineating the dynamics of the competition, as it begins to play itself out between three insiders—Horner, Harcourt, Dorilant—and three outsiders—Sir Jasper Fidget, Pinchwife, and Sparkish. The criteria that distinguish the two factions are compactly summed up in a word that character after character invokes as talismanic touchstone: *wit*. Hobbes defines wit as in part "the swift succession of one thought to another" (*Leviathan* 1.8). In *The Country Wife*, that succession most often takes the form of quick comparison, metaphor- and analogy-making that operates (among the insid-ers) as a kind of competitive leapfrog. When Harcourt proposes that "mistresses are like books," to be taken up and put down at whim, Dorilant promptly retorts that "a mistress should be like a little country retreat," to be visited but not steadily inhabited. The point of both similes is that women are only diversions, while men are each other's true companions. The "mistress" becomes almost an abstract counter in a competition where the men perform similes for each other's delectation and defeat (my simile's better than yours). Throughout the play, the wit works to seal those bonds between men that Eve Kolsofsky Sedgwick reads so astutely in her famous exploration of the play ("*The Country Wife*: Anatomies of Male Homosocial Desire," in *Between Men* [Columbia University Press, 1985]). In Wycherley's world, she argues, wit, like cuckoldry, "is an important mechanism for moving from an ostensible heterosexual object of desire to a true homosocial one" (61). *As* and *like*, the syntactic lynchpins of similitude, become for these characters the currency in this mix of contest and companionship. The play's very first lines abound with *as*'s, as Horner launches an elaborate and fairly sickening analogy, worth unpacking, among quacks, pimps, midwives, and bawds. The insiders have secured that status by their wit, but they must renew it with virtually every utterance; their competition is continuous, and demanding.

The outsiders are by contrast comparatively witless. Sir Jasper Fidget repeatedly declares himself a man of business, not pleasure. Pinchwife prefers plain self-assertion over anything more intricate: "I know the town," he avers repeatedly upon his first appearance; Horner echoes the sentence once in order to mock both the repetition and the deluded self-confidence it proclaims; by his own witty responses, he makes clear that he knows the town much better than does Pinchwife. Sparkish, unlike Pinchwife, is a wit wannabe, but he wants wit in both senses of the word: he desires it, and lacks it. At his first appearance he retells a long, strained joke ostensibly at Horner's expense but actually at his own: though he jests about shop signs (and about Horner as the "sign of a man"), he makes clear that he cannot manipulate linguistic signs—puns, metaphors, the slippery convergences of realities and representations—with anything like the dexterity or economy habitually displayed by his exasperated interlocutors. When Horner slyly supplies Sparkish with the opening for a *real* witticism—"Look to't, we'll have no more ladies"—Sparkish misses the opportunity entirely, so absorbed is he in telling a joke that is more self-praise than skilled performance.

As Sedgwick points out, both wit and cuckoldry, as practiced by the insiders, are modes of exchange between men: my simile will supplant yours in the chain of jests; I will supplant you in your wife's favors. The act of exchange, displayed in its varied and nearly numberless manifestations, accounts for most of what's hypnotic in the play: its comedy, its ruthlessness, and Wycherley's entwining of the two. Horner's scheme aims at an infinite succession of interchangeable bedmates. Sparkish eagerly but obliviously delivers up his fiancée to the tender attentions of the amorous Harcourt. Changes of identity abound (Harcourt dresses up as a parson, Margery as her own brother, and then as Alithea). The play's pivotal scene (3.2) takes place at the New Exchange, London's first and fabled shopping center; the most notorious scene (4.3) takes place in more private quarters, but still construes sex as a mode of shopping.

Most of these exchanges are prompted by the competition among the men, but their outcomes are shaped by the ingenuities of the women. It is Lady Fidget who devises the cover story of the "china house" (2333), and she plainly enjoys cuckolding her husband amid a barrage of sexual puns and at the narrow remove of one locked door; her female cohorts want to traffic in Horner's china too. In their two great conversation scenes (2.1, 5.4), this "virtuous gang" (2345; the oxymoron is wonderfully worth unpacking) lament and redress other modes of exchange—notably the male preference for "common and cheap" women over "women of quality" like themselves (5.4).

Margery Pinchwife is in effect traded on the New Exchange, passing from her husband to Horner, and returning with a hatful of fruit that is as expressive in its way as is all the imaginary china in the ensuing act. Before long, though, she manages to sustain such exchanges less passively, substituting, in her letters to Horner, a new, amorous, adventurous, London self for the submissive role in which her increasingly desperate husband still hopes to confine her, eventually, with Lucy's help, dispatches herself in the same direction, enveloped in Alithea's cloak and delivered by her unwitting spouse. One of the play's strongest running jokes is the mechanism by which Pinchwife, in his efforts to constrain his wife, repeatedly produces the very consequences he seeks to forestall. Every attempt at power produces new loss of power, and every loss ups the ante of attempt, so that the more vehement he becomes ("I will write 'whore' with this penknife in your face," 2330), the more he connives in his own catastrophe. In the early stages of this process (2.1) Alithea functions as observant and sardonic commentator. She herself embodies perhaps the play's most puzzling instance of exchange: displayed as marital ware by Sparkish, coveted by Harcourt, she delivers herself from the one to the other in the play's final, chaotic moments.

These acts of exchange pose questions aplenty. Are we to admire Margery and Alithea for making a break with the ways of this world (Pinchwife's power, Sparkish's folly) or to ridicule them for their abiding roles in it (country wife, town lady)? Students often value Alithea (and sometimes Harcourt) as the only figures of acuity and moral clarity in the play; many rejoice, too, at watching Margery work her way out of bondage in the letter scenes. Whether Restoration audiences may have felt the same is problematic. Milhous and Hume's chapter, and Pat Gill's *Interpreting Ladies: Women, Wit, and Morality in the Restoration Comedy of Manners* (U of Georgia P, 1994), can help navigate the questions if not answer them. In any case, the range of student responses usually affords a terrific opportunity for exploring the differences between the mindsets of seventeenth- and twenty-first-century audiences.

The play's ending is so unusual, so various in its implications and impacts, that a good class hour can be launched by the simple question, "What did you think?" In comedy, the culminating moment of recognition usually resolves problems (*Twelfth Night* offers a superb example, as indeed does *School for Scandal*, but almost any romantic comedy will serve). Margery's unmasking, by contrast, compounds difficulties, producing an effect queasily poised between the comic and the catastrophic. The frantic attempts of other characters to shut her up (even when they don't fully understand what she intends to say) clinches Wycherley's satiric point, that this social realm *requires* such secrets, and that revelation would be its unmaking. And the dance confirms (like Sedgwick) that cuckoldry, with all its tricks and lies, may be the only form of harmony this world can know. But Wycherley focuses enough on individual miseries to temper his satire perhaps (readings vary) with something like pathos. Margery acknowledges her own immuring: "I must be a country wife still." Pinchwife, so ridiculous and repellent throughout the play, comes closer than any other character to possessing a quasi-tragic knowledge, seeing clearly that he is deceived, that he is alone (no one will confirm his deception), and that he must henceforth contrive somehow to deceive himself. The aborted verse-line at the center of his final speech ("But—[sighs]") is strangely powerful, and the dance of cuckolds ensues with ominous immediacy.

The characters who escape scot-free may fare little better. The virtuous gang may still romp with Horner, but as the china equation quietly implies, there may be something smooth, cold, sterile, and ornamental about their revels. Horner is free to continue his pursuits, though in this last scene he has seemed a bit weary of them, cornered by the gang and exasperated by Margery ("a silly mistress is like a weak place, soon got, soon lost"). In his last line, he acknowledges that his successful trick has sundered him from the society of men that, at play's start, he seemed most to enjoy. Pinchwife and he are the last to speak; though different in many ways, they are similar in their solitudes. Harcourt and Alithea, embarked on matrimony, may map a way out of all this gloom, but Wycherley pays them scant attention, so absorbed is he in darker developments elsewhere.

The play will teach well in concert with the other texts that trace the progress and regress of rakes (Rochester, Gay, Hogarth, Boswell, Sheridan) and of women (Cavendish, Behn, Chudleigh, Astell, Finch, Swift, Leapor, Montagu, Piozzi). It will also work tellingly as the first in a sequence of three plays, alongside *The Beggar's Opera* (where the world-as-Exchange again constitutes the core motif and satiric point), and *The School for Scandal*, in which Sheridan deliberately recalls and recasts crucial moments from Wycherley's play. For suggestions and comparisons, see the commentary on Sheridan below.

Mary Astell

Francis Atterbury, Bishop of Rochester, complained about Astell: "Had she as much good breeding as good sense, she would be perfect; but she has not the most decent manner of insinuating what she means, but is now and then a little offensive and shocking in her expressions; which I wonder at, because a civil turn of words is what her sex is mistress of. She, I think, is wanting in it. But her sensible and rational way of writing makes amends for that defect, if indeed anything can make amends for it. I dread to engage her" (quoted in Astell, *Political Writings*, ed. Patricia Springborg [Cambridge UP, 1996], Introduction, xiv). A bit unclear on the concept, Atterbury separates out Astell's mind from her gender, and implies, in the tradition that Astell so acerbically parodies, that Gender in the end matters more than Mind. As Catherine Gallagher argues, it is precisely the mind—rather than the body or soul—that interests Astell, that for her forms the basis of a consistent and rational identity (see "Embracing the Absolute: The Politics of the Female Subject in Seventeenth-Century England," *Genders*, No. 1 [1988]: 25, 34). Astell's pugilistic prose is her way to fight into the heart of the matter. She clearly is not much interested in decently insinuating meanings and civilly turning words—such placatory tricks are precisely the forms that traditionally reified women's (self-) subjection.

Astell plays beautifully with those forms; much of the rhetorical force of *Reflections* turns upon the demure presentation of the accepted line, and then its wide-eyed disembowelment: "But how can a woman scruple entire subjection, how can she forbear to admire the worth and excellency of the superior sex, if she at all considers it? Have not all the great actions that have been performed in the world been done by them? . . . They make worlds and ruin them, form systems of universal nature and dispute eternally about them, . . . they recount each others' great exploits, and have always done so" (2360, 2364). Students might see why Atterbury would dread to confront her, and work up his own verbal thrust-and-parry in defensive retreat. How would Astell respond to Atterbury?

Astell neatly combines traditional political and rationalist argument to simultaneously upset and secure the status quo. As Ruth Perry argues, Astell's "conclusions about women are inseparable from her religious faith, her belief in political authority, and her commitment to philosophical rationalism" ("The Veil of Chastity: Mary Astell's Feminism," *Studies in Eighteenth-Century Culture* 9 [1979]: 25). On the one hand, Astell points out, "tyranny . . . provokes the oppressed to throw off even a lawful yoke that fits too heavy. And if he who is freely elected, after all his fair promises and the fine hopes he raised, proves a tyrant, the consideration that he was one's own choice will not render more submissive and patient, but I fear more refractory" (2365). Echoes of the Civil War, the Commonwealth, and the Restoration might all resonate in the contemporary mind, and be introduced into the students'. On the other hand, "if man's authority be justly established, the more sense a woman has the more reason she will find to submit to it" (2361); therefore it is "very much a man's interest" that women should be educated intellectually, spiritually, and politically (2363). At the end of the treatise she speaks directly first to her male and then to her female readers. Towards whom does the weight of her argument lie? In riling, instructing, threatening, and soothing the men? In prodding, poking, and promising the women? Her last sentence suggests both: "the man's prerogative is not at all infringed, whilst the woman's privileges are secured" (2366); does this balance adequately resolve the tensions within the argument as a whole?

Daniel Defoe

Defoe loved to play among the boundaries between fact and fiction: his novels are filled with lists and measurements and dates; his nonfiction with characters and conversations. One useful way of approaching *A True Relation of the Apparition of Mrs. Veal* and the excerpts from *A Journal of the Plague Year* is to get students to work out how Defoe constructs the appearance of historical truth. As one of Defoe's nineteenth-century critics claims of the *True Relation*: "It is one of the most remarkable exhibitions ever seen of a power of giving an exact air of reality to imagined facts. Its old formal precise air . . . meant it to convince" (from an 1856 review; quoted in *Defoe: The Critical Heritage*, ed. Pat Rogers [Routledge and Kegan Paul, 1972] 147). A gathering of authorities, an accumulation of physical details, a reproduction of dialogue, all shore up a sense of authenticity and at the same time offer a sense of a full human world; the boundaries between fiction and fact are at once delineated and blended.

What counts as evidence? In *A True Relation*, for example, the clock striking, the hand of Mrs. Veal continually drawn across her eyes, the sense of fabric, of upstairs and downstairs, of intimate detail, are first related in Mrs. Bargrave's account to the "editor," and then *repeated*, in a classic Defoean move, with the recapitulation of the pros and cons of the story (2373). For Defoe, it's as if a fact gets stronger in repetition—which, in scientific theory, may be methodologically true, but which in human discourse works two ways: just because I say it's true five times doesn't mean it's five times truer; on the other hand, if I don't deviate from my story in five retellings, the officers of the law are a bit more likely to believe me.

Another criterion of belief or verifiability that the student might look for, in the larger context of Restoration and eighteenth-century preoccupations, is the reading of faces in both texts. Mrs. Bargrave is not only reliable because she doesn't take money for her story (a particularly apt criterion in our own time); her veracity is also established, for the "editor," by her face, in which "there is not the least sign of dejection" (2369). H. F.'s account of Robert the waterman wins his own conviction by the sight of the man's "countenance that presently told [him, he] had happened on a man that was no hypocrite, but a serious, religious good man" (2385)—though the narrator, in his habitual skepticism, finds a little extra empirical evidence not amiss: "'Well, but,' says I to him, 'did you leave her the four shillings too, which you said was your week's pay?' 'YES, YES,' says he, 'you shall hear her own it'" (2386). And she dutifully does.

On the other side of things, how does Defoe play with imaginative elements to advantage? In some ways, *A True Relation* reads like a proto-mystery: the paragraph beginning the narrative itself opens with a place and time ("In this house, of the eighth of September last") and closes with a temporal chime that ushers in its own form of suspense ("At that moment of time, the clock struck twelve at noon" [2370]). It's only later the reader finds out when Mrs. Veal died; it's only the next paragraph that she makes her very physical entrance; the narration of the visit emphasizes its reality in its mundane details. The reader is geared, by knowing beforehand that Mrs. Veal is indeed an "apparition," to look for "signs" of her ghostliness—the "long journey," the unwillingness to touch lips, the shadowed eyes, the heavenly assurances, the demands for promises, the disposing of the worldly goods.

Ultimately, students should also be clear about the good-faith use that Defoe sees in these accounts (a use that doesn't always have a current parallel), and where such use is carefully spelled out, either by the narrator or by the characters. Fact is used to support faith; there is a life hereafter, and we should acquit ourselves accordingly. As with the Royal Society members such as Hooke, Boyle, and Sprat, precision in empirical detail comfortingly grounds spiritual abstractions. Whatever the nineteenth-century critical skeptics thought, Defoe's religious upbringing and convictions operated every bit as powerfully as his love of fictional identity-exploring and his love of a buck—or a guinea, so to speak.

PERSPECTIVES

Reading Papers

We live lives enmeshed in media, and students generally find it fun to trace long-used forms (the breaking news-bulletin, columns of advice and opinion, letters to the editor, etc.) back to their origins in the seventeenth and eighteenth centuries. The pieces here assembled can yield both entertainment and a salutary alienation. To read these familiar genres as they were first devised and manipulated, in a culture three centuries distant from our own is often to become more aware of cultural force fields and media tactics that we tend to take for granted. These brief texts can raise big questions: In what ways do the new print modes mirror the community they addressed? In what ways, and for what purposes, do they seek to reform the community they address? And in what ways do they *create* the communities they address, so that the community defines itself, at least in part, as that group of people which reads these particular texts? For investigating such questions, the passage from Anderson (*Imagined Communities* [Verso, 1991], 35), quoted in the section headnote (2387), furnishes an eloquent place to start.

Two particularly rich resources for teaching the periodical essay are Kathryn Shevelow's *Women and Print Culture* (Routledge, 1989), with compact, perceptive chapters on the *Athenian Mercury*, *Tatler*, *Spectator*, and *Female Spectator*, and Erin Mackie's anthology *The Commerce of Everyday Life* (Bedford, 1998), which presents the most thorough sampling available of eighteenth-century periodical literature (including many of the pieces printed here), surrounded by copious and useful commentary on the papers' political, social, and economic positions, purposes, and contexts.

The texts here are arranged into five clusters wherein the selections, drawn from a variety of papers, are meant to speak to each other, exploring the same topics from different vantages of format, rhetoric, genre, gender, and social position. Read as clusters, these pieces can simulate (and stimulate?) the kinds of conversation that the papers sought to prompt among their customers at tea tables and in coffee houses (the section frontispiece, Bowles's *Medley*, makes clear how copiously such texts could accumulate, even interact, on any available surface). Here I'll sort things a little differently, beginning with comments on each of the major periodicals in chronological order, then offering some suggestions about the clusters as they appear in the anthology.

The Papers

The Athenian Mercury: This paper, the birthplace of one of the formats students will find most familiar, can make a useful starting point for the whole section. What relationship does the paper perform between its inquiring readers and knowledgeable responders? At first, the Athenians figure as learned lawgivers, answering at length the brief questions put to them (often in the formulation "whether it be lawful . . ."). Later, the proportions change, as readers' narratives occupy more space (2428). One question about this pioneering periodical concerns subsequent refinements: How did later papers—*Review, Tatler, Spectator*—manage to include and respond to their readers without relying exclusively on the letter-response, question-answer format? (For some suggestions, see ensuing comments.) Comparisons with current columns of advice and information may also prove fruitful: what relations do contemporary audiences demand between the print "authorities" (Ann Landers, Cecil Adams) and their correspondents? How are these relations encoded in the columns' language and format? How are the transactions of the Internet (e-mail, bulletin boards, etc.) reworking and redistributing textual authority?

A Review of the State of the British Nation: Defoe had written (anonymously, of course) for the *Athenian Mercury.* In the *Review* he devised the least anonymous of all periodical personae, a readily recognizable version of himself: beset, pugnacious, exasperated, and undaunted. The paper's title implies retrospect, but the *Review,* more than any subsequent paper, presented the ongoing spectacle of a single journalist vehemently engaged with breaking news. Defoe's ways of performing this engagement collate interestingly with his other writings in the anthology, both fiction and non-. His alertness (in *Mrs. Veal*) to the way dress and other commodities encode both social class and private predicament becomes, in the *Review* (1.43, 2416–17), a socio-economic analysis of the changes in trade that remake a neighborhood. His imaginative evocation of a real-life duellist's tormented conscience (*Review* 9.34, 2424–26) has much in common with his conjuration of Crusoe's despair (Perspectives: Spiritual Self-Reckonings), and of the desperate solitudes in *A Journal of the Plague Year.*

The Tatler: The *Tatler* attracted readers by supplanting the *Review*'s stringency with Bickerstaff's gregariousness. What perhaps distinguishes the paper most is its sheer populousness: all those crowded coffee houses in the opening salvo (No. 1), the dispossessed society of news writers and the long list of characters who occupy the *Tatler* (No. 18), and the copious cast of walk-ons (comparable in some ways to the recurrent guest roles in situation comedies) who crop up (*Seinfeld*-like) even in the precincts of "My Own Apartment": Partridge (No. 1), Jenny Distaff (No. 104), the Political Upholsterer (No. 155). The paper, from its title onward, undertook to mimic talk and to critique it. Dunton's "Athenians" read and responded to letters, and Bickerstaff does that too. But he derives much of his authority, as the vaunted Censor of Great Britain, from the skill with which he hears, dissects, and prompts ongoing conversation.

The Spectator: The *Spectator,* by contrast, mimics silence. (The paper pervaded its culture, and crops up correspondingly in other parts of the anthology: alongside *The Man of Mode;* and in the Perspectives sections Mind and God and Landscape, Pleasure, Power.) A key passage for the reading of any *Spectator* is the fictive author's initial self-portrait, as a "silent man" suddenly determined "to print my self out," in the form of a "sheet-full of thoughts every morning" (2402).

He construes capacity for silent observation as both a means of pleasure and a mode of power (see for example No. 69, where he takes effectual possession of the Royal Exchange by admiring it in action). The plan "to print my self out"–to multiply himself daily, not only on paper but in the minds of his readers–may constitute the largest power play of all, a way of monitoring and instructing that works less by overt instruction than by osmosis. By its fusion of silence with diurnal form, the Spectator fosters a fiction of reciprocity between itself and its readers, in which each party not only mirrors the other but appears to occupy the other's place in space and over time. Readers occupy Mr. Spectator both as objects of his attention and as presences in his paper: writers of letters, performers of actions, recipients of counsel. He occupies them–or rather "informs" them–as the figure of that silent part of themselves which they, as gregarious social beings, least recognize; in a constantly recurring phrase, he offers them the "secret satisfaction" (2410) that arises from the precise observation of self and others. These strategies of self-figuration inflect the style and the argument of nearly every paper: How does Mr. Spectator take possession of his public (No. 10)? How does he celebrate the appropriations of commerce (No. 69) while critiquing its inhumane excesses (No. 11)? How does his modelling of silent self-containment inform his paean to the expressive silence of the cosmos (No. 465, pp. 2670-71)? How does osmosis operate in his program of moral instruction, and particularly in his address to female readers (Nos. 10 and 128)? He clearly acknowledges and reinforces gender boundaries; does he also in any way transcend them, by cultivating identification with his female as with his male readers?

Some of the Spectator's impact can be discerned in Boswell's admiring comments fifty years later (2829), and some of its most important origins can be traced in the excerpts from Locke (2660-65), whose account of ideas and associations underlies both the form and the substance of Mr. Spectator's silent thought. Another useful companion reading is Pepys's diary, whose transactions between self and world the paper effectually inverts. From the vantage of its first readers, the Spectator's most surprising innovations–its diurnal timing and its silent persona–gave it the salient features of a diary, but of a diary turned inside out: the work not of a public or social figure (like Pepys), composing a more secret version of the self in a single sequestered manuscript, but of a wholly secretive sensibility imparting itself entirely through print, to be read by a wide and varied public in the daily rhythm and at the running moment of its making.

The Craftsman: Much of the Craftsman's craft consists in pointedly alienating its readers from their own familiar (albeit unacceptable) political predicament, by transposing their circumstances into an alien milieu, so that Walpole becomes a "vampyre" (2393-96) and South Sea stock a comically potent set of nonsense syllables, capable of inducing frenzy in the hearer (2422). In the Craftsman, Walpole's censorship produces an extraordinary traffic between news and fiction (note, for example, the use of a genuine London Journal piece to launch the economic satire on the vampires). Only by careful deflection, and by outright lying, can Amhurst and colleagues tell the truth as they see it.

The Female Spectator: In an astute reading of the first paper's second paragraph (2402–3), Kathryn Shevelow points out a central difference between Haywood's approach to periodical didacticism and that of her male predecessors. They propose to teach their readers from a position of patriarchal authority and innate rightness, whether grounded in learning (the Athenians), savvy (*Review*), sociability (*Tatler*), or inborn, enlightened eccentricity (*Spectator*). The Female Spectator, by contrast, undertakes to teach from her *mistakes*. "Hers is the voice of error rather than propriety, experience rather than innocence . . . [S]he has been guilty herself of the conduct she is to criticize." By thus "basing her persona's claims to authority upon her culpability rather than her superiority, Haywood rewrote the moral essay" (*Women in Print Culture*, 168–70). The tactic operates throughout. Quickly discovering her own "infinite deficiency" as author, the Female Spectator seeks out collaborators, with whom she works closely from the start (2403–4); later, she yields to the "superior judgment" of her collaborator Mira and ends her own argument early rather than running it into "dangerous" excess (2435). The collaborators' response to their reader's letter (2436–37) smacks more of community and collaboration than of the condescension and counsel that mark the *Athenian Gazette* (and that filter also through the *fair-sex* texts of the *Tatler* and the *Spectator*).

The Clusters

News and Comment: Students will be struck first by the blatancy of bias in government-sponsored papers (*Mercurius*, *Gazette*) that during the Restoration were often the only print-news sources legally available. The *Gazette*'s account of the fire quickly becomes a paean to His Majesty's solo efforts; the accounts by Pepys and Evelyn (2096–2102) offer instructive contrast. The important difference is not between private emotion and objectivity but among the different sorts of feeling (panic, piety, patriotism) that each narrator strives to evoke. The later, independent *Daily Courant*, by contrast, grounds its claims of impartiality in scrupulous documentation of sources. The passions bestirred by news furnish the *Spectator* and the *Tatler* with a steady source of comedy (2404–8).

The mix of plausible fact and intense feeling shaped both newspapers and novels—the two most lasting narrative modes the period produced. For a sketch of their relations, see the general introduction (2079–80). Students can here track the traffic between fact and fiction in the *Craftsman*'s use of the *London Journal* item (itself of questionable veracity) as prompter for the satiric discourse of Caleb D'Anvers and his friends. They can also watch Defoe deploy one narrative device—the "to the moment" reportage of significant sounds—in several narrative contexts: firsthand reports of fact (the cannonade announcing Union, 2391–92); the secondhand "relation" of a tale (the bell that tolls Mrs. Veal's arrival—and death, 2270, 2372); the projecting of fictional experiences onto a historical background (H. F.'s recollection of the mourner's groans as his family disappeared into the plague pit, 2383).

Periodical Personae: For comments on the personae, see discussions of the individual periodicals (above). A useful question in each instance: In what ways do the personae cultivate an identification with their readers, and by what means do they set themselves apart? The answers play out differently in the Athenians' aloofness, Mr. Spectator's busy but almost invisible movement among his readers (No. 10), the Female Spectator's consortium of collaborators.

Getting, Spending, Speculating: As J. G. A. Pocock has shown, Addison, Steele, and Defoe write both to celebrate commerce and to restrain it; to remedy the newly speculative culture's fixation on the fictitious future (where stocks will rise, debts will be paid, and profits accrue) by prescribing a prudent focus on the present (see Pocock's *Virtue, Commerce, and History* [Cambridge UP, 1985], 113–16). The time form of Augustan journalism did much to abet these economic interventions. The close succession of dates at the top of the thrice-weekly *Review* and the daily *Spectator* consistently grounded their "speculations" (in Addison's frequent term) about trade (and everything else) within the local limits of the present.

The first three essays here can be read profitably in conversation with each other, and in conjunction with several of Pope's poems which subject the nation's new prosperity to varied scrutiny: *Windsor-Forest*, *The Rape of the Lock* (particularly Canto 1), and the *Epistle to Burlington*. What are the bounties that empire brings forth? An expanded community, new national centrality, all those ornaments for women (*Spectator* No. 69). What are the costs that commerce incurs? A starkly reduced humanity (No. 11); an unthinking obsession with luxury (*Review* 1.43).

In the little collection called "A Bubbler's Medley," ambivalence about the new commerce runs another way. Each of these pieces critiques the South Sea catastrophe, and yet each in some measure exploits it, making it (by widely varied rhetorical strategies) the occasion of entertainment and instruction for the reader, and profit to the author. This assortment of takes on the South Sea Bubble should teach very well with the Thomas Bowles engraving of the same title that serves as frontispiece to the whole section (2060). In his quasi-scrapbook of printed papers casually scattered across the picture's plane, Bowles manages to cram many of the culture's most pressing and durable preoccupations: with money, trade, and empire; with miscellany; with evanescence; with "memorial." But most of all he suggests a cultural addiction to text itself, a world in which print representations (and misrepresentations) of reality are at once the most common and the most prized commodities; in which readers (like the invisible assembler of this collage, and like the denizens of the coffee house in the upper-right corner) are perpetually engaged in assembling their own ephemeral anthologies.

Women and Men, Morals and Manners

For a sketch of the periodicals' role in the propagation of "politeness," see the general introduction (2070–71). The essays on duelling by Steele and Defoe afford one of the most instructive contrasts in the section. Steele seeks to laugh duelling out of fashion by looking at its language: the ludicrous incongruity between the words used and the actions they describe serves as shorthand for the folly and waste of the entire enterprise. Defoe sermonizes. The imaginative, casuistical method that would later drive his fiction prompts a kind of fiction here. Projecting from his own "*unhappy experience*," he "guess[es]" at the "perturbed thoughts" of Hamilton on the eve of his death. What would it be like (he asks and answers), to be this person in this predicament?

In the papers on relations between men and women, the author's arguments are clear enough. What is more interesting, and sometimes more elusive, are the gestures by which the papers *perform* (as opposed to preach) those relations, in the gendered transactions between persona and audience. In the *Athenian Mercury*, a woman is permitted to pray to God for a husband, just as the (putatively female) inquirer has been permitted to *ask* permission for such a prayer from the Athenians, who here offer a male-written script for women to "use . . . if they are not better furnished already" (2427; the *if* clause offers a little room for autonomy). Bickerstaff describes his sister's moral progress after marriage in terms that plainly sketch the kind of influence that this confirmed bachelor hopes to wield over female readers: "upon talking with her on several subjects, I could not but fancy that I saw a great deal of her husband's way and manner in her remarks, her phrases, the tone of her voice, and the very air of her countenance. This gave me an unspeakable satisfaction . . ." (2430)—a satisfaction which *not* be spoken, in part because the desired male-female ventriloquy ("the tone of her voice") has already been so successfully accomplished. The *Female Spectator*'s tale of Seomanthe, by contrast, quietly ironizes the authority of its female narrator, who writes to show the danger "of laying young people under too great a restraint," only to discern that she is exerting too little restraint over her own "expatiat[ing]" argument; she promptly seeks to redress the discursive balance (2435). The episode performs wisdom more as process than as pronouncement.

Jonathan Swift
Poems *and* The Journal to Stella

An "aubade" is "a musical announcement of dawn, a sunrise song or open-air concert" (OED), and that's exactly what "A Description of the Morning" sets out to corrupt. (Some call this poem "The Hangover.") It's a pleasure to work with this poem's structures of order and disorder. The poem begins in and reiterates the sense of the present, and a constant, eternal presence: "Now, Now, Now." What, in fact, does the morning reveal? What spaces are lit up by the sun? Something not unlike cockroaches when the kitchen light turns on. It's as if the underside of London, the things that live and bloom in darkness, shape the daylit contours: Betty rumples her bed, the duns dog the lords for their debts, the prisoners pretend once again to be imprisoned, the boys head listlessly towards the semblance of an education. What is the order of the aubadic revelation? We see the servants, who imply their masters; we see the public places that imply the private ones; the morning is defined not by its soft colors and sweet scents but by the sights and sounds of urban activity, by the people who work to make appearances work. Morning brings, not decency, not beauty, but the false, fragile semblance of order.

"A Description of a City Shower" offers a similar satiric rumpling of poetic and psychological expectations. As a "georgic," the poem is supposed to tell us what to do: know the signs, recognize the patterns, learn the tricks. The rain, like the city's morning sun, reveals the social contours of London even as it obscures physical ones: venting spleens (a physiological complaint or a metaphorical gripe?), vomiting clouds, dust indistinguishable from rain, Tories cowering with Whigs. Physical proximity threatens social distance: "Here various kinds by various fortunes led, / Commence acquaintance underneath a shed" (ll. 39-40). Finally, the kennel itself "in huge confluent" carries the whole literal and symbolic mess that pretends to distinguish itself topographically ("Filths of all hues and odors, seem to tell / What streets they sailed from by the sight and smell" [ll. 55-56]), but ironically, of course—who's going to sort garbage by smell? Students often liven up at the sight of a map; tracing the course of the city's garbage adds to the ferocious concreteness of the poem. The poem—as poem—offers a specious sense of structure and order that comes most beautifully undone in the last triplet, which reads aloud now as richly and rudely and ringingly as it must have done for Swift's Londoners, spilling its wonderfully fetid imagery into readers' awareness. The triplet itself, despised by Swift as a cheap trick of prosody, pushes the sense of overflow in repetition. The Alexandrine hexameter (as opposed to the loose heroic couplets of the rest of the poem) gives extra rhyme, extra sounds, extra room, extra time to all these disgusting, mingled things that all lead to a kind of parodic purging. But to what end? What happens, figuratively speaking, to the "pensive cat" (l. 3) by the last line? What kind of purging is possible in this post-diluvian poem?

Stella's birthday poems come rather sweetly among these selections of Swift's characteristic explorations of fetidness; they help students understand that Swift was not a sick, twisted mind (often their first delighted or appalled conclusion), but a very caring, committed man who spent a rather large amount of time showing us our darker, filthier sides in the distant hope of reform. The Stella poems, like the coterie poems in the Behn section, presume an intimate audience but also speak to a larger one. How do the poems create that sense? Look at the parentheticals, the asides, the direct addresses. How does the speaker work with his tone? Different students might try out different ways of reading this poem aloud, imagining their Stella in front of them. Which lines would be read "straight," and which with a half-smile? Which affectionately, which teasingly, which ironically, which sadly, which admiringly?

Students should try to keep the Voice of the Stella poems in mind as they find themselves trapped in "The Lady's Dressing Room." This poem shocks students, and asking them to read particularly revolting lines aloud increases the general queasiness, but no one sleeps through this one, and it can open up wonderful discussions. The poem works delightfully on the level of close structural analysis: the first couplet, almost but not quite iambic pentameter, has its last foot cut off, so to speak, in a limping "feminine" or unstressed-syllable ending; it plays mischievously with puns ("void" [l. 5]) and sounds ("issues" and "tissues" are like onomatopoeic sneezes). But of course the big question is "Why?" Why all this intimate dwelling on the disgusting? The question applies not only to Strephon, but also to the narrator, and by implication, that appalled but fascinated voyeur, the reader ("Strephon bids us guess the rest" [l. 16]). It's useful to ask: can things *really* be this disgusting? Or, as "Celia's magnifying glass" (l. 60) suggests, is the poem playing on the psychological implications of perspective? Neither the worm nor the squeezing of it, for example, is really there—thing and act are extrapolated by Strephon or the narrator. The voyeurism magnifies the horror; the very act of seeing what one's not supposed to see lends a darker luster to things that would probably shift to some extent into ordinariness if openly offered. Have a few signs of female physicality been magnified by Strephon into a Brobdingnagian horror-show of Femaleness? Or is Celia particularly filthy in her personal habits; if so, why generalize to all women? Do we think Strephon keeps his own room any better? Who is the real object of satire here? Who's punished?

That last question is a good opener for *Verses on the Death of Dr. Swift*, that lively, wicked, fascinating poetic autobiography that pairs so richly with Pope's *Epistle to Dr. Arbuthnot*. How does the poet construct an image of himself, of his work, of his world? How does Swift use the initial bit of Rochefoucauldian cynicism to present in the end a picture of human generosity? Why does the speaker imaginatively kill himself off as the premise for the poem? How does the poet's image shift within the various constructions? In the fourth stanza, for example, the poet is One of Us: "I love my friend as well as you, / But would not have him stop my view" (ll. 17–18); not too much further along, however, he inverts Pope's "damning with faint praise" to praise with faux-envy, thereby revealing himself as a pretty generous-hearted guy: "In Pope, I cannot read a line, / But with a sigh, I wish it mine: / When he can in one couplet fix / More sense than I can do in six" (ll. 47–50). How does dialogue enter and operate? Think especially of the end, when "One quite indifferent in the cause / [His] character impartial draws" (ll. 305–06). It's a long, long character being drawn, and given its quite favorable review, and given that it is, after all, Swift creating Swift's voice that gives over to the anonymous biographer, there's a lovely subtle irony to be worked out here.

The *Journal to Stella* entry gives us yet another Swiftian voice—playful, cooing, boyish, happy, chatty, silly. What does the genre of a private, *journalized* correspondence permit the writer to say and do in offering a self-portrait, a virtual dialogue, a "converse of the pen", as Richardson calls it? As Stuart Sherman shows, Swift tries to render contemporaneity, a sense of the immediate, living moment, by constructing scenes that he in London and Stella and Rebecca Dingley in Dublin can share: "He contrives, for example, to simulate second sight and inform the women of what they are doing at the exact instant of his writing, and then later gloats at having done so" (*Telling Time: Clocks, Diaries, and English Diurnal Form 1660–1785* [U of Chicago P, 1996], 176). Political events and social gossip, large thoughts and small speculations, a day's acts and a day's inaction, are all presented as if unsorted, in a jumble that represents the full skein of daily life. The journal can recreate, represent, and stand in for living, speaking, sharing, joking; the journal can be self, other, life.

A Modest Proposal *and* Petty's Political Arithmetic

Satire depends upon a sense of humor (gallows or otherwise); the success of something like A Modest Proposal depends upon the reader's understanding the precise distance between the narrator's voice and the author's—something that often got satirists in trouble. Swift here introduces a narrator who *cares* about the poverty, the overpopulation, the underemployment of Ireland; his "compassion" moves towards an objective, scientific means of alleviation, parodying at once the bizarre optimism of projectors and the callousness of the larger (English and even Irish) world towards the calamity at home. He uses the language of the political arithmetic of Petty—"reckoned," "calculate," "subtract," "number" (2467)— in order to introduce a scheme that "will not be liable to the least objection" (2468). Cannibalism, of course, just happens to be one of the deepest human taboos. The charity depends on depravity, the humanity on inhumanity. The speaker goes on for several pages in a mild, reasonable, hopeful voice about the particular delicacies of infants' flesh, its seasonability (like game), the overall expenses involved. The suggestions—in the same mild, benevolent tone—get more and more gruesome: flaying (2469), for example. The elderly, offered as another reasonable concern, are reasonably dealt with: "they are every day dying, and rotting, by cold, and famine, and filth, and vermin, as fast as can be reasonably expected" (2469-70). The whole project is offered as something that will economically, socially, and politically advantage the troubled country of Ireland. The end of the piece reiterates the horrifying reality: how will anyone "find food and raiment for an hundred thousand useless mouths and backs"? (2471). The last lines declare the narrator's disinterestedness: his own youngest child is nine, his wife is past child-bearing. Much as he'd like to, he can't offer one of his own.

What do any of us do with this? The aching humanity behind this friendly inhumanity makes this text utterly unforgettable. It makes the William Petty reading all the more striking. Petty has it all figured out—the numbers, the reasons, the effects: "then the said people, reckoned as money at 5 percent interest, will yield 3 millions and a half per annum" (2472). England will then be "enriched"; and that's what counts. Petty's postscript argues, much like Swift's narrator, that the overall good includes Ireland as well, offering "a competent livelihood" to all able and interested parties (2473). The sheer emphasis on numbers, on bodies over persons, renders this straightforward text as least as chilling as A Modest Proposal itself. We might ask, which should be the "context" piece here?

Alexander Pope

In his Life of Pope, Samuel Johnson wrote of the poet: "From his attention to poetry he was never diverted" (Lives of the Poets, 1781). Pope's life, in many ways, was spent in shaping his poetry and at the same time was shaped by the various effects his poetry had on the world around him. Johnson's details suggest a life spent listening, observing, poised for writing: "If conversation offered anything that could be improved he committed it to paper; if a thought, or perhaps an expression more happy than was common, rose to his mind, he was careful to write it; an independent distich was preserved for an opportunity of insertion, and some little fragments have been found containing lines, or parts of lines, to be wrought upon at some other time." The continuity Pope created in a life committed to writing—an intensely solitary task—was at the same time the product of a close-knit community of friends. From his days in the Scriblerus Club, Pope created in his writings a confident sense of an always-present, always-understanding audience, intrinsically different from the legion of dunces, hacks, and small-minded critics festering in vast numbers outside the magic circle. This implicit sense of audience that began among a community of authors ties together the community of Pope's writings, from the freshly confident *Essay on Criticism*, the saucy *Rape of the Lock*, the nostalgic *Windsor-Forest*, the pensive *Eloisa to Abelard*, all the way to the ringing *Essay on Man* and the raging *New Dunciad*. How Pope draws the line between inside understanding and outside idiocy, how he teaches the reader to read and creates a space for reform, is always a useful way to begin ranging around in the vast literary fields of Pope.

A second overarching strategy for approaching Pope is to spend some detailed time on the nature and phenomenon of the heroic couplet. Pope wrote almost *everything* in rhymed iambic pentameter couplets; it's a staggering thought. He says, "As yet a child, nor yet a fool to fame, / I lisped in numbers, for the numbers came" (*Epistle to Arbuthnot*, ll. 128–29, 2539). One tends to believe him. Students should work on getting a good grasp on the couplet from within and without. Getting them to write some heroic couplets helps (although it's odd how often the idea of scansion seems utterly elusive); there finally (usually) comes a point where the precise, rhythmic, alien form suddenly crosses over into natural speech patterns (one of the form's virtues, according to eighteenth-century poets), and students "get it." Then they find they can read the poetry much more clearly; the form no longer gets in the way but—pretty much as Pope claims ("But true expression, like th' unchanging sun, / Clears and improves whate'er it shines upon, / It gilds all objects, but it alters none" [*Essay on Criticism*, ll. 315–18, 2483])—*clarifies* the sense of the subject. Students' readings then, both internal and oral, tend to open them up oratorically to nuance, pause, and emphasis, away from the metrically monotonous and intellectually unintelligible "da DA da DA da DA da DA da DA."

Once students understand both the complexity of writing heroic couplets and the equally unexpected ease of reading them, they can begin to apply some formal analysis to the different ways Pope uses the couplet, reproducing "the grandeur and the sonority of the lines in which ancient poets composed their epics" in order "to encompass all the things and actions of the world" (see the period introduction, 2079). By the time they come through on the other side, they should be dazzled.

An Essay on Criticism

"The things I have written fastest have always pleased most. I wrote the *Essay on Criticism* fast, for I had digested all the matter in prose before I began upon it in verse"—so Pope said to his friend Joseph Spence in February or March 1735

(Spence, *Observations, Anecdotes, and Characters of Books and Men, Collected from Conversation*, ed. James M. Osborn [Clarendon Press, 1966], #107). Yet as Johnson illustrates in his *Life of Pope*, this boast can be misleading; Pope may sometimes have been fast in his creation, but never *hasty*. As Johnson puts it, "To make verses was his first labor, and to mend them was his last." The *Essay on Criticism* is a study of the art of writing, the art of reading, and the art of analyzing literature (very useful for the instruction and delight of young persons). It enjoyed virtually all of the success for which the young aspiring poet hoped; Dennis hated it, but for Dennis, *all* things Popean "[looked] yellow to [his] jaundiced eye" (EC, ll. 558–59, 2488). Addison, on the other hand, praised the poem in almost the same terms that the poem determines for praise: "*The Art of Criticism* [i.e. *An Essay on Criticism*] . . . is a masterpiece in its kind. The observations follow one another like those in Horace's *Art of Poetry*, without that methodical regularity which would have been requisite in a prose author. They are some of them uncommon, but such as the reader must assent to, when he sees them explained with that elegance and perspicuity in which they are delivered. As for those which are the most known, and the most received, they are placed in so beautiful a light, and illustrated with such apt allusions, that they have in them all the graces of novelty, and make the reader, who was before acquainted with them, still more convinced of their truth and solidity" (*Spectator* No. 253, 20 December 1711). What oft was thought but ne'er so well expressed? Sorting out the basic precepts makes a good basic exercise that can be highlighted with marking and paraphrasing those phrases and epigrams that made their way into proverbial status and still have currency today ("fools rush in," etc.). (A brief look at *Bartlett's Familiar Quotations*, in print or online, produces instant respect.) And perhaps the most pointed place to begin is with the criterion: "A perfect judge will read each work of wit / With the same spirit that its author writ"; and with the advice: "In every work regard the writer's end" (EC 233–34, 255, 2481).

The most famous passage is typically the most pleasurable and profitable for students to play with—the stanza in which Pope teaches by example: "A needless Alexandrine ends the song, / That like a wounded snake, drags its slow length along" (ll. 356–57; the passage begins "But most by numbers judge a poet's song" [l. 337, 2483]). Precisely what students often expect of and dread in Pope's poetry is anticipated and dissolved in this passage; Pope teaches us to read his poetry by distinguishing the subtle from the unsubtle ways of doing the job. The *effort* put into the art of writing heroic couplets emerges briefly here—the effort that, once mastered, disappears back into a now-complicated sense of fluid ease: "True ease in writing comes from art, not chance, / As those move easiest who have learned to dance" (ll. 362–63).

The eighteenth-century preoccupations with politeness as well as learning and sense are addressed in lines 572–83 (see period introduction, 2070); to what extent does this poem follow its own moral and pedagogical precepts as well as it does its poetic principles?

The "little learning" passage (ll. 215–32, 2480–81) is a good place to see how Pope builds the couplet into verse arguments (see J. Paul Hunter, "Form as Meaning:

Pope and the Ideology of the Couplet," *The Eighteenth-Century: Theory and Interpretation*, 37:3 [Fall 1996], 257–70). It also connects well with the fissures of doubt that attended the new realms of scientific "enlightenment" illustrated by the selections in Perspectives: Mind and God:

> While from the bounded level of our mind,
> Short views we take, nor see the lengths behind,
> But more advanced, behold with strange surprise
> New, distant scenes of endless science rise!
> So pleased at first, the towering Alps we try,
> Mount o'er the vales, and seem to tread the sky;
> Th' eternal snows appear already past,
> And the first clouds and mountains seem the last:
> But those attained, we tremble to survey
> The growing labors of the lengthened way,
> Th' increasing prospect tires our wandering eyes,
> Hills peep o'er hills, and Alps on Alps arise!

Issues of perspective, of changing lenses, connect a number of texts in this period selection, and Pope's poetry, historically as well as ideologically central and reflective, offers a good point for summary and anticipation.

Windsor-Forest

This poem was written, in its two stages, to celebrate a number of pasts (England's and Pope's) and a number of futures (Britain's and the world's). Pope pieces together memory, imagery, history, mythology, and prophecy in complicated ways; students might pick one strand, follow it through, and describe how it relates to the poem as a whole. It's often helpful to have them write a very brief explication of a short passage; one close reading can open up key issues of meaning, form, and context. How does the poem use hunting as a displaced image of war throughout the poem? What varying perspectives does the poem offer on both hunting and war? The hunting of the partridge is compared parenthetically—"(if small things we may with great compare)" (l. 105)—to England eagerly bent on taking "some thoughtless town, with ease and plenty blessed" (l. 107); the perspective is that of the hunter moving closer and closer until he seizes the surprised prey, and "high in air Britannia's standard flies" (l. 110). But then the perspective suddenly shifts in the next stanza: the invocation "See!" is to the reader, who then "sees" the scene from the perspective of the victim. The pheasant's triumphant flight ends in a graphic, lingering death ("he feels the fiery wound, / Flutters in blood, and panting beats the ground" [ll. 113–24]). We get to "know" that whirring pheasant in some detail—his colors, his crest, his eyes, his feathers, his wings, his breast. Then scene follows scene of hares, lapwings, perch, eels, carp, trouts, pikes, harts, unceasingly hunted. The final shift from country pastime into familiar mythology moves us into identification with a human figure: Lodona pursued by Pan, his "sounding steps" catching up with her, his shadow overtaking her, his breath on her neck—all the panic of the chase and the complicated implications of escape and release. How does the poem work all these different perspectives into its accounts of English history and a British future? Although the image of Britannia's standard waves over a number of stanzas, does this poem present an unambivalent imperialism?

This poem, particularly the episode of the whirring pheasant, is also useful for illustrating a particular brand of eighteenth-century poetic detail. "Nothing can please many, and please long, but just representations of general nature," said Johnson (2755), who elsewhere counselled against numbering the stripes of a particular tulip (2749). A visual image must capture the "general nature" of something with one powerful adjective: "whirring pheasant," "scarlet-circled eyes," "clam'rous lapwings," "leaden death," "quiv'ring shade," "scaly breed"—the scene abounds with model tags. The poetic world is colorful, memorable, distinctively drawn and universally applicable. This kind of visual detail smooths the move from particular to general, from scene to analogy; the world of things and the world of interpretation are poetically entwined.

The Rape of the Lock *and* Sarpedon's speech from The Iliad

In 1818 William Hazlitt commented about the *Rape*: "It is like looking through a microscope, where every thing assumes a new character and a new consequence, where things are seen in their minutest circumstances and slightest shades of difference; where the little becomes gigantic, the deformed beautiful, and the beautiful deformed" (*Lectures on the English Poets* [London, 1818], 4:142). Making connections with the selections from Boyle's *Meditations* and Hooke's *Micrographia* can show how the "new science" offered new opportunities for poetic experiment and imagery. The microscope and the telescope (the latter makes an actual appearance within the poem as "Galileo's eyes" [5.138]) supply images through which to analyze the exaggeration and miniaturization of the poem, to see how the "mock" transforms in paradoxical ways the "epic."

This poem can be approached in so many ways. The most obvious beginning is to sort out the precise distances between "the trivial *matter* and the heroic *manner*," as the introduction suggests. Comparing Sarpedon's speech to Clarissa's is an excellent beginning. Pope had much earlier than the publication of the *Iliad* itself published a translation of Sarpedon's speech in the 1709 *Miscellany*, so Clarissa's speech (added in 1717 to "*open more clearly the* MORAL *of the poem*") was already a parody of his own text. Where does he strike out differences? What is the difference in the contexts of the two speeches? in their intended audiences? and in their effects? Why does Pope make the speaker of the moral the same character who hands the Baron the scissors in the first place (3.127–30)?

Pope's poetic technique is at its most dazzling here. Take students through the rich connections of zeugma: "Or stain her honor, or her new brocade" (2.107); "Dost sometimes counsel take—and sometimes tea" (3.8). And through the interpretive prisms of metonymy: Belinda's dressing table, on which India and Arabia

are reduced (1.129-36), or Japan and China on "the board" (3.105-12), the poem
at once celebrating and satirizing the symbols of imperialism. Visit the dark corners of the mind in the Cave of Spleen, where boundaries of gender and identity
blur: "A pipkin there like Homer's tripod walks; / Here sighs a jar, and there a
goose pie talks; / Men prove with child, as pow'rful fancy works, / And maids
turned bottles, call aloud for corks" [4.51-54]). And what do students think
Belinda means when she cries out, "Oh hadst thou, cruel! been content to seize /
Hairs less in sight, or any hairs but these!" (4.175-76)? (John Dennis was incensed
at the implicit obscenity here; students don't have to worry that they're "reading
into" the poem some 1990s sexual sophistication or deviance.)

That last question can lead into the overarching and contested issue of the "rape"
itself. The Latin word *rapere* means to "carry away"; the lock is literally stolen. But
"rape" then as now had its violent sexual meaning; of what else is Belinda "raped"?
How do the genderless—or cross-gendering—sylphs fit into the scenario? Why does an
"earthly lover lurking at her heart" (3.144) become the crux of vulnerability? What,
in this central interpretive issue, are the "epic" meanings and the "mock-epic" exaggerations? *Windsor-Forest* ends with the poet modestly asserting a humble Muse, un-
ambitious strains, careless days, and retired content; but the last line does remind us
of the "I [that] sung the sylvan strains"; the end of *The Rape of the Lock* (and of *Eloisa
to Abelard*, and the whole of *Epistle to Arbuthnot*) sings the power of the poet in the
scheme of representation. It's always worth studying Pope's construction of the poet
in his poems; in his life he did much both to professionalize the poet—to pull away
from the system of private patronage and move into the public world of booksellers
and publishing—and to privatize the realm of poetry, to authorize the writing of self
along with monarch, national events, philosophical issues. (Aphra Behn is another,
earlier figure in this development of the professionalized writer—one who writes for
bread—publicly writing about a private self.) The final stanza recommends, with an
implicit "I," that Belinda cease to mourn her ravished hair; she should instead cheer
up because the Muse is about to make her immortal; the story is about the rape of
Belinda's lock, but it's also very much about the telling of the rape of the lock.

Eloisa to Abelard

In this poem Pope assumes the voice and perspective of a woman to explore the
experience of anguished, solitary love. In some ways this poem is biographically allegorical: politically disenfranchised, religiously marginalized, and sexually disadvantaged, Pope himself was immured and wounded; he was also at this time writing half-witty, half-anguished letters of "epistolary gallantry" to Lady Mary Wortley
Montagu as she travelled in Europe towards Turkey with her husband. At some
points he would be imagining her "soul stark naked, for I am confident 'tis the
prettiest kind of white soul, in the universe" (1 September 1718); other times he
would confess, "I can't go on in this style: I am not able to think of you without
the utmost seriousness, and if I did not take a particular care to disguise it, my letters would be the most melancholy things in the world" (October 1716). It's a toss-
up whether Pope gives "Eloisa" a voice, or Eloisa gives Pope one.

The form of heroic epistle allows Eloisa to create the fiction of a dialogue with her absent lover, or attempt the reality of a dialogue with God, but the very presumption of the form underscores a sense of isolation, futility, and silence engulfing the voice, the constructed "conversation." How does the poem formally and imaginatively negotiate the tensions between the "erotic and pious, gothic and tender"? Spend some time on the rhyme, for example. "Love" frequently ends a line, and yet is never matched up with an exact rhyme; the oral union of sound, like the intellectual union of resolution, always slips away ("remove," "prove," "move"). "God," too, never finds an exact rhyme (it's always "abode," an implicitly unstabling housing of thought), and in fact "God" appears much more rarely than "love" in the authoritative position of an end rhyme. The key rhymes, like Eloisa's earthly/divine dilemma, find no resolution.

The story, in fact, is passed into mediation: Eloisa imagines "some future bard" who, also condemned to lovers' separation, will join his own griefs to hers and tell the story. The poet thus once again emerges in the final lines, simultaneously appropriating Eloisa's voice as he voices her story.

Epistle to Burlington

"In the greatest literary document of the neo-Palladian movement, the *Epistle to Burlington*, Pope moves naturally from the pompous utility of Roman architecture (ll. 23–24) to the old English patriarchal ideal of rural landownership (ll. 181–86), and then, in the remaining verses to the end of the poem, just as naturally to an expansive vision of healthy national cultural renewal expressed in great and noble civic building" (James Sambrook, *The Eighteenth Century: The Intellectual and Cultural Contexts of English Literature, 1700–1789* [Longman, 1990], 161). Pope's poetry and Pope's world-view always look for integration, coherence, a fundamental relationship between form and content, inside and outside, appearance and function. "'Tis use alone that sanctifies expense, / And splendor borrows all her rays from sense" (ll. 179–80).

This poem could be taught along with other "country house poems" in this anthology, and/or with the "Perspectives: Landscape, Pleasure, Power" in this period section. What is the ideology of wealth here? In some ways Pope's poem departs from the usual requirement of the country house poem—that owner and tenant, house and land, all coexist in mutual obligation and support; tenant works for owner, owner protects tenant, owner hunts and fishes, game and fish leap onto owner's table. Pope's vision here is primarily aesthetic; "sense" is to be applied to the owner's and visitor's use and pleasure, not to a larger social ecosystem. (One brief stanza excepted: in Timon's villa, that "huge heap of littleness," at least "the poor are clothed, the hungry fed; / Health to himself, and to his infants bread / The lab'rer bears: what his hard heart denies, / His charitable vanity supplies" [ll. 169–72]. In an odd move, even senseless wealth, architecturally depicted, has its justification.)

Students can sort out first the aesthetic requirements and then their stated or implicit social and political correspondents. If possible, illustrations of some of the real Palladian "villas" would help tremendously; particularly for American students, the traditional descriptive language of country house poetry (even the terms "house" or "villa" themselves) conjures up something almost cozy in size and appearance—nothing remotely like Penshurst, Prior Park, Hagley, or Stowe. Pope's poem witnesses a change in aesthetic preference; at Timon's villa the garden is in the formal Versailles style: "Grove nods at grove, each alley has a brother, / And half the platform just reflects the other" (ll. 117–18). What is the aesthetic (i.e. conceptual) advantage in "pleasing intricacies" and "artful wildness"? As the texts in "Landscape, Pleasure, Power" suggest, perspective was shifting from the owner's architectural self-statement to the observer's interpretation; the ideas of solitude and individuality were investing all aspects of life. And in this poem, as in all of Pope's poems, there's at least one couplet that could be used to define Pope's poetic art itself: "He gains all points, who pleasingly confounds, / Surprises, varies, and conceals the bounds" (ll. 55–56). Following his own instructions in the *Essay on Criticism*, Pope carefully constructs his art and just as carefully conceals its artfulness, "as those move easiest who have learned to dance." How does this poem, in overall structure and local detail, conform to its own precepts for use and beauty and sense in architecture and landscape design?

from An Essay on Man

Pope published this poem anonymously, and watched with wicked interest as his enemies, while assiduously attacking his other works and the patently evil mind behind them, praised the *Essay on Man* to the skies for its wisdom, probity, freshness, and moral inspiration. (Later editions of the *Essay* include portions of those rave reviews.) Few thought there was anything original in the work, but that was scarcely the point; most praise closely conformed to the precepts in the *Essay on Criticism* in finding it "true wit"—"What oft was thought, but ne'er so well expressed" (EC, ll. 297–98).

Pope himself had long mulled over the basic claims of perspective, human inconsistency, divine order, and the interconnectedness of things. In an early letter to Joseph Addison he wrote: "Good God! What an incongruous animal is man! how unsettled in his best part, his soul; and how changing and variable in his frame of body? . . . What is man altogether, but one mighty inconsistency! . . . What a bustle we make about passing our time, when all our space is but a point? . . . Our whole extent of being no more, in the eyes of him who gave it, than a scarce perceptible moment of duration. Those animals whose circle of living is limited to three or four hours, as the naturalists assure us, are yet as long-lived and possess as wide a scene of action as man, if we consider him with an eye to all space, and all eternity. Who knows what plots, what achievements a mite may perform in his kingdom of a grain of dust, within his life of some minutes? and of how much less consideration than even this, is the life of man in the sight of that God, who is from Ever, and for Ever!" (14 December 1713).

The opening stanza of the *Essay on Man* sets up the perspective—and the issues of perspective—for the whole poem: the speaker and the philosopher Bolingbroke will together explore the "scene of man" which turns out to be "A mighty maze!

but not without a plan" (l. 6). The image of the maze is deliberate: a garden fancy, a popular human construction, a very earthbound and recognizable image. The perspective is consistently human, grounded, looking down towards insects and mites, or up towards God and angels, but never assuming omniscience in all its assertions of God's omniscience. Students can trace the consistency of this perspective and discuss the ways it connects to the overall argument of design.

In the "Design" of this poem, Pope explains that he chose verse instead of prose to distill and present the argument. How does he explain the advantages of verse in philosophy? As the selections in the "Mind and God" section show, philosophy doesn't typically represent itself poetically. How does Pope's "design" fit in with "God's"? This poem works perhaps best of all for students' understanding of the relationship between form and function. This is a poem about ontological order that employs the ultimate in poetic order not only to explain but to illustrate—almost to prove—the "argument by design." Each word, each line, each stanza, each section relates to every other. It's an architectural masterpiece, and students tend to enjoy finding and explicating those connections. All those connections must, in the end, lead to the intensely controversial claim (then as now): "Whatever IS, is RIGHT" (l. 294). How do students debate that claim? Do any feel that this confident, assured poem has any interesting fissures in its (assertions of) plenitude? The same kind of rhetorical analysis that was suggested for the selections in "The New Science" can work well here in precisely these intersections of perspective, assertion, and implication.

An Epistle from Mr. Pope, to Dr. Arbuthnot

This formal "apology" is in one sense Pope's autobiography, and in another a biography of his time, in which "many will know their own pictures" (2550). It is perhaps the most fully grounded in precise, local, unexaggerated detail of all his poems, almost novelistic in its use of dialogue and the immediate intersections of time and space: "Shut, shut the door, good John! fatigued I said, / Tie up the knocker, say I'm sick, I'm dead" (ll. 1–2). What other details throughout the poem contribute to the creation of a real, believable, concrete world? To what extent does a "real world" contribute to the "reality" of the self-construction and self-explanation here?

Compare this poem to Verses on the Death of Dr. Swift. How are the major sections of the poem arranged? The breathlessness of the opening lines suggests Pope has just barely made it inside, hotly pursued by hordes of would-be poets. "What walls can guard me, or what shades can hide? / They pierce my thickets, thro' my grot they glide" (ll. 7–8). Pope has become a spectacle in his own time. Once "inside," he has time and space to analyze the problem, consider the causes (going back through his own childhood), study his actions and others' reactions, ponder the unfairness of it all, utter a few last wan words of blessing on his friend and a wish for peace for himself and his mother, and in the whole process create a kind of textual protection that reveals the "true" Pope and wards off both attacks and unreasonable appeals. What is the image of Pope created and offered here? What "evidence" does Pope use to support that image? In an unexpected way, the methods of this poem intersect with those of Defoe: historical data—names and places and numbers and lists—play a powerful part.

One particularly useful approach to understanding this self-construction pivots on Pope's deformity. Pope was haunted all his life by enemies playing viciously on his humped back and shortened stature, calling him toad, spider, ape. Pope first marches painfully through the "helpfulness" of "friends": "There are, who to my person pay their court, / I cough like Horace, and though lean, am short, / Ammon's great son one shoulder had too high, / Such Ovid's nose, and 'Sir! you have an eye—' / Go on, obliging creatures, make me see / All that disgraced my betters, met in me" (ll. 115–20). Helen Deutsch argues: "In Pope's literary self-fashioning . . . deformity and poetic form create the ultimate couplet, guaranteeing the author, if not possession of his text, at least a kind of patent on it. . . . [A]n ability to anticipate and manipulate such responses [informs] Pope's career-long strategies of self-authorization" ('The Truest Copies' and the 'Mean Original': Pope's Deformity and the Poetics of Self-Exposure," *Eighteenth-Century Studies* 27:1 [Fall 1993]: 6). Watch for the ways Pope uses animal imagery back: particularly with Sporus (Lord Hervey), that insect, that spaniel, that familiar toad who "Half froth, half venom, spits himself abroad" (ll. 319–20), and even worse, that "Amphibious Thing! that acting either part, / The trifling head, or the corrupted heart!" (ll. 356–27).

The *Epistle to Arbuthnot* draws local portraits as well as the poet's own. Perhaps one of the most famous in the gallery of insults is Pope's portrait of Addison (Atticus, ll. 193–214), who so memorably damns with faint praise, and assents with civil leer. Have students take this apart, to see its own deft balance of faint praise, civil leer, attack and regret. And the brief, sharp portrait of Gay, or rather, Gay's career (ll. 256–60)? In some sense Pope's portraits, indeed the entire poem, answers his own apparently rhetorical question: "Heav'ns! was I born for nothing but to write?" (l. 272). Well, of Gay's "blameless life the sole return" seems to have been Pope's epitaph on his tomb; and much of his poetry seems designed to have a real, concrete effect upon the world, to change things by rewriting them. This poem, unlike many, does not end with the poet reinscribing the ultimate powers of poetry in the last line; but then, this whole poem is the autobiography of a poet.

from The Dunciad, Book 4

The New Dunciad is the darkest and harshest of all of Pope's works; Pat Rogers sums up a frequent critical suspicion that there is "something ill-proportioned" about its shape, that the new events in the new book are not fully integrated into the poem as a whole. The scope of the satire widens considerably, from the original "plague of authors and a publishing ecodisaster" to "a vision of ubiquitous moral, political, and social decay" ("Literature," *Eighteenth-Century Britain: The Cambridge Cultural History*, ed. Boris Ford [Cambridge UP, 1991, 1992], 177). Students of course won't be able to analyze such a formal criticism with the selections here, but they should have a sense of apocalypse, of a poem very different in tone and structure from, say, *The Rape of the Lock*. What are the elements of darkness, of stasis employed in these stanzas? How do the different parts feed into and upon each other? Rogers's term "ecodisaster" seems apt: Pope has always used poetic structures to illustrate ontological infrastructures; here, the interconnections of education, travel, experimentation, natural philosophy, religion, law, politics, and art all damage each other, all need each other to die. And this poem ends without even the hope of Poetry and the Poet for future reclamation: the hand of the Anarch, not the pen of the poet, closes the poem, and "Universal Darkness buries All." Students might choose a particular passage, a particular image, and sort out the realistic from the surrealistic detail, using other texts in the period as bases for measurement. The texts in "The New Science" or "Mind and God," for example, can help plot a cultural and imaginative trajectory that leads to Swift's Academy in Book 3 of *Gulliver's Travels*, or to the point in the *Dunciad* where the Goddess reminds her sons: "Yet by some object every brain is stirred; / The dull may waken to a humming-bird; / The most recluse, discreetly opened find / Congenial matter in the cockle kind; / The mind, in metaphysics at a loss, / May wander in a wilderness of moss; / The head that turns at superlunar things, / Poised with a tail, may steer on Wilkins' wings" (ll. 445–52). What does Pope find missing from such attention to detail? In what ways do the contemporary religious and scientific "explanations" of the world lead to the dismantling of it? How does the *Dunciad* portray an anti-world, a structure of dissolution, the very opposite of that produced in *An Essay on Man*? And how can the world-order so confidently asserted in the *Essay on Man* permit the world of the *Dunciad* to come into being?

Lady Mary Wortley Montagu

The selections from Montagu's writings presented here—the kinds of things she chose to write about and the ways she chose to present them—permit a brief but accurate glimpse into a very complex mind. Lytton Strachey, with typical sweep, called it a mind of an age: "She was, like her age, cold and hard; she was infinitely unromantic; she was often cynical, and sometimes gross" ("Lady Mary," *Biographical Essays*, 1907). Presumably not only the Montagu selections here, but the selections for the "age" belie Strachey's characterization; still, Lady Mary was at once stoic and sensual, serious and witty, learned and graceful, careful and contemptuous. She knew her Newton, but at times could say: "I allow you to laugh at me for the sensual declaration that I had rather be a rich Effendi with all his ignorance, than Sir Isaac Newton with all his knowledge" (Letter to Abbé Conti, 19 May 1718, in Robert Halsband's edition of her letters [Clarendon Press, 1965], 3:23). On the other hand, she was committed to the rigors of honest self-scrutiny; she knew her Locke as well: "The most certain security would be that diffidence which naturally arises from an impartial self-examination. But this is the hardest of all tasks, requiring great reflection, long retirement, and is strongly repugnant to our own vanity, which very unwittingly reveals even to our selves our common frailty, though it is every way a useful study. Mr. Locke (who has made a more exact dissection of the human mind than any man before him) declares he gained all his knowledge from the consideration of himself. It is indeed necessary to judge of others" (to Lady Bute, 1 March 1754; Halsband, 3:48). All of Montagu's writings here reveal sharp powers of observation and analysis of both self and others.

What does Montagu's choice of the epistolary form as vehicle for her travel narratives permit her, that a straightforward essay would not? (In other words, why might she choose to retain the epistolary form for the entire collection to be published posthumously?) What kind of a cultural and social critic is she? How does she approach foreign customs and habits? How "fair" does she seem to us? One way of approaching these questions is to look at the way she balances perspective: sometimes she is the observer (her entrance into and description of the bagnio), sometimes the observed ("I believe in the whole there were two hundred women, and yet none of those disdainful smiles or satiric whispers that never fail in our assemblies when anybody appears that is not dressed exactly in fashion" [2574]). To what extent does she familiarize the foreign by translating it into English terms ("'tis the women's coffee house" [2575]), and to what extent does she let things remain alien? And what is her tone towards unassimilable difference? ("I own I cannot *accustom myself to this fashion* to find any beauty in it" [2576; emphasis added].)

It is also worth pursuing Montagu's talent with detail—the luxuriance and precision of the Turkish ladies' dress (2576) makes that distant world present, fresh, vivid, *real*—the whole point of legitimate travel narratives.

Analyzing Montagu's discussion of women and gender-related issues will discover more layers of intellectual and rhetorical complexity. Compare the account of the veiling of Muslim women (2576–77), the advice to her daughter suggesting that a woman should "conceal whatever learning she attains" (2579), and the point in the "Epistle from Mrs. Yonge to her Husband" when the speaker notes that though "I hide my frailty from the public view," her vindictive, philandering husband pursues her even "to this last retreat" (ll. 47, 52, p. 2581). In what ways are the veils, masquerades, concealments of women liberating? Self-generated? Counter-productive? Paradoxical? Futile?

Montagu observes and records a female world constructed of imposed contradictions, a world in which it becomes virtually impossible to live straightforwardly. The poem "The Lover: A Ballad," for example, even as it constructs an ideal, implicitly acknowledges the limits of even imaginative possibility. (This speaker, after all, imagines a clandestine lover, not a *husband*—though marriage, as Astell, Finch, and others point out, is the culturally produced dream of every girl, the chance of finding a good husband is, according to Montagu, one in ten thousand [2580].) And most poignantly, why is "The Lover" a *ballad*? The form predetermines the futility of the vision.

In "The Reasons that Induced Dr. S. to write a Poem called *The Lady's Dressing Room*," how does Montagu play with male/female perspectives to show in yet another form the kinds of contradictory expectations and interpretations of women that men employ? Isobel Grundy argues that the poem is "a virtuoso pattern-book of Swiftian technique: rapid narrative, ruminative digression, pedantic analogies, scatological or titillating detail. But one weapon of Pope [Montagu] avoids; her rebukes to [Swift], unlike her rebuke to Bathurst, make no use of idealizing self-construction" (Lady Mary Wortley Montagu, *Essays and Poems and* Simplicity, A Comedy, ed. Robert Halsband and Isobel Grundy [Clarendon Press, 1993], xviii). Like Behn's "The Disappointment," this poem shows a "reality" of male inadequacy that male prose and male posturing will try to efface or explain away ("The fault is not in me. / Your damned close stool so near my nose . . . / Would make a Hercules as tame" [ll. 69–72, p. 2585]). But in a way the poet does make some use of idealizing self-construction. The last line of the poem takes up, in a rather new way, the literary tradition of privileging the author, of giving the poet the final word, the final power of creation: "She answered short, 'I'm glad you'll write. / You'll furnish paper when I shite'" (ll. 88–89). The speaker, in conversation, and the poet, in the final couplet, pronounce in chorus their comment on the literal and poetic future of the frustrated male poet's textual revenge.

John Gay

In order to grasp the pleasures and intricacies of the *Opera*, students need to hear the music. It's a good idea to make available to them a full recording, and to play a few of Gay's most artful arias as part of the lecture and/or discussion (a few suggestions follow). Many recordings distort the music with patently twentieth-century re-orchestrations. Jeremy Barlow's rendition, by contrast, is scrupulously authentic and gloriously vivid (*John Gay's The Beggar's Opera*, The Broadside Band, Hyperion CDA66591/2); it comes complete with dialogue (brilliantly performed), and is ardently recommended. Two of the arias are included on our new audio CD accompanying Volume I of the anthology.

It is worthwhile in class to attend to the *Opera*'s opening moments fairly carefully, in order to show how deftly Gay disorients his audience. The piece's title promises an opera, and the opening night audience (including, according to the next day's papers, "a prodigious concourse of Nobility and Gentry") would surely have expected to hear music from start to finish. Instead, Gay gives them two men talking—they establish, among other things, that in this "opera" recitative will be supplanted by talk. (One consequence is that the songs contrast their "surroundings" more sharply than in opera: they burst in with heightened energy and artifice. The modern "book" musical derives, of course, from Gay's strategies here.)

Only now does the overture commence, followed by Peachum's opening number. It's worth hearing in class, because it states compactly (and to an interestingly melancholy tune) one of the arguments central to the whole. In the punch line, Peachum makes clear that he is more "honest" than the great men in the world (and in the audience) because, while he practices the same chicaneries as they, he knows (unlike them) who he is and what he's up to. For an audience so freshly set adrift amid the genre-disorientations of the past few minutes, Peachum's confident knowingness must exert a strong appeal, but at a semi-comic cost. In grabbing on to his witty and persuasive outlook as a spar amid the muddle, they become complicit in calling their own bluff.

In fact the whole musical strategy of the ballad opera is well-designed to keep the audience off balance, oscillating rapidly between knowingness and uncertainty. They would know each familiar tune within the first bar or two, but would be unable to forecast what new lyrics Gay would supply—what new tone and texture he'd import. A famous instance is Air 6 (worth playing), sung to music by Henry Purcell whose original lyric was a deeply conventional love-lament sung by a young suitor about the object of his desire: "What shall I do to show how much I love her? / How many millions of sighs can suffice?" Gay reverses the gender and immeasurably complicates the situation. Polly sings the song, in an attempt to persuade her father that she is as calculating as he wants her to be—teasing presents out of Macheath without surrendering "what is most material," her chastity. And yet the new lyric smacks more of vulnerability than of avarice. "Virgins are like the fair flower," capable of attracting "gaudy butterflies" (like the young lover of Purcell's aria?), but susceptible to rapid ruin. In the song's second half, Polly traces the "plucked" flower to Covent Garden, site of theaters, floral markets, and prostitutes, where the flower (like the deflowered virgin) "rots, stinks, and dies, and is trod under feet." The downward motion is Swiftian in its savagery (compare the last lines of "City Shower," the whole of "A Lady's Dressing Table"), and runs directly counter to Purcell's original, in whose second half (with its brightening from minor into major), the young man redoubles his idealistic amorous resolve: "I will love her more than man e'er loved before me. . . ." And yet all the while, Polly's litany of cynicism and fragility, decay and despair, is suffused with the sweetness of Purcell's original air, and with the echo of its young lover's passionate, hollow protestations. Gay's song, wrote the musicologist Charles Burney, quickly became "the favorite tune in the *Beggar's Opera*," perhaps because it epitomized the whole. Here and throughout, the audience is prompted to move rapidly (even concurrently) among a wide range of emotions and responses, sometimes conflicting, but curiously coinciding. Disorientation has by now become a source of fascination, a rich and various form of pleasure.

Much of the pleasure and fascination centers on the figure of Macheath. His name suggests a "son of the open field," and more than any other character he embodies the volatility of genre—the free, rapid, and inspired shifts from mode to mode—that Gay had built into the entire structure. Macheath is both dashing and easily duped, brilliant and a bit of a jerk. But his passion for remaining at large, for exercising his liberty to the fullest, for exploiting others at no cost to himself, made him attractive to many in Gay's time and after (James Boswell was perhaps the Captain's most ardent hero-worshipper). Macheath's charisma as a gallant comes through most clearly perhaps in the gorgeous Air 16, where Gay enacts remoteness in various ways: by the song's fantastical geography; by retaining the tune's famous refrain ("Over the hills and far away") but delaying it to the very end (two lines later than in the original); by implying the remoteness of any possibility that Macheath actually means anything he sings to Polly. For sheer volatility, nothing surpasses the near-lunatic sequence of airs (58–67) which Macheath sings, one after another, while in prison awaiting execution. Here the operatic predicament and the mostly homespun melodies collide head-on. The heroes of opera and tragedy, Gay suggests, are really no more than this: scared, self-interested scoundrels singing their torment in a fancier dress. At the same time, the speed with which Macheath shifts from tune to tune makes his panic palpable, even pitiable (and comic too, in his devotion to drink). Sending up the heroes of grander genres, he manages also to join their number—not so much a mock hero as an anti-hero, a genuine hero for degenerate times. Macheath makes real the paradox implicit in Swift's original hint about a "Newgate pastoral." Newgate is a place of confinement, the pastoral a genre devoted to celebrating the exuberant freedom of shepherds' lives. Macheath is that freedom principle incarnate and rerouted: moved into—and finally out of—the walls of Newgate.

The "happy ending" that sets him free affords one last instance of Gay's ingenious doubling. (Weill and Brecht rework it compactly and brilliantly in The Threepenny Opera, and a recording of that work's final song is worth playing too.) On the one hand, we know the ending to be "false," generated by the characters' desires and our own rather than by any likelihoods in the narrative. On the other hand, we know the ending to be true: the "great men" for whom Macheath and Peachum here serve as figures do indeed get away with this sort of thing (and worse) every day. By now, after some two hours of Gay's sublime and subliminal tutelage, we have perhaps become masters of disorientation, able to navigate it for all the multiple and intricate pleasures it affords.

Three points about the play as satire:

The political satire is worth noting, explaining, and enjoying, but not perhaps obsessing over: point-for-point correspondences between Macheath's world and Walpole's are in fact rather elusive, and if students come to think of the whole thing as "code," more crackable by its contemporaries than by us, they will surrender some of their capacity to savor other features of Gay's exuberant mockery. Colin Nicholson sketches the underlying politics succinctly: "Within a parody of currently fashionable Italian opera, [Gay's] immediate joke, of course, lay in the projection of London as a den of thieves, with the political bite of the satire coming from the implicit and wholesale indictment of the Whig administration in general and Walpole in particular. If we had no further evidence that the ascendant Hanoverian Whigs who rode to power on the back of the new finance and stayed there after the collapse of the South Sea Company appeared to some contemporaries as no more than a state banditry, then Gay's manipulation of the comic-opera would remain convincing testimony" (Writing and the Rise of Finance [Cambridge UP, 1994], 123-24).

Gay's sendup of crime literature is less often attended to but very fruitful. What made crime writing so popular was the writer's implicit promise to show readers a profoundly "other" world, a world concurrent with their own in time and space, but virtually invisible to them in daily life. Gay's counter-argument: the criminal world is neither a parallel world nor an invisible world; it is instead the very world we live in, work in, and profit by every day. Hogarth's painting, in which audience and actors occupy the same Newgate space, helps drive the point home.

Finally, Gay writes a satire of gender relations at times almost Wildean in its inversions, forthrightness, and surprises. One of the easiest ways into the piece is to spend some time on the early dialogue among Peachum, his wife, and Polly on the subject of marriage. It plays out Peachum's earlier assertion that he (and by extension, his clan) are more honest and astute than most about who they are, what they're about, and the commercial fabric of which their lives are woven. But Polly's knowledge (as Air 6 makes clear) is a complex thing, a mix of cynicism and sadness. How does her knowingness operate—how does it conduce to power and to powerlessness—in her relations with her lover and her rival?

The Beggar's Opera will teach well in tandem with Swift's poems (particularly "Morning" and "Shower": how do Swift's genre-mixes differ from Gay's? For one thing, Swift mixes ancient with modern; Gay remains mainly in the modern— opera, criminal biography, etc.) and with Gulliver (the satiric management of mirrored worlds); with Mary Carleton, who comes off at times as a gender-reversed Macheath, autonomous and free-moving and involved with a family bent on "securing" her one way or another; with Rochester; with The Man of Mode (Macheath works new variations on the by-now remote model of the Restoration libertine); with Hogarth (how does his satirical mirroring resemble and differ from Gay's?); and with James Boswell, Macheath's ardent emulator at a remove of several decades.

COMPANION READINGS
The Beggar's Opera, Influences and Impact

Thomas D'Urfey, from Wit and Mirth. D'Urfey's lyrics can help students savor one of the Opera's most elusive but important original effects: the delicious double play that Gay stimulated in the auditors' minds as they instantaneously collated the new lyrics they were now hearing with words they long knew. In each of the four instances presented here, Gay reworks not only the song's words but also its situation: singer, auditor, purpose. One of his subtlest performances (Air 6) has already been discussed in detail above, but the same metamorphic artistry operates everywhere. In "Why is Your Faithful Slave Disdained?" a seducer praises his beloved in earnest and protracted pursuit of what, with calculating delicacy, he "dare not name." In Gay's version, a fretful mother cuts right to the point: such blandishments promise pleasure but produce a victim; the closing line accordingly shifts referent, from sexual bliss in the original to whore in the redaction. Macheath's triumphal closing tune (Air 69) reverses gender in the opposite direction. In D'Urfey's original, a young woman recounts her copious pleasure in food and then (subsequently, comparably) sex. Macheath supplants this sensual linearity with a more compact reckoning of both variety ("black, brown, and fair") and mutability ("The wretch of today may be happy tomorrow"). Here and throughout the Opera, the play between the original and the revision is intrinsically dramatic, producing not merely a change of content but a deepening of character. D'Urfey's "Would Ye Have a Young Virgin?" works as a rather cynically confident rhymed advice manual on how to bed a variety of women. Macheath by contrast construes sex for once as solace rather than accomplishment, in a lyrical conjuring of a single amorous encounter and the "soft repose" that follows it. He emerges, unexpectedly, as a far tenderer lover than D'Urfey's sexual predator—and his capacity for ardor was clearly part of his intricate appeal.

One consistent change Gay makes in his originals usually goes unremarked, but must have mattered hugely to his original audience. His airs are brief, not only in comparison with the operatic arias for which they were serving as comic surrogates, but also with the ballads whose tunes they borrowed. The brevity must have formed part of the novelty and part of the pleasure. Songs were suddenly punctuating speech, swiftly deepening situation, in ways unprecedented on stage or street.

Daniel Defoe, *from* **The True and Genuine Account of the Life and Actions of the Late Jonathan Wild.** The section on "Tactics" works well as a companion to the *Opera's* opening scenes, where Peachum and Filch lay out the techniques of thief-taking; here, Defoe's somewhat labored exposition and Gay's spritelier dialogue can illuminate each other. Defoe's prose also allows for a comparison of textures. Defoe emphasizes details that will depict Wild's life as nasty and brutish, if not short enough. He measures out Wild's folly and tragedy, for example, in the doses of laudanum the thief-taker ingests on the verge of execution: "as he lived hardened, he seemed to die stupid." Defoe's evocation of Wild's last days and moments (even compassing a catastrophic imaginary reprieve) bears comparison with the scenes displaying Macheath on the verge of execution. The deliberate and moralized squalor that suffuses Defoe's whole *Account* gives way in Gay's *Opera* to an airier mixture, still moral but more playful. Even Mr. Peachum, for all his faults, is more engaging, more comic, and more sympathetic (in his panic as a father, his affections as a husband) than the Wild depicted here.

Henry Fielding, *from* **The Life of Mr. Jonathan Wild the Great.** Fielding's narrative, published fifteen years after the *Opera's* premier, testifies to the lingering power of Gay's conceits, by echoes both direct (the borrowed name of "Mr. Bagshot") and subtle. In the second excerpt, where Fielding compares public life to a perpetual playhouse in which the spectators half-consciously collude in the Great Man's chicaneries, he works an interesting variation on the *Opera's* finale, where audience whim dictates the arrant fiction of Macheath's reprieve. Gay's masterpiece had left an indelible mark on Fielding's career and memory. Fielding's first play had opened in London in the same week as the *Opera*, and was utterly eclipsed by it; after that, Fielding produced several ballad operas of his own. *Jonathan Wild*, probably begun around 1740, catches Fielding on a later cusp, between the play-writing he gave up in 1737, when Walpole's Licensing Act (aimed directly against Fielding's own satires) drove him from the theater, and the novel-making that he would soon take up with *Shamela* (1741) and *Joseph Andrews* (1742). Both the past playwright and the nascent novelist are detectable in the encounter between Wild and Bagshot. Fielding crafts the whole episode as a dialogue (contrast Defoe's nearly conversationless narrative), punctuated by occasional "stage directions," but too detailed and discursive for the confines of the playhouse. It requires instead the roomier precincts of prose fiction.

Anonymous, *from* A Narrative of All the Robberies . . . This first-person account may help students pinpoint some of the audacity and insouciance that Gay borrowed from Sheppard to make Macheath—and some of the practicalities he deliberately dispensed with. Sheppard's tale of his escape evinces an almost *Crusoe*-like fascination with the material means—locks, holes, leads, cuffs, shackles—by which the deed is done. Gay's Newgate is more ethereal: friends feast and drink, convicts dance, and lovers woo. To escape, Macheath need hardly touch the hardware; he need only convince Lucy that he loves her still, and she'll bring back the key. At such moments, Swift's originary suggestion that Gay write a "Newgate pastoral" tips firmly away from prison toward Arcadia, and stark documentary gives way to pleasing fantasy.

John Thurmond, *from* Harlequin Sheppard. This tail-end of a failed afterpiece can give students a glimpse of some theatrical practices that may seem both odd and at least partly recognizable: pantomime, and the long evening's entertainment. Pantomime dispensed with speech, but mingled action, instrumental music, and song. (Music videos recombine some of the same elements, and the recent movie *Moulin Rouge* seems at times to be reaching backwards for the some of the same effects.) Pantomimes, afterpieces, curtain-raisers, and other such fare catered to an audience for whom a single play was not quite enough. Eighteenth-century playgoers expected a sequence of shows, sometimes lasting as long as five or six hours. The *Beggar's Opera* navigated an unprecedented path between paucity and plenitude. From its title onward, it is pointedly more restricted in its resources than is the grand genre it parodies; at the same time it dealt, as the Beggar boasts, in all the materials of opera—songs, dances, similes, divas—and so smuggled into the playhouse a more varied menu of delights than the audience was accustomed to expect.

Frisky Moll's song points up another of Gay's innovations. Moll imports the exotic "cant" of the criminal underworld into the ordinary world of the playgoer, who can thereby savor the privilege of being momentarily let in on this secret language. Gay works the other way. From Peachum's first song on, he informs the audience that their world *is* the criminal world—that "all employments of life" are in this respect indistinguishable. Criminal transactions transpire at every level every day, and require no cant.

Charlotte Charke, *from* A Narrative . . . This episode shares with Gay's play (and with much else in Charke's autobiography) a peculiarly eighteenth-century sense of the world-as-stage, and the stage-as-world, the resemblance resulting not so much from poetic melding (as in Shakespeare's oft-quoted lines) but from hard circumstance: power, punishment, and questions of cold cash. (Hogarth's painting of the play [Plate 27] confirms this view: all the world's a prison.) Charke insists that she was put into jail "only for a show," to satisfy the potentate who controlled the court. Once imprisoned, she seizes the chance, unavailable hitherto, to sing Macheath's most troubled and impassioned songs "IN CHARACTER." Those small caps count: the momentary reality of her incarceration may even underwrite the heightened realism of her gender-crossing (at another point in her career, Charke passed as a man full time for several years). The moment invites a revisiting of Gay's anarchic coda, where the *Opera*'s "epilogue" (the dialogue between Beggar and Player) concludes before the play does, and alters all that follows. Here, as in Charke's anecdote, reality and theatricality converge with such force as to outlast and push past conventional constraints: the familiar frame of prologue and epilogue, the customary boundaries between world and stage.

James Boswell, Journal Entries. Why does Macheath prove so persistently hypnotic for Boswell? These short extracts can suggest several answers, particularly if read in tandem with some of Boswell's longer entries later in the anthology. Clearly, the diarist covets the privileges the character enjoys, notably the pursuit of promiscuity without consequence. But he seems even more possessed by Macheath as a *performance*, as a role that he might play. He had once actually performed it, in his teens, and for decades remains almost as obsessed by West Digges, his favorite interpreter of the role, as he is by Macheath himself. (In the *London Journal*, Digges looms as favorite alter ego; see Boswell's entries for 1 December 1762 [2829] and particularly 12 January 1763 [2831], when en route to consummating his affair with the actress Louisa, Boswell passes himself off as Digges's cousin.) In one of the entries here, he stages a tavern scene to match Macheath's (he even inveigles a waiter to serve as approving audience). In another, he casts a genuine criminal, Paul Lewis, in the role, and wishes "to relieve him" from the terror of execution scheduled for the next day (Boswell attended the hanging, and wrote it up). Macheath himself, of course, *does* find such relief: by *Opera*'s end, he has so charmed his audience that the Beggar reluctantly grants him his reprieve. It is precisely because of his success as a *theatrical* being that he attains immortality both within Gay's play and beyond it. For Boswell, obsessed alike with theater and with death (see his deathbed discussion with Hume [2835–38], and his talk with Johnson *about* Hume [2845–47]), this convergence exerted enormous appeal. In the last entry here, "thoughts of mortality and change" contend with the excitements aroused by the play, and with evidence of the performer's immutability: though Boswell may have changed, "Digges looked and sung as well as ever." The songs by now must have seemed immutable as well. In their many echoes throughout these entries, we can hear something of how they had come to function as part of the audience's vocabulary for desire, exuberance, and emotions more complex— as one of the ways the culture talked to itself about itself.

William Hogarth

A Rake's Progress provides glorious opportunities for close reading. Each detail speaks, and by working out what it says and how it says it, students may develop a sharper eye for the speaking detail in works of prose, drama, and poetry produced in a world where the relations among *minds*, *words*, and *things* were newly charged for everyone from scientists to novelists to philosophers to graphic artists (for more on these relations, see the discussions of Sprat, above, and Locke, below).

For reading Hogarth's details, the most compendious companion is Ronald Paulson's *Hogarth's Graphic Works* (Alan Wolfsy Fine Arts, 1989); the most convenient is Sean Shesgreen's inexpensive *Engravings by Hogarth* (Dover, 1973), with its large reproductions and copious captions (from which most of the information accompanying the anthology's plates was distilled). Shesgreen's volume makes it easy to compare the *Rake's Progress* with its closest antecedent, *A Harlot's Progress*; and to compare the engravings in their first state (printed here) with Hogarth's later revisions, of which the most notable appear in Plate 3 (where he added in the lower-right-hand corner a cluster of children busily mastering the vices of their elders), and in Plate 8 (where the madmen's activities became more global in implication).

The *Rake's Progress* will teach well with all the other literature of libertinage in the volume: Rochester's poems and some of Behn's; Boswell's *London Journal*; and above all *The Beggar's Opera*, close in date and content. As Jenny Uglow observes, Plate 4 might almost serve as an illustration for that moment in the *Opera*'s Act 2, Scene 4 (2605–07) when Macheath cavorts among his wenches on the verge of being betrayed by one of them (*Hogarth: A Life and a World* [Farrar, Straus and Giroux, 1997] 251–52). Like Macheath, Tom Rakewell is a rake transported (and thereby translated) from the glittering Restoration court to a new, drabber, and perhaps more precarious world of commerce. He is, Uglow points out, "no dashing blade, conquering fashion, decoying women, and terrorizing the town with nonchalant, demonic arrogance. He is a young bourgeois, first seen as a trembling youth with a fresh face haloed in curls, attractive, open, innocent—and weak. . . . Tom is less a seducer than an outsider who is himself seduced, ruined and killed by the city" (244).

Like earlier commentators, Uglow deftly writes out as verbal narrative the story that Hogarth's sequence suggests to her (244–59), thereby confirming the widespread sense that he worked like and in league with the satiric novelists—with Swift, Fielding, Sterne, Smollett. Authors and artists of the period cherished Horace's dictum *ut pictura poesis*: poetry is [or ought to be] like a picture (for a signal instance, see Dryden's ode to Anne Killigrew [ll. 88–141]). Such comfortable conflations, however revelatory, are worth testing in class discussion. Do we really follow Rakewell's progress exactly as we do Christian's, or Crusoe's, or Gulliver's, or Pamela's, or Tom Jones's? What differences obtain between the ways pictures and prose fiction work in time—between the freeze-frame of the one and the verbal flow of the other? (For purposes of comparison, it may be useful to consult the verse commentary that Hogarth engraved beneath each picture, legible in Shesgreen's large reprints but irreproducible here.) Hogarth's *tableaux* were first published as plates which could be displayed all at once, rather than riffled through as pages in a book. Such a design renders the eight stages of the story abidingly and perhaps concurrently present, a simultaneity rather than a sequence—as though each were always there and always true. How does such an effect differ from our experience of prose fiction, and how does it contribute to our sense that Rakewell's decline may be both mechanical and inexorable, a foregone conclusion determined by cultural forces over which he (and we?) have culpably lost control?

Mind and God

This section invites questions that parallel those raised by "The Royal Society and the New Science"—as Newtonian physics and Lockean psychology seemed to chart with some clarity and even reliability the outer and inner universes of human experience, what was going to happen to God? What does the privileging of sensory experience displace? How does each writer here use *text*—the written word in a chosen shape—to negotiate territories apparently resistant to empirical approach? How are many of these writers engaged directly or indirectly in persuasive or argumentative discourse with each other? Note the generic divisions among the texts included here: while religious argument is often couched in philosophical discourse, philosophical argument is pointedly left behind in the religious poetry. What *are* the various rhetorical merits of the letter, the essay, the dialogue, the hymn, the psalm, the poem?

The selections in this section are all, in their various methodological and rhetorical ways, trying to do the opposite of what Sprat declares the Fellows of the Royal Society are up to: where the Fellows' "purpose was to heap up a mixed mass of experiments, without digesting them into any perfect model," these writers look for *completion* and *wholeness*, either in the mechanical workings of the universe, the epistemological workings of the mind, or the divine workings of God. One might ask of these authors in what ways—and for what reasons—their texts complicate this agenda by insinuating doubt, disorder, counter-example, pointlessness, and rhetorical flourish in their prose and prosody.

Two Pope selections would work well with this section: the *Essay on Man* for its poetic distillation of philosophical argument, and the excerpts from the *Dunciad* for the apocalyptic vision of cosmic inertia and centrifugal destruction. The *Essay on Man*, Pope says, he might have done in prose, but he "chose verse, and even rhyme," in order to "strike the reader more strongly at first" and to achieve the most powerful concision in his argument (2542). The poem, then, sells itself on Lockean principles (association, memory) in order to sell Newtonian ones (order, harmony). The *Dunciad* ushers in the goddess Dullness, whose main plan is "to destroy *Order* and *Science*" (2561), the same fine, strong heroic couplets that built up a conceptual universe in the *Essay on Man* describe its destruction in the *Dunciad*: "Physic of Metaphysic begs defense, / And Metaphysic calls for aid on Sense! / See Mystery to Mathematics fly! In vain! they gaze, turn giddy, rave, and die. / . . . Thy hand, great Anarch! lets the curtain fall; / And Universal Darkness buries All" (2572).

Isaac Newton

The choice of genre is always a useful way to begin discussion. In some ways, of course, Newton's "choice" here is predetermined: he's responding by letter to Bentley's epistolary request for help in adequately transmitting a Newtonian convergence between science and faith. So what does the *form* of a letter permit him to do? He can, and does of course, essentially write a small essay, but that essay takes on the qualities of dialogue, of a "converse of the pen" (to use Richardson's phrase) in which doubts, implicit or explicit, can be answered directly. There are several "minds" here, Newton's and various real or imagined others: the "public," to which he has done or may do some service; Bentley, of course, to whose queries he directly responds, point by point; other natural philosophers such as Descartes (when Newton discards a "Cartesian hypothesis" [2658]); the even more imaginary second-guesser that any good thinker anticipates in an argument ("it may be represented" [2659]); and the vague combination of all three ("unless you will urge it" [2660]). The textual creation of a participating audience characterizes several of the selections here: Berkeley's religious dialogue; Watts's hymns, implying a congregation; Hume trying to catch himself in a moment of identity; Smart speaking to and with Jeoffry as he chants to and with God; Cowper in an imagined broken dialogue with the castaway's comrades, with the world, and with God.

Newton's letter begins with the assertion of an explicit agenda ("I had an eye upon such principles as might work with considering men for the belief of a Deity"), and then follows that agenda with carefully qualified statements: "I do not think"; "I know no reason but"; "I see not why"; "I see nothing extraordinary." He does not say: it is, only, I think it is. His prose manages to set up two universes, one which would not permit things-as-they-are, and one which does; and the latter, he says several times, he does not think "explicable by mere natural causes" but must be ascribed "to the counsel and contrivance of a voluntary agent" (2658). God is fitted within the epistolary constructs of a rational argument based on known facts, rejected alternatives, and reasoned truths. Order is established; but the very sense of being "forced to ascribe" one answer is precisely what someone like Hume, in other contexts, will insist he is forced not to do. The answers are plausible, but not irrefutable. As the introduction to this section points out, "for Newton, Locke, and countless other inquirers, empiricism promised to explain the ways of God; but they had begun a process which, in other hands, might threaten to explain God away" (2656).

John Locke

Locke's epistemology is crucial for understanding, among other things, the eighteenth-century fascination with things, with lists, with a compartmentalizing of the universe at the same moment of attempting to unify it. Locke breaks down "ideas" into things, arguing that our epistemological operations spring from the perception of individual sensations and of various psychological processes such as "perception, thinking, doubting, believing, reasoning, knowing, willing" (2661). Ideas of substances "are nothing else but a collection of a certain number of simple ideas, considered as united in one thing" (2663). Not until the advent of twentieth-century phenomenology would human psychology be argued back towards wholes perceived first, details later artificially abstracted out. Locke argues that when an English person sees or thinks of a swan, she sees or thinks of a "white color, long neck, red beak, black legs, and whole feet, and all these of a certain size, with a power of swimming in the water, and making a certain kind of noise" (2663); the human mind puts these things together to construct a whole. The "whole" comes second to the parts. And for Locke, it appears, we put together the *idea of God*, composed of bits of what we know magnified to an imagined perfection (2663).

What does this form of epistemology tell us about the penchant for *lists* in Swift and Defoe? Gulliver's lists of the causes and weapons of war in Book 4 of *Gulliver's Travels* unite into an epistemological and ethical horror of human nature; Defoe's lists of graveyard measurements and body counts amount to a different horror of human experience. Locke's epistemology sorts, separates, categorizes—and leaves room for new fictions, not always comforting.

Isaac Watts

The selections here show two very different minds, one rhythmical and orderly, one symbolically as well as rhetorically free-verse. "A Prospect of Heaven Makes Death Easy" offers a simple metrical and rhyme scheme that opens with a promise ("There is"), and that opening offers us everything we habitually dream about: no pain, no night, no faded flowers. Its middle describes the timorous Us, fearful of the impeding isthmus; its end describes the larger, telescopic perspective that would and should nudge us into faith. Try having students analyze the poetic form, the rhyme scheme, the simple meter and rhymes that set up psychological expectations that get quickly and firmly answered by those very poetic schemes. This hymn offers a structure of reassurance fundamentally different from the structure of argument, which argues with doubt in such a different way. This hymn *records* the experience of doubt but displaces it swiftly with the promise of a different, larger perspective.

Watts's "The Hurry of Spirits" is a very different animal; the free verse permits the doubt; little is "closed" between lines; much spills over into the next. Clauses or even sentences often end in the middle of lines; form as well as content is in a relative uproar, only relatively contained by a basic pentameter. Students could linger over the choice of forms here, and think about the ways that form expresses mind: "Abrupt, ill-sorted" abruptly stops a line and asks for sorting (l. 20).

"Against Idleness and Mischief" returns to smooth sorting (it's a lovely idea to reproduce Carroll's version ["How doth the little crocodile"] to demonstrate another of Locke's ideas, not reproduced here, about the association of ideas). The whole idea of *form* is so crucial here: when to bolster with meter and rhyme and music and a general sense of congregational *chorus* to support an idea, and when to let the idea bleed itself out in other ways.

Joseph Addison

Addison's *Spectator* essay raises its own questions: what's the relative importance of solitude in negotiating the difficulties of faith? The eighteenth century was an age of conversation, but as the introduction points out, it was also an age of solitude (2083). Addison observes that the world is too much with us; as Hume says, "our eyes cannot turn in our sockets without varying our perceptions" (2675). Precisely *because* knowledge was coming to be perceived as the product of sensory experience, we need time to sort things out, to watch the operations of our own mind, to "reflect" in Locke's sense. The very obviousness of God, on Newton's argument from design, requires an observer who is not too caught up in the empiricism of her own daily life.

Speculate on Addison's switch from prose to poetry: the difference in typesetting on the page is something to consider in class as a call to a different mode of thinking. We are forcibly moved from the engulfing prose of the page to the spatially isolated ode; the large margins of page-space itself give room for reflective thought. (One might compare this in form and intent with Finch's poem "A Ballad to Mrs. Catherine Fleming in London" [2228-30].)

George Berkeley

Berkeley chooses dialogue for his form; why? How does it help to have two persons on the stage? What is the difference between expounding and discussing? The reader, in a dialogue, is given voice, so to speak, and even a choice of voices—with whom will she identify? The choice is programmed, of course, towards the mind-loving Philonous, but at least the reader is offered an outlet, a way of asking those embarrassingly obvious questions. Jules David Law argues: "Far from making language into a transparent window onto the empirical world, Berkeley's philosophy seems almost to render the sensory world transparent before language" (The Rhetoric of Empiricism: Language and Perception from Locke to I. A. Richards [Cornell UP, 1993], 94). How does Berkeley work to make Philonous's position seem the right, the sensible, the transparent choice? How does conversation itself work to make abstract ideas concrete, to make philosophical peculiarities seem common-sensical?

Even some great minds of the eighteenth century never felt fully satisfied with Berkeley's system. Boswell recounts Samuel Johnson's distinctive form of refutation: "After we came out of the church, we stood talking for some time together of Bishop Berkeley's ingenious sophistry to prove the non-existence of matter, and that every thing in the universe is merely ideal. I observed, that though we are satisfied his doctrine is not true, it is impossible to refute it. I shall never forget the alacrity with which Johnson answered, striking his foot with mighty force against a large stone, till he rebounded from it, 'I refute it thus'" (Life of Johnson [Oxford UP, 1980] 333). How would Philonous answer Johnson?

David Hume

However much ignored when it was first publicly articulated, Hume's theory of identity—basically, that we have none, it's all convenient psychological construct—perhaps still offers the best theoretical insight into much of eighteenth-century literature. The deceptions and disguises in The Country Wife, the multiple voices in Rochester's poems, Behn's play with identities, and the general cultural preoccupation with masks, all suggest a search for some sort of identity, some sort of stability, a shift in epistemological and ontological underpinnings. Hume's connection between personal identity and the theater is apt; one might call in those Restoration voices to confirm the uncertain cultural sense of self that Hume puts in theatrical terms: "The mind is a kind of theater, where several perceptions successively make their appearance: pass, re-pass, glide away, and mingle in an infinite variety of postures and situations" (2675). If Hume did, in fact, articulate a larger cultural sense of epistemologically disenfranchised selves, how might this work towards explaining the explosion of new genres of self-hood? In a way, biography, autobiography, familiar letters, travel narratives, and the novel itself might all be part of a culture trying to enter most intimately into what it calls the *self*, trying to catch a self grounding all those perceptions and ideas.

The issues of solitude and society surface prominently in Hume, but where Addison (and Finch) recommend retirement for self-study, self-composure, and acquaintance with God, Hume finds himself "ready to throw all [his] books and papers into the fire" and find a sociable game of backgammon (2676). Hume discovered and bequeathed an uncomfortable paradox: he "is convinced that skepticism is logically irrefutable; nevertheless, he is convinced also that scepticism is psychologically untenable" (James Sambrook, *The Eighteenth Century: The Intellectual and Cultural Context of English Literature, 1700–1789* [Longman, 1990], 60). The path of philosophy, of solitary contemplation, when truly steadily pursued, leads the pursuer into skeptical darkness; careful questions and honest answers discover the dissolution of the idea of self, of cause and effect, of an external world, of God. But human beings cannot live in this cold darkness; with a hallmark Humean twist of sense and humor, "after reasoning away reason, Hume turns his irony upon himself" (Sambrook, 60). Fortunately for us, we simply do not have the psychological stamina to be full-time philosophers. So why does he keep going back to it? One can see the appeal of a Newtonian project that seems mathematically to guarantee order, beauty, and divinity; but if, as Hume suggests, one keeps pushing that project further and the world disintegrates, what happens to the value and point of truth? Is he really saying, okay, read your serious Saturday issue of the *Spectator*, think quiet solemn thoughts on Sunday, but don't think too much?

Christopher Smart

In Oxford in the 1740s, Robert Lowth (1710-87) delivered lectures on *The Sacred Poetry of the Hebrews* (published in Latin in 1753 and English in 1787), in which he demonstrated the differences between Old Testament prose, marked by regular word order ("correct, chaste, and temperate"), and poetry, in which "the free spirit is hurried along, and has neither leisure nor inclination to descend to those minute and rigid attentions. Frequently, instead of disguising the secret feelings of the author, it lays them quite open to public view; and the veil being as it were suddenly removed, all the affections and emotions of the soul, its sudden impulses, its hasty sallies and irregularities, are conspicuously displayed" (*The Sacred Poetry of the Hebrews*, trans. by G. Gregory [1787], lecture 14; quoted in Sambrook, 188). Such a description offers a perfect entry into discussing the form and content of Smart's amazing poem *Jubilate Agno*. With strategies utterly unlike mathematical or philosophical discourse—without argument, without formulas, without deduction, without induction, but instead with religious history, with linguistic puns, with hebraic parallelism, with public emotion, with sudden impulses, with moving irregularities—Smart con-

structs a God-warmed universe as intimately bound and breathtakingly structured as Newton's gleaming mechanical one.

This poem demands to be read aloud, and it can be a great pleasure simply to
begin by going around the room, each student speaking a line. As a sort of chorus emerges, students might "consider" the poem and watch for all the linguistic, historic, emotional, religious, and imaginative connections that sustain its all-
encompassing prayer. How are the sacred and the secular arranged? How are they
combined? ("For there is nothing sweeter than his peace when at rest. / For there
is nothing brisker than his life when in motion" [ll. 738–39].) What does the
word "for" mean, and what is the effect of its ceaseless repetition? What is the
power of the last line: "For he can creep"?

William Cowper

As with Watts, it is revealing to watch the change in generic form as Cowper
changes his poetic perspective. The three selections here offer different attitudes,
different tones, different structures, different visions. What is the difference between the kind of vision or observation made possible by "philosophic tube" (the
telescope) and by poetry, by the word of God? What does it mean to "baptize" philosophy? How does poetry itself work into that process?

Pat Rogers suggests that Cowper's verse "rises in technical control when he approaches matters of close personal concern," most poignantly in the Calvinistic allegory of "The Cast-away" ("Literature," in *Eighteenth-Century Britain: The
Cambridge Cultural History*, ed. Boris Ford [Cambridge UP, 1991, 1992], 170). Have
students analyze how the choices of structure, rhyme scheme, meter, stanzaic pattern, all contribute to the power of the anguish and loss first of the "real" story,
and then of the "realer" one—the speaker's religious despair. In a way, like the
other writers in this section, Cowper moves from experience to reflection, from
empirical data to philosophical implication, from a story current in the world
around him to a darker story within himself. Cowper's poems reveal both the
promise of hope and the thread of doubt occasioned by the very "advances" in science and reason in the eighteenth century.

James Thomson

"Ah, what shall language do?" Thomson asks at one point in *The Seasons* (*Spring*, l.
475). "Ah, where find words," he continues, to render all the sensual plenitude of
nature—its sights, sounds, smells? His own solution: to arrange words in ways that
saturated the senses, particularly sight and hearing (note *Winter's* first word, "See!,"
and the many like imperatives that follow). Blank verse abetted this purpose. In a
world crowded with heroic couplets, blank verse suggested boundlessness, an impulse to track the data of the world, the train of thought, wherever it might lead,
unfettered by the bonds of rhyme. Students who find the poem peculiar on the
page are often surprised to feel it take possession of the tongue and ear. They
should first read or hear swatches of it aloud (the Penguin collection includes a

complete performance of Thomson's first *Winter*), and then savor analytically the abundance of particular lines. When Thomson asserts that the autumn woods "the country round / Imbrown; a crowded umbrage, dusk and dun" (2692), what effects does he achieve by the enjambment of words that nearly rhyme? by the surprises of wording ("Imbrown," "umbrage")? by the array of words fashioned from the same few sounds (*ow, c, d, r, n*)? by the correspondence between the aural texture he thus creates and the monochrome he describes? At times Thomson's blank verse seems not so much a banishment of rhyme as rhyme run riot: sounds everywhere echoing sounds, and thereby transmitting nature's plenitude.

The poem's boundlessness extends beyond its blank verse structure. *The Seasons* celebrates metamorphosis (note how Thomson wedges in an account of autumn early in his first version of *Winter*), enacts metamorphosis (as in the changes rung around "Imbrown"), and undergoes a metamorphosis of its own, through the poet's numerous revisions; it was proffered to the public, over the course of twenty years, as a poem almost without end. The cross-references in the footnotes should help make possible a close comparison of Thomson's first and final versions of some passages. In the earlier version, the evocation of "philosophic melancholy" (l. 66, 2690) preceeds a list of conventional feelings, conventionally expressed ("the tender pang," "the pitying tear"). In the revision, Thomson transmutes abstraction into personification ("Philosophic Melancholy" [l. 1005, 2693]) dramatically described: "He comes! he comes!" and there follows in his wake a far more intricate account of the traffic between nature's abundance ("Ten thousand thousand fleet ideas," i.e. images) and "the mind's creative eye"—in short, a theory of the processes that have produced the poem, and that should suffuse the reader. Typically, Thomson soon veers elsewhere. He is borne once again to "embowering shades," but promptly recoils ("Or is this gloom too much?") and betakes himself to Stowe, the best (and most politically significant) of Britannia's gardens. In Thomson's poem, motion perhaps matters most, because every move delivers a new piece of the whole picture, demonstrating humanity's "fragmentary perception of the beauty and sublimity of the world and leading to an act of faith in God's love and wisdom," which alone comprehends the whole (Ralph Cohen, *The Unfolding of* The Seasons [Johns Hopkins UP, 1970], 247).

"Rule, Britannia" was first performed in a garden, and students won't fully get it until they hear the music (an authentic version is available on the Broadside Band's *English National Songs* [Saydisc CD-SDL 400], which contains many other tunes useful for transmitting eighteenth-century ethos). But don't allow Arne's vaulting melody to obscure the argument. The last verse collates well with the passage from *Winter* (2692) where Thomson envisions the British Muse in the company of Homer and Virgil. And the penultimate verse is particularly instructive in relation to the last part of *Windsor-Forest*: where Pope envisions commerce supplanting conquest, Thomson finds the two more intertwined, with both sea and shore "subject" to Britain's imperial power (and the "fair" of the final line exalted and subjected all at once). How sharp a line does the song draw between subjection and slavery? Thomson manages to make "generous" (l. 19) mean both itself ("bountiful") and something like its opposite: ferocious, retributive.

The Seasons *and Its Time: Poems of Nightfall and Night*

Anne Finch, A Nocturnal Reverie   This poem is best read alongside (or aloud with) the dialogue it echoes from Shakespeare's *Merchant*. All the love affairs that Jessica and Lorenzo invoke end in disaster. So, in a sense, does Finch's poem, with the return of daylight and distraction. But night, the site of delusion for all those ancient lovers, affords Finch a respite from delusion, a respite expanded by the poem's long-stretched periodic structure (all those *Whens* and *Ands*), which finds a too-brief resolution ("let me abroad remain" l. 47) on the very verge of morning's breaking. The poem invites comparison with both Thomson's and Cowper's busier evenings, with Gray's *Elegy*, and with three poems more remote: the opening of the *Canterbury Tales* (similar in its syntax and suspense), and Wordsworth's *The World is Too Much with Us* and *Westminster Bridge*, written by one of the first poets to acknowledge Finch's power.

Edward Young, *from* Night Thoughts   Thomson and Finch portray themselves as so immersed in the world's sensations that darkness itself can promote, rather than interrupt, their cherished communion with nature. In Young's poem, by contrast, night cuts off the speaker from the world—but in doing so it only intensifies a depression and alienation that he plainly feels by day as well. Enclosed in night's "opaque of nature," Young must (to adapt Thomson's phrasing, l. 1016, 2693) disperse the unwanted thoughts that "crowd" him, and deploy his "mind's creative eye" a different way: in hatching visions more than rendering realities. The argument of the excerpt runs along similar lines: the repose that "Nature's sweet restorer" can't supply (l. 1), he must attain for himself; the passage dramatizes his resolve to do so. If the students have *Hamlet* in their heads, they can hear him speak anew in the two passages here: ll. 61–67 echo "To be or not to be"; ll. 66–87 replay "What a piece of work is a man!" What changes does Young ring on Shakespeare? The dreams that may come are initially (as for Hamlet) dreadful (l. 8) but ultimately wondrous (ll. 90–103). They (and not nature, as in Thomson) form the basis of the visionary power that the poet will deploy throughout his poem.

William Collins, Ode to Evening *and* Ode on Thomson   The "Ode to Evening" contrasts with most contemporary odes in its brevity and in its blank verse (compare Dryden's odes); still, the poem harbors a Pindaric variability of its own. As Richard Wendorf argues, the *Ode to Evening* enacts a learning curve. In the first twenty lines, the speaker beseeches Evening to become his teacher and his muse (note the lovely pun, l. 19); as if to confirm her consent, he then "dares to introduce Evening in the company of her traditional machinery," clothing "his elusive figure in classical and native superstitions" (ll. 21–40); finally (ll. 41–52) he makes a pledge of enduring fealty, confident where his first lines were tentative, and couched (like Thomson's allegiance to all of nature) in the language of the shifting seasons (*William Collins and Eighteenth-Century English Poetry* [U of Minnesota P, 1981], 127–33). In the ode to Thomson, Collins again seeks to clothe his "elusive subject in classical and native superstitions" (the lament of the shepherds, the evocation of the Druids). This time the subject is Thomson himself, elusive in death, and the poem's exquisite balance inheres in the way Collins brings in all that mythology while adhering (Thomson-like) to the actual geography of

Thomson's world (the river at Richmond), and to the actual texture of Thomson's lines (see, e.g., l. 33).

William Cowper, from The Task Students may find it worthwhile (and something of a relief) to work out the differences between Thomson's more elaborate and Cowper's more colloquial blank verse. In the passage on the newspaper, a curious thing happens: with the world outside occluded by night, the newspaper itself becomes a kind of landscape, marked by a "mountainous and craggy ridge" (in the news about ambitious city big shots); adorned with "roses" and "lillies" (in the advertisements). Cowper's semi-comic, semi-satiric use of the newspaper as an index of retirement, as a measure of his remoteness (ll. 88–119), contrasts with Collins's more conventionally idealized conjuring in "Ode to Evening" of "the sylvan shed" (l. 49) from which he'll adore his muse. Cowper too invokes Evening in verses clearly influenced by Collins (ll. 243–66), but here she too is domesticated, a "matron" rather than a mythic shape-shifter, "not sumptuously adorned, nor needing aid . . . of clust'ring gems." Blanketing both nature and man for the night, she bears some relation to the comforting, caretaking "fair" (l. 53) who allow the poet to read his paper in silence.

Thomas Gray

Of the four poems presented here, three concern actual deaths; the fourth (*Eton College*) traces a metaphorical death, of hope and joy. It may be useful to teach all four as elegies—tonal and technical variations on the theme of loss.

The sonnet on West focuses relentlessly on the plight of the speaker abandoned and alone after his friend's death. It bears comparison with the emergent poetry of solitude represented (in the section just preceding) by Finch's "Nocturnal Reverie," Young's *Night Thoughts*, and Cowper's *Task*. At the same time, it contrasts sharply with earlier pastoral elegies—Milton's *Lycidas*, Collins's ode on Thomson—where the poet joins with nature and its mythical embodiments (nymphs, naiads) in a community of mourning. In Gray's own subsequent elegies, too, mourning entails communion: with the boys at Eton, with the owner of the "favorite cat," with the dead themselves in the *Elegy*. "I fruitless mourn to him that cannot hear," Gray laments in the sonnet; in the *Elegy* he will enact a less despairing and more "fruitful" conversation between the living and the dead.

Familiarity may have flattened the final pronouncement of the ode on Eton College, and made the whole poem seem an exercise in wistfulness, far more sentimental than it actually is. Vincent Newey points out the near-Hobbesian darkness of Gray's vision: "The impulses that seemingly enhance childhood—the courage of the 'bold adventurers' who seek out 'unknown regions,' 'Gay hope,' the 'tear forgot'—are in truth but a training for subsequent devastating vulnerability, where, for example, to aspire is to be a sacrifice to 'grinning infamy' (ll. 71–74), unfulfilled desire 'inly gnaws the secret heart' (ll. 61–70), and 'Unkindness . . . mocks the tear it forced to flow' (ll. 76–77). In the long run, delight and liberty are a delusion. . . . No poet has put more graphically on parade the evils of living." ("The Selving of Thomas Gray," in *Thomas Gray: Contemporary Essays*, ed. W. B. Hutchings and William Ruddick [Liverpool UP, 1993], 28). In fact, the darkness touches Gray's early stanzas on the children's pleasures, where even "joy" is "fearful," where tears, though soon forgot, are shed nonetheless, and where things desired are "less pleasing when possessed."

How, then, in the ode on Walpole's cat, does the poet manage to make death seem comic? Mostly through the mock-epic matrix of allusions, to ancient practices ("Tyrian hue"), venerable proverbs ("Nor all that glisters, gold"); and global grandeurs ("China's gayest art"); but also through the stringent gendering of Selima's error. Walpole and Gray laugh together at a woman's mistake; the disappointment of desire, tragic in the Eton College ode, is cast as comic here. The poem invites comparison with Pope's *Rape of the Lock*, many of whose topics and strategies Gray compactly reworks. Pope suffuses the *Rape*'s last lines with intimations of death and pathos. Does Gray here wholly laugh death away? A short companion reading may help with the question: the epic episode of the warrior-queen Camilla's death (*Aeneid* ll. 768-835)—a chief source for Selima's misadventure—will heighten students' sense of both the comedy and the possible tragic undertow in Gray's antic poem.

The *Elegy* begins with a fading of light and sound and an assertion of silence ("All the air a solmen stillness holds"), which Gray immediately complicates with a haunting litany of exceptions ("Save where . . ."). The opening stanzas enact in miniature the motion and argument of the poem, where the silence of obscure lives—and of death itself—modulates into utterance through the ventriloquy of the poet's voice. "Ev'n from the tomb," Gray insists, "the voice of nature cries," but it is the elegist who makes that voice heard, first on behalf of others, and finally (in the closing stanzas) for himself. Gray offers the reader a kind of ear-training, a heightened attention to the way sounds emerge from silence. Partly for this reason, the poem's actual sounds repay careful hearing (beginning perhaps with the vowel rhymes, closely allied but sharply distinguished, of the opening stanza). The poem's quatrains were themselves an innovation in a world dominated by couplets; they too enhanced the sense, memorably noted by Johnson (at the end of his life of Gray) that the poet had achieved something new: "The four stanzas beginning 'Yet even these bones' are to me original: I have never seen the notions in any other place; yet he that reads them here, persuades himself that he has always felt them." Roger Lonsdale has defined Gray's innovation more specifically. The *Elegy* is "in one aspect a sustained struggle to find decorous ways of talking about the self and the meaning of one's life"—and about a self more sequestered than that "idealized, public self" which Pope "dramatized" and made fashionable in his Horatian poems (*The Poetry of Thomas Gray: Versions of the Self* [London: Oxford UP, 1973], 9).

In Gray's letters to Walpole about the *Elegy* (2710-11), the poem as object travels a course parallel to that of its own argument, from the quietude of manuscript to the noise of publication. Gray's final metaphor for the poem is antic and pointed: the published *Elegy* is his *misfortune*, an infant he had no desire to bring forth into the world; the publisher Dodsley is its incompetent nurse, Walpole its generous relation. In these letters, and in the others gathered here, Gray's strategies of intimacy involve both playful figuration, and—as Bruce Redford points out—a pervasive allusiveness to knowledge the correspondents share ("The Allusiveness of Thomas Gray," in *The Converse of the Pen: Acts of Intimacy in the Eighteenth-Century Familiar Letter* [U of Chicago P 1986], 95–132). Note, for example, the way Shakespeare, Congreve, and Cibber converge in Gray's early reproach to Walpole for not writing (2708-9), and the way typology heightens his biblical lament to West about life at Cambridge (2709).

Samuel Johnson

Reading Johnson, like reading Shakespeare, takes some practice. Students become more familiar and more comfortable over time with the motion of his sentences, the range of his diction, and the thrust of his arguments. I like to begin with a few "graduated" exercises, short texts or passages for close reading and basic training. Among the likeliest (here listed in rising order of "challenge"): the poem on Levet; the letter to Chesterfield; the opening sentence of *Rambler* No. 60; and the opening sentence of *The Vanity of Human Wishes* (for suggestions about each of these, see the individual discussions below). In grappling with Johnson's sentences, students need ear-training in parallel structure and periodic suspense; old-fashioned sentence diagramming can help with this, and the *Rambler* sentence is tailor-made for the purpose (though virtually any paragraph will supply samples). They also need alerting to the pleasures and purposes of Johnson's well-timed shifts in diction (often from high and Latinate at a passage's or paragraph's outset, to plain and punchy at its conclusion). Examples: the last stanza of the Levet elegy; the punch line of the "Short Song of Congratulation"; the plain speaking in the Chesterfield letter ("I never had a patron before"; "encumbers him with help"); the lists in *Vanity* ("Toil, envy, want . . ." [l. 160]); the famous (and almost self-contradictory) injunction about "the streaks of the tulip" (*Rasselas*, ch. 10). It is valuable, even important, to establish from the start that Johnson's style is not all parallelism and orotundity. The power of plain words matters everywhere in his writing, and in his conversation (the dialogues from Boswell's *Life* can make for an interesting comparison here).

As students become familiar with Johnson's style, they will learn also to recognize his sense and substance. Johnson is an anthology in himself. His versatility across genres was one of the main means by which he established himself as the "Great Cham" (Khan, or emperor) of eighteenth-century letters. The Johnson selections here are organized by a combination of genre and chronology, but they work well when taught thematically too. Johnson's central arguments recur throughout his writings; I'll touch on some of them here (listing particularly relevant selections) before treating the works one by one. An enormously useful handbook for teaching both the central themes and the individual texts is *Approaches to Teaching Samuel Johnson* (hereinafter *Approaches*), edited by David R. Anderson and Gwin J. Kolb (Modern Language Association, 1993).

"The dangerous prevalence of imagination": The phrase comes from *Rasselas*, the point recurs throughout: in *Vanity*; in the *Rambler* (Nos. 4, 5) and *Idler* (No. 31); in Pope's and Jenyns's complacent self-delusions about human suffering (review of Jenyns); in the account of disappointments in the Preface to the *Dictionary*, and in the definition of *imagination* itself (2767-68); in the history of Imlac (*Rasselas*). By imagination mortals delude themselves ruinously about their capacities and their prospects; the proper counter-measure is a combination of religious faith and close attention to the plain truth. "The use of traveling," Johnson remarks in a letter to Thrale (2798), "is to regulate imagination by reality, and instead of thinking how they may be, to see them as they are." For Johnson, this was also the proper use of writing, and a central purpose of living.

Time: "Time is," Johnson remarks in the Preface to Shakespeare, "of all modes of existence, the most obsequious to imagination" (2790). In context, this sentence makes a very specific point: Shakespeare's audiences can readily accommodate his rule-breaking leaps in time. The proposition also works well as a touchstone for Johnson's abiding preoccupation with the problem of the way time operates on the human mind. People enmeshed in present dissatisfaction (or "vacuity") delude themselves with the promise of future prosperity; the delusion produces both immobilizing passivity (with so pleasing a prospect, why work?) and inevitable disappointment. Time, then, is *dangerously* "obsequious to the imagination": the seeming plasticity of the future lets imagination run riot, rendering the actual future a kind of wasteland. The theme recurs in all the works mentioned under "imagination," above; in Johnson's *Dictionary* definition of *future*, with its striking quotation from *Macbeth* (2737-38); in the letter to Chesterfield; and in the remarkable paragraph on Pope's pace in translating the *Iliad* (*Life of Pope*, 2767). As *Idler* No. 31 suggests, Johnson's admonitions on this topic were often self-directed. Boswell records that Johnson had inscribed on his watch-dial the first words of "our Savior's solemn admonition to the improvement of that time which is allowed us to prepare for eternity: 'The night cometh, when no man can work'" (John 9.4).

Suffering: "From first to last," observes John Wain (in a sentence quoted in the headnote), Johnson "rooted his life among the poor and outcast," to whose plight he returned obsessively throughout his work: in his esteem for the charity of an impoverished doctor (the poem to Levet); in his fictional, first-person account of the prostitute Misella (*Rambler* Nos. 170, 171); in his furious demolition of the argument that the pains of the poor can be explained by a proposition like Pope's, in the *Essay on Man* (l. 1.294, 2550), that "Whatever Is, is RIGHT" (the Review of Jenyns, 2749-53; *Lives*, 2817-18); in his analytic reconstruction of the lost culture of the Highlands (*Journey*, 2804-7).

Connection and loss: "Our social comforts drop away," Johnson laments near the start of the poem to Levet. The line touches at once on two of his prevailing concerns: first, his deep investment in the satisfactions of friendship; second, his profound susceptibility as a mortal, and his fascination as a moralist, with the experience of loss, with the severing of human connections through alienation or through death. His impassioned but analytic eloquence on loss emerges in the *Ramblers* on Misella and on ending (Nos. 170, 171, 207); in the peroration of his Preface to the *Dictionary*; in the "Annals" of his own life; throughout his letters (and particularly in the final sequence to Hester Thrale); and in the writings of Boswell and Piozzi (notably their discussions of Johnson and death, 2846-47; 2872-73).

Experience and authority: At first, many students hear in Johnson's voice an impenetrable smugness, an unwavering self-certainty. But close attention to his arguments reveals a tendency to question almost everything, including tenets he himself has articulated in past years or in the previous paragraph. A devotee of the New Science, Johnson values ongoing experience over fixed authority (in this respect he bears interesting comparison with Chaucer's Wife of Bath, as well as with Hooke, Newton, et al.). He wields experience *against* authority in his demolition of Jenyns (*Review*), in his dismantling of the Aristotelian unities (Preface to Shakespeare), in his innovative insistence on deriving his *Dictionary* definitions from demonstrable usage rather than earlier dictionaries. We can watch him questioning his own previous stances in the Preface to the *Dictionary* (where he details and disavows his earlier conception of the project), in the chapters from *Rasselas* (where he projects a sequence of self-debunkings onto Imlac), and in many of his periodical essays (for more detail, see the discussion of them below). Waging battle against the human propensity for self-delusion, Johnson uses (and recommends) self-interrogation—an abiding *uncertainty*—as an indispensable weapon.

The general and the particular: The movement between these two categories accounts for much that is most compelling in both Johnson's style and his thought. Johnson's arguments favor the general. "The business of a poet," Imlac remarks, "is to examine, not the individual but the species; to remark general properties and large appearances" (2779); Shakespeare establishes his mastery through "just representations of general nature" (2785); biographers trace those universal arcs of experience that the emperor and the laborer traverse in common (2739). At the same time, Johnson makes clear at every turn that, to carry conviction, the "general" must be embodied in the judiciously portrayed "particular": Imlac promptly invokes "the streaks of the tulip" (2779); Johnson as editor pays obsessive attention to the details by which Shakespeare composes his "just representations"; biographers, he argues, must traffic abundantly in the "domestic particularities" and "minute details" of their subjects' lives. Details, though, pose the greater danger. Travel writers overdo them, and thereby lose sight of larger truths and plainer purposes (*Idler* No. 97); and even biographers can choose incorrectly (see the instance of Addison's pulse, 2740). Johnson often seems to have devised his own intricate style as a means of mingling, within a single sentence, forceful generalizations and sharp discriminations, with each concurrent activity lending credence to the other. (Again, the opening sentence of *Rambler* No. 60 affords a striking instance.)

Poems

The Vanity of Human Wishes: In the opening sentence, Johnson's initial personification produces in the reader a mix of detachment and engagement that he will play
upon throughout the poem. Technically, it is "Observation" who is to "survey
mankind," but as the long sentence advances, the verbs come to seem directly imperative: it is *our* job to "remark," "watch," and "say," with the goal of avoiding the
errors we witness. Meanwhile, ominously, the intricacy of the sentences themselves
(particularly the second) may involve us in a syntactic labyrinth to match the fatal
mazes that Johnson here describes: we prove susceptible to confusion, even as we're
being urged towards clarity. (Garrick complained that the poem was "hard as
Greek," but Johnson arranges his difficulties with a purpose.) In the poem's great
peroration (ll. 343–68), Johnson urges again our disengagement from the horrors
we have witnessed, as we renounce the instabilities of desire for the firmer ground
of Christian faith. (His renaming of the cardinal virtues, "faith, hope, and charity,"
works interestingly: for "hope," whose perils he has exposed throughout the poem,
he substitutes "patience," a merit more in keeping with the pains the poem has
shown.) Between the general arguments of the first and the final lines, Johnson presents a welter of particulars, calculated to involve us with the folly and anguish of
the aspirants he names (Hester Thrale reports that when he read the poem aloud
many years after composing it, Johnson himself "burst into a passion of tears"). The
exemplum of the ambitious student (ll. 135–64) is particularly rich: here Johnson
builds a swelling best-case scenario with all those parallel, desirable "Shoulds," only
to puncture it with a bitter summation ("Yet hope not . . ."). Other instances likely
to hit home: the account of Wolsey (99–128) and of beauty (319–42).

To read Johnson's poem alongside Juvenal's (perhaps in the excellent Penguin
translation by Peter Green) is to learn much about the eighteenth-century art of
imitation, and about Johnson's particular tactics and purposes here (for a brief
comparison, see 2078). Another excellent resource is Thomas Jemielity's essay on
"*The Vanity of Human Wishes* in the Classroom," in *Teaching Eighteenth-Century
Poetry*, ed. Christopher Fox (AMS Press, 1990); among many other points, Jemielity
argues that the teacher should start by mapping the poem's structure: opening argument, specific examples of aspirants towards Preferment, Power, Intellectual
Eminence, Military Fame, Beauty; and, in conclusion, an urgent question (l. 343)
and "dynamic, affirmative" answer. Also useful is Michael Pennington's lucid
recorded reading of the poem (in the Penguin *English Verse* collection; see "Ways
in," above). *Vanity* teaches interestingly with Gray's *Elegy*, which surveys lives led in
the absence of aspiration.

Couching deep feeling in plain syntax, reworking private loss into both a tender portrait and a larger lament ("As on we toil from day to day"), Johnson's poem
"On the Death of Robert Levet" affords a particularly rich introduction to all his
writing. The metaphors ("Hope's delusive mine"), the personifications, the mix of
empathy, esteem, and instruction ("Nor, Lettered Arrogance, deny . . ."), all deeply
characteristic of the author, here take a particularly clear and compact form.
Christ's parable of the talents (Matthew 25.14–30) is worth reading aloud in class;

Johnson touches on it lightly here (as in many other of his works), but its import pervades the poem.

"A Short Song of Congratulation" works as counterpoint: attack, not tribute, plainly couched and artfully caustic.

Periodical Essays *and* The Review of Jenyns

The selections from *The Rambler* and *The Idler* may usefully be read as a set, and in conjunction with the periodical essays in the Perspectives section—particularly *The Spectator*, whose immensely successful model Johnson both esteemed and re-worked. In the epigraph to the first *Rambler* presented here (No. 4), Johnson invokes Horace's injunction that writers must supply both "profit" and "delight." One way into a comparison might be to ask what kinds of profit and what modes of delight each periodical undertakes to provide (*Spectator* No. 10 and *Rambler* No. 207 may prove particularly useful here). Addison, Steele, and Johnson all undertake to serve (in Hawkins's phrase) as "instructors of mankind"—but what differences obtain between the kinds of instruction they offer, and the language in which they offer it?

The comparison can work to Johnson's disadvantage: students will often find him complacent, even overweening, in the weight and seeming certainty of his pronouncements. It pays to show them (slowly, not stridently) how often Johnson deals in human *uncertainty*, not only as his topic but as his method. His essays often live up to the original meaning of the term: they are *attempts* and (partly, at least) improvisations; they opt to enact a search rather than to present "finished" findings. (They are in fact far more elastic, less "authoritative" in form, than the symmetrical, "inverted triangle" essays we tend to require of our students: thesis, demonstration, conclusion.) As an analysis of the extraordinary *movement* of Johnson's essays, and as a useful companion in the teaching of them, nothing surpasses Paul Fussell's superb chapter "'The Anxious Employment of a Periodical Writer'" in his *Samuel Johnson and the Life of Writing* (Norton, 1971), 143-80.

Among the Johnson essays presented here, a grouping of those on writing may prove fruitful: *Rambler* Nos. 4 (fiction) and 60 (biography); *Idler* Nos. 84 (autobiography) and 97 (travel writing).

Rambler No. 4, about the "comedies of romance" (i.e., novels) newly fashionable at the time, will work well in conjunction with almost *any* novel being read in the same course. What elements of the new genre does Johnson pinpoint accurately—perhaps surprisingly? What are his assumptions about the ways such fiction operates upon the reader? What alarms him about the "mixed" characters, compounded of good and evil traits (one thinks of *Pamela*'s Mr. B.), which the novel presents with new ingenuity and abundance?

Rambler No. 60 is perhaps the essay worth spending the most time on. A compact, enormously influential investigation of the purposes and methods of biography, it opens approaches to many other texts, within this section (Pepys, Aubrey, Carleton, Cavendish, Montagu, Boswell, Piozzi) and beyond (Kempe, Coleridge, Strachey). The opening sentence compasses many of Johnson's most important stylistic and conceptual moves: as Johnson signals by his initial "All," he aims at a comprehensive pronouncement on human nature. But he writes as though the only hope for accuracy in such utterance lies in the careful drawing of distinctions: between experiences (the *ors*), among degrees (the *howevers*), within modes of cognition (the temporary "deception" as against the abiding, implied reality). The elaborate architecture of the sentence works (as so often in Johnson) to sort things out in the very act of pulling them together. After this magisterial opening, the essay moves with ease and suppleness. Biography, it emerges, is one instance of this pleasing and potentially useful "deception"; its value derives from the universality of basic human experiences (that "all" again); its proper management requires close investigation into the "domestic privacies" and "minute details," followed by tact in their selection and display. By such modulations, Johnson works his way from the "deception" of the opening sentence to the valuable "truth" of his final word.

Idler No. 84 makes a useful pendant: it argues the much more surprising claim that autobiography is reliable because disinterested. Is Johnson merely "talking for victory" here, defending an untenable point? Or is he arguing from his own limited experience as an unusually frank, even brutal, autobiographer? The essay invites comparison with his own "Annals" (2818–22).

Idler No. 97 meshes well with Johnson's travel writing and with Boswell's. Here, Johnson takes to task those travel writers (their number was growing almost exponentially) who "crowd the world with their itineraries," and fill their books with too many details of their trip, too little analysis of the country and culture they visited. To what extent does Johnson in his *Journey* live up to his own precepts here? What about Boswell, in his *Journal* of the same trip (2839–43)?

Another grouping of essays (*Rambler* Nos. 5 and 207; *Idler* Nos. 31 and 32) centers on self-delusion. The theme is consistent, the tone and presentation different in each instance, from the eager anticipations of *Rambler* No. 5 to the valedictory broodings of No. 207; from the semi-comic "case study" of *Idler* No. 31 to the more acerbic reproaches of No. 32. Johnson is at all times moralizing against a propensity towards inattention and delusion to which he considered himself deeply susceptible. One interesting question to ask of these essays (as of much of Johnson's prose) concerns the place of the first person: Where does the "I" appear explicitly? How is the author's investment in the topic couched or redirected in larger pronouncements, about "he" ("poor Sober" in *Idler* No. 31) and "we"? How does Johnson persuade his readers that he is speaking accurately of both himself and them?

The essays purportedly by Misella (*Rambler* Nos. 170 and 171) present a striking counterpoint in this regard. Johnson writes in a ventriloquized (and cross-gendered) first person, from the point of view of a woman who (in fulfillment of one of his favorite precepts) "instead of thinking how things may be, [sees] them as they are" (2799). To what causes does Misella attribute her plight? How accurate and thorough (by Johnson's standards, by ours) is her analysis—economic, familial, psychological—of her predicament? How does Johnson's creation of this character fit or diverge from the precepts for moral fiction that he sets forth in *Rambler* No. 4?

Johnson has long stood accused of misogyny—though not, interestingly enough, by Mary Wollstonecraft, who resolutely admired him. (The case against has often boiled down to one notorious quotation from Boswell's *Life*: "Sir, a woman's preaching is like a dog's walking on his hinder legs. It is not done well; but you are surprised to find it done at all.") How, if at all, do the Misella essays complicate this claim? The female-voiced essays in the Perspectives section "Reading Papers" may serve as useful touchtones here: see the excerpts from *Athenian Mercury* (esp. 2427-28) and the *Female Spectator*. Boswell considered Johnson's ventriloquy a stylistic failure: "Johnson's language . . . must be allowed too masculine for the delicate gentleness of female writing. His ladies, therefore [including Misella], seem strangely formal, even to ridicule" (*Life of Johnson* [Oxford UP, 1980], 160). For questions of Johnson and gender see also his letters to Thrale, her accounts of him in *Thraliana*, and James G. Basker, "Dancing Dogs, Women Preachers, and the Myth of Johnson's Misogyny" in *The Age of Johnson* 3 (1990): 63-90.

The Review of Soame Jenyns's *Free Inquiry*: Students who love a good debunking may well take pleasure in Johnson's powerful dissection—painstaking and pugilistic at the same time—of Jenyns's errors in logic and distortions of language. See, for example, Johnson's careful readings of *want of riches* (2750) and of *inconceivable* (2752), and his sardonic impromptu on Jenyns's "consoling" argument that human sufferings may provide entertainment for some order of superior beings. Johnson ends by turning the analogy directly against Jenyns: in its presumption, his book has proven "very entertaining" (though not at all useful) for Johnson and (through Johnson's arts of argument) for us as well. The review is noteworthy for the ways in which it melds cold logic with caustic laughter.

Boswell declared this "Johnson's most exquisite critical essay," and students may enjoy attempting an imitation: taking a short passage from some piece of social argument with which they vehemently disagree, and exposing its error through close attention to both the logic and the language by which it's made.

The review may be read in conjunction with the selections from Pope's *Essay on Man* (especially ll. 23-32, 43-48), and with Johnson's critique of that poem in his *Life of Pope* (2717-18). In an excellent article on teaching Johnson's review of Jenyns (*Approaches*, 92-98) Thomas F. Bonnell gives a useful guided tour to Johnson's piece and to all the texts that prompted it.

A Dictionary of the English Language

Like Johnson's periodical essays, much of his *Dictionary* (Preface and body) concerns the ways in which experience impinges on expectation. In the Preface, Johnson confronts the discrepancy between his original ambitions for the project and the limits of the actual book he has now produced (see especially the paragraph beginning "Of the event of this work . . ." [2764]), as well as the losses he has incurred along the way (see the Preface's final paragraph).

As for the definitions themselves, Allen Reddick, in his excellent article on teaching the *Dictionary* (*Approaches*, 84-91), emphasizes the insistence and innovation with which Johnson derived these too from experience—from England's continual reworking of its own language, and from Johnson's own sustained and (in the years of the *Dictionary*) systematic encounter with English literature: "Johnson's

Dictionary became the first to rely to a large extent on a criterion of word *usage*, written usage, for establishing meaning." Students, Reddick suggests, can profitably test for themselves the methods by which Johnson derives each definition from the quotations that follow it.

At the same time, even so scant a selection as the one presented here may support a reckoning of the *Dictionary* that is gaining increasing attention: as a work of literature, even of polemic. In what ways do the clusters of passages operate as a running anthology of English writing? What forms of pleasure and instruction do they proffer? (The definitions of *knack* and *imagination* provide interesting cases.) To what extent can an entry constitute an *argument* about the word or concept being defined, and how do sequence and selection contribute to the shape of argument? The notably "Johnsonian" quotations under *future* and *vacuity*, and the distinctions and elaborations under *imagination*, *judgment*, and *substance* all repay close scrutiny.

Rasselas

Like the entire tale, the short excerpt printed here radiates outward to touch on virtually everything that Johnson ever wrote. Recounting his own history, Imlac quickly and memorably sounds many of Johnson's central themes: the inevitability of self-delusion, the necessity of self-correction, the elusiveness of firm conclusion, the difficulties that beset "the choice of life." Johnson intertwines two skeins of error: the errors Imlac makes in projecting his future, and the errors Rasselas makes (as listener) in his responses—first eager, then renunciatory—to each of Imlac's choices (he will soon make similar errors in respect to his own). En route, Imlac takes up some of Johnson's most writerly concerns. The "Dissertation upon Poetry" has long served as the *locus classicus* for critical tenets about the general and the particular that Johnson would later expand and illustrate in his Preface to Shakespeare and his *Lives of the Poets*. The form of Imlac's history, however exotic in locale and genre, bears comparison with Johnson's other ventures into life-writing: the brutal biographical catalogue in *The Vanity of Human Wishes*; *Rambler* No. 60; the *Life of Pope*; and his autobiographical "Annals." To what extent can Pope's life and Johnson's (to say nothing of the vain wishers who populate Johnson's poem) be seen as travelling the selfsame arc of choice and disappointment that Imlac sketches here?

The Plays of William Shakespeare

For Johnson, Shakespeare's achievement is transhistorical. The playwright has produced "just representations of general nature," recognizable by all audiences in all cultures; "his characters are not modified by the customs of particular places." Such assertions sort oddly but fascinatingly with the historically localized Shakespeare set forth by recent scholarship (and by this anthology). On the other hand Johnson's account meshes quite comfortably with the "immediate" Shakespeare who surfaces in class discussion whenever a student says something like

"Oh, I can really relate to this speech. Just yesterday I was talking to my father . . . ." In short, our real conversations about Shakespeare—our real experience of Shakespeare?—oscillates between Johnson's "take" and the New Historicist's (what's more, the two are not sharply distinguishable; elsewhere in the Preface, Johnson is keenly alert to the cultural circumstances in which the playwright worked). So: In what ways, by our lights, is Johnson right about Shakespeare? And what elements of the plays, by our lights, does Johnson miss or misapprehend? (He condemns, for example, the very "quibbles"—the puns—which we have learned to treasure as some of Shakespeare's richest moments.)

The dismantling of the unities (2789-92) makes for delicious reading. The appeal is immediate: Johnson is refuting critical pieties that now seem remote and absurd, in a culture weaned on the rapid cross-cuttings of film and video. His demonstration here has all of the efficacy, some of the comedy, but little of the violence conspicuous in his review of Soame Jenyns; he is simply describing the audience's experiences not (to borrow again his words to Thrale) "as they may be" in the minds of theorists, "but as they actually are" in the seats of the theater. Johnson (like Shakespeare) rates the audience's dexterity of imagination far more highly than does the theory from which he dissents. He describes our experience, and measures our capacities, both accurately and flatteringly.

The notes to *Othello* will work best in a course where that play has been read—and will work with particular energy *while* it is being read. Even within this small selection, Johnson performs many of the actions that all readers of Shakespeare undertake: collating the play with real life (1.3.141-42); paraphrasing Shakespeare's lines, expanding his compressions, plumbing his obscurities (5.2.1-3); responding with raw feeling (5.2.67-69); assessing moralities and meanings (3.3.206-08, and the summation). Much of what Johnson does as editor overlaps with what we do as readers. Again, then: Is his Shakespeare our Shakespeare? What are the differences between these tasks as he performs them and as we do—in method, and in result? Much might be gained by comparing Johnson's notes and Preface with the apparatus (headnotes, footnotes, companion readings, etc.) surrounding the text of *Othello* in this anthology. What information does each convey? What presuppositions about Shakespeare, *Othello*, literature, and history does each embody?

Travel Writing

These selections will work best when read in conjunction with Johnson's *Idler* No. 97 (see comments under Periodical Essays, above) and with the excerpts from Boswell's *Journal of a Tour to the Hebrides* (see further comments under Boswell below). In the *Idler* essay Johnson mocks the personal details that had come to inundate contemporary travel writing. By comparing his journal-letter to Thrale and his *Journey* account of the same stretch of days, students will be able to detect the distinctions Johnson draws between the kinds of details proper in a letter to a beloved friend, and the modes of narrative and thought valuable in a published account; readers may also be struck by the difference between Johnson's "private" and his "public" voice (even the shapes of his sentences change markedly). These comparisons can make for a good paper topic; a particularly intriguing parallel transpires between the two accounts of Johnson's pause for rest in a "small glen" (2796; 2803). Johnson's gesture towards the Thrales in the letter, and towards the reader in the book, coupled with his different description and analysis of his responses to the scene, say much about his alertness to audience, and his conception of travel.

Travel writers, Johnson argues in the *Idler*, ought to pay less attention to themselves and more to the culture they encounter. Ever since the *Journey's* first appearance, the degree and precision of Johnson's attention to the Highlands has remained a matter of dispute. Scots readers and others found Johnson's preoccupation with paucity (the absence of trees and other amenities) insultingly reductive; for them, his comic comment about the inn at Glenelg—"of the provisions the negative catalogue was very copious"—might stand as a damning emblem of his attitude through the book. In travelling to Scotland, Johnson the empiricist was eagerly participating in the newly productive and powerful pursuits of ethnography and geography—in the careful delineation (often with a view towards dominion) of distant lands and peoples. At the same time, Johnson finds in the Highlands much confirmation for arguments he has waged all his life—about mutability, about the human capacity for self-delusion, about human life being "every where a state in which much is to be endured, and little to be enjoyed" (*Rasselas*, 2781). How, then, do Johnson's presuppositions inform and inflect his ethnography here? Thomas Jemielity's article on teaching the *Journey* (*Approaches*, 99–106) is helpful on this and many other points.

The Lives of the Poets

The excerpt on Pope's *Iliad* can be read most profitably in conjunction with the selections from that work (2523-27; how does Johnson's account of Pope's purposes square with the one offered by Pope himself?), and with Johnson's own *Rambler* No. 60. To what extent does Johnson here follow the precepts on biography that he there articulates—the stipulation about "minute details," the argument about universal usefulness? At the end of the *Iliad* excerpt, Johnson defends the particularity of his history of this, "the noblest version [i.e., translation] of poetry which the world has ever seen." But how has he deployed the details he has selected? And by what means has he managed (in keeping with the *Rambler* essay) to suggest points of correspondence between the lives led by this matchless writer and by the ordinary reader? The paragraph on Pope's pace of translation (2814) provides a compact instance of Johnson's method. It begins with a small observation ("When we find him translating fifty lines a day . . .") and ends with a universal pronouncement ("He that runs against time . . ."); the modulations in between are worth attending to.

Also worth noting is Johnson's attention not only to the processes by which books get written and read, but to those calculations by which they are made and marketed: price, size, press run, profit, subscription, competition. A bookseller's son, Johnson is here (as elsewhere in the *Lives*) melding literary biography with a cultural history of the book as commodity and artifact.

The critical excerpts, on *Paradise Lost* and Pope's poems, are best read in conjunction with the works themselves. "I rejoice to concur with the common reader," Johnson once remarked, and students may rejoice in turn to collate his judgments with their own. Johnson invites such collation at the end of his comparison between Pope and Dryden, and the last paragraph of the excerpt on Milton provides another well-trod testing ground.

Lawrence Lipking, in his splendid essay on teaching the *Lives* (*Approaches*, 114-20), suggests another apt companion reading: Johnson's poem "On the Death of Dr. Levet." Throughout the *Lives*, Lipking points out, Johnson asks of each poet and each poem the question he answers so confidently in his memorial to Levet: how well was the allotted talent here employed?

Annals and Letters

The "Annals" contrast interestingly with the excerpts from the *Life of Pope*. Here Johnson extenuates nothing and elaborates little; instead he focuses rigorously on "domestic privacies" and corporeal facts—eyes, sores, jack-weight, dog, cup, spoons, frock, books. Only occasionally does he expand from the particular to an analysis of emotions and relationships, as when his problems of sight open out into a quick and sharp account of his parents' marriage (2819). There is in Johnson's procedure here a confidence in the revelatory particular, the speaking object, comparable to Aubrey's and to Hooke's. Beginning from his precarious emergence ("I was born almost dead"), he is investigating the raw materials of his own difficult life and writing them up for himself alone.

In his letters, he writes for someone else—for a reader specifically circumstanced and artfully addressed. In tone and tactics, the letters included here proffer first antithesis, then synthesis. In the one to Chesterfield Johnson crafts a dazzling and audacious rebuke: no aristocratic patron had been dismissed this way before. In his letter to Hester Thrale from Skye (2796-2800), as in so much of their correspondence, Johnson performs gestures of intimacy across removes of space and time; in his last letters to her (2823-25), Johnson mingles reproach and tenderness, in measures intricately moving because his stance itself (against a marriage she deeply desires) now seems so unsympathetic (the excerpts from *Thraliana*, discussed in her section below, provide an impassioned counterpoint). In the letter of 19 June 1783, Johnson faces down two abiding fears: of losing Thrale, and of losing life. In his account of his "paralytic stroke" and its aftermath he attempts uneasily to renew his cherished connection with his friend ("How this will be received by you, I know not"), and he enacts once more the tenet he had earlier pronounced to her, struggling to see his illness and her alienation "as they are" (the Latin lines he wrote after the stroke "were not very good, but I knew them not to be very good"), while hoping against hope that they might be otherwise. In his superb article on teaching Johnson's letters (*Approaches*, 78-84), Bruce Redford argues that they "richly merit, and abundantly repay, the kind of close scrutiny we automatically accord the 'major' works"; he makes the claim convincing in close readings of the letter to Chesterfield and the final missive to Hester Thrale.

James Boswell

Five strands mingle vividly in nearly everything Boswell wrote: theatricality, nationality, filial attachments, gender, and genre. A question about any one of these matters will open up the wonders of the text—and carry you quickly to the other four, so inextricably are they intertwined.

Nowhere is their mingling more apparent and entertaining than in the *London Journal*. Boswell's early discovery (quoted in the headnote) "that we may be . . . whatever character we choose" makes a useful touchstone. Fascinated by the power, he found the choice perpetually perplexing; he worshipped actors because they possessed the power in full, with their "choices" both simplified and multiplied by the requirements of each successive role. Freshly arrived in London from Edinburgh, Boswell resorts immediately to role-playing as a way to define and redefine his perpetually confused cultural affiliations. This propensity comes through clearly enough in the early excerpts here, where he both confirms and counteracts his Scottishness by playing a "true-born Old Englishman" for a day (15 December), and by imagining himself longingly as West Digges, the Edinburgh actor famously capable of transforming himself into the London kingpin Captain Macheath (1 December); Boswell invokes this fantasy in order to soothe himself for the rapidity with which he has fallen back into the milieu of a Scots family visiting London—only a week or so after his own bold advent.

Boswell's passion for playacting shows clearest of all in the account of his intrigue with the actress Louisa, who, he is gratified to note (in a passage not in the anthology) "has played many a fine lady's part"—including Gertrude in *Hamlet*. En route to his assignation (12 January) Boswell dines with the actor Thomas Sheridan and debates the merits of superstar David Garrick, in his performance as the dying King Henry confronting his wayward son (like Prince Hal, Boswell is leading a London life deeply displeasing to his father). Arriving at the appointed inn, Boswell pretends to be the cousin of West Digges; following consummation, he solicits his actress-lover's applause for his performance(s). Eight days later (20 January), he presents his culminating confrontation with Louisa as a playtext, and after his ruffled departure from her he seeks out the paternal blessing of Garrick himself. Functioning simultaneously as playwright, actor, and director, Boswell is also his own most ardent, anxious audience.

Boswell's tendency to transmute autobiography into theater—to build a proscenium in prose—persisted throughout his career. Students may enjoy comparing the *Journal* passage on the first meeting with Johnson (16 May) with this revision in the *Life*: "Johnson unexpectedly came into the shop; and Mr. Davies having perceived him through the glass-door in the room in which we were sitting, advancing towards us,—he announced his awful approach to me, somewhat in the manner of an actor in the part of Horatio, when he addresses Hamlet on the appearance of his father's ghost: 'Look, my Lord, it comes.'" Boswell becomes the prince, Johnson his spectral father.

The deathbed interview with David Hume extends the father-son strand. Boswell seeks and assesses the views of a formidable figure, "just a-dying." A glance back at his fervent account (2830-31) of the father-son scene in *Henry IV* may prove worthwhile here. But the richest comparisons will arise with the selections by Hume in Perspectives: Mind and God (2674-80), and with the "Conversations about Hume" excerpted from the *Life of Johnson* (2845-47). Johnson firmly dismisses Hume's heresies. Boswell, by contrast, cannot let them go. In his talks with Johnson, he resumes the topic again and again over the course of years, seeking reassurance from this most authoritative father figure, but unable quite to absorb it. In his account of the deathbed interview itself, Boswell does uneasy battle with Hume's views even as he transcribes them, and returns to the narrative field of combat twice after the death of his "opponent"—once by revising his first account, once by supplying "additions from memory." (Contrast Hume's own far more comfortable approach to self-revision: "I shall leave [my] history . . . as perfect as I can" [2808]) Much of Boswell's fascination arises from the perceived incongruity between Hume's cheerfulness (deeply attractive to the diarist) and his predicament (deeply dreadful): "There was no solemnity in the scene." This is not death as *Boswell* would script it. (For a fuller reading, see Redford).

The Journal of a Tour to the Hebrides again dramatizes the complexity of Boswell's chameleonic allegiances. A proud Scot, he cannot "refrain from tears" (1 September) when re-hearing the defeat of the Highland rebels at the culture-crushing battle of Culloden—and then plunges into a partly dismissive analysis of his response ("with which sober rationality has nothing to do"). Proud companion of a supereminent Englishman, he is embarrassed by what he sees as the peasant woman's price-gouging, and he laughs loud and long at the condescension displayed by escort Hay to "*Dr. Samuel Johnson*"—but he laughs at Johnson too.

These excerpts from the *Journal* work best when read in company with Johnson's accounts of the same days in his letters to Hester Thrale and in his published *Journey*; Boswell's competition with Thrale for the privilege of Johnsonian intimacy arises in his very first entry here. Competition is a keynote in the *Journal*. The sequence of composition, revision, and publication (sketched in the first footnote to these excerpts) prompted Boswell to argue, implicitly and explicitly, that now, ten years after the appearance of Johnson's *Journey*, he had something new and valuable to impart about the trip: the portrait of Johnson himself, in energetic motion through an alien land. One version of the argument crops up in the contrast Boswell draws (1 September) between Johnson's "great mind," unsuited to "minute particulars," and the "neat little scales" of his own mind, well-suited for weighing mundane details. Though Boswell purports here to be defending only his rude conduct on a Highland hillside, he is in fact arguing for his whole new narrative enterprise. He lightly echoes Johnson's famous tenet (in *Rambler* No. 60) that all biographers should deal in "domestic privacies, and the minute details of daily life." But Boswell also emphasizes that he is dealing in such particulars on a scale and in an abundance that Johnson never implemented—and consequently (so he implies) giving us "more" of Johnson than we have had of any human subject hitherto. In transmuting the minutely detailed daily record of his own life into the published portrait of another, Boswell was making a new kind of biography, a kind open then and now to buzzing questions: How much of any given passage is really about the biographer rather than the biographee? And how does our knowledge (or illusion) about each man inflect our knowledge about the other, "relativizing" the whole so that we move among uncertainties rather than travel directly to biographical "truth"?

These questions arise everywhere in The Life of Johnson, for which the Journal served as prelude. The Life excerpts here will perhaps work most productively if read in company with Johnson's own precepts about biography (Rambler No. 60, Idler No. 84), and with his practice in the lives of Pope and Milton. In the Life of Johnson's opening sentence Boswell makes it clear that Johnson is not only his subject but also his model—the best biographer (and potential autobiographer) who ever lived. This sentence, cast pointedly as an elaborate period in Johnson's own most ornate style, is worth reading aloud in class, by way of decoding and of pondering: Boswell is subliminally arguing that, even in the shapes of his prose, he has absorbed (as he elsewhere asserts, in a passage omitted here) the Johnsonian ether. A comparison with the Johnson excerpts, though, will reveal how much the two biographers differ. At one of the most striking points of divergence, Boswell in his introduction resolves as biographer to "'live o'er each scene' with [Johnson], as he actually advanced through the several stages of his life" (2844; emphasis added). As the diction suggests, this is essentially a dramatist's dream, of rendering a life now ended so that it unfolds before us in what feels like the "real," present time of the theater, rather than the retrospect of the reading-chair (for more on Boswell's tactics, see Ralph W. Rader, "Literary Form in Factual Narrative: The Example of Boswell's Johnson," in Boswell's Life of Johnson: New Questions, New Answers, ed. John A. Vance [U of Georgia P, 1985] 25–52). The fascination with prose-as-stage that first emerged in Boswell's journals now shapes his Life.

In the famous "Dinner with Wilkes," Boswell not only lives o'er the scene; he stages it in the first place. As usual with Boswell, the audiences are multiple: Johnson and Wilkes perform for each other, and for the other guests at the dinner, and (thanks to Boswell's intricate mediation) for us as well. Boswell, of course, is everywhere, as scripter and prompter (see in particular his management of Mrs. Williams), director and actor, guiding the performances of others and assessing and interpreting his own. By letting us into his scheme from the first, Boswell gives us the sense that, in this situation at least, we know more about Johnson than does Johnson himself. Yet Boswell allows us, like spectators at a play, to shift identifications readily: Johnson as "dupe" emerges (as usual) as Johnson triumphant. All Boswell's tactics as manipulator and narrator converge in the dialogue near the end of the episode, when Johnson and Wilkes collude in witticisms at Boswell's expense—"and we ashamed of him" (2852). The two antagonists have (to literalize Lennon) come together over Boswell; without him they would not have come together at all.

The conversation at Streatham (2853–54) affords a fascinating instance of the way the men in Boswell's circle "gendered" the privileges of life-writing. Boswell's proud remark that "as a lady adjusts her dress before a mirror, a man adjusts his character by looking at his journal" suggests 1) that (as Pope wrote in his Epistle to a Lady) "most women have no characters at all"; hence 2) that the writing of journals occupies no proper place in a lady's life. Yet Boswell presses on, with much complacency and not a trace of irony, to mention with esteem the diary of Lady Cutts; at this point, all the gendering analogies get interestingly and precariously muddled. Hester Thrale, of course, is listening, and one of her *Thraliana* entries (10 December 1780, 2866–67) affords the perfect counterpoint to this passage.

The conversation at the Club (2855–58) conveys both the range and the mode of many similar exchanges throughout the *Life*. The speakers move through many topics, and reveal as they do so how clearly the art of conversation was construed as a mix of competition and collaboration. They are working with and against each other to produce a shapely, pleasurable flow of talk, one worth savoring in the moment, and living o'er afterwards. The *contrast* between Johnson as talker (his sentences generally short and punchy) and Johnson as writer (often more elaborate) is worth dwelling on. And Boswell's gifts as drama-tist—as selector, shaper, reviser—remain in evidence: did a real-life conversation *ever* run so smooth as this?

The Boswell selections are closely linked (as I've already suggested) with those by Johnson and Thrale. Read with Rochester, Wycherley, Gay, and Hogarth, Boswell completes a kind of mini-history of the London rake. His journals will work well also with Addison (whose overwhelming influence Boswell explicitly ac-knowledges) and with Pepys. The *Spectator*'s model of a daily essay, and of the pow-erful observer recording both the ways of the world and the workings of his own mind, accounts for much of the difference between Boswell's diary and Pepys's, a century apart. Boswell also compares interestingly with Mary Carleton and Margaret Cavendish; like him, but working from different positions and using dif-ferent techniques, they seek to construct identity and achieve authority in the records of their lives.

Hester Salusbury Thrale Piozzi

Piozzi's life-writing is *sui generis*—fascinating in itself (students generally take to it im-mediately), and even more revelatory when read against the men's journals ex-cerpted elsewhere in the anthology: Pepys's and Boswell's, Crusoe's and H. F.'s (in Defoe's *Journal of the Plague Year*). Like Boswell, Piozzi pursued self-recording in many modes, from the calendrical regularity (at least in the first pages) of the *Family Book*, to the more sporadic effusions of *Thraliana*, a record of observations, reflec-tions, conversations, and anecdotes composed at moments when leisure and im-pulse converged. But she never worked in the time-form characteristic of Pepys and Boswell: the continuous daily journal, temporally regular and exact. She herself drew the distinction in a *Thraliana* entry of spring 1778: "Mr. Boswell keeps a regu-lar literary journal I believe of everything worth remarking; 'tis a good way, but life is scarce long enough to talk, and to write, and to live to rejoice in what one has written—at least I feel that I have begun too late." Piozzi's sense that she has started "too late" registers a difference not of age (she is thirty-seven, Boswell thirty-eight) but of situation. Piozzi has something like Boswell's appetite for self-recording, but nothing like his opportunities. Over and over within her texts, Piozzi makes clear how randomly, plentifully, and at times exasperatingly the predicaments of her children and the peremptoriness of her husband punctuate her days, precluding the long stretches of solitary time desirable for more systematic writing. For Piozzi and for other women similarly situated (including her dear friend, the copious but sporadic diarist Frances Burney), diurnal form is hardly an option: by circumstance, family obligation, and social pressure, they *must* write selectively and intermittently, leaving days and moments (however reluctantly) unrecorded.

Among the excerpts here, several passages invite particular attention: her agonizing record of the short sequence of her son's death, from the complacency of the morning to the catastrophe of the night (her detailed retraversal of that stretch of time, from ignorance to loss and anguish, bears comparison and contrast with Pepys's account of the London Fire). In her *Thraliana* entry about the rough drafts for Pope's *Iliad*, she genders her metaphors intricately and caustically. The male readers of the manuscript (Johnson among them) intrude violently and obtusely into woman's province: into "the cradles and clouts" of the nursery (Pope momentarily becomes yet another frail infant under Thrale's watchful care); into the naked vulnerability of the bath. At the same time, Thrale aligns herself with Pope as a kind of literary stage manager, anxiously wielding "wood and wire" behind the scenes in a bizarre game of performance and concealment ("stranger still that a woman should write such a book as this . . ."). The passage reads well as a retort to the Streatham conversation recorded in Boswell's *Life* (2853).

In her courtship narrative (2869–72) the circle of intruders expands to include not only men like Johnson, but women of her own blood—the very daughters whose early accomplishments she had chronicled in the *Family Book*. A reading of Johnson's letters to her during this period (2823–25) will convey a fuller sense of the pressures she was resisting; but only a close reading of her own prose can map the tackings between deference and defiance, diffidence and pride, by which she navigated a route to hard-won happiness.

The elegy on Johnson (2872–73), rueful, evocative, and searching, makes for an interesting contrast with Boswell's more aggressive claims to possess a kind of monopoly on the man he writes about (see the Introduction to the *Life* [2843–44], and his attack on Piozzi as biographer [2854]). Such claim-staking is anticipated and gently mocked by both Piozzi and Johnson in her reminiscence here—though of course, the very fact that they share such inside jokes works to enforce her own claim of intimacy with him.

Oliver Goldsmith

At one point in *The Deserted Village*, Goldsmith recalls "The varnished clock that clicked" in the local tavern (l. 228). Time of several kinds makes a useful touchstone when teaching the poem. Goldsmith grounds his argument in the stark contrast between a prosperous "then" and a barren "now," whose conflicting pressures he often weaves into the texture of his verse. In the line just quoted, the onomatopoeia makes the clock-sound present, while "varnished," by the omission of a single letter, ghosts Goldsmith's point that both sound and clock have vanished, like the whole small world whose time they told.

Goldsmith grounds his nostalgia in another trick with time. Conjuring up Auburn's lost loveliness, he dwells less on the villagers' labor than on their leisure. As early as the fifteenth line, "toil remits" in favor of "play," "sports," and "pastime" (the only sustained toil the poem depicts—that of the "wretched matron" gathering cresses [l. 129-36]—takes place in the bleak present, not the remembered past). This elision of the laborer's actual labor helped prompt Crabbe's critique (see below); it also compares interestingly with the sketch of village life in Gray's *Elegy*.

The poem moves, too, along wider arcs of time. Celebrating the past, foredooming the future, Goldsmith hoped to intervene in history, to warn Britain away from a ruinous course. As he anticipated in his dedicatory letter to Reynolds, many readers found his specific doctrine dubious: "England," wrote an anonymous and generally admiring reviewer, "wears now a more smiling aspect than ever she did; and few ruined villages are to be met with except on poetical ground." Recent historians generally concur, emphasizing that enclosure, though it often reduced the *number* of farms, actually increased both the population and the food supply of rural villages. Still, Goldsmith wages an argument grounded in poetics as much as politics. "The pastoral and georgic modes," writes Roger Lonsdale, "are devastated within the poet's imagination"; the new economics of empire simply won't allow for such celebrations of idyllic leisure and labor. "The whole poem negates the familiar 'Whig' panegyric of English commerce and liberty" ("'A Garden and a Grave': The Poetry of Oliver Goldsmith," in *The Author in his Work*, ed. Louis L. Martz and Aubrey Williams [New Haven: Yale University Press, 1978], 27).

The Deserted Village inhabits another kind of history as well: the literary history of landscape verse. In important ways, Goldsmith borrows and differs from important predecessors. In *Cooper's Hill*, Denham views the Windsor landscape from on high, and reads from it monarchic history and present dangers (ancestral voices prophesying rebellion). In *Windsor-Forest*, Pope finds in the same terrain new cause for celebration in the triumphs of Queen and commerce. Unlike Denham and Pope, Thomson and Cowper tend to be absorbed into the landscapes they record: there Thomson finds occasion for praise of brilliant human accomplishments (notably Newton's), Cowper for satire (of foolish urban bustle). Goldsmith dwells both inside and outside sweet Auburn—in by way of memory, out by way of his painful exile in present time. Like Pope he reads economy into landscape, but like Denham he finds foreboding. Like Cowper he honors rural leisure and castigates the depradations of commerce. He seeks a reabsorption into landscape (here construed as a place of human community rather than natural wonders) but, unlike Thomson, cannot achieve it.

Crabbe's attack on Goldsmith is both political (Goldsmith is actually colluding in a rich man's fantasy of rural life) and poetic: Goldsmith participates unthinkingly in a pastoral tradition which for centuries has ignored the facts (or does he? see the remark by Lonsdale above). Crabbe pointedly inverts the "timing" of Goldsmith's poem; he focuses sharply on the time of labor in "the midday sun" (p.

2855), and describes village pastimes ("the riots of the green," p. 2856) so caustically as to make them seem another, brutal form of toil.

Richard Brinsley Sheridan

In *School for Scandal*, students will likely recognize the origins of a world we almost
helplessly inhabit: the world of commercial gossip, of "private" revelations, factual
or fictitious, profitably retailed for public consumption. The *Town and Country
Magazine*, cited in the play's first moments, was the Adamic ancestor of today's
People and all its numberless cousins and clones, print and electronic. The magazine had commenced publication only seven years earlier; in its success, Sheridan
and many others saw the signs of a cultural shift, a whole new mode of fashionable consumption and preoccupation.

"All the world's a stage," Jacques famously intoned in *As You Like It*, but the advent of the news media over the two ensuing centuries radically complicated
Shakespeare's formulation. By the late eighteenth century, all the world might make
its way onto the page too, whether in the form of foreign news or of London gossip, on a sheet of newsprint available for all the world to read. In the play's prologue
(worth a close read in class), David Garrick conjures up just such a world, where
readers savor print gossip as a kind of second theater; such an audience, he jokingly
suggests in defiance of the play's title, needs no further schooling in scandal. But
Sheridan, whom Garrick depicts as a combination Hercules and Quixote, bent on
slaying the "Hydra Scandal," plainly thought otherwise. One of the things that
makes the play at once so pleasurable and so teachable is the dexterity with which
Sheridan navigates, early and perceptively, a maze we now know well, marked by the
overlapping paths of gossip, entertainment, consumption, commerce, and desire.
What kind of audience, he asks by way of comedy, do our gossip and our media
make of us, and what kind of audience might we aspire to become?

Sheridan knew more intimately than most the workings of the new gossip enterprise. His father was a famous actor, his mother a well-known novelist and playwright. A few years before *School* capped off his first season as manager at Drury
Lane, the newspapers had made much of Sheridan's elopement with a young
woman who had been previously betrothed to a much older man, and of his two
half-farcical duels with a rival suitor (her earlier betrothal had even been transformed into a successful comedy, *The Maid at Bath*, by Samuel Foote). Sheridan in-
corporated elements of these experiences in both of the two linked but separate
manuscript sketches that eventually took shape as the *School for Scandal*. In "The
Slanderers," a group of gossips convenes to mock and plot; in "Sir Peter Teazle" a
middle-aged man newly and ruefully married does combat with his young, defiant
country wife. (Both manuscripts are reproduced and transcribed in Bruce
Redford's *The Origins of the School for Scandal* [Princeton UP, 1986] which can serve
as sourcebook for some terrific assignments: what was the playwright striving for
as he rewrote these early sketches into the scenes we know now?) Soon enough,
Sheridan worked out a way to make the two parts mesh.

He begins with the slanderers, and the best route into his opening scene is to savor the buzz and the sting of it, the malicious pleasure that the characters take in their own machinations, and the more complex pleasure, at once satirical and collusive, that Sheridan invites us to take in observing them. Snake and Lady Sneerwell relish scandalmongering as a mode of art, almost a form of painting, that requires "coloring," "outline," "delicacy," "mellowness." Sheridan, in turn, analyzes the art, anatomizing the different techniques and brushstrokes the slanderers deploy. Students may enjoy following suit, cataloging (by way of an initial assignment or opening question) all the different tactics on display: the planting of paragraphs, the circulating of rumors, the propagation of errors (in Crabtree's game of eighteenth-century "telephone" concerning the Nova Scotia sheep), the protestation against gossip as a cover for purveying gossip (this is Mrs. Candour's specialty), the profession of sympathy (this is Joseph's) for the very victim one is currently skewering. Sheridan works the customary satirist's double play of exaggerating bad behavior in such a way as to allow the audience both identification and self-distancing: we've been bad this way ourselves, but surely not *this* bad (or have we?). Still, by placing the slanderers first in the play, he partly cultivates our alliance with them. We depend on their gossip for exposition—for the story of Charles, Maria, Sir Peter and the rest on which the play will turn. Even while anatomizing the tactics of tattle, Sheridan addicts us to their operations.

After this initial helping of scandal, all characters in the play will be gauged in part by their involvement with, and distance from, Lady Sneerwell's circle. Maria, in the first scene, gains the first exemption. Her few lines and her hasty exit show her critical of the school's machination, but helpless in the face of them. (Sheridan conspicuously pares back her role throughout the play; the actress was new, and to his mind unimpressive). By a strategy of staging at the start of the second scene, Sheridan confers on Sir Peter a subtler distance from the pack. Peter first appears alone (not in conference with co-conspirators), baffled by his own predicament but incapable of self-criticism, and possessed by a genuine if troubling emotion: the love he asserts, at soliloquy's end, for his recalcitrant new wife. Sheridan writes into the role a shifting mix of comedy and sympathy, and different students will differently reckon up the proportions. Peter is (as his wife well knows) deeply invested in the illusion of his own "authority," but is also awakening (as the audience learns) to other priorities: "how pleasingly she shows her contempt of my authority," he remarks once she's left. To what extent does the investment make him preposterous, the awakening appealing?

In Lady Teazle, the country wife newly enamored of town ways, Sheridan embodies the most ambivalent response to the Scandal School, and the one that the audience may most recognize as its own. Lady Teazle is both drawn to the group and at least incipiently wary of it. Sheridan sequences the scenes so as first to show Sir Peter and Lady Teazle in short, sharp combat with each other (2.1) and then to move them quickly into Sneerwell's circle (2.2), where the conflict unfolds in a larger world and a longer scene. Like Maria earlier, Sir Peter tries to confront the slanderers; he proves more vociferous than she but no more effectual, and (again like Maria) departs in haste, leaving his wife and (as he jokes) his reputation behind. In Lady Teazle's lingering, the School would seem to have scored a palpable hit, but Sheridan takes pains to deflect it. When Lady Teazle confronts her would-be seducer Joseph Surface, she makes clear that while she has some taste for scandalous talk, she has none for scandalous (sexual) practice. She remains, alert and clever, on the cusp.

Joseph forms half of the other most expressive pairing in the comedy. In tandem with his brother Charles, he plays out Sheridan's mixed response to the theory of moral sentiment. Throughout its elaborations by thinkers from the Earl of Shaftesbury to Adam Smith, the fundamental proposition remained simple. Doing good *feels* good; the best criteria for evaluating actions are the feelings that prompt them, and the feelings they produce. It followed, by extension, that generous impulses might constitute a kind of virtuous action in themselves. In plays, novels, and treatises, writers had long explored the idea's potential as a source of beneficence and of self-absorption (sentimentalists being apt to congratulate themselves on the pure intensity of their own emotions). Sheridan recasts both possibilities as a kind of fraternal binary. Joseph compulsively spouts "sentiments" in the old root sense of the word: high moral sentences, generalizations about proper feeling, to which (as his condemnatory surname implies) he adheres not at all in practice. (It is one of Sir Peter's saving graces that, though he falls for Joseph's sentimental act hook, line, and sinker, he cannot quite bring himself to replicate it. In the very first and very last lines of his first scene [1.2], he attempts to launch a Joseph-like generalization, but promptly gives it up as a bad job.) Charles, by contrast, acts on the genuine feelings themselves, free of their verbal formulation. The propensity first appears at his drinking-party (3.3), a mid-play counterpart (all festivity and no cunning) to the Sneerwell circle, and culminates in the auction scene (4.1), where affinities of fellow feeling abound and prevail. At the comic climax of that scene, where Charles decides *not* to sell the portrait of his beneficent Uncle Oliver at any price, Sheridan clinches his point visually and theatrically. Uncle Oliver's good nature is at this point doubly concealed, by his present disguise as Mr. Premium, and by the "stern" expression of the portrait that belies his benevolence. Yet Charles's intrinsic good nature responds to Oliver's despite all these barriers, and so secures his inheritance ("The rogue's my nephew after all!"). As Frank Ellis points out in his book *Sentimental Comedy* (Cambridge UP, 1991), one of the things that sentimentalists most often sentimentalized was money. Fellow feeling trumps monetary desire (Charles will not sell the picture), and thereby garners monetary rewards (Charles is set for life). "Knock 'em down," cries the auctioneer as he sells off the other pictures, but at scene's end what have really been knocked down are the barriers of reputation and appearance so useful to the Sneerwell circle, and so inimical to the affinities that Charles and Oliver discover by the mysterious operations of sentiment.

The auctioneer's key phrase proves prophetic of both the play's structure and its performance history. The *School for Scandal* climaxes in a subsequent knock-down—the falling of the screen in Joseph's library (4.3)—that by all accounts nearly brought the house down too. The audience response on opening night was such that one boy, passing the playhouse at the crucial moment, believed in terror that the edifice was actually collapsing, and discovered only "the next morning that the noise did not arise from the *falling* of the house, but from the *falling* of the screen in the fourth act; so violent and so tumultuous were the applause and laughter" (Frederic Reynolds, *The Life and Times of Frederic Reynolds* [London, 1826], 1.110).

What accounted for all this tumult? Perhaps it was the quick ricochet of revelation, in one of the best-managed moments of recognition in all comedy: Charles's and Peter's twinned reactions, ending in opposite adjectives ("Lady Teazle, by all that's wonderful/horrible"); Joseph's protracted silence, followed by convulsive, ineffectual self-defense. (Silence, specified in the stage directons, matters hugely to the scene's success, making room not only for the "applause and laughter" but for Charles's acute and almost tender interrogation of the other three, who stand stock still.) The core of the scene's power, though, lies not in any of these three characters but in the two parties at opposite ends of the revelatory spectrum: Lady Teazle and the audience, now freshly linked by Sheridan's stagecraft. During her time behind the screen, Lady Teazle has become an audience too, in fact pure auditor (all ears, no eyes). She has heard things—about Peter's warmth, and Joseph's coldness—that the audience has long understood. At the fall of the screen, the audience can laugh at the stupefaction of the stage witnesses, but can savor what those onstage are too surprised to contemplate: Lady Teazle's self-recognition, her sorting-through of the delusions she's done with and her working-out of how to proceed from here. Sheridan stages things so that we suddenly see her at a moment when she is suddenly seeing herself; during the ensuing dialogue he deftly gives her reaction considerable time to develop.

Such is one reading, in any case. The scene allows for several interpretations, and students will likely discover a variance among their own responses. Lady Teazle, for example, has overheard Sir Peter devising generous and unconditional bequests for her; are her motives for reform then more mercenary than emotional? (Again, money is being sentimentalized, but which exerts the stronger tug, the money or the sentiment?) The scene is worth plenty of class time, perhaps an entire session, commencing with the pivotal moment (and the anecdotes of its success) and opening out onto the ingenuities by which Sheridan leads up to and away from the pivot. Much of the pleasure beforehand consists in watching Joseph construct his own trap in a series of encounters with characters more authentic and estimable than himself, working hard against the effects of Lady Teazle's crackling retorts, Sir Peter's newly self-critical self-revelations, Charles's confident and rather wide-eyed banter. Sheridan makes props work hard too. Joseph arranges the screen, at the scene's start, to block a window; here as always he is energetic in pursuit of opacity. But in the end, the screen becomes a medium of transparency, a means of seeing-through ("you make even your screen a source of knowledge," Peter remarks, in one of the scene's exquisite little self-prophecies). Sheridan sustains the motif of enclosures and openings into the later reconciliation scene (5.2), where Peter approaches his wife through a door she has deliberately left open.

In *School* as in many comedies, the moment of recognition breaks a spell for audience as well as characters. We spend almost all of Act 5 in the company of the Scandal School, but find no trace of our earlier expository dependence on them.

They are in the wrong and we are in the know, because we have witnessed the events that they now elaborate into preposterous fiction. Sheridan here sends up the fuss the newspapers made of his own amorous activities and abortive duels, but he makes a larger point too, about the medium he works in and the media that compete with it. Gossip, whether spoken or in print, depends on absence; we purvey malicious news, and contrive malicious fictions, only when the person under scrutiny is safely elsewhere. Theater, by contrast, insists on presence. We *saw* the screen scene, and Lady Sneerwell's ignorant clique did not. Simply by entering the room, Peter explodes their fantasy that he's near death ("Egad . . . this is the most sudden recovery!"). At a moment when the *Town and Country Magazine* and many other venues proffer a kind of secondary theater in which readers can titillate themselves with narratives only putatively true, Sheridan makes an argument for the primacy of the playhouse, for the pleasures of an audience rendered healthy and acute by the privileges of witness rather than the dependency of report.

The *School for Scandal* teaches wonderfully well alongside *The Country Wife*. In fact, that pair of plays (with perhaps *The Beggar's Opera* wedged between) offers one solution to the recurrent problem of how one might cram the Restoration and eighteenth century into a few tight weeks towards the end of a first semester survey. In themselves, and in their contrast with each other, Wycherley's and Sheridan's comedies can epitomize for students, in a few class sessions, many of the most striking and important cultural developments in the period. As the headnote to *School* remarks, Sheridan began his career as theatrical manager by reviving and revising Restoration comedies. The contrast with Wycherley a century earlier can suggest much about his art and about the different audience it was aimed at.

One of the chief changes during the intervening decade centered on the reckoning of the rake. The components that mingled so confusingly in a libertine like Horner—wit, self-possession, rapacity, malice—had long since been tempered and redistributed in response to new audiences, mercantile rather than aristocratic, that saw themselves as valuing politeness over predation. (A short account of these new audiences appears in the Introduction's section on "Money, Manners, and Theatrics"; a few of the rake's mutations can be traced in the selections by Behn, Rochester, Steele, Gay, and Boswell; brilliant fuller accounts of rakes and audiences can be found in Laura Brown's *English Dramatic Form, 1660–1760* [Yale UP, 1981] and Richard Braverman's *Plots and Counterplots* [Cambridge UP, 1993].) In various ways, the Restoration rake had been rendered nearly innocuous (by the mid-eighteenth-century, revivals and revisals of the *Country Wife* had completely dropped Horner from the proceedings). Charles, designated "that libertine" (1.1), turns out to be, by Restoration standards, no such thing; his imprudence with money seems mostly the consequence of compulsive generosity, and he is obsessively devoted to the ingenue Maria. Joseph, ostensibly the play's secret libertine, barely fills the bill himself. He takes cover behind false sentiment as Horner did behind false impotence, but where Horner's disguise was at odds with his priapic essence, Joseph's fits him almost like a second skin. He is so cold at core that even Sir Peter rejoices, momentarily, to suspect that this seeming milquetoast has acquired a mistress. Details of structure help highlight the contrast. In the notorious china scene of Wycherley's fourth act, Horner consummates adultery energetically and audibly behind a locked door. In Sheridan's fourth act, the obstacle is flimsier, the consequences less drastic: the screen comes down, Lady Teazle stands alone and uncorrupted, and Joseph's scheming is exposed. Sheridan recovers the wit of Restoration comedy while annulling some of its dangers.

Perhaps the best payoff for comparing these comedies comes from the contrast between the two country wives. Margery Pinchwife is the naïf in her play; Lady Teazle (strikingly enough) is the wit in hers. In scene after scene, Sheridan shows her trumping everyone she talks to (2.1, 2.2, 3.1, and especially 4.1, where she atomizes Joseph's logic of seduction: "so . . . I must sin in my own defense, and part with my virtue to preserve my reputation?"). Margery Pinchwife at her writing table, Lady Teazle behind the screen, both undergo fourth-act awakenings out of an old way of life into a new. They move, of course, in opposite directions: the one towards adultery, and the other towards fidelity. (One of the most striking moments in the screen scene comes when Lady Teazle momentarily renounces her quick wit for hard truth, in the pointed plainness of her first line after the screen falls: "For not one word of it, Sir Peter.")

Margery's unmasking in the *Country Wife*'s final moments produces that comedy's unprecedented, unresolved sense of closing crisis, as the other characters move in to shut the woman up while her husband begins to reckon with the burden of knowledge (about Horner, about cuckoldry) that no one else on stage will willingly accept. Lady Teazle's umasking, by contrast, produces resolution, neutralizing the Scandal School and affirming marital happiness. Students will differ as to both the actual and the intended impacts of these two denouements. By what means, and to what ends, does Sheridan tease redemption out of a situation so comparable at some points with Wycherley's darker structures and strictures? And did Sheridan's audience really *want* to swallow his affirmations whole? Colman's brilliant epilogue to the play suggests otherwise, as Lady Teazle conjures up her future confinement in country life ("With dogs, cats, rats, and squalling brats surrounded") and echoes Othello's lament for his lost powers and pleasures. Colman's epilogue bears comparison with Wycherley's, where Lady Fidget confidently punctures male self-delusion and wittily asserts female discernment.

Finally, as a way of reckoning up all the energies, affinities, and oppositions between these two comedies, students may want to look once more at Reynolds's portrait (Plate 23) of Frances Abington in the role of another would-be country wife, Congreve's Miss Prue. The painting adumbrates, a few years in advance, the mix of elegance and audacity, wonder and defiance, male gaze and female retort, that would help make Lady Teazle the definitive role of Abington's career and the *School for Scandal* the crowning achievement of Sheridan's. In both the portrait and the play, the late eighteenth century revisits its Restoration origins, and remakes them in its own self-pleasing image.

The Romantics and Their Contemporaries

Anna Letitia Barbauld

Note in several of the selections the combination of an easy, even comic, tone with graver issues: in *The Mouse's Petition*, "liberty" and "freedom," charged terms in the era (see Perspectives: The Rights of Man and the Revolution Controversy), and the contrast in *Washing-Day* between the subject of the "domestic Muse" and the formal invocations ("Come, Muse"), Latinate diction ("impervious," "propitious"), and mythological and historical allusion ("Erebus," "Guatimozin"). One might compare the memory of the childhood self that emerges in this context (58 ff.) with Wordsworth's *Tintern Abbey*. One might also ask students to compare Barbauld's picture of, and distance from, "red-armed washers" (l. 14) with Wordsworth's positioning of himself *vis-à-vis* those of a lower social class whom he encounters and the class considerations in the works included in Perspectives: The Rights of Man and the Revolution Controversy. Barbauld's ameliorative view of the poor in *To the Poor* and at the close of *The First Fire*, in which she invokes the "assist[ance]" of "ye / On whose warm roofs the sun of plenty shines" so that they may "feel a glow beyond material fire" (ll. 79–81), as eighteenth-century sympathetic moralists urged, should likewise be compared to the social restructurings urged by the authors in that section and in Perspectives: The Wollstonecraft Controversy and the Rights of Women. *Inscription for an Ice-House* similarly juxtaposes tones and genres: playing "fair Pleasure" against "the giant" stern Winter, and asking the reader to see in the lightest delicacies (the frozen berries and "sugared hail") the sublime power that has produced them. The lofty couplets of *Eighteen Hundred and Eleven* mix panorama and prophecy, personifications ("Luxury" and "Want") with a roll-call of the heroes of the liberal Whig tradition (Locke, Milton, Clarkson, Fox, Priestley). Barbauld patriotically declares her love for her country (67) and attacks its current policies. The eighteenth century had hailed "Commerce" (62, 228, 273) as the engine of wealth and the nurse of manners, but feared that as oppressive empire replaced free trade, decadence and retribution were inevitable. Barbauld envisions a Britain that is the latest example of this cycle of self-corrupting success (205–320); her poem is at once a review of the progress of Liberty to the New World and a warning of Britain's decline. The imaginative projection into a future in which "wanderers" from the New World, the new seat of Liberty, inspired by Britain's past glories, will view contemporary Britain, mart and metropolis of the globe, as "gray ruin and . . . mouldering stone" (124), produces a startling double vision that, as Croker's review confirms, could only offend those for whom resistance to Napoleon (4) mandated uncritical praise of Britain. Barbauld's view of the misery that Empire has brought London (316–20) can be compared to Blake's *London* and her impersonal manner to the self-portrayal that grounds Byron's development of similar themes in *Childe Harold's Pilgrimage*.

Barbauld builds *On the Death of the Princess Charlotte* on the surprising shift from the moment of general mourning to the King who cannot feel, whose insensitivity is a death-in-life that uncannily repeats with even greater poignancy the death that overtook his grand-daughter. The image of the King as a "scathed oak" (l. 26) draws on a long tradition that identified the monarchy with that tree. In his *Reflections* Burke, for example, had scornfully dismissed the insignificance of the Revolution Society and their fellow radicals:

> Because half a dozen grasshoppers under a fern make the field ring with their importunate chink, whilst thousands of great cattle, reposed beneath the shadow of the British oak, chew the cud and are silent, pray do not imagine that those who make the noise are the only inhabitants of the field; that, of course, they are many in number, or that, after all, they are other than the little, shrivelled, meager, hopping, though loud and troublesome, insects of the hour. (Unprinted here)

Barbauld gets full value from the contrast between the fixed tree and the signs of "time's incessant change": "leaves bud, and shoot, and fall" (ll. 29, 27), an image that plays against the death of the Princess and her stillborn child. See also the remarks on the poem in this manual (Perspectives: The Sublime, the Beautiful, and the Picturesque, p. 297).

Charlotte Turner Smith

Although Smith's two long poems, *The Emigrants* (1793) and *Beachy Head* (posthumous), are returning to critical attention today, we have focused our selection on Smith's sonnets for two reasons. First, there is the rationale of the Romantic era: these are the poems, collected in *Elegiac Sonnets* in all their performative pathos and intertextual display, that brought Smith to public attention in the 1780s, and continued to play well for decades after, influencing Wordsworth and Coleridge, and then Keats and Shelley, as well as setting an example for many women poets, most remarkably Mary Robinson. Smith defined the female poet as a kind of torch singer, whose theatrical melancholy created the readers and commercial success by which she was to be enjoyed. Second, there is a pedagogical appeal: sonnets are quite teachable, in their compactness and in relation to sonnet traditions.

Smith is both working within and reworking the conventions of sonnet-writing. *To Tranquillity* and *To Melancholy* use Petrarchan structure, both in the rhyme pattern and the strong turn (or *volta*) at line 9. *Far on the Sands* is Shakespearean, with the intricacy of the *d* rhyme in the second quatrain (*glows/repose*) echoing the *b* rhyme of the first (*flow/blow*), and the final couplet plays a standard Shakespearean off-rhyme (*prove/love*) that here might reflect the way love never really gets partnered, but remains alone—alone, too as, an extra iambic foot (in the alexandrine last line). Yet in the structure of thought, the second movement, the questions inaugurated by *Alas!* seem almost to accelerate a Petrarchan pattern at line 7, as if Smith could not wait for the conventionally allotted time to announce her pain, but wanted to interrupt her second quatrain to do so. *Written in the church-yard* works Shakespearean patterning, with an even tighter closing couplet, and a nicely interlaced second and third quatrain (see the first 8 lines of *On being cautioned* for another instance of interlacing). But the form as a whole is dilated by a long footnote (Smith's) that is part of the poem's paratext. *To the Shade of Burns* is more dazzling still (ask students to trace the rhyme pattern and the units of argument: where is the volta?). No less impressive is *The Sea View*, where in a pattern of interlaced rhymes, the first sentence drives a steadily more sinister drama of description right into the middle of line 12, followed by two short declarative sentences, linked by a couplet rhyme and the spoil of the last line extended further with the alexandrine measure. Notice here, too, the paratext of Smith's note.

The accumulating story of melancholy and world-weariness can be studied not only across Smith's sonnet-sequence, but also in a comparison of Smith's representations of these themes and their emblematic images to other poets': *To Melancholy* with Coleridge's *Dejection Ode*, Wordsworth's *Resolution and Independence*, and Keats's *Ode on Melancholy*; *Far on the sands* with Wordsworth's '*Tis a Beauteous Evening* (also a sonnet on the beachside) and Smith's announced intertext, the dialogue from *Macbeth* (is Smith giving a tragic dimension to her moods?). *To the Shade of Burns* and *The Sea View* show Smith turning her melancholy outward into political commentary and protest, on the model of Milton. The loss of Burns occasions elegy, but also political anger. Students may not realize how difficult it was to champion "Liberty" when this term, with its capital L, was taken to indicate support for the principles of the French Revolution; and to lament a world at war in the years when England was at war with France risked, no less then than now, seeming anti-patriotic. *The Dead Beggar* is also political poetry, here satirically noting that in death the democratic principles of the revolution will be fulfilled; Death is the great leveler. Smith's address to "a Lady" is not just a woman speaking to a woman, but one woman fallen from her former luxury (Smith) speaking to a woman whose title "Lady" designates a member of the gentry. Is this a poem of religious consolation? To what degree is the language of religious consolation also carrying a political critique? Compare to William Wordsworth's various beggars (the veteran soldier, the beggar in London), Dorothy Wordsworth's encounters with beggars, Robinson's *The Old Beggar*.

The selection from the end of *Beachy Head*, an example of Smith's much admired mastery of blank verse (also the measure of her two-book mini-epic, *The Emigrants*), reflects a theme in other Romantic-era writing: the lonely recluse still bearing a human heart. Students might study this selection alongside Wordsworth's *Michael*, to study these figures of human sympathy and their acute "reading" of the world of nature.

The Rights of Man and the Revolution Controversy

These excerpts make up a debate that is carried as much by the level of style as by disagreement over the key terms of nature, reason, and rights. The content does not always align neatly with the manner; students can be asked to consider the tensions between points made in the texts and the implicit assumptions about the audience of the texts.

Note **Williams's** attempt to balance her enthusiastic faith in the Revolution with her revulsion at the execution of the king. Her insistence that despite the outcome "the foundation was laid in wisdom" can be set against **Burke's** *Reflections*: her defense of "Principles . . . however unsuccessful may be the attempt to carry them into practice" should be played against his argument for judging practices rather than illusory principle. Williams's response to the successive phases of the Revolution can be paired with Books 9 and 10 of Wordsworth's *The Prelude*.

For Burke the Revolution is a "monstrous tragic-comic scene" that simultaneously violates the hierarchy of society and the order of genres. The section "Liberties as an Entailed Inheritance" illustrates the elevated language that Burke believed appropriate to the conduct of politics, and its endorsement of the seeming paradox of a "choice of inheritance" ("choice" introduces will into the tropes of organism and family Burke also employs), in which rights are defined as traditional and conventional rather than as the conclusions of abstract reason, memorably focused the debate. His opponents charged that in choosing "the freedom of epistolary composition" (*Reflections* is cast as a letter to a young Frenchman) and elevating feeling over reason, Burke epitomized the hysteria he ascribed to the Revolutionaries. The portrait of Marie Antoinette, saturated with echoes of *Othello*, aroused the scorn of **Wollstonecraft** and **Paine**: their replies sharpen the questions of literary representation (narrative, rhetorical style, scene-painting) inseparable from the debate. Invoking the model of tragedy, Burke defends artifice as appropriate to represent the natural and the true, as before he insisted that it is the "wardrobe," the clothing of "pleasing illusions" that makes men civilized. (Consider the tropes of architecture in the various writers.) Wollstonecraft attacks this rhetoric of elaboration as the symptom of "pampered sensibility"; her "sober" style enforces the distinction between appeals to reason and to passion. She develops the ethos of a plain speaker, countering Burke with specific challenges to his general formulations ("What do you mean by inbred sentiments?") and economic instances ("Why cannot large estates be divided into small farms?"), insisting on the actual "continual miseries" Burke's system perpetuates.

The appeal to a seemingly neutral observation of "fact" and the evidence of individual observation to arouse sympathy for the Revolution may be seen in Young's *Travels in France*, as with Williams. Yet note that despite Young's critique of the absence of papers and political discussion in France, his own (not cheap) work and implied audience suggest the confining of political discussion to men of property. His readers are more like Burke's than like Paine's, and as *The Example of France* demonstrates, the advance of the Revolution from the reform that Young welcomed to the specter of a universal attack on property hardened class lines. His responses to France and the trajectory of his politics offer a telling parallel to Wordsworth's narrative in Books 9 and 10 of *The Prelude*.

Paine's plain style is yet more democratic in its intended audience than Wollstonecraft's or Young's; the accessibility marks the expansion of political discussion beyond men of property and leisure. Paine's insistence that "Man has no property in man: neither has any generation in the generations which are to follow" epitomizes the break with the continuity of history that Burke affirms; in place of the historical process of English liberty, Paine returns to the "origin" of the rights of man at the creation: "Here our inquiries find a resting-place, and our reason finds a home." Burke sees history as an accumulation of meaning, Paine as an encrustation that must be stripped away, but note that his demystification requires an anchor that is more mythological, less demonstrable, than the particular documents Burke invokes. Likewise, if Paine charges that Burke has become "a composition of art," his climactic sentence brilliantly deploys parallelism, assonance, and alliteration: "the real prisoner of misery, sliding into death in the silence of a dungeon." The conflict is not between "the real" and the rhetorical, but between two forms of rhetoric.

The conjunction of Paine and **Godwin** illustrates the shifting relations among thinkers classed as radical. Paine's espousal of the "universal" truths of reason accords with Godwin, but whereas *The Rights of Man* was written in a plain style and cheaply disseminated, Godwin's *Political Justice* was published in an expensive format and addressed to an audience of intellectuals more elite than Burke's. The notorious thought experiment in which Godwin argued for saving the reputedly great public benefactor rather than one's own family member or particular friend, like his critique of marriage, abolishes the claims of the individual that Paine and Wollstonecraft urge. The contrast with Burke's affirmation of what he called (in passages not printed here) "just prejudice" and the legitimate claims of "the little platoon" to which we are allied by experience could scarcely be clearer. Moreover, Godwin's objection to "inflaming" the people rather than "informing" them and his patient faith in "sober thought, clear discernment and intrepid discussion" led to quietism rather than revolution.

Such cross-currents resonate with the poets. Some examples to consider: to what degree is Wordsworth's "nature" co-ordinate with history, as in Burke, and to what degree opposed? To what degree does the simplicity of Wordsworth's language align him with the radicals? and his cherishing of local domestic affections with Burke? Burke's evocation of chivalry underlies the medievalising *Childe Harold's Pilgrimage*, but how does Burke's corporate, traditional sensibility accord with the radically personal effect of Byron? The *Anti-Jacobin* parody of Southey repeats the opposition of the delusions of speculative philanthropy (Burke's charge against the Revolutionaries) versus particular action. Note that the debate hinges on shifting notions of particular and general: Burke charges that those who derive rights from universal reason indulge in fantasy and insists that systems can be judged only by results; the radicals urge against him the reality of misery that his system produces; here the conservative parodist invokes a particular instance against the ideological preconceptions of the speaker. The parody can usefully be set against Wordsworth's poems (for example, *The Solitary Reaper*): how much does imagination depend on suppressing the voice of the other, here permitted to speak? To what degree is imagination a speculative and self-congratulatory sympathy divorced from engagement and action?

More's *Village Politics* has been called "Burke for Beginners," but the social situation of the pamphlet is complex. Burke wrote for the literate and well-off; More's work acknowledges that in times of crisis political discourse had to address the lower class—Burke's ideas in Paine's style, as it were. The dialogue reveals itself as loyalist catechism when Jack tendentiously redefines Tom's radical terms one by one: liberty, democrat, equality, and so forth, finally reducing them to "gibberish." More's use of catechism may be set against such Blake poems as *The Lamb*, and her use of the dialogue form against *The Marriage of Heaven and Hell*: what response does each hope to arouse in the reader? Her effort at common speech may be compared with his *Songs* generally (as well as the much-mocked simplicity of Wordsworth's "real language of men"). More's pious conservatism contrasts Blake's liberatory religion, but students might be asked to weigh the restricted availability of his handmade, expensive works with the cheap broadcast of hers. Though faced with the problems that arise when one class presumes to speak for another, More dramatizes the characters and idioms of the lower orders whose independence she opposes. If More did not teach the poor writing for fear of its insurrectionary potential, and her character Tom learns that he is unhappy only through reading, her tract assumes and perpetuates the spread of debate she wishes to stop.

William Blake

Note how *All Religions Are One* uses the form of logic to argue for a poetic genius that transcends empiricism and "experience," and *There Is No Natural Religion* counters the Deist rational/empirical propositions of (a) in their own form with (b). One might compare Blake's "Reason is the ratio of all we have already known," associated with the "bound," to the honorific sense of Reason in Paine, Wollstonecraft, and Godwin. The missing plate iii creates, whether intended or not, a crucial upsetting of linearity. The revolution for Blake will not proceed from reason, rights, and the stripping away of tradition, but from creative perception and desire. This emphasis might also be posed against the suspicion of desire in Wollstonecraft's *Vindication of the Rights of Woman*.

The illuminated books raise several important questions. These expensive, hand-produced, limited editions may be compared with popular caricatures such as Gillray's *Smelling Out A Rat* and Cruikshank's illustrations for Hone. The relationships between text and plate require the beholder both to read sequentially and view the design as a whole, thus escaping from what Blake elsewhere called the tyranny of "single vision and Newton's sleep," a linear, materialist perception of the world. Moreover, sometimes word and image support each other, and sometimes diverge, as in the portrait of the unthreatening Tyger, so that reading becomes a complex interpretative challenge rather than the smooth, uniform, reception of argument sought by the wielders of the plain style. Because each copy was unique, and available only from Blake, reading became an individual encounter with the artist. Compared to the purchase of a mass-produced book, the form thus suggests a radical enfranchising of individual perception; but to consider the tensions between the liberatory content of *The Marriage of Heaven and Hell* and the mode of production, which restricted availability to the few, is to trigger a fruitful exploration of the terms "radical" and "democratic" in the period.

Much of the discussion of *Songs of Innocence* has turned on the possible ironies of the speaker's voice. Although the poems reflect contemporary interest in children's literature, and are written in simple forms with simple, traditional language, their world is not limited to that of children. The speaker of *The Lamb* is sufficiently instructed to know that Christ is Agnus Dei, the Lamb of God. The last line of *The Chimney Sweeper*—"so if all do their duty they need not fear harm"—reflects the consolatory pieties of its child speaker, but can also generate a wider understanding that indicts those who expect the sweepers to do their duty while ignoring their own to the suffering poor. Likewise, *The Little Black Boy* may be seen as part of the humanitarian campaign against slavery, but also plays the awaited heavenly moment in which both children are "free" of color against the hint that the white child can love only one white like him, and the black boy's fears that he can be loved only if white. The plates play out the problem in varying the tint of "black." (See the color section.)

These instances suggest that even before Blake added *Songs of Experience* the poems of Innocence acknowledged the perspective of Experience; insofar as Innocence and Experience are the "contrary states of the human soul" they are both available at all times, rather than forming an irreversible progression. Blake's schema can thus be set against the dynamics of individual memory in such Wordsworth poems as *Tintern Abbey*. Once Blake had joined the two—and Experience was never available alone—he produced pairs (such as the two *Holy Thursday* poems or *The Lamb* and *The Tyger*) in which the latter work may alter the meanings of the former. When Blake produced the joined volume, he moved *The School-Boy* from *Songs of Innocence* to *Songs of Experience*. Students may want to ponder the logic of this recategorization as well as the intertextual thickening by other songs of "Experience."

Blake's world may be pointedly juxtaposed with Burke's: when to the repeated insistence on "charter'd" in *London*, as the term signalling constraint and limit just as it signals granted right and commercial opportunity, Blake adds the unfeeling Palace and Church he stigmatizes the network of institutional power that Burke lauded. Once unpacked by engaged readers, freed from the "mind-forg'd manacles" that led them to accept the social order as just or natural, the extreme metaphoric compression of the poem reveals a cityscape "marked" as the crystallization of an oppressive system. Its inclusive effects invade domestic relations, poisoning the infant's health with the diseases of prostitution. Blake's city, everywhere the product of historically specific conditions, may be compared with Wordsworth's *Composed upon Westminster Bridge*, where the beauty of the city depends on the suspension of the usual indices of urban activity, and his emblematic "Harlot" with the ambiguous social status of the subject of Wordsworth's *Poor Susan*, trapped in the city but precariously endowed with restorative memory.

Blake's linking of the social hierarchy to the relations between men and women is most visible in *Visions of the Daughters of Albion*, where Bromion figures both as a tyrant and the rapist of Oothon, whose lover Theotormon (literally, "god-tormented") is so enmeshed by conventional notions that he sees her as defiled by an action in which her will took no part. Neither man is capable of responding to the cry of innocent desire that characterizes her. The situation thus illustrates the convergence of the movements against slavery and for women's rights in the literature of the period, though Blake's emphasis on the body and desire distinguishes him from those who argue for women's equal intellectual capacity and status within marriage. The Proverbs of Hell in *The Marriage of Heaven and Hell*, where emphasis on excess, desire, and the body is reinforced by rejection of the Burkean terms of respect for the dead, prudence, and restraint, make Blake's antinomian impulses clear. But in this composite form, where the Proverbs mix with prophecy, dialogue, and satire, Blake does not simply invert the traditional associations of Good and Evil. As the declarations that "opposition is true friendship" and "without contraries is no progression" suggest, Blake rather sets in motion a continuing dialogue of competing perspectives. If, as he tells the Swedenborgian angel, "all that we saw was owing to your metaphysics," his own point of view too is that of a dramatic speaker within the text rather than a privileged authority outside its play of argument. The revisionary interpretation of *Paradise Lost*, the conversation with Old Testament prophets, and the allegory of cultural transmission figured in the sequence from visionary dragon-men and eagles to library shelves, all suggest the necessity for readers to question for themselves. The task of the *Marriage* is both to demystify, by the corrosive fires of satire that parallel the acid etching of Blake's printing, and to regenerate: cleansing the doors of perception is to set free the poetic genius of each reader. The intent of Blake's drama can be set against the didacticism of Hannah More's *Village Politics* and the implications of her wide dissemination weighed against the very few known copies of the *Marriage*.

PERSPECTIVES

The Abolition of Slavery and the Slave Trade

In 1771 James Somerset, a black slave from Virginia brought by his owner to England, refused to return. Lawyers for Somerset argued that "slavery is not a natural, 'tis a municipal relation, an institution therefore confined to certain places, and necessarily dropt by passage into a country where such municipal regulations do not exist." As one put it: "Will not all the other mischiefs of mere utter servitude revive, if once the idea of absolute property, under the immediate sanction of the laws of this country, extend itself to those who have been brought over to a soil whose air is deemed too pure for slaves to breathe in it [?]" In his ruling, William Murray, Earl of Mansfield, chief justice of the King's Bench Court, declared that "the state of slavery is of such a nature, that it is incapable of being introduced on any reasons, moral or political, but only positive law, which preserves its force long after the reasons, occasion, and time itself from whence it was created, is erased from memory: It's so odious, that nothing can be suffered to support it, but positive law. Whatever inconveniences, therefore, may follow from a decision, I cannot say that this case is allowed or approved by the law of England, and therefore the black must be discharged."

The ruling did not ban the slave trade, nor slavery in the colonies, but in freeing Somerset Mansfield sharpened the discrepancy between what Britain permitted at home and what it encouraged abroad. The distinction between "positive" or "municipal" law, that is to say man-made law, and "natural" law, resonates throughout the selections in this section, and with the other Perspectives sections: the claims of property as opposed to individual right, in "The Rights of Man and The Revolution Controversy", and the relation of men to women in "The Wollstonecraft Controversy and The Rights of Women". Consider how the language and ideas of of the Revolution controversy—liberty, freedom, tyranny, oppression—function in the abolitionist controversy, and how the abolitionists shift categories such as "savage," "brutal," "barbarous," "slave," "human," and "inhuman" from their conventional associations. Similarly, one might ask students to consider the ways in which the racist vocabulary of black, white, light, and sable gets spun, from skin to soul. (The link to Blake's Little Black Boy is obvious.) One might also study the biblical allusions and the rhetoric of Christian morality in the texts, available for advocates of either side of the question, as indicated by the convergence with the notion of "benevolence" in Bellamy; with him the parallel with the conflict between the Painite discourse of rights and the Burkean discourse of "natural" individual feeling is particularly suggestive. Against such moral arguments one can set the force of detail in Dorothy Wordsworth, the selection from The Edinburgh Review, and particularly in Clarkson's reports. The vocabulary of "seeing" and "beholding" to arouse sympathy is one tactic; the emphasis on the exemplary endurance and forbearance of the oppressed another. Newton's well-known hymn, students might be surprised to learn, was written by a former slave-trader turned evangelical Christian abolitionist. This is but one instance of the way the evils of the slave trade were felt to extend beyond the misery of the enslaved Africans to the moral corruption of their purchasers. In Cowper's The Negro's Complaint ("complaint," students may need to be told, does not indicate whining; it's a literary genre akin to "the blues"—of singing one's heart out, in pain, the "lover's complaint" being a standard Renaissance genre), at once indicts the "slaves of gold" (the purchasers, and, by implication the nations that support slave-trading and enjoy the goods and wealth produced by slave labor) and insists on the humanity of the enslaved. A standard dualism of a free mind and soul and a tortured body is politically motivated to make a case for a common moral and spiritual humanity. **Southey's** ballad, *The Sailor, Who Had Served,* is sometimes read as the historically situated version of Coleridge's *Rime of the Ancient Mariner.* Southey and Coleridge were brothers-in-law (both married to Fricker sisters); their poems were published the same year (1798), and begin in similar forms: a little explanatory headnote, similar first lines, and ballad stanzas. Like Coleridge's *Rime,* too, Southey's ballad makes the possibility of redemption questionable for a sailor so haunted. His sailor is forced into a kind of slavery himself aboard ship, turned into a "wretched" man by his forced torturing of a resistant slave, a "poor wretch." The memory of torture is lurid, horrifying the reader even as it conveys the horror by which the sailor is haunted. For one who feels as irredeemably damned as Milton's Satan (whom he echoes), the status of the conversion narrative at the ballad's close is debatable: it does stage a scene dear to abolitionists who have been converted from their former lives of sin, and in so doing allegorizes the desired conversion of sinning (even if unconsciously) citizenry. But the language of ministry is very sing-song, pat, and perhaps ultimately inadequate to the horrors it means to address. The constructions of the slaves by the abolitionists play against the voices of the ex-slaves themselves, **Equiano** and **Prince,** often within a single text; fables of patience and deliverance jostle against impulses of rebellion. The figure of the suffering woman is often exploited to focus outrage or pity: how does this work with or against the complex representation of women? Such tropes also point attention toward the common ground between the representation of women in the abolitionist literature and the poetry of sympathy generally, and the employment of slavery as analogy in the feminist critique of the marital relationship.

Mary Robinson

Poems such as *January, 1795, The Camp,* and *London's Summer Morning* remind us that within the Romantic period poems in couplets, filled with crisply observed social detail and wit, continued to be written. The urban pastoral of *London's Summer Morning* may be compared to Jonathan Swift's *A Description of the Morning* and *A Description of a City Shower* (in volume 1); the panoramic view and play with classical conventions can then be set against *Poor Susan* to underscore Wordsworth's focus on a single, lower-class consciousness. *Lyrical Tales,* an early response to *Lyrical Ballads,* shows the widespread interest in the poor and in unusual states of mind: comparison between Robinson's *The Old Beggar* and Wordsworth's *Old Man Travelling* discloses the differences between her emphasis on the scene, the sufferer, and the evoking of a sympathetic response, and his understated, cryptic handling of encounter. If *Lyrical Tales* suggests debt to Wordsworth and Coleridge, the indebtedness runs the other way with *Sappho and Phaon;* contemporary women poets (see also Charlotte Smith), and not alone his rereading of Milton's sonnets in 1802, showed Wordsworth the power of the compact form. Robinson's sequence endows the female protagonist with dignity and analytic power as well as passion, and combines the lyrical intensity of the single sonnet with narrative development.

Written just a few years after Wollstonecraft's *Vindication of the Rights of Woman*, this sonnet sequence, itself the display of a woman of learning and education, contests Wollstonecraft's conviction that women may call on "Reason" to thwart and discipline the chaos of destructive passions, especially the erotic passions. In the productive discipline of sonnet form, Robinson sets love in conflict with Reason, even addressing two sonnets, 7 and 11, to this capacity. In 7, the octave seems promising in its call; students can ably list the informing oppositions, but if they sense a desperation of tone, they will have anticipated the second act staged in the sestet, where the closing lines "dreary labyrinths of mental night" repeat rather than redeem "the wayward wand'rings of [the] mind," and itself seems phantasmic. Still, they may want to ask if the poem sounds reasonable in its argument, and whether it is reason or passion that is managing the intricate poetic form. Robinson's Critique of Reason (if that's not too formal a term) continues in the string of questions that evolve from 7 to emerge as the primary rhetoric of protest and complaint in 11. With this unresolved conflict and contradiction in mind, students will be prepared to address Wollstonecraft's ideology of "Reason" with some attention to how the biographical facts of Wollstonecraft's life and times (movie-of-the-week passions, political and personal) have driven her to this standard. At the same time, students may also see a rather seamless continuity between Wollstonecraft's critique of youthful physical beauty as the ephemeral measure of a woman's value and Robinson's earlier satirical *Ode to Beauty*, its sarcasm involving, as Wollstonecraft's would, the iconography of Milton's Eve, especially in the first stanza. The "fall" of Robinson's beauty is wrought not only by social corruptions (ill-nature, jealousy, slander, flattery, and so forth) but also by the mere, and devastating inevitability of aging.

To the Poet Coleridge possesses a great deal of contextual interest. Robinson's *Lyrical Tales* is an acknowledged response to *Lyrical Ballads*, but Robinson's fame was such that Wordsworth briefly considered altering the title of the second edition to "Poems by W. Wordsworth" to avoid the "great objection," as Dorothy Wordsworth put it, of confusion with a rival volume also published by Longman (Letter of 10-12 September 1800). In *To the Poet Coleridge* Robinson positions herself not merely as a member of the Coleridge circle, privy to Coleridge's unpublished poem (as those who also recognized the echoes would realize), but as the senior established poet, the SAPPHO who welcomes him, and "weave[s] a crown" for him (l. 51) to offset Coleridge's lost vision of an Abyssinian maid. In so doing Robinson converts the sublime aloneness of Coleridge's speaker into a social experience: "with thee I'll wander" (l. 2), "with thee I'll trace" (ll. 5 and 27), "With thee . . . I'll listen" (ll. 29-30). The sympathy that marks the action extends also to the form of the poem: Robinson adroitly mimics the "meander" and "varying sounds" (l. 4, ll. 7 and 57) of Coleridge's poem, testimony to the compelling rhythm, the "wondrous witcheries of song" (l. 64), that gave Coleridge's "airy dreams a magic all [their] own" (l. 72) at a level beneath meaning. In claiming to be "wake[d] . . . in ecstatic measures" by Coleridge's nymph (l. 61)—and demonstrating by her verse that she has been—Robinson fulfills the role of the ideal Romantic reader, inspired by a poem to repeat the poet's imaginative act.

Mary Wollstonecraft

In calling for "a revolution in female manners," Wollstonecraft's *Vindication of the Rights of Woman*, published in 1792, extends the debate over rights provoked by the French Revolution to the private sphere of the relations between men and women—but her polemic is energized by the refusal to separate private from public in that fashion. Her figurative language repeatedly joins the treatment of women to the largest topics of the day—slavery, tyranny, injustice, power, rights—and proceeds in part by provocative rereadings of canonical writers, such as Milton, lauded (and condemned) radical ones, such as Rousseau, and the popular handbooks of female education. Her independence of mind emerges in her treatment of her two audiences: men, whom she would persuade to live up to their ideals by renouncing their illegitimate authority, and women, whom she satirizes, often harshly, in order to free them from complicity with the system of values which keeps them in subjection. A deceptively unflashy style thus serves a variety of rhetorical ends. Her work may be situated against several other texts: compare, for example, Wollstonecraft's specific critique of female education with the treatment of children in Blake (who knew and admired Wollstonecraft) and Wordsworth's visions of childhood in *There was a Boy* and *Three years she grew in sun and shower*. All these reflect the recent sense of the child as a particular stage of human development, shaped by environment, and hence improvable by changes in that environment, or, conversely, corrupted by experience rather than innately guilty. Wollstonecraft makes clear the contemporary gender demarcations of such social construction: one might ask students to consider what Wollstonecraft would have remarked about the social ideal of (girl) "Child," "Maiden's form," and "Lady" shaped in Wordsworth's *Three years*, and the implicit authority of the implicitly male narrator. Teasing out the relations between Lucy's education by "nature" and the actual education of young girls in eighteenth-century society that Wollstonecraft criticizes reveals the intellectual toughness of Wollstonecraft's dissenting tradition and the mythology of the private, inner life in Wordsworth's poetry. With Wollstonecraft as a triangulating third party, the differences between the childhood Wordsworth accords the Boy of Winander (in early drafts a first-person recollection) and that he gives to Lucy in *Three Years* emerge. How does the "natural" foundation for the education of the boy differ in its lessons from that for the girl? One might also compare Blake's sense of innocence as a precarious and vulnerable ignorance to Wollstonecraft's aspersions on "innocent" as a term of praise for girls or women, and her exposure of the cultural ideal of keeping women in a state of innocence, or a state analogous to childhood, as a covering for the self-serving male ideal of deferral to and blind dependence on male authority.

But Wollstonecraft is too forceful a writer to figure only in relation to her male contemporaries. Jemima's story, from her unfinished novel *Maria, or the Wrongs of Woman*, published posthumously by Godwin in 1798, demonstrates at once her powers of fiction and of polemic. Its strength grows from its belief in the representative case: Jemima, though a compelling voice, is not a unique creation, in the way later novelists excelled in the creation of individual, often idiosyncratic, characters. Rather she stands as the embodiment of conditions that Wollstonecraft presents as actual and typical. She speaks for herself, but of, and from, the social and material circumstances that have produced her. Her voice is the outcome of Wollstonecraft's compression: she is at once character and argument. Students might be asked to compare the sense of the social situatedness of the individual, in Jemima as in the *Vindication*, with the representation of character in other texts of the period.

The Wollstonecraft Controversy and the Rights of Women

Much of the material in the selections from *Vindication of the Rights of Woman* is literary or literary-critical in nature, inviting productive treatment in courses of literary study. Wollstonecraft frequently writes as a literary critic: she notes keywords of description, and demystifies their habituated meanings and values; with the pressures of protofeminist critique, she reads literature from *Paradise Lost*, to Rousseau's *Émile*, to Reverend Fordyce's and Dr. Gregory's advice manuals for young women, tracing out the informing and debatable ideologies of gender; she views cultural practices ("the prevailing opinion" and the systems of education that nurture it) as if these were structured and readable as a text, a system of language that might be illuminated and submitted to critical review. And across all these events, explicitly in *Maria*, she uses techniques of literary representation: characterizations and caricatures of deficient men and women, romances of idealized women, symbolic anecdotes and scenes, systems of metaphor and image, allusions to literary precedents from the Bible to contemporary poetry, all punctuate her polemic.

This textual emphasis is no less on display in the readings in this "Perspectives" section. **Macaulay** develops her argument for "No Characteristic Difference in Sex" (the document behind Wollstonecraft's chapter, "The Prevailing Opinion of a Sexual Character") with reference to the same text from Alexander Pope (*Epistle II*) that focuses Wollstonecraft's irritation. Like her, too, she finds Rousseau, Addison, and Chesterfield useful antagonists. Students may want to ponder the emergence of a "canon" of anti-feminist literature that comes to stand for the prevailing social text in these polemics, and compare the critiques developed of these influential works. **Barbauld's** explicitly allusive poem, *The Rights of Woman*, is motivated in part by personal anger over Wollstonecraft's criticism of her as a dismaying instance of a woman of sense writing poetry that is part of the problem. Like many male antagonists of women's rights, Barbauld "misreads" Wollstonecraft as promoting a battle of the sexes for superiority. In a parody of conduct book instruction, Barbauld cautions that the battle may be won, but at the price of love and affection, where powerplays must dissolve in mutual love. Students may want to consider the suspension of political contexts in this idealization, and whether a privacy of mutual affection is sufficient in a world of unequal rights and opportunities. The political woman is on **Southey's** mind, when he writes a sonnet urging Wollstonecraft not to be insulted by traditional terms of praise, and such figures (political and traditional) inform **Blake's** verses on *Mary* as a kind of Blakean twin, despised and slandered for her rebelliousness.

Polwhele's satire in Augustan couplets shows that Blake is not just being self-referential. His *Unsex'd Females* (unsexed by a lack of modesty; otherwise entirely too sexy) are monsters that defy fathers, nature, and even patriotic Englishness. Polwhele's voluminous footnotes may look daunting and unattractive to students, but urge them to have a look, because in many ways the diatribe Polwhele conducts here is just as important, and on the subject of Wollstonecraft quite nasty and virulent. As the development of his poem makes clear, not only Wollstonecraft but any woman of public opinion, including many in our anthology (Barbauld, Williams, Smith, Yearsley, Hays, and Robinson) is prime for whipping. Polwhele's hystericized but nonetheless credible (to conservative culture critics) polemic helps students see why the case for women's rights virtually died away for more than half a century, and why **Wheeler** and **Thompson's** tract was as risky as it was important when it appeared in the 1820s. The only cases possible by the end of the 18th century were twofold: more sensible education and respectable employment for women who had no other means of support. **Wakefield** cautiously positions her tract in behalf of the progress of Christian civilization and relies on almost novelistic scenes of abjection and dishonorable male usurpation of female opportunities to make her case. **Radcliffe** appeals to the values of Christian charity to argue for these opportunities for women, and like Wakefield relies on the techniques of novel-writing to paint scenes of abject misery. She also boldly invokes the parallel to slavery to describe women as "Christian slaves at home," and hazards the rhetorical gambit that these women are more miserable than actual slaves. Students who want to put differential pressure on the feminist analogues between female oppression and chattel slavery will not want to skip over Radcliffe's remarkable claims. **More's** *Strictures* may strike students as patently conservative not only in its positioning against Wollstonecraft's political argument but also in its insistence that women be educated on Christian principles of humility, patience, and service. Yet it is a sign of how ready even conservatives were for some changes that More shares with Wollstonecraft a critique of "sensibility" (a cultivation of emotional responsiveness) and the literary genres (especially the novel) that sustain it, and a desire for more rational education. One contradiction that More attempts to address is her own status as a woman (and a novelist, even) writing for the public sphere. **Lamb,** like More, was childless, unmarried, and a sometime author. Her essay on needlework takes up a female pastime that Wollstonecraft and other women regarded as mindnumbing, and in Lamb's case, so aggravating as to spark fits of madness. Lamb recognizes that some women depend on such work for a living, so that the culture of needlework as a pastime is doubly pernicious. Not framed as an abstract economic tract, however, Lamb's letter could almost be a draft for a chapter in a novel, setting a scene, populating it with characters, and unfolding the cultural and economic issues out of that fabric. Finally, Thompson and Wheeler offer a reprise not only of all these issues, but also of the techniques of literary representation. In their protomarxist document, they discuss female authorship, Wollstonecraft and Hays, the analogies of female oppression to slavery (the 1820s were a hot decade in the abolition movement), and deploy techniques of novel-writing to advance a case for women's rights that involves fundamental questions of political and social reform.

Joanna Baillie

Baillie's "Introductory Discourse" can be compared to Wordsworth's 1800 Preface to *Lyrical Ballads*, which it anticipates in its emphasis on the analysis of passion and unadorned style; one might then also contrast Baillie's manner of address to the reader with Wordsworth's edgy critique of current taste, and consider the effects of Wordsworth's connection of simplicity of language with the way of life of the north country small-holder. Baillie's poems can also be inserted into comparisons: her *London* with Wordsworth's sonnet, *Composed upon Westminster Bridge*, and Book 7 of *The Prelude*, or Blake's *London*, or Byron's account of Juan's approach to the city (*Don Juan*, 11), as instances of the poets' efforts to represent the unprecedented impact of the metropolis; the domesticity of *A Mother to Her Waking Infant* and *A Child to His Sick Grandfather* with the poems of childhood and age in Blake and Wordsworth. The vernacular of "Dad" in the latter, like the Scotticisms of *Woo'd and Married and A'*, shows the familiar end of Baillie's stylistic range, but *Thunder*, like her *London* (or Barbauld's *Inscription for an Ice-House*), demonstrates that the sublime was not closed to the woman writer.

Literary Ballads

The revival of interest in the Romantic poets in the 1960s, after the denigration of them by modernist poets and critics (such as T. S. Eliot) who elevated wit and the precise, dry image over what they saw as Romantic vagueness of emotion and loose-ness of form, was nurtured by a revaluation upwards of terms such as imagination, vision, and apocalypse. To an older literary history Romanticism sprang not from its affinities with the infinite and the inexpressible but with the folk, with tradi-tional communal life, and with elliptically understated narrative. Though ballad scholars divided between those who saw ballads as the product of the people and those who ascribed them to court minstrels, they agreed in emphasizing the con-trast between the cryptic, often vernacular style of the ballads and the polish of Augustan poetry. Instructors may wish to consider how the tangy native particu-lars of *Sir Patrick Spens* and *Lord Randal* play against the universal affirmations of the Enlightenment; tradition here seems counter to the abstract prescriptions of reason that fuelled the Revolution. These aristocratic stories differ from the em-phasis on peasant, or at any rate, traditional agricultural, life in Burns, which Wordsworth was also to emphasize in *Lyrical Ballads*. Here too an instructor may wish to play the democratizing implications of Burns's language and sentiments, and his cheerful bawdiness, against the conservative, stabilizing qualities of such regionalism. As Burns's familiarity with high-culture forms and language suggests, his earthiness was a sophisticated gambit, a choice of genre rather than the un-mediated transcription of experience: Wordsworth admired how Burns "avail[s] himself of his own character and situation of society, to construct out of them a poetic self." His lexicon may be placed against Wordsworth's "language really used by men," but "purified indeed from what appear to be its real defects, from all last-ing and rational causes of dislike or disgust," as the Preface to *Lyrical Ballads* puts it, and with Clare's dialect; likewise the range of experience he narrates against that of the Wordsworth known for "plain living and high thinking," to use his own words. Moore adapts the regional to the polite: Wordsworth confessed that Moore had "great natural genius," but complained that his "poems smell of the per-fumer's and milliner's shops. He is not content with a ring and a bracelet, but he must have rings in the ears, rings on the nose—rings everywhere."

William Wordsworth

Reviewing Wordsworth's *Descriptive Sketches* (1793), the radical Thomas Holcroft exclaimed: "More descriptive poetry! Have we not yet enough? Must eternal changes be rung on uplands and lowlands, and forests, and brooding clouds, and cells, and dells, and dingles? Yes; more, and yet more: so it is decreed." The debt to the picturesque tradition remained large in Wordsworth; his poetry may be seen to present as spontaneous personal experience what was already a highly codified, impersonal response to landscape (see the variant cited in the headnote to *Tintern Abbey*). Holcroft's exasperation points to an issue recently contested in Romantic studies. The instructor who has followed the suggestions of tensions in earlier en-tries in the manual may wish to ask students to consider whether Wordsworth's in-vocation of "nature" constitutes a withdrawal from the political issues of the pe-riod. By not including Tintern Abbey in the poem that bears its name, for example, Wordsworth avoids mentioning the beggars found there, noted in con-temporary guidebooks; the "smoke" (18) reads as an evocative detail, divorced from the poor charcoal-burners in the neighborhood; the "vagrant" (21) becomes a surmise, interchangeable with a "hermit" (22), rather than a victim of injustice asking redress. If the date in the title, one day before the anniversary of the fall of the Bastille and the eighth anniversary of Wordsworth's arrival in France (see *The Prelude* 6:339 ff.), suggests an allusion to the Revolution, contemporary violence and political disillusionment are distanced and generalized into the "still, sad music of humanity" (92). Likewise, the specific social ills Wordsworth enumerates in the letter to Fox accompanying *Michael* are not to be found in the poem, and the action is set in the past where intervention is no longer possible. To many these gestures have marked Wordsworth as a neo-conservative. Against this line of argu-ment the instructor can set the excerpt from Francis Jeffrey's comments on "the new poetry" as evidence of how subversive an intelligent contemporary found Wordsworth's power to unsettle conventional hierarchies, literary and social. The address to the reader in *Simon Lee*, placing the burden of understanding on his or her capacity for "silent thought" (74), urges a reformation in attitudes in a form that may be the most effective available after the reaction to Jacobin excess, not an abandonment of revolution but a change in strategy. Students may be asked to consider the contrast between the discourse of rights in Paine, for example, with the extensions of sympathy in *Simon Lee* (clinched by the surprise of "gratitude" instead of the stock "ingratitude") and *Old Man Travelling*, triangulating these against Burke's respect for tradition and feeling. Wordsworth's project of reforming the reader—a process not always pleasant to undergo, as the Preface declares, and analogous to the Christian pattern of the necessity of humbling pride in order to enable exaltation—thus substitutes the formation of the individual's power of silent, inward meditation for systematic social reform, and disguises its agenda by presenting it (as in *Expostulation and Reply* and *The Tables Turned*) as the mere outcome of the "nature" that Holcroft scorns, rather than as the abstract, conscious program of the rationalists that Burke lambasted. (Compare Burke's scorn of "sophists and calculators" with the insistence on counting of the narrator of *We Are Seven*.) *Tintern Abbey*, the final poem of the 1798 *Lyrical Ballads*, witnesses the new reflective sensibility.

The "experiment" of *Lyrical Ballads* thus challenges readers to become sensitive and skilled enough to fill in their gaps, understatements, and indirections. The difficulty of poems such as *A Slumber* or *Lucy Gray* does not arise from allusion to classical learning, but from an audacious minimalism and refusal to point to a moral or a conclusion; consequently, good reading depends not on high education, but on qualities of soul. The process is self-confirming: to be capable of reading Wordsworth is to have joined a new sort of elite, independent of class. Lamb's indignant reply to Wordsworth's pride in his union of "Tenderness and Imagination" makes clear the qualities the poet sought to form in his readers. As a term "lyrical ballads" had already pointed in two directions: toward the narrative of ballad and the inwardness of emotion in lyric, away from action and toward the quality of response. One might ask students to consider how the emphasis on "silent thought" affects narrative impulse. Instructors may also want to compare the relations between language and revolution in Wordsworth with other writers, particularly Wollstonecraft. How does the issue of gender enter in Wordsworth's description of the poet as "a man speaking to men"? in his portrayal of women? Questions of gender and of narrative often converge: fruitful assignments spring from comparisons of the representation of male narrator and female subject in *Poor Susan* and *The Solitary Reaper*. Revision often highlights the issues: consider the effect of the omitted last stanzas of *Poor Susan* or of *Strange fits of passion*.

After *Lyrical Ballads* Wordsworth's rejection of traditional literary artifice relaxes; students may compare the formalism of the sonnets with the earlier poems. Note also the sequence from *Tintern Abbey*, which Wordsworth did not "venture" to call an ode, to *Ode: Intimations of Immortality*, to *Elegiac Stanzas*. In all, the comparison between what one used to see and what one now sees spells the crisis of the poem, but the conclusions, the attempted resolution of the crises, differ. Students might be asked to compare the "abundant recompense" of *Tintern Abbey* or its last line with the last lines of the two later poems—"Thoughts that lie too deep for tears" and "not without hope we suffer and we mourn"—and the processes by which these resolutions, if they are resolutions, are reached. What is the relationship between affirmation and mourning in the three texts? How does the mediation through art in *Elegiac Stanzas* signal a change in Wordsworth's relationship to nature? How do we understand the difference in the treatment of landscape in *Tintern Abbey* (located, dated) from the general scene in the *Ode*? and of the speaker of *Tintern Abbey*, with a history and a sister, and that of *Elegiac Stanzas*, with a specific loss to grieve, from the "I-representative" of the *Ode*? Wordsworth placed the *Ode* as the closing poem in every collection that he published in his lifetime: students might consider the meaning of that gesture, and gauge its effectiveness. (The comparisons can be reordered by inserting the more *Lyrical Ballad*—like *Resolution and Independence*.)

Our companion reading, Mary Shelley's lyric, *On Reading Wordsworth's Lines on Peele Castle*, counterpoints this sequence in suggestive ways. Students might be asked to consider how Shelley's "dirge" (l.6), her fixed grief, contrasts with the consolation Wordsworth seeks in his *Elegiac Stanzas*, and still more in *Tintern Abbey*, *Resolution and Independence*, and *Ode: Intimations of Immortality*. Crossing, of course, Shelley's re-reading of Wordsworth is her awareness of Percy Shelley's elegy for Keats, *Adonais* (1821), whose plot and imagery are echoed in the waves and calling voice (lines 6–10) of her poem, tropes given retrospective poignance by Percy's drowning in 1822. The intertextual density exemplifies the ongoing, charged conversation Romantic poems generate among themselves. If in 1814 Mary and Percy could declare that Wordsworth had become "a slave" (see p. 322 of this manual) it is through an encounter with his poem that she articulates her own sorrow a decade later.

Instructors will choose their own paths through the wealth of *The Prelude*, but a few general points may be helpful. Despite the chronological narrative flow that reflects the age's interest in human development, of character as proceeding in stages from its beginning rather than as (in Aristotelian terms) that which shows the moral character of the fully formed adult in action, the poem is written in retrospect. If the *bio* moves forward, the *graphy* is thoroughly after the fact. Several consequences follow: the shifting spacing between the Wordsworth-narrated (the child of the early books) and the Wordsworth-narrator should not lead one to overlook that the Wordsworth-narrator is always remembering/writing in his present, aware of the constructedness of what he recounts: see, for example, his acknowledgment of "conjectures" in his tableau of the Blessed Babe (2.238) and, in a passage we don't print, his recognition of Coleridge as one who understands that it is a "Hard task to analyse a soul, in which, / Not only general habits and desires, / But each most obvious and particular thought, / Not in a mystical and idle sense, / But in the words of reason deeply weigh'd, / Hath no beginning" (2.232–37). The overlay and interplay of past and present animates virtually every passage: the instructor should show students how fractured and multiple is the "I" of, for example, 2.28–33, where the "I" of the narrator observes the "two consciousnesses" in his own mind. The extended simile of the autobiographer as one trying to see into the depths of a lake (4.247–64) is another self-reflexive trope. The drama of the poem repeatedly depends upon a saving reinterpretation, in which the present narrator comes to understand a previous formulation as inadequate: the sudden recognition, in the act of writing, in 6.535–49, is thus representative of typical patterns. Note the affirmation at the close that "in the end / All [is] gratulant if rightly understood" (13.385), which counterbalances the dynamic in which the potent events come as shocks, or surprises in a moment of calm, of which the meaning can be grasped only later: for example, the episodes of ice-skating, the stolen boat, the drowned man, unwittingly crossing the Alps, or *There was a boy*, when it becomes part of *The Prelude*.

Moreover, as the composition of the poem stretched over many years, it inevitably entailed shifts in perspective on what was already written. Though we do not print Book 8, entitled "Retrospect," it may be useful to instructors to mention it: a retelling of what had just been told, in a kind of feedback loop in which the revision of old material was needed to unlock the future, it epitomizes the rhythm of the poem as a whole. Important to remember is that the writer is always posterior to the events he narrates: if the "spots of time" in Book 11 are out of chronological order, the late placement is true to a central feature of Wordsworth's experience: the Wordsworth who wrote them, even he of the *Two-Part Prelude*, was one who had lived through the French Revolution, and students may profitably be asked to consider how the accounts of childhood terror and abandonment, of guilt and chastisement, may have been inflected by what happened *subsequently* to their experience, but *prior* to their writing. The titling of Book 5, "Books," points to the centrality of writing in the construction of memory. Wordsworth's assertion that he was not frightened by the apparition of the drowned man because he had read about such sights before (450–81) may suggest a reversed truth: that by writing them up Wordsworth gains control of potentially traumatic experiences. Instructors might ask students to compare lines 473–481 to the version of the episode in the *Two-Part Prelude*, which concludes: "I might advert / To numerous accidents in flood or field, / Quarry or moor, or 'mid the winter snows, / Distresses and disasters, tragic facts / Of rural history, that impressed my mind / With images to which in following years / Far other feelings were attached—with forms / That yet exist with independent life, / And, like their archetypes, know no decay" (1.279–87). The exercise shows Wordsworth's intention as less to recover what the child "really" felt than to subject "experience" to continuing revision, according to the aims and needs of his present; the differences between the accounts should precisely focus lively discussion. Similarly, it is provocative to compare the accounts of the 1790s given by *The Prelude* with the poems written in that period; the apostrophe to Burke we print from *1850* can start a discussion of whether it is a late graft that contradicts what went before or a belated recognition of loyalties ignored at the time.

Central to Wordsworth's enterprise is the wresting of the high, inclusive cultural form of epic to the narrative of his own growth, a wresting that involves narrating the French Revolution not as a momentous event in itself, to be grasped from the perspective of a grand authority (contrast Burke's "History will record . . ."), but as it appeared to him. The poem thus insists on the individual nature of truth: on truth as it is felt by the individual witness. Wordsworth's experience nonetheless participates in the debate of his generation, and *The Prelude* should be placed next to the writers in our Perspectives section: his account of events in France with Helen Maria Williams and Arthur Young, his account of the dispiriting effect of pure "Reason" in Book 10 with Godwin, and his restoration through feeling, Nature, and a "beloved Woman" with the Burkean emphasis on domestic affections. The commitment to change and growth as an overarching value—"a something evermore about to be" (6.542)—renders conclusion problematic. Students may be asked whether the sublime vision on Mt. Snowdon, the record of a 1791 excursion that occurred *before* events narrated in the previous books, seems adequate to them, and to explore the relation between their sense of the poem and Wordsworth's assertion that the "Song" has "centr[ed] all in love" (13.384). The importance of love and of the friendship with Coleridge signalled at the close can be played against the "Fraternity" celebrated by the Revolution; likewise the degradation of "revolutions in the hopes / And fears of men" to a parenthesis (13.449-450) in comparison to the "lasting inspiration" to be sung by "Prophets of Nature" (13.442-43) can spark a reconsideration of the relationships between "nature" and "history." One might ask students to ponder throughout the poem how Wordsworth's emphasis on childhood, intimacy (e.g., the Blessed Babe passage), friendship, nature, and values traditionally associated with the feminine adjusts the traditionally masculine, public form of the epic. Note, for example, 13.204ff.: "he whose soul hath risen / Up to the height of feeling intellect / Shall want no humbler tenderness, his heart / Be tender as a nursing Mother's heart, / Of female softness shall his life be full. . . ." Such passages, congruent with the emphasis on feeling in the Preface to *Lyrical Ballads*, spring the question whether the Romantic poet colonizes the feminine, displacing women writers from their place by appropriating their materials or risks seeming too feminine, unmanly.

The trajectory of *The Prelude* enables readers to see that the values of nature that the poem affirms (perhaps especially those applied to Wordsworth's own growth: "Fair seed-time had my soul" [1.306]; compare Burke's tropes of nature) always existed against the backdrop of the Revolution, the urban, the disturbing modern. One set of tropes Wordsworth employs is that of the consecrated soul, but another perspective is given by that of the writer seeking to found his authority, his professional position, in a post-revolutionary world without fixed sources of appeal. Wordsworth's account of London as an unknowable community in Book 7 should be juxtaposed with the representations by Robinson, Blake, and Baillie. Wordsworth's most profound experiences tend toward solitude, or of such withdrawal from social life that he is virtually solitary. Hence his strategies when confronted by a crowd—compare Burke on the mob—are particularly telling. Lines 593-622 raise important questions about the relationship between identity and recognition by others, and the blind beggar seeking to explain the story of his life furnishes a particularly fraught commentary on Wordsworth's own autobiographical enterprise. Wordsworth's anxiety at finding himself "Living amid the same perpetual flow / Of trivial objects, melted and reduced / To one identity, by differences / That have no law, no meaning, and no end" (702–05) repeats the stig-matizing of city life in the Preface to *Lyrical Ballads*, where it is not inertness but excitement, spectacle, and distraction that dull the mind. *The Prelude* thus makes clear the connection between the threatening urban anonymity and the need to develop the "discriminating powers of the mind" and the self-sustaining powers of inward meditation described above. Students might contrast the isolation and con-fusion that characterizes London and the treatment of "crowd" and "solitude" in *I wandered lonely as a cloud*.

Dorothy Wordsworth

Dorothy Wordsworth's repeated declarations that she would not consider herself a poet—in her letters, in *Irregular Verses*, in *Lines Intended for my Niece's Album*—evidently resonate with the expectations for women delineated (and contested) by Mary Wollstonecraft and the writers in "Perspectives: The Wollstonecraft Controversy and the Rights of Women". With her the gender distinctions can be brought to bear on the vocation of the poet. Wordsworth proclaims that the "ap-pointed close" of *The Prelude* is "the discipline / And consummation of a Poet's mind" (1850, 14.30–04); in some ways, the poet of *Irregular Verses* unfolds a neg-ative version of this story, that of someone who "*might have*," but did not, become a poet. What are the important elements of this anti-history in Dorothy's ac-count? What sort of imaginative impulses did she display as a girl? What was ex-pected of her as a girl and woman-to-be? How are we to understand her present poem: its motivation, title, and self-representation? These questions point toward a general one about the figure of the poet: is a "poet" someone endowed with a certain sensibility, as the Preface to *Lyrical Ballads* puts it, or is the figure of the poet something constructed: public, hence unequally available to men and women in the period? Is to be a poet not simply to write poems, but also to shape a visible self, accumulating over time into a career? One might compare Dorothy's *Floating Island* with the treatment of things that are no more in her brother's poetry. Some of his poems even involve "island"-like images: isolated figures, poets on mountain tops (islands in the sky), or the charged "spots" that are everywhere in his poetic landscapes. Students might be asked to consider how Dorothy writes about this image (the island and its disappearance), and the per-sons who speak of it, against William's representations. How do they each han-dle fragments and disappearances? Accounts in Dorothy's journals of scenes and images that William represents in his poetry form evident points of contrast: stu-dents may be asked to compare a few of these, with an eye to similarities and dif-ferences in imaginative orientation: what is important for Dorothy? What is the focus of her writing? Where is she as a figure in the scene? Where is he as figure in the scene? Some possibilities: his *I wandered lonely as a cloud* and her account of the daffodils; his encounter with a discharged soldier (*Prelude* 4.400–504) and a blind beggar in London (*Prelude* 7.593–623) and her encounters with beggars in the Lake District.

The difference between private journal and published poem should not be ignored in these comparisons; rather, the influence of gender on the distinction should be weighed. The much-praised realism of Dorothy's observation of the world around her is not inseparable from the historically conditioned self-suppression of the female author, and can be set against the "egotistical sublime" of William's representations. In the Preface to *Lyrical Ballads* William asserted that he had "at all times endeavoured to look steadily at my subject"; the much greater detail in the observation of the other in Dorothy's accounts suggests that William's subject was his own responsiveness. Likewise, the tangy vernacular she records sets off his claims to the "language really used by men." Her eye and ear for the particular mark Dorothy's distance from the generalized and conventional vocabulary of the picturesque, but in judging that her account of her Scots tour "far transcend[s] Gilpin," De Quincey located the literary tradition that underlay Dorothy's quicksilver response to nature. In light of the comments made above on William's power to suggest that responsiveness to nature was the hallmark of the sensitive soul, Dorothy's realism and spontaneity can be seen as epitomizing the new sensibility: in her what seem to be "merely" description and transcription emerge as radiant values in themselves. Students may be asked to consider how Dorothy's emphasis on the particular contrasts with the "philosophic mind" William claims for himself in the *Intimations Ode*: in what ways is the particular marked as feminine?" One might also place William's *Tintern Abbey* next to Dorothy's *Thoughts on my Sickbed* to ask how Dorothy's poem answers William's prayer for his sister 35 years earlier, and in what ways she may be seen as saying something different.

So too one might ask students to consider the perspectives our readings in Mary Wollstonecraft and *Perspectives: The Wollstonecraft Controversy and the Rights of Women* cast on the descriptions of Dorothy's vivacity, sensitivity, and innocence by Coleridge and De Quincey. One might also consider De Quincey's speculations on professional possibilities for Dorothy in connection with the anxieties of other woman writers in the volume. An instructor might tease out the ways these accounts of the woman play against William's literary representations of his sister: if Coleridge's letter precedes the publication of most of these, De Quincey's memoir echoes *Tintern Abbey* and *The Prelude* (which he knew well long before its appearance in 1850). The large questions of the situation of any biography between "fiction" and "representation" on the one hand and "actuality" on the other can be raised by asking students to compare De Quincey's *Recollections* with the praise of Dorothy in *Prelude* 10 (1805, 908 ff.). William resented as a violation of his domestic privacy the magazine publication of De Quincey's "scandalous, but painfully interesting" essays, as the frank details of Coleridge's opium-taking and of the marriages, habits, and persons of the Wordsworth-Coleridge circle led Crabb Robinson to characterize them. Crabb Robinson reported that "He said with great earnestness: 'I beg that no friend of mine will ever tell me a word of the contents of those papers' & I dare say he was substantially obeyed" (See John E. Jordan, *De Quincey to Wordsworth: A Biography of a Relationship*, 1963). That such accounts were published and popular attests to the prominence William and Coleridge had acquired, and exemplifies the mechanisms of celebrity that further magnified the image of the Romantic author. William's resentment can thus be understood in part as a desire to control his representation, aggravated by his having withheld publication of *The Prelude—his* representation of his life, now anticipated by De Quincey—as a legacy to his family, to ensure copyright-protected income after his death.

PERSPECTIVES

The Sublime, the Beautiful, and the Picturesque

The reader of this manual will already have encountered in the section on Literary Ballads two different ways of configuring the Romantic period: through the ballad tradition, or through the prominence given to terms such as imagination, vision and apocalypse. Opening our volume with Anna Barbauld suggests another starting-point: the reconstellation of the period resulting from the restoration of the women writers important in their own day but lost in the modern critical tradition: Barbauld, Smith, Hemans. The clustered terms sublime, beautiful, and picturesque likewise effect a return: to a contemporary critical vocabulary that undoes any absolute distinction between the eighteenth century and the Romantic period. **Burke's** *Philosophical Enquiry* is the earliest text (1757) in our volume, yet it remained a touchstone for generations of writers and painters, in Britain and abroad.

The instructor might further compare the two versions of the anecdote in the introduction to draw out the social valence of the terms. The woman's unpublished journal is filled with detail suppressed in the man's philosophic *Principles.* Note how Coleridge chooses the more dignified "travelers" over Dorothy's confessed "tourists," and eliminates any reference to the particular place that might have revealed the accuracy of the latter designation. "Accidental party" is also interesting: the meeting of the Coleridge-Wordsworth party with the hapless speaker was chance, but their visit to Cora Linn was not random. If Coleridge obscures his motives, his account shows him thoroughly conversant with formal landscape description: note how carefully the "cataract of great height, breadth, and impetuosity" is stationed, its summit blending with the clouds, its lower part hidden by rocks and trees. Height and depth, light and dark make a careful pictorial composition that marks the connoisseur of "sublime object[s]," less "natural" than composed as deliberately as the "bench" and "station" of Dorothy's account indicate.

These maneuvers, and the joke itself, confirm that by 1814, when *On the Principles of Genial Criticism* was published in *Felix Farley's Bristol Journal,* the play of terms was of long standing but still charged. Burke's grounding of the sublime (to follow our excerpts) in *Terror, Obscurity, Power, Privation, Vastness, Infinity,* and *Difficulty* furnishes the code of representation of an event as terrific as the French Revolution—in which under Robespierre and St. Just "terror" was state policy— and, at the other extreme, of Barbauld's sympathy for the isolated "apath[etic]" George III, deprived of the capacity for sympathy (*On the Death of Princess*

Charlotte), or of Wordsworth's depiction of the protagonist of *Old Man Travelling*, "insensibly subdued / To settled quiet . . . by nature led / To peace so perfect, that the young behold / With envy, what the old man hardly feels." Burke's terms provide the language that shaped both the efforts of authors and the articulated responses of readers. Consider, for example, Coleridge's description of *A slumber did my spirit seal* as "a most sublime Epitaph," where the *genre* Epitaph crosses the effects of privation, terror at sudden loss, and difficulty—the reader's difficulty in grasping the potent minimalism of the poem. Burke's memorable expression "[a] clear idea is therefore another name for a little idea," is an antecedent of many typical Wordsworthian formulations:

> I deem not profitless those fleeting moods
> Of shadowy exultation: not for this,
> That they are kindred to our purer mind
> And intellectual life; but that the soul,
> Remembering how she felt, but what she felt
> Remembering not, retains an obscure sense
> Of possible sublimity, to which,
> With growing faculties she doth aspire,
> With faculties still growing, feeling still
> That, whatsoever point they gain, they still
> Have something to pursue.

We do not print this passage (1805 *Prelude* 2.331-41), but an instructor might point to a characteristic moment in *Resolution and Independence*: "Dim sadness—and blind thoughts, I knew not, nor could name." Here it is worth remarking that beyond the obvious connection between Burke and the countless forbidding mountain landscapes, Welsh, Lake District, and Alpine, of Romantic literature—consider Wordsworth's climactic laborious ascent of Snowdon, capped with a vision of sea, clouds, and a "deep and gloomy breathing-place thro' which / Mounted the roar of waters, torrents, streams / Innumerable, roaring with one voice" (1805 *Prelude* 13.57-59)—and despite his materialist emphasis on phenomena as if they automatically caused certain responses (in Part One, Section 19, not printed here, he writes "[a] low, tremulous, intermitting sound . . . is productive of the sublime"—Burke concludes the *Enquiry* with a Part devoted to Words and Poetry. His singling out of the effect of Milton's phrase "of Death" (p. 504) marks an attention to linguistic particulars that can fruitfully open up close attention to Wordsworth and other poets. Note in the excerpt from *The Prelude*, above, Wordsworth's characteristic double negative (how does "not profitless" differ from profitable?), the unfolding syntax of which Donald Davie has written "[i]t seems to be explaining, while in fact it is meditating, ruminating, at all events *experiencing* more fully than one does when one explains" (*Articulate Energy*, published 1955, rpt. 1976), and the repetitions that tug against but found the evolution of the argument. Note too how the line from *Resolution and Independence* becomes suggestive by refusing specification. Burke's analysis of the effects of Milton's description of Sin and Death

(p. 501) resonates for the next half-century and more, as its reappearance in the crucial chapter 13 of Coleridge's *Biographia Literaria* (p. 574), witnesses.

For Wordsworth the picturesque was a suspect mode, but one in which he was steeped. By 1796 he owned both "Gilpin's tour into Scotland, and his northern tour" and if he later tried to sell them second-hand (Letters of 21 March 1796 and 28 August 1798) that did not preclude his taking Gilpin's *Wye Tour* with him when he and Dorothy Wordsworth went on the trip that produced *Tintern Abbey*. In a note appended to an elaborate description of a sunset (ll. 332–47) in his 1793 *Descriptive Sketches* he wrote: "I had once given to these sketches the title of Picturesque; but the Alps are insulted in applying to them that term. Whoever, in attempting to describe their sublime features, should confine himself to the cold rules of painting would give his reader but a very imperfect idea of those emotions which they have the irresistible power of communicating to the most impassioned imaginations. The fact is, that controuling influence, which distinguishes the Alps from all other scenery, is derived from images which disdain the pencil." In *The Prelude* he mounts the same charge against those "disliking here, and there / Liking, by rules of mimic art transferr'd / To things above all art," and asserts that this "strong infection of the age, / Was never much my habit—giving way / To a comparison of scene with scene, / Bent overmuch on superficial things, / Pampering myself with meagre novelties / Of colour and proportion, to the moods / Of time or season, to the moral power, / The affections, and the spirit of the place / Less sensible" (1805, 11.152–64, not printed here). Two celebrated anecdotes involving his patron Sir George Beaumont illustrate the rules Wordsworth inveighed against: Beaumont kept an old fiddle in his sketching-case to calibrate the shade of brown to give his images, and once, looking at a canvas by John Constable, whose career he supported, demanded "Where's your brown tree?"

What Wordsworth repudiated he was nonetheless saturated by, and his response points to a deepening rather than a simple rejection. Gilpin and his fellows taught Englishmen how to see landscape, taught them that they *should* turn to nature, and the picturesque emphasis on variety, irregularity, roughness, and contrast is everywhere in the subsequent literature. Moreover, Gilpin's insistence that "[w]e are most delighted, when some grand scene . . . rising before the eye, strikes us beyond the power of thought—when . . . every mental operation is suspended," producing "a deliquium of the soul" (p. 509), points straight to such intense moments of feeling as that in Wordsworth's *Tintern Abbey* (ll. 36–50). As Gilpin continues to argue, it is "the imagination, active and alert" in the absence of "all objects of sense" that transforms the scene (p. 510), giving it what he elsewhere calls "the brilliance of a dream." Gilpin's distinction between "the original sketch" and the "adorned sketch" already enacts within the medium of art the difference between fidelity to the actual, the matter of fact, and the power of imagination which Wordsworth and Coleridge emphasize (p. 510). But Gilpin claims only "amusement" for the picturesque: for Wordsworth the landscape can disclose a "presence . . . something far more deeply interfused" (*Tintern Abbey*, ll. 95–97); the imagination creates "moral power" (see *The Prelude* excerpt above), and new intensities and compositions of feeling. It is as if Wordsworth and Coleridge had foregrounded what was merely potential in the Picturesque; compare Gilpin's absence of objects of sense to the inwardness of poems such as Coleridge's *Frost at Midnight* (and the discussion in later sections of this manual), or Gilpin's dependence on landscape and the comparative timidity of his invocation of imagination with Wordsworth's resistance to "the tyranny of the eye," to Blake's contempt for "Natural Objects" and exaltation of the "Poetic Genius," to Shelley's austere mental audacity in the aptly named *Mont Blanc*, and Coleridge's declaration: "I meet, I *find* the Beautiful— but I give, contribute, or rather attribute the Sublime."

Keats followed a similar pattern: visiting the Isle of Wight in July 1819, he told Fanny Brawne he planned to "spy at the parties about here who come hunting after the picturesque like beagles"; a month later, from Winchester, where he was soon to write *To Autumn* (which instructors might approach by asking about its difference from the picturesque) he told her that he was "g[ettin]g a great dislike of the picturesque; and can only relish it over again by seeing you enjoy it," a phrase that repeats the gendering in the anecdote with which this section begins. The sense of the picturesque as a state to be passed through to a more masculine and strenuous encounter emerges most sharply in Keats's disappointment in the Isle of Wight: having lost his "cockney maidenhead" to "lake and mountain" on the Scottish walking tour a year previously, he wrote Fanny "I may call myself an old Stager in the picturesque, and unless it be something very large and overpowering I cannot receive any extraordinary relish." Tellingly, this boast arose from a good-humored competition with Charles Brown to sketch Shanklin Church. (Keats letters of 16 July, 16 August, and 31 July 1819.) Moving in the circle of artists and amateurs such as Benjamin Robert Haydon, Leigh Hunt, and William Hazlitt, Keats became familiar with the painters from whom picturesque taste sprang. In his Epistle *To J. H. Reynolds, Esq.* (1818, not printed here), he casually observes "You know the Enchanted Castle," surrounding the reference with details (ll. 20–29) that suggest Claude's "Landscape with the Father of Psyche sacrificing at the Milesian Temple of Apollo," exhibited at the British Institution in 1816: "The sacrifice goes on; the pontiff knife / Gleams in the sun, the milk-white heifer lows, / The pipes go shrilly, the libation flows," a scene that resonates in *Ode on a Grecian Urn*. The survey of the "art garniture" in Leigh Hunt's cottage in Hampstead that closes *Sleep and Poetry* (ll. 354–404) recalls the same Claude, Poussin's "Bacchus and Ariadne," and Titian's "Diana and Actaeon," singled out in Hazlitt's "On Gusto" (p. 936). Those interested in pursuing these relations should consult Ian Jack's *Keats and the Mirror of Art* (1967).

Burke's discussion of Beauty reveals the interplay of aesthetic categories and female manners, as **Wollstonecraft** inclusively named the complex of gender stereotypes, the gendered distribution of power, and eros. Burke's fantasia on the woman's beautiful throat (p. 503) makes clear as well his investment in the values of sensibility (p. 504) and her commitment to reason. Wollstonecraft's critique of Burke's proposition that love "relax[es] the solids of the whole system" should also be compared with the active force of sympathy in Hazlitt and Keats. In Burke, beauty—associated with smallness, smoothness, and weakness—has no capacity to inspire: the values of harmony, proportion, and symmetry, the intellectual achievements of neo-classicism, have been evacuated. This perspective suggests why Burke could seem as lurid as the French revolutionaries he denounced, and why his prose continued to appeal to his political opposites, such as Hazlitt (see p. 941).

If the language of Burke and Gilpin furnishes the genealogy of British Romantic treatment of nature, the contemporary philosophy of **Kant**, already making itself felt in Britain by the turn of the century, has been seminal for subsequent discussion of Wordsworth and Coleridge. Kant's insistence that "the sublime is not to be looked for in things of nature but only in our own ideas" (p. 514) freed discussion of the term from all pettily precise "comparison of scene with scene," and turned it forcefully to the categories of mental activity. Kant's identification of the "feeling of displeasure, arising from the inadequacy of the imagination in the aesthetic estimation of magnitude" (p. 514) economically states the unease attendant on the mind's attempt to grasp that which exceeds its capacity, and his sketching of the *dynamic* sequence through which an initial failure or sense of vulnerability—even "humiliation" (p. 516)—is recuperated by the mind's consciousness of its superiority to "the seeming omnipotence of nature" (p. 515) tracks and conceptualizes the experience narrated in many paradigmatic moments of Romantic poetry. Kant's vocabulary of "attraction and repulsion," "vibration," and "abyss in which [the imagination] fears to lose itself" (p. 515), of "challenge" and final "exalt[ation]" (p. 516), helps unpack Wordsworth's recounting of his first entry into London:

> On the Roof
> Of an itinerant Vehicle I sate
> With vulgar men about me, vulgar forms
> Of houses, pavement, streets, of men and things,
> Mean shapes on every side: but at the time
> When to myself it fairly might be said,
> The very moment that I seem'd to know,
> The threshold now is overpass'd—Great God!
> That aught external to the living mind
> Should have such mighty sway! Yet so it was—
> A weight of Ages did at once descend
> Upon my heart, no thought embodied, no
> Distinct remembrances, but weight and power,
> Power, growing with the weight: alas! I feel
> That I am trifling: 'twas a moment's pause,
> All that took place within me, came and went
> As in a moment, and I only now
> Remember that it as a thing divine.

We do not print this passage from Book 8 of the *The Prelude* (1805, 694–710), but it may serve as a template for reading the crossing of the Alps in Book 6 (1805, 488–572). Note how the narrative displaces the expected traveler's high point—Crossing the Alps!—into a "sadness" (l. 492) and "dull and heavy slackening" (l. 549) that reveal their meaning years later in the act of writing. The "downwards"

(l. 520) course of the traveler springs in reflection the counter-movement of reve-lation: "Imagination! Lifting up itself / Before the eye and progress of my Song / Like an unfather'd vapour" (ll. 525–27). The "perplex'd" traveler in the conven-tionally sublime mountainscape of 1790 (l. 514) is repeated in the poet of 1804 "lost" in his own mind, who can "now recognize" in his own bafflement and the extinction of the "light of sense" the "invisible world" of Greatness, destiny, and infinitude, of "hope that can never die, / Effort and expectation, and desire, / And something evermore about to be": the power of the "Soul" (ll. 529–42). The structure and the potent after-recognition govern also the two "spots of time" in Book 11 (258–389). The first begins with the six-year-old Wordsworth separated from his guide, "stumbling" into a scene of past violence, and confronted by a pri-vative "bare Common" and "naked Pool," and a girl "who . . . with difficult steps . . . force[d] her way / Against the blowing wind." In the second the teen-age Wordsworth finds himself straining to see the horses that would bring him home, alone amidst "the wind and sleety rain / And all the business of the elements, / The single sheep, and the one blasted tree," only to have his anticipated Christmas cheer interrupted by the death of his father. In both these episodes "visionary drea-riness" and defeated expectation, violence and death, yield by rebound "renovat-ing Virtue," the "deepest feeling that the mind / Is lord and master, and that the outward sense / Is but the obedient servant of her will." These are the experiences that undergird the program that Wordsworth invokes for himself and Coleridge to conclude *The Prelude*:

> What we have loved
> Others will love: and we may teach them how,
> Instruct them how the mind of man becomes
> A thousand times more beautiful than the earth
> On which he dwells, above this frame of things
> (Which 'mid all revolutions in the hopes
> And fears of men doth still remain unchanged)
> In beauty exalted, as it is itself
> Of substance and of fabric more divine. (1805, 13.444–52)

From this perspective even the upheavals of the French Revolution dramatically narrated in the previous books become a parenthesis in—but a productive stage of—the "Growth of a Poet's Mind," as the sub-title of the 1850 *The Prelude* has it.

Ruskin placed on the title-page of the first volume of *Modern Painters* an epi-graph from Wordsworth's *The Excursion*:

> Accuse me not
> Of arrogance, unknown Wanderer as I am,
> If, having walked with Nature threescore years,
> And offered, far as frailty would allow,
> My heart a daily sacrifice to Truth,
> I now affirm of Nature and of Truth,

Whom I have served, that their DIVINITY
Revolts, offended at the ways of men
Swayed by such motives, to such ends employed;
Philosophers, who, though the human soul
Be of a thousand faculties composed,
And twice ten thousand interests, do yet prize
This soul, and the transcendent universe,
No more than as a mirror that reflects
To proud Self-love her own intelligence. (4.978-92)

Ruskin described Wordsworth as his "guide, in all education," and quoted *The Excursion*, little read today, more than any other of his works. This frequency is a salutary reminder that "Wordsworth" in the nineteenth century was far more the observer who invested nature with a passionate "moral power" (see the quotation from Book 11 of *The Prelude* above) than the poet of ruptures, discontinuities, contradictions, and aporias of our own time. Ruskin's Calais Church can be placed in several contexts: the elevation of the connection with the past of the Continent against a triumphalist English faith in progress can be set against a traditional contempt for France the Revolution had intensified a generation earlier; the unconscious dignity of the Church points back to Wordsworth's *Old Man Travelling* (p. 351) and *The Old Cumberland Beggar* (1800; unprinted here), in whose title character the villagers who sustain him "Behold a record which together binds / Past deeds and offices of charity, / Else unremembered" (ll. 89-91), as the church stands as an "infinite of symbolism," the "epitome" of all "which binds the old and the new into harmony"; this figural reading of the concrete can also be juxtaposed with Carlyle's scorn for the "picturesque Tourist" in *Past and Present* (1843; pp. 1035 ff.) and insistence on "the eternal inner Facts of the Universe" over the "transient outer Appearances thereof . . . the Outer Sham-true" (*Past and Present*, Chapter 2, not printed here). The reader who finds the spiritual weight given to a piece of architecture should consider, on the one hand, Coleridge's definition of the symbol in *The Statesman's Manual* (pp. 568-69), and on the other, that it was Ruskin who in *Modern Painters*, vol. 3, chapter 12, defined the "pathetic fallacy":

> I want to examine the nature of the other error, that which the mind admits when affected strongly by emotion. Thus, for instance, in *Alton Locke*,—
>> They rowed her in across the rolling foam—
>> The cruel, crawling foam.
> The foam is not cruel, neither does it crawl. The state of mind which attributes to it these characters of a living creature is one in which the reason is unhinged by grief. All violent feelings have the same effect. They produce in us a falseness in all our impressions of external things, which I would generally characterize as the "pathetic fallacy."
>> Now we are in the habit of considering this fallacy as eminently a character of poetical description, and the temper of mind in which we allow it as one eminently poetical, because passionate.

Ruskin's unattributed citation of the epigraph on the Greek philosopher Epictetus (AD 55-135)—"poor, and sick in body, and beloved by the Gods" (p. 519) reminds us too that the values he praises have deep roots in Stoicism.

Samuel Taylor Coleridge

The instructor unafraid of confronting students with a daunting text might begin with "Once a Jacobin Always a Jacobin." Coleridge's patient sorting through the shades of meaning borne by the key term of opprobrium not only offers a concise synopsis of the issues in "Perspectives: The Rights of Man and the Revolution Controversy"; it is also a wonderful introduction to Coleridge's characteristic devotion to the "duty to have clear, correct, and definite conceptions," no matter how subtle and extended the process of discrimination necessary to achieve clarity. His contempt for the "gallican" style of brief sentences or pointed antitheses as a manner in which it was impossible to do justice to the truth is the corollary of his own recursive prose, which goes over ground ever more finely, turning and turning topics. The consequent elaboration of his sentences, reconditeness of vocabulary (and Coleridge was fertile of neologisms), and almost panoramic allusiveness—a defeated biographer once confessed that if a book, any book, was available in England, it was safe to assume that Coleridge, whose borrowings and annotations were notorious, had read it—should be assessed in the light of the remarks on the politics of style in the manual for that Perspectives section. Comparison of Coleridge's prose to Paine's, say, on one side, and Burke's or Godwin's on the other, will illuminate the audience at which he aimed. His prose is that of the man of letters: it is neither that of a philosopher—"Once a Jacobin" is topical, and published in a newspaper—nor that of a journalist seeking to attract a transient attention; it models, and thus forms in its readers, a mind engaged with public affairs yet claiming a reflective station above them.

Coleridge's distinction between the broad sense of Jacobin as one "interested in the cause of general freedom" and one who "in *our* sense of the term" adheres to the specific tenets of the sovereignty of the people, of the supremacy of individual rights to the preservation of property, and of the equality of each individual, so that representation is made to depend on a kind of evacuated interchangeability of persons without regard to merit, determined solely by voting ("*numbered*"), with universal suffrage, typifies his search for the fundamental principles in a dispute. His own commitment to the maxim that "*that government was the best, in which the power was the most exactly proportioned to the property*" reveals his continuity with Burke; at the same time, his scorn for those alarmed that peace with France would revive the dangerous seductiveness of Jacobin ideas—the essay was published during the Peace of Amiens, and the "Mr. W" referred to is William Windham, the Secretary of War in Pitt's Tory cabinet, who had resigned rather than negotiate a treaty—mounts a Burkean argument for the wisdom of experience, of "our common sense and common feelings," against the hysterical reaction identified with Burke. This supple middle position, in which Coleridge defends the possibility of change over time, so that "once a Jacobin" (in the specific political sense he attaches to the term) does *not* mean "always a Jacobin," since "the young, and the inexperienced," in a phrase that Coleridge repeats for emphasis, "grow wiser," accords with the revisionary autobiography of *Biographia Literaria* (and *The Prelude*). Such moves remind us that if Romanticism is commonly associated with the perspective of childhood, a fuller understanding casts the balance toward the ambiguous drama of growth, of gain and loss, of "emotion recollected in tranquillity," of the "philosophic mind" reshaping or imagining an origin from which it is always distant.

Beginning with a piece of political prose will also enable the instructor to open the question of the relationship between Coleridge's sociopolitical position and his literary and aesthetic criticism. What is the relation between "organic form" as Coleridge discusses it in our next selection from the *Lectures on Shakespeare*, including the tropes of natural growth and the affirmation that "a living body is of necessity an organized one; and what is organization but the connection of parts in and for a whole," with the function of such language in the Burkean discourse of the organically growing, hierarchically ordered state? Similarly, how is Coleridge's notion of the *unity* of the aesthetic object, as instanced in his description of the poet as one who "brings the whole soul of man into activity, with the subordination of its faculties to each other, according to their relative worth and dignity . . . diffus[ing] a tone, and spirit of unity, that blends, and (as it were) *fuses*, each into each, by that synthetical and magical power to which we have exclusively appropriated the name of imagination" (*Biographia Literaria* 14), to be situated against the Burkean vision of the nation, neutralizing the real differences in its members by the compelling force of its symbolic attractiveness? Students might be asked to juxtapose the psychology of "that willing suspension of disbelief for the moment, which constitutes poetic faith" that Coleridge formulated in defending his contributions to *Lyrical Ballads* and amplified in his comments on stage illusion from the *Lectures on Shakespeare*, with Burke's defense of the monarchy and of "pleasing illusion" (not delusion) as the self-conscious fictions of the civilized, moral imagination. How does Coleridge's image of a hierarchy that preserves differences in "worth and dignity" but "magical[ly]" resolves them into harmony play against the eighteenth-century language of the ranks and orders of society, and against the emerging language of division between classes? How does Coleridge's immersion in and dissemination of German philosophical traditions (idealist and pietist), then largely unknown in Britain, relate to the distaste for things French, particularly French rationalism, brought on by the course of the Revolution and protracted war?

Beginning with "Once a Jacobin" may also prevent Coleridge from being absorbed into discussions of Wordsworth in the classroom, as Wordsworth absorbed Coleridge when he affixed his name alone to *Lyrical Ballads* in 1800 and afterwards. *The Eolian Harp* shows Coleridge's achievements before the collaboration. *The Eolian Harp*, *This Lime-Tree Bower*, and *Frost at Midnight* exemplify Coleridge's development of the conversation poem. Out of the eighteenth-century loco-descriptive poem, usually addressed to a place or its resident genius, or to a muse, and usually long, Coleridge developed a compact meditative form, addressed to wife, child, or friend, domestic in setting, and giving the impression, abetted by low-key blank verse, of intimate conversation. The conversation poems seem devoid of formal constraint, being shaped only by "the drama of reason—and present the thought growing" (as Coleridge described them) rather than being poured into predetermined rhyme or stanza pattern (see his animadversions on "mechanic" form), but are carefully constructed. Coleridge subtitled one work "A Poem which Affects not to be Poetry," but in them one can detect the back-and-forth movement of the ode, hidden as the spontaneous flow of thought, and an overall roughly circular pattern: a quiet beginning, a rise into a more elevated or even vexed mood, a return to the opening calm, with some new advance in knowledge or self-understanding.

The situation of *This Lime-Tree Bower*, in which Coleridge imagines the walk with his friends of which injury has deprived him, and through this act of sympathy heals his own regret, epitomizes the social value of imagination the poems celebrate. The image of the Aeolian harp that permits the speculation that "all of animated nature" responds to "one intellectual breeze" (4447) is one of the polar tropes of the Romantic imagination: the figuring of the imagination as "indolent[ly] and passive[ly]" (41) responsive to a universal spirit is the opposite of the figure of Prometheus, the emblem of the imagination as creative, assertive, even daemonic, that one finds in Byron and Shelley. Coleridge's affirmation of "the one life within us and abroad" (26) provoked charges of pantheism, embodied in the imagined rebuke from Sarah (49 ff.), but students might be asked to situate this vision of universal harmony against the rhetoric of brotherhood in the Revolution, and to consider Coleridge's tableau of marital "Innocence and Love" (6) as a rejoinder to the charges of violating sacred bonds levelled by the conservatives against the radicals. To John Thelwall, a radical friend, Coleridge wrote in 1796: "We have an hundred lovely scenes about Bristol, which would make you exclaim— O admirable *Nature*! and me, O gracious *God*!" For the mature Coleridge, a Trinitarian, mind or spirit rather than matter was the necessary starting point for all analysis, and students can be asked to consider the differences between the more theological language of his visions of nature with the carefully ambiguous language of "presence," say, in Wordsworth's *Tintern Abbey* (95).

Comparisons between Wordsworth and Coleridge in the period of their intense mutual stimulation are inevitable, and to be welcomed, in part as showing that even when Romantic rhetoric invokes the individual genius it does so within the exchanges of a group. If the Pantisocratic project failed, the impulse to build an ideal community, as a miniature of the new society, remained, whether in the proximity of the poets at Nether Stowey and Alfoxden, or in the public image of the life lived by the Wordsworths in Grasmere. Coleridge's declaration in *This Lime-Tree Bower* that "Nature ne'er deserts the wise and pure" (60) is echoed in *Tintern Abbey*: "Nature never did betray / The heart that loved her" (123-24). The eddying structure and extraordinary fluidity in the representation of time in *Frost at Midnight*, as for instance in the sequence beginning at line 24, in which the narrating Coleridge remembers his schoolboy self, who (flashback within flashback) had been dreaming of his birthplace, remembering the bells that had fallen on his

ear "like articulate sounds of things to come," finds its counterpart in the treatment of past, present, future, and present as remembered past in *Tintern Abbey*. In
both poems such representations of mental activity—an observer of the speakers of
Frost at Midnight or *Tintern Abbey* would see no action—create the rich inwardness
that is the hallmark of "romantic" poetry. To follow the drama of consciousness
requires readers alert to the associative logic that governs the poems: skilled
enough, for example, to grasp that what returns Coleridge to his son, sleeping next
to him in the present, in *Frost at Midnight*, is the culmination of his multi-layered
retreat into the past: "My playmate when we both were clothed alike!" (43). The
turn to the younger figure, and the concluding blessing invoked for his or her future, is parallel in *Frost at Midnight* and *Tintern Abbey*, but the instructor, having
pointed out the similarities, should be able to ask students to ponder the differences as well. For instance: in the context of the poems of which they form a part,
what are the different valences of Coleridge's "Nature ne'er deserts the wise and
pure" and Wordsworth's "Nature never did betray / The heart that loved her"?

Commenting on the lines "and the deep power of joy, / We see into the life of
things" in *Tintern Abbey* (49-50), Coleridge observed: "By deep feeling we make
our *ideas dim*, and this is what we mean by our life, ourselves. I think of the wall—
it is before me a distinct image. Here I necessarily think of the *idea* and the thinking *I* as two distinct and opposite things. Now let me think of *myself*, of the thinking being. The idea becomes dim, whatever it be—so dim that I know not what it
is; but the feeling is deep and steady, and this I call *I*—identifying the percipient and
the perceived." The dimming out of the outside world is often a precondition of
the liberation of imagination: note the "strange / And extreme silentness" (9-10),
and "the numberless goings on of life / Inaudible as dreams" (12-13), at the opening of *Frost at Midnight*. This sensorily deprived state frees the mind to range, and
the sense of the union of percipient and perceived, of subject and object, to swell.
(A comparison of Bowles's *To the River Itchin* with Coleridge's *Sonnet to the River
Otter* reveals that Bowles draws the river and the speaker as distinct, but Coleridge
parallels the river rising in memory to the bedded sand rising through the river's
"bright transparence" [11]: the same phenomenon spills over the border between
subject and object, "fusing" them. See also Coleridge's elevation of symbol over allegory in the selection from *The Statesman's Manual*.) Coleridge's interest in this
state links imagination, dream, and reverie, and provides a link between the conversation poems and the three supernatural poems: *The Rime of the Ancient
Mariner*, *Kubla Khan*, and *Christabel*.

Coleridge's description of the *Rime* as a "poem of pure imagination" in his re-
buttal of Mrs. Barbauld's criticism that it had no moral has not stopped critics
from reading it as an allegory of sin and redemption as well as a demonstration of
the salvific power of the sympathetic imagination: the Mariner is freed from the
Albatross around his neck at the moment that he "blesse[s]" (285) the water
snakes. In what seems to embody the mysterious workings of grace, the unmotivated shooting of the bird is offset by an equally sudden "spring of love," a motion
of the spirit that occurs "unawares," beneath the level of conscious choice
(284-85). However consoling such a plot, and the final words of the Mariner—"He

prayeth best, who loveth best / All things both great and small; / For the dear God who loveth us, / He made and loveth all" (614–17)—most readers are more struck with the nightmarish guilt and isolation of the Mariner's voyage than with this comforting moral lesson. A ballad writ large—its self-consciously literary medieval-ising quality most apparent in the first version—the *Rime* offers a narrative that proceeds from the certainties of land, to the uncharted territories of ocean, returning to land from a quality of experience that exceeds the conventional faith of the Hermit and even the Mariner's ability to grasp the meaning of what he has undergone. We include Cowper's *The Castaway* as a kindred instance of the conversion of a narrative of adventure into a sudden, shocking glimpse of fearful abandonment; the workings of the *Rime* exemplify the double focus of the terms in the title of the collection, shifting emphasis from ballad-story to psychological response. In that perspective the crucial character of the poem is the Wedding Guest, the destined but unwilling auditor—"I know the man that must hear me: / To him my tale I teach" (589–90)—who is blocked from attending a wedding, a fundamental ceremony of human communion, by the tale. The Mariner's experience does not lead to final absolution—"at an uncertain hour, / That agony returns" (582–83)—and his sharing of the tale unsettles as much as it enlightens its hearer; in the words of the concluding quatrain, "He went like one that hath been stunned, / And is of sense forlorn: / A sadder and a wiser man, / He rose the morrow morn" (622–25). Coleridge's poem thus offers a vision of literary transmission as contamination as much as education, repetition compulsion as much as gain in wisdom, in which the figure of the poet, the Mariner, appears less like the bringer of relationship and love, in the words of Wordsworth's Preface, than as the *poète maudit* of later tradition. Students should be asked to consider the tensions between the disruptive operations of the Mariner's "strange power of speech" (587) and the affirmations of the Preface to *Lyrical Ballads*, and the similarities and dissimilarities between Wordsworth's manner of revising his reader's expectations and sensibilities and the image of the relationship between poet and reader implicit in Coleridge's pairing of Mariner and Wedding Guest.

The obvious instance of horrific voyages in the period would have been the Middle Passage of the slave trade, certainly familiar around the port of Bristol, and to readers generally, as our Perspectives section establishes. The *Rime* might be seen as drawing on topical materials, magnifying their import into a seemingly universal drama of guilt by suppressing a particular referent. In this light, the *Rime* would appear as a displacement, or denial: a poem deliberately *not* about the slave trade, a historically contingent text, willfully *unknowing*, consciously or unconsciously, a contemporary abuse. But the Mariner's plight resonates more widely: the unmotivated shooting of the Albatross raises the general question of the origins of violence, a problem that the age had had to confront. Enlightenment thinkers had attacked the notion of sacrificial violence as a primitive residue, and extended their critique to the Christian narrative itself, an intellectual background that may contribute to the way the *Rime* echoes (but not quite) Christian symbology. To many Englishmen the French Jacobin justification of violence as politically necessary had been vitiated by the excesses of the Terror. The *Rime* may thus be seen as asking what language, what explanatory scheme, is adequate to explain violence, and what gain can persuasively be posited as arising from it. Asking, but not answering, Coleridge deepened the interpretive puzzles when he added the marginal glosses. Students should be asked how they handle the glosses as they read: some will follow the narrative, and only occasionally switch to the gloss; those who alternate poem and gloss as they proceed can be asked to describe the effects thus produced. The notion that the glosses are a privileged authorial explanation of the text will give way to recognition that the discrepancy between text and gloss rather complicates than simplifies understanding. (A good instance of the distance between the medievalising ballad and the elaborate, beautiful seventeenth-century prose of the gloss comes at 265.) *Within* the poem the Wedding Guest is helplessly gripped by the Mariner—"He holds him with his glittering eye—/ The wedding-guest stood still, / And listens like a three years' child: / The Mariner hath his will" (13–16)—but readers *of* the poem are both gripped by the spell and escape it into reflection as they negotiate the layers of competing interpretation attached to the act at its center.

Coleridge also brilliantly exploited the potentials of editorial apparatus, as it were, in the presentation of *Kubla Khan*. Poem and prose introduction together enact the quintessential fiction of the so-called fragment. Considering the opposition between the spontaneous composition recorded in the Preface, and its interruption "by a person on business from Porlock," and its parallel in the poem, that between Kubla Khan, a figure of absolute power whose "decree" [2]) immediately produces an Edenic garden ("So twice five miles . . . were girdled round" (6–7), and the speaker who laments the loss of vision, reveals that interruption and loss are the necessary guarantors, by contrast, of ideal vision: the fragment is the form that artfully intimates a whole beyond human potential to achieve. Note that the "I" enters the poem only at 42, concurrent with the admission of a plenitude impossible to "revive": self-consciousness appears precisely as the loss of vision. *Kubla Khan* should be read with the description of "the poet, described in ideal perfection" of *Biographia Literaria* 14, whose imaginative power is demonstrated in "the balance or reconciliation of opposite or discordant qualities" (cf. Kubla's "sunny pleasure-dome with caves of ice" [36]) and the contrary images of "turmoil" (17), "war" (30), and barely contained violence that the poem also witnesses. At play is the placing of emphasis in Coleridge's formulation in *Biographia Literaria* 13 that the imagination "struggles to idealize and to unify": emphasis on unity will lead readers to organic form and the internally balanced, coherent aesthetic object; emphasis on struggle will highlight rather the "chasm" (12) of the poem (and the gap between poem and gloss in the *Rime*), the division between introduction and poem, the division of the poem into two irregular parts, and the fracture of Coleridge himself between the figure in his poem and the several of his introduction, where he describes "the Author" in the third person, quotes his own poem, *The Picture*, an image of dissolution "without the after restoration," points to a future that "is yet to come" and substitutes for an unrealized harmonious vision a "dream of pain and disease." To account for these effects the instructor may ask students to place against the descriptions of the ideal poet from *Biographia Literaria* the passage from *Lectures on Shakespeare*: "The grandest efforts of poetry are where

the imagination is called forth, not to produce a distinct form, but a strong working of the mind, still offering what is still repelled, and again creating what is again
rejected: the result being what the poet wishes to impress, namely, the substitution
of a sublime feeling of the unimaginable for a mere image."

As the *Rime* produces the Mariner and his "glittering eye" (13), so *Kubla Khan*
concludes with a vision of the poet as dread, sacred figure: "And all should cry,
Beware! Beware! / His flashing eyes, his floating hair! / Weave a circle round him
thrice, / And close your eyes with holy dread" (49–52). Students may be asked to
explore the relationship between these quasi-Gothic images of potency, with the
poet at the center of the circle, and the experience of isolation and loss the narratives record, and the figure of the poet as sensitive, socially useful, and professional
developed in the Preface to *Lyrical Ballads*. The complementary treatment of
woman in *Kubla Khan* can also be highlighted: how do the "woman wailing for her
demon-lover" and the "Abyssinian maid" (16, 39) figure in relation to the poet?

Kubla Khan is a deliberate "fragment", *Christabel* an incomplete poem, but the
interpretive puzzles posed by the romance, with its disturbing overtones of maternal loss, homoerotic seduction, and paternal violence (emphasized in the conclusion to Part 2) are no less deliberate. Coleridge explicitly casts *Christabel* as a story:
the tale-teller has a voice that solicits our responses, and the tale has numerous affiliations with already encoded literary conventions and genres. Coleridge may be
seen repeatedly to present unresolved moments of reading and interpretation *in*
the poem for the reader *of* the poem. A sample crux: Bard Bracy reports his dream
(523 ff.) in terms quite charged for the reader, not least because he connects the
"dove" of his dream to Christabel, invoking Sir Leoline's own naming of the bird
by his daughter's name. Yet when Sir Leoline listens to his account, he assigns the
dove to another referent: Geraldine (569–70). Such a moment not only focuses
questions of the relationship of the two women—doubles? split selves? opposites?—
but stages the interpretive dilemma of understanding the texture of the poem itself, *in toto* as well as in its details. As with the *Rime* (and with Wordsworth's *The
Thorn*) we may note how lurid materials are set in a narrative frame that checks absorption in sensationalism by demanding active interpretive engagement from the
reader. (But the particular nature of the materials should not be ignored: students
can be asked to track the treatment of women in Coleridge's poems in *Lyrical
Ballads* and elsewhere—the wailing woman, the (be)witching Geraldine, the specter
Life-in-Death—especially in relation to the figure of the poet.)

Sir Walter Scott, hearing the "striking fragment" of *Christabel* recited, was so
struck by the "singularly irregular structure of the stanzas, and the liberty which it
allowed the author to adapt the sound to the sense," that in his notes to his *Lay of
the Last Minstrel* he admitted himself "bound to make the acknowledgment due
from the pupil to his master." The accentual meter that works by stress rather than
syllable to which Coleridge calls attention in his preface anticipates what Gerard
Manley Hopkins was later to call "sprung rhythm," and it had the same startling effect on Byron. This piece of literary history suggests that what distinguished the
poem was not so much its words as its rhythm, underlying or prior to any meaning:
as with the "meandering with a mazy motion" of *Kubla Khan* (25), Coleridge pro-

duced his effect by a characteristic sound pattern. Though Coleridge ascribes the unpublished status of *Christabel* to his moral failure—"I have only my own indolence to blame"—the instructor may consider the ways in which the delays in publishing both *Kubla Khan* and *Christabel* operated to keep the poems out of the market-place and attached to the voice of the poet himself (cf. the figure of the poet at the end of *Kubla Khan*). As the denunciation of "the *trade* of authorship" in Chapter 11 of *Biographia Literaria* makes clear, Coleridge resisted (even as his employment as journalist and book-maker exemplified) the growing commercialization of literature. Not to publish may be seen as a strategic decision to avoid the stigma of seeming a mere "*compositor*," Coleridge thereby ensuring his status as man of integrity (not profit) and genius, the begetter of works unsoiled by market concerns, works which magically, as it were, produced effects on major poets even before they were completed or existent themselves, and whose status grew in exact proportion to their invisibility to readers at large. Coleridge's creation of such cultural capital by these means can usefully be juxtaposed with Blake's restricted production.

Students may be asked to think critically about all of Coleridge's self-representations. The title *Dejection: An Ode*, for example, points to both a personal psychological crisis and a literary construction. The succession of addressees of the poem as it evolved from a verse-letter to "Sara" to the Ode of *Sybilline Leaves* (1817) suggest the dangers of trying to read back too directly from the poems to the life: "Wordsworth" and "William" in a version of the poem Coleridge sent to a friend (July 1802), "Edmund" in the *Morning Post* (October 1802), "William" in another letter (August 1803), "Edmund" (a transcript of 1804–05), "Lady" (published texts of 1814 and 1817). "Dejection" is the necessary stage for the growth of self-consciousness in the pattern repeatedly traced by the literature of the period. Coleridge's account of his passage from joy and hope to affliction, and particularly the opposition formulated in "by abstruse research to steal / From my own nature all the natural man" (89–90), epitomizes a widespread vision of the life-cycle: "We Poets in our youth begin in gladness, / But thereof come in the end despondency and madness" (Wordsworth's *Resolution and Independence*, 48–49); "who would not give, / If so he might, to duty and to truth / The eagerness of infantine desire" (Wordsworth's *Prelude*, 2.24–26); "No more—no more—Oh!! never more, my heart, / Canst thou be my sole world, my universe! / . . . / The illusion's gone for ever, and thou art / Insensible, I trust, but none the worse, / And in thy stead I've got a deal of judgment, / Though heaven knows how it ever found a lodgement" (Byron's *Don Juan*, 1. 215). Rather than accept this pattern as a natural truth of human nature, we might study it as a construction, subsequently naturalized by our psychologies of maturation, and interrogate it historically. (Blake's insistence on desire is a forceful counter-example.) What is the relation between this plotting of the individual life and the experience of the period, excited and then disillusioned by the French Revolution? As always, the identification of similarities permits the instructor to ask about differences: what is the relation between Coleridge's emphasis in *Dejection* on the "shaping spirit of Imagination" (86) and his declaration that "we receive but what we give, / And in our life alone does Nature live" (47–48) to the artfully equivocal representation of the exchange of mind and nature in *Tintern Abbey*?

The interplay of texts should remind us that even the most seemingly intro-spective poems enter into and emerge from a dialogue that the instructor will find it easy to explore. Coleridge heard the first four stanzas of *Ode: Intimations of Immortality* before writing *Dejection: An Ode*; *Resolution and Independence* plays against *Dejection: An Ode*; *Ode: Intimations of Immortality* sets the stoic "philosophic mind" (189) and its "thoughts too deep for tears" (206), self-composed, without an ad-dressee, against the "joy" Coleridge continues to wish for the "friend devoutest of my choice" (138). (Compare these conclusions with those of *Tintern Abbey* and *Frost at Midnight*.) As our introductory note suggests, the climax of the mutual and anxiety-laden self-definitions of Wordsworth and Coleridge occurs in *Biographia Literaria*, which may be seen in part as Coleridge's reaffirmation of his position in their relationship after the publication of Wordsworth's *Excursion* (1814) and *Poems*, with a substantial new theoretical essay (1815). Throughout discussion of the book one may ask students to consider how Coleridge's discussion of Wordsworth reveals Coleridge himself. The instructor will not need prompting to consider the rela-tionship between, for example, Wordsworth's discussion of language in the Preface to *Lyrical Ballads*, suggesting that language is "derived" from "objects," and Coleridge's insistence, in Chapter 17 of the *Biographia*, that the "best part of human language, properly so called, is derived from reflection on the acts of the mind it-self. It is formed by a voluntary appropriation of fixed symbols to internal acts." Questions may also be raised about the differences of class involved in the two dis-cussions of language, and what they imply about the composition and sympathies of the audience for poetry. It may be worthwhile to suggest that the contrast can be developed by consideration of the treatment of *things*, of objects represented as out-side and independent of consciousness, in the two poets: could one imagine Coleridge as the author of "It was, in truth, / An ordinary sight; but I should need / Colours and words that are unknown to man / To paint the visionary dreariness / Which, while I look'd all round for my lost Guide, / Did at that time invest the naked Pool" (*Prelude*, 11.308-13) or of "the wind and sleety rain / And all the busi-ness of the elements, / The single sheep, and the one blasted tree, and the bleak music of that old stone wall" (*Prelude*, 11.376-80)? If not, why not? This line of in-quiry can be connected to Coleridge's remarks on the dimming of the idea of ob-jects, quoted above, and his account in Chapter 14 of the design of *Lyrical Ballads*, in which he was to concentrate on "persons and characters supernatural" and Wordsworth to "give the charm of novelty to things of every day."

The definitions of imagination and fancy in Chapter 13 have proved a corner-stone of modern criticism, but by printing them in context we enable instructors to consider how their luminously declarative character when read by themselves—as usually anthologized—forms part of a familiar Coleridgean drama. Embedded in a sequence in which Coleridge interrupts himself by a letter from himself, masked as a friend, rife with allusions to the Gothic, to his own *Christabel*, to the Miltonic sub-lime, to his own past words on Wordsworth and allusions to Bishop Berkeley, with a (self-vaunting) glance at the commercial futility of his enterprise, in short, a se-quence that is anything but an instance of imaginative unity, the famous distinc-tion emerges not simply as the proclamation of indubitable aesthetic truths, but as a *fiat* made necessary by the impossibility of persuasive argument. If this ruse is a comic confession of Coleridge's having "been obliged to omit so many links" in his demonstration, it is by the same token a critique of the actual book-buying "*PUB-LIC*" incapable of following philosophical argument, and an enactment of the tenet that the truths of imagination can be reached only by intuition, not by sequential thought. Ending by deferring explanation to a never-published essay, Coleridge slyly exploits—within a two-volume work of discursive prose, at a moment of intense philosophical definition—the suggestive power of the fragment.

Lectures on Shakespeare

To the notes on our selections and the headnote to "Coleridge's Lectures in Context" one might merely add that attention should be given to the phenomenon of the public lecture itself. The rise of the lecture, whether literary as here or scientific, practical, or philosophic, attests to the public hunger for education, and the existence of an audience, or more properly, diverse audiences according to the subject, sharing common interests. Students may need to be reminded that education past the age of eight was an uncommon opportunity for boys, and an even rarer opportunity for girls (unless home tutoring was provided). English literature, students should also be reminded, whether Shakespeare or the contemporary writers on whom Coleridge and Hazlitt also lectured, did not form part of the university curriculum, nor were the restricted enrollments and objectives of Cambridge and Oxford capable of satisfying the numbers of new, non-university trained readers, chiefly but not exclusively middle class. Conversely, one might argue that the process by which lecture-going became fashionable created the audience it seemed to satisfy. However one balances cause and effect, the lectures were potentially lucrative and added to the celebrity of the lecturer, who for the mediation of print substituted the sense of presence. The lecturer was a contemporary version of the old oral poet, immediate rather than manufactured, performing directly for his hearers, and thus a component of the image of the author as the source of ideas, opinions, authority, perhaps even genius. In this formation Shakespeare was prominent, as a national poet whose genius was to be defended against the (French-influenced) neo-classicists, as it had been in the eighteenth century, but also as the central figure around whom the mission of civilizing those new readers ignorant of Latin and Greek, and hence barred from all the influence the classics were still held to exert in shaping the military hero, the civil servant, and the gentleman, could coalesce. As our headnote suggests, this project was not without its embarrassments, but pronouncing on Shakespeare was a particular form of the effort to instruct and to mold their audiences to which the Romantics and their successors were committed.

In so doing they created a "Shakespeare" who mirrored their own concerns and exemplified many of their most cherished aspirations. One might compare the paean to Shakespeare of De Quincey—a written essay, not a public lecture—beginning "Oh! mighty poet!" to other representations of genius in the period, and to its artful maskings of form and distrust of artifice in representative works: for example, the Preface to *Lyrical Ballads*, Chapters 13 and 14 of *Biographia Literaria*, the figure of the poet in Coleridge's poetry, *Tintern Abbey* and the conversation poems. Historical (and generic) difference is elided in such panegyrics, as will be revealed by posing Coleridge's praise of natural "organic form" against the conventionality of the Elizabethan stage. As Shakespeare is reworked into a psychological poet, emphasis on him as a practicing playwright, shareholder in an acting company, proportionately recedes. Although reading this criticism only in excerpts should make judgment cautious, the instructor might still ask students to consider how much attention Coleridge actually gives to form, understood as the shape of a whole work, and how much to soliloquy, local insight, and character analysis. The emphasis on character, reversing the Aristotelian primacy of plot, issues in such exclamations as Lamb's "we see not Lear, but we are Lear" and Hazlitt's "It is *we* who are Hamlet." Hazlitt makes Shakespeare the epitome of sympathetic imagination— "He had only to think of anything in order to become that thing, and with all the circumstances belonging to it"—and so makes viewing/reading the capacity to repeat the same power of sympathetic identification, thereby demonstrating one's own sensitivity. If Hamlet, the speaker of more and longer soliloquies than any other character in Shakespeare, is the privileged instance of psychological depth— and as the son seeking to find his place in a world out of joint, the one closest to the anxieties of the male poets of the era—the fascination with unusual mental states expands to take in the villains too, whether it is Coleridge on Iago, or De Quincey on Macbeth. In the latter the emphasis on the moment of suspension, which is also the suspension between the aesthetic and the ethical, has widespread affiliations that the instructor may wish to explore: forward to the timeless moment in Keats's odes and the Keatsian complexity of emotion, backward toward the questions of the representation of violence in Burke, or to comparison with the sanity of "feeling" in Wordsworth's Preface to *Lyrical Ballads*. What happens when the value given to emotion modulates into "intensity"?

George Gordon, Lord Byron

The critiques of Wilson and Scott highlight the novelty of *Childe Harold's Pilgrimage*: the sense of an author "speaking in his own person" (in Sir Walter Scott's phrase), revealing emotions disturbing as well as sublime, the more fascinating because the reputation of the man fed the poems and the poems fed the reputation of the man across the unstable border between them, making Byron himself into a myth, a star. The gloominess of the "Childe" owed much to the Gothic tradition, but also to Burke's glorification of chivalry, an idealization that the disillusioning course of the French Revolution and decades of conflict had rendered hollow to many. That Harold was not all of Byron the first letter, to Moore, makes clear, but as a melodramatic exaggeration of parts of Byron's character he spoke to a wearied generation. Students can be directed to instances of Byron's self-dramatization: the identification with the storm in our first excerpt, and the centrality of the meditating and declaiming "I" in canto 4, where Byron's affinity to the oratorical, including his exploitation of the commonplace, understood as a rhetorical trope already shared by poet and audience, can be contrasted to the domestic and self-effacing rhetoric of Coleridge and Wordsworth. In an episode such as that of the dying gladiator (4.139–45) Byron stands as our guide, animating for us a piece of classical sculpture, enacting a response on which we can model our own. One might further contrast Byron's apostrophe to his daughter (3.111–18) to similar gestures in *Frost at Midnight* and *Tintern Abbey*, drawing attention to the Coriolanian frame that dominates his passage and the fact that the turn to the younger other does *not* here close the poem. Byron instead concludes with an apostrophe to the vastness of the ocean. *Childe Harold* 4 becomes the Longinian "echo of a great soul" and a schooling in a cultural heritage: Murray quickly exploited excerpts from his most celebrated author in the guidebooks he published in the 1830s. In Byron (and after cantos 1–2 Harold and Byron converge) readers encountered both a melancholy sense of human limitation and the renewed hope of personal grandeur on the broad stage of history. The instructor might ask students to draw out the full range of implications of Byron's jibe at Wordsworth, Coleridge, and Southey in the Dedication to *Don Juan*: "You—Gentlemen! . . . / through still continued fusion / Of one another's minds, at last have grown / To deem as a most logical conclusion / That Poesy has wreaths for you alone: / There is a narrowness in such a notion, / Which makes me wish you'd change your lakes for ocean" (5). Byron's cosmopolitanism can be contrasted to the domesticity and localism celebrated in the poetry of Wordsworth and Coleridge.

The description of Lord Byron by former lover Caroline Lamb as "mad, bad, and dangerous to know" encapsulates the celebrity as well as the transgressive thrill of the character type that Byron embodied and bequeathed, "the Byronic Hero." By the time *Manfred* was published, in 1817, this type had been tainted by the scandalous "Separation" of Lord and Lady Byron in the spring of 1816: the causes were mysterious and overdetermined, but among the rumors was Lord Byron's incestuous liaison with his half sister Augusta. That Byron was willing to tease this rumor in *Manfred*, in the hero's tormented memories of some unnamable past sin involving his intimate Astarte, suggests the commercial potency that even this level of Titanic transgression could anticipate. Not only its eponymous protagonist, as self-tortured as any, but the closet drama *Manfred* itself figures a kind of Byronic Hero, a secretly motivated, sin-flaunting, self-consciously extreme, and extremely self-indulgent work. Students' reactions may vary as much as critical reactions and assessments. Some may love its modern existential heroics, its deepening of mental anguish into metaphysical angst, refusing all accommodation to the solaces of nature, of religion, of family, and inspiring modern antiheroes such as Brontë's Heathcliff, Melville's Ahab, and the alienated souls of *film noir*. Others may see these dynamics complicit with disease, pathology, and narcissism (a critique voiced within *Manfred*, too). And still others may giggle at the nearly self-parodic excess, reacting to *Manfred* as a kind of gothic comedy, a mannerist, over-the-top exhaustion of the character type. It is possible that Byron deliberately pushed this formation to such extremes in order to kill it off and liberate himself for the altogether different, steadily ironized heroics of *Don Juan*, the serial epic he had started to imagine and begun to compose the very next year, in 1818, in which the old-style Byronic Hero survives only in parody.

But the durability of the type survived even Byron's own execution, suggesting the deep attraction of its constituent elements and tantalizing composition. Part of this appeal is the way this character type drew on, but refused to moralize, a genealogy of darkly attractive self-torturers, allowing their own remorse to preempt any necessity for a reader's moral judgment. Part of the imaginative power of this character type draws on the way Byron did not so much invent it as crystallize it for his modern moment. Its lineage includes Shakespeare's tragic heroes (Hamlet, Macbeth, Othello, Edmund [in *King Lear*]), especially the voices of their tormented soliloquies, Marlowe's *Dr. Faustus* and Goethe's recent reprisal (its first part published in 1808), Milton's Satan (considered as a psychological and existential, rather than theological figure), and such contemporaries as the writer of self-torturing passion Jean-Jacques Rousseau and vanquished world-conqueror Napoleon, a "spirit antithetically mixt" to an "extreme in all things." All these figures defy tidy, coherent moral evaluation, their dramatic appeal and psychological fascination prevailing over easy judgments, but it is important to note that readers such as Coleridge took a more critical view, especially in reference to actions in the world. Coleridge's moral judgments (equating Napoleon and Satan and leaving Byron out of it) set the stage for Poet Laureate Southey's attack on the Byronic hero and his contemporary fraternity as the population of a "Satanic School" of literature. Even P. B. Shelley's Preface to *Prometheus Unbound* is sensitive to the ignoble aspects of Satanic lineage, differentiating the heroics of his god-tormented and heroically defiant Prometheus from the Satanic taints that Byron is happy to weave into the delineation of his heroes. A retreat to a mythological idiom that is historically antecedent to Milton's Biblically based drama assists Shelley in this differential refinement.

Our unit opens with Byron, who launched this modern hero with the overnight success of "Childe Harold" (the mysterious sinning, passionately tormented protagonist of *Childe Harold's Pilgrimage*, 1812). Tracking the career of this figure, students might be asked to note how *The Giaour* presents this hero in a theater of "the Mind"—a psychology that refigures the damnation of Milton's Hell, where "hell" is ultimately, and permanently, within, and where the torture is self-inflicted. In *The Corsair* the hero is shaped by disappointments in the world, but is tormented by his need to maintain and prosecute his opposition rather than seek a separate peace. The poem's neatly antithetical heroic couplets, far from effecting what Coleridge would call a reconciliation of opposite or discordant qualities, becomes the pattern of a relentless antagonism: almost every sentence involves a pivot on "but." Having read two of these selections, students will begin see the delineation of a character type, one whose name and circumstances may vary, but whose construction is basically the same. When they turn to *Lara*, they will see the degree to which Byron's delineations are now "by the book," indeed explicitly textualized: Lara is a figure of "lines" to be read, of feelings to be traced, and so forth—not necessarily into clear understanding, but into a familiar tale of advertised depths and secret passions. Byron's *Prometheus* not only shares an intertextual network with the Shelleys (Mary Shelley's subtitle for *Frankenstein* was *The Modern Prometheus*; Percy Shelley's political-metaphysical drama of 1819 is titled *Prometheus Unbound*), but is also contextualized in Byronism (Prometheus is a Titanic version of Byron's own torments) and Napoleonism, all enhanced with a sympathetically rendered Satanic defiance.

That the form of the Byronic hero that does survive in *Don Juan* is the tormented heroine (Donna Julia in her life-sentencing to a convent; Haidée gone mad with passion) suggests why women writers were fascinated by this character, too. Caroline Lamb's *roman a clef* produced her own, critically inflected version of the Byronic Hero, emphasizing his madness and destructiveness. Mary Shelley parses the Byronic Hero into two, ever more Satanically inwrought figures in *Frankenstein*, the transgressive, overreaching creator, Victor Frankenstein and his miserable, then vengeful Creature. The first excerpt from the novel shares with Coleridge a reading of Promethean defiance as colossal self-idolatry, even as Victor Frankenstein's narration of his enthusiasms and success may sweep the reader up in its passions. Students may note the way this self-involved, self-infatuated record still manages to expose some critical lineations, especially in marks of self-wasting pride. The Creature, by contrast, grasps his own fraught relation to Milton's Satan, like him, irrevocably damned to alienation, but unlike him, guiltless of original sin. Students may already be familiar with the novel or the fable; if so, they can be asked about how their sense of its two key figures is affected by a review in this discursive context. Shelley and Lamb, though writing as women, define this character type in male form. Hemans, using the octosyllabic couplets that shaped Byron's first romance of this hero (*The Giaour*) tries it out in a qualified female form, a vengeful heroine disguised (as some of Byron's heroines are) as a page, and displaying, indeed advertising, the iconography of the Byronic hero. Students can be invited to see how the wealth of obvious verbal echoes almost constitute an allusion to Byron's several texts.

Southey memorably set himself up for ridicule when he used his preface to his brief epic, on the ascension of George III to heaven, to damn the modern vogue of Byronic heroics. In an era when unexpurgated Shakespeare was being eclipsed by Reverend Bowdler's edition of *The Family Shakespeare* (which no less a Byron enthusiast than Francis Jeffrey said should prevail over the profane and bawdy original), Southey's policing seems less a cranky piece of hysteria than it might seem today. He claims, in his capacity as the kingdom's chief poet, to worry that the panache of Byronism is being used by all sorts of young men to justify reprehensible behavior. However this may be, it is important to remember that Southey, a Tory, was also exercising political differences with liberals Byron and Shelley and calling for censorship of their work on "moral" grounds. Byron retaliates by putting the patron saint of the Byronic hero, Satan himself, in his satire of Southey, where the devil appears as no archfiend but as a courtly ironist who stands for Byron himself. The difference between the regent of Heaven, St. Michael, and the viceroy of Hell, Satan, is staged as a difference of fashion rather than morals, an encounter between "his Darkness and his Brightness," with Satan showing a little aristocratic disdain at the more recently elevated Michael. That

Byron could spoof the whole discourse of the Byronic hero suggests both his ironic regard of his success as well as his enduring affection for the figure that continued to define it.

Don Juan, too, emphasizes the comic over the sublime, but there are notable continuities with the earlier poetry. The Dedication, though unpublished in his lifetime, marks his unrepentant politics, while canto 1, in refracting his autobiography, even more thoroughly makes his personal experience the point of reference—though demonstrating that "experience" is not a simple given, but a complex category built up from the narrator's reflections on history, literature, religion, genre, and contemporary society. The flaunted artifice of Don Juan, from its ottava rima stanza, outrageous rhymes, authorial interventions, mixture of satire and epic, and fictionalized self-representation, can be compared to the blank-verse "poem to Coleridge," Wordsworth's intimate revision of epic. Nothing more quickly underscores Byron's habitual resort to the theatrical multiplication of aspects of his character than the contrast between Wordsworth's arduous effort to integrate his "two consciousnesses" in The Prelude and Byron's splitting of his experience into Juan and the narrator, whose different perspectives he plays against one another. Wordsworth, who declared that "Don Juan will do more harm to the English character than anything of our time," in his bitterness located two features of the poem that instructors may wish to explore: its perspective on what it means to be English, and its attitude toward character, toward that goal of growth toward, and consolidation of, moral personality that Wordsworth's works exemplify (a contrast that made him Poet Laureate, and Byron a scandal).

Contemporary readers so drawn in by the love story of Juan and Julia that they overlooked the adulterous frame on which Byron insists were shocked by the naturalistic violence of the shipwreck scenes in canto 2. Our sequence from Cantos 2 and 3 shows Byron again following sentimental indulgence with debunking worldliness; to many readers the sequence seemed a brutal trifling with emotions, and its possible motives—defensive, self-correcting—can be fruitfully explored. "Sequence" points to a cardinal quality of Byron's verse; as W. H. Auden observed, "What Byron means by life—which explains why he could never appreciate Wordsworth or Keats—is the motion of life, the passage of events and thoughts. His visual descriptions of scenery or architecture are not particularly vivid, nor are his portrayals of states of mind particularly profound, but at the description of things in motion or the way in which the mind wanders from one thought to another he is a great master." Such strengths require space for their realization, as Auden recognizes: Byron's verse, compared to a lyric such as A slumber did my spirit seal or the concentration of Keats's odes, can seem relaxed. To appreciate Byron's effects, students can profitably be asked to look closely at any sequence of ten or so stanzas in Don Juan that appeals to them, and then to consider the different understanding of temporality in Byron, in Wordsworth and Coleridge, and in Keats. The commitment to passage and motion in Byron can be set against the practice of "emotion recollected in tranquillity" in Wordsworth and the older poet's subordination of action to reflection, or the circling around a central symbol in Keats. Though the "mind wander(ing) from one thought to another" describes Tintern Abbey and

Frost at Midnight as well as *Don Juan*, students will quickly see that Byron's wandering is along the surface—of cognition, intellectual reflection, "pro-ing and con-ing," to use a phrase of Keats—and hence seems immediate and realistic—rather than towards mysterious inwardness, the quality identified by the "unawares" of the *Rime*, and the subtle freedom from linearity. *Don Juan* proliferates a metonymic chain rather than the metaphoric and symbolic unity lauded by Coleridge. The instructor might ask students to consider *Don Juan* in terms of the distinction between fancy and imagination in Chapter 13 of *Biographia Literaria*: it is the great work of the aggregate and the "counter." Auden's observation on style may also start an interesting discussion: "What had been Byron's defect as a serious poet, his lack of reverence for words, was a virtue for the comic poet. Serious poetry requires that the poet treat words as if they were persons, but comic poetry demands that he treat them as things and few, if any, English poets have rivaled Byron's ability to put words through hoops." Byron's acceptance of the social continuities of language can be juxtaposed with the discussion of language in the Preface to *Lyrical Ballads*.

Byron's letters on *Don Juan* reveal his deliberate insistence on the many-sidedness of experience (this too may be compared with Wordsworth's "egotistical sublime," or as Shelley put it, Wordsworth's concentration on always grounding "contemplation" at the point at which he stood). Of the first two cantos he insisted: "I maintain that it is the most moral of poems—but if people won't discover the moral that is their fault not mine"; three years later he declared: "D[on] Juan will be known by and bye for what it is intended a *satire* on *abuses* of the present *states* of Society—and not an eulogy of vice;—it may be now and then voluptuous—I can't help that—Ariosto is worse—Smollett (see Lord Strutwell in vol 2d of R[oderick] R[andom]) ten times worse—and Fielding no better." Students may be asked to test this claim against the anarchic or comic impulses of the poem; more subtly, to ponder what Byron might mean by "moral." To what degree is the term restricted to the notion of *a* moral, and to what degree does "morality" for Byron require the power of extended discrimination among a variety of perspectives, a refusal to be taken in by cant (including one's own smugly self-serving fictions) or to settle for premature judgment? The complex array of perspectives in the episode of the trimmer poet (3.78--8) offers a rich instance of Byron's ironic intelligence, at once an affirmation of values, a satire on opportunistic authors, and an oblique self-portrait, since Byron himself, in love with Teresa Guiccioli, was not untouched by feelings of having abandoned ideals for pleasure.

The sudden switches of tone that offended many readers—perhaps even more than the charges of "voluptuous[ness]"—are inseparable from issues of gender. Students will have seen Byron's ambivalent attitude to women from the beginning. "Alas! the love of women! It is known / To be a lovely and a fearful thing" (2.199), laments the narrator, and this double aspect of Byron's representation of women, from the portraits of Inez, Julia, and Haidée, down to the level of rhyme—"ladies intellectual" / "henpecked you all" (1.22)—should provoke lively discussion. (The attitude is articulated in Juan's later immersion in the "gynocracy" of English society, rhymed with "hypocrisy" in 12.66 and 16.52.) The letter of 26 October 1818

[1819], like the defense that "No Girl will ever be seduced by reading D[on] J[uan]" quoted above, points to the gendering of audience that Byron's poetry illuminates: the letter of 6 April 1819 discloses Byron's uneasy awareness that his magnetism had made the "ladies" a substantial part of his audience, and hence of his commercial success; the charges of indecency his poetry now generated closed Don Juan to women in a world much more concerned with gender propriety than the aristocratic Regency circles in which Byron had flourished; students may consider how much Byron courted outrage, as a mark of his freedom from the audience of women that was increasingly the audience of poetry. Class too enters into the picture: Childe Harold, sublime, poignant, a cultural monument, was the image of Byron that held middle- and upper-class readers of Byron throughout the nineteenth century; Don Juan, radical, satirical, and published in cheap editions, had a wide readership among lower classes. The social critique of the English cantos, admired even by T. S. Eliot, shows that Byron remained an English poet—but from the perspective of an expatriate aristocrat, at once inside and outside the world he anatomizes. The importance of his aristocratic status should be drawn out: that Byron was Lord Byron matters in several ways—to readers seeking to live vicariously, or to acquire cachet by imitating; or as an emblem of transgressive power; or of freedom from bourgeois values. In what ways, students reading Wilson's critique might be asked to consider, is Byron the antithesis of bourgeois experience, and in what ways the very model for the isolated, alienated reader? How do we understand the fact that romance became the best-selling genre of the book trade, the very symbol of the conditions that brought the world of romance to an end? How do we understand the Europe-wide phenomenon of the aristocratic author, after Burke had declared that the age of chivalry was dead?

The paradoxes that underlie Byron's force were capped by his death while aiding the Greek revolution, the refuge for all the hopes ended by the metamorphosis of the French Revolution into Napoleonic empire, followed by the fall of Napoleon and restoration of the conservative monarchies. Coming after the critique of military glory in cantos 7 and 8 of Don Juan, Byron's fate can be seen as either a final instance of theatrical self-delusion or as an admirable constancy to principle. The two late lyrics we print demonstrate his ability to maintain an ironic play of viewpoints even on enterprises for which he was willing to give his life. "On This Day," widely reprinted in the newspapers after his death, was influential in shaping the final image of Byron.

Percy Bysshe Shelley

An older literary history grouped Blake (born 1757), Wordsworth (born 1770), and Coleridge (born 1772) as the first generation of Romantic poets; Byron (born 1788), Shelley (born 1792), and Keats (born 1795) as the second. One aim of this anthology is to challenge such categorizations (see the remarks on "the difficulty of specifying the term 'Romantic'" in our introduction to the period), and students might be asked to reflect how adequately a natural term—"generation"—describes a process of canon formation—while at the same time recognizing that the conventional resort to it is itself evidence of the prevalence of Romantic thought and its typical representation of cultural practice as natural phenomenon. The chronological division does serve to distinguish those writers formed by the swell and ebb of enthusiasm for the French Revolution and those who came to notice well afterwards, in the post-war reaction and economic downturn. To these distinctions one might add others, asking students to consider the explanatory weight to be ascribed to them: the varied but modest origins of Blake (hosier's son), Wordsworth (steward's son), and Coleridge (vicar's son, charity-boy school), as opposed to the aristocratic status of Shelley (son of a Member of Parliament, later Baronet) and Byron (inheritor of a title, a Baron); Blake and Keats apprenticed, the others studied at the ancient universities, with all that implies about status and connection; Wordsworth and Coleridge identified with the north, an area where traditional ways survived; Byron and Shelley with the south, in Italy, a land that to English eyes had always seemed dangerously seductive and morally lax ("An Englishman Italianate is the Devil incarnate," ran a Renaissance tag), in the Mediterranean, which in the 1820s still fermented with revolution. And where fit Keats, tarred as a "Cockney" of the Hunt coterie and in straitened circumstances, but drawn to Italy for his health, invited by Shelley? When Byron, Shelley, and Hunt collaborated on The Liberal, the title spoke to a new term in a political terrain previously divided into Tory and Whig, radical, democrat, Jacobin, and conservative.

Overlapping publication dates further complicate any simple alignment of "generations": Byron's Childe Harold's Pilgrimage 1–2 (1812), Shelley's Queen Mab (1813), Wordsworth's Excursion (1814), Wordsworth's Poems (1815), Shelley's Alastor (1816), Byron's Childe Harold's Pilgrimage 3 (1816), Coleridge's Sibylline Leaves and Biographia Literaria (1817), Keats's Endymion (1818), Byron's Childe Harold's Pilgrimage 4 (1818), Coleridge's The Friend (1818), Byron's Don Juan 1–2 (1819), Wordsworth's Peter Bell and The Waggoner (1819), Shelley's Prometheus Unbound (1820), Keats's Lamia, Isabella, The Eve of St Agnes, and Other Poems (1820), Shelley's Adonais (1821), Wordsworth's Ecclesiastical Sketches and Memorial of a Tour on the Continent, 1820 (1822), Coleridge's On the Constitution of Church and State (1830), and—well after the deaths of all the other poets—Wordsworth's Yarrow Revisited (1835).

This interweaving alerts us to a complexity of feelings in the relations of Byron and Shelley to the older poets. In one sense Coleridge and Wordsworth were already established precursors, figures whose achievements one could learn from, as poets have always learned from tradition, defining themselves by the gestures of acknowledgment and rejection through which they shape their own writing. Coleridge and Wordsworth were not comfortably removed, however, and hallowed by the authority of time that (to choose a salient instance for all these writers) rendered Milton an imposing mark of excellence for which to strive, but preserved one from daily rivalry. They were contemporary writers with whom one had to compete for attention and praise, whose press of ongoing publications could not be ignored. Hence we begin our selection from Shelley with "To Wordsworth" and in our notes underline the recurrent play of allusion and echo. Instructors will hear others, and can make of them entries into comparative analysis: consider, for example, "Reality's dark dream" in Coleridge's *Dejection* (95) and Shelley's "lest the grave should be, / Like life and fear, a dark reality" in his *Hymn to Intellectual Beauty* (47–48), as focusing the differences in the narratives of life in time that the two poems sketch. Underscoring the echoes should trigger provocative questions: what do they suggest about the role of emulation, and how does emulation accord with a poetics of inspiration? What do they suggest about tradition, revision, and self-definition? What anxieties—literary? personal?—might they disclose?

The charged observations ran in both directions across the generation gap. Two years before *To Wordsworth* Mary Shelley noted in her journal: "Shelley . . . brings home Wordsworth's *Excursion*, of which we read a part, much disappointed. He is a slave" (14 September 1814). The savage conclusion of the sonnet—"to grieve, / Thus, having been, that thou shouldst cease to be" (13-14)—warrants unpacking in class: in what sense did Wordsworth, who lived for another 34 years, outliving Shelley by 28, "cease to be"? Would the denunciation be as sharp if Shelley did not feel Wordsworth's continued presence? How should one understand the connection between the death sentence and the way Shelley builds his poem by taking over Wordsworth's own language throughout (two instances: that of *Ode: Intimations of Immortality* in the quatrain, of *Peele Castle* at 9-10)? Wordsworth, for his part, was recorded long after Shelley's death as believing that "Shelley had the greatest native powers in poetry of all the men of this age" but "Saw in Shelley the lowest form of irreligion. . . . Named the discrepancy between his creed and his imagination as the marring idea of his works." Shelley's philosophic radicalism, including his violent anti-clericalism, is evidently in the line of Enlightenment rationalism, and instructors may find it helpful to return to our selections from his his father-in-law Godwin. The continuities raise questions about the relationship between debate among intellectuals and working-class organization, between the genteel reformers and the new force of the people in the 1820s, that bear on *The Mask of Anarchy*. Instructors may want to ask students to address the widespread admiration for the poem's protest against tyranny, in the "masque"-like parade of its agents and in its phantasmatic internal oration, which takes up the last three-fifths of the poem, in relation to some contrary elements: that Shelley remained in Italy, sending the poem to Leigh Hunt, who would have borne all the risks of charges of sedition had he published it; that the dreaming poet of the opening stanzas never wakes up, but merges into the fantasy oration; the peculiar mystery by which Anarchy dies and the visionary Shape arises; the efficacy of non-violent resistance, and whether the concluding exhortation "Rise like lions after slumber" (372 ff.) is or is not non-violent.

Put bluntly, one might ask whether Shelley's radicalism constitutes fidelity to the principles of the Revolution (and students might ponder the revision of the Christian "Faith, Hope, and Charity" into "Love, Hope, and Self-esteem" in *Hymn to Intellectual Beauty*, 37), undimmed by the reaction that marks Wordsworth and Coleridge, or the radical chic of an aristocrat safely living on his inheritance in Italy? Whether his politics constitute a holdover of an earlier radical discourse rendered irrelevant by the shifting locus of actual political power since 1790, or a prescient forecast of the Chartists and the Marxists, both of whom found his writings inspirational? A thoughtful response to this avowedly irritating antithesis might begin by noting that it assumes exactly the historical linearity that Shelley challenges. The first chorus from *Hellas* is exemplary: "Worlds on worlds are rolling ever / From creation to decay," but against this image of ceaseless mutability Shelley posits that "*they* are still immortal / Who through birth's orient portal / And death's dark chasm hurrying to and fro, / Clothe their unceasing flight / In the brief dust and light / Gathered around their chariots as they go" (197–98; 201–06). Beneath the flux of forms the ideas endure: "New shapes . . . / New gods, new laws" are but the temporary embodiments of uncontingent truths. As the final chorus, "The world's great age begins anew," proclaims: "Another Athens shall arise, / And to remoter time / Bequeath, like sunset to the skies, / The splendour of its prime" (1084–87). Instructors may want to compare the commitments to the Greek Revolution of Byron, who fought and died for it, and of Shelley, who never set foot in Greece; but distinguishing them is more fruitful than using one to depreciate the other. " 'I do think the preference of *writers* to *agents*," wrote Byron in an early journal (24 November 1813), "the mighty stir made about scribbling and scribes, by themselves and others—a sign of effeminacy, degeneracy, and weakness. Who would write, who had anything better to do? 'Action—action—action'—said Demosthenes: 'Actions—actions,' I say, and not writing,—least of all, rhyme." The distinction appears to focus the difference between Byron's involvement in immediate circumstance, and Shelley's rhetorically persuasive celebration of ideals, but a more capacious understanding of the relationship between *writing* and *agency* will suggest that Shelley's writings might too have their effect.

The importance for Shelley, however, is that the validity of an ideal does not depend on its outcome. In the final words of *Prometheus Unbound*, unprinted here: "To suffer woes which Hope thinks infinite; / To forgive wrongs darker than Death or Night; / To defy Power which seems Omnipotent; / To love, and bear; to hope, till Hope creates / From its own wreck the thing it contemplates; / Neither to change nor falter nor repent; / This, like thy glory, Titan! is to be / Good, great, and joyous, beautiful and free; / This is alone Life, Joy, Empire and Victory." Ideals thus stand as a perpetual *potential*, self-renewing from their own defeat as the world goes "rolling ever." Shelleyan time is apart from the determinism that came to dominate much nineteenth-century thought about history. Its determining feature is a refusal to be wholly of the time, wholly timely. In its elegiac mode it sounds much like Wordsworth, a resonance instructors will want to explore: "We look before and after, / And pine for what is not" (*To a Sky-Lark*, 86–87). In its prophetic mode it epitomizes Romanticism as an anachronistic disruptive power, too late or too soon (Godwin or Marx?), a rejuvenating excess that refuses to be contained by any teleological scheme, whether of historical progress or individual growth. (Compare how Wordsworth assimilates "something evermore about to be" [6.542] to the narrative line of *The Prelude*—or does he?)

As these instances suggest, the rude question just put to Shelley is met—not answered, but enacted—in his poetry. The sonnets furnish a compact site in which to study the inseparability of questions of Shelley's politics from his formal agility (as well as providing comparisons between his handling of the form with Wordsworth's or Charlotte Smith's). *Lift not the painted veil* offers a compressed version of the metaphysics that animate *Mont Blanc*, *Hymn to Intellectual Beauty*, *Adonais* and numerous other Shelley poems strung across a dualism of the physical, temporal world, and the mysterious spirit world of eternity. Given Shelley's sense that the temporal world is composed of deceptively unreal images, students may not register the "not" in line 1—the injunction not to trespass into the beyond. The risks become apparent at the volta, or turn, which Shelley places at the start of line 6, thus inverting the usual 8/6 organization of the Petrarchan sonnet. *Ozymandias* neatly nests historical existence and representational modes, subtly culminating with the power of poetry: Ozymandias's rule, Ozymandias's boast, the representation of Ozymandias, in sculpture and the text on the pedestal, the fragmentation of the sculpture, the communication of the text (now ironic) by a traveller's anecdote, and then the poet's sonnet. The date of composition and the journal of publication suggest multiple ramifications in post-Napoleonic Europe: Napoleon, who had invaded Egypt, had been defeated, but was still a hero to many, while his fall had revived the conservative monarchs Shelley and Hunt deplored.

In *England in 1819* Shelley defies the formal patterns of both the Italian and Shakespearean sonnet, increasing the syntactic pressure of his list of ills toward the predicate, finally appearing in the blunt statement "Are graves" (13). Even here the postponed declarative syntax does not close, but initiates a couplet that drives past the rhyme toward *Burst* (14). In this climactically enjambed "may / Burst," Shelley allows two incompatible senses of *may*: if it implies "perhaps," it is tentative, whether with cautious optimism or sad skepticism; if it means "is enabled to," it is energized as a promise of inevitable emergence. Students may be asked to consider whether the "may" yields to the explosion of "burst," or whether the emphasis placed by the rhyme on "may" exposes a hesitation, the weakness of a politics of miraculous agency, or whether it marks a tough-minded assessment that in the current conditions redemption is unlikely. The divergent readings show that the question is one Shelley's form produces as unresolvable. A letter to Hunt pivots interestingly on the point: "I do not expect you to publish it, but you may show it to whom you please," he wrote of the sonnet. Publication would provoke two audiences, the oppressed for whom the sonnet articulates political grievances and the oppressors for whom it articulates a political threat. The compromise of giving the poem to Hunt with no demands, but with yet another calculated overload on *may*, places the agency on him: either with Shelley's permission, or from his own judgment, he "may" show the poem to readers in England in 1819.

This gesture confronts readers with the question of audience. *England in 1819* was not published until 1839, *Lift not the painted veil* until 1824, *The Mask of Anarchy* until 1832; *Adonais* was printed in Pisa and sold so poorly in England that Shelley's publisher merely disposed of the copies he had received (1821); *A Defence of Poetry* appeared for the first time in 1840. In some instances failure to publish was prudent, as we have just seen, and in other instances merely unfortunate, but compared both with Wordsworth's initial confidence that poetry written in "the real language of men" could be widely accessible and with Byron's best-sellerdom. Shelley's relation with his audience(s), like Blake's, should be explored. *The Mask of Anarchy*, a topical poem targeted for the *Examiner*, drew forth a simpler style than, for example, *Adonais*, but was too inflammatory to publish; the poet who, in the Preface to *Prometheus Unbound*, declared that his "purpose has hitherto been simply to familiarise the highly refined imagination of the more select classes of poetical readers with beautiful idealisms of moral excellence" (1820) evidently conceived of his task, and his readership, quite differently from the Wordsworth who defined the poet as "man speaking to men." The difficulty that students often feel when confronted by Shelley should not be explained away, but seized as the portal to twin questions: why is it difficult? and what does it mean to intend difficulty?

With *Mont Blanc* it often helps to suggest that Shelley has organized his language in part to frustrate understanding, as if to mime his own overwhelming by the spectacle of Mont Blanc, the glacier, the ravine, and the river Arve. Notice, for instance, the tumult of nearly anagrammatic words that spills over the blank verse of stanza 1 and the top of 2—ever/river/raves/Ravine/Arve/cavern—a linguistic transformation that reflects the dynamic power of the scene. Even the rhymes of the first stanza—things/springs/brings—are enjambed, so that form is visible, but not strongly. The letters twisting into new words and the tension between the rhymes and the enjambments convey a sense of language at the limits of its power to represent the object of its attention. Crucial to Shelley's aim is a double critique, of the seemingly solid "universe of things" (1) and of the capacity of language to represent it. The river is not a material entity, but rather "Power in likeness of the Arve" (16), itself a kind of figure for, or the temporary likeness assumed by, "Power"; seeking to represent the "clear universe of things" with which it is in "unremitting interchange" (39–40), the mind does not enjoy a language derived from objects (as the Preface to *Lyrical Ballads* put it), but turns inwards, where in "the still cave of the witch Poesy" (44) it finds only the figures of language: "seeking among the shadows that pass by, / Ghosts of all things that are, some shade of thee, / Some phantom, some faint image" (45–47).

Shelley's lyric thus forces the reader to examine questions both of "Power" and of representation. Does the sensation of power stirred by Mont Blanc confirm the existence of "Power" apart from and transcending human consciousness? (A question the more loaded historically, insofar as the sublimity of the Alps was conventionally taken to demonstrate the existence of God.) How does such power manifest itself to consciousness, and with what sort of intelligibility, information, consequences, or mystery? What power might the human mind have in its naming of this power in the first place, even if the effect is to diminish, or annihilate, the importance of any one mind? The questions climax in Part 5, a description in which the repeated deictic "there" is both the home of power and frighteningly privative: still, calm, dark, moonless, lone, silent, voiceless, where "none beholds." The question that closes the poem ("And what were thou . . .") is often read as a rhetorical question, in the cliché usage of the term, as if it implied that without a human mind to project and confer value, Mont Blanc would be merely a "vacancy" (144)—punningly, a blank—rather than a symbol of a powerfully mysterious silence and solitude. But Shelley's conjunction *And* (instead of, say, *Yet*, which would assist this implication) lets the question seem apposite, rather than contrary, to the preceding statement—namely, that there *is* something outside of thought which governs thought.

Shelley, in the registers of the hotels at which he stayed on the tour during which he saw Mont Blanc, declared his occupation (in Greek) as "Democrat, Philanthropist, and Atheist" and his destination as "L'Enfer." Whether he was maddened by stock piety or tourist gush, the bravado was risky; Byron, coming upon one of the entries, crossed it out to protect his friend, but the others remained, reprinted in guidebooks, feeding the demonic image of himself Shelley no doubt courted. Shelley's gesture is theatrical but uncomplicated; the rhetoric of his poem, suspending closure on a question, between "the secret strength of things" and "the mind's imaginings," between "silence and solitude" as plenitude or as "vacancy," operates a powerfully suggestive doubt.

Instructors may want to ask students to compare Shelley's treatment of this landscape with Byron's Alpine vistas (in *Manfred* and *Childe Harold III*); with Wordsworth's report of his first view of Mont Blanc in Book 6 of *The Prelude* or his account of the mind's transactions with nature at the top of Mount Snowdon in Book 13 (neither of which the Shelleys would have known), or his treatment of mind and nature in *Tintern Abbey*.

Shelley was imbued with the classics, and our notes signal some of the influence of Plato, whom he translated. The Platonic insistence on the deceptiveness of appearance produces a structure consonant with that of eighteenth-century skepticism, a tradition, as we have seen, in which Shelley was also well read. In either case essential reality remains unknowable to man's limited perceptions, though the balance shifts across the spectrum from affirmation of transcendence to doubt of its existence—exactly the drama of *Mont Blanc*. To illustrate further the consequences of this philosophical position for Shelley's language it may help to concentrate on *"To a Sky-Lark."* The critical element of the bird is that it should be invisible (compare the "viewless gales" of *Mont Blanc* [59], the "unseen Power" of *Intellectual Beauty* [1], and the "unseen presence" of *West Wind* [2]), known only by its song. Thus absent though producing an effect, the bird stimulates the mind. Shelley responds to what may be seen as a specimen case of his epistemology with a series of similes. "What thou art we know not" confesses the speaker, but proceeds: "What is most like thee?" (31–32). What follows is a series of approximations, or rather, figures, for what cannot be stated directly: "Like a Poet hidden . . . Like a high-born maiden / In a palace tower . . . Like a glow-worm golden / In a dell of dew, / Scattering unbeholden / Its aerial hue . . . Like a rose embowered" (36–52). Serial simile rather than metaphoric compression is the hallmark of the verse; as the mind rushes to comprehend an elusive reality, figures will accumulate, generate each other, dissolve and give way to the next, as they do when Shelley apostrophizes the "wild West Wind" (*Ode to the West Wind* [1]). Mental action, not mimesis of an external world is the aim. Instructors may ask students to compare this process to Byron's "passage," to use Auden's term, and to consider the relationship between metonymic style and philosophic skepticism; on the other hand, one might compare Shelley's mode to Coleridge's poetics of symbol and the privilege granted poetic unity in *Biographia Literaria*, or, contrastingly, to the description of imagination as a "strong working of the mind" from the *Lectures on Shakespeare*.

For a display of Shelley at his most typically and technically accomplished, one might carefully examine the *Ode to the West Wind*, tracking the terza-rima sonnet stanzas (four tercets and a couplet) and their interlocking rhymes, the energetic enjambments that evoke the force that Shelley evokes, the rush of assonance and alliteration, the repetitions. The first three stanzas convey the force of the wind on the earth; in the fourth stanza, the poet seeks participation in this energy and realizes his exclusion; in the fifth he imagines, and prays for inspiration, to make his poetry a force aligned with the prophetic, life-bearing wind, bringing spiritual and possibly political rejuvenation. Like *Mont Blanc*, the ode ends on a question: "If Winter comes, can Spring be far behind?" (70). This has been called the most famous rhetorical question in English poetry. Yet given that the first draft was a statement ("When Winter comes Spring lags not far behind"), Shelley's revision to interrogative syntax may pose a genuine question about the symbolic parallel—can the logic of seasonal renewal in the natural world be extended to spiritual renewal in human existence?—and its suspense acts powerfully on the reader. The ode invites comparison to other poems that invoke natural forces and human circumstances (Baillie's *Thunder*, Wordsworth's *Tintern Abbey*, the thunderstorm in canto 3 of Byron's *Childe Harold's Pilgrimage*), with Keats's *To Autumn*, and with other poems that invoke the wind as an agent of transformation, such as the opening of Wordsworth's *Prelude* or Coleridge's *Dejection*. More generally, one might ask students to compare the means through which Shelley impedes his reader's comprehension, forcing a heightened attention, and the means Wordsworth employs to the same end. Some telling discussion of the differences between difficulty produced by minimalism, as in *A slumber did my spirit seal* (syntactic simplicity, unremarkable vocabulary, cryptic reduction), and that produced by virtuoso interweaving and elaboration should emerge.

Shelley's virtuosic remaking of tradition is most evident in *Adonais*. The sense of composing out of a high literary heritage is evident from the very beginning, in the epigraphs from Plato and Moschus's *Elegy on the Death of Bion*. Students might be asked the effect of introducing a poem with bits of untranslated Greek: as they mark a tradition, as they define an elite audience. Among models closer in time is Milton's pastoral elegy, *Lycidas* (printed in volume 1 of the anthology). If the instructor has organized the course chronologically, *Adonais* may be the occasion to look back on the Preface to *Lyrical Ballads*, asking students to measure the distance between Wordsworth's repudiation of poetic artifice and Shelley's embrace of it: the literariness of *Adonais* (in contrast, too, to Coleridge's poems which "affect not to be poetry") shows a conception of genius as difference-within-a-tradition, as opposed to (the fiction of) spontaneous originality. The earliness of the reference to Milton (stanza 4) confirms that Shelley wanted the comparison to *Lycidas* to be made by the reader. Note that Milton is described as "the Sire of an immortal strain" but also placed in opposition to "The priest, the slave, and the liberticide": it is Milton as republican hero, as well as Milton the epic poet, whom Shelley summons. To draw out the political implications of this stanza the instructor may adduce stanza 10 of the Dedication to *Don Juan*, where Byron makes Milton the moral antipodes of the despised Castlereagh. Modern readers may also need to be reminded that for Shelley to place Keats together with Milton and the other "sons of light" (presumably Homer and Dante) was an affront to conservative critics. To Byron he confessed: "I need not be told that I have been carried too far by the enthusiasm of the moment; by my piety, and my indignation, in panegyric. But if I have erred, I console myself with reflecting that it is in defence of the weak— not in conjunction with the powerful." Shelley's elegy is oppositional, not merely monumental; "I have dipped my pen in consuming fire to chastise [Keats's] destroyers," he wrote to friends; "otherwise the tone of the poem is solemn and exalted." Students might be asked how Shelley handles this complexity of emotion in the poem, or to consider *Adonais* as a group manifesto: in what ways does Shelley use the death of Keats to establish a counter-orthodox lineage and solidarity among Milton, Keats, Byron (stanzas 27 and 30; *not* the Byron of *Don Juan*), the much-scorned Leigh Hunt (stanza 35), and most of all himself (stanzas 31–34)?

The images of the poet in *Adonais* may also be juxtaposed with those noticed in writers discussed above. Keats is both "made one with Nature" (stanza 42) and so "a portion of the loveliness / Which once he made more lovely" (stanza 43) and elevated into one of the "splendours of the firmament of time" (stanza 44), seemingly both returned to earth, his individual identity reabsorbed into nature, and immortalized as a great poet. Shelley's conceptions of the relation of language and the world, and of the one and the many, cast light on this doubleness. To state that "There is heard / His voice in all her music" (stanza 42) is to point to the poet's power to transform our apprehension of reality: the world is different to us (note the agentless passive of "there is heard") because of Keats. And by extension, Keats "doth bear / His part, while the one Spirit's plastic stress / Sweeps through the dull dense world; compelling there / All new successions to the forms they wear" (stanza 43), because the world is built up by the collective, cumulative, co-operative efforts of those who have imagined it, who together form "one Spirit." The remarks on the choruses from *Hellas*, above, and on *A Defence of Poetry*, below, amplify this argument. Shelley may thus be seen to offer a particular reconciliation of the poet as Aeolian harp and the poet as Prometheus described in the section on Coleridge. A more engrossing comparison is supplied by *The Rime*: students might be asked to consider the relation between the final vision of Shelley himself (stanzas 53–55) and the Ancient Mariner (and also the poet-figure of *Kubla Khan*). As our headnote suggests, *Adonais* seems to subvert the customary function of elegy to provide consolation; at the very least it sails right past "'t is Death is dead, not he; / Mourn not for Adonais" (stanza 41) to the drama of the speaker's own end, fearful and desiring. The question whether the conclusion constitutes apotheosis, suicidal self-destruction, or romantic fulfillment through death ought to provoke lively discussion. The challenge of Shelley's charged indeterminateness may be revealed by comparing this figure of dissolution with the consolidation of identity at the close of Wordsworth's *Ode: Intimations of Immortality*.

Other exercises will have suggested themselves. One might cast discussion forward, by asking students to consider how Keats would have reacted to being memorialized in this fashion. One might also compare *Adonais* with *Childe Harold 4*, with which it shares the Spenserian stanza form and in which Rome plays a significant part.

After the urgencies of Shelley's earlier poems, the lyrics "To Jane" produced in the last year of his life (there are two others: *To Jane: The Invitation* and *To Jane: The Recollection*) show a new calm. Shelley found in Shakespeare's Miranda, Ferdinand, and Ariel a script through which to figure in *With a Guitar, to Jane* his infatuation with Jane Williams. "I think," he wrote in 1822, "one is always in love with something or other; the error, and I confess it is not easy for spirits cased in flesh and blood to avoid it, consists in seeking in a mortal image the likeness of what is perhaps eternal" (Letter of 18 June). Students might be asked to consider the various purposes served by representing through *The Tempest* what in another perspective was a married man's love for another man's (common-law) wife. Casting himself as the spirit Ariel who both submissively "serve[s]" (l. 34) and actively "guides" (l. 29) Jane/Miranda, Shelley desexualizes the relationship, but at the cost of acknowledging himself outside the "humbler happier lot" (l. 35) of Jane and Edward/Ferdinand. If the drama thus re-enacts the split between the spirit/ideal and physical/material/historical worlds that energizes Shelley's great poems (and his poem on love, unprinted here, *Epipsychidion*, the 1821 work to which the letter just quoted refers as "an idealised history of my life and feelings"), it also offers middle terms. Ariel provides Shelley with a part, distanced and not overwhelmed by his feelings (or disillusionment, when the mortal proves mortal after all, as happened repeatedly in Shelley's life), and the guitar, the "slave of Music" (l. 2) is a material body that will speak to those who "question well / The spirit that inhabits it" (ll. 80–81), and reveal its "highest holiest tone / For our belovèd Jane alone" (ll. 89–90). As the next poem gracefully puts the compliment, Jane's voice reveals the "world far from ours, / Where music and moonlight and feeling / Are one" (ll. 22–24), an emblem of artistic success unimagined for a human in the more intractable oppositions of, say, *To a Skylark*, *Lift not the painted veil*, or *Hymn to Intellectual Beauty*. Students might be asked to consider the contrast also between the guitar, traditional instrument of the love serenade, and the Aeolian harp of Coleridge's poem. (See Jerome McGann, "The Scerets of an Elder Day: Shelley after *Hellas*," *Keats-Shelley Journal*, 1966).

Discussion of A *Defence of Poetry* gains by being joined to reconsideration of Wordsworth's Preface to *Lyrical Ballads* and Coleridge's various reflections on language and poetry. Particular points of comparison include: the role of pleasure; the poet as "a man speaking to men" and the poet as a "nightingale, who sits in darkness to cheer its own solitude"; and the role of will in composition. The famous last sentence of the *Defence*—"Poets are the unacknowledged legislators of the world"—stakes a high polemic claim against the denigration of poetry in the essay by Peacock that provoked it, but students might be asked to consider how "legislator" functions in Shelley's text. Undoubtedly Shelley is throwing the mantle of the lawgiver around the poet, but a thoughtful reading of Shelley thus far will also suggest that he is employing *legislate* in a special sense: poets are the *legislators* of the world not because they make law, but because it is their imaginings of it which shape our perceptions of the world itself. This is both the highest possible status, and a far cry from the civil power "legislator" connotes in political discourse. As always, Shelley is provocatively ambiguous: the poet is more exalted than civil lawmakers, but also removed from their world. As the final paragraph develops the argument, poets are both the Promethean shapers and the "astonished" vessels of "the spirit of the age," speakers of "words which express what they understand not." Figurative gain is finely balanced against the potential loss of role in the public sphere. Shelley's rhetoric does not answer Peacock's charge that in an age of "mathematicians . . . historians, politicians, and political economists" poets have lost the pre-eminence they once had, when bards and epic poets were a culture's source of wisdom. Rather, Shelley shifts the grounds of the argument, and thus brings to clarity the issue of shifting the configuration of poetry and its antagonists that runs through our selections, from *Literary Ballads* through Wordsworth's Preface to *Lyrical Ballads* to Coleridge on the reviewers and literature as a trade to Shelley on the reviewers in *Adonais*.

Most interesting perhaps, as Shelley is compelled by the increasing pressures of utilitarian, practical, scientific thought, on the one hand, and a narrow moralism on the other, to defend poetry as the potent power of figure (extending it, but perhaps also diluting it, from literature per se to all forms of thought), is an echo in his declaration that "We have more moral, political and historical wisdom than we know how to reduce into practice. . . . The poetry in these systems of thought is concealed by the accumulation of facts and calculating processes. . . . We want the creative faculty to imagine that which we know; we want the generous impulse to act that which we imagine; we want the poetry of life; our calculations have outrun conception. . . . " In this compelling peroration one unmistakably hears Burke's famous lament from his *Reflections*: "But the age of chivalry is gone. That of sophisters, economists, and calculators, has succeeded: and the glory of Europe is extinguished for ever. Never, never more shall we behold that generous loyalty to rank and sex. . . ." As the plea for a world of imagination and generosity rather than calculation, and for a world conceived symbolically rather than literally and instrumentally, swings from an avowed conservative to an avowed radical, the instructor will be able to bring students to recognize the need to think to those terms historically, and to use them discriminatingly.

Felicia Hemans

First among the issues raised by Jeffrey's review of Hemans (1829)—which Jeffrey reprinted in his selected *Contributions to the* EDINBURGH REVIEW (1843), thus ensuring its continued dissemination—is the elaborate differentiation between genders. Students might be asked to consider how much Jeffrey ascribes the difference between "the rougher and more ambitious sex" and the "delicacy" of women to innate characteristics and how much to upbringing. Is women's "substantial and incurable ignorance of business" an essentialist statement or a recognition of social exclusion: "[t]his, however, we are persuaded, arises entirely from their being seldom set on such tedious tasks." Whatever the cause, in Jeffrey's world women are excluded from "the great theatre of the world": "their proper and natural business is the practical regulation of private life." Instructors may wish to juxtapose

Jeffrey's certitudes—and the unsigned articles of the *Edinburgh Review* spoke as with the voice of authority—with earlier readings from Mary Wollstonecraft and in Perspectives: The Wollstonecraft Controversy and the Rights of Women. Jeffrey's literary history involves a certain suppression; it may be true that "it has been . . . little the fashion . . . to encourage women to write for publication"—think of Richard Polwhele—but as our selections from Anna Letitia Barbauld, Mary Robinson, Charlotte Smith, and Hannah More demonstrate, the immediately precedent period was distinguished by a number of eminently successful women writers. Casting these authors into the shade, Jeffrey also obscures the *kind* of poetry that they did write: Barbauld, for example, appears as the author of "Hymns and Early Lessons," not of the extended and political *Eighteen Hundred and Eleven*. Students might be asked to weigh Jeffrey's review against their own readings—and against the claims of Wollstonecraft that intellectual strength knows no gender. The exercise suggests that the separation of spheres became more rigid as the century advanced.

Jeffrey's contrast between masculine ambition and feminine "perception of character and manners," masculine "commanding genius" and feminine "elegance and neatness . . . exactness of judgment," conventionally conceding to women keenness in the analysis of "manners," unfolds within the well-developed opposition of the sublime and the beautiful. The superimposition of gender distinctions on aesthetic categories, familiar at least since Burke's *Philosophical Enquiry into the Origin of our Ideas of the Sublime and Beautiful* (see the unit above), raises questions more suggestive than Jeffrey's schematism first promises. One might note the contrast between the various strategies taken by the male poets to roughen their work, to make comprehension more difficult, as noted in previous sections of this manual, with the qualities Jeffrey praises in Hemans's verse: "regulated and harmonized by the most beautiful taste . . . finished throughout with an exquisite delicacy, and even serenity of execution." Instructors might first ask students to contemplate to what degree Hemans's eclipse, after a century's popularity, stemmed from the triumph of critical standards that subordinated "finish"— whether to the provocative fragment, read as the sign of an unattainable wholeness (Coleridge); to the cryptic text, built on gaps (*A slumber did my spirit seal, Strange fits of passion, Lucy Gray*); to flow, as a sign of passionate immediacy (*Childe Harold* or *Don Juan*) or meditative intimacy (*Tintern Abbey*); to simplicity and even awkwardness, as power (*Simon Lee, The Thorn*); to difficulty as well as elusiveness (*Mont Blanc*). One might then ask to what degree this cultural preference for the unfinished and for the striving it betokens in both poet and reader, insofar as it defines Romanticism, is not gender-neutral, but marks Romanticism as a masculine project. Any such line of argument would immediately encounter complicating evidence—such as Wordsworth's emphasis on emotion in the Preface to *Lyrical Ballads* and the union of "Tenderness and Imagination" of which he boasted to Charles Lamb (see *Lyrical Ballads*: Companion Reading)—which in turn would lead the class into the complexities of an issue too often treated rigidly. Second, the instructor might ask students to sketch a shift in critical approach that would enable Hemans's strengths to emerge. Note that in his mapping of his age Jeffrey forecasts that Samuel Rogers and Thomas Campbell will outlive Shelley, Keats, Wordsworth, and Byron because of their "fine taste and consummate elegance," thus aligning them with Hemans. Their absence from our current configuration of the age, even as Hemans has been revived, throws light on the notion of a period as something retrospectively constructed by a network of current interests. Is it Hemans's "execution" that has restored her, or her subject matter or her presence in the age? Without Rogers and Campbell in the anthology one cannot ask students whether they too merit restoration, but one can ask students self-consciously to test Jeffrey's account of Hemans against their experience of her poetry, and, if they find him inadequate, to work out the grounds of their judgment.

Wordsworth's commentary may also be used to sharpen discussion of the category of "Female Poetry," as Jeffrey puts it. Wordsworth observed in 1829 that he had once thought of writing "an Account of the Deceased Poetesses of Great Britain—with an Estimate of their Works—but upon mature Reflection I cannot persuade myself that it is sufficiently interesting for a separate subject." He nonetheless remained "of opinion that something is wanted upon the subject—neither Dr Johnson, nor Dr Anderson, nor Chalmers, nor the Editor I believe of any other Corpus of English Poetry takes the least notice of female Writers—this, to say nothing harsher, is very ungallant. The best way of giving a comprehensive interest to the subject," he continued, "would be to begin with Sappho and proceed downwards." In the same year he congratulated Alexander Dyce on his *Specimens of British Poetesses* (1825)—suggestively misremembering the title as *Selections from the Poetry of English Ladies*—telling Dyce that were there to be a second edition he wished to be consulted about the work of Anne Finch, Countess of Winchelsea. The mixture of interest and condescension in this "gallant[ry]" is worth exploring, since at issue is the question of the "separate subject": not just the relation of English women writers to women writers generally, but of whether there is: a) only poetry, inclusively, or b) poetry, and "Female Poetry," a condition in which true poetry is men's, the more thoroughly because unmarked as such, and women's thus inevitably secondary. Wordsworth's commentary appears to inhabit (b). Students might be asked about the existence of a possible third category (c), in which men's and women's poetry are distinct, but equal. (And also whether Jeffrey's elevation of the "fine" Rogers and Campbell over poets of "fiery passion, and disdainful vehemence"—Byron is undoubtedly meant—designates a poetry that rises above the usual gender antitheses, or whether he too inhabits [b].) Instructors may also want to consider the degreee to which Wordsworth's remarks are informed by anxiety that he and Hemans occupied not "separate" spheres but overlapping ones. As noted above, Wordsworth was identified as a poet of domesticity, an identification that his life at Rydal Mount visibly enacted. When, in *To the Poet Wordsworth* (1826), Hemans hailed him as a "True bard and holy!" whose "calm" poems should be heard "by some hearth where happy faces meet, / . . . / While, in pleased murmurs, woman's lip might move, / And the raised eye of childhood shine in love," she specified a prominent and much cherished component of his reputation. Denying that Hemans could manage either the spear of Minerva or her needle, Wordsworth denies Hemans competence in either the public or the domestic realm, and we may wonder whether the need to mark his superiority even in the realm to which women had been relegated not only acknowledges rivalry but also betrays a worry that in an age of "mathematicians . . . historians, politicians, and political economists," as Peacock had characterized it (quoted in the headnote to Shelley's *Defence of Poetry*), *all* poetry risked being stigmatized as feminine. (Compare Lockhart's disdain of Keats as a boy, a "bantling" and a "stripling," and Matthew Arnold's retailing of the image of Shelley as a "luminous and ineffectual angel.")

The readings from Jeffrey and Wordsworth amplify questions that a reading of Hemans's poetry will have already suggested. One might ask students to compare the construction and valuation of the domestic in the male writers (for example, in Coleridge's *Eolian Harp* and *Frost at Midnight*, Wordsworth's *Tintern Abbey* or *The Prelude*, Byron's evocation of his daughter in *Childe Harold 3*) with its treatment by Hemans. Remember that Wordsworth placed some of his most celebrated works in the classification *Poems Founded on the Affections: Strange fits, She dwelt among th' untrodden ways*, and *Michael*. Similarly, one might ask how her representations of history and glory, the fields traditionally assigned to men, stand against her contemporaries, particularly Byron's *Childe Harold's Pilgrimage*. The discussion can be pointed by drawing attention to the interplay between Hemans's epigraphs from men's writings and her own narratives: Byron's anti-heroic heroic drama *Sardanapalus* for *The Bride of the Greek Isle*, Scott's chivalric romance *Marmion* for *The Homes of England*, Plutarch, the epitome of humanist history, for *The Last Banquet of Antony and Cleopatra*. More broadly: what happens when a woman writer wields the pen? how does Hemans represent men, women, and their social relations and expectations? what values does she define as "masculine" and "feminine"? how do Hemans's representation of women willing to die for their passions compare with what leads men to death? More formally: what is the relation between Hemans's "historical scenes in verse" and the contemporary understanding of Shakespeare's plays witnessed in our section "*Lectures on Shakespeare* / Coleridge's Lectures in Context"? *Casabianca*, *The Homes of England*, and *The Graves of a Household* might lead one to ask how Hemans's handling of the ballad-stanza and ballad-like material compares with Literary Ballads and Lyrical Ballads. The juxtaposition of *Graves* with Wordsworth's *We Are Seven* will highlight the difference between Hemans's "finish" and Wordsworth's drama of stubborn cross-purposes, not least by bringing into focus the question of what effect the poems seem intended to have on the reader. A kindred debate has recently been aroused by *The Homes of England*: is Hemans's blend of domesticity and nationalism a pious restatement of the themes and tropes of Burke's *Reflections*, a work of art whose ideological *work* is precisely to erase class differences in a vision of a united "England," or does it rather demonstrate by the very conventionality of its gestures that the symbols of cultural continuity to which it appeals are always only conventional? A prime display of stock responses, or a sophisticated, as it were second-order, performance of them? Looking forward as well as back, the instructor might want to place *The Homes of England* into dialogue with Tennyson's *Mariana*, and Hemans's portrait of the woman artist with Elizabeth Barrett Browning's *Aurora Leigh*.

John Clare

Discussion of Clare might begin by asking students to consider the tensions in the term "peasant poet" that was both Clare's entrée into the literary marketplace and his straitjacket. Clare was actually an agricultural laborer, and the experiences he voices, and the voice in which he speaks, offer a counterpoint to the representation of rural life in the Preface to *Lyrical Ballads* and throughout Wordsworth's work, to Coleridge's critique in *Biographia Literaria* of that aspect of Wordsworth's theory of language, and to Hemans's view of the "cottage homes of England." But insofar as Clare was a *poet*, he was also a reader who worked in poetic traditions: the contrast is less between an unlettered man and literature than it is between those who by training and social position feel confident of their relation to tradition, even when they may choose to flout it, and someone who stands outside the works he nonetheless knows. *Written in November*, for example, does not announce itself as a sonnet, but it plays against the form: its odd force arises partly from the tension between its vernacular lexicon and unpunctuated structure and the intricate form that stands behind it, half-acknowledged and half-denied. The unusual rhyme pattern, neither Shakespearean nor Petrarchan, and the unexpected syntactic division (5-5-4)—even as cleaned up by Clare's publisher—might be viewed as a deliberate take on sonnet form, a free variation that rejects the conscious literariness of, for example, Wordsworth's *Nuns fret not* or *Scorn not the sonnet*. The couplets that compose *The Mouse's Nest*, including the reversed repetition of the "hay / away" rhyme, reaching, after the sudden actions of the first twelve lines, the spacious stability of the image in the concluding line, also surprise.

Instructors will easily find pairings to highlight Clare's innovations-appearing-as-ignorance: *Written in November* might be matched with Wordsworth's *Surprized by joy*, or Coleridge's *Sonnet to the River Otter*, or any of Keats's sonnets. Clare summons up a world of "songs eternity," natural melodies that he represents as outlasting and transcending the world of "books" that he wanted to enter, but the pressure of books is everywhere evident in our selections: "Clock a Clay," beginning with an echo of *The Tempest*, is as much an imitation of Shakespeare as proof of Clare's attentiveness to unregarded nature. The Romantic sympathetic imagination, the desire to think one's way into the other, can have had fewer more striking outcomes than Clare's personification of Swordy Well, which startles by delivering a social history as an individual's speech. The discourse of property and "nature" begun in "Perspectives: The Rights of Man and the Revolution Controversy" resonates through the poem, and the instructor might well place Clare's vivid ventriloquizing of exploited nature against the vision of property in Wordsworth's *Michael*. Michael's vision of Luke's possession of the land "free as is the wind / That passes over it" (256–57), and Wordsworth's argument for the importance of their land to the north-country small-holders, can be set in contrast to Clare's bitter and elegiac account of the fate of the land when it falls to the parish. *I am* asks to be set next to other Romantic poems of troubled adulthood, such as Coleridge's *Dejection Ode* and his late *Work Without Hope*. Clare's poem, like Wordsworth's *Tintern Abbey* in the words of Keats quoted below, "explor[es] . . . the dark Passages [in which] We feel the 'burden of the Mystery'" (letter of 3 May 1818, rearranged) and gains in force from its uncanny echoing of its precursors. *Childe Harold* and *The Rime of the Ancient Mariner* lurk behind the second and third stanzas, and behind them the half-heard reverberations of Elizabethan plaints and the formulaic adjective + noun pattern of much eighteenth-century verse ("stifled throes," "waking dreams," "vast shipwreck," "vaulted sky"). The six-line stanza is common from the Elizabethan period onward, but Clare's use is irregular: the first stanza lacks the closing couplet of the last two, and enjambs into the second. The uncertain introduction of the rhyme scheme and the floating of bits of poetic diction and abstractions ("oblivion's host," "life's esteems") adjacent to prosier lines ("even the dearest, that I love the best / Are strange") produce an instability that seems to enact the disorientation and final dissolution of the declarative "I am" that opens the poem.

The Mores is dominated by the historical fact of the enclosure of Helpston between 1809 and 1820, which converted the open-field landscape of Clare's youth into the rectangular, discrete plots of the new agriculture. The poem exploits the former openness both as exemption from restriction (in politically charged language): "Unbounded freedom ruled the wandering scene / Nor fence of ownership crept in between" (ll. 7-8) and as intimating infinity: "One mighty flat undwarfed by bush and tree / Spread its faint shadow of immensity / And lost itself which seemed to eke its bounds / In the blue mist the orison's edge surrounds" (ll. 11-14). On this last effect one might direct students to Burke's remarks on *Vastness* and *Sublimity* as characteristics of the sublime (p. 502), while at the same time emphasizing how thoroughly Clare avoids the conventional attributes of the picturesque, insisting that the old landscape was a "mighty flat" (is this Burke's *Privation?*), but filling it with everyday agricultural activity: free-ranging sheep and cows, swains and shepherds, corn fields, mulberry bushes where a boy (Clare's younger self) "would run / To fill his hands with fruit" (ll. 41-42). The vision of lost freedom and of the sharp division between a rich past and a constricted present, relayed in couplets, suggests a rewarding comparison to Wordsworth's *Tintern Abbey*, where the scene provokes a sinuous blank verse that interweaves past, present, and future. In Clare "Fence now meets fence in owners little bounds" (l. 47); in Wordsworth property markers are carefully softened: "hedge-rows, hardly hedge-rows, little lines / Of sportive wood run wild" (ll. 17-17). For Clare loss is absolute—"Moors loosing from the sight . . . / Are vanished now with commons wild and gay / As poets visions of lifes early day" (ll. 37-40)—whereas Wordsworth seeks "abundant recompense" (l. 89), inspirited by "pleasing thoughts / That in this moment there is life and food / For future years" (ll. 64-66). Clare's identification of his "boyish hours" (l. 15) with the landscape leaves him vulnerable; Wordsworth's developing inwardness, though mournful, is compensatory. The difference is in part one of status: Wordsworth is a tourist in the Wye landscape, Clare is one of "the poor" (l. 20)—occluded by Wordsworth's exclusion of any description of Tintern Abbey itself—and questions of "labours rights" (l. 20) are crucial for him as they are not for Wordsworth. The terms of the 1790s resonate in *The Mores*—"freedom," "bondage," "hope," "tyrant," "lawless laws"—and asking students to compare the terms here with their use in Perspectives: The Rights of Man and the Revolution Controversy will be productive. *Tintern Abbey* concludes by affirming human bonds, *The Mores* with the grim revelation that no one benefitted from enclosure. As John Barrell explains: "The financial crisis of the period after 1815, and the notorious failure of the country banks, made it extremely difficult for farmers to obtain credit, and as a new enclosure demanded an immediate and fairly extensive outlay of capital to be properly successful, the enclosure of Helpston, first conceived at a time of high wartime prices, but paid for at a time of poor credit facilities and low prices, must have made large inroads into the capital of the Helpston landowners" (*The Idea of Landscape and the Sense of Place*, p. 208). *Tintern Abbey* has seemed to many readers to record the birth of a remarkably layered inner life, but Clare's "flat" despair is lit by memories of his, nature's, and the villagers' freedom, vivid details, such as the sweeping "plover in its pleasure free" (l. 38), and as vivid, precise renderings of current oppression: "A board sticks up its notice 'no road here'" (l. 70). *The Mores* is not merely specific detail: it surprisingly trembles on the verge of myth ("these are all destroyed / And sky bound mores in mangled garbs are left / Like mighty giants of their limbs bereft" [ll. 44–47]) and powerful personification ("This with the poor scared freedom bade good bye" [l. 75]). Here as elsewhere Clare's irregular syntax and non-standard spelling and pointing poignantly intensify the sense of a mind and way of life under siege.

John Keats

To the extensive notes in the body of our text a few general considerations may be added here. Instructors might dwell on the emblematic significance of *On First Looking into Chapman's Homer*. Wordsworth attended a grammar school famous for instruction in the classics, and later translated portions of the *Aeneid*; Coleridge and Shelley were adept in Greek; Byron translated a portion of Aeschylus's *Prometheus Bound* as a school exercise, and as the allusions incessantly and casually scattered across his writings attest, had more than a gentleman's familiarity with Greek and Latin literature. That Keats's career should begin with an excited response to a translation of Homer signals a difference in position in regard to the tradition, for Keats and his audience. Students overwhelmed by Keats's mythological references might have their dismay alleviated by being asked to consider the richness as an extravagant display designed to establish the high cultural credentials of someone who (feared that he) didn't possess them. Lockhart's attack on Hunt's suburban muse, stripped of its contempt, can be taken as a provocative analysis of Keats's situation. "As a vulgar man is perpetually labouring to be genteel," pronounces Lockhart, "in like manner, the poetry of this man is always on the stretch to be grand." The attitude, which survives in Yeats's image of Keats as a boy with his nose pressed against a sweet-shop window, may be unpacked in a number of ways. For Lockhart (and for Yeats), Keats's infatuation with *literature* (with mythology, with Shakespeare, Spenser, and Milton) betrays his exclusion from a world that others already enjoy. *On First Looking into Chapman's Homer*

records the discovery as "new" wealth of the old "realms of gold" (Homer)—a discovery that remains mediated through the voice of another (Chapman), and a
"wild surmise" (13) of a territory ahead, not (one might implicitly fill in) the secure
knowledge of those who know Homer in the original. For the aristocracy culture
is an inheritance—aristocrats, it has been wittily remarked, are born old—upstarts
must acquire it. Keats's substitution of Cortez for Balboa (the first European to see
the Pacific from Darien in 1513) may be a "mistake" or may be allegorically fitting:
the seeker for culture discovers for himself the paths blazed by others. Lockhart
seeks to dismiss Keats by fixing him in two congruent contexts: personally, he is
young—a boy, not a man; culturally, he is lower middle class, and his attempts at
"honorable elevation" only manifest his ignorance. Hunt's addressing Lord Byron
as "My dear Byron" is insufferably presumptuous, and Keats's juxtaposition of
Hunt, "the most vulgar of Cockney poetasters," with Wordsworth, "the most classical of English living poets," exposes a failure to distinguish, a failure that broadcasts Keats's lack of the distinction by which he would seek, in his ostentatious display of the trappings of culture, to establish his title.

Lockhart's attack, if patiently explored and not merely dismissed as a conservative's failure to recognize genius, may have the reverse effect of making Keats more
sympathetic to students by leading straight to several of the chief preoccupations
of the poetry. Most users of this Anthology will be in positions analogous to Keats's:
young college students with nothing like the familiarity with the classics assumed
by Lockhart (or Byron, or Shelley, or Coleridge, or Wordsworth). The instructor
may wish to contextualize Keats's relation to tradition by returning to Burke's discussion of inheritance, or to contrast Keats's approach to it with that of Clare, also
outside, or of Blake, another apprentice, who counters classical tradition by drawing on the Bible and Christian tradition, and inventing his own mythology or with
women poets, whose learning was similarly scattershot and eclectic. The *literariness*
of Keats's imagined worlds forcefully contrasts with the terrain of *Lyrical Ballads*,
and students should be asked to consider the implications of Keats's embrace of
the artifices of language that Wordsworth rejected. Wordsworth sought to naturalize the imagination by locating its "birth-right" in the sensibility of the child
(*Prelude*, 1.286), and to employ (a "purified" version of) "the language really used
by men"; Keats returns to mythology and Elizabethan richness, the formal reposi-
tories of "fine fabling" (see the introduction to our section "Literary Ballads") in
elaborately worked language and forms. His advice to Percy Shelley to "'load every
rift' of your subject with ore" (16 August 1820) is the hallmark of his own richest
practice. One may set Coleridge's goal of "A Poem which Affects not to be Poetry,"
and the works of his and of Wordsworth that it describes, against the virtuosic lay-
ering of season, day, and life on which Keats built *To Autumn*. In the Preface to
Lyrical Ballads Wordsworth argues that there can be no essential difference between the language of poetry and the language of prose; for him the poet is "a man
speaking to men." Students might be asked to consider how Keats's "realms of
gold" alter the continuity between literature and other forms of writing evident in
the earlier sections of the *Anthology*: Barbauld's *Eighteen Hundred and Eleven* is a political intervention, *Don Juan* is topical and engaged, Shelley's *Ode to the West Wind*

glances at revolution, and *Hellas* and *The Mask of Anarchy* confront it directly.
Overt politics are less telling, however, than the conviction (sometimes stronger,
sometimes weaker) of all these writers that poetry can contribute to matters of national moment. With Keats poetry moves closer to *the poetic*, a separate sphere, that
of the seemingly autonomous aesthetic object and *belles-lettres*. One might ask students to weigh the connections between an age of "mathematicians . . . historians,
politicians, and political economists," as Peacock defined it (quoted in the headnote to Shelley's *Defence of Poetry*, and discussed in the Shelley section of this manual), and the rise of the specialized domain of art. Presented as monument, Keats's
poetry may seem daunting; presented as the exuberant product of a young man uncertain of his class status, eager to display the badges of learning and genius, the
characteristic too-muchness becomes immensely appealing.

Lockhart's critique can thus be read against the grain to found a contextual understanding of Keats's enterprise. Note, for instance, the characterization of
Wordsworth as "the most classical of living poets," a characterization that will surprise those students who remember the denunciation by the *Anti-Jacobin* and
Francis Jeffrey of the "childish" simplicity, which they read as radicalism, of the
Lake Poets. Lockhart touches not only on the understatement of Wordsworth's
ballad style and the stoicism of his elevated one, but also on his attachment to the
land, a political position in which peasant and aristocrat meet, joined by a common opposition to the world of "getting and spending," the urban world of new
wealth and commercial activity Wordsworth excoriated in his sonnets of 1802, his
portrait of London in *Prelude 7*, and the Preface to *Lyrical Ballads*. One might ask
students to consider to what degree the contempt expressed by Lockhart, educated
at Balliol College, Oxford, for the "Cockney" and the "Plebeian" and the "vulgar,"
usefully marks an expanding middle-class audience, untrained in but aspiring to
the classics, whose taste Keats would have to win if he were to earn a living by poetry, so that the very removal of his style from the colloquial and his matter from
the everyday would be the sign of his response to current conditions. Instructors
may set the manifestly literary ballad *La Belle Dame*, with its deliberate archaism
("wretched wight") and a stanza form metrically sophisticated by an abbreviated
last line, against those in our "Literary Ballads" section (*Lord Randal*, *Sir Patrick
Spens*, the work of Burns) or *Lyrical Ballads* to underscore Keats's particularly self-
conscious, perhaps even coterie, use of the form.

Lockhart's scorn for Keats as a "boy" likewise disengages a central theme. In
the Preface to *Endymion* Keats wrote: "The imagination of a boy is healthy, and the
mature imagination of a man is healthy; but there is a space of life between, in
which the soul is in a ferment, the character undecided, the way of life uncertain,
the ambition thick-sighted: thence proceeds mawkishness, and all the thousand
bitters which those men I speak of ["men who are competent to look, and who do
look with a zealous eye, to the honour of English literature"] must necessarily taste
in going over the following pages." Keats here thematizes adolescence: awkwardness is not his failing, it is his subject. The instructor may compare this formulation with the poems of his contemporaries on the stages of life: for example,
Wordsworth's *Tintern Abbey* and *Prelude*, Coleridge's *Dejection Ode*. To do so is to

recognize that a heightened awareness of the "space of life between" characterizes the period. Looking back in 1874 on this "burst of creative activity in our literature," Matthew Arnold decided that it "had about it, in fact, something premature." He summed up: "the English poetry of the first quarter of this century, with plenty of energy, plenty of creative force, did not know enough" (*The Function of Criticism*). Accepting the description but reversing the evaluation, one can argue that the character of the era, coming after the Revolution had destroyed the old certainties but left uncertainty in its wake, and before the evolution of a new order (after Waterloo, after the 1832 and 1867 Reform Bills), was precisely its unsettledness. The age saw itself, in the phrase of John Stuart Mill, as an age of transition.

One might therefore note the congruency between "transition" (in sociocultural terms), "space of life between" (in individual psychological terms), and the kinds of narrative suspension devised by the Romantics. The fragment (*Kubla Khan*), the dialogue of poem and gloss (*The Rime of the Ancient Mariner*), and the self-interrupting letter (*Biographia Literaria* 13) are among Coleridge's modes of leaving the imagination hovering, converting the lack of "not know[ing] enough" into a provocative staving-off of the finality of closure; Byron's proliferating "passage" in *Don Juan* converts epistemological uncertainty into exfoliating speculation—seventeen cantos on, the poem continues in a perpetual middle; Shelley's chains of similes raise from the failure of language ever to reach reality a strenuous intellectual energy. That Keats shared with his contemporaries the sense of human life as growth is shown by his analogy of human life to a series "of Many Apartments" that the awakening of the "thinking principle" impels us successively to explore (3 March 1818), and by his spring 1819 letter to George and Georgiana Keats on "*Soul-making*," perhaps its fullest articulation: "I will call the *world* a School instituted for the purpose of teaching little children to read—I will call the *human heart* the *horn Book* used in that School—and I will call the *Child able to read*, the *Soul* made from that *school* and its *hornbook*. Do you not see how necessary a World of Pains and troubles is to school an Intelligence and make it a soul?" In this letter Keats observes that "[t]hough a quarrel in the streets is a thing to be hated, the energies displayed in it are fine," surprisingly linking this instinctive "animal eagerness" to poetry: "our reasoning may take the same tone—though erroneous they may be fine This is the very thing in which consists poetry; and if so it is not so fine a thing as philosophy." The ranking of philosophy over poetry coordinates with the drive toward the development of identity elsewhere in the letters, but more characteristic is Keats's suspension of closure in order to "widen speculation" (3 May 1818; see also the "speculative Mind" of spring 1819) in "the space of life between." This drama is acted through Keats's close reading of Wordsworth, the epitome of the "egotistical sublime" to which Keats opposes his own kind of "poetical Character": the "camelion poet" who "has no Identity—he is continually in for[ming?]—and filling some other Body" (27 October 1818). (The contrast might be amplified by recurring to the "Lectures on Shakespeare".) From the extended comparison of Milton and Wordsworth that Keats conducts by means of his analogy of "Many Apartments" he recovers a Wordsworth to admire: "many doors are set open—but all dark—all leading to dark passages—We see not the ballance of good and evil. We are in a Mist—We are now in that state—We feel the 'burden of the Mystery.' To this point was Wordsworth come when he wrote 'Tintern Abbey' and it seems to me that his Genius is explorative of those dark Passages." Keats's definition of "*Negative Capability*" encapsulates the transformation of the confession of the Preface to *Endymion* into a virtue: "that is when man is capable of being in uncertainties, Mysteries, doubts, without any irritable reaching after fact & reason—Coleridge, for instance, would let go by a fine isolated verisimilitude caught from the Penetralium of mystery, from being incapable of remaining content with half knowledge" (December 1818).

Keats repeatedly bends traditional forms toward the self-questioning these quotations suggest. *The Eve of St. Agnes*, for example, is a chivalric romance of the kind popular ever since the series of Scott's narratives beginning with *The Lay of the Last Minstrel* (1805) and *Marmion* (1808); Wordsworth's *The White Doe of Rylstone* (1815) and Coleridge's *Christabel* (published 1816) were more recent instances of the genre. But *The Eve of St. Agnes* is more like an episode from a romance than a complete romance action, and its abrupt ending, with the surprising shift in tenses that sidesteps the question of the future happiness of the lovers by remanding them to the distant, completed past, caps the series of oppositions and puzzles that surround the story: the white of virginity linked with the ice of death versus the purple and red of erotic passion with the violence of conflict, Porphyro as satanic seducer versus agent of growth. The story, recounted by a narrator who can see his heroine as both "thoughtful" and the dupe of a "whim" (55), "Hoodwinked with fairy fancy" (70), offers intense wish-fulfillment and chastens wishing in its conclusion, leaving readers to ponder their own investments in romance. Of the odes we may note here their interrogative conclusions: the question at the end of *Ode to A Nightingale* ("Do I wake or sleep?"), the enigmatic distich at the end of *Ode on a Grecian Urn* ("Beauty is truth, truth beauty,—that is all / Ye know on earth, and all ye need to know"), the reversal at the end of *Ode on Melancholy* that makes the energetic pursuer of Melancholy her victim ("His soul shall taste the sadness of her might, / And be among her cloudy trophies hung"). To borrow a phrase from the *Ode on a Grecian Urn*, these poems "tease us out of thought" (44) rather than offer firm resolutions, and the instructor may wish to compare them with the kindred works enumerated in the paragraph above, or contrast them with the closure on the "philosophic mind" in Wordsworth's *Ode: Intimations of Immortality* or the consolatory pronouncement that resolves his *Peele Castle* ("Not without hope we suffer and we mourn"). The tension between narrative movement and speculation, action and meditation, that Keats shares with his contemporaries (consider the exhortations of the narrator of *Simon Lee* to "silent thought" or the presentation of the story of the Ancient Mariner as the drama of its telling and reception in *Lyrical Ballads*, a title that itself poses contraries) can be illustrated by two repeated words. "Generation" occurs in both the *Ode to a Nightingale* (62) and *Ode on a Grecian Urn* (46), "cease" in both the *Ode to a Nightingale* (56) and *To Autumn* (10): in the latter poem the tension between the ongoing flow of life and the arrest that enables contemplation is ratcheted to its highest in the poising of autumn between maximum fullness and impending death.

To return to the exclusion from tradition enforced by Lockhart's review: if to Lockhart the tradition brands Keats as a vulgar upstart, permanently crippled by ignorance, to Keats the tradition provokes emulation, and the opportunity for enlargement. "I was never afraid of failure," Keats told his publisher after *Endymion*, "for I would sooner fail than not be among the greatest" (8 October 1818). A week later, still absorbing the harsh reviews his ambitious poem had aroused, he declared to George and Georgiana: "This is a mere matter of the moment—I think I shall be among the English Poets after my death" (14 October 1818). The past, a massive obstacle, may also serve as inspiring model. The very last paragraph of the Preface to *Endymion* runs: "I hope I have not in too late a day touched the beautiful mythology of Greece, and dulled its brightness: for I wish to try it once more, before I bid it farewel." In this confession Keats acknowledges his distance from the world of antiquity, an acknowledgment dramatized in his ode to Psyche, the "latest born and loveliest vision far / Of all Olympus' faded hierarchy! / . . . / . . . too late for antique vows, / Too, too late for the fond believing lyre" (24-25; 36-37). Instructors will have noticed that in Keats distance from the cultural past largely occupies the role of distance from their own past in Wordsworth and Coleridge: in Keats memory is not personal but cultural, and the fate of mythology is a more explicit subject than the mind of the boy. It is worth therefore emphasizing that if Keats was not university educated, he lived in a circle of art and artists, a phenomenon that should then be studied. William Hazlitt, whose "depth of Taste" Keats declared one of the "three things to rejoice at in this Age" (10 January 1818), was both a painter and an art critic; Leigh Hunt, in whose *Indicator* Keats published *La Belle Dame*, was an enthusiastic guide to old work as well as a genial sponsor of new; and the painter Benjamin Robert Haydon (whose pictures constituted a second in Keats's trio) was a principal in *Annals of the Fine Arts*, the first quarterly devoted to the fine arts in England, in which both *Ode to a Nightingale* and *Ode on a Grecian Urn* first appeared.

The separation of Hunt's aesthetic *Indicator* from his political *Examiner* foretells the modulation of middle-class radicalism into depoliticized general culture in his later periodicals. As our note to Keats's *On Seeing the Elgin Marbles* conveys, Haydon championed the purchase of the Elgin Marbles against establishment connoisseurs in a dispute that eventually led to a government committee having to determine the sum to be paid Elgin, a fascinating instance of the conundrum of the relationship between aesthetic value and market price. Keats's *On Seeing the Elgin Marbles* seems to explode the confines of sonnet form by making it the vehicle of "dim-conceived glories of the brain" (9), a phrase that signals the sublime. The paratactic structure and fragmentary abstract images of the last two lines ("Wasting of old Time—with a billowy main / A sun—a shadow of a magnitude") mime the dissolution of formal "Grecian grandeur" (12) in the immediacy of an experience too powerful to organize syntactically. Instructors may wish to point out that the natural images are evoked by statues, and ask students to weigh the difference between the sublimity of nature (and the mind's response to nature) and the agency of art in Keats: the marbles, the representation of the gods in the two *Hyperions* that they underlie, and the Grecian urn. Keats's romanticism is romantic classicism, and parallels the rise of the museum. Keats's pictorialism may be contrasted with Wordsworth's resistance to the tyranny of the eye, exemplified by his disappointment at first seeing Mont Blanc: he "grieved / To have a soulless image on the eye / Which had usurp'd upon a living thought / That never more could be" (*Prelude* 6.453–56). Wordsworth's characteristic bare "visionary dreariness" (*Prelude*, 11.311) could not be more different from the visuality of Keats, steeped in Nicolas Poussin (1593/94–1665) and Claude Lorrain (1600–1682); it was dissatisfaction with a painting, Benjamin West's *Death on a Pale Horse*, that provoked Keats to formulate "negative capability." The Pre-Raphaelites seized on the sensuousness of surface and display of objects in Keats, repeatedly illustrating his poems. The instructor can usefully highlight this quality by bringing into class reproductions of John Everett Millais's *Lorenzo and Isabella* (1849) and *Eve of St. Agnes* (1865), Holman Hunt's *Eve of St. Agnes* (1848) and *Isabella and the Pot of Basil* (1867), and Frank Dicksee's *La Belle Dame Sans Merci* (*circa* 1902)—and then asking students to consider what aspects of Keats's self-questioning and intense appeals to other senses painting inevitably scants. (A specimen: "Then will I pass the countries that I see / In long perspective, and continually / *Taste* their pure fountains," *Sleep and Poetry*, 99–101; "Oh, for a draught of vintage . . . / . . . / *Tasting* of Flora and the country green," *Ode to a Nightingale*, 11–13; "Though seen of none save him whose strenuous tongue/ Can burst Joy's grape against his palate fine; / His soul shall *taste* the sadness of her might," *Ode on Melancholy*, 27–29; and—synaesthetically— "Oh, turn thee to the very tale, / And *taste* the music of that vision pale," *Isabella*, 391–92.)

When Keats declared of the mythology of Greece that he "wish[ed] to try once more, before I bid it farewell" he specified a gesture of assumption followed by rejection that he would rehearse again and again. *Sleep and Poetry* inaugurates the rhythm: "First the realm I'll pass / Of Flora and old Pan. . . . / And can I ever bid these joys farewell? / Yes I must pass them for a nobler life, / Where I may find the agonies, the strife / Of human hearts" (101–02; 122–25). In Keats's short life the movement from pastoral to tragedy was never quite completed, and instructors may ask students to reflect on whether the cause lies in the accident of Keats's early death or is not fundamental to the Romantic inhabiting of "the space of life between." Repeatedly Keats seeks escape in bowers (*Endymion*), in imaginative leaps to the idealized world of the unseen nightingale ("I will fly to thee, / Not charioted by Bacchus and his pards, / But on the viewless wings of Poesy," 31–33), or the perfection of the Grecian urn, its figures "All breathing human passion far above" (28). Repeatedly the ideal world discloses a lack, and Keats returns to a reality that is virtually defined by its capacity to say "farewell" to the temptations of the ideal. The nightingale is dismissed, with a telling use of the lesser of Coleridge's terms in the hierarchy Imagination/Fancy: "Adieu! the fancy cannot cheat so well / As she is fam'd to do, deceiving elf" (73–74). The Grecian urn reveals itself as a "Cold Pastoral" (45). The consummation of Porphyro and Madeline is immediately followed by, or by the logic of poetic sequence, seems to produce, a storm: "Solution sweet: meantime the frost-wind blows / Like Love's alarum, pattering the sharp sleet / Against the window-panes: St. Agnes' moon hath set" (stanza 36). The instructor may wish to juxtapose these texts with earlier ones: the *Ode to a Nightingale* with Shelley's *To a Skylark*, Keats's treatment of Madeline and Porphyro with Byron's of Juan and Haidee. More generally, one might ask about the relations between skepticism and idealism in Shelley, Byron, and Keats.

In sending his analysis of Wordsworth to Reynolds, Keats comments that it is "to show you how tall I stand by the giant" (3 May 1818). His wrestlings with his eminent older contemporary in turn involved a still weightier precursor: "My Branchings out therefrom have been numerous: one of them is the consideration of Wordsworth's genius and as a help, in the manner of gold being the meridian Line of of worldly wealth,—how he differs from Milton." (See the remarks on generational rivalry in the section of this manual on Shelley.) Keats's early sonnet "To one who has been long in city pent" purchases a famous epic simile in *Paradise Lost* (Satan's temporary delight in Eden) to describe a holiday of reading and relaxing in the country. Part of this holiday is a knowing suspension of Milton's epic import and metaphysical urgency. Keats's two *Hyperions* represent his most sustained effort to conquer poetic tradition on its highest ground, the epic. To our headnote we may just add here that *Paradise Lost* unfolds in a three-leveled symbolic space: Hell, Eden, and Heaven. Keats's narrative in its first form recounted the humanizing of the Titans by their fall, and the rapid education of Apollo, his rise from pastoral innocence toward humanity. Milton's scheme, which Keats follows in Books 1 and 2, thus collapsed toward the middle level of human experience. Recasting the poem as *The Fall of Hyperion: A Dream*, Keats refocused the narrative (at least as far as he managed to take it) on his own agonized poetic initiation, exchanging Miltonic epic for Dantean spiritual drama. (But which, one may note, edged Keats away from the Shakespearean poet without identity and toward the egotistical sublime of Wordsworth—and Milton.) Perhaps no work better illustrates the pattern of the period by which objective forms turned inward, and action bent into signifying stasis, narrative into lyric responsiveness: note that the poet gains illumination by looking on the epic action before him (372 ff.), which recedes before the drama of his capacity to bear "The load of this eternal quietude" (390). The revision thereby sharpened the questions of the role of the poet and of the meaning of suffering rather than alleviating them, and Keats could not complete it. In setting the *Hyperion* project against the two other Romantic revisions of epic in the anthology, Wordsworth's *Prelude* and Byron's *Don Juan*, the instructor may wish to situate the discussion at the level of style. What style was appropriate for representing the drama of a mind that does not "see the ballance of good and evil," for uncovering the "dark Passages" in which Keats found Wordsworth superior to Milton and to which he too committed himself: "Now if we live, and go on thinking, we too shall explore them"? In *Hyperion*, Byron commented, Keats had "contrived to talk about the gods of late, / Much as they might have been supposed to speak" (*Don Juan* 11.59, quoted in the companion reading to *Adonais*), but the question was whether a style apposite for gods, even fallen, was sufficiently supple to talk about human questions, about the painful education of a soul into an intelligence. Even in its revised form as *The Fall of Hyperion: A Dream*, Keats's poem remained elevated, its very stylistic brilliance, testimony to Keats's determination to enter the tradition, a stumbling block. In *The Prelude* Wordsworth crossed epic with epistle, gaining the stylistic flexibility to write about childhood and domestic intimacy as well as the Revolution; repudiating Murray's desire that he write "'a great work' an Epic poem I suppose or some such pyramid" Byron demanded "you have so many *'divine'* poems, is it nothing to have written a *Human* one? without any of your worn out machinery" (6 April 1819). Liberated from the aspiration that hobbled even as it inspirited Keats, Byron found in *ottava rima* a middle style whose "pedestrian Muses" (Dedication, 8) enable him successfully to mutate epic, narrating the ordinary that Keats indicates only as the gap between the taking up of a style and its abandonment. One might consider the distance between the style of Keats's poems and the staccato immediacy of his letters, and the closing in *Don Juan* of the similar gap between *Childe Harold* and Byron's letters. To contrast Keats's artifice (for example, the evolution of the stanza forms of the odes from his experiments in the sonnet) with the theory of language embodied in *Lyrical Ballads* and its preface should throw light on the latter not available earlier in the semester.

Questions of gender are inseparable from questions of imagination in Keats. What happens, the instructor might ask, when the aesthetic category of the "imagination" converges with the condition of a man who confesses that he has "not a right attitude towards Women"? (18 July 1818). The sequence of erotic fulfillment and immediate chastening in *The Eve of St. Agnes*, the triumph of Melancholy, and Autumn, carrying the scythe that associates her with death, have already been noted, and students might be asked also to consider Keats's gendering of literary "Romance" as a dangerous temptress to the masculine poet, and (as with Byron) the pressures of a readership of women on his sense of independence. How too shall we understand the threatening figure of Moneta? No simple answers will, or should, emerge from "a gordian complication of feelings," but they point towards the issues that drive the poems: is La Belle Dame the merciless figure the title suggests, or is the knight's despair a product of his own blinded and willful interpretations of her, perhaps even a self-fulfilling fantasy of betrayal that leads to solidarity with other self-pitying men? Or one might suggest a thematic issue: compare Keats on fame (in the letters, in *Hyperion*, in *When I have fears*) to Hemans's assessments of "Women and Fame" and famous women.

PERSPECTIVES

Popular Prose and the Problems of Authorship

Here is the conclusion of Thomas Love Peacock's *The Four Ages of Poetry* (1820), cited in part in the headnote to Shelley's *A Defence of Poetry* and commented upon in the Shelley section of the manual. Peacock proclaims the imminent death of poetry:

> and this not from any decrease either of intellectual power, or intellectual acquisition, but because intellectual power and intellectual acquisition

have turned themselves into other and better channels, and have abandoned the cultivation and the fate of poetry to the degenerate fry of modern rhymesters, and their olympic judges, the magazine critics, who continue to debate and promulgate oracles about poetry, as if it were still what it was in the Homeric age, the all-in-all of intellectual progression, and as if there were no such things in existence as mathematicians, astronomers, chemists, moralists, metaphysicians, historians, politicians, and political economists, who have built into the upper air of intelligence a pyramid, from the summit of which they see the modern Parnassus far beneath them, and knowing how small a place it occupies in the comprehensiveness of their prospect, smile at the little ambition and the circumscribed perceptions with which the drivellers and mountebanks upon it are contending for the poetical palm and the critical chair.

A *tour de force* of exaggeration, surely, for Peacock combined working for the East India Company under the quintessential Utilitarian James Mill with the authorship of satirical novels and mythological poetry, and his complimentary citation of political economists here did not stop him from lampooning them in *The Paper Money Lyrics* (1837). But Peacock's jest is just as surely an index to a shift in the ordering of knowledge, or at least to the emergence of newly professionalizing fields with which poetry had to compete for authority and prestige. By the 1820s the costly quartos in which Scott's *The Lay of the Last Minstrel* (1805) and his subsequent chivalric romances, Byron's *Childe Harold's Pilgrimage* (1812–1818), and Wordsworth's *Excursion* (1814) were published had become a thing of the past, and a crash in the world of publishing in 1826 tightened market conditions still further. By 1830 most major publishers were declining to publish new poetry. Concomitantly, as P. G. Patmore, a friend of **Lamb** and **Hazlitt** and a fellow contributor to the *London Magazine*, noted, magazines "have changed their place in the system of literature" and risen "aloft into higher spheres," publishers having discovered it was worth their while handsomely to remunerate writers who attracted readers. Coleridge, responding to the criticism of Barbauld, spoke of *The Rime of the Ancient Mariner* as "a work of pure imagination" (see Coleridge companion reading); the essayists in the magazines aimed at no such goal. In the deliberately informal sketch they depicted city life, or gave rein to an idiosyncratic persona; even more elaborate forms fit into the mixture of serious reviewing, political opinion, and current news or scandal that in varying proportion made up the appeal of the magazines to their different readerships. Looking back in 1855 on "The First Edinburgh Reviewers," Walter Bagehot, editor of *The Economist*, author of *The English Constitution* (1867) and other still valuable works of social analysis, declared with his characteristic flickering irony: "The *Edinburgh Review* . . . may be said to be, in this country, the commencement on large topics of suitable views for sensible persons." The magazines did not seek the authority of the quarterlies, but they helped to form another cultural image: the reader they project is abreast of current affairs, and equally *au courant* in art and literature, a man (other periodicals aimed at women) of taste rather than a scholar (scholarship could look too much like pedantry), whose wit tended more to genial enthusiasm than to sharp satire. As we note in our introduction to the section, personality, as conveyed in style, was the key. The essay was an elastic genre, in style and subject, accommodating both reportage and reflection, and in it one can recognize the ancestor of today's columnists, personal journalism, and creative non-fiction.

In the selections in this section the instructor will find many of the themes and techniques already commented on in the manual. The sequence of narrators in the *Introduction to TALES OF MY LANDLORD* (obviously not a magazine piece), for example, can be connected to all the devices by which the Romantic poets complicate the notion that a story has a single authoritative origin, and convert straightforward narrative into a Chinese-box structure of tale-telling and tale-hearing. Scott embeds his stories in a differentiated social world, and turns to comedy the debate (see "Literary Ballads") between those who seek "authentic" folk material and those who condescend to, or refine, or sentimentally idealize it. Intensely nationalist, pedantically learned (note the Latin tags), Jedediah richly dramatizes the traffic between Scots local color and British readers, an unfamiliar, vivid tradition and the current book market. Scott's allegory of cultural transmission can be set against Blake's in *The Marriage of Heaven and Hell*; Jedediah's quarrels with Peter Pattieson over style offer a miniature of the wrestlings with their heritage of Wordsworth, Byron, and Keats. Looking forward, the *Introduction* can be set against Carlyle's narrative use of an editor in his *Sartor Resartus*. Lamb's *Oxford in the Vacation* even in its title indicates the condition of suspension the Romantics sought in order to free the imagination: the university vacation "falls in so pat" with Elia's respite from business that he can try on identities: "play the gentleman, enact the student," recover if only briefly (but therefore more sweetly) the freedom he knew "as long back as I was at school at Christ's." Lamb's style, allusive, irregular, colloquial and archaic both, is just such a freedom from the business-like prose of the clerk. Wordsworth narrates his own childhood in *The Prelude*; Lamb turns to a persona, Elia, and simultaneously concedes, as it were, Peacock's charge that literary studies had become irrelevant to contemporary reality and defends the "liberal pursuits" by embodying them in the figure of G——, whose absent-mindedness is a sign of the freedom of imagination from constraint: "For with G.D., to be absent from the body is sometimes (not to speak it profanely) to be present with the Lord." Low-key, ironic, moving in the realm of fancy rather than imagination, Lamb wields a style that brilliantly reconciles artifice and the everyday. *Dream Children* plays on the Romantic themes of childhood, memory, and imagination, and its darkening of tone at the conclusion, when the prior fantasy, teetering on the edge of the sentimental, is revealed as preparation for the announcement of a real loss, that of the death of Lamb's brother, and so becomes yet more painful, may be set against the kinds of closure commented on before in these pages. *Old China* likewise resumes several themes: art and artifice (compare Keats's *Ode on a Grecian Urn*), the relations of brother and sister (compare *Tintern Abbey*), gender construction, and domesticity generally, the relation of past and present, youth and age, and the fluid operations of memory figured by the lack of perspective on the china (*Tintern Abbey* again). Lamb offers a *diminuendo* replay of the concerns of the poets, their emotional intensity held within the scale typified by the old china. In Lamb the Romantic passes from unique experience to cultural pattern, available even to the unremarkable Elia and Bridget at home. But the modesty of the form is deceptive: teaching the essay, one should not underplay its canny awareness of the passions of memory, or the way in which Lamb brackets (with the kind of irony Byronists recognize) the powerful recovery of the past accomplished in the breathless rush of the last paragraph by the steady introduction—"It is true we were happier when we were poorer, but we were also younger, my cousin"—and the light self-mocking conclusion: "And now do just look at that merry little Chinese waiter. . . ."

"It is not easy to write a familiar style," Hazlitt observed. "Many people mistake a familiar for a vulgar style, and suppose that to write without affectation is to write at random. On the contrary, there is nothing that requires more precision, and, if I may so say, purity of expression, than the style I am speaking of. It utterly rejects not only all unmeaning pomp, but all low, cant phrases, and loose, unconnected *slipshod* allusions. It is not to take the first word that offers, but the best word in common use; it is not to throw words together in any combinations we please, but to follow and avail ourselves of the true idiom of the language. To write a genuine familiar or truly English style, is to write as one would speak in common conversation, who had a thorough command and choice of words, or who could discourse with ease, force, and perspicuity, setting aside all pedantic and oratorical flourishes" (*On Familiar Style*, 1821). The instructor may set this ideal against Lamb's, and also carry the works of this section back to "Perspectives: The Rights of Man and the Revolution Controversy" and ask students to consider the contrast in prose styles between Hazlitt and, for example, Burke, Paine, or Wollstonecraft. The writers of the 1820s evolved prose styles responsive to a new audience, less formal and hortatory, more flexible and conversational, more individual than those of their predecessors; to borrow Wordsworth's phrase in the Preface to *Lyrical Ballads*, such prose as Hazlitt's is an instrument deft enough to follow "the fluxes and refluxes of the mind."

Hazlitt's *On Gusto* identifies a key term in the aesthetics of the period. Neoclassicism had valued order, harmony, decorum, proportion; the immediately precedent aesthetic vocabulary had been the sublime, the picturesque, and the beautiful. These are categories of the object, or of nature perceived within artistic categories. "Gusto" is rather an alacrity and intensity of responsiveness than a formal property, a quality that an artwork intimates about its creator. Note that Hazlitt does not argue from general propositions, but accretively builds up his definition by particular instances, moving from the concrete instance to his recreation of it for his reader. Gusto is shown to be both a quality of Titian and Michelangelo, and of Hazlitt, who proves his own gusto by his enthusiasm for that of others. The essay is a list of examples crossing genres—painting, poetry, opera—from which the reader must induce the general term, or rather, we will understand "this delicate subject" if we are capable of it. Like many another work in the period, the essay covertly challenges the reader to rise to the state of the author. Hazlitt's impact on Keats can be seen by juxtaposing this essay with Keats's pronouncements that "the excellence of every Art is its intensity" (December 1818) and that "every mental pursuit takes its reality and worth from the ardour of the pursuer" (3 February 1818), and with Keats's poems (particularly useful is the *Ode on Melancholy*).

My *First Acquaintance with Poets* exemplifies Hazlitt's precepts. Irresistible as it is to read the essay as a source of biographical information about Wordsworth and Coleridge, instructors should show students that the essay performs, unobtrusively, what it recounts. A recollective essay, written when Wordsworth and Coleridge had both, from Hazlitt's point of view, turned regrettably conservative, the essay summons up a golden and long since departed past. Ideas condense into telling physical details, as in Hazlitt's notice of Coleridge's manner of walking: "I observed that he continually crossed me on the way by shifting from one side of the foot-path to the other. This struck me as an odd movement; but I did not at that time connect it with any instability of purpose or involuntary change of principles, as I have done since. He seemed unable to keep on in a strait line." By the time the essay concludes, the reader knows as much about Hazlitt (and Hazlitt's father and childhood) as about his nominal subjects, but one should point out to students how such essays contributed to the image of the poets. In his middle years Wordsworth declared that "I wish either to be considered as a Teacher, or as nothing"; teachers need pupils if they are to succeed; Hazlitt's memoir is the evidence that already in 1798 Coleridge and Wordsworth had captured the next generation. No longer simply the (invisible) authors of works, they come before the public as vividly colored presences; the essay witnesses their already established celebrity and spreads it further—carrying Hazlitt, in all his gusto, along with them.

De Quincey's *Confessions of an English Opium-Eater* best illustrates the perpetuation and modulation of romanticism in the magazines. Students will recognize familiar topics, transposed into the setting of a rapidly expanding and labyrinthine London: a suffering child; a redemptive mother, here the child-prostitute Anne, lost in "Oxford-street, stony-hearted step-mother"; the fracturing of identity, played through De Quincey's transactions with the Malay, in the infinite recessiveness of the Piranesi plates, and in the return of the other, in this instance the Asian as private nightmare; the recursive interpretive process that turns the "Pleasures of Opium" into the "Pains of Opium"; the darkening of Coleridge's definition of the ideal poet as one who "balance[s] or reconcil[es] . . . opposite or discordant qualities" (*Biographia Literaria* 14) into De Quincey's sensational "I was the idol; I was the priest; I was worshipped; I was sacrificed." The *Confessions* evidently ask to be read with Wordsworth's (then unpublished) *Prelude*, Coleridge's *Rime*, and, say, Keats's *Ode on Melancholy*: all explore autobiography, guilt, imagination turned perverse, and gusto as self-tormenting intensity. Compare for example, the inseparability of pleasure and sorrow produced in Keats's *Ode* by the very fervor of the speaker's perception of joy, and in Moneta's charge against the narrator of *Hyperion*—"Every sole man hath days of joy and pain, / Whether his labors be sublime or low—/ The pain alone, the joy alone, distinct: / Only the dreamer venoms all his days" (1.172-75)—to De Quincey's "involute" of emotion, to use his term: "wherever two thoughts stand related to each other by a law of antagonism, and exist, as it were, by mutual repulsion, they are apt to suggest each other. On these accounts it is that I find it impossible to banish the thought of death when I am walking alone in the endless days of summer."

The episode of the Piranesi plates, a close look reveals, has a suggestively multiple origin. De Quincey records himself as looking only at Piranesi's *Antiquities of Rome*; the reading of the *Carceri* that follows is introduced by the parenthetical confession "I describe only from memory of Mr. Coleridge's account." While we supply a sample of what Coleridge means, the students' visual encounter should not eclipse their attention to the way, by a series of intense addresses and imperatives, the reader is urged to enter into the world of the plate: "you perceived . . . follow the stairs a little further, and you perceive . . . whatever is to become of poor Piranesi, you suppose. . . . But raise your eyes. . . . Again elevate your eye . . . until the unfinished stairs and Piranesi both are lost in the upper gloom of the hall." But just as Piranesi disappears into his plate, so the plate itself loses reality. Where is it, and who is talking? Is this Coleridge's accurate description of Piranesi's self-portrayal? (In fact it corresponds to no specific plate in the *Carceri*, conveniently available in paperback to show students.) Is De Quincey retailing Coleridge's fantasy? Is this De Quincey's own fantasy? De Quincey has never seen the plate, and we cannot tell, cannot separate one voice from another. "With the same power of endless growth and self-reproduction did my architecture proceed in dreams," continues De Quincey, but this instance suggests that the unconscious is not the place of an authentic self, but a network built up from myriad other figures and texts. De Quincey's dreams enact the transmission of culture as a repetition without a causal origin. Or, to put that another way, effect is all.

This episode can be fruitfully juxtaposed with the Arab dream in *Prelude 5* (49–165), a dream of which Wordsworth too obscures the origin, ascribing it in *1805* to "a Friend," but claiming it as his own in *1850*, though in either case, as our footnote indicates, it echoes a dream of René Descartes centuries earlier. It is worth developing the continuities and differences between the handling of dreams, visions, and terrors in De Quincey and Wordsworth. Immediately after the Piranesi episode De Quincey quotes 18 lines from Wordsworth's *Excursion* (1814), introducing them with the comment: "From a great modern poet I cite part of a passage which describes, as an appearance actually beheld in the clouds, what in many of its circumstances I saw frequently in my sleep." One might note the many functions of this seemingly innocuous comment. It is, first, significant as a document in the history of Wordsworth's reception. *The Excursion* had been savagely reviewed, and, an expensive quarto, had sold poorly; the second, cheaper but still small, edition had appeared only in 1820, the year before the *Confessions*. Wordsworth's other recent publications, from the two-volume *Poems* of 1815 through *The White Doe of Rylstone* (1815), *Peter Bell* and *The Waggoner* (both 1819), and *The River Duddon* (1820), had received at best mixed notices; Coleridge's extensive discussion in *Biographia Literaria* (1817) attested to his importance, but Coleridge's criticisms and declarations of disagreement had been sharp, and by 1817 Coleridge himself was suspect in many quarters. Of the readers who undertook *Biographia* many shared Byron's exasperation: "And Coleridge, too, has lately taken wing, / But like a hawk encumber'd with his hood,—/ Explaining metaphysics to the nation—/ I wish he would explain his Explanation" (*Don Juan*, dedication, 2). To Wordsworth's chagrin, the poems of Byron, Scott, and others had certainly elbowed his aside in the marketplace: as noted in the period introduction, the 3,000 guineas his publisher paid Moore for *Lalla Rookh* (1817) represented a sum of which he could scarcely dream. In ordaining Wordsworth a "great modern poet" in a publication of much wider circulation than Wordsworth's own editions attained—and attaching his praise to one of his most maligned works—De Quincey was not so much repeating received opinion as assisting Wordsworth's canonization. In doing so he also advanced his own claims: quoting throughout his works from the still-unpublished *Prelude*, De Quincey both built up Wordsworth's reputation and advertised his own intimacy with the "great modern poet," a double process on which he explicitly capitalized with the publication in *Tait's Edinburgh Magazine* of his *Recollections* of the Lake Poets (1834-40). Moving into Dove Cottage after the Wordsworths had relocated—it is the setting for "A Picture of the Opium-Eater"—De Quincey marked himself as the secondary figure who establishes the primacy of his predecessor.

But a close look at the introduction of the lines from *The Excursion* reveals, as does the relation to Coleridge in the Piranesi episode, an obscuring of the hierarchy of primary and secondary. *The Excursion* had been published seven years before, but do De Quincey's dreams anticipate or follow the poem? The paragraph immediately following the quotation reverses the elevation De Quincey has given Wordsworth: "The sublime circumstance—'battlements that on their *restless* fronts bore stars,'—might have been copied from my architectural dreams, for it often occurred." The "great modern poet" is now no more than a copier of De Quincey's independent imagination. Suppose, however, that the reverse is the case, and that, as we have repeatedly seen in the manual, Romanticism is a mode in which cultural transmission is rewritten as original experience. As Wordsworth transforms the picturesque into a psychological account of his childhood, so De Quincey then presents Wordsworth's prior, written sublime text as a description of, rather than the inspiration for, his own dreams.

In *The Prelude* Wordsworth exclaims: "Ah me! that all / The terrors, all the early miseries, / Regrets, vexations, lassitudes, that all / The thoughts and feelings which have been infus'd / Into my mind should ever have made up / The calm existence that is mine when I / Am worthy of myself. Praise to the end!" (1.356-62). Wordsworth's goal is "the end," the composed self who will have become The Poet. Though readers may most prize Wordsworth's accounts of his childhood experience, Wordsworth's project is integrative. "There is a dark / Invisible workmanship that reconciles / Discordant elements," he affirms in the lines just before these, "and makes them move in one society" (11.353-56). In one sense the workmanship is not invisible at all: it is the task of growing up, as Wordsworth understands it, and therefore the work of interpretation the poem performs, to achieve "harmony" (1.353). Wordsworth desires to become "worthy of [him]self," to demonstrate that he is "in manhood now mature" (1.653) and capable of undertaking the great work to which he is dedicated—by writing it. Though he did not name it, *The Prelude* is a faithful title for a poem Wordsworth conceived of to himself as preparatory (cf. 1.158-59).

With De Quincey the visions have become sufficient for themselves. *Confessions of an English Opium-Eater: Being an Extract from The Life of A Scholar* signals De Quincey's text as a fragment; moreover, its success fixed De Quincey ever afterwards as "the Opium-Eater." Though it may seem that De Quincey anticipated Freud in his archaeology of the layers of the mind, an instructor might wish to propose a counter-model: that in De Quincey the "unconscious" matters less than the canny discovery that the intense psychological exploration that Wordsworth pioneered could be exaggerated, "dark"ened, and worked up into salable articles (to pun intentionally), divorced from any model of growth. Students who incline to attribute De Quincey's visions to opium should be reminded of his initial *caveat* that "If a man 'whose talk is of oxen' should become an opium-eater, the probability is that (if he is not too dull to dream at all) he will dream about oxen," and the proposition can be developed. As De Quincey's ease of obtaining the drug shows, there was no difficulty of access: laudanum was uncriminalized and the most widely used sedative in Britain. Rather than presenting opium as the sufficient cause of De Quincey's visions, one might argue that it is rather a literalization of imagination: De Quincey was not in fact transgressing in purchasing opium, he was creating in his writing (with more than a little pride and pretense to professionalism) the type of the imaginative writer as a transgressive, suffering figure. Instructors will have seen for themselves the line of descent in which De Quincey stands: Keats's *Ode on Melancholy* and citation of "Bacchus and his pards" in *Ode to a Nightingale* (32), Coleridge's *Rime*, *Kubla Khan*, and *Dejection: An Ode*. The materializing of imagination corresponds to its commercial success: the Opium-Eater is, fittingly, both an addict and a scholar with a particular expertise in political economy, who earns his living by prolifically manufacturing out of his ununified knowledge a prodigious number of essays for the periodicals. (One might compare Coleridge on "literature as a trade" and his alarm at the risk of turning into a mere compositor in *Biographia Literaria* 11, and consider how De Quincey blazons his imagination and integrity by his invalid incapacity for regular employment; or consider De Quincey the scholar/periodical writer as a figure who mediates Peacock's opposition of real knowledge and outdated poetry.)

"Imagination" in the *Confessions* thus disguises the economic exigencies of the author: De Quincey had "created the taste by which he is to be enjoyed," as Coleridge (and Wordsworth) declared that every great writer must do: he had secured his market niche. To pose the two languages—of imagination and economics—thus polemically is not to devalue the former, but to turn attention from De Quincey's lurid confessions to the art of the *Confessions*. "Paint me, then," begins "A Picture of the Opium-Eater," and students should be asked to consider the careful construction of De Quincey's writing, from a tableau such as this one down to the shape of his paragraphs and the rhythm of his sentences. (De Quincey was interested in the repetitions and elaborations of musical fugues). In *Selections Grave and Gay*, the collected edition of his writings (1853-60) begun under his supervision at the end of his life, De Quincey commented on those passages where "amusement passes into an impassioned interest" and alerted readers to their craftsmanship: "Two remarks only I shall address to the equity of my reader. First,

I desire to remind him of the perilous difficulty besieging all attempts to clothe in words the visionary scenes derived from the world of dreams, where a single false note, a single word in a wrong key, ruins the whole music; and, secondly, I desire him to consider the utter sterility of universal literature in this one department of impassioned prose." An instructor might easily set this ideal, and the "impassioned prose" it inspired, against Hazlitt's "familiar style."

It would be hard to pick styles more divergent than **Austen's** measured understatement and **Cobbett's** tirade of invective. Except to epitomize the range of writing that flourished in the "Romantic" period, the instructor ought to resist any attempt to force the two together. It nonetheless may be worth noting that Austen's style is premised on the virtual unavoidability of miscommunication: the comedy of the social interactions she minutely tracks depends on the repeated failure of her characters quite to understand the nuances of the world in which they must function. In the Preface to Lyrical Ballads Wordsworth had insisted that "the human mind is capable of being excited without the application of gross and violent stimulants; and he must have a very faint perception of its beauty and dignity who does not know this, and who does not further know, that one being is elevated above another in proportion as he possesses this capability." The more pellucid the style, the more attentive readers must be so as not to miss its acute but delicate discriminations; readers who mistake Austen's clarity for transparency will blunder badly. Irony separates the sheep from the goats, within and outside her texts; like Wordsworth, her simplicity is a challenge to the capacity of readers. Students might be asked to triangulate Wordsworth (the preface to and poems in Lyrical Ballads), De Quincey ("gross and violent stimulants" personified, and baroque style), and the tactics of "the most unlearned and uninformed female who ever dared to be an authoress," as Austen described herself in asserting her independence against the Prince Regent's chaplain and librarian (11 December 1815).

On the other hand, Cobbett, who drives his points home relentlessly, in our passage self-consciously and slyly concentrates on a Semaphore, that is, a device for signalling. Cobbett constructs a symbol, reversing the function its builders intended: for the government the semaphore had been part of a necessary defense against a French invasion, for Cobbett it is the sign of corrupt policies far more dangerous to English liberty than the French. "And to that place a story appertains," wrote Wordsworth in Michael of the "straggling heap of unhewn stones" that when attended to by the sympathetic imagination—first the poet's, then of the tourist/traveller who enters Greenhead Ghyll, then of the reader he figures—releases the tragic story of the shepherd (18; 17). For Cobbett as well the landscape discloses a story of human action to the keen eye: his "nature" is man-made, and the story it tells is of economic and political injustice. Students might be asked to recall various aspects of Lyrical Ballads and its Preface: to compare Wordsworth's "real language of men" to Cobbett's vernacular, Wordsworth's vision of "low and rustic life" to Cobbett's experience, Wordsworth's characteristic displacement into the past or into the sensitivity of the respondent to Cobbett's immediacy and anger, and Cobbett's observation—"the soil is a beautiful loam upon a bed of sand"—to Wordsworth's "matter-of-factness," as Coleridge criticized it in Biographia

Literaria 22 (a passage not printed here). Clare will provide a useful third term. Considering the differences between "pastoral" (the generic subtitle of *Michael*) and political rhetoric should deepen appreciation of both, for Cobbett's is an imaginative style too, one that can be measured against Hazlitt's and De Quincey's, as suggested above. "The principal object" proposed by *Lyrical Ballads*, Wordsworth wrote in the preface, "was to chuse incidents and situations from common life . . . and . . . to throw over them a certain colouring of imagination, whereby ordinary things should be presented to the mind in an unusual way." The semaphore, and nature generally, will never look the same to one who has learned from Cobbett to read from their appearance the social structure that has shaped them. Cobbett's indignation may return students to Blake's *London*.

Readers may be puzzled by the geography of Mary Shelley's *The Swiss Peasant*. The title locates the story in Switzerland, and the description of Fanny as "one of those lovely children only to be seen in Switzerland" (p. 995) reinforces the setting. But Soubiaco, where the narrator encounters her, is in Italy (see fn. 4) on "the river Anio" (p. 995), near Rome. The same uncertainty recurs at the close of the story, when Fanny takes up residence at Soubiaco, which Louis "passe[s] through . . . in his way" "into Italy" (p. 1006). One explanation suggested for this discrepancy is that because the stories in *The Keepsake* were often commissioned to accompany the illustrations, Shelley may have assumed an Italian setting from the dress in the painting by Henry Howard (1769–1847), engraved by Charles Heath, the proprietor of the annual, with which the story was published, and imperfectly adjusted her text. The editors welcome any light that users of this anthology can shed on the problem.

The representation of Switzerland in *The Swiss Peasant* is anomalous in another way as well. In the poem based on his tour of Switzerland, *Descriptive Sketches* (1793), Wordsworth had adopted the standard view that the Swiss mountaineers represented primeval man, free and independent. Napoleon's invasion of Switzerland in 1798 particularly affected the English, as may be seen in Wordsworth's *Thought of a Briton on the Subjugation of Switzerland*, the twelfth of the "Sonnets Dedicated to Liberty" in *Poems, in Two Volumes* (1807):

Two Voices are there; one is of the Sea,
One of the Mountains; each a mighty Voice:
In both from age to age Thou didst rejoice,
They were thy chosen Music, Liberty!
There came a Tyrant, and with holy glee
Thou fought'st against Him; but hast vainly striven;
Thou from thy Alpine Holds at length art driven,
Where not a torrent murmurs heard by thee.
Of one deep bliss thine ear hath been bereft:
Then cleave, O cleave to that which still is left!
For, high-soul'd Maid, what sorrow would it be
That mountain Floods should thunder as before,
And Ocean bellow from his rocky shore,
And neither awful Voice be heard by thee!

Byron's *Prisoner of Chillon* (1816), cited by the narrator, is introduced by a sonnet apostrophizing Liberty—"Eternal Spirit of the chainless Mind!"—and the Chamois Hunter of *Manfred* sets "the free fame of / Of William Tell" (2.1.39–40) against Manfred's gloomy *hauteur*. Closer in time to Shelley's tale, Wordsworth filled his *Memorials of a Tour on the Continent, 1820*, with praises of Aloys Reding, "Captain-General of the Swiss forces, which . . . opposed the flagitious and too successful attempt of Buonaparte to subjugate their country," of William Tell, and of "the genuine features of the golden mean; / Equality by Prudence governèd," liberty and serenity, to be found in Berne, the canton of Fanny's birth (p. 996).

In contrast to these idealizing images of Switzerland, Shelley's narrator observes that "those of the Swiss who are most deeply planted among the rocky wilds are often stultified and sullen" (p. 996), an opinion that may mirror that held by the readers of *The Keepsake* attribute to the target audience of the annual (see p. 22). Monsieur de Marville, presented as a bigoted aristocrat (p. 996), and his impetuous and condescending son Henry, behave like figures from *ancien régime* France rather than stereotypically republican Switzerland, and Madame de Marville, though benevolent, is relentlessly class-conscious and afraid of a misalliance: she offers Fanny "a bourgeois education, which would raise her from the hardships of a peasant's life, and yet not elevate her above her natural position in society" (p. 996). Students might be asked to ponder the phrase "natural position," especially in opposition to Switzerland as the land of equality and natural grandeur and the nature invoked decades earlier by, for example, Wordsworth or Paine or Burke. The plot bears out Madame de Marville's "project," joining the intrepid and self-sacrificing Fanny to the chastened and devoted Louis. Instructors may wish to compare the way in which Louis's former radicalism is presented as a matter of "guilt" to be "expiated" by "his return to [domestic] virtue" (p. 1006) with the radicalism of the 1790s and of the young Percy Shelley, and with the philosophically radical but anti-violent Godwin. The wager of "a louis" that introduces Fanny (p. 995) turns in part on the character of Louis.

The Victorian Age

1832–1901

Thomas Carlyle
Past and Present (1843)

One might start with some background about the 1843 Poor Law, explaining that this supposedly rational legislation was based on Malthus: the thinking was that subsidizing the poor would lead them to multiply, and then they would be even more miserable. Instead they were incarcerated in workhouses and segregated by sex. The "crime" of poverty was apparently regarded as worse than felony, since workhouse inmates received a diet of fewer calories than criminals in prisons. Carlyle was scathing about the irony of a system of "workhouses" in which no work could be done.

The Poor Law was intended as a deterrent to poverty, on the assumption that its causes were not unemployment and low wages but idleness. A distinction was made between the "deserving poor" (the aged, the blind, orphans) and the able-bodied, who were punished and stigmatized for their condition. By forcing shirkers into honest labor, the Poor Law aimed at the moral reform of the pauper population.

Carlyle expresses his outrage with every rhetorical strategy at his command, comparing the workhouses to the Bastille and to Dante's hell. The analogy to Midas is central, and one should spend time exploring the implications of this vivid allusion, since students may be confused about the nature of the Enchantment from which England suffers; some will think Carlyle is saying that England is an enchanting place with terrible problems. This isn't too far off, but it misses the eerily frozen quality that Carlyle stresses, and the idea of enchantment as imprisonment.

Carlyle writes in the style of a biblical prophet, exhorting his readers in impassioned prose to wake up and reform their society. He is furious, sarcastic, appalled. He drives home his arguments with the most shocking examples he can find, such as the horrible story of the parents who were tried at the Stockport Assizes for poisoning their own children to collect the insurance money.

Past and Present accuses the entire economic and social system which permits such atrocities to take place. Carlyle points to the division between rich and poor (cf. Disraeli's notion of Two Nations in *Sybil* in the Industrial Landscape perspectives section). The Master Worker whom he indicts is the laissez-faire capitalist (not a skilled laborer, as some students believe), concerned only with profit, indifferent to the social fallout from his self-serving policies. (The Master Idler or Unworker is the parasitic Aristocrat—not a workhouse pauper.)

On the subject of class division, one might go over Carlyle's allusions to the Corn Laws, protectionist legislation that drove up the price of grain, and the Game Laws, which inflicted brutal punishments for poaching on the hunting preserves of the wealthy. (In 1823 William Cobbett estimated that one third of English prisoners were in jail for killing hares or game birds).

Ask students to discuss the story of the poor Irish widow who infects her neighbors with typhus in the "Gospel of Mammonism." In what sense would it have been "economy" to help her? (Those who clutch their padlocks and money-safes while claiming she is no business of theirs suggest Scrooge and Marley's attitude towards charity.) How does she "prove her sisterhood"? Contagion serves as a powerful symbol of brotherhood, for no one, rich or poor, is immune to infection. Gaskell's *Mary Barton* and Dickens's *Bleak House* also use disease as a metaphor for human interconnectedness. Carlyle condemns the lack of leadership in a society where the rich do not acknowledge any responsibility for the poor.

In "Labour" Carlyle reiterates the Gospel of Work (articulated earlier in *Sartor Resartus*). In the context of his belief in the sacredness of work, the picture of an England full of unemployed workers, of paupers prevented from working, and of idle aristocrats takes on even greater resonance. Students might be interested in seeing Ford Madox Brown's famous painting, *Work* (1852). Inspired by Carlyle's injunction to "Produce!" it includes a portrait of Carlyle observing a group of laborers.

In "Democracy" Carlyle elaborates on the implications of the Irish widow's story, specifically the way the worship of wealth results in human isolation: even the "savages" in Africa would help a stranger, whereas supposedly civilized people in Edinburgh spurn their own neighbor. Even "Gurth, born thrall of Cedric," could count on being looked after by his master. This is the thorny heart of Carlyle's argument: that it is better to be a medieval serf whose master takes care of him than to be a supposedly free Englishman of the nineteenth century, whose freedom consists of the liberty to starve. Unlike the modern industrial worker, Gurth had clean air, the certainty of food, and, most important of all, "social lodging," i.e. a place in the social scheme of things.

Why did Cedric "deserve" to be Gurth's master? Because Cedric did not shirk his responsibility for Gurth, as contemporary capitalists and industrialists shirk their social obligations. Carlyle's arguments, of course, are paternalistic and antidemocratic. One could ask students whether they find Carlyle's example about preventing a madman from jumping off a cliff a convincing rationale for the abrogation of liberty. He expresses a nostalgic longing for an ordered society in which everyone knew his place, in which everyone *had* a place, was "related indissolubly, though in a rude brass-collar way, to his fellow-mortals." The brass collar that symbolizes slavery and the rule of force does not trouble Carlyle.

Harking back to the Middle Ages in his search for an ideal polity, Carlyle echoes Pugin, who had pointed out the abominations of nineteenth-century industrial society in *Contrasts* (1836). Have students look at *Catholic Town in 1440/Same Town in 1840* for another example of the contrast between past harmony and present horror implicit in Carlyle's title. One might use *Past and Present* as a starting point for the topic of the Gothic Revival and the uses of medievalism in Ruskin's *Stones of Venice*, Tennyson's *Idylls of the King*, Morris's *News from Nowhere*, etc.

Finally, in "Captains of Industry" Carlyle develops his notion that strong leaders are the solution to society's ills. Democracy is not the answer; Parliament cannot solve the "Condition of England" crisis by enacting laws (although progressive legislation throughout the century *did* gradually improve conditions, reducing hours of factory work, and so on). Rather, Carlyle optimistically urges the industrialists to take command and regulate themselves. They must become "noble," a new kind of benevolent aristocracy—wise fatherly heroes who will put profit and self-interest aside and revitalize the chivalric ideal of leadership.

In their novels Gaskell and Dickens reiterated Carlyle's appeal, showing factory owners (Carson in *Mary Barton* and Thornton in *North and South*) and businessmen (Scrooge and Marley) coming to a new understanding of their duties towards their employees. In each case this requires a traumatic personal wake-up call (Carson's son is murdered, Scrooge is visited by ghosts), and in *Past and Present* Carlyle makes explicit the threat of national trauma, in the form of revolution: "will not one French Revolution and Reign of Terror suffice us, but must there be two?"

To prevent this the Captains of Industry must find ways to lead that go beyond "cash-payment." To exist only in the relation of employer and employee is soul destroying. The feudal baron felt it "a necessity, to have men round him who in heart loved him." He is to be the model because his leadership was based on mutual esteem, not on hire-for-money. Without such bonds of loyalty and emotional connection, each individual is alone—and "isolation is the sum-total of wretchedness to man." (Cf. Teufelsdröckh, who suffered from "a strange isolation" in which "Invisible yet impenetrable walls, as of Enchantment, divided me from all living" like "the tiger in his jungle.") Carlyle's message about the deadening and chilling effect of human isolation became the central theme of Dickens's *Christmas Carol*, where Scrooge lives "solitary as an oyster."

These excerpts from *Past and Present* can be paired very fruitfully with the *Carol*, and they also serve as an excellent introduction to the Industrial Landscape perspectives section. However, even if one has no time for anything else, it would be worthwhile to read Dickens's *A Walk in a Workhouse* (1850) alongside Carlyle's analysis of the workhouse system.

PERSPECTIVES

The Industrial Landscape

This perspectives section is designed to suggest some of the ways in which machine work and machine-made products affected every aspect of Victorian life, from ordinary household objects to social relations, economic systems, and even basic notions of space and time. It is also designed to give the instructor flexibility: some or all of the selections can form a separate unit on the Industrial

Revolution, or individual selections can be taught in combination with texts elsewhere in the anthology.

The section as a whole works well with *Past and Present*: Carlyle's grim picture of the human consequences of industrialism can be considered along with the testimonies of child workers, and with the excerpts from **Engels** and **Mayhew**. The class alienation illustrated by the inability of Carlyle's Irish widow to find charity, and Carlyle's insistence that "isolation is the sum-total of wretchedness to man," can be compared with **Disraeli's** passage on a divided nation, and with Engels's claim that "isolation of the individual . . . is everywhere the fundamental principle of modern society." Such themes lay the groundwork for Dickens's *Christmas Carol*, enabling the student to bring a more informed awareness of contemporary social and economic issues to that familiar text.

Similarly, the illustration from **Pugin's** *Contrasts*, the portrait of Coketown from **Dickens's** *Hard Times*, Engels's description of Manchester, and the lives of the child laborers recorded in the Parliamentary papers can all be read along with Ruskin's *The Nature of Gothic*. Taken together, they form the basis of a discussion of the degradation of the workers from craftsmen to "hands," the changed face of the landscape, the monotony of factory work, and the various ways in which the middle classes were implicated in the plight of the workers.

The radically altered landscape appears vividly in the excerpt on "The Coming of the Railway" from *Dombey and Son*, as well as in Pugin's *Catholic Town in 1440/Same Town in 1840*, and in Engels, who evokes the rural past that has given way to slums in the industrial north. Pugin's illustration serves not only as a jumping off point to discuss the industrial landscape, but also as an introduction to the notion of Victorian Gothic. The pervasive nostalgia for an imagined medieval past can be traced from Pugin to *Past and Present*, *The Stones of Venice*, *Modern Manufacture and Design*, the *Idylls of the King*, *The Lady of Shalott*, and on through William Morris's writings and designs. A Catholic convert, Pugin went even further by insisting that only a return to Catholicism would restore medieval values. The staunchly Protestant Ruskin denied being influenced by Pugin, but between them they sparked the revival of the Gothic arch that has left its mark on public institutions and college campuses throughout England and America.

The texts gathered in this section include not only indictments of industrialism, but also expressions of pride and wonder at the accomplishments of technology. Along with the pro-technology voice of **Macaulay**, *The Steam Loom Weaver* captures the pure energy and exuberance of this new world of machines, as does **Fanny Kemble's** enthusiastic delight in the marvel of the railroad. In conjunction with these readings one might talk about the Great Exhibition of 1851 (see the photograph of the Crystal Palace), and the ways in which ideas of social and material progress were linked with ideas of scientific progress (cf. Darwin, and some of the passages in the Religion and Science perspectives section).

Both Kemble's letter and the excerpt from *Dombey and Son* give a sense of the sheer strangeness of the railroad. One might look at Tennyson's *Locksley Hall* (1842): "Let the great world spin for ever down the ringing grooves of change." Like Kemble, Tennyson also rode the Liverpool to Manchester line in

1830—though his recollection of the technical details of the experience was less precise than hers!

Kemble's conceit—the train engine is like a mare or a she-dragon—illustrates the tendency to naturalize the mechanical. Compare this to Dickens's famous image for the monotonous motion of a steam-engine piston: it is "like the head of an elephant in a state of melancholy madness." *The Steam Loom Weaver* uses the rhythmic movement of the steam-powered loom as a metaphor for the natural processes of sex. Today, we still attempt to humanize the complexities of technology through analogies to natural functions: computers think, get viruses, talk to each other, enjoy "downtime."

As well as being fascinating social documents, these selections are literary texts in their own right. Mayhew, for example, crafts the narratives that he has collected on the street in such a way that they become mini-autobiographies. In his introduction to the Dover edition of *London Labour and the London Poor*, John D. Rosenberg writes of Mayhew's superb artistry: "he edits, shapes, and intensifies, until we are stunned by the slang beauty and inventiveness of the spoken voices he recreates." Comparing him to Browning, Rosenberg suggests that Mayhew "should be credited with evolving a new art form, a kind of dramatic monologue in prose."

Mayhew was presenting a world as unfamiliar to most middle-class Victorians as "Darkest Africa"—yet it was a world right at their own doorstep. As Thackeray put it, "these wonders and terrors have been lying by your door and mine ever since we had a door of our own. We had but to go a hundred yards off and see for ourselves, but we never did. . . . You and I—were of the upper classes; we have had hitherto no community with the poor." In his own way, Mayhew was teaching the Victorians to see freshly just as much as Ruskin was.

Individual readings in this perspectives section can also be combined in countless ways with material elsewhere in the anthology, material that may have little to do with the Industrial Revolution. For example, *The Steam Loom Weaver* could form part of a unit on ballads, oral tradition, work songs, and so forth. Or, in a discussion of autobiography and/or childhood, the voices of children preserved by Mayhew and the Parliamentary commissioners might be compared to the excerpts from the autobiographies of Mill, Ruskin, Cobbe, and Gosse. The conditions of life for the young mill or mine workers and the London street children might be juxtaposed with the portraits of children's lives in Blake, *Aurora Leigh*, *Tom Brown's School Days*, the Brontës, or *The Child in the House*.

John Stuart Mill
On Liberty (1859)

This is the classic defense of the individual's right to resist governmental constraints and social pressure to conform. For Mill, freedom of speech and press are not unquestionable rights but reasoned principles worth defending: "freedom of opinion" is necessary "to the mental well-being of mankind," the freedom "on which all their other well-being depends." It is important to remember that the

British have no written constitution or Bill of Rights guaranteeing these liberties. Characteristically, Mill undertakes to show the benefits that accrue to all if free speech is maintained, and the consequent injury to all if it is not. Free speech will ultimately serve the interests even of those whose beliefs are questioned, he says, because it will strengthen their convictions if they are proven correct, and will give them new insight if they are shown to be wrong. (Note that Darwin relies on this scenario in the testing of scientific theory; see the opening paragraph of the selection from *The Descent of Man*.) Ask students what Mill would think of current efforts to restrain free speech so as not to give offense.

Mill ties freedom of thought and expression to the notion of individuality, and he fears that in modern times mass culture and the increasing powers of censorship and social control have led to a situation wherein "society has now fairly got the better of individuality; and the danger which threatens human nature is not the excess, but deficiency, of personal impulses and preferences." For Mill, individuality and eccentricity are not simply aberrations to be tolerated, but the sources of all social improvement ("the amount of eccentricity in a society has generally been proportional to the amount of genius, mental vigor, and moral courage which it contained"), and must therefore be vigorously defended against the pressures of conformity. Since most Americans have strong views about individual freedom, demonstrating the continuing relevance of these issues should not be difficult.

Because the role of the individual in modern society was an issue that engaged all the great Victorian writers in one way or another, Mill's carefully articulated views can be compared to the more emotive or empathetic ideas of his contemporaries. He was almost certainly reacting against Carlyle's more conservative stance: Carlyle argues for individual self-awakening in *Sartor Resartus* (1833), but then in *Past and Present* (1843) calls for "Government by the Wisest," suggesting that the wage-slave's "liberty to starve" would be better surrendered to "Captains of Industry." Mill's views were in turn challenged by Matthew Arnold in *Culture and Anarchy* (1869), where Arnold condemns the English habit of "doing as one likes" as a practice that selfishly destroys the whole social fabric. Oscar Wilde, in *The Soul of Man Under Socialism* (1891), returned to Mill's basic point: "In proportion to the development of his individuality, each person becomes more valuable to himself, and is therefore capable of being more valuable to others."

A Millian celebration (or defense) of individual liberty comes up more obliquely in the free-market pleading of Macaulay's *Review of Southey's Colloquies*, in Ruskin's concern for the artistic freedom of workers in *The Nature of Gothic*, in Pater's stirring anthem to self-fulfillment in the "Conclusion" to *The Renaissance*, and in Oscar Wilde's trials. One can find counterpoints in Dickens's biting portrait of Scrooge in *A Christmas Carol* and in Engels's grim view of industrial poverty in "The Great Towns." Note that the individuality of capitalist and worker are often at odds.

Be on the lookout for Mill's subtle irony: in *On Liberty*, for example, he claims that the "collective mediocrity" of the English press is fine with him, since "I do not assert that anything better is compatible, as a general rule, with the present low state of the human mind." In *The Subjection of Women* he notes wryly that men base claims about women's nature on their wives, yet "most men have not had the opportunity of studying in this way more than a single case."

The Subjection of Women (1869)

In conjunction with this selection, assign Mill's brief "Repudiation" of his marriage rights, and Caroline Norton's *Letter to the Queen* in the perspectives section on Victorian Ladies and Gentlemen. Norton directly addresses the legal status of Victorian women. Other important Victorian statements on "the Woman Question" include Elizabeth Barrett Browning's *Aurora Leigh* (Book II), Tennyson's *The Princess*, Florence Nightingale's *Cassandra*, and George Eliot's *Margaret Fuller and Mary Wollstonecraft*. Eliot, like Mill, compares the current situation of women to slavery, and asserts that men too suffer by enforcing such inequality.

Mill begins by pointing out that all arguments urging the logic of male dominance are weak because the alternatives, equality or matriarchy, have never been tried: "The present system, which entirely subordinates the weaker sex to the stronger, rests upon theory only." Moreover, the system is maintained in the face of the very meaning of modernity, "that human beings are no longer born to their place in life . . . but are free to employ their faculties." For Mill, the "subordination of women thus stands out an isolated fact in modern social institutions," sustained by unexamined custom rather than rational analysis. Citing other historical prejudices that have since been overturned, he asks tellingly, "was there ever any domination that did not appear natural to those who possessed it?"

Mill strategically uses the language of Victorian laissez-faire economics to shake the foundations of gender stereotypes. He first contends that women should be left to decide what roles they will play in society: "Whatever women's services are most wanted for, the free play of competition will hold out the strongest inducements to them to undertake." But then he uses this conservative, commercial premise to ask whether "the vocation of wife and mother" is truly natural for women. If so, then why do men force them into it? The free-market implication, Mill says, is that women would naturally rather do anything else, if they had the economic and personal freedom to do so. Far from being natural, the inequality of Victorian marriage is based on coercion and men's fear that women would not stand for it, except on equal grounds. Thus, one might add, the fictional Aurora Leigh, as well as Florence Nightingale and Christina Rossetti, refused proposals of marriage in order to live and work alone.

Anticipating twentieth-century feminist theory and gender studies, Mill pushes his argument further by saying that all speculation about the essential qualities of women is moot because of the social construction of personality: it is impossible to know in our society what the true nature of men and women is since "what is now called the nature of women is an eminently artificial thing—the result of forced repression in some directions, unnatural stimulation in others." Even when compared to slaves women are in a unique position, since "Men do not want solely the obedience of women; they want their sentiments. . . . They have therefore put everything in practice to enslave their minds." Here Mill implicitly calls for the discipline of Women's Studies: women's true character will remain unknown until women are free to reveal it, "until women themselves have told all that they have to tell." Interestingly, he compares a woman's unwillingness to be open with her husband to a son's reticence with his father—there is more than a hint of his own biography here.

Deborah Epstein Nord has an intriguing article, "Mill and Ruskin on the Woman Question Revisited," in *Teaching Literature: What Is Needed Now*, ed. James Engell (1988): 73-83. Nord contrasts Ruskin's enormously popular *Sesame and Lilies* (1865) to Mill's *Subjection*, which was "roundly criticized by contemporary reviewers as social heresy," and reconstructs the Victorian debate about woman's "true nature" and gender difference.

Autobiography (1873)

Mill's unique education now seems inseparable from his famous mental crisis. But did the second invalidate the first, or merely indicate that a sound pedagogical approach had been mismanaged on the human level? Mill contends that he was not unusually gifted, but simply avoided "the wretched waste of so many precious years" of conventional schooling; "if I have accomplished anything, I owe it . . . to . . . the early training bestowed on me by my father." Certain aspects of James Mill's approach have found their way into the contemporary curriculum, such as flash cards (though not in ancient Greek) and the practice of having advanced children tutor the others. Half a million American families now homeschool their children, often with superior results. Can Mill be seen as a model and not just a dire example?

It may be said that all the great Victorian autobiographies center around a crisis in faith, and in Mill's case the faith in doubt was Utilitarianism. But the *Autobiography* provides ample evidence that the roots of his breakdown lay in his childhood. Like Ruskin, who confessed in *Praeterita* that "I had nothing to love," Mill had no playmates. He had a distant, if intense, relationship to his father; his mother is never once mentioned. He also had little other "mental activity than that which was already called forth by my studies." When he catastrophically discovered at the age of twenty-one that "my love of mankind . . . had worn itself out," the chief obstacle to his recovery was his inability to take pleasure in anything for its own sake. Raised on the principles of Bentham's moral calculus that sought to magnify "associations of pleasure with all things beneficial to the great whole, and of pain with all things hurtful to it," Mill suddenly saw how artificial his attitudes were. His insight casts doubt on the wisdom of reward-and-punishment approaches to child rearing or teaching. But it is a sign of how deeply balanced a mind Mill possessed that, even when he perceived that "the habit of analysis has a tendency to wear away the feelings," he did not reject his learning, his family, or his political work. Compare this early realization with Darwin's similar discovery about analytical thinking (described in his autobiography).

Mill's recovery has two turning points. The first comes when reading Marmontel's memoir about the death his father. In *The Evolution of a Genius*

(1985), Peter Glassman examines this passage in detail: Mill not only imagines how he will be able to act (freely) when James Mill dies, but he also sees this death as James's punishment for being so unrecognizing of his son's separate existence and needs (38-43). With the death of a father, "the oppression of the thought that all feeling was dead within me, was gone." Deciding that happiness comes "by the way" when "aiming at something else," Mill was now in a receptive frame of mind for reading Wordsworth, the second stage in his recovery.

Compare Mill's crisis to Teufelsdröckh's in *Sartor Resartus*. Mill's dissatisfaction with Byron ("The poet's state of mind was too like my own") echoes Carlyle's famous injunction "Close thy Byron." But Mill opens Wordsworth, not Goethe, and finds consolation not in a philosophy of work, but in cultivating, through "the love of rural objects and natural scenery," "a source of inward joy, of sympathetic and imaginative pleasure, which could be shared in by all beings." Do students who have just read Wordsworth share this view? (Note that here, as in almost all his writings, Mill—perhaps because he was so conscious that he had an exceptional background—makes every effort to convince his readers that his proposals and discoveries are dedicated to the *common* good.)

Finally able to imagine that people can enjoy life even if all their wants are satisfied, Mill is able to return to his work, the delight he takes in poetry showing him he has "nothing to dread from the most confirmed habit of analysis." Curiously, he does not rate Wordsworth very highly as a poet, saying he values him "less according to his intrinsic merits, than by the measure of what he had done for me." Ask students if they think the merit of literature can be divorced from its effect on the reader. Mill's experience would seem to prove the truth of William Carlos Williams's remark that "It is difficult to get the news from poems, but people are dying every day for lack of what is found there."

Elizabeth Barrett Browning

In *The Second Common Reader* (1932) Virginia Woolf wrote that people were more interested in Barrett Browning's biography than they were in her works: "'Lady Geraldine's Courtship' is glanced at perhaps by two professors in American universities once a year; but we all know how Miss Barrett lay on her sofa; how she escaped from the dark house in Wimpole Street one September morning; how she met health and happiness, freedom, and Robert Browning in the church round the corner" (182). While renewed critical interest in *Aurora Leigh* makes it harder for professors to remain aloof from Barrett Browning's texts, student curiosity about the interplay of her love life and her love poetry still tends to dominate discussion. Yet this is as Barrett Browning would have had it: unlike her husband, she valued highly the open, personal quality of poetic expression. All the poems included here touch on Barrett Browning's double sense of herself as woman and writer.

Barrett Browning said that the French novelist George Sand, known for her masculine attire and passionate love affairs, was "eloquent as a fallen angel." Her two sonnets addressed to Sand are ardent fan letters lauding and defending her tarnished heroine. Both poems mingle male and female attributes, and progress through purgatorial fire from a state of blame (for sexual freedom) to redemption (because of the writer's great soul). The concluding image of A Recognition is especially provocative, suggesting that the immense tension between being "True genius, but true woman!"—a veritable paradox for most Victorians—can be resolved only in death, by God's finally "unsexing" the pure artist. Whether artistic genius has any intrinsic sexual identity, male or female, is a question that occupies Barrett Browning throughout her work.

The urgent, often conflicting demands of sexual desire and poetic drive give Sonnets from the Portuguese much of their passionate power. Written as the Brownings' secret love affair progressed, the sequence has the immediacy of a private diary: will the brilliant, aging invalid be used by the younger, unknown poet? Does he really love her? The author herself is not quite sure. (A Year's Spinning, from the same period, also confronts the threat sex poses to women and their work.) In the first sonnet Love arrives suddenly, warding off the deathly shadows of the poet's past. But in contrast to harmless Theocritus, whose Greek text she is able to control through her learning, Love grabs her by the hair—symbol of a Victorian woman's sexuality—and masters her. He seems as ready to ruin as to save her. The danger recurs in Sonnet 13: despite her lover's urging, the poet strongly refuses to speak her love. Yet her "voiceless" silence "rend[s] the garment of my life"—an image suggesting that her deepest self, the private woman who is also an outspoken poet, will be violated whether she speaks or not.

The battle for verbal and erotic mastery continues in subsequent poems. Sonnets 14 and 21 seek reassurance but play with "love" as word, sound, and entity, reiterating it into a silence that will wordlessly, paradoxically, say even more. By Sonnets 22 and 24 the lovers struggle less against each other than against heaven and earth. In 22 the "erect" lovers turn their aspirations from heaven to delight in standing out among ordinary mortals, while in 24 they shut the world out as if closing a pocket-knife, so that free of "the stab of worldlings" they can become pure lilies in the care of God. In Sonnet 28 the poet plays again with texts, words, and silence, rereading her lover's letters, only to balk at revealing some secret phrase that all his words have taught her not to betray. The most private words she now guards are his, not hers.

But the poet's lover is in control once again in Sonnet 32: she becomes a "worn viol," a defaced instrument that his "master-hands" can turn to wonderful music. While the metaphor suggests sexual surrender, it also retains the poet's artistic integrity; her lover speaks through her, relying on her voice. The ambiguous epithet "great souls" can thus apply to both of them. The poet returns to writing and speaking in Sonnet 38, her hand, head, and lips blessed and enabled by her lover's kiss. But with characteristic wit Barrett Browning makes gentle fun of herself (not letting people shake that hand) and also of Robert Browning (whose kiss misses her brow and lands on her hair) in order to explore the nature of sexual power by which his third kiss grants her possession of him.

The most famous of all her love lyrics, Sonnet 43 (How do I love thee), is even more remarkable when read in this context. We see how hard-won is its impetuous rush of passion, its unreserved declaration of love that breaks the rules of sonnet form by refusing the customary "turn" of idea and attitude in lines 9 to 14. But there is a subtle play, as images of spiritual love are succeeded by more physical, personal images. The shift implies not only that the poet has lost conventional religious faith, but also that love has replaced it; now her God is love.

The question of how a woman can love, write, and do God's will is raised most extensively in *Aurora Leigh*, where the heroine recounts her growth as poet and lover, undergoing experiences that loosely parallel Barrett Browning's own life. *Aurora Leigh*, she said, was a book "into which my highest convictions on Life and Art have entered," and she focussed her efforts on making an epic of *her* moment: "my chief *intention* just now is the writing of a sort of novel-poem . . . running into the midst of our conventions, and rushing into drawing rooms and the like . . . meeting face to face and without mask the Humanity of the age, and speaking the truth of it out plainly." Reversing the mask-obsessed poetic strategy of Robert Browning, she presents Aurora's quest as a successive stripping away of masks—all the preconceived notions of what a woman is and should do. Aurora begins with her own dawning, describing her childhood and parents (mother first), starting to construct a modern, psychologically informed autobiography. The dominant event is the early death of her mother (Barrett Browning's mother did not die till the poet was twenty-two), and the dominant pattern of imagery is maternal: pregnancy, birth, nursing, caring for children. She then describes the mystery built about her mother's picture, a disturbing concatenation of the stereotypes applied to women, ranging from Muse and Madonna to the Medusa.

These are the conceptions she must contend with, first suffering through her miserable aunt's idea of a proper Victorian gentlewoman's education, and then confronting the condescending prejudices of her rich cousin and lover, Romney Leigh. The description of Aurora's education is a classic (I:372–498); to set it in a larger context, students can read selections in the Ladies and Gentlemen perspectives section, particularly Mrs. Ellis on women's necessary submission to man, and Cobbe and Martineau on women's education. Though savagely scornful of British social convention, Aurora withers in this cold, unloving climate, saving herself only by discovering poetry's power to transcend petty materialism and human weakness (I:815–80).

Having dedicated her future to art, she is outraged when Romney proposes that they marry so she can help him with his grand plans to cure society's ills. Echoing Jane Eyre's rejection of St. John Rivers (Brontë's novel was published in 1847), their great debate explores the conventional ideas about women's characters and capabilities. But unlike *Jane Eyre*, it also offers crushing feminist rejoinders to these views, particularly II:359–61: "am I proved too weak / To stand alone, yet strong enough to bear / Such leaners on my shoulder?" Aurora's views quarrel in important ways with Tennyson's widely quoted passage from *The Princess* (1847), "The woman's cause is man's," and anticipate Mill's systematic attack on sexism in *The Subjection of Women* (1869).

In Book 3, set seven years later, we see the results of Aurora's defiance. She has found "a room of one's own" in London, and earns her living as an independent literary woman. In a kind of interior monologue she comments on her mail—the ludicrous advice of critics, the bizarre requests from strangers, and an intriguing note from an artist friend, Vincent Carrington, asking her opinion of how to best represent Danae's sexual encounter with Jove. Aurora comments that the two versions of Danae's response, one active, one passively self-negating (III:121-43), represent "Two states of the recipient artist-soul." Surprisingly, she appears to opt for the passive response. Is the poet being ironic? Or is the ambitious Aurora's quest for a feminist poetry, with Jove as male muse, as fraught with contradictions as the masculinist views she opposes?

The visionary, oddly violent passage that follows (III:167-203), one of the rare descriptions of an *urban* sunset in Victorian poetry, also stresses how humans can be blotted out by superior forces of nature or God. As she "view[s] the city perish in the mist," the poet safe in her garret compares Londoners to the Egyptians swallowed by the Red Sea, and herself to Moses's sister Miriam, who celebrated the Hebrew victory. This alternating classical/biblical frame of reference—poet as ravished Danae, poet as virgin Miriam—indicates the complex, sometimes contradictory way Barrett Browning seeks to clarify the experience of the woman artist, and her all-out search for metaphors to sustain her quest.

Her poetic ambitions come through most clearly in Book 5 of *Aurora Leigh*, where she presents her rationale for a modern, feminist epic. In his Preface to *Poems* (1853) Matthew Arnold had insisted that contemporary life had little to offer poets, and here Barrett Browning responds at length by asserting that the poet's duty is "to represent the age, / Their age, not Charlemagne's,—this live throbbing age" (202-03). Having read the social satire of Pope, Swift, Johnson, Blake, and Byron, and conditioned by American culture's obsession with the present, students may not have noticed how wary the Victorians were about dealing with contemporary life in poetry—and thus how bold Barrett Browning's words were. But a quick run-through of Tennyson, Browning, Arnold, and others will turn up very few poems that directly address the looks, clothes, fashions, events, issues, and technology of the day. Almost every theme was treated obliquely through a historical parallel, a static rural setting, or the borrowing of some earlier story. Asserting that "every age / Appears to souls who live in't (ask Carlyle) / Most unheroic" (155-56), Barrett Browning rejects the Victorian tendency—from Carlyle and Pugin to Morris and Pater—to denounce the present by reimagining the past. Moreover, in what is probably a rebuke of Tennyson's *Idylls of the King*, she feminizes this iconoclastic perspective: "King Arthur's self / Was commonplace to Lady Guenever" (209-10).

Her aim is to reinvent the epic poem—and even the "man's world" of Victorian culture itself—on matrilineal terms: "unscrupulously epic," she will capture "the full-veined heaving, double-breasted Age" in a "living art" that will suckle future generations (216-22). In *Cassandra*, Florence Nightingale complains, quoting from *Othello*, that women are expected to "suckle their fools and chronicle their small beer;" rejecting this confining familial role she turns to a *metaphoric* nursing and makes a worthy profession of it. Barrett Browning, however, uses her epic to stress repeatedly the value of suckling as a *literal* as well as metaphoric act, an image of female creativity and cultural transmission—like poetry itself. Nightingale compares wives to prostitutes, but Barrett Browning claims that if a woman is true to her art, genuine love and marriage are possible.

Although *Aurora Leigh* insists on the noble, even sacred function of art, some of the later poems emphasize an important undertone in the epic—the painful nature of artistic creation, whether prompted by angels or gods, Christian or classical muses. *A Curse for a Nation* explores the poet's unwillingness to turn her writing into cursing, even against slavery, and *A Musical Instrument* examines the brutality of "the great god Pan" who rips the reed from its home by the river, violating nature and changing its being forever, in order to produce life-giving art. In Barrett Browning's poetry, disturbingly, writing is never very far from coercion and rape.

An interesting biographical aspect of Barrett Browning's abolitionist writing is that she appears to have considered herself as, in part, descended from slaves. Discussing her family name and background (her father's family were rich slave-holders in Jamaica) in a letter to her future husband, she wrote: "Nevertheless it is true that I would give ten towns in Norfolk [where an ancestor was governor] . . . to own some purer lineage than that of the blood of the slave!—Cursed we are from generation to generation!" In *Dared and Done: The Marriage of Elizabeth Barrett and Robert Browning* (1995), Julia Markus explores the significance of Barrett Browning's writing *The Runaway Slave* on her honeymoon, and suggests that the reason her father allowed none of his children to marry was his fear of continuing black blood in the Barrett line (88–115). Like Elizabeth Barrett, Robert Browning was considered "dark" in complexion; his paternal grandmother was Creole, and this may have been a further bond between the two poets.

Alfred, Lord Tennyson

The Victorians embraced Tennyson as their national poet because almost everything he wrote seemed to be about their inmost selves, and yet also applicable to their times and destiny as a people. In the vast library of Tennyson criticism that seeks to reconcile the brooding, private lyricist with the resolute and timely public voice, a good starting place is *Critical Essays on Alfred Lord Tennyson*, ed. Herbert F. Tucker (1993). The volume contains recent essays, both formalist and contextual, by leading critics on the major works and poems. Tucker's introduction surveys the poet's evolution into Victorian sage, his fall from popular grace by the turn of the century, and his subsequent resurrection.

But one could equally begin with the insights of Tennyson's first reader. Arthur Hallam's review of Tennyson's first book—"On Some of the Characteristics of Modern Poetry" (1831)—remains unsurpassed. If in death Hallam, the "hero" of both *In Memoriam* and *Idylls of the King*, turned into Tennyson's most elaborate literary creation, in life he was the poet's most astute critic. Calling Tennyson a Poet of Sensation, Hallam summarized "five distinctive excellencies" of his verse that are still worth pointing out: 1) "his luxuriance of imagination and . . . his control over it;" 2) "his power of embodying himself in ideal characters, or rather moods of character" such that the narration evolves naturally from the predominant feeling; 3) "his vivid picturesque delineation of objects . . . fused . . . in a medium of strong emotion;" 4) "the variety of his lyrical measures, and exquisite modulation of harmonious words and cadences to the swell and fall of the feelings expressed;" and 5) "the elevated habits of thought" and "mellow soberness of tone" that does not so much "instruct the understanding" as "communicate the love of beauty to the heart."

These qualities emerge distinctly in the early verse, mellifluous poems that seem to undercut mainstream Victorian values. All the earlier poems included here, from The Kraken to The Eagle (mirror versions of one another) concern themselves either by their music or subject with a passivity and lack of will that challenge Victorian earnestness and the Carlylean Gospel of Work. They are lyrics of isolation and desolation, their topics chosen from literature rather than life, seeking release from life's cares and duties.

Mariana, whose dense psychological landscape caught the attention of Mill and Edgar Allan Poe, piles an eerie array of thickly textured description ("With blackest moss the flower-plots . . ."), sound ("The blue fly sung in the pane"), and vocal silences ("unlifted was the clinking latch") upon a nearly static refrain that emphasizes Mariana's solitude and helplessness. The poem is driven by a certain sexual tension (the shadow of the gnarled poplar on her moonlit bed), but the overall effect is one of inertia and passivity. Ruskin grumbled over Millais' beautiful painting of the poem, Mariana in the Moated Grange (1850): "If the painter had painted Mariana at work in an unmoated grange, instead of idle in a moated one, it had been more to the purpose—whether of art or life" (qtd in Houghton's Victorian Frame of Mind [1957] 243).

In an age of energy, the young Tennyson appears strangely fatigued. This is most obvious in Tithonus, where the misguided quest for too much life has undone the once-impassioned speaker, who now mourns for the brief simplicity of ordinary human life succinctly presented in line 3. Similarly, The Lotos-Eaters is a soporific tour-de-forcelessness whose initial resolve, like an old-fashioned phonograph, runs down under the weight of Tennyson's long, heavy vowels. The "island home" and attendant responsibilities that the debilitated mariners cannot rouse themselves to regain would seem to be not just ancient Ithaca, but also modern Britain.

Even Ulysses, so often read as a stirring call to action (Matthew Rowlinson's "The Ideological Moment of Tennyson's 'Ulysses,'" Victorian Poetry 30.3-4 [1992]: 265-276, traces this view) is sabotaged by the language the speaker uses to convince himself and his men to set off: the pauses of the last few lines appear less emphatic than simply weary, Ulysses trailing off redundantly with "that which we are . . . we are" and finally lurching to a halt amidst his closing monosyllables. As Christopher Ricks asks in his immensely helpful guide to the poems, Tennyson (1972), why aren't there any verbs in the future tense? Ricks cites one Victorian reviewer who said that Ulysses only "intends to roam, but stands for ever a listless and melancholy figure on the shore." Attuned to Tennyson's floundering meter, Matthew Arnold commented that the three lines beginning "Yet all experience is an arch . . ." (19-21) "by themselves take up nearly as much time as a whole book of the Iliad" (see Ricks 122-25).

Why does the poet dwell on incapacity and inanition? Why does a great hero like Ulysses dismiss the Victorian virtues of hearth, family, and public duty? Why does Tennyson admit later that even his tears are "idle"? *The Lady of Shalott*, probably Tennyson's most complex and elusive early poem, provokes a range of possible responses. Because the Lady is an artist, we see more clearly the poet's likely identification with characters who feel trapped by the spell of life or circumstance. The poem casts a spell with its ornate musicality, which struck reviewers in 1832 and which the poet carefully refined before republishing the work in *Poems* 1842. Tennyson sets the poem in the realm of fairy tale, and in section 1 heightens the unreality of the Lady's existence, occupation, and isolation. Traditionally, readings have focused on the Lady's curse (which Tennyson himself added, along with the mirror, to the story he found in Malory) as a sign that art and life are incompatible. Regarding the world only indirectly through her mirror, the Lady inhabits a sort of Plato's cave, one which it is fatal for her to break out of, since both her art (the web) and she herself are destroyed—and then, tragically or ironically, her great sacrifice is puzzled over by an uncomprehending public downstream in worldly Camelot.

But as soon as one foregrounds the fact that this artist is a *woman*, a new series of possible readings opens up. Since Tennyson links artistry to a passive, patient, shadowy, cloistered femininity, is he suggesting that poets occupy a woman's place in Victorian society? and what would that role be, exactly? The poem's form provides some clues: the two worlds of embowered Shalott and towered Camelot, female and male, are separated by the rest of the stanza, yet linked by rhyme. The whole thrust of the narrative is to bring them together, creating a further tension between the magic of the poem's music and its tragic topic. Ignorant of the Lady's plight and the action his appearance precipitates, Lancelot may be read as a figure of oblivious indifference ("tirra lirra") or sympathetic understanding (his final words). Visual potency and sexual attraction ("the helmet and the plume") seems to bring them together momentarily in her fatally unmediated gaze. But the shadow-world of art and isolation have already failed to satisfy the knightless Lady—although she perhaps realizes that even visual contact with Camelot is deadly. Is Tennyson saying that women or poets have no scope of action in masculine Victorian society; that action is death for woman or poet; that romantic self-sacrifice or sexual knowledge brings death for women (who might well die in childbirth if they acted on that knowledge)?

In "'Cracked from Side to Side': Sexual Politics in 'The Lady of Shalott,'" Carl Plasa contends that the supposed separation of art and life in the poem is really an illusion, since that separation is an issue historically grounded in Tennyson's own society, and thus the poem is itself an example of how art and life really *are* inextricably mixed. He reads it as a fractured, self-contradictory addressing of "the Woman Question." Plasa takes the mirror as "the ideological status quo" which is overturned by the Lady's daring, iconoclastic gaze; but it is a only a short-term victory over patriarchy, since marriage, figured as death, "is tantamount, for women, to a form of self-annihilation" (*Victorian Poetry* 30.3–4 [1992]: 258, 260; the entire issue is devoted to essays on Tennyson).

Julia Sackville reads the poem against its many Victorian illustrations, Holman Hunt's chief among them. In "'The Lady of Shalott': a Lacanian Romance," she regards the distinction between "real" Camelot and faery Shalott as a misconception that has deluded readers as much as it deludes the Lady: "In order to read Camelot as representing 'life' . . . one is surely forced to close one's eyes to its long-established literary role as the context for romantic fiction" (76). Mistaking the world of romance (in both senses) as a true "beyond," a way out of the mediated world she inhabits, the Lady attempts to "experience the revelation of direct contact with the real" (78). But in so doing, she collapses the double mystery (what she imagines about Camelot, what Camelot imagines about her) upon which her art and life depend. Portraying the moment at which mediation becomes revelation, Hunt focuses on the disarray of hair and web to show how the Lady's bold delusion has "undone" her both sexually and artistically (*Word and Image* 8 [1992]: 83).

Was Tennyson an imperialist? a sexist? gay? Poems of the middle period, such as *Locksley Hall, The Princess,* and *In Memoriam* may prompt students to ask these questions—to which the answers are complicated, both biographically and textually. Not surprisingly, Tennyson seems more interested in exploring a range of possible attitudes to war, women, and love, than in committing himself to one position. The dramatic monologue (or tirade) *Locksley Hall* is a kind of reverse *Ulysses* (his comrades are urging the speaker to go) that cuts a wide swath through major Victorian issues (including commercialism, gender roles, evolution, imperialism, racial characteristics, human destiny, and divine providence). Like *The Charge of the Light Brigade,* it may seem a sabre-rattling endorsement of masculine self-fulfillment in action, duty, and world domination—or else the story of "someone [who] had blunder'd."

The strong caesura of the unusual octameter line implies a self-divided mind that is only partially reconciled by the distant rhymes at the end of the lengthy couplet. Is the speaker justly or unjustly laying blame for the ruin of society and his own aspiration when he lashes out against materialism, social hierarchy, his conventional cousin Amy and her loutish upper-class husband? Does his fulminating against women ("woman is the lesser man") and other races or religions ("I count the gray barbarian lower than the Christian child") suggest that their lower evolutionary status will have to be subsumed in that of the Victorian male in order to attain his idealistic, Providential, science-fiction view of a universal peace to come, with him as "heir of all the ages"?

One could say that the poem is most concerned with exploring social, sexual, racial, and evolutionary *levels,* through the troubled hopes, grudges, and prejudices of a young man trying to find his own level emotionally. In "Tennyson and the Savage" Gerhard Joseph points out that in his treatment of other lands and races Tennyson was torn between a pastoral/utopian tradition of the Noble Savage and Edenic landscape, and an evolution-oriented Victorian ideology: "His literary heritage and romantic bent may have inclined him to extol the virtues of the native and his natural setting, but his cultural heritage and belief in progress in the guise of imperialist ideology led him to extol the virtues of civilization" (*Tennyson Research Bulletin* 6.1 [1992]: 38). While both these attitudes jostle uneasily in *Locksley Hall,* Lynne B. O'Brien sees Tennyson endorsing a way out of the speaker's confusion through the "beneficial function" of alienation and war, which initiate "a quest for personal growth which benefits the entire society" ("Male Heroism: Tennyson's Divided View," *Victorian Poetry* 32.2 [1994]: 180-181; see also Marion Shaw's "Tennyson's Dark Continent" in the same issue, 157-168).

The Princess seems equally ambivalent in its response to "the Woman Question." Eve Kosovsky Sedgwick points out in "Tennyson's *Princess*: One Bride for Seven Brothers" (reprinted in Tucker from her book *Between Men: English Literature and Male Homosocial Desire*, 1985) that formally the poem has a "direct and explicit link to the division of gender; for the narrative, feminist content and all, is attributed entirely to the young men [who narrate it], while the ravishing lyrics that intersperse the narrative, often at an odd or even subversive angle to what is manifestly supposed to be going on, are supposed to be entirely the work of women in the group" (134). Such a structure implies, like *The Lady of Shalott*, that while the process of ideological construction is male, mere "ornamental" (though perhaps oppositional) work belongs to women and poets. In the speech that has come to be called "The Woman's Cause Is Man's," the Prince claims attention as a visionary "feminist" by prophesying a more androgynous narrowing of sexual difference, even as he conceives it under the aegis of a traditional marriage that helps the sexes differentiate themselves. As he says later to the Princess: "Accomplish thou my manhood and thyself; / Lay thy sweet hands in mine and trust to me" (Book 7, lines 344-45). This strategy is reminiscent of Barrett Browning's comment that Victorian culture grants women the "Potential faculty in everything / Of abdicating power in it" (*Aurora Leigh* I: 441-42).

Many of the lyrics reinforce this feminine passivity or masculine call for surrender, particularly "Sweet and Low" and "Come Down, O Maid," but others, such as "Now Sleeps the Crimson Petal," require the male listener to lose himself in a woman's body. J. Hillis Miller's essay "Temporal Topographies: Tennyson's Tears" (*Victorian Poetry* 30.3-4 [1992]: 277-289) reads "Tears, Idle Tears" as Tennyson's attempt to "express the human sense of time" in genderless spatial images (280), so that the poem transcends its immediate dramatic role within *The Princess* as a marker of feminine idleness and nostalgia at odds with masculine efforts to build the future. As Miller notes, the poem "expresses Tennyson's own obsession with what he called 'the passion of the past'" (280), a generalized feeling of human mortality and temporality, a distance in time figured as spatial distance. As Tennyson said, his boyhood feeling for the past "is so always with me now; it is the distance that charms me in the landscape, the picture and the past, and not the immediate today in which I move."

Tennyson is enamored of distance: perhaps that explains why a poet who makes readers uncomfortable with his far-off resolutions to religious and social problems should be so immensely effective on a personal level. In fact, it is probably the appeal to the emotions that makes his wispy case for political or spiritual evolution more convincing. We may have difficulty crossing the physical distances of empire or the dizzying perspectives of the distant future (*Locksley Hall*) or the psychological frontiers of a re-gendered society (*The Princess*), but we all know, and feel, losses that we inevitably image to ourselves as a distance from time past. That is why "Tears, Idle Tears" (and *Break, Break, Break*, which treats similar themes) works so subtly to translate images of what is before our eyes, but just out of reach, into images of "the days that are no more."

Building on this impulse, Tennyson managed in *In Memoriam* to put his tears to good use. "Much soothed and pleased with Tennyson's *In Memoriam*," Queen Victoria wrote in her diary on January 5th, 1862: "Only those who have suffered as I do, can understand these beautiful poems" (*Dear and Honoured Lady: The Correspondence Between Queen Victoria and Alfred Tennyson*, ed. Hope Dyson and Charles Tennyson [1969], 67). The Queen had reason to be soothed: the poem's structure and technique are built around an ultimately reassuring pattern of loss and recuperation. The poem's memorable lines seem to solve the dilemmas they propose: on the personal level, the "hand that can be clasp'd no more" of section 7 is offset by "'Tis better to have loved and lost / Than never to have loved at all" (section 27, repeated in 85); on the religious and evolutionary level, the presciently pre-Darwinian horror of godless "Nature, red in tooth and claw" (section 56) is allayed by section 118's confident injunction, "Move upward, working out the beast / And let the ape and tiger die." The poem gains additional continuity and a consolatory narrative drift from the poet's contrasting reactions to key images (such as the old yew tree in sections 2 and 39), places (Hallam's house in 7 and 119), dates (the anniversaries of Hallam's death in 72 and 99), and larger topics, such as the spiritual implications of evolution, first despaired over in sections 54, 55, and 56, but then re-viewed in a positive light in 118, 120, and 123. Even the fact of Tennyson's having doubted is recuperated: "There lives more faith in honest doubt / Believe me, than in half the creeds" (section 96).

In his helpful book *Reading 'In Memoriam'* (1985), Timothy Peltason calls Hallam "a vivid absence" at the heart of the poem, and this may well be a large part of the poem's lasting appeal, allowing readers to project their own losses into that emotionally charged void, as did Queen Victoria. As J. Hillis Miller comments in the article cited above, "Hallam's death did not generate Tennyson's feeling of loss. Rather the death gave Tennyson an occasion to personify a loss he already felt" (282). And as John D. Rosenberg notes, Tennyson invited this practice; in the course of the poem he compares his love "to that of mother, father, fiancée; wife and husband; friend, brother, mate, comrade, widow, and widower; a ghost seeking a ghost; a poor girl in a great man's house; a dog that loves its master; a father giving away a bride" ("Stopping for Death: Tennyson's *In Memoriam*," *Victorian Poetry* 30.3-4 [1992]: 305). Thus, in a famous comment, an early reviewer wrote that the poem (published anonymously) revealed the grief "from the full heart of the widow of a military man."

But this polyvalence of mourning can also be disturbing. In reviews of the first edition, Gerard Manley Hopkins's father was troubled by the "amatory tenderness" of one man for another, and the Rev. Charles Kingsley compared the poem to Shakespeare's sonnets in treating "love passing the love of woman." Exploring the homoerotic aspects of the poem, Christopher Craft ("'Descend, and Touch, and Enter': Tennyson's Strange Manner of Address" in Tucker 153-73) contends that the poet, addressing a desire perhaps born of death, treats "homosexual desire as indissoluble from death" (158); he produces a "discourse of homosexual longing" (170) whose satisfaction, or even expression, death and social norms combine to make impossible. Craft concludes that "in the sheer ferocity of its personal loss . . . Tennyson's elegy manages to counterspeak its own submission to its culture's heterosexualizing conventions;" it is a "desiring machine whose first motive is the reproduction of lost Hallam" (170).

Rosenberg disagrees that this desire is homosexual. Pointing to the range of readers who grieve along with the poet, he views the poet's feeling for Hallam as part of a "freely gendered sexuality" which is "so primal and all-encompassing that it lacks gender specificity or constancy" (303). But he does agree that "the most startling effects of In Memoriam all have a transgressive quality, a crossing of borders that normally separate the living from the dead, the natural from the supernatural, one sex or species from another" (295). Rosenberg notes that when Tennyson seeks to "grow incorporate" with the yew tree in section 2 he is striving to possess the corpse of Hallam that the yew's roots now embrace more fully than he (295). Rosenberg also takes seriously Tennyson's remark that the poem was "a sort of divine comedy—cheerful at the close," arguing that Hallam is Tennyson's Beatrice, and that "the marriage that overrides all others and is both the origin and end of In Memoriam is the marriage of Alfred Tennyson to Arthur Hallam. This union, the true Epithalamion of In Memoriam, is consummated in the last third of the Epilogue and takes place in heaven" (323).

Students interested in the strange compound of physical and spiritual longing in the poem can look at the pervasive hand imagery (such as the clasp broken by death that is figured in the white space between stanzas one and two in section 7, but re-established mentally in section 119); the mingled desire for the rebirth of Christ and Arthur (figured in the ambiguity of "he" that starts section 107, that at first seems to refer to Christ, the last noun in section 106); and the ghostly consummation Tennyson so devoutly wishes in section 93 ("Descend, and touch, and enter") and in section 95, which many readers take as the poem's climax ("The dead man touched me from the past, / And all at once it seemed at last / The living soul was flashed on mine").

Idylls of the King

A central difficulty of the Idylls is the ethereal quality of its Arthur. The king emerges out of dark rumor, struggles with shadows, and passes into a distant dawn. In "The Coming of Arthur" Tennyson deliberately clouds the question of Arthur's birth to emphasize both the king's supra-human qualities and the morally revealing responses they elicit from the other characters. The King's uncertain origins and strange proofs of legitimacy also suggest anxiety over patriarchal authority and the credibility of Christianity, for Arthur's elusiveness stems in part from his Christlike embodiment of ideals unattainable in a fallen world. This is a theme stressed repeatedly in "The Passing of Arthur," whose conclusion can be read as a dirge for Christianity itself, "a broken chancel and a broken cross." Most contemporary readers readily grasped the parallels between the shattered spiritual aspirations of

Victorian society and the Round Table's self-ruin through sensuality and faithless-ness. But partly, too, Arthur is so much the "once and future king" of Tennyson's own life that the pain of his passing and the yearning for his return leave the poet little room to savor his presence as a vigorous, living human being. As the resigned yet hopeful conclusion of the *Idylls* makes clear, the return of Arthur, his "Second Coming," is just as "far off" here as at the ending of *In Memoriam*.

Of the many larger patterns of imagery in the poem (including the reciprocity be-tween the natural world and human one, figured most strongly in the changing sea-sons), humanness and beastliness are central. Throughout the poem, as beasts (and heathens) are extirpated, human (and spiritual) qualities flourish; but by the end, as it was in the beginning, the reverse is also true. In "The Coming of Arthur" Britain is a wilderness where "the beast was more and more" till Arthur arrives and eventu-ally remakes the land: "the old order changeth, yielding place to new." The gather-ing storm is symbolized by the animality of "Pelleas and Ettarre." Ettarre is a biting ant, her knights are hounds, Gawain is a dog, and the disillusioned Pelleas invokes foxes, wolves, and rats before finally becoming a hissing snake at Arthur's court.

Finally, in "The Passing of Arthur," as the "realm / Reels back into the beast" this savage devolution is figured by traitorousness, civil war, and "the last weird bat-tle in the west," one of the most dark, despairing, and eerie passages in all of Tennyson. Arthur's own doubts ("I know not what I am . . . I seem but King among the dead") are followed by Bedivere's questioning of the legend ("empty breath / And rumours of a doubt") until "the whole round Table is dissolved / Which was an image of the mighty world." But in slaying Modred, Arthur casts a temporary otherworldly peace over the wasted landscape; the sheep and goats of Judgment Day are the last beasts mentioned in the epic. On the poem's overarch-ing themes, see John D. Rosenberg, *The Fall of Camelot: A Study of Tennyson's "Idylls of the King"* (1973).

Yet one of the things that separates man and beast is terribly equivocal: the use of weapons. From the mystic arrival of Excalibur, which proves Arthur's legitimacy, to Pelleas's Freudian lament, "I have no sword," when he loses all hope of Ettarre's love, to the protracted trial of Excalibur's return to the Lady of the Lake, swords are of vital interest to Tennyson, his knights, and his ladies. Looking at visual in-terpretations of Tennyson's text in "To Take Excalibur: King Arthur and the Construction of Victorian Manhood," Debra N. Mancoff argues that the sword, with its commands in ancient and modern tongues, requires the Victorian gentle-man "to bring ancient, honorable standards to life in the modern world" (258), and she concludes that "to take Excalibur was to be a man" (*King Arthur: A Casebook*, ed. Edward Donald Kennedy [1996], 278). In a very different reading of the poem's "modernity," entitled "Commodifying Tennyson: The Historical Transformation of 'Brand Loyalty'" (*Victorian Poetry* 34.2 [1996]: 133–148), Gerhard Joseph connects the imposing physical and symbolic power of Excalibur and the medieval "brand" or sword with the birth of "brand-name" proprietorship in commerce and bookselling. We are all Bediveres, he says, idealist-consumers tantalized into covetousness by both the author's unadulterated text and his signi-fying sword.

But how male is this masculine-seeming signifier? Linda Shires examines how the "maleness" of the sword depends on its relation to a female donor or recipient ("Take me" / "Cast me away") in such a way that "the poem asserts a definition of manliness as the letting go of literal objects of masculine authority" ("Patriarchy, Dead Men, and Tennyson's Idylls of the King," Victorian Poetry 30 [1992]: 408). One might look at this in conjunction with Newman's feminized ideal gentleman in our perspectives section on Victorian Ladies and Gentlemen. Moving from sword to society, Elliot Gilbert's article, "The Female King: Tennyson's Arthurian Apocalypse" (in Tucker; also PMLA 98 [1983]: 863-78) considers how the unstable patriarchy of Idylls, even as it seeks to punish female transgression of Arthur's hopelessly ideal laws, projects authority as chastely female: "the Arthurian credo of passionlessness embodies the early Victorian belief in the benevolence and controllability of . . . nature. But just as the Victorians' famous efforts to suppress female sexuality only succeeded in generating a grim and extensive sexual underground, so Arthur's naive manipulations of nature conclude in the society of the Round Table being swept away on a great wave of carnality" (213).

Scenes from Julia Margaret Cameron's classic photographic edition of Idylls of the King (1874-75) are worth bringing into class. How—and why—would one go about photographing a work of poetic fiction? Some answers can be found in Helmut Gernsheim's beautifully illustrated Julia Margaret Cameron (1975) and in Victoria Olsen's "Idylls of Real Life," Victorian Poetry 33.3-4 (1995): 371-89.

Edward FitzGerald
The Rubáiyát of Omar Khayyám
(1859, 1868, 1872, 1879, 1889)

The author was born Edward Purcell, but his whole family took on the name "FitzGerald" on the death of his maternal grandfather in 1818. A graduate of Trinity College, Cambridge, where he became friends with Thackeray and Tennyson, FitzGerald lived the life of a country gentleman, puttering on his estate, sailing, writing letters, and above all making the many free translations or adaptations from Greek, Persian, Spanish, and other languages that he is known for today. He rarely allowed his name on a title page, and was not known publically as the author of the Rubáiyát until 1875. But by 1900, it had become one of the most popular poems in English; it was printed in over 200 editions in the century following its first publication. The first major review of poems, published by Charles Eliot Norton in the U.S., did not appear until 1869, a year after the second edition, but most people agreed with Norton's conclusion: "It has all the merit of an original production." In many ways, FitzGerald's poem anticipates Oscar Wilde's resolution to take the serious things of life trivially and trivial things seriously.

Like his friend Tennyson, FitzGerald seems to speak to his audience intimately of private feelings on big questions. And as Tennyson had done in The Lotos Eaters, he proposes a subversive, drugged inertia as a response to life's most urgent demands. His self-deprecating tone and penchant for pondering the larger meaning of life fit in well with the late-Victorian backlash against the moral earnestness of earlier generations. But what is his message, exactly? Is the final effect a longing for rest, certitude, a structure and meaning to life? Or a Paterian affirmation that "experience itself" is all that matters? Stanza 96 circles round to the themes and images of the opening stanzas, mourning the passing of Spring, Youth, the Rose, the song of the Nightingale. But Stanza 99 suggests neither resignation nor a simple quest for understanding; rather, Omar and his love want to "grasp this sorry Scheme of Things entire" in order to "shatter it to bits" and then "Re-mould it nearer to the Heart's Desire!" His form of address to his lover—"Ah Love!"—reminds one of the conclusion to Arnold's *Dover Beach*, but what does FitzGerald/Omar want to be true to? Wine alone?

Claiming to have toned down the "Drink and make merry" aspects of the original, FitzGerald insisted that his text was not a frivolous one: "Either way, the Result is sad enough: saddest perhaps when most ostentatiously merry." One might sense in the music of the poem something of this underlying sorrow. The distinctive four-line stanzas of the *Rubáiyát* recall another, equally beloved poem of similar stanza length, similarly constructed around the author's musings about life, death, and the place of humans in the universe. Tennyson's *In Memoriam* mournfully fights its way toward Christian orthodoxy even as FitzGerald's poem flippantly proclaims a *carpe diem* outlook. But both struggle long and hard with mortality and the apparent unknowability of any divine plan, either for individuals or for the entire human race. The aural strain of bridging the symbolic and emotional gap between the rhymes of lines one and four in *In Memoriam* may actually be easier to handle than the gap between lines two and four in the *Rubáiyát*. Tennyson's opening and closing lines embrace a couplet, just as Tennyson longs to embrace Hallam; but FitzGerald's triple rhyme makes the unrhymed third line all the harder to bear—it has a lonely individuality, and no mate.

Though he may have had Tennyson's poem at least partly in mind—he did call the poem "a sort of Consolation"—FitzGerald denied any extenuating symbolism in Omar's text: "Worldly Pleasures are what they profess to be without any pretense at divine Allegory: his Wine is the Veritable Juice of the Grape: his Tavern where it was to be had: his Sáki [wine bearer] the Flesh and Blood that poured it out for him." Although he hints that he has ruined his life and reputation with wine, Omar appears to prefer the world of drink to that of sobriety, as in Stanza 94— "Indeed, indeed, Repentance oft before / I swore—but was I sober when I swore?" The poem's final comment on Wine—"I wonder often what the Vintners buy / One-half so precious as the stuff they sell" (Stanza 95)—reaffirms one of the poem's underlying themes, that drink offers greater, and surer, insight into "the one True Light" (Stanza 77) than religion. In this sense, the *Rubáiyát* could be seen as a very curious part of the nineteenth-century fascination with "the derangement of the senses" promulgated by Poe, Baudelaire, Rimbaud, Verlaine, and others.

A good locus for classroom discussion is the "Colloquy of the Pots," Stanzas 82–90. Note that FitzGerald marked off this section with stars so that it would stand alone, yet he precedes it in Stanzas 77–81 with a discussion of the apparent absurdities of the Bible's rationale for human existence, including an attack on the doctrine of predestination. Thus when the pots speak the theological stage is set for their musings on the motivations of their Maker. In his notes to the third and fourth editions, FitzGerald commented: "This Relation of Pot and Potter to Man and his Maker figures far and wide in the Literature of the World, from the time of the Hebrew Prophets to the present; when it may finally take the name of 'Pot theism,' by which Mr. Carlyle ridiculed Sterling's 'Pantheism.'" There are six speakers, and it may be useful to have students offer a precis of each pot's "theology"—what position does each take, what thinkers or doctrines might each one represent? Despite their variety of opinions, the pots all turn eagerly toward the arriving porter and his wine. What's the point? Perhaps that all humans need physical fulfillment, even of a most literal sort, as in food and wine. Or if the wine is to be taken symbolically despite FitzGerald's disclaimer, then perhaps it represents thirst for God's Word or the reanimating infusion of some life-force greater than ourselves. Because Omar's exploration of key religious issues is situated in a foreign culture, English readers would have found themselves able to indulge his ideas without too much threat to their own beliefs, even as they saw Judeo-Christian attitudes relativized by reference to images and ideas shared with other traditions.

Look also at the role played by pots elsewhere in the poem. In Stanza 36, Omar drinks from a vessel that was once a man; in Stanza 37 a pot on the wheel seems to speak to its Potter, and in 38 readers are reminded that in Genesis God made Adam from clay. Thus when the pots speak later on, they are not just metaphors for humans, but human material themselves.

FitzGerald adds in his note that a friend has written him with this corroboration of his "pot theism": "Apropos of old Omar's Pots, did I ever tell you the sentence I found in 'Bishop Pearson on the Creed'? 'Thus are we wholly at the disposal of His will, and our present and future condition framed and ordered by His free, but wise and just decrees. Hath not the potter power over the clay, of the same lump to make one vessel unto honour, and another unto dishonour? (Rom. ix. 21). And can that earth-artificer have a freer power over his brother potsherd (both being made of the same metal), than God hath over him, who, by the strange fecundity of His omnipotent power, first made the clay out of nothing, and then him out of that?'"

One could opine that all this textual buttressing of pot-and-pan-theism just renders the whole subject ridiculous. Having proposed what he knew would strike readers as an untenable philosophy based on immediate gratification and the rejection of religious doctrine, and then having put this philosophy in the mouths of wine-jars, FitzGerald goes one step further: he uses his notes deliberately and ironically to exaggerate the theological pedigree of his argument. Maybe that is the point—outside of "A Book of Verses underneath the Bough, / A Jug of Wine, a Loaf of Bread—and Thou," all the rest *is* nonsense.

In Salman Rushdie's *Shame* (1983) the hero is named Omar Kayyam Shakil. The narrator comments: "Omar Khayyam's position as a poet is curious. He was never very popular in his native Persia; and he exists in the West in a translation that is really a complete reworking of his verses, in many cases very different from the spirit (I say nothing of the content) of the original. I, too, am a translated man.

I have been *borne* across. It is generally believed that something is always lost in translation; I cling to the notion—and use, in evidence, the success of Fitzgerald-Khayyam—that something can also be gained" (23). Ask students if they sense anything "lost" behind FitzGerald's "original" translation. What do they think he may have added? What is that "something" that Rushdie thinks "can also be gained" in translation?

A good paper project would be to investigate how FitzGerald's depiction of Persian leisure squares with other popular Victorian representations of the Islamic world, including the travel books of Eliot Warburton and Alexander Kinglake (see *Perspectives: Travel and Empire*) and the painted images of William Holman Hunt, Edward Lear, and Frederic Leighton. Lear and FitzGerald in particular make a fascinating pair.

Charles Darwin
The Voyage of the Beagle (1845)

From *Tierra del Fuego*:

Instructors may wish to assign the selection from Darwin's *Autobiography* first; even though it was written much later, the story of Darwin's being chosen to go on the *Beagle* voyage helps prepare students for reading the *Voyage* itself. The *Autobiography* also contains Darwin's reflection that "the sight of a naked savage in his native land is an event which can never be forgotten," a remark which may serve as a useful introduction to the Tierra del Fuego section, with its meditation upon the differences between "savage and civilized man."

The *Voyage* is interesting not only for what it tells about the development of Darwin's scientific theories, but also as a work of travel and exploration. Have students compare this book with the selections from Burton, Stanley, and Kingsley in the Travel and Empire section. One might also situate Darwin's first contact with the Fuegians in the context of other well-known moments of "first contact," such as Columbus's arrival in the New World, or Montaigne's essay "Of Cannibals," or *The Tempest*'s portrayal of the mariners' encounter with Caliban. In Darwin's case, the notion of "first contact" is complicated in odd and interesting ways by the fact that the *Beagle* actually carried three Fuegians aboard, with whom Darwin had had daily contact for nearly a year. It is fascinating to see Darwin waver between his perception of Jemmy Button as fully human, and his incredulity that Jemmy could be "of the same race . . . with the miserable, degraded savages whom we first met here." There is a similar disjunction between Darwin's description of Fuegia Basket ("a nice, modest, reserved young girl") and his undisguised horror at the sight of "absolutely" naked women in the rain.

In *Darwin's Century* (1958) Loren Eiseley claims that the account of the *Beagle*'s departure, and Jemmy's last signal fire, "contains the pathos of great literature" (265). Indeed, the story of Jemmy Button, a person whose emotions we can comprehend and with whom we can sympathize, works against Darwin's portrayal of the Fuegians as wretched, abject, sub-human beings. Darwin seems on the brink of suggesting that the differences between "savages" and "civilized" peoples might in fact be cultural rather than natural or biological. In a footnote, Darwin wrote: "I believe, in this extreme part of South America, man exists in a lower state of improvement than in any other part of the world. The South Sea islander of either race is comparatively civilized. The Esquimaux, in his subterranean hut, enjoys some of the comforts of life, and in his canoe, when fully equipped, manifests much skill. . . . But the Australian, in the simplicity of the arts of life, comes nearest the Fuegian. He can, however, boast of his boomerang, his spear and throwing-stick, his method of climbing trees, tracking animals, and scheme of hunting. Although thus superior in acquirements, it by no means follows that he should likewise be so in capabilities. Indeed, from what we saw of the Fuegians, who were taken to England, I should think the case was the reverse."

Eiseley quotes from Darwin's diary: "It was quite melancholy leaving our Fuegians amongst their barbarous countrymen. . . . In contradiction of what has often been stated, three years has been sufficient to change savages into, as far as habits go, complete and voluntary Europeans" (*Charles Darwin's Diary of the Voyage of H.M.S. "Beagle,"* ed. Nora Barlow [1933], 136).

Despite this apparent insight, Darwin declared in the penultimate paragraph of *The Descent of Man* that he would as soon be descended from a baboon as from "a savage who delights to torture his enemies." In *Rule of Darkness* (1988) Patrick Brantlinger writes that throughout *The Descent of Man*, Darwin "emphasizes the distance between savage and civilized peoples," adding that "in general, Darwinism lent scientific status to the view that there were higher and lower races" (187).

In *Victoria's Year* (1987) Richard Stein has an essay contrasting Darwin's description of the *Beagle* voyage with Captain Fitz Roy's, tracing the ongoing debate in their writing (211–35). Stein says that although Darwin initially can scarcely make himself "believe that they are fellow-creatures," he recognizes that nature has fitted the Fuegians to their environment. This thought, an early speculation on the path to the theory of evolution, presupposes a common ancestor for the educated Englishman and the "savage." Stein writes that Darwin "is beginning to experience, with some of Kurtz's 'horror' but a far greater measure of pure fascination, that the savage Other is in reality his own double" (224). The notion of savages as animals in fact defines our essential kinship with them—once we have recognized ourselves as animals, too. Stein notes that such an idea stands in stark contrast to Captain Fitz Roy's view of "savages" as fallen from "some originally perfect form;" he could not accept that different cultures might be at different stages of development. Fitz Roy saw only degradation, where Darwin came to perceive adaptation (the Fall vs. evolution).

In *Open Fields* (1996) Gillian Beer writes that "Darwin's encounters with Fuegians in their native place gave him a way of closing the gap between the human and other primates, a move necessary to the theories he was in the process of reaching" (67). In a sense, though, the Fuegians raise as many questions as they answer. One that can never be answered is what the experience of being taken to England meant to the three Fuegians themselves. Beer writes that it is "as sentimental to imagine that they enjoyed nothing as that they relished everything and were grateful for their kidnap. . . . The reader can know el'leparu, o'rundel'lico, and yok'cushlu, if at all, only under the sign of the their Western sobriquets as York Minster, Jemmy Button, and Fuegia Basket. . . . Trying to understand the sensibil-ity expressed by the British sailors in that act of re-naming the Fuegians . . . is likely to make us register our baffled distance from the shipboard community of the 1830s more intensely than does anything in the rest of Fitzroy's urbane or Darwin's ardent prose" (70).

From *Galapagos Archipelago*:
    In *The Flamingo's Smile* (1985) Stephen Jay Gould has a chapter called "Darwin at Sea—and the Virtues of Port" (347-59) in which he cautions us to avoid "the myth of the *Beagle*." Debunking the notion that Darwin miraculously "discovered evolution" by simple observation of natural phenomena in the Galapagos, Gould reminds us that "Darwin functioned as an active creationist all through the *Beagle* voyage" (359); Darwin "did not appreciate the evolutionary significance of the Galápagos while he was there" (348). Indeed, Darwin wrote in 1877 that "when I was on board the *Beagle* I believed in the permanence of species" (350). In *The Voyage of the Beagle* Darwin admits that while in these islands he was told that the tortoises differed, but that he did not "pay sufficient attention to this statement" for he "never dreamed that islands, about fifty or sixty miles apart . . . would have been differently tenanted."
    Gould explains that "evolutionists see variation as fundamental, as the raw ma-terial of evolutionary change," whereas "creationists believe each species is en-dowed with a fixed essence" and "variation is a mere nuisance" (353). The distinct species of finches found on the Galapagos were in fact evolutionary descendants of colonists from the mainland. Ultimately, these insights formed the basis of evo-lutionary theory. The discovery was exciting, but also embarrassing, since Darwin had so utterly failed to realize this on the spot that "he didn't even bother to record or label the islands that had housed his specimens" (353). As a result, "Darwin's finches are not mentioned at all in the *Origin of Species*" (356).
    Gould wishes to counter the romantic view of Darwin as a lone genius, and of the process of scientific creativity itself as a matter of sudden flashes of inspiration. Rather, he argues for a vision of science as "a communal activity, not a hermit's achievement" (359). Compare these ideas with Darwin's own memorable image in the *Autobiography* for the difficulty of seeing phenomena that have not been no-ticed before: on their geological trip to Wales, he and Professor Sedgwick did not notice that they were in a valley formed by glacial action, though "a house burnt down by fire did not tell its story more plainly."

On the Origin of Species (1859)

One might spend some time in class sketching the state of scientific thought at the time Darwin undertook his *Beagle* voyage, and the conflict between natural theology and natural selection. Our headnote to the Religion and Science perspectives section briefly describes Paley's analogy about the watchmaker (an argument that Darwin explicitly rejects in his *Autobiography*). For more detail, Tess Cosslett's *Science and Religion in the Nineteenth Century* (1984) anthologizes excerpts from William Paley, Robert Chambers, Hugh Miller, and Darwin himself. Philip Appleman has compiled a useful anthology of "companion readings" ranging from Charles Lyell and Thomas Henry Huxley to Carl Sagan and Noam Chomsky (*Darwin*, Norton Critical edition, [1970], 1979). Our bibliography for the Religion and Science perspectives section includes many titles that would be helpful to the student of Darwin.

In *The Panda's Thumb* (1980) Stephen Jay Gould summarizes the story of publishing the *Origin*; Gould writes that Darwin set forth his theory of natural selection "in two unpublished sketches of 1842 and 1844," then, "afraid to expose its revolutionary implications, he proceeded to stew, dither, wait, ponder, and collect data for another fifteen years" (48). Darwin finally rushed the *Origin of Species* into print when it appeared that Alfred Russel Wallace might preempt him. (The rest of Gould's essay explores the differences between Wallace's position and Darwin's). In her introduction to the Oxford edition of *The Origin of Species* (1996) Gillian Beer outlines various theories as to why Darwin waited so long to publish; her essay also situates the work in its intellectual context and traces the impact of Darwin's ideas on his contemporaries.

Have students look at the paragraph on the struggle for existence, with its description of songbirds "constantly destroying life" and being themselves destroyed by "beasts of prey." To illustrate the shock of this violent depiction of nature, read the famous passages from Tennyson's *In Memoriam* about "Nature, red in tooth and claw" (sections 55 and 56). Although these lines pre-date the *Origin*, they convey the emotional impact of a Darwinian vision of nature, not divinely ordered for mankind's use, but indifferent to human concerns. Darwin's observations about the brutal struggle for reproductive success negate comforting thoughts of a God who is aware of the fall of every sparrow. Nature is not the visible evidence of God's handiwork, but rather an amoral force, "careless of the single life."

Darwin uses vivid images to portray the competition for survival, yet students may find these excerpts rather dry; they may not grasp the larger implications of Darwin's work, and how it was that *On the Origin of Species* raised such frightening questions for the Victorians. By arguing that species change over time, Darwin undermined the belief in a single Creation, as described in Genesis, and thus indirectly cast doubt not only on the truth of Christianity, but even on the existence of a beneficent Creator.

The book shook people's sense of themselves and their place in the divine scheme of things as radically as Copernicus had done in saying that the earth was not the center of the universe. Richard Altick writes: "The ancient metaphor of the great chain of being therefore had to be revised. . . . It gave the impression now of a vertical zoo in a state of eternal flux rather than a structure of classic design raised by the Creator and enduring unchanged to the end of time" (*Victorian People and Ideas* [1973], 229). For many, the result was a profound crisis of faith. Despite the upbeat last sentence of the chapter, most Victorians were *not* "consoled." As Tennyson's lines illustrate, Darwin's vision of nature as a battleground seemed bleak, random, and purposeless.

Look at the excerpt from Edmund Gosse's autobiography, *Father and Son* (Religion and Science perspectives) in which Gosse describes his father's "omphalos" theory. In 1857, in a vain attempt to reconcile Darwin's theories with traditional religion, Philip Henry Gosse proposed that God had created the world with fossils already in the rocks, even though no dinosaurs had ever lived, just as He created Adam with a navel, even though Adam had no mother. Gosse was laughed at for his efforts, but his book suggests the intense resistance to Darwin's ideas.

Another approach to Darwin is taken by Gillian Beer in *Darwin's Plots* (1983) and George Levine in *Darwin and the Novelists* (1988), works which treat the *Origin* as a work of imaginative literature in its own right. Beer's book looks closely at the influence of Darwin on George Eliot and Hardy, while Levine explores the ways in which Darwinian assumptions permeated the culture: "Darwin's vision, his great myth of origins, was both shaping the limits of the Victorian imagination of the real and being tested in the laboratories of fiction as well as in scientific argument" (4). Levine's chapter, "Darwin's Revolution," analyzes how "Darwin's language helped his ideas subversively enter the culture" (95).

Finally, one might discuss the ways in which Darwin's images of natural struggle and survival of the fittest echo metaphors of social and economic competition. Gould believes "that the theory of natural selection should be viewed as an extended analogy—whether conscious or unconscious on Darwin's part I do not know—to the laissez faire economics of Adam Smith. The essence of Smith's argument is a paradox of sorts: if you want an ordered economy providing maximal benefits to all, then let individuals compete and struggle for their own advantages. The result, after appropriate sorting and elimination of the inefficient, will be a stable and harmonious polity" (*Panda's Thumb*, 66). In other words, not God but rather the struggle among individuals produces order. As the title of an essay by Robert M. Young puts it, "Darwinism *is* Social."

Darwin's ideas have, of course, been much misunderstood and abused, with the notion of "survival of the fittest" used to justify the exploitation of the poor by the rich. Social Darwinism has been used to sanction oppression, war, tyranny, imperialism—after all, Darwin had "proved" that "might is right" (as he himself observed ironically in a letter to Lyell in 1860, quoted in Walter E. Houghton's *Victorian Frame of Mind* [1957], 209). As Altick puts it, "The history of animals, from amoeba to man, gave warrant to the assumption by analogy that cutthroat competition was an ineradicable fact of economic life and that the prizes were reserved for those best equipped to survive—the tough-bargaining employer, the hard-working employee" (*Victorian People and Ideas*, 232).

The Descent of Man (1871)

In *On the Origin of Species* Darwin carefully avoided placing mankind in the picture; twelve years later he spelled out the implications: those who look at the facts "cannot any longer believe that man is the work of a separate act of creation." Even more explicitly, "man is descended from a hairy quadruped, furnished with a tail and pointed ears."

Students might be interested in a description of the now-legendary confrontation between Huxley and Bishop Wilberforce on the question of descent from a monkey (described briefly in our headnote on Thomas Henry Huxley in the Religion and Science perspectives section, and more fully in many other places, including Robin Gilmour's chapter, "Darwin and Darwinism" in *The Victorian Period*, 1993).

In *The Descent of Man* Darwin used a detached, rational tone to describe the processes of sexual selection in human beings. Sexual selection is not quite the same thing as natural selection. "Sexual selection means the selection of mates by individual animals: the preference for particular variations could cause them to become inherited, at the expense of characteristics that were not attractive to the other sex. This process would account for characteristics that were of no use or survival value to the species" (Tess Cosslett, *Science and Religion in the Nineteenth Century*, 156).

Even people who could accept that human beings were descended from animals found difficulty in accounting for the moral and spiritual qualities of mankind. Darwin argues here that faculties such as conscience derive from the same social instincts that we share with animals; had he our degree of intelligence, a pointer dog would arrive at the same moral conclusions. Such claims could not fail to antagonize many; Tess Cosslett quotes a reviewer of 1872: "We do not see how to reconcile with our Christian faith the hypothesis . . . that our moral sense is no better than an instinct like that which rules the beaver or the bee; that He whom we have been accustomed to regard as the Creator of all things, is a creature of our imagination, and that our religious ideas are a development from the dreams and fears of anthropomorphous apes."

Autobiography (1876)

Compare the tone and style of the *Autobiography* to Darwin's scientific works; here, the object of study is himself, and he attempts to view his own life with the same dispassionate objectivity that he brought to any other subject. Note the extraordinary statement in the opening paragraph about writing "as if I were a dead man in another world looking back at my own life." One might ask students to reflect on this narrative stance: is it really possible to write about oneself with such detachment? If so, does this defeat the "purpose" of autobiography?

The simile warns us not to expect intimate revelations; Darwin's *Autobiography* is concerned, rather, with tracing the development of his own scientific mind. He apparently regards himself as an example, on a small scale, of the evolutionary process at work: in explaining how he lost his taste for shooting Darwin writes that "the primeval instincts of the barbarian slowly yielded to the acquired tastes of the civilized man."

As a reliable guide to the stages by which Darwin arrived at his theories, the autobiography must be treated with caution: Gould calls it "maddeningly misleading." For example, Darwin recalls his reading of Malthus as a eureka providing the sudden key to natural selection, yet "the notebooks belie Darwin's later recollections—in this case by their utter failure to record, at the time it happened, any special exultation over his Malthusian insight" (*Panda's Thumb*, 64).

In devoting himself so exclusively to science, Darwin gradually lost his capacity to enjoy most aesthetic and emotional pleasures; his mind became "a kind of machine for grinding general laws out of large collections of facts." (Contrast this with Mill's belief that it was the discovery of poetry that saved him from being a mere thinking machine.) Like many of his contemporaries, Darwin also lost his faith. These passages in the *Autobiography* make a good introduction to the Religion and Science perspectives section, for they lay out in clear and simple language many of the issues that led to the widespread Victorian crisis of faith. Students may be interested, for example, in a fuller discussion of Paley's argument from design, and the ways in which Darwin claimed to have refuted it.

Darwin's wife Emma found certain of his remarks in this section "raw" and shocking, and they were omitted when the *Autobiography* was first published. For example, she disapproved of his reference to the "damnable doctrine" of eternal punishment, and of his comparing the difficulty in throwing off belief in God to that of a monkey ridding itself of "its instinctive fear and hatred of a snake." The full text did not appear in print until 1958 (in his granddaughter Nora Barlow's edition of the *Autobiography*, from which our text is taken).

The modesty of Darwin's self-assessment in the final paragraphs has occasioned much comment. Was it hypocrisy? Or had he so internalized his father's low opinion of him that, even after spectacularly proving his father's predictions wrong, Darwin still on some level accepted his father's estimate? If Darwin—the child stealing fruit from the garden—was an Adam in relation to his uncannily omniscient Father, he went on to undo his "Father's" creation and re-write the story of Genesis. Possibly he felt both triumphant at this supplanting of the father's authority, and yet also profoundly ambivalent and full of unresolved anxiety about his relationship to his father.

In "Mr. Darwin Collects Himself" (possibly the best single article on the *Autobiography*) John D. Rosenberg writes: "It is difficult not to see in his theft of fruit from his Father's garden shades of the primal transgression in Eden. . . . Ancient archetypes are embedded just below the surface of Darwin's narrative, as if in his own childhood he were naturalizing or secularizing our culture's central myth of guilt, as he was later to naturalize the central myth of our Beginnings in *The Origin*" (*Nineteenth-Century Lives*, ed. Lockridge, et al. [1989], 88).

In "Darwin's Comedy: The *Autobiography* as Comic Narrative" (*Victorian Newsletter* 75 [Spring 1989]), Eugene R. August suggests another interpretation: "Darwin created a comic portrait of himself as an unpromising dimwit who evolves into an unlikely hero, a klutzy innocent who confounds the stolid wisdom of the ages" (15). Like the folk hero of traditional comedy, Charles the "troublesome bumbler" redeems himself "by undertaking a perilous journey-quest" that leads first to self-discovery, then to a return "with saving knowledge for humanity" (17). Analyzing the humor throughout the book, August notes that "while Darwin eschewed the sublime and the tragic, he never abandoned the comic" (19).

The note on marriage (published for the first time as an appendix to Nora Barlow's edition) provides a fascinating glimpse of Darwin's mind. Note the distancing use of the second person: "Only picture to yourself a nice soft wife"; "poor slave, you will be worse than a negro"; and "Never mind my boy—Cheer up." Darwin addresses himself as though he were someone else, and concludes that a wife will be "better than a dog anyhow."

Have students compare Darwin's autobiographical writings with his *Biographical Sketch of an Infant* (his eldest son) in Perspectives: Imagining Childhood.

PERSPECTIVES

Religion and Science

This section is designed to introduce students to some of the key debates among the Victorians on the changing roles of science and religion. It was an era when both subjects were passionately interesting to the educated layman, and neither had yet become the exclusive province of the specialist. Just as Darwin read Milton aboard the *Beagle*, so novelists and poets followed scientific and theological developments, and what they read permeated their own creative work. The section can accompany Darwin or Tennyson's *In Memoriam*, but some or all of the selections can certainly be taught independently. The Macaulay passage provides a starting point for consideration of the wide range of attitudes towards science. Strauss and Colenso will give students an idea what the "Higher Criticism" was, and why it had such an impact on fundamentalist religious beliefs. The selections from Dickens, Brontë, Clough, and Gosse offer a glimpse of Evangelicalism and the hostility it aroused in some quarters (here one might also assign our excerpts from *Praeterita*, both for Ruskin's portrait of an Evangelical childhood and for his famous description of his loss of faith). Newman recounts the most famous spiritual crisis of the century—although, unlike many of his contemporaries, his was not an *unconversion* prompted by scientific upheavals, but an embracing of Catholicism at a time when the Protestant ascendancy was still strong. For a general overview of the issues, Robin Gilmour has interesting chapters on religion and science in *The Victorian Period* (1993).

Thomas Babington Macaulay
from Lord Bacon (1837)

This excerpt is a fruitful starting point for discussion of nineteenth-century attitudes toward science. Contrast Macaulay's cheerful confidence in the benefits of science with the anxieties expressed in *Frankenstein* about science getting out of control and unleashing monsters. Was Macaulay's faith in progress justified? Ask students to think about twentieth-century scientific developments and the controversies surrounding them. On the one hand, there have been extraordinary advances in medicine, computer technology, and space exploration; on the other hand, the atom bomb, Chernobyl, global warming, and chemical warfare make it harder to assume that the fruits of science will always be applied wisely, for the greater good of humanity.

Point out how the piling up of clauses in this paragraph suggests the inevitability, even inexorability, of the "march" of progress (or, given the imagery of "goal" and "starting-post" in the last line, the *race* of progress). Compare this passage with the views on progress that Macaulay voiced in "A Review of Southey's *Colloquies*" (Perspectives: Industrial Landscape). In contrast to Macaulay's materialistic notion of what constitutes human happiness, Newman ridiculed the idea that "education, railroad travelling, ventilation, drainage, and the arts of life, when fully carried out, serve to make a population moral and happy" (note on "Liberalism" in *Apologia pro Vita Sua*; qtd. Houghton, 41).

In *Victoria's Year* Richard Stein points out that Darwin was "reading Macaulay's essay on Bacon at the time he was revising the *Journal of Researches* [later *The Voyage of the Beagle*] for publication" (233). Did Macaulay's ideas about progress influence Darwin's formulation of his theories? (In "Darwin's Reluctant Revolution," George Levine writes that while he denied "that natural selection is necessarily progressive . . . Darwin *believed* in progress." See *South Atlantic Quarterly* 91:3 [1992]: 547).

Charles Dickens
from Sunday Under Three Heads (1836)

Dickens returned to the subject of Sunday closings several years later in *A Christmas Carol*, where Scrooge reproaches the second spirit for preventing the poor from getting a hot dinner on Sundays: "I wonder you, of all the beings in the many worlds about us, should desire to cramp these people's opportunities of innocent enjoyment." The Spirit may not be personally guilty of seeking Sunday closings, Scrooge admits, but "it has been done in your name." The Spirit objects that there are those "who lay claim to know us, and who do their deeds of passion, pride, ill-will, hatred, envy, bigotry, and selfishness in our name."

Contrast Dickens's conviction of the importance of pleasure (e.g. the Christmas festivities in *A Christmas Carol*) with the Evangelical suspicion of it. The selections from Ruskin's *Praeterita* and Gosse's *Father and Son* portray two families intent on Sabbath observance: in the Ruskin household, pictures were covered or turned to the wall on Sundays; Gosse's father regarded the keeping of Christmas as "nothing less than an act of idolatry" and indignantly threw the servants' illicit Christmas pudding on the dust heap.

Dickens was hardly alone in his resentment of Evangelical attempts to legislate morality: Frances Trollope detested Evangelicalism and its effects on the arts (see Travel perspectives); Walter Besant called it a "Wretched, miserable creed!" and George Eliot wrote in *Middlemarch*: "The Vincys had the readiness to enjoy, the rejection of all anxiety, and the belief in life as a merry lot, which made a house exceptional in most county towns at that time, when Evangelicalism had cast a certain suspicion as of plague-infection over the few amusements which survived in the provinces."

Dickens is particularly cutting on the ill-concealed class condescension implicit in the proposed legislation. He pulls no punches in spelling out the myriad ways in which the bill is designed to keep "the lower orders" in line; it is social control

dressed up as religion. Infuriated by such sanctimonious hypocrisy, Dickens concludes by asking what could possibly motivate Agnew's self-serving fanaticism?
Only "an envious, heartless, ill-conditioned dislike, to seeing those whom fortune
has placed below him, cheerful and happy." Compare this reading to the excerpt
from *Jane Eyre* below.

David Friedrich Strauss, (trans. G. Eliot) 1846
from The Life of Jesus Critically Examined (1835)

This reading may strike students as dry until they realize how new and shocking
such ideas were. Have them look at the first two sentences: the very notion of
using words such as "mythical," "legendary," and "fiction" in the same breath
with the Gospels was offensive to many people. In a brief but useful discussion of
Biblical history, Robin Gilmour points out that "myth" was the most contentious
term of the Higher Criticism: people were not ready to accept the notion "that
an episode in the Bible could be both fictional (i.e. unsupported by history and
science) and . . . also be a true embodiment of genuine religious insights."
Strauss's work thus led to "a predictable outcry," for he did not accept miracles,
found the Gospel narratives unreliable, and worked to discover the historical
Jesus, an entirely human figure. That Jesus was not the Messiah did not, for
Strauss, "invalidate Christianity, for the ethical teachings remained as well as the
profound symbolic truth about human destiny expressed in Christ's life and
death" (*The Victorian Period* [1993], 55).

Richard Altick also has several pages on the Higher Criticism; he writes that
the higher critics regarded the Old Testament not as divinely inspired "but as a
mixed bag of human documents—tribal histories, genealogies, digests of laws,
erotic songs, biographies, and folk myths . . . quite fortuitously assembled, and endowed long after the fact with divine authority." As for the Gospels, they "comprised several versions of a biography of a historical figure named Jesus whom an
early group of disciples believed to be the Son of God. . . . Thus the New
Testament was a record of a particularly memorable episode of hero-worship in
Hebrew-Roman times. In brief, the Bible was not what it was taken to be, the pure
Word of God and from Genesis to Revelation the infallible factual basis of
Christian faith." As for Strauss, "he himself concluded that the abiding value of
the Bible resided not in its 'facts' . . . but in its character as a body of symbol and
myth. . . . Stripped of its vulnerable historicity, Scripture retained its spiritual and
ethical significance" (*Victorian People and Ideas* [1973], 220–21).

Students may find helpful some explanation of Christian typology, the practice
of seeking parallels between events in the Hebrew bible and the Christian gospels,
and arguing that the earlier events foreshadow the later. Far from seeing these parallels as evidence of divine providence dropping hints to prepare the world for the
Messiah, Strauss argues that "when we find details in the life of Jesus evidently
sketched after the pattern of [Hebrew] prophecies and prototypes, we cannot but
suspect that they are rather mythical than historical." In other words, the gospel
writers shaped the story of Jesus's life so as to reflect earlier stories—men, not God,
are the authors of the scriptures.

Have students read Clough's *Epi-strauss-ium* for a contemporary commentary on Strauss.

Charlotte Brontë
from Jane Eyre (1847)

Victorian novels are full of caricatures of Evangelical clergymen, from Chadband in Dickens's *Bleak House* to Obadiah Slope in Trollope's *Barchester Towers*. But the worst is undoubtedly Brocklehurst, a real-life figure whom Brontë had good reason to detest. Yet it is worth pointing out, as Richard Altick does in *Victorian People and Ideas* (1973), that since "fanaticism and absurdity always make good copy," we may have a somewhat exaggerated image of Evangelicalism based on these fictionalized portraits (178). Not everybody was a hypocrite or an extremist: "there were plenty of Evangelical families who laughed and played," and Evangelicals were responsible for much real and useful social reform (e.g. abolishing flogging, opposing slavery). Gilmour also has a helpful discussion of Evangelicalism in *The Victorian Period*, 71ff.

Students may be amused by Brocklehurst's resemblance to the Big Bad Wolf ("What a face he had . . . what a great nose! and what a mouth! and what large prominent teeth!"), and horrified by the sadistic threat of hellfire and damnation with which he torments Jane. His hypocrisy emerges in his praise of the Psalm-reciting little boy, whose insincerity earns him extra ginger-nuts. One might also tell students about the comic episode later in the novel, where Brocklehurst allows his own daughters to curl their hair, but forbids the Lowood schoolgirls to wear curls—even natural ones! His daughters appear "splendidly attired in velvet, silk, and furs" immediately after he has reproved the headmistress for allowing the charity girls more than one change of clothes a week. These incidents underline the complacent snobbery of a certain sort of insufferable Evangelical, focused on the moral reform of those "beneath" him socially; thus Brocklehurst emphasizes Jane's dependent position, and calls Mrs. Reed (Jane's own aunt) her "excellent benefactress." As in the proposed Sabbath laws so bitterly opposed by Dickens, religion is used to reinforce class distinctions and keep inferiors properly "humble."

Arthur Hugh Clough

Although he died at 42 after a fairly undistinguished career, Clough (pronounced *cluff*) was in the thick of things during his short life: he was Dr. Thomas Arnold's star pupil at Rugby; he was Matthew Arnold's best friend at Oxford; he married a cousin of Florence Nightingale's; he was good friends with Carlyle, Emerson, and Tennyson; he was the subject of Arnold's famous elegy, *Thyrsis*. American students might be interested to learn that as a boy Clough lived for several years (1823-29) in Charleston, South Carolina, where his father worked as a cotton merchant. Most of his poetry was not published until after his death.

Dipsychus means "of two minds" and the title conveys Clough's own unsettled state of mind on religious questions: he seemed unable either to reject Christianity or to embrace it fully. This quintessentially Victorian tension emerges everywhere in his poetry: note the negative formulations expressive of doubt in the lines "It may be that in deed and not in fancy, / A hand that is not ours upstays our steps" (from *Poems*, 409).

But if he freely confessed his own uncertain agnosticism, Clough was nonetheless wryly observant of the hypocrisies of others, as *The Latest Decalogue*'s satire of money-grubbing Pharisees makes plain. Note the resolutely practical nature of these revised Commandments—no wasted effort or energy, just a steady focus on the main chance, on ends not means. Students will appreciate the dry humor: "Thou shalt not steal; an empty feat, / When it's so lucrative to cheat." Compare this ironic exposé of the materialist and self-serving aspects of Evangelicalism with Dickens's and Brontë's attacks. *"There Is No God,"* the *Wicked Saith* is similarly knowing and humorous about the complacency of those who are well-off.

Epi-strauss-ium, of course, refers to David Friedrich Strauss, author of *Das Leben Jesu,* and students who have read Strauss will be amused at Clough's mock-horror: "Matthew and Mark and Luke and holy John / Evanished all and gone!" Clough wrote to his sister in 1847 that the contemporary furor over Strauss was an overreaction: "I do not think that doubts respecting the facts related in the Gospels need give us much trouble." The poem seeks to capture the public dismay but also the poet's reassurances. Earlier, reverential attitudes toward the four Gospel writers, or evangelists, have punningly "evanished" in the light of common day. The sun, the light of God's truth, when rising in the east helped color their "gorgeous portraits" as it shone through stained glass ("pictured panes"). Now setting in the west, it shines directly through plain glass. The "luster" on the Gospels is lost, but Clough suggests that the Church is now "more sincerely bright" for this naked Straussian light of inquiry. As proof, he concludes that the Son/Sun of God ("the Orb") continues visible in the heavens. The allusion in the poem's title (which means "On Strauss-ism") to Spenser's *Epithalamium* ("On the Marriage-bed") gives an intertextual clue to the poem's origin, imagery, and outlook. In Psalms 19:1–6, the sun is both bridegroom (Spenser) and proof of God's existence (Clough): "The heavens declare the glory of God; and the firmament sheweth his handywork. . . . In them he hath set a tabernacle for the sun, which is as a bridegroom coming out of his chamber." For close readings of these and other poems by Clough, see Anthony Kenny's *God and Two Poets: Arthur Hugh Clough and Gerard Manley Hopkins* (1988).

John William Colenso
from The Pentateuch and Book of Joshua Critically Examined (1862–1879)

Colenso can usefully be paired with Strauss as another example of the sort of biblical criticism that caused enormous controversy in the nineteenth century. A fellow mathematician, J. B. Young of Belfast University, implied that Colenso must be crazy: "If Bishop Colenso be really in a condition of mind which renders him fully accountable for what he writes (and there is reason to suspect otherwise), then we say that a more reprehensible instance of scientific *guess-work,* deliberately promulgated as established scientific truth, has rarely been witnessed" (qtd. in Michael Brander's *The Victorian Gentleman* [1975], 114).

In "Colenso's 'Intelligent Zulu': A Rhetorical Trick?" (*Victorians Institute Journal* 11 [1982–83]: 33–43) Ben Varner argues that the notion that Colenso's doubts were suddenly triggered by the innocent questions of a Zulu was merely a clever rhetorical device. "The clear implication is that if an intelligent but untutored Zulu native found these biblical stories impossible to believe, then the inhabitants of one of the most cultured nations in the world could hardly assent to them." Colenso, in fact, had a long history of unorthodox views and involvement in controversies: for example, in 1855 he'd published a book which "seemed to condone the Zulu practice of polygamy." The Zulu himself, William Ngidi, apparently held perfectly conventional beliefs.

Varner quotes some hilarious Victorian limericks about Colenso that demonstrate the currency of the story:

> A Bishop there was of Natal
> Who took a Zulu for his pal.
>   Said the Kaffir, "Look here,
>   Ain't the Pentateuch queer?"
> And converted the Lord of Natal.

> There once was a Bishop of Natal
> Whose doubts on the Deluge were fatal;
>   Said the infidel Zulu,
>   "D'you believe this—you fool, you?"
> "No, I don't," said the Bishop of Natal.

John Henry Cardinal Newman
from Apologia Pro Vita Sua (1864)

Even students for whom the religious issues in the *Apologia* remain obscure might be intrigued by Newman's description of his childhood vision of himself: "I thought life might be a dream, or I an Angel, and all this world a deception, my fellow-angels by a playful device concealing themselves from me, and deceiving me with the semblance of a material world." In essence, the young Newman was raising the question of human identity; as he put it elsewhere in the *Apologia*, "Who can know himself, and the multitude of subtle influences which act upon him?" It is the fundamental question at the heart of every autobiography.

For many Victorians reason and faith were at loggerheads (think of Ruskin hearing the clink of the geologists' dreadful hammers "at the end of every cadence of the Bible verses"). But Newman professed himself untroubled by the contradictions that were keeping his contemporaries awake at night: "Many persons are very sensitive of the difficulties of Religion . . . but I have never been able to see a connexion between apprehending those difficulties . . . [and] doubting the doctrines to which they are attached." Newman distrusts reason, for if reason can convince you to believe, it can as easily convince you *not* to believe: reason tends "towards a simple unbelief in matters of religion." Faith, therefore, must be beyond reason.

Newman's vision of a fallen world is striking: since he is more certain of the existence of God "than that I have hands and feet," he is filled "with unspeakable distress" to see no evidence of God in the world of men: "If I looked into a mirror, and did not see my face, I should have the sort of feeling which actually comes upon me, when I look into this living busy world, and see no reflexion of its Creator." It is a remarkable image, worth spending time on in class, and it suggests the essentially personal—some might say egotistical—nature of Newman's religious belief. The self must prove the existence of God, since the world so obviously doesn't (Newman was unpersuaded by Paley's "argument from design" in *Natural Theology*; he refers to "the tokens so faint and broken of a superintending design"). One might set Newman in the context of the Romantic stress on the individual self in reaction to eighteenth-century rationalism.

Newman was not a liberal; he did not share Macaulay's faith in human progress and the unlimited capacities of human reason to solve our problems. He believed that mankind is in a fallen and sinful state, and he saw "the defeat of good, the success of evil, physical pain, mental anguish, the prevalence and intensity of sin" as "a vision to dizzy and appal." He can only conclude that "either there is no Creator, or this living society of men is in a true sense discarded from His presence." He argues therefore that "*if* there be a God, *since* there is a God, the human race is implicated in some terrible aboriginal calamity."

Newman is defending himself against a charge of untruthfulness, but he is also, in a broader sense, defending his conversion to Catholicism. (His conversion was gradual, not sudden and dramatic; in fact, the actual moment is omitted entirely from the *Apologia*.) Thus he is led to defend the Catholic Church, and particularly its doctrine with regard to papal infallibility, which Protestants found especially hard to swallow. Newman, however, calls it "a provision, adapted by the mercy of the Creator, to preserve religion in the world, and to restrain that freedom of thought . . . and to rescue it from its own suicidal excesses." Infallibility is "a working instrument . . . for smiting hard and throwing back the immense energy of the aggressive, capricious, untrustworthy intellect."

Students who wish to know more about the *Apologia* might begin with David DeLaura's Norton Critical edition (1968), Walter Houghton's *The Art of Newman's Apologia* (1945), and Blehl and Connolly's collection of essays, *Newman's "Apologia": A Classic Reconsidered* (1964). More recent collections include Ker and Hill's *Newman After a Hundred Years* (1990), Block's *Critical Essays on John Henry Newman* (1992), and Magill's *Discourse and Context: An Interdisciplinary Study of John Henry Newman* (1993).

Thomas Henry Huxley
from Evolution and Ethics (1893)

Huxley may have been "Darwin's bulldog," but he also voiced late-nineteenth-century fears about where evolution might lead. Selective breeding? Degeneration of the species? In *The Time Machine* (1895) H. G. Wells (who was Huxley's student) imagined a future in which human beings had devolved into two distinct species, the decadent Eloi and the cannibalistic Morlocks who feed off them. *Brave New*

World (1932), written by Huxley's grandson, Aldous Huxley, seems to dramatize a scenario envisioned in *Evolution and Ethics* by depicting an authoritarian future in which selective breeding is the law.

Evolution and Ethics opens with a vision of nature, apparently unchanging, but in reality in constant flux. As Darwin had already shown, the living world is in a perpetual struggle for existence. Huxley then draws a distinction between the processes of nature and the artificial works of man, such as the creation of a garden: nature is antagonistic towards that garden, in the sense that "if the watchful supervision of the gardener were withdrawn" natural forces would overrun and eventually destroy it. He then draws an analogy between the garden and a settlement of English colonists who must similarly "conquer or be vanquished" in the struggle for existence. Human morality, as expressed in maxims such as the golden rule, has nothing whatsoever to do with this cut-throat competition for survival: evolution is unconcerned with ethics. The golden rule amounts to a "refusal to continue the struggle for existence." As Huxley memorably formulates the question: "What would become of the garden if the gardener treated all the weeds and slugs and birds and trespassers as he would like to be treated, if he were in their place?"

Thus, although mankind is part of nature, we are inescapably at war with it. Survival of the fittest refers only to those who are best adapted to the environment; it has nothing to do with those who are morally superior. Evolution demands self-assertion; ethics demand self-restraint. As Huxley says elsewhere in the lecture, ethics aim "not so much to the survival of the fittest, as to the fitting of as many as possible to survive."

The notion that moral conduct—not extirpating the "unfit" among us—runs counter to the very evolutionary processes of adaptation that ensure our survival as a species raises deeply troubling questions. One might wish to bring up twentieth-century issues such as Hitler's desire to breed a master race, or current debates about the rationing of medical care and the wisdom of allowing very sick infants to survive. At the very least, Huxley's lecture serves as a caution against a naive and optimistic faith that evolution is synonymous with progress.

For further reading, see the introduction and essays in James Paradis and George C. Williams's edition of *Evolution and Ethics* (1989).

Sir Edmund Gosse
from Father and Son (1907)

Even if one has time to teach nothing else from this perspectives section, this excerpt can be read in conjunction with *Origin of Species* to give students a sense of the extreme resistance Darwin's theories met in some circles. Look at Gosse's use of the language of science ("test," "experiment") in the comic description of worshiping the chair: even as a child, Gosse employed scientific methods to test the claims of religion—in contrast to his father, who asserted the infallibility of revelation even at the cost of rejecting a lifetime of patient scientific observation. Students who are intrigued by Philip Henry Gosse's theory might wish to read the original: *Omphalos: An Attempt to Untie the Geological Knot* (1857).

These passages also suggest what it meant to grow up in an Evangelical household; here, one might compare Gosse to Ruskin, and also look at the excerpts from Dickens and Brontë. The Evangelical distrust of art shaped many a Victorian upbringing, but perhaps nowhere is it so memorably depicted as here, where the book-loving child is sternly kept from the knowledge of any form of story. Gosse was eleven years old before he discovered the existence of fiction, and he described the shock and intoxication as like being given "a glass of brandy neat."

One of the best articles on Gosse is Vivian and Robert Folkenflik's "Words and Language in *Father and Son*," *Biography* 2 (1979): 157-174. In *The Victorian Self: Autobiography and Biblical Narrative* (1989) Heather Henderson has a chapter on the autobiographer as idolater in Gosse. Those with an interest in autobiography, or in portraits of Victorian childhood, might compare our excerpt from *Father and Son* with *Sartor Resartus*, Mill's *Autobiography*, *Aurora Leigh*, Newman's *Apologia*, Darwin's *Autobiography*, *Praeterita*, and *Cassandra*, all linked by themes of education, conversion, vocation, and self-realization.

Robert Browning

Browning labored to find—or create—a reading public that would take pleasure in his strange viewpoints and unexpected juxtapositions of sounds and images. With his grotesque details and sudden disjunctions, his eccentric characters and their tangled motivations, Browning prepared the way for the discontinuities of twentieth-century poetry. But his demanding allusions, twisted, elliptical syntax, and abrupt transitions make for difficult reading: John Ruskin complained to Browning, "The worst of it is that this kind of concentrated writing needs so much *solution* before the reader can fairly get the good of it, that people's patience fails them, and they give the thing up as insoluble."

George Eliot warned that one should expect no "drowsy passivity in reading Browning." His poetry "requires the reader to trace by his own mental activity the underground stream of thought that jets out in elliptical and pithy verse" (*Westminster Review*, 1856). Extending this insight, Oscar Wilde claimed that "It was not thought that fascinated him, but rather the processes by which thought moves" (*The Critic as Artist*).

Browning gets at that thought by presenting his characters in intense moments where self-justification mixes with anger, fear, and daring self-betrayal. By turns cramped, explosive, lyric, or commonplace, Browning's language simultaneously builds and exposes character through apparently chaotic self-revelation. The first nineteen lines of *The Bishop Orders His Tomb* are a masterpiece of disorganized thinking about the Bishop's children, his mistress, his rival Gandolf, his anxieties about death, and his concern for eternal life—in the form of a marble tomb. It is a stream-of-consciousness barrage three-quarters of a century before Joyce's *Ulysses*, winding up in cacophony: "Shrewd was that snatch from out the corner south / He graced his carrion with, God curse the same!"

Claiming that Browning's ability to invent and project character though idiosyncratic language was second only to Shakespeare's, Wilde wrote: "If Shakespeare
could sing through myriad lips, Browning could stammer through a thousand
mouths." Some good examples of this awkward, illuminating density of speech include the schizophrenic end of *Soliloquy of the Spanish Cloister* ("Ave Virgo! Gr-r-r—
you swine!"); stanza 12 of *Childe Roland*, remarkable for the way the thickly textured sound evokes the mutilated landscape; the deliberate contraction of swelling
hopes in alternate lines of *Love Among the Ruins*; and the irresolute fits and starts
that conclude *Andrea Del Sarto*.

James Mason's chilling, urbane reading of *My Last Duchess*, included on our
audio CD, beautifully brings out the intense drama of Browning's verse. For
Wilde, Browning was not so much a poet as "a writer of fiction, the most supreme
writer of fiction, it may be, that we have ever had. His sense of dramatic situation
was unrivalled." The monologues are often delivered in outrageous situations:
Porphyria's lifeless head resting on her lover's shoulder, the Duke negotiating for
the hand of his *next* duchess. The dramatic monologue forces the reader into uneasy intimacy with these speakers—we become "you," listening just inches away.
The form enables these speakers to solicit our sympathy, and causes us to suspend
evaluation and moral judgement.

What does Browning want us to learn about them, and how does he expect us
to react? Is Porphyria a representative victim of male possessiveness and anxiety
about female sexual freedom? Students alert to the class barriers that divide
Porphyria and her lover (sketched in lines 24–29) may decide that Porphyria was
trifling with the speaker, and got what she deserved—or at least what she may literally have been asking for, to be his forever. Similarly the Duchess may be an innocent victim of brutal patriarchy, or else have boldly flirted in front of the Duke
once too often. A formalist reader might point out that Browning is the artist who
has drawn her "as if she were alive" and argue that her vitality cannot be contained
by the Duke's masterful rhetoric, even in death. Although the Duke now limits access to the image of the duchess and boasts about his other artistic possessions
(lines 54–56), he cannot control curiosity about her portrait's wayward gaze, its
"spot / Of joy," any more than he controlled his wife while she lived. But then
should Fra Lippo Lippi, with his roving eye, be seen as a laudable contrast to the
Duke, as the masculine embodiment of the duchess's fatal freedom? Is he a courageous artist struggling to bring a hidebound medieval church into an enlightened
Renaissance awareness of the true spirituality of the flesh? Or is he a sensual, self-
serving opportunist who now hypocritically paints "saints and saints / And saints
again" (48–49) for an equally unenlightened secular patron?

Our access to the cagey ventriloquist behind these characters is rigorously controlled. The poet is very much like his dominating Duke: "since none puts by / The
curtain I have drawn for you, but I." Whatever Browning's speakers confess, their
words appear to be grounded as much in the historical moment as in the speakers' or
poet's own personal passion. Hence the difficulty not only in deciding what the author thinks of his creations as individuals, or the Renaissance as an epoch, but also
what the poem might be implying about Victorian manners and mores. Is Browning

suggesting that the Duke and Porphyria's lover are intentionally provocative versions of how Victorian men treat women? Browning's audience was divided over his ability to communicate effectively, and even his wife wished he would step out from behind the mask. Perhaps the quest for interpretive control within the poems—by dukes, lovers, painters, knightly questors—is meant as a self-revelatory but cautionary tale of Browning's own artistic and sexual searching. Maybe the point is that all forms of domination or control are misguided, morally wrong, and ultimately impossible.

Reflecting on the active but uncomfortable role of the reader in these poems, John Maynard singles out the last line of *Porphyria's Lover* as emblematic of the responsibility Browning places on us. The assertion that "God has not said a word" underlines "the interpretive problem at the very beginning of the Browning dramatic monologue: God doesn't offer definitive reader responses and interpretations. In his silence, we will rush forward with our own interpretations. But if God won't, who will authorize the one standard reading?" ("Reading the Reader in Robert Browning's Dramatic Monologues," *Critical Essays on Robert Browning*, ed. Mary Ellis Gibson [1992], 74). Students might also look ahead to Swinburne's lurid sex-and-murder poem *The Leper*, which deliberately picks up on *Porphyria's* strategy of daring God and reader to judgment.

In effect, however, Maynard says, the reader occupies a non-theistic "third position" between the poem's speaker and its auditor: "the envoy's silence and compliance in *My Last Duchess* allow us to objectify and criticize our own tendency merely to submit to the strength of the Duke's rhetoric—thus provoking us to a middle position, combining respect for hypnotically powerful language and moral distance and criticism" (75). Collectively, the monologue's readers produce a multiplicity of responses that further constructs, in our own images, the intricate personality who addresses us.

Yet for all that reading Browning is a sort of mirror experience, there is very much an actual, historically minded poet writing these portraits into being, shading the light in certain ways. As the poems show, love, art, class, money, and sexual or artistic control are recurring topics in Browning. But the monologue form turns them into moving targets, figured dynamically as a struggle between past and present, between textual and actual life. Taking *The Bishop Orders His Tomb* as his prime example, Herbert Tucker usefully distinguishes between two historicisms in Browning's dramatic monologues—the first, such as impressed Ruskin (see opening footnote), reads the individual speaker as a manifestation of his historical moment (all the paraphernalia of Renaissance greed, classicism, ambition, amid a Christian outlook), while the second explores "the truth of subjective experience" (what Elizabeth Barrett admired when she called *The Bishop* a poem "full of the power of life"). The first historicism is "what history *means*" while the second historicism is "how history *feels*" ("Wanted Dead or Alive: Browning's Historicism," *Victorian Studies* 38 [1994]: 25).

Bringing these two perspectives together, Tucker focusses on line 13, the bishop's query to himself and to his "nephews:" "Do I live, am I dead?" The Bishop is worried about his corporeal status, but he is also asking about his own fictive life as a character in literature. Tucker argues that "through these auditors the poem makes its appeal to a different posterity: the one comprising its readers, whose curiosity or fascination with the past mirrors the Bishop's bemusement or obsession with the future. Our desire for the past that was the Bishop's matches, and so to speak fulfills, his desire for the future that will be ours" (32). Thus the poem is both literally and figuratively about the desire for burial and resurrection—of the past (for us) and of the future (for the bishop). In an interesting essay on "Browning's Corpses," Carol Christ points out a number of poems that reveal Browning's "need to appropriate the dead body to the use of the living" (*Victorian Poetry* 33.3-4, 399).

The lump of lapis lazuli (lines 40–48) is a key image in the Bishop's transhistorical scenario. "Bedded" in fig leaves, buried, dug up, and set between the bishop's (statue's) knees as a symbol of the omnipotency of God, the stone is further complicated by associations with the fertile, nurturing Madonna, and martyred, symbolically castrated John the Baptist. It functions as an image of rebirth for the bodily Bishop and his sexuality, but also for classical learning, for the unearthing of new life and the construction of a glorious tomb to mark the end of an old one. For the Bishop, the tomb *is* eternal life, and he is literally dying to become his own monument, an iffy effigy which turns from marble to gritstone to text before the reader's eyes. As Elizabeth Barrett wrote to the poet in 1845: "You force your reader to sympathize positively in his glory in being buried!"

Even as he explores historical attitudes and timeless literary themes, Browning is also interested in contemporary Victorian parallels. In contrast to Pugin, Carlyle, Ruskin, Tennyson, and Morris, all of whom are entranced by the Middle Ages as a model for social and cultural reform, Browning appears to revel in the corruption and worldliness of the Renaissance. Is it because it seems a time like his own? Does Browning, like Ruskin in *Stones of Venice*, see Victorian Britain on the verge of a moral and political decline? Or does the era's exuberance outweigh its immorality? Browning went beyond suggesting a merely general relevance for *The Bishop Orders His Tomb*: trying to sell the poem to its first publisher in 1845, he wrote that it was "just the thing for the time—what with the Oxford business" (a reference to the Tractarian Movement at Oxford University).

Love Among the Ruins and *Two in the Campagna* would also be good poems to consider when addressing Browning's uses of the past. Both are love lyrics whose dramatic monologue form renders them unreliable as professions of pure affection. In the first poem love is counterpointed to yet allied with empire, whose glory is in turn connected to gold. The awkwardly short even-numbered lines truncate the ambition, the emotion, the "plenty and perfection" (line 25) that build in the long lines preceding them, thereby evoking the empire's reduction to a few broken stones. The woman waiting in the turret is a Lady of Shalott figure, held motionless till the arrival of the narrator-lover, who perhaps glories in his own power no less than in the civilization he condemns. After all, who is he talking to here? Is he boasting to male friends? (The mobile male narrator and the waiting woman also appear in *Meeting at Night* and *Parting at Morning*).

A similar undercutting of emotion occurs in *Two in the Campagna*. The old tomb in stanza 3 and the ghost of Rome in stanza 5 connect the speaker's fleeting love to the vanished empire, suggesting that his rejection of the earth-bound woman is historically inevitable. Meanwhile, the narrator pursues his free, darting intellect into the ether, transcending (or having satisfied) the worldly passion of "the good minute" (line 50). Both poems can be compared to Rossetti's *The Burden of Nineveh* as reflections on what builds and destroys empires or love affairs, and what sort of things, such as art, might outlast them.

Most of the poems included here can be construed as being about "maleness," as assertions of masculinity in which quests for verbal, artistic, social, or intellectual control of a situation are tied up in a sexual, or sexualized, power struggle. The Duke, the Bishop, Porphyria's Lover, Childe Roland, Fra Lippo Lippi, and Andrea Del Sarto all define themselves through their imagined standards of male behavior and their ability to construct in life or art a place for themselves in a man's world. Critics have long pointed to Browning's frustration that he was unable, before or after marriage, to make a living wage in the marketplace. In *Dared and Done: The Marriage of Elizabeth Barrett and Robert Browning* (1995) Julia Markus explores some of the crueler ironies of his position: while living comfortably, Browning's parents had little money to spare because his father had refused to profit from the family's slave-dependent business in the West Indies. But the only way Browning could afford to flee to the continent with Elizabeth was by living on *her* inheritance from the extensive Barrett family sugar plantations in Jamaica. Both poets were painfully aware of the moral compromise involved. See Markus's chapter, "The Runaway Slave," 88-115.

Browning's uneasiness about the financial insecurities of the artist emerges in both *Fra Lippo Lippi* and *Andrea Del Sarto*. Herbert Sussman argues that, as compared to Tennyson's or Arnold's depiction of the artist's world as romantic, passive, and feminized, Browning projects an artistic "manliness" defined by sexual and commercial activity: "Lippo exemplifies the 'successful' artist not merely because he has moved from medieval formalism to a more modern sacred realism. This formal 'progress' is also inseparable from his moves from the patronage of the Church to that of a merchant prince and from the imprisoning male celibacy of the monastery to energetic heterosexual activity. Within the gendered, historicist categories of mid-century aesthetics, this highly sexed artist-monk represents the possibility of creating a popular realist religious art while maintaining a truly 'manly' gender identity" ("Browning and the Problematic of a Male Poetic," *Victorian Studies* 35 [1992]: 189).

Yet, as Sussman points out, "the conditions of artistic production within a mercantile society generate new constraints upon male desire" (192). Lippo works long hours for his "master" (the term Victorians used for factory owners), fulfilling repetitive, moralistic commissions (lines 47-49). Is his escape to the brothel the inevitable and necessary consequence of artistic self-prostitution? Is Browning using Lippo to sanction the Victorian double standard, his excess of sexual/artistic energy needing "natural" release outside his unsatisfying work? *Fra Lippo Lippi* establishes the potent masculine artist only to subvert him; in *Andrea Del Sarto* the protagonist is already married, and thus that much further tangled in the commodification of sexual and artistic energies.

One can read "*Childe Roland to the Dark Tower Came*" as a further chapter in the search for masculine and/or artistic self-definition. Notice that the poem opens with uncertainty about the narrator's honesty: "the working of his lie / On mine." My lie or my eye? The ambiguity suggests that knight and poet may not be telling the truth about this cryptic quest, in which Roland's friends have already perished shamefully (stanzas 16 and 17). Is this a poem of deep faith or radical doubt, honor or futility? The nature of the quest seems to depend on the nature of the critic: the blighted (post-industrial?) landscape interests contextualizers, while Freudians see a psycho-sexual journey to the dark tower of *eros* and *thanatos*, and intertextualists may find a nightmarish reworking of Byron's *Child Harold's Pilgrimage*. Victorians (and many readers since) regarded the poem as detailing the trials of a bracing spiritual quest. When a friend asked if the poem meant "he that endureth to the end shall be saved," Browning responded "yes, just about that" (W. C. DeVane, *A Browning Handbook* [1955], 229-231).

Read this way, Childe Roland's blast on the horn could signal Browning's self-assertion as poet against all odds. One might talk about the poem as a metaphoric journey through Browning's work, probing (as Roland does with his lance) for answers, endings, or closure. But even then the poem arrives only at its origin, giving narrative "sense" to nonsense words uttered by someone pretending to be crazy (Edgar as "Poor Tom" in *King Lear*). So Browning is speaking like Edgar, or Hamlet, insinuating that there is method to the madness he adopts. It is instructive to compare this strategy to how Tennyson uses a line from *Measure for Measure* to generate *Mariana*. Both poets take a gap in the Shakespearean text and fill it, but Tennyson deepens his character by describing her time alone, waiting for the play to return to her. Browning on the other hand *creates* a whole new character who exists entirely in his own dream—or nightmare—animated and motivated by words outside his world. As with the Bishop's maunderings, these last words are his only destiny, his verbal attempt to break into fictive life.

Intriguingly, *The Last Ride Together* can be seen as a sort of mini-*Childe Roland*, having a similarly broad range of meaning. It might be an allegory of the poet's relation to his muse—one Victorian saw it as "the noblest of all Robert Browning's love poems"—and for Robert Altick it describes the "fulfillment of God's purpose for man in the simple process of living" (*Victorian Poetry* 1 [1963]: 64). Readers who want to bring the poem down to earth will note that horses are never mentioned. Their ride is sex.

Caliban upon Setebos (1864) was written 1859-60, close to the time Darwin's *Origin of Species* was published. Caliban muses upon the source and meaning of the natural world in a way that bears on Darwin, but he is as much concerned with the evolution of religion and thought as biology and organic form. In "Upon *Caliban Upon Setebos*" Barbara Melchiori argues that physical evolution is not what bothers Caliban. He seems to accept it, based on evidence of fossils: he mentions the newt "turned to stone, shut up inside a stone" (lines 214-15) and does not view this phenomenon as questioning the existence of God. Rather, says Melchiori, Caliban asks, "how did God evolve? And he answers the question by showing the thought processes by which a concept of God could, or would, come into being" (*Browning's Poetry of Reticence* [1968]; rpt. in *Caliban*, ed. Harold Bloom [1992], 96).

The poet is also concerned with the birth of art, and of human art's uneasy relation to a jealous God's power of creation. Caliban uses reeds to make bird sounds, and imagines his pipe mocking him, saying, as Caliban might say to God: "I am the crafty thing, / I make the cry my maker cannot make / With his great round mouth; he must blow through mine"; he then comments: "Would I not smash it with my foot? So He" (lines 123-26). (Elizabeth Barrett Browning also takes up this topic in *A Musical Instrument*.)

As a shaper of words and maker of music, Caliban is obsessed by the dangerous possibility that God might overhear him, and "hides" himself by avoiding personal pronouns. In his fears, Caliban is rather like his poetic creator, Browning. It was J. S. Mill who said that poetry was not so much heard as overheard, and Mill whose penetrating analysis of the anonymous author of *Pauline* confirmed the poet's desire to mask his lyric utterance. As Melchiori notes, Caliban's sin against Setebos is most obviously his speech, and his anxiety about God hearing him expresses Browning's own uneasiness as a writer: "This poet's fear of offending God by his speech is . . . the simplest reading of *Caliban upon Setebos*, to which the opening quotation from the Psalms gives a clue" (99).

The epigraph—"thou thoughtest that I was altogether such a one as thyself"—is worth lingering over. Not only does it suggest that Caliban is making God in his own image, and that Browning is audaciously doing the same, but also that Browning is making Caliban in his own image, and that his readers will be caught in a similar stance. In *Open Fields: Science in Cultural Encounter* (1996) Gillian Beer comments that this "double-faced" epigraph signals a poem that "disturbs any easy developmental patterning": "Ethnocentrism, cultural imperialism, anthropomorphism are jangled in that biblical rebuke" (90). Thus it could be Caliban or God speaking to each other or to us about their or our perceptions of humans, God, or savages—or poets. Beer points out that "Unlike in most of Browning's monologues, there is no dramatized listener within the poem. We are caught into the mind of Caliban and into the brooding reflexivity of his attempt to manage the universe" (91). Wilde grasped the range of Browning's implication when, in the Preface to *The Picture of Dorian Gray*, he projected all nineteenth-century readers as Calibans.

Charles Dickens
A Christmas Carol (1843)

The *Carol* is sometimes thought of as a sentimental fable about the spirit of charity at Christmas. But students who have read *Past and Present* and a few of the selections in the Industrial Landscape section (particularly Engels and Mayhew) will be better prepared to appreciate the ways in which *A Christmas Carol* "was born out of the very conditions of the time" (Peter Ackroyd, *Dickens* [1990], 407). Through the figure of Scrooge, Dickens was addressing the inadequacy of contemporary attitudes towards the poor or feeble—those whom Scrooge regards as "surplus population." Like Carlyle and Pugin, Dickens was angry about the 1834 Poor Law and the callous Workhouse system (instructors might assign *A Walk in a Workhouse* along with the *Carol*).

Scrooge was not an anomaly; his views were fully in keeping with political and economic theory of the day. Having paid his taxes to maintain the prisons and workhouses, he is quite satisfied that he has fulfilled his obligation to society. Edgar Johnson writes that with the growth of industry in the nineteenth century "political economists had rationalized the spirit of ruthless greed into a system claiming authority throughout society." Scrooge, he says, "is nothing less than the personification of 'economic man'" (*Charles Dickens: His Tragedy and Triumph* [1952], 256). Profit is Scrooge's only goal, and he acknowledges no bonds between human beings except those of economic exchange, of what Carlyle had termed the "cash-nexus."

Carlyle was an enormous influence on Dickens, even a hero to him (see Michael Goldberg's *Carlyle and Dickens* [1972], 32–44). In *A Christmas Carol* Dickens adapted Carlyle's call to the Captains of Industry to exercise paternal leadership rather than merely pursuing gain. Scrooge is thus not only a private miser but, more importantly, a capitalist businessman. He and Marley form part of what Carlyle termed in *Past and Present* "a virtual Industrial Aristocracy as yet only half-alive, spell-bound amid money-bags and ledgers." In awakening to the possibility of becoming a compassionate employer, Scrooge acts out Carlyle's injunction to "Arise, save thyself, be one of those that save thy country."

Part of the great popularity of *A Christmas Carol* is that it is a "feel good" story, and readers may sympathize uncritically with Scrooge's transformation. But teachers might wish to talk about the limitations of benevolent paternalism as a solution to deplorable economic and social conditions.

Another *Christmas Carol* theme that echoes *Past and Present* is human alienation. Scrooge is "solitary as an oyster," while Carlyle proclaimed that "isolation is the sum-total of wretchedness to man." Marley has no mourners; Scrooge has no children. Material suffering is not the only consequence of laissez-faire capitalism; Scrooge's notion that the lives of others are "not my business" illustrates his estrangement from all of humanity. Fezziwig, in contrast, invites everyone to his party, including not merely his own employees and servants, but even the half-starved "boy from over the way." He is generous with food and drink, but even more importantly, he shakes hands with each guest individually, a gesture suggestive of the social responsibility and enlightened paternalism that Carlyle longed for.

As in so much of Dickens's work, childhood is a major theme. The impulse to write *A Christmas Carol* grew out of a visit Dickens had paid earlier in 1843 to a "ragged school": "I have very seldom seen in all the strange and dreadful things I have seen in London and elsewhere, anything so shocking as the dire neglect of soul and body exhibited in these children." The child-like figures of Ignorance and Want are allegorical representations of the lives of children such as those interviewed by Mayhew and the Parliamentary Commission (see Industrial Landscape perspectives).

There are also psychological and autobiographical elements in the depiction of Scrooge's childhood. The Spirit succeeds in evoking sympathy for another being, not by showing Scrooge scenes of misery and suffering, but by reminding him of his own lonely boyhood (point out how the description of the solitary boy in the silent schoolroom echoes the psychological landscape of Tennyson's *Mariana*: the mice, the poplar, the creaking door). Scrooge has to recall his deeply repressed past, and to feel for himself, before he can begin to feel for others (though the chapter ends with his snuffing out the spirit's light with an "extinguisher cap"—a striking pre-Freudian image of repression). The unexplained neglect of the boy Scrooge, his virtual abandonment by his family, coupled with his refuge in books and the imagination, suggest that Dickens was tapping into the secret sources of his own inner grief. As Michael Slater puts it, "The longed-for school and the dreadful blacking-factory are deftly merged (with considerable assistance from Tennyson's "Mariana") into one house of desolation" (*Dickens and Women* [1983], 33).

In other ways, too, the grouchy old miser shares surprising traits with the jolly young novelist (his inability to resist a pun, for example); Dickens was perhaps trying to exorcise the fear that his own determination never to be poor again might turn him into a Scrooge. (See Ackroyd's *Dickens* for more on the circumstances of composition of the *Carol*, and on the biographical aspects of Dickens's identification with Scrooge and his preoccupation with money, 407–14).

In addition to its prevailing imagery of cold and fire, A *Christmas Carol* seems to antedate twentieth-century "magic realism" in startling ways. Harry Stone describes how the world inhabited by Scrooge comes to life: "Dickens builds an atmosphere dense with personification, animism, anthropomorphism, and the like. The inanimate world is alive and active; every structure, every object plays its percipient role in the unfolding drama. Buildings and gateways, bedposts and door knockers become sentient beings that conspire in a universal morality. Everything is connected by magical means to everything else" (*Dickens and the Invisible World* [1979], 121).

The most complete discussion of A *Christmas Carol* can be found in Paul Davis's illustrated *Life and Times of Ebenezer Scrooge* (1990). He describes the *Carol* as an essentially urban text that transforms nostalgia for an idealized rural past by reclaiming Christmas for the city. Davis explores the *Carol*'s place in popular culture from 1843 until now, and the history of theatrical representations of it, from Dickens's own public readings through a long line of dramatic adaptations that have constituted a virtual "Carol industry" (215). (Even the Muppets got into the act with *The Muppet Christmas Carol* in 1992.) One reason for its enduring relevance is that "contemporary America, like Victorian England, is two nations" (229); those engaged on both sides of the economic debate in the *Carol* continue to enlist Scrooge on their side.

Instructors who wish to read further might look at the special issue of *The Dickensian*, 89.3 (1993), devoted to A *Christmas Carol*; it includes articles by Kathleen Tillotson, Philip Collins, Edwin Eigner, J. Hillis Miller, and others. Michael Slater's contribution, "The Triumph of Humour: The *Carol* Revisited" (184–92), traces the comic facets of the work, arguing that one way of expressing Scrooge's conversion "might be to say that he begins as a Wit and ends as a

Humorist." Certainly it would be a shame to focus on the economic and social message of A *Christmas Carol* without taking pleasure in its exuberant jokes and verbal playfulness.

A Walk in a Workhouse (1850)

Even though it was written several years after A *Christmas Carol* and Carlyle's *Past and Present*, this essay's first-hand account of workhouse conditions provides an excellent background for these texts. One might also pair it with the interviews conducted by Mayhew or with the Blue Book reports of the Parliamentary Commission (in the Industrial Landscape perspectives section).

Dickens made a lifelong habit of touring places where the destitute and disadvantaged were incarcerated—prisons, orphanages, hospitals, lunatic asylums—and writing exposés about the conditions he encountered. Most middle-class people steered clear of such places, but Dickens's investigative reporting brought them vividly before his readers. He published much of this writing in *Household Words*, a journal he had founded in 1850 at least in part to crusade for radical social reform. For further examples of Dickens's social journalism see A *December Vision*, a collection edited by Neil Philip and Victor Neuburg (1986).

Dickens had already vented his hatred of workhouses in *Oliver Twist* (1837–39), and he would return to the subject in *Our Mutual Friend* (1864–5) where old Betty Higden pleads "Kill me sooner than take me" to the workhouse. In between the two he published A *Walk in a Workhouse* (1850). As this piece demonstrates, Dickens the journalist had a great deal in common with Dickens the novelist. In both themes and language, much of this essay could come straight from the pages of one of Dickens's novels. There is his abiding concern with social justice, with the plight of the weakest and most neglected members of society. There is his characteristic mixture of pathetic sentiment and ironic anger. There is his restless play of language and imagery. And there is his almost magical ability to animate a scene, so that out of these endless wards of colorless misery emerge the voices of individual paupers.

For example, the scene with which A *Walk in a Workhouse* opens might be straight out of *Macbeth*, with its assembly of ancient paupers, crouching, drooping, leering, and its "weird old women, all skeleton within, all bonnet and cloak without." The "ugly old crones . . . with a ghastly kind of contentment upon them which was not at all comforting to see" might figure in *Oliver Twist*, just as "the dragon, Pauperism, . . . toothless, fangless, drawing his breath heavily enough, and hardly worth chaining up," inhabits the same imaginative realm as the Megalosaurus with which *Bleak House* begins.

Yet these toothless dragons *are* chained up, and their loss of liberty is one of the pervading themes of the essay. Why should children, guilty only of being poor or crippled, be locked away with no hope of a better future? Why should dying old people, whose only crime is being unfit to go on drudging for a pittance, have to spend their last days in confinement? Although Dickens does not propose concrete alternatives, the thrust of his article is that surely a healthy and sane society could find some better way to provide for these innocents.

Dickens interviews the paupers, asks why the nurse of the Itch Ward is crying, whether the chattering, witch-like old women get enough to eat, whether the feeble old men are comfortable. Like Mayhew and the Parliamentary Commissioners, he records their answers, preserving their idiom and their thoughts on their lives. Obviously their responses are shaped by the questions that have been posed, and by the social gulf between the paupers and their questioner; we can no more get an unmediated glimpse of their inner world than we can of Darwin's Fuegians. Yet even if we see them only through a glass, darkly, certain qualities come through: the humble, even obsequious, note of the aged paupers' gratitude; the mustn't-grumble mentality ("I have no complaint to make, Sir"); the flicker of enthusiasm over the fate of Charley Walters.

Dickens is morally outraged that criminals receive better treatment than the poor. Of the epileptic girl imprisoned with noisy madwomen, he writes: "If this girl had stolen her mistress's watch, I do not hesitate to say she would, in all probability, have been infinitely better off." He observes bitterly that the only way for workhouse boys to improve their lot in life would be "by smashing as many workhouse windows as possible, and being promoted to prison." The workhouse system was administered on the theory that people are indigent because of idleness (rather than unemployment, low wages, etc.), and so they should not be indulged with easy living but spurred to useful activity. See M. A. Crowther's *The Workhouse System, 1834–1929* (1981) and Beatrice and Sidney Webb's *English Poor Law Policy* (1910, rpt. 1963).

Dickens's walk takes him through Dantesque scenes of gloom and suffering. He uses animal imagery to convey the degradation of the inmates: crippled children are lodged in a "kennel" and they slink about "like dispirited wolves or hyaenas." It would be better to be a "big-headed idiot . . . in the sunlight outside" than to be caged up like these castoff youths. The people thus shut away are so numerous as to constitute "groves" of babies, mothers, and lunatics, and "jungles" of men. It takes Dickens two long hours to survey them all.

He takes care to praise where he can: "I saw many things to commend. It was very agreeable . . . to find the pauper children in this workhouse looking robust and well." He notes with pleasure the "two mangy pauper rocking-horses rampant." Yet the very presence of these meager toys is itself a poignant detail; the thought that children might actually try to play in this grotesque setting is painfully incongruous.

The most striking section may be the spectral old men, too inert to reply when spoken to. In a scene reminiscent of Grandmother Smallweed's outbursts in *Bleak House*, they are briefly roused by the interesting topic of death, only to subside into apathy again. Dickens flirts with comedy here, but he's already established that the old men are virtually starving. It is not remarkable that they should be listless, but rather that they should bother to go on living at all. The pathetic yet dignified request to be allowed a bit more fresh air dramatizes the needlessness of their privations—air, after all, is free.

The ability of these old men to endure such a bleak and hopeless existence arouses Dickens's curiosity, and he tries to make a leap of imaginative sympathy into their consciousnesses, wondering "whether Charley Walters had ever described to them the days when he kept company with some old pauper woman in the bud, or Billy Stevens ever told them of the time when he was a dweller in the far-off foreign land called Home!"

The essay ends with the burnt child, as it began with the dropped one. As he had done with Tiny Tim, Dickens evokes the potential death of a sick child as the ultimate indictment of a sick society: he looked as if he thought it best, "all things considered, that he should die." Tiny Tim's fate, the Spirit implied, hung in Scrooge's hands; the burnt child's is in the hands of Dickens's readers.

Elizabeth Gaskell
Our Society at Cranford (1851)

Perhaps it is Gaskell's apparent switch from the serious social themes of *Mary Barton*, published only three years earlier, that has led many critics to dismiss *Cranford* as a bit of nostalgic fluff. Yet *Cranford* can be situated in relation to the contrasts between past and present, rural and industrial, that animate the work of Carlyle, Pugin, Ruskin, and others. The narrator draws a sharp distinction between Cranford and "the great neighbouring commercial town of Drumble," and repeatedly asks, "Do you ever see that in London?" The question implies the singularity of Cranford's eccentricities, but also a sense of loss, since the eventual dominance of London and all it stands for can hardly be in doubt.

Contemporary readers would easily have seen how out-of-date the Cranford ladies were. For one thing, the story (published in December 1851) is backdated fifteen years: the famous literary quarrel must take place in November 1836 if *Pickwick* is hot off the presses. Fashion provides another clue: they are the last in England to cling to the outdated styles of their youth. The railroad which kills Captain Brown was still very much a symbol of innovation in the 1830s, and Gaskell conveys through many nuances that this is a community on the edge of enormous changes.

For background on the social world the Cranford ladies inhabit, have students read Mrs. Ellis and Mrs. Beeton in the Ladies and Gentlemen perspectives section: Beeton's rules about limiting social calls to a quarter of an hour clarify Miss Jenkyns' advice to the young narrator, and Ellis's notions of female self-sacrifice illuminate the choices made by Gaskell's characters (such as Miss Jessie's devotion to her sister) and yet suggest how surprisingly utopian this fellowship of independent women really was, with no husbands and children to cater to. Florence Nightingale, who relished novels in which the heroines had "no family ties," must have enjoyed this one.

Students who have not yet encountered both Johnson and Dickens will need some explanation of the literary dispute. Johnson, like everything else Miss Jenkyns admires, belongs to the previous century. She has formed her style upon his, and the letters of which she is so proud are elaborate, artificial, and full of multisyllabic words. It is fun to read the extract aloud and translate into more modern English her grand expressions ("communicated to me the intelligence," "quitted," "quondam," "you will not easily conjecture"). Dickens represents the other side of Gaskell's contrast between past and present: he is lively, colloquial, and full of jokes. His style is popular, not elevated, and Miss Jenkyns is deeply hostile to it, as she is towards all things newfangled.

Since Dickens was the editor of *Household Words*, in which this story first appeared, his reaction to the praise of his own early work is interesting: he insisted that Captain Brown be killed while reading the poems of Thomas Hood instead. Gaskell was annoyed at the change, and reinstated the references to *Pickwick Papers* when she republished the collected sketches as *Cranford*. (She also dropped the final sentence: "Poor, dear Miss Jenkyns! Cranford is man-less now.")

In *Scheherezade in the Marketplace* (1992), Hilary Schor argues that *Cranford* "rewrites marginality to form its own kind of experiment with narrative" (84). Critics "have assumed, simplistically, that Gaskell was only describing from *within* the village life she missed" but in fact the narrator also "becomes a kind of anthropologist, an ethnographer visiting an alien culture" (86). Schor observes that the first number "offers an extended meditation on women and their relationship to male texts" (89), and analyzes the composition of *Cranford* partly in terms of Gaskell's complicated relationship with Dickens. (Schor suggests that having Captain Brown killed while reading *Pickwick* "makes Dickens himself seem the murdering engine").

What does Gaskell mean by calling the ladies of Cranford "Amazons"? Initially, it appears ironic: these women are not fierce in battle but in upholding small gentilities and economies. They may seem quaint, even ridiculous, in their preoccupation with trivial matters, but when put to the test, they display courage and moral integrity. Miss Jessie is heroic, despite her dimples, and Miss Jenkyns forgets her anxiety about the carpet in the face of real tragedy. It is sometimes objected that their self-sufficiency is illusory, that in critical moments they always rely on outside male assistance (e.g. Miss Jessie's fairytale rescue by Major Gordon). But Miss Jessie is quite prepared to go to work and support herself—one could say that she is rewarded, but hardly that she is rescued.

Some see these isolated spinsters and widows as ultimately sterile: they are stuck in a bygone era, and have no future in the form of children. Are they really happily self-reliant single women, regarding men as merely a nuisance, or are they putting a brave face on a dismal situation? In "Gaskell's Feminist Utopia" (1994), Rae Rosenthal maintains that the Amazons "do battle with and defeat the succeeding invasions of patriarchal forces, and . . . ensure the preservation of their utopian society through the education and assimilation of the narrator, Mary Smith" (74). Captain Brown's violent end might seem harsh, but it is necessary for "the future of their utopia" (85), for *Cranford* "is much less innocuous than it first appears" (92). In *Nobody's Angels* (1995), Elizabeth Langland argues that the spinsters are not stagnant and moribund, but brimming "over with engaged life;" they are constantly "creating meaning rather than slavishly following rigid social formulas" for "the very conventions that seem, in the abstract, to bind them, prove enormously flexible in their practice" (123).

Carlyle's paternalist Captains of Industry represent a top-down solution to the evils of the new industrial society; in contrast, Gaskell's feminist Cranfordians represent a very different kind of organic community. They too take care of one another, and are bound by loyalty and compassion, not the cash-nexus—but they manage this without resorting to the brass collar. They practice neither laissez-faire economics nor feudal magnanimity but "elegant economy." One can read *Cranford* as a celebration of a feminine alternative, or a mourning for its disappearance—just as one can read Captain Brown's death as the triumph of the Amazons, or the triumph of the modern era, with its railroads and novels by Boz.

Thomas Hardy
The Withered Arm (1888)

In *Wessex Tales* Hardy was consciously striving to preserve a record of a way of life that was passing; *The Withered Arm* is set in humble rural surroundings in the years about 1826-32. But Hardy's rustics enact dramas on the scale of Greek tragedy; in the opening scene the anonymous milkers comment on the lives of the protagonists like a Greek chorus. Hardy himself made the connection in the preface of 1912, writing of "our magnificent heritage from the Greeks in dramatic literature" which had found sufficient scope in a geographical area not much larger than Wessex.

With its portrait of intertwined lives drawing inexorably towards catastrophe, *The Withered Arm* echoes Greek tragedy. But it also echoes the classic triangle of the folk ballad, such as the one where Lord Thomas chooses "fair Annie" over the "nut brown maiden," who takes her revenge by killing them both. As Kristin Brady points out in *The Short Stories of Thomas Hardy* (1982), Rhoda's questions about Gertrude "directly invoke the conventions of the ballad or folk tale," underlining the two women's "opposing physical, social, and moral attributes: dark and fair, tall and short, strong and weak, poor and wealthy, rejected and beloved" (25). The contrast between the virginal blonde and the passionate dark woman is familiar, but Rhoda and Gertrude are more than stereotypes: Brady describes the "complex interplay" of strength and weakness between the women, who "continually fluctuate between affection and hostility" (25-26). The initial polarity dissolves as Gertrude's emotional isolation comes to mirror Rhoda's social isolation.

Unlike *The Mayor of Casterbridge* (written two years earlier), *The Withered Arm* does not make the working out of the man's destiny its central focus. The choices Farmer Lodge makes—to seduce and abandon Rhoda, to marry Gertrude—set events in motion, but we get scarcely a glimpse of his thoughts and feelings. Our attention is first directed to Rhoda, the spurned woman, jealous of her rival, and then to Gertrude, the insecure newcomer and neglected wife, anxious to recapture her husband's faded affection. Interestingly, the women are not really enemies: they strike up a friendship, and fate grinds forward to the dénouement *in spite of* their actions, not *because* of them. (Students may argue that on a moral level, this makes the story merely depressing—all the characters are punished far beyond what they have conceivably deserved).

As in Hardy's novels, the past is inescapable: Lodge ignores his castoff mistress and their illegitimate son—the evidence of his earlier misdeeds—but they blight his new marriage. His wife's withered arm destroys his desire for her, and he fears their childlessness "might be a judgement from heaven upon him." There are no fresh starts in Hardy.

One should ask students about the symbolism of that arm: it is the external sign of Gertrude's coming-to-consciousness, or loss of innocence, as well as of her husband's impotence. The arm dramatizes the power of the unconscious, for while Rhoda gives up any conscious desire to harm Gertrude, her unconscious is clearly working overtime. As Brady puts it, "the power of Rhoda's mind over her rival is so strong that it can only be expressed in an image which challenges belief" (23). On a psychological level, the story is set up so as to fulfill *both* women's deepest wishes: the contrived coincidence of the ending enacts Gertrude's suppressed longing to erase her husband's past, embodied in his son.

Hardy's reliance on elaborate coincidences has troubled many readers. In *Thomas Hardy in Our Time* (1995) Robert Langbaum argues that Hardy sacrifices verisimilitude "to set up highly concentrated scenes that permit the explosive revelation of internal states of being. . . . Hardy's coincidences . . . allow his characters to fulfill their desires and destinies." Langbaum adds that "what appears to be chance turns out to be design—that of fate and/or the characters' unconscious" (25).

Brady notes that the implausible elements in Hardy preserve "the mood and substance of a rural community's belief in the improbable" (18). Harold Orel concurs, arguing that Hardy relied on "bizarre events as a means of stimulating reader interest" (*The Victorian Short Story* [1986], 105). Hardy—who said that "'realism' is not Art"—was interested not in the grey details of everyday life, but in "spectres, mysterious voices, intuitions, omens, dreams, haunted places" (Orel 106). As Julia Briggs puts it in *Night Visitor* (1977), "his Wessex novels are deeply imbued with local legends, superstitions, omens, techniques of divination and sympathetic magic. Hardy had seen cures and curses made, knew the tricks of 'conjurors' (white witches) and the many signs and portents that directed the lives of country folk before the coming of the railways and agricultural mechanization radically altered their way of life. The supernatural of his novels is commonly susceptible of rational explanation and can often be attributed to accident or coincidence, but in his short stories such as *The Withered Arm* the events speak for themselves, and the inexplicable is presented with that terseness, that refusal to abide our question, which also characterizes the ballad" (100). Hardy said that "a story dealing with the supernatural should never be explained away" (Brady 22).

One may want to talk specifically about Egdon Heath, that ancient and mysterious place where Conjurer Trendle lives in remote solitude. It is a symbolic and fearful landscape, into which Gertrude undertakes a kind of mythic journey into the unknown (or the unconscious). She ventures forth to find the guardian of primitive powerful folk wisdom, hoping to gain access to his secret knowledge. Here again Hardy melds classical and folk sources, for her quest seems to echo Aeneas's visit to the sibyl at the gate of the underworld.

Hardy may not have cared for realism, but in *The Withered Arm* he carefully delineates the class distinctions that structure this rural world. The dairyman who employs the milkers has to pay the prosperous Farmer Lodge rent for every cow. Lodge wouldn't stoop to marry a milkmaid: he prefers "a lady complete." Rhoda

wonders whether the new wife "seems like a woman who has ever worked for a living, or one that has been always well off, and has neer done anything, and shows
marks of a lady on her." Rhoda's thatched mud cottage contrasts to Lodge's "white
house of ample dimensions." Riding in his fancy gig past his trudging son, Lodge
remarks condescendingly that "these country lads will carry a hundredweight once
they get it on their backs." Clothes are another class indicator: Gertrude wears "a
white bonnet and a silver-coloured gownd," while the boy who observes this dies
"wearing the smockfrock of a rustic, and fustian breeches."

Brady makes an important point about the ending of the story: just "when the
two women finally enact the physical struggle of Rhoda's dream, the narrator shifts
the reader's attention to the real victim of the story: the boy who earlier had been
pitifully attracted to Gertrude and her position of elegance in the parish."
Suddenly we realize that we too have neglected the solitary child, viewing him
merely as the evidence of his parents' illicit union. Our final recognition implicates
us in "the shared guilt of having allowed the boy to come to such an end" (26-7).

Like Jo in Dickens's *Bleak House*, this nameless boy represents the failure of the
rich to take responsibility for the poor, and their own resulting sterility. Like the
typhus widow in Carlyle's *Past and Present*, the boy proves his connection at last.
Remind students of Hardy's words about the eighteen-year-old whom his father
saw hung merely "for *being with* some others who had set fire to a rick. . . . Nothing
my father ever said to me drove the tragedy of Life so deeply into my mind."

Another aspect of the story is its treatment of the "fallen woman." As in
Thrawn Janet, a woman who has borne a child out of wedlock lives as a semi-out-
cast in a rural world of suspicious gossips. Neither Janet nor Rhoda intentionally
harms anyone, but their previous sexual transgressions place them sufficiently beyond the pale that they are suspected of possessing threatening unnatural powers:
Janet is "sib to the deil" and Rhoda is "a sorceress [who] would know the where-
abouts of the exorcist." Their neighbors project their own fears onto these female
scapegoats, isolated by disgrace. Powerless, they are perceived as dangerously powerful. (In *The Woman Warrior* Maxine Hong Kingston portrays a community's
atavistic fear of a woman who violates its taboos: she is stoned by the villagers for
becoming pregnant while her husband is away).

Hardy returned to the figure of the fallen woman (another milkmaid) in *Tess of
the d'Urbervilles* (1891). He writes sympathetically, with no moral condemnation. In
fact, the "fallen woman" would actually make Farmer Lodge a better wife than the
"virgin," for Rhoda is both vital and fertile, whereas Gertrude is tame and sterile.
Despite her profound isolation, Rhoda is a survivor; Gertrude dies when her husband rejects her, but Rhoda outlives them all, fiercely independent to the last.

Sir Arthur Conan Doyle
A Scandal in Bohemia (1890)

Watson tends to be neglected in discussions of the Sherlock Holmes stories, but
in *Murder Will Out* (1989) T. J. Binyon calls the creation of Watson "a stroke of

genius," for "however outré the events he describes, the fact that they are mediated through his prosaic, stolid personality gives them a reality and a plausibility
which they would otherwise lack" (9–10). Many critics have noted the parallels
between Watson and Boswell, each an admiring chronicler of the doings of a
great man.

The portrait of Holmes is more complex. Despite his cozy name and respectable lodgings, Holmes is recognizably "a product of the Romantic tradition.
He is another proud, alienated hero, superior to and isolated from the rest of humanity; a sufferer from *spleen* and *ennui*, who alleviates the deadly boredom of existence with injections of cocaine and morphine" (Binyon 10). Students are often
surprised by this side of Holmes, and they aren't the only ones: Julian Symons
writes that it seems "astonishing that this Victorian philistine [Doyle] should have
created an egocentric drug-taking hero so alien from his own beliefs" (*Mortal
Consequences* [1972], 65).

Holmes is a sufficiently fin-de-siècle figure that instructors might want to pair
A Scandal in Bohemia with some of the selections from the Aesthetes and
Decadents perspectives section. In his introduction to the Oxford World's Classics
edition of *The Adventures of Sherlock Holmes* (1993), R. L. Green calls Holmes a "domesticated aesthete" in the tradition of Poe, Baudelaire, Huysmans, and Wilde,
who yet "falls short of true decadence" (xvi). Ian Ousby notes that in later stories
Holmes becomes more conventional and "the cocaine, surely Holmes's most bla-
tant venture into Decadence, all but disappears" (*Bloodhounds of Heaven* [1976],
158–59). (For more on Holmes as aesthete, see Paul Barolsky's "The Case of the
Domesticated Aesthete" in *Critical Essays on Sir Arthur Conan Doyle*, ed. Harold
Orel [1992]).

Near the beginning of the story, Holmes demonstrates his trademark ability to
guess what others have been up to, observing that Watson has resumed practice
and has had a wet walk recently. He had already claimed in *A Study in Scarlet* (1887)
that "by a man's finger-nails, by his coat-sleeve, by his boots, by his trouser-knees,
by the callosities of his forefinger and thumb, by his expression, by his shirt-cuffs—
by each of these things a man's calling is plainly revealed." This aspect of Holmes's
character was modelled on Joseph Bell, one of Doyle's professors of medicine at
Edinburgh University. Doyle wrote that Bell "would sit in the patients' waiting
room with a face like a Red Indian and diagnose the people as they came in, before even they had opened their mouths" (For more on the legend of Bell, see
Green xvii-xxi).

The essence of Holmes's method is to make readers feel that we could do it,
too; there's nothing arcane or supernatural about his skill. Watson says, "When I
hear you give your reasons . . . the thing always appears to me to be so ridiculously
simple that I could easily do it myself." Yet "the reader cannot preempt Holmes's
deductions, for the evidence on which they are based . . . is usually displayed only
after the deductions have been made" (Binyon 63). Nonetheless, Holmes's ability
to "place" people is comforting. In the worlds of *Cranford*, *Brother Jacob*, *Thrawn
Janet*, and *The Withered Arm*, events hinge upon the arrival of a stranger—but in
London, *everyone* is a stranger. Amidst the disorienting flux of urban life, jostled by

crowds of people we can't possibly know, we feel soothed by the idea that *someone*, at least, can make sense out of chaos, can "read" the city. Holmes's airy deductions suggest that identity is visible, that bodies give clues and can be deciphered.

However, while Holmes's deductions depend on the stability of other people's identities, he himself has a chameleon's gift for metamorphosis: he moves freely through different levels of society, breaking the rules of class in order to uphold the social system. Thus, Holmes is not merely a reader or detached observer; he is also an actor, a master of different roles. Even Watson scarcely recognizes him when he appears as a drunken groom or an amiable clergyman, writing that "his expression, his manner, his very soul seemed to vary with every fresh part that he assumed." Holmes further aspires to become director and stage manager when he orchestrates the theatrics outside Irene Adler's house: he hires the actors, assigns them their parts, and prepares to take the lead role himself. In *The Valley of Fear* Holmes said, "Some touch of the artist wells up within me and calls insistently for a well-staged performance."

Holmes's ability to transform himself makes the King's feeble attempt at disguise look pathetic. But, oddly, Holmes seems to forget that Irene Adler is a professional actress. He gloats to Watson that she "responded beautifully," as though she were his creature, unknowingly playing her part in his play. Irene, of course, outwits him by taking charge from behind the scenes, adopting her own disguise, and arranging her own drama. (Ask students why she says good-night when she passes Holmes.)

Holmes underestimates Irene Adler, not merely because she is a better actor, but because she is a woman. Holmes confidently assumes he knows all about women; for example, he informs Watson that "women are naturally secretive" (neither sees any irony in a bachelor preaching to a married man). But in fact Holmes neither knows nor loves women. He has no interest in "the softer passions;" emotions "were abhorrent to his cold, precise" mind. For Holmes, love would be like "grit in a sensitive instrument." (*Star Trek*'s Spock seems descended from Holmes, another "perfect reasoning machine" without feelings.) One might ask students about the significance of such dichotomies. Do they represent a basic distrust of intellect?

Sherlock Holmes is not infallible. At the beginning we may imagine that he will be duped by falling in love with Irene, but he's blinded by patriarchal convention, not desire. Before she outsmarted him, Holmes "used to make merry over the cleverness of women." He believes that they are ruled by passion: her "instinct is at once to rush to the thing she values most. It is a perfectly overpowering impulse." In short, he sees women as precisely opposite to himself, all heart and no head. His ignorance of women is his Achilles heel.

Irene Adler unmans Holmes. Look at the verbs when he realizes she's beaten him at his own game: staggered, pushed, rushed, tore, plunged—Holmes is no longer cool and precise. She had already unmanned the King, placing him in the vulnerable (female) position of fearing that his reputation might be ruined by scandal; in contrast, Irene emerges unscathed, conscience untroubled and respectable marriage secured. These role reversals are symbolized by the question of who controls access to her safe and photographs, images of her sexuality. In her letter, she takes control of her story by narrating it herself. (In the 1990s Carole Nelson Douglas has published a series of detective novels with Irene Adler as the protagonist.)

One might argue that A Scandal in Bohemia is thus a feminist text dramatizing the dangers of stereotyping women. But in that case, why does Holmes call Irene Adler "the woman"? By emphasizing her singularity, Holmes avoids learning anything about women in general. He solves the problem of her threatening female competence and sexuality by concluding that this one woman "eclipses and predominates the whole of her sex." She is the exception that proves the rule.

Furthermore, her boldness and cleverness are always described as male qualities. The King says she has "the mind of the most resolute of men." Adler adopts male disguise to verify Holmes's identity, and writes that "male costume is nothing new to me. I often take advantage of the freedom which it gives." She beats Holmes at his own game, but does so by adopting his terms (after all, she could have disguised herself as a nursemaid or washerwoman). One might ask students whether a feminist reading of the story is undermined by the fact that Irene Adler only enters the masculine sphere of action and initiative in the guise of a man.

Finally, ask why Holmes coolly ignores the King's outstretched hand. Although he began as the King's agent, working to defeat Irene Adler, by the end Holmes feels himself allied with her. He recognizes her as an equal—but the King still maintains she is "not on my level." Holmes despises the false values of the aristocrat: the King is arrogant and selfish; he's not very bright, but relies on his inherited wealth and position. In contrast, Adler and Holmes live by their wits; they are self-made masters of their craft. Middle-class readers would applaud the triumph of merit over birth. Steven Knight adds that "the King of Bohemia is a fairly thin disguise for the Prince of Wales, that great antagonist of Victorian respectability" ("The Case of the Great Detective," in Critical Essays, ed. Orel, 57).

Edith Nesbit
Fortunatus Rex & Co. (1901)

Originally fairy tales were passed on orally, but in the nineteenth century collectors began recording them. The brothers Grimm tales, for example, were translated into English in 1823. English writers, including John Ruskin, Charles Kingsley, Christina Rossetti, George MacDonald, and Oscar Wilde, adopted the form, producing literary fairy tales. English Puritanism disapproved of stories of elves and sprites, however, and some authors argued that children's literature should be strictly factual. Maria Edgeworth asked: "Why should the mind be filled with fantastic visions, instead of useful knowledge? Why should so much valuable time be lost?"

Fairy tales play with the border between the everyday world and the fantastic. In Lewis Carroll's Alice's Adventures in Wonderland (1865), a well-bred little girl finds herself talking to a White Rabbit, a Mad Hatter, and a Cheshire Cat—and occasionally correcting their manners. In Fortunatus Rex the familiar schoolroom world is transformed by a battle between rival magicians. Part of the fun of the story is that the King and Queen are such models of unimaginative respectability that they scarcely notice this injection of sorcery into their lives. The Queen goes right on making preserves and knitting stockings. The King concludes that the whole mad adventure shows "you cannot go far wrong if you insist on the highest references!"

This preposterous obsession with references—even the ruling sovereign is required to supply them—highlights Nesbit's mockery of all sorts of bourgeois conventions. The comedy begins in the second sentence, where Miss Robinson realizes she is "insufficiently educated" to do anything but teach. Have students read Cobbe's account of her own fashionable boarding school for background; Nesbit takes the genteel pretensions of Cobbe's school to a ludicrous extreme by having *all* the pupils be the daughters of "respectable monarchs."

The reliance on references also suggests a society where the basis of trust has been eroded, where everyone (including Miss Robinson, whose references are phony) is a sham. How can Miss Robinson be sure of her customers? How can they be sure of her? When the King asks, "But can I trust you?" she reminds him starchily that "We exchanged satisfactory references at the commencement of our business relations." Her no-nonsense answer is *no* answer, of course. But since their *only* relations are "business relations"—defined by the King's ability to pay ten thousand pounds a year—the King is forced to be satisfied.

In his grief, the King embarks on an entrepreneurial frenzy. Far from feeling any patrician disdain for money-grubbing, he eventually hangs the six princes, maintaining that "business is business after all." He floats a company of land developers (hence the title), making a fortune by building ugly little suburbs and destroying "all the pretty woods and fields." In lines that seem to come straight out of John Ruskin's *Modern Manufacture and Design* (1859) or William Morris's *The Beauty of Life* (1880), Nesbit remarks: "It is curious that nearly all the great fortunes are made by turning beautiful things into ugly ones. Making beauty out of ugliness is very ill-paid work." On one level, then, the story represents a showdown between money and magic, between the destructive forces of the capitalist (who makes beautiful things ugly) and the creative forces of the artist (who makes beauty out of ugliness).

The wealthy princesses "don't require the use of magic, they can get all they want without it." But Miss Robinson, a woman of modest means, must rely on her talent for magic—as Nesbit herself relied on writing to support her family. In real life, the middle-aged spinster with no money and limited education would be a hopeless downtrodden governess; here, in a comic fantasy of female empowerment, Nesbit cleverly transforms the schoolmarm into a powerful magician who invests in land and defeats the King's voracious building schemes. Miss Robinson drives a hard bargain: her price for restoring the princesses is to "make the land green again," thus fighting off the "greedy yellow caterpillars" of speculative building. On a mythic level, she accomplishes the redemption of the Waste Land; the blight upon the land, caused by the loss of the King's daughter, is reversed by Daisy's restoration. (The echo of the legend of Proserpine, who also returns to make the land green, may be ironic, in that housing development is hardly seasonal.)

Nesbit's satire has other targets as well. In *Forbidden Journeys* (1992) Auerbach and Knoepflmacher write that Nesbit was "a critic of imperialism, which she persistently identified with male domination." Thus in *Fortunatus Rex* "modern geopolitics are deliciously mocked." The imprisoned magician shouts: "Open up Africa!" or "Cut through the Isthmus of Panama" or "Cut up China!" Meanwhile, "the six princes assume that they are being asked to colonize the globe, and protest that they have no such imperialist ambitions" (135–37).

In "Of Babylands and Babylons: E. Nesbit and the Reclamation of the Fairy Tale," U. C. Knoepflmacher suggests that *Fortunatus Rex & Co.* "provides a self-mocking commentary on [Nesbit's] own imaginative enterprise by thematizing a female imposter's magical recovery of a threatened girlhood world" (*Tulsa Studies in Women's Literature* 6.2 [1987]). He argues that Nesbit "often saw herself as an impostress of sorts." Like Nesbit, Miss Robinson is a "dispenser of illusions [who] profits from her ability to make others believe in her fictions." Miss Robinson's restoration of the princesses and the land ("a female terrain") is both literal and literary, for it also represents Nesbit's "own reappropriation of a literary province," that of children's fantasy and fairy tales, which had been usurped by men (such as Perrault and the brothers Grimm, who had taken over the "folk-tales that had once been the pre-eminent possession of women story-tellers").

But if Miss Robinson embodies aspects of the adult writer, so Princess Daisy embodies aspects of Nesbit's childhood: "Daisy" was her own nickname. Nesbit's father died when she was four, and her mother was emotionally distant; Knoepflmacher points out that her fiction reenacts the trauma of abandonment and the fantasy of loving reunion. When Daisy disappears in *Fortunatus Rex*, her mother carries on with the housekeeping and has "not much time for weeping," while her father immerses himself in business. The story is partly about parental—and especially maternal—neglect, about being in trouble while one's mother is too busy to notice. The happy ending fulfills the frustrated wish to reconstruct a harmonious nuclear family. Autobiographically, then, Nesbit is both Miss Robinson *and* Daisy—the powerful artificer and teller of tales, but also the lost child reunited with her family.

John Ruskin
Modern Painters (1843-1860)

The critic John D. Rosenberg has called *Modern Painters* "perhaps the finest" book on art by an English writer; it is "the last great statement of the English Romantic renovation of sensibility, as the *Lyrical Ballads* is the first." He traces its genesis to the patterned carpet in the nursery upon which the solitary child developed his powers of observation (*The Genius of John Ruskin*, 18).

Ask students about Ruskin's definition of painting as a language, and "nothing more than language"—his point is that a painting's subject counts more than its style. He never abandoned this conviction, though he came to feel that he may have stated it too categorically, thus encouraging inferior artists to imagine they could get away with poor workmanship as long as they chose a noble subject. But Ruskin wasn't saying that style doesn't matter: on the contrary, he believed that a thorough mastery of technique was the starting point, not the goal, of great painting. Much later he said that while "there are few who enjoy the mere artifices of composition or dexterities of handling as much as I . . . the pictures were noblest which compelled me to forget them."

The Art for Art's Sake movement rebelled against the privileging of subject-matter, asserting the centrality of form and color. Students might like to hear about the Ruskin-Whistler trial (described briefly in our headnote to Whistler), and to read the excerpts from Whistler's "Ten O'Clock" lecture, which argues that art has "no desire to teach" and deplores people's habit of looking "not *at* a picture, but *through* it, at some human fact, that shall, or shall not, from a social point of view, better their mental or moral state" (see Perspectives: Aestheticism, Decadence, and the Fin de Siècle).

Turner was an enormous influence on Ruskin, and one might bring some reproductions of his work to class. The young Ruskin was inspired to begin *Modern Painters* as a defense against accusations that Turner's paintings distorted nature. Ruskin owned *The Slave Ship* for many years, eventually selling it because he found the subject "too painful to live with." But in contrast to the definition of greatness in art, this passage is sheer aestheticism; Ruskin confines mention of the painting's subject—slavery—to a footnote! It is all light, shadow, color, with scarcely a word about the immorality of slavery, about guilt or human suffering. But, as Oscar Wilde put it in *The Critic as Artist*, "who cares whether Mr Ruskin's views on Turner are sound or not? What does it matter? That mighty and majestic prose of his, so fervid and so fiery-coloured in its noble eloquence, so rich in its elaborate symphonic music . . . is at least as great a work of art as any of those wonderful sunsets that bleach or rot on their corrupted canvases in England's Gallery."

In *Ruskin and the Art of the Beholder* (1982) Elizabeth Helsinger points out the sheer energy of Ruskin's seeing: describing *The Slave Ship*, Ruskin puts "figure, story, and literary allusion last instead of first . . . meaning does not emerge easily or at once; it seems to come only out of energetic visual exploration" (181).

Like Carlyle, Pugin, Tennyson, and Morris, Ruskin contributed to the ongoing contrasts the Victorians made between their own century and the Middle Ages. Ruskin's angry sarcasm echoes Carlyle's: "whereas the mediaeval never painted a cloud but with the purpose of placing an angel in it, and a Greek never entered a wood without expecting to meet a god in it . . . [o]ur chief ideas about the wood are connected with poaching." Ruskin uses art now as a launching pad from which to analyze the flaws of the times, the ugliness, the want of solemnity, the ennui, the dull "modern principles of economy and utility."

The Stones of Venice (1851-53)

Just as Tennyson's *Idylls of the King* trace the rise and fall of Camelot, so the three volumes of *The Stones of Venice* recount the rise and fall of the Venetian empire— and both epics warn Victorian Britain of a similar fate if this latest empire doesn't mend its ways. The central theme is "the relation of the art of Venice to her moral temper" and this theme is most famously expressed in "The Nature of Gothic," the chapter where Ruskin relates "the life of the workman to his work."

Bring in pictures of Gothic architecture to give students an idea what Ruskin has in mind when he writes of pointed arches, vaulted roofs, flying buttresses, and grotesque sculptures. Also, have students look at our illustration from Pugin's *Contrasts* (though the evangelical Ruskin did not accept Pugin's linking of the Gothic revival to a Catholic revival). The argument of *The Stones of Venice* is that the very imperfections of the Gothic style were evidence of a moral society; the Renaissance represented degeneration and corruption. A memorable example (from the chapter "Roman Renaissance") is the carved statues on tombs who are propped up on one elbow, looking about instead of reclining peacefully—the worldly pride and vanity of the sixteenth-century soul "dared not contemplate its body in death" (one thinks of Browning's bishop ordering his tomb, apparently imagining that he'll still be around to enjoy it; Ruskin's comments on *The Bishop Orders His Tomb* are quoted in the first footnote).

For the pure pleasure of Ruskin's prose, read aloud the long passage about the bird's-eye view of Europe as it flies north from the Mediterranean to the polar north. Point out how even the language gradually modifies, with latinate words and geographical features (lake, promontories, volcano, variegated, lucent) giving way to Anglo-Saxon ones (clefts, heathy moor, wood, ice drift). The landscape, the human beings who inhabit it, and their artistic productions are all inextricably entwined: there is a "look of mountain brotherhood between the cathedral and the Alp." The capacity to appreciate both—the barbaric remnants of the Dark Ages, the ugly blister on the face of the earth—represented an important shift of taste. But more important, for Ruskin, is his conviction that art and architecture are expressions of religious principle, a kind of visible bodying forth of the inner moral temper of a people.

Thus the very perfection and symmetry of ancient Greek architecture are evidence that the Greek workman was in fact a slave. Medieval Christians, however, did away with this slavery, "Christianity having recognized, in small things as well as great, the individual value of every soul." The very rudeness of Gothic sculpture attests to the greater nobility of spirit that lay behind it, and Ruskin sees in the goblins and monsters of the old cathedral "signs of the life and liberty of every workman who struck the stone." This liberty modern industrial Europe has lost, and Ruskin sees the "degradation of the operative into a machine" as one of the leading causes of nineteenth-century political upheavals, even revolutions.

The argument about Gothic architecture thus segues into an indictment of the Industrial Revolution. Modern Englishmen, like ancient Greeks, desire an inhuman perfection that is nowadays only possible with machines. Compare Ruskin's depiction of a brutalized factory worker with Dickens's description of the monotonous lives of Coketown "hands" in *Hard Times*. Ruskin argues that the medieval craftsman was freer than the nineteenth-century operative: "there might be more freedom in England, though her feudal lords' lightest words were worth men's lives . . . than there is while the animation of her multitudes is sent like fuel to feed the factory smoke." (These words seem to echo Carlyle's about the brass-collared serf, Gurth, and might be a starting point for a discussion about the true nature of liberty, bringing in not only Carlyle but also Mill's On Liberty and Arnold's thoughts about "Doing as One Likes" in Culture and Anarchy). Ruskin's concerns about both the value of work and the plight of workers anticipate twentieth-century issues surrounding the nature of work, consumer advocacy, and human rights in a global economy. His indictment of materialist and consumerist society still resonates: "It is not that men are ill fed, but that they have no pleasure in the work by which they make their bread, and therefore look to wealth as the only means of pleasure." Discuss his claim that "every young lady . . . who buys glass beads is engaged in the slave-trade" (one might draw a contemporary parallel with current efforts to boycott the products of third-world sweatshops).

Ruskin did not invent the Gothic Revival, which began in the late eighteenth century, but he did more to popularize it than anyone else, even Pugin. As Kenneth Clark put it in The Gothic Revival (1928; 1962), Ruskin "disinfected" Gothic architecture for an audience wary of Catholicism. The success of the revival can be seen in buildings all over England—and on many American college campuses—but Ruskin himself was appalled at the unintended consequences of his own influence; in the preface to the 1874 edition of The Stones of Venice he wrote: "I would rather . . . that no architect had ever condescended to adopt one of the views suggested in this book, than that any should have made the partial use of it which has mottled our manufactory chimneys with black and red brick, dignified our banks and draper's shops with Venetian tracery, and pinched our parish churches into dark and slippery arrangements for the advertisement of cheap coloured glass and pantiles." For more on this topic see Michael Brooks's John Ruskin and Victorian Architecture (1987).

Modern Manufacture and Design (1859)

Invited to address the citizens of Bradford on art, Ruskin instead inveighed against the horrors of unrestrained industrial development. By this point in his career he had turned more towards social criticism than ever before; the lecture expands on the themes of The Nature of Gothic and prepares the way for Unto this Last (1860). Ruskin was ahead of his time in sounding warnings about the destruction of the environment, and he was vigorously denounced by a hostile audience; as Rosenberg explains, "If the uproar over Unto this Last now seems excessive, we need only recall that Ruskin attacked every principle held sacred by the economists and industrialists of the age" (The Genius of John Ruskin, 219).

The lecture begins with a ghastly futuristic vision of an England covered from shore to shore with chimneys, mine shafts, and engines, a landscape so clotted that there is no longer "even room for roads"—travel takes place on viaducts or in tunnels (an unfortunately prescient intuition!). Ruskin contrasts an imaginary seventeenth-century cottage with an industrial suburb, the one a pastoral paradise, the other a fallen wasteland. The imagery is biblical (a blighted garden, a blackened stream), suggesting an Eden transformed into Hell, or the New

Jersalem become Coketown ("the furnaces of the city foaming forth perpetual plague of sulphurous darkness").

Ruskin then creates a gorgeous word-portrait of fourteenth-century Pisa (with "bright river" and "brighter palaces"), another set-piece worth reading aloud for the hypnotic and poetic quality of the prose. Note the single 200-word sentence (beginning "Above all this scenery of perfect human life . . .") that piles clause upon clause to evoke a world where mankind lived in harmony with nature, and where nature incarnated the sacred; the sentence culminates with the word "God." In contrast to this fantasy of dazzling medieval splendour Ruskin reminds us of the "depressing and monotonous circumstances of English manufacturing life"—not, he says, from any hope that Bradford can become another Pisa, but to urge indus- trialists to "surround your men with happy influences and beautiful things."

For, Ruskin argues, "all that gorgeousness of the Middle Ages" was founded upon "the pride of the so-called superior classes." The fine arts have "been sup- ported by the selfish power of the noblesse" but now it is time to extend "their range to the comfort or the relief of the mass of the people"—to bring "the power and charm of art within the reach of the humble and the poor." The lecture closes with a plea not to allow greed and consumerism to destroy the arts, the virtues, and "the manners of your country."

Praeterita (1885–1889)

Victorian autobiographies have some notable omissions: just as Mill leaves out his mother, so Ruskin never mentions his six-year marriage to his cousin. But he warns us in the preface that he will pass over "in total silence things which I have no pleasure in reviewing." *Praeterita* offers one of the most famous depictions of an evangelical childhood, one in which his mother had it "deeply in her heart to make an evangelical clergyman of me." He describes the tedious Sundays, the long hours spent memorizing the Bible, and the prohibition on toys or companions. It was a childhood where the "chief resources" consisted of the carpet and the pat- terns on the wall-paper; the greatest misfortune was "that I had nothing to love." Yet, although Ruskin does not mitigate the errors of his well-intentioned elderly parents, the dominant impression is somehow one of richness, not of deprivation. If he was brought up in an Eden where it was forbidden to eat the fruit, it was, nonetheless, an Eden, a place of clear streams and marvellous summer excursions.

The passages in which Ruskin recalls his travels might be compared with some of the readings in our Travel and Empire section. Ruskin was no audacious ad- venturer roughing it in the wilderness; even as an adult he almost always travelled with his parents, and they travelled in style. They carried the comforts and rou- tines of home with them, for they were seeking neither excitement nor novelty: we "rejoiced the more in every pleasure—that it was not new." The Ruskins, who had not been born to wealth, felt a certain social insecurity that led them to keep to themselves, both at home and abroad. Their isolation further reinforced the pri- macy of Ruskin's pleasure in looking: wishing to be a "pure eye," his "entire de- light" was "observing without being myself noticed." His nostalgic contrast between the old days of travel by private carriage and the contemporary system of mass travel by rail echoes Thackeray's remarks (quoted in the headnote to Perspectives: The Industrial Landscape).

In "The Grande Chartreuse" Ruskin traces the "breaking down of my Puritan faith," and one might juxtapose this account with some of the selections in Perspectives: Religion and Science. Clearly these recollections were not among those which gave him pleasure because he begins to digress, as though to postpone the moment when he will reluctantly describe his "unconversion." At the time of writing, he was battling episodes of madness: "He suspended publication for six months," Rosenberg writes, then issued the superb chapter, "The Grande Chartreuse," "one of the most exquisitely written passages in all of *Praeterita*." In it, the lifelong conflict between Evangelicalism and Art sharpens into crisis—first there is the drawing made on a Sunday, then the urban pleasures of Turin, and finally the dreary sermon contrasting so powerfully with the glorious painting of Paul Veronese. Finally, the arbitrary life-denying restrictions of the evangelical Sabbath drive him to his "final apostasy from Puritan doctrine." Yet, ironically, the embrace of the aesthetic also marked its decline in his life, for Ruskin wrote that "the real new fact in existence for me was that my drawings did not prosper that year, and, in deepest sense, never prospered again." The decisive turn from art criticism to social criticism dates from this period, as though on some level Ruskin was atoning for his unconversion by dedicating himself to duty.

Students who would like to read more Ruskin, without tackling the brilliantly indexed 39 volumes of the Cook and Wedderburn edition, should see *The Genius of John Ruskin*, an anthology edited by John D. Rosenberg. For a good introduction to the somewhat confusing subject of Ruskin's views of earlier painters see Patrick Conner's "Ruskin and the 'Ancient Masters' in *Modern Painters*" (*New Approaches to Ruskin*, ed. Robert Hewison [1981], 17–32). The same volume contains an essay on "The Nature of Gothic" by John Unrau. A more recent collection, *John Ruskin and the Victorian Eye* (1993), has readable introductory essays and is lavishly illustrated.

Florence Nightingale
Cassandra (1852)

Myra Stark's introduction to the Feminist Press edition of *Cassandra* (1979) addresses the contradiction between the popular view of Nightingale as "the prototype of the saintly nurse" and the reality of her work as a reformer. Stark situates Nightingale's writing in the context of contemporary Victorian thinking about women's lives, and provides interesting biographical background. Stark focuses closely on *Cassandra*; for a more general introduction to Nightingale's career, students will enjoy the chapter on her in Elizabeth Longford's *Eminent Victorian Women* (1981).

Many of the selections in the Ladies and Gentlemen perspectives section relate closely to the issues that concern Nightingale. For example, Ellis, Cobbe, and Beeton illustrate the social expectations for middle- and upper-class women against which Nightingale was rebelling. Reading these three excerpts before turning to *Cassandra* helps make vivid the sort of world in which Nightingale lived, with its ideology of separate spheres and female subordination. Without some sense of this social setting, students may see her passionate complaints as merely neurotic.

Compare, for example, Nightingale's description of society—"you are not to talk of anything very interesting"—to Mrs. Beeton, who informs us that social calls "should be short, a stay of from fifteen to twenty minutes being quite sufficient," and the subjects of conversation "such as may be readily terminated." Similarly, the narrator of *Cranford* observes that "As everybody had this rule in their minds, whether they received or paid a call, of course no absorbing subject was ever spoken about. We kept ourselves to short sentences of small talk, and were punctual to our time." No wonder Nightingale felt herself stifled by the obligation "to drop a remark" every two minutes, unable "to follow up anything systematically."

Cobbe's description of life in a fashionable boarding school illuminates the difficulties that even wealthy girls faced in acquiring a serious education or putting it to some practical use; the very notion would have been regarded by Cobbe's headmistresses as "a deplorable dereliction." It was the duty of women in Nightingale's rank of life to be "Ornaments of Society," a duty her sister and mother embraced without question: as Nightingale wrote scathingly, "The whole occupation of Parthe and Mama was to lie on two sofas and tell one another not to get tired by putting flowers into water."

In *Cassandra* Nightingale astutely makes the connection between female infirmity and free time: "A married woman was heard to wish that she could break a limb that she might have a little time to herself." It does seem that illness was managed creatively by some Victorian women; think of Isabella Bird, an invalid at home, an adventurer abroad. Five years after writing *Cassandra*, Nightingale apparently employed this strategy herself: "Florence took to her 'deathbed' at the age of thirty-seven, and remained there on and off—mostly on—for another fifty-three years" (Longford, 86). She lived to be 90 and performed heroic amounts of work, all the while maintaining that she was too frail for any social engagements. In *Creative Malady* (1974) George Pickering argues that her illness was a socially acceptable way to protect herself from her family.

Nightingale wrestles with the question of how the needs of the individual—particularly the female individual—can be met within the confines of the family. Conventional wisdom urged women to sacrifice themselves on the altar of family life, but Nightingale likens the inevitable consequence of psychological repression to the foot-binding endured by Chinese girls. Directionless young women daydream over novels, whose secret charm is that the heroine has "no family ties (almost *invariably* no mother)." As if these images were not revealing enough, Nightingale's stinging parable of the lizard and the sheep proclaims her intense alienation from her family.

Although both Nightingale's essay and her career now serve as feminist inspirations, she herself was emphatically not a supporter of women's rights. In a letter to Harriet Martineau in 1861 Nightingale said: "I am brutally indifferent to the wrongs or the rights of my sex." Like George Eliot, she refused to sign the petition for female suffrage. "That women should have the suffrage, I think no one can be more deeply convinced than I," she wrote to J. S. Mill; nonetheless, she was reluctant to lend her influence and prestige to the cause. Wondering how we can "place Nightingale in the context of nineteenth-century feminism," Elaine Showalter asks whether she was "a great leader or merely a great complainer?" ("Florence Nightingale's Feminist Complaint: Women, Religion, and *Suggestions for Thought,*" *Signs* 6.3 [1981]). Myra Stark suggests that Nightingale was impatient with women who did not work as hard as she did, seeing their failure "as a failure of will."

Both Mary Poovey and Nancy Boyd explore how the Nightingale mystique was built upon powerful gender myths. In *Three Victorian Women Who Changed Their World* (1982) Boyd says, "The legend of Florence Nightingale contained much that people wanted to hear. . . . It centred on two folk heroes—the British soldier and the woman who serves him. . . . It epitomized what the Victorians believed to be the ideal relationship between man and woman" (186–87). In *Uneven Developments* (1988) Poovey writes that "the mythic figure of Florence Nightingale had two faces . . . the self-denying caretaker [and] . . . the tough-minded administrator. . . . These two versions of Florence Nightingale most obviously consolidated two narratives about patriotic service that were culturally available at midcentury—a domestic narrative of maternal nurturing and self-sacrifice and a military narrative of individual assertion and will" (168–69). What was not available at mid-century was *Cassandra* itself, which has given twentieth-century readers new insights into the private despair that launched the public figure.

PERSPECTIVES

Victorian Ladies and Gentlemen

This section serves as an introduction to some of the debates about gender and class in Victorian culture. The views of the different authors are by no means uniform: one imagines that neither Caroline Norton nor Harriet Martineau would have had much use for Mrs. Ellis and Mrs. Beeton. These passages on women's lives interact with one another in provocative ways: Norton's description of how married women forfeited virtually all rights might lead students to wonder why women ever agreed to marry; the Brontës' accounts of the miserable lives of governesses suggest at least one answer.

These selections can be paired with other texts throughout the anthology: contrast the conventional wisdom urged on women by Ellis and Beeton to the unconventional lives led by Isabella Bird, Frances Trollope, and Mary Kingsley (Travel perspectives). Ellis on separate spheres, and Cobbe and Martineau on women's education, provide good preparation for Nightingale's *Cassandra,* Barrett Browning's *Aurora Leigh,* and Eliot's *Margaret Fuller and Mary Wollstonecraft.* Norton on women's rights makes an excellent companion reading to Mill's *Subjection of Women.* Ellis's notions of female inferiority counterpoint Gaskell's portrayal of an all-female society of "Amazons," and Beeton's advice about social calls sets the

Cranford ladies' standards in context. Compare Nesbit's fanciful description of a fashionable boarding school in *Fortunatus Rex & Co.* with Cobbe's real-life recollections of just such a school.

Juxtapose these readings with the Industrial Landscape perspectives: where the earlier section offers glimpses of working-class lives and attitudes towards the family, childhood, and education (or lack of it), this one provides insight into the middle-class world. There, we read about women and children in factories and mines; here, we see how female inactivity becomes a status symbol. In Mayhew, boys and girls work the streets; here, they torment governesses and attend expensive schools.

The notion of what constitutes a "gentleman" or a "lady" was intensely fascinating to the Victorians, with their newly expanded middle classes. What did it take to belong? Could one lose caste? Only ladies could become governesses, but were governesses still really ladies? Such questions pervade Victorian literature: in Gaskell's *North and South* Margaret Hale, whose family has sunk into poverty, insists that she is still "a born and bred lady;" in Dickens's *Great Expectations* the convict Magwitch "makes" both a lady and a gentleman with his money.

Inevitably, questions of rank are linked not merely to birth and money, but to occupation and education. Women's educations might be trivial, but they were designed to ensure status. One could assemble a unit on Victorian education, reading not only this perspectives section but also chapter 1 of Mill's *Autobiography*, book 2 of *Aurora Leigh*, and the selections from Darwin's and Ruskin's autobiographies.

Frances Power Cobbe
[A Fashionable English Boarding School]

The memorable image of the girls "in full evening attire" being punished in the corner illustrates how upper-middle class women were educated to serve a largely decorative function as "Ornaments of Society." Cobbe gives a good picture of the nature of genteel female "accomplishments": foreign languages, music, dancing were essential, while "Morals and Religion" were at the bottom of the scale.

Cobbe writes in a lively, humorous way, for she has a keen sense of the ridiculous. Yet she's also outraged at the recollection that these girls, "full of capabilities," were expected to do nothing useful with their lives: "all this fine human material was deplorably wasted." Compare Cobbe's amused regret to Nightingale's passionate anguish in *Cassandra*: Cobbe was writing at the end of a long life in which she had, in fact, accomplished a great deal, while Nightingale wrote before she had found her vocation.

For an overview of nineteenth-century women's education, see Lee Holcombe's chapter, "Women and Education," in *Victorian Ladies at Work* (1973). Reviewing the findings of the Taunton Commission, which investigated the state of middle-class education in 1867, Holcombe notes that the majority of girls' schools were small boarding schools in converted private houses, that "snobbery was rampant," and that since chaperoned walks were the schoolgirls' only form of exercise, "pallor and crooked spines were supposedly their distinguishing marks" (23–24).

Academic achievements were not considered feminine; they might even be a hindrance in the marriage market, for who would care to marry a "bluestocking"?

As Joan Burstyn puts it in *Victorian Education and the Ideal of Womanhood* (1980), "No father wanted to be accused of educating his daughter so as to make her unsuited to marriage and motherhood; better to ignore the possibility of her remaining unmarried and in need of supporting herself than to run the risk that her very education would make her an old maid" (37).

Sarah Stickney Ellis
from The Women of England (1839)

Charlotte Brontë described her efforts to live up to the feminine ideal: "Following my father's advice . . . I have endeavored not only attentively to observe all the duties a woman ought to fulfil, but to feel deeply interested in them. I don't always succeed, for sometimes when I'm teaching or sewing, I would rather be reading or writing; but I try to deny myself; and my father's approbation amply rewards me for the privation" (qtd. in Joan Burstyn, *Victorian Education and the Ideal of Womanhood* [1980], 106). That even so gifted a woman as Brontë should regard reading as self-indulgence and force herself "to feel deeply interested" in housework suggests how pervasive—and potentially destructive—such attitudes were. Many more women than Brontë and Nightingale must have been led to distrust their own deepest instincts, to wonder what was wrong with them when they couldn't find fulfillment in home-making and self-denial.

Mention the famous title of Coventry Patmore's popular poem, *The Angel in the House* (1854-63), which has come to serve as shorthand for the domestic ideal promoted by Ellis (T. H. Huxley complained that girls were educated "to be either drudges or toys beneath man, or a sort of angel above him"). Although dated, Walter Houghton's chapter on "Love" (*The Victorian Frame of Mind*, 1957) and Richard Altick's chapter on "The Weaker Sex" (*Victorian People and Ideas*, 1973) provide brief introductions to Victorian attitudes concerning middle-class women and the sanctity of the home.

Mrs. Ellis aimed her books at a specific readership: those families "connected with trade or manufacture, as well as the wives and daughters of professional men of limited incomes." Davidoff and Hall's chapter on "Domestic Ideology and the Middle Class" (*Family Fortunes*, 1987) devotes several pages to Ellis (180-85); they point out that while "she addressed herself first and foremost to women who did not need to earn," she herself "clung with some guilt to her financial independence." They suggest that "a tension between the notion of women as 'relative creatures' and a celebratory view of their potential power lies at the heart of Mrs Ellis's writing and helps to explain her popularity." Nonetheless, "the moral panic engendered in the 1840s by the vision of women working in the mines, mills and factories of England was fuelled by the view that women's duty was to care for home and children"—a view that Mrs. Ellis "played a part in rigidifying."

In *Nobody's Angels: Middle-Class Women and Domestic Ideology in Victorian Culture* (1995) Elizabeth Langland analyzes gender ideology in terms of class (71-76). She notes that Ellis's "mystifying rhetoric" of ministering angels "effects at once a justification of the status quo and a concealment of the class issues as gender ones." Pointing out that "the myth of the home as a harmonious refuge from external strife and storms was daily in jeopardy from the discontent of servants," Langland argues that "supervision and control become a mistress's unacknowledged and mystified agenda, which is accompanied by a rhetoric of concern whose purpose is to reinscribe bourgeois women within a domestic ideology that posits the home as refuge from the workplace it refuses to recognize that it is."

Charlotte Brontë
from Letter to Emily (1839)

Anne Brontë
from Agnes Grey (1847)

Elizabeth Longford tells us that "Charlotte was stoned by a small Sidgwick of Stonegappe Hall. Nevertheless, her influence over this child was to develop satisfactorily until he burst out at dinner that he loved her; whereupon Mrs. Sidgwick barked, 'Love the governess, my dear!'" Brontë got her revenge: Mrs. Sidgwick became the model for Mrs. Reed in Jane Eyre (Eminent Victorian Women [1981], 30). Brontë returned to the governess in Shirley (1849), where a man is horrified at the thought that his niece might become one: "While I live, you shall not turn out as a governess, Caroline. I will not have it said that my niece is a governess." In The Victorian Governess (1993) Kathryn Hughes cites this passage as eloquent testimony "of the way in which middle-class women were responsible for reflecting and confirming the status of their male relatives" (33–34).

Show students how the details of Richard Redgrave's painting, The Poor Teacher (1844), convey visually many of the same points that the Brontës were making concerning the governess's misery, isolation, and ambiguous social position.

The Victorians were fascinated and troubled by the governess, although M. Jeanne Peterson remarks in "The Victorian Governess" that her suffering "seems pale and singularly undramatic when compared with that of women in factories and mines" (Suffer and Be Still, ed. Martha Vicinus [1973]). (Brontë, however, declared that "I could like to work in a mill. I could feel mental liberty.") The governess's difficulties arose principally because, as a contemporary observer put it, she "is not a relation, not a guest, not a mistress, not a servant—but something made up of all. No one knows exactly how to treat her." Elizabeth Eastlake defined the ideal governess: "Take a lady, in every meaning of the word, born and bred, and let her father pass through the gazette [bankruptcy], and she wants nothing more to suit our highest beau idéal of a guide and instructress to our children."

The fact that being a governess was an acceptable occupation at all is connected with the ideology of separate spheres—at least she was working in the home, engaged in the feminine task of caring for children. The lack of alternatives meant that "for much of the nineteenth century, the supply of governesses far exceeded the demand" (Hughes, 37). Precisely because they were easier to replace than good servants, "employers frequently placed their parlourmaid's comfort and contentment above that of the two-a-penny governess" (154).

The governess features frequently in Victorian novels: after Jane Eyre one thinks of Becky Sharp in Thackeray's Vanity Fair (1847). In Daniel Deronda (1876)

Gwendolyn marries a detestable man to avoid becoming a governess. Yet Hughes points out that "it is one of the great ironies of Victorian history that we know virtually nothing about the 25,000 women who actually worked as governesses" (xi). We do know, however, that the lunatic asylums were "supplied with a larger proportion of their inmates from the ranks of young governesses than from any other class of life" (Lady Eastlake, qtd. by Hughes, 163). In *Uneven Developments* (1988) Mary Poovey has a chapter called "The Anathematized Race: The Governess and *Jane Eyre*" (126–163).

John Henry Cardinal Newman
from The Idea of a University (1852)

From the first sentence, Newman's notion of a gentleman contrasts sharply with the manly, fighting ethos of Hughes, Kingsley, and Newbolt, for how could a fighter avoid inflicting pain? Further, how could soldiers treat an enemy "as if he were one day to be our friend"? Muscular Christians would have seen effeminacy in every sentence of Newman's (as they had seen it in the entire Oxford Movement). The adjectives Newman uses to define a gentleman—tender, gentle, merciful, patient, forbearing, resigned—could easily apply to the model Victorian woman. What sort of man "submits" and rarely "takes the initiative"? What sort of man can be compared to "an easy chair or a good fire"?

While Newman himself hardly disdained a good fight (as his triumphant rejoinder to Kingsley in his *Apologia Pro Vita Sua* demonstrates), he clearly endorses a less aggressive ideal of male behavior. In *Dandies and Desert Saints* (1995) James Eli Adams writes: "there is no question that Newman from the outset understood his Christian discipline to be an affront to prevalent, broadly aristocratic norms of masculinity" (85); "in his 1843 sermon, 'Wisdom and Innocence' . . . Newman cannily anticipates the dynamics of Kingsleyan manliness well before its public manifestation" (99).

In *The Idea of the Gentleman in the Victorian Novel* (1981) Robin Gilmour says that Newman's "is a superb, searching definition, feeling its way . . . into the nuances of the gentlemanly character. Justice is done to the courtesy and stoicism of that character, but Newman also mercilessly lays bare the pride at the heart of the gentleman's self-effacement. Behind the seeming selflessness lies a real selfishness; the gentleman will surrender the outworks of his personal convenience in order to preserve the citadel of his self-esteem intact. Newman acutely perceives that there is an exquisite vanity at work in the gentleman's courtesy which works against deep commitment or self-surrender. Hence the strikingly negative character of the definition. . . . Newman's gentleman is not a man who does but a man who refrains from doing" (91).

In *The English Gentleman* (1987) David Castronovo proposes that the entire definition is in fact a parody of extravagant idealizers of the gentleman: "He reduces the gentlemanly ideal to absurdity by writing his own purple passage, a stretch of prose that destroys the ideal—for the careful reader—by parodying its pomposity and confusion." Castronovo calls it "an ironic bravura performance staged to show the inflated claims of the gentleman and the inadequacy of gentlemanly traits when they are compared to a higher good" (64). The gentleman is a hollow man, all surface, embodying the poverty of worldly values; for Newman, he is "a grand illusion, a marvellous spectacle" (65).

Caroline Norton
from A Letter to the Queen (1855)

Norton's writings are of interest, not merely because they so dramatically portray the legal situation of Victorian married women, but because of the assumptions those laws reveal about women's very nature. The title of an essay by Frances Power Cobbe concerning married women's property rights says it all: "Criminals, Idiots, Women, and Minors: Is the Classification Sound?" (*Fraser's Magazine* [1868]). In *Uneven Developments* (1988) Mary Poovey has a good chapter entitled "Covered but Not Bound: Caroline Norton and the 1857 Matrimonial Causes Act." Poovey writes: "The point that Norton makes indirectly is that women's legal incapacities are a function of their social *position*, not of natural, biological inferiority" (65).

Poovey notes that the debates surrounding reform called attention to women's paradoxical "nonexistence" in the eyes of the law, and also, by "acknowledging the fact of marital unhappiness . . . inevitably exposed the limitations of the domestic ideal." Further, "in publicizing the economic underpinnings of many marital disputes, the parliamentary debates threatened to reveal the artificiality of separate spheres" (52). If class stability depended on "the morality of women and the integrity of the domestic sphere," then "allowing anyone to petition for divorce would imperil the social order" (59–60).

Although Norton played a central role in the debates about women's rights, she did not herself demand equality; she merely asked for protection. In this sense, "her challenge actually reinforced the idealized domesticity she seemed to undermine." Nonetheless, her story made it clear "that women were not necessarily protected in exchange for their dependence" (81).

The story of reform is told by Lee Holcombe in "Victorian Wives and Property: Reform of the Married Women's Property Law, 1857–1882" (A *Widening Sphere*, ed. Martha Vicinus [1977]) and in *Wives and Property: Reform of the Married Women's Property Law* (1983). Although the 1857 Matrimonial Causes Act began to improve the legal position of women, until the 1880s they could legally be sent to prison for denying their husbands "conjugal rights."

George Eliot
Margaret Fuller and Mary Wollstonecraft (1855)

Eliot used the occasion of an anonymous book review to offer her own views on the position of women, arguing for "that thorough education of women which will make them rational beings in the highest sense." To put her essay in context, one might assign Wollstonecraft's *Vindication of the Rights of Woman* (1792), J. S. Mill's *The Subjection of Women*, and also some of the selections concerning women's rights and education in the Ladies and Gentlemen perspectives section, particularly Cobbe, Ellis, Norton, and Martineau. Florence Nightingale's passionate *Cassandra*, which was also written in the 1850s, makes an excellent counterpart to Eliot's carefully reasoned review.

The essay has troubled readers eager to enlist George Eliot in the ranks of nine-teenth-century feminists. On the one hand, she argues in favor of women's educa-tion, and quotes approvingly Margaret Fuller's words about letting women be sea captains, or letting girls saw wood and use carpenter's tools. On the other hand, she writes: "Unfortunately, many over-zealous champions of women assert their ac-tual equality with men—nay, even their moral superiority to men." Students are likely to have difficulty with this passage, and to assume that Eliot does not believe equality to be either possible or desirable.

However, her logic is more subtle: "If it were true, then there would be a case in which slavery and ignorance nourished virtue, and so far we should have an argu-ment for the continuance of bondage. But we want freedom and culture for woman, because subjection and ignorance have debased her." In other words, if women, lack-ing education and opportunity, are nonetheless *already* equal or even superior to men, then what are the grounds for granting women the things they lack?

Kathleen McCormack discusses how Eliot's novels enact various aspects of *The Rights of Woman* ("The Sybil and the Hyena: George Eliot's Wollstonecraftian Feminism," *Dalhousie Review* 63.4 [1983–84], 602–14). She says that these connec-tions "help explain many of the problems . . . that have led to feminists' percep-tion of Eliot as an awkward nineteenth-century puzzle piece rather than as a force in the development of feminism. Point for point, Eliot's novels illustrate Wollstonecraft's feminist arguments, possibly most importantly the argument rel-evant to Rosamund [in *Middlemarch*]: that the education that society currently de-signs for girls ultimately produces not an angel in the house but an adulteress."

The male voice in which Eliot writes, both in this essay and in many of her nov-els, has often been noted. Here, for example, she refers to "our wives," and the last sentence presumes a male reader, one likely to be but half-interested in this whole business of women's lives. In adopting a masculine stance, is Eliot distancing herself from her sisters, as some critics have claimed? Or is she employing a rhetorical strat-egy calculated to play on the fears of the male audience? For instance, she suggests that men "are really in a state of subjection to ignorant and feeble-minded women," for weakness always triumphs over strength, "as you may see when a strong man holds a little child by the hand, how he is pulled hither and thither." Eliot cleverly transforms the familiar sexist comparison of women to children into an unsettling image of male vulnerability. She is arguing, in essence, that man will strengthen his own position by strengthening woman's: better to deal openly with a "rational being" who will "yield in trifles" than to be yoked to an "unreasoning animal."

Eliot's novels demonstrate her awareness of the debilitating effects of limited ed-ucation and opportunities on talented women, such as Maggie Tulliver and Dorothea Brooke. Even a vain and selfish woman like Rosamund Vincy might have been better off if she'd had a real education instead of a finishing school, and if she had had something to do all day. Eliot warns in this essay that "men pay a heavy price for their reluctance to encourage self-help and independent resources in women. The precious meridian years of many a man of genius have to be spent in the toil of routine, that an 'establishment' may be kept up for a woman who can understand none of his secret yearnings, who is fit for nothing but to sit in her drawing-room like a doll-Madonna in her shrine." In *Middlemarch* she would later dramatize this warning in Lydgate's appalling fate: an intelligent man's ambitions are wrecked by his own insistence on having an ornamental wife who cannot begin to sympathize with his dreams. Eliot's heroines suffer from having no outlets for their energy and abilities, but it is not *only* the heroines who suffer: as she insists here in *Margaret Fuller and Mary Wollstonecraft*, when Woman is debased, then so is Man.

Yet Eliot was not herself an active champion of women's causes; she refused, for example, to sign the petition for female suffrage that J. S. Mill presented to Parliament in 1866. No doubt she felt hampered by her own anomalous position as an unmarried "wife." McCormack suggests that Wollstonecraft's life would have served Eliot as a cautionary tale, for she read *The Rights of Woman* at a critical juncture in her own life: "Just back in England after her elopement with George Henry Lewes, she was experiencing constant humiliation and rejection for having pursued precisely the same course that Wollstonecraft had followed." Her strong identification with Wollstonecraft might, somewhat paradoxically, explain her "adopting the low feminist profile for which she is often criticized today."

Thomas Hughes
from Tom Brown's School Days (1857)

Tom Brown's School Days introduces the American student to the world of the English public school and to the schoolboy code that governed the conduct of the Victorian gentleman. The whole question of what constituted a "gentleman" was hotly contested among the Victorians (perhaps most famously in Dickens's *Great Expectations*), but it was generally agreed that the product of a public school such as Eton, Harrow, Winchester or Rugby was a gentleman, no matter what his social origins might have been.

In *The Return to Camelot* (1981) Mark Girouard observes that Hughes's philosophy of life "owed much to Carlyle: life was a constant fight between good and evil; strength of intellect was useless and even dangerous without strength of character. But *Tom Brown's Schooldays* . . . went far beyond Carlyle in suggesting that the best way to moral prowess was physical prowess, in actual fighting or in sport" (166). Tom, for example, voices his ambitions thus: "I want to be A 1 at cricket and football, and all the other games. . . . I want to carry away just as much Latin and Greek as will take me through Oxford respectably. . . . I want to leave behind me . . . the name of a fellow who never bullied a little boy, or turned his back on a big one."

Not everybody endorsed this conception of the gentlemanly ideal; in *Jane Eyre* Charlotte Brontë conveyed her disdain by putting a version of it in the mouth of the arrogant and disagreeable Blanche Ingram: "as to the *gentlemen*, let them be solicitous to possess only strength and valour: let their motto be:—hunt, shoot, and fight: the rest is not worth a fillip."

Ask students to analyze the values implicit in Brooke's speech to "the dear old School-house." Why would he rather "win two School-house matches running, than get the Balliol scholarship"? Those interested in learning more about the gentlemanly ideal might turn to Girouard's book; for more on the public schools themselves, see Jonathan Gathorne-Hardy's *The Public School Phenomenon* (1977),

J. R. de S. Honey's *Tom Brown's Universe: The Development of the English Public School* (1977), J. A. Mangan's *Athleticism in the Victorian and Edwardian Public School* (1981), and John Chandos's *Boys Together* (1984). Instructors may want to teach Kingsley and Newbolt in conjunction with Hughes.

Isabella Beeton
from The Book of Household Management (1861)

The growing popularity of etiquette books beginning around the 1830s attests to the rise of the middle class and the fluidity of social caste. Clearly there was a large market for books that would tell women how to pay a social call or manage servants. Yet in *Nobody's Angels* (1995) Elizabeth Langland argues that "it is a popular misconception that these etiquette manuals helped to facilitate the movement of individuals from a lower to a higher sphere in society. In fact, they . . . consolidated an image of the genteel middle class" (28). "The very popularity of the etiquette manuals reveals a pervasive awareness of and commitment to the class distinctions they create and reinforce" (32).

These manuals offer fascinating glimpses of the intricate maze of duties, manners, and social codes that defined middle-class womanhood. They also demonstrate that, despite the carefully constructed impression of cultivated leisure, Victorian middle-class women were not lounging about; the home was a workplace where genuine labor was done and servants had to be hired, trained, and supervised. Beeton compares the housewife to the Commander of an Army; another etiquette guide compared her to the "captain of a seventy-four" gun warship (Langland 47). With her emphasis on the housewife's multitude of duties, "Beeton underscores only what is generally accepted in the etiquette guides and household manuals, but often mystified in the novels, tracts, and sermons: the mistress's key management role" (45).

Beeton stresses the moral as well as administrative dimension of being a good commander: the housewife must serve as an exemplar for her servants. If she sleeps late, her servants "will surely become sluggards." Beeton reinforces her precepts with an implicit threat: a woman must perform up to snuff or risk losing her man to the rival attractions of clubs and taverns. The suggestion that the feminine domain of the home was in competition with the masculine domain of dining-houses—rather than a refuge from it—is a revealing twist on the ideology of separate spheres.

Queen Victoria
Letters and Journal Entries on the Position of Women

Read against the stereotype of the Victorian woman as selfless and uncomplaining, the letters of the Queen—who supposedly embodied the domestic ideal—are almost comical. She dwells on her own sufferings, she resents the births of her children, and she grumbles that her husband never sympathizes when she bemoans the lot of women. In one startling epistle, she calls the news of her daughter's first pregnancy "horrid"—and grimly predicts a miscarriage. Nor did her acute awareness of women's trials make the Queen a supporter of efforts to improve their legal and educational position: she terms the suffrage movement "mad, wicked folly."

Queen Victoria was nothing if not outspoken. Yet if her character did not quite match the feminine ideal, she nonetheless provided a compelling, if paradoxical, image of female power. The competent presence of a woman at the head of an enormous empire seemed to undermine the prevailing orthodoxy about the home being the only proper sphere for females—an orthodoxy Victoria herself seemed all the more determined to uphold. She was always troubled by her dual roles of monarch and matriarch: in 1852, after fifteen years on the throne, Victoria wrote, "I am every day more convinced that *we women, if* we are to be good women, *feminine* and *amiable* and *domestic,* are not *fitted to reign.*" The contradictions that both Victoria and her subjects perceived as inherent in her position make a good starting point for discussions about nineteenth-century domestic ideology.

Students interested in Victoria might like Elizabeth Longford's 1964 biography, which has been called "the envy and despair" of subsequent biographers; these include Stanley Weintraub (1987) and Dorothy Thompson (1990).

Charles Kingsley
from Letters and Memories

In *Dandies and Desert Saints: Styles of Victorian Masculinity* (1995) James Eli Adams writes that Kingsley's "ideal of 'muscular Christianity,' formulated largely in antagonism to Newman's ascetic discipline, has long been seen to codify a crucial shift in Victorian conceptions of masculinity, through which an earlier paradigm of spiritual discipline gave way to a celebration of unreflective bodily vigor." Interestingly, Adams argues that "Kingsley's 'muscular' ideal of manhood is structured by the very asceticism he insistently attacked" (17); "Newman's ideal of priestly celibacy . . . was a standing affront to Kingsley's celebrations of marital bliss" (84). Adams associates Kingsley's popularity with British anxieties about upholding its farflung empire, as well as with the public schools' glorification of "success on the playing fields" (109).

Mark Girouard suggests that Kingsley's obsession with manliness "was probably inspired by his friendship with Thomas Hughes" (*The Return to Camelot*, 136). While the term "muscular Christian" may have struck Hughes and Kingsley as slightly ridiculous, Girouard points out that it "caught to perfection" the flavor of their doctrine. "Emotionally they found physical prowess gloriously exciting . . . they preferred a strong man to a clever one" (143). Girouard notes, however, that "under his surface aggressiveness [Kingsley] was neurotic, morbid, and liable to frequent collapses; his heroes were what he would like to have been, not what he was. There is a hysterical edge to his writing that can be very distressing." Girouard adds that "Kingsley's enthusiasm for working men's causes diminished as he grew older. . . . In 1865, when Governor Eyre's prompt but savage suppression of disaffection in Jamaica divided the English Establishment into two camps, Kingsley supported Eyre, and lost Thomas Hughes's friendship in consequence" (144).

For further reading see *Muscular Christianity* (1994), a collection of essays edited by Donald E. Hall.

Sir Henry Newbolt
Vitaï Lampada (1897)

Newbolt's poem merges the language of the playing fields with the language of the killing fields: the "Captain" is at once a schoolboy heading his rugby team, like Brooke in *Tom Brown's School Days*, and an officer urging his men on in battle. The schoolboy who "rallies the ranks" echoes Brooke's rousing speech to his teammates. Newbolt's glorification of bloodshed may shock modern American students—or strike them as naive—but it is the logical extension of the credo proclaimed forty years earlier in Hughes's novel: "From the cradle to the grave, fighting, rightly understood, is the business, the real, highest, honestest business of every son of man." When one of the boys in *Tom Brown's School Days* chooses a career as an army officer in India, the master says, "He'll make a capital officer," and Tom exclaims, "Aye, won't he! No fellow could handle boys better, and I suppose soldiers are very like boys."

Writing about World War I in *The Public School Phenomenon* (1977), J. Gathorne-Hardy says: "Letter after letter from the front says how glad the writers are not to have let school or house down. . . . And these themes are echoed again in the school obituaries. The public school ethos had gone beyond the grave. . . . To play well for your school meant to die well for your country" (199–200). One might think that the horrors of that war put an end to such glamorizations, but as late as the 1920s the American sportswriter Grantland Rice wrote, "when the One Great Scorer comes / To write against your name / He marks—not that you won or lost—/ But how you played the game."

In *The Return to Camelot* (1981) Mark Girouard has a chapter called "Playing the Game" where he reproduces Baden-Powell's 1908 adaptation of *Vitaï Lampada* for performance by Boy Scouts (233–34). Girouard adds: "It is still widely believed that the Duke of Wellington said, 'The Battle of Waterloo was won on the playing fields of Eton.' He never said anything of the sort, but the legend . . . had been taking shape since the 1850s."

Girouard traces the rise of sports in the nineteenth century, and links the Victorian code of the sportsman with the concept of gentlemanliness and with chivalry. Ask students to reflect on how phrases taken from sports, such as "it's not cricket," "the whole nine yards," "par for the course," and so on, became part of the language. How do sports come to serve as metaphors for character and moral conduct?

For more on the connections between public school sports and the work of empire, see J. A. Mangan's *The Games Ethic and Imperialism* (1986).

Matthew Arnold
Poetry

Though poets and critics have found fault with the style of Arnold's poetry, they have always taken seriously what he has to say about a central problem of modern life: the difficulty of achieving true communion with another person, or even one-self. In "Matthew Arnold," in *The Use of Poetry and the Use of Criticism* (1933), T. S. Eliot commented on Arnold's forthrightness: "With all his fastidiousness and su-perciliousness and officiality, Arnold is more intimate with us than Browning, more intimate than Tennyson ever is, except at moments, as in the passionate flights of *In Memoriam*. . . . His poetry, the best of it, is too honest to employ any but his genuine feelings of unrest, loneliness and dissatisfaction" (106). Most readers tend to agree with Eliot, whose essay is harsh but fair on Arnold's techni-cal limitations and murky definitions. W. H. Auden, on the other hand, felt that Arnold's openly acknowledged difficulty in penetrating his "buried life" meant that his own inhibitions "thrust his gift in prison till it died // And left him noth-ing but a jailer's voice and face," so that "all rang hollow but the clear denuncia-tion" of his times ("Matthew Arnold," 1940).

From early to late, Arnold's poems thus raise a tortured question: if we cannot know ourselves or others, how can we discover and communicate our true feelings about this underlying alienation? The "Marguerite" poems speak with conviction about human longing, the capacity for both self-deception and disillusionment, and the deep-rooted loneliness of each individual. In the second poem Arnold im-plies, in the face of Donne, that every man is an island. His beautiful concluding line suggests that a sea of tears divides us all, and that, in a kind of abortive gene-sis, God separated lands and waters without ever continuing on to make an Adam and Eve who could couple to compensate for this estranging process.

The poems have provoked keen speculation as to Marguerite's identity. "Marguerite, at best, is a shadowy figure," writes Eliot, "neither very passionately desired nor very closely observed, a mere pretext for lamentation. His personal emotion is indeed most convincing when he deals with an impersonal subject" (107–108). Arnold's biographers and editors, however, such as Hugh Kingsmill, Park Honan, and Miriam Allott, have sought an actual woman as the source of Arnold's poems—a French waitress, a well-educated Englishwoman and family friend named Mary Claude, or "a pious and rather literary, though appealing, young holiday friend," respectively. How important is it that the poems be about a real love affair? Is it more important to see them as the self-revelation of the *speaker*, who need not be Arnold at all? Is Arnold conveying an insight into the na-ture of human experience, the catalyst for which is relatively insignificant? The "Marguerite" debate, along with the issue of how relevant biographical informa-tion should be to literary interpretation, is taken up by Wendell Harris and Bill Bell in the Fall 1989 and 1991 issues of *The Victorian Newsletter*.

Dover Beach is one of the great poems of the era, and, with its irregular lines, rhymes, and stanzas, which seem to echo "the turbid ebb and flow" of its subject, it is Arnold's finest foray into modernist poetics. Stefan Collini even calls it "the first major 'free-verse' poem in the language" (*Matthew Arnold* [1988], 41). Likely written in 1851, perhaps on Arnold's return from his honeymoon, the poem pon-ders the withdrawing tide of religious faith in a way that links it to *Stanzas on the Grande Chartreuse*. The overall tenor of the poem has been read variously as a clas-sic expression of Romantic self-sufficiency, or of Victorian doubt. Note the apparent contradiction of the injunction, "Ah, love, let us be true / To one another" in a world that, the speaker claims, has no love in it. Is this a dubious come-on, a Victorian agnostic's version of *To His Coy Mistress*? Or is it a heartfelt appeal to romantic love as the one stay against confusion in a brutal post-Darwinian world?

The speaker is usually assumed to be Arnold (or, in Clough's words, "someone very like him"), although much attention has been given to the possible situation in which the narrator addresses his "love." Most notable is Anthony Hecht's satiric poem *The Dover Bitch* (*The Hard Hours* [1960]), which depicts the auditor as an impatient prostitute. But recently Eugene R. August has argued that the poem is "gender neutral," and that "every line of the poem could just as plausibly be spoken by a woman as by a man. . . . For all we know, the poem's speaker may be a recreation by Arnold of what a woman (Marguerite? Mary Claude? Frances Lucy Wightman? someone else?) said to *him*" ("The Dover Switch, Or the New Sexism at 'Dover Beach,'" *Victorian Newsletter* [Spring 1990]: 36). August says the poem should seen as "an expression of a *human* feeling shared by women and men alike" (37). His article follows from a lively debate over the poem's meaning by Gerhard Joseph, Nathan Cervo, and Tom Hayes in *The Victorian Newsletter* (Spring 1988 and Fall 1989).

Whoever is speaking, the text is haunted by echoes, including much-disputed possible references to Sophocles in stanza 2 (*Antigone* 583ff or *Trachiniae* 112ff), and to Thucydides or Tennyson in the last line (*Peloponnesian War* 7.44 or "The Passing of Arthur," lines 90ff). In *Matthew Arnold and the Betrayal of Language* (1988), David G. Riede offers a fine overall discussion of the poem (196–203). He points out how the poem's opening parallels that of Wordsworth's sonnet *It is a Beauteous Evening*, while there are significant echoes of Milton's *Paradise Lost* toward the end: "neither joy, nor love" is what Hell holds for Satan (*PL* 4:509), and "the world, which seems / To lie before us" revises the epic's concluding passage "The world was all before them" (*PL* 12.646). Riede also summarizes Ruth Pitman's important article ("On Dover Beach," *Essays in Criticism* 23 (1973): 109–136), which makes a strong case for the insubstantiality of the landscape in the poem (due to geological erosion and metaphysical doubt—perhaps picking up on section 123 of *In Memoriam*). Pitman also notes that there are ghosts of two sonnets in the first twenty-eight lines, and the eroded octet of a third at the conclusion. As Riede puts it, "like 'The Buried Life,' it is a poem that in subtle ways is about its own decomposition" (196).

The poem's fame and emotional appeal have caused it to function in contemporary culture as something of a high-art symbol of the crisis of belief in the self, nature, or science. There have been sightings in Pynchon's *Gravity's Rainbow* and in cyberpunk novels. See Robin Roberts, "Matthew Arnold's 'Dover Beach,' Gender, and Science Fiction," *Extrapolation* 33.3 (1992): 245–257.

Dating from the same period (early 1850s), *Lines Written in Kensington Gardens*, *The Buried Life*, and *Stanzas from the Grande Chartreuse* are built around inside-outside contrasts, written from a momentary vantage point wherein Arnold, presenting himself as an estranged outsider, gains a privileged glimpse into the bosom of nature, self, or faith. In postlapsarian *Kensington Gardens* the poet stresses the physical contrasts between country and city, park and street, in order to make an emotional and spiritual opposition between nature's peace and the city's deathly uproar. In a variation on Cowper's famous eighteenth-century dictum "God made the country, and man made the town" (alluded to in the penultimate stanza), Arnold uses a sequestered nook in the park to cast himself, Wordsworth-style, into a more vital relationship with himself and his past. But the revealing images of nurse, cradle, child, and broken toy posit not simply a further contrast, but also an underlying connection, between frazzled adult poet and helpless child. Both can only pray that Mother Nature will look after them.

The Buried Life employs Arnold's characteristic river and sea imagery to channel its way to his inmost self. It is as if he were a geological formation concealing an underground stream that might, if plumbed, buoy him toward that deeper calm he strains for in Kensington Gardens. For many readers, the search for "the buried life" is the quintessence of Arnold's poetry, and of the modern condition in general. But how do we know when we are (or aren't) in touch with our "true" feelings? (Note how little Arnold actually tells us about his). Consider the validity of the archeological (or funereal) metaphor the poem is built on: how useful or misleading is our cultural predisposition to value depth over surface? In an essay that is itself rather lofty and Arnoldian, Philip Davis writes of the centrality of the poem and its sentiment for the whole of nineteenth-century poetry: "in what seem to me the greatest lines written by anyone in the century, Arnold captures what (in retrospect) we can see it would take to turn Thomas Hardy back towards William Wordsworth, when suddenly 'A bolt is shot back somewhere in our breast / And a lost pulse of feeling stirs again'" ("Arnold's Gift: The Poet in an Unpoetic Age," Essays and Studies, special Arnold issue, ed. Miriam Allott [1988]: 78).

In Stanzas from the Grande Chartreuse Arnold situates himself within the famous community of monks, not—he is at pains to point out—"as their friend, or child," but as a fellow seeker who leaves worldly paths "to possess my soul again." Here he finds himself in the company of those whose faith is as out of favor with the world as his melancholy introspection; he declares himself ready "to die out with these / Last of the people who believe!" (lines 111–112). In the poem's central stanza, the speaker presents himself as "Wandering between two worlds, one dead, / The other powerless to be born" (lines 85–86). These lines epitomize the Victorian sense of living in "an age of transition," when Christianity appears to have lost its power to console and guide, and nothing convincing has appeared in its stead. Arnold captures the feeling of frustrated postponement and self-division that wracks Carlyle in Sartor Resartus, Tennyson in In Memoriam, and even Hopkins in his late sonnets.

It is typically Arnoldian to want to wait out this period somewhere isolated, while still feeling that his life is driven onward "To life, to cities, and to war" (line 180). Yet his concluding remarks (beginning with line 169) are couched in a strange, extended simile in which Arnold compares his Victorian, post-Romantic generation to children who live in an abbey in the forest (not mountains). Like Ladies of Shalott, they catch gleams "Of passing troops in the sun's beam" (line 177), but they resist the charm of "bugle music on the breeze," instead answering that this call has come too late for such "shy recluses" as they. Thus the poem ends by turning Arnold and his fellow orphans into monks after all, perhaps suggesting that even if a new world were to be born soon, they would be unable to inhabit it.

The Scholar Gipsy (is the title a contradiction in terms?) presents the scholar as having been spared the disease of modern life because centuries ago he had the good sense to anticipate Arnold's advice: "fly our paths, our feverish contact fly!" He is a romantic version of the monks' religiously based renunciation of the world in *Stanzas*. But the rejection of an Oxford education brings questionable success: is the ex-scholar perhaps fatally deluded, doomed to wander enchanted in his time-warp, forever unsatisfied, because of his misguided quest? Is he a victim of the gipsies' magic, rather than the master of it? His professed intention to reveal their secrets to the world when he finds them out may have been his undoing. His desire to communicate hidden knowledge is one of the many features in the poem that link the gipsy-scholar to the poet, and may echo Coleridge's promise at the end of *Kubla Khan* to rebuild the pleasure dome himself *if* he can "revive within me" the song of the Abyssinian maid.

In his rich, densely descriptive Keatsian stanzas, Arnold seems to be positing a vague, solitary identification with the natural world as an alternative to modern angst and alienation. He also implies that the source of this angst has at least two historical locations. The first is when the scholar joins the gipsies, the moment in the seventeenth century when the Hebraism of Puritan England won out over the Hellenistic spirit of the Renaissance (see *Culture and Anarchy*). The second source of civilization's woes, it is suggested in the complex final simile, can be found in ancient times, when the "merry," intrusive Greeks first came into Tyrian waters. Thus the "repeated shocks" of change that "wears out the lives of mortal men" are as old as Western culture, and what seem the Victorian poet's particular woes are those of introspective, solitary souls in every era. For more on the way in which Arnold grounds (and ungrounds) his poem historically, see Antony Harrison, "Matthew Arnold's Gipsies: Intertextuality and the New Historicism," *Victorian Studies* 29 (1991): 365–383; and Alan Grob, "Arnold's 'The Scholar Gipsy': The Use and Abuse of History," *Victorian Poetry* 34.2 (1996): 149–174.

Thyrsis is unusual as a pastoral elegy. It relies less on the classical pastoral tradition of Milton or Shelley than on an earlier poem of Arnold's own. In *Thyrsis* Arnold inserts the figure of Clough into the framework of *The Scholar Gipsy*, employing the same stanza form, and changing the search for the gipsy into the quest for a glimpse of "the signal elm" whose existence proves "Our friend, the Gipsy-Scholar, was not dead." Through Arnold's act of poetic will, Clough thus metamorphoses into an already immortal literary character who haunts the Oxford countryside as Clough did in his youth. But the later poem also seems to confirm the earlier one's warning that contact with modern life is fatal; ironically, what turns Clough into the Gipsy-Scholar is his failure to act as the Gipsy did: Clough made the mistake of leaving Oxford for London where "his piping took a troubled sound." The search for the tree, triumphantly located at the last moment, images the poet's quest to believe in his dead friend Thyrsis's continuing life, whether in nature or art. The tree functions as a symbol of the afterlife, but also of lost youth, and of phallic power or poetic potency (Arnold's perhaps more than Clough's). As in most elegies, the poet uses the task of resuscitating a dead friend as a means of insuring his own literary immortality. The poem ends with the poet reaffirming the value of the Scholar's search, and rededicating himself to the same pursuit, urged on by Thyrsis's otherworldly words. But Arnold wrote no more poetry, and Clough is remembered mostly for his spectral role in this valediction. The tree and Scholar provide the final, active images, suggesting that Corydon and Thyrsis have been subsumed by them.

Prose

In 1849 Arnold wrote to Clough complaining "how deeply *unpoetical* the age and all one's surroundings are. Not unprofound, not ungrand, not unmoving;—but *unpoetical*." Within a few years Arnold all but gave up trying to deal with his "unpoetical" times in verse form. In the literary and social criticism that followed, he sought to reconcile his high-minded poetic concern for eternal verities with the more down-to-earth demands of timely, topical commentary on the shortcomings of Victorian culture. In his most famous essay, *The Function of Criticism at the Present Time*, he suggested that, in an era where great creative activity was impossible, criticism could stand in as "a free creative activity," one that could both improve society at large and still satisfy the intellect of the gifted observer.

But to have genuine authority, Arnold contends, criticism must preserve its "disinterestedness" or objectivity "by keeping aloof from what is called 'the practical view of things.'" If criticism does not pursue "the law of its own nature" as "a free play of the mind on all subjects which it touches," it will end up serving private interests, not the public's. Only non-sectarian, purely intellectual analysis can enable critics to pursue their fundamental goal: "to see the object as in itself it really is." For Arnold, then, criticism has little to do with the prophetic denunciations of Ruskin, or even the closely reasoned defense of human rights offered by Mill. Instead, Arnold stresses that criticism is not so much a toting up of faults and merits as it is a continuing process, dedicated to producing "a current of true and fresh ideas."

Arnold's claims for the necessity of critical open-mindedness can be compared to Mill's position regarding the benefits of free speech in *On Liberty*. Like Mill he asserts that an unimpeded entertaining of all ideas, including those that challenge convention, is "an essential provider of elements without which a nation's spirit . . . must, in the long run, die of inanition." What Arnold adds to Mill is the explicit championing of an ideal intellectual position—a "disinterested love of a free play of the mind on all subjects, for its own sake"—that sets the true critic above the fray of political contention, so that he can dedicate himself to pursuing "the best that is known and thought in the world, irrespective of practice [and] politics." Claiming that "practical considerations cling to it and stifle it," Arnold recognizes that his brand of criticism may be "slow and obscure," but contends that such a careful, collected transcending of the "inadequate ideas" of the masses is the only way "that the critic can do the practical man any service."

But Arnold's own rhetoric often seems to undermine his argument: why is it so insistent yet so vague, so repetitive, so ungrounded by examples of what "fresh and true ideas" really are? And don't you have to have an interest in disinterestedness in order to practice it? Moreover, Arnold clearly delights in attacking people by name, attempting to expose fallacious reasoning or uninformed opinions. One might respond that Arnold is proposing a critical method whose benefit lies in its refusal to take sides or to spare anyone, liberal or conservative, bishop or working man. It could also be said of his criticism that, like his poetry, it sets up standards it cannot reach, and that the perhaps noble aspiration is more important than the failed execution.

Arnold himself does not seem to question whether the critical objectivity he calls for is genuinely possible, just as he does not seem to doubt his ability to see "the object as in itself it really is." Does he purposefully avoid raising these vexed questions because he expects his audience to recognize that *all* critical theory depends, to a greater or lesser extent, on some sort of universalist claim? He would no doubt have vehemently rejected Baudelaire's view that criticism should be "passionate, partisan, personal." Since current critical sympathies seem to lie more with Baudelaire than Arnold, it is interesting to examine just how Arnold carries out his difficult task. The essay's most famous passage deals with the news item ending "Wragg is in custody." By contrasting the bombast of self-congratulatory political rhetoric about "our old Anglo-Saxon breed" to the sensational crudity of tabloid journalism, Arnold attempts to moderate, in a double sense, the discourse of British national life. Wragg's sad example casts doubt on the country's economic health, the fineness of its landscape, the legitimacy of its citizens, the equality of its laws, its respect for women, and even the dignity of its names. Appearing to lay his own views aside, Arnold sets one aspect of his culture against another, in order to "get rid of what in them is excessive and offensive, and to fall into a softer and truer key."

The essay therefore provides a good opportunity to ask what the ideals of social commentary ought to be, and if critical "disinterestedness" is a laudable goal or an impossible dream. Eugene Goodheart provides a strenuous defense of the concept in "Arnold, Critic of Ideology" (*New Literary History* 25 [1994]: 415–428), arguing that in "Function," as in *Culture and Anarchy*, Arnold realistically strives to develop "the human capacity for the transcendence of narrowly conceived self-interest." Susan Walsh, however, portrays a very different Arnold in her article "That Arnoldian Wragg: Anarchy as Menstrosity in Victorian Social Criticism" (*Victorian Literature and Culture* 20 [1992]: 217–241). Viewing the story of Wragg in the context of Victorian tendencies to connect menstruation, factory work, soiled rags, and female biological determinism, Walsh writes that "it is Arnold who completes the transformation of Wragg into a thing, a tattered cast-off of a commodity culture. . . . Elizabeth Wragg comes to stand, not for herself, but for an anarchical social political economy whose factories spawn abominations. . . . While it may appear as if Arnold means to liberate the working class from Roebuck and Adderley's sentimental portrait of the happy non-exploited laborer, he actually works to reestablish Victorian classism with his ugly, jarring portrait of Wragg."

Culture and Anarchy remains relevant for many reasons, among them its concern to identify the factors that make up a culture and shape its public discourse; its effort to defuse class hostility and promote mutual tolerance and political cooperation; and its questioning of whether "our worship of freedom in and for itself" is not detrimental to the public good. *Culture and Anarchy* evolved from a series of lectures and articles Arnold wrote in 1867–68, during debates over the Second Reform Bill. Passed in August, 1867, the bill doubled the electorate to include about one-third of adult males, among them many members of the working class. Filled with apprehensions about the direction that modern mass democracy would carry his nation, Arnold attacked the central British notion of "Doing As One Likes"—an anarchical tendency he found throughout society, but especially in the middle and working classes. His remedy, the cultivation of a trans-class "best self" based on education and located in the authority of the State, remains as controversial today as it was during Victorian times. To set Arnold's social analysis within its initial context, see the complete editions edited by J. Dover Wilson (1950) and Samuel Lipman (1994). Lipman reprints the original 1869 text, and includes important new essays by Gerald Graff, Maurice Cowling, and Steven Marcus. On Arnold's use of irony, satire, and humorous language, see Robert Altick's "The Comedy of Culture and Anarchy" in *Victorian Perspectives: Six Essays*, ed. John Clubbe and Jerome Meckier (1989), 120–144.

There is much to grapple with—and argue about—in this text, including the two main structural premises: 1) Arnold's vision of British intellectual and social history as a struggle between an active Puritan "Hebraism" and a reflective secular "Hellenism"; and 2) Arnold's division of society into three warring, self-serving factions: aristocratic Barbarians, middle-class Philistines, and an uneducated working-class Populace. When he suggests that the current predominance of the individualistic Hebraic strand is in fact causing society to unravel, he raises the question of what can bind a nation together, particularly in an increasingly secular age. The media? Shared political or economic values? If something more uplifting, such as the "pursuit of perfection," is desired, then how is this "sweetness and light" to be defined, and how best promoted? Can genuine culture ever be attained in the absence—or in the presence—of individual liberty? In "*Culture and Anarchy* Today," (*The Southern Review* 29.3 [1993]. 433–452, rpt. in the Lipman edition), Steven Marcus points to Arnold's foresight regarding the social ferment and challenges to tradition that strong group affiliation generate: "Arnold sensed or intuited in the matrix of nineteenth-century Dissenting British Protestantism a very early precursor of what nowadays goes by the temporary name of multiculturalism" (434).

Ironically, where Arnold comes under the heaviest attack from both Victorians and Moderns is where he is most idealistic, calling on people "to rise above the idea of class to the idea of the whole community, the State, and to find our centre of light and authority there." Even if one were to second his hopes for enlightened universal education, and temporarily forget the uneven results of that effort in the past century, the notion that a "disinterested" government could direct the enterprise successfully smacks too much of Plato's *Republic* and various totalitarian states ever since. But as Marcus concludes (speaking for many of Arnold's critics),

Culture and Anarchy is difficult to reject in its entirety. Education, open-minded critical debate, and social cooperation remain essential values of the democratic culture Arnold feared would overthrow them: "What Arnold is in effect saying, with historical perspicacity, is that class life is in itself alienated life, and hence culture once again represents a project of transcendence. . . . Arnold's culture represents a permanent contribution to an evolving ideal of what may be thinkable if not possible for modern humanity. . . . And unlike Arnold's biddings about the state, it has not been either superseded or altogether defeated by historical experience" (449).

In *The Study of Poetry* Arnold seeks, in a sense, to apply his social and critical principles to the activity of reading. He proposes what might be called a "disinterested" evaluation of what constitutes "the best poetry," poetry that, more than religion or philosophy, has the "power of forming, sustaining, and delighting us, as nothing else can." In his opening paragraphs Arnold thus lays the groundwork for the Modernist worship of the religion of Art. Having placed an immense responsibility on poetry as a "criticism of life" that can guide humanity, Arnold tries to show readers how they can find the "really" best poetry; they must rule out "fallacious" estimates of poetic value based on historical significance or personal appeal. But can we read poetry apart from these relativistic considerations? Why do we care about poetry, if not because of its impact on us? Consider Pater's famous challenge to Arnold in the Preface to *The Renaissance*, where Pater places the personal response foremost: "What is this song or picture . . . to *me*?"

Rejecting such subjectivity, Arnold elaborates his famous doctrine of objective "touchstones"—readers should always have in mind examples of "the truly excellent" lines of "the great masters" so that they can "apply them as a touchstone to other poetry." Arnold provides many examples, from many languages, of what he considers the best poetry, and then proceeds to evaluate the major English poets on the basis of how their work measures up to the "higher truth and higher seriousness" of the very greatest poetry. T. S. Eliot, so harsh on Arnold elsewhere, says "you cannot read his essay on *The Study of Poetry* without being convinced by the felicity of his quotations: to be able to quote as Arnold could is the best evidence of taste." The Victorian critic John S. Eells noted in 1880 that Arnold favors quotations dealing with pathos, pain, and loss; Eells finds that what Arnold most admires is "contemplation, profoundly earnest, of the grimness and darkness of the human adventure."

The contemporary student of poetry may well quarrel with this taste, and hence the whole idea of touchstones. Though furnishing concrete examples, Arnold is still maddeningly vague, since he never says *why* these are great lines, contenting himself with reiterating that they are of "the very highest quality." Refusing to acknowledge "the historical estimate," Arnold does not consider how timebound his own choices are. Modern readers may feel that what makes a text classic is its instability: very different lines within the same poem may acquire "touchstone" status over the years. Frank Kermode has remarked that a classic is a work that changes its meaning every generation.

Yet one of the things that keeps Arnold's essay interesting is the way in which it stimulates thought not only about what poetic greatness involves, but also about how contextually determined any definition—or later response to that definition—is likely to be. Sensing this, Arnold leaves it to his readers to say (or intuit) why his touchstones have been chosen: "if we are asked to define this mark and accent [of greatness] in the abstract, our answer must be: No, for we should thereby be darkening the question, not clearing it." He challenges his readers to grapple with Arnoldian standards of taste, to try and appreciate poetry as he does, and in the process to provide for themselves the fresh readings that will, provokingly, keep his dated essay up to date.

Dante Gabriel Rossetti

In *The Symbolist Movement in Literature* (2nd. ed., 1919), Arthur Symons wrote: "What would French poetry be to-day if Baudelaire had never existed? As different a thing from what it is as English poetry would be without Rossetti." While it's hard to credit such an extravagant claim today, fin-de-siècle poets like Symons, Wilde, and Yeats took Rossetti as a model because he had dedicated himself steadfastly to the pursuit of Beauty and Art for Art's Sake. Whether one regarded it as lurid or laudable, his devotion to idealized images of beautiful women caused "Aestheticism" to be called "Rossetti-ism" in its early stages. He took inspiration from his Florentine namesake, but paid little heed to the conventions of Victorian art, literature, or society.

The Blessed Damozel, his earliest important work, was written while he was still a teenager. It can be read not only as the poet's self-dedication to an unworldly, unattainable muse, but also as a rejection of the religiously and socially informed art of the day. Readers have always been amazed at the sensuous audacity of Rossetti's conception of heaven, particularly the tangibility of the Damozel's trappings and desires, and her daring plan to ask Christ "Only to live as once on earth / With Love,—only to be, / As then awhile, for ever now / Together, I and he." Meanwhile, her egotistical earthly lover cannot conceive that the Damozel could be happy without him, even in heaven: "I heard her tears."

But the poem challenges orthodoxy in subtler ways as well. Rossetti flattens out the religious or symbolic depth of his vision even as he complicates it formally and psychologically. Although they invoke the mystic numbers three and seven, the lilies and stars that adorn the Damozel seem less relevant to her situation than the weight of her golden hair or the heat of her bosom. (*The Woodspurge* is another example of Rossetti shifting potential religious significance—the "cup of three"—into the realm of visual fact and concrete observation.) Neither is it clear who presents the Damozel to the reader: is the earthly lover, who speaks in his own voice in parentheses, confidently fantasizing about her current position? or is there an omniscient narrator who describes her and sets her words in ironic juxtaposition with a bereft, earthbound lover who is just talking to himself?

The intertwined narrative—or is it two independent visions?—seems to progress toward a reunion, but death and life, represented by the gold bar and its typographical equivalents, the parentheses, conspire to keep the lovers apart.

Maybe Rossetti is projecting his own frustrations as lover and poet onto the imprisoned Damozel, as Tennyson does with the Lady of Shalott. What would it have meant for the Victorian artist to see himself as a passive, sequestered woman, hemmed in by otherworldly expectations about love? With her penchant for imagining future heavenly scenes, is the Damozel an artist figure, and "I" an inert caricature of the powerless, lovelorn Victorian maiden? The lovers' sense of separation is reinforced by the well-known painting also titled *The Blessed Damozel* that Rossetti did much later. Begun in 1871, it was not "finished" until 1879 when the artist, at the request of a patron, added a predella depicting the earthly lover gazing upward. Those interested in poetry/painting comparisons can relate the parentheses of the poem to the actual "gold bar" of the painting's frame, noting the painter's use of embracing couples in the background to visually "narrate" the Damozel's loneliness.

The brief selections from *The House of Life* give a sense of Rossetti's approach to the sonnet as a timely yet timeless work of art ("a moment's monument"), fraught with life-giving emotion. Using the sonnet sequence to enshrine bodily passion in sacramentally tinged language, Rossetti continues to explore the tensions that animate *The Blessed Damozel*. Some may feel that by investing so much in melding body and spirit, Rossetti has written himself into a sonorous sameness. (The notorious *Nuptial Sleep*, with its Adamic revelation at the end, is an exception.) In *The Fleshly School of Poetry* (1871) Robert Buchanan savaged what he called "this protracted hankering after a person of the other sex," and complained about the "inference that the body is greater than the soul, and sound superior to sense; and that the poet, properly to develop his poetic faculty, must be an intellectual hermaphrodite." Without accepting all Buchanan's objections, one can still see how Rossetti's sense of spiritual sexuality (or vice versa) produced artistic challenges for the author as well as his audience.

The Burden of Nineveh shows Rossetti at his wittiest. Taking his title from the opening words of the biblical book of Nahum, Rossetti plays on the many intertwined meanings of the word "burden." First, it refers to the sheer bulk of Assyrian statuary whose awkward entrance into the British Museum prompts the poem. This physical grappling with an outlandish ancient object introduces the idea of the museum as an imperial storehouse, to be stocked by armies and aristocrats, then culturally raided by the public (Keats's visits to the British Museum provided material for the *Ode on a Grecian Urn*). But "burden" also refers to the metaphorical weight of empire, both Assyrian and British. Then there is the formal "burden" or refrain of a poem—its central theme—and this meaning leads the poet to end each stanza with the word "Nineveh." Finally, the dominant biblical meaning is "oracle," a heavy lot or fate; the King James Bible thus speaks of "the burden of Babylon" in addition to "the burden of Nineveh," since both cities are destroyed by the Lord because of their worldliness.

The revolving door through which the poet passes suggests the cycles of history that have brought Nineveh low and sent its remains to London. Britain may follow this fate, for the winged bull is also John Bull, the popular caricature of Britain. But Rossetti hints that Nineveh enjoys a certain post-mortem triumph in the survival of its mighty icons, and raises the amusing possibility that future ar-chaeologists might conclude that the bull was an idol worshipped by Victorian civ-ilization. The vision of London as a ruin to be viewed nostalgically by a visitor from the South Pacific would have reminded Victorian readers of Macaulay's cautionary image of a New Zealander coming to sketch the ruins of London after the center of civilization had moved further west. Rossetti's concluding question, suggesting Britain's misplaced values, anticipates Kipling's doleful warning in *Recessional* (1897) about the transitory rewards of empire. But the chipper tone of Rossetti's poem, its brisk rhythms and rhymes, implies that the poet takes some delight in the prospect. The incongruity and semantic unruliness of the bull, its imagined carousings in the symbolic china-shop of history, seem to interest him more than dire prophecies about the fall of Victorian London.

Rossetti's poems provide a good starting place for discussing the Pre-Raphaelite movement. The original "Brotherhood" included Rossetti and the painters William Holman Hunt, John Everett Millais, and James Collinson; the sculptor Thomas Woolner; and the critics F. G. Stephens and William Michael Rossetti, Dante's brother. Christina Rossetti and Ford Madox Brown were closely allied with the group. Later, as the initial group grew apart, the term "Pre-Raphaelite" expanded to cover the highly-colored, medievally inspired works done by friends and associates. These included the poets Swinburne, George Meredith, and Coventry Patmore, the artists Edward Burne-Jones and Arthur Hughes, and painter-poets such as William Morris and William Bell Scott.

There is a great deal of Pre-Raphaelite material to be found on the World Wide Web. Jerome McGann's Rossetti Archive at the University of Virginia is useful, along with the Pre-Raphaelite sites at the University of Indiana and the more gen-eral information on the Victorian Web at Brown University. There are many good print collections of PRB documents and images; in addition to those listed in the Bibliography, the new *Anthology of Pre-Raphaelite Writings*, ed. Carolyn Hares-Stryker (1997), is especially rich. Crammed with intriguing anecdotes, William Gaunt's *The Pre-Raphaelite Dream* (1966) remains the most lively introduction to the group. For illustrations and background, the best inexpensive book is still Timothy Hilton's *The Pre-Raphaelites* (1970), though the text is somewhat dated.

We were unable to include Rossetti's long dramatic monologue *Jenny*, spoken by a poet to a prostitute who has fallen asleep in his lap. Students or teachers might find it interesting to seek out the poem because the situation—a male speaker spec-ulates on life and love to a silent/dead woman—seems characteristically Victorian, recalling *The Blessed Damozel*, Swinburne's *The Leper*, Arnold's *Dover Beach*, and Browning's *Porphyria's Lover* and *Andrea del Sarto*.

Christina Rossetti

Stylistically, Christina Rossetti's poems have a purity and grace, a quirky bemused intelligence that may remind readers of Emily Dickinson (whom she admired) or Edna St. Vincent Millay (who admired her). Her deceptive simplicity of language

and phrasing make her in many ways the most modern of Victorian poets, and an
opening line like "Something this foggy day, a something which" seems right out
of e. e. cummings. But Rossetti was rarely light-hearted in her choice of subjects;
her lyrics are almost always addressed to an estranged lover-listener. Speaking in
the voice of a slighted or forgotten lover, they often tell of a lonely yearning that
persists even in the grave.

According to her older brother William, Christina Rossetti's first poetic composition, spoken because she was still too young to write, was: "Cecilia never went
to school / Without her gladiator." William comments that "She understood this
much—that a 'gladiator' would be a man capable of showing some fight for 'Cecilia'
upon an emergency." He adds that the euphonious, carefully metered lines forecast her future work, "hinting at a certain oddity or whimsicality of combination
which (mingled indeed with qualities of a very different kind) can be not unfre-
quently traced in verse of her mature years" (The Poetical Works of Christina Rossetti
[1904], xlix).

It could be said that, in spite of her whimsy, the mature Rossetti never wrote a
lyric poem without missing that gladiator. Whether we call her "Cecilia" (the patron saint of music) or "Christina" (a female Christ), the speaker appears vulnerable and sinned against; she must become her own gladiator, providing her own
protection against the wounds of love. Her weapons are the subtle ones of wit,
irony, self-denial and above all an unsentimental, clear-eyed detachment.

Renunciation is in many ways Rossetti's central theme, the tone becoming playful and arch in the few poems where the speaker suggests that others do the renouncing (such as No, Thank You, John and Promises Like Pie-Crust) and painfully resolute when it is she who appears forgotten (cf. When I am dead, my dearest, Remember,
After Death, A Pause, and Echo). Unrelieved by the bursts of passion, classical allusions, and domestic, nurturing metaphors that characterize Barrett Browning's love
lyrics, Rossetti's poems have a sort of bare lucidity, a "bleak mid-winter" quality;
they seem to be written mostly after, rather than during, the relationships described. Some of the poems meditate on the idea of a life not fully lived (Dead Before
Death and In Progress); the striking sonnet on what it was like to model for Dante
Rossetti's paintings (as Christina did before Elizabeth Siddal became his favorite
subject) suggests that even when a woman has a man's full attention, the sense of
fulfillment belongs to him rather than her. Though her brother William's famous
assessment—"she was replete with the spirit of self-postponement"—does not take
into account the ways in which Christina Rossetti validated her life through her art,
it does capture an essential part of her poetic approach (lxvii).

In an equally influential reckoning, however, Virginia Woolf astutely noted
the tug-of-war between the keenness of the poet's desires and perceptions and the
stern religious outlook that held them in check: "your eye . . . observed with a sensual, pre-Raphaelite intensity that must have surprised Christina the Anglo-
Catholic. But to her you owed perhaps the fixity and sadness of your muse. The
pressure of a tremendous faith circles and clamps together these little songs" ("'I
Am Christina Rossetti,'" The Second Common Reader [1932], 219). Woolf continues, "You were not a pure saint by any means. You pulled legs; you tweaked noses.

You were at war with all humbug and pretense. Modest as you were, still you were drastic, sure of your gift, convinced of your vision . . . in a word, you were an artist" (220).

In *Christina Rossetti: The Poetry of Endurance* (1986) Dolores Rosenblum grapples with the tension between worldly and religious attitudes in Rossetti's poetry, concluding that "the religious poems 'correct' without cancelling the experiences of the fallen world rendered in the so-called secular poems, and that Rossetti's rewriting or doubling of her own poems, as well as the texts of biblical and Romantic literary tradition, contributes to a female myth, and ultimately, a female aesthetic" (84). Those looking for a briefer but still detailed introduction to Rossetti's work might consult Virginia Woolf's famous essay, as well as Sandra Gilbert and Susan Gubar's chapter on Rossetti in *The Madwoman in the Attic* (1979) and their headnote in *The Norton Anthology of Literature by Women*. See also *Victorian Women Poets: An Anthology*, ed. Angela Leighton and Margaret Reynolds (1995), a book which provides an excellent overview of its subject, and fine introductions to individual women poets, Rossetti and Browning chief among them.

In recent years, probably no Victorian poem has generated more interest than *Goblin Market*. It is unsurpassed for sheer energy and narrative drive, for accessibility of language and haunting quirkiness of image and action. The first edition featured line illustrations by Dante Rossetti, intense close-ups of furry-faced goblins and embracing sisters that did little to resolve the Victorians' still pertinent questions: who is this poem meant for? and what is it about? Is it a fairy tale, a religious allegory, a meditation on rape, money, or sexual repression?

Leighton and Reynolds point out the poem's "transgressive playfulness" and how, "like the wayward, perverse metres in which it is written, it constantly slips its own moral framework." They also note some interpretive possibilities: "The goblins' fruit may . . . represent original sin, Eucharistic redemption, sexual desire, prostitution, the nurturing south, economic power, imperial capitalism, masculinity, or even, as Gilbert and Gubar suggest, language and poetry. All of these are 'marketed' in the poem's extraordinary changes and exchanges of meaning. The fruit may even just be fruit, literally, and the poem about 'shopping'—that new popular pastime for women in the early 1860s" (355). Rosenblum includes a good chapter on *Goblin Market*, in which she suggests that the "goblin men" might be Christina's brothers, Dante and William Rossetti. She views the poem as built on a structure of acting, suffering, and recovering. Two other thought-provoking articles are: Elizabeth K. Helsinger's "Consumer Power and the Utopia of Desire: Christina Rossetti's *Goblin Market*," *ELH* 58.4 (1991): 903-33 and Dorothy Mermin's "Heroic Sisterhood in *Goblin Market*," *Victorian Poetry* 21.1 (1983): 107-18. Teachers can also compare the poem to Barrett-Browning's *Aurora Leigh* as a poetic narrative of women's education.

One of the most fascinating aspects of the poem is the way it seeks to control the conditions of its own reception via the final stanza, in which Laura relates the story—and the moral she draws from it—to her own daughters. The coda appears to tidy up and gloss over the desperate spiritual or psychosexual struggle of the narrative by proclaiming tritely that "there is no friend like a sister." Yet at the same time, the poem seems destined as a cautionary tale for precisely this pre-adolescent female audience. Pulling no punches, it warns vulnerable young misses about the dangers of desire and strange men with tempting fruits, and the need for sisterly solidarity to resist them. What may be the most unsettling thing about *Goblin Market* is its status as a classic Victorian children's story: it is a tale whose darkly disturbing scenes really do seem *intended* to trouble children's minds, even as the fairy-tale elements allow "respectable" adults to read it aloud without ever explicitly raising the subjects of temptation, transgression, and fall.

Rossetti also wrote strangely affecting short stories. Students looking for paper topics may want to consider *Goblin Market* or the love lyrics in light of her curious fables: see especially *Nick* in *Commonplace and Other Short Stories* (1870), (rpt. *Forbidden Journeys: Fairy Tales and Fantasies by Victorian Women Writers*, eds. Nina Auerbach and U.C. Knoepflmacher, 1992). Though quite short, *Nick* bears close comparison with Dickens's *A Christmas Carol* for the way in which its central character is bludgeoned into goodness; see also Rossetti's collection of nursery rhymes (1872) and the children's tale *Speaking Likenesses* (1874).

William Morris
The Defence of Guenevere (1858)

Morris's celebration of Guenevere's sexuality and energy contrasts with Tennyson's portrayal in *Idylls of the King* of a shamed and guilt-ridden queen responsible for Camelot's ruin. Unlike Tennyson, Morris is not concerned with moral disapproval. One might discuss other Victorian portrayals of "fallen women," such as the bourgeois adulteress in Augustus Egg's trilogy of paintings, *Past and Present* (1858).

Have students look at Morris's painting of Jane Burden as *Queen Guenevere* (1857). Carole Silver comments on how it "emphasizes the queen's heroic force and transcendence of conventional morality. . . . The power of the queen is manifest . . . in the strong vertical lines of her body which almost break through the patterns that enclose her. . . . Her dignity and calm make us perceive her not as 'fallen' but as risen, albeit from a bed of love" ("Victorian Spellbinders," *The Passing of Arthur*, eds. Christopher Baswell and William Sharpe, 1988, 253).

In *The Return to Camelot* (1981) Mark Girouard has a chapter called "The Return of Arthur," which details the Victorian reinvention of the legendary king. Jonathan Freedman writes that "for Morris, Arthurianism conjured forth a romance-world whose authenticity, intensity, and vitality stood in vivid contrast to the industrial ugliness of Victorian England, and at the same time evoked a privileged heterocosm whose squalor and violence ironically mirrored that of his contemporary world" ("Ideological Battleground," *The Passing of Arthur*, 236).

Interpretations of *The Defence of Guenevere* turn on the subtleties of the queen's argument: she seems to deny having committed adultery, yet her evocation of passionate love seems in itself a confession. In *The Romance of William Morris* (1982) Carole Silver suggests that "the queen does not know whether she is morally guilty;

she is uncertain of the rightness of her position, certain only of the strength of the love that has placed her in it" (20). Silver argues that "the poem's title is ironic. Guenevere intends a speech of self-vindication, but her words and actions persuade the reader of her adultery" (24).

Virginia S. Hale and Catherine Barnes Stevenson disagree. They argue in "Morris' Medieval Queen: A Paradox Resolved" that the apparent contradiction can be resolved by seeing Guenevere in the medieval context of courtly love: Morris portrays a woman who, "accused of treason, mounts a rhetorically sophisticated defense, in which she contemptuously dismisses that charge, while at the same time offering a celebration of her love in the medieval tradition of the 'defense d'amor'" (*Victorian Poetry* 30.2 [1992]: 171-78).

Freedman maintains, however, that Guenevere's assertion that Gauwaine lies "is clearly true: Gauwaine does not, cannot pierce the mystery of the love she and Lancelot share." But he adds that while this is "a brilliant equivocation," it is a flimsy defense; Guenevere's performance is in fact "a defense in a different sense: a knightly defense, a parrying, by the use of language, of the thrusts of her accusers—a holding action, while she awaits the intervention of Lancelot" (243).

Instructors will also want to call attention to Morris's use of the dramatic monologue, and to his language. Paul Thompson writes: "The poems must be read slowly, with each syllable given its full value, avoiding any strong rhythmic beat. Read like this, the apparently naïve defects in the poems, the odd deviations from the normal iambic beat, the unexpected rhymes and the curious overlapping of the lines, become masterly devices for creating tension, for suggesting a deeper meaning. . . . Morris had in fact created a new verse form, like stammering direct speech, which parallels the effects of Gerard Manley Hopkins" (*The Work of William Morris* [1991], 182-83). For more on the art of Morris's language see W. David Shaw's "Arthurian Ghosts: Phantom Art of *The Defence of Guenevere*" and Karen Herbert's "Dissident Language in *The Defence of Guenevere*," both in *Victorian Poetry* 34.3 (1996).

The Haystack in the Floods (1858)

The inspiration for this bleak poem lay not in Malory's *Morte Darthur* but in the *Chroniques* of Jean Froissart, a history of the Hundred Years' War between France and England.

Cecil Lang calls Morris's poetry a hybrid of Rossetti and Browning: "Browning can be seen in the dramatic technique (abrupt openings, omitted transitions, harsh meter, etc.), Rossetti in the vivid, concrete detail." Morris's own contribution "was in the directness, bluntness, and violence—the brutality—with which he rendered his pictures of the Middle Ages. English poetry had seen nothing like it" (*The Pre-Raphaelites and Their Circle* [1975], 507-8).

As in *The Defence of Guenevere*, a woman's sexuality—and her right to control it herself—forms the crux of an emotional drama that mingles images of violence and passion. In each poem, a woman faces a male accuser who threatens to punish her illicit love affair with death. Yet in each case, the woman's "guilt" is really beside the point; for example, it isn't entirely clear why the "Paris folks" are clamoring to kill Jehane (presumably they regard her as a traitor for having an English lover, and wish to scapegoat her for the recent French defeat). Carole Silver points out that "Jehane, unlike Guenevere, does not reveal the inner workings of her mind" and "her passive strength . . . is sharply opposed to Guenevere's histrionic power" (*The Romance of William Morris* [1982], 34).

The impact of this poem lies in the horrific impasse in which Jehane finds herself. Students may feel she makes the wrong "choice"—but does she really have one? Would the sadistic Godmar have spared Robert if she had yielded to him? The very first lines betray the outcome, suggesting that the point is not what choice she makes—or even, as Silver proposes, "her ability to stick to it despite the pressure put upon her" (34)—but rather the stark *lack* of choices she faces. *The Haystack in the Floods* may be the only significant Victorian poem that offers no redemptive possiblities whatsoever.

In "Cataclysm and Pre-Raphaelite Tragedy: Morris' *The Haystack in the Floods*," Antony Harrison writes: "This poem, with its dominant tone of morose inevitability symbolically reinforced at every turn, austerely depicts for its characters life's apocalyptic hour." He notes the poem's surreal quality: "The pervasive horror, the sublimated sexuality, the violence and paranoia that are normally relegated to nightmares, here alone constitute reality." Jehane does not go mad at the end, for "doing so would be an escape that Morris does not allow from his wrenchingly tragic universe." In the end, Harrison concludes, Pre-Raphaelite poetry such as this "attempts to redeem the tragic by emphasizing the sensory and sensual" (*South Atlantic Review* 47.4 [1982]: 43–51).

The Beauty of Life (1880)

Beginning in the late 1870s, Morris began lecturing on the decorative arts, bringing to the people his message about the necessity of art and beauty for a meaningful life. In its concern for the working classes, *The Beauty of Life* foreshadows Morris's decision to join the Socialists several years later, for he came to believe that only under socialism would the renewal of society he envisioned become possible. Many of the essay's themes—preserving green spaces, providing decent housing, reducing air pollution, saving historic buildings—strikingly anticipate twentieth-century preoccupations.

Ruskin's "The Nature of Gothic" (*The Stones of Venice*, 1853) was a kind of manifesto for Morris & Company and the Arts and Crafts movement (Morris called it "one of the very few necessary and inevitable utterances of the century"). To Ruskin's theories Morris added his own years of practical experience as a craftsman and designer. Compare Ruskin's credo in *Modern Manufacture and Design* (1859)—"Beautiful art can only be produced by people who have beautiful things about them, and leisure to look at them"—with Morris's dictum in *The Beauty of Life*: "Have nothing in your houses that you do not know to be useful, or believe to be beautiful."

Like Ruskin, Morris insists that this is not an elitist project: just as Ruskin, disdaining "the selfish power of the noblesse," claims "the loftier and lovelier privilege of bringing the power and charm of art within the reach of the humble and the poor," so Morris argues that "the civilization which does not carry the whole people with it is doomed to fall." Morris wants a Democracy of Art, "Art made by the people and for the people."

Have students read Nesbit's *Fortunatus Rex & Co.* along with Morris's essay; Nesbit's own socialism and environmentalism led her to satirize unhindered development as "eating up the green country like greedy yellow caterpillars." Paul Thomson describes Morris's pioneering effects on British town planning, particularly "the restriction of advertising hoardings to towns, the protection of ancient buildings, the clean air acts and attempts to control litter, and the garden cities and new towns" (*The Work of William Morris* [1991], 73).

Algernon Charles Swinburne

Even in the bizarre world of the Victorian dramatic monologue, populated by charlatans, lechers, lunatics, and murderers, *The Leper* stands out. Students will be fascinated and horrified to discover that this tale of unrequited passion is told by a necrophiliac who begins to satisfy his desires only when his beloved is too wasted with leprosy to resist. The poem offers a good occasion to ask why any poet would want to impersonate such a character: what could he hope to say either about human psychology or—since Swinburne's narrator is a medieval scribe—about the nature of writing? Toward the end of the poem the scribe muses: "It may be all my love went wrong—/ A scribe's work writ awry and blurred, / Scrawled after the blind evensong—/ Spoilt music with no perfect word." Is writing a poem like making love to a corpse? Students may be quick to see parallels with the half-crazed confessional monologues of Browning, especially *Porphyria's Lover* (which also invokes God's judgment at the end) and *My Last Duchess*. To suggest the extent of Victorian poetic fetishizing of the dead or inert woman, remind them of Tennyson's *Mariana* and *The Lady of Shalott*, Dante Rossetti's *The Blessed Damozel*, and Christina Rossetti's *When I Am Dead My Dearest* and *After Death*.

But Swinburne goes further than any of these in literalizing the idea of physical love after death. Moreover, while the speaker's hunger for the lady's diseased body has its own perverse purity of devotion (he is "maddened" by her worn-off eyelids), Swinburne triangulates this desire by suggesting in stanza 7 that the narrator had earlier also been enamored of his rival—the golden-haired knight who "shames" the lady sexually and possibly gave her leprosy in the bargain. The knight's hair and mouth are one of the "three thoughts" the speaker takes "pleasure" in; of the other two "thoughts" one is the lady's thanking the scribe for acting as a go-between, and the third is his glad response to her subsequent disease. The lady's leprosy functions as an outward sign of her secret liaison, so that everyone, including the knight who once covered her with kisses, now shuns her. But the lowly scribe can now shelter her, performing what he cryptically calls "the service God forbids."

Perhaps sensing how outrageous this plot was, Swinburne not only made up a sixteenth-century French source for his tale (see first note), but also distanced the action by using archaic or awkward formulations ("it is meet," "this was well seen"). In addition, he generates a great deal of symbolic and aural density—while keeping the action vague—by repeating key words and concepts that resonate with religious, feudal, and modern meanings: service, forbiddeness, golden hair, kisses, blindness, sweetness. The poem's final question ("Will not God do right?") attempts to cast the whole situation in a theological light, but right to and for whom? Is the question a sign of the scribe's craziness? Or of the poet-creator's desire either to mollify or further scandalize a devout Victorian readership?

If *The Leper* reveals Swinburne's twisted genius for shocking monologues, the oft-recited passage from *The Triumph of Time, I Will Go Back to the Great Sweet Mother*, gives the full flavor of his sonorous style. It is a wonderful piece to read aloud. The dactylic rhythms (long short short) seem to emulate the surge of the sea. The rhyme scheme is a variation of *ottava rima*, such as Byron used in *Don Juan*, but with the normally concluding couplet inserted between the second and third group of *ab* lines—perhaps to suggest the unconventional or frustrating nature of the speaker's love affair. There is more than a hint of incest in this passage, as the speaker seeks to forget his lover by merging with the sea. As a way of getting into Swinburne's sensibility as well as his method of constructing a line, ask the class to distinguish between "the pain of pleasure" and "the pleasure of pain," and to consider how that concept-construction operates in this passage (and in *The Leper*) as an underlying principle. John D. Rosenberg notes that Swinburne made "compulsive use of alliterating antitheses" because he was "obsessed by the moment when one thing shades off into its opposite, or when contraries fuse. . . . Swinburne *perceived* in paradoxes" ("Swinburne," *Victorian Studies* 11 [1967]: 131-152). Two examples from the last stanza are "The hopes that hurt and the dreams that hover," and "Thy depths conceal and thy gulfs discover."

Itylus is a beautiful, disturbing, and at first confusing poem. In the Greek legend Philomela, raped and mutilated by her sister's husband Tereus, turns into a swallow; her sister Procne, who kills their son Itylus in revenge, turns into a nightingale. Latin versions reverse the sisters' fates. The Greek version is perhaps sounder ornithologically, since the nightingale is thought to sing sweetly to mourn its dead child, while the tongueless swallow merely chatters. But the Latin version, which most English poets follow, suggests how the deepest art, the fullest song, is born out of the sexual violence and voicelessness endured by women.

Not till the end does Swinburne specify who is singing, and yet the impact of the poem depends on whether it is Procne (the mother of Itylus) or her sister who mourns. The death of Itylus and the feast where he was eaten by his father are not mentioned until the third-to-last stanza. The penultimate stanza alludes to the tapestry revealing Tereus's crime, and the result of Procne's seeing it: "the small slain body" of the boy she has killed. The only clue as to which sister is the suffering nightingale haunted by this death and which the forgetful swallow comes at the start of the last stanza: "O sister, sister, thy first-begotten!" By obliquely leading up to this revelation, Swinburne seeks to convey not only the lingering horror of the boy's murder, but the raped sister's grief that the mother who did it has now forgotten her son. It is typical of Swinburne to focus on the violence of act and affection that destroys families, and also typical that, by giving voice and body to Itylus as well as Philomela, he manages to suggest a surprisingly intense bond between them.

Because of his licentious topics and flagrant disregard for Christian morality, Swinburne was often called "pagan" by Victorian critics. In the dramatic monologue *Hymn to Proserpine* he speaks in the voice of a Roman writer who mourns the death of his own ancient faith as the era of Christianity begins. (The attempt to view the Christian era from a perspective and time outside it anticipates Yeats's poems *The Magi* and *The Second Coming.*) The situation gives Swinburne latitude to compare pagan gods, oriented towards fertility and natural abundance, to a self-denying Christ and Madonna. The poem's most famous line, "Thou hast conquered, O pale Galilean; the world has grown grey from thy breath," yields victory to the Christians, but in such a way as to suggest that life on these grim terms is not worth living. Anapests (short short long) usually create a light, rapidly tripping meter, but here Swinburne manages though word choice and his long, six-beat alexandrine line to suggest the world weariness of the pagan poet who—having pronounced an eventual death sentence for the new Christian faith—is ready to sleep forever in the Underworld.

The Forsaken Garden is a postDarwinian fantasy that may derive from memories of Swinburne's childhood home of East Dene on the Isle of Wight. Its supple anapestic rhythms, its narrative of lost love and passion's vulnerability amidst the fleeting vista of years, are typically Swinburnian, as are the coupling of contrasts and aggressive liminality of the opening lines. Sometimes it seems Swinburne collapses opposites to the point of muddle, as in "Here death may deal not again forever" (line 65), and the lovers embedded at the heart of the poem have far less definition than those in a similar poem, Browning's *Love Among the Ruins.*

But Swinburne's aim seems to be to create a sort of anti-Eden, a garden at the end of time where geological forces have outdistanced theological concerns. A master of evoking what is gone or to come, Swinburne projects a landscape where Adam and Eve, and all human history, are irrelevant: "Not a breath of the time that has been hovers / In the air now soft with a summer to be" (lines 59-60). The poet anticipates the cosmic perspective of Thomas Huxley's *Evolution and Ethics* (see the Religion and Science perspectives section): "nothing is more certain than that, measured by the liberal scale of time-keeping of the universe, this present state of nature, however it may seem to have gone and to go on for ever, is but a fleeting phase of her infinite variety." Swinburne's concluding lines gain in power and shed some of their showy paradox when read as part of a vast natural process. With the passage of aeons, the world crumbles and in the absence of any animal or vegetable life, even Death, born in Eden and now a mere remnant of transitory organic epochs, finally perishes. What Swinburne adds to Darwin and Huxley is a nostalgia of barrenness, the idea of lifeless places haunted by imperceptible ghosts of memory.

Aware of his own reputation for vagueness, Swinburne was adept at locating it in other writers. His parody of Tennyson's *The Higher Pantheism*, called *The Higher Pantheism in a Nutshell*, strikes to the heart of Victorian religious confusion; it is a funny poem to read aloud. But in its nonsensical parallels and contrasts the poem makes fun of Swinburne's own style as well. He parodied himself at greater length in *Nephelidia* (Little Clouds), whose first line reads "From the depth of the dreamy decline of the dawn through a notable nimbus of nebulous moonshine." Swinburne once said of his work, "If we insist on having hard ground under foot all the way we shall not get far." But readers who wade in after him, surfing in the waves of words, inevitably have a good time.

Walter Pater

It could be argued that the most important word in Walter Pater's work is "me." But far from being an egotist, Pater produced an impressionistic, subjective criticism whose emphasis on the relativity of experience and knowledge seems to dissolve the human personality along with the absolutes his fugitive consciousness challenges. In doing so, Pater helped spark the transition from High Victorian morality to the Aesthetic creed of "art for art's sake." Pater begins his attack immediately at the start of the Preface to *The Renaissance*. First he questions the underlying project of Ruskin's *Modern Painters* (and of classical aesthetics) by claiming that attempts to define beauty in the abstract are not very helpful; rather, "the true student of aesthetics" seeks to define beauty "in the most concrete terms possible," because the experience of beauty, like all human experience, is relative.

Then Pater deliberately undercuts Arnold's critical aim of seeing the object "as in itself it really is" by suggesting that the most one can be sure of is "one's own impression as it really is." The "primary data" of aesthetic response, says Pater, exist only in relation to the observer: "What is this song or picture, this engaging personality presented in life or in a book, to *me*? What effect does it really produce on me? Does it give me pleasure? and if so, what sort or degree of pleasure? How is my nature modified by its presence, and under its influence?" For Pater, the critic registers the "pleasurable sensations" that beautiful art produces, and it is important for him to have "a certain kind of temperament, the power of being deeply moved by the presence of beautiful objects." Pater thus might be said to be the original embodiment of Wilde's "critic as artist," a man whose "sole aim is to chronicle his own impressions."

Students may enjoy—or be outraged by—the danger Pater poses to the Academy. Is there such a thing as objective criticism, then? If it is philosophically impossible, should it exist as a laudable goal? If a student paper bears little relation to the text we have read and taught, should we protest—or encourage the further cultivation of this creative sensibility? Why is it all right for Pater to daydream on paper but not all right for students and art critics to do the same? Wilde works through Pater's ideas with dazzling logic in *The Critic as Artist*, concluding that the task of the critic is "to see the object as in itself it really is not."

By his choice of topic, Pater shifts the home ground of beauty from the Middle Ages to the Renaissance, countering those such as Ruskin and Morris who denounced the Renaissance as too corrupt, sensual, pagan, and materialist. The Victorian prejudice against the Renaissance was so strong that only in the 1860s did it begin to get critical attention, thanks to Pater's efforts; the first entry on the Renaissance in the *Encyclopedia Britannica* does not appear until 1885. But Pater's full title, *Studies in the History of the Renaissance*, raises the question, what kind of history is this? He speaks vaguely in the Preface of the "general spirit and character" of an age, and of its "aesthetic charm," yet his description of painters and their works is so intensely idiosyncratic that all the history it seems to supply is a history of Victorian taste, or maybe just the poetic "history" of Pater's own evanescent appreciations and imaginings.

In *Stones of Venice* Ruskin viewed art as an index of morality, the lasting evidence of the spiritual health or sickness of a society. And in Pater's emphasis on recreating the experience of art through imaginative prose, he seems to follow Ruskin: compare Pater's *Mona Lisa* to Ruskin's description of Turner's *Slave Ship*. But as Harold Bloom notes, Pater's "great achievement was to empty Ruskin's aestheticism of its moral basis" (*Walter Pater: Modern Critical Views* [1985], xxxi). For Ruskin, Turner's painting expresses divine wrath at slavery; for Pater, the *Mona Lisa* is a catalogue of supposedly timeless and definitely fantastic notions of womanhood, ranging from Greek goddesses to vampires. Compared to Ruskin's moral humanism, which sees art as objectively shaping and responding to human behavior, Pater offers a hedonistic humanism implying that art does not exist or matter apart from our sensations of it.

In "Arnold and Pater," T. S. Eliot insists that since Pater uses his rhapsodic prose to tell people how to live, Pater is indeed a moralist after all. "A writer," says Eliot, "may be none the less classified as a moralist, if his moralizing is suspect or perverse" (*Selected Essays* [1950], 389). Eliot complains that "the degradation of philosophy and religion, skilfully initiated by Arnold, is competently continued by Pater" (388), and he denies Pater's aestheticism: "The right practice of art for art's sake was the devotion of Flaubert and Henry James; Pater is not with these men, but rather with Carlyle and Ruskin and Arnold" (393).

Pater did seem troubled by the impact of his work. He chose not to reprint the "Conclusion" to *The Renaissance* in the second (1877) edition because he thought it might "mislead" impressionable young men, and though *The Renaissance* brought him recognition, it also precipitated a crisis in his own life. In 1874 it appears that Benjamin Jowett, master of Balliol, blocked Pater's routine promotion to University Proctor because Pater's writing made it impossible for Jowett to ignore Pater's relationship with a Balliol undergraduate. See Billie Andrew Inman's "Estrangement and Connection: Water Pater, Benjamin Jowett, and William M. Hardinge" in *Pater in the 1990s*, ed. Laurel Brake and Ian Small (1991), 1–20, and William F. Shuter's "The 'Outing' of Walter Pater," *Nineteenth-Century Literature* 48.4 (1994): 480–506. Pater was also satirized as the hedonistic "Mr. Rose" in W. H. Mallock's *The New Republic* (1877). Together, the two events brought pain to Pater and prevented him from being considered for Professor of Poetry in 1877. After 1874, the theme of victimization and suffering becomes pronounced in his works.

Despite the homoerotic current to his thought, Pater's attitude toward sexuality remains notoriously elusive. On Pater and "manliness" see James Eli Adams's chapter in *Dandies and Desert Saints: Styles of Victorian Masculinity* (1995), 183–228. More directly useful in the classroom is Herbert Sussman's detailed reading of the "Conclusion" in *Victorian Masculinities* (1995), 173-202: "these famous words are wholly self-contained, a call not for a particular formal program but for a particular practice of regulating male desire. Rather than an essay on style, the 'Conclusion' is a sermon on manhood" (193). After an early "trajectory of unmanning" (196) that deals with the dissolution of the personality ("that strange perpetual weaving and unweaving of ourselves"), the essay shifts, says Sussman, to "figures of . . . structuring, control, agency" culminating in the famous phrase, "To burn always with this hard, gem-like flame, to maintain this ecstasy, is success in life."

Sussman comments that "for Pater as for his predecessors" (such as Carlyle) "the crucial act in achieving manhood lies in imposing form on the formlessness of male desire by a virile act of will." Seeking "tight control of the internal current of male potency," the image is "not only Pater's but his age's vision of manliness as contained power" (198). One might also connect Pater with the "hard" science of Darwin and Huxley. Pater's starting point—"our physical life is a perpetual motion"—is the evolutionary principle writ small. Pater applies the concept of the variability of species to the individual body and personality, and in a speed-up of biological time urges us to grasp fleeting impressions that are in "perpetual flight," for they will never come again.

Sussman makes an interesting connection to Hopkins's *That Nature is a Heraclitean Fire* which "also moves along the trajectory of the masculine plot" to end in "immortal diamond," thus outdoing Pater's image for hardness and durability in the face of worldly flux (199). Yet, Sussman concludes, Pater is not merely appropriating "the vocabulary of normative Victorian [heterosexual] masculinities;" rather, "Pater subverts this formation by foregrounding the erotics always present within the practice of psychic restraint for earlier Victorians" (202). In other words the flame and the burning are what count most. Point out, however, that Pater concludes by saying that of all passions "the love of art for its own sake" is what makes for the fullest life.

This shading of eroticism into aestheticism, of experience into sensation and perception, continues in *The Child in the House*. Here Pater probingly explores the gradual process of how we come to be ourselves, and the role played by specific places and sensations in that development. According to Arthur Symons, Pater told him the story was designed to show "'the poetry of modern life,' something, he said, as Aurora Leigh does" (see Gerald Monsman, *Walter Pater's Art of Autobiography* [1980], 10). Though there is something outrageous in Pater likening his lush, measured prose to Barrett Browning's fitful, bristling pentameter, they are both concerned with how visual stimuli shape child psychology. Aurora's reaction to her mother's portrait in Book I not only parallels Florian's relation to his house, it is also a striking anticipation of (and perhaps a source for) Pater's famous rendering of the *Mona Lisa*.

While the story has traditionally been viewed as a thinly veiled autobiography, in *Walter Pater: Lover of Strange Souls* (1995) Denis Donoghue writes that such a reading is "no good" since "Pater never lived in such a house, his father didn't die abroad, the actual moves from Stepney to Enfield and later to Canterbury didn't at all resemble the move in the story" (181). Noting that *A Child* is framed as a dream parable, Donoghue argues that "the purpose of memory in his fiction is not to recall an old experience but to create a new one" (182), and he points to the chain of sensations in the story as being not so much shaped by a historical causality as by a psychological predisposition, "a kind of tyranny of the senses," in the narrator's words, that rules over the boy. For Florian, the memoir has the perhaps liberating goal of self-exploration, "the noting . . . of some things in the story of his spirit—in that process of brain-building by which we are, each one of us, what we are." As William E. Buckler says in *Walter Pater: The Critic as Artist of Ideas* (1987), *The Child in the House* is "the poetic myth of a man whose mental house is furnished forever in the first twelve years of his life. . . . It is the paradise from which his very eagerness to depart visits on him a piercing and eternal sense of loss" (187).

Gerard Manley Hopkins

If one wanted to prove the truth of Ruskin's famous pronouncement that "seeing clearly is poetry, prophecy, and religion, all in one," the work of Hopkins would be a fine place to start. His impassioned combination of visual acuity and spiritual intensity not only produced great religious poetry, but prophetically opened the way for the dazzling leaps of sound and image that mark the most innovative poems of the twentieth century. Reading the selections from journals of 1871–73, when Hopkins was silently meditating on his new way of seeing the world and recasting its language, we discover how keenly he observed ordinary objects, and how carefully he sought to convey their exact appearance. He captures their particularity through a combination of minute, objective description and subtle references to the human body and activity—a sky is "frowning," buds on a branch remind him of a finger tied with string, clouds in motion are like tossed napkins falling. His descriptive language thus emulates the interpenetration of human and natural worlds, and their infusion with God's beauty and power—themes the poems present even more urgently.

Much fuss has been made about the terms "inscape" and "instress." But as the journal entries show—like the wonderfully detailed one on bluebells (May 9, 1871)—Hopkins is simply trying with "inscape" to get at the complex "thisness" of the thing he observes, its look, feel, and structure. In *As Kingfishers Catch Fire* he clearly states his belief in the individuality of every entity: "Each mortal thing does one thing and the same: / Deals out that being indoors each one dwells; / Selves—goes itself; *myself* it speaks and spells; / Crying *Whát I dó is me: for that I came.*" Often he is frustrated that he can't more readily bring outside, to everyone's attention, "that being" that "indoors . . . dwells" in each thing. The entry on the beautiful roof structure hidden inside the barn (July 19, 1872) might serve as a metaphor for his mission as a poet, bringing inscapes to the world's notice. It also anticipates his own lack of an audience for this undertaking: "I thought how sadly beauty of inscape was unknown and buried away from simple people and yet how near at hand it was if they had eyes to see it and it could be called out everywhere again."

As for "instress," it projects the uniqueness of the inscape toward the observer, but only if he or she is receptive and attentive—i.e., most likely alone. See the entry for Dec. 12, 1872: Hopkins comments that despite the presence of a friend, "I saw the inscape [of tufts of grass] though freshly, as if my eye were still growing, though with a companion the eye and the ear are for the most part shut and instress cannot come." As it conveys the inscape outward, instress enables the poet's eye to keep "growing" in maturity and power.

The letter to Bridges clarifies what principles of composition Hopkins had in mind when he finally began, in the late 1870s, to arrange these perceptions in words and sound. It is important to note that he never abandons form; although he wrenches syntax, makes up words, revises the rules of meter and diction, and violates the grammatical integrity of the poetic line, rhyme is always sacred for him. Moreover, most of his best poems are sonnets, with conventional Petrarchean octets (*abbaabba*) followed by a sestet (usually *cdcdcd*, his favorite conclusion) that registers the traditional "turn" in the poet's attitude toward his topic.

Students will enjoy reading Hopkins aloud, once they have had a chance to work through each poem and familiarize themselves with the unusual words and constructions. Remind them of what Hopkins says to Bridges about accents in nursery rhymes and the natural rhythms of prose. If we let the stresses fall where they may, then most lines will scan pretty nicely.

God's Grandeur is a good introduction to Hopkins's outlook and technique. The internal rhyme in the first stanza augments the bleariness of human toil, as contrasted to the flaming "grandeur of God" that worn-out mortals cannot feel. But after the turn, the world's combined inscapes, the "dearest freshness deep down things" burst out irrepressibly (cf. "What is all this juice and joy?" in *Spring*). The startling break between lines 13 and 14 should be pointed out: Hopkins separates adjective and noun forty years before William Carlos Williams attempted it. In so doing he generates a suspense that is partially resolved in the image of the brooding dove and then transformed into sheer wonder with the heartfelt interjection—one of Hopkins's trademarks—at the close.

The Windhover is a classic whose airborne energy, assonance, and alliteration seem to rip the sonnet form to shreds ("king- / dom" doesn't survive the first line intact). But fragmentation is never Hopkins's goal: his stress marks on "shéer plód," for example, make the line scan and emphasize the mundane toil that can reveal—"no wonder of it"—God's grandeur in ordinary, unlooked-for places. He reassembles the poem around the earthbound realization in the final tercet that the beauty of Christ's sacrifice is emulated in the bursting open of soil or embers with their radiant self-rending. What happens in lines 9-11, however, is not clear: "Buckle" suggests conjunction, battle (a "buckler" is a shield), and collapse. Perhaps the Falcon is diving toward a sinner, creating a turmoil that, as Hopkins shows at length in the later dark sonnets, is indeed both "lovely" and "dangerous." Compare this ecstatic Christ-the-Falcon to Yeats's out-of-control predator in *The Second Coming*.

Pied Beauty is a good poem in which to examine Hopkins's love of dense descriptive words conveying the multicolored and textured quality of "dappled things." The final lines slow the pace to dwell on each adjective. The short last line metrically joins the previous two to create a measured six-beat concluding couplet, while visually standing on its own to drive home the poem's appreciation of the unchanging God who made this bountifully variegated flux.

As befits a season of plenty, *Hurrahing in Harvest* is full of gorgeous language, such as "has wilder, wilful-wavier / Meal-drift moulded ever and melted across skies?" Line 7 ends in a way unprecedented in English poetry, with the indefinite article "a." But it works as a rhyme: the last three words are pronounced "gave ya" to rhyme with a cultivated British pronunciation of "Saviour." The poem closes by insisting on the double, dynamic quality of observation. Nature needs to come together with a beholder to realize God's greatness—"him" in the last line can be Christ for whom the heart hurls (exults).

Binsey Poplars and *Spring and Fall: to a young child* could be used to build a case for the "ecological" Hopkins, who feels the loss of trees as not simply a blight on the landscape but the destruction of their personality—in dying they "unselve," robbing the world of their specialness and that of the landscape they inhabited. Compare the final journal entry (April 8, 1873) on the felling of an ashtree: "I heard the sound and looking out and seeing it maimed there came at that moment a great pang and I wished to die and not to see the inscapes of the world destroyed any more." In *Spring and Fall* the child Margaret's sorrow over the leaves falling from the trees reminds the poet, as it does Frost in *The Oven Bird*, of "that other fall we name the fall." One of Hopkins's most moving poems, *Spring and Fall* mixes the theological framework of original sin with basic human experience, claiming that our grief over calamity in the world beyond us is finally grief over our own mortality and deathly ways.

Exhausted and lonely at his final post in Ireland, Hopkins turned his sense of creative impotence and spiritual angst into unforgettable religious poetry. The Christ that is "lovely in limbs" in *As Kingfishers Catch Fire* now turns a "lionlimb" against him in the "terrible" sonnets. As Eliot said of Tennyson's *In Memoriam*, it is "the quality of the doubt" that makes these works so compelling. In *Carrion Comfort* the opening line renders "Despair" as both noun and verb, setting up the engulfing, tortured language to come. Amid the violence of image there are echoes of Shakespeare's *The Tempest* (II,ii) where Caliban and Trinculo cower under a cloak to avoid the coming storm: "in turns of tempest, me heaped there; me frantic to avoid thee and flee." (See also "Here! creep, / Wretch, under a comfort serves in a whirlwind" in the equally bleak *No Worst, There Is None*). The shattering conclusion evokes Jacob wrestling with the angel, registering confusion and horror at the poet's conflict with God, but what makes it most vivid is the interjection "my God!" that is also a recognition, an acknowledgement, a confession.

No Worst, There Is None and *I Wake and Feel the Fell of Dark, Not Day* continue to grapple with the darkness of the soul. The irrepressible morning of *God's Grandeur* fails to come: night never ends and day is only redeemed by its death in sleep. In deepest misery, unable to communicate with God, the poet becomes gall, Christ's bitter drink at the crucifixion, galling himself in a bitter parody of those revelatory embers at the end of *The Windhover*. Bodily, bloody imagery now predominates as Hopkins imagines himself scourged like Christ, but all this suffering only places him among the damned and "their sweating selves"—"but worse."

That Nature is a Heraclitean Fire offers a momentary reprieve, its thickly textured description of nature recalling the early poems. Its mid-poem doubts give way to a final vision of the resurrection. But the overall effect is wrenching. The lines are broken (like the poet's spirit?) into roughly three-beat halves, and after a sonnet-like opening, *abbaabba*, with no pause for a turn, the sonnet form explodes; first comes a typical sestet, *cdcdcd*, then another *d* rhyme, and finally a complete new unit with an alternate pattern to conclude: *ccceeefff*. This desperate search for closure parallels the poet's quest for Judgement Day, his desire to turn "This Jack, joke, poor potsherd" into "immortal diamond."

Thou Art Indeed Just, Lord seems written to disprove the title, arguing that no enemy could wound as deeply as this heavenly friend. Sinners, plants, and animals prosper, but not "Time's eunuch," who builds no nest and breeds no lasting work. Perhaps Hopkins's most sexually conscious work, the poem is a mini-*Waste Land* whose agonized plea for rain generates poetic fertility out of spiritual barrenness. Despite these harrowing last poems—or maybe in view of the agony they express—Hopkins's dying words were "I am so happy, so happy."

Lewis Carroll

What makes a good story? One of the basic elements is a journey from the security of home out into regions of conflict and danger. When Carroll precipitated Alice "straight down a rabbit hole . . . without the least idea what was to happen afterwards" he launched her and his readers on a curiously epic adventure. Curious because of the tiny rabbit hole, the funny falling, the safe landing, the inverted or at least vertically tilted version of Arthurian medieval chases after a Questing Beast. Epic because Carroll has linked Alice's adventure to that of the human race, as represented in the Judeo-Christian tradition. Like Adam and Eve, she has a *felix culpa* or "fortunate fall." But it is a literal fall that leads her *to* a garden, not out from it. Moreover, what she eats enables her (eventually) to get into the garden, not get banished from it.

One of the hallmarks of Carroll's inventiveness is his eagerness to turn things around, to entertain all possibilities, to look at the flip side of the rules laid down by society, religion, school. There is a poem by W. H. Auden, about the need for commitment, entitled "Leap Before You Look." And while Alice has moments of conscientiousness, both she and her author leap into situations and explanations without being constrained by "normal" ways of thinking. When Alice falls and doesn't hit the ground right away, it could be because she is falling slowly, rather than falling far. When she drinks and grows smaller, it seems logical that she might eat and grow larger. Reversibility is a key element in Wonderland, whether it is verbal ("Do cats eat bats?" "Do bats eat cats?") or physical (opening and shutting like a telescope) or narrative (first the fall, then the eating, then the garden). If Adam and Eve fall into knowledge (of sexuality, of difference, of alienation from each other, God, and the Garden), Alice falls into perplexity and wonder. Hers is no clear progress from light to darkness, or, as in spiritual autobiography, from darkness to light. Instead, she must try to make sense of the strangely mundane, the mundanely strange aspects of wonderland. One might ask students if Carroll's sense of her confused perceptual and moral "education" is not finally more "realistic" than that presented in conventional literature.

The poems play an important role in this grappling with the unknown. Like the fall down the rabbit hole, they contain familiar components, but keep coming out "wrong." "You are old, Father William" comes from Chapter 5 of *Wonderland*; a parody of Robert Southey's "The Old Man's Comforts and How He Gained Them" (1799), it is recited by Alice at the command of the Caterpillar, who afterwards comments that "it is wrong from beginning to end." In place of sententious moral instruction, the poem views old age as vigorous, fantastic, and foolish. Because it comes from Alice herself, it shows how her inner world has become as topsy-turvy as her outer one. We learn not only that received wisdom and school lessons can be undone by Wonderland experience, but also how implanted structures help create new ideas and images. In this regard, Carroll is anticipating some of Freud's work on how dreams are generated.

The Mock Turtle sings "The Lobster Quadrille" in Chapter 10 of *Wonderland*. As with so many of the creatures Alice meets, there is the question of eating in the air (Alice stops herself from saying that she knows all about whitings from her experience at dinner). But if "The Spider and the Fly," which it parodies, is about taking care not to be eaten, "The Lobster Quadrille" purports to be pure fun; it deliberately holds off on its moral, perhaps to entice the pale snail into a trap. It makes a good lead-in to "The Walrus and the Carpenter," where (in the meter of Hood's "The Dream of Eugene Aram" [1832], about a murderous schoolteacher) Tweedledee tells the story of some unfortunate little oysters. In Victorian times as now, children were taught to love animals that they sooner or later found on their dinner plates. By anthropomorphizing the food ("Their coats were brushed, their faces washed, / Their shoes were clean and neat"), Carroll brings together these two aspects of childhood education, the cuteness and the consumption. Students may have strong opinions on whether this is humorous or shocking, as well as reminiscences about their own culinary encounters with Peter Rabbit, Chicken Little, and the Three Little Pigs.

Finally, "Jabberwocky," from Chapter 1 of *Through the Looking Glass*, where it first appears as a backwards mirror-image, also begins and ends with food. As we and Alice learn later from Humpty Dumpty: "Twas brillig. . . ." means that it is the hour for "broiling things." In the middle of the poem, we learn that the Jabberwock has "jaws that bite" so the hero must slay the beast first, with a sword that goes "snicker-snack." The eat-or-be-eaten side of the Alice stories, the conjunction of primeval struggle and childhood anxiety, is to be found everywhere, from the "cats eat bats/bats eat cats" and "EAT ME /DRINK ME" episodes of Chapter 1 to Alice's promise to her kitty on the last page of *Through the Looking Glass*: "All the time you're eating your breakfast, I'll repeat 'The Walrus and the Carpenter' to you, and then you can make believe it's oysters, dear!" Food, hunger, appetite, absence. Ask students why the jar of marmalade that Alice picks up as she falls turns out to be empty. Is this a frustrated foretaste of the world of loss and mortality that Carroll builds around Alice and that he explicitly addresses in "Child of the Pure Unclouded Brow"?

"The White Knight's Song" uses the stanza form of Thomas Moore's "My Heart and Lute," but its content parodies Wordsworth's "Resolution and Independence." Wordsworth's "leech-gatherer on the moor" has been replaced by the "aged man / A-sitting on a gate." Before the Knight starts singing, Carroll comments: "Of all the strange things that Alice saw in her journey Through the Looking Glass, this was the one that she always remembered most clearly. Years afterwards she could bring the whole scene back again . . . the mild blue eyes and kindly smile of the Knight—the setting sun gleaming through his hair, and shining on his armour in a blaze of light that quite dazzled her . . . all this she took in like a picture . . . listening, in a half-dream, to the melancholy music of the song." Carroll saw himself as the White Knight, but then so did John Tenniel, the illustrator, who gave the Knight his own features. Both were old(er) storytellers who try to entertain a young girl with tales (or pictures) of inconsequential nonsense. They are allied with the speaker in the poem, a searcher for knowledge who shakes the aged man to wring from him the truth of life, but is so caught up in his own crazy world of invention that he cannot focus on the bizarre answers he receives.

One of the best books on Alice is Jackie Wullschläger's *Inventing Wonderland* (1995), full of useful illustrations, which situates the Alice books in the context of Victorian images of childhood, and also has chapters on Edward Lear, J. M. Barrie, Kenneth Grahame, and A. A. Milne. The Norton Critical Edition of *Alice in Wonderland* (revised 1992) gives a good sense of the variety of critical approaches to the Alice books, ranging from the mathematical to the psychoanalytical.

PERSPECTIVES

Imagining Childhood

This section contains a wide variety of writings for and about children—and even, in the case of Daisy Ashford's novel, by a child. Time permitting, the instructor might assign the entire Perspective in conjunction with the readings from Lewis Carroll. But it would also be possible to single out, for example, the nonsense verse of Carroll, Lear, and Belloc for a class session devoted to the whimsical and humorous aspects of Victorian poetry. Or one might focus on autobiographical recollections of Victorian childhood, linking some of the readings here with excerpts elsewhere in the anthology (from Newman, Mill, Darwin, Gosse, Ruskin, Cobbe, Pater, etc.).

Other depictions of childhood can be found in Parliamentary Papers and Henry Mayhew (*Perspectives: The Industrial Landscape*), Book I of *Aurora Leigh*, our excerpt from *Jane Eyre* (*Perspectives: Religion and Science*), *A Christmas Carol*, and several of the readings in *Perspectives: Victorian Ladies and Gentlemen* (notably, Cobbe, the Brontës, and *Tom Brown's School Days*, though Queen Victoria's letters on child-bearing might also be relevant). Other writings for children include Edith Nesbit's *Fortunatus Rex & Co.* and Rudyard Kipling's *Just So Stories*. Thus, the instructor who wished to use Childhood as one of the unifying themes of a course on the Victorians would find ample resources within this anthology, perhaps to be supplemented with some full-length works such as *Oliver Twist* or *Great Expectations* or *Peter Pan*.

Antony and Peter Miall's *The Victorian Nursery Book* (1980) is excellent for giving students a sense of the visual world of Victorian children. It is heavily illustrated, with everything from pictures of bassinets and other nursery furniture, to the illustrations in children's books, to pictures of their toys and clothing. The book also contains a wonderful chapter on "The Photograph Album" which reproduces numerous photos of middle-class Victorian children all dressed up to have their pictures taken.

Students who wish to know more about the lives of working children should consult E. Royston Pike's *Human Documents of the Victorian Golden Age* (1967), which has many accounts of the lives of working children, as well as arguments for the necessity of child labor. A particularly compelling passage is the testimony of the Nottingham master sweep, which Pike quotes at length:

> No one knows the cruelty which a boy has to undergo in learning. The flesh must be hardened. This is done by rubbing it, chiefly on the elbows and knees with strongest brine . . . . You must stand over them with a cane, or coax them by a promise of a halfpenny, etc. if they will stand a few more rubs.
>
> At first they will come back from their work with their arms and knees streaming with blood, and the knees looking as if the caps had been pulled off. Then they must be rubbed with brine again, and perhaps go off at once to another chimney. In some boys I have found that the skin does not harden for years.

The master sweep claims that although the best age to teach boys is about six, he has known them start as young as four or five. He recalls trying to accept no work in the afternoons so the sweeps could go to school, but "a lady complained to me because she could not get her chimney done, and said, 'A chimney sweep, indeed, wanting education! what next?'" Yet the boys became unemployable at fifteen or sixteen, and those who survived cancer or lung disease often went into the workhouse.

Without education, the chimney sweeps faced a grim future. But the education of children in nineteenth-century Britain was a wildly diverse and inconsistent affair. Have students examine the range of educational situations described or implied in this Perspective section, and elsewhere in the anthology. At one extreme was the absolute ignorance of the watercress girls (Miller's and Mayhew's) or the Blue Book girls. At the other was the expensive boarding school experience described by Cobbe or fictionalized by Hughes. Some children—these included Mill, Ruskin, Gosse, Robert Browning, and Stevenson—were educated at home by their parents; others—like Carroll's Alice, or Henry James's Maisie—had governesses (for a description of what this could be like from the point of view of the governess, see Charlotte and Anne Brontë's writings in *Perspectives: Victorian Ladies and Gentlemen*). For middle-class children, there was an intense emphasis on proper behavior and manners (see, for example, *Alice*, *Moral Verses*, and *Peter Rabbit*). Memorization played a larger role than it does today, as illustrated in both the brutal schoolroom satirized by Dickens in our excerpt from *Hard Times* (in *Perspectives: The Industrial Landscape*), and Alice's preoccupation with recalling the words of poems she has learned by heart.

Charles Darwin
from A Biographical Sketch of an Infant (1839–41; 1877)

One might ask students to consider how far modern beliefs about child development coincide with Darwin's—in what ways have we followed his thinking, and in what ways have we diverged? Notice how frequently he compares his child to various animals—this might have been thought radical at a time when suggestions that human beings are essentially animals provoked outrage. To a naturalist, such comparisons no doubt came easily to mind, and students who have read the readings from Darwin earlier in this anthology might recall his unromantic thoughts on a wife: "Better than a dog, anyhow." Does Darwin emerge as a monster, dispassionately noting the reactions of his baby just as he would those of a laboratory animal? Or as a loving father, fascinated with every aspect of his baby's emerging capacities and personality? Have students compare Darwin's autobiographical description of his own childhood with his biographical sketch of his son's childhood.

Moral verses

To Darwin, his baby was an object of study; to many Victorians, the child was an object to be improved upon. Where Darwin was curious to note vestiges of "savage" responses, the moralists were intent upon taming the savage by teaching it table manners. The earnest "Table Rules for Little Folks" is an excellent example of this sort of preoccupation. The Victorians continued to produce heavily moralistic literature for children at the same time that they mocked such writing. *Alice in Wonderland* has been called "the first fantasy entirely free of moralizing" (*Victorian Britain: An Encyclopedia*); compare the verses in this section with the garbled nonsense Alice recites ("How doth the busy bee" for example) as she attempts to recall the lessons she has been obliged to learn by heart in the schoolroom. It is sometimes difficult to know where sincerity ends and mockery begins: if Eliza Cook's greedy little mouse dies merely to teach children a lesson about unselfishness, is Heinrich Hoffman's Augustus in quite the same category? It is hard not to detect irony in the wildly exaggerated punishments Hoffman's characters endure. Those wishing to know more about Heinrich Hoffman will find a chapter on him in Frey and Griffith's *The Literary Heritage of Childhood*.

There is an obvious pairing to be made between Thomas Miller's poem and Henry Mayhew's interview with the watercress girl (in *Perspectives: The Industrial Landscape*); perhaps a student might find a paper topic in comparing the two treatments of the same subject. On first reading "Willie Winkie," students may assume that Willie is the name of a child who won't go to sleep. But a moment's reflection suggests how unlikely it is that a toddler would be scampering about the village at bedtime. Rather, Willie Winkie is the name given to Sleep—perhaps analogous to the Sandman?—whose nightly visits help children nod off. Point out how light it stays on summer evenings in Scotland—children in northern countries have to go to bed in broad daylight, a situation described by another Scottish poet, Robert Louis Stevenson, in "Bed in Summer."

Edward Lear

In *Children's Literature: An Illustrated History* (1995) Peter Hunt points out that "Lear was a unique phenomenon": not until his *Book of Nonsense* (1846) did nonsense become an accepted literary genre. He was "a talented artist, but it was his children's books . . . which gave him lasting fame, particularly for such surrealistically absurd narrative poems as "The Owl and the Pussy-cat." "The rhythms of the verse, word coinages such as the 'runcible spoon', and Lear's use of extravagant imagery are wonderfully effective, even though a note of unease, almost panic, can often be felt even in the slightest lyrics" (94). His "limericks rarely preach Victorian morals but aim to make their readers laugh, while his black-and-white drawings often display adults as amusing eccentrics rather than figures to be respected" (95).

Instructors wishing to focus on nonsense as a genre should read an essay by X. J. Kennedy, "Strict and Loose Nonsense: Two Worlds of Children's Verse" (*School Library Journal*, 1991; rpt. *Only Connect: Readings on Children's Literature*, eds. Sheila Egoff et al, 1996). Kennedy writes that, far from being "merely lunatic and disorderly," the nonsense of Lear and Carroll is "fearsomely reasonable"; these writers imagine a "strictly logical universe controlled at all times by cause and effect" (226). Lear, for example, gives us "a whole zooful of imagined beasts and even invented a 'Nonsense botany,'" while in *Sing-Song* Christina Rossetti "gives us fish who carry umbrellas to protect themselves from the rain." Kennedy adds that "a further rule of strict nonsense is . . . emotional detachment"; hence, "some find an apparent cruelty and indifference in those limericks wherein poor old characters are humiliated, publicly ridiculed, beaten, and even put to death" (229). But Lear "strives for total unreality. He banishes his characters to a nutty world all their own, and he stakes out the boundaries of that world in bouncing metre and jog-trot rhyme," which along with the "loony" drawings advertise "the fact that a poem is a game" (230).

Some students have trouble with the violence in Lear (and in Carroll, for that matter). In *Secret Gardens* (1985) Humphrey Carpenter writes that Lear "was the first to realize that Nonsense is inextricably associated with violence, destruction, annihilation, and that any Nonsensical proposition, if pursued logically to its conclusion, must end in Nothing. And this realisation underlies *Alice*" (60). Carpenter argues that Lear's message was that the public world was vindictive and intolerant, and the true artist must alienate himself from society and pursue a private dream" (11-13). Lear's own alienation from society is thus the real subject of his Book of Nonsense. His later verses for children consist of explorations of the possibilities of escape and strange journeys—a theme that became central to the great children's writers: the search for a mysterious elusive Good Place.

Inventing Wonderland (1995) by Jackie Wullschläger elaborates on these themes of alienation and escape: "Edward Lear, whose secret homosexuality set him at odds with society and whose love affair with a judge ended in disappointment and rejection, wrote fantasies about mismatched couples—the Owl and the Pussy Cat, the Duck and the Kangaroo—living happily ever after" (6). Victorian fantasies "employ images which call attention to a sense of psychological release. *Alice's Adventures in Wonderland* opens in a pool of tears. Edward Lear's characters—the Owl and the Pussy Cat, the Daddy Long-legs and the Fly, the Jumblies—sail away to sea and freedom. . . . In fantasy, unconscious or repressed desires could be expressed, and this is why strict and sombre Victorian England inspired so great an outburst of anarchic, escapist, nonsensical children's books" (26, 27). One of the great pleasures of such books is that "they celebrate rebellion and chaos, point no morals, rejoice in freewheeling thought. That liberty, however, is framed and made possible by their concentration on child and child-like characters" (27). Wullschläger points to contrasts between Carroll and Lear, however: whereas Carroll's nonsense "is rooted in the Victorian England of trains and furniture dealers and Darwinian debate, Lear's nonsense emerged out of the Mediterranean landscape [where he had settled in later life] and is full of the joys of sailing away to exotic, calm, distant seascapes." And "where Carroll's nonsense is intellectual and logical, Lear's is poetic and emotional" (83, 85).

For a nineteenth-century view of Lear and his work, see Sir Edward Strachey's "Nonsense as a Fine Art" which originally appeared in *The Quarterly Review* in October 1888 (rpt. Lance Salway, ed. *A Peculiar Gift: Nineteenth Century Writings on Books for Children*, 1976).

Christina Rossetti
from Sing-Song: A Nursery Rhyme Book (1872, 1893)

Christina Rossetti and Lewis Carroll knew each other fairly well: Carroll, in the person of Charles Dodgson, photographed Christina and her family, and he sent her a copy of *Alice in Wonderland* when it first came out in 1865. But U. C. Knoepflmacher, in his *Ventures into Childland: Victorians, Fairy Tales, and Femininity* (1998), speculates that Rossetti saw Carroll as a literary rival in the expanding children's book market, and may have suspected him of borrowing her ending from "Goblin Market" (see Knoepflmacher's chapter on Rossetti, "Razing Male Preserves: From 'Goblin Market' to *Sing-Song*" pp 312–349). Carroll's conclusion does indeed follow Rossetti's in seeking to resituate what has turned into a wildly transgressive tale within Victorian social structures; it emphasizes how the story would be lovingly passed down to Alice's own children. One might also hazard that the "Eat Me" and "Drink Me" episodes of Chapter 1 of *Alice* were inspired by the memory of a climactic moment in "Goblin Market" (1862) when Lizzie tells her sister Laura "Eat me, Drink me, love me" (line 471). But *Alice* made by far the bigger splash with the public, and when in 1872 Rossetti and her illustrator Arthur Hughes (whose little girls look like Tenniel's Alice) brought out *Sing-Song*, they "entered a market in which their competition with Carroll and Tenniel had to be openly confronted" (Knoepflmacher 339).

On the surface there seems little enough in common. However imaginative Rossetti may be, she finds ways to corral her wild ideas and set them in an instructive context. The book seems to be written for a double audience, a child who will wonder (or simply sit still and absorb the lesson) and an adult who will read, explain, and guide. In the best essay on Sing-Song, "Sound, Sense, and Structure in Christina Rossetti's Sing-Song," (Children's Literature 22 [1994]: 3–25), Sharon Smulders writes that the poem unfolds "a narrative from cradle to grave, from winter to fall, from sunrise to sunset," inviting readers "to understand life as an ordered totality" (3). Nothing could be further from the anti-structure of the Alice stories, which career from place to place, character to character, only to end with the abruptness of a bad dream. Moreover, the enclosed nursery world of Sing-Song is clearly very different from the ever-changing landscape that Alice roams without help from adults. While Knoepflmacher writes that "Sing-Song . . . allowed [Rossetti] to realize an 'adult' agenda that she had previously been unable to disseminate" (xiv), one contemporary reviewer of Sing-Song asked whether "Miss Rossetti would have done more for the children if she had done less for us."

But there are enough patches of nonsense to warrant comparison, as well as an overlapping of animal characters and situations. Alice encounters the King and Queen of Hearts, who upset her emotionally till she upsets them physically, declaring them "nothing but a pack of cards." In Rossetti's "If I were a Queen" the little girl speaker on her heart-shaped throne yields to the importunate little boy—both the poem and illustration reinforce the way in which gender can redistribute power. In "When fishes set umbrellas up" Rossetti's semi-human fishes and lizards sport umbrellas and parasols, but only in the conditional tense, showing what is not likely or possible—on the order of "if wishes were horses beggars would ride." Carroll's Bill the Lizard, on the other hand, makes direct contact with Alice, and gets kicked up the chimney by her (see Knoepflmacher 330–331; 347–348). Or compare the linguistic oddities explored in "A pin has a head but no hair" with those in the Alice books. Rossetti concludes that "baby crows, without being a cock," but in Wonderland when Alice tells a baby not to grunt, it turns into a real pig.

One way to approach this material is to ask where the reader is supposed to be located in relation to the story—identifying, distanced, threatened, amused? Does one emerge from the reading feeling bewildered, empowered, chastened, superior?

The series is framed by dead and sleeping babies. The same year that Sing-Song was published Parliament passed the Infant Life Protection Act to fight the rising rate of unexplained baby deaths. Why does Rossetti think that mortality belongs in her nursery rhymes? One might sense a "that's the way the world is and you'd better accept it" strain to these poems, whether it's gender roles ("What does the bee do?"), household duties ("A pocket handkerchief to hem"), or human limitation ("Twist me a crown of wild-flowers"). Yet the two poems about flint, for example, hint at a different Rossetti, the fiery personality hidden within the drab exterior: "Stroke a flint, and there is nothing to admire: / Strike a flint, and forthwith flash out sparks of fire." Is this the "true" Christina, the powerful poet seemingly imprisoned by chains of respectability and responsibility? One feels that elemental energy also in the most famous of the lyrics, "Who has seen the wind?" Like the wind, Rossetti's poems cause us to feel the force of emotions and contingencies we cannot see.

Robert Louis Stevenson
from A Child's Garden of Verses (1885)

Darkness and light: whether part of the daily cycle or symbols of the moral universe, these are the double center of Stevenson's literary world. There is barely a year between the publication of these child-oriented poems and the very grown-up tale of *Dr. Jekyll and Mr. Hyde*. Both hinge on the fluctuating nature of human behavior and the physical world. If the adult horror tale alternates between respectability and depravity, dark streets of crime and mundane interiors of drab respectability, the Garden of Verses harbors both good and bad children, cozy bedclothes and troubling night shadows. "Bed in Summer" struggles with the incongruity of going to bed in daylight and rising in the dark. "The Land of Counterpane" is a daytime topography of toys dominated by the child-giant who controls them, while "The Land of Nod" contrasts that daytime comfort with the strange autonomy of dreamland that one can reach only alone and by night.

Daytime seems to bring out the moralist in Stevenson—or at least his moralizing poems have no specific location or temporal dimension; they are uttered as absolutes: "The world is so full of a number of things, / I'm sure we should all be as happy as kings." And rather like a king, the child-moralizer has definite ideas about private property ("Looking Forward"), manners ("The Whole Duty of Children"), naughtiness and poverty ("System"), and the superiority of his kingdom to that of anyone else ("Foreign Children").

Darkness, on the other hand, can bring out the adventurous child, as in "Escape at Bedtime," when the narrator sneaks outside to get an eyeful of the stars, a vision so powerful that even being "packed off to bed" cannot dim "the stars going round in my head." Similarly, in "The Lamplighter"—of all the poems the most evocative of Stevenson's childhood infirmity and the rhythm of late Victorian domestic life—the housebound speaker longs to join the lamplighter outside on his mission: "when I am stronger and can choose what I'm to do, / O Leerie, I'll go round at night and light the lamps with you!" But the attractive symbolic resonance of the lamplighter's task and the child's pride in his social standing ("for we are very lucky, with a lamp before the door") are mitigated by the poignance of childhood aspiration and the emotional vulnerability revealed at the end: "O Leerie, see a little child and nod to him to-night."

It can be easy to overlook the verbal artistry of the poems; like Christina Rossetti's they have a simple transparency of form that handles big ideas effortlessly. "Shadow March" is a good poem to focus on for some rhythmic analysis. The first and third lines of each stanza move forward briskly in a march-like tetrameter, while the second and fourth lines advance more slowly, in a hesitating trimeter. The shadows come rapidly "tramp, tramp, tramp" but the boy who is carrying his shadow-producing candle up the stairs dares not move too fast (he's scared, and the candle might blow out if he runs). The poem's final line—"With the black night overhead"—brings everything to a stop with heavy stresses on four out of the last five syllables.

It might be interesting to look back to Blake's "Songs of Innocence" to see how Stevenson's middle-class vision of a sheltered childhood compares with the harsher world of Blake's little workers and orphans. So many children's works are written from the point of view of an adult that it is a rare achievement to speak in a child's voice and from a child's perspective. It may be that Blake, like James's Maisie, focuses on the difference between what a child lives through and what he or she can understand, thus making room for an adult reader to link the worlds of innocence and experience, while Stevenson's sickly, sensitive child is so preternaturally aware of his hopes, fears, and duties that one is touched by the amount of innocence in the experience, the level of anxious experience in the cosseted innocence.

Hilaire Belloc
from The Bad Child's Book of Beasts (1896)
from Cautionary Tales for Children (1907)

Like Carroll and Lear, Belloc brilliantly juxtaposes the bizarre and the ordinary, as in the zany image of the yak on a leash at the art gallery, or the deadpan assumption that "mothers of large families" will appreciate a word to the wise about the value of keeping a tiger for a pet. The bouncing nursery-rhyme rhythms of the verse are hilariously at odds with the violence of the texts.

By the *fin de siècle*, a title such as *Cautionary Tales for Children* no longer could be taken straight. To illustrate the difference in tone, pair "Table Rules for Little Folks" with Belloc's explanation of why he calls the little child "bad." Then pair "The Mouse and the Cake," or "The Story of Augustus" with Belloc's "Jim, Who ran away from his Nurse, and was eaten by a Lion." Belloc is in a different universe entirely, and should be taught in conjunction with Carroll and Lear. His verse, like theirs, is often violent, and comically cruel: the tiger swallows up the baby, but the mother is expected to regard this a helpful reduction of household expenses; Jim is eaten by a lion, but his complacent mother—already drying her eyes!—takes comfort in being unsurprised that such a fate should befall a disobedient son.

The poet takes a diabolical pleasure in detailing Jim's demise, as he is devoured bit by bit, "shins and ankles, calves and knees." One senses that—unlike the authors of "Table Rules" and "The Mouse and the Cake"—Belloc is fundamentally on the child's side. What child wouldn't relish such a description? The adults in the poem are of no use: in addition to the easily consoled parents, there is the lionkeeper: "Though very fat he almost ran / To help the little gentleman." The "almost" is delicious. And Belloc shows his hand in the last line, when he points the moral of the story: "always keep a-hold of Nurse / For fear of finding something worse." Sticking to Nurse's side, in other words, is a fate only *slightly* less to be dreaded than being eaten by a lion! As the *Dictionary of Literary Biography* puts it: "The sense of ironic distance from the voice and attitudes of the Establishment, represented by the adult authority figures of his children's verse, is the key to the appreciation of that verse. Belloc implicitly sides with the child reader against the pompous, didactic person in charge, revealing the absurdity of that person's values and attitudes" (volume 141).

Beatrix Potter
The Tale of Peter Rabbit (1893, 1902)

Peter Hunt observes in *Children's Literature: An Illustrated History* (1995) that although Beatrix Potter was initially admired primarily as "one of the greatest of all animal artists," recent criticism has "laid increasing emphasis on the elegance and wit of her prose, with its humorous understatement . . . and its balanced, almost biblical rhythms" (186).

The Tale of Peter Rabbit seems at first to belong to the tradition of moralizing writings for children: Peter disobeys his sensible mother and muddles into a near-disaster (though, unlike Eliza Cook's mouse, or Heinrich Hoffman's Augustus, Peter Rabbit gets off with nothing worse than a fright and perhaps a cold). But in *Inventing Wonderland* (1995) Jackie Wullschläger places Peter in a more satiric world:

> Before Carroll and Lear, children's books preached convention and duty, and criticised stupidity and bad manners. Since, children's writers have been on the side of the radicals. Edwardian writers shot their Arcadian visions through with irony as Carroll had done. . . . The rebelliousness and waywardness of the Wonderland creatures . . . can be traced in the irresponsible heroes of Edwardian children's stories—Peter Pan, Toad, Peter Rabbit (103-4)

Graham Greene has a wonderful brief essay tracing Beatrix Potter's literary career (rpt. *The Lost Childhood and Other Essays*, 1952). In it he calls *Peter Rabbit* "the second of the great comedies" (the first being *Two Bad Mice*, 1904). Greene writes: "In Peter and his cousin Benjamin Miss Potter created two epic personalities. The great characters of fiction are often paired: Quixote and Sancho, Pantagruel and Panurge, Pickwick and Weller, Benjamin and Peter. Peter was a neurotic, Benjamin worldly and imperturbable. Peter was warned by his mother, 'Don't go into Mr. MacGregor's garden; your father had an accident there; he was put in a pie by Mrs. MacGregor.' But Peter went from stupidity rather than for adventure. He escaped from Mr. MacGregor by leaving his clothes behind, and the sequel, the story of how his clothes were recovered, introduces Benjamin, whose coolness and practicality are a foil to the nerves and clumsiness of his cousin. It was Benjamin who knew the way to enter a garden: 'It spoils peoples' clothes to squeeze under a gate; the proper way to get in is to climb down a pear tree.' It was Peter who fell down head first" (108).

Students may be surprised, even dismayed, to hear Peter treated in such a portentous manner—an "epic personality"? But *is* Peter truly a stupid neurotic, an incompetent bumbler? In their chapter on *Peter Rabbit* in *The Literary Heritage of Childhood* (1987) Frey and Griffith put a more positive spin on the story. They see it as a pastoral romance, a tale of illicit adventure in which the hero begins his initiation towards maturity.

In *Secret Gardens: A Study of the Golden Age of Children's Literature* (1985) Humphrey Carpenter devotes a chapter to Beatrix Potter, placing her in context (she knew Millais and Gladstone, for example, and kept a detailed journal commenting on the political and social events of the day). He takes issue with the popular view of her as a lonely spinster writing primarily out of nostalgic yearning for a childhood paradise: while "Peter Rabbit and his fellows certainly move through a landscape . . . perfect in terms of physical beauty," Potter "used the Arcadian setting as an ironic contrast and background to the blackly comic themes of her stories" (140-1). *The Tale of Peter Rabbit* is the first in a series, "a connected body of writing" with a "very adult view of the world." And although it is one of the "least ambitious" of her works, "its single theme is a dark one, familiar in folk-tales: the pursuit of a hapless individual (Peter) by a vengeful giant (Mr McGregor the gardener)." Carpenter adds: "Strikingly, his eventual escape is utterly unheroic; no folk-tale hero would arrive home in a pathetic condition and be put to bed by his mother." Thus, "the expectations of the folk-tale or fairy story have been upset. . . . *Peter Rabbit*, though slight, is an ironic comment on the giant-killer stories" (145).

Daisy Ashford
from The Young Visiters; or, Mr Salteena's Plan (1890, 1919)

The Young Visiters is an extraordinary mixture of innocence and knowingness. For example, Ashford never questions or explains why "quite a young girl . . . of 17" is staying with "an elderly man of 42." Adult readers may raise an eyebrow at Mr. Salteena's leave-taking of Rosalind the housemaid—why are they so bashful and blushing, and why does he give her money?—or at Bernard's obliging distribution of guest rooms: "I have given the best spare room to Miss Monticue said Bernard with a gallant bow and yours turning to Mr Salteena opens out of it so you will be nice and friendly." Best of all—for the amused grown-up reader—"Ethel and Bernard returned from their Honeymoon with a son and hair."

Yet if Daisy Ashford betrays not the slightest awareness that such goings-on might be open to misinterpretation, she displays an almost frighteningly clear-sighted knowledge of the workings of other aspects of the adult world. The women in her novel trade openly on their looks to get what they want, and the men comment unabashedly on the women's appearance and desirability. Social or class distinctions are portrayed with a no-holds-barred frankness. Ashford has a keen eye for the trappings of wealth, and her characters take an uninhibited pleasure in them: Ethel admires the "violets in a costly varse" and Mr Salteena rolls over "in the costly bed"; he enjoys his "sumpshous" bathroom with its "good dodges of a rich nature."

Her grownups behave in many ways like children, tearing open letters and parcels avidly, running and skipping upstairs, sulking and sneering and bickering with one another. They exchange insults as casually as children in a playground: "You will look very silly"; "Well so will you"; "She has a most idiotick run." They say out loud things which grownups customarily express in a more roundabout way: "Please bring one of your young ladies whichever is the prettiest"; "I am parshial to ladies if they are nice"; "I am not quite a gentleman but you would hardly notice it"; "he is inclined to be rich."

Yet the innocence of the author mingles disturbingly with a certain shrewdness—Daisy Ashford is wise beyond her years in ways that might make us uncomfortable were it not for her rollicking sense of fun and insouciant misspellings. Mr Salteena and Ethel are upstarts on the make: Ethel's frock "had grown rarther short in the sleeves" and neither one is at ease in the world of "very exalted" footmen and country houses with indoor plumbing. They are unsure whether to tip the servants, but very clear about the power of money: "Well I am paying for the cab said Mr S. so I might be allowd to put my feet were I like." The Earl who undertakes the task of transforming Mr Salteena into a gentleman pulls no punches either: "Have you much money he asked and are you prepared to spend a good deal. . . . the point is that we charge a goodly sum for our training here but however if you cant pay you need not join."

Peter Hunt notes that The Young Visiters "is probably unique as an adults' book written by a child" (Children's Literature: An Illustrated History, 1995, xi). In his preface to the 1991 Academy Chicago edition of the book, Walter Kendrick argues that for many years the book was mistakenly pigeonholed as a children's book:

> This was a gross injustice. . . . Ashford did not have nine-year-olds in mind while she wrote. What she had in mind was the truth of human experience, as she had seen it and read about it in novels written for adults. . . .
> The Young Visiters has two themes: love and social advancement. So does Pride and Prejudice. It has a double plot, the specialty of Dickens, George Eliot, Trollope . . . . And her viewpoint throughout is strictly unsentimental. You may laugh with joy, but you dare not patronize her (x–xi).

The Young Visiters was a huge success when it was finally published, decades after Ashford wrote it; it was reprinted eighteen times in the year of its first publication. Yet although the author lived to be 90, she wrote nothing after 1894. The Young Visiters was made into a musical in 1968 (while Ashford was still alive) and a film in 1984. Students who wish to learn more about Ashford should consult R. M. Malcomson's Daisy Ashford: Her Life (1984).

Henry James
from What Maisie Knew (1897)

Daisy and Maisie make a good pairing, and could easily be taught together. Each shows the adult world through the eyes of an innocent young girl. James relished the challenge inherent in his use of such a limited narrator: in his Preface he noted that "small children have many more perceptions than they have terms to translate them; their vision is at any moment much richer, their apprehension even constantly stronger, than their prompt, their at all producible, vocabulary." The child's understanding of what was going on around her would inevitably be confused and partial, so much so that James felt his novel would be "strangled" if he really restricted himself "to what the child might be conceived to have *understood*"; rather, he decided, "I should have to stretch the matter to what my wondering witness materially and inevitably *saw*; a great deal of which quantity she either wouldn't understand at all or would quite misunderstand." The innocence of her perspective enabled James to explore ironic depths: James called her "the ironic centre."

Since we have had space to print only the Prologue and first chapter, students may wish to know what happens next. Briefly, the parents who initially fought to gain custody of Maisie both remarry, and soon can't be bothered with her. As James put it: "The wretched infant was thus to find itself practically disowned, rebounding from racquet to racquet like a tennis ball or a shuttlecock." Yet although her parents treat her with relentless selfishness, Maisie somehow emerges unscathed. James felt that "for satisfaction of the mind . . . the small expanding consciousness would have to be saved . . . rather than coarsened, blurred, sterilized, by ignorance and pain" (Preface). *The Dictionary of Literary Biography* (Vol. 12) adds: "What Maisie gradually gains knowledge of is the baseness of some adults, the morality of one eccentric governess, and something which ought to be called love for her father's second wife's lover, who has become Maisie's mother's second husband. Poignant ambiguity results from the innocent little Maisie's incomplete ability to verbalize her bewildering conceptions."

In *The Image of Childhood* (1967) Peter Coveney has a chapter called "Innocence in Henry James." Coveney writes that the "symbol of the sensitive child developing into an awareness of the complexities of life seems to have been specially attractive" to James; "Most of the greater James novels are in fact an inquiry into the fate of innocence, an investigation of the dramatic and moral possibilities of innocence confronted with life" (194). "The child's psyche, claustrophobic, contained, gazing out upon the mysteries of adult life, had particular relevance to the kind of sensibility he was so often concerned to convey. The moral perceptions of *What Maisie Knew* are in fact the perceptions of a unique sensibility" (198). Coveney makes an interesting comparison to Pansy in James's earlier novel *The Portrait of a Lady* (1881): she "suggests James's distinctive image of childhood. She is the innocent 'blank page,' . . . the victim . . . of her father's egotism. . . . [However], she is a victim with a frank, and very wide-eyed awareness. It is a forecast of a characteristic which he developed so brilliantly in *What Maisie Knew*" (198). Coveney also compares Maisie to Dickens's *David Copperfield*: "Maisie's phantasmagoric world is given in a way reminiscent of David Copperfield, with its keenly felt and disconnected sensations of a child thrust into an adult environment, with its wilful, and casual, sadism towards children" (201).

Yet for all his *fin de siècle* irony, James is still typically Victorian in his vision of the child as morally spotless; he fits right in with earlier portrayals of the child as a spiritual redeemer. As Jackie Wullschläger puts it, a favorite Victorian theme "was childhood as morally redemptive, with adult men cared for and spiritually rehabilitated by children. Mean miserly Scrooge is saved by Tiny Tim, a crusty old earl by Little Lord Fauntleroy" (*Inventing Wonderland*, 19). Thus James calls Maisie "our little wonder-working agent" who is "really keeping the torch of virtue alive" (Preface).

For further reading, Edward Wagenknecht has several good pages on *What Maisie Knew* in *The Novels of Henry James* (1983). Paul Theroux has written an interesting introduction to the Penguin edition of the book. There are also three essays on this novel in *New Casebooks*, ed. Neil Cornwell and Maggie Malone (1998). Students who wish to read all of *What Maisie Knew* and perhaps write a paper on it might follow up U. C. Knoepflmacher's suggestion of pairing it "with *A Little Princess*, the novel written by James's brash neighbor Frances Hodgson Burnett" (*Ventures into Childland*, xiv).

Rudyard Kipling
Without Benefit of Clergy (1890)

The history of colonialism is full of stories of white men and their native mistresses. The most familiar scenario is the one Ameera so jealously predicts, in which the man jilts his mistress, either to marry a white woman, or simply to return home to Europe. Here, in contrast, the devotion of the lovers is entirely reciprocal, and the story does not moralize about interracial relationships—an unusual attitude for the period. *Without Benefit of Clergy*, then, works against a too-ready labelling of Kipling as a racist imperialist, despite his portrayals elsewhere of Indians as childlike. Somerset Maugham called it "a beautiful and pathetic tale . . . the best story Kipling ever wrote."

J. M. S. Tompkins notes the concentric circles that structure the narrative: "At the centre is the native house; all the pictorial details, the colours, the little homely sounds belong to the centre; here we listen to the language of love and grief. Outside . . . is John Holden's official life, the Club, the Office, the 'unlovely' bungalow, open to any visitor, the unsparing short phrases of order and criticism, edged with irony by the unseen facts of the native house. . . . Enclosing everything is the India of swarming life and terrifying epidemics, generating the menace and finally the certainty of separation" (*The Art of Rudyard Kipling* [1959], 115).

In *The Good Kipling: Studies in the Short Story* (1971) Elliot Gilbert offers a detailed reading of *Without Benefit of Clergy*, a reading that all subsequent critics have had to take into account. Gilbert describes Holden's constant visions of death and disaster, and the random, hopeless universe he inhabits. The secrecy of Holden's life with Ameera "testifies to the power of convention. The British, who stand ready at any hour to give their lives for the Indian people, nevertheless balk at accepting them as equals, and drive men like Holden into the pointless subterfuges of a double life" (25). Yet Holden relies upon the rigidity of English customs to hold himself together. He participates in native ceremonies, and Ameera learns many of the English ones, yet finally their "elaborate and hopeful" rituals turn out to be "of no use at all" (28). Gilbert claims that this failure of ritual is central to the story's meaning, for ritual is an effort "to achieve order in a chaotic world"—like the British administration's efforts to order the violence and chaos of India.

Ritual is a form of haggling with the universe, but "nothing can be gained, Kipling points out, from bargains like this. . . . It is a man's business . . . to live as fully as he can, postponing nothing" (35). In these terms, Ameera's refusal to go to the Himalayas is not foolishly willful; rather, "it represents her passionate commitment . . . to the idea that life . . . is meaningful only when it is being lived" (33). Gilbert argues that Ameera is "absolutely honest. . . . She is not Madame Butterfly, building her life on self-deception" (36). In fact, she may be "the shrewdest person" in the story. With the death of her child she realizes "that sorrow is not the ultimate disaster of life" and she is freed "of the drag of ritual with its useless self-sacrifice, free to live without fear" (38). The title thus reinforces the "uselessness of ceremony," and represents "Kipling's approval of the couple, of their life together and, perhaps especially, of Ameera's courageous death" (40).

Jeffrey Meyers disagrees, writing that Gilbert "surely misinterprets the story." He contends that the lovers' sufferings, culminating in the "total annihilation of their house," are "a fatal retribution for breaking every rule and law of the white man's code" ("Thoughts on *Without Benefit of Clergy*," *The Kipling Journal* 36 [1969]: 8–11). Meyers writes that "Kipling is neither willing to permit Indians to marry whites nor to allow Indians a viable emotional and cultural life of their own. Wife-beating is the *sine qua non* of his native marriages." Holden and Ameera are "doomed to destruction, not by fatal fever and cholera, but rather by Kipling's sanction of the 'colour prejudice' and 'superiority complex' of his age."

Martin Seymour-Smith also takes issue with Gilbert's reading of the universe in this story as hostile, arguing rather that it is Holden who is a pessimist. Gilbert "has got it the wrong way round: it is Holden's perception of the universe that we are really being shown, not the universe. It may be like that or it may not, and in India it does seem so to foreigners; but we are seeing it through Holden, and we are seeing it because he has entered into a socially forbidden love" (*Rudyard Kipling* [1989], 97).

Seymour-Smith is unhappy with the dialogue in *Without Benefit of Clergy*, calling it an "ineffective and unconvincing semi-Biblical English, stilted and poetical, and not at all as vigorous as the words [Kipling] put into the mouths of his private soldiers." Students, too, may find the characters' speech, with its "thee" and "thou" and "my lord," awkward and unreal. Gilbert contends, however, that while the dialogue has misled some critics "into reading the story as a quaint, rather sentimental love idyll," we should see these lines "as translations into English of expressions which, in the original, are completely idiomatic and unselfconscious" (36n).

Harold Orel suggests that what marks Kipling's "distinctive contribution to the short-story genre, and his arrival as a literary force to be reckoned with . . . comes at the moment that Holden, awed by his introduction to the fact of the physical existence of his son, reaches out to touch the hand of Tota, and learns something new about himself." Quoting the passage, Orel writes appreciatively: "The author of *that* has imagined greatly." For Kipling, who did not marry or have children himself until several years later, accurately captures the tumultuous emotions of the new father. "Kipling's best short stories . . . show a character in the process of change, and very frequently of growing in his or her understanding" (*The Victorian Short Story* [1986], 148).

In *Narratives of Empire: The Fictions of Rudyard Kipling* (1993) Zohreh Sullivan locates *Without Benefit of Clergy* in "a familiar nineteenth-century colonial discourse that fetishizes the Other as fixed sterotype. The colonial object and the native woman, then, are both objects to be recognized and disavowed, appropriated and defamiliarized. . . . The details of Ameera's life, background, appearance, and destiny are all charged with Orientalist anxieties. The native 'wife' has been 'bought' from her mother . . . [who is] an Orientalist stereotype of the Eastern beauty as one who ages easily and hideously." The same things happens to Ameera, who "gradually dissolves from beautiful desired body to a corpse, even as the rain dissolves walls, roads and graves" (96–97). "The marginalized and otherwise silent native female is idealized and denigrated, given presence and voice, yet finally erased" (94). "Structures of forbidden sexuality and desire, troped in terms of mastery and pleasure, fetishize the woman in order to counter male fear of self loss" (96).

Instructors might find Norman Page's A Kipling Companion (1984) a useful reference, with its chronology of Kipling's life and its plot summaries of all Kipling's works. The Illustrated Kipling (ed. Neil Philip [1987]) is a good place to send students who would like to read more of Kipling.

Just So Stories (1902)

Parental love is one of the themes of Without Benefit of Clergy, and Kipling himself went on to be a devoted father of three. He wrote the Just So Stories for his daughter Josephine, the "Best Beloved" (who died in 1899 at the age of six). A friend of Josephine's recalled "the fun of hearing them told in Cousin Ruddy's deep unhesitating voice" (qtd. in The Illustrated Kipling). They are still best read aloud.

The charm of the Just So Stories lies in their whimsical humor, and their mingling of the homely details of nursery life with exotic far-off worlds and talking animals. Angus Wilson admired the first seven stories, pointing out that "they are all united by the same little joke," namely "the pleasing little Darwinian send-up" (qtd. Norman Page, 55). Actually, as Gillian Beer has noted in Darwin's Plots (1983), the explanations are more of a throwback to Lamarck's theory of evolution (24); ultimately, comic absurdity seems more the point than any realistic account of causation.

J. M. S. Tompkins writes: "They are fables about how things came to be as we see them, the elephant's trunk, the camel's hump, the whale's throat, the armadillo's scales, the alphabet that children learn." She describes the idiom as "Oriental grandiloquences embedded in colloquial narrative" (58). "There are manners and morals in the fables, but they are not at all oppressive" (58–59).

Jacqueline S. Bratton analyzes the verses at the end of each story: some "take up the implicit relationship between the adult and the child to whom he tells the fantastical tales and bring their domestic life into focus. An example is 'When the cabin portholes are dark and green,' the vignette from the life of a travelling family which appears at the end of the story of How the Whale Got its Throat. This domestication of the story by the verse can have a moralizing effect, as in The Camel's Hump, where the fun of chanting and the relation of the story to the world of the nursery combine to drive home the moral point" ("Kipling's Magic Art," Critical Essays on Rudyard Kipling, ed. Harold Orel [1989], 58).

In *Kipling the Poet* (1994) Peter Keating remarks on "the subtle air of intimacy with a youthful audience in *Just So Stories*," adding that "whether the balance falls in favour of instruction or entertainment, Kipling's main concern is to communicate a pleasure in the rhythms and meanings of words, often revealing a delight in nonsense verse . . . that demonstrates his deep admiration for Lewis Carroll" (164).

Students who are interested in Victorian children's literature might like to read Edward Lear's *Book of Nonsense* (1846), Lewis Carroll's *Alice in Wonderland* (1865), and Kipling's *Jungle Books* (1894, 1895) and *Puck of Pook's Hill* (1906).

Poetry

In *Kipling the Poet* (1994) Peter Keating writes that Kipling's poetry "offers an insight into early modern Britain, unique in its social range, linguistically adventurous, emotionally powerful, and deeply personal. Kipling's poetry should not be regarded as simply an outward chronicle of public events: it is more a record of his personal responses to those events, and of his thoughts and feelings on a range of other matters, not least the art of poetry" (xiv). Keating adds: "Many of the poems are tantalisingly subtle; quite a number are allegorical; others are syntactically complex and disclose their full meanings through literary, Biblical, and topical allusions" (xv).

Keating notes that the soldier "whose life is so famously saved" by Gunga Din "speaks in a slightly modified Standard English which thickens at moments of emotion or tension and, more strikingly, is distinguished by the speaker's linguistic inventiveness." Keating argues that "the opening of *Gunga Din*, staled by countless mechanical recitations, is one of the finest moments in *Barrack-Room Ballads*. . . . The mood is quiet and thoughtful, with the opening line made up entirely of monosyllabic words, and the speaker remains calm as he tries to find the right terms to express his scorn for those of his listeners who have never experienced the ultimate test. As the terms are not ready to hand, he makes some up: 'penny-fights' for small frontier wars, and, with true poetic flair, he turns Aldershot, the name of the army training camp in Hampshire, into a verb. With his audience fixed as people who are used to having an easy time of it, he tells them (with the help of a heavy rhyme and an emphatic long line) that moral values are determined by necessity, and, until they realise that, they might as well sit safely in quarters drinking their 'gin and beer'. The hero of the ballad is, of course, not the speaker, but Gunga Din, who proves himself to be brave, loyal, intelligent, and even courteous under fire: he is 'white, clear white inside'. . . . *Gunga Din* has become something of a by-word for racial condescension . . . but if the speaker comes over as condescending it is because of his determination to assert his own inferiority" (72).

Norman Page has a chapter on Kipling's verse (161–174) in which he observes that "even though *The Widow at Windsor* and many of the other poems . . . are monologues, there is no attempt to present the speaker as a unique individual: rather he is a representative and communal voice, and in this respect Kipling is closer to the traditional ballad and street-song than to the mainstream of poetic tradition in the late Victorian period" (168). Page suggests that in *The Widow at Windsor* "the loyal tribute to the Queen is undercut in two ways: first by the colloquial fa-

miliarity with which Victoria is referred to ('the Widow at Windsor / With a hairy
[famous, splendid] gold crown on her head'; 'Missis Victorier's sons'), and then by
the parenthetical refrain that echoes the tribute with significant variations that shift
the centre of interest from the Queen to her soldiers. . . . The effect is to turn a patriotic poem into one that has as its real theme not monarch or Empire but the sufferings of the ill-paid, unsung common soldier" (167–68). Page proposes that *The
Widow at Windsor* "may in the matter of tone be compared with Housman's '1887'
(the opening poem of A *Shropshire Lad*) later in the same decade, and contrasted
with the unqualified patriotism of Newbolt's poetry in the same period" (168).

Keating writes that the tone of *The Widow at Windsor* "is one of a boastfulness
at the extent and power of the British Empire that is constantly undercut by a
melancholy refrain recalling the human price demanded by imperialism. The final
stanza extends this echoing discontent to open criticism." Keating points out that
it contains "an allusion to Psalms 139:9 ('If I take the wings of the morning / And
dwell in the uttermost parts of the sea'). But the biblical meaning, that even here
the Lord's hand will be a guiding influence, is overturned and the soldier transformed into some kind of grotesque wounded bird of prey, 'flopping' directionless
around the globe. His guiding light should be the Union Jack, but this becomes
merely 'a bloomin' old rag', that, like the Indian sun, is out of reach and impervious to the suffering it causes. It is hardly surprising that readers pondered the effect this particular poem might have on Queen Victoria, and, taking into account
the range of attitudes and points of view presented in *Barrack-Room Ballads*, debated among themselves whether the young author from India was a flag-waving
imperialist or a dangerous radical" (75).

Recessional (1897) only added to the confusion; like Bruce Springsteen's *Born in
the USA*, Kipling's poem has found itself at the center of debate about its political
and patriotic content. Norman Page calls it "one of the ironies of literary history"
that *Recessional*, "actually a warning against the arrogance to which a world power
is inevitably prone, should have come to be regarded by many as jingoistic and im-
perialistic. Kipling does not *celebrate* the imperial idea—and to this extent he was,
of course, distinctly out of line with the public mood of 1897—being rather intent
on reminding the mother country of its burden of duty" (181–82).

In *The Good Kipling* Elliot Gilbert devotes several pages to this controversial
poem, noting that critics have long been offended "by the contempt for dark-
skinned natives" that seems implicit in what has been called Kipling's most notorious line: "Or lesser breeds without the Law." Gilbert quotes George Orwell (who
believed that Kipling was referring to the Germans, not to colonized peoples): "It
is assumed as a matter of course that the 'lesser breeds' are 'natives,' and a mental
picture is called up of some *pukka sahib* in a pith helmet kicking a coolie"
("Rudyard Kipling," *Essays* [1954]).

Gilbert reminds us that patriotic celebrants of Victoria's Jubilee "waited in considerable suspense" to see what Kipling would write for the occasion, for his voice
"had become almost synonymous with" Britain's imperial destiny. But what Kipling
produced shocked admirers and critics alike: the title suggests "not triumph and
glory, but rather withdrawal, waning, a going-away. And the rest of the poem, with

its clear references to the impermanence of power and to the need for humility in an uncertain world, surprised Kipling's countrymen" (17–18). Nevertheless, the poem still strikes readers as "extraordinarily arrogant." Its "regular tread and comfortingly familiar cadences" suggest "the security and self-congratulatory clubbiness of a not-very-demanding religion" (19). The discrepancy "between the announced and the implicit subject of the poem" jars. Ultimately, Gilbert says, it doesn't matter which race or nation is intended by the word "breeds," for "what is dismaying about the line is its inherent act of 'presuming to judge' in the context of a poem whose ostensible subject is the arrogance of such judgments" (19). In other words, the poem is an aesthetic failure because it never achieves artistic wholeness.

Keating points out that *Recessional* is "virtually a compilation of Biblical allusions, quotations, and echoes. . . . It is based on the assumption that God has made a special covenant with England . . . [but] *Recessional* points to its possible collapse. The principal text, from which Kipling took the refrain of his poem ("Lest we forget—lest we forget!") is Deuteronomy 6:12: 'Then beware lest thou forget the Lord, which brought thee forth out of the land of Egypt'" (116). As for "lesser breeds without the Law," both Germans and non-white races are outside the Law, "though in different ways. The Germans have turned their backs on it deliberately: the non-white races have still to be shown the benefits of living within the law. . . . *Recessional* suggests that even England is in danger of losing God's favour" (117).

If–, which appeared in the children's book *Rewards and Fairies* (1910), "escaped from the book, and for a while ran about the world" on its own, wrote Kipling in his autobiography, *Something of Myself* (191). Keating says "it was copied, parodied, recited, and reproduced in a variety of ways—needlework samplers being a favourite—until its eminently sensible, skilfully articulated maxims became a byword for unacceptable cloying moralism" (168). Zohreh Sullivan suggests that "repeated collapse under excessive pressure is, in a way, the repressed text lying just beneath the surface bravado of such poems as *If* "; Kipling's "fascination with breakdown" was his way of "internalizing the unacceptable, the terror of annihilation or boundary slippage in the troubling structures of gender, race and identity" (79).

Finally, one might compare Kipling's attitudes towards empire—and the men doing the work of colonizing, trading, fighting, and administering—with Stanley and Burton (in the Travel and Empire perspectives section). Also, Kipling provides an excellent lead-in for many of the twentieth-century readings in this anthology, including *Heart of Darkness* and the various perspectives on the Great War (in which Kipling's only son was killed).

PERSPECTIVES

Travel and Empire

For the middle and upper classes the British empire was, according to the critic Robin Gilmour, "a global playground where they could enact the fantasies inspired by a classical education, and become the Romans of the modern world."

Though warnings by moralists such as Ruskin and Tennyson made Victorians mindful that Britain might soon imitate Rome's decline and fall, images of the glorious sacrifices they were making for their nation, culture, and religion kept the empire-builders going. As Rudyard Kipling wrote, "The idea is a pretty one, and men are willing to die for it."

There was also the more individual but still politically important glory of exploration. Scaling the highest peaks in the Alps during the 1850s and 1860s, mountain climbers used the rhetoric of conquest to recount their perilous ascents. In the 1870s and 1880s, British explorers like Stanley, Speke, and Burton survived daunting adventures to map the continent; the Scottish missionary David Livingston was the first European to cross Africa from coast to coast, locating and naming Victoria Falls in the process. Their exploits and best-selling accounts led the way for the dividing up of Africa by European colonizers.

Discuss with students the contradictions and complications of being a traveller. While any outsider remains inevitably "other," some travellers made intense efforts not to be mere spectators, but to participate as fully as possible in the culture they were visiting: Trollope opened a business in Cincinnati, Bird joined in the work of Western settlers, Kingsley set herself up as an African trader, and Burton succeeded in passing himself off as a Muslim pilgrim. From our perspective, these undertakings are hardly unproblematic. But they suggest the complexity of cross-cultural encounters—particularly between representatives of the world's most powerful empire, and members of its colonies, former, actual, or potential.

While many Victorian explorers, missionaries, and colonial administrators saw themselves as bringers of light to dark places, not every traveller fully shared the imperialist ideology of the era or the assumption of moral and cultural superiority. At the very least, some travellers were more nuanced in their approach. Mary Kingsley, in particular, seems to have approached West Africans with an intriguing blend of panache and humility: she wrote that "we gradually educated each other, and I had the best of the affair; for all I had got to teach them was that I was only a beetle and fetish hunter, and so forth, while they had to teach me a new world, and a very fascinating course of study I found it."

Instructors might teach this entire perspectives section as a unit, comparing the different travellers with one another, and perhaps also with Darwin's *Voyage of the Beagle*. If lack of time makes this impossible, individual excerpts can be taught in conjunction with other readings in the anthology: Stanley and *Heart of Darkness*, for example, or Burton and Kipling. The women travellers can be taught in conjunction with the selections on Ladies and Gentlemen, illustrating that not *all* middle-class Victorian women were finding fulfillment in domesticity, whatever the prevailing dogma about women as angels in the house. One might also contrast these travellers to distant and "exotic" places with the more conventional Continental travel experienced by the Brownings, Arnold, and Ruskin (see, for example, the excerpts from *Praeterita* evoking the remembered pleasures of Ruskin's European tours). British writing exercised enormous influence throughout the world, but was influenced in turn, not only by literary currents in Europe, but also by the tales brought back by adventurers further afield.

Frances Trollope
from Domestic Manners of the Americans (1832)

As travel writing, *Domestic Manners* has never lost its appeal, in part thanks to the grouchy persona Mrs. Trollope adopts (a bit like Paul Theroux nowadays). She's a lively writer, with an ear for dialogue and colloquial speech. She combines the dramatic story of a woman venturing into wild territory with domestic and social analysis based on her two-and-a-half year residence in Cincinnati. Her method involves a constant comparison of England and America, sometimes direct, sometimes implied.

Trollope's opening description of voyaging upriver into uncharted territory conveys her initial unease. It is an almost apocalyptic scene of desolation. She compares the landscape to Dante's inferno (instructors might look ahead to Conrad's *Heart of Darkness*, with its ominous trip upriver into a nightmare landscape). But when Trollope meets her first Americans, she regains her equilibrium, and her tone quickly changes from foreboding to satiric. Taking comfort in social condescension, she mocks both American table manners and the American presumption of equality: in this new society, *everyone* professed to be a "lady" or a "gentleman." Students familiar with the readings in Perspectives: Victorian Ladies and Gentlemen will be better able to see why an English gentlewoman like Frances Trollope found such claims preposterous.

At every turn Trollope mercilessly exposes American pretensions: the proliferation of inflated military titles, the granting of worthless "degrees" after a smattering of instruction, the boasts of literary scholarship by a man who scarcely recognizes the most famous English authors. If nineteenth-century American readers were enraged by *Domestic Manners*, contemporary American students sometimes feel almost equally insulted. It can be uncomfortable to find one's own country subjected to the same patronizing attitudes that Western travellers have often displayed abroad.

Trollope's opinions, of course, tell us as much about her and her milieu as they do about America in the 1820s. It's helpful to situate this book against the backdrop of both the American Revolution (hostility towards English paternalism still lingered, and Trollope was often treated rudely) and the impending Reform Bill of 1832 in Britain. Taking democracy for granted, students find it difficult to see how anyone could have opposed the extension of the franchise. But the British, fearful of mob rule and a levelling of society, felt a mixture of admiration and anxiety as they watched the American experiment with democracy. Trollope—like Dickens a decade later—arrived with an idealized image of America that took a beating from the rough-and-tumble reality, and both authors reacted by painting sour portraits of the young country's flaws.

Americans, in turn, have always had complicated attitudes towards Europe: Mark Twain's *Innocents Abroad* (1869), for example, wavers uncertainly between awe towards the monuments of European culture and contempt for effete European traditions. Mrs. Trollope's hilarious conversations with her servant girl provide a good starting point for a discussion of cultural assumptions: Americans, suspicious

of class privilege, are likely to applaud the girl's assertive spirit and refusal to humble herself; English readers would have been as astounded at her impudence as at
her attire. A world in which a servant considers herself "a young lady," wants
money for a silk dress to go to a ball, and tells her employers "I never seed such
grumpy folks as you be" must have seemed to Mrs. Trollope's English readers to be
a kind of bedlam of misrule.

But Trollope's satire was not purely mean-spirited. One theme running
throughout is her concern for the position of women. She believed that American
women were undervalued by their men, a disregard powerfully symbolized by the
universal habit of spitting which made it impossible to keep their dresses clean.
She felt that early marriage, lack of education, and "the servant problem" condemned American women to narrow lives as household drudges. Women were
thus denied their proper role as civilizing and uplifting influences on society. Seen
in this light, her remarks about leisure seem less frivolous: without it, there can be
no "great development of mind" (for background on these topics, see the readings
about separate spheres and female education in Perspectives: Victorian Ladies and
Gentlemen).

Trollope deplored the lack of opportunity for cultivated social life, not merely
because she herself missed dinner parties, concerts, and the theater, but because
she could see that American women had few outlets except church. She detested
the evangelical distrust of pleasure and of the arts, which she saw as largely responsible for the sad state of society in Cincinnati. (In a passage we do not excerpt,
Trollope described a revival meeting; she was horrified by the impropriety and excess she witnessed, particularly the lack of respect for women). Her views on
"Amusement" can be compared with evangelical attitudes described in the
Religion and Science perspectives section.

Thomas Babington Macaulay
Minute on Indian Education (1835)

Both popular and problematic, Macaulay has never lacked for readers or critics.
Many Victorians shared Lord Acton's assessment: "He remains to me one of the
greatest of all writers and masters, although I think him base, contemptible and
odious." While the "Minute on Indian Education" does not show Macaulay's
style or narrative drive to full advantage, it does give even the casual reader a sense
of his personality: the essay is clear, confident, assertive, energetic, high-minded
in tone and ruthless in pressing home its arguments. It might be a good idea to
start with Macaulay's overstatements—"a single shelf of a good European library
was worth the whole native literature of India and Arabia"—and questionable assumptions: "The literature of England is now more valuable than that of classical
antiquity." If proven false, do these generalizations make any difference to his
overall argument? It might be demonstrated that other languages have made great
contributions to world culture and scientific progress, but Macaulay insists that
English is the language of the moment, the one best calculated to satisfy the dou-

ble charge of the vague legislation that he is trying to interpret: "the revival and promotion of literature" and "the introduction and promotion of a knowledge of the sciences."

For Macaulay, it is English that will open minds, teach history, and advance science. Moreover, English is politically and economically expedient, since the "ruling class" of Indians already speak it, and English is also the language of South Africa and Australia, important trading partners. Macaulay found a good deal of local support; when he says in his summation that "the natives are desirous to be taught English" he could have pointed to the work of the Hindu social reformer Raja Rammohan Roy (1772–1833), who asked that educated Europeans "instruct the natives of India in mathematics, natural philosophy, chemistry, anatomy, and other useful sciences, which the natives of Europe have carried to a degree of perfection that has raised them above the inhabitants of other parts of the world." Finally, the other languages proposed, Arabic and Sanscrit, are studied chiefly for their religious texts, and Macaulay ridicules these texts as sources of "false history, false astronomy, false medicine" at the same time that he maintains that Britain should "be not only tolerant, but neutral on all religious questions." Thus, he says, "we abstain, and I trust shall always abstain, from giving any public encouragement to those who are engaged in the work of converting natives to Christianity."

The rest of his argument is built around two historical analogies, those of Britain and Russia. But the analogies work in different ways. Renaissance England was right not to focus its reading on what was written locally in the late 14th and early 15th centuries, for the ancient languages of the Greeks and Romans contained . . . what? Macaulay does not say, but he asks rhetorically, "would England have now been what she is" if education had centered on Norman or Anglo-Saxon? In those days, dead languages apparently had more to offer than living ones. So what about Sanscrit today, Macaulay's opponents might well ask. He has an answer ready: more recently, in 18th and 19th century Russia, huge progress was made by "teaching . . . those foreign languages [of Western Europe] in which the greatest mass of information had been laid up." Having claimed that English literature has now surpassed that of classical antiquity, Macaulay is in a position to argue that modern English carries with it the special something of the classics as well as the information of the Western European tongues. Ask students if these analogies are logical, convincing, or even fair.

Macaulay's final two paragraphs are masterful summaries of his position that make explicit the long-term goals of his policy: "We must at present do our best to form a class who may be interpreters between us and the millions whom we govern; a class of persons, Indian in blood and colour, but English in taste, in opinions, in morals, and in intellect." This apparent effort to govern a colony through conversion or subversion has been much discussed. Gauri Viswanathan's *Masks of Conquest* (1989) is one of the better known analyses of how the British used the study of English as "a blueprint for social control in the guise of a humanistic program of enlightenment" (10); she asserts that English was "incredibly–the most substantial weapon in the colonial arsenal" (145). Others have argued that such a view fails to take into account how colonized Indians understood or resisted the imposed texts, how they eventually remade the language in their own image—just as Americans have done. Today English is one of the official languages of India; along with Hindi it functions as a link-language in a multilingual society.

Alexander Kinglake
from Eothen (1844)

Although Kinglake faced genuine discomforts and even dangers on his jaunt through the Near East, he saw himself not as an adventurer but as a tourist following wellworn paths. Indeed, so self-conscious was he about his predecessors—both actual and literary—that his first concern in writing *Eothen* was to stake out his own territory by announcing what his book was *not*: geographical, antiquarian, historical, scientific, political, or moral. The humor of Kinglake's approach depends on our picturing rows of these dusty tomes full of Useful Knowledge. But rather than be discouraged by not being the first to describe these regions, he chooses to be liberated. *His* contribution will not be further instruction, but merely a description of his own sensations: "as I have felt so I have written."

Eothen makes us aware of the ways in which the apparently simple encounter between the observer and the observed is rarely so straightforward. What each traveller sees is almost always mediated by what he or she has already read. Kinglake is explicit about this process, informing us that it was the "rapturous and earnest reading of my childhood which made me bend forward so longingly to the plains of Troy." Books do more than inspire travellers, they also shape their perceptions: Kinglake travels not to meet contemporary Turks or Egyptians but to see the landscapes of the *Iliad* and the Bible. Of course, by doing so he sets himself up for disappointment when reality doesn't measure up to his expectations: Kinglake watches with "vacant unsatisfied eyes" the Homeric waters of "divine Scamander." Sometimes *not* seeing for oneself is preferable, he concludes, finding that only later, now that "I am away from his banks," does the river recover "the proper mystery belonging to him as an unseen deity." Memory happily colludes in erasing the prosaic realities of travel: "One's mind regains in absence that dominion over earthly things which has been shaken by the rude contact." The traveller's feelings are bruised by "the material presence of a mountain or a river . . . but, let these once pass out of sight, and then again the old fanciful notions are restored."

Often, Kinglake would rather daydream about home than work himself up into the "right" frame of mind for appreciating "important" places. His reflections on the unpredictable interaction of imagination and landscape suggest some anxiety over not feeling what he thinks he's supposed to feel: "it is only by snatches, and for few moments together, that I can really associate a place with its proper history." Being well-read imposes an uncomfortable obligation to react in particular ways—he can't respond freshly to scenes when he knows so much about their past.

Kinglake's consciousness of the many ways in which the countries he visited were already-written inhibited not only his on-the-spot responses but also his ability to write his own book. Twice he tried and failed; only when Eliot Warburton asked for advice was Kinglake finally able to produce *Eothen*. Writing casually and humorously, as if to his friend, Kinglake composed not what he called "a regular book of travels" but instead "a sadly long strain about Self." His approach set the tone for much travel writing that has come after him: as F. A. Kirkpatrick observed in 1916, "the better travel-books of the nineteenth century . . . deal less with monuments, museums, churches and institutions: they deal more with men and women in relation to their surroundings. Sometimes, this human interest lies in the pleasant egotism of the traveller" (*The Cambridge History of English Literature*, vol. 14, 240–56). Jan Morris approves, remarking that "*Eothen* is a thoroughly self-centred book, that is half its charm." Edward Said disapproves, complaining in *Orientalism* (1979) that Kinglake "is more interested in remaking himself and the Orient . . . than he is in seeing what there is to be seen."

But Kinglake declines the traveller's usual duty to report back as impartially as possible. His solution to the problem of describing places that have already been much described is to turn inward, writing less about the places themselves than about the impression they made upon him. He acknowledges that focusing on feeling rather than fact opens him to the charge of egotism, and he embraces the charge: his very subjectivity will vouch for his truthfulness. He places himself at the center of each scene, arguing that ultimately we can only know our own sensations. Travelling vicariously through his words, seeing through his eyes, the reader—he claims—may be "slowly and faintly impressed with the realities of Eastern Travel" (For a more detailed version of this argument, see Heather Henderson's "The Travel Writer and the Text" in *Temperamental Journeys: Essays on the Modern Literature of Travel*, ed. Michael Kowalewski [1992], 230–48).

Sir Richard Francis Burton
from A Personal Narrative of a Pilgrimage to El-Medinah and Meccah (1855)

Like Kinglake, Burton prefaced his book by acknowledging its personal nature: to some, it may appear "mere outpourings of a mind full of self." Yet Burton was a voracious scholar and prolific writer, and his two dozen travel books are crammed with hundreds of pages of cultural detail and scientific information. In the three-volume *Pilgrimage to El-Medinah and Meccah* Burton recounts how he journeyed to the holy cities of Islam, disguised first as a dervish (a Muslim holy man), then as an Afghan physician. He travelled in a spirit of adventure, longing "to set foot on that mysterious spot which no vacation tourist has yet described," and he claimed that "when entering the penetralia of Moslem life my Eastern origin was never questioned." Had he been discovered, he would probably have been killed. In *Rule of Darkness: British Literature and Imperialism, 1830–1914* (1988) Patrick Brantlinger notes how Burton dramatizes "the dangerous role of anthropological spy" and "revels in the Protean ambiguity of his various roles" (161, 162).

Burton is one of the most famous examples of a traveller who used a disguise to reach a forbidden destination, but he's hardly alone: during the 1860s, William Gifford Palgrave spent a year in Arabia in the guise of a Syrian doctor; in the 1920s the Frenchwoman Alexandra David-Neel undertook a gruelling trek to Lhasa (closed to foreigners) masquerading as a Tibetan beggar; in the 1970s a young Englishwoman, Sarah Hobson, explored Iran dressed as a boy, entering people's homes, mosques, and religious discussions. What motivates travellers to cast off their own identities and assume the clothing, language, and manners of another culture, sometimes at the risk of their lives? How does a disguise alter the way in which one perceives others—and oneself? And what ethical dilemmas do such impostures present?

Clearly, such travellers are attracted by the idea of freeing themselves from the codes and customs of "civilization," of shedding their own nationality, language, class, religion, even gender. Think of Lady Mary Wortley Montagu's pleasure in adopting Turkish dress to pass unnoticed through the streets of Constantinople in the early eighteenth century. Brantlinger argues that for Burton "Disguise was a means of crossing the gulf between superior and inferior races, civilization and barbarism—a means that led to ethnological knowledge as well as to adventure. Disguise also allowed Burton to criticize western society while permitting him eventually to return to it" (163–64).

Disguise offers a temporary liberation from oneself, and also new perspective on one's own privilege: wasting days in a frustrating effort to obtain a passport in Alexandria, Burton notes that as an Englishman he would have had no trouble—only as an "Asiatic" does he encounter rebuffs and delays. On the steamboat to Cairo he travels third class, disguised as a dervish, and the European passengers avoid him. Nick Danziger, a contemporary travel writer, found it similarly eyeopening to wear Afghan clothing on the streets of London in the 1980s: "Everywhere I went I was either shunned or regarded with undisguised suspicion" (*Danziger's Travels* [1987]). Only her disguise admitted David-Neel into the hovels of poor Tibetans; ordinarily, no foreigner would have glimpsed their interiors. Such experiences afford genuine insight into the lives of others. But doesn't the secret knowledge thus obtained represent a betrayal of trust and a form of cultural aggression?

Burton relished the challenge of creating and sustaining a difficult part; proud of his linguistic and acting skills, he invites the reader to admire his performance. Yet his disguise raises troubling questions: his quest was a morally dubious undertaking, an invasion of the privacy and sacred sites of another culture. When Burton finally glimpses Mecca, he thinks, "how few have looked upon the celebrated shrine!" Of course he means, how few Europeans. And although he shares the deep emotion of his fellow pilgrims, he admits that "theirs was the high feeling of religious enthusiasm, mine was the ecstasy of gratified pride." Brantlinger points out how "In a sea of Muslim pilgrims . . . Burton remains isolated by his consciousness of difference, by his sense of personal and racial superiority. Yet the superior man has stooped to deception to reach his goal." His gaze is not that of the "worshipful pilgrim" but that of western science "prying into the deepest, most sacred mysteries of every culture" (162–63). Brantlinger argues that disguise is ultimately an exercise in power and imperial domination: it "entails a double arrogance characteristic of Burton's entire career: contempt for the peoples among whom he travels and upon whom he spies or anthropologizes" (164). "All of the information he gathered . . . he viewed as a form of power over nonwestern peoples" (166).

Reading our selection from Burton's *Narrative* thus gives students not merely a taste of the popular Victorian genre of swashbuckling travel adventures, but also a jumping-off point to discuss nineteenth-century attitudes toward nonwestern cultures and people. Instructors might invite students to discuss Brantlinger's arguments; is he being fair to Burton? Have students look, for example, at Burton's description of the contrast between Eastern and Western manners, such as drinking a glass of water. How does he portray cultural difference? Some might contend that to observe the ways of others as minutely as Burton argues for a certain sensitivity and even respect for difference; others might point to ways in which a conviction of cultural superiority is embedded in the very language Burton chooses.

Isabella Bird
from A Lady's Life in the Rocky Mountains (1878)

Travel offered women an escape from the restrictions of genteel lives at home; students who have read Nightingale's *Cassandra*, and our excerpts from Mrs. Ellis and Mrs. Beeton (Perspectives: Ladies and Gentleman), will have a clearer sense of what Bird was getting away from. Rejecting domestic comforts and responsibilities, she preferred to climb mountains, ride through blizzards, round up cattle, and flirt with a celebrated outlaw.

Bird's invalidism bears some discussion. The search for better health provided a respectable "excuse" for travelling, which women needed more than men. But Bird was not simply a hypochondriac; in *Across New Worlds: Nineteenth-Century Women Travellers and their Writings* (1990) Shirley Foster explains that "as an adolescent she underwent an operation to remove a tumour on her spine and suffered from back trouble for the rest of her life." Foster quotes Bird's obituary in the *Edinburgh Medical Journal*: Bird presented "many characteristics of a physical type which can hardly be considered as common. . . . The Invalid at Home and the Samson Abroad do not form a very usual combination" (13). A psychological interpretation is hard to avoid: illness bought Bird privacy, freedom, and time (just as it seems to have done for Christina Rossetti, Elizabeth Barrett Browning, and even Charles Darwin). The advantages of ill health were acutely perceived by Nightingale, who remarks in *Cassandra* that "A married woman was heard to wish that she could break a limb that she might have a little time to herself."

Instructors might compare Bird's depiction of life at the Chalmers' with Trollope's depiction of life in Cincinnati. In each case, a cultivated Englishwoman recoils in horror and wry amusement at the narrowness of American horizons: graceless manners and tedious patriotism, self-righteous religion, devotion to work and money-grubbing, lack of intellectual and artistic pastimes, reduction of wives and daughters to mere drudges. And just as Trollope passed through scenes of appalling desolation, so Bird's scorching Sunday at the Chalmers', with its snakes and dust and blazing heat, becomes a hellish waste land.

Fortunately for Bird, these infernal horrors are but a prelude to the paradise of Estes Park, and her depression vanishes in exuberant exclamation points. Although her first experiences of the American West undercut romanticized myths about life on the frontier, she goes on to live a Western dream—driving cattle with real cowboys in the crisp air of the Rocky Mountains, acknowledged as one of the boys by the cattlemen.

These letters may surprise those who believe that all Victorian middle-class women aspired to be the "Angel in the House." Bird, in fact, actively resisted the ideal. Although she found Estes Park to be a sublime Shangri-la, she wasn't inclined to settle down there. Marriage to Mountain Jim—quite apart from his problem with whiskey—would have meant housekeeping. And when Evans offered her a job for the winter, she turned it down, unwilling to exchange her glorious freedom for cooking and chores. It was a question of independence, particularly from women's traditional homemaking: "it would suit me better to ride after cattle," she wrote cheerfully.

If the duties of home defined most women's lives, then travel—leaving home—could liberate them in ways unimaginable in Britain. But not if they recreated home in a new land: Bird's letters are full of portraits of hard-working settlers' wives. All Western women, even "ladies," worked hard; Bird writes that Evans's wife worked like a "squaw." She was not about to spoil her exhilarating adventure by joining their ranks.

Travel "unsexed" Victorian women, in ways Bird is both eager for (she relishes the fact that the cattleman "had forgotten that a lady was of the party") and anxious about: early in her book she adds a footnote describing her riding costume as thoroughly feminine and, according to Dorothy Middleton, when *The Times* of London described her as riding in "male habiliments" she told her publisher "that as she had neither father nor brother to defend her reputation, she expected him personally to horsewhip the *Times* correspondent" (*Victorian Lady Travellers* [1965], 8). As Maria Frawley writes in *A Wider Range: Travel Writing by Women in Victorian England* (1994), "Women who flaunted their physical fortitude and vitality abroad . . . seemed to challenge their own 'natural' limitations and to invite" portrayals of themselves as "aggressively sexualized" (113).

Frawley devotes a chapter to "The Social Construction of the Victorian Adventuress" in which she argues that travellers like Bird "created a kind of imaginary 'wild zone,' one that enabled them to accomplish feats of physical endurance and courage that would be inconceivable for a middle-class woman in England." At the same time, these writers found ways "to translate adventure into an essentially womanly activity" (38). One such way was "to position themselves as mother figures in relation to the natives," as Bird does when she deplores "the extinction of childhood" in the Western States (117–18). Such an analysis posits Victorian women travellers as both in flight from patriarchal authority back home, and yet reinscribing its values.

Nor did the patriarchy welcome them home unequivocally; Frawley writes that "when a few women—led by Isabella Bird Bishop—began to agitate for admittance as fellows into the Royal Geographic Society, the debate took a nasty turn. In a letter to the editor of *The Times*, the influential MP George Curzon wrote: 'We contest *in toto* the capability of women to contribute to scientific geographic knowledge. Their sex and training render them equally unfitted for exploration, and the genus of professional globe-trotter is one of the horrors of the later end of the nineteenth century'" (111).

Sir Henry Morton Stanley
from Through the Dark Continent (1878)

Stanley is the only one of the six travellers excerpted here who could claim to be discovering new terrain or geographical features. In *Imperial Eyes: Travel Writing and*

Transculturation (1992) Mary Louise Pratt writes drily that "As a rule the 'discovery' of sites like Lake Tanganyika involved making one's way to the region and asking the local inhabitants if they knew of any big lakes, etc. in the area, then hiring them to take you there, whereupon with their guidance and support, you proceeded to discover what they already knew" (202). In fairness to Stanley, even the Africans with whom and among whom he travelled apparently had no idea where the Congo river led. Given the immense obstacles his expedition encountered, his claim to be the first to descend the entire river is probably truer than similar Western claims to be "the first" to find or view a particular place in "unknown" territory.

Stanley writes that the object of his "desperate journey is to flash a torch of light across the western half of the Dark Continent." In a chapter entitled "The Genealogy of the Myth of the 'Dark Continent'" Patrick Brantlinger examines the origins and implications of this imagery (*Rule of Darkness: British Literature and Imperialism, 1830–1914* [1988]). By envisioning Africa as a dark and savage place, the Victorians justified their own intervention in the name of bringing civilization and light: "By the time of the Berlin Conference of 1884–85, which is often identified as the start of the Scramble for Africa, the British tended to see Africa as a center of evil, a part of the world possessed by a demonic darkness or barbarism, represented above all by slavery, human sacrifice, and cannibalism, which it was their duty to exorcise. . . . The obverse of the myth of the Dark Continent was that of the Promethean and, at least in Livingstone's case, saintly bestower of light" (179, 180).

Books by Livingston, Stanley, Burton, Speke, and others "took the Victorian reading public by storm. . . . Although such accounts of African exploration do not figure in standard histories of Victorian literature, they exerted an incalculable influence on British culture and the course of modern history. . . . The great explorers' writings are nonfictional quest romances in which the hero-authors struggle through enchanted, bedeviled lands toward an ostensible goal: the discovery of the Nile's sources, the conversion of the cannibals. . . . The humble but heroic authors move from adventure to adventure against a dark, infernal backdrop where there are no other characters of equal stature, only bewitched or demonic savages" (180–81).

Stanley is one of the possible models for Conrad's Kurtz, and instructors planning to teach *Heart of Darkness* will certainly want to assign this excerpt from *Through the Dark Continent*. In an autobiographical essay Conrad recalls his own disillusionment at Stanley Falls in 1890: "A great melancholy descended on me . . . there was . . . no great haunting memory . . . only the unholy recollection of a prosaic newspaper 'stunt' and the distasteful knowledge of the vilest scramble for loot that ever disfigured the history of human conscience and geographical exploration." Brantlinger explains that "The stunt was Stanley's 1871 trek . . . in search of Livingstone for the *New York Herald*, the scramble for loot that Conrad saw at first hand King Leopold's rapacious private empire in the Congo" (239–40).

Stanley repeatedly images Central Africa as a blank white space: he tells Frank Pocock that "this enormous void is about to be filled up." Indeed, Stanley has "already mentally peopled it, filled it with most wonderful pictures of towns, villages, rivers, countries, and tribes—all in the imagination." Yet—as Stanley knew perfectly well—Africa was *already* full of people and villages. Ask students to consider the implications of this imagery; how does it serve to free the European explorer to write himself across the blank paper? how does it serve to justify European colonial expansion?

Elsewhere in the book, Stanley exclaims—apparently without irony—"Think what a benefit our journey will be to Africa!" What sort of benefits did Stanley have in mind? Have students look closely at his heroic rhetoric: is the conversation with Frank Pocock really likely to have taken place in such elevated language? Stanley presents himself as a confident, resourceful commander with a grand vision and the courage to carry it out; meanwhile, the Africans are irrational and bloodthirsty savages. Frightful as they are, it takes the superior abilities of Englishmen but "five minutes work" to clear the river of "the filthy, vulturous ghouls." On a more personal level, Stanley's stupendous efforts to gain fame in Africa may also be seen as a lifelong attempt to overcome the poverty and obscurity of his own origins, to recreate himself on an epic scale.

There is a disturbing ruthlessness about Stanley, and what may most strike a reader of the entire two volumes of *Through the Dark Continent* is the horrifying loss of life he was prepared to accept in pursuit of his goal: "Nine men lost in one afternoon!" he pauses to lament, before pushing on. Perhaps only Odysseus returned home with fewer of his followers. In *Loneliness and Time: British Travel Writing in the Twentieth Century* (1992) Mark Cocker writes: "If ever there were an archetypal travel book, then surely this is it. Yet it contains an account, as Stanley bludgeoned his way down the Congo, of thirty-two battles between the white explorer's Zanzibari retainers and the indigenous Africans—thirty-two episodes in what was, in effect, one long, continuous, private armed conflict" (105). Stanley's private conflicts, however, had international consequences, as—for better or worse—his explorations helped bring Africa to the forefront of European consciousness.

Mary Kingsley
from Travels in West Africa (1897)

As her famous defense of "the blessing of a good thick skirt" indicates, Kingsley joined Isabella Bird in insisting on proper female attire as evidence of her own womanliness. Maria Frawley writes that "More than any other adventuress, Kingsley bristled at . . . implications of anomalous sexuality and aberrant womanhood. She publicly retaliated against being labeled a 'new woman,' and . . . claimed she could not have accomplished anything without help from 'the superior sex'" (*A Wider Range: Travel Writing by Women in Victorian England* [1994], 113–14).

This sort of thing makes it easy to treat Kingsley as a slightly ludicrous figure poking crocodiles on the nose with her umbrella; as Evan Connell writes of Victorian lady travellers in *A Long Desire* (1979), "They give the impression of being mildly batty, these upright, energetic, innocent, valorous, polite, intelligent, prim, and condescending British females in long skirts, carrying parasols" (24). Kingsley, at first glance, seems to lend herself to this sort of caricature, but she was in fact a complex and elusive personality.

Dorothy Middleton's *Victorian Lady Travellers* (1965) is a good starting place for students who would like to know more about both Bird and Kingsley. Though her book is short on literary analysis, Middleton provides biographical background and she summarizes in detail the works of these and other travel writers. Another good source is the lengthy chapter on Kingsley in Catherine Barnes Stevenson's *Victorian Women Travel Writers in Africa* (1982), particularly useful for details of Kingsley's role as a spokeswoman for Africa once she was back in Britain.

Kingsley's life until the age of thirty was the classic story of the dutiful but solitary unmarried daughter at home; she later wrote of "the dreadful gloom of all my life before I went to West Africa." Biographers always mention her resentment that two thousand pounds were spent on her ne'er-do-well brother's schooling, while nothing at all was spent on hers. Those who have read Nightingale's *Cassandra* might see parallels: a sense of confinement and futility, coupled with a longing for some meaningful work. Stevenson concludes that Kingsley's years of service to others "fostered a radical sense of insignificance bordering on anonymity" (94). In her 1976 introduction to the Everyman edition of *Travels*, Elspeth Huxley quotes from a revealing letter written when Kingsley was thirty-seven: "The fact is I am no more a human being than a gust of wind is. I have never had a human individual life. I have always been the doer of odd jobs—and lived in the joys, sorrows and worries of other people. It never occurs to me that I have any right to do anything more than now and then sit and warm myself at the fires of real human beings." In this letter she also said: "I went down to West Africa to die." Kingsley's jaunty insouciance about heading off for "the white man's grave" reads rather differently in light of these words—the notion that she was not so much defying death as courting it gives an unsettling edge to her jolly comic send-up.

Kingsley's low-key approach and self-deprecating humor contrast vividly with Stanley's heroics and macho swagger, as do her humility and openness to new experience. Compare her portrayal of cannibals to his: for Stanley, they are ferocious primitives, but for Kingsley they are just people whose domestic habits happen to be a bit different from her own—she registers no moral disapproval, merely lively curiosity and willingness to learn. Unlike both Stanley and the missionaries, she doesn't see herself as a cultural superior conferring benefits upon Africans. There is a sense of wonder in her writing that might remind us of Mandeville. Never does she employ Dark Continent imagery, or suggest that she is a bringer of light. The Africans whom she meets are not unknowable and savage Others, but real people—fellow participants in the absurd drama of life.

Furthermore, as Mary Louise Pratt notes in *Imperial Eyes: Travel Writing and Transculturation* (1992), "The masculine heroic discourse of discovery is not readily available to women." However, "through irony and inversion, [Kingsley] builds her own meaning-making apparatus out of the raw materials of the monarchic male discourse of domination and intervention. The result . . . is a monarchic female voice that asserts its own kind of mastery even as it denies domination and parodies power" (213). Pratt notes that "the domain she chose to occupy" was not the large-scale one of male conquest, but the small-scale one of mangrove swamps, through which Kingsley sloshed zestfully, "up to her neck in water and slime."

Glossing the passage in which Kingsley recalls those blissful nights "dropping down the Rembwe" in a makeshift sailboat, Pratt writes: "What world could be more feminized? There shines the moon lighting the way; the boat a combination bedroom and kitchen; Kingsley the domestic goddess keeping watch and savoring the solitude of her night vigil. . . . Kingsley creates value by decisively and rather fiercely rejecting . . . fantasies of dominance and possession." Instead, she foregrounds the workings of her own imagination. "Far from taking possession of what she sees, she *steals* past" (214).

While Pratt goes on to argue that Kingsley's playfulness and comic irony constitute "her own form of mastery," she concludes that Kingsley ultimately "seeks out a third position that recovers European innocence. Politically she argued for the possibility of economic expansion without domination and exploitation." Her "bumbling, comic innocence . . . proposes a particular way of being a European in Africa" (215)—a utopian mode that Pratt contrasts to the fearful, threatened mode experienced in night scenes on the river in *Heart of Darkness*.

Finally, one might look at *Penelope Voyages: Women and Travel in the British Literary Tradition* (1994), in which Karen Lawrence discusses Kingsley's "complex relation to imperialism and the individualism of adventure." Lawrence observes that Kingsley "deliberately eschews the search for identity thematized in much nineteenth-century travel literature." Her "protean narrative performance" "frustrates our attempts to chart the narrator or traveler as a unified psychological 'self.'" While inevitably implicated in colonial discourse, Kingsley sought "to represent the rich and complex African cultures that were being trampled by" colonialist policy. She "opposed both the blatantly aggressive policies and rhetoric of imperialism practiced by the Belgians and the more ostensibly liberal but still aggressive ethos of the British, who sought to 'civilize the natives.' . . . Although she never questioned the British presence in Africa, she argued that its Crown colony ideology and practice were both stupid and insensitive" (128–29).

The White Man's Burden (1899)

The poem was first published in *McClure's Magazine* in early February 1899, and immediately reprinted in newspapers across the U. S. It appeared just as the United States formally assumed control of Puerto Rico, Guam, the Philippines, and Cuba in the wake of the Spanish-American War. While Kipling lay near death from pneumonia in New York (he eventually recovered), debates, testimonials, diatribes, and eulogies swirled in the press. One scathing parody, "The Brown Man's Burden" by Henry Labouchère, appeared in London in the same month. It runs, in part:

> Pile on the brown man's burden
>   To gratify your greed;
> Go, clear away the 'niggers'
>   Who progress would impede;

Be very stern, for truly
     'Tis useless to be mild
With new-caught, sullen peoples
     Half devil and half child.

Pile on the brown man's burden;
     And, if ye rouse his hate,
Meet his old-fashioned reasons
     With Maxims up to dae.
With shells and dumdum bullets
     A hundred times made plain
The brown man's loss must ever
     Imply a white man's gain.

Pile on the brown man's burden,
     Compel him to be free;
Let all your manifestoes
     Reek with philanthropy.
And if with heathen folly
     He dares your will dispute
Then, in the name of freedom
     Don't hesitate to shoot.

This, and many other texts of the day, can be found on a helpful website called "'The White Man's Burden' and its Critics." Written by Jim Zwick, the website can be found at *www.boondocksnet.com/ai/kipling/* There one can also view an advertisement placed in *McClure's Magazine* in October, 1899 by the ever-opportunistic proprietors of Pears Soap. A white-haired ship's captain is seen washing his hands in his private cabin, while at the lower right a missionary offers a bar of soap to a dark man clad in a loincloth. The caption reads, "The first step towards lightening The White Man's Burden is through teaching the virtues of cleanliness. Pears Soap is a potent factor in brightening the dark corners of the earth."

Was the vilification or praise of Kipling's poem fully deserved? Is there a middle ground between the imperialist assumption that the burden was necessary and the cynical view that American intervention meant nothing but violence and exploitation? Kipling himself speaks of no profit to be had from assuming the burden, only hardship and ingratitude. But he also makes it clear that civilization is a process of maturing from child to man. Since the poem anticipates what might be seen as a century of American imperialism, whether political, economic, or cultural, in the wake of the British Empire's decline, how has Kipling's prophecy—or Labouchère's—been borne out? This may take class discussion far from Victorian literature, but it can be reined in by comparing the poem to Kipling's other important poem about imperial power and responsibility, "Recessional" (1897), to be found near the end of the main Kipling entry in the anthology. "The White Man's Burden" rouses an empire on the rise to acknowledge and fulfill its new responsibilities; "Recessional" warns an empire on the wane to heed God and ask for mercy: "Judge of the Nations, spare us yet." In his advice to the Americans, has Kipling forgotten the lessons apparently learned by a country soon to be "one with Nineveh and Tyre"? In 1899 an anonymous contributor to the *New York World* succinctly forecast the evolution of both British and American foreign policy in the century to come:

> We've taken up the white man's burden
> Of ebony and brown;
> Now will you kindly tell us, Rudyard
> How we may put it down?

Robert Louis Stevenson
The Strange Case of Dr. Jekyll and Mr. Hyde (1886)

The story was born out of Stevenson's desire to explore "that strong sense of man's double being which must at times come in upon and overwhelm the mind of every thinking creature." Or, as G. K. Chesterton put it in *Robert Louis Stevenson* (1928), "The real stab of the story is not in the discovery that the one man is two men; but in the discovery that the two men are one man." Victorians felt very intensely the truth of Stevenson's assertion, and would likely have agreed with Chesterton's assessment. But is that "sense of man's double being" universal or historically conditioned? Is it a particular product of Victorian repression, of a society so tightly bound by conventions of moral and social behavior that many 'natural" impulses—sexual, violent, self-indulgent impulses—must go "underground" only to coalesce around a dangerous alter-ego? Is our post-Freudian society less prone to generate Mr. Hydes? The story's continuing popularity might suggest otherwise.

Moreover, as the widening circle of his impact implies, Hyde need not be seen as having importance only for the body that harbors him. In the edition of *The Strange Case of Dr. Jekyll and Mr. Hyde* edited by Susan Wolfson and Barry Qualls (2000), the editors provide a range of responses to the text, from its initial reviews to recent criticism by contemporary authors and critics. They cite the critic Edwin M. Eigner who in 1966 wrote that "Hyde does not appear purely evil in this adventure, but he does seem to bring out all the cruelty and malice in those who judge him . . . . Enfield, the bystanders, and the other narrators are rejecting a part of themselves when they reject Hyde, and the more strenuously they excise him, the more thoroughly they come to resemble their notion of him . . ." (Wolfson/Qualls 94). In other words, one man's Hyde may bring out the Hyde—and hatred—in others. There are few women glimpsed anywhere in the story (hence the novelist Valerie Martin was able to make a fascinating narrative called *Mary Reilly* out of the imagined experiences of Jekyll's maid—the book is far better than the film), but those that encounter Hyde in the opening episode are turned "wild as harpies."

In one of the most perceptive early reviews, Julia Wedgwood noted in 1886 that "Whereas most fiction deals with the relation between man and woman . . .

the author of this strange tale takes an even narrower range, and sets himself to investigate the meaning of the word *self*. No woman's name occurs in the book, no romance is even suggested in it; it depends on the interest of an idea. . . ." (Wolfson/Qualls 87). But what idea, exactly? In this male world of closely guarded emotions and long but distant friendships, where is the self to be located—in the daily dull discourse of law and medicine, in the few social gatherings between aging bachelors? Fairly early in the story, Utterson thinks, "If he be Mr. Hyde . . . I shall be Mr. Seek." As the narrative follows Utterson's efforts to penetrate Hyde's secrecy, Stevenson may be suggesting that a man's task is to get to know better both self and other. Mr. Hyde gives Utterson a new identity, that of "Mr. Seek." It is a more salutary personality shift than that undergone by Dr. Jekyll, for the more one Hydes, the more one comes to the attention of others. The story finally favors openness; it seems the opposite of Poe's "The Man of the Crowd" (1840) where an aged version of Mr. Hyde totally baffles all attempts that the narrator makes to discover his suspected secrets.

And yet many secrets remain. For twenty-first century readers—and possibly for nineteenth-century readers, too—Julia Wedgewood's review raises another set of questions: Is Dr. Henry Jekyll homosexual? Is Mr. Hyde the tortured expression of that heavily repressed desire or fear? Mr. Enfield remarks near the story's opening that "I make it a rule of mine: the more it looks like Queer Street, the less I ask." The narrative fluctuates between moments of hiding, moments of seeking; it seems unwilling to uncover the dark story it nevertheless propels the reader headlong into. Of the two Victorians cited in the headnote to the story as having their own inner Hydes, J. A. Symonds was openly gay and G. M. Hopkins, a Jesuit priest, was likely privately so. Are the adventures of Mr. Hyde a foreshadowing of the more comic Bunburying we hear about in Wilde's *The Importance of Being Earnest*, or the more tragic trial and imprisonment of Wilde himself because of his own hidden life?

It would help to know more about Mr. Hyde. As Elaine Showalter writes in *Sexual Anarchy* (1990), "Stevenson was the fin-de-siècle laureate of the double life," but "in the multiplication of narrative viewpoints that makes up the story . . . one voice is missing: that of Hyde himself." Unlike Frankenstein's monster, "we never hear his account of the events, his memories of his strange birth, his pleasure and fear." We don't, she says, because "Hyde's story would disturb the sexual economy of the text, the sense of panic at having liberated an uncontrollable desire." His power and potency may be felt so frighteningly precisely because his motives and most of his activities are so heavily veiled. Still, he is present in two ways, Showalter argues, "in the representation of his feminine behavior" and in his body language: "Hyde's reality breaks through Jekyll's body in the shape of his hand, the timbre of his voice, and the quality of his gait." To this should be added the impression that he conveys of an indefinable deformity. His twisted vagueness, his vague twistedness, seem to exude evil; he is a sort of spontaneous combustion of noxious repression.

A good way into the novel is through the light-dark imagery and the shifts between cozy, cold, and foreboding locations, and from interior to exterior. Like Dr. Jekyll himself, his house has two "outlets"—the front door manned by servants and

the rusty side door to which Mr. Hyde holds the key. In this regard it might be useful to make some links to Stevenson's "A Child's Garden of Verses" (see *Perspectives:
Imagining Childhood*). If they haven't made the connection already, students might
find it fascinating to realize that the author of a classic horror novel is also the classic author of nostalgic evocations of childhood—themselves composed upon a dark
vs. light theme. Underlying the happy boyhood portrayed in the poems are lurking
fears of the dark and the night, death, shadows and strange creatures.

There is a lot to be done in class exploring the narrative technique of *Dr. Jekyll*.
The novelist Vladimir Nabokov wondered how Stevenson can manage to convey
to his readers the full horror of Hyde when he has made the decision to bolster
the story's plausibility by passing it through the matter-of-fact lens of Enfield and
Utterson. Nabokov concluded: "I suggest that the shock of Hyde's presence brings
out the hidden artist in Utterson" (Wolfson/Qualls 93). At first, Utterson seems
about as artistic as Dickens's prying but tight-lipped "oyster of the old school," Mr.
Tulkinghorn in *Bleak House*, surely one of the formative elements in his literary
genesis. But Utterson's sheer patience and reticence allow the story to come to
him, to the extent that we forget that he actually has no narration of his own. He
asks questions but never, unlike Enfield, Lanyon, or Jekyll, or even Poole the servant, recounts his experiences in the first person. His artistry lies in the spider-web
of narrative that he permits to be spun around him. The son rather than father of
utterance, he has the story literally handed to him at the end. Stevenson allows
Utterson to disappear entirely once the letters from Layton and Jekyll are in his
hand; the author never returns to his frame; we never learn if Utterson gets back
before midnight to relieve poor Poole and notify the police.

Is there a point, a moral to the tale? Wolfson and Qualls point out that the
wine that brings out the humanity in Utterson at the beginning of the tale is akin
to the blood-red potion that transforms Dr. Jekyll into Mr. Hyde. Both Utterson
and Jekyll deny themselves and then indulge themselves, but Utterson manages to
let himself out in little steps (the shift from solitary gin to social wine, for example, lights up his eye) while Henry Jekyll does it with a devastating cocktail of
chemicals that wracks his whole body. Mr. Utterson's most pronounced trait, we
learn in the story's first and second paragraphs, is his unusual tolerance for those
"down-going men" of his acquaintance. Perhaps the story favors tolerance over
condemnation, expression over repression, wine and companionship over gin and
solitude. A late Victorian joke about pipe tobacco began, "do you have Prince
Albert [brand tobacco] in a tin?" If the smoker or tobacconist said yes, then the
prankster replied, "Well, why don't you let him out!" Stevenson may be saying the
same thing about Mr. Hyde.

Oscar Wilde

Writing a half century after Wilde's death, Jorge Luis Borges claimed to have made
a discovery: "the provable and elementary fact that Wilde is almost always right."
Fifty years later, Borges seems right too. Readers today praise Wilde's astuteness as

a critic, his brilliance as a dramatist, his insight as a social analyst, his proleptic genius as a one-man media event, and his theatrical understanding of gender as performance. Wilde was exceptionally versatile as a writer, perhaps more skilful in
more genres than any other author. Our selections give a sense of the poet, critic,
playwright, political theorist, autobiographer, and public man; students might also
want to investigate his novel, stories, fairy tales, lectures, letters, other plays, and
incidental journalism. The best introductions to the current discourse on Wilde
are *Critical Essays on Oscar Wilde*, ed. Regenia Gagnier (1991), and the *Cambridge
Companion to Oscar Wilde*, ed. Peter Raby (1997). Richard Ellmann's *Oscar Wilde: A
Collection of Critical Essays* (1969) remains valuable for its survey of earlier responses
to Wilde, including those of Pater, Yeats, Joyce, Shaw, Auden, Alfred Douglas,
Hart Crane, and Borges.

In some respects Wilde's poems are his shakiest claim to greatness, and the
elaborate stylistic pastiche of Baudelaire, Swinburne, and Browning that dominated his first publication, *Poems* (1881), has troubled critics ever since. But the
three poems included here represent a different Wilde: simple in diction, restrained in manner, they are characteristic of the early modernist fascination with
London. *Impression du Matin* begins with allusions to Whistler's paintings; like the
painter, Wilde stresses the insubstantiality of the city and the subtle transformations of light and color as night yields to day. Stanza 3 suddenly changes the
tempo. Compare these bolder images of dawn with a probable source, Tennyson's
final lines of sections 7 and 119 of *In Memoriam* (whose stanza form Wilde also emulates). Wilde's lurid final stanza undercuts both Whistler's refusal to moralize in
his paintings and Tennyson's presentation of dawn as spiritually uplifting. Is the
harlot an artistically "legitimate" feature of this morning impression, or does she
function as a jarring, sensational note that breaks up the "harmony" and emphasizes the "clang" of early morning?

Each of the other two poems elaborates an aspect of *Impression du Matin*.
Symphony in Yellow is an exquisite Whistlerian tone-poem that wavers between yellow and green, artificial and natural (bus to butterfly, fog to scarf), and motion
and stasis (Thames to rod of jade). The poem could be regarded as an aesthete's
version of Wordsworth's sonnet *Westminster Bridge*, Wilde substituting languid,
fashionable details (the trendy color yellow, the allusion to Whistler's butterfly signature, the Wildean silk scarf, the orientalist taste for jade) for Wordsworth's spiritually charged wonder; where Wordsworth's sleeping city seems ready to burst
into life, Wilde's urban activity gradually turns to stone. *The Harlot's House* reverses the emphases of *Impression du Matin*, exploring the harlot's world first, then
bringing in the dawn in the last stanza. Is the harlot's house an image of death,
of carnal knowledge, a sort of Goblin Market that entices all who pass by? Wilde's
narrator keeps aloof, but his "love" enters, with mysterious results. Does the
dancer's tune turn false for the speaker or for his love? Is it her arrival that breaks
up the waltz of the "dead" dancers, bringing relief in the form of silver-sandaled
dawn? Or does his lover's defection give the speaker a new perspective that contrasts the (properly) "frightened girl" of dawn to the worldly woman who has left
him in the night?

In 1891 Walter Pater wrote that "*The Decay of Lying* . . . is all but unique in its half-humorous, yet wholly convinced, presentment of certain valuable truths of criticism." Wilde turns Platonic philosophy on its head by asserting not only that art should be enjoyed for its own sake, regardless of mimetic accuracy, but also that art is the original creation and nature merely the belated, inferior imitation. "Life imitates Art far more than Art imitates Life," Wilde concludes, and even "external Nature also imitates Art." Therefore lying, the refusal to take Nature or Reality on its own terms, "is the proper aim of Art."

Many of Wilde's theories, such as the artist's independence from his historical moment, and the foolishness of imitating nature, can be found in Whistler's "Ten o'clock" lecture (see the "Aesthetes and Decadents" section), and Whistler in fact charged Wilde with plagiarism. Wilde does acknowledge "the Master," as Whistler liked to be called: contending that life imitates art, Wilde attributes "the extraordinary change that has taken place in the climate of London" to Whistler's paintings of the Thames. Students might compare the style, substance, and imagery of Whistler's lecture and Wilde's dialogue (their common source was Gautier's famous Preface to *Mademoiselle de Maupin* [1835]).

Whatever Wilde's intellectual debt to Whistler, *The Decay of Lying* sparkles with critical and comedic genius. First Wilde shocks his readers by assaulting their preconceptions: he doesn't like *nature*? He's going to defend *lying*? Then, instead of retreating from his attention-getting start, he pushes further, charging poets with "careless habits of accuracy," and claiming that Hamlet proves his madness when he says, "Art should hold the mirror up to nature." And yet, by logical exposition and constant reference to literary history, Wilde gradually makes us see how important it is that life—the raw material of art—be transformed by the artistic process (lying) into something more beautiful and expressive. Moreover, "life is the mirror, and art the reality," since "a great artist invents a type, and Life tries to copy it." Women imitate the Pre-Raphaelite look; frustrated lovers shoot themselves as did Goethe's Werther; Impressionist paintings create London fogs. How can this be? Because "things are because we see them, and what we see depends on the Arts that have influenced us." Ask students to come up with examples of this phenomenon—have they noticed a kind of landscape, a style of dress, a time of day or type of weather as a result of having been taught to see by a book, painting, or film? By the last lines of the dialogue, the sympathetic reader is ready to entertain the outrageous claim, unthinkable at the start, that nature's "chief use is to illustrate quotations from the poets."

In one of the most amusing passages, Wilde provokingly traces American commercialism (perceived then, as now, to be a major threat to European culture) to George Washington's inability to tell a lie. Why *has* the cherry tree story assumed mythic status? Has public veneration of "the truth" contributed to the "materializing spirit" of the U.S. and its indifference to poetry? One could use this passage as a way into Wilde's theory about lying. Point out that he carefully distinguishes *lying* from the mere "misrepresentation" of politicians and lawyers, who actually try to convince people of their veracity. For Wilde, lying should be practiced for its own sake, with no pretence of plausibility. Thinking particularly of Zola, he argues that when Fact invades the realm of Fancy and Romance, art becomes vulgar and wearisome. But lying looks to art itself for a model, and can thus produce works of beauty and imagination. Why does Wilde use the word "lying," instead of imagination or creativity, as do the Romantics? In *Oscar Wilde* (1987) Richard Ellmann suggests that imagination is "too natural" a word—for Wilde, lying is more conscious, sinful, and willful (302).

The Soul of Man under Socialism belongs to the tradition of Victorian social prophecy that includes Carlyle's *Past and Present*, Ruskin's *Nature of Gothic*, and Morris's *Beauty of Life*. Meditating on "the condition of England," each author stresses the interconnection of aesthetics and politics, and how beauty cannot flourish in an ugly, unjust society. But Wilde begins his surprising essay with a challenge to conventional definitions; instead of calling for collective action, he asserts a startling preference for individualism, and the means of achieving it: "Socialism would relieve us from that sordid necessity of living for others." As he says later, individualism "does not try to force people to be good. It knows that people are good when they are let alone." Gagnier points out that this is "Wilde's best-known work in the world at large" and belongs "clearly with a long tradition of socialist aesthetics," that ranges from Schiller and Marx to Morris, Trotsky, Marcuse, and Foucault, who wondered in a late interview, "couldn't everyone's life become a work of art"? (7–9).

Reenvisioning both society and human nature, Wilde combines a faith in spontaneous personal development with a bold, deliberately impractical case for abolishing private property; he turns over to machines "all the necessary and unpleasant work." Anticipating the objection that his views are utopian, Wilde offers one of his brilliant rejoinders: "A map of the world that does not include Utopia is not worth even glancing at, for it leaves out the one country at which Humanity is always landing."

Compare the style and structure of the essay to Mill's method in *On Liberty*. Both authors try to work through the vast body of received wisdom surrounding their topic, but while Mill carefully debunks common misconceptions, Wilde embraces conventional maxims so that he can turn the clichés inside out and then argue seriously from his apparently thoughtless one-liners. The essay moves rapidly through a series of unexpected insights which constitute almost a line of reasoning in themselves: "Charity creates a multitude of sins;" "disobedience is man's original virtue;" "as for the virtuous poor, one can pity them but one cannot possibly admire them. They have made private terms with the enemy;" "agitators are a set of interfering, meddling people. . . . That is why they are absolutely necessary;" "wealthy people are, as a class, better than impoverished people;" "there is nothing necessarily dignified about manual labour." Each of these formulations forces a reconsideration of Victorian social policy and its platitudes; any one of them might spark discussion on how poverty and social inequality should be addressed.

At the heart of Wilde's program is his claim that private property gets in the way of individual development, encumbering the privileged even as it starves the poor. He criticizes the social conditioning that focuses people on "gain not growth," and to end this obsession with ownership he proposes an enlightened self-reliance (he admired Emerson). Some lines now read ironically in view of his experience in Reading Gaol: "Public opinion is of no value whatsoever. . . . After all, even in prison a man can be quite free." Most remarkable, though, is the long passage reinterpreting the Gospels, where he imagines Jesus saying "You have a wonderful personality. Develop it. Be yourself." Wilde apparently thought constantly about the implications of the Gospel stories, as many people who recalled his conversation, including Yeats and Gide, attested. Just as Wilde foresees the limitations of a planned economy ("under an industrial barrack system, or a system of economic tyranny, nobody would be able to have any such freedom at all"), in his reading of Christianity he anticipates the ego-centered approach of late twentieth-century psychology and religion. Ask students if they think Wilde is correct in assuming that the road to self-realization lies through the shedding of possessions. Does his message seem today to be more personal than social, more "self-help" manual than political manifesto? Or is that analysis itself a proof of Wilde's point that individual and political philosophies need to converge?

Wilde added the Preface to *The Picture of Dorian Gray* in angry response to critics of the novel. For example, "Those who find ugly meanings in beautiful things are corrupt without being charming. That is a fault." But, as Richard Ellmann points out, the Preface provokingly "flaunted the aestheticism" that the book's own moralistic ending indicts ([1987], 315) Indeed, two inflammatory lines from the Preface would later be used against Wilde during his trials: "There is no such thing as a moral or an immoral book. Books are well written or badly written. That is all." Ellmann comments that "To prevent the book's being treated as immoral, Wilde excluded morality from its province, although it exposed the follies of a false and excessive aestheticism" (322). Ask students if books (or other works of art) are really beyond moral judgment. Can literature that appears racist, sexist, treasonous, or threatening to public safety be evaluated only on the grounds of literary style? Is the denunciation of "dangerous" ideas the exclusive province of jittery dictators and intolerant moralists? In his essay "Why Write?" (1949), Jean-Paul Sartre offers an unexpected defense of Wilde's position. For Sartre, reading requires a voluntary collaboration of reader and writer to produce meaning (cf. Wilde's "it is the spectator, and not life, that art really mirrors"), and any attempt on the writer's part to restrict the reader's freedom diminishes the work of art. "Thus," says Sartre, echoing Wilde, "there are only good and bad novels . . . the moment I feel myself a pure freedom [in the process of reading] I can not bear to identify myself with a race of oppressors. . . . I'd like to know a single good novel whose express purpose was to serve oppression, a single good novel which has been written against Jews, Negroes, workers, or colonial people."

  Wilde's remark about Caliban's rage over seeing (or not seeing) his face in the mirror raises the question, why do we read? How much like daily life do we want our literature and literary characters to be? Since, for Wilde, art mirrors the spectator, his warning about the dangers of interpretation (going beneath the surface, reading the symbol) acquires a sort of Oedipal urgency. We have to beware of what art will tell us about ourselves. His stance recalls Mark Twain's "Notice" at the start of *Huckleberry Finn* (1884): "Persons attempting to find a motive in this narrative will be prosecuted; persons attempting to find a moral in it will be banished; persons attempting to find a plot in it will be shot." If, as Wilde claims (and Twain implies), art is not to be put to conventional uses, perhaps it serves a different purpose. In Wilde's case, his defiantly amoral attitude functions as a Victorian class indicator in its "gentlemanly" disdain for anything that smacks of business and trade.

The Importance of Being Earnest can be read as a seriously comic, or comically serious, dramatization of the social theories Wilde had earlier presented in *The Soul of Man Under Socialism* (Lady Bracknell denounces land ownership as a nuisance; Algernon chastises the lower classes for not providing a good moral example). The play also explores the aesthetic issues Wilde had raised in *The Decay of Lying*, particularly the connection between art and lying, and the dictum that life imitates art. Wilde's characters invent alter egos, lie without hesitation, and play their social roles with utter sincerity, ultimately confirming the reality of their own pretenses. While earnestness is a vital asset to the talented liars who transform social routine into an aesthetically satisfying spectacle, truth is simply irrelevant. It belongs to the dull realist novel, to Life, not Art. Jack begs Gwendolen's pardon at the end: "it is a terrible thing for a man to find out suddenly that all his life he has been speaking nothing but the truth. Can you forgive me?"

What counts is the free-play of wit and imagination; as Gwendolen remarks: "In matters of grave importance, style, not sincerity, is the vital thing." Or, as Lady Bracknell says, "We live in an age of surfaces. . . . Algernon has nothing, but he looks everything. What more can one desire?" In such a world, "success in life," to use Pater's phrase, depends on performance and the outward manifestations of class, gender, or character (gestures, etiquette, the rituals of social intercourse); a substantive, private, inner self is nowhere to be found. Every action is to be performed as if before an audience. When Jack proposes, Gwendolen says, "I hope you will always look at me just like that, especially when there are other people present."

Wilde's presentation of such self-consciously creative personas inevitably reminds the audience of the play's immensely clever author, and his own double life as self-fashioning Bunburyist. As Peter Raby writes in the best single introduction to the play, *The Importance of Being Earnest: A Reader's Companion* (1995), "Wilde's characters are all scriptwriters and storytellers: Chasuble's sermons, Prism's novel, Cecily's and Gwendolen's diaries, Lady Bracknell's list of eligible young men. Jack and Algy invent characters . . . to enable them to escape the restrictions of Victorian life and morality. . . . The dual fictions allow each bachelor to live a double life. The young women, in contrast, cannot wait to be married so that their double life can begin. . . . The play, so far from suggesting that the double life will be dispelled by marriage, suggests that it is a permanent and inescapable part of it" (89). Wilde took the "double life" theme closer to his own situation in the earlier four-act version of the play, when Algy is nearly sent to debtor's prison because of Jack's unpaid bills at the Savoy hotel; students might wish to compare versions in an annotated edition such as that edited by Russell Jackson (1980).

One of the many paradoxes of the play is that self-invention is also a quest for self-discovery. The play culminates with Jack's question, "Would you kindly inform me who I am?" Some critics have compared *Earnest* with *Alice in Wonderland* as a quintessentially Victorian search for self amid the elaborate, arbitrary conventions of society, while others link Wilde with Beckett, Ionesco, and Stoppard as an explorer of the Absurd. Joseph Bristow, for example, writes that in its rejection of realism and obsession with artifice, "Wilde's comedy marks . . . the beginnings of a theater of alienation or estrangement which would become a cornerstone of European modernism" (cited in Raby, 22). Yet it is equally possible to read *Earnest* back into the history of Western theater: Jack's question, echoing King Lear's "Who is it can tell me who I am?" was first posed by Sophocles in *Oedipus Rex*. Both plays deal with heroes who have "carelessly" lost both parents early in life, both are raised in ignorance of their true families, and both feel compelled to establish their genealogy in order to resolve social crises and penetrate the mysteries of identity. Oedipus's discoveries have the effect of forcing him out of society, while Jack's bring him further in; Wilde comically rewrites Sophocles to make the intolerable doubleness of Oedipus—his being both son and husband to Jocasta—become an admirable, "brotherly" social trait that the male leads share: "the vital Importance of Being Earnest." Like a cheerful Freud, Wilde presents the Oedipal state as a universal human condition.

Other trappings of Greek tragedy are also revised. Lady Bracknell is, as Mary McCarthy once remarked, "Olympian" (see Ellmann [1969], 109); she is the *dea ex machina* whose unshakable observance of social ritual propels the marriage plot. The Aristotelian fatal flaw turns into mild gluttony for cucumber sandwiches, and the expiation of sin is also expressed as a form of consumption: "They have been eating muffins. That looks like repentance." Parodying the convention of the lost baby, Wilde focuses on the trappings, not the child: Miss Prism is delighted to have her handbag back, never mind the baby whom she had mistaken for the manuscript of her novel. The Greek Chorus is implicit in the preoccupation with what "Society"—represented by the audience (and Lady Bracknell)—will think.

But do the "doubleness" of the characters and their preoccupation with fictive selves prevent what for Aristotle was a key feature of Greek drama, the audience's involvement with the characters? Do we have sympathy with Algy and Jack, with Cecily and Gwendolen? Is the play too clever to be humanly felt? George Bernard Shaw, for example, was unmoved by it, though he admired Wilde. Or does it strike too close to home in the sense that it shows how much our notions of "self" have to do with self-presentation and performance?

The play inverts other longstanding social norms: the servants are more polished than their masters; the women are more forthright and commanding than the men. The scene shift in Act II further emphasizes the topsy-turvyness of this world: it deceptively suggests a move from urban sophistication to rural innocence, but *this* country place isn't pastoral at all—the outdoor garden is as fully constructed and aesthetic an environment as any interior (books, chairs, tables, tea service). As Lady Bracknell puts it, "A girl with a simple, unspoiled nature, like Gwendolyn, could hardly be expected to reside in the country."

Lady Bracknell merits special attention. One of Wilde's greatest creations, she is an authoritarian representation "of all that is most obstructive, conservative, and negative in Victorian society. But as the play unfolds, it becomes clear that she herself has manipulated life for years" (Raby, 65). She is prepared to change the fashionable side of Belgrave Square, and with a sort of ruthless perspicacity she pronounces smoking a suitable occupation for a gentleman, recognizes that education poses "a serious danger to the upper classes," and advises Jack to "acquire some relatives as soon as possible" if he hopes to marry. Her frequent references to revolution, violence, and anarchy reveal her awareness of the fragility of upper-class privilege. She assesses social position with the acuteness of a former bounder: "When I married Lord Bracknell I had no fortune of any kind. But I never dreamed of allowing that to stand in my way." She is pleased with Jack's income and excited about Cecily's fortune: looking out for Algernon and Gwendolyn, she wishes to assure the class status that only money can buy.

Thus, as Raby comments, the world of the play "is a mixture of the reassuringly stable and the chaotically surreal. Society, led by its spokesperson Lady Bracknell, offers the appearance of respectability, but the respectable has a disconcerting habit of vanishing, like the Cheshire Cat, leaving only a grin behind. . . . The individual characters are capable of rapid transformations" in affection and manner, and have none of the familial or moral stability that Victorian society prided itself upon. Lady Bracknell's difficult role is "to impose some kind of order on a society intent on dissolving before her eyes" (81–82). Marriage, the social glue of high society and the goal toward which all the characters race, is portrayed as dispiriting and divisive: Lane finds that "in married households the champagne is rarely of a first-rate brand," Lord Bracknell's ill health may be a Bunburyish fiction through which Lady Bracknell manages her own life; Gwendolen is likely to marry often; General Moncrieff was a man of peace except in his domestic life; and "a man who marries without knowing Bunbury," Algy remarks, "has a very tedious time of it."

Does the play finally challenge or confirm the social conventions that it mocks? "Why should there be one law for men and another for women?" Jack asks seriously; but he asks his momentary "mother," Miss Prism, and this misprision is characteristic of how Wilde deliberately ironizes all of his serious points. Do social structures inevitably triumph over individual witticisms, or does the clear-sighted reinforcement of tradition and hierarchy, in all their glorious folly, ultimately undermine their credibility? Critics tend toward the latter position. Raby points out that although the play was written when Britain's prosperity and empire were at their peak, "Wilde's jokes surreptitiously draw attention to the impermanence, and absurdity, of the prevailing social and political structures and to the inherited complacency that cocoons them" (7). Ellmann comments that "In *The Soul of Man Under Socialism*, Wilde had repudiated marriage, the family, and private property; in his play, he repudiated them by pretending they are ineradicable, urging their enforcement with a mad insistence which shows how preposterous they are" ([1987], 422). And Katharine Worth concludes that *Earnest* is Wilde's "supreme demolition of late nineteenth-century social and moral attitudes, the triumphal conclusion to his career as revolutionary moralist" (155).

In addition to Raby, significant criticism of the play includes Katharine Worth, *Oscar Wilde* (1983); Harold Bloom, ed., *Modern Critical Interpretations: Oscar Wilde's The Importance of Being Earnest* (1988); and the *Earnest* section of Gagnier's *Critical Essays*. For a fascinating contextualization, see Kerry Powell's *Oscar Wilde and the Theatre of the 1890s* (1990): "Like its hero, *The Importance of Being Earnest* can be said to have lost its 'parents'—those forgotten farces that in a real sense gave birth to Wilde's play" (124). Powell's genealogy includes *Godpapa* (1891), a play which contains a character named Bunbury who is prone to fictitious ailments (127). Life took revenge on Art: Bunbury was played by an actor who later helped collect evidence used against Wilde during his trials.

Contemporaries instantly recognized Wilde's uncanny skill at turning conversational clichés into provocative, show-stopping aphorisms. But they also claimed it was a trivial occupation, something anyone could do. Reviewing *An Ideal Husband* in 1895, G. B. Shaw wrote: "They laugh angrily at his epigrams. . . . They protest that the trick is obvious, and that such epigrams can be turned out by the score by any one lightminded enough to condescend to such frivolity. As far as I can ascertain, I am the only person in London who cannot sit down and write an Oscar Wilde play at will" (cited in Beckson, *Oscar Wilde: The Critical Heritage* [1970], 176). For Shaw, the key was Wilde's sensitivity, as an Irishman, to English seriousness, to "the Englishman utterly unconscious of his real self" (Beckson 177).

Building on this insight, Regenia Gagnier writes that Wildean wit springs from the author's status as "an outsider—Irish, homosexual, artist—to Victorian imperial, commercial, and polite society." Wilde used the linguistic rituals of group affiliation to expose the instability of the social structure, and the shallowness of group identity. "His legendary wit consisted in practice of a talent for inverting Victorian truisms. . . . Yet the astonishing thing about his wit is not that he could always . . . find the right word to substitute for the key word of the platitude, but rather that he knew the platitudes so well to begin with. His mind was stocked with commonplaces, and these seem to have been there for the sole purpose of their subversion" (*Idylls of the Marketplace: Oscar Wilde and the Victorian Public* [1986], 7–8).

De Profundis might have been called "The Soul of Man Under Lock and Key." It has, according to Gagnier, a vast—and growing—readership who relate directly to its emotional accuracy in describing prison life ([1991], 17). In this undelivered letter to his ex-lover, Wilde veers between bitter accusation and even more bitter self-accusation, trying to understand how he came to be in prison, and how he might live to get out. While the epistle reads at first as a venting of anger and anguish, it returns consistently to the theme he had addressed more hopefully in *The Soul of Man Under Socialism*, namely the necessity of self-understanding. Wilde twice repeats his call for painful introspection: "the supreme vice is shallowness. Whatever is realized is right." The line carries with it an echo of Edgar's pronouncement in *King Lear* in the midst of *his* distress and desperate soul-sifting, "Ripeness is all."

Yet even as he catalogues Bosie's vanities, and proclaims his own arrival at "absolute Humility," Wilde expands on his genius and his achievements: "I was a man who stood in symbolic relations to the art and culture of my age." Claiming for himself even greater representative status than Byron, Wilde stunningly conducts his own apotheosis, writes his own epitaph: "I awoke the imagination of my century so that it created myth and legend around me: I summed up all systems in a phrase, and all existence in an epigram." Unhumble as it may seem, this grandiosity could be regarded as in keeping with Wilde's gnostic intent: "It is only by realizing what I am that I have found comfort of any kind," he remarks. "To reject one's own experiences is to arrest one's own development. . . . It is the denial of the Soul." But in "realizing what I am," Wilde produces a mélange of recrimination, moralizing, and self-aggrandizement. It sometimes seems that Wilde's personal dealings with Bosie are less important to his quest than the assessment of his own artistic potential and accomplishment. Is it personal remorse or a sort of Faustian dramatization of his talent that leads him to write, "I was so typical a child of my age that in my perversity, and for that perversity's sake, I turned the good things of my life to evil, and the evil things of my life to good"? One could argue that the letter is Wilde's last great dramatic work, a biblical melodrama in which he creates a Satanic Bosie who tempts Eve/Christ/Oscar, precipitating a fall (from public grace), a crucifixion (at and after the trials), and finally a moral/literary resurrection.

Companion Reading

When discussing the transcript of the trials (used as the basis of the recent play, Gross Indecency), debate the issues raised in the cross examination. Is Wilde justified in dismissing "Philistine" or "illiterate" responses to art? Does the artist bear any responsibility for the public's (mis)interpretation of a work that may defy mainstream views? Wilde commented in the second trial that "one man's poetry is another man's poison." Why did Douglas's poems, or Wilde's poetic letters to him, seem so disturbing to Wilde's opponents? Any trial is a sort of drama, a morality play in which guilt and innocence are meted out by judge and jury. The series of Wilde's trials came about because Queensbury accused Wilde of "posing" as a sodomite; Carson questioned Wilde about his artistic "pose." Should we read the trials—and Wilde's performance at them—theatrically, as exploring a role that first Wilde, and then British society, had created for the errant artist?

See Ed Cohen's Talk on the Wilde Side (1993) for an illuminating reappraisal of the received view of Wilde's "tragic downfall." Cohen reexamines the original newspaper reports on which H. Montgomery Hyde based The Trials of Oscar Wilde, showing how Hyde constructed a version of the trials that has been perpetuated by contemporary critics, including Richard Ellmann in his 1987 biography. Rather than regarding the story as that of the personal downfall of a genius who made a "fatal mistake," Cohen situates it in a larger social and political context, elucidating the underlying assumptions about normative masculinity, and "Wilde's emergence as a paradigmatic figure for a discernibly nonnormative male sexuality at the end of the nineteenth century."

Aesthetes and Decadents

Closely identified with the idea of "art for art's sake," the literary and artistic movement of Aestheticism flowered in England during the 1880s and early 1890s. By
then the concept of moral, didactic art had been under attack for several decades
from those who thought that books and pictures should be judged on their own intrinsic merits, rejecting any claim to utility, social relevance, or the education of a
wide audience. Announcing the independence of artists from their times, figures
such as Whistler, Wilde, and Symons scorned practicality and progress; heroically—
in their eyes—they faced isolation as dandies and Bohemians cast out by a bourgeois
world. Creating amoral art became their sacred mission. Whereas Ruskin had said
that apprehension of beauty leads to apprehension of God in the world, Aesthetes
argued that perceiving beauty was in and of itself a religious experience. Claiming
that "Life is terribly deficient in form," Oscar Wilde encouraged his readers to de-
vote themselves to the perfections of art rather than questions of conduct:
"Aesthetics are higher than ethics. They belong to a more spiritual sphere."

Aesthetic ideas—and the reaction to them—coalesced in the early 1880s, when
they were parodied in George DuMaurier's cartoons in Punch (1879–81), spoofed in
Gilbert and Sullivan's light opera Patience (1881), and sympathetically appraised in
Walter Hamilton's book, The Aesthetic Movement in England (1881). As we learn
from W. S. Gilbert's If You're Anxious for to Shine, Aesthetes were conspicuously
fond of "Queen Anne" architecture, medieval art, bits of stained glass, Japanese
furnishings, and rarified conversation. Many of their favorite articles could be
found at the Liberty department store that had opened in London in 1875.
Among the "vegetable" motifs Aesthetes sported were sunflowers, lilies, peacock
feathers, and green carnations, the last invented by Wilde. The art of book-making
also enjoyed a revival; authors demanded that the page be as thoughtfully conceived as the words upon it. Whistler, Wilde, Yeats, Symons, John Gray, and many
others published their works in graceful editions employing distinctive type and a
maximum of white space on every page. Thus in books as in interior design, architecture, and illustration, Aesthetes drew on the resources of both Art Nouveau
and the Arts and Crafts Movement to create a taste for elegant simplicity that was
diametrically opposed to the usual Victorian clutter.

The ostentatiousness of Aesthetic beauty-worship signalled to Gilbert that the
Aesthetic manner was an elaborate pose designed to draw attention to egotistical
bounders, who had a flair for self-promotion. Many commentators have seen in
the flamboyant gestures and conversation of Whistler and Wilde the birth of the
modern cult of celebrity, of fame as a media event based more on image than accomplishment. George DuMaurier is less cynical than Gilbert, and his clever, detailed cartoons seem designed to present the Aesthetes anthropologically, as if he
were a bemused Mayhew chronicling a strange new tribe of Londoners. Against a
trendy backdrop of Japanese and Chinese elements, The Six-Mark Tea-Pot features a
drooping man and an imposing, sweepingly gowned woman with the long neck

and thick hair that characterize Rossetti's portraits of Jane Morris. "Six-mark" blue-and-white pottery of Chinese origin was highly prized, and the couple's aspiration to "live up to it" proceeds from one of Aestheticism's central tenets, that Life should imitate Art.

But not everybody's life had artistic potential. Whistler makes it clear in the *Ten O'Clock* lecture that art is not for the multitude, and that the middle-classes would be better off if they ceased to regard art as a fashionable status-symbol or a source of moral instruction. Divorcing art from history, national culture, and even nature, Whistler asserts the artist's autonomy, his indifference to politics, social organization, or mimetic obligation: "To say to the painter, that nature is to be taken as she is, is to say to the player, that he may sit on the piano." Does art then have *any* relation to its moment or context? Students may pick up on the ways in which Whistler's vision of a universal, eternal art released from Victorian notions of morality or progress is in itself quite Victorian. His contradictory gendering of Art and Artist is especially interesting; the "Master's" quest to win the favor of the "cruel jade" of inspiration seems to assert male supremacy at the same time that it proves it to be useless, since Art herself will decide whom to favor.

As the selections from Gilbert, Whistler, DuMaurier, Leverson, and Beerbohm show, the *fin-de-siècle* was an era of wit and witticism, in which caricatures and cartoons flourished alongside self-absorbed rhapsodies over art and artificiality. Leverson's short story *Suggestion* is a nuanced parody not only of Aesthetic self-involvement (in the person of "Cissy," its narrator), but also of upper-class family life and values. The first sentence announces the theme of gender definition and confusion, and the story ends with a word Leverson has done her best to problematize, "home." Leverson, like her great friend Wilde, delights in exploring contemporary social types through the lens of a sophisticated gay consciousness dedicated to cultivating pleasurable impressions and suggestive appearances. "Cissy" is an engagingly selfish teen-aged Prospero who seeks to arrange his own domestic happiness by stage-managing the love lives of his father, his sister Marjorie, and Marjorie's friend Laura (representing Victorian patriarchy, the New Woman, and the Aesthete, respectively). Cissy is a charming but ruthless egotist, particularly in the way he disposes of Marjorie, yet he can also be seen as a curiously moral figure whose desire for revenge upon his faithless, self-absorbed father seems motivated more by aesthetics than by ethics.

A public discomfited by male characters like "Cissy" was equally shocked by "manly" women. Feeling itself on the defensive, British society policed the borders of hitherto more fluid sexual identities with new medical and legal definitions of normalcy. Confronted with a growing openness about women's bodies and their desires, doctors lent credibility to the idea, found in many *fin-de-siècle* works, that women could become vampiric sexual predators, who endangered the human race when they cultivated either their intellects or feminist alliances. Bram Dijkstra's *Idols of Perversity: Fantasies of Feminine Evil in Fin-de-Siècle Culture* (1986) covers this ground in fascinating detail, and is especially strong on visual images of the femme fatale.

The emergence of the word "lesbian" at this time conveniently served to stigmatize women's friendships that appeared to threaten male power. In *Studies in*

Sexual Inversion (1897), Havelock Ellis, one of the first sexologists, assigned for the first time a deviant, "lesbian" identity to all women who "show some traits of masculine simplicity, and . . . a disdain for the petty feminine artifices of the toilet." He also singled out "brusque energetic movements," and "especially the attitude towards men, free from any suggestion either of shyness or audacity." But because Parliament did not dare to address female sexuality, declaring women "passionless," sexual relationships between females did not undergo any legal definition and prohibition, as did relationships between men.

Katharine Bradley and **Edith Cooper**, the aunt and niece who created the composite poet **"Michael Field,"** lived quietly; but though they did not ally themselves with the attention-getting tactics of Wilde, Douglas, Beardsley, or Symons, their lyric poems challenge received wisdom about women's art and desires. After decades of neglect, their reputation is recovering: for an overview of their career, see David J. Moriarty, " 'Michael Field' and their Male Critics," *Nineteenth Century Women Writers of the English-Speaking World*, ed. Rhoda B. Nathan (1986); on their lesbianism and the complex issues raised by "poems written by two women writing as a man writing as Sappho," see Yopie Prins, "Sappho Doubled: Michael Field," *Yale Journal of Criticism* 8 (1995): 165-86, and "A Metaphorical Field: Katherine Bradley and Edith Cooper," *Victorian Poetry* 33.1 (1995): 129-145. In the same issue of *Victorian Poetry* see also Holly Laird's "Contradictory Legacies: Michael Field and the Feminist Restoration," which argues intriguingly that "there is an uncanny parallel between the archival creativity which was the hallmark of Field's career and that of the contemporary feminist scholar/teacher" (112).

Field's rendition of DaVinci's *La Gioconda* follows from Pater's description of her in *The Renaissance* as predatory and vampiric, but for Bradley and Cooper the keynote becomes the lady's power and self-restraint. In *A Pen-Drawing of Leda*, they give Leda, "wild and free," control over her encounter with the swan, who yields to *her* will (line 7). Readers accustomed (especially from Yeats's poem) to regarding Leda as a victim are forced to reconsider. On Michael Field's pictorial strategy in these and other poems, see Kenneth R. Ireland, "*Sight and Song*: A Study of the Interrelations between Painting and Poetry," *Victorian Poetry* 15.1 (1977): 9-20. Their later lyric, *A Girl*, mingles the descriptive qualities of *La Gioconda* with the passionate embrace of *Leda*. In this "portrait," the poet's apparently detached rendering of her subject collapses in line 10 into a common identity ("our souls so knit"), a moment of consummation that momentarily stalls the act of poetic creation. But the author(s) can still give birth to a divine poetic "conception" if the girl will "come" into some further relation to "the work begun"—whether it be the poem, their love, or even a sexual act.

Few critics agree on just where Aestheticism—often regarded as an attitude toward art—shades over into Decadence, a term frequently used to describe both artistic style and personal behavior. "Decadence" literally means a "falling away" from an earlier standard. Walter Pater used the word in 1873 to praise some poems of the late Renaissance, and many find the seeds of decadence in his famous conclusion to *The Renaissance*, where he spoke yearningly of "any stirring of the senses, strange dyes, strange colours, and curious odors." As a literary term, "décadence" gained currency in France during the 1880s to designate the elaborately crafted works of the Symbolists. Yet by the 1890s, the word, often with its French pronunciation intact, had become in England a vague and fashionable label of both moral censure and avant-garde respect. The decadent object or action is usually highly artificial, abnormally developed (or thought to be so, such as an intellectual woman), and unnaturally stimulated by physical disease or spiritual decay. The original literary decadents had been Latin poets of late Roman antiquity, so the emergence of English Decadents suggested that the decline and fall of the British Empire was imminent. The various strains of decadence—the spiritual and the sensual, the stylistic and the behavioral—are summed up in Wilde's *The Picture of Dorian Gray* (1890) when Dorian reads J.-K. Huysmans's *A Rebours* [*Against the Grain*] (1884), the infamous "Bible" of French decadence: "it was written [in] that curious jewelled style, vivid and obscure at once, full of *argot* and archaisms, of technical expressions and of elaborate paraphrases, that characterizes the work of some of the finest artists of the French school of *Symbolistes*. There were metaphors in it as monstrous as orchids. . . . One hardly knew at times whether one was reading the spiritual ecstasies of some medieval saint or the morbid confessions of a modern sinner."

These days, when "Decadent Delight" is apt to refer to an extra-rich chocolate dessert, it may be useful to ask students to explore contemporary meanings of the word, and then direct their thoughts toward **Arthur Symons's** definition of decadence in *The Decadent Movement in Literature* as "an intense self-consciousness . . . a spiritual and moral perversity." "Healthy we cannot call it," he says. How does his approbation of literary unhealthiness relate to current ideas about bodily and moral health? How do the advantages Symons finds in this malady—such as a loosening of literary forms, a fresher kind of language—manage to spring from the "over-luxurious" sophistication of the 1890s? Curiously, Symons implies that artistic decadence is simply an honest response to the times he lives in, and that the two branches of Decadence, Impressionism and Symbolism, result from a genuine effort to capture the truth of the visible world or the "soul" of "things unseen." Wouldn't that make Decadence a fairly moral artistic enterprise, after all? In his Preface to *Silhouettes* he seems to be arguing for a more tolerant form of criticism that would allow room for both natural and artificial pleasures, and both moralistic and aesthetic responses to works of art. Perhaps what Symons wants is simply freedom to practice his nocturnal art without fear of moral censure or preconceived notions of what a poem should be.

In *Pastel* his emphasis is almost purely visual, with a minimum of commentary; he describes the sudden lighting of a cigarette in a vivid way that forecasts the thousands of such scenes that soon became a part of movie history. In *White Heliotrope*, the equally acute visual details of a one-night stand are presented in order to be condensed, à la Proust, into a sensation that the same perfume may release at a later date. Mixing Impressionism and Symbolism, Symons brazenly uses the *In Memoriam* stanza not to mourn a dead friend, but to package a memory of casual sex for future resurrection. Symons's reduction of the female object of desire into a hand, a ring, a hair-pin also anticipates Eliot's technique in *Preludes*, *Prufrock*, and *The Waste Land*; the young Eliot assiduously read Symons as an undergraduate at

Harvard. The best single book on Symons is probably Karl Beckson's *Arthur Symons: A Life* (1987).

The obsession with what Symons elsewhere called "perversity of form and perversity of matter" sometimes slips over into deliberate self-parody, with writers and artists such as Wilde, Johnson, Beardsley, and Beerbohm producing works that distressed the public while amusing insiders. **Richard LeGallienne's** *A Ballad of London* walks a fine line between celebrating its subject and denouncing it. It should be compared to Rossetti's *The Burden of Nineveh*, since the poems share an ironic appreciation of Britain's current imperial status and inevitable decline. Yet Le Gallienne's tone is far from the dire urgency of Kipling's *Recessional*; he seems to revel in London's role, shared with Paris, as a blazing gas-lit capital of modern Babylon, where lilies turn to iron, and humans into moths fatally attracted by the artificial light. There are the seeds of social critique, however, in stanzas five and six, the hint of an underground world of the oppressed (as in H. G. Wells's *The Time Machine*, published the same year, or Fritz Lang's *Metropolis*) working to support all this gaiety on the surface. Curiously, the doomed human moths of stanza 4 return to "eat up all" at the end; they become Time's agents, suggesting that human appetites will bring about their own demise. Vanquished nature, in the form of a desert, will return to reclaim London's night, as the poem moves from initial flower to final blight.

Lionel Johnson's poem *A Decadent's Lyric* joins the author's voice even more closely to the feverish behavior he might be condemning. Is the poem sincere? Is it a parody? Or a dramatic monologue containing both elements? Parody is a treacherous form because it requires the writer to inhabit the very literary body he rejects. Johnson comes so close in this poem to the vocabulary of Douglas (flame/shame) and the technique of Symons (the terse, unrepentant melding of steamy sex and musical metaphor) that only the intriguing grotesqueness of the final line suggests the poet's distance from the speaker. The choice of subject is significant, for like many writers of the 1890s, Johnson was torn between the longing to recover lost innocence and the need to express his sexual desires.

This tension, with its current of repressed homoeroticism, underlies Johnson's tortured poem, *The Dark Angel*. Though the poem ends with a renunciation of the Dark Angel of gay desire (displaying a bit of the bravado of Donne's *Death Be Not Proud*), the intensity of the struggle is unmistakable, and the first forty lines show the Dark Angel dominating every area of the poet's life. All dreams, thoughts, sights, sounds, and delights are transformed into poisoned desires, and only the rhetoric of otherworldly punishment and salvation in the final stanzas can deliver the poet from the tempting corruption he finds everywhere in nature. As if to confirm the newly conceived "norms" of sexual orientation, such a poem shows how sexuality can indeed become the central component of identity—when one is thrust into the position of deviant outcast. (In "The Poetry of Lionel Johnson," *Victorian Poetry* 28.3-4 [1990], M. G. H. Pittock suggests that the Dark Angel is both drink and poetry. See 47-49).

Ironically, Johnson himself had tried to brand Wilde this way a few years earlier when he accused him in *The Destroyer of a Soul* of corrupting Lord Alfred Douglas. Because sonnets traditionally speak of love, this "hate sonnet" gains additional force from its Petrarchean form, barely controlling the venomous rage of the poet. Like *The Dark Angel*, the poem focuses on the health of the soul as the measure of true life. Johnson's feeling that a "living body" now hides the "dead soul" of his friend not only evokes the vampiric strain of 1890s thought, but also *The Picture of Dorian Gray*, which Johnson had lent to Douglas in 1891. Johnson may have felt he had unwittingly helped Wilde create a real-life Dorian Gray whose physical beauty masked a deathly spirit.

If Johnson was tormented by his desires (and those of his friends), **Lord Alfred Douglas** seemed determined to celebrate his own passions boldly. *In Praise of Shame* uses the sonnet form to affirm his preference for "sweet" and "lovely" Shame (note how the diction and vocabulary of desire echo Swinburne's *The Leper*). Douglas explores Dantesque territory, but his flames seem harmless and unremorseful; indeed one might criticize the poem for the lack of tension in its structure, especially compared to the poems of Johnson. Perhaps the poet expects tension to emerge from the reader's surprise or shock that shame merits praise at all. But then doesn't such shameless approval of shame undo the very meaning of the word?

Douglas presents the topic more complexly in *Two Loves*, where the narrator hears, as if he were sitting in judgment, a smiling rosy youth accuse a "sweet" but pale youth of usurping the name of Love. The poet allows the youth who sings of heterosexual love to insist that *he* is "Love" and to designate the other as "Shame." The figure of "Shame" advertises nothing; he speaks of no partners; he simply sighs in a way that moves the narrator, conceding, "I am the love that dare not speak its name." While Douglas effectively conveys how righteously prescriptive a heterosexist world can be, he does not try to make "sweet" unspoken love look like a natural, everyday sort of thing. The terza rima suggests Dante's journey, and while words like "bright," "joy," "ivory," "gold," and "roses" describe the first youth, the second is "pallid" and "wan," associated with serpents and flame. One might ask if Douglas is not so much challenging conventional views as reiterating them, in order to stress the alluring difference of outlawed desire. One could even read *Impression de Nuit: London* as an effort to transform the whole of London, figured as a monstrous woman, into his own object of desire, turning her breasts into towers, and her dark lanes into a brain haunted by stealthy men.

The idea of a masculine identity built upon the dominance of homoerotic desire is a late Victorian construct, coinciding roughly with the criminalization in 1885 of any activity suggestive of male-male desire. Persecution led to activism: J. A. Symonds and Edward Carpenter defended the naturalness of homosexual attraction, citing the ancient Greeks and modern "comradeship." At boarding schools there continued to be room for same-sex romance under the guise of friendship—and the single-sex institutions of schools, clubs, and Parliament helped shield active homosexuality from the public eye. In the 1890s the new field of sexology sought to naturalize homosexuality and open the way for its decriminalization. But it did so by designating male-male love as a pathological state, thereby marking its "victims" as diseased. Richard Dellamora's *Masculine Desire* (1990) provides valuable background on efforts to define hetero- and homosexuality during the 1890s (see chapter 10, 193–217).

It has been suggested that **Olive Custance's** scandalous elopement with Lord Alfred Douglas, in defiance of her father's wishes, was meant to emulate the flight of the Brownings almost sixty years earlier. Like the Brownings, Custance and Douglas each respected the other's poetic talent, but the note of frustration and fatigue in Custance's work marks the *fin-de-siècle*'s distance from the idealized, energetic *amours* of mid-Victorian times. *The Masquerade* seems intended as a comment on Wilde's *The Harlot's House*. Custance universalizes the dance in her poem and, unlike Wilde, does not allow her speaker to remain aloof from it. Wilde, guarding his distance, makes his dancers ghostly and grotesque, while she gives her reluctant dancers a weary dignity as they go through their repressed paces. The same sense of fatigue turns her poem *The White Witch* from conventional praise of female sexual magnetism into a decadent portrait of love-weariness. The idea of a woman's imprisonment in empty gestures of love comes through most strongly in *Statues*, where human passion is unable to awaken a reciprocal longing on the part of deified stone. Because the subject is plural, this seems less a love poem than a generalized complaint about the inaccessibility of sculpted male bodies. Is Custance asking herself, "why am I always falling in love with gay men?" or should the poem be read more symbolically (and heterosexually) as a revisionary text about art and inspiration, treating the relation between aspiring female poet and elusive male muse? Why is the speaker unable to achieve the favor of the gods, as did Hyperion, or Pygmalion?

Produced as a sort of prospectus, **Aubrey Beardsley's** *"J'ai baissé ta bouche, Iokanaan"* won him the commission to illustrate Wilde's *Salome*. Here Salome floats in a dream-space with the object of her desire, the severed head of John the Baptist. There is a narcissism to Salome's gaze, and the disembodiment of her victim is oddly echoed in her own floating posture. Beardsley generates an eerie cross-projection of mirrored desire and sexual traits by giving Medusa-like hair to the Baptist, raising horns of hair on Salome, and not so much grounding as sinking the whole scene in the fluid sexual signification of water lilies and their phallic/vulvic flowers and tendrils. On how the Wilde/Beardsley text/images compliment each other, see Elliot L. Gilbert, "'Tumult of Images': Wilde, Beardsley, and *Salome* in *Victorian Studies* 26 (1983) 133-159; for arguments that the illustrations work disruptively against or disjointedly with the text, see, respectively, Jeffrey Wallen, "Illustrating *Salome*: Perverting the Text?" *Word and Image* 8.2 (1992): 124-132, and Robert Schweik, "Congruous Incongruities: The Wilde-Beardsley 'Collaboration,'" *English Literature in Transition* 37 (1994): 9-26.

Though the story of Salome might seem to reverse the terms of *The Ballad of a Barber*—here a woman commits violence upon a sexually unavailable man—in both cases one can read the woman as responsible for a man's execution, expressing the Nineties' preoccupation with the castrating, predatory female. Linking the Wilde/Beardsley protagonist with Ibsen's threatening female characters, lately arrived on the London stage, the Scottish drama critic William Archer called Salome "an oriental Hedda Gabler." A good overview of the free-thinking "new woman" and the uneasiness she caused even among Aesthetes and Decadents can be found in Karl Beckson, *London in the 1890s* (1992) 129-159, and in Patricia Marks, *Bicycles,*

Bangs, and Bloomers: The New Woman in the Popular Press (1990); Marks usefully deals with American as well as British attitudes. In *Dorian Gray* Wilde summed up the male artist's pervasive anxiety about feminine beauty: "Women inspire us with the desire to do masterpieces and always prevent us from carrying them out."

Max Beerbohm
Enoch Soames

Beerbohm's reflective and self-reflective story provides both a fitting close to the 1890s and also an excellent transition toward the modernism that was blossoming when he wrote his retrospective story in 1914, at the very end of "the long nineteenth century." Beerbohm wrote *Enoch Soames* in Rapallo, Italy, where he had moved in 1910 and where he spent the rest of his long life, sketching caricatures, writing verbal sketches, and maintaining a flow of witty, self-mocking conversation—most memorably recorded by the playwright S. N. Berhman in his *Portrait of Max* (1960).

Even in 1896, when he published his collected *Works*, the twenty-four-year-old Max liked to think of himself as a relic of a bygone era: "Already I feel myself a trifle outmoded. I belong to the Beardsley period," he wrote in his prefatory essay, *Diminuendo*. Yet he maintained a keen interest in contemporary life and literature throughout the modernist era and beyond, and on his bedroom wall he sketched a portrait of Joseph Conrad, in a mural of his favorite modern authors.

Enoch Soames shares both themes and formal devices, in fact, with *Heart of Darkness*, with which we begin our twentieth-century section. Both works involve complex frame-tales that play up the constructedness of the societies they portray, and suggest the ways fiction shades over into reality; and both involve a relatively innocent narrator who encounters a mysterious character who makes a pact with the Devil—literally in Soames's case, only barely metaphorically in the case of Kurtz. Kurtz is a Decadent character in his own right—a would-be painter and writer, making his way in rarified and finally fatal venues where he hopes to transcend his origins, much as Soames tries to leave behind the "plain, unvarnished Preston man" he used to be.

Beerbohm's tale is, of course, radically different in effect from Conrad's; one value in the juxtaposition is to show students how varied the modernism of these years really was. Beerbohm displays his virtuoso abilities in social satire and in parody—the sly way he works in the title of *Fungoids* is a classic moment. He parodies the Faust myth as well, in a way that is still all too apt today: Soames sells his soul not for knowledge or for sex, like his predecessors, but for *fame*: a classic 1990s lust, presciently planned to be fulfilled in the 1990s themselves.

Beerbohm draws freely on the supernaturalism favored in many of the popular stories of the later nineteenth century (as seen in some of the tales in our section on "Popular Short Fiction"), but at the same time he insists on the determining force of everyday realities. His satire is different in kind from the comedy of ideas that Shaw favored, for instance; in a review of one of Shaw's plays, Beerbohm criticized Shaw for creating characters who are "disputative machines," adding that "Mr. Shaw's penetrating eye is of great use to him in satire or in criticism. He is one of those gifted observers who can always see through a brick wall. But the very fact that a man can see through a brick wall means that he cannot see the brick wall." The absurd futuristic world that Soames encounters when he gets his wish to look himself up in the British Museum is none other than the world made in Shaw's image: everyone dresses "in Jaeger"—Shaw's favorite clothing—and people write an incomprehensible phonetic spelling that parodies Shaw's rationalist agitation for spelling reform. Contemplating Shaw, Beerbohm approached Orwell's vision of the future.

Soames's comic tragedy is that he comes up against a series of brick walls: his own lack of talent; his inability to claw his way from provincial Preston into the social circle of aesthetes like Rothenstein; the world's refusal to provide any opponent more glorious than the devil-as-vulgarian—Pater and Wilde's worst nightmare brought to life.

Enoch Soames was published in Beerbohm's collection *Seven Men* (1919), a book that tells the stories of only six characters. The seventh is Beerbohm himself, present both as narrator and as refracted through his protagonists. At the start of *Enoch Soames*, Beerbohm fails initially to find Soames in Holbrook Jackson's *The Eighteen Nineties*; he neglects to mention that he himself is the subject of an entire chapter in that history, which is also dedicated to him. Soames's evanescence may be Beerbohm's own, or the evanescence of the period that he paradoxically immortalized in verbal and visual sketches alike. According to the story, in exchange for his soul Soames gets to visit the British Museum reading room on June 3rd, 1997. On that day, Professor Laura Frost of Yale was doing research at the British Library. Just after two o'clock, a vague figure in a long cloak rushed in, looked wildly through the "S" section of the card catalogue, uttered a cry of despair, and left. "Assuredly," as Beerbohm says, "truth was stranger than fiction."

The Twentieth Century

Ways In

The instructor who turns to this last section of the instructor's manual, devoted to the twentieth century, will either be fresh and sparkling as a new semester or a year-long course unfolds, or else catching a second wind after traversing prior centuries or periods. You may be teaching a course with the relative luxury of being focussed on the twentieth century alone, as for example in surveys of Modern British prose and poetry, or in classes on modernist literature, both of which generally begin with Joseph Conrad or possibly let Oscar Wilde get in under the century's wire; or you may be perusing these pages rather breathlessly and short on time, with twentieth-century literature only part of a longer course with a syllabus encompassing several centuries—for you, this literary period, like the twentieth century itself, quickly draws to a close. Whether your course has the comparative freedom of the former in terms of time and pace, or if it is on the tight schedule of the latter, with no time to dawdle over lesser lights, there are a few general principles to keep in mind in addressing the twentieth-century section of the *Longman Anthology of British Literature*, and some common pedagogical goals on the fast track or the slower, leisurely path, that we hope will invigorate your teaching.

Modern British literature (that is, post-Victorian, twentieth-century British literature) rejoins or embraces world literature, in a way that British literature accomplished at several of its peak periods, but not at all. William Shakespeare is an English writer, to indicate the obvious, but Shakespearean drama and poetry have had and continue to have world-wide audiences, scholarship, and cultural implications. The epic poetry of John Milton has had similar, if slightly less powerful, reverberations across many other literatures and tongues; the British Romantic poets opened up Romanticism for Europe in general and then, as Romanticism spread as a movement, they created a literary style, and a cultural politics, which traveled across the globe. Twentieth-century British literature in many of its facets—its prose, poetry, and drama—has the same global distinction and global dissemination, and the same innovative stature, as these past exemplars. Stating this fact is not meant to create a hierarchy within British literature, labeling some of its periods or productions "greater" than others by virtue of their being more widely read, or more influential, outside Britain itself. All questions of value aside—and it would be absurd to judge Donne's poetry or Johnson's prose or Austen's novels as less great, or even less "universal," than they manifestly are, only for not having leapt over the divisions of language and nation quite as nimbly—it is still the case that twentieth-century British literature happens to contain many of the premier names in modernism regardless of nation or language: Conrad, Joyce, Woolf, Eliot, Beckett, Yeats, and Lawrence. They constitute a formidable line-up no other single country can match across the key genres—and genders—of modernism.

Teaching the twentieth-century section of the *Longman Anthology*, then, has as a great plus the chance to watch British literature set many of the standards that ultimately will count as "modernist art" around the world, and to see English literature in action as a foremost innovator on the world scene. One common thread in the following guides to teaching the individual works or authors of the last section will emphasize ways the selections from this period can stand alone as a study in modernism, a compact modernist lineage. The changes occurring in the novel, in poetry, and in drama in the twentieth century—how they become "modern" in formal terms—can all be witnessed at their height in the authors of this section, who offer a lexicon of modernist literature just as experimental, powerful, and influential as Picasso's paintings or Einstein's physics for the lexicon of modernist art and modern science, respectively. The most dynamic—and true—way to present the century's literature is at that high level of technical innovation and lasting human import: British literature in the twentieth century alters the forms and the roles of art.

Modernist form is by no means the only hallmark of twentieth-century British literature, but it is to be meaningfully discerned even in writers whose works, however monumental, might appear to have more than one foot set in a previous century. The two extraordinary writers in the section who most bear this out are George Bernard Shaw and Thomas Hardy, both Victorianists by birth, education, and literary training, yet each of whom stakes a claim to modernism in unique ways: Shaw in the de-centered, ensemble nature of his drama, and Hardy in the old-fashioned echoes within his very modern poetry. What makes something "modern," then, whether work of art, idea, or even person, is and should be a constant refrain in teaching the twentieth-century canon. One path through the *Anthology* selections, then, would involve extracting the modernist nugget—the works of Conrad, Hardy, Yeats, Eliot, Joyce, Woolf, Beckett, and Lawrence—and using the Perspectives sections as surrounding and deepening contexts: in other words, foregrounding the era's literary experimentation and achievements. Exploring the modernist "nugget" just described need not be only a formal enterprise—if the basis for our anthology holds, aesthetic choices are never divorced from cultural, historical, and political roots. One of the most exciting approaches to the modernist canon embedded in the section would be to tease out the complex literary geographies modernism contains, starting with Conrad's foreignness and tracing modernism through the diverse cultures, classes, genders and regions of its development. Another pathway to adopt as a supplement to the primarily literary-historical route would focus on key issues emerging in the period, which spill over into the literature and also arise from within it: one such issue is the encounter with difference and diversity brought about by the loss of empire, through the challenges of independence movements and struggles, including women's suffrage and trade unionism. Under such scrutiny, "British" modernism quickly reveals its fragmentation and its "otherness"; consider a syllabus which investigates how modernism came to be such an off-center movement in cultural terms, and why the greatest modernist writers in its tradition are women, or Irish, or working-class, or foreign-born. Modernism stands revealed as a veritable encounter with difference—in some cases literally, as in encounters across race, culture, or class; in some cases metaphorically, as Virginia Woolf insists on the productive silences of women's voices and lives. Wyndham Lewis's work sketches a modernist recoil from the masses; D. H. Lawrence's writing explores the intertwining of sexuality and power in class terms. England's cultural "opposite" for six hundred years had been its colony Ireland; in the twentieth century, Irish writers are the fountain of British modernism. The writing of these modernist giants—Wilde, Shaw, Joyce, Yeats, Beckett—is itself an encounter with the Other, as their works hold up "the cracked looking-glass of a servant," in Joyce's phrase quoting Wilde's, in which to mirror the history of English literature and the legacy of colonialism. A course set up in this way, in other words one that took modernism as a complicated and a divided phenomenon, a series of rich encounters with differences inside and outside, would flow quite readily into the post-World War II and the contemporary parts of the *Anthology*: Conrad's modernist lineage could (and should) be traced through Naipaul, Rushdie, and Churchill, while Yeats's poetic modernism travels through to Auden, Larkin, the Irish poets Heany and Ni Dhomhnaill, ending with Derek Walcott's voyage back to Conrad.

At the heart of the twentieth-century section is Virginia Woolf's work: she is at the center of the volume because its editors see her writing as the quintessential representative of British modernism. Woolf's *Mrs Dalloway* gives students the best example of the trajectory of the modernist novel, in a work that refers repeatedly to Conrad's *Heart of Darkness*, within a narrative that highlights the global predicament of modern Western societies, and underscores the place of women in modern culture. Moreover, Woolf's intricate prose and the audacious structuring of the novel stand as a model of modernist experimentation. In addition to including this novel, the *Anthology* provides an extensive selection from Woolf's well-known works of social thought, *A Room of One's Own* and *Three Guineas*, and several short fictions. The amplitude of the Woolf selections, allows an instructor to link Woolf's writing with the lineage of female writers who precede her in the anthology, and to connect her prose writing with the important documents of cultural thought—Milton, Johnson, Wollstonecraft, Mill, Carlyle, Arnold, Wilde, Pearse—that form a major current of British letters, sometimes oppositional, sometimes not. Gender is an explosive feature of the twentieth-century section and now has its own Perspectives section, Regendering Modernism; male writers like Bernard Shaw, who argues for women's equality no less passionately than Woolf does, D. H. Lawrence, whose story *The Horse Dealer's Daughter* centers on female sexuality, or Caryl Churchill, who depicts fluid sexualities and the pressures on immigrant women in particular, can be read with Woolf, West, Bowen, Mansfield, Rhys, Gordimer, and others for a multi-faceted exploration of gender and sexuality as a profound force in modern literature and life.

As any instructor knows, one of strongest techniques for teaching is the creation of cross-references, so that issues or themes or styles accumulate force as they are repeated with a difference in works that cross-reference or allude to others. The twentieth-century section has a built-in engine for cross-reference in its first selection, Joseph Conrad's *Heart of Darkness*. Critically accepted as the first modernist literary work, *Heart of Darkness* reverberates through all the prose fiction, much of the poetry, and some of the drama, even including the play, *Cloud 9*. Conrad's brief but monumental novella refers back to the travel writing of the nineteenth century in its narrative thrust, points forward to the postcolonial voices narrating their own further journeys, incorporates in its astonishing style of poetic density the developments in imagery and rhythm made by poets like Hopkins, Hardy and others, and draws on the visual sophistication of the modern painters revealed and revered in the art criticism of Ruskin, Pater, and, later, painters in the color illustrations such as Vanessa Bell. Most of the streams of critical interest in the twentieth century converge in Conrad's work, and those that seem to remain frustratingly outside it—for example, the modern awakening of women's self-awareness and self-determination—can be provocatively introduced by virtue of their absence in this rich text.

Britain is one of the few European countries to experience a revolution on its own soil during the twentieth century: the revolt for Irish independence reached its goal in the formation of the Irish Republic in 1922. The twentieth-century section of the *Anthology* provides ample selections from Irish literary and political documents—many of the latter works of literature in their own right—in order to allow the specificity of its Irishness to emerge from writing often lumped under the sanitized heading of British literature. The *Anthology* consistently emphasizes the linguistic, cultural, and political complexity of Great Britain from medieval times, and illustrates in its selections, commentaries, maps, and perspectives sections the complicated traffic between and among England, Scotland, Wales, and Ireland, and, later, farther-flung colonial possessions in Africa, the Caribbean, Southern Asia, Australia, and the subcontinent. The Irish case is perhaps the most fully developed one in the *Anthology*, and since it did lead to the formation of a separate nation in the twentieth century, a thoughtful literary case history centering on Irish/English literary relations could make a powerful, interesting, and coherent syllabus in and of itself. Wilde, Shaw, Parnell, Collins, Pearse, Yeats, Joyce, Bowen and Beckett could form an internal unit on modernism in art and politics. Wilde's defiant aestheticism and flouting of bourgeois norms takes on a different light when seen as a form of artistic polemic against English social norms and control; Yeats and Joyce offer two completely distinct paradigms of what political "action" might mean, and conceive of modernity in oppositional ways; Beckett's Irishness takes him to Paris and to a hiding place within the French language.

The relationship between literature and national identity, or between literature and politics, could also be a strong focus for teaching this section. Wyndham Lewis's *Manifesto* articulates a politics—verging on fascism—no less than an aesthetic program; Shaw's *Pygmalion* is a political essay in charming disguise, which counters Lewis with a form of pragmatic democratic socialism. The poetry of Owen, Sassoon, Rosenberg and others in response to the Great War is especially resonant seen in this light. The two *sui generis* memoirs of that section—David Jones's *In Parenthesis* and Robert Graves's *Goodbye to All That*—are luminous interconnections of the artistic and the political, the self and history. Evelyn Waugh's stories *Cruise* and *The Man*

Who Liked Dickens scathingly etch the decline of what he saw as England's natural aristocracy; P.G. Wodehouse vaults over social unrest to make class distinctions mostly a hilarious matter of language on holiday. George Orwell comments on the role of the committed or partisan writer, and the modern self in light of fractured or tormented histories, as do W. H. Auden, V. S. Naipaul, Ni Dhomhnaill and Heaney, in divergent ways. The vivid multiculturalism of Britain today, with its "Black British" citizens, its non-white immigrants, its openness to Europe as well as its Irish, Scottish, and Welsh communities, is signaled in works by Caryl Churchill, Angela Carter and James Kelman.

The above paragraphs have described several pathways into the rich materials of the section, suggesting modes of organization—literary language and form, cultural issues and themes, historical contexts and events, and their dynamic interaction around specific texts, writers, or even styles. In what follows, ideas for teaching individual works intersect with these broader agendas, even as they harken back to other periods or literary forebears.

Joseph Conrad
Heart of Darkness

This deceptively slim text was a fateful event in the history of fiction, a novel that set modern fiction on an entirely new course. To teach the novel is to examine what makes this a radically new narrative style, and how its innovations are linked to the historical circumstances of its production, to the story of how it came to be. The global history of imperialism that engenders this novel and pervades it is inseparable from the distinctive techniques of writing that distinguish it as a specifically modernist novel. The two tracks in pursuit of *Heart of Darkness* ultimately converge and tie together. Because the novella is so pivotal to the twentieth-century section, inaugurating post-Victorian literature, announcing British modernism, and reverberating in literary or thematic ways in virtually all the writing that follows it in the *Anthology*, this entry in the manual is longer than most, and includes a full-fledged interpretive reading of the text, as well as background for understanding it in critical and historical terms, to provide a possible paradigm for teachers of the text in the context of twentieth-century British literature.

Heart of Darkness is the story of a voice, of Marlow's voice as it issues forth from the gloom of the shipboard of the *Nellie* as she lies becalmed, waiting for the turn of the tide to begin traveling back to London, where she is moored. His voice seemingly issues from the darkness—first of all, because it is growing dark on ship, with night falling as the story unfolds. Moreover, Marlow is left in partial darkness as a character—never fully described, never given a personal history—so that human personality and character is shadowy and "flat," a silhouette. He has become nothing more, and nothing less, than a ribbon of sound. Conrad's tale moves back to one of the oldest forms of narrative, the personal tale, the story of the eyewitness, the testimony of memory, and in that sense *Heart of Darkness* certainly is a return to an old-fashioned mode, to what Walter Benjamin called "the art of the storyteller."

In that same move, however, Marlow's "living voice" is also directed toward an audience, the mostly silent companions he has on ship, the men who go by the names of their professions, the Director (a version of the CEO), the Lawyer, the Accountant. Tell students to imagine that Michael Eisner, Bill Gates, and Michael Jordan are all listening to Marlow on the deck of Steven Spielberg's yacht, to get the effect of power and privilege Conrad intends. Marlow's voice, then, is as hallowed in narrative history as the voice around the campfire, telling tall tales, or the tradition of the seaman's "yarn" that begins in literature with Homer's *Odyssey*; Conrad intends these parallels too. Yet in being a voice out of the darkness, directed to a shadowy assemblage of the forces of power in modern society in the "greatest city in the world," Conrad also gives the ancient tradition a very modern twist: Marlow's voice is like the disembodied sound of the gramophone, Edison's new invention that was taking the world by storm. Marlow is an ancient mariner or a troubador type, but he is also a phonograph recording, a piece of modern technology, a technical "ghost." The ear is emphasized over the eye—just as it will be in other modernist writing, as for example in Joyce's *Dubliners* and *Ulysses*. As the narrator says, "we knew we were fated, before the ebb began to run, to hear about one of Marlow's inconclusive experiences." Hearing and telling are the ground of the story, while seeing is always a precarious achievement and a much less certain business. Marlow doesn't claim to be an eyewitness to Kurtz's and imperialism's crimes, although he was, because seeing is not believing. He relies on telling, listening, hearing.

Conrad's narrative "trick" is to make us, his readers, feel as if we are listening to the story, not reading it with our eyes. We have to "hear" its voice, just as Marlow's listeners did. One fascinating project for students is to trace the references to sight and sound, to the "oral" versus the "written" across the whole novel. The narrative, then, could be looked at abstractly as the alternation of presence and absence; the *presence* of spoken words in time makes absent their written version, or at least postpones the sense that they are written—that's the "trick"; a speaker takes over the narrative with his voice, and his voice overrides the fact that he is absent or unseen to his listeners as he speaks. Paradoxically, the goal here is "to make [us] see," as Conrad's famous preface states. "Only make them see," he yearns of his readers, who have to "hear" first in order to then "see" in their mind's eye, to transcend the absence of everything but words so that we may pass into a realm of vision beyond the words. Conrad tries to use prose in a negative fashion, in order to transcend writing and thereby embody direct utterance and vision—in other words, the voicing or sound that is so crucial to *Heart of Darkness* is a way of proposing a path out of words, written words with their inability to open out and to tell. Written words threaten to lie flat and inert and ignored on the page; spoken words can thrill, persuade, or horrify as they almost enter the body of the listener. Every experience begins with the relation of speaker to hearer and hearer to speaker: we are listening as much as we are reading, our reading is meant to take us through to a point where what we hear is Marlow's voice. Conrad's complex book leads us through sound to sight, taking the "long way around," in a sense, because the mark of modernity is a doubt that words can capture and reproduce reality. The problem lies not only with words, which suddenly are seen to be much more than transparent windows onto ideas or thoughts—words are playing their own complicated game with us, as the philosopher Nietzsche among others discerned, whose thought about language was a strong influence on Conrad. "Reality" also is no longer felt to be certain, has vanished as a possibility. This arises partly because modern life makes reality hard—if not impossible—to determine: images are more real than real things at times, space and time are altered by technology, "reality" could be microscopic or telegraphic or x-rayed, or hidden in the unconscious. And, most perplexingly of all, a sense of what is real, or true, is not necessarily shared by people, whose perspectives or blindness can create their very reality. *Heart of Darkness* envisions a sharing of "truth" between speaker and listener that could escape some of the blindness of language. That attempt, though, seems bound to fail; Kurtz, for example, is reduced to a talking insubstantiality, rather than a man: "he was just a voice." The darkness we are asked to enter in *Heart of Darkness* is a dark space where Conrad hopes that the language humans so excruciatingly use as a barrier to truth, and an obstacle to sharing what is real between ourselves, will somehow vanish, leaving in its place the complete absorption of teller and listener into an imaginative truth they share. This is one important sense of the darkness that so pervades *Heart of Darkness*: it is also a way of pushing beyond the constraints of language to suggest a shared substance, a negativity that becomes something, a darkness that can be inhabited as the shared space of memory and truth. And nonetheless, as is of course obvious, the novel is made up of words, and cannot escape using words to try to effect the very escape from them. This impasse or paradox begins to account for the importance of the voice, which helps to insist that the words are entering our minds in some other, almost telepathic way. "After *Heart of Darkness*," the critic Marvin Mudrick says, "the recorded moment—the word—was irrecoverably symbol."

Conrad embeds the method of this story into its own frame. Let's step back for a moment and acknowledge how complex that frame is; we don't have Marlow as a first-person narrator who takes over at the beginning of the story and operates ever after with authorial control, narrative certainty, perfect knowledge or at least self-knowledge. We're taken off-balance from the start by the fact that the narrative of Marlow's voice is framed by another narrator, never named, who sets up Marlow's discourse for us. The narrative makes concentric circles, with Marlow's in a sense being surrounded or circumscribed by that of the narrator. This invisible narrator is not a "voice," but a presence on the page, and has no omniscience, no authority, no ability to testify that language can convey truth and total exposition. This narrator who establishes the opening for Marlow's voice is not superior in knowledge to Marlow or to us; he is also a listener—and he is decidedly not Joseph Conrad. Students can be shown how unusual the lack of authorial omniscience is—the vanishing of the eighteenth-century asides like "Dear Reader," and the nineteenth-century moral commentary of Eliot or Hardy or Dickens is decisive. In this way the novel thoroughly sets aside any internal claim to total knowledge, to capturing reality, to presenting a wholeness that can be completely revealed in the language of the work. Instead, we are insinuated into the text and reminded of its provisionality. This move has many consequences: authorial omniscience is abandoned—even the text is seemingly dependent on what Marlow will say next. A passage has been made from the "closed text" of realism, as many literary critics have described it, i.e. the realist novel that can be finished, or summed up with a moral, or provided with a clearly tragic or happy ending, to the open text, where what is being told or narrated cannot be finalized, closed, or defined, since the meandering voice narrates a journey without a definitive ending, or final meaning.

The famous lines about how Marlow's open-ended story differs from the "seaman's tale," a tale with a kernel of meaning inside it like a nut within a shell, are the best single source for explicating Conrad's new method. A reader of *Heart of Darkness* can't hope to bore in and extract a nugget of truth, to peel away a husk and extract the solid meaning within. The almost mystifying image Conrad's narrator gives for the nature of Marlow's storytelling is that of a moonlit glow bringing out a shimmering haze, where two insubstantialities are set in conjunction with one another. The meaning that surrounds what is being told like a vapor is, then, greater than the individual words within the sentences. The impression, in the sense of sensory impression, that is imparted by teller to listener, or reader, relies on the consciousness of the teller, not on some supposedly external reality, firm and fixed. When one probes this language, tries to open it up or make it a formula, one puts one's hands into a retreating mist. This isn't because Conrad is being opaque or deliberately difficult; his new mode of writing, which even his early readers recognized as "modern," casts a net of words that fans out in a diaphanous way. To use another simile—Conrad's style is like the many ripples passing over the surface of a pond when a stone has been thrown, because he conceives of language and knowledge in new ways. *Heart of Darkness* lodges us within a voice that knows that the teller is not separate from the tale, that what is told is the stream of consciousness. These impressions are not easily available, straightforward, complete, true or false. The Preface to *The Nigger of the "Narcissus"* included in the volume states some of these artistic intentions directly.

Every word, then, in *Heart of Darkness* becomes a kind of charged particle, receiving its valence from the words that surround it and also from its repetition over time. Individual words accrete meanings that shift and change in this work, that are as indeterminate as the misty halo, not because of some obscurity or desire to thwart the reader, but because the process of arriving at the "truth," insofar as that is possible, must shake language, or words, from their fixed moorings, must let words open out the way a radiance surrounds a misty reflection. The words in the book are "symbolic," but not in the older critical understanding of the symbol as a permanent meaning carried by a word or image throughout a work. Conrad's words are incredibly important—none of them is chosen casually, none of them is "merely" descriptive. When we talk about symbols in the older way, we usually envision going on some kind of a symbol hunt, tracking down the meaning of a word or image and then fixing it in amber, or stuffing it and mounting it on the wall in order to say— yes, this symbol eluded us for a while, but we finally bagged it. The metaphor of charged particles opening the paragraph was meant to evade this sense of finitude or completion. For example, taking the images of light and dark that naturally sug-

gest themselves as vitally important to Conrad's text, one can see that they are indeterminate, unfixed, never resolving themselves into neat identifications or discrete meanings, but instead operating as fields of force in the text, moving in and
through Marlow's account, where the "meaning" is never stated or defined, because
it is being made, being spoken. "Dark" and "light," "white" and "black," seemingly
clear-cut terms that are opposites to one another, in Conrad's lexicon reverse their
meanings, or subtly exchange places. "Whiteness" can become an immensely dark
moral blankness, while "blackness" can suggest revelation and truth. We have to
hang on Marlow's every word, because with each word the story is created anew, the
relations of the words and images to one another is altered and transformed.

The narrative form of *Heart of Darkness* makes a deliberate havoc of any simple
scheme based on the quest, because the quest presupposes a final ending, reaching
the goal or grail at some point. Marlow has set out on a quest of a sort—to make a
trip up the river, incidentally encountering the Kurtz he has come to hear so much
about—but the narrative doesn't rest on the unfolding of that search. Instead, the
narrative becomes retrospective, a looking back over in memory, to find in memory an understanding of what the experience might have meant. Unlike a quest,
where the hero finds what he is looking for, or at least, like Ulysses, finds his way
back home, Marlow's journey is incomplete, fragmentary, and inconclusive. At the
same time it is crucial for Marlow to make us see, as he sees or doesn't see. The
journey of the telling takes precedence over and displaces the actual journey to
Africa and back, because it is not a matter of recounting an incident and then producing a moral out of it, but rather exploring the nature of the perception and the
memory of that event, whose moral is only achieved in group awareness. Marlow
is as much in the dark as we his listeners are; what the novel is built out of, then,
is its words. Just as the mist surrounds the halo, so will Marlow's words, his voice,
become ghostly, until he is described as an ivory fetish, a blankness himself as he
speaks the tale; just so will all aspects of the journey as they are described also take
on a spectral glow, phantom-like at some level, unreal in the sense that their meaning is being made out of the ghostly medium of words. In that mist of interconnection we look to find what we can see behind the words of this text. Thus as
one moves through it, much of the account can be read as having the unreality of
a dream—"we live, as we dream, alone," Marlow says. The *Anthology* includes the
song lyric "We Live, As We Dream, Alone," by the important punk band Gang of
4, in part to cite how widespread the cultural references to Conrad's masterwork
are, in high art and in popular art, in fiction, film, and even popular music. The
song zeroes in on one profoundly modern, or modernist, aspect of *Heart of Darkness*,
which is the feeling of loneliness experienced by Marlow and, by extension, all
modern people. No human community shares his, or our experiences, and
Marlow, like the singer of Gang of 4's ballad, must provide whatever meaning or
truth will emerge from his life on his own. Modern loneliness is summed up too
in the phrase T. S. Eliot borrowed from Conrad for his poem on modern existence
"The Hollow Men." In the absence of shared values and common goals, in the face
of ambiguity, alienation, and solitude, human beings become hollow, become
empty. Marlow, however, is not an example of a "hollow man"—he is still trying to

tell the story which, if his listeners hear it, will redeem such loneliness and replace the hollowness of amorality. The question for Marlow, as it is the question for Joseph Conrad, is whether artful language can draw people together long enough to accomplish ethical community.

The book spins out a ghostly line of narrative, with a shimmering, poetic surface of words, but is also completely rooted in historical detail—thoroughly realistic, if we want to use that word. In teaching the book in relation to the *Anthology* as a whole, emphasizing the historical particularities is as important as giving full recognition to Conrad's stylistic daring and modernist methods. Instructors should make use of the maps, which show the extent of the British empire by the turn of the century. The travel writing section of the nineteenth-century section is replete with the overtures to imperialism which bore fruit later in the century, and makes a strong companion piece with Conrad. Many of the subsequent selections—those by Forster, Waugh, Woolf, Greene, Bowen and Mansfield and Sackville-West no less than those by Naipaul, Rushdie, Rhys, Gordimer, Heaney and Walcott—are vital intertexts with the history and ideology recorded so enduringly in *Heart of Darkness*. For what Conrad writes about in *Heart of Darkness* is true history: Marlow's journey replicates the exact and horrifying conditions to be found in the Belgian Congo as they actually existed at the time, despite the fact that neither he nor Conrad ever names the country or its colonial rulers; every aspect down to the nuances of tribal differentiation is present in Conrad's work. How are these two aspects of the text compatible: its radical inconclusiveness and yet its precise realism, meticulously and subtly conveyed? Moreover, Conrad himself had made a voyage up the Congo nine years before the writing of *Heart of Darkness*, as a ship captain commissioned by a trading company in Belgium, much as Marlow happens to be given a job. Conrad's trip lasted six months, and involved bringing back a trader, Klein, who had become sick at his "station" and then died on board the ship Conrad commanded. The history of the so-called Congo Free State Conrad writes of but does not name is as follows: In 1876, King Leopold of Belgium who, in response to the smallness of his kingdom and the spirit of the age, had been looking around for an empire for some time, promoted the formation of the "International Association for the Suppression of Slavery and the Opening up of Central Africa." At its founding international conference in Brussels, he announced: "To open to civilization the only area of our globe to which it has not yet penetrated, to pierce the gloom which hangs over entire races, constitutes, if I may dare to put it this way, a Crusade worthy of this century of Progress."

Leopold had in mind a crusade in the only large area of Africa not already claimed by the chief colonial powers—England, France, Germany, and the Netherlands—and in the journalist-explorer Henry Morgan Stanley he found a comrade and co-conspirator to help him acquire it. Stanley set up a chain of stations along the upper reaches of the Congo River. The association's concern with free trade, human betterment and the abolition of slavery was purest propaganda; as soon as possible, Leopold used shameless economic and political exploitation to carve out this territory, setting the other great powers against each other, and then in Berlin in 1885 won international recognition as the sovereign ruler of the

Independent State of the Congo. He became the sole ruler of an empire of a million square miles; so ruthless was this empire that three million African lives were lost; finally, in 1906, Leopold was forced to divest himself personally of his holdings in the face of international outcry.

That is not to imply that there was a happy ending as a result, or self-determination for the Congo; merely that this style of individual or private imperialism was ended. Leopold had maintained the Congo Free State under completely different conditions than the other African colonies held by England, Germany, France and Holland. All exports from the Congo ports, and imports too, were so heavily taxed that trade could not be set up by any other countries; this turned the Congo into a warehouse of wealth for Leopold, whose intentions were not to colonize the Congo but essentially to strip it bare of all its resources, in particular ivory, wood, and important minerals. To accomplish this Leopold simply turned every "subject" into a slave; the men who Marlow sees dying under the trees in such numbers are those who had been rounded up as slave labor to create the railroad Leopold hoped would facilitate the emptying of the country: it had no use as a means of modernization, as there was no place to "go." The laborers were not fed, and so died in massive numbers when they had worked as long as they could. The very railroad Conrad describes in Marlow's reminiscences took eight years to build and was, interestingly, masterminded by a brilliant black engineer from the United States, George Washington Williams. Conrad, who was active in anti-imperialist circles, wrote often about the cause in journals and newspapers, and spoke in lectures before professional and humanitarian societies, was to call Leopold's sixteen-year reign "the vilest scramble for loot that ever disfigured the history of human consciousness." Heart of Darkness shows these slaves or workers dying of starvation and overwork, holding thin pieces of wire, whose meaning seems to mystify Marlow; Conrad knew well what he was writing about, as Leopold had established these lengths of wire as a form of fake currency, having bundles of wires handed out to the slaves, and thereby claiming to pay them as workers, when in fact there was no food to buy, and no value to the wire currency even if there had been any food. The tone of harsh irony Marlow adopts at the absurdity of these cruel manipulations of language—slaves as "workers," men who won't accept slavery as "criminals," useless wire as "money"—anticipates all modern critiques of politics and language, from Orwell to Rushdie. No settlements other than the stations were set up; other than these stations the primary force in the country was the militia sent out to conscript workers by burning their villages and destroying tribal living areas. The enormity of this genocidal process is hard to take in, hard to register, and it is that difficulty which Conrad speaks to in Heart of Darkness.

Marlow refers in a famous passage to the nature of the imperial project, that it is nothing more nor less than taking land away from those who have flatter noses than most white Westerners: "Only the idea redeems it." Recall that this is early on in his oral narrative, at a point when it is still crucial to keep the attention of his listeners, to draw them in by articulating a notion they might be thought to share. The first section of his tale is, in fact, an attempt to connect and then to reverse the trajectory of imperialism as it begins to be his subject; looking out over the Thames, he recalls that England, too, now a seat of imperial power, was once a "place of darkness," that it, too, was a wilderness conquered, invaded and penetrated by the Roman empire and civilization. He imagines two possible personas for this Roman stage, one a confident boat commander, the other a young citizen forced to travel out to wild Britain because of financial problems at home in Rome, and of their sense of the savagery and darkness of the England they visit. The unnamed narrator in the prologue articulates the glories of Britain in the first flush of imperialism, when adventurers and explorers like Sir Walter Raleigh and Sir Francis Drake set sail to bring back loot, or to found colonies, when imperial exploits were part of dazzling personal adventures and discoveries. It is Marlow, and of course Conrad, who suggests that present-day imperialism bears little resemblance to those days of buccaneering glory, ironically reversing the terms of light and darkness so that the sheen of Renaissance golden treasure becomes the dark heart of modern British empire.

Conrad took great pains to differentiate the types of imperialism present in his time, the height of British empire-building, when Britain quite literally ruled the majority of the world. Leopold's gangster imperialism he deemed the worst type, whereas he found somewhat better the colonial type practiced by Britain in India, for example, where British people settled, and cities, railroads, schools, and courts were built, ostensibly for the benefit of some of the native subjects, as well as the ruling British. At the time, the support for empire was near universal, so that by making such thoughtful distinctions Conrad was already branded a radical. Fifty years later, making any distinction whatsoever in the degrees of harm caused by imperialism struck many people as intolerable acceptance of a vile political practice, and Conrad received blame as an apologist for imperialism, even though he had worked so hard to confront it, study it, and criticize it. Historical hindsight is responsible for many such judgments, and these are understandable, especially when imperialism was being challenged and overthrown. Conrad's book cannot be read as simple imperialist apology, though, if it is looked at in fairness as the extraordinary work of anti-imperialism it was in its day, and if its bitter ironies are fully understood. Class discussions which revolve around the simple binary of Heart of Darkness as imperialist and racist, or neither of those things, will probably not resolve much. A better approach arises in and through the literary selections which follow in the Anthology—especially those post-World War II—as they enter into vibrant dialogue with Conrad, sixty or more years later. It should be noted, too, that while the major African writer Chinua Achebe branded Conrad's book "racist" in the 1950s, at the dawn of the African novel in English, on the grounds that Conrad had spoken for Africans but had not let them speak for themselves, subsequent African writers and theorists of postcolonial literature and culture have acknowledged that Conrad had little choice. He wrote in a vacuum, from the only possible "side" he could know. The many adaptations of Heart of Darkness by contemporary African and African-diaspora writers from Achebe to Ngugi wa-Thiongo, Soyinka and Emecheta among others, have been the most fruitful and productive response to the issue of voice.

Still, Marlow holds out the slim hope that those forms of imperialism that sincerely are motivated by an idea—of improvement, justice, or "civilizing mission"—

may be better than those forms awash in murder and hypocrisy. But if it is "the idea behind it [imperialism] that redeems it," what is that idea, who has it, where is it confirmed? Marlow makes a distinction among imperialisms when he remarks on the colorful world map of empire hanging in the otherwise sepulchral offices of the Company that "a jolly lot of work gets done" in the red areas. Work is sacred to Marlow, and red is, of course, England's color in the imperial banner sweep-stakes—the very notion that the spaces on a map are colored according to whom they "belong" is an extraordinary inversion of the logic of color, and this para-graph about the map is, with the exception of the description of the Russian's har-lequin clothes, the only outburst of color in the somber chiaroscuro of the text. The book discriminates among imperialisms, not to support or admire one or the other, but to show the differences that exist, and perhaps to express hope that Britain will change its views on the efficacy of the "work" done in imperial con-texts. Marlow describes his early boyhood relation to the map of the world and how he wanted to inscribe himself on the blankness at the heart of the imperial map. His desire to do so is also a fateful one; the snake-like river virtually uncoils itself from two-dimensionality and snares him, charms him, as he says. Here one can see the crossing over of the two tracks of analysis: the utter factuality of that imperial map, rendered precisely as it existed in history, and yet the dynamization of that map by the psychic forces of memory and consciousness at the same time. Conrad through Marlow shows us how seductive the very "blankness" was to Western eyes, who sought to know it in boyish innocence, leading to effects as grave and ghastly as the Belgian Congo takeover.

The railroad scene at the company station juxtaposes the crisply insane European clerk, who has made a fetish of whitening his laundry and wearing daz-zlingly white garb no matter what the hardships on his African laundress, with the dying African men, diversely given the label of enemy or criminal by the Europeans at the station, one of whom has tied a bit of white yarn around his neck as a fetish or talisman, Marlow presumes. Marlow's narrative shows that the white station clerk's infernal whiteness is no less a "fetish" or primitive talisman than is the piece of yarn, which is no less ambiguous than any European self-decoration. He must move under the cliches of imperialism and racism, which would equate "black" with "savage," tunnel into it by using these phrases ironically, as a way of getting to the heart of colonial language. The indeterminacy of darkness as the trope of Africa is the metaphor for its unknownness, the location of moral ab-sence, the site of plenitude and discovery. Only against the darkness can one see the mist that makes the halo, or the spectral moonshine. The difficulty and the challenge to language in this first modernist work in English, is to make it at one and the same time both clear and fuzzy, both darkly ambiguous and brilliantly lucid, and brilliantly ambiguous and darkly apparent. Only out of a negativity can anything be revealed, a negativity so complex it shifts the entire terms of the mod-ern novel. The people in the book, at least the Europeans, are negative too, as Marlow says of the bricklayer he meets, "empty inside, with nothing but a little loose dirt" there, or "they were nothing," as he says of the pilgrims. Language takes on uncanny forms, or is described in talismanic or fetishistic ways, as if Conrad

were deliberately adopting the worst criticisms Europeans made against African natives and colonial others and turning them against Western customs; for example,when Marlowe describes the way the word ivory rings in the air "like a god to
be prayed to"; or the way the "little smile of the manager of the inner station is a
kind of seal set on his words"; or the ways that, since they have no shared language,
Marlow regards the Africans as gestural hieroglyphs, whose every movement of the
hand is a carefully wrought form of speech.

As Marlow makes his way along the river, heading toward Kurtz's station, with
several of the pilgrims irritably and gun-happily in tow, his crew made up of pre-
sumed cannibals and their dwindling stores of dead hippo meat, again and again
the landscape that surrounds them, the wilderness, as Marlow thinks of it, is described as having a face, a face whose features cannot be seen, but a face nonetheless. The anthropomorphizing of the jungle, turning it into a human figure with
an implacable face, is crucially related to the voice that is Kurtz's "gift." "I could
see through a sombre gap glittering, glittering, as it flowed broadly by without a
murmur. All this was great, expectant, mute, while the man jabbered about himself. I wondered whether the stillness on the face of the immensity looking at us
two were meant as an appeal or a menace." And a little later, "Somehow it didn't
bring any image with it." The face that isn't a face; this figural language begins to
establish the wilderness as a mysterious place that will not speak itself, that refuses
to reveal itself by any act of voice, and the silence that surrounds Marlow is not at
all the silence of, let's say, the proverbial forest when no one is there to hear the
tree fall, but a silence that is utterly meaningful because it constitutes a refusal to
speak. This form of silence is evidence that the wilderness could speak, because
against its majestic and even pregnant pauses the speech of humans is a jabber, an
irrelevance, a mistake. So desirous of breaking through to the meaning of that silence does Marlow become that the novel begins to use the words that derive from
the vocabulary of truth and knowledge—there is a veil that Marlow wants to pierce,
a veil that hides the face he wants to gaze upon for the truth that presumably lies
behind. These aspects introduce the gender questions an instructor will want to
highlight, and to connect to selections by Bowen, Woolf, Lawrence and others, in
terms of the relationship between women and truth.

This dialectic of speech and silence, of darkness and revelation, is complexly
mapped out in the novel; one place to look for its complication is in the painting
Kurtz has left with the young aristocrat at the central station, which he shows to
Marlow. This painting is an allegory, in the style of that period's salon painting,
but it is also an allegory that reverses expectations. "Then I noticed a small sketch
in oils, on a panel, representing a woman, draped and blindfolded, carrying a
lighted torch. The background was somber, almost black. The movement of the
woman was stately, and the effect of the torch-light on the face was sinister."
Traditionally, it is the figure of Justice who is depicted blindfolded, carrying the
scales, while the figure of Truth with her torch looks out with unfettered gaze from
her representations in paint or in stone. Nietzsche's *Genealogy of Morals* pointed out
that the icon of truth veiled as a woman was the impetus behind philosophical
speculation; here that image is extraordinarily changed, the woman blindfolded

while her torch is nonetheless carried aloft. Something is awry with the "truth" of what Europeans, and Kurtz, are doing in Africa. A woman symbolizes truth (light) turned to blind darkness. The Western white women in the novel—Marlow's Aunt, Kurtz's Intended—are "blind" to the truth, because they have been prevented from seeing it. They live, blindfolded in a sense, within the "beautiful lies" of imperialism, never recognizing the actual truth revealed by the lit torch of Marlow's story. Their very morality and goodness is a kind of screen or shield, keeping them from seeing "the horror, the horror" beyond.

The mask, too, is an important substitute for the desired speaking face of truth: a mask figures that possibility, but also implacably takes it away. As Marlow approaches the village where Kurtz has been living, under the guidance of Kurtz's disciple, the young Russian seaman, he makes a visual discovery. Using a pair of binoculars, he scans the enclosure ahead, where he had seen a series of poles topped with what he thought were ivory balls, totems on a stick. As the super-visual acuity of the binoculars permits him to see, these balls are actually heads Kurtz has had impaled around his encampment, dead faces, if you will, all of whom—and the personal pronoun is unavoidable—have their heads turned away from Marlow's gaze, withholding themselves from it. Except one. That head he does indeed gaze upon, but this head's eyes are closed. However, it is smiling; "the shrunken dry lips showing a narrow white line of the teeth . . . smiling continually at some endless and jocose dream. . . ." Another dead end, in a sense: despite the aid of the binoculars, Marlow cannot succeed in entering that line of sight, and the head keeps its own secret, its own dreamy counsel. The binoculars too are not irrelevant to the dynamic of the entire book; almost cinematically, we are swept across Marlow's line of vision, we see with him through these devices, distanced from what is to emerge by technological power.

In this anthropomorphic landscape, where the world refuses to speak itself, Kurtz's voice is the sole source of truth; Kurtz is voice, is speech, is talk, against the stillness of the wilderness for Marlow and the others—whereas for those on the other side of the bank, the Africans, there is no wilderness, there is no silence. Again and again the text refers to the presence of the colonizers, to the pilgrims and even to Marlow himself as a "fantastic invasion." Out of the jabber of their speech Kurtz, however, is said to be all eloquence, to have the gift of expression, and it is to this hope and indeed fetish that Marlow begins to cling. His world of rivets and hard work had kept him safe from the hallucinatory strangeness and indeed the horror of his encounter with what the company has made of this place, for a time; Marlow uses the Victorian ethos of the nobility of work to forget the silence; he vanishes into the world of rivets as long as he can, until that world is punctured as truly as the helmsman's side is punctured by the spear. Marlow comes to suspect that even work is conforming to a system whose grasp is so vast it cannot be comprehended by individual effort, which holds out no redemption—what has Marlow's devotion to the duty of repairing the ship's bottom done but bring them to Kurtz's outpost, to replace Kurtz's "unsound methods" with the equally brutalizing corporate extractions of ivory the manager is going to institute? Kurtz, then, is not just a single "bad apple," to be weeded out so that the merry work of imperializing can go on. Kurtz is the voice of that imperial project speaking itself and knowing itself—he is the one person who will admit to the horrible truth of what is being done.

Kurtz is a voice—we need to take that very seriously. What he has done has consequences, yes, but they aren't neatly identifiable as timeless or universal patterns, and especially not as some kind of regression to "savagery." The novel explores the notion of regression, of going back in time to some primordial state, when, for example, it says: "we were wanderers on a prehistoric earth"; its use of such metaphors results from its collision with and against the theory of progress that had arisen out of Social Darwinism, a theory Darwin himself argued against. Kurtz is a mouth—the first time Marlow actually lays eyes on him, from afar, he is being carried on a stretcher, shouting, and his mouth is a black hole. "He wanted to swallow this, swallow all the air, swallow all the earth." Marlow can barely hear his voice, but it reaches him faintly, and he sees Kurtz physically as having become an ivory fetish, a piece of the ivory his gaping mouth has wanted to swallow.

One of the most famous quotes in the book addresses the nature of Kurtz: "All Europe contributed to the making of Kurtz." He is one-quarter English and one-quarter French, with the other halves of each parental side left mysteriously missing; all Europe has made him, though, because all of Europe's imperial discourses have combined in him. His eloquence consists in intermingling all the discourses of Sweetness and Light, Civilization, Power, Truth, and Good which the English, French, Germans and so on had employed to justify the progress of empire. Kurtz specialized in "burning noble words," a "magic current of phrases." These words belong, Marlow says, with the dustbin of progress, among the "sweepings and the dead cats of civilization." Marlow can scarcely remember what Kurtz says after he hears him talk, and can hardly remember the speech of Kurtz's he reads after the latter's death: it's all a cloud of verbiage. What he does remember, and so does everyone who reads Conrad's book, is what Kurtz scrawled as the postscript, so electrifying, simple, and "true" it is like a lightning bolt, a phrase that flashes up against the rhetoric and illuminates it: "Exterminate the brutes." Notice the postscript is in the grammatical form of a command, an exhortation, an order: Kurtz "forgot" to pretend that there was an idea behind it to redeem it—he just wrote what was happening—"kill them all." Marlow hates this postscript, but recognizes he must tell the story of extermination everyone else, besides himself and Kurtz, is denying. When this passage arrives in the story Marlow, sitting on the boat deck, lights a match, and it goes flickeringly out. And Marlow, too, as the bearer of this terrible news, yellows and withers and becomes ivory-like, a hard fetish, an idol before his listeners. The tale, and the novel, is a flickering illumination; Marlow is trying to tell the untellable, the catastrophic, where no one can believe it. Marlow describes his audience, as well as the readers of the text, when he refers to them as lodged "between the butcher and the policemen, afraid of the gallows, the insane asylum, and of scandal." Will they listen? Will we?

The Intended is described as "the echo of Kurtz"—she is the echo of his voice, not really a person. As Kurtz speaks his final words, "the horror, the horror," Marlow again experiences the tearing of the veil over truth, and pledges his loyalty to Kurtz, because he has uttered the truth. After this, Marlow is an outcast among the other pilgrims, and he has to return to Europe, taking the relics and effects of Kurtz with him, as if in expiation. It is there he learns that Kurtz is, in a sense, the figment of an imperial imagination, a figment of language; no one can even tell him what Kurtz was famous for—journalism? painting? or for being a speaker, a fascist mass speaker without any particular politics except those of extremism? Marlow has gone to see the Intended; her apartment is as tomb-like as the Company offices, and as sinister: not because the Intended is evil, but because she is an allegory come to life. The Intended is the woman in the picture at the station, painted by Kurtz, blindfolded Truth in a glare of horrible whiteness. When Marlow yields to her pleas and tells her that Kurtz's last words were "her name," one might think that this is the lie Marlow hates to tell, a face-saving fiction that operates to keep a woman in the beautiful, blind world of truth. Marlow in fact tells the literal truth: her name—blindfolded Truth—is the horror; horror is the name for her. The horror isn't just in Africa, in the Congo, in Kurtz's outpost: the horror is back home, here in our language, in the words we use to name or to conceal what we are doing. Marlow temporizes for the sake of his audience, but it is as imperative that they hear, as well, what he has told the Intended and why. The Intended is "an ashy halo out of which dark eyes glowed"—she is the story itself, the glow around the haze, that "seems to lead into the heart of an immense darkness."

Conrad did not learn English until he was twenty, and yet we start the formation of the modern British novel with his work. Why? Because all Europe went into the making of it; because the linguistic exile or displacement effected on Conrad as a writer is in fact the displacement, the sundering, of speech that *Heart of Darkness* enacts. Marlow is one individual seaman, the most old-fashioned of narrators, the storyteller, and yet it is his burden to tell what is kept silent, to tell of a new world of immense power, exerted in language a world away. Joseph Conrad brings this new modern story into English, and correspondingly brings English literature into modernism.

(George) Bernard Shaw

Bernard Shaw's work almost teaches itself: the "didactic" tendency of all his writing draws its readers (and, in the case of his plays, his viewers) directly into the debates and issues he finds at the heart of art. The effervescent brilliance of his didactic streak makes Shaw's educational mission a delightful experience, and Shaw never writes as if he is preaching to the already converted. His writing seldom if ever devolves into simple moral admonitions, but Shaw did truly believe that the words of verbal art could make things happen in society. His plays, reviews, and essays put him at the forefront of a society in change. The Shaw section is rich with teaching opportunities that connect his work to other parts of the *Anthology*. A teacher will want to point out the subtlety of Shaw's arguments for art, and his careful adjudication of realism and Romanticism. Shaw should accompany Wilde, Yeats, and Joyce as an example of Irish writing in exile, or in extremis; Shaw's satirical gifts shine with their truest glow when placed with Swift's essays, since Swift's passionate defense of Ireland in the face of its incredible poverty and misery was shared by Shaw.

Pygmalion

Pygmalion is an utterly fascinating play, and the teaching opportunities it sparks are as manifold as those of the twentieth century volume as a whole. Shaw's play is that rich: it is an important, indeed classic, commentary on modernity and gender, focusing as it does on the tutelage of Eliza Doolittle, flower girl turned cultivated, independent modern woman; it is as innovative in its own way about language, authorship, and the work of art as are the modernist experiments of Eliot's *The Waste Land*, Joyce's *Ulysses*, and Woolf's *Mrs Dalloway*. Pygmalion echoes the modernist form of those works as well by its use of the "mythic method"—after all, the story of the sculptor Pygmalion and his statue turned to life Galatea was a pivotal myth of art and its creation for more than a thousand years, and it resonates in the twentieth century both formally and in terms of its revised content: it begins to mean something new when the Galatea figure, in this case Eliza Doolittle, chooses not to marry her Pygmalion, Henry Higgins, and in fact is more necessary to him than he to her by the end of their relationship. And then there is the modern fact of Shaw's play and its transmutation from literature to film. Well within Shaw's lifetime, and with his ardent approval, *Pygmalion* was made into a celebrated film; even before that, though, Shaw's clever stage directions embrace the cinematic and underscore the modernist blurring between genres and media. Of course *Pygmalion* had yet another popular cultural incarnation in the stage musical and then hit film *My Fair Lady*, with Audrey Hepburn and Rex Harrison becoming the archetypal Liza and Henry Higgins in the public mind.

Pygmalion looks forward and backward in the anthology, and among the twentieth century offerings. It gives an uncanny glimpse into a London still beset by Victorian mores even into the Edwardian age, a city that has new motor-cars and buses on its streets and an underground railway, even as horse-drawn carriages continue to transport the aristocracy. The phonograph and the telephone are crucial to its plot, and even newer media like the cinema are apparent, just as class distinctions and accents are as rigidly drawn as before. Women are agitating for their freedom and independence (with Shaw's vociferous political support), and suffragettes and shop girls alike insist on moving around the city and earning their own income; *Pygmalion* reveals that at the very same time, women are considered to be a form of male property, passing from father to husband, whose independent acts cause them to be viewed as prostitutes or eccentrics. The first public performances of *Pygmalion* took place in German in Vienna, Austria in 1913, rather than in England in English, because Eliza's vehement curse "Not bloody likely" in Act III was so shocking for the period, and Shaw's whole point was to have a woman's voice articulate an "unwomanly" but commonplace oath for all to hear. Shaw's plays insist on displaying what is real, what people really say and do, not out of an old-fashioned "realism," but with as much boldness as the theater of Ibsen, Artaud, or Brecht. His anti-idealism was meant to uncover in particular the gender and class oppression that keeping things "out of sight, out of mind" helped to further.

Eliza Doolittle is an adorable character most people find deeply endearing; Shaw's play has her make as violent, unsentimental, and un-idealized a transformation as that of Nora's slammed door in *The Doll's House*. When times seemed ripe to present *Pygmalion* in London, the beginning of World War I prevented its opening, but by 1914 it had become a huge success. Students should be shown that Shaw's play is as modern a "blast" as Wyndham Lewis's *BLAST*, and that it is as much a manifesto, too. The difference between these manifestoes is that Shaw was dialectical—he liked to share power with his characters and his audiences, and he considered stage plays to be the occasion for a shared, even if conflicted, conversation.

Among the many things to get across to a class about *Pygmalion* is how much the text of the play subverts expectations. Shaw takes his readers and his audience into the play, and with great wit and incisive seriousness he withdraws as the authority figure. Shaw's fingerprints seem to be all over *Pygmalion* and his other plays, but in fact this theatrical work is a philosophical experiment in undercutting the supposed absolute authority of the author, the stability and "truth" of the written text, and the inferiority of the reader or audience. On the contrary, *Pygmalion* is an interactive play, one that begins with a preface and ends with an extraordinary non-dramatic prophecy of how things will end after the events of the play. At times the stage directions almost give up, asserting that only the cinematic can convey the atmosphere of the scene; at other times, the page looks as graphically playful as a comic strip, as when Pickering and Higgins "speak together" in Act III in a point-counterpoint of dialogue that was later turned into one of *My Fair Lady's* songs, because it is like spoken chamber music. There is no absolute ending, no closure, and no simple villains or virtuous characters. Students need to be shown that Shaw's experiments with language and with form are radical and breathtaking, and the opposite of "didactic." Instead, his play is a strange hybrid, a modernist work that although it bows to realism is as transgressive and eerie as a Beckett play.

The primary reason for this revolutionary effect is Shaw's emphasis on the mutability of language. The core of *Pygmalion* is what various characters call "new speech." This is an elastic term that encompasses a kind of speech that transcends class boundaries and gender roles, an imaginative, radical mode of self-expression. When students read the Preface to *Pygmalion*, its preoccupation with phonetics and pronunication and new alphabets might seem dusty, fussy, or even crackpot. Persuade them to hold on, though; Shaw joined a line of nineteenth-century language experimenters who dreamed of a universal language, a common alphabet, or at least a global, shared dialect. This dream has never been realized, and perhaps it never could be. The point is, though, that Shaw's interest in language and in "new speech" was revolutionary: he saw how much language created self, and the divisions between people, whether of class or gender or race. All of these were anathema to him, and so in the charming fable of a Cockney flower girl who learns to speak anew, and be someone new as a result, is a powerful critique of the idea of an unchanging "essence," of fixed identities, and of levels of hierarchy.

That is at the heart of the play in the figure of Eliza Doolittle, whose speech change transforms her into an entirely different person. One theory of language prevailing until the twentieth century derives from Plato; it claims that truth is fixed and eternal, and that language merely mirrors or copies truth, but can never become it. Henry Higgins is a Platonist about language at some points in the play, as for example when he declares that Eliza was always a duchess underneath—it only took his art and his science to make that "visible" in her speech. Shaw's play has neither pure heroes/heroines nor absolute villains: Henry Higgins is an example of this, in that he brings about a life-transforming event, and offers a brilliant contribution to modernity, yet remains something of a chauvinist brute, a snob, and a manipulator. Eliza sees through him, and protests his exploitation of her with all the passion Shaw advocated that the oppressed—whether workers, women, colonized peoples or the poor—draw upon in trying to change their circumstances. Nonetheless, Eliza must love Henry Higgins, in a daughterly way, it would seem. Audiences began to hope for and, in the film versions, to demand that Eliza and Henry become a romantic couple at the end of the play. A wonderful pedagogical tactic is to stage yet another debate wherein students argue for or against this kind of "happy" ending. Why did Shaw leave the matter unresolved in the stage play, yet add his long, almost short-story-like appendix recounting Eliza's marriage to Freddie and her gradual success in all her endeavors? Here too, Shaw puts the emphasis on dialectics—on complex ideas that shift back and forth, rather than on absolutes or one, singular "truth."

A facet of *Pygmalion* that ties it to almost all the selections in the twentieth century anthology, and that also makes it as modern and contemporary as it can be, is Shaw's realization that fashion, style, performance and costume are the basis of modern personal and social identity. Instead, in play after play, with *Pygmalion* as perhaps the most lasting cultural example, (harmlessly apolitical in the later musical and film *My Fair Lady*), Shaw showed how women could aspire to modernity, equality, and self-fulfillment.

Shaw, despite his Fabian socialism and his prominent political role as a founder of the Labour Party, never believed that instant joy and harmony would emerge with the destruction of private property. Far from it—he saw that all the foibles, selfishness, desires, and aggressions people have in such abundance would always exist, and that we have to forgive each other for these. What is needed is a *modus vivendi*, a way of living whereby people can achieve the maximum amount of freedom without impinging on other people—and that means freedom for all, inside and outside the home. Shaw very perceptively viewed the modern world as too complex and layered for instantaneous revolutions, or for the triumph of the proletariat. Instead, he realized that changes would come by alterations in how the middle classes live, love, and work. This strand of Shaw's thinking has affinities to the essays by Orwell which follow, and is the mirror opposite to Wyndham Lewis's disgusted response to the masses and their tastes in his *Manifesto*. If one goal of modernism was to shock the everyday person, or to raise art to an elite, difficult plateau, Shaw's writing refused to become modernist. He seems to have been confident that however "difficult" the art or the ideas behind it, it could be shaped so that ordinary people might understand it, or begin to. Dialogue, not manifesto, is the hallmark of his art.

Faith in dialogue led Shaw to his true calling, as a dramatist. In theater he saw the formal conditions for bringing language alive on stage, and for setting up confrontations in language that could explore the inherent conflict in ideas as dialogue. To bring the difference between Shavian drama, for all its magnificence, and modernist drama into the starkest perspective, teach Shaw's play with the theater work of his fellow Irishman, Samuel Beckett. While Shaw's drama is unsentimental, and is highly innovative in its lack of full-fledged "characters" and its decentered musicality, look to Beckett for a dramatist who questions Shaw's fundamental dramatic premise: that drama *is* dialogue, communication. Beckett's plays ask whether "communication" between people in general, between characters on stage, and even between a play and its audience is possible in any sense. Rather than the talky, dense fabric of Shaw's dramatic writing, he strips theater down to its silences, to the gaps in communication, and to the essential loneliness of human beings in language. If Shaw's plays are like symphonic music, with many dissonant sounds, Beckett's plays are like avant-garde jazz, each character condemned to an improvisatory solo the other characters may never understand, or even hear. Shaw's playwrighting style shows that he had a fundamental compact or contract with his audience: the argument of the play, however unresolvable or complex, would be transmitted in all its complexity. Beckett's theater illustrates a more somber view of the possibilities of art: we may feel trapped or stuck on stage, waiting for an argument that can never really begin. Surprisingly, though, the dark quixotic humor of Beckett's theatrical world owes a great debt to Shavian repartee—the cosmic comedy of being at cross-purposes was transmitted directly from one Irish playwright to the other.

Shaw's glorious humor is on display both in the play and in the letters included in the section, and it would be a loss not to explore the nature of his comedy by way of comparison. In the twentieth-century section the very different comic modes of Evelyn Waugh and P. G. Wodehouse could be compared to Shaw. Shaw's comedy is more Shakespearian, in fact—it embraces the world and hopes to revitalize it through laughter, while Waugh's admittedly hilarious work is an acid-tongued denunciation of what he saw as inferior and grotesque. Wodehouse's endlessly pleasing verbal mirth lacks a satirical or transformative thrust at all—one doesn't go out to change the world high on "Plum's" humor, whereas one very well might after a dose of Shavian wit. These comic pieces of Shaw's are rife with the most sophisticated intellectual and artistic theory, and yet they are staggeringly funny, perhaps because Shaw considers us all to be in the same human boat. If we can laugh at our common predicament, we may then be able to stop fighting long enough to change it.

Thomas Hardy

Thomas Hardy's poetry was far less formally bold or innovative than his fiction had been, or at least it seems so on the surface: the appearance is deceptive, however, and therein lies the challenge in teaching it. His poetry has a Victorian flavor, even those poems he wrote late in his long life, penned simultaneously with the great modernist poems, such as Eliot's *The Wasteland*, which we know was tapped out on the typewriter, and which changed the poetic landscape. Why are Hardy's poems important, given their anachronistic quality? What makes Hardy a great poet of the twentieth century, when his fellow Victorian poets, Tennyson and Browning, had long since been replaced by poets mapping a new poetic territory? And perhaps most pressing for the instructor, how to best teach Hardy's poetry when it may strike a student reader as either quaint or hard to read?

One successful route of entry into Hardy's poetry might be to show students the extent to which it creates a self-sufficient world, a poetic universe following the natural laws of the imaginary countryside he invented in his masterful novels. His first collection, *Wessex Poems*, supposedly takes root in this same creative landscape. Help students get the lay of this land, and they are likely to sympathize with Hardy's poetic project: preservation and reclamation, almost ecological goals of recycling and nourishing a place and a tradition. The old-fashioned aspects of Hardy's poetry arise in homage to the old-fashioned aspects of England's rural countryside; the poetry preserves a vanishing age, a vanishing vocabulary, and a vanishing culture. To preserve a poetic past in the amber of one's own making is clearly a far different thing than to be a relic of a bygone poetic age. Hardy's poetry can look and read at first glance as if it were "left-over," traditional poetry that has been taken out of its author's drawer many years after composition. In fact, Hardy's poems deliberately hover in a past time, as his novels deliberately unfold in a past place.

A constant feature of the Wessex novels involves a character or characters walking across one of the myriad tracks or pathways devised for foot travel, a spiderweb of paths connecting obscure villages and solitary cottages with one another. Hardy invented his own geography for Wessex, but the footpaths really existed, and were the most important trails carved into the landscape by travelers over many years. Such footpaths are called ley lines in folk culture; ley lines are not only a means of getting from place to place on foot, they are thought to be lines of energy drawn across the land. Ley lines gather their energy over time, as hundreds of people gradually wear down a shared path, and leave traces of themselves in the form of memory and tradition. Ley lines are often celebrated in folk songs and in oral tales, and they are part of a religious or spiritual approach to the land itself. Referring to a pre-Christian folk mythology of spirits animating the land, ley lines are tracks of wisdom and sometimes even magic power. The pagan customs of worshipping land as a living being were sustained in rural England, as in virtually every rural region, even as late as the nineteenth century. When Hardy's characters walk the ley lines of Wessex, they are doing more than walking—they are communing with the gods of the earth.

We can circle back to Hardy's poems through the ley lines. Poetry has long had an association with walking, after all; the meter of a poetic line is measured by its *feet*, and the meter of a poem, or its rhythm, is often called its *gait*, as if the line itself were doing the walking. The lines of Hardy's poetry are extremely carefully measured, and cut with precision—Hardy is not a writer of "free verse" or blank verse. To unfold the metaphor of walking further is to imagine Hardy's carefully designed lines (he was an architect once) as ley lines made of words. With architectural care, Hardy's words are wrapped into complicated structures, lines with precise foot counts, lines whose poetic paths are well-trodden and well-used.

And then there is the nature of the words Hardy uses. Many critics of Hardy's poetry comment on his "archaic diction" or the "ancient word-store" of his poems. An instructor should make sure that students are not put off by Hardy's use of "hath" and "doth" and so on, imagining these to be stilted remnants of upper-class British diction. Hardy's "haths" and so on were more often country speech, a gentler rural dialect. For a writer whose novels were accused of indecent subject-matter and undue frankness, this may seem paradoxical. However, if we take seriously Hardy's aim of preserving the key lines of his British rural past, by preserving them in literary form and by translating them into poetic stanzas, we can also see his impetus toward the preservation of the rural treasure-house of words. This does not mean, of course, that Hardy was a naive poet, or that Hardy was simply copying down folk poetry. His poetry is sophisticated and learned, and is part of the British Romantic tradition, with a strong influence by Wordsworth. Romantic poetry had privileged the usages of the vernacular too, as his famous collection of *Lyrical Ballads* makes clear: the "ballads" were an oral, sung folk poetry, turned into lyric poems by the alchemy of the poet's written words.

One of the monumental cultural events Hardy encountered as a young man in London was the controversy over Charles Darwin's revolutionary scientific text, *The Origin of Species*. Published in 1859, Darwin's book charted the development of species over time, which he famously termed evolution. His discovery altered forever the modern relation to time, and destroyed the narratives of divine providence and human uniqueness. In many ways, Hardy's novels register the Darwinian revolution, as these ideas (which Hardy, like most others, fundamentally accepted) set off on a collision course with older notions of a divine plan for individual human beings. Evolutionary ideas became pervasive in many fields of study; linguistics was one such field that also caught Hardy's attention. Linguists like Max Muller proposed that languages also underwent evolution, and that rural areas were places where adaptations in language could be seen as they happened. Industrialization and urban life changed what Muller and Hardy saw as the organic relationship of country language to country life. Thomas Hardy's poetry contains the words that once were as organic and vivid as the practices of country life, words whose energy has been altered by the passage of time and changes in a rural way of life. Show students the signs of Hardy's erudition—his scientific, architectural, technological and critical sophistication is apparent throughout his poetry. He juggles this scholarship and modern knowledge with the folk knowledges and the intense sense of animated, almost pagan wonder at life and landscape he found in country folk.

Hardy's magnificent body of poetry refers to a landscape (Wessex) whose counterpart is fast disappearing; leafing through the pages of Hardy's vast *Collected Poems* (1919), for example, one finds lyric poems predicated on hearthside embers (when, in London, electricity and coal were the fuels), thorn birds and vixens (rarely encountered in cities), circles of "elders," "sweet maids" in a time of women's suffrage and coquettish modern girls, "cyder" spelled in the old way, and "hostelry." The tight lines Hardy uses, the ley lines of yore, hold fast and bind up words that also threaten to vanish or lose their meaning outside the context of a living, thriving countryside.

An astonishing poem like *During Wind and Rain* exhibits all these features of Hardy's wonderful poetry. In four symmetrical stanzas, with precise scansion and strict meter, the poem is built around a repeated line "Ah, no; the years O!" or "Ah, no; the years, the years." Gesturing toward the song-form of a country reel, even the first line of the poem establishes lyric or song as the heart of an oral culture: "They sing their dearest songs—." The action of the poem involves a host of quaint, outmoded activities, as "elders and juniors" and "men and maidens" interact in a landscape whose paths and gardens they collaborate on making "neat" and "gay." Weather and the flight of storm-birds are the markers of time and place; summer trees and rotten roses delineate the passage of seasons and years, as they do for country folk. The very vocabulary of the poem sings of a communal life whose harmonizing voices are no match for the snatching hand of time, nor for the "high new house" whose furniture sits incongruously out on the lawn, even including the ominous clock, whose measurement of time had never been needed before, when the sun and the moon gave time its compass. The "brightest things that are theirs" cannot suspend the losses of time, and as the poem ends, its lament "Ah, no; the years, the years" segues into a picture of the carved names of the merry men and maids as raindrops trace their shapes on the gravestones marking their places in the earth: "Down their carved names the rain-drop ploughs." It is not an accident that Hardy chooses "plough" as the word for the course of the raindrops. Ploughing is the agricultural labor which was the basis of this way of life, now gone along with its people. Ploughing also makes marks or inscriptions in the earth, as do ley lines or pathways, as do written words in the lines and feet of poetry. Hardy allows us to momentarily see these tombstones with their carved names as the substitute for the poem itself, and the poem, incorporating time, death, and loss into its words, as a tombstone. His poetry hallows what is gone, as it traces the names on the blank page before us.

Thomas Hardy's poetry lyrically laments what time has done to England: made it unrecognizable. Because it performs this act of preserving the rhythms and the words of another time and place, turning away from modernity while knowing poetry is not strong enough to stop time, Hardy's poetry became important for all the modern poets writing in English, especially those, like Thomas, Eliot, Larkin and Heaney, who emphasize landscape. The hallmarks of modern identity students have captured in reading Joseph Conrad are invoked in Hardy's poetry, too: the lonely human subject, self-aware, floats over the poems, many of which are lyrics. That is, they are said (or sung) by an "I," a self who takes stock of his impressions, an "I" who feels lonely in the universe. As Hardy's novels make clear, his is a world without providence or faith, a secular vista whose scientific developments and scientific truths he accepts, but whose bleak rationality gives no comfort. Hardy's poetry articulates the sense of loss and loneliness as human beings are thrown back onto themselves, in a universe whose machinery does not include their happiness, or even their significance. Hardy's poetry may be most richly appreciated if his poetic forebears—Herbert, Donne, Cowper, Gray, even Clare—are referred back to by the instructor, and his inheritors, like Auden with his scrupulous poetic form and yet modern ease of diction, are set alongside his poems.

The poem *Convergence of the Twain* is a superb starting place in Hardy's corpus for today's students, since it is the greatest poem ever written about an event made topical and urgent again—the sinking of the Titanic in 1912. As a poetic subject it is perfect for Hardy's style, and as an event it captures the very issues which crystallize in all his work: the operation of blind fate or destiny, the inevitability of suffering, the inhuman reaches of technology, the need to commemorate what has been lost. Memory is the strongest human power, for Hardy the source of all creation, and Hardy the poet devotes his poetry to the task of remembering. This becomes achingly poignant in his war poetry, as in his elegies. Hardy was appreciated as a fine war poet, yet his verses on World War I are rarely taught in conjunction with the young English poets of our World War I section, many of whom were soldiers who died in the trenches. In part this is because Hardy's poetry does make a world—a world riven by the war, just as his society was, but a world able to encompass his specific war poems as part, not all, of its landscape. Thomas Hardy was elderly when World War I arrived, and could not himself have served. But his poetry, like his prose before it, had anticipated in its bleak rigor the mechanization of life and the absence of the gods that became so clear and so shocking to the society at large when war began. Hardy's poetry has the unenviable distinction of having known in advance how much would be lost—human lives, a way of life, a well-trodden human path. "Down their carved names the rain-drop ploughs."

The Great War: Confronting the Modern

Blast

One way to begin talking about Ezra Pound and Wyndham Lewis's *Vorticist Manifesto* is to talk a little bit about manifestos generally, and literary manifestos more specifically. In this volume of the *Longman Anthology*, it is possible to trace a brief history of literary manifestos beginning with Wordsworth's *Preface to Lyrical Ballads* and Shelley's *A Defense of Poetry*, and including (later in the century) texts like Eliot's *Tradition and the Individual Talent*, Woolf's *Three Guineas*, and the debate across the years between Orwell and Rushdie, *Inside the Whale* and *Outside the Whale*. Among modernist manifestos that we did not have the space to include, most important would probably be the manifesto establishing the poetic movement called Imagism, also written by Pound (*A Retrospect*).

Manifestos always throw down the gauntlet, issue a kind of challenge: they announce that, according the issuers of the manifesto at least, the rules of the game have changed. Part of the fun in the *Vorticist Manifesto* is that it takes advantage of modern developments in typography and printing to make concrete its challenge to the British artistic establishment. To wit: the *Vorticist Manifesto* isn't simply a declaration of artistic revolution; in the audacity of its design, and the rhetorical excess of its language, it seeks to enact that very rebellion within its oversized pages.

While we have sought to reproduce *Blast's* striking design, students will appreciate the opportunity to see a copy of the genuine article. Fortunately, this is fairly simple since the Black Sparrow Press has produced an inexpensive, good-quality oversized facsimile, complete with puce covers and bold, blocky, broken type.

One piece of evidence that the challenge issued by Pound and Lewis has been taken up by later artists—and taken up only half-seriously, even as the manifesto itself has its tongue firmly in its cheek—can be found on Morrissey's solo debut, *Viva Hate* (Sire/Reprise, 1988). Morrissey, former front man of the influential '80s British band The Smiths, sings in "Hairdresser on Fire" about the emotional and metaphysical import of his hairdresser in terms that recall Pound and Lewis's praise in the manifesto:

> Can you squeeze me
> Into an empty page of your diary
> And psychologically save me?
> I've got faith in you.
> I sense the power
> Within the fingers
> Within an hour the power
> Could totally destroy me
> (Or, it could save my life).

While Lewis and Pound praise the hairdresser because he is a working-class prototype of the new Vorticist artist, "trim[ming] aimless and retrograde growths / into CLEAN ARCHED SHAPES and / ANGULAR PLOTS," Morrissey at the same time turns the hairdresser into a kind of therapist/personal advisor.

Rupert Brooke
The Great Lover

In this poem Brooke weds the delight in the sensual physicality of life, which he would have experienced in the poetry of Gerard Manley Hopkins, with the celebration of earthly existence one finds in the early poetry of Yeats, in a poem like "The Stolen Child." Brooke rolls out a litany of life's blessings, or "benisons" as he describes them in the poem; in its overabundance of material detail, "The Great Lover" recalls as well the poetry of the American Walt Whitman, himself a great lover of life. The opening lines make clear that this celebration of life's gifts takes place under the shadow of death, and Brooke wrote it while shipping out to the military service which would claim his life; but the message of the poem is, in the phrase that another American poet, Ezra Pound, would later use in one of the most beautiful of his *Cantos*, "What thou lov'st well remains, / the rest is dross / What thou lov'st well shall not be reft from thee / What thou lov'st well is thy true heritage" (Canto LXXXI).

The Soldier

If you have discussed a number of other sonnets during the term, you will want to consider the implications of Brooke's use of the form for his tribute to the British Tommy. The insistent patriotism of the poem is perhaps its most noteworthy feature; it helps to suggest the zeal with which Britain entered into the war, and sets a high-water mark against which we can read the disillusionment and bitterness of the remainder of the section's poems.

Sigfried Sassoon
Glory of Women, They, The Rear Guard, Everyone Sang

While Lawrence's wartime writing is irreverent toward British pieties—he takes special delight in the disgust occasioned among the British officers by his "native" costume, for instance—Sassoon's poetry introduces a bitterly ironic note into the perspectives section. *Glory of Women* makes its ironic points about the inhumanity of modern warfare by attacking a group of faceless, naive women; one issue the class may want to discuss is whether or not the poem's misogyny is necessary for its success. Was it only women who misunderstood the true nature of the war, and unthinkingly prolonged it by celebrating a myth rather than reality? Is this misogyny the bitter harvest of what T. E. Lawrence calls *diathetics*—propaganda?

"They" is similar to "Glory of Women" in a couple of respects. First, it reiterates the complete separation of the rhetoric deployed on the home front from the realities of the Western front; in hearing the (presumably well-meant) information disseminated by the Bishop, we begin to have a better idea where the half-baked notions of the women in "Glory of Women" might have come from. And like that other poem, "They" depends on a mordant irony to make its point, only here it's more dramatically staged: one verse paragraph, without authorial intrusion, gives the propaganda view of the soldiers' experience, and the second—with no kind of transition furnished—gives the lie to the first.

"The Rear-Guard" consists primarily of the first-person narrative of a common foot soldier, making his way through underground tunnels rather than the more celebrated trenches. In the poem, Sassoon employs the symbolic journey through the underworld so important in much modernist literature—the most prominent example, perhaps, being Ezra Pound's "In a Station of the Metro" in which travel on London's underground subway is economically likened to Persephone's journey in the underworld. Part of what this short poem accomplishes is to make quite vivid the idea that "War is hell."

Everyone Sang serves to balance somewhat the presentation of Sassoon; though hardly an upbeat poem, it does suggest the possibility of at least a momentary retreat from the horrors of war in nature, and places the "unnatural" military activity within a larger, natural context.

Wilfred Owen
Anthem for Doomed Youth, Strange Meeting, Disabled, Dulce et Decorum Est

Like *Glory of Women*, *Anthem for Doomed Youth* is a sonnet: but while Brooke's poem employs the form in a straightforward manner, Owen derives a certain ironic charge by playing off the traditional associations (love, beauty) that cling to the form. Likewise, the poem plays traditional religious imagery off against the realities of war; church bells are usurped by machine-gun fire, bugles replace the choirs. The poem's closing lines do suggest, however, that though the anonymity of modern warfare threatens to reduce death to a simple beastly fact, nature herself keeps vigil and keeps (after a fashion) rites for the dead.

Strange Meeting borrows its macabre tone from the ancient tradition represented by Lucian's Dialogues of the Dead (though the poem is properly a monologue), and recalls scenes like Odysseus's visit to Hades in the Odyssey. In a letter to his father, Ezra Pound had announced that "Live man goes down into world of Dead" was to be one of the three recurring motifs of his magnum opus, The Cantos; James Joyce, too, includes a "Hades" encounter in his twentieth-century versions of the Odyssey, Ulysses, and the opening section of T. S. Eliot's most famous poem, The Waste Land, closes with the image of a dog digging up the bodies of the dead. Clearly, something about this topos was powerful for modernist writers.

This wrenching poem should require little in the way of contextualization; the "disabled" war veteran—tucked away conveniently out of sight, so as not to make the civilian population uncomfortable—has become a common figure in subsequent literature, including the figures of Luke Martin (John Voight) in the 1978 film Coming Home and Lt. Dan (Gary Sinise) in the 1994 box-office smash Forrest Gump.

Perhaps the best-known of all the poems to emerge from World War I, Dulce et Decorum Est skillfully weaves together a brief but compelling battle narrative while at the same time seeking to impose an ethical imperative on its readers. Warfare, when it is not brutally violent and sadistic (as in the gas attack of stanza 2), is instead brutish and dreary. Again, T. E. Lawrence's enthusiastic support of the military use of propaganda (diathetics) has severe repercussions here—in part because the propaganda is most effective when not limited to the enemy, but used against one's own people as well. British singer/songwriter Kate Bush has explored these themes in a number of her songs—most notably "Experiment IV," in which the military experiments with musical propaganda: "They told us all they wanted was a sound / That could kill someone from a distance." This track, along with another song critical of British militarism, "Army Dreaming," is included in her "greatest hits" compilation The Whole Story (EMI, 1986). The British comedy troupe Monty Python presents a comic take on military propaganda in a sketch included in the very first episode of their television series Monty Python's Flying Circus, called "The Funniest Joke in the World" (The Complete Monty Python's Flying Circus: All the Words NY: Pantheon [1989], vol. 1, 10–14).

Isaac Rosenberg
Break of Day in the Trenches, Dead Man's Dump

The overriding tone of Break of Day is again irony, though an understated, situational irony, very different from the bitter tone of Dulce et Decorum Est, for instance. In the war to save civilization, apparently, it is only vermin that can act civilized; this rat's-eye view of the war (and of course, the speaker has been reduced to inhabiting dank muddy trenches, himself like a rat) suggests that while humankind is locked in a blind fury, only inhuman creatures retain any wisdom.

"Dead Man's Dump" eschews the quiet understatement of "Break of Day in the Trenches" for a more aggressive, violent presentation. The scene again invokes, though indirectly, the tortures of the damned: a scene from Dante's *Inferno*, seemingly, though set in Western Europe. The suffering of these men suggest one reason that T. S. Eliot chose as an epigraph to *The Waste Land*—a poem which, while set in a post-war Europe, is saturated with the war's horrors—the words of the Sibyl of Cumae: "I want to die."

David Jones
from In Parenthesis

Jones's piece is quite difficult for most beginning students to get a handle on; its mixture of "voices"—the voices of the military establishment, of British and Celtic mythology and legend, of factual newspaper reportage, etc.—makes the poem every bit as difficult for a first-time reader as Eliot's *The Waste Land*, the poem to which it owes its most obvious debt. One way to help students through the textual confusion of the poem is to have the students "dissect" an especially dense passage: take a pen or pencil and draw angle brackets around the various voices or textual threads that make up a given paragraph. This exposure of the polyphonic nature of the text should lead quite naturally into a discussion of both the various sources that Jones employs, as well as the goals of such a strategy. Given Jones's acknowledged use of Eliot's poem, some side-by-side comparison may prove helpful; one possible result of such a procedure is not simply an explication of *In Parenthesis*, but simultaneously a discovery of just how much World War I imagery and anxiety is buried beneath Eliot's classical façade.

Virginia Woolf's *To the Lighthouse*, published in the same year (1928) that Jones began working on *In Parenthesis*, uses the same image (the space of the war as a parenthesis, as Jones writes in the footnote to his title) in the novel's middle chapter, "Time Passes." A brief examination and discussion of Section VI of that chapter (198–202 in the Harcourt edition)—which includes, for instance, the rather clinical observation that "[A shell exploded. Twenty or thirty young men were blown up in France, among them Andrew Ramsay whose death, mercifully, was instantaneous.]"—may help to suggest what Jones was trying to accomplish both with this metaphor, and with the relatively distanced and flat affect that the poem largely adopts.

Finally, this may be the first opportunity of the semester to discuss the modernists' use of what T. S. Eliot called the "mythical method"—"manipulating a continuous parallel between contemporaneity and antiquity" ("*Ulysses*, Order, and Myth"). This aspect of the poem suggests obvious links with *The Waste Land*, Joyce's *Ulysses* and *Finnegans Wake*, and a number of Yeats's poems.

Robert Graves
from Goodbye to All That

If we might have jumped to the conclusion that the war seemed folly primarily to the enlisted men, Graves helps to correct that impression. The tone of these selections is "semi-facetious," to use the term Graves employs to describe his lecture to the troops on "How to be happy though in the trenches." The writing is irreverent toward the pieties of the British propaganda effort, especially coming from one of the British army's best and brightest; and Graves's writing derives much of its power from the stark contrast between the life of an officer and that of a Tommy in the trenches. As he writes, "We [in the officer's mess tent] talked more freely there than would have been possible either in England or in the trenches."

The notion of propaganda, introduced explicitly in Lawrence's writing, is again operative here; without labeling it as such, Graves quietly juxtaposes Western Front propaganda and reality, attempting to revisit some of the fictions visited upon the British public by the British war propaganda machine. Similarly, he damns the prejudice and brutality of British officers and soldiers not by outright condemnation, but rather through silent, dramatic presentation of the men's thoughts and deeds, presented (seemingly) in their own words.

Speeches on Irish Independence

Charles Stuart Parnell
At Limerick (31 August 1879)

One of the great documents suggesting the impact of Parnell on early twentieth-century Irish thought and art is the famous Christmas dinner scene in Joyce's *A Portrait of the Artist as a Young Man*; in the characters of Mr. Dedalus and Mr. Casey, on the one side, and in the family friend Dante on the other, students will see quite dramatically what the two sides of the debate looked like, and sounded like. An audio recording of this scene is available on the Caedmon set *James Joyce: Readings* (Caedmon 71–6527).

This speech at Limerick is of course quite early in Parnell's political career, but is remarkable for both its firm resolve and simultaneously the gentle tactics it urges upon the farmers of Limerick. Parnell is well on his way to becoming an imposing nationalist leader, but both the tenor and content of these remarks mark him as a gentleman. The strategy adopted is what we would now call "economic sanctions"; it is in fact that old Irish strategy of the boycott, which derives its name from Charles C. Boycott (1832–97), the English estate manager in Ireland against whom the practice was first put in place.

Before the House of Commons (23 February 1883), At Portsmouth, After the Defeat of Mr. Gladstone's Home Rule Bill (25 June 1886)

In the speech before the House of Commons, Parnell tries to defend himself against the campaign being waged against him by conservative MP's; by branding him as an extremist, these opponents hoped to silence Parnell and stop the momentum enjoyed by his Home Rule movement. At this stage Parnell remains, as he had declared himself in the speech delivered at Limerick, "confident as to the future."

In the speech delivered at Portsmouth Parnell, perhaps surprisingly, remains optimistic about the future of his Home Rule movement; while they have experienced a temporary setback, victory, he believes, will ultimately be theirs. The scandal over his affair with Kitty O'Shea, however, put a stop to all progress for some time. In this address, Parnell rather cleverly addresses the British working citizen, and stresses, through coded language, the fact that members of the British working class have more in common with their Irish brothers than with their English masters (hence the strategic trotting out of titles: Lord Beaconsfield, Lord Carnarvon). This almost Marxist rhetoric was employed, much more explicitly, by participants in the Easter Rising, especially James Connolly.

Easter 1916. Proclamation of the Irish Republic

An obvious exercise here, for American students, is to compare the Irish declaration of independence to ours, one of its obvious sources and inspirations. While taking the courageous step of addressing itself to all Irishmen and Irishwomen—and explicitly insuring voting rights for women within its short compass—the document is at the same time a product of the Irish nationalist iconography which depicted Ireland as the *shan van vocht*, the "poor old woman" who must be rescued from British oppression and persecution by Irish martyrs, themselves always men; thus a very traditional gender hierarchy is reinscribed.

Padraic [Patrick Henry] Perse
Kilmainham Prison (2 May 1916)

Perse's speech is characterized most strongly by its courage, a feature no reader should need underscored. That courage is underwritten in part by Christian imagery of innocent sacrifice; whether consciously or no, Perse frames his discourse with references to the sacrificial lamb, even to the point of suggesting in the last sentence that if they kill him, the spirit of freedom which lives in him will be resurrected within the Irish people.

Michael Collins
The Substance of Freedom (5 March 1922)

A wonderful tie-in for this selection is Neil Jordan's 1996 film *Michael Collins*. The film is helpful not only for the light it casts on Collins himself, but it provides wonderful background for the independence movement as a whole; Liam Neeson, as Collins, delivers passages from this speech in the film. And for as long as it's up, make sure to visit the Warner Brother's Web site dedicated to the film: http://www .MichaelCollins.com. It's beautifully put together, with a detailed biography, a photo archive of Collins's life, as well as an illustrated tour of Dublin locales important to Collins's life and career.

William Butler Yeats
The Lake Isle of Innisfree

One of Yeats's best-known and most beautiful poems, *Innisfree* owes an obvious debt to Romantic poems like Wordsworth's *Tintern Abbey* and Coleridge's *This Lime-Tree Bower My Prison*, in which the poet laments the fact that he has been separated by circumstance from the consolations of the natural landscape—only to discover, by poem's end, that he has gained the power to travel there imaginatively. Yeats here begins to makes something distinctly Irish of this English genre, introducing Irish vocabulary and geography to the England of the Romantic imagination.

Who Goes with Fergus?

In this poem, Yeats blends the torpid feel of the British poetry of the '90s—an artistic scene in which his father, John B. Yeats, was a minor participant—with Irish mythology, in the process making something vital and contemporary of Ireland's founding narratives. In this project, he joined folklorists like Douglas Hyde and his friend Lady Augusta Gregory, attempting to instigate a Celtic Revival for Ireland—a literary and artistic project which was always meant to stir a nationalist political conscience within the Irish people, as well.

No Second Troy

Yeats here uses what T. S. Eliot would later call the "mythical method"—"manipulating a continuous parallel between contemporaneity and antiquity" ("*Ulysses,* Order, and Myth")—to talk about his love for, and exasperation with, his obscure object of desire Maud Gonne. In this particular case, the mythic overlay serves to suggest a framework for understanding Gonne's penchant for "rhetoric" and violence, and to hint as well that such a stance is a matter of fate rather than personal will. Yeats's use of myth in the poem, though relatively simple, can be compared to similar strategies in *The Second Coming, Leda and the Swan,* and *Byzantium,* as well as texts by other authors like Eliot's *The Waste Land* and Joyce's *Ulysses.*

The Fascination of What's Difficult

This poem from 1910 sounds a theme that Yeats will repeat with variations until he dies: the day-to-day concerns that keep the poet from his true work. His resolution to "find the stable and pull out the bolt," however, was in retrospect premature: he continued to be involved in the common public life until the very end of his life, knowing in part that the myth of the ivory tower was no life at all.

September 1913, An Irish Airman Foresees His Death

Both these poems are deeply rooted in specific historical circumstances, which it will help students to have illuminated. "September 1913" is part of a sequence of five poems (the others being "To a Wealthy Man. . . ," "To a Friend Whose Work Has Come to Nothing," "Paudeen," and "To a Shade") connected to a controversy involving the art dealer Hugh Lane, who was also a nephew of Yeats's friend Lady Gregory. Lane wanted to donate his important collection of modern European painting to the city of Dublin, on the condition that the city would construct a suitable gallery for hanging the pictures; the city refused for a number of reasons, not least of which the fact that Lane himself, the paintings, and the architect who had designed the gallery, were less than pure Irish. For Yeats, the controversy (like the Irish people's treachery against Charles Stewart Parnell) was yet another instance of the narrow parochialism of the Irish.

The Wild Swans at Coole

There is a logic for comparing this poem, too, with *Tintern Abbey*, for both articulate the poet's changing response to a beloved place over time; in both poems, the unchanging aspect of the landscape serves as a still point by which the growth, or aging, of the poet can be measured. When Yeats declares in lines 14–16 that "And now my heart is sore. / All's changed since I, hearing at twilight, / The first time on this shore . . . ," we can hear an echo of *Easter 1916*—a poem which, though written just before *Wild Swans*, was not published until a few years later; the similar wording suggests that the Easter Rising has changed Yeats—changed, changed utterly—while the natural beauty of Coole Park remains unchanged.

An Irish Airman Foresees His Death

"Irish Airman" is in a sense a belated WWI poem; the airman in question, Major Robert Gregory, was the son of Lady Gregory, who was shot down in Northern Italy in January 1918. The attitude of the Irish in general to WWI was somewhat distanced, and the rebels used the circumstance of the British being distracted to launch the Easter Rising; Major Gregory here represents for Yeats the kind of olympian indifference to one's fate best expressed in "Lapis Lazuli." Hence the poem is both philosophically and politically polemical.

Easter 1916

Perhaps the best-known and best-loved text associated with Irish independence, there is no small irony in the fact that while the poem counsels against blind adherence to any ideology and myopic worship of any nationalist martyrs and heroes, these are the purposes for which the poem is most often recited. The poem is on one level about the ways in which Ireland was changed by the revolutionary violence of Easter 1916; but it is also about the human cost exacted by participation in such violence, where flesh-and-blood human beings are "Enchanted to a stone / To trouble the living stream." The final "change" comes at the poem's conclusion, where Yeats predicts, with stunning accuracy, that the names of the rebels will be repeated as a litany by the Irish schoolchildren of the future whom they helped to make free—and in being reduced to a simple honor roll, the human complexity of their lives, the contradictory motives that propelled them, are lost. The final irony, which Yeats perhaps could not foresee, is that it's not just the names of these patriots that are recited: it is, precisely, Yeats's poem which counsels against the unthinking "murmur[ing] of name upon name."

The Second Coming

This short poem probably rivals Conrad's *Heart of Darkness* as a source of phrases and metaphors with which we describe our experience of modernity. In this poem, of course, one is confronted head-on with the problem of Yeats's complicated mythology; *The Second Coming* is the first of Yeats's poems presented here which may appear virtually indecipherable without making some reference to Yeats's occult system, as enunciated in *A Vision* (1925). Two elements of that mythology will probably suffice to explicate the poems we've included here. First, Yeats understood human history to be constructed of alternating 2000-year cycles, each new cycle characterized by values and beliefs antithetical to those of its predecessor. One era runs from 2000 B.C. to 1 A.D.; it begins with Zeus's rape of Leda (see *Leda and the Swan*), and is brought to an end—and its successor, the Christian era, announced—by a structurally parallel "annunciation," the conception of Christ in the womb of the Virgin Mary by the Holy Spirit, who comes to Mary in the form of a dove. In 1919 this Christian era is, according to Yeats's reckoning, nearing its end; the era to come, announced no doubt by some other kind of birth, will be of a nature completely antithetical to the values we currently hold near and dear. The second important point of Yeats's mythology for student readers of these poems is that Yeats envisioned these cycles of history as interlocking three-dimensional cones; students will benefit from looking at the illustration of "The Gyre & Its Images" in T. R. Henn's *The Lonely Tower: Studies in the Poetry of W. B. Yeats* (London: Methuen [1965]). Yeats's reliance on these cones suggests a good deal of the imagery of this poem in particular: the widening gyre, for instance, as well as the lack of a center.

A Prayer for My Daughter

It may be interesting to discuss with your students to what extent they find *A Prayer for My Daughter* a sexist, or even a misogynist, poem; one way to get at this would be to consider what Yeats might have said differently were the prayer instead for his son. According to a strange kind of logic, this poem about the birth of his daughter becomes gradually something like a eulogy, or elegy, for Maud Gonne. In effect, the best advice Yeats can give his young daughter is not to be like Gonne.

Sailing to Byzantium

Clearly a poem of Yeats's middle age, it might be interesting to contrast it to the earthy discourse of Crazy Jane, who is not ashamed, nor stoops to make apology, for her body—its wants, needs, desires.

Meditations in Time of Civil War

This poem is Yeats's great argument for the importance of tradition, and for the need for a monied and educated aristocracy that would keep such traditional values alive. Together with Yeats's peasant poems and plays, this suggests two important poles in Yeats's thinking; and while he was Romantic in his interest in the life of common people, he was not so Romantic as to wish away all distinctions of class and merit. Like the poem that follows in the *Anthology*, the Civil War backdrop seems to have suggested to Yeats the possible annihilation of all that was best in Irish culture, in the name of a misguided "democracy."

Nineteen Hundred and Nineteen

The poem remains striking for its honesty: for Yeats the Civil War, as World War I that had preceded it, serves as a powerful reminder of the dark side of human nature—a potential, even penchant, for evil that Romantic philosophy had failed to account for. One of Yeats's most powerful poems, it is marred by an unnecessarily outré reference at the close: a concrete example for students of the perils of an over-reliance on myth and legend.

Leda and the Swan

Yeats sees Zeus's rape of Leda as another (anterior) version of the visitation of the Virgin Mary by the Holy Spirit—an interpretation which seemingly excuses the violence of the scene depicted here. Two rhetorical features of the poem, at least, will engage the students' interest (or fury). First, his insistent use of rhetorical questions will strike some readers as a dishonest way of disguising his own sympathies in the poem; crudely put, at least one strain of the poem asks whether Leda was asking for it, and whether she enjoyed it. The connection to contemporary debates about rape and other intimate violence should be clear; more and more of my students every year object to the poem's seeming sanctioning of the rape. Second feature: the poem is surely one of the century's most unromantic sonnets (it's a somewhat disguised sonnet, but a sonnet nonetheless). Does Yeats intend an ironic comment by couching the poem as a sonnet—the quintessential love poem? Or, again, does he use the sonnet form to make a covert argument about right and wrong in this rape case?

Among School Children

Another of Yeats's meditations on aging—on the costs exacted, and on the benefits of mature wisdom. In the last stanza, especially, we can see Yeats feeling toward the great synthesis of mind and body that characterizes his feisty, energetic last poems.

Byzantium

Yeats worked hard to make this later poem parallel very closely, in its structure, the earlier "Sailing to Byzantium"; the main difference, as John Unterecker has shown, is that the scene in the earlier poem is described from the position of an outsider, while in "Byzantium" the point of view is that of an initiate. For Yeats, Byzantium represents the full flowering of the culture of the first millennium A. D., one of the end-points in his interlocking gyres of history.

Crazy Jane Talks to the Bishop

Crazy Jane is one of the strongest and most vivid of Yeats's female characters; unlike the various incarnations of Maud Gonne in the poetry, however, she is not criticized but admired. Unimpressed by the pieties of traditional religion, she quests for a bodily wisdom, and eschews all purely intellectual abstractions—a position that Yeats himself, at this point in his life, is trying to emulate.

Lapis Lazuli

Perhaps the greatest of Yeats's poems—a perfectly cut gem, like the stone it describes. This poem clearly marks itself out as a product of Yeats's mature years; the almost stoic acceptance of the whole range of what life has to offer strikes a new note in Yeats's *oeuvre*. The thinking in this poem is much indebted to the Nietzschean doctrine of tragic wisdom—that one must learn to love, rather than to resist, one's fate (the opposite of the disease Nietzsche called *ressentiment*). Unfortunately, students will perhaps have to be reminded that "gay" does not (in 1936) connote "homosexual," but again is probably taken from Nietzsche, whose influential volume *Die Frölische Wissenschaft* is normally translated *The Gay Science* (i.e., philosophy).

The Circus Animals' Desertion

Probably one of the best poems about writer's block in the language. The poem is useful for the truncated tour of Yeats's poetry that it provides, as well as running commentary; in this very late poem, Yeats makes the courageous decision to strip away the fantastic and Romantic trappings that have brought him so much success in the past, and to return to basics: the foul rag and bone shop of the heart. It was a decision he had announced as far back as A Coat (1914), in which he declared that it was time to put off his "coat / Covered with embroideries / Out of old mythologies / From heel to throat," resolving instead to "walk naked"; this poetic nakedness, however, proved to be the work of a lifetime.

Under Ben Bulben

Traditionally the last of Yeats's poems, and the one containing his epitaph, which was indeed carved on his headstone in Drumcliff churchyard. The poem reaffirms Yeats's belief in the ongoing presence of the dead—in the memories of the living, if not in more tangible form; and in writing what amounts to an elegy for himself, Yeats helps to insure that he will continue to live in the Irish mind. He leaves, too, what amounts to a set of instructions to the writers who would succeed him, in section 5. Considering the poem an elegy for argument's sake, it makes an interesting contrast to Auden's rather grudging elegy, *In Memory of W. B. Yeats*.

James Joyce
Araby

A few general strategies will help students come to terms with these difficult stories. To begin with, Joyce said in correspondence that his goal was to betray the paralysis of the Irish people; all of the stories touch on some form of paralysis, whether emotional, psychological, physical, or moral, and none more explicitly than "Araby," especially its closing tableau. Second, Joyce sometimes used the concept of "epiphany"—roughly, "revelation"—to talk about one of the major strategies of the stories. In the second and third stories presented here, the only possible "epiphany" would seem to take place in the reader: the protagonists of these stories clearly remain blind to their own paralyses until the end. More controversy surrounds the conclusion of *The Dead*, which we will discuss in due course.

It makes sense with "Araby"—indeed, perhaps with all the *Dubliners* stories—after having read it through, to start at the end. The conclusions of these stories are uniformly vexing, and yet seem as well to bear a great deal of interpretive weight: with "Araby," its fair to ask what the protagonist has learned, or what has happened to him, to wring from him the overwrought final sentence of the story. What, precisely, is vanity—and what about his experiences leading up to the bazaar, and at Araby itself, has forced this conclusion upon him? What about the protagonists's relationship to women—his aunt, "Mangan's sister" (whose name we, and perhaps even the protagonist, never learn), the shopgirl at the bazaar? Can students detect any passages in which the protagonist is being criticized, his foibles being treated ironically? Finally: Joyce said that the narrative goal of these stories was to give the Irish people a look at themselves in his nicely polished lookingglass. In looking at the mirror this story holds up to us, do we recognize ourselves? In what ways might we be like the story's callow narrator?

Dubliners: Eveline

A few general strategies will help students come to terms with these difficult stories. To begin with, Joyce said in correspondence that his goal was to betray the paralysis of the Irish people; all of the stories touch on some form of paralysis, whether emotional, psychological, physical, or moral, and none more explicitly than *Eveline*, especially its closing tableau. Second, Joyce sometimes used the concept of "epiphany"—roughly, "revelation"—to talk about one of the major strategies of the stories. In the first three stories presented here, the only possible "epiphany" would seem to take place in the reader: the protagonists of these stories clearly remain blind to their own paralyses until the end. More controversy surrounds the conclusion of *The Dead*, which we will discuss in due course.

One simple strategy for engaging students in the moral and ethical problems that the story poses is to have them answer one question: Should Eveline have gone with Frank, or was she right to stay behind? Why? Careful exploration of the story should show that in fact Eveline has probably done the right thing—we readers don't really know much about this guy Frank, and Eveline doesn't seem to either—but she makes her decision for all the wrong reasons (primarily fear of the new). No explicit moral judgments are pronounced in the story; instead, throughout the collection, Joyce uses the characters' language, or the language used to describe the characters, to suggest to readers where our sympathies should lie. In this story, for instance, when Eveline at the quay asks God to show her what her duty is, the jig's up: she's already made her decision. No one elopes with an exciting young man out of "duty."

Dubliners: Clay

The stylistic device called "free indirect discourse" is important to a full appreciation of this story. In free indirect discourse, the (ostensibly) third-person, objective narration takes over the thought patterns and speech idioms of the character being described; in this fashion, the writer is able to convey the qualities and contours of a character's mind, without having to resort to first-person narration, and to having the character give voice to all kinds of observations that she would never make to herself in real life. The first four paragraphs of Clay are written in free indirect discourse; part of what's fascinating about the story is that after this "biased" introduction, it's very difficult to tell what, of the rest of the story, may have been influenced by Maria's own desires—such as, for instance, the story's close, which attempts to let Maria out of an embarrassing situation with the minimum of fuss.

Dubliners: The Dead

This closing piece from Dubliners is Joyce's best-known story; it's also the collection's longest by a good bit, and dividing the story into three main parts helps to focus class discussion. The first section is made up of the conversation and events leading up to the dinner (the night of the story is the Feast of Epiphany, or Twelfth Night); the story's middle section comprises the dinner, and Gabriel's after-dinner speech; and the closing section includes the breaking-up of the party, Gabriel and Gretta's journey to the Gresham Hotel, and the climactic scene that plays out there.

In the opening section, the main points of interest are the three blows that Gabriel's quite substantial ego suffers at the hands of women at the party. First, his indelicate questioning of Lily, the caretaker's daughter, is coolly rebuffed; next, Gretta playfully makes fun of Gabriel's love of all things European to his two aunts—and the playfulness is lost on Gabriel; and finally, Gabriel endures some teasing at the hands of an old schoolmate, Molly Ivors, on the subject of the Celtic Revival, and Gabriel's somewhat less patriotic political convictions.

Still hurting from these slights, Gabriel launches into the speech he has prepared, ostensibly to honor his aunts. Perhaps because his ego has been bruised, however, we see that the speech serves primarily to shore up his own sense of self-importance; the aunts, and their hospitality and generosity, are really of no particular interest to Gabriel—as we see when he praises them in classical imagery that they cannot understand. Part of Gabriel's irritation during the speech seems to be due to the fact that Molly Ivors, against whom Gabriel wishes to score points during his speech, has fled; indeed, he has changed the text precisely to put her down—but she has escaped into the night.

In the final section, Gabriel hopes to repair the damage of the day through a romantic tryst with Gretta at the fashionable Gresham hotel, away from the distractions of home and children, and away from the criticism of friends and family and the party. When Gretta confesses that Mr. D'Arcy's song has called to mind a boy she once loved, Gabriel's romantic scenario is shattered, and the story comes to an emotionally powerful, but rather ambiguous, climax.

The controversy over the story's conclusion centers on whether or not Gabriel has had an "epiphany"—whether the day's events, and his wife's revelation, will show him that a change of heart is needed; or whether, instead, he is hardening his heart against his wife and against anyone who would challenge his image of himself. Recent critics are more inclined toward this cynical reading; for many years, however, the trend was to see in this closing story an optimistic ending to an otherwise bleak and despairing collection.

Ulysses: [Chapter 13. "Nausicaa"]

Chapter 13, the "Nausicaa" chapter of *Ulysses*, is unique for its split personality: halfway through the chapter, the narrative point of view switches abruptly, and without warning, from the young Gerty MacDowell to the novel's protagonist whose wanderings the final fifteen chapters trace, Leopold Bloom. As a result, the chapter offers a perfect opportunity to talk about voice, style, and point of view, as well as (Joyce's take on) the differences between female and male perspectives on fashion, sexuality, love and desire.

Joyce is famous for adopting a different literary style for each chapter of *Ulysses*; for this chapter, which takes as its mythical prototype Odysseus's encounter with the Phaeacian princess Nausicaa in Book 6 of *The Odyssey*, Joyce adopted for Gerty what he dubbed a "namby-pamby jammy marmalady drawersy (alto là!) style with effects of incense, mariolatry, masturbation, stewed cockles, painter's palette, chitchat, circumlocutions, etc. etc." Gerty's section is narrated in that first-person/third-person hybrid that Joyce learned from Flaubert, called "free indirect discourse"; we do not get Gerty's narrative with Gerty as the narrator, quite, but instead seem to have an intimate access to Gerty's thought process mediated by the commodified languages of fashion and advertising, as well as the turgid prose characteristic of late-nineteenth century women's fiction. Critics seem almost evenly divided regarding the tone of Gerty's section: some feel the "shopworn" prose belittles and diminishes Gerty as a character, and even suggests that women's consciousness in general is a pastiche of second-hand opinions and sentiments. Other critics—among whom the editors of this section would count themselves—believe instead that a careful reading of the chapter shows Gerty's consciousness to be no more, no less commodified than anyone else's, and this is one of Joyce's great achievements in *Ulysses*: to suggest that we're all beholden to the narratives we consciously or subconsciously invest ourselves in, be they the narratives of fashion and romance (Gerty MacDowell), or those of cuckoldry and jewishness (Bloom), or those of Irish nationalism (the unnamed "Citizen" of the "Cyclops" chapter), or those of anti-Semitism (Mr. Deasy in the "Nestor" chapter), and so on. In fact, we would argue, Joyce's depiction of Gerty

MacDowell is not at all derriere-guard, but instead evidences a postmodern understanding of the constructedness of all identity, and the complicated role that commodity culture plays in such a process.

The prose of the second half of the chapter is recognizably the "stream of consciousness" style of Leopold Bloom—but recognizably such only to those who have encountered it earlier in *Ulysses,* and hence not to students reading chapter 13 in isolation in this anthology. So while students encountering Gerty's narration in the first half of the chapter will be at no greater disadvantage than other readers of the novel, they will perhaps need some background on Bloom, background that would have been assembled in reading chapters 4-12 (chapters 1-3 focus on Stephen Dedalus). Bloom is a salesman, selling advertising space in two Dublin newspapers to various merchants and commercial concerns. More important, perhaps, he is a Jew in turn-of-the-century Dublin, where less than 1% of the population was Jewish, and quite virulent anti-Semitism was not uncommon. But even without a detailed knowledge of Bloom's character, students can infer a great deal by juxtaposing the two very different perspectives on the beach scene presented by Gerty and Bloom. And if Bloom's background in merchandising tends somewhat to turn Gerty into a "piece of (damaged) goods," the larger logic of the chapter suggests that this isn't a personal foible alone, but part of the reification of the human that inevitably takes place under capitalism.

Finnegans Wake

Our audio CD includes a recording that Joyce himself made of the conclusion to the most beautiful chapter in the *Wake,* "Anna Livia Plurabelle." Joyce's high tenor voice conveys the quarrelsome speech of the two old Irish washerwomen in a tour de force of verbal music.

T. S. Eliot
The Love Song of J. Alfred Prufrock

Eliot's first "famous" poem, like the rest of Eliot's work, has attracted a great deal of critical commentary; by all accounts (excepting, perhaps, that of Arthur Waugh, below), the poem is a remarkable achievement for a young man recently graduated from Harvard (the poem was written in 1910–11). Too often, though, the "undergraduate" nature of the poem is overlooked, as it is read through later work like *The Waste Land;* and surely it's worth pointing out that Prufrock is a figure not just of pity but of comedy. "I should have been a pair of ragged claws / Scuttling across the floors of silent seas"—indeed!

The Canadian band Crash Test Dummies have a playful but finally respectful version of the song—reading its themes of ennui and alienation into a contemporary context, with echoes of the poem thrown in as grace notes—called "Afternoons and Coffee Spoons," on the album *God Shuffled His Feet.*

COMPANION READINGS

Arthur Waugh: Cleverness and the New Poetry; Ezra Pound: Drunken Helots and Mr. Eliot

These readings are salutary primarily as a reminder of how very much this new poetry threatened the literary establishment when it was first published—and the venom with which Pound and others were willing to strike back when attacked. Irreverent literary texts were seen as a potent threat in the 'teens and twenties, in a way that perhaps only rock-and-roll and film are perceived in our time (the religious controversy over Salman Rushdie's *The Satanic Verses* notwithstanding).

Gerontion

Like Prufrock, Gerontion is an old man, created and inhabited by a young poet; this contrast explains in part the power and fascination that both poems hold. In the draft materials for *The Waste Land* that Eliot sent to Ezra Pound for his consideration, Eliot had considered using *Gerontion* as a preface to *The Waste Land*; though the decision was ultimately made to separate the two poems, they do share some obvious stylistic and thematic connections, and a discussion of *Gerontion* might be used to prepare students for the greater difficulty of *The Waste Land*. Looking back to Prufrock, students might be encouraged to think about the differences, as well as similarities, in the situations and outlooks of these two aging gentlemen.

The Waste Land

The Waste Land is of course vast and complex, and a tremendous challenge to teach in the course of a British Literature survey. There are many different possible, and fruitful, approaches; themes to be emphasized will depend to some extent on what texts and themes the course has emphasized to this point, and what will be important in the second half of the course.

The poem's textual history is not only important but quite interesting; Valerie Eliot's edition of the manuscript, complete with Ezra Pound's marginal comments, will help students to appreciate that Eliot's masterpiece didn't come to the marketplace immaculate and fully formed, but instead went through a difficult birth, with Ezra Pound as midwife. This insight can be especially valuable to student writers, who sometimes suspect that "real" writers work in complete isolation.

As with Joyce's *Anna Livia Plurabelle*, hearing the text in the author's own voice(s) is a wonderful aid to comprehension. In an earlier draft Eliot had called the poem "He Do the Police in Different Voices"; and his recording helps to distinguish some of the many voices that wander in and out of the poem. One interesting approach to Eliot's orchestration of various and varied voices is to have the students "dissect" an especially dense passage: take a pen or pencil and draw angle brackets around the various voices or textual threads that make up a given paragraph. This exposure of the polyphonic nature of the text should lead quite naturally into a discussion of both the various sources that Eliot employs, as well as the goals of such a strategy. If you have made such an analysis of Jones's *In Parenthesis*, you may want to have your students turn back to that poem to consider the similar strategies the two poems employ.

Students may want to talk about the status of Eliot's notes: with the exception of the strange marginalia that Coleridge added to *The Rime of the Ancient Mariner*, no well-known precursor of Eliot's notational strategy comes to mind, and students may well want to debate the "validity," as well as the efficacy, of all of Eliot's extra-poetic apparatuses: the notes, but also the epigraph, dedication, and section titles. What are we to think of a poem that embeds so much of its interpretive apparatus within the poem itself?

For teachers interested in the influence of modernist texts on artists in other media, the early '70s rock band Genesis (headed up by Peter Gabriel) did a song on their album *Selling England by the Pound* called "Cinema Show"—a loose adaptation of the scene in *The Waste Land* between the typist and the young man carbuncular, as well as Tiresias's commentary upon that scene. The song succeeds quite well in capturing the feeling of the passage, in the form of a miniature rock opera.

Journey of the Magi

In Eliot's version, we are privy to all the contradictory feelings as the wise men of the New Testament nativity story realize that the epiphany they have had, of the newborn Christ, makes them somewhat discontent to return to life as usual. The story of the wise men is the source for the term "epiphany" that Joyce liked to use: the wise men (or magi) arriving at the stable at Bethlehem is the original epiphany. As the speaker of *Gerontion* asks, "After such knowledge, what forgiveness?" The scene described here can be productively compared to the scene of epiphany at the close of Yeats's *The Second Coming*, as well as his own poem on this same story, *The Magi* (which may have influenced Eliot).

Four Quartets: "Burnt Norton"

Eliot's *Four Quartets* are supremely the work of a mature poet. When he comes to write the quartets Eliot is solidly middle-aged, and has become solidly Christian in his beliefs, after an earlier syncretism made popular by the comparative anthropological work of scholars like Sir James Frazier and Jessie Weston, both acknowledged influences behind the religious amalgam of *The Waste Land*. Whereas Eliot used the writing of Christian mystics in his earlier poetry, here he approaches, experientially, a kind of mystical stance; whereas the earlier poetry excelled at hard-edged, almost clinical description and diagnosis of his times ("like a patient etherised upon a table"), in *Burnt Norton* Eliot dreams of transcending language through language. The result is some of the most beautiful poetry Eliot ever wrote—not a poet often associated with the celebration of beauty; the poem's recurrent image of the rose-garden, for instance, helps to make solid what otherwise threatens to disappear in clouds of vaporous generalizations.

One way to measure how far Eliot's poetry (and philosophy) had come since *The Waste Land* is to compare the conclusion of the earlier poem—which counsels a stoic detachment from the fallen world of the Waste Land, with the similar counsel at the end of section 3 of *Burnt Norton*. The opening of section 5, and the image of the Chinese jar, owes an obvious debt to Keats's Grecian urn and Yeats's lapis lazuli, and can be fruitfully set alongside those poems for the sake of comparison.

Tradition and the Individual Talent

It has been suggested by some that this essay is the most influential text in twentieth-century Anglo-American literary criticism, and the most influential text Eliot ever wrote; if one or both of those claims overstate the case, it's not by much. Very early in the modernist period, Eliot's essay served not just to reiterate the modernist battle cry of "make it new," but to remind his readers, as well as his fellow writers, that the only way to make it new was to keep always in one's sight the monuments of the tradition. The essay is a masterpiece of persuasive critical writing, produced by a poet who (not yet thirty) has at this point written almost no important poetry, and is newly arrived in England as well.

The essay's two most important and suggestive points are, first, the argument that the new work proves its importance by reconfiguring our understanding of its forebears, and second, that the artist, when doing his work properly, maintains a perfectly "impersonal" stance toward his material. This latter notion owes something to Keats's concept of negative capability.

Virginia Woolf

The editors of the *Longman Anthology* hope that Virginia Woolf will be a pivotal part of any course that includes the twentieth-century material. She is one of its major female authors, if not *the* major woman writer across the two volumes, and her work is central to modern British literature by any measure. As has been mentioned in the introduction to this section of the instructor's manual, if one additional novel can be assigned for this period, it is hoped that it will be one by Woolf. The section is set up so that *Mrs Dalloway* would fit with virtually all the literary and critical agendas animating the *Anthology*, thematically encompassing for the century which saw Britain's empire wane and the cultural margins of empire return to constitute its center. *Mrs Dalloway* prophesies this change, and in a sense enacts it, making its major character a British woman in the thick of the social turbulence of war, empire, immigration, urbanization, and class warfare. The book has a further element to recommend it, in that a film adaptation of it starring Vanessa Redgrave as the eponymous heroine, written and directed by the actress and Woolf scholar Eileen Atkins, has been released. While the film does not in any way substitute for a reading of the novel, it can nonetheless supplement the Woolf section by the visual excitement of its London and country settings, allowing students to grasp the modernity of Woolf's themes.

Virginia Woolf is a triple or quadruple threat as a writer, since she is a prose master in fiction and nonfiction, a lyrical poet in her style, and was an arbiter of English literary history and style as an essayist and as an autobiographer in her superb *Diaries*. As a diarist she has ties to Defoe, to Pepys, and to the great nineteenth century autobiographers, such as Cardinal Newman. As an essayist and reviewer she stands with Dr. Johnson, with John Stuart Mill and Mary Wollstonecraft, with Thomas Carlyle, Matthew Arnold, John Ruskin and several of her Bloomsbury cohort. As a novelist and short story writer her peers are Joseph Conrad, James Joyce, George Eliot, D. H. Lawrence and few others in English. As a specifically modernist writer, only Joyce and perhaps Beckett can compare in the English language modernist tradition for formal innovations. Virginia Woolf is an astounding writer, and the *Anthology* attempts to showcase most of these facets of her work.

Woolf's gender is critical to studying her work, if only because as her literary writing accumulated in her lifetime she also had to argue for the right to be taken seriously as a writer. Nineteenth-century writers like Jane Austen, the Brontë sisters, George Eliot, and others had decisively entered the canon of English literature during Woolf's lifetime, so she was not arguing in a vacuum or a wilderness. Instead, she saw and pointed out the cultural lag which allowed those female authors entry into the pantheon of serious writers, yet perpetuated a hierarchy of female inferiority in education, employment, and personal freedom. It is an irony that many of Woolf's phrases for this gap or lag continue to be household words long after her death: to have a "room of one's own" is still a political and cultural goal of women in Britain and the United States, and the words crop up in newspaper headlines, in journalism, and on the Web, despite all the social changes and accomplishments in equality since Woolf wrote her essay. In other words, genuine equality for women is an ongoing issue, and Woolf's two long essays on the subject remain pertinent in political terms, no less than in the history of social thought to which they belong as sterling examples. Students should read Mrs. Pankhurst's speech to get a sense of Woolf's own context, and they will want to read Mary Wollstonecraft, J.S. Mill and the introductions to the Romantics section and the nineteenth-century volume for much more edification.

Partly because Woolf was a woman, her writing has sometimes been seen as less universal, less political, or less strong for often centering on what look like domestic settings: the room of one's own, the family house of *To the Lighthouse*, the party Mrs Dalloway spends the day preparing, and so on. Jane Austen's books experienced the same criticism; swirling around plots of marriage and located in country houses or resort towns, Austen's work was thought to ignore the important historical issues of its time—the Napoleonic wars, and so on. Later critics have caught up with readers in discovering the acute immediacy of Austen's plots, and the ways her prose style and narratives alike investigate the economic and social arrangements of the rising British middle class. Virginia Woolf's fiction is every bit as imbricated in the major issues of its period: imperialism, class conflict, women's independence, and sexual autonomy are only some of its concerns. Woolf argued that the British literature of the later nineteenth and the early twentieth century was retrograde in holding to the certainties of realism. Influenced by and fascinated with new discoveries in science, with socialist politics, with psychological models of the personality that accepted the importance of fantasies, dreams, and memories, Woolf developed a style that was anti-realist. She avoided neat and tidy endings, abhorred moral or sentimental judgments, and argued that a fluid sense of self, open to dreams, to sexual feelings, and to the darker sides of human character, should find its way into open-ended literary works. Woolf believed that an aesthetic style was also a politics: the breaking down of authorial authority was as powerful to her as questioning the unquestioned domination of a family by the father—in fact, these were one and the same action to her. Literary "rules" had no basis other than custom, and in the main literary rules upheld a straight and narrow, masculine notion of the world and women's place in it. By defying literary rules, and by creating literary spaces within language where the rules were of her own making, Woolf was convinced that both the individual readers of that writing, and the society surrounding those individuals, could be changed. She also wanted to challenge the unspoken rules, the rules of silence and taboo. Woolf's prose is lush and sensual; her characters inhabit a fluid sexuality, where desires are freely voiced, and often break the rules of social and sexual convention.

Woolf's story The Lady in the Looking-Glass: A Reflection shows her style at its most poetic and most sophisticated literary height. Remind students that one of the oldest, if not the oldest, metaphors for art is the mirror—art "holds up the mirror to nature," and so art is a reflection, or a representation, of reality. This story is a meditation on art and its powers, and a commentary on the mimetic or mirroring view of art. It should be read in tandem with the great Romantic theories of art as mimesis, including Coleridge, and the influential theories of art produced by Ruskin and Pater, among others. In a deceptively "ordinary," domestic scene Woolf stages a complex rumination on art's power to create, and to destroy. She focuses on a scene without any characters in it—the "lady of the house" is not in sight at the beginning, and she never receives a name. It is Woolf's language which, in its rich metaphors, brings personification and animation to the garden, the hall glimpsed from the doorway, and the mirror hanging in the hall, the fatal lens of art-making. Nothing in this very short story is actually "seen" in straightforward description. Woolf tricks and seduces us by her language into accepting a "reflection" of language as if it were reality—the reality of the setting and the woman in it. The imagery and metaphors of the convoluted sentences she uses begin to contain indirect, oblique hints of violation, of violence, and even of rape. Woolf's story implicates its readers in the spellbinding power of reflection, since a reader is aching to know what is in the letters on the little table in the hall, dying to know who the woman is, what her story may be—even how she looks. All of this is accomplished solely through words, as if by magic. Woolf implicates herself as a writer too—this eery fable about art and representation is not a simple gender parable, where the "male gaze" of writing has harmful aspects which female writing would not share. It seems crucial to point out to students that Virginia Woolf never makes such simplistic dichotomies; The Lady in the Looking-Glass: A Reflection illustrates that Woolf does not contrast male with female writers per se. She sees all art, and all writing, as potentially insidious or dangerous, as much as it is creative and productive: what, after all, gives us the beautiful garden, its flowers and vines, the absent lady and the gleaming mirror, if not literary art? One explanation for this paradox at the heart of her ghostly story (with links in theme to Christina Rosetti's *Goblin Market*) is Woolf's appreciation for the flip side, or back side, of language: she wants to give silence its due. Virginia Woolf's literary style embraces the silence behind language. Silence was equally important for Joseph Conrad's *Heart of Darkness*; Woolf mentions his novel innumerable times in her own writing. Conrad's understanding of silence was more one-sided than Woolf's; since women have been silenced so literally in the cultural record, Woolf saw great potential in silence, along with death and darkness. Fruitful things can dwell in silence, just as the earth gives rise to a riot of flowers and fruits from its silent, invisible depths. Woolf's story provides a metaphor for silence as the handmaiden of literary art. The only twentieth-century writer to create as much from silence as Woolf was Samuel Beckett. Woolf recognized that many things of immense cultural value had been lost to silence—virtually anything or anyone which fell outside the "rules," including not only women, although women most of all, but also the lower classes, colonial subjects, homosexuals, Jews, people of color. Woolf did not rush to "represent" all of these in her writing, since, as her story shows, she is suspicious of the urge to represent others in art. She does, however, leave open spaces in her writing, so that the silences which mark such people as outside the norm, outside the "rules," can gather.

Her novel *Mrs Dalloway* indicates how sensitive Woolf was to London as the center of a commercial and a political empire, and to the complexity of everyday life as a whirl of impressions, fantasies, memories, and even resistances. While Mrs Dalloway is merely "shopping"—an activity scorned by many as a feminine frivolity—Woolf's writing style compares itself to a shopping expedition: creative, fragmentary, open to suggestion. The tiny details are what makes shopping, and the tiny details of Woolf's prose gather momentum and strength. Ultimately, Woolf proposes that literature, like life, is not a solid, fixed reflection, but a quicksilver mirror, dappled and darkened, a mirror in motion. T. S. Eliot's poem *The Waste Land* had contemplated just such a fragmentary view of modern life and modern art; the poet laments that his poem is a collection of scraps, "these shards I shore up against my ruin." Virginia Woolf sees ruin in war, in social inequality, in violence and in enforced silence. Yet her diagnosis of modernity, despite these terrible evils, and her literary response to it, is entirely different. Woolf and women like her had very little stake in a system that had placed them outside politics, education, cultural achievement, and the public sphere. Whereas Eliot saw the collapse of tradition and religion, the downfall of the father (in church, state, and family) as sole authority, as responsible for the ruinous conditions of fragmentation, Woolf exulted in the fragmentary, the momentary, the new. Her writing begins on the scrap heap of modern culture—she couldn't have written what she did in Victorian times. Her gender had long been thrown onto the cultural scrap heap, in any event, so for all her love of the English literary tradition and its great masters, Woolf seizes on fragmentation as an opportunity. Virginia Woolf's modernist writing puts aside literary dreams of control, mastery, or totality—which is not to say that it isn't ambitious, political, and intense. Instead, in exquisitely lyrical and yet rigorous prose, she explores the silences, the neglected spaces—park benches, shops, parties, hospital rooms— and the momentary, fragile links between human consciousnesses.

Mrs Dalloway

Modernism is envisioned as an international, primarily European, urbanism, in other words the idea of modernity is the idea of the city, a city rooted in national identities, myths, and power, but breaking free of that horizon precisely at the level of modernist cultural practice. The place of women in the city, and the city seen as a space by and for women, however, considerably complicates modernism's urban focus. Concentrating on Virginia Woolf's *Mrs Dalloway*, but also with reference to "A Room of One's Own" and *Orlando*, this entry for the Instructor's Manual is meant to illuminate Woolf's great novel, but also to show how the modern(ist) city is figured there in ways at odds with the now customary notions of metropolitan experience under modernity—shock, fragmentation, dissolution, nostalgia. With an emphasis on consumption, viewed as an active, even productive or creative process, Woolf's texts are a prism of the multiple presences of women in the metropole, or capital city of London, and consequently this major emblem of modernist Europe, the city, is viewed quite differently in her novel. Within this difference there is by no means a singular "woman's" city *or* a single "female" modernism—instead, the richness of urbanity, of the presence of the city in Woolf's writing, establishes new directions for modernism, and multiple vectors for the women within the modern metropole implies liminality of identity, and its multiplicity: the ultimate result of the fluidity of identity, sexuality, and consciousness in *Mrs Dalloway* is the destabilizing of our conceptions of the metropole/periphery split. Woolf's novel recasts our ideas of what is central, what on the margins, whether that be in terms of gender and its masculine/feminine division, or of empire, where "center" and "periphery" are technical terms referring to the power at the heart of the imperial city; of nation or region, as in London appearing to be the very center of England, but shot through with the marginal—Scottish servant girls, Irish landladies, working-class intellectuals, Italian war brides; in regard to sexuality, where "proper" heterosexuality would seem to inhabit the center, yet in the novel is knocked off-center by the same-sex desires that infiltrate so many relationships. Finally, *Mrs Dalloway* questions the impregnable center of the English literary tradition, the British novel, and the English language, by Woolf's writing from the margins—female, unorthodox, uncompromisingly lyric prose.

If, as Raymond Williams persuasively demonstrates, modernism is characterized by an international, cosmopolitan metropole, with a floating bohemia or avant-gardist cafe society, a migratory modernist work force, then Virginia Woolf's greatest work decisively fails to register this, since her book is set squarely in one place, London, on one June day, occupied largely with the doings of a middle-to-upper class matron preparing for a party that evening. Some critics have been deceived by this appearance, and relegate Woolf's novel to the domestic settings or the embroidery hoop of narrative circumference within which her texts work their inscriptions. We may choose, however, to envision her writing as a material modernism engaged throughout with the dilemmas of the urban and of modernity, concerned actively with politics, the city, the empire, the world. Mrs Dalloway spins around the core of consuming, often very literally in the form of shopping, a female-coded activity that is thought to be the opposite of manly production. In Mrs Dalloway "production" in the sense of masculine order, heritage, and power has led to World War I, to the inequities of the British empire, and to the dominating theories of its villainous doctors, theories personified by Woolf as the social forces of Conversion and Proportion. To this "center" of coercion and control—London's economic power, its government, its male arbiters of social and psychic health—Mrs Dalloway escapes to the margins, to seemingly trivial acts of consuming, fraught with all its mysteries, its possibilities, its sacred rites.

We are led to expect "shock" as the objective correlative for the modernist urban experience; certainly a work like T.S. Eliot's The Waste Land creates an atmosphere of shock and dislocation for its vision of modern London, and "shock" was the term that both Georg Simmel and Walter Benjamin, two of the most important theorists of modernity, gave to the new experience of urban modernity. The poet Charles Baudelaire, for example, used the metaphor of an electric shock to describe the confusing, painful, and yet often pleasurable intensity of the modern city and human reaction's to the modern world. In The Transparent Society Gianni Vattimo links shock with Heidegger's term for the modernist art work's effect, Stoss, or the blow, and arrives at a definition for modernist aesthetic experience: "the focal point for art corresponding to this excitability and hypersensitivity is no longer the work, but experience. . . the phenomenon Benjamin describes as shock, then, does not concern only the conditions of perception, nor is it to be entrusted to the sociology of art. Rather, it is the manner of the work of art's actualization." In other words, Vattimo claims that modernist works of art are themselves experiences, and that their "shock value" lies in showing the positive sides of modernity. Woolf's novel embraces this experience and enters the fray, taking sides in one of the primary disputes of modernism by repudiating the notion that modernity and its shocks are only alienating, dehumanizing, or degrading, and that the nature of mass culture, modern spectacle, and consuming behaviors is always negative or "fallen."

The character of Septimus Smith is indeed a victim of modernity, suffering from a mental illness brought on by the war, whose very name "shell-shock" would seem to undercut the idea that shock or the modern metropole can be anything other than destructive. The book's sympathy with Septimus, and its covert praise of his suicide as an act against the forces of "normality" in the form of Dr. Bradshaw, however, depends on seeing the city and modernity in new ways and from new perspectives: Septimus's "insane" point of view, his working-class background and his apparently unimportant life are all celebrated in the book, as he becomes a stand-in for Eliot's Fisher-King, a force of renewal. This transpires because of the obliquity, or off-centeredness, of Woolf's approach to the urban and to modernity in general: her metropole, unlike, say, Walter Benjamin's, has women and other marginal people at the heart of it, and thus reconfigures the stage of the commodity, consumption, and gender. The society of the spectacle is not simply a society of appearance manipulated by power, where the refraction of goods in myriad shop windows makes for a dazzling, illusionary surface over the stark reality of hegemony. "This is also the society in which reality presents itself as more fluid, as weaker, as soft, where experience can acquire the characteristics of oscillation, disorientation, and play," Vattimo notes, and since he is speaking of modern social form, or "reality," and not of Woolf or her writing, the adjectives fluid, weak and soft are not any summing up or privileging of the "feminine," but descriptive of an alternative understanding of the effects of the advent of mass culture and the media. Essentially, Woolf's writing already contains or enacts just such an exploration.

The dual possibility—both negative and "alienating" and positive or creative—of this cultural terrain is brought out in the famous episode of collective transfixing as a scattered group of people in a London park look up to watch as a skywriting plane emits its puffy, magic script across the sky, "Glaxo. . . Creemo. . . Toffee," writ large in the air for the wonderment and puzzlement of the onlookers in the park. "The clouds to which the letters E, G, or L had attached themselves moved freely, as if destined to cross from West to East on a mission of the greatest importance which would never be revealed, and yet certainly so it was— a mission of greatest importance." The words West and East are capitalized, a portentous reminder of the pan-European nature of the first World War and the importance of airplane technology to its devastation. But this airplane is not the mere replica of that other engine of destruction, the war-plane. Here the airplane, for good or ill, is an ineluctable feature of modernity, capable of hieroglyphic play, of hierophantic writing, and able to draw people together. "It was toffee; they were advertising toffee, a nursemaid told Rezia. Together they began to spell t . . . o . . . f . . ." This fluid sky-writing, emblematic of all writing under the sign of mass culture, and a figure for the modernist writing of Woolf's own book, prompts an unfurling of the personal history of various women in this city, especially Mrs Dempster, a figure left out of most accounts of modernity, urbanism, and shock, but decisively included here: "Ah, but that aeroplane! Hadn't Mrs Dempster always longed to see foreign parts? She had a nephew, a missionary. It soared and shot. She always went to sea at Margate, not out o' sight of land, but she had no patience with women who were afraid of water. It swept and fell. Her stomach was in her mouth. Up again. There's a fine young feller aboard of it, Mrs Dempster wagered, and away and away it went, fast and fading, away and away the aeroplane shot; soaring over Greenwich and all the masts; over the little island of grey churches, St. Paul's and the rest till, on either side of London, fields spread out and dark brown woods where adventurous thrushes hopping boldly, glancing quickly, snatched the snail and tapped him on a stone, once, twice, thrice." Mrs Dempster's experience is not comfortably to be written off in the vocabulary of reification or alienation, nor is she just a victim of the modern mass cultural spectacle. On the contrary: via the unexpected medium of the evanescent toffee advertisement Mrs Dempster has entered a geopolitical reverie. Her metropole is sexed by way of the skeins of consumption, which are not riveted, mechanical, or restricting, but offer a cast-out line to another way of envisioning her circumstances.

Woolf reverses the expected trajectory of international metropolitan modernism in fascinating ways. A pivotal refrain in the book is the rather garbled crooning song, "the voice of an ancient spring spouting from the earth," emitted by the chthonic old woman who sits at the park entrance, one of Woolf's old woman figures, half working-class crone, half mythologized primal earth mother. The song she sings has thankfully been identified for us by numerous commentators as "Allerlei Seelen" or "All Souls," a European high art fragment that recirculates through the old woman, a sexing (in the sense of grafting onto) of the metropole. The old woman's "ee um fah um so, foo swee too eem oo" refrain is the transformation through consumption of the otherwise abstract modern artifact, and its re-entry in the culture of London on that day, in the form of an old woman's song, as another form of currency.

Clarissa Dalloway has a special relationship to the metropole or "center," in part because she lives in the heart of London, is married to a diplomat, and grew up on a classic 18th-century estate in the countryside. Her name, too, is borrowed, perhaps, from Samuel Richardson's *Clarissa*, one of the first novels. Clarissa Dalloway also has a special role in the book as a hostess—she is a shopper and a consumer, exactly the modern gender roles assigned to women of her class. However, while consumers and especially female consumers are the subject of much cultural disapproval, one thing that is so exciting and fresh about *Mrs Dalloway* is its refusal to do so. What is often labeled a marginal, trivial act—shopping, consuming, preparing for a party, taking care of a family's needs, and so on—becomes the heart of this novel. Clarissa's parties, it goes without saying, are bound up in extensive acts of literal consumption, the purchase of flowers and candles and food and clothes. But of greater significance is the placement of Clarissa at the core of the book, a meditation on urban modernity. Clarissa tentatively and tenuously reverses the "disenchantment of the world" characteristic of modernity, according to the great sociologist Max Weber, who argued that the nature of modernity was an ever-encroaching rationality, bureaucracy, and calculation. The world becomes "disenchanted," in his lovely phrase, in that everything that doesn't concern money or statistics or power politics slips away, whether it be personal touches or rural customs or belief in fairies and folklore. Clarissa re-enchants her world, or at least tries to defy its disenchantment, by the generosity of her gendered acts of consumption, where consumption is reformulated as the nature of the gift.

This appears paradoxical, in that gift-giving looks like the reversal of consumption, the taking in or appropriation of something through an act of exchange. Nonetheless, Clarissa's consumption has this perverse or unexpected valence, and it is linked by the text to the nature of modernist writing and Woolf's writing in particular. "I threw a coin once into the Serpentine," Clarissa famously says, comparing this to the suicide of Septimus Smith as a form of sacrifice, giving the gift of his death to the city of London not as a soldier in the European war, but as an ex-centric denizen of the city itself. And on the verge of his suicide, Septimus is gendered female, when he decorates the party hat as his penultimate creative offering. The sexing of the metropole in this fashion is not meant at all to suggest that, for example, men are unable to take up this relation to the city or to consumption. Rather, this is a way of figuring the dynamics of the modernist city, where, to put it very baldly, shopping is not the root of all evil—nor, one hastens to say, is it utopian. The processes and procedures of modernity, however, are accorded weight and positive possibilities, in contradistinction to the dehumanization often attributed to the modern city. The city of women—Clarissa's London, for instance—is the site not only of all the hierarchies and divisions of the gendered social world, but also their liquefaction in gifts of consumption.

In Mrs Dalloway the English subjects depicted throughout the book are ex-centric to the metropole in multifarious ways, whether by dint of having spent twenty years in India like Peter Walsh, repatriating as a World War I veteran in the case of Septimus Smith, being Italian, coming down from Scotland in hopes of escaping poverty there, or in less tangible ways, as for Richard Dalloway, pillar of the metropolitan establishment, but secretly wishing to be a farmer, a man with rural longings. Even Sally Seton, Clarissa's dearest friend and for one brief moment the object of her romantic love, is marginal, unusual; she is at the time of the story a married mother of five sons, living in the country, but she was an intellectual, a radical, a bold and brilliant young woman who even now has defied the class system by marrying a business man who worked his way up in life. People all over the world are linked to London because of the British Empire; Mrs Dalloway diagnoses the injustices and wrongs of the empire, but shows that even people and cultures pushed to the margins are central in their significance and experience to modernity. London is a shadowy city of great power and exclusion, yet also a city of joy, of transformation, of women. Clarissa's daughter Elizabeth travels the city on the open-air upper deck of a bus in the memorable next-to-last scene; she, unlike her mother, seems headed toward a profession, is uncomfortable with the role of debutante her father wants her to play, loves the city and its freedom, has compassion for those who, like her mentor Miss Kilman, are unloved and on the outskirts.

The novel ends with the party Clarissa gives; in it, through her, her friends and even foes have come together, spark memories and find themselves anew in talking about her. She is almost magical in her "sea-green silver" dress, like a mermaid as well as a middle-aged woman. Clarissa's party is also her life, a whirling shimmering scatter of conscious moments, possibilities, gifts of love and thought she showers. "It is Clarissa, he said. For there she was," are the last two lines, the first spoken by Peter Walsh and the second perhaps by us, the readers. What Clarissa "is" is as uncertain as are all our individual selves. This book encompasses so much historical loss, dislocation, personal compromise, grief and yet exultation. Clarissa's party is a gift whose recipients don't even recognize it—the truest form of gift there is, tossed without expectation of thanks or of reciprocation, like the coin into the Serpentine. Not all truth and knowledge comes from production, ruling, coercing, defining. Clarissa's consuming gift is her gift to the world she inhabits, priceless and beyond measurement.

Regendering Modernism

Virginia Woolf's *Orlando*

The brief excerpt from the middle of Virginia Woolf's famous book, *Orlando*, serves as the introductory and exemplary text to this Perspectives section on gender and modernism. It does so not only because Woolf is quite clearly herself the exemplary modernist writer who "regendered" modernism by the sheer power of her texts, and the centrality of gender to her work; the section of her novel *Orlando* is in some ways an allegory of the process of re-gendering, in a sense, taking gender newly into account.

Modernism was by no means the first literary movement or school to carry implicit or explicit questions of gender, nor the first where female writers participated as creative and ground-breaking innovators. The rest of the anthology amply demonstrates how important women writers have been to canonical and non-canonical literature, and even in their absence, the degree to which gender is a formative structure within language and literature as a whole. We include this special Perspectives section to highlight the special relationship modern writing has with, on the one hand, broad social and cultural changes in the understanding of men and women, and on the other, the paralleling of modernist literature with revelations and revolutions in gender roles and the knowledge of sexuality and desire. In a general way modernist writing is characterized by its movement into interior, psychic space, its rendering of the quicksilver patterns of consciousness and the equally powerful force of unconscious drives and wishes. Freud made it evident that, as he described it, conscious awareness of the self was but the visible part of a far more extensive iceberg, whose underwater dimensions are an apt analogy to the superior role of unconscious elements in the mind. Human beings, Freud showed, are "split" subjects, split into unequal parts and forever blocked from complete self-awareness or self-knowledge. Selfhood became for modernity a fluid affair, an almost literary, ever-fluctuating script that drew no distinctions between conscious and unconscious, present and past, self and other. Freud's theory mapped the movements of desire, as desire went undercover and returned in the form of memories, wishes, thoughts, repressions, dreams, sublimated creativity, and the ability, as Freud put it, "to work and to love," a more realistic hope than simply expecting to be "happy." Desire can be viewed as simply the most available source of human energy, and far from being used up in sexual activity, its primary reason for being is to keep human beings directed toward life and away from death. The interior fiction of identity each person constructs, then, circles importantly around gender, since the bottom line of self-definition, in social and cultural scripts that control even one's entry into language, is to be able to say "I am a girl" or "I am a boy." Freud's psychoanalytic work illustrated that such declarations are not only comprised of constant performances of what such gendered identities mean, but also that they take place along a spectrum, where the "normal" shades into the so-called "perverse," and where both sexes share gender elements and fantasies.

This fluid model of the self and necessarily of gender becomes pivotal to modernist writing, writing that tries to capture the evanescence of self-awareness just as it turns away from fixity and absolutes. This section contains separate works that address the innovations in language, style and subject that marked a renewal of interest in gender, as contrasted to biological sex. Much of the rest of the anthology, however, is as deeply invested in experiments with gender: Shaw's *Pygmalion* has rich affinities with Woolf's *Orlando* and with Caryl Churchill's *Cloud Nine*; D.H. Lawrence is as alert to the flow of desire and the gendering of power as is E. M. Forster or Thom Gunn; Eavann Boland experiments with the gender of language with the same intensity as does Angela Carter. This Perspectives section teaches as a distinct and discrete grouping, though, in that each of the pieces emanates from the investigation of gender and self-hood so well-represented by Virginia Woolf's *Orlando*, whose main character is both man and woman, heterosexual and homosexual, self and other.

Virginia Woolf's father, Leslie Stephen, was most famous for his writing and direction of a vast Victorian project, the *Dictionary of National Biography*, a reference work in numerous volumes that provided a capsule biography of the great and important figures who were seen as making up British social life: its major writers, its political figures, its educators, explorers, reformers and journalists, its diplomats and its scientists. The *Dictionary* turned lives into neat formulations of achievement and into standard evaluations of greatness, both linked to the desire to compile a national list that could also be said to define a national identity. Lives were seen as part of a larger cultural project or destiny, and the idea of placing these biographical sketches in alphabetical, dictionary form is, if you think about it, also something quite strange. Listing people in place of words, the dictionary then gives the impression that, for example, there are no other famous lives between f and g, that there is a kind of fictitious totality which the alphabet format provides. In some ways, it helps to form the very idea of a nation, where it even makes sense to compile a collection of these life stories under one heading. This major life's work gave enormous cultural power to Leslie Stephen, in the sense that he could be an arbiter of someone's importance to the national life; the connection to an imperial consciousness is also very direct, because it only became necessary to have such a reference work at the point that Britain was through its empire spreading itself out over the globe. People have often read *Orlando* as a *jeu d'esprit*, concentrating on its playfulness, its dedication to Vita Sackville West, its glossy surface and constantly ironic tone. If we consider, though, as we must, that Woolf is taking on a form brought to its national, imperial, Victorian height by her own father, then the textual politics of *Orlando* becomes something else again. Its status as a spoof is a serious one, for it takes on, seemingly in jest, all the principles of such biographies and really looks at what they do to constitute a sense of a person's life. Along the way, Woolf's novel presents an intertwined investigation of sexual, international and textual politics.

Orlando is subtitled "A Biography," and clings to that premise throughout its improbable unfolding, improbable because it becomes apparent that a biography of a person who won't neatly die within one historical "age," won't even conform to the ultimate sanctity of biography, that is, identifiable sexual identity. This throws a huge monkey wrench into the works, since Orlando the character begins as a man and is described in those terms, but then becomes a woman and opens up all the established categories of representation. Moreover, the "biography" is wrapped around the literary tradition of England, since Orlando is a writer, whose writings we never really get to read, and is involved in the lives, if only in passing, of the writers who are said to "sum up" their respective periods, to stand in for them, almost. Finally, the biography also is from its opening words interlaced with Britain's imperial identity, with its gradual building up of a mercantilist empire to its ultimate political installation of an imperial state—Orlando doesn't just witness this, but takes part in it in many ways. This construction of the mock biography helps to show us how indissolubly linked these elements are in cultural discourse. *Orlando* is not a text in which we identify with the hero/heroine, or are moved by the characters' losses and courage, as happens in *Mrs Dalloway*; we are kept on the surface of this life because the process of biography itself is in question, the ways that selves and genders are put together in culture. And running throughout this is the interrogation of patriarchy—simply put, why it is that the "norm" has been taken to be male, and that all the positive cultural terms—rationality, art, power, action, strength, purpose, and even fame are taken to be masculine traits.

Orlando begins with the character Orlando as a boy, slicing off the head of a Moor, a desiccated severed head, we soon learn, part of the family bounty from the grandfather's trips to foreign places. This head grins at Orlando with its shriveled lips, and in that gaze begins to confound the placement of self and other the text will set thoroughly at odds. The questioning continues, for example, in the section where Orlando goes to Constantinople as the Ambassador. This part is reflected to us in bits and pieces only—as the very vocal narrator says, only "charred fragments" of history remained. The opulence and merriment of the Arabian court where the male Orlando enjoys his time as Ambassador, the extravagance of the royal party leading even to his marriage with the gypsy Rosita Pepina, are all obliterated in a very significant stroke, wherein this male Orlando is looked back at, as it were. Following a strange courtly allegory, a Masque that one could show students is an ironic take-off on courtly masques in Shakespeare and other early writers, three graces come before Orlando and then withdraw, upon which Orlando stands revealed as a woman. It seems not to be a coincidence that this transformation should have taken place on foreign, exotic soil, in the land of the Other, since after all, Woman is seen as the ultimate Other in patriarchal culture. Orlando suddenly becomes a beautiful object, drawn out almost magically (or through literary magic) of the immensely beautiful surroundings and their lavish strangeness. It is as if this splitting off of Orlando into femininity has come about because of a kind of surplus of exoticism, of which femininity can readily become a part. It also signals that the biography of this supposed person, Orlando, is not going to rest content with the exploits of a swashbuckling Duke; suddenly we are on the other side of the looking glass, an unfamiliar place, except perhaps in fiction. It is clear how hard it is to tell the story of the British empire and its noble deeds if the protagonist is a woman, how hard it is to connect the elusive self with a national identity when in a foreign place. Orlando goes out to the gypsies in her new incarnation, as a woman, although what she seeks is solitude and contemplation. But her desire for England drives her back home, and she leaves on the ship The Enamoured Lady, anything but in love.

While the newly female Orlando will survey, from the deck of the ship, an England suddenly made orderly by the arrival of the 18th century, there is more disorder now in the text than it can cope with, because the issue of sexual identity cannot easily be resolved. Initially, Orlando is simply no different, except anatomically, but then an internal doubling occurs, and Orlando knows life from two sides—prompted, in fact, by being back in England, where there is a need to see how much a woman is created by the social order and how much stems from some innate "womanliness." The argument of this text, or what it enacts, at any rate, is the costumed nature of sexuality, its performative aspects. Gender is like a form of theater; obviously there are unique biological experiences, such as giving birth for women, or experiencing sex with different physical organs, but beyond those, the display of sexuality is a matter of clothing, in a sense. A woman's experience is not created by any innateness, nor by an "essence" that is womanly, but by the social construction of women. Orlando even feels a rush of anger against her own former category, the male side of things, while at the same time the text suggests a double state for all human beings. More sex changes occur further along in the novel, when Orlando has been wearing women's garb for a considerable period of time, and the book ends in the modern period, with Orlando in love with modernity and the city, waiting for a husband who likes to wear pearls.

These flips back and forth across the central divide of gender are also played out in the main "plots" of the biography, in order to suggest the difficulty of making even a simple statement about someone's love affairs or their desires. The Archduchess Harriet is a case in point. She comes on the scene early on in the Elizabethan period, an ungainly 6'2" of love for Orlando (then a man), laughing rather maniacally, and evaded by Orlando in his then repulsion from her. Later in the 18th century the Archduchess is back, except this time it is revealed that she had been playing a part, and was really the Archduke, madly in love with Orlando as a man and adopting this ruse to be able to woo him. Now that Orlando is a woman, the Archduke is willing to propose marriage, although this little performance is not accepted by the female Orlando. There is a confetti of sexual positions and desires going on here, on both sides of the Archduke's masquerade. Orlando almost prophesies transgendered and transsexual identities that had not become surgically or socially possible until very recently.

The entire biography of Orlando, male and female, is wrapped up with writing; ironically, Orlando carries the manuscript of her poem "The Oak Tree" around in one form or another for several hundred years. The work is begun in the Elizabethan age in Orlando's flush of enthusiasm for the immortality of literature, until he is rudely disabused of this notion by the poet Nick Greene. Greene is scathing about the literary value of the present age and criticizes Shakespeare, Donne, Jonson, Marlowe, and so on for their inability to hold up next to the great classical past. Literary value is shown to be as subjective and fluid as gender. The text oscillates wildly back and forth between the act of writing and the act of being written, the act of writing and the act of reading. There is a hilarious scene when Orlando goes with Sasha, his early love, to a street fair, there to see a puppet show of Shakespeare's *Othello*; in the very next passage, without knowing it, Orlando acts out *Hamlet* in his obsession with death and the futility of all action. But Orlando won't die, can never die or reach closure, and thus allow the act of biography to really begin. Obviously, one of the most important features of biography is that the life it traces has ended, making a narrative complete. In *Orlando*, no final judgment is able to be made, and this stymies the whole operation of fixing and embalming an identity. Modernism, too, refuses closure, refuses simple endings, whether they be "happy" or sad. Modernist works like *Mrs Dalloway* end on an open note; Joyce's *Ulysses* famously ends without punctuation and in a passionate rush with Molly Bloom's "yes I will Yes" and then is over.

The fetishizing of men leads to the denigration of women's lives and the repetition or the reproduction of a social system that uses the worship of art for conservative rather than liberating ends.

The Victorian age is horrific to Orlando, and points to a kind of constricting, narrowing, dominative aspect that in *Mrs Dalloway* was presented as Proportion and Conversion, an age where his/her liminal status as man—woman is even less tolerable than before. The empire is ushered in, and this has everything to do with the conditions of sexuality under Victorianism. Soon, imperceptibly, Orlando the woman finds herself subject to the blushing fits which characterize the age and, much worse, to the desire to marry, the ultimate paradigm of conformity. The book takes up most savagely its critique of the ways that an ideology of marriage and the family came to be so dominant, with such appalling results, and how this was related to the spectacle of Britain as an imperial society.

Orlando does succumb to the pressure to marry, but is able to do this in such a unique way that it obviates all the control mechanisms of the century, since Marmaduke Bonthrop Shelmerdine (obviously a playfully ironic name) is more like a woman than a man, is never in England, and is not part of Orlando's real life, her writing. The book ends with an open future, an open page, before her, an allegory for the regendering that perhaps only literature can accomplish in the modern age.

Vita Sackville-West
Seducers in Ecuador

In some ways, *Seducers in Ecuador* is the perfect cautionary tale for Western tourists and even students and faculty off to acquire spring-break tans in tropical places like Key West and Aruba, wearing RayBans to ward off the fierce glare, and, in that sense, becoming like Arthur Lomax in Vita Sackville-West's tale, a prisoner of spectacles. Lomax's trip to foreign ports of call leads inexorably to his death by hanging back in a grimmer and greyer England; most tourists have nothing like this to worry about as they contemplate much-needed voyages to tropical climes. Still, the relation of this text to travel, empire, and gender is one of the compelling reasons for including it in the anthology and in the Regendering Modernism Perspectives section. Vita Sackville-West's tale is an ironic parable of an empire, England, in the process of regendering itself.

There are other key contexts that help to situate this work an instructor needs to embroider upon first. It may seem that after *Ulysses* or *Mrs Dalloway* that writing itself had undergone an apocalypse and nothing remained to do with words on a page. The revolutionary reverberations of Joyce's and Woolf's texts are still ringing in students' ears, but an important thing to point out is that their modernist textual experimentation was a highly specific cultural act, that it had meaning not just as an experiment in modernist art but as very committed political texts originating out of the colonial context and its collision with language. One of the main lines of change we have been tracing in the anthology has been what makes British literature British, in other words, why is this tradition composed so strikingly of people from non-British or at least non-English backgrounds, or by those with a highly marginal relation to the nation itself, whether by politics or sexual orientation or by gender or race or class. Joyce's *Ulysses* went as far as it is perhaps possible to go with a challenge to the English language as an instrument of oppression and an instrument of change and renewal—his very mode of writing has been called a version of *écriture féminine*, women's writing, by French feminist theorists including Julia Kristeva, who is under no misapprehension about James Joyce's biological masculinity, but whose claim is that the fluidity of the language in his texts approaches a feminine, rather than masculine, sensibility. Vita Sackville-West is not mounting a challenge to the supremacy of English nor tunneling inside writing itself to carve out a new consciousness of modernity. Next to that project this story is somewhat slight. It is, however, revelatory of a kind of displacement that enters all British modernist writing and that is especially valuable to investigate as the product of a female writer, perhaps only possible emanating from a female sensibility.

Far from being an outsider figure like Conrad, or Lawrence, or Joyce, Sackville-West was brought up in, literally, the largest house in England, an Elizabethan estate called Knole that is approximately *Brideshead Revisited* times two. Set squarely in the ruling elite of Britain, poised within its aristocracy with all the feudal trappings of merry old England on a vast acreage, she grew up as a confident possessor of what may be the ineffable quality of Britishness, which was her birthright. She later lost the house when, on her father's death, it went to her male cousin by the immutable laws of gender and property. That sense of usurpation—of having something taken away solely because, in this case, one was female, became paramount to Vita Sackville-West. Her entitlements remained almost unimaginable to most of us; she had a perfectly fine, enormous house called Sissinghurst instead, was wealthy in the extreme, and, through her marriage to Harold Nicholson, was part of ruling circles socially and diplomatically until she died in 1962. But her intersection as a writer with the world of modern British literature, her occupation of a strange niche within the Bloomsbury group, and her accomplishments as a female writer who helped to change the texture and aims of British literature are key to the section: her work shows how much this modernist literature was predicated on a relationship, suppressed or acknowledged, with the rest of the world, with Britain's status as an imperial power and as such, as the ruler of an empire of English, too—since under the British flag English was disseminated to the colonies and was taught rigorously there. The first advanced college courses in English literature were, in fact, developed in India for Indian students, meant to teach them to absorb Englishness and thus loyalty to the British culture that ruled them. Vita Sackville-West spent a large part of her adult life in Persia, now Iran, and wrote some of the first and best books and essays about that culture in English, a part of the vast imperial administration of English, but a marginal, insidious voice within its world of writing. Even at the veritable center of power and empire, there is margin, at the metropole, there is periphery, to use two terms from the theory of colonialism that help to describe the uncanny as well as exploitative ties between the ruling country and its colonies. The center comes to depend on the margin, in linguistic and psychological ways, and one could argue that if the modernist center was also masculine, it depended on its female or queer margins for much of its energies. *Seducers in Ecuador* is a neat presentation, unconsciously perhaps, but delivered with great zest, of this predicament.

Show students that the story is dedicated to Virginia Woolf, one of West's closest friends, so close indeed that, according to her, they went to bed together twice. The physical extent of their relationship is unimportant; certainly its emotional intensity was powerful, and even more so, Sackville-West's debts to her friend Virginia's writing. *Orlando* is dedicated to and "about" Vita; it is, as is everything Woolf wrote, lyrical, rich, and extraordinary. Sackville-West realized her strengths did not lie in style or writerly genius. Instead, she could offer something to the modernist table, too, a small gift, but crucial, the gift of her elite sensibilities put to subversive use by her ironic stance as woman, a bi-sexual, a feminist, and a critic of Britain's empire. Sackville-West had a propensity for donning men's clothes and, with her ample checkbook in hand, leaving her husband and two sons for a month or two of deliciously decadent rampaging in Europe and the Middle East; she lived out an aristocratic version of the sexual and intellectual freedoms commanded by Bloomsbury circles.

Bloomsbury is an important phenomenon within the study of 20th century British literature, and other than West both E.M. Forster and Virginia Woolf on our anthology syllabus have to be rooted within it too—not to wholly explain their literary being nor as the only way of reading their texts, but to help to explain in the larger historical sense what a language community can provide, what work it can do in generating literary responses. It's hard to pin down the elusive Bloomsbury Group or to give any definitive explanation for what they were about, because of course one is dealing with a group of people with loose alliances over time, not an institution or a group that can be pinned down. This group of friends, rivals and colleagues was centered in London as an outgrowth of friendships made at Oxford and Cambridge that then also expanded to include the non Oxbridge-educated, especially the Stephens sisters, Virginia Woolf and Vanessa Bell. Other prominent members besides Forster were Lytton Strachey, the biographer, Maynard Keynes, the economist, Leonard Woolf, Roger Fry and Clive Bell, who worked in art and art criticism, Duncan Grant, Bertrand Russell, Lady Ottoline Morell, and students of the philosopher G.E. Moore. These people don't cluster to form one school or one program, but nonetheless, with their iconoclasm and their anti-imperialism within limits, their prolongation of a kind of university life well past its ending, with their sexual nonconformity—Bloomsbury as such is reported to have begun when Vanessa Bell said to someone else entering the room where a group was gathered to talk—"Is that sperm on your skirt?"—homosexuality and round-robin affairs, their devotion to free thought and to an anti-national, anti-Victorian stance, they do constitute a strong cultural force within British life, one that has been thoroughly mythologized.

Arthur Lomax's life is transformed by the wearing of sunglasses, first the blue pair he buys in London to prepare for going to Egypt on Bellamy's yacht, and then the amber, green and black pairs he acquires at Cairo. Ultimately, he is unable to look at the world without them, and they do provide him with an entirely new insight into things, into truth, however much the colors of the lens change what seem to be the real hues of life. It is in fact the saddest thing that happens to him, even worse than being tried and hanged, when the police take his spectacles away when he is arrested in Paris. Twice in the tale the adjective "quixotic" is applied to Lomax's extraordinary behavior under the sway of the glasses, and this is a giveaway of sorts. Lomax is a new incarnation of Don Quixote. "Quixotic" is now used to mean an attempt to do something idealistic, despite the obvious impossibilities. Lomax is a Don Quixote because just as the Don picked up the romances of chivalry, was overwhelmed by them, and then read the world through the lens of the romantic page, treating the world as text, and in the blunt encounters that resulted, saw the power of the text to utterly transform and even refigure the "real," so the colored glasses produce a new sense of the world. This world is one where chivalrous behavior or loyalty and honor go without saying—Lomax will marry Miss Whitaker in a flash because she merely sets him up to believe that she is pregnant with the child of a bounder who has gone off to Ecuador to hide amongst his exploits, and he will agree to poison Bellamy because Bellamy has begged him to put him out of his supposedly terminal misery. So far, there are indeed echoes of the behavior Don Quixote engaged in that made him thought to be so mad, but other aspects also enter in. The world becomes skewed by an altered sense of vision, by a covering or veil that makes everything different—Lomax even says that he thinks he would go mad without the spectacles, and cannot bear to take them off, even when he has returned to England. Don Quixote imbibed his world view from literature, and then was himself turned into a piece of writing, as he and Sancho Panza became characters in a text whose author they meet on the road. Nothing quite so metaphysical happens to Lomax, but his story encapsulates a kind of encounter that is earth-shaking. This is not just an accident of sunglasses, but that it is precisely because he has to shield his eyes from the hot colonial sun, as it were, that he is given this vision, a vision that, on the one hand, turns him into a person others think is mad, bad, and dangerous to know (famously said about Oscar Wilde) and that, on the other, gives him the "half-dozen pictures" he wants to remember out of the seventy or eighty pages or years of life most people have. His changed vision is the product of the colonial eyestrain, or the sun that only mad dogs and Englishmen go out to confront. Once you think of it that way, everything in the story is hooked to that inexorable logic, because there are intimations everywhere of what it is like to go elsewhere, to see other things, under the auspices or the regime of the imperial flag—even when the people are not in the slightest degree aware of it. For example, Arthur Lomax is as distant from Frantz Fanon, the theorist of colonial revolution, as it is possible to be—he hasn't broken through to any glimpses about empire or its problems at all. He accepts the status quo unquestioningly. What has happened, though, is that under the urgency of taking in these other sights and places he has been thrown out of the life course, the almost zombie life course, of his previous existence, and is set in a shattered world where anything can happen. Under the spectacles, Lomax is utterly without ego—it is egoism that, Mr. Bellamy tells him, he himself suffers from, and one can also see that Miss Whitaker partakes of this as well.

All these British people are in need of the tropics or of exotic locations in some way: Miss Whitaker must use them to invent a lover who has romantically taken advantage of her, to escape from the desolation of her bed-sitting room and her lack of friends and prospects. Bellamy is a Nietzschean figure who is so colossally bored he steers the yacht into a deadly storm off the Mediterranean coast, and sets up Lomax to kill him when, in fact, there is nothing the matter with him at all. This egotism is important to the Bloomsbury connection, because one of the key touchstones for the Bloomsberries, as they were called, was G. E. Moore's ethical philosophy, which posited a detached, secular ethics that involved an understanding of the self's position in relation to the social. This story works out some of that—in a completely non-philosophical way, to consider how it is that Lomax could stand on the other side of egotism altogether—he almost has no personality at all.

When Lomax gets his glasses he sees Miss Whitaker, for example, as having tears like Ethiopian jewels, whereas we know she is quite ordinary and plain; when he stands on the deck in the storm off the Illyrian coast he wears his amber ones, and the world is bathed in the mists of Elizabethan conquests and the glamour of gold—like the opening evocation of *Heart of Darkness*. One of the most salient scenes in the novella, and a scene to discuss with students, is set in Artivale the scientist's Parisian workshop; he studies butterflies, and has turned his basement into a simulacrum of the tropics, with butterflies and their larvae disporting about. He talks to Lomax about Bellamy and the fortune, and then Artivale—whose name seems to refer to "art" and "truth" or its "veil" at once—demonstrates his most crucial link to the unquestioned assumptions of empire, class, race and gender. This basement tropical zone contains black female workers, "imported," so the text says, and the echo of slavery and empire is there, several black women to serve him, since only they can stand the heat of this work in the warmth needed to preserve the butterflies. As blue butterflies circle about their heads Lomax tells Artivale that he will give his fortune to him to use for "the good of humanity," another abstraction that Artivale and we the reader must question, especially given the ways that the two men think nothing of exploiting black women, who are as invisible to them as they can be. Of course the text contains another irony, in that the money supposedly left to further scientific progress will be taken away by some old maiden aunts who will use it to advance the civilizing missionary work of British empire. Lomax's attempt to divert the money to another cause—the science of blue butter-flies— has fallen back to perpetuating empire. What is so ironic is that Artivale's laboratory in Paris is empire writ small—science masquerading as impartial, but de-pending on the labors of "others"—black, female, subservient—to accomplish. Note for students how the word "civilized" constantly appears in the early sections of the text, and show them how it accumulates irony. The company of British strangers keeps together only because they see each other as examples of the "civilized" world. In their inevitable brush with what lies outside themselves everything is, through Lomax, unveiled.

Miss Whitaker speaks of Lord Carnavon, the real-life discoverer of Tutankamen's tomb: "He would be alive today if he had not interfered with the tomb." This tossed-off reference to one of the great archaeologists and accompa-niers of empire has fateful echoes, since Lomax will be hanged, and it is in his trial that Bellamy's tomb is interfered with. But how is Lomax like Lord Carnavon? He doesn't even find the antiquities of Egypt exciting—he hates the Sphinx, for exam-ple, but the installation of the sphinx in the text is deliberate and important. The Sphinx is traditionally given female gender, and women's wisdom is referred to cul-turally as mysterious, or "sphinx-like." Vita Sackville-West quietly disputes this, and shows how for English people so culturally blinkered, that oracular icon can no longer give off knowledge in a world that has been eviscerated by tourism, by the empire, by these differences and displacements. These colonial places are now en-tirely like tombs. Lomax and the others stay with their own kind, go with the tourists to the hotels and so on, but they don't have a life that isn't made up out of these encounters with sameness. Miss Whitaker is a debased version of the sphinx herself, with her silence and her riddles about pregnancies and brothers and friends that don't exist.

It is a high point of the text when, as a result of the trial, she is submitted to an examination and is found to be *virgo intacta*. Her body and also Bellamy's corpse and then Lomax's body are subjected to the Law, to the surveillance of the rules that don't take into account the tropical world that glimmers behind the glasses. Her virginity is the final disproof of marriage, used by the court to demon-strate, ironically, the final proof of Lomax's guilt. The fortune that Bellamy wills to him had been made through colonial speculations; it is thus in a manner of speaking like the tomb that Carnavon entered. The fortune was tainted with em-pire, and Miss Whitaker's virgin body was "unconquered" by a male seducer, hid-ing in Ecuador or anywhere else. She told a lie that paradoxically revealed the truth underneath British law and propriety—better to be a seduced and "fallen" woman than a person who dares to put on "queer spectacles" and see the world in new ways. When Artivale tries on Lomax's spectacles, he doesn't like them, but says "By Jove, what a queer world! Every value altered!" He means that things look strange or queer with the spectacles on, and that their color alters the color "values" one ordinarily sees. Vita Sackville-West's wonderful story, however, contains a hidden meaning for this line. The "queer world" opened up is just the world as other eyes see it, a world whose values and meanings are diametrically opposed to the confident propriety of those who refuse to at least try to see things from another perspective. Nietzsche made a famous claim about philosophy and its search for truth—"truth is a woman!" he declared, meaning that philosophy was largely an attempt in words to see beyond the "veil" of female mystery, to conquer and control, to dictate values and propose absolute knowledge. There is none of that masculine truth, that singular white Civilization available in *Seducers in Ecuador*. Things break down, go queer, turn blue or amber or misty mauve. The female writer Vita Sackville-West casts a cold eye on British "truth" and offers up a new world through the lenses of her powerful and mordantly funny tale.

E. M. Forster
The Life to Come

E. M. Forster's literary writing has the same fidelity to subjective experience and the dawning of awareness. While Forster did not make the same experimental leaps in style that Woolf did, in order to convey the momentariness of consciousness and the elasticity of time, he nonetheless took "standard" Victorian plot lines and stretched them beyond recognition. In his novels the British social classes do not stay in their places, but converge and conflict, breaking ranks for love or sex or politics' sake. His many female protagonists are not content with marriage proposals or childbirth; he daringly makes one female main character an intellectual and—gasp—a German; he traces the erotic bonds of men across class lines; he takes his characters to places like Italy or India where their British propriety and timidity about life is subjected to rude shocks, which produce painful growth and even glimpses of happiness. Forster was like his fellow Bloomsburyites in being strongly critical of British empire and imperialism in general, and Forster didn't just speak this, he lived it. Venturing to Alexandria, Egypt as a Red Cross worker during World War I, and later on his many extended professional trips to India, he saw firsthand the execrable toll of imperialism, on those it dominated and on the dominating culture itself. The hypocrisy of the British Empire maintained that its mission in the colonies was a beneficent one—noble, just, kind, and imbued with the British sense of "fair play." Forster's writing, whether literary or critical, sniffed out these hypocrisies at home and abroad and challenged them. Like Virginia Woolf in *Three Guineas*, he judged that the hierarchy that elevated the British above their supposedly inferior subjects in the empire was the same one that denied rights to women, proscribed homosexuality, and kept the underclass in its place at home in Britain. His writing on India, then, with its sparkling, deft prose, joins his magical literary work in mounting a subtle but general critique of the social forces that have erected a false god: the white, male, upperclass, heterosexual, rugby-playing, cigar-smoking Briton as the supreme peak of humankind. Sir William Churchill brought the stereotype to life, yet transcended it in his command of the victorious World War II forces. Afterward, Britain repudiated Churchill despite the victory, voting in a Labour government. E. M. Forster's lifework predicted the transition in values, as Britain as a whole became just that much closer to Bloomsbury's ideal.

"The Life to Come" should make it clear to students that gender relations and their transformation also includes gender and sexuality, and the rupture of negative views of homosexuality. Forster died just as the Gay Liberation movement began, but his literary work throughout the century was an enormous intellectual and artistic contribution to a revisionary understanding of men, women, heterosexuality and homosexuality. Forster's story was among many of his explicit works that could not receive publication earlier in his life, when despite the sexual revolutions apparent in Joyce, Lawrence, and many other writers, overt homosexuality remained coded and secret, in part no doubt because the laws that sent Oscar Wilde to prison simply for "being" gay were still on the books.

The story explores its subject with quiet irony—that is, it argues indirectly that hatred of homosexual desire stems from the same hatred of Otherness that lies behind colonial racism, because it too operates out of a fear of finding the loathed quality of Otherness in oneself. Students may not get the tone at first reading, since the story is filtered through the self-deluding perspective of the missionary preacher who comes to this colonial outpost to convert the natives to Christianity, but finds himself struggling to control his own truest desires. The Reverend Paul is a naïve young man who does not at first see how much the Christian missionary project he pursues is linked to imperial control of the native population and their valuable land. In reality, the religious conversions he is directed to get for the British church are paving the way for British political control and economic penetration. The story exposes the ugly underside of what many supporters of empire liked to call its "civilizing mission." The mission to "civilize" is bogus both because the native culture and religion are perfectly civilized already, without white, British interference, and also because the church missionaries are just the thin edge of the wedge of colonial takeover. Read this story with Ngugi wa Thiong'o's account of his boyhood missionary education, for example. To imagine that one is civilizing people requires a racist notion that they are inferior savages; the story shows that this is the basis of the missionary intervention, but it backfires on the Reverend.

The Reverend never has enough enlightenment or self-awareness to admit to his own racism. Confident that the native chief Vithabi is inferior to him in every way, he is nonetheless instantly sexually drawn to him, and they become lovers without the Reverend ever naming their actions to himself. It is important to stress that what is morally flawed in the story is NOT the homosexual activity and indeed love between the missionary and the native chief, but instead the inability of the Reverend to acknowledge this love and the equality of his lover. Instead, he retreats from him in fear and self-loathing, and casts all his self-hatred into redoubled energy to convert these heathen inferiors. To admit that he is a gay man with desires for the chief would be to have the whole precarious construct of male superiority, colonial conquest, racism and sexism collapse.

The amazing ending or climax of the story is also an allegory of self-deception. The Reverend has settled for his closeted, self-hating life of missionary activity that largely serves to make the native community pliant and childlike. When Vithabi is dying, his fears recede a bit and he goes to try to get this man, his own former lover, to deny their past. This Vithabi will not do—in fact, in his religious universe, he wishes to free the Reverend from his bonds and to allow the two of them to unite after death in a return to the love they once shared. The Reverend finds himself in a last moment of shock and, one hopes, self-realization, the object of a "sacrifice"—but not a sacrifice on the altar of savage violence. The blade that comes down to kill him where he lies is a repetition of the sexual act that once promised to free the Reverend to see things differently—native peoples, his nation and church colluding in empire, and above all, himself. He didn't then, and lived a life of repressed conformity and actual destruction of the native culture. There is, then, an ironic kind of poetic justice in his death at Vithabi's hands, a poetic justice for what he has done to them but also to himself. "The Life to Come" plays on both senses of this phrase: in Christian terms, the "life to come" is heaven, and it is thought to be more important than life on earth, which is just its prelude. The life to come is equally important in Vithabi's theology, but it is a life that honors the genuine love expressed on earth. Finally, Forster's title, with its echoes of both sexual climax and religious resurrection, makes a political point, too. In the life to come on earth, perhaps there will not be such waste of love, solidarity, and community as has happened in the homophobic, racist and imperial society constructed so unwittingly by the poor Reverend Paul.

Rebecca West
Indissoluble Matrimony

Since the plot of Indissoluble Matrimony is set in motion by marital tensions caused by the women's suffrage movement, West's story can be taught fruitfully in conjunction with Virginia Woolf's famous text on women's rights, A Room of One's Own, as well as Emily Pankhurst's Address, included as a Companion Reading. West's story also raises many of the same issues as does Woolf's Mrs Dalloway; on the other hand, while many of the interpersonal tensions are similar to those raised in D. H. Lawrence's stories like The Horse-Dealer's Daughter, students will quickly see that these two authors have very different sympathies and loyalties in the battle of the sexes. The revulsion that George Silverton betrays for his wife's self-confident sexuality, for instance, is held up by West for ridicule; Lawrence's men feel this same revulsion, but we're invited to share, rather than criticize, it.

Katherine Mansfield
Daughters of the Late Colonel

One productive way of reading Mansfield's story is to contextualize it with Nietzsche's 1882 declaration, "God is dead." Daughter of the Late Colonel functions at least in part as an allegory: the daughters, like all twentieth-century citizens, find their "father," the "colonel"—the one from whom they had been used to taking orders, the one who imposed rules and a structure that made life meaningful and rewarding—suddenly dead. The story can thus be read as a parable of the loss of certainty, the loss of a "center" that Yeats laments in The Second Coming, that has seemed to many of the century's most prescient writers to characterize our age. The story is also reminiscent in its atmosphere of Henry James's haunting The Beast in *the Jungle*, as well as looking forward to Samuel Beckett's landmark drama of inactivity, *Waiting for Godot* (1953).

Jean Rhys
Mannequin

Jean Rhys is a fascinating writer in twentieth century British literature, in part because well before the "wave" of commonwealth reintegration she emigrated to England from her Caribbean birthplace. While Rhys was nominally "white," her life in the Caribbean marked her forever as a Creole in British eyes, an outsider who was suspicious as an Anglo-Caribbean with perhaps black blood in her family's past, as a woman who had an outspoken cultural affinity (explored wonderfully in her novels) with all things Caribbean, from the people to the landscape, and certainly as a woman making her own way in the world. Like the characters in her story, Rhys came to England with no money and no education, and worked as a model, a dancer, an "escort," a typist and so on, all while she avidly wrote the stories and novels that only in her old age were seen as the vital contributions to literature and women's writing they are.

Jean Rhys is most famous for her novel *Wide Sargasso Sea*, a book that rewrites *Jane Eyre* from the point of view not of Jane Eyre, shy governess, but of Bertha Mason, the Creole first wife of Rochester, the one who goes mad when taken back to England and who haunts the estate and finally burns down Rochester's English country house. For Charlotte Bronte this madwoman in the attic was simply that, a threat from outside, from the wild Sargasso Sea, a possibly black "savage" woman who keeps Rochester from all that is white, English, and good (namely, Jane herself). Rhys shifted the lens, an act that is characteristic of every writer in this Perspectives section. She demanded that new angles of vision, new sorts of narratives, and points of view once despised as Other for their gender, class or race come into literary voice.

"Mannequin" has the sour, understated quality of all Jean Rhys's prose. Students should be made aware that even its subject matter was considered outrageously risqué at its time—these are girls and women who are working, making money, and under their own control. That they are constantly subjected to male exploitation and violence is made evident, but that they have to live and do what it takes, despite so-called "morality," is paramount.

Mannequin is of course the French word for model, and Jean Rhys's story has a wonderful continental flavor. She shows that women on their own financially could hardly get adequate jobs in sexist England; there is consequently much circulating back and forth from France to England to the rest of Europe on the part of these restless girls. Happy endings—the typical fictions of marrying a rich man or finding true love—are shown up in Rhys's daring prose for what they are—fictions. She speaks through the voice of her heroine, Anna, who is as lost and desperate and strong as the other girls. The kind of social morality that would label her a "loose woman," a "slut" or prostitute, because she is a woman on her own, is exactly the logic *Pygmalion* puts on display and explodes. It is also clear that having sex for money is something these models have to do—and it differs only in degree from traditional marriage. "Mannequin" is a much quieter piece of work, but it too probes the gender inequality that makes the female point of view almost invisible culturally and literarily, too. Anna is struggling for a "room of her own," barely managing, and yet her desires, ideas, and inadequacies are never idealized or sentimentalized. That is perhaps the break-through of Jean Rhys's fiction: it refuses to sentimentalize women or men. The emphasis on clothes, costume, and self-fashioning we have seen from Shaw to Woolf to Churchill suffuses this story about fashion models, clothes, style, and gender. Models are "objectified" by the fashion industry and by male approval, yet modeling also permits Anna and the others to change their identities, and to have whatever freedom and creativity they can grab onto. A mannequin is in some senses a silent, effaced statue, something like the statue Galatea, who nonetheless came to life. There's no magical Pygmalion or Henry Higgins figure for most women, the story adds. Anna's life is both frozen and objectified by her mannequin staus, a wax doll, and yet her non-idealized woman's voice is also on display in Jean Rhys's subtle and bitter story.

Angela Carter

Angela Carter was a contemporary of the playwright Caryl Churchill, although Carter died in her early fifties and thus had her writing life cut short. She ends the Perspectives section because her fiction so wonderfully pursues the regendering theme; while Carter wrote in a postmodernist period, from the late 1960s until the 1990s, she was a self-declared feminist writer, exploring the gender divide and directing her work to its erasure. She self-consciously followed in Virgina Woolf's literary footsteps, not by writing like Woolf, but by placing gender questions at the heart of her work. Her story "The Heart of the Forest" is just such an excursion.

Angela Carter's mode of writing descended through Gothic foremothers—there is a large strain of Gothic plots and non-realist characters flowing in her stories especially. The Gothic has been known to be related to women from its inception, not only because many of the first Gothic novelists were women, but because the Gothic is pervaded with questions of the family and women's place in it, with reproduction, incest, and death. Carter's other main literary source came from fairy tales. She saw these tales as incredibly powerful in creating social scripts that people clung to subconsciously—Little Red Riding Hood, for example, may be dismissed as "merely" a fairy tale, but it is repeated so widely throughout the culture that rare is the woman who doesn't hear the refrain "beware the big bad wolf" when she sets out on independent adventures. Carter wanted to deconstruct fairy tales and generate new ones with a gender twist. Her fairy tales were so vivid that many were adapted for the screen; "The Company of Wolves" is the film made from her re-telling of "Little Red Riding Hood."

"The Heart of the Forest," then, is not a realist or naturalistic story, but an allegory and a fairy tale, another way, as morbid and sexy as Carter's work often was, to tell the story of origins. The forest is in some ways the Garden of Eden, for whose loss Eve's supposed curiosity and "weakness" has been made culturally responsible. Carter is having none of that. She makes her characters, the sister and brother pair, both versions of a fairy-tale like Hansel and Gretel, going into a menacing forest, and Adam and Eve. In the blender of her mordant, audacious wit, she seeks new patterns that are not gendered in old ways, to account for knowledge and power. Another influence on the story is Mozart's opera *The Magic Flute*; transformation and enchantment are also possibilities in this gender fable.

The story is a fable, a parable, and an allegory all at once. It compresses many of the narratives of knowledge or truth that have been told in literature and folklore for thousands of years. Carter brings in philosophers of the Enlightenment, for example, not by name but by allusion, as in calling her male character Emile. Emile was the title of a work by Jean-Jacques Rousseau, an exploration of education. In it, Rousseau claims that only men need education, and that the best education starts in early childhood with exposure to nature. Carter pokes holes in this paradigm—"nature" is rarely pure or even untouched by culture, and in fact Emile is learning what men have been taught for aeons. Carter's twist on the tale is to give the "fruit of the tree of knowledge" an incest motif. The story is not meant to be a shocking "real" description of brother/sister incest—it's an allegory of arriving at knowledge shared between men and women, where women are not the culprits. Take all the details of the story and consider them not as realist details, but as part of a fable that seeks to retell the education into truth. For Angela Carter, in the past "truth" has come at too high a price—whether by eliminating women altogether, blaming them, or ruining their adventures. Her incestuous pair go to the heart of the family and propose an androgynous solution to the mystery of what lies at the heart of the forest. Along the way, the power over nature and supposedly inferior beings, whether these are women or animals or native Others, is questioned. The mysterious ending leaves the allegory open—does there exist a way to tell the story anew? Can truth and knowledge be recognized in a egalitarian way? Carter's tale becomes an almost religious parable by its close—beckoning us into a forest we would rather avoid.

D. H. Lawrence

D. H. Lawrence's writing can still shock. The flavor of scandalous modernity surrounding his work makes him both an easy sell and a hard sell to students. Some may batten on the "bad boy" image his writing conveys, with its whiffs of class rage and its glamorous foreign settings; others may be incensed by his sexual and cultural politics, or at least by what may appear to be their flagrant political incorrectness. In either event it should be possible to prompt lively discussions on Lawrence's artistic methods, on his pivotal role in modernism, and on the lasting shock waves of his uncompromising art. There isn't a tame version of D. H. Lawrence to be had; his new readers need to be prepared for its invigorating outrage as much as its aesthetic power.

The *Anthology* includes all four facets of Lawrentian modernism: his poetry, his "travel writing," his fiction, the latter in the form of two short stories, "The Horse Dealer's Daughter" and "Odour of Chrysanthemums," and a snippet (in *Surgery for the Novel—Or a Bomb*) of his considerable and important critical writing. Even in his criticism Lawrence's voice is wild and untamed: works like his *Studies in Classic American Literature* or *Study of Thomas Hardy and Other Essays* might sound dry and scholarly, but are in fact as outrageous and idiosyncratic as Lawrence's fiction. Of the latter Lawrence wrote in a letter in 1914, just as he was starting the book: "Out of sheer rage I've begun my book on Thomas Hardy. It will be about anything but Thomas Hardy I am afraid—queer stuff—but not bad." "Sheer rage" was the motive for much of Lawrence's writing on every subject, as was his propensity to make his subjects "anything but" what they nominally appeared to be.

"I *don't* like little islands," Lawrence once wrote with typical spleen. He wasn't referring to England in that comment, but might as well have been, since the relatively small island of Great Britain was incapable of holding him. Among the modernists collected in the *Anthology* Lawrence is the sole world traveler: Joyce and Beckett lived in self-imposed exile in Europe, Auden took American citizenship, T. S. Eliot took British citizenship, but no one else traveled the globe as if they had been shot cannonball-fashion right out of their native land. Lawrence didn't live in England, but he didn't live anywhere else either, or not for long. His restlessness and peripatetic writing practice is important to stress to your students, if only so that they can identify with his search for places to become himself. Surely they will have sympathy with what Lawrence stated was his desire "only to *be*." The pilgrimages so many Westerners now make to Nepal or the Ganges, for example, the treks to Macchu Picchu or Tibet, the interest in Eastern religions and in spiritual guides like Carlos Castaneda, have a serious counterpart in Lawrence's searching art. Lawrence was modernism's rolling stone: his special places were Italy, specifically Sicily and Sardinia (he was called by the Italian name *Lorenzo*), Greece, Australia, Mexico, New Mexico, and a host of other ports of call. He wrote: "One can no longer say: I'm a stranger everywhere, only 'everywhere I'm at home.'" To emphasize the rootlessness of much of Lawrence's life underscores something special about his literary art—it moves rapidly and even dangerously across the landscape of English literature. The first sentence of Lawrence's *Sea and Sardinia* is "Comes over one an absolute desire to move." The subject of Lawrence's writing is to trace the movements of desire wherever they may lead.

The center of his circle of wanderings was Eastwood, his birthplace, a grim mining town in Nottingham, England. The pervasive ugliness of life there—ugliness in a spiritual sense as well as in the physical surroundings of poverty and grim, grueling labor—injected Lawrence with his life-long rage, as it did with his understanding of beauty. People condemned to such lives as his parents and relatives hungered for beauty, even when they couldn't afford it or didn't understand it. The unplayed piano sitting in many working-class parlors was a mute symbol of this longing, a longing which had brought Lawrence's own art into being. "What was the piano but a blind reaching out for beauty?" he asked. The point of this reference makes clear that beauty and art were not, for Lawrence, simply the luxurious icing on the cake of life: they were part of a life and death struggle in which art and beauty *were* life; a struggle most people, through no fault of their own, were going to lose. Lawrence's anger makes more sense when it is seen as the flash point of creation.

The first poem included in the *Anthology* is *The Piano*, and when read in light of Lawrence's comments on his home life, the picture of a small boy positioned beneath the piano is far more than an endearing childhood memory. The poem speaks of "the old Sunday evenings at home, with winter outside," and of "the hymns in the cosy parlour, the tinkling piano our guide." If students imagine a pampered middle or upper class parlor where a family is gathering, they need to think again. Only on Sunday is there time for the piano, since every other day is a working day; on Sundays the only music permitted is hymns. The power of those hymns played on the parlor piano by "the mother who smiles as she sings" is not merely religious. The intensity of the poem rests on how special and rare the music was in the life of its narrator and his family; the instrument of the music, that is, the piano itself, provides a refuge from the everyday that is also highly charged with desire: the small boy hidden underneath it is in intimate contact with his mother as he presses her "small, poised feet" on the pedals. The rich delight of their intimacy melds with the infusion of music and song: mother and son share a moment out of time—out of the daily grind of time, that is—transfigured by the homely art of her music-making. The poem refers to "the glamour of childish days is upon me" not because, as students may think, those childhood surroundings were glamorous or wealthy. "Glamour" means the power of fairies to cast a spell; in other words, the potent memory of those days casts its spell of reverie over the narrator, who is locked in the enchantment of memory, impervious to the singer who has now "burst into clamour with the great black piano appassionato." The rhyming of "clamour" and "glamour" is inspired—literally. Clamourous, loud music is transmuted into the spirit of past days as if by fairy magic. The "flood of remembrance" he experiences is as passionate, if not infinitely more so, than the musical marking of the unheard, if clamorous, score being sung in the present. The sensual and even ejaculatory "flood" of memories casts down the narrator's "manhood" in several senses—he no longer is conscious of his present age and maturity, since the past of his boyhood has him in its spell; his adult sexuality is overmastered by the pull of the past, so that he is not aroused by the passionate singer but wholly present in a memory of his mother's warmth and closeness. The closing line continues the ambiguity: "I weep like a child for the past" suggests that, like a child unashamed of its tears, he weeps for what is now gone, but also that he weeps as a child does for what is past in its short life. The confusion is intentional—the poem suggests that we can't sort out the present from the past, nor resist the past's "glamour."

Thomas Hardy's poetry is the best comparison to Lawrence's in general, not only because Lawrence considered Hardy his master in both poetry and prose, but also because the differences between these two past-worshipping, memory-obsessed poets is so striking. Hardy's poetry doesn't dissolve the thin membrane between present and past. For Lawrence, it is porous, because the man of the poem is really no more than the exalted child under the piano, forever banished now from his mother's skirts and the pure sway of her music, weeping for the comfort and wholeness he has lost. Hardy like Lawrence was a self-educated artist; Hardy like Lawrence was "rescued" by his mother when she recognized his intelligence and got him placed in school, instead of sent out at an early age to labor. Both owed their literary art to the prescience of their mothers and to the maternal bond; only Lawrence is willing to so explicitly sexualize that all-important tie to the mother. His poem moves into a past where a socially deprived mother and son create a self-sufficient world unto themselves in and through a piano, a symbol of both art and desire. The piano (as an extension of the mother's music) both "mans" and "unmans" the narrator simultaneously. Formal similarities are just as important between these two poets. Show students how much Lawrence accomplishes within the four-line stanza format; spend time looking at the rhymes he makes out of the homely vocabulary of simple language. This poem and Lawrence's others have the same fidelity to form and to rhyme that Hardy's perhaps grander poems do; Lawrence is willing to emphasize the singing voice in his poetry, as was Hardy, but less willing than Hardy to bring abstractions and complex references into the poems. What he does include in the "insidious mastery of song" that "betrays him back" is direct reference to desire, to sexuality, and to rage. For example, the title of the poem *Tortoise Shout* refers mind-bogglingly to the male tortoise's cry of orgasm. The "tortoise in extremis" is a symbol of the power of sex to "crucify" us: the round wholeness of a tortoise shell deceptively hides its reliance on another being—a female tortoise—for completion and wholeness. Yet the moment of completion and union is far from serene or fulfilling—the tortoise's cry at their moment of consummation is reminiscent of Christ's agony on the cross, because it manifests the terror of separateness at the heart of our being. Lawrence boldly juxtaposes the natural world (turtles) with transcendent myth (Christ on the cross) to hint at the human state. No more than tortoises are humans able to be complete and whole in and of themselves. Sexuality is necessary, but it is a form of "crucifixion," in that humans are left hanging (the horrible pun is inevitable) in their desire for one another. "Sex" is at the heart of the mystery of human existence, in this poem as in Lawrence's work as a whole, not because of any focus on the sexual act or on sexual pleasure for its own sake. Lawrence deplored sexual hedonism—he wrote about his relationship to his wife Frieda that "Fidelity to oneself means fidelity single and unchanging, to one other one." No, sex is metaphysical, going beyond the physical to the spirit: it "breaks us into voice." In other words, sexuality is at the core of our being, and giving voice to ourselves, like the tortoise's shout, is a painful yet triumphant shout. Sex is the empowering ground of our being, but it is also always godforsaken—we can never be complete within ourselves, and will always long and yearn for a completion by another that never arrives. The darkness of this view returns in *Snake*, whose narrator confronts an ominous snake come to drink at his water-trough. Debating internally whether to kill the snake, yet drawn by its majesty—"he seemed like a king to me"—the narrator clumsily throws a log at it, and the snake retreats, leaving the poem's speaker guilty of "a pettiness" he longs "to expiate." The pettiness lies in his fear of the snake and his need to get rid of it; the snake itself, like a "dark king of the underworld," is that part or principle of life we fail to honor and confront at the peril of our own petty natures.

"Cypresses" is a good example of Lawrence's "primitivism"—his romantic fascination with premodern peoples and cultures. In his essay "Indians and an Englishman," for instance, Lawrence writes: "I don't want to live again the tribal mysteries my blood has lived long since. I don't want to know as I have known, in the tribal exclusiveness. But every drop of me trembles still alive to the old sound, every thread in my body quivers to the frenzy of the old mystery. I know my derivation. I was born of no virgin, of no Holy Ghost. Ah, no, these old men telling the tribal tale were my fathers. I have a dark-faced, bronze-voiced father far back in the resinous ages. My mother was no virgin. She lay in her hour with this dusky-lipped tribe-father. And I have not forgotten him." Cypresses are, among other things, famous for their longevity; healthy trees can live as long as a thousand years. Lawrence imaginatively stretches this life-span even further, and imagines that the trees he views were looking on during various classical scenes, including the suppression of the "primitive" Etruscans by the civilizing Romans. Lawrence's fascination with the primitive can be fruitfully compared to Conrad's, as can his belief that we "civilized" people have to some degree lost the ability to comprehend the primitive, to decipher its secret language: "Is there a great secret? / Are our words no good?"

Bavarian Gentians is perhaps a poem about following the snake, dangerous as it might be, into that underground, the realm where art gets made. Lawrence rewrites the myth of Persephone in this short poem. Persephone's mandatory stay underground with the lord of Death is usually thought to be the tragic part of her narrative; the happy and fruitful part of the cycle occurs when she emerges each spring into the light and into her mother's arms. Lawrence suggests that creation, like sex, partakes inevitably of the dark side. He proposes that the flowering blooms of poetry—of literary art—owe as much to the workings of death and to what is unseen or unconscious in our natures, as creative art does to the illumination of conscious awareness.

Lawrence's "The Horse Dealer's Daughter" makes an interesting companion piece to Katherine Mansfield's "Daughters of the Late Colonel"; Lawrence and Mansfield were friends, and both stories deal with the coping strategies of young women who suddenly find themselves in radically altered family circumstances. If Mabel's strategy in this story is a desperate one, it is at least a strategy—something the sisters in Mansfield's story can't seem to muster for the life of them. Then too, the dramatic climax of the story, when Mabel is rescued from a rather banal drowning by the young doctor Fergusson is just one of many memorable scenes in Lawrence's writing in which women, water, and sexuality are woven together in provocative ways. For another, less happy incident, you may want to screen the "Water-Party" scene from Ken Russell's film adaptation of Women in Love—in which a newly wed bride helplessly pulls her groom down while he's trying to save her from drowning. In both instances, a woman's love—or is it lust?—is the undoing, the "drowning," of an innocent man.

"Odour of Chrysanthemums" is perhaps Lawrence's best-known short story, and is as well one of his most unsettling. One of Lawrence's famous laws for readers of fiction is "Trust the tale; don't trust the teller." But "Odour," strangely enough, is precisely the kind of story in which the "teller" (the story's narrator) and the "tale" (the plot-level events) are at loggerheads. For while the history of Walter and Elizabeth suggests she's more sinned against than sinning, by the end of the story Lawrence has turned Walt into a sinless lamb of God without blemish—a very obvious Christ figure. It will be useful to have students explore their shifting responses to Elizabeth as the storyline unfolds, and to think through the fictive methods by which Lawrence attempts to win us to Walt's side in this battle of the sexes.

P. G. Wodehouse
Strychnine in the Soup

The exuberant dialogue and witty narration of this story recall the work of Oscar Wilde; like Wilde's plays, *Strychnine in the Soup* functions primarily as a light-hearted social satire, and comically makes the point that in the modern world, it is the thinkers (and artists) rather than the women and men of action, who have ascendancy. Indeed, there is a kind of reverse Darwinism at work in the story's plot: for it is not the strong who survive and triumph, but instead our pipsqueak protagonist, who exploits Lady Bassett's weakness for popular fiction to his own ends.

Graham Greene
A Chance for Mr Lever

The theme of Greene's *A Chance for Mr Lever*—or one of its themes—is again the British imperial exploitation of remote areas of the globe; the story resembles Conrad's *Heart of Darkness* in important ways. The story presents no unusual difficulties for students until its strange closing paragraph, which probably merits some discussion; the irony of the story's closing rivals the bitter cosmic irony of some of Hardy's best poems.

PERSPECTIVES

World War II and the End of Empire
Sir Winston Churchill
Blood, Toil, Tears and Sweat (May 13, 1940)

This first major speech of Churchill's teaches us a great deal about what made him such a powerful and charismatic leader during the darkest days of World War II. The speech contains a number of features you may wish to discuss with your students. Most prominent, perhaps, is the way he urges the serious nature of the engagement to come: it is a "crisis," promises to be "one of the greatest battles in history," perhaps "an ordeal of the most grievous kind." In the face of this great challenge, Churchill both counsels and exemplifies "buoyancy and hope." The final paragraph emphasizes especially the threat not just to the nation, but to the British Empire—an entity which of course will survive the war only in part, and much weakened.

Reading a speech is rather like reading a play: while the most powerful oratory remains powerful in transcription, it was created as a performance, and is most fully appreciated in performance. We have included excerpts from this and another great speech by Churchill on our audio CD.

Wars Are Not Won By Evacuations (June 4, 1940)

This speech provides an opportunity, if one be desired, to connect back to the materials in the perspectives section "The Great War: Confronting the Modern"; for what Churchill is engaging in here is, in the very best sense of the word, *propaganda*, discussed by T. E. Lawrence in *The Seven Pillars of Wisdom* (and which will be one of the objects of Orwell's scrutiny in *Politics and the English Language*, below). Students might be asked to compile a list of the terms and phrases used to describe the German people, the German army, and Hitler; they are, not surprisingly, highly-charged, emotionally evocative descriptions playing on longstanding stereotypes of the Germans. The suggested power of language and of names is implied even in the name of the newest British fighter plane, which Churchill proudly announces will be called the Defiant.

When it comes to recounting episodes of British valor in combat, Churchill proves himself a masterful storyteller. The various engagements of the British Expeditionary Force are told with an air of great suspense; and the fact that, in Churchill's telling, these stories all have a more or less happy ending helps to reinforce the idea that Great Britain is God's favored combatant (a notion that language like "a miracle of deliverance" makes quite explicit). The quotation from Tennyson calls our attention to the ways that Churchill employs British literature and mythology in order to assert the nation's preeminence in the current conflict; in the manner of Tennyson in *The Charge of the Light Brigade*, perhaps, or in some of Kipling's nationalistic writing, Churchill combines reportage with legend, history with mythmaking. A keen student of history, Churchill realized that history is made, not simply recorded, and must have recognized as well that his simple chronicles of the British military experience in World War II will set the model for subsequent writing about the war. Furthermore, while his immediate audience is the members of the House of Commons, more importantly (through the press) Churchill is talking to, reassuring and calming the fears of, the British people; and the down-home storytelling style that he adopts ("I will tell you about it"), reminiscent of FDR's fireside chats, is clearly better-suited to the populace than members of Parliament. More importantly, perhaps, it is, because of Churchill's unabashed narrative bent and his gift for the memorable phrase, language that history has remembered.

Part of what that powerful language was able to accomplish, of course, was the kind of internal exile of "enemy aliens and suspicious characters of other nationalities" that Churchill advises toward the end of the address. American students may better understand what is being proposed here (in a rather understated way) by reference to the internment of Japanese-Americans in this country after the bombing of Pearl Harbor, as well as (in his comments about "Fifth Column activities" and a "malignancy in our midst") an obvious similarity to the Communist "witch hunts" of the 1950s led by Senator Joe McCarthy.

Stephen Spender
Icarus

The poem in some ways plays a trick on readers' expectations; only when we arrive at the final couplet do we realize that Icarus has been the vehicle, and not the tenor, of the poem's controlling metaphor, and the subject of the poem, who is compared to Icarus, remains unnamed. It was a subject which also proved attractive to Auden, whose later *Musée des Beaux Arts* (1938) approaches the myth rather differently, and makes an interesting comparison. The American poet William Carlos Williams also has an Icarus poem, which can be pulled in to make a triptych, and provoke a discussion on the role of the Icarus myth in modern poetry. One might argue, for instance, that Icarus plays the part in the modern imagination that Prometheus played for the Romantics; in this way, a link could be forged to both Shelley's *Prometheus Unbound* and Byron's *Prometheus*, as well as more generally to the figure of the Byronic hero. Indeed, if one is willing to make a stretch, Icarus in these poems becomes a type of Lucifer, whose pride goeth before his fall; Stephen Dedalus makes this linkage explicit in Joyce's *A Portrait of the Artist as a Young Man*, and a number of pertinent texts are included in the "*Frankenstein* and Its Time" cluster. The Spender and Auden poems, then, can be used as a kind of case study in the modernist mythical method.

What I Expected

The poem expresses quite effectively the disillusionment felt so poignantly by so many during the years leading up to World War II. The poem can be opened up for students by posing one simple question: what led the speaker to expect "thunder, lightning," and all the rest? What is the paradigm, or ideology, that seems to be coming apart in the face of the '30s?

The Express, The Pylons

These two poems, together, suggest Spender's complex and somewhat contradictory attitude toward what might broadly be called "modernization." In *The Express*, the powerful train is an object of worship; she is mysterious, powerful—almost a "great black god" in a world without god. The poem's closing verse sentence goes so far as to invert the Romantic valuation of nature over culture, arguing instead that nature can never equal her beauty. In *The Pylons*, however, the ugly concrete pillars used to suspend electrical or telephone lines throughout rural England are "giant girls that have no secret"; they clearly represent the wave of the future, "so tall with prophecy," and yet they retain no mystery, and are anything but beautiful: more like a scar on the natural beauty of the land.

Elizabeth Bowen
Mysterious Kôr

Mysterious Kôr is a mysterious story—mysterious in the sense that it acknowledges that there is something ineffable, not accessible to logical analysis, at the core of all human relationships. The foci of the story are two, and both are of historical, cultural, and literary interest: the position of two single, working women in London during the war; and, more generally, the strange inversions and privations of life during wartime. Pepita and Arthur—Pepita most especially—walk through the moonlit, war-ravaged landscape of London like automatons, seemingly bereft of their life scripts, and separated from their instinctual reactions and behaviors by the new rules imposed by the war.

The story's opening paragraphs quite graphically demonstrate the ways in which wartime realities have usurped the natural rhythms of life: the moonlight of the story's opening sentence "drenche[s] the city and searche[s] it," like an enormous, infinitely bright searchlight; in the second paragraph, the clouds metamorphose into "opaque balloons"—seemingly the zeppelins introduced by the Germans during World War I. And the military atmosphere takes over not just the natural, but the human, environment; Pepita and Arthur, attempting to complete a romantic stroll through the city as though nothing had changed since their courtship began (before the war), suddenly "faced round to look back the way they had come . . . as though a command from the street behind them had been received by their synchronized bodies."

The story does make use of the mythical method, after a fashion; the difference is that the "myth" that Pepita, and Bowen, exploit is not an ancient one, but instead part of the plot of H. Rider Haggard's extremely popular adventure story *She* (1887). Teachers may want to reproduce the short passages describing Kôr from the novel, or perhaps show a short scene or two from the 1965 film *She*, starring Ursula Andress. A couple of suggestions: the "shell shock" that Bowen witnessed first-hand during World War I seems to become in this story a moral condition; even the women who remain at home during World War II seem to be suffering from a kind of shell shock (or Pepita, at least; Connie, by contrast, is an old-fashioned sort of woman, who seemingly doesn't let any of the spiritual malaise touch her). In what ways might "going to Kôr" be like the psychological retreat that shell-shock victims make? The story also demonstrates to some degree the ways in which the power relations between the sexes have been changed by the wartime economy.

Evelyn Waugh
Cruise

Two of the stories in this cluster of short fiction of the '30s—those by Waugh and Wodehouse, as well as the Monty Python sketch—are intended to remind students of an aspect of British writing that is too often lost in scholarly anthologies: there's a lot of tremendously funny British writing. Indeed, many of the students in lower-division literature courses, especially students with majors outside the humanities, will have had as their first exposure to British literature the likes of Monty Python, Benny Hill, Fawlty Towers, and other British comedies (not to mention the music of the British Invasion and beyond).

Waugh's *Cruise* is a wonderfully lighthearted satire on the self-satisfied stupidity of some members of the privileged classes. Our postcard writer is a culture vulture of the worst kind; she wanders from port to port taking in whatever Daddy's money is sufficient to buy, without letting anything that she sees change her: indeed, she seems primarily interested in a shipboard romance (as, in fairness, do the rest of the members of her party). The story helps to suggest that the ugly Brit is every bit as potent a stereotype as the ugly American.

It is also possible to do a darker reading of the story, however. The boorishness of our correspondent and her family parallels, in important ways, the brutal insensitivity of British imperialism as it lingers into the 1930s, '40s, and '50s; the cruise ship sails through the Suez Canal, a largely British project completed in 1854 and paid for by 120,000 Egyptians who died in forced labor while digging the canal. In Waugh's story, the British penchant for travel and travel writing merges almost imperceptibly into the imperial quest for land; our postcard writer seems to be master of all she surveys—and a wholly incompetent, and disengaged, master. In her postcards, all the lands she visits are reduced to the stereotypes convenient to hand: "This is a photograph of the Holyland and the famous sea of Gallillee." Indeed, all the foreign lands, and their peoples, are reduced precisely to postcards: the leisure class's equivalent of colonial possession.

COMPANION READING
Monty Python: "Travel Agent"

The connection between the Waugh story and the Monty Python sketch should be readily apparent; the tourist in the sketch wants to go on holiday not to learn about places and people different from himself, but to have his prejudices confirmed, and to taste the comforts of home however far from home he might be; Great Britain seems to have devolved from the empire on which the sun never sets to a seemingly endless string of Watney's Red Barrel franchises. Comic actor Eric Idle puts in a virtuoso performance as the tourist, Mr. Smoke-Too-Much; it can be heard on a few different Monty Python compilation recordings, and (even better) seen on volume 3 of the *Monty Python's Flying Circus* videotape collection (Paramount Home Video 12545).

The Man Who Liked Dickens

The first connection to make with this story is its pretty explicit parallel to *Heart of Darkness*. For while its setting is South America rather than Africa, "The Man Who Liked Dickens" explores life in one of the unexplored areas of the world map, a "white space," in which the invading white man is king. In place of Kurtz we find Mr. McMaster, whose name means, fittingly, "son of the master"; and the story's opening pages, when McMaster nurses Henty back to health, turn the narrative of *Heart of Darkness* on its head. McMaster's rather improbable Dickens library, in the heart of the primeval Brazilian forest, is an oasis of "civilization" in the midst of "barbarism"—not unlike the hut of the accountant Marlow meets at the middle station in *Heart of Darkness*. In this story McMaster, who believes in no god, believes instead in Dickens: the narratives of Dickens's novels become a vicarious form of (quintessentially British) life in this alien environment. That McMaster can treat Henty with such complete barbarity—as, apparently, he has treated his previous "reader," Barnabas Washington—ironically gives the lie to the notion that reading the Great Books improves one's moral character. In *Apocalypse Now*, Francis Ford Coppola's re-telling of *Heart of Darkness*, his Kurtz (Marlon Brando) reads T. S. Eliot's poetry while carrying out genocide; McMaster, in "The Man Who Liked Dickens," is likewise representative of the British imperial mind-set, disguising his selfish designs behind a façade of British "culture."

Evelyn Waugh's first wife was named Evelyn; she also happened to be the daugh-ter of Lord Carnarvon, the man who discovered King Tut's tomb. Through this close association and many others, such as his own journalistic jobs around the world, Waugh was connected to the map of otherness I have contended is such an integral part of modernism. Although Waugh upheld the traditional virtues, as he saw them, of Western culture, he was always "ready to be startled" by the spectacle of barbarism wherever he found it, and he spent much of his time going places in order to glimpse that spectacle, looking for examples of man's disregard of civilized society. Believing barbarism was " a dog to be stalked with a pinch of salt," he " went to the wild lands where man had deserted his post and the jungle was creeping back to its old strongholds." It was in "distant and barbarous" places that his literary sense came alive, " at the borderlands of conflicting cultures and states of develop-ment, where ideas, uprooted from their traditions, became oddly changed in trans-plantation." He stalked this division of savagery and civilization in Abyssinia, in Kenya and in Brazil, as well as in England; he later felt he had found its epitome in California, in Forest Lawn cemetery and the celluloid castle of Hollywood. "The Man Who Liked Dickens" is set at that razor's edge between savagery and civiliza-tion, its modernism in dialogue with both Joyce and Woolf, and with its recreation of Conrad, its own quite obvious undertaking of a journey to the heart of darkness. Especially, I want to read the impulses that set this text on the track of the wilder-ness, and to explore the satiric modernism which is at its heart.

In quite different ways, and at the risk of simplifying, Conrad, Joyce, Lawrence and Woolf are preoccupied with the excess of rationality or the deadness of intel-lectuality which had left Western European culture without spontaneity, the will drained. In each there is an attempt to suggest a route to immediate experience, to a realm of sensation and depth that is figured as sexuality, or the unconscious of writing, or the loosening of the bonds of rational thought and convention. In Waugh's work, the analysis is different— it is the inability to sustain a dialect be-tween reason and will which has led to the stalemate of modern culture, the divi-sion between mindless action and an enfeebled reflection tied to a nostalgia for what is past. The gusto with which the "savage" comes to infiltrate Waugh's work is on the one hand a diagnosis of a problem in modern society and on the other a leaning toward that which isn't accomodated in his system.

Waugh referred to himself once as a "pure aesthete," and despite his later de-nunciations of modernist art his own quicksilver narratives are purely in the mod-ernist vein, with their poised artificiality, their utterly withdrawn narrator, their dizzying changes of scene, and, as in Lawrence, the absence of any "stable ego of character." Waugh's text makes a flat canvas across which these figures are drawn, taking up the glossy linguistic artificiality of Ronald Firbank, camp novelist extraordinaire. While Waugh wants to avoid what he felt to be modernism's perilous Scylla and Charybdis of the overly abstract and the ludicrously mimetic, there is never any return to traditional narrative style, to "realistic" characters, to narratorial commentary. And the major influence on the technique of his story is without doubt the cinema. His primary charge against modernist aesthetics, and in particular the work of Woolf and Joyce, was that it was overly subjective, and one can see how ruthlessly the subjective is scooped out in favor of the energy of satire, which can propose another underlying assessment of the matter at hand. Woolf and Waugh begin writing from exacxtly the same premise: the nineteenth century novel has died. Woolf's response to this knowledge is to move inward, to what she calls for in this passage: "Examine for a moment an ordinary mind on an ordinary day. The mind receives a myriad of impressions—trivial, fantastic, evanescent, or engraved with the sharpness of steel. From all sides they come, an incessant shower of innumerable atoms . . ."

"For moderns, " she also says, " the point of interest lies very likely in the dark places of psychology." Their subject, one could say, was the self at the very moments where, by accident or by design, it eludes the conventions of society. The mind has no access to objective truth, and what can be charted are the moments of subjective longing, of desire transfigured in language. Waugh just as scrupulously avoids the fiction of the "complete" or rounded personality of 19th century fiction, and despises the 19th century novel for its sentimentality and the worn-out furniture of realism. Waugh's modernist technique is stripped away from an ideology of modernism, and deployed for other purposes; it uses scattershot scenes, a lack of realist detail and an absence of transitions, implausible characters who are linguistic costumes more than anything else, to mount a diagnosis of the conditions of modern life. An algebra of fiction, in Waugh's words. One of the chief concerns or problems for modernist writers was the lack of a belief that their world was intelligible or coherent, that it could be written about. Woolf's response to this, for example, was to privilege the subjective moment of consciousness, not for its coherence or for its ultimate truth, but as the evanescent register of consciousness. Waugh avoids any register of consciousness; with a surreal narration, a counterpointing of innumerable tiny scenes, paper-thin characters and the dissolving of any claims of verisimilitude, Waugh pitilessly looks on at the world. Woolf had urged, in a classic passage on the character Mrs Brown in the fiction of the Victorian novelist Arnold Bennett that this fictional character should be released from realist fiction by a smashing and crashing of the furniture of the novel; in Waugh's fiction the houses are falling left and right, among them Hetton in A Handful of Dust. The fictional Mrs Brown also dissolves and fades into "the kaleidoscope of dimly discerned faces" which made up, for Waugh, the truth of the modernist age.

Tony is, in a sense, deserting his post, refusing to confront the savagery at the heart of British life and instead vanishing into the outposts of another world, eager to put the present behind him. "The seemingly-solid, patiently built, gorgeously ornamented structure of Western life was to melt overnight like an ice castle, leaving only a puddle of mud." The aimlessness and restless movement of the modern world that made a concerted, heroic effort seem impossible was also, clearly, favored by an economic system that is run for the circulation and accumulation of ever more commodities, goods and sensations, and the world of Waugh's characters is an unceasing round of the dictates of such an economic system, with parties and movies and redecorating and airplane rides and frenzied travel for the sake of it. For those who want to resist this, it is imperative that they not pursue an idealized and outmoded notion of Western culture, as Tony does; such an idealization causes petrifaction, it removes the possibility of actually resisting conditions and tends to turn these figures into completely disaffected and thus ineffectual wanderers. Without conviction, such characters can only be doomed, as is Tony, to the assaults of modernity.

The story's very construction is cinematic. Take in particular the use of montage—the sudden juxtaposition of utterly different scenes which is a primary technique of film, so that we can "go" from viewing one scene unfolding to seeing something else that is happening elsewhere at an adjacent or the same time. In Conrad's *Heart of Darkness* the voyage is ironized by the words Marlow uses to recount it; the irony is provided by these sudden cross-cuttings which undermine the stability of place or time and rocket the reader back and forth between these spaces with the greatest alacrity. Scenes are spliced together with associational rather than linear logic, and with radical editing as a trope of modern life. The discontinuity and unreality of such life was virtually cinematic, for Waugh.

Film is ideally suited to the relativist, satirical sensibility, capable of suggesting the shifting, fluid perspectives of a world without any fixed center and periphery, actually or in ethical terms.

The relation of film to primitivism was also a direct one for Waugh; the text shows that modern technocracy unwittingly promotes the reversion to a barbarous sensibility, which for Waugh is characterized, quite unanthropologically, as an immersion in the here and now incapable of perspective, distance and civilized thought through time. Film fascinates at least in part because it seems to subvert those very structures, and thus is also linked with a primitivism of sorts. Europe can't keep its pretense at civilization.

Waugh's primitivism was unsound and ethnocentric, to be sure, but it is also mythical, not a real assessment of other cultures, since what preoccupied Waugh was the condition of the west, which he can't, however, depict without invoking all these other places, and putting them into counterpoint.

Waugh's take on the question of subject and object can be compared to Woolfs—in Woolf's work, the two come ever closer and closer, so that the object is penetrated by subjectivity and becomes an expression of it. Waugh holds these resolutely separate, and in fact uses his figurative language, the use of similes, to do so—his similes, in contrast to Woolf's, are classical ones, intended to keep compartments between subject and object, rather than figuratively blurring them

The riveting closing of "The Man who Liked Dickens" puts that juxtaposition of the savage and shows that Tony's fate is to be evicted from time. When last seen, he has just awoken from two days of drugged sleep, having missed the search party of Englishmen who have come looking for him by Mr. Todd's clever ruse; his watch is also gone, given to those same men as proof, along with the wooden cross, that he has actually died. The search party returns to England where Tony is declared officially dead, and Tony becomes the permanent captive of Mr. Todd, who will keep him to read and reread the works of Dickens to him endlessly. Tony is trapped in one of the barbarous borderlands of the 20th century, between the menace of an illiterate madman who has a sentimental attachment to Dickens. Mechanized speed and the manipulation of goods for profit—this text is absorbed in these forces as thoroughly as Woolf or Lawrence's are. Last's final fate is that of Western society—the eye held hostage to the ear, a civilized man trapped because he can read, not by primitive so-called savages, but by a barbarous man who is backed up by the technology of a gun. History is annulled, time and tradition swept away.

Tony has vanished into the far away, living the life of a Dickens novel.

George Orwell
Politics and the English Language

Like *Inside the Whale*, Orwell's *Politics* essay is at its most effective as a critique of what Orwell called "group think" in *1984*: the ways that party-line thinking results in foolish writing—which, in turn, reinforces foolish thinking. The argument Orwell makes here—especially the stylistic foibles that he catalogs in the middle of the essay—make up the backbone of Richard Lanham's famous composition textbook, *Revising Prose*; and it's not difficult to see how Orwell's prescriptions here could be used as a sort of abbreviated *Strunk and White*.

An interesting exercise is to turn back a few pages and see how well Orwell's diagnosis of political language serves to describe the speeches of Winston Churchill—or going back further, those of Perse, Parnell, and Collins. Students are likely to conclude that the speeches anthologized here are memorable because they largely avoid the solecisms Orwell outlines.

If the teacher is interested in suggesting the points where Orwell's argument is vulnerable, this can be done inductively by having students think for a minute about the word "extramarital," which Orwell singles out as one of his examples of "pretentious diction." What he has in mind, apparently, is that the good old-fashioned English word "adulterous" will do just as well; if it was good enough for Chaucer, it ought to be good enough for us. One might argue, though, that there are good reasons for a new formation like "extramarital": "adulterous" cannot help but carry connotations of Biblical morality along with it, whereas a new formation like "extramarital" is, at least for a time, free from such associations. In other words: "adultery" is, literally, a sin; but an "extramarital" affair is simply one which takes place outside the bounds of marriage—and its morality would be left up to others to decide; it is surely a more objective, less evaluative term. Similarly, students of literature who have spent a good portion of the term reading British poetry and prose of the early nineteen century may well want to argue that words like "romantic," "sentimental," and "natural" have important philosophical meanings, though Orwell writes them off as "meaningless words."

Shooting an Elephant

Orwell's brief essay is a classic exploration of the perverse logics of imperialism and colonial domination—and, Orwell's particular interest in this piece, the ways that neither colonizer nor colonized is entirely free in this most unnatural of civil arrangements. What is perhaps most remarkable is the complete honesty of the writing: Orwell is willing to reveal his own racism ("sneering yellow faces") and the vanity which values saving face over the preservation of animal, and even human, life ("I was very glad that the coolie had been killed; it put me legally in the right"). Orwell is able to write with such disarming honesty about his role as an enforcer of empire because he understands the situation structurally: he recognizes that he is part of an evil system, and that his possible responses are tightly proscribed by his circumstances. Orwell's awareness—"I had already made up my mind that imperialism was an evil thing and the sooner I chucked up my job and got out of it the better"—might be fruitfully compared with the attitude of Marlow in *Heart of Darkness*, who also got a look at "the dirty work of Empire at close quarters."

Salman Rushdie
Christopher Columbus. . . .

In "Christopher Columbus," Salman Rushdie employs a fictional technique much in evidence in postmodern writing: he reanimates the historical record with a farcical fictional imagination, and succeeds at the same time in exploring the power struggles evident in the *un*-colonial enterprise of the Western imagination, Columbus's "discovery" of America. The story is comprised in part of the question-and-answer pattern characteristic of the religious catechism; James Joyce, perhaps the most important influence on Rushdie's writing, was the first to bend the catechism to fictional ends, in the penultimate chapter of *Ulysses*, the "Ithaca" chapter. (One might also hear a faint echo of the famous ending of Joyce's famous novel—"yes I said yes I will Yes"—in the close of Rushdie's story, in words spoken by Columbus: "'Yes,' he tells the heralds. *Yes. I'll come.*" Thus, in Rushdie's twisted version of imperial history, Columbus must "come" (as Molly Bloom may indeed "come" at the end of *Ulysses*) before he can go; sexual consummation prefigures imperial consummation. Among other things, Rushdie's story makes the point that even the great knight of empire Columbus was a foreigner, an outsider, in Isabella's court.

Dylan Thomas

Dylan Thomas's poetry usually appeals immediately to its first-time readers; its lyric intensity and its musical rhythms galvanize even neophyte readers of poetry, while the personal and yet universal issues Thomas's poems raise are immediately recognizable. His incantatory reading of *Do Not Go Gentle Into That Good Night*, included on our audio CD, provides a compelling introduction to his voice and verse. The poetry meshes beautifully with other poets' offerings in the twentieth-century section—Hardy, Yeats, and Boland in particular—while it is a superb complement to readings in the Romantics, especially Keats and Wordsworth, and to Hopkins later in the nineteenth century. The medieval and early modern Welsh poetry is extremely apposite, since Dylan Thomas was furthering a long tradition of Welsh poetry, as well as fostering the English lyric poem, where John Donne and Andrew Marvell are the best comparisons and companions for his work.

The Force That Through the Green Fuse Drives the Flower is one Thomas poem that can center a discussion radiating out into all the poetic forebears and styles sketched above. The passionate "I" of its lyric speaks repeatedly of (his) "dumb-ness" before the natural world's force, a force which itself speaks through many "mouths" of stream and wind and blood. Nature is personified, and yet impersonal. The poem seems to refer directly to Wordsworth's *The Leech Gatherer* in its line "The lips of time leech to the fountain head," where time too is a human agent, a speaking subject or mouth with lips, lips that greedily try to adhere themselves to the fountain head at life's source, just as the "I" of the poem does. At the same time the line echoes the concerns with temporality found in Keats's *Ode on a Grecian Urn* and in Marvell's *To His Coy Mistress*. While it rewrites the pastoral genre in an almost violent vein—a post-Darwinian view of nature's harshness infuses the poem—there is an ecstatic element very akin to Hopkins's divine landscapes, imbued with God's animating power. Thomas Hardy's verse forms seem to cling to the lines "And I am dumb to tell the hanging man, How of my clay is made the hangman's lime," and their aura of fatalism resembles Hardy's poetic sensibility too. Yeats' poetic presence can be glimpsed throughout the poem—which is not to say that it is derivative of Yeats, or any of the other poets cited, but that it is, like all poetry, a complicated hybrid of things that came before—in the majestic way a whole world can be summoned up in the image of "the crooked rose," in the bow to the destructive side of an empowering nature, and in the cosmic implications of humanity's position: when the "I" looks up to the heavens at the end of the poem, it is a speechless "I" in the face of time's relentless pace, "how time has ticked a heaven round the stars."

If at all possible, the best way to teach the extraordinary radio play *Return Journey* is to get a recording of it. Without hearing it in that form, one might forget that it uses modern technology to create a crucial part of its meaning. A radio broadcast transmits disembodied voices, voices floating through time and space without definite location. This piece is about a definite location—Swansea, Wales, where the narrator is returning to find out if anyone remembers him in the town he has left for good. He finds many who remember him, but none who recognize him as the young man he inquires about, and in fact his last interlocutor tells him with great authority that the boy is "dead." Of course, the boy *is* dead, or at least that version of his identity seems dead. The peculiarities of radio can convey the sense of disappearance or death as no other medium could. Thomas's formal brilliance in this work is reminiscent of the *sui generis* art form created by David Jones in *In Parenthesis*, and the latter work would be terrific to read in conjunction with it. Jones fuses poetry, narration, and drama in his memoir of World War I, and many of the artistic issues of style, and the political issues of Welsh history, emerge in Thomas as in Jones. Both writers need to find a style which can include elements from the great English literary tradition, while inflecting these with the different and in many ways oppositional artistic legacy of Wales. Welsh art was often literally suppressed and censored over the centuries by the English, as were attempts at Welsh independence, and by the twentieth century the Welsh language was primarily relegated to cultural uses—songs, church music, poetry, and ballads. Welsh identity was constructed, in English eyes, as fanciful, overly emotional, and even magical—shading into the demonic. Welsh writers in English of the stature of Jones and Thomas had to take into account the threatening power of Welsh language for English speakers, who saw it as alien and transgressive, and had to reckon with the still disturbing force of Welsh accents in English. Southern accents in the United States, or what is called "Black English" dialect, are analogous in conveying negative connotations or stereotypes to some American English speakers' ears. So the sound of the voices in Dylan Thomas's *Return Journey* is all-important, and cannot be fully captured on the page. National radio broadcasts, like national television, demands that a standard English be spoken—we know this phenomenon in the United States media as regional or ethnic dialects are suppressed in favor of standard, "accentless" speech for news anchors or television hosts. Dylan Thomas's radio play is formally ingenious in linking its ghostly themes of self-forgetting and death to the specificities of radio; Samuel Beckett, among others, would follow and imitate his ingenuity. There is also a political aspect to the use of the radio medium, however. The narrator in *Return Journey* cannot go back to Swansea and inquire about the ghost of himself without encountering the Welsh "accents" that BBC English forbids. The narrator has adopted a less regional form of speech, as his life has taken him away from his community—he has lost his "accent," and his dialect as well. No wonder no one recognizes him—his voice patterns are as much of a disguise as his age and his social status. *Return Journey* summons up the dialect and accent of the narrator's youth, as all the folks he speaks to respond to him unself-consciously in their regional speech forms; the melange of Welsh voices make up the play being broadcast on the BBC, which tended whenever it could to eliminate accents. The British Broadcasting Network has only very recently begun accommodating regional accents and dialects on its programs, and even now rarely allows these to be heard on its news broadcasts. Its announcers speak a standard upper-class British, whether they be from Scotland, Wales, or Yorkshire. *Return Journey* is a sly and yet immensely poignant radio play, making a political point in disguise by capturing the lost voices of Dylan Thomas's youth and broadcasting them in all their regional glory to an English nation never comfortable with the audible marks of difference. Speech is a force that through the fuse of radio waves drives the nation toward sameness, and death. Dylan Thomas's writing certainly insisted upon raging against the dying of that linguistic light.

The second edition of the anthology adds among other things Thomas's astonishing poem "Fern Hill." Among the approaches to this poem that would surely captivate students is reading it aloud with an emphasis on the way the description of a very local place—Fern Hill itself—with very specific memories for the poet is enlarged as a space or zone for the intersection of consciousness with place.

Compare Thomas's technique of what could be called "poetic geography" to the more sweeping, abstract landscapes in poetry by Hughes, Auden, Hardy or Larkin. A crux of Dylan Thomas's poetics lies in making a small spot on the Welsh countryside, a gentle, fern-covered hill, surge with lyric intensity and general application. Students should pay special attention to the words for landscape features Thomas draws upon, and how the poem almost burrows into the ferny hill of its title to invest the local with sublimely immediate passion. Cultural geography and the intense relation humans have to place is becoming ever more engaging in current thinking; Thomas's gorgeously detailed topographic poetry inscribes an absent place with surging fervor, and by doing so invests his poem with the forces of place and time. Dylan Thomas in "Fern Hill" writes like a green fuse driving the flowers of mind and memory back to a location its readers now forever share.

Samuel Beckett
Krapp's Last Tape

Like most of Beckett's work, *Krapp's Last Tape* works by bringing an unusual amount of pressure to bear on a minimal amount of verbal material. The text of *Krapp's Last Tape* is short and quite repetitive; indeed, the plot is primarily about repetition—about our inability to avoid repeating the past, even our compulsion to play again and again the "tapes" (as contemporary psychologists would say) of our past, thus effectively erecting barriers to any more satisfactory future.

In a strange way, *Krapp's Last Tape*, despite all the differences in *mise en scéne*, could easily be a James Joyce, *Dubliners*-style story. In playing over and over the birthday recording from his 39th birthday, Krapp is presented with the opportunity to look himself in the eye—to see himself for the vain and selfish person that he is, and to attempt to grow in consequence of that awful knowledge. But like Joyce's characters, he refuses that "one good look" in the looking-glass; continued self-delusion—even if it requires a lifetime of alienation and loneliness—is easier than admitting one's faults and honestly facing them. Thus the play's close, with the 69-year-old Krapp insisting that he wouldn't want the past back, finally suggests the awful price he has paid for the macho "no regrets" philosophy he has lived by.

A brilliant performance is available on videocassette, from Smithsonian Institution Press, in the *Beckett Directs Beckett* series: a production by the San Quentin Drama Workshop starring Rick Cluchey. Watching the play, more than anything else, will drive home its pathos, as well as underscoring the genuine humor that underlies the play, including Beckett's debts to Charlie Chaplin and vaudeville.

Texts for Nothing

All of Beckett's narrators are obsessed with the fact of their narrating; this is nowhere more evident than in the *Texts for Nothing*. Text 4 performs an inquiry into the nature of the self, and suggests that the "self," the "I," is simply a story that we tell ourselves in order to create the illusion of unity of being—the sense of a whole, integrated self. "Who says this, saying it's me?," our narrator wonders in the first sentence. The suggestion is that some portion of one's experience is always sacrificed in the forging (in both senses of that word) of the self; some part that doesn't seem to fit in with the overall story one wishes to tell ends up on the cutting-room floor, edited out of the final text. But those censored passages that the "self" tries to keep out have a nasty way of reasserting their rights, as Freud taught us. Thus the monologue we overhear in Text 4 might almost be narrated in the voice of Krapp—that part of Krapp that the self-confident, vain man who works the tape recorder can't allow, that thing of darkness he is unable, or simply unwilling, to acknowledge his. This human tendency—the way that the host ego that keeps our narrator down "tells his story every five minutes, saying it is not his"—is the focus of Beckett's late play *Not I*, in which the psychological mechanism of repression is able to create a seemingly healthy self with which to meet the world, but only at the cost of saying "not I" to a number of things that the whole person had experienced. Text 4 is then, on one level, a parable about the unavoidable but costly process of creating a self—about the violence and violent forgetting that a life narrative visits upon lived experience. The "self," Beckett reminds us, is a fiction—a character whom we create but, that creation accomplished, can no longer see.

Text 8, while continuing the focus of Text 4 on the creation of the self, broadens its horizons somewhat to talk about the more general human drive to tell stories. Throughout Beckett's writing there is the strong message that humans are condemned to tell stories, condemned to speech: to go silent is all that many of Beckett's characters dream of, but it is a dream that is approached but never quite realized. To cease telling stories is to die; but as long as we have the breath of life in us, that breath will be used to tell stories—and far too often, Beckett suggests, used to tell stories about ourselves that prevent us from honestly facing who we are and what we have done.

The Expelled

The Expelled, we learn in this story, includes all of us: we all suffer the originary act of being expelled from the mother's body at birth—an ouster which Beckett here compares to the Christian notion of the Fall, through the narrator's comic series of falls—and spend the remainder of our time here on earth trying to get back on our feet, and to write the story that will make sense for us of our being tossed out of our ancestral home.

Making reference to *Paradise Lost*, and the doctrine of the fortunate fall, may help students to see the paradigm that Beckett is playing with here; in this story, of course, the Fall is made quite literal, our protagonist lying in a gutter as he begins to tell his story, and he proceeds to fall and fall again throughout the brief story (one of Beckett's plays for radio is called *All That Fall*).

Like the characters in the *Texts for Nothing*, our protagonist here seems to be forced to tell his story, punished by being forced to describe ("How describe this hat? And why?"; "I have always greatly admired the door of this house. . . . How to describe it?"); like Charlie Marlow in Conrad's *Heart of Darkness*, life seems to our protagonist a stiff sentence indeed, and he hopes to shorten his stay—to earn time off for good behavior—by dutifully telling the stories that he thinks are demanded of him.

W. H. Auden

W. H. Auden provided the skeleton key for reading his poetry in the many essays and books of literary criticism he also wrote. The *Anthology* includes just such a critical essay, *Writing*, in order to facilitate the interpretation of Auden's poetic mission, and to compare his ideas of the goals of art to the critical writings other poets produced in past eras. William Wordsworth's "Preface to the *Lyrical Ballads*," Samuel Taylor Coleridge's *Biographia Literaria*, Percy Shelley's *Defense of Poetry*, and even William Blake's poetic rationales make productive companion readings. Auden was a literary scholar along with being a practicing poet; his erudite understanding of the English literary tradition extended even to his passionate explications of its precursor forms in the medieval sagas. Within the twentieth-century section itself, Auden's essay, like his poetry, ought to be compared to T. S. Eliot's critical essay on poetic form and modern writing. The two critics, like the two poets, have an intriguingly different diagnosis of modern poetry, and a similarly divergent prescription for writing.

Eliot is famous for having insisted on the necessary impersonality of art. He called for an impersonal style which sought an "objective correlative" to the subjective emotion of the artist. In other words, a poetic object was sought to correlate with, and to replace, the explicit mention of subjective inner states. Out of this prescription Eliot also created a canon of his favorite poets, those who had adopted the "objective correlative" he championed—for example, the "metaphysical" poets, like John Donne, who had been relatively ignored. The knotty conceits and cerebral metaphors of poets like Donne exemplified the refined, impersonal poetry Eliot mandated. While many critics have lately insisted that Eliot's poetry, far from impersonal, fairly seethes with references to his own experiences and emotional states, there is nonetheless a huge contrast between Eliot's criteria for poetry and Auden's. W. H. Auden kept the lyric or personal voice alive in his poetry. This is not to say that it was openly confessional or autobiographical: Auden's poems are not at all like Anne Sexton's or Sylvia Plath's, for example. Still, poems like *In Memory of W. B. Yeats* or *September 1, 1939* hinge on personal experience and the voice of a person narrating the history of his own time. Eliot's poetry contains myriad splintered allusions to all sorts of historical and personal experiences, of course, yet these are filtered through a mesh of "objective correlatives"—quotes from other poems, images that refract the experience. W. H. Auden by contrast seems to stand or hover in back of his poetry, not just a witness but an actor in its events.

The famous *Musée des Beaux Arts* does not revolve around a strikingly *personal* personal experience, yet it exhibits Auden's poetic signature. The poem transcribes a visit to an art museum, where the viewer—the poetic voice—is looking at a well-known painting by Brueghel, yet is not fully aware of an ominous detail of it. Hidden in a corner of the painting, the boy Icarus falls into the sea, the wings his father Daedalus molded from wax having melted when Icarus brought them too close to the sun. The Greek myth of Daedalus and Icarus is a cautionary tale about art: the father's artifice was so skillful that the son, borne aloft on artificial wings, overreached himself, and was drowned. So much else seems to be happening in the painting, so much else draws the eye, that the poignant tragedy of Icarus unfolds unseen. Auden's poem draws a word-picture of the painting—this is a favorite technique of the Renaissance, when the Latin phrase *ut pictura poesis* referred to the ability of verbal art to mimic or imitate visual art. The classical and early modern rivalry between poets and painters was intense, and long-standing, with painters claiming to be able to imitate the real, and poets claiming supremacy because their art, the art of language, could introduce the element of time. Keats's *Ode on a Grecian Urn* brings this old quarrel of *ut pictura poesis* into Romanticism, when the frieze on the Grecian urn he depicts in his poem freezes time—the figures on its surface are forever dancing to the music of "slow time," and the maiden who is on the verge of her marriage yet who never gets there in the frieze is a "still unravished bride of quietness." Neither Keats nor Auden is interested in whether painters or poets are better—they have entirely given up on that ancient and somewhat silly debate. What interests them both is the question of time: how poetry relates to time, and staves off death by filling the void of time with language. Auden's words are able to draw our attention to a new part of the picture; there, unlike anything that can actually happen on a picture's surface, Icarus is in the process of falling, as if the picture had become a motion picture. Does knowing that Icarus is falling allow him to be rescued? Unfortunately, no. Words have the power to "give life" to Icarus for an instant, just as his father's ingenuity gave him the wings to soar. Both modes of artifice or art, however, have no power to change things in the face of time. Icarus will fall, the painting will remain, and Auden's poem asks, what will the poem have changed?

Musée de Beaux Arts shows how adept Auden is at borrowing things—in the case of that poem, borrowing a *topos* from Renaissance defenses of poetry, and from Romantic defenses of those defenses, and making it new. The highlight of Auden's poetic method is his love of, and talent for, pouring new wine into old bottles; that is, using older metrical forms, like the sonnet and the aubade, and infusing them with new poetic life. A serious inquiry into Auden's poetry would require a rigorous grasp of the techniques and the technicalities of English verse forms. Auden may have violated T.S. Eliot's idea of poetic protocol by inserting himself into his poetry in a lyrical Romantic fashion, but he has no argument with Eliot's love of classical form, and no modern peer in his facility for remaking the patterns of English poetry to fit the age of anxiety, atomic bombs, and free love. For example, *Lullaby* follows its model poem Herrick's *To the Virgins, to Make Much of Time*, echoing its line "Gather ye rosebuds while ye may" with the same scrupulous meter and tight prosody. Auden is strict, never sloppy, and exacting in his verse and vocabulary. By borrowing the older poem's form, yet not its words and images, he imbues that paean to love—and sex—with a heady modern sexiness, and an equal poignance at the fleeting wings of time.

Love is perhaps Auden's best poetic subject. This has been proven in popular terms, anyway, in the pop culture of the 1990s, when Auden had a huge posthumous success with his love poetry. After a scene in the British film *Four Weddings and a Funeral* featured a character reciting an Auden poem aloud at a friend's funeral service, audiences found the poem overwhelmingly moving, and tried to find out who had written it. Auden's publishers heard about the demand for the poem and reprinted it, along with others, as a new volume, *Four Love Poems by W. H. Auden*, sold at bookstores and discount stores, with "includes the poem from *Four Weddings and a Funeral*" emblazoned on its cover. It may seem ironic or even a little seedy that it took a film to revive interest in Auden's work for a wider public. However, Auden would have appreciated the happy accident of coming to public notice, whatever the circumstances. The poet who wrote *Musée des Beaux Arts* worried about how, and if, people would notice what art tried to show them. It is no more strange that Auden's poem proved to be so moving and powerful when read by an actor in a movie, than that Icarus might fall to earth in a stationary painting. Life is always going on, and time hastening along; Auden believed that if the words of a poem were strong enough, they could "stop time." So precise and strong were Auden's words that they overpowered the film around them, and took on a new life of their own.

Stevie Smith

Stevie Smith's poetry almost teaches itself, especially when read where it is embedded, within the largely male poetry of post-war poets such as Auden, Larkin, and Hughes. Sylvia Plath's individual poems, like those of the poets just mentioned, demand individual glosses, whereas Smith's poems are best taught as a group. This is not meant to imply that she is an unserious poet, but rather that her greatest worth lies in the poetic voice she brought to the fore, a voice that insists on an "I" without enlarging its own importance.

Smith boldly violated one of the unspoken taboos of modern poetry when she added her sprightly, tensile line drawings to her poetry. For a thousand years or more an artistic "war" has been waged between poets and visual artists, the latter claiming that only they could render "reality," the former insisting that the advantage literature has over poetry, in addition to the almost infinite permutations of words, is its incorporation of time. Paintings can only freeze or stop time, the critical argument went, whereas words need no secondary clues or illustrations of what they can so elastically show to the mind's eye. Into this long debate waltzes Stevie Smith, who matches her poems up not only with visual art, but with representational or figural drawings that dare to be personal, almost decorative, additions. Help students see how their immediacy, their almost improvisatory nature is meant to collaborate with her poems—Stevie Smith is not intent, as was Auden, for example, on establishing herself as a witness to the major historical events of her time, nor was she interested in maintaining a lofty seriousness nor a "purity" of poetic word. My headnote in the anthology compares her instead to the recent singer-songwriters Alanis Morissette and Chrissie Hynde, among others—Smith's poetic lyrics are about herself, her loneliness, her pain, her observations, her grasp of everyone's ordinariness. They dramatize and, with her sketches, bring to life a persona that while desperate, is never bitter, while suffering is never just a victim. "Not Waving But Drowning" attributes its own main line to someone else, and then flips the poetic line to have the poet's persona voice this scary but still comical plaint. Waving, after all, is such a sweet interpretation to make of a flailing hand stretched above the waves—and of course Smith uses the play on hand-waving and ocean waves, too. Like her sketches, the poems are stripped down to the tightest, thinnest line, the most economical stanzas, and despite this self-effacing economics her poetry bursts with casual flair and immediate rapport with a reader. Stevie Smith's work does not articulate a "theory" of feminism, as perhaps could be said of Sylvia Plath's incisive poetry, with its controlled rage against Fathers everywhere. Smith doesn't rail or dramatize, she just insists on putting her heart on the page, certain that others—women, yes, but men too, who are as lonely in this life as anybody else—will have been struck by the absurdity, the sadness, and yet the "pretty" aspects of the world. The poem "Pretty" is as bold as her others in the same fashion—here is a female poet who dares to deploy the word "pretty," when the only proper poetic subject, according to the tradition of poetics, is beauty. Prettiness is not ugliness, but not beauty either—it stands there unrecorded, seemingly not a part of art, never reaching the heights of Beauty, where Truth also resides. Pretty is in the eye of the beholder, much more so than beauty is, because "prettiness" isn't valued in the same way, and has to be given value by those who find it and name it.

Stevie Smith's poetry was highly popular, and that too was a strike against her. Without in the slightest taking away from the admittedly great poets—Yeats, Eliot, Thomas, Hardy and so forth—who occupy center stage in the tradition of modern poetry, Stevie Smith makes room for herself and room for other readers, sophisticated and not so, to read poetry differently. Well before it was fashionable, Stevie Smith developed a kind of "confessional" poetry that honored her own emotions, her own observations, her solidarity with others. She never, however, used poetry to highlight herself or for narcissicistic purposes. Just as the vibrant female singer-songwriters of today yoke words and music, so too did Stevie Smith yoke words and image. Her poetry and her line drawings are both as light as air and inscribed like a diamond, in recognition of what is both "pretty" and "drowning."

Philip Larkin
Church Going

Much of Larkin's poetry is concerned with the creation of a meaningful life after the death of God; in Church Going, the speaker wonders why he is attracted to houses of worship, largely empty, when he does not believe in the God they were built to honor. The interior is described in terms that emphasize its emptiness and silence; clearly, these empty churches are meant to symbolize the death of an older order, one which, for all its shortcomings, did help to explain to people their place in the creation, and a purpose for their lives. For the speaker, not just belief, but even "unbelief," has disappeared; both can create a kind of energy, a kind of passion, that he in his agnostic torpor cannot capture. In the poem's conclusion the speaker reaffirms the church's importance—which lies not in its fulfilling the purposes for which it was originally constructed, but rather serving as discrete, physical links in British history and tradition, another system of belief within which one can find one's place and purpose.

High Windows

The curse word in the second line of *High Windows* may present problems for teachers of some students, in some parts of the country; though texts from Beckett and Kelman are by turns vulgar and profane, there is something especially troubling and unexpected about the "f-word" cropping up in a poem, especially in verse as classically disciplined as Larkin's. And that, of course, is precisely the point: there's nothing adventitious or cheaply sensationalistic about Larkin's "fucking," but instead the harsh language suggests the violence of the speaker's reaction to what he thinks he sees. It's important to point out that the speaker's indictment of this "couple of kids" is purely conjectural, borne of his own prejudices and envy; a perfectly parallel passage, and one which may give students a better understanding of the way that Larkin is here criticizing his speaker, occurs in the opening paragraphs of Don DeLillo's novel *White Noise*, where a middle-aged college professor, envious of his students' monied families and healthy, tanned bodies, imagines luggage full of all kinds of prohibited substances. Both DeLillo's Jack Gladney and Larkin's speaker owe something to Eliot's Prufrock, indulging themselves in "pity parties" and imagining that while the mermaids sing each to each, they will not sing to them.

Thus the speaker's palpable self-pity is meant to undercut, at least to some degree, the critique of modern sexual mores that the poem presents. In the same way the speaker, with a disarming honesty, recalls as the poem closes that this is a timeless strategy employed by the older generation against the younger; every generation of parents have thought their kids' music was too loud, etc. The poem achieves a fine balance between criticism of contemporary morality and a critique of the nostalgia that helps the older generation sustain the illusion of its ascendancy. Larkin has little time for either of these comforting illusions.

Talking in Bed

This brief and poignant poem is in part an indictment of sex without love—an indictment which, unlike that delivered in *High Windows*, focuses primarily on the speaker's own life. The slippage of values is suggested economically in the last two lines, where the quest to find and speak words "at once true and kind" devolves to the depressing attempt only to speak words "not untrue and not unkind."

MCMXIV

Looking back over the distance of half a century, the speaker considers images of the Edwardian and Georgian life that MCMXIV—1914, and World War I—brought suddenly to an end. The closing stanza suggests what many other poets of the War, including W. B. Yeats, had proposed—that the Great War marked the end of innocence for the British Empire, and made post-War life a pale shadow of Great Britain's heyday. In another sense, the poem can almost be read as an epitaph for Larkin himself; born in 1922—traditionally considered the banner year for British Literary modernism—Larkin here (and much more explicitly in his preface to *All What Jazz*) suggests that he was born into a world with which he had no sympathy, and longs instead for a pastoral and traditional British culture which had disappeared permanently by the time of his birth.

Sylvia Plath

As the anthology's headnote to Plath's work suggests, it is for all practical purposes impossible to read Plath's poetry apart from her tragic life story; her "confessional poetry" makes lasting art of that tragedy. The first three poems collected here, "The Colossus," "Daddy," and "Lady Lazarus," are fruitfully read and discussed as a coherent cluster, picking up and enriching through repetition a group of images related to suicide, death, and patriarchal authority. The poems suggest, for instance, that an accidental near-death experience at age ten was followed by a more deliberate suicide attempt at twenty—and that the every-ten-years pattern would play out again. "Dying / Is an art, like everything else," Plath writes in "Lady Lazarus"; "I do it exceptionally well." The fact that Plath connected much of her despair to the death of her father suggests connections to Mansfield's "Daughters of the Late Colonel" and even, perhaps, Lawrence's "The Horse Dealer's Daughter"; in those texts, as in these three poems of Plath's, the death of the father is both literal and hugely metaphorical—the death of the father signifying the death of God, the death of law and order and reason and purpose. The deliberately shocking use of Holocaust imagery in "Lady Lazarus" (chillingly read by Plath on our audio CD) can be seen within the wartime context provided by Churchill's speeches.

The final Plath poem, "Child," is every bit as dark as the first three—but melancholy where the others are angry or bitter. The poem manages three perfectly beautiful and poignant stanzas, buoyed by the hope of innocent new life, before grinding to a dark halt in the despairing final stanza.

Ted Hughes

In the poetry of Ted Hughes, human beings learn what it means to be human only through encounters—often painful, or disturbing, or violent encounters—with the inhuman. In "Wind," the speaker is reduced to cataloguing the evidence of the violent energy of nature; the poem's final line echoes Christ's famous claim that the very stones call out God's identity, though for Hughes they testify more to an impersonal natural force than a personal God. "Relic" gives Hughes's version of Tennyson's nature, "red in tooth and claw"; Hughes's vision of nature is not that of the Romantics—or better, perhaps, it's Shelley's nature, or Blake's, not Wordsworth's. These themes are further developed in his powerful reading of his *Second Glance at a Jaguar*, included on our audio CD. "Theology" takes its place in a long and venerable tradition of retelling the story of the Fall from Genesis; in Hughes's version, pride and effrontery (that of the serpent) is rewarded rather than punished. "Dust As We Are" bears comparison to some of the poetry emerging from WWI, including some of the poetry in this anthology, detailing the after-effects of war on those fortunate enough to survive. The poem also depends on a stark contrast between the masculine and feminine principles, the nuturing of the mother and the hard-won wisdom of the father, as does "Leaf Mould," which figures both the knowledge of nature and the feel for poetic language as emanating from the mother. "Telegraph Wires" conveys an apt image of the collision of the natural and the human worlds, telegraph wires hung across "a lonely moor." And though communication is thus enabled, it's a complex mix: for while "towns whisper to towns over the heather," so too natural forces use the telegraph wires to communicate their inhuman messages, the lines "picked up and played" by the winds like the aeolian harp celebrated by the Romantic poets. Unlike the Romantics, though, there's no suggestion that this is spirit music: these are "the tones / That empty human bones."

Thom Gunn

If Hughes's poetry is largely about the agency of the inhuman, and human beings' powerlessness in the face of it, Gunn's poetry is intimately human in scale and scope. In "Lines for a Book," he celebrates the active life of the body over the contemplative life of the mind, admiring those in history who have backed up thought with action—"those exclusive by their action." This admiration immediately distinguished Gunn from most of his contemporaries in the British poetry scene. "Elvis Presley" celebrates a popular culture figure who succeeds in marrying thought and deed, art and action, turning "revolt into a style," and paving the way for a generation at war with the proprieties of their elders. In "A Map of the City" Gunn revisits the topos of a poem like Wordsworth's "Tintern Abbey," but privileges the city and its dangers and possibilities over the hill upon which he stands; what others would call "urban decay" Gunn sees as "ground of my delight"—"I would not have the risk diminished." This romantic, indeed implicitly erotic, love of danger boils below the surface of "Black Jackets" as well. The fact that this biker bar is virtually indistinguishable from one of the Bay Area's gay leather bars is not an accident, for while Gunn had not yet publicly come out as a gay man, his poems dealt increasingly with homoerotic material. But even in his openly gay poems like "The Hug," love and desire and sex are universalized, so that every reader can read him- or herself into positions which finally aren't "gay" or "straight," but instead profoundly human.

"From the Wave" represents Gunn's growing infatuation with his adopted Californian home, celebrating as it does the hedonist, active lifestyle he champions starting with "Lines for a Book." For teachers interested in spending time on prosody, it's worth making the point that Gunn here combines a "slack," pop-culture topic with carefully controlled prosody: a poem of classical proportion, singing the praises of surfing. Indeed, the overall effect of Gunn's worship of the surfers is to turn them into classical gods, marbled bodies "half wave, half men," underscoring the discipline involved in this seemingly spontaneous activity. "The Hug" comes from Gunn's first book focusing on the AIDS epidemic, *The Man With Night Sweats*; and while the context, both historical and biographical, make clear that the lovers are men, the poem exploits gender ambiguity (as does Auden's beautiful "Lullaby") to emphasize what's universal about this emotional experience. "Patch Work" works as an allegory of the poetic process, suggesting that poets are mocking birds, patching together bits and pieces of others's songs; as if to prove the point, Gunn gestures broadly to Shelley's "To a Sky-Lark" and Keats's "Ode to a Nightingale," both echoing and redirecting those poets' work. "The Missing" again makes the point that we are defined by those with whom we are in relation and that, as Donne wrote centuries before, implicitly indicting the "straight" audience's indifference to AIDS: "Any man's death diminishes me, because I am involved in mankind, and therefore never send to know for whom the bell tolls; it tolls for thee." We are all incalculably diminished by "the missing."

V. S. Naipaul

All the selections from V. S. Naipaul's work stem from his autobiographical writing. They will connect well with other selections that stress the memoir or the first-person story; what is especially important for students is to recognize what is so unusual about Naipaul's narrative. He writes in majestic English prose about the arrival in England of a young man who is the product of a complex colonial history. This is a return journey of sorts—Conrad's character Marlow, a British seaman, travels to Africa and then makes his way back to tell a harrowing story of what empire has wrought. Naipaul starts "out there," and finds his way to the heart of darkness at the imperial center, where he makes his way as a writer.

It's not only what he writes about, but how he writes, that makes Naipaul so distinctive and distinguished. Unlike his younger colleague in distinction, Salman Rushdie, who also came from "elsewhere" to make a lasting mark on modern British literature, Naipaul's prose models derive from classically British models. Rushdie's writing is self-evidently modernist; a cosmopolitan in style as well as in background, his influences are James Joyce, William Faulkner, and Gabriel Garcia Marquez, whereas Naipaul's writing displays no modernistic pyrotechnics. His prose is nourished by nineteenth-century realist writers—Eliot, Austen, Thackery and Dickens among them—and by the scrupulous style of Matthew Arnold, Cardinal Newman, and Thomas Carlyle. Joseph Conrad is a major influence running through Naipaul's writing, since it is symbolically charged and rich with poetic imagery. If Naipaul were being placed in a modernist category, it would be in the Conradian section, where realist narrative is still discernible under the narrative innovations, rather than in the company of out-and-out experimentalists like Woolf, Joyce or Beckett. The chiseled gravity of his essays owes something to T.S. Eliot's crisp prose in *Tradition and the Individual Talent,* and his polemical tartness owes something to the moral urgency of George Orwell's voice in *Politics and the English Language.*

Naipaul has refused to be categorized as a postcolonial writer, although he is one in a sense, and has refused the mantle of multiculturalism. Nonetheless, the settings for many of his novels, and of his nonfiction, have been places still found "exotic" by many Westerners, British and Americans alike. Naipaul has not avoided or ignored these places—the Caribbean, Africa, India, Latin America—in his writing, but he has not made a simple division between the evils of imperialism—the British—and the virtues of resistance—Britain's colonial subjects. Contrast Graham Greene's story with V. S. Naipaul's writing: both writers are animated by ethical questions, above all, and see writing as a calling of moral seriousness. Greene's stories and novels, like a latter-day Conrad's, are mostly set in exotic places, where the Greene anti-hero, a flawed but good man, is finally able to express his religious and political solidarity with the oppressed local population. Naipaul's exotic locales just do not include this opportunity for romanticized self-redemption; his colonial characters usually throw the request for solidarity with them right back into the startled British face, often at gunpoint. Well-meaning British travel writers, and sometimes would-be heroes, from Richard Burton to T. E. Lawrence, make an excellent contrast to Naipaul's literary universe too. Naipaul's monumental writing emanates from an in-between place, neither here nor there. He has witnessed the end of British empire as one of its subjects, yet he neither idealizes nor glamorizes the aftermath of the national independence movements.

One fascinating pairing would contrast V. S. Naipaul and Derek Walcott as Caribbean writers who have enlarged the territory of English literature in differing ways. Walcott's Caribbean heritage melds white British and African diaspora ancestors, and his writing parlays those roots; Naipaul's Caribbean inheritance is by way of a further or double dislocation, since his Indian ancestors had been brought from one British colony to serve in another, far away. As a Trinidadian, his ethnic background put him at some distance from the Afro-Caribbean majority, yet was no less colonial in its origins. Putting them together will demonstrate conclusively that no singular identity as a British Caribbean or Anglophone (English-speaking) Caribbean writer exists. Their styles, their subjects, their genres, their influences, and their politics could not be more diverse.

Another great Caribbean writer, the political theorist and physician Frantz Fanon, wrote a hugely influential book on colonialism called *Black Skins, White Masks.* His thesis was that colonialism was so dehumanizing and dominating a system that it affected the personal identity of everyone it touched: it caused some colonial subjects to denigrate themselves as the colonizers had, and thus to idealize them and even imitate them, while hating themselves. Fanon, a psychiatrist from Martinique, described the psychological condition of putting on a "white mask" inside the self, identifying with whiteness, with colonial values, and even with colonial superiority, in a distorted form of self-hatred of what the colonizers had rejected as "bad." V.S. Naipaul has written (in *Mimic Men* especially) of this distorted mimicry, and of how destructive it has been individually and socially in a postcolonial world. However, his entire body of work stands as a refutation of those who would claim that his artistic gifts are in themselves an "imitation" of Britishness, and not "authentically" Caribbean or third world. Naipaul's work never feels the need to disguise its own power, nor to pretend not to be "British"—in the sense of being part of the central tradition of the finest British literature. The pressures on him to do and think otherwise, which come from both sides of the colonial division, and both sides of the political fence, are evident in his work, and in his memoir. It is a testament to his lasting place in British letters that V.S. Naipaul has made a literature out of resisting those pressures either to conform or to mimic.

Caryl Churchill

Churchill's *Cloud Nine* is a comic maelstrom of racial, sexual, gender, religious, and imperialist energies and antagonisms; it touches on some of the most troubling aspects of post-Cold War, post-Imperial British life and culture, while deploying a theatrical style sometimes bordering on farce (reminiscent of Joe Orton). The highly stylized result is one of the period's most incisive texts, juxtaposing the restrictive Victorian-era colonial project with the 1970's "permissive society" within which Churchill wrote the play. One of the points of comparison Churchill is able to bring out is that for all its vaunted "permissiveness," the 1970s was indeed a good deal like the 1870s in one important respect: the British Empire, under the symbolic leadership of a strong, humorless, and seemingly asexual female political leader determined to set a high moral tone, was in fact seething with barely repressed and anarchic sexual energy.

A teacher using *Cloud Nine* as one of her concluding texts in a British literature survey would do well to take a cue from Churchill's own prefatory note to the play, in which she expresses her interest in "the parallel between colonial and sexual oppression." For convenience sake, we will break down the remainder of discussion here to those topics indicated in our opening sentence:

Race. Set in "a British colony in Africa in Victorian times," Act I contains the bulk of the play's meditation on the politics of race under empire. Joshua, the family's black servant, is played by a white actor—because, as Churchill explains, white is what Joshua wants to be. He is both treated as an inferior by members of the ruling British family, and is full of self-loathing: his divided consciousness finds no point of similarity or kinship with the other African household servants, as Joshua instead identifies wholly with his oppressor (even to the point of refusing to grieve the death of his own parents). Joshua's sexuality is somewhat ambiguous; by some characters, he is treated as a "savage," and since less than human, not a sexual being; so that the extramarital affairs of the whites are barely hidden from him. At the same time, when the polymorphously pleasure-seeking Harry Bagley suggests a tryst, Joshua seems neither very interested nor repelled: "That's all right, yes." Joshua is a prime example of the deeply contradictory images ascribed to black men in western culture: both outside the ken of appropriate sexual desire and, at the very same time, a deeply fetishized "primitive" sexual object (with obvious parallels to the situation in E. M. Forster's "The Life to Come").

Sexuality and Gender. Most remarkable for its time, when homophobia was perhaps the most acceptable form of discrimination in Thatcherite Great Britain, *Cloud Nine* dwells with real intensity and insight on questions of sexual identity, the social construction of sexual roles, and sexual politics. In Act I, the famous (if stereotypical) outlines of "Victorian morality" are ostensibly in place—everywhere respected in appearance, everywhere violated in private. Clive, steadfast and stalwart husband, carries on a sexual relationship with the widow Mrs. Saunders; meanwhile his wife, Betty, attempts in vain to inflame the ardor of the bisexual Harry Saunders, and at the same time keeps at arm's length the advances of her maid Ellen—only to leave Clive in the second act, and explore a lesbian relationship with Lin. For each of the play's women—with the possible exception of Betty's mother Maud—must discover, in the course of their maturing, that desire is an active force that can be claimed by a woman for herself; this in contradiction to the widespread Victorian belief that sexual pleasure is exclusively a man's prerogative. (Betty's extended description of her post-divorce discovery of the pleasure of masturbation would have to be read in this context.) Both Betty and her daughter's friend Lin—and seemingly, by the play's end, Victoria as well—have thrown off marriage partners who dominated and subordinated them, much as (by 1972) most of the former possessions of the British Empire had thrown off their protective "spouse." Like the Dark Continent, men secretly realize that women, with their own appetites, are "voracious," as Clive says of Mrs. Saunders—voracious, and threatening: "You are dark like this continent," he tells her, "Mysterious. Treacherous." The uncertain boundary between child and adult sexuality—so troublingly evidenced in a figure like Lewis Carroll, author of the *Alice* books, but also photographer with a penchant for slightly risque (by contemporary standards) portraits of little girls—also crops up in *Cloud Nine*; the sexual relationship between Harry Bagley and young Edward is a clear example, but even the matronly Maud's nursery rhymes carry a pederastic (and incestuous) edge: "Clap hands, daddy comes, with his pockets full of plums. All for Vicky."

In one of the play's keener insights into the sexual mores of the swinging sixties and seventies Churchill shows, through the adult relationship of Edward and Gerry, that gay relationships, though ostensibly outside the strict boundaries of traditional morality, can quickly fall into the very same cliched gender dynamics as heterosexual relationships. This failure—though at the play's end Gerry, who had walked out on Edward in disgust over his traditional domesticity—is but one aspect of the larger problem the play points toward: how to build satisfying modes of personal relationships after having torn down the unsatisfactory models of our forebears. As Betty, of all people!, says in her last extended speech: "If there isn't a right way to do things you have to invent one."

Religion. Though the references are brief, Churchill succeeds in suggesting that the western Judeo-Christian tradition is complicit in the patriarchal oppression seen throughout the play; Joshua's alternative cosmogony, sketched out in the first act, points the way to a different understanding of man's and woman's place in the larger scheme of things than that suggested in the creation stories of Genesis, while the Biblical story of the Fall is invoked in Act II as proof positive of women's moral and intellectual inferiority.

Imperialism and Empire. The play opens, in Act I, with a somewhat ironic paean to the British Empire, "Come gather, sons of England"; the speeches then given by the principal characters give undisguised voice to the patriarchal politics which play out both within the microcosm of the British family and the macrocosm of the British Empire ("The empire is one big family," Clive blithely declares). The disguised motives behind imperial conquest are rendered in the same double register in which Conrad speaks of the Europeans bringing to Africa both a lamp and a sword; here, all sing of how "the forge of war shall weld the chains of brotherhood secure"—a dramatic irony that prepares an audience for the riot of contradictory and hypocritical statements and actions to follow. Then too, Harry's description of British settlements "up the river" which are distinguished by "a lot of skulls around the place but not white men's I think" must call to mind Marlow's horrified description of Colonel Kurtz's compound at the Inner Station in *Heart of Darkness*. In one of the plays most scathing suggestions, the entire imperial project is likened to a confidence game, a con: "Come along everyone," Clive exclaims, "you mustn't miss Harry's conjuring trick"; whence from his sleeve Harry produces the union jack, to "general acclaim."

There are quiet suggestions that the Empire is in decline—that, as Betty innocently suggests, "sometimes sunset is so terrifying I can't bear to look." Clearly, Clive's reign over the Africans is somewhat precarious, even if he stiffly insists that he "look[s] after Her Majesty's domains." At the same time, though—and following hard on the heels of this speech of Clive's—we learn that Edward is "minding" a baby doll for "Vicky" (his sister Victoria, not Queen Victoria—and yet the ironic parallel is clearly suggested). On some level, Clive's imperial rule is another version of Edward's caring for his sister's doll.

PERSPECTIVES

Whose Language?

Seamus Heaney

Though it's a truism about poetry in general, it's probably especially important to say about Heaney: that poetry is meant to be *heard*, and that his poems need to be read aloud. Audio tapes of Heaney reading some of these poems are available; but even more simply, students should be encouraged to read these poems to one another, for much of what fascinates Heaney, especially in the early poems, is the sound of words, the feeling of words shaped and held in the mouth.

"The Toome Road" juxtaposes the human scale of small-town life in rural Ulster with the military transport used to enforce the peace and sustain the Union. The "omphalos" in the poem's final line is both "navel," as the footnote suggests, but perhaps more specifically a reference to the tower occupied by Stephen Dedalus and Buck Mulligan in the opening chapter of Joyce's *Ulysses*: like Yeats's tower at Thoor Ballylee, a symbol of Irish art. "A Postcard from North Antrim" also deals with the Northern Irish "Troubles," and the inextricable way that the personal and the political are entangled one in the other.

"The Singer's House" indulges one of Heaney's recurrent interests, that in place names: specifically, the possibility that the sound of a place name might evoke some essential reality about the place, through repetition and meditation. In "The Skunk," Heaney manages the very tricky proposition of analogizing his wife to a skunk, and succeeds in having the comparison come off as affectionate, even apt. The poem is probably richer for those who know Robert Lowell's "Skunk Hour," as Heaney clearly does.

"Punishment" is one of Heaney's most powerful and disturbing poems, one of a loosely affiliated series of poems growing out of his encounter with P.V. Glob's work on the "bog people"—immaculately preserved human bodies brought out of peat bogs in England, Germany, and Denmark, some of them dating back nearly two centuries. Some of the bodies seem to have been ritually prepared human sacrifices, as for example that evoked in Heaney's poem; more information about these archaeological finds, and some haunting photographs, are to be found in Don Brothwell's *The Bog Man and the Archaeology of People*. In "Punishment," the similarities between the (inferred) circumstances surrounding the death of this bog woman and the sectarian terrorism carried out by the IRA in Northern Ireland. Like Boland's poem "The Journey," *Station Island* reprises Dante's journey to the underworld with his guide Virgil—though in this instance Heaney's guide is the shade of the nearly blind James Joyce. The attitude toward the Irish language, and the appropriateness of English for the Irish writer, might be compared to that of Boland in "Mise Eire"—and contrasted to that of Nuala Ní Dhomhnaill in her essay, "Why I Write in Irish."

"In Memoriam Francis Ledwidge" explores the logic of an Irish solider fighting in support of British interests in WWI; the wisdom of this decision is not as easy to decide as the narrowly nationalist rhetoric Heaney is surrounded by would suggest. The poem makes an interesting companion piece to Rupert Brooke's "The Soldier," who is made proud at the prospect of dying in foreign parts as a forfeit for his country's freedom. Finally "Postscript" returns to the Hughes-like nature poetry of Heaney's earliest work, suggesting the capacity of the natural landscape to astonish and to revivify—to "catch the heart off guard and blow it open." The terrorist echo of the poem's closing line serves to make the advice both more powerful and more menacing.

Nuala Ní Dhomhnaill
Feeding a Child

Ní Dhomhnaill here plays on a couple of meanings of the phrase "feeding a child": her child is literally fed at her breast, but is also, or will soon be, literarily fed on the stories of her people and her culture: no less important food, the poem suggests. In the poem's repeated questions "Do you know . . . ?", "Of all these things are you / ignorant?", the mother/poet/speaker paradoxically is able to give voice to the stories she fears her child needs to hear. The importance of these stories is suggested especially in the closing lines, where the speaker insists that the myths and legends of the Irish people are not about other people and other times, but about themselves.

Parthenogenesis

The concept of parthenogenesis—the development of an egg without fertilization—is here the concept that links immaculate conception of the Virgin Mary to the Irish legend, in its many variants, of the childless woman got with child by the sea-shadow. Standing between these two versions of the same archetypal story, at least for an Irish poet, is Yeats's retelling in *Leda and the Swan*; it's worthwhile to direct students back to Yeats's poem at this point, as well as to the account in the Gospel of Luke (1:26–38) of Mary's visitation by the Holy Spirit in the form of a dove. The Irish poet Yeats demonstrates the universal quality of Mary's conception, by comparing it to the Greek myth of Leda and Zeus; Ní Dhomhnaill here allies the myth to a uniquely Irish version. The "sea people" that the poem speaks of—the half-human, half-seal selkies of Celtic myth—were the subject of the John Sayles film *The Secret of Roan Inish*—hardly required viewing in this context, but a delightful film, and one which evokes quite vividly the rugged beauty of the West of Ireland, and the Gaeltacht.

Labasheedy (The Silken Bed)

The genre of this poem might be made clear by comparing it to Christopher Marlowe's *The Passionate Shepherd to His Love*; at the same time, the poem depends in part for the vividness of its imagery on the Old Testament *Song of Solomon*, with its rich sensual images translated into an Irish landscape and an Irish idiom.

As for the Quince

This puzzling poem partakes of an air of mystery which, as Ní Dhomhnaill explains in her essay *Why I Write in Irish*, may be a unique feature of writing in Irish; it is a mode that has been employed quite successfully by Paul Muldoon, for instance in the poem *Why Brownlee Left*. Such poetry insists, finally, that there is something ineffable, a-rational—mysterious—about experience (and in this case, human behavior and motivation), and that it is not the job of the poet to make mystery comprehensible, but rather to bear articulate witness to it.

The poem also has a humorous pop culture motif running through it; the brand-name reference (Black & Decker), the slangy feel of the language ("left me so zonked"), and the Raymond-Chandleresque tough talk that the "bright young thing" spouts all give the poem a refreshing colloquial energy.

Why I Choose to Write in Irish, the Corpse That Sits up and Talks Back

Ní Dhomhnaill's essay is at once so confident and so self-deprecating that it's hard to see where students might need any real explication. Instead, you may wish to locate the essay's central claim—that "minority languages like Irish" have a "unique and unrepeatable way of looking at the world"—and ask your students whether or not they find it compelling. Does Ní Dhomhnaill's analogy to biological diversity seem reasonable?

Ngugi wa Thiong'o

To approach Ngugi's polemical argument about the need for African literature to be written in African languages, an excerpt from his passionate book on postcolonialism, *Decolonizing the Mind*, it might help to turn to an earlier section of the Longman Anthology and find one of the poems that Ngugi refers to in his essay. Wordsworth's "Ode on a Daffodil," a poem that describes a quintessentially English landscape, is among the choices, although a Shakespearean sonnet, a selection from Chaucer's *Canterbury Tales*, or a Tennyson poem will do as well. Have students imaginatively enter the subjective position of a young student from a village in colonial Kenya, surrounded by the African landscape, its unique animals and plants, its huts and unpaved roads and herds of cattle, sitting in a dusty missionary school under scorching sunlight, memorizing such a poem. If they perform this "thought experiment" they will be closer to seeing what Ngugi means about the sheer distance between African realities and the assumptions and expectations of English poetry. In general, such poetry assumes a middle-class, white audience, or takes on the lyric voice of such a person, unlike the everyday life of a young African boy like Ngugi, for whom the issues of survival, hunger, poverty, and encounters with a hostile if stunning natural world are commonplace. Ngugi's intention is not to critique British literature as out of touch, inferior to indigenous oral traditions, or a thin veil over an ideology of conquest. Nonetheless, his essay describes how alienating and humiliating the imposition of even the greatest literary heritage can be, when it is accompanied by the certainty that everything African is inferior, degraded, or even sub-human. The violent ways that his school—and the entire British colonial government in Kenya—prohibited speaking in his native Gikuyu, and rewarded only the study of English, has parallels in the anthology in the experience of Irish, Scottish, and Welsh writers also, whose languages were either forbidden by law or extirpated by years of privileging English. The Irish, the Scottish, and the Welsh peoples, however, shared a landscape, a climate, certain ways of life, customs, and folklore with the English, which doesn't of course mitigate the pain and the violence of their cultural conflicts with the latter, nor the loss of their languages. It does mean that there were always fewer echoes of home present in English literature to the Africans who learned English and became intellectuals, writers, and artists in a tongue not their first. By contrast to Ireland or Wales or Scotland, Africa as a whole had symbolized darkness and savagery to Europe, and in Conrad's *Heart of Darkness* students will have read how Conrad reverses the stereotypes of light versus dark, white versus black that remained unreversed stereotypes that were fully in place in Ngugi's boyhood homeland.

The title of Ngugi's work of political theory provides another glimpse of what is at stake—for if most African nations had succeeded by the second half of the twentieth century in becoming independent nations, and throwing off the colonial yokes of Britain, France, Belgium, the Netherlands and Portugal, to name a few, to truly "de-colonize," Ngugi argues, requires an inner independence, a freedom of the mind and soul. Ngugi seeks this in language itself. Until the once-suppressed languages of African colonies become the vehicles for literature and thought at the highest level of excellence, he says, there will still be a colonial flag planted in the minds of Africans. The great modern works of literature and theory from Africans in the later twentieth century have been written in English, French, Portuguese and sometimes in Arabic, rather than in Swahili or Yoruba or Gikuyu. It is not a problem of having too few outstanding writers, but of having the majority of African literature be written in European languages. Ngugi himself came to prominence as an African writer in English, as did Chinua Achebe, Wole Soyinka and many others. He suggests that for Africa to genuinely step beyond the old colonial legacy, writers like himself will need to put theory into practice and adopt their native African languages as their literary tongues.

Nuala ni Dhomhnaill argues something quite similar in her essay in this volume, and follows her desire to keep Irish alive by writing poetry in Irish and having others translate it. There are political reverberations to her argument as well, but students may find some stark differences. Irish is now a mandatory subject in Irish schools, and while few speak it as a mother tongue, the Irish-English facing pages of a poetry collection like ni Dhomhnaill's can be read by many and appreciated by a wide circle of English-only readers. Ngugi's stance has been applauded by many in Africa and outside it, yet there are also many who question the realism behind his position. For one thing, Africa is a vast continent with so many languages and dialects that even within the body of African languages none is dominant; in Kenya, not everyone can read or speak Gikuyu, for example, so Ngugi's work in that language will have to be translated multiple times for African audiences. A lively discussion could be prompted among students by having a debate with members of the class assigned each side of the argument. Critics of the Ngugi side have commented that what is lost in the attempt to emphasize African languages, however laudable the goal, is a sense of cosmopolitanism, a mission to exchange culture, literature, thought and so on around the globe by acknowledging the impossibility of nativist or provincial enclaves. On the one hand, the attitude that English is global may lead to complacency and smugness in countries like the U.S., famous for its xenophobia, its lack of interest in the outside world, and its confidence that American English should be the world's lingua franca by fiat. That non-cosmopolitan world-view is obviously narrow, blinded, and arrogant—and calls for Ngugi's decolonization process.

The result of European colonialism is that modern African literature is written in European languages like English. This is a different predicament from that of British writers such as Naipaul and Rushdie; Naipaul's first language was English, and although it was disconcerting to have English literature taught as the standard of beauty, truth, and realism in his diverse Caribbean birthplace, there is no other language Sir Vidia can or would turn to—and he has given British English his own sounds. The same is true for Salman Rushdie, whose audience in English is global, even in Pakistan and India. What Ngugi wa Thiong'o points out is another lesson, another struggle altogether, a battle for independence that may entail abandoning English. There may be more people who read Ngugi's newest literary work in English than read it in Gikuyu, but for him, it makes a world of political difference which language his writing is translated into: English has become that secondary language, with Gikuyu the proudly original source of his creativity.

Nadine Gordimer
What Were You Dreaming?

Part of what's so engaging about this story is that at several points along the way, we're sure we know what kind of story this is. And we're constantly being proved wrong. The first section, narrated by the "Coloured" hitchhiker, creates the impression of a somewhat cunning young African, and the two well-meaning, if somewhat naive, Britons who stop for him out of some condescending sense of "white liberal guilt." The hitchhiker, having summed up his hosts quite quickly, plays up to their expectations, telling probable stories rather than the sometimes improbable truth about his life and situation.

But if the passenger suspects that the whites' heads are full of stereotypes about black (and coloured) South Africans, we quickly learn that he operates out of just as narrow a set of assumptions about these whites—assumptions which, in the case of the white woman, turn out to be quite unfounded. She knows who he is, and what he's doing; while the passenger sleeps in the back seat, after the story breaks midway and the narrative point-of-view shifts to third person, we hear both the simplified version of the truth that she tells her tourist companion, as well as the more complex truth that she figures out for herself. She realizes that their passenger isn't what he appears to be; but she also knows that if he's lying, he's doing so in an attempt to "translate" the hardship of his life into an idiom that will be comprehensible to English men and women unfamiliar with the realities of life in South Africa. The only solution, seemingly, is for both the Africans and the English to take the time to live in one another's cultures, to gather knowledge about one another first-hand; while she is thinking about the half-truths that she must concoct for her companion that he might understand better, if not perfectly well, she thinks, looking at his tourist's sunburned arm: "there is the place through which the worm he needs to be infected with can find a way into him. . . . Complicity is the only understanding."

James Kelman
Home for a Couple of Days

One thing that the common comparison of Kelman to both Beckett and Kafka overlooks is that both Beckett and Kafka present a vision of human despair undergirded with a fundamental humor; "Don't presume," Beckett would say, "one of the thieves was damned; don't despair—one of the thieves was saved." Kelman's is an altogether darker vision; even if his characters don't face the extreme, even allegorical, misery that Beckett's characters come up against (buried up to one's neck in a pile of sand, exposed to the hot sun, watching one's husband crawl up the pile with a pistol), their options, and their resources, seem if anything more strained. A more apt comparison on this score would be James Joyce, to whose story A Little Cloud Kelman's Home for a Couple of Days bears more than a surface resemblance.

The dialect, and Kelman's representation of it, may prove something of an obstacle at first; you may want to have students try their hand (or tongue) at reading some dialogue aloud, to get a feel for Kelman's Glaswegian speech rhythms. With a little practice, one develops an inner ear for the writing.

There is of course an air of mystery hanging over much of the story—Why did Eddie leave for London? Why has he come back? Has he in fact been in prison? Kelman is careful not to dispel these mysteries, and students should be encouraged not to spend too much time on fanciful solutions to problems the story itself refuses to answer.

Instead, Kelman seems to want us to stay on the literal level of the story: a world in which men of all ages sit in pubs drinking, waiting for the next dole check to come through; where new curtains in a pub, and a friend drinking in a different establishment, signify that a city like Glasgow has changed tremendously in three years. By the story's conclusion, we're apt to believe not that Eddie Brown has just been released from prison, but that he's just landed back in it.

Eavan Boland

In "Anorexic," Boland adopts the persona of a young woman suffering from *anorexia nervosa*, disciplining the unruly and unholy female body by starving it into submission, and in the process effacing the secondary characteristics of female sexuality. The poem is an acerbic exploration of the strange logic of anorexia, in which a woman carries out the sexualized torture which the culture at large both sanctions and absolutely denies. Instructors may wish to introduce Muldoon's poem "Aisling," as well, which moves the act of self-starvation into both the male and the Irish political realms.

Boland's "The Journey" allies itself with the great journey poems of the Western tradition: Virgil's *Aeneid* (explicitly through the epigraph), Dante's *Divine Comedy*. As Dante is guided in his journey through hell, purgatory, and heaven by the poet Virgil, so Boland imagines herself in the capable hands of Sappho, the classical forebear of women's poetry. The poem might be discussed in light of Woolf's suggestion in *A Room of One's Own* that women writers must learn to think back through their poetic mothers, and construct a useable women's literary history.

"The Pomegranate"—beautifully read by Boland on our CD—also imaginatively reinhabits mythic terrain, in this case the story of Persephone and Hades (hence another myth of the underworld), which Boland implicitly likens to the story of the Fall in Genesis by her focus on the pomegranate—a version of Eve's apple. Imaginatively identifying herself both with the lost daughter and the bereaved mother (and with Hades as well?), Boland writes again about the power of thinking through literary history and through myth. So too with "A Woman Painted on a Leaf," which adopts and adapts the story of the Sibyl of Cumae. The sibyl foretold the future and inscribed her verse prophecies on leaves; they were set at the mouth of her cave and, if not collected and read, were scattered by the winds. The poem closes with Sibyl's words, "Let me die": she was granted by the god Apollo eternal life, but not eternal youth. In wishing for a poem "I can die in," the speaker echoes the Sibyl's words—and we come to recognize that the poet is herself "a woman painted on a leaf," in this case the leaves of her books of poetry.

In teaching "Mise Eire"—a poem as resolutely set against the kind of sentimental, nationalist nostalgia as is Yeats's "Easter 1916," or the writing of Joyce—
teachers may want to present an English translation of Padraic Pearse's "Mise
Eire," to which Boland's poem responds:

I am Ireland:
I am older than the Old Woman of Beare.

Great my glory:
I that bore Cuchulainn the valiant.

Great my shame:
My own children that sold their mother.

I am Ireland:
I am lonelier than the Old Woman of Beare.

Great my pain:
Enemies ever torturing me.

Great my sorrow:
Dead the people in whom I put hope.

Joyce said of this kind of sentimentalized nostalgia, that the Irish too much loved
to hug their chains; in her poem Boland rejects the notion that a return to the
Irish language itself will somehow undo the historical suffering of the Irish people:
"I won't go back to it."

Paul Muldoon

Paul Muldoon's poems will pose pretty significant difficulties for many students—especially, perhaps, those who are good readers of poetry, adept at "translating" a poet's
elusive or seemingly ambiguous language into a more-or-less coherent "reading."
Muldoon's work largely resists this kind of paraphrasing; his poetry is most often
structured around scenes of real mystery, and insists that the mystery be experienced,
and accepted, rather than mastered. When we agree to wrestle with Muldoon's
poems, we must do so knowing that we will lose (and therein, we will win).

"Cuba" takes as its occasion the famous Cuban Missile Crisis—the "missiles of
October," 1962. The first two stanzas of the poem unfold rather smoothly: a narrative in which the small daily events that make up a life (a dance, breakfast-table
quarreling) are juxtaposed against a crisis of world-historical dimension; Muldoon
derives some mild humor from the fact that the Irish seem to have less confidence
in one of their own (JFK) than even the Americans do. The poem takes an unexpected turn in the last stanza, where those same everyday acts—in this case, a ca-
ress—turn the tables on the prurient inquest conducted by the priest.

"Aisling" takes a traditional Irish poetic form and deploys it to explore a very
contemporary problem—the hunger strikes carried out in Northern Ireland in support of the IRA's demands for independence from the United Kingdom. The
poem manages successfully to combine the graphic, clinical details of slow death

by starvation ("a lemon stain on my flannel sheet") with the mythological air of the traditional *aisling*; the fact that advanced states of starvation cause the sufferer to hallucinate serves in the poem as a kind of physiological bridge between the body and the spirit. Instructors will probably want to connect discussion of this poem to another poem about anorexia, Boland's "Anorexic."

In "Meeting the British" Muldoon reflects contemporary concerns about the British role in Northern Ireland through the colonial experience of the Americas. Similar in some ways to Rushdie's "Christopher Columbus," the poem imagines its way back to a still-innocent moment in the British imperial project, before the full force of its domination had been experienced. Marlow, in heart of darkness, talks about the Roman ships that had sailed up the Thames, bearing with them "The dreams of men, the seed of commonwealths, the germs of empires"; Muldoon's poem closes with a very literal rendering of this last phrase, with the British introducing to the French-speaking native Americans smallpox, against which they had no resistance.

"Sleeve Notes" is a loosely organized and loosely associational group of lyrics provoked by twenty-one rock albums. Muldoon himself was born right around the birth of rock & roll, and the history of rock largely parallel to his personal and poetic history; in this cycle of short poems, then, he explores the cultural, political, historical and aesthetic influence of rock on his poetry. The albums referred to are listed chronologically, from 1967 through 1994, and by registering his reactions to each of them, Muldoon creates an imaginative personal, national (note the presence of the Irish band U2, Ulsterman Van Morrison, and Irish "wild goose" Elvis Costello, born Declan MacManus), and international history of the period. Since much of this music was made before our students were born, it will be helpful to audition some of this music, and display some of the cover art, to fuel classroom discussion. As you move toward the end of the sequence, some of the albums—beginning, perhaps, with Nirvana's *Bleach*—will evoke a more personal response from at least some of your students, which can be put in dialogue with Muldoon's poems.

Derek Walcott
A Far Cry from Africa

Walcott's punning title suggests both that the speaker hears, from afar, the anguished cry of Africa, but also that the Africa of the western imagination is often "a far cry" from the reality of Africa. The poem dwells and does its work in the space between these two meanings, investigating the ways in which propagandistic language allows us to commit violence against others, and how Walcott's own dual allegiances force upon him an awareness of this hypocrisy.

Wales

Describing the Welsh landscape in grammatical and poetic terms, Walcott asserts a similarity between the way that language is used in Wales—with its native Welsh falling into disuse, the linguistic situation of Wales is similar to what Ní Dhomhnaill describes in Ireland—while asserting that "a language is shared / like bread to the mouth," ultimately holding the people together. This faith is based on the fact that the English-speaking Caribbean, like Wales, will continue to forge an identity simultaneously through its two linguistic traditions.

The Fortunate Traveller

The word "fortunate" of the title comes to have a number of ironic resonances by the poem's end, and not just because it plays on Thomas Nashe's *The Unfortunate Traveller*: the speaker of the poem is "fortunate" in that his creature comforts are well attended to both by the government agencies that support him and by the foreign bodies that attempt to bribe him, but the sharp contrast between the luxuries he enjoys and the misery he sees all around him makes it difficult for him to feel especially fortunate. ("'You are so fortunate, you get to see the world—' / Indeed, indeed sirs, I have seen the world. / Spray splashes the portholes and the vision blurs.") His simple charge is to show mercy, or charity, as the New Testament teaching requires; the protagonist realizes, however, that it is quite possible to dispense charity (aid, relief) without a spirit of charity undergirding the operation—and in fact, the more suffering one sees, the more one is deadened to the pain of others, and the more difficult true Christian charity becomes.

The poem brings up the false charity that has propped up various colonial projects throughout history, including the Belgian ivory trade in the Congo that is the subject of Conrad's *Heart of Darkness*; various of Conrad's pilgrims, too, spoke of charity, but instead robbed the continent blind. "The heart of darkness is not Africa. / The heart of darkness is the core of fire / in the white center of the holocaust."

Midsummer: 50 ("I Once Gave My Daughters, Separately, Two Conch Shells")

The writing of youth is compared to separate stones dropped into the sea, which lie separate on the sandy bottom; but as one's career and life progress, those separate stones start to form lineaments between themselves—form constellations that surprisingly resemble those of the tradition one has (unconsciously) inherited, or, as in Walcott's case, those of parents that we have imbibed at a pre-logical level.

Midsummer: 52 ("I Heard Them Marching the Leaf-wet Roads of My Head")

The invasion of the English language is imagined as a military invasion, trampling the native language into the mud; Walcott, the poet, declares that his occupation "and the Army of Occupation / are born enemies." Thus the poet with dual linguistic citizenship, like Walcott, is in a difficult position, as he had explored in *A Far Cry from Africa*. The solution, in this poem, is to appropriate the materials of English into his own language—to pin the poppies of English to his blazer, to let them bleed and stand by, articulating their death.

Midsummer: 54
("The Midsummer Sea, the Hot Pitch, this Grass, These Shacks That Meet Me")

Another poem on the same theme: Walcott's vexed relationship to the English language and to the British literary tradition. The reference to "the sacred wood" in the third line is, among other things, a veiled allusion to T. S. Eliot's criticism, and the way that his critical pronouncements for decades set the fashion, and made and broke reputations, among British poets; his first critical volume was called *The Sacred Wood* (and contained the essay *Tradition and the Individual Talent*).

Teaching with Audio

Voices of British Literature
Volume 1

Literature is first and foremost an art of the ear: throughout most of history, literature was written to be read aloud, or recited, or sung. Volume 1 of *Voices of British Literature*, the CD accompanying the first volume of *The Longman Anthology of British Literature*, presents spoken and musical selections from the beginnings of British literature to the close of the 18th Century, from the medieval period's Anglo-Saxon, Middle English, and Middle Scots poetry to the wittily pointed couplets of Alexander Pope and the rollicking songs of *The Beggar's Opera*. These performances do much to bring out the nuances of meaning—and the sheer drama—of the works we include in *The Longman Anthology of British Literature*.

The verbal music of British literature is given literal form in the musical settings we have included for works in each period. Our unaccompanied selections make compelling listening as well. We have searched for the most beautiful and gripping performances we could find for each work: Richard Burton reading John Donne with an intense intimacy; Dylan Thomas relishing his role as Milton's Satan; the poet and translator Tim Murphy giving a rousing rendition of his brilliant alliterative translation of *Beowulf*. In this and several other instances, particularly for several selections from recently rediscovered women writers, we have commissioned our own readings.

Like the *Longman Anthology* it accompanies, this CD opens up a range of cultural contexts for the writing and reading of literature. From the Middle Ages, for example, we give popular songs together with Chaucer and Dunbar. From the Early Modern period, along with poems by Wyatt and Shakespeare on betrayal and loss, we include an anguished speech by Queen Elizabeth I on the death sentence given to her cousin, Mary Queen of Scots—paired with a haunting motet by the Catholic composer Thomas Tallis. For the Restoration and 18th Century, selections include Samuel Pepys's eyewitness account of the great Fire of London and a satiric response by Lady Mary Wortley Montagu to a misogynist poem by Jonathan Swift.

Most of our selections can be found in the pages of the full *Longman Anthology of British Literature*, 2/e (LABL), starting on the page given following each title in the notes that follow. Many of these texts are also available in the anthology's Compact Edition (CE). Occasionally, we have taken the opportunity to extend the anthology's range with a compelling recording of a work not in the anthology itself. The texts for these selections are printed following the listing of works, so all these texts can be studied in detail. These great performances can readily stand on their own as well: they are a delight to hear.

–David Damrosch

Track Listing
The Middle Ages

+ Music

The Restoration and the 18th Century

Notes

Track	Page in Anthology

1   *BEOWULF:* The Dirge, in Anglo-Saxon (1:12).
    Read by Tim Murphy.

2   *BEOWULF:* The Dirge, in English (2:20).   LABL 1:91 CE 94
    Read by Tim Murphy.

3   *SUMER IS ICUMEN IN* ("The Cuckoo Song") (1:22). LABL 1:550 CE 341
    Performed by Roxbury Union Congregational
    Church Choir. *A celebration of fertility and renewal
    as summer approaches.*

4   GEOFFREY CHAUCER: The Canterbury Tales: LABL 1:302 CE 221
    The General Prologue, lines 1–29 (1:51).
    Read by J. B. Bessinger, Jr. *Springtime inspires a
    varied–and talkative–group to go on pilgrimage.*

5   GEOFFREY CHAUCER: The Canterbury Tales: LABL 1:312 CE 231
    The General Prologue, lines 447–78 (1:59).
    Read by J. B. Bessinger, Jr.

6   *THERE IS NO ROSE* (4:31).   See text below.
    Performed by Oxford Camerata. *"There is no rose of
    such virtue, as is the rose that bare Jesu." An ethereal mix
    of English and Latin, this 15th century carol celebrates the
    Virgin Mary.*

7   WILLIAM DUNBAR: In Secreit Place This Hyndir   LABL 1:592 CE 357
    Nycht (3:48). Read by Patrick Deer (NYU). *A lover's
    dialogue–humorous, tender, and starkly physical–by the great
    Middle Scots poet.*

The Early Modern Period

8   SIR THOMAS WYATT: They Flee from Me (1:37).   LABL 1:672 CE 383
Read by Edward DeSouza. *A moving recollection of lost*
love in a time of political disfavor.

9   QUEEN ELIZABETH I: *from* a speech on Mary,   LABL 1:1088
Queen of Scots ("On Mary's Execution") (5:47).
Read by Elizabeth Richmond-Garza (Univ. of Texas).
Queen Elizabeth's response to Parliament's death sentence on
her cousin displays her deep sorrow, her resolve to protect her
country and her own reputation, and her striving not to be
forced into irrevocable action in a treacherous situation.

10 THOMAS TALLIS: *from* Lamentations of   See text below.
Jeremiah (3:02). Performed by Oxford Camerata.
Both a devout Catholic and a loyal subject of his patron
Queen Elizabeth, the great composer Thomas Tallis
(c. 1510–1585) turned to the biblical Book of Lamentations
to express the anguish of Queen Mary's fall from grace. Whereas
in Lamentations *a destitute woman is a metaphor for a fallen*
Jerusalem, in this powerful motet sequence, the fallen Jerusalem
stands in for the imprisoned Mary.

WILLIAM SHAKESPEARE: Sonnets
Read by Alex Jennings. *Six sonnets from the most famous*
sonnet sequence in English, written to both a mysterious lady
and an endlessly attractive young man. Jennings's performance
of these poems shows them as intimate dramas of passionate
debate and self-analysis.

11 Sonnet 18: Shall I compare thee to a summer's day   LABL 1:1226 CE 553
(1:03)

12 Sonnet 29: When, in disgrace with fortune and   LABL 1:1227 CE 553
men's eyes (1:00)

13 Sonnet 55: Not marble nor the gilded monuments   LABL 1:1229 CE 554
(0:59)

14 Sonnet 73: That time of year thou mayst in me   LABL 1:1230 CE 554
behold (1:03)

15 Sonnet 126: O thou, my lovely boy, who in thy   LABL 1:1235 CE 556
power (1:00)

16 Sonnet 130: My mistress' eyes are nothing like the   LABL 1:1236 CE 556
sun (0:59)

17 WILLIAM SHAKESPEARE: Opening monologue   LABL 1:1239
from Twelfth Night (1:19). Performed by Robert Hardy.
The languid Count Orsino wants to be done with music and
with love.

18 HEVENINGHAM/PURCELL: If music be the food   See text below.
    of love (3:44). Music by Henry Purcell (c. 1659-1695).
    Performed by Howard Crook. *In this gorgeous setting
    by one of England's greatest composers, Heveningham's song
    turns Orsino's theme on its head, in a passionate celebration
    of music and love.*

19 JOHN DONNE: The Sun Rising (1:39).   LABL 1:1650 CE 665
    Read by Richard Burton. *A classic "aubade," or dawn-song,
    in which the speaker chides the sun for intruding on himself
    and his beloved.*

20 JOHN DONNE: A Valediction: Forbidding   LABL 1:1657 CE 668
    Mourning (2:04). Read by Richard Burton. *One of
    Donne's most moving poems, said to have been written for
    his wife just before a voyage to France in 1611.*

21 KATHERINE PHILIPS: To Mrs. Mary Awbrey   LABL 1:1743
    at Parting (2:58). Read by Elizabeth Richmond-Garza.
    *The poet asserts that her intimacy with her friend will only
    increase with distance and even death: "our twin souls in
    one shall grow, / And teach the world new love."*

22 ANDREW MARVELL: To His Coy Mistress (2:22).   LABL 1:1730 CE 687
    Read by Patrick Deer. *One of the most famous of all
    poems on the theme of "carpe diem": seize the day.*

23 *WHEN THE KING ENJOYS HIS OWN AGAIN* (2:49).   See text below.
    Words and music by Martin Parker. Performed by
    John Potter. *Composed in support of Charles I during
    the first phase of the civil wars, this exuberant song long
    outlasted its initial occasion. It was revived and revised at
    the Restoration, when the return of Charles II partly fulfilled
    its prediction. The tune remained popular throughout the
    eighteenth century, as a setting for lyrics announcing good
    news or hopeful prognostications.*

24 JOHN MILTON: Paradise Lost, Book 1,   LABL 1:1843 CE 791
    lines 242-70 (2:13). Read by Dylan Thomas.
    Satan rouses his fallen angels in hell and defies God.

The Restoration and the 18th Century

25 SAMUEL PEPYS, *from* The Diary: The Fire of   LABL 1:2096 CE 934
    London (3:50). Read by Ian Richardson. *The sharpest
    observer of Restoration life records London's most devastating
    natural disaster.*

26 JONATHAN SWIFT: *from* The Lady's Dressing   LABL 1:2445 CE 1075
Room (3:38). Read by Patrick Deer. *A love-smitten*
shepherd tiptoes into his beloved Celia's dressing room,
where he finds more than he has bargained for.

27 LADY MARY WORTLEY MONTAGU: *from* The   LABL 1:2583 CE 1078
Reasons that Induced Dr. S to Write a Poem called
"The Lady's Dressing Room" (3:05). Read by Elizabeth
Richmond-Garza. *Matching Swift witticism for witticism*
and obscenity for obscenity, Montagu reveals the "true"
story behind Swift's poem.

28 ALEXANDER POPE: *from* An Essay on Criticism   LABL 1:2483 CE 1153
lines 337–83 (3:18). Read by Max Adrian. *"The sound*
must seem an echo to the sense," Pope asserts at the start of
this selection. Easier said than explained or done. But Pope
proceeds to explain and do, simultaneously and dazzlingly.

29 APHRA BEHN: To the Fair Clarinda, Who Made   LABL 1:2223 CE 1015
Love to Me, Imagined More than Woman (1:36).
Read by Stella Gonet. *Behn declares that her beloved*
friend combines the virtues—and the attractions—of both sexes.

30 JOHN GAY: *from* The Beggar's Opera: Air 6 (2:10).   LABL 1:2594
Lyrics by John Gay. Performed by Bronwen Mills and
Charles Daniels. *"Virgins are like the fair flower in its*
luster." In most of his airs, Gay evokes a mix of feelings in
both singer and auditor. Here Polly assures her parents of her
cunning and competence, but gives voice also to her vulnerability.

31 JOHN GAY: *from* The Beggar's Opera: Air 21 (2:19). LABL 1:2604
Lyrics by John Gay. Performed by Adrian Thompson.
"When the heart of a man is oppressed with care." Besotted
with his own prowess and promiscuity, Macheath nonetheless
sings a song of swooning, of surrender. It will shortly prove
prophetic; before the evening is out, several of the women
he savors will help put him in jail.

Texts for Selections Not in The Longman Anthology

Track 6: There Is No Rose

There is no rose of such virtue,
as is the rose that bare Jesu.
There is no rose of such virtue,
as is the rose that bare Jesu.
Alleluia.

There is no rose of such virtue,
as is the rose that bare Jesu.
For in this rose contained there,
was heaven and earth in little space.
Resmiranda.

There is no rose of such virtue,
as is the rose that bare Jesu.
For by that rose we may well see,
that he is God in persons three.
Pariforma.

There is no rose of such virtue,
as is the rose that bare Jesu.
The angels sungen the shepherds to:
Gloria in excelsis Deo.
Gaudeamus.

There is no rose of such virtue,
as is the rose that bare Jesu.
Leave all this worldly mirth,
and follow we this joyful birth.
Transeamus.

There is no rose of such virtue,
as is the rose that bare Jesu.

Track 10: Thomas Tallis: Lamentations of Jeremiah (Latin, with translation):

Quomodo sedet sola civitas	How desolate lies the city
plena populo;	once thronged with people;
facta est quasi vidua domina gentium:	the queen of nations has become as a widow:
princeps provinciarum	once a ruler of provinces,
facta est sub tributo.	she is now subject to others.
. . . .	
Ierusalem, Ierusalem, convertere	Jerusalem, Jerusalem, turn back again
ad Dominum Deum tuum	to the Lord your God.

Track 18: Henry Heveningham: If music be the food of love

If music be the food of love,
Sing on, till I am fill'd with joy;
For then my listening soul you move,
To pleasures that can never cloy;
Your eyes, your mien, your tongue declare
That you are music everywhere.

Pleasures invade both eye and ear,
So fierce the transports are, they wound;
And all my senses feasted are,
Though yet the treat is only sound;
Sure I must perish by your charms,
Unless you save me in your arms.

Track 23: When the King Enjoys His Own Again

What Booker can prognosticate,
or speak of our Kingdom's present state?
I think myself to be as wise,
as he that looks most in the Skies.
My skill goes beyond the depth of the Pond,
or Rivers in the greatest Rain.
By which I can tell, that all things will be well,
when the King comes home in peace again.

There is no Astrologer then say I,
can search more deep in this than I,
to give you a reason from the stars,
What causeth Peace or Civil Wars.
The Man in the Moon may wear out his shoon,
in running after Charles his Wain.
But oh to no end, for the times they will mend,
when the King comes home in peace again.

Though for a time you may see White-hall,
with Cob-webs hanging over all,
instead of Silk and Silver brave,
as formerly it us'd to have.
And in every Room, the sweet Perfume,
delightful for that Princely Train,
the which you shall see, when the time it shall be,
that the King comes Home in Peace again.

Till then upon Ararat's-hill
my Hope shall cast her Anchor still,
Until I see some Peaceful Dove
bring Home that Branch which I do Love,
Still will I wait till the Waters abate,
Which most disturb my troubled brain
For I'll never rejoice, till I hear that Voice,
That the King's come Home in Peace again.

Teaching with Audio

Voices of British Literature
Volume 2

Literature is first and foremost an art of the ear. Throughout history, literature was usually written to be read aloud, or recited, or sung, and in the twentieth century as well writers continued to be intensely aware of the aural dimensions of their writing. Volume 2 of *Voices of British Literature*, the CD accompanying the second volume of *The Longman Anthology of British Literature*, presents spoken and musical selections of British literature from the nineteenth and twentieth centuries, from Barbauld, Byron, and Jane Austen in the Romantic era to modernists like Yeats and Virginia Woolf, ending with major contemporary figures reading their own works. These performances do much to bring out the nuances of meaning—and the sheer drama—of the works we include in *The Longman Anthology of British Literature*.

The verbal music of British literature is given literal form in the musical settings we have included for works in each period. Our unaccompanied selections make compelling listening as well. We have searched for the most beautiful and gripping performances we could find for each work: Jean Redpath singing tender and erotic songs of Robert Burns; Claire Bloom reading Jane Austen with cool irony; James Mason giving a chilling rendition of Robert Browning's "My Last Duchess." In several instances, to provide selections from recently rediscovered women writers, we have commissioned our own readings. When possible, we have included writers performing their own works, from Tennyson reading "The Charge of the Light Brigade" on a historical Edison wax cylinder, to Yeats, Joyce, and Eliot in the modernist period and Eavan Boland today.

Like the *Longman Anthology* it accompanies, this CD opens up a range of cultural contexts for the writing and reading of literature. From the era of the Romantics and their contemporaries, for example, we include songs by Robert Burns along with the poetry of Wordsworth, Keats, and John Clare; from the Victorian period we have a song by Gilbert & Sullivan satirizing Oscar Wilde's aestheticism, together with a scene from Wilde's *The Importance of Being Earnest*; from the 20th Century, we include BBC broadcasts by Winston Churchill in the darkest moments of World War Two, together with postwar poems of violence, loss, and recovery.

Most of our selections can be found in the pages of the full *Longman Anthology of British Literature*, 2/e (LABL), starting on the page given following each title below. Many of these texts are also available in the anthology's Compact Edition

(CE). Occasionally, we have taken the opportunity to extend the anthology's range with a compelling recording of a work not in the anthology itself. The texts for these selections are printed in these notes following the listing of works, so all these texts can be studied in detail. These great performances can readily stand on their own as well: they are a delight to hear.

—*David Damrosch*

Track Listing

The Romantics and Their Contemporaries

Track		Time
1.	ANNA LETITIA BARBAULD: The Mouse's Petition to Dr. Priestly	(2:21)
2.	ROBERT BURNS: A Red, Red Rose	(1:50)+
3.	ROBERT BURNS: The Fornicator	(1:55)+
4.	WILLIAM WORDSWORTH: Strange Fits of Passion Have I Known	(1:29)
5.	WILLIAM WORDSWORTH: Composed Upon Westminster Bridge, Sept. 3, 1802	(1:03)
6.	GEORGE GORDON, LORD BYRON: *from* Don Juan	(3:59)
7.	PERCY BYSSHE SHELLEY: Ozymandias	(1:09)
8.	FELICIA HEMANS: The Wife of Asdrubal	(4:44)
9.	JOHN CLARE: I Am	(1:45)
10.	JOHN KEATS: When I Have Fears	(1:05)
11.	JOHN KEATS: This Living Hand	(0:38)
12.	JANE AUSTEN: *from* Pride and Prejudice	(3:45)

The Victorian Age

13.	ELIZABETH BARRETT BROWNING: *from* Aurora Leigh	(3:46)
14.	ROBERT BROWNING: My Last Duchess	(3:37)
15.	ALFRED, LORD TENNYSON: *from* The Charge of the Light Brigade	(1:20)
16.	ALFRED, LORD TENNYSON: *from* In Memoriam	(1:36)
17.	CHARLES DICKENS: *from* A Christmas Carol	(3:35)
18.	OSCAR WILDE: *from* The Importance of Being Earnest	(2:50)
19.	W. S. GILBERT/A. SULLIVAN: If You're Anxious For to Shine	(2:36)+

The Twentieth Century

20.	BERNARD SHAW: *from* Pygmalion	(2:07)
21.	WILLIAM BUTLER YEATS: The Lake Isle of Innisfree	(1:10)
22.	JAMES JOYCE: *from* Finnegans Wake	(3:22)
23.	T.S. ELIOT: *from* Wasteland	(3:31)
24.	VIRGINIA WOOLF: *from* Mrs Dalloway	(4:16)
25.	SIR WINSTON CHURCHILL: Speech to the House of Commons, May 13, 1940	(0:44)

+ Music

Notes

The Romantics and Their Contemporaries

Track		Page in Anthology

1 ANNA LETITIA BARBAULD: The Mouse's   LABL 2:31 CE 1339
   Petition to Dr. Priestly (2:21). Read by Elizabeth
   Richmond-Garza (Univ. of Texas). *Barbauld's poem
   wittily used a mouse's perspective to plead for liberty and
   the rights of all sentient beings.*

2 ROBERT BURNS: A Red, Red Rose (1:50).   LABL 2:330 CE 1517
   Performed by Jean Redpath. *Set to the Scottish folk tune
   "Major Graham." Burns wrote this love song in the style of
   the melody, which he called "simple and wild."*

3 ROBERT BURNS: The Fornicator (1:55).   LABL 2:331 CE 1519
   Performed by Jean Redpath. *Set to the Scottish folk
   tune "Clout the Cauldron." Burns wrote this lusty song in
   celebration of fathering a child out of wedlock with one of
   his father's servants.*

4 WILLIAM WORDSWORTH: Strange Fits of   LABL 2:363 CE 1539
   Passion Have I Known (1:29). Read by Sir Cedric
   Hardwick. *One of Wordsworth's Lyrical Ballads, this poem
   illustrates Wordsworth's efforts to embody profound emotion
   in the rhythms and the events of everyday life.*

5 WILLIAM WORDSWORTH: Composed Upon   LABL 2:386 CE 1561
   Westminster Bridge, Sept. 3, 1802 (1:03). Read by
   Sir Cedric Hardwick. *One of Wordsworth's greatest sonnets,
   this poem triangulates between nature, the city, and the poet's
   observing mind.*

6 GEORGE GORDON, LORD BYRON: *from* Don   LABL 2:693 CE 1685
   Juan (3:59). Read by Tyrone Power. *In this excerpt
   from Canto 1 (stanzas 104–5, 109–12, and 115–17),
   young Juan and his (unfortunately married) first love struggle
   in the throes of illicit yet strangely innocent passion.*

7   PERCY BYSSHE SHELLEY: Ozymandias (1:09).   LABL 2:760 CE 1710
    Read by Michael Sheen. *Shelley's famous sonnet*
    meditates on antiquity, on art, and on the frailty of power.

8   FELICIA HEMANS: The Wife of Asdrubal (4:44).   LABL 2:813 CE 1736
    Read by Elizabeth Richmond-Garza. *A dramatic*
    recreation of an ancient scene at Carthage in North Africa.
    As the Romans conquer the city, the governor's wife scorns
    her husband's accommodation to the invaders, to fatal effect.

9   JOHN CLARE: I Am (1:45). Read by Michael Sheen. LABL 2:849 CE 1749
    Early promoted as a model "peasant poet," Clare lost his
    patrons as his social criticism sharpened. He was eventually
    confined to an insane asylum, where he wrote this troubled,
    self-affirming poem.

10 JOHN KEATS: Sonnet: When I Have Fears (1:05).   LABL 2:865 CE 1752
    Read by Samuel West. *Already suffering from the*
    tuberculosis that would kill him three years later, in 1818
    Keats wrote this poem about his hopes and fears as a great
    poet with little time left for poetry.

11 JOHN KEATS: This Living Hand (0:38). Read by   LABL 2:899 CE 1771
    Samuel West. *A late fragment. "Hand" can mean either*
    the physical hand or a person's handwriting.

12 JANE AUSTEN: *from* Pride and Prejudice (3:45).   LABL 2:982
    Read by Claire Bloom. *This reading from Austen's*
    opening chapter captures her dry wit and her acute social
    and psychological insight.

The Victorian Age

13 ELIZABETH BARRETT BROWNING: LABL 2:1124 CE 1876
    from Aurora Leigh (3:46). Read by Diana Quick.
    In this extract from Book 2 of Browning's verse novel
    (excerpted from lines 343–508), the aspiring poet Aurora
    rejects the restrictive security of the life offered her by her
    suitor Romney.

14 ROBERT BROWNING: My Last Duchess (3:37).   LABL 2:1311 CE 1961
    Read by James Mason. *This famous "dramatic monologue"*
    was based on the life of the 16th-century Italian duke
    Alfonso II, who remarried a few years after the sudden death—
    possibly by poison—of his young bride, Lucrezia de Medici.

15 ALFRED, LORD TENNYSON: *from* The Charge   LABL 2:1195
    of the Light Brigade (1:20). Read by Lord Tennyson.
    In 1889, at the age of 80, Tennyson recorded his poem

*about military folly and bravery during the Crimean War.
Tennyson's incantatory reading comes through powerfully,
despite the poor sound quality of this pioneering recording
on one of Thomas Edison's newly invented wax cylinders.*

16 ALFRED, LORD TENNYSON: *from* In Memoriam   LABL 2:1172
    (1:36). Read by Dame Sibyl Thorndike. *A poem
    from Tennyson's great sequence in memory of his
    beloved friend Henry Hallam, who had suddenly died in
    Vienna while still in his twenties. Here the poet envisions
    Hallam's body being transported across a deathly calm
    ocean to be buried in England.*

17 CHARLES DICKENS: *from* A Christmas Carol (3:35). LABL 2:1391
    Read by Anton Lesser. *Fantasy and sharp social realism
    mingle in this scene, in which the Ghost of Christmas
    Present forces Scrooge to contemplate two wretched children
    named Ignorance and Want.*

18 OSCAR WILDE: *from* The Importance of Being   LABL 2:1907 CE 2108
    Earnest (2:50). Performed by Lynn Redgrave,
    Alec McCowen, and Jack May. *In this scene from Act 2,
    the hero, Algernon Moncrieff, a free-living aesthete, is visiting
    a country house under the assumed name of Ernest. Here
    he suddenly declares his love for the daughter of the house,
    Cecily, whom he has just met, only to find that she had
    already recorded their entire future romance.*

19 W. S. GILBERT/A. SULLIVAN: If You're Anxious   LABL 2:1943 CE 2144
    for to Shine (2:36). Music by Sir Arthur Sullivan, from
    the operetta *Patience*. Performed by Orva Hoskinson
    (circa 1975). *In this satire of Oscar Wilde and his friends,
    a canny young aesthete named Bunthorne explains how he
    poses as an aesthete simply in order to attract women.*

The Twentieth Century

20 BERNARD SHAW: *from* Pygmalion (2:07).   LABL 2:2110
    Performed by Michael Redgrave, Lynn Redgrave,
    and Michael Horndern. *The opinionated Professor Henry
    Higgins gives the bewildered flower-seller Eliza Doolittle a
    crash course in elocution.*

21 WILLIAM BUTLER YEATS: The Lake Isle of   LABL 2:2246 CE 2325
    Innisfree (1:10). Read by W. B. Yeats. *Living in London
    in 1890, where he was trying to establish himself as a poet,
    Yeats wrote this warm evocation of the West Irish landscape
    of his mother's family origins.*

22 JAMES JOYCE: *from* Finnegans Wake (3:22).   See text below.
    Read by James Joyce. *In these concluding paragraphs from*
    the chapter called "Anna Livia Plurabelle," two old Irish
    washerwomen meet by the banks of the River Liffey in the
    growing dusk and talk about Anna Livia and her ubiquitous
    husband HCE. Joyce's poetic prose imitates the flow of the
    river, which in turn becomes an image of the recirculating
    flow of stories upon stories.

23 T. S. ELIOT: *from* The Wasteland (3:31).   LABL 2:2360 CE 2429
    Read by T. S. Eliot. *In this excerpt from Part 2 of the*
    poem, a non-conversation between husband and wife gives
    way to two women talking in a pub about the tangled sexual
    and emotional aftermath of the Great War.

24 VIRGINIA WOOLF: *from* Mrs Dalloway (4:16).   LABL 2:2387
    Read by Elizabeth Richmond-Garza. *The novel's opening*
    pages: both a prose poem to London and an overture to the
    book's many themes.

25 SIR WINSTON CHURCHILL: Speech to the House   LABL 2:2701 CE 2523
    of Commons, May 13, 1940 (0:44). *In this excerpt*
    recorded by the BBC, the new Prime Minister takes up the
    struggle against the Nazi onslaught.

26 SIR WINSTON CHURCHILL: Speech to the   See text below.
    House of Commons, November 10, 1942 (3:28).
    As the Allied forces begin to make headway against the
    German army, Churchill asserts a lasting commitment to
    winning the war and to preserving both civilization overall
    and the British Empire in particular. His apt quotation of
    Byron at the speech's end gave the United Nations its name.

27 SYLVIA PLATH: Lady Lazarus (3:29).   LABL 2:2812
    Read by Sylvia Plath. *With its deliberately shocking imagery*
    drawn from Nazi anti-Semitism, Plath's poem reads the
    century's history into the speaker's inner turmoil.

28 DYLAN THOMAS: Do Not Go Gentle Into   LABL 2:2762 CE 2554
    That Good Night (1:41). Read by Dylan Thomas.
    The poet's sonorous, Welsh-accented voice bring out the
    verbal music of his famous 1951 poem about resilience in
    the face of old age and death.

29 TED HUGHES: Second Glance at a Jaguar (1:54).   See text below.
    Read by Ted Hughes. *An exploration of the violence,*
    inscrutability, and inner perfection of animal creation.

30 EAVAN BOLAND: The Pomegranate (2:57).   LABL 2:2938
    Read by Eavan Boland.

Texts for Selections not in The Longman Anthology

Track 22: James Joyce, Finnegans Wake

Ah, but she was the queer old skeowsha anyhow, Anna Livia, trinkettoes! And sure he was the quare old buntz too, Dear Dirty Dumpling, foostherfather of fingalls and dotthergills. Gammer and gaffer we're all their gangsters. Hadn't he seven dams to wive him? And every dam had her seven crutches. And every crutch had its seven hues. And each hue had a differing cry. Sudds for me and supper for you and the doctor's bill for Joe John. Befor! Bifor! He married his markets, cheap by foul, I know, like any Etrurian Catholic Heathen, in their pinky limony creamy birnies and their turkiss indienne mauves. But at milkidmass who was the spouse? Then all that was was fair. Tys Elvenland! Teems of times and happy returns. The seim anew. Ordovico or viricordo, Anna was, Livia is, Plurabelle's to be. North-men's thing made southfolk's place but howmulty plurators made eachone in person? Latin me that, my trinity scholar, out of eure sanscreed into oure eryan! Hircus Civis Eblanensis! He had buckgoat paps on him, soft ones for orphans. Ho, Lord! Twins of his bosom. Lord save us! And ho! Hey? What all men. Hot? His tittering daughters of. Whawk?

Can't hear with the waters of. The chittering waters of. Flittering bats, field-mice bawk talk. Ho! Are you not gone ahome? What Thom Malone? Can't hear with bawk of bats, all thim liffeying waters of. Ho, talk save us! My foos won't moos. I feel as old as yonder elm. A tale told of Shaun or Shem? All Livia's daughtersons. Dark hawks hear us. Night! Night! My ho head halls. I feel as heavy as yonder stone. Tell me of John or Shaun? Who were Shem and Shaun the living sons or daughters of? Night now! Tell me, tell me, tell me, elm! Night night! Telmetale of stem or stone. Beside the rivering waters of, hitherandthithering waters of. Night!

Track 26: Winston Churchill, Speech to the House of Commons, November 10, 1942

We have not entered upon this war for profit or expansion but only for honor and to do our duty in defending the right.

Let me, however, make this clear, in case there should be any mistake about it in any quarter: we mean to hold our own. I have not become the King's First Minister in order to preside over the liquidation of the British Empire. For that task, if ever it were prescribed, someone else would have to be found, and under a democracy I suppose the nation would have to be consulted.

I am proud to be a member of that vast commonwealth and society of nations and communities gathered under and around the ancient British monarchy, without which the good cause might well have perished from the face of the earth.

Here we are and here we stand, a veritable rock of salvation in this drifting world. And all undertakings, in the east and in the west, are parts of a single strategic and political conception which we had labored long to bring to fruition and about which we are now justified in entertaining good and reasonable confidence. Thus taken together they wear the aspects of a grand design, vast in its scope, honorable in its motive, noble in its aim. And should the British and American affairs continue to prosper in the Mediterranean, the whole event will be a new bond between the English-speaking people and a new hope for the whole world.

There are some lines of Byron which seem to me to fit the event, the hour, and theme:

> Millions of tongues record thee, and anew
> Their children's lips shall echo them and say,
> Here where the sword united nations drew
> Our countrymen were warring on that day.
> And this is much and all which will not pass away.

Track 29: Ted Hughes, Second Glance at a Jaguar

Skinful of bowls, he bowls them,
The hip going in and out of joint, dropping the spine
With the urgency of his hurry
Like a cat going along under thrown stones, under cover,
Glancing sideways, running
Under his spine. A terrible, stump-legged waddle
Like a thick Aztec disemboweller,
Club-swinging, trying to grind some square
Socket between his hind legs round,
Carrying his head like a brazier of spilling embers,
And the black bit of his mouth, he takes it
Between his back teeth, he has to wear his skin out,
He swipes a lap at the water-trough as he turns,
Swivelling the ball of his heel on the polished spot,
Showing his belly like a butterfly
At every stride he has to turn a corner
In himself and correct it. His head
Is like the worn down stump of another whole jaguar,
His body is just the engine shoving it forward,
Lifting the air up and shoving on under,
The weight of his fangs hanging the mouth open,
Bottom jaw combing the ground. A gorged look,
Gangster, club-tail lumped along behind gracelessly,
He's wearing himself to heavy ovals,
Muttering some mantrah, some drum-song of murder
To keep his rage brightening, making his skin
Intolerable, spurred by the rosettes, the cain-brands,
Wearing the spots off from the inside,
Rounding some revenge. Going like a prayer-wheel,
The head dragging forward, the body keeping up,
The hind legs lagging. He coils, he flourishes
The blackjack tail as if looking for a target,
Hurrying through the underworld, soundless.

About the Editors

Christopher Baswell is Professor of English at the University of California, Los Angeles. His interests include classical literature and culture, medieval literature and culture, and contemporary poetry. He is author of *Virgil in Medieval England: Figuring the "Aeneid" from the Twelfth Century to Chaucer* which won the 1998 Beatrice White Prize of the English Association. He has held fellowships from the NEH, the National Humanities Center, and the Institute for Advanced Study, Princeton.

Clare Carroll is Chair of the Comparative Literature Department and Director of Irish Studies at Queens College, CUNY. Her research is in Renaissance Studies, with particular interests in early modern colonialism, epic poetry, historiography, and translation. She is the author of *The Orlando Furioso, A Stoic Comedy*, and editor of Richard Beacon's humanist dialogue on the colonization of Ireland, *Solon His Follie.* Her most recent book is *Circe's Cup: Cultural Transformations in Early Modern Ireland.* She has received Fulbright Fellowships for her research and the Queens College President's Award for Excellence in Teaching.

David Damrosch is Professor of English and Comparative Literature at Columbia University and President of the American Comparative Literature Association for 2002/03. A specialist in ancient, medieval and modern literature and criticism, he is the author of *The Narrative Covenant, We Scholars: Changing the Culture of the University, Meetings of the Mind,* and *What Is World Literature?* (2003).

Kevin J. H. Dettmar is Professor and Chair of English at Southern Illinois University Carbondale, and President of the Modernist Studies Association. He is the author of *The Illicit Joyce of Postmodernism,* and editor or co-editor of *Rereading the New, Marketing Modernisms,* and *Reading Rock & Roll.*

Heather Henderson is a freelance writer and former Associate Professor of English Literature at Mount Holyoke College. A specialist in Victorian literature, she is the recipient of a fellowship from the National Endowment for the Humanities. She is the author of *The Victorian Self: Autobiography and Biblical Narrative.* Her current interests include homeschooling, travel literature, and autobiography.

Constance Jordan is Andrew W. Mellon Professor of Humanities and Dean of Arts and Humanities at Claremont Graduate University. She is the author of *Renaissance Feminism: Literary Texts and Political Models, and Shakespeare's Monarchies: Ruler and Subject in the Romances.* Her current interests include the literature of contact in the Atlantic World, 1500–1680.

Peter J. Manning is Professor and Chair of English at Stony Brook University. He is the author of *Byron and His Fictions* and of *Reading Romantics*, and of numerous essays on the British Romantic poets and prose writers. With Susan J. Wolfson, he has co-edited *Selected Poems of Byron*, and of *Beddoes, Hood, and Praed*. He has received fellowships from the National Endowment for the Humanities and the John Simon Guggenheim Memorial Foundation, and the Distinguished Scholar Award of the Keats-Shelley Association.

Anne Howland Schotter is Professor of English and Chair of Humanities at Wagner College. A specialist in medieval literature, she has written articles on Middle English poetry, Dante, and medieval Latin poetry, and co-edited *Ineffability: Naming the Unnamable from Dante to Beckett*. She has received fellowships from the Woodrow Wilson and Mellon Foundations.

William Sharpe is Professor and Chair of English Literature at Barnard College. A specialist in Victorian poetry and the literature of the city, he is the author of *Unreal Cities: Urban Figuration in Wordsworth, Baudelaire, Whitman, Eliot, and Williams*. He is also co-editor of *The Passing of Arthur* and *Visions of the Modern City*. He is the recipient of Guggenheim, National Endowment of the Humanities, Fulbright, and Mellon fellowships, and is currently at work on a book on images of the nocturnal city.

Stuart Sherman is Associate Professor of English at Fordham University. He received the Gottschalk Prize from the American Society for Eighteenth-Century Studies for his book *Telling Time: Clocks, Diaries, and English Diurnal Form, 1660–1775*, and is currently at work on a study called *News and Plays: Evanescences of Page and Stage, 1620–1779*. He has received the Quantrell Award for Undergraduate Teaching, as well as fellowships from the American Council of Learned Societies and the Chicago Humanities Institute.

Jennifer Wicke is Professor of English at the University of Virginia, having previously been a professor of English and Comparative Literature at Yale University and at New York University. Her teaching and research areas include nineteenth and twentieth century British and American literature, comparative and international modernisms, literary and cultural theory, and studies of mass culture, aesthetic value, and global culture. She is the author of *Advertising Fictions: Literature, Advertisement, and Social Reading*, and the forthcoming *Born to Shop: Modernity, Modernism, and the Work of Consumption*; she co-edited *Feminism and Postmodernism* with Margaret Ferguson; she has written widely on Joyce, feminist theory, celebrity, and the academy.

Susan J. Wolfson is Professor of English at Princeton University and series editor for Longman Cultural Editions. A specialist in Romantic-era literature and criticism, she is the author of *The Questioning Presence: Wordsworth, Keats, and the Interrogative Mode in Romantic Poetry* and *Formal Charges: The Shaping of Poetry in British Romanticism*. She is the editor of *Felicia Hemans: Selected Poems, Letters, Reception Materials*, and *The Cambridge Companion to John Keats*. With Peter J.

Manning, she has coedited *Selected Poems of Byron*, and *Selected Poems of Thomas Hood, W. M Praed and Thomas Lovell Beddoes*. She has received fellowships from the American Council of Learned Societies, the National Endowment for the Humanities and the John Simon Guggenheim Memorial Foundation, and was the 2001 recipient of the Distinguished Scholar Award of the Keats-Shelley Association of America.

Index of Authors*

---

* For authors who appear in perspectives sections, see the perspectives entry; for discussions of
Companion and Contexts authors, see the principal author listing with which they appear